THE
COMPLETE
PLAYS

Russian Dramatic Theory from Pushkin to the Symbolists

Anton Chekhov

The Chekhov Theatre:
A Century of the Plays in Performance

Russian Satiric Comedy (translator)

Russian Comedy of the Nikolaian Era (translator)

Gordon Craig's Moscow Hamlet

Serf Actor: The Life and Art of
Mikhail Shchepkin

National Theatre in Northern and
Eastern Europe (editor)

THE
COMPLETE
PLAYS

ANTON
CHEKHOV

TRANSLATED, EDITED, AND ANNOTATED BY

Laurence Senelick

W. W. NORTON & COMPANY

NEW YORK | LONDON

Copyright © 2006 by Laurence Senelick

For information about permission to reproduce selections from this book, write to Permissions,
W. W. Norton & Company, Inc., 500 Fifth Avenue, New York, NY 10110

Manufacturing by RR Donnelley, Harrisonburg
Book design by JAM Design
Production manager: Devon Zahn

Library of Congress Cataloging-in-Publication Data

Chekhov, Anton Pavlovich, 1860–1904.
[Plays. English]
The complete plays / Anton Chekhov; translated, edited, and annotated by Laurence Senelick.—
1st ed.
p. cm.
ISBN 0-393-04885-3 (hardcover)
1. Chekhov, Anton Pavlovich, 1860–1904—Translations into English. I. Senelick, Laurence.
II. Title.
PG3456.A19 2006
891.72'3—dc22   2005024362

ISBN 978-0-393-33069-4 pbk.

W. W. Norton & Company, Inc.
500 Fifth Avenue, New York, N.Y. 10110
www.wwnorton.com

W. W. Norton & Company Ltd.
Castle House, 75/76 Wells Street, London W1T 3QT

2 3 4 5 6 7 8 9 0

These translations are dedicated to the directors, designers, casts, and crews of all the productions of their earlier versions, who, from 1967 to the present, have demonstrated that fidelity to an author and stageworthiness are not incompatible qualities.

CONTENTS

PREFACE

*C*omplete is a weasel word. No sooner does a complete edition of any-thing appear than it is trumped by new discoveries. However, if one may mod-ify an absolute, this edition is the most "complete" collection of Anton Chekhov's plays in English. It contains all the plays performed during his life-time and posthumous works, performed or not. The former include the first version of *Ivanov*, never before translated into English, and the latter the farce by Ivan Shcheglov cobbled together from his collaboration with Chekhov, which has never been published in any language since 1911.

I have also included a number of dialogue pieces that Chekhov wrote for comic journals in the 1880s. Throughout that decade, Chekhov published stories which are virtually one-act plays or monologues and which he often called "scenelets" (*stsenki*). They were frequently adapted for the stage. The Moscow Art Theatre, for instance, played "Surgery," a dialogue between a country doctor and a sexton, as one of its recital pieces; and other stories, such as "The Witch" and "Robbers," were produced by the Art Theatre studios and amateur groups. I have chosen not to list these stories among his plays, because they were not typographically distinguishable as such, and because they are readily available in collections of Chekhov's prose. Similarly, I have not included the dialogue captions he wrote to cartoons, since these make little sense without their drawings. On the other hand, I have included every journalistic squib that he did write in the form of a play, including his paro-dies of popular drama.

This edition contains a number of features intended to improve the read-ers' understanding of Chekhov and his writing. First, the plays are heavily annotated, not merely to provide explanations of obscure names and terms, but also to point out jokes and subtleties in the original and to explain why I made the translation choices I did.

Next, I have included a choice of variants. Plays in pre-Revolutionary Rus-sia had to undergo two censorships, one for publication and one for performance. Occasionally, the censorship required deletions or rewrites of lines that, in the case of speeches about Arkadina's liaison with Trigorin in *The Seagull* or Trofimov's remarks about social conditions in *The Cherry Orchard*, were never restored in Chekhov's lifetime. In other cases, such as in *Ivanov*, Chekhov kept tinkering with the play for years, the final published version being quite distinct from the two different stage versions of 1887 and 1888. Often a Chekhov play will have been published in a magazine before it was produced, or, in rehearsal, the director required or suggested changes. For example, it was Konstantin Stanislavsky who insisted that Act Two of *The Cherry Orchard* end with a love scene between Anya and Trofimov. Here the variants may coincide more exactly with Chekhov's ideas than the final versions do. The fewest variants appear in *Uncle Vanya*, since it was a thoroughgoing revision of a pre-existing play, *The Wood Goblin*.

I have seen no reason to include variant inversions of words or minor changes that do not involve the sense and would be of interest chiefly to Slavic specialists who have access to the Russian originals. Those interested in the minutiae can consult the notes to Ronald Hingley's *Oxford Chekhov*. However, I have left in anything that can provide more information about a character or an insight into Chekhov's working methods. Except when the changes were made at the instigation of third parties, I do not recommend spatchcocking these remnants from Chekhov's waste-paper basket back into the plays. He was a shrewd editor of his own work, regularly deleting lines that were too explicit or repetitive or caricatural. In his case, less is definitely more.

Over the years, my translations of Chekhov have benefited greatly from the directors and companies who have staged them. My thanks go to all of them for enhancing my understanding. Of the many individuals, scholars, and theater people who deserve my gratitude, I shall name only Martin Andrucki, John Emigh, Donald Fanger, Spencer Golub, André Gregory, Michael Henry Heim, John Hellweg, Simon Karlinsky, Nils Åke Nilsson, Emma Polotskaya, Sasha Popov, Herta Schmid, Virginia Scott, Julie de Sherbinin, Anatoly Smeliansky, Jurij Striedter, Richard Trousdell, and the late Irene Worth.

ANTON CHEKHOV'S
BRIEF LIFE

*A*nton Pavlovich Chekhov was born in the town of Taganrog on the sea of Azov in southern Russia on January 17, 1860,[1] the third of six children, five boys and a girl. He might have been born a serf, as his father, Pavel Yegorovich, had, for the Emancipation came only in 1861; but his grandfather, a capable and energetic estate manager named Yegor Chekh, had prospered so well that in 1841 he had purchased his freedom along with his family's. Anton's mother, Yevgeniya Morozova, was the orphaned daughter of a cloth merchant and a subservient spouse to her despotic husband. To their children, she imparted a sensibility he lacked: Chekhov would later say, somewhat unfairly, that they inherited their talent from their father and their soul from their mother.[2]

The talent was displayed in church. Beyond running a small grocery store where his sons served long hours—"In my childhood, there was no childhood," Anton was later to report[3]—Pavel Chekhov had a taste for the outward trappings of religion. This was satisfied by unfailing observance of the rites of the Eastern Orthodox Church, daily family worship, and, especially, liturgical music. He enrolled his sons in a choir that he founded and conducted, and he aspired to be a pillar of the community.

Taganrog, its once-prosperous port now silted up and neglected, had a population that exceeded fifty thousand during Chekhov's boyhood. Its residents included wealthy Greek families, the ship-building interests, and a large number of Jews, Tatars, and Armenians. The town benefited from such public amenities of the tsarist civil administration as a pretentious-looking *gymnasium*, which the Chekhov boys attended, for one of Pavel's aims was to procure his children the level of education needed for entry into the professions. The upward mobility of the Chekhov generations is reflected in the character of Lopakhin in *The Cherry Orchard*, a self-made millionaire whose ancestors had been serfs on the estate he succeeds in purchasing. Chekhov's father, born a serf, had risen from *meshchanin*, or petty bourgeois,[4] to be the member of a merchant guild; and Chekhov himself, as a physician and writer, became influential on the national scene. He was a model of the *raznochinets*, or person of no settled rank, who began to dominate Russian society in the latter half of the nineteenth century.

To impede mass advancement, the tsarist curriculum laid great stress on Greek and Latin. One recalls the schoolmaster Kulygin in *Three Sisters* chuckling over the fate of a classmate who missed promotion because he could not master the *ut consecutivum* construction. Schoolmasters are usually portrayed by Chekhov as narrow-minded, obsequious, and unimaginative, no doubt the result of his own observations as he studied the classics, German, Russian, and, for a brief time, French. His best subject was Scripture. School days were lightened by the fairy tales of his nanny, the picaresque reminiscences of his mother, vacations spent on the estate his grandfather managed, fishing, swimming, and, later, visits to the theater.

As a boy, Chekhov was stage-struck. Although it was against school regulations, he and his classmates, often in false whiskers and dark glasses, frequented the gallery of the active and imposing Taganrog Playhouse. He was also the star performer in domestic theatricals, playing comic roles such as the Mayor in *The Inspector* and the scrivener Chuprun in the Ukrainian folk opera *The Military Magician*. While still at school, he wrote a drama called *Without Patrimony* and a vaudeville (a farce with songs) called *The Hen Has Good Reason to Cluck*. Later, while a medical student, he tried to revise them, even as he completed another farce, *The Cleanshaven Secretary with the Pistol*, which his younger brother Mikhail recalls as being very funny. Never submitted to the government censorship office, which passed plays or forbade them from performance, it is now lost.

By 1876 Pavel Chekhov had so mismanaged his business that, fearing imprisonment for debt, he stole off to the next town, where he took the train to Moscow. There his two elder sons, Aleksandr and Nikolay, were pursuing their studies. He had already stopped paying his dues to the merchant guild and had reverted to the status of *meshchanin*. Whether Anton suffered a psychic trauma at this loss of caste, as had the young Henrik Ibsen when *his* father went bankrupt, is matter for speculation. Certainly, the repercussions felt at the sale of the home left their trace on many of his plays, including *Platonov* and *The Cherry Orchard*. Dispossessed of home and furniture, his mother and the three youngest children also departed for Moscow, abandoning Anton in a house now owned by a friend of his father's. He had to support himself by tutoring during the three years before he graduated. He did not rejoin his family until Easter 1877, his fare paid by his university-student brother Aleksandr. This first visit to Moscow and its theaters set standards by which he henceforth judged the quality of life in the provinces. Suddenly, Taganrog began to look provincial.

Just before Anton Chekhov left Taganrog for good, a public library opened. This enabled him to read classics such as *Don Quixote* and *Hamlet*, a work he was to cite recurrently, and, like any Victorian schoolboy, *Uncle Tom's Cabin* and the adventure stories of Thomas Mayne Reid. Heavier reading included philosophic works that enjoyed a high reputation at the time, such as Thomas Henry Buckle's positivist and skeptical survey of European culture, *The History of Civilization in England.* Later in life, Chekhov took a wry view of this omnivorous autodidacticism, and had the clumsy bookkeeper Yepikhodov in *The Cherry Orchard* allude to Buckle's works as a token of self-improvement.

It was at this time that Chekhov began writing prose, sending comic pieces to Aleksandr in Moscow in the hope that they would be accepted by the numerous comic journals that had sprung up in the capitals. He made friends with actors, hung around backstage, and learned how to make up his face. Two of his school fellows did enter the profession: Aleksandr Vishnevsky, who would become a charter member of the Moscow Art Theatre, and Nikolay Solovtsov, who was to create the title role in *The Bear.*

In 1879 Chekhov moved to Moscow to enter the medical school at the university, funded by a scholarship from the Taganrog municipal authorities. He arrived to find himself the head of the family, which was still in dire straits and living in a cramped basement flat in a disreputable slum. His father, now a humble clerk in a suburban warehouse, boarded at his office; Aleksandr, a journalist, and Nikolay, a painter, led alcoholic and bohemian lives; his three younger siblings, Ivan, Mariya, and Mikhail, still had to complete their educations. Lodging at home, Chekhov was compelled to carve out a career as a journalist at the same time that he was taking the rigorous five-year course in medicine.

At first, he wrote primarily for humor magazines, contributing anecdotes and extended jokes, sometimes as captions to drawings by Nikolay and others; these brought in a niggardly ten to twelve kopeks a line. Gradually, he diversified into parodies, short stories, and serials, including a murder mystery, *The Shooting Party,* and a romance that proved so popular it was filmed several times in the days of silent cinema (*Futile Victory*). He was a reporter at the trial of the CEOs of a failed bank. He became a close friend of Nikolay Leykin, editor of the periodical *Splinters of Petersburg Life,* to which he was a regular contributor from 1883. He conducted a theatrical gossip column, which won him entry to all the greenrooms and side-scenes in Moscow. And he partook of his brothers' bohemianism. He wrote to an old school chum in a letter his Soviet editors provided only in expurgated form: "I was on a spree all last night and, 'cept for a 3-ruble drunk didn't . . . or catch . . . I'm just about to go on a spree again."[5] His writing at this time was published under a variety of pseudonyms, the best known being Antosha Chekhonte, from a schoolboy nickname. He also found time to revise *Without Patrimony*, which he seriously hoped would be staged; turned down by the leading actress to whom he submitted it, it was burnt by its author. Chekhov always took failure in the theater hard. However, two variant copies survived, minus the title page. It was first published in 1923. It has since become known as *Platonov*, after the central character.

The year 1884 was critical in Chekhov's life. At the age of twenty-four, he set up as a general practitioner and, influenced by reading the English social critic Herbert Spencer, began research on a history of medicine in Russia. That December he had bouts of spitting blood, which his medical expertise might have led him to diagnose as a symptom of pulmonary tuberculosis. No outside observer would have suspected this active, well-built, handsome young man was suffering from a mortal illness. Only in his last years did he become a semi-invalid, and, until that time, he kept up the pretence that his symptoms were not fatal. This subterfuge was not carried on simply to allay his family's anxieties. He wilfully strove to ignore the forecast of his own mortality and regularly discounted the gravity of his condition.

Eighteen eighty-four also saw the publication of his first collection of stories, pointedly entitled *Fairy Tales of Melpomene*: the muse of tragedy compressed into pithy anecdotes of the life of actors. Chekhov had found more prestigious and better-paying periodicals to take his stories and was now an expert on Moscow life.

He had an opportunity to amplify his subject matter when he and his family began to spend summers in the country, first with his brother Ivan, master of a village school, and then in a cottage on the estate of the Kiselyov family. It was during those summers that Chekhov gained first-hand knowledge of the manor house setting he employed in many of his plays, and made the acquaintance of the officers of a battery, who turn up as characters in *Three Sisters*. Chekhov's artistic horizons also expanded, for the Kiselyovs, intimates of the composer Chaikovsky, were devoted to classical music. Another summer visitor to become a lifelong friend was the painter Isaak Levitan, whose impressionistic landscapes are graphic counterparts of Chekhov's descriptions.

The following year Chekhov's literary career took a conspicuous upward turn. On a visit to St. Petersburg, Chekhov had been embarrassed by the acclaim that greeted him, because he recognized that much of his output had been hasty and unrevised. "If I had known that that was how they were reading me," he wrote his brother Aleksandr, on January 4, 1886, "I would not have written like a hack." Such stories as "Grief" and "The Huntsman," both from 1885, had already displayed a new care in technique and seriousness in subject matter. Shortly thereafter, he received a letter from Dmitry Grigorovich, the *doyen* of Russian critics, singling him out as the most promising writer of his time and urging him to take his talent more seriously. Although Antosha Chekhonte continued to appear in print for a few more years, Anton Chekhov made his first bow in the powerful Petersburg newspaper *New Times*. Its editor, Aleksey Suvorin, had risen from peasant origins to become a tycoon and a leading influence-monger in the conservative political camp. He and Chekhov were to be closely allied, although their friendship would later founder when Suvorin promoted the anti-Semitic line during the Dreyfus affair.

During the years when he was winning recognition as a writer of short stories, Chekhov made two further attempts to write for the theater. With the first, *Along the Highway* (1885), he came up against the obstacle of the censor, who banned it on the grounds that it was a "gloomy, squalid play." The other piece, the monologue *The Evils of Tobacco*, was, like many of his early "dramatic études," written with a specific actor in mind. It first appeared in 1886 in a St. Petersburg newspaper, and Chekhov kept revising it, publishing the final version, virtually a new work, in his collected writings of 1903. Farces he sketched out with collaborators never got beyond the planning stage.

Between 1886 and 1887, Chekhov published one hundred and sixty-six titles while practicing medicine. Such fecundity boosted his fame but wore him out. His health and his temper both began to fray. Profiting from an advance from Suvorin, Chekhov returned to southern Russia in 1887, a trip that produced remarkable work. The stories that ensued signaled his emergence as a leading writer of serious fiction. The novella "The Steppe" (1888) was published in *The Northern Herald*, one of the so-called fat, or weighty, journals that had introduced the writing of Ivan Turgenev and Lev Tolstoy and served as organs of public opinion. That same year, Chekhov was awarded the Pushkin Prize for Literature by the Imperial Academy of Science for his collection *In the Gloaming*. One of the most enthusiastic instigators of this honor had been the writer Vladimir Nemirovich-Danchenko, who would later play an important role in establishing Chekhov's reputation as a dramatist.

The Northern Herald was liberal in its politics, its editor, Aleksey Pleshcheev, a former prisoner in Siberia with Dostoevsky. Typically, Chekhov was able to be friendly with Pleshcheev and Suvorin at the same time, and he continued to contribute to *New Times*. His reluctance to be identified with any one faction exposed him to much acrimonious criticism from members of both camps, and especially from the progressive left. The writer Katherine Mansfield pointed out that the "problem" in literature is an invention of the nineteenth century. One of the legacies of Russian "civic criticism" of the 1840s was the notion that a writer had an obligation to engage with social problems and offer solutions, making his works an uplifting instrument of enlightenment. This usually meant espousing a doctrinaire political platform. Chekhov, perhaps fortified by his medical training, treasured his objectivity and steadfastly refrained from taking sides, even when his sympathies were easy to ascertain. "God keep us from generalizations," he wrote. "There are a great many opinions in this world and a good half of them are professed by people who have never had any problems."

Between 1886 and 1890, his letters discuss his objectivity and his "monthly change" of opinions, which readers preferred to see as the views of his leading characters. To his brother Aleksandr he insisted on May 10, 1886, that in writing no undue emphasis be placed on political, social, or economic questions. In another letter to Suvorin, on October 27, 1888, Chekhov wrote that the author must be an observer, posing questions but not supplying the answers. It is the reader who brings subjectivity to bear. Not that an author should be aloof, but his own involvement in a problem should be invisible to the reader, he explained to Suvorin, on April 1, 1890:

> You reproach me for my objectivity, calling it indifference to good and evil, absence of ideals and ideas, etc. You want me to say, when I depict horse thieves: horse-stealing is a bad thing. But that's been known for a long time now, without my help, hasn't it? Let juries pass verdicts on horse thieves; as for me, my work is only to show them as they are.

The year before "The Steppe" appeared, Chekhov had at last had a play produced; the manager Fyodor Korsh had commissioned *Ivanov* and staged it at his Moscow theater on November 19, 1887. It was a decided if controversial success. As Chekhov wrote to Aleksandr, "Theater buffs say they've never seen so much ferment, so much unanimous applause *cum* hissing, and never ever heard so many arguments as they saw and heard at my play" (November 20, 1887). It was taken up by the Alexandra Theatre, the Imperial dramatic playhouse in St. Petersburg, and produced there on January 31,

1889, after much hectic rewriting in an attempt to make the playwright's intentions clearer and to take into account the strengths and weaknesses of the new cast.

The theme of a protagonist fettered by a sick wife and want of money was a distorted reflection of Chekhov's own situation. His family obligations kept his nose to the grindstone, and he felt guilty whenever he traveled away. Yet the success of *Ivanov* and the curtain-raisers *The Bear* and *The Proposal* (1888–1889) had put Chekhov at a premium as a dramatist. Urged on by Korsh and others, and unable to make headway on a full-length novel, Chekhov hoped to collaborate with Suvorin on a new comedy; when the publisher begged off, Chekhov completed it himself as *The Wood Goblin* (1889). It was promptly turned down by the state-subsidized theaters of Petersburg and Moscow, which regarded it as more a dramatized story than an actable play. They recommended that Chekhov give up writing for the stage. A production at a private theater in Moscow was received with apathy bordering on contempt, and may have helped provide the impetus for a decision Chekhov would soon make to go to Sakhalin, ten thousand miles away. Throughout 1888 and 1889, Chekhov also tended to his brother Nikolay, who was dying of tuberculosis; after Nikolay's death, Chekhov experienced both guilt and a foreboding of his own mortality, which brought on the mood conveyed in "A Dismal Story" (1889), in which a professor of medicine contemplates his frustrated ideals and imminent demise. The author's mood was at its lowest ebb.

Secure in his reputation and income at the age of thirty, Chekhov sought to cast off this despondency by traveling to Sakhalin, the Russian Devil's Island, in 1890; the eighty-one-day journey was arduous, for the Trans-Siberian railway had not yet been built. The enterprise may have been inspired by a Tolstoyan wish to practice altruism or it may have been an ambitious project to write a magnum opus of "medical geography." In any case, the ensuing documentary study of the penal colony was a model of socially engaged field research, and may have led to prison reforms. On a more personal level, it intensified a new strain of pessimism in Chekhov's work, for, despite his disclaimers, he began to be bothered by his lack of outlook or mission.

No sooner had Chekhov returned, via Hong Kong, Singapore, and Ceylon, than he made his first excursion to Western Europe, accompanying Suvorin. His initial enthusiasm for Vienna, Venice, and Naples began to wane by the time he visited Nice, Monte Carlo, and Paris, and he was eager to get back to work. In Russia, with the writing routines resumed, the sense of enslavement returned. This mood was modulated by a flirtation with a family friend, Lidiya (Lika) Mizinova, who invested more significance in the relationship than he did. Her subsequent affair and illegitimate child with the married writer Ignaty Potapenko would be exploited by Chekhov in *The Seagull* (although he hoped his own circle would not spot the similarities).

The steady flow of royalties enabled Chekhov in 1891 to buy a farmstead at Melikhovo, some fifty miles south of Moscow, where he settled his parents and siblings. There he set about "to squeeze the last drop of slave out of his system," (as he wrote to Suvorin on January 7, 1889); "a modern Cincinnatus," he planted a cherry orchard, installed a flush toilet, and became a lavish host. This rustication had a beneficial effect on both his literary work and his humanitarianism. He threw himself into schemes for building roads and schools and opened a clinic to provide free medical treatment, improving peasants' minds and bodies. During the cholera epidemic of 1892–1893, he served as an overworked member of the sanitary commission and head of the famine relief board. These experiences found their way into the activities of Dr. Astrov in *Uncle Vanya*.

During this period, Chekhov composed masterful stories that explored the dead ends of life: "The Duel" (1891), "Ward No. 6" (1892), "The Black Monk," "A Woman's Kingdom," "The Student" (all 1894), "Three Years" (1895), "The House with the Mansard," "My Life" (both 1896), and "Peasants" (1897), carefully wrought prose pieces of great psychological subtlety. They recurrently dwell on the illusions indispensable to making life bearable, the often frustrated attempts at contact with one's fellow man, the inexorable pull of inertia preventing people from realizing their potential for honesty and happiness. Chekhov's attitude is clinically critical, but always with a keen eye for the sympathetic details that lead the reader to a deeper understanding.

For several years, Chekhov abandoned the theater, except for some monologues and one-act farces. Not until January 1894 did he announce that he had again begun a play, only to deny it a year later, in a letter to V. V. Bilibin: "I am not writing a play and, altogether, I have no inclination to write any. I am grown old, and I have lost my burning ardor. I should like to write a novel 100 miles long" (January 18, 1895). Nine months after that he was to break the news to Suvorin, "Can you imagine, I am writing a play which I shall probably not finish before the end of November. I am writing it not without pleasure, though I swear horribly at the conventions of the stage. A comedy, three women's parts, six men's, four acts, a landscape (view of a lake); a great deal of conversation about literature, little action, five tons of love" (October 21, 1895).

The comedy was *The Seagull*, which had a rocky opening night at St.

Petersburg's Alexandra Theatre in 1896: the actors misunderstood it, the audience misapprehended it. Despite protestations of unconcern to Suvorin ("I dosed myself with castor oil, took a cold bath—and now I would not even mind writing another play"; October 22, 1896), Chekhov fled to Melikhovo, where he renounced playwriting. Although *The Seagull* grew in public favor in subsequent performances, Chekhov disliked submitting his work to the judgment of literary cliques and claques. Yet barely one year after the event, a new drama from his hand appeared in the 1897 collection of his plays: *Uncle Vanya*, a reworking of the earlier *The Wood Goblin*. It was widely performed in provincial capitals, where the residents found it reflected their dreary lives.

It was during this year that Chekhov's illness was definitively diagnosed as tuberculosis, and he was compelled to leave Melikhovo for a milder climate. For the rest of his life, he shuttled between Yalta on the Black Sea and various French and German spas, with occasional business trips to Moscow. He had a house constructed in the Yalta suburb of Autka. To pay for it, and to cover the new expenses his multiple residences created, Chekhov sold all he had written before 1899, excepting the plays, to the publisher Marks for the flat fee of 75,000 rubles (in current purchasing power, approximately $81,000), along with the reprint rights to any future stories. It was an improvident move. Marks had had no idea of the size of Chekhov's output and had underpaid. The error in calculation may have induced Chekhov to return to playwriting as a more lucrative activity.

The remainder of his dramatic career was bound up with the fortunes of the Moscow Art Theatre, founded in 1897 by his friend Nemirovich-Danchenko and the wealthy dilettante K. S. Alekseev, who acted under the name Konstantin Stanislavsky. Chekhov was one of the original shareholders in the enterprise. He admired his friends' announced program of ensemble playing, their serious attitude to art, and a repertory of high literary quality. At the opening production, Aleksey Tolstoy's blank-verse historical drama *Tsar Feodor Ioannovich*, his eye was caught by Olga Knipper, the young actress who played the tsarina. With only slight misgivings Chekhov allowed the Art Theatre to revive *The Seagull* at the close of its first season. Stanislavsky, as co-director, had greater misgivings; he did not understand the play. But a heavily atmospheric production won over the audience, and the play was a resounding success. The Moscow Art Theatre adopted an art-nouveau seagull as its insignia and henceforth regarded Chekhov as its house dramatist. When the Imperial Maly Theatre insisted on revisions to *Uncle Vanya*, which had been playing throughout the provinces for years, Chekhov withdrew the play from them and allowed the Art Theatre to stage its Moscow premiere. *Three Sisters* (1901) was written with Art Theatre actors in mind.

Chekhov's chronic reaction to the production of his plays was revulsion, and so two months after the opening of *Three Sisters*, he was declaring, to Olga Knipper, "I will never write for the theater again. One can write for the theater in Germany, in Sweden, even in Spain, but not in Russia, where dramatists get no respect, are kicked by hooves and forgiven neither success nor failure" (March 1, 1901). Nevertheless, he soon was deep into *The Cherry Orchard* (1904), tailoring the roles to specific Moscow Art players. Each of these productions won Chekhov greater fame as a playwright, even when he himself disagreed with the chosen interpretation of the Art Theatre.

Chekhov languished in Yalta, which he called his "warm Siberia," feeling that he had been shunted to an outpost for the moribund. At the age of forty, in 1900, to the great surprise of his friends and the temporary dismay of his sister Mariya, who had always been his housekeeper, he married the Art Theatre actress Olga Knipper. Chekhov's liaisons with women had been numerous, ranging from a brief engagement in 1886 to Dunya Efros, a Jewish woman who refused to convert to Orthodoxy, to a one-night stand with a Japanese prostitute and a fling with the flamboyant actress Lidiya Yavorskaya. He exercised an involuntary fascination over a certain type of ambitious bluestocking and his fan mail from female admirers was considerable. Some women friends, such as Lidiya Avilova, projected their desires on to an ordinary relationship, casting themselves as Chekhov's Egeria. Whenever the affair became too demanding or the woman too clinging, Chekhov would use irony and playful humor to disengage himself. In his writings, marriage is usually portrayed as a snare and a delusion that mires his characters in spirit-sapping vulgarity. His relationship with Knipper was both high-spirited—she was his "kitten," his "horsie," his "lambkin," his "darling crocodile"—and conveniently remote, for she had to spend much of her time in Moscow, while he convalesced at his villa in Yalta. On those terms, the marriage was a success.

Chekhov's villa, today a museum, became a Mecca for young writers, importunate fans, touring acting companies, and plain freeloaders. Such pilgrimages, though well meant, were not conducive to Chekhov's peace of mind or body, and his health continued to deteriorate. Despite this rapid decline, and the disappointment of a miscarriage Olga suffered in 1902,[6] a deeply lyrical tone suffuses his last writings. His late stories, "The Darling" and "Lady with Lapdog" (both 1899) and "The Bishop" (1902) and "Betrothed" (1903), offer more acceptance of the cyclical nature of life. They also reveal an almost musical attention to the structure and sounds of words, a quality to be remarked as well in the last "comedy," *The Cherry Orchard.*

In December 1903, a failing Chekhov came to Moscow to attend rehearsals of *The Cherry Orchard.* The opening night, January 17, 1904, concided with his nameday and the twenty-fifth anniversary of the commencement of his literary activity. Emaciated, hunched over, gravely ill, he did not show up until the second act and sat through the third, after which, to his great bemusement, a ceremony to honor him took place.

In June 1904 the Berlin doctors Chekhov consulted ordered him to Baden-weiler, a health resort in the Black Forest. There the forty-four-year-old writer died on July 2. Shortly before his death, the doctor recommended putting an ice pack on his heart. "You don't put ice on an empty heart," Chekhov protested. When they suggested a glass of champagne, his last words came, "It's been a long time since I've drunk champagne." Unconsciously, he echoed the line of the old nurse Marina in *Uncle Vanya*: "It's a long time since I've had noodles."

Chekhov's obsequies were a comedy of errors he might have appreciated. The railway carriage bearing his body to St. Petersburg was stencilled with the label "Fresh Oysters," and, at the Novodevichy cemetery in Moscow, the bystanders spent more time ogling the controversial author Maksim Gorky and the bass singer Fyodor Shalyapin than in mourning the deceased.[7] Finally, and inadvertently, Chekhov's cortège became entangled with that of General Keller, a military hero who had been shipped home from the Far East. Chekhov's friends were startled to hear an army band accompanying the remains of a man who had always been chary of the grand gesture.

NOTES

1 The date given by Chekhov himself, although he would appear to have been born on the 16th. The 17th was his "saint's day" or "name day," the day of St. Anthony after whom he was christened. Dates given here are "Old Style," in accord with the Julian calendar, twelve days behind the Gregorian.

2 M. P. Chekhov, *Vokrug Chekhova* (Moscow: Moskovsky rabochy, 1980), p. 44.

3 Quoted in Ernest Simmons, *Chekhov, A Biography* (Boston: Little, Brown, 1962), p. 6.

4 Peter the Great had established a table of ranks that stratified social status into civil, military, naval, and ecclesiastical hierarchies. In the civil hierarchy, *meshchanin* (literally, townsman) came just above peasant. In *The Seagull*, Treplyov complains that his father had been classified as a *meshchanin* of Kiev, even though he was a famous actor, and the same rank appears on his own passport. He finds it particularly galling since the term had come to imply philistinism.

5 Letter to Dmitry Savelyov, January (?) 1884. All translated quotations from Chekhov's writings and letters are based on *Polnoe sobranie sochineny i pisem*, the complete collected works and letters

in thirty volumes published in Moscow in 1974–1983. On the cuts made by Soviet editors, see A. Chudakov, "'Neprilichnye slova' i oblik klassika. O kupyurakh v izdaniya pisem Chekhova," *Literaturnoe obozrenie* (November 1991): 54–56.

6 Olga's miscarriage is described in a letter of hers to Chekhov (March 31, 1902). However, a controversy has arisen among scholars as to whether it was a miscarriage, an ectopic pregnancy, or something else; moreover, the paternity of the child has been questioned. See the articles of Hugh McLean and Donald Rayfield in *The Bulletin of the North American Chekhov Society* XI, 1 (Summer 2003), and letters in subsequent issues.

7 Maksim Gorky, *Literary Portraits*, trans. Ivy Litvinov (Moscow: Foreign Languages Publishing House, n.d.), pp. 158–159.

CHRONOLOGY OF CHEKHOV'S LIFE

1860. *January 17* (Old Style) / *29* (New Style). Anton Pavlovich Chekhov, third son of the shopkeeper and choirmaster Pavel Yegorovich Chekhov and Yevgeniya Yakovlevna Morozova, is born in Taganrog, a port of the Sea of Azov. He is the grandson of a serf who managed to purchase his liberation.

Aleksandr Ostrovsky's play *Thunderstorm* wins an award from the Academy of Sciences.

1861. Tsar Alexander II abolishes serfdom, but without providing enough land for the emancipated serfs.

1862. Ivan Turgenev's *Fathers and Sons* is published.
Academic freedom restored to Russian universities.

1863. Flogging with birch rods abolished by law.
Konstantin Stanislavsky is born, as Konstantin Alekseev, son of a wealthy textile manufacturer.

Nikolay Chernyshevsky's *What Is to Be Done?*, the gospel of nihilism, is written in prison.

1864. *Zemstvos*, self-governing rural councils, are created.

1865. Lev Tolstoy begins to publish *War and Peace*.

1866. An attempted assassination of the tsar prompts a wave of political reaction, especially in education and the press. Chekhov, as a student, will suffer from the new emphasis on Greek, Latin, and grammar.

Fyodor Dostoevsky's *Crime and Punishment* published.

1867–1879. Chekhov's primary and secondary education in Taganrog in very rigorous schools. He gives lessons, frequents the theater, edits a student newspaper, writes plays now lost.

1868. Dostoevsky's *The Idiot* is published serially.

1871. Dostoevsky's *The Devils* is published.

1872. Special court set up to try treason cases.

1873. Only 227 factories in all of Russia.
Nikolay Nekrasov begins to publish his populist poem *Who Can Be Happy in Russia?*

1874. Trade unions made illegal.

All males over twenty-one, regardless of class, now liable for conscription into the armed forces.

1875. Chekhov writes comic journal *The Stutterer* to amuse his brothers in Moscow.

Tolstoy begins to publish *Anna Karenina*.

1876. Chekhov's father goes bankrupt and moves the family to Moscow, leaving Anton in Taganrog.

1877. Chekhov visits Moscow where he finds his family in penury.

The Russians fight the Turks in the Balkans, ostensibly to free the Christian Slavs from Moslem oppression. An armistice, signed in 1878, greatly reduces the Turkish presence in the Balkans, but the Congress of Berlin humiliates Russia by reducing its spoils to part of Bessarabia.

1878. Chekhov writes plays now lost: *Without Patrimony*, *He Met His Match*, and *The Hen Has Good Reason to Cluck*.

Public outcries against the government and acts of terrorism increase.

1879. Chekhov finishes high school and in June moves to Moscow, where he enrolls in the medical school of the University of Moscow on a scholarship. Starts to write cartoon captions for the humor magazine *Alarm Clock*.

Dostoevsky begins to publish *The Brothers Karamazov*.

1880. *March*. Chekhov's first short story, "Letter of a Landowner to His Learned Neighbor Dr. Friedrich," is published in the comic journal *The Dragon-fly*.

1880–1887. Chekhov writes for Moscow and St. Petersburg comic journals under pen names including Antosha Chekhonte, Doctor Who's Lost His Patients, Man without a Spleen, and My Brother's Brother.

1881. Chekhov writes play later known as *Platonov* (not published until 1923).

Tsar Alexander II is assassinated; his son, Alexander III, initiates a reign of political repression and social stagnation.

Dostoevsky dies.

1882. *Platonov* is turned down by the Maly Theatre. Chekhov publishes "Late-blooming Flowers."

The imperial monopoly on theater in Moscow and St. Petersburg is abolished. Several private theaters are opened.

Troops are used to suppress student uprisings at the Universities of St. Petersburg and Kazan.

1883.   Chekhov publishes "Fat and Lean," "At Sea," and "Christmas Eve."

1884.   Chekhov finishes his medical studies and starts general practice in Chikino, outside Moscow. Publishes his first collection of stories, *Fairy Tales of Melpomene*, under the name Antosha Chekhonte. His only attempt at a novel, *The Shooting Party*, serialized in *Daily News*. Writes one-act play, *Along the High Road*, which is censored and not published until 1914.

December. Symptoms of Chekhov's tuberculosis diagnosed.

1885.   Chekhov's first trip to St. Petersburg. Meets the publisher Aleksey Suvorin and the painter Isaak Levitan, who become close friends. Romances with Dunya Efros and Nataliya Golden. Publishes "The Huntsman," "Sergeant Prishibeev," and "Grief."

1886.   Chekhov begins writing for Suvorin's conservative newspaper *New Times*. Puts out a second collection of stories, *Motley Tales*, signed both An. P. Chekhov and Antosha Chekhonte.

The eminent Russian writer Dmitry Grigorovich encourages him to pursue his literary career in a more serious fashion. Publishes "The Witch," "The Chorus Girl," "On the Road," and the first version of the comic monologue *The Evils of Tobacco*.

1887.   Chekhov publishes third collection of short stories, *In the Gloaming*, and fourth collection, *Innocent Conversations*, which include "Enemies," "Typhus," "The Siren," and "Kashtanka." Also writes one-act *Swan Song*.

November 19. Ivanov, a full-length play, performed at Korsh's Theatre, Moscow. It receives a mixed press.

1888.   First serious long story, "The Steppe," published in St. Petersburg magazine *Northern Herald*, initiating a new care taken with his writing. One-act farces *The Bear* and *The Proposal* produced to acclaim. *In the Gloaming* wins the Pushkin Prize of the Academy of Sciences.

Student uprisings at the Universities of Moscow, Odessa, Kharkov, and Kazan are put down by the military. The government decrees that all Jews must live within the Pale of Settlement in Eastern Poland and the western provinces of Russia.

Tolstoy publishes his play of peasant life *The Power of Darkness*, but the censor will not allow it to be staged.

Maksim Gorky is arrested for subversion, and is henceforth under police surveillance.

1889. The Social Democratic Working-man's Party is founded.

"A Dismal Story," one of the first of Chekhov's mature stories, published in *Northern Herald*.

January 31. Premiere of the revised *Ivanov* at Alexandra Theatre, St. Petersburg.

October. Chekhov's play *The Wood Goblin* finished. Played at Abramova's Theatre in *December.* The play is poorly received by the critics; he is scolded for "blindly copying everyday life and paying no attention to the requirements of the stage."

1890. According to a letter to Sergey Dyagilev, Chekhov reworks *The Wood Goblin* into *Uncle Vanya*, which will not be published until 1897. Chekhov publishes collection *Glum People*, which includes "Thieves" and "Gusev." Writes one-act comedies, *The Involuntary Tragedian* and *The Wedding*.

April–October. Travels through Siberia to Sakhalin Island, where he visits prison camps and carries out a census. Sails in the Pacific and Indian Oceans.

1891. Six-week trip to Western Europe. Publication of the novella *The Duel* and "Peasant Women." Buys a small farmstead in Melikhovo.

1892. Chekhov settles in Melikhovo with his family.

Work begins on the Trans-Siberian Railway, to be completed in 1905.

Sergey Witte becomes Minister of Finance, and turns Russia into a modern industrial state, increasing industrialism, railways, and Western trade by 1899.

1892–1893. Severe famines in the grain-growing provinces in the south and along the Volga.

Chekhov acts as head of the district sanitary commission during the cholera epidemic, combats the famine, treats the poorest peasants for free.

Publishes eleven stories, including "My Wife," "The Grasshopper," "Ward No. 6," as well as the one-act farce *The Celebration*.

1893. Dalliance with Lika Mizinova, whom he decides not to marry, but who sees herself as a prototype for Nina in *The Seagull*. *The Island of Sakhalin* published serially. Publishes "An Anonymous Story" and "Big Volodya and Little Volodya."

1894. Second trip to Italy and to Paris. Health worsens. Publishes "The Student," "Rothschild's Fiddle," "The Head Gardener's Story," "The Literature Teacher," "The Black Monk," and "At a Country House."

Alexander III dies and is succeeded by his son, the conservative and vacillating Nicholas II.

1895.   *The Island of Sakhalin* published. Chekhov meets Lev Tolstoy at his estate Yasnaya Polyana.

Chekhov writes *The Seagull*, publishes "Three Years," "Ariadne," "His Wife," "Whitebrow," "Murder," and "Anna Round the Neck."

1896.   Chekhov sponsors the construction of a primary school in the village of Talezh. Serial publication of "My Life" and "The House with a Mansard."

October 17. The premiere of *The Seagull* at the Alexandra Theatre in St. Petersburg fails. Chekhov flees during the second act.

October 21. Relative success of the play at its second performance.

1896–1897.   Strikes of factory workers lead to a law limiting adult work to eleven and a half hours a day.

1897.   The first All-Russian Congress of Stage Workers meets in Moscow to argue questions of trade conditions and artistic principles.

Stanislavsky and Nemirovich-Danchenko found the Moscow Art Theatre.

Chekhov sponsors the construction of a primary school in the village of Novosyolky. Participates in the All-Russian census of the population. Father dies.

March–April. Hospitalized with first acute attack of pulmonary tuberculosis. Reads Maurice Maeterlinck.

September. Travels to France for medical treatment.

Uncle Vanya, Ivanov, The Seagull, and one-act plays published, as well as stories "Peasants," "The Savage," "At Home," and "In the Cart."

1898.   Thirteen thousand students at Moscow University go on strike to protest repressive moves on the part of the administration; orders are given to enlist them in the army.

May. Chekhov returns from abroad. Relations with Suvorin strained in connection with the Dreyfus trial.

September. Settles in Yalta after suffering a pulmonary hemorrhage. Publishes the stories "Calling on Friends," "Gooseberries," "About Love," "A Case History," and "Ionych."

December 17. The Seagull, staged by Stanislavsky, is revived with great success at the Moscow Art Theatre.

1899.   Theatres in Kiev, Kharkov, and Nizhny Novgorod play *Uncle Vanya.* Chekhov decides to turn it into a short novel, but does not. Offered to the Maly, *Uncle Vanya* is considered offensive to professors and is turned down.

Tolstoy's *Resurrection* and Gorky's *Foma Gordeev* published.

Chekhov attends a performance of *The Seagull* in Yalta. Sells all rights to his works to the publisher A. F. Marks for 75,000 rubles (in current purchasing power, approximately $81,000). Begins to edit his complete works. Awarded Order of St. Stanislav, second class, for work in education. Publishes "On Official Business," "Lady with Lapdog," "The Darling," and "The New Villa."

June. Sells his estate in Melikhovo. Has a house built in Yalta.

October 26. Premiere of *Uncle Vanya* at the Art Theatre.

1900. *January.* Elected to honorary membership in the Literary division of the Academy of Sciences. Publishes "In the Ravine" and "At Christmas."

April. The Art Theatre plays *Uncle Vanya* and *The Seagull* in Sevastopol, in the presence of the author.

August–December. Writes *Three Sisters.* Finishes the play in Nice.

1901. *January–February.* Trip to Italy.

January 31. Premiere of *Three Sisters* at the Moscow Art Theatre with considerable success.

May 25. Marries the actress Olga Knipper, who plays Masha.

The Marxist journal *Life*, which publishes Gorky, is banned. Gorky is expelled from Nizhny Novgorod.

1902. Chekhov publishes "The Bishop." Complete works published in eleven volumes. Awarded Griboedov Prize of Society of Dramatic Authors and Opera Composers for *Three Sisters.* Begins *The Cherry Orchard.*

March. Olga Knipper suffers miscarriage.

August. Resigns in protest from the Academy of Sciences when Gorky's election is nullified at the tsar's behest.

Gorky writes *The Lower Depths.*

1903. At a Congress in London, the Social Democratic Working-man's Party is taken over by the radical Bolshevist wing, led by Vladimir Lenin.

Second edition of Chekhov's complete works published in sixteen volumes.

Publishes his last story, "Betrothed," in the magazine *Everybody's.*

June. The censor rules that his plays cannot be performed in people's theaters, low-priced theater for the working class.

September. *The Cherry Orchard* is finished. Nemirovich-Danchenko and Stanislavsky are enthusiastic. Chekhov attends rehearsals.

An atrocious pogrom occurs in Kishinyov, with 47 dead and 2,000 families ruined.

1904. Chekhov's health deteriorates.

January 14 or 15. Attends a rehearsal of *The Cherry Orchard*.

January 17. Premiere at the Art Theatre, where a celebration in his honor is held.

Spring. A new, grave attack of tuberculosis.

April 2. First performance of *Orchard* in St. Petersburg a great success, greater than in Moscow, according to Nemirovich and Stanislavsky.

June 1. Publication of the play in a separate edition by Marks.

June 3. Departure for Germany with Olga Knipper.

July 2/15. Dies in Badenweiler.

July 9/22. Buried in Novo-devichy cemetery in Moscow.

The Mensheviks drive the Bolsheviks from the Central Committee of the Social Democratic Working-man's Party, but drop out the following year, leaving the field to the Bolsheviks.

The Russo-Japanese war breaks out.

1909. First performance of a Chekhov play in English: *The Seagull*, translated by George Calderon, at the Glasgow Repertory Theatre.

A NOTE ON THE
TRANSLATION

The texts on which these translations are based are those in A. P. Chekhov, *Polnoe sobranie sochineniy i pisem v tridtsati tomakh* [*Complete Works and Letters in 30 Volumes*], ed. N. F. Belchikov et al. (Moscow: Nauka, 1974–1984). The Russian texts of the plays were drawn from the latest versions published in Chekhov's lifetime and subject to his revision.

Chekhov had his doubts about the efficacy of translation and, after reading some Russian prose translated into French, concluded that transmission of Russian literature into another language was pointless. Later, when his own plays began to be translated, he lamented that purely Russian phenomena would have no meaning for foreign audiences. To offset these misgivings, the translator of Chekhov must be as sedulous in making choices as the author was in composing the original work.

From his earliest farces, Chekhov wrote plays with an eye to their being performed. He often had specific actors in mind, and, despite his discomfort with histrionic convention, he expected his dialogue to be recited from the stage. Therefore, translating his plays entails problems different from those encountered in translating his prose fiction. At first sight, the vocabulary and sentence structure seem straightforward enough. Under scrutiny, however, the seeming simplicity turns out to be illusory.

The literary psychoanalyst Gregory Zilboorg, initiating American readers into Russian drama in 1920, stated point blank that Chekhov was fundamentally untranslatable, more so even than Ostrovsky and Gorky. "Chekhov's plays lose their chief element in translation into whatever other language: the particular harmony and rhythm of the original. The student must bear in mind that studying Chekhov's drama in English he actually studies only some elements of them, the rest being lost in a foreign language."[1]

The "harmony and rhythm" so lost derive from a number of sources. First, Chekhov uses language to consolidate his major plays: recurrent phrases echo off one another, often for ironic effect. George Bernard Shaw was another playwright well aware that it was precisely this adhesive repetition of key words that knit a play together. He scolded his German translator:

The way in which you translate every word just as it comes and then forget it and translate it some other way when it begins (or should begin) to make the audience laugh, is enough to whiten the hair on an author's head. Have you ever read Shakespear's Much Ado About Nothing? In it a man calls a constable an ass, and throughout the rest of the play the constable can think of nothing but this insult and keeps on saying, "But forget not, masters, that I am an ass." Now if you translated Much Ado, you would make the man call the constable a Schaffkopf. On the next page he would be a Narr, then a Maul, then a Thier, and perhaps the very last time an Esel.[2]

This was such a salient principle for Shaw that he hammered at it the following month: "I tell you again and again most earnestly and seriously, that unless you repeat the words that I have repeated, you will throw away all the best stage effects and make the play unpopular with the actors. . . . Half the art of dialogue consists in the echoing of words—the tossing back & forwards of phrases from one to another like a cricket ball."[3]

What is true for Shaw is equally true for Chekhov. In Chekhov, a commonplace uttered in the first act may return to resonate with fresh significance. For example, in *Uncle Vanya*, Astrov complains that when people can't understand him, they call him "peculiar" (*stranny*); later, Yelena uses that very word to describe him, thereby revealing that she doesn't understand him. To translate it as "peculiar" in its first occurrence and "odd" in its second would be to lose Chekhov's thematic irony, the cement he employs to bind the play together. The same holds true for *chudak* (crackpot) and its derivatives. Similarly, in *Three Sisters*, the phrases *vsyo ravno* (it doesn't matter, it's all the same) and *nadoelo* (fed up, sick and tired) recur regularly, and in *The Cherry Orchard*, changes are rung on *neschastye* (unhappiness, misfortune, trouble). It is the translator's obligation to preserve these verbal leitmotivs as much as possible.

Next, lexical and etymological elements subliminally affect the atmosphere. In *Uncle Vanya*, words based on *dush*— (implying psyche and soul) and *dukh*— (implying breath and spirit) help create a sense of stifling and suffocation. In *The Cherry Orchard*, earthy terms such as *nedotyopa* (half-chopped) contribute to the theme of hewing the cherry trees. Literary allusions to the Russian classics (Aleksandr Pushkin, Mikhail Lermontov, Nikolay Gogol, Ivan Krylov, Aleksandr Ostrovsky) enrich the cultural context. For the educated Russians of Chekhov's time, they would have been immediately familiar.

However, the translator must be alert to what I call imbedded quotations, less obvious than the explicit citations from literature. In *The Seagull*, Treplyov refers to Pushkin's unfinished verse play *Rusalka* in regard to Nina, and later Nina says that both he and she have fallen into the *omut*. In this context, it might be translated as "whirlpool" or "maelstrom," but its use in *Vanya*, the suggestion that Yelena dive—plop!—into an *omut*, reveals that an alternative meaning is intended: a "millrace," precisely the body of water into which Pushkin's heroine threw herself to become a *rusalka* or water-nymph. Similarly, when Astrov remarks of Yelena, "*Ona prekrasna, spora net*," he is quoting Pushkin's version of *Snow White*, the "Tale of the Tsar's Dead Daughter and the Seven Warriors"; the evil tsarina turns to her mirror with the question whether she is really the fairest in the land and the mirror replies: "*Ty prekrasna, spora net*," "Fair art thou, no contest there; but the Tsar's daughter's still more fair . . ."

In his last plays, Chekhov is extremely careful in choosing his words. A French translator has pointed out that in *The Seagull*, Chekhov employed three separate words for *why*: *otchego, zachem,* and *pochemu*. I have been very careful to observe those choices, translating them by "how come," "what for," and "why." Hence, in this translation the famous opening line is not "Why do you always wear black," but "How come you always wear black?"—which distinguishes Medvedenko's way of asking a question from that of others.

Every character in Chekhov speaks in a particular cadence. Compare Pishchik's short asthmatic phrases with the run-on grandiloquence of Trofimov or with Anya's iambic meters. Although both Vershinin and Tusenbach spout speeches about the future, one can tell merely by the tone and phrasing which one is speaking. When Nina Zarechnaya starts picking up Arkadina's phrases, we are given insight into her character.

Third, and this is harder to pin down, the "specific gravity" of a statement may reside in its structure. Since Russian can reassemble the elements of a sentence to make a particular emphasis, English has to find a way of reproducing this. Mere literal translation, offering a direct statement, may conceal the subtle emphases of the original. To render Charlotta Ivanovna's "*Uzhasno poyut éti lyudi*" as "These people sing horribly" is to miss her idiosyncratic syntax and the course of her thought as a foreigner, which imply, "It's awful the way these people break into song at the drop of a hat" (although to spell that out explicitly would be to over-translate).

Finally, certain words and phrases which held a special meaning in Chekhov's time may require that an explanation be imbedded in the translation, particularly if it is meant to be performed. *Nado delo delat* should not be rendered literally as "It is necessary to do something" or even as the customary "We must work," because it has to convey the idea that it is an outdated and platitudinous slogan of liberalism. The quotations from Nekrasov's poems have to reflect the pseudo-progressivism of the person doing the quoting. Who is the unpronounceable Poprishchin referred to in two of the plays? Just what sort of food are the *raznye kabuli* that the Professor imposes on the Voinitsky household? (Spicy Central Asian stews, which account for his dyspepsia and offer a vivid contrast to the nanny's homely noodles.)

The same applies to jokes. Chekhov often imbeds *jeux de mots* and facetious phrasing as depth charges; the translator's first task is to be aware of them, and then to find a way of making them detonate properly. At the beginning of *Ivanov*, Count Shabelsky complains that Anna has no more musical ear than a *farshirovannaya ryba*. This is invariably rendered as "stuffed pike" or "stuffed trout," which misses the point. Shabelsky is always teasing Anna about her Jewish origin; the fish in question is therefore not a piece of taxidermy but *gefilte fish*.

These particularities of Chekhov come in addition to the usual problems experienced in translating from Russian: the passive constructions, such as *Tyazhelo mne* (literally, "it is heavy to me"); the distinction between verbs of imperfect and perfect action (the difference between *strelilsya* and *zastrelilsya*, Konstantin's having shot himself and having shot himself for good); and onomatopoeic sounds that are overlooked or scanted. The last lines of *Uncle Vanya*, the repeated *my otdokhnyom*, consist of soft, aspirated sounds, easily drawn out and wafted into the air. "We shall rest" (or worse, "we will rest"), with its terminal dental sound, cannot be manipulated by an actress in the same way.

"The shock of the new" in Chekhov's handling of dialogue contributed mightily to his reputation in his lifetime, but this aspect also tends to be lost or overlooked. As the Swedish scholar Nils Åke Nilsson pointed out, Chekhov is an unacknowledged precursor of the Futurists and their launching of a *zaumny* or transrational language. He cites as examples the phrase "You've Gavrila-ed it up enough" in *Ivanov*, the trom-tom-tom exchange in *Three Sisters*, and Gaev's billiard jargon, calling this a "new dramatic syntax."[4]

The American critic Stark Young, when he set out to translate *The Seagull* for the Lunts in 1938, singled out "those balances, repetitions for stage effect, repetitions for stage economy, theatrical combinations and devices, time-patterns, and so on, that are the fruits of much intention and technical craft, and that are almost totally absent from the translation."[5] Yet even he trembled before Chekhov's linguistic audacity: "Chekhov's dialogue is perhaps a trifle more colloquial than mine. Certainly it is more colloquial than I should ever dare to be; for in a translation any very marked colloquialism is always apt to hurt the economy of effect by raising questions as to what the original could have been to come out so patly as that" (p. xix).

Young took as an example Trigorin's remark that when he gets a whiff of heliotrope *skoree motayu na us*, "quickly I wrap it around my moustache." Any good Russian dictionary will tell you that this is a figure of speech meaning "I make a mental note of something." Perhaps, as Stark Young feared, it is as wrong to translate it literally as it might be to translate "he got my goat" literally into Russian. Nevertheless, to translate it as he does, "Quickly I make note of it" is to substitute the bland for the colorful. My own solution, bearing in mind first Chekhov's fascination with facial hair (every one of his major plays contains remarks about whiskers) and next that Trigorin is an avid fisherman, is "I instantly reel it in on my moustache." Trigorin's following phrase *Lovlyu v sebya i vas na kazhdoy fraze* Young renders awkwardly as "Every sentence, every word I say and you say, I lie in wait for it." However, it ought to continue the piscatorial imagery, since Chekhov may have had in the mind the biblical idiom "to fish in troubled waters," in Russian *lovit' rybu v mutnoy vode*. It helps to know that from his long boyhood experience as a chorister under his father's tutelage, Chekhov's mind was well-stocked with scriptural commonplaces. My solution goes "I'm angling in myself and you for every phrase."

Finally, I have not tried to pretend that Chekhov is anything other than Russian. Although I have converted weights and measures into Western equivalents, so that an audience can more easily gauge distances and density, I have left currency, beverages, and, in particular, names in their Russian forms. Modern readers and audiences rapidly adjust to patronymics, diminutives, and nicknames. If one is to turn Pavel into Paul and Yelena into Helen, then one must go the whole hog and refer to *Uncle Jack* instead of *Uncle Vanya* and, to be consistent, *Ivanov* as *Mr. Johnson*.

NOTES

1 Gregory Zilboorg, "A course in Russian drama," *The Drama* (November 1920): 69.

2 *Bernard Shaw's Letters to Siegfried Trebitsch*, ed. Samuel A. Weiss (Stanford: Stanford University Press, 1986), p. 30 (December 26, 1902). The words translate as "sheep's head," "fool," "muzzle," "beast," and "ass."

3 Ibid., January 15, 1903, p. 36.

4 Nils Åke Nilsson, "Two Chekhovs: Mayakovskiy on Chekhov's 'futurism,'" in Jean-Pierre Barricelli, ed., *Chekhov's Great Plays: A Critical Anthology* (New York: New York University Press, 1981), pp. 251–261.

5 Stark Young, "Translating *The Sea Gull*," in *The Sea Gull, A Drama in Four Acts*, translated from the Russian of Anton Chekhov by Stark Young (New York: Samuel French, 1950), pp. xii–xv.

GUIDE TO TRANSLITERATION
AND PRONUNCIATION

When a Russian name is a Cyrillic transliteration of a European name, I have used the European form—for example, Mühlbach, Sonnenstein, Tusenbach, Charlotta, Maupassant, Buckle.

Cyrillic	*System used in this book*	*Pronunciation*
Аа	a	*f*ather
Бб	b	*b*ank; (at the end of words) to*p*
Вв	v	*v*et; to*w*el; (at the end of words) dea*f*
Гг	g	*g*et; (at the end of words) brea*k*
Дд	d	*d*addy; (at the end of words) ve*t*
Еë	e, ye (when it begins a name)	m*e*t; m*i*tt; *y*eah
Ë	yo	b*or*der; *y*ore
Жж	zh	vi*s*ion; pu*sh*
Зз	z (except when it indicates a German *s*)	*z*eal
Ии	i	ch*ee*se; *i*f
Йй	i; y (at the end of names)	unstressed vowel
Кк	k	*k*ept
Лл	l	*l*og
Мм	m	*m*ama
Нн	n	*n*o
Оо	o	(stressed) *or*der; (unstressed) *a*rtistic
Пп	p	*p*age
Рр	r	*r*ake
Сс	s	mi*ss*
Тт	t	*t*en
Уу	u	sp*oo*n
Фф	f	*f*orm

Хх	kh (except when it indicates a German *ch*)	*h*ah; a*ch*
Цц	ts	i*ts*
Чч	ch	*ch*ief
Шш	sh	*sh*oe
Щщ	shch	fi*sh ch*owder
Ъъ	Omitted	No sound value
Ыы	y	ph*oo*ey
Ьь	Omitted	No sound value
Ээ	é	v*e*t; d*a*y
Юю	yu	*you*; s*ue*
Яя	ya	*ya*hoo

Combinations of vowels

-ай	ay	*eye*
-ый	y	*i*ts
-ий	y	*e*ven
-ия	iya	tri*age*
-ье	ye	*ye*ah
-ьи	yi	*yi*p

STRESSED SYLLABLES
OF THE NAMES IN THE PLAYS

Abrám	Andréevich	Babelmandébsky
Abrámovich	Andréevna	Baikál
Abrámovna	Andréy	Balabálkina
Abramsón	Andrúsha	Basmánny
Afanásevich	Andrúshenka	Bátyushkov
Akáky	Anfísa	Berdíchev
Aléko	Ánna	Berezhítsky
Aleksándr	Ánya	Bóbik
Aleksándrovich	Anyúta	Bolshóy
Aleksándrovna	Aplómbov	Borís
Alekséevich	Arínushka	Bortsóv
Alekséevskoe	Arísha	Bortsóvka
Alekséy	Arkádina	Búdkin
Aleútov	Ástrov	Bugróv
Altukhóv	Babakálkina	Chádin
Anastásy	Babákina	Charlótta

Chátsky	Gerásya	Kirpichyóv
Chebutýkin	Glagólyev	Kirsánovsky
Chekharmá	Glínka	Kocháne
Cheprákov	Gógol	Kokóshkina
Cheremshá	Grékova	Kólya
Chitá	Grendilévsky	Kolotílin
Chubukóv	Grigóry	Konstantín
Dárya	Grísha	Konstantínovich
Dásha	Grokhólsky	Korchágin
Dáshenka	Grúzdev	Korólkov
Dávid	Gúsev	Kóstya
Denís	Hánsen	Kosýkh
Derigánov	Ignátyevich	Kotélnikov
Dmítry	Ilyá	Kozoédov
Dobrolyúbov	Ilyích	Kózyrev
Dostoévsky	Irína	Krasnúshkina
Dúdkin	Iván	Krylóv
Dunyásha	Ivánov	Kubán
Dyádin	Ivánovich	Kulýgin
Dýmba	Ivánovka	Kúritsyn
Elizavetgrád	Ivánovna	Kuzmá
Fédenka	Izmáilov	Kuznetsóv
Fedótik	Izmáilovka	Lébedev
Fédya	Kanítelin	Ledentsóv
Ferapónt	Kardámonov	Lénochka
Fílka	Kárlovich	Lénsky
Fínberg	Kárp	Lentóvsky
Finíkov	Kashalótov	Leoníd
Finíkova	Kashkinázi	Lérmontov
Fírs	Kátya	Lezgínka
Fonvízin	Khamónyev	Líka
Fyódor	Kharlámov	Lomonósov
Fyódorovich	Kharlámpy	Lómov
Fyódorovna	Khárkov	Lopákhin
Gáev	Khírin	Luká
Gavríla	Khrápov	Lukích
Gavrílych	Khrushchóv	Lukínishna
Gavrúsha	Kíev	Lvóvich
Gerásim	Kiríllych	Lyónya

Lyóv	Murométs	Pável
Lyúba	Múshkino	Pávlovich
Lyubóv	Nastásya	Pávlovna
Lyubvín	Natáliya	Pávochka
Lyudmíla	Natásha	Pelagéya
Máikov	Nazárka	Pétrin
Mákar	Nazárovna	Petrúshka
Málitskoe	Nekrásov	Pétya
Mamashyóchkina	Nemétskaya	Pirogóv
Mánka	Nikíta	Pisaryóv
Marína	Nikítych	Platónov
Maríya	Nikodímovich	Platónovka
Márkel	Nikoláevich	Plátoshka
Márko	Nikolásha	Plésniki
Máshenka	Nikoláy	Polikárpov
Másha	Nikólka	Polína
Máshenka	Níl	Potápych
Matryóna	Nílovich	Poltáva
Matvéev	Nína	Pólya
Matvéevich	Nóvo-Dévichy	Popóva
Matvéich	Nóvo-Petróvskoe	Porfíry
Matvéy	Nyúkhin	Pravdolyubóv
Mazútov	Nyúnin	Protopópov
Medvedénko	Odéssa	Prózorov
Mérik	Olénin	Púshkin
Merchútkina	Olénina	Pýzhikov
Mikhaíl	Ólenka	Ragúlin
Mikhaílo	Ólga	Raísa
Mikhaílovich	Ólya	Ranévskaya
Mikhaílovna	Onégin	Rasplyúev
Mikíshkin	Orlóvsky	Répina
Mirónov	Ósip	Revunóv-Karaúlov
Mísha	Ostróvsky	Rossítsky
Míshenka	Ovsyánov	Rozhdéstvennoe
Molchánovka	Panteléich	Rýblovo
Moskóvsky	Pásha	Sabínin
Mozgovóy	Páshenka	Sadóvsky
Múehlbach	Patrónnikov	Samára
Muráshkin	Páva	Samovár

Sánichka	Sófya	Ványa
Sarátov	Sónechka	Varsonófev
Sárra	Sónya	Varvára
Sásha	Sórin	Várya
Sáshenka	Soúsov	Vasíl
Sáshurka	Spártakov	Vasílych
Sashúrochka	Spiridónovich	Vasíly
Sávishna	Sprút	Vasílyevich
Sávva	Stanisláv	Vasílyevna
Schrífter	Stepán	Vengeróvich
Semyón	Suvórin	Véra
Semyónovich	Súzdaltsev	Vershínin
Semyónovna	Svetlovídov	Víkhrin
Sénya	Svobódin	Vladímir
Serebryakóv	Talié	Vladímirovich
Sergéy	Tamára	Vlásin
Sergéevich	Tamárin	Vlásov
Sergéevna	Tarantúlov	Voinítsev
Seryózha	Tarnóvsky	Voinítseva
Seryózhenka	Tatyána	Voinítsevka
Seryózhka	Telégin	Voinítsky
Sevastópol	Telibéev	Vólga
Shabélsky	Téstov	Vólgin
Shamráev	Tíkhon	Volódya
Shcherbúk	Tolkachóv	Yaroshévich
Shekhtél	Tolstóy	Yaroslávl
Sherventsóv	Treplyóv	Yásha
Shimánsky	Trífon	Yáshnevo
Shipúchin	Trigórin	Yefímovna
Shipúnov	Trilétsky	Yéfim
Shúra	Trófim	Yefímushka
Shúrka	Trofímov	Yegór
Shúrochka	Tsytsykár	Yegórka
Simeónov-Píshchik	Túla	Yegórov
Skvortsóv	Turgénev	Yegórovna
Smirnóv	Túsenbach	Yegórushka
Solomónovich	Upryámov	Yeléna
Solyóny	Valentínovich	Yeléts
Sónnenstein	Válts	Yelizavetgrád

Yepikhódov	Zaimíshche	Zhílkovo
Yermoláy	Záitsev	Zína
Yevdokím	Zákhar	Zinaída
Yevgény	Zaréchnaya	Zínochka
Yevstignéev	Zárev	Zipunóv
Yevstignéy	Zarévsky	Zmeyúkina
Yúlechka	Zásyp	Znóikin
Yúlya	Zheltúkhin	Zyúzyushka
Yusnóvka	Zhigálov	

INTRODUCTION

$\mathscr{A}$nton Chekhov's plays occupy a unique place in the history of drama. They derived from no obvious forerunners and produced no successful imitators. Despite his obvious influence on any number of important playwrights, there is no school of Chekhovian playwriting. Yet somehow, within the space of a few years, Chekhov managed to bring together elements that created, to paraphrase Maksim Gorky, a new kind of drama, which heightened reality to the point at which it turned into a profoundly inspired symbol.

Chekhov himself approached the theater and playwriting with a deep distrust, a fear that the demands of the stage would coarsen or distort his carefully wrought perceptions. As a boy in Taganrog, he delighted in the melodramas and operettas performed at the local playhouse, but as a young journalist in Moscow in the 1880s he poured vials of scorn on what he saw to be the ingrained mediocrity of professional theater practitioners. According to his friend Ivan Bunin, he regarded most actors as "vulgarians, thoroughly steeped in vanity."[1] Still, his attraction to the theater persisted. The backstage world appeared in many of his stories, and, significantly, his first published collection was called *Fairy Tales of Melpomene* (1884), comic anecdotes dedicated to the Muse of Tragedy.

Chekhov's early plays, written with an eye to stage production, clearly display his sense of the conflict between the pedestrian demands of the theater and the need to express his own concerns dramatically. His farces are extremely stageworthy, but differ from the run of most curtain-raisers only in their shrewd observation of human foibles. Chekhov's discomfort with having to use traditional dramatic conventions is more apparent in the disjointed and contrived nature of *Ivanov* (1887; revised 1888) and *The Wood Goblin* (1889). They emerge from a period in his life when he was striving to perfect his skill as a short-story writer, to increase the subtlety of the techniques available to him, to depict states of unfulfilled desires, misconstrued ambitions, and futile endeavor. Transferring these concerns to writing for the stage, aware as he was of its fondness for platitudes and cheap effects, drove him to agonies of frustration.

Yet, when he gave advice to would-be playwrights, he limited himself to matters of technique. For instance, in 1889, he offered these adages to a young novice:

> "If you have hung a pistol on the wall in the first act, then it has to be shot in the last act. Otherwise, don't hang it up."
>
> "It is unconscionable of authors to bring on stage messengers, bystanders, policemen. Why force the poor actor to get into costume, make himself up, while away hours on end in a nasty draft backstage?"
>
> "In drama you mustn't be afraid of farce, but philosophizing in it is disgusting. Everything goes dead."
>
> "Nothing is more difficult than writing a good vaudeville. And how pleasant it is to write one."[2]

Essentially, there were two prevalent traditions of nineteenth-century playwriting upon which Chekhov could draw. One was the mode of the "well-made play," which dominated European and American stages. Based on strict rules of construction, the well-made play involved a central intrigue, intricate manipulation of the hero's fortunes, contrived episodes of eavesdropping, revealing soliloquys, and misdelivered letters, and a denouement in which good would triumph and evil receive its just deserts. Its leading exponent, the French playwright Eugène Scribe, declared that the function of such a play was solely to entertain, not by mirroring real life, but by providing an improved surrogate for life. Many of the greatest "box-office hits" of all time have been enacted within the constraints of the well-made play.

Later on, the well-made play attempted to encompass social problems, setting forth in its neat five-act structure a "burning question of the day," such as women's rights, divorce, or unemployment, and just as neatly resolving it by the fall of the curtain. As the Russian critic Vasily Sleptsov pointed out, the social question and the mechanical plot seldom bore an organic relationship to one another. The question was usually embodied in the *raisonneur*, a character like a doctor or lawyer who, in Sleptsov's image, is a bottle brought on, uncorked, its message poured out, and then packed away until needed again.

The other dramatic tradition available to Chekhov was a purely Russian one. From Gogol onward, Russian playwrights had composed open-ended dramas, loose in structure and combining elements of comedy and pathos. The most prolific dramatist of Chekhov's youth, Aleksandr Ostrovsky, used such plays to depict *byt*, the everyday life of merchants and civil servants, and to capture the rhythms and idioms of vernacular speech. Many of Ostrovsky's types recur in a modified shape in Chekhov: the dispossessed and victimized young girl seeking to make a life for herself reappears as *The Seagull*'s Nina; the boorish peasant who buys the estate in *The Forest* is refined into *The Cherry Orchard*'s Lopakhin. However, Ostrovsky and his imitators took a definite moral stance. The apportionment of good and evil in their plays is as strict as in melodrama. Chekhov's view of life was too complex to allow such a simplistic viewpoint and his sense of form too sophisticated for him to adopt Ostrovsky's lax principles of construction.

In practice, Chekhov repudiates his predecessors in radical ways. Chekhovian drama has been defined as imitation of stasis, with action so gradual and non-progressive as sometimes to be imperceptible. Nevertheless, even though central actions, such as Treplyov's attempted suicide or the sale of the cherry orchard, take place off stage, a sense of development is produced by the sequential placement of characters and their concerns. Chekhov creates an illusion of life in motion by juxtaposing apparently static elements, implying relationships in objects by aligning them in a kind of "montage." The authorial point of view is not invested in any one character, but a spectrum of attitudes is provided, which reflect on each another and offer ironic counterpoint. The dialogue eludes the characters themselves to be transmitted along an underground railway of subtext and hidden motivation. Often, the conversation breaks off just when the characters are about to declare themselves. As Patrice Pavis puts it, the peculiar power of Chekhov's text originates in a sort of teasing, never explaining, never providing the key to the quotations or to the characters.[3]

Given the uniqueness of Chekhov's plays, the rise of his reputation is something of an anomaly. Shortly before his death in 1904, if you asked anyone who was the greatest living Russian writer, the answer would no doubt have been Tolstoy. Tolstoy's imposing position as a moralist and reformer, his eminence at the panoramic novel, the genre most honored by the nineteenth century, which preferred monumentality, his political stance as the unassailable opponent of autocracy—these and other features made the sage of Yasnaya Polyana the voice of humanitarian culture to the world at large.

Chekhov, on the other hand, was regarded as a purely local phenomenon. Within the Russian Empire, his reputation was fragmented among various publics. The common reader remembered him chiefly as the author of a number of funny stories. The intelligentsia saw him as a chronicler of its own malaise, particularly in the plays staged by the Moscow Art Theatre. Political factions on the right and left dismissed him as a fence-sitter, too cowardly to take sides in ideological battles. The literary avant-garde deplored his lack of religious uplift and "sublimity."

Outside Russia, Chekhov was viewed at best as an exotic *petit maître*, trading in doom and gloom. The Poles patriotically neglected him, the Germans interpreted him as another exponent of the tragedy of fate, and the Georgians noted sarcastically that only ethnic Russians would fritter away their time as trivially as his characters do. In France, the standard works on Russian literature around 1900 shrugged off Chekhov: Kazimierz Waliszewski described his drama as "completely devoid of action and psychological differentiation of characters," while the critic and novelist Melchior de Vogüé declared the full-length plays too pessimistic for the French, full of impotent heroes with "enigmatic Slavic souls."[4] In the first two English-language reference books to include Chekhov, both published the year before his death, those same dramatic characters were cited as "fit subjects for the psychiatrist" and "a strange assemblage of neurotics, lunatic and semi-lunatic," obsessed with solving the riddle of life.[5]

In Russia, too, the respect and affection Chekhov's memory had accrued began to evaporate. At the jubilee celebrations in 1910, some dissenting voices could be heard above the chorus of praise. At a meeting of the St. Petersburg Literary Society, the prominent feminist author Olga Shapir renewed the charge that he was a poet of gray, humdrum depressives, and added the complaint that his women especially lacked clear outlines or strong emotion, despite the fact that since the 1880s he had been in the vanguard of political reform movements.[6] In a period of activism and engagement, Chekhov's deliberately peripheral stance grew increasingly distasteful. It would culminate in the Bolshevik rejection of Chekhov after the October Revolution.

That rejection was due in part to Chekhov's inextricable association with the Moscow Art Theatre, a symbiosis rich in ironies. It was ironical that Chekhov, who deeply admired skilled acting technique, should have been imposed on the cultural consciousness of his times by a troupe of amateurs and semi-professionals. It was ironical that Stanislavsky, who had cut his teeth as an actor and director on Shakespeare, Schiller, and operetta, and whose dearest ambition was to stage historically accurate productions of the classics, should find his most important challenge and success in re-creating the dreary world of his contemporaries and, along the way, inevitably ennoble Chekhov's characters. It was ironical that a theater whose founders intended it to be a school for a mass public should find itself explicating the intelligentsia to the intelligentsia. It is perhaps the irony of ironies that the Art Theatre, having discovered its most successful modus operandi in its staging of Chekhov, tried to apply this technique to all sorts of unlikely authors with the to-be-expected failure; while Chekhov himself chafed at what he felt were wilful departures from his meaning and intention.

He complained that, "at the Art Theatre, all those prop-room details distract the spectator, keep him from listening. [. . .] Let's take *Cherry Orchard* . . . Is this really my *Cherry Orchard*? Are these really my types? . . . With the exception of a couple of performers, none of it's mine. . . . I write life. . . . This gray, everyday life. . . . But that does not mean annoying moaning and groaning. . . . They make me lachrymose, a really boring writer. [. . .] It's starting to get on my nerves. . . ."[7]

Whatever the discrepancy between Chekhov's vision and that of the Art Theatre, what struck the spectators of the original productions most forcefully was that company and author seemed to be totally and intimately amalgamated; the plays seemed to be written and staged by the same person. When the actors at provincial theaters simple-mindedly played Chekhov in a dismal monotone, the result was boredom; whereas the Art Theatre revealed the covert, repressed feelings underlying the bad jokes and banal conversation. What distinguished Chekhov's drama from all other plays at the time was what Stanislavsky called the "submarine" course of the through action, which renders the dialogue nearly allegorical. Every individual scenic moment was carefully worked out in terms of the integrity of the entire production, to create an effect of seamlessness. Everyday or material reality went beyond mere naturalism to achieve the famous *nastroenie* (mood). Stanislavsky's layering of "mood" or "atmosphere" is essentially a symbolist technique. Just as the words "Balzac was married in Berdichev" overlay another, more profound emotion significance, so the tableaux of ordinary life, abetted by sound and lighting effects, opened into a "beyond" of more intense reality.

Those who saw Chekhov as a realist were deceived by Stanislavsky's atmospheric and detail-crammed productions and the seeming looseness of the plays's dialogue and structure. Like all great artists, however, Chekhov was highly selective in what he chose to take from reality. The director Vsevolod Meyerhold recalled an occasion in 1898 when *The Seagull* was in rehearsal at the Moscow Art Theatre, and an actor boasted to Chekhov of how backstage "frogs were to croak, dragon-flies were to buzz, dogs to bark."

"What for?" Anton Pavlovich asks in a surly voice.

"Realism," replies the actor.

"Realism," repeats A. P., with a grin, and, after a brief pause, says: "The stage is art. There's a genre painting by Kramskoy, with the faces magnificently painted. What if the nose were to be cut out of one of the faces and a real one stuck in? The nose is 'realistic,' but the painting is spoiled."

One of the actors tells him proudly that at the end of the third act of *Seagull*, the director wants to bring on stage the whole domestic staff, some woman with a crying child.

Anton Pavlovich says:

"It isn't necessary. It's the same as if you're playing a piano *pianissimo*, and meanwhile the lid of the piano collapses."

"In life it often happens that a *forte* breaks into a *pianissimo* quite unexpectedly," one of the acting company tries to object.

"Yes, but the stage," says A. P., "demands a certain conventional quality. We have no fourth wall. Nevertheless, the stage is art, the stage reflects the quintessence of life, you don't have to put anything extraneous on stage."[8]

This succinctly expresses Chekhov's belief in the selective detail and the need to edit reality to make an artistic point. Perhaps the symbolist writer Andrey Bely put it best when he described *The Cherry Orchard* as "loops from the lace of life," realistic details scrutinized so closely that the dimension beyond them is revealed. He suggested that Chekhov became an unwitting Symbolist as his surface layer of reality turned transparent and disclosed the hidden profundities beneath. A similar analogy might be made with pointillist painting. Up close, the individual specks of color make no sense, create no discernible pattern; but at the proper distance, the shapes reveal themselves in new and often striking ways; their relationships fall into place. In this respect, Chekhov's plays fit Goethe's prescription for a stageworthy drama: "each incident must be significant by itself, and yet lead naturally to something more important."[9]

This scenic extension of the Russian tradition of literary realism enabled the intelligentsia to behold its hopes and fears on stage in terms it readily adopted. As the poet Osip Mandelshtam wrote in 1923:

> For the intelligentsia to go to the Moscow Art Theatre was almost equal to taking communion or going to church. . . .
>
> Literature, not theater, characterized that entire generation. . . . They understood theater exclusively as an interpretation of literature . . . into another, more comprehensible and completely natural language.

. . . The emotional zeal of that generation and of the Moscow Art Theatre was the emotional zeal of Doubting Thomas. They had Chekhov, but Thomas the intellectual did not trust him. He wanted to touch Chekhov, to feel him, to be convinced of his reality.[10]

The illusion of life created by Stanislavsky, his emphasis on subtext and context, provided that reality, and gave Chekhov a novel-like amplitude that satisfied the intelligentsia's need for theme and tendentiousness.

The Bolsheviks had extra-literary uses for the theater. No less tendentious, they fomented performance that was stark, immediate, and viscerally compelling. The new demands made on art in the aftermath of the October Revolution had a Medusa-like effect on the Art Theatre: it froze in place. Locked into its aging repertory, it found itself and Chekhov both repudiated as irrelevant excrescences of an obsolete bourgeois culture. Sailors at special matinees for workers shouted, "You bore me, Uncle Vanya," while ideologues and journalists called for Chekhov's suppression in favor of a vital, swashbuckling, romantic drama. "Is it really necessary to stir up such feelings?" émigrés reported Lenin complaining about *Uncle Vanya*. "One needs to appeal to cheerfulness, work, and joy."[11] Such vital creators of Bolshevik theater as Yevgeny Vakhtangov and Meyerhold turned to the one-act farces when they sought to stage Chekhov, and the only full-length play of his to be performed regularly in this period was *The Cherry Orchard*, treated as a satiric farce mocking the estate owners and their parasites.

While Chekhov languished at home, abroad he was promulgated by a diaspora. The 1920s and 1930s are the decades of the émigrés' Chekhov; fugitives from the Revolution saw themselves as Ranevskayas and Gaevs, expelled from a tsarist Eden. Outside Russia, the tours of the Moscow Art Theatre and its offshoot, the self-exiled Prague Group, disseminated the style and look of the original, but aging, productions, while resident actors and directors who left the Soviet Union perpetuated a Stanislavskian approach in Europe and America. Even those refugees who had never practiced the Art Theatre approach, such as Theodore Komisarjevsky in England and George Pitoëff in France, carried on under its banner. Their Chekhov was lyrical, enigmatic, moonstruck, and, above all, steeped in romantic nostalgia. European and American audiences accepted this without demur. After all, if Chekhov was a particularly Russian author, then who better to interpret him than a Russian, any Russian? Chekhov, a man of sorrows acquainted with grief, came to be seen as elegiac and wistful.

After the Second World War, in countries under Soviet hegemony, Chekhov and the Art Theatre interpretation, now heavily adulterated by Socialist Realism, were thrust down the throats of Czech, Polish, East German, and Hungarian audiences. Little wonder if, left to their own devices, directors and critics found him indigestible and sought to supplant the Stanislavsky legacy.

The rehabilitation of Chekhov's drama in Europe after World War II is due to a Czech and an Italian—Otomar Krejča and Giorgio Strehler, both leftists, but of quite different stripes. At his theater near Prague, Krejča worked in collaboration with his actors to realize what Gorky had once called the cold, cruel Chekhov, an impassive creator who flung his characters into an absurd world. There, in his interpretation, they beat their wings futilely against the meaninglessness of existence. Without being either a programmatic existentialist or a doctrinaire absurdist, Krejča distilled his own experiences as a victim of postwar Soviet domination into an interpretation of Chekhov that administered the shock of recognition to audiences throughout Europe. They could identify with the blighted hopes of his characters.

Strehler, for his part, employed elegance and metaphor in his 1956 *Cherry Orchard*, arguably the most influential Chekhov production of modern times. His white-on-white decor, with its overhead membrane of petals in a diaphanous veil, was copied from Bucharest to Indiana. Strehler sought to conflate all the levels of meaning in the play: the narrative, the socio-historical, and the universally metaphoric. The toys in the nursery, for instance, went beyond realistic props to become emblems of the characters' lost innocence and retarded emotions. Strehler universalized the nostalgia of Komisarjevsky and Pitoëff by enlarging it beyond the private sphere, while Krejča's productions grew ever more schematic, insisting on the collective grotesque of the Chekhovian world.

In Soviet Russia during the 1960s, Chekhov was co-opted by a generation of idealists opposed to one of cynics. *Ivanov* became the play for the times, repeatedly revived. Antidomesticity was proclaimed by scenery that lacked walls and doors; manor houses were made to look like skeletal prisons and the branches of the cherry orchard became sterile and gnarled.

The English-speaking world has been the most resistant to extreme reforms in the performance of Chekhov. Psychological realism remains the preferred format, and the Chekhovian estate has become as familiar as the old homestead or the derelict country house. "Chekhov has been ennobled by age," says Spencer Golub. ". . . He is as soothing and reassuring as the useless valerian drops dispensed by the doctors in all his plays . . . an article of faith, like all stereotypes . . . the Santa Claus of dramatic literature."[12] This may account for the large number of plays about Chekhov's life, in which he turns into Drs. Dorn, Astrov, or Chebutykin, depending on the playwright's bent. It is also the case that the English-speaking theater has, until very recently, been dominated by playwrights rather than directors. A Chekhovian resonance can be found more in the plays of leading dramatists from Rodney Ackland to Tennessee Williams than in extraordinary stagings.

Anywhere else in the world, the reinterpretation of Chekhov, defying the conventional homilies and exploding the traditional conventions, was the work of directors. At least until the end of the nineteenth century, one could trace the stage history of Shakespeare or Molière through the actors and their treatment of individual roles. Chekhov's career as a dramatist, however, coincides with the rise of the director as prime mover in the modern theater; and the nature of his last plays derives in part from his awareness—if not his full approval—of what a director's theater was capable of. Following the Wagnerian notion of *Gesamtkunstwerk*, it required the integration of every component: the actors had to become an ensemble led by a virtuoso conductor. We can compare the Hamlets of great actors to some advantage and insight; but to compare the Ranevskayas of individual actresses makes no sense outside the context of the directorial visions for the productions in which they appeared.

Writing in 1960, Harry Levin pointed out that the opening of a New York apartment building called The Picasso signaled the domestication, and hence the end, of modernism.[13] When the enfant terrible becomes the elder statesman and new coinages turn into commonplaces, efforts have to be made to recapture the original effect. The acceptance of Chekhov as a readily recognizable cultural totem makes him available for all kinds of co-optation. In the 1970s, the process of dismantling the Soviet icon of Chekhov continued: Anatoly Éfros converted *The Cherry Orchard* to a graveyard and Yury Lyubimov flung open the wall of the Taganka Theatre during his *Three Sisters* to reveal the Moscow streets outside: "You yearn for Moscow?" he seemed to be saying, "Well, there it is, in all its noise, grubbiness, and squalor." Fifty years of false aspiration were debunked in a moment.

Later, Yury Pogrebnichko re-created *Three Sisters* behind a velvet rope as a museum exhibit, cluttered with the detritus of the past, forcing the post-Soviet spectator to come to terms with a regime that left him washed up on the shoals of the present. Henrietta Yanovskaya put her *Ivanov* on roller-skates to show him attempting to evade the responsibilities of his sordid situation. In the United States, the experimental Wooster Group dismantled *Three Sisters* by means of video screens and improvisation to evoke the modern world of mass media and create a hybrid theatrical language. The seamless web of the Stanislavskian simulacrum is fragmented into jagged shreds of interrupted meaning and faulty recollection. Dramatists remote from Chekhov's sensibility, language, and concerns, such as Pam Gems, Edward Bond, David Mamet, Trevor Griffiths, Lanford Wilson, David Hare, Brian Friel, and Richard Nelson, transmogrify him in new versions, refracting their own preoccupations. This need of the English-speaking playwright to wrestle Chekhov to the mat has become a rite of passage. There is something compulsively Oedipal in this recurrent grappling with the one universally admitted patriarch of the modern stage.

Chekhov as patriarch may be a jarring image. Let us return to Chekhov's replacement of Tolstoy as the Russian man of letters par excellence. Even as late as the 1940s, the Communist critic György Lukács could point to Tolstoy as the paradigm of universal genius who transcended his otherwise crippling bourgeois milieu through the power of his demiurgic creativity. In our less heroic age, however, Tolstoy seems unsympathetic; like Blake's old Nobodaddy, he glowers at us dispprovingly from beneath his beetling brows. Tolstoy's creative achievements and his moral demands on us seem the titanic labors of some mythic era, impossible to us puny mortals. They also exude a kind of confidence and self-righteousness that are luxuries too costly for the spiritually impecunious survivors of the twentieth century. Even his death was exemplary: Tolstoy's solitary demise in the railway station at Astapovo is the stuff of tragedy, Lear succumbing on the heath, this time unreconciled with Cordelia.

Chekhov's death, which has been so often retold and reworked as fiction, is, in contrast, a comedy of errors. It too is exemplary, but as farce, from his alleged last words, "It's been a long time since I've drunk champagne" (which echoes *Uncle Vanya*'s nanny: "It's a long time since I've had noodles") to the transport of his corpse in a freight car marked "Oysters," to the military band straying from a general's funeral to double in brass at his graveside. Chekhov is the more accessible and more familiar figure. His irony has greater appeal than does Tolstoy's moral absolutism. His vaunted objectivity, not all that objective under scrutiny, is more welcome because less judgmental. His inability to write a novel and his preference for small forms, open endings, and ethical ambiguities appeal to our postmodern fondness for the marginal, our wary distrust of the grand gesture. Tolstoy the schoolmaster stands over his text, ferule in hand, to make sure we have learned the lesson; Chekhov endears himself by modestly bowing out, protesting that it's all in the words.

Yet, for all this modesty, over the course of a mere century Chekhov has reached the rank of Shakespeare. They are bracketed together as the greatest playwrights of all time. The Polish director Andrzej Wajda has remarked, "Theatre in our European tradition derives from the word, from literature, the Greeks, Shakespeare, Chekhov."[14] Note the absence of Ibsen, who might deserve better, with his endeavors to raise everyday experience to an epic level. Ibsen's grandiosity takes risks: when he succeeds, the effect is breathtaking; when he fails, it is involuntarily ludicrous. Chekhov regularly avoided the grandiose, the overtly poetic, the tragic pose; or else he undercut them when they arose inadvertantly.

Despite what Wajda says about the word, part of Chekhov's special appeal comes from what he leaves out, another legacy from the Symbolists, the pregnant pause. Often what is left unsaid—the awkward gaps in conversation, the sentences that trail off in the air, the interstices of pauses—matters most in Chekhov's plays. Of course, Stanislavsky, who distrusted understatement, amplified and multiplied the Chekhovian pause, turning it into a pretext for veristic stage effects. An actor who worked at the Art Theatre in 1908–1909 recalled that the pauses "were held precisely by the numbers and the actors were recommended to count the seconds mentally during the duration of the pauses."[15] This mechanical rendition loses touch with the essence of the Chekhovian pause, itself a precursor of what Beckett referred to as the transitional zone in which being makes itself heard.

What then justifies this coupling of Shakespeare and Chekhov? I would suggest that John Keats, in a famous letter of 1818, put his finger on it. Reacting to a performance of Edmund Kean as Richard III, Keats mused on Shakespeare's protean brilliance:

> at once it struck me, what quality went to form a Man of Achievement especially in Literature & which Shakespeare possessed so enormously—I mean Negative Capability, that is when man is capable of being in uncertainities, Mysteries, doubts, without any irritable reaching after fact & reason.[16]

Walter J. Bate paraphrases this: "in our life of uncertainties, where no one system or formula can explain everything . . . what is needed is an imaginative openness of mind and heightened receptivity to reality in its full and diverse concreteness."[17] Shakespearean mastery requires a negation of the writer's own ego, a sympathetic absorption into the essential significance of the writer's object. Chekhov seems to have attained that state of authorial absence.

For Keats, as for the other English Romantics, Shakespeare's brilliance at negative capability was shown in his extensive gallery of characters, all equally vivid, multi-faceted, and imbued with idiosyncratic opinions, idioms, behavior. Chekhov can hardly exhibit the Bard's variety or plenitude in his plays; the narrow, seemingly repetitive nature of his dramatic world was a ready target for satire even in his lifetime. But another, earlier letter of Keats comes to our aid; in it he divided ethereal things into three categories: "Things real— things semireal—and no things—Things real—such as existences of Sun Moon & Stars and passages of Shakspeare—Things semireal such as Love, the Clouds &c which require a greeting of the Spirit to make them wholly exist— and Nothings which are made Great and dignified by an ardent pursuit."[18]

Chekhov admits the existence of real things in his writings and endows them with a significance beyond their material status; however, the existence of semireal things such as love remains problematic and nebulous for his characters. Yet, the confines of the Chekhovian world teem with Keats's "Nothings" to be made great and dignified by an ardent pursuit. As Stanislavsky intuited, a samovar in Chekhov was not the same as a samovar in Ostrovsky; it, along with the pauses and sound effects and changeable weather, bespoke the overall tone, reflected the inner life of the characters. Leonid Andreev named this interrelationship of everything in Chekhov "panpsychism." The same soul animates whatever appears on stage:

> On the stage Chekhov must be performed not only by human beings, but by drinking glasses and chairs and crickets and military overcoats and engagement rings. . . . it all comes across not as items from reality or true-to-life sound and its utterances, but as the protagonists' thoughts and sensations disseminated throughout space.[19]

This goes beyond the sympathetic fallacy; it creates a distinctive microcosm, instantly recognizable whatever the vagaries of directors. It is the unifying factor that ties together even the most seemingly non-communicative dialogue and solipsistic yearnings.

When Mariya Knebel, Stanislavsky's last pupil, came to the Abbey Theatre in Dublin in 1968 to direct *The Cherry Orchard*, the actors were surprised that she did not require a samovar on stage.[20] The samovar had always been the indispensable token of Chekhov's foreignness. In the last decades, however, in production after production, the samovar has been supplanted as emblematic prop by an old Victrola with a morning-glory horn. Chekhov is still associated with the past, but not a specifically Russian or historic past. His "pastness," like that of any great dramatist, is part of a continuum with the present. The suggestion is that somehow the screechy recorded voices played back on a turntable return the past to us in distorted, nostalgic form, which we interpret as our needs require.[21]

In his book *The Theatrical Event*, David Cole refers to *illud tempus*, an archetypal realm that the theater must depict, "not so much when it first occurred as where it is always happening."[22] Beyond the reality the estates and garrison towns of Chekhov's plays held for their original audiences, they have now taken on a polysemic existence. They transcend a specific society to become archetypal realms. The spellbinding lake of *The Seagull* has more in common with the island of *The Tempest* than with a landscape in Turgenev. The rooms in the Prozorov home can expand to the dimensions of Agamemnon's palace or dwindle to the claustrophobic cells of Beckett. The early critics of Chekhov could not have been more wrong when they condemned him as the poet of an obsolescent set, circumscribed by its own eccentricity. Just as the Shakespearean *illud tempus* shines through modern dress and radical transpositions, the Chekhovian *illud tempus* gains in eloquent meaning from its disguises, even when Thomas Kilroy transfers *The Seagull* to the Ireland of the Celtic Twilight or Tadashi Suzuki plunges the officers of *Three Sisters* into absurdist baskets or the Irondale Ensemble Project turns *Uncle Vanya* into a 1940s radio announcer in Charlevoix, Michigan. Without shedding its specificity, the world of the Chekhovian intellectual has become as remote as Camelot and as familiar as Grover's Corners, as exotic as Shangri-La and as homely as Kasrilevka. It instantly conjures up a long-vanished way of life that nevertheless compels us to adduce current counterparts. The persistence of the identifiable and idiosyncratic world suggests that he never stopped being Chekhov our contemporary.

NOTES

1 Ivan Bunin, *O Chekhove [About Chekhov]* (New York: Chekhov Publishing House, 1955). Translations are mine unless otherwise stated.

2 Ars. G., in *Teatr i Iskusstvo [Theater and Art]* 28 (1904). The author's real name was Ilya Yakovlevich Gurlyand (b. 1863?), a student at the time he met Chekhov in Yalta in 1889, later a journalist and professor.

3 Patrice Pavis, "Commentaires et notes" to Antoine Tchékhov, *La Mouette*. Traduction d'Antoine Vitez (Paris: Actes Sud, 1985), pp. 99–103.

4 K. Waliszewski, *Littérature russe* (Paris, 1900), p. 426; de Vogüé, quoted in Yu. Felichkin, "Rol teatra v vospriyati tvorchestva Chekhova vo Frantsii," in *Literaturny Muzey A. P. Chekhova: sbornik statey i materialov [The Chekhov Literary Museum: a collection of articles and documents]*, vyp. V (Rostov, 1969), p. 155.

5 Leo Wiener, *Anthology of Russian Literature* (New York, 1903), II; A. Bates, *The Drama* (London, 1903), p. 73.

6 "V Peterburge," *Chekhovsky yubileiny sbornik* [*Chekhov Jubilee Anthology*] (Moscow, 1910), p. 530.

7 Yevtikhy Karpov, "Dve poslednie vstrechi s A. P. Chekhovym" [My last two encounters with Chekhov], *Ezhegodnik imperatorskikh teatrov* [*Yearbook of the Imperial Theaters*], vyp. V. (1909). It should be noted that Bunin considered Karpov's reminiscences to be a tissue of lies.

8 V. E. Meyerhold, "Naturalistichesky teatr i teatr nastroenii" ["The Naturalistic Theater and the Theater of Mood"], in *Teatr. Kniga o novom teatre: sbornik statey* [*Theater: A Book About the New Theater. A Collection of Articles*] (St Petersburg: Shipovnik, 1908): 136–150.

9 J. P. Eckermann, *Conversations with Goethe in the Last Years of His Life*, trans. S. M. Fuller (Boston: Hilliard, Gray, 1839), p. 168 (July 26, 1826).

10 Osip Mandelshtam, in *Teatr i muzyka* [*Theater and Music*] 36 (November 6, 1923).

11 *Moskovsky Khudozhestvenny teatr v sovetskuyu épokhu. Materialy, dokumenty* [*The Moscow Art Theatre in the Soviet Era. Materials, Documents*], 2nd ed. (Moscow, 1974), p. 124; V. A. Nelidov, *Teatralnaya Moskva (sorok let moskovskikh teatrov)* [*Theatrical Moscow (Forty Years of Moscow Theaters)*] (Berlin-Riga, 1931), p. 436.

12 In *Newsnotes on Soviet and East European Drama and Theatre*, III, 3 (November 1983): 2–3.

13 Harry Levin, "What Was Modernism?" (1960), in *Varieties of Literary Experience*, ed. S. Burnshaw (New York: New York University Press, 1962), p. 307.

14 Quoted in Maciej Karpinski, *The Theatre of Andrej Wajda*, trans. C. Paul (Cambridge: Cambridge University Press, 1989), p. 124.

15 A. A. Mgebrov, *Zhizn v teatre* [*A Life in the Theater*], ed. E. Kuznetsov (Leningrad, 1920), I, pp. 224–225.

16 *The Letters of John Keats*, ed. H. E. Rollins (Cambridge, Mass.: Harvard University Press, 1958), I, 184.

17 W. J. Bate, *John Keats* (New York: Oxford University Press, 1966), p. 249.

18 Letter to Benjamin Bailey (March 13, 1818).

19 Leonid Andreev, *Pisma o teatre* (1912), trans. as "Letters on Theatre," in *Russian Dramatic Theory from Pushkin to the Symbolists*, ed. and trans. L. Senelick (Austin: University of Texas Press, 1981), pp. 240–241.

20 Mariya Knebel, "'Vishnyovy sad' v Irlandii," *Teatr* 5 (1969): 158–166.

21 Even the first production of *Three Sisters* in 1901 gave the critic Innokenty Annensky the sense of a phonograph reproducing his own world: "the phonograph presents me with *my* voice, *my* words, which, however, I had been quick to forget, and as I listen, I naively ask: 'who is that talking through his nose and lisping?'" I. F. Annensky, "Drama nastroeniya. Tri sestry," in *Knigi otrazhenii* [*A Book of Reflections*] I (St. Petersburg: Trud, 1906), p. 147.

22 David Cole, *The Theatrical Event: A Mythos, a Vocabulary, a Perspective* (Middletown, Conn., 1975), p. 8.

EARLY

EXPERIMENTS

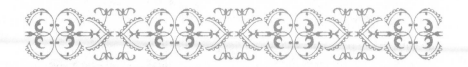

UNTITLED PLAY

$\mathcal{W}$hile still in high school Chekhov wrote a four-act play so full of incident, "with horse-stealing, a gunshot, a woman who throws herself under a train,"[1] that a family friend described it as a "drrama," the two *r*s bespeaking its sensational quality. The critical consensus today sees it as the early stage of a work that may or may not be identical to a play called *Without Patrimony* or *Disinherited* (*Bezottsovshchina*). The hopeful neophyte sent it to his literary brother Aleksandr in Moscow. He got back a very negative critique, and may either have shelved it or else launched into the work now usually known as *Platonov*. This play also underwent intense rewriting, probably between 1878 and 1879. Chekhov toned down the dialogue, dropped two characters (Shcherbuk's ugly daughters), and omitted a lurid scene in which Voinitsev pulls a dagger on Platonov, who disarms him with the shout, "Stand back!" and a torrent of rhetoric. Even with cuts, it was over twice the length of an ordinary play of the period.

Chekhov took it to Mariya Yermolova, one of the stars of Moscow's Maly Theatre, an ill-considered move since the part suitable for her would have been the merry widow Anna Petrovna. Yermolova, noted for her heroic Joan of Arc, never played roles of sexual laxity. She returned the play, and the chagrined young playwright tore up the manuscript. However, his younger brother Mikhail had made two copies for submission to the censorship; and one of these survived in a safety-deposit box, to be published in 1923. Since then, actors and producers have tried to reconstitute it for the stage as a "newly discovered play by Chekhov." Cut to the bone and drastically rewritten, it was first staged in German as *Der unnützige Mensch Platonoff* (*The Superfluous Man Platonov*) in 1928, and since then has appeared as *A Country Scandal*, *A Provincial Don Juan*, *Ce Fou Platonov*, *Fireworks on the James*, *Untitled Play*, *Comédie russe*, *Wild Honey* (Michael Frayn's version), *Player Piano* (Trevor Griffith's version), and *Platonov* (David Hare's version). None of these adaptations has managed to secure a place for the protracted piece of juvenilia in the repertory. Its interest lies primarily in its being a storehouse of Chekhov's later themes and characters: the cynical doctor, the cynosure attractive woman, the parasitic buffoons, the practical housewife, and the failed idealist. Most intricately reworked of all, the threat of losing the estate to debts was to become the connecting thread and constitutive symbol of *The Cherry Orchard*.

The characters are neatly divided into debtors and creditors. The older generation corrupts and suborns the younger generation through mortgages, loans, bribes, and gifts. Many of them are shown as *nouveaux-riches*, upstarts whose incomes derive from such suspect sources as leasing out dramshops and ruining old, established families. Yet their juniors are easy prey, depicted as wastrels and profligates. In Act Two, the clownish young doctor Triletsky puts the touch on an enriched grocer "just because," and then hands out the cash he has received, ruble by ruble, to anyone who comes along. The passing of the banknotes from hand to hand graphically illustrates the mindless prodigality of Chekhov's nobly born contemporaries.

Whether or not this play is identical to *Without Patrimony*, the obsession with paternal relations and dispossession runs through it. Platonov has descended in status from gentleman to village schoolmaster. Voinitsev loses his estate through his own and his stepmother's extravagances; a deceased general looms over their lives as one will in *Three Sisters*. A bleak picture is drawn of fathers and sons on a moral level: Platonov's recollections of his late father are contemptuous; Glagolyev Jr. heartlessly tricks his father and goads him into a stroke; both Glagolyevs woo the same woman and drown their disappointment in Parisian debauchery. The Triletskys are ashamed of their drunken father, whom they treat as a kind of wayward child. Shcherbuk hates his two daughters. Only the Vengerovichs seem to preserve a mutually respectful alliance, and they are Jews, outsiders in this society.

Chekhov was unable to pursue all the hares he started in this play, or to find the proper angle from which to view his protagonist. Awkwardly, he puts his own opinion in the mouth of Glagolyev Sr. shortly before Platonov's first appearance, setting him up as "the finest exponent of modern infirmity of purpose." This rural Don Juan is irresistible to women, but he is also a cracker-barrel Schopenhauer whose alleged idealism and skepticism appeal to the men. Shallow and vacillating, he has a silver tongue, not unlike Turgenev's Rudin, the exemplar of superfluous man. He bears all the earmarks of the type: alienated, hypersensitive, and mired in inertia.

Irony swamps Platonov's claims to heroic stature; with ambitions to be Hamlet, "a second Byron," "a prospective cabinet minister and a Christopher

Columbus," he is shamefaced to reveal his paunchy schoolmaster status to a former girlfriend. He has not even graduated from the university, which does not prevent him from lecturing others on their spiritual and moral failings. Since most of the men in the community are grotesque clowns or flaccid weaklings, he seems in contrast a paragon, and hence a lodestone to women.

Four of the *mille e tre* this village Don Giovanni numbers in his catalogue of conquests contradict Glagolyev's notion that a woman is a paragon. Platonov's wife, Sasha, is a long-suffering homebody whom he forces to read Sacher-Masoch's *Ideals of Our Times*; her two attempts at suicide, both thwarted, are not to be taken seriously. Twenty-year-old Mariya Grekova is shown to be a hypocritical bluestocking, whose highminded scorn melts into infatuation when Platonov writes her a love letter. The sophisticated widow Anna Petrovna manipulates the men in her circle for financial security, and sees Platonov as a better quality of plaything, although her feelings may run deeper than she is willing to admit. Sofiya, her daughter-in-law, commits adultery with Platonov in hopes of a "new life" but shoots him when he shrugs off the affair. If Mariya is the Donna Elvira, then Sofiya is the Donna Anna of this opera.

Osip the thief does not play Leporello to Platonov, however; rather, he is a kind of double. He tries to set himself above his fellows by being a "bad man." He is a Nietzschean superman on a plebeian plane. Platonov harms others by manipulating their emotions; Osip harms them physically and materially. And they are both destroyed by their victims. When the two men grapple in the schoolroom, it is like a man fighting his shadow or *Doppelgänger*.

For all its overstatement, what makes this play a real portent of Chekhov's mature work is the unsteady listing from the comic side to the serious. It bespeaks a view of the cohesiveness of life, in which critical issues and meaningless trivia coexist. Chekhov's career as a professional humorist made him alert to the grotesque detail, the absurd facet of any situation; but more important is his ingrained awareness that the current of life, awash with the banal flotsam of everyday, carries away heroic poses and epic aspirations. A comic effect is natural when grandiose philosophical questions and emotional crises have to share space with the inexorable demands of the humdrum.

NOTE

1 M. P. Chekhov, "Ob A. P. Chekhove," *Novoe slovo* 1 (1907): 198.

UNTITLED PLAY

Пьеса без названия

sometimes known as

WITHOUT PATRIMONY (DISINHERITED) *or* **PLATONOV**

Безотцовщина **or** Платонов

Play in Four Acts

C H A R A C T E R S

ANNA PETROVNA VOINITSEVA, *the young widow of a general*

SERGEY PAVLOVICH VOINITSEV, *General Voinitsev's son by his first marriage*

SOFYA YEGOROVNA, *his wife*

PORFIRY SEMYONOVICH GLAGOLYEV SR.

KIRILL PORFIRYEVICH GLAGOLYEV JR.

GERASIM KUZMICH PETRIN

PAVEL PETROVICH SHCHERBUK

MARIYA YEFIMOVNA GREKOVA, *a girl of 20*

IVAN IVANOVICH TRILETSKY, *a retired colonel*

NIKOLAY IVANOVICH, *his son, a young physician*

ABRAM ABRAMOVICH VENGEROVICH SR, *a rich Jew*

landowners, neighbors of the Voinitsevs

ISAK ABRAMOVICH, *his son, a university student*

TIMOFEY GORDEEVICH BUGROV, *a merchant*

MIKHAIL VASILYEVICH PLATONOV, *a village schoolmaster*

ALEKSANDRA IVANOVNA (SASHA), *his wife, daughter of I. I.*
Triletsky

OSIP, *a fellow about 30, a horse thief*

MARKO, *messenger for the Justice of the Peace, a little old geezer*

VASILY

YAKOV — *servants of the Voinitsevs*

KATYA

GUESTS, SERVANTS

The action takes place on the Voinitsevs' estate in
one of the southern provinces.

ACT ONE

A drawing-room in the Voinitsevs' home. A French window to the
garden and two doors to the inner rooms. A mixture of both old-
and new-fashioned furniture. A grand piano, beside it a music-
stand with a violin and sheet music. A harmonium. Pictures
(oleographs) in gilt frames.

SCENE I

ANNA PETROVNA is sitting at the piano, her head bowed over
the keys. NIKOLAY IVANOVICH TRILETSKY enters.

TRILETSKY (*walks over to Anna Petrovna*). What's the matter?

ANNA PETROVNA (*raises her head*). Nothing . . . Just a little bored . . .

TRILETSKY. Let's have a smoke, *mon ange!*[1] My flesh is itching for a smoke.
For some reason I haven't had a smoke since this morning.

---

1 French: my angel.

ANNA PETROVNA (*hands him hand-rolled cigarettes*). Take a lot so you won't be pestering me later.

They light up.

It's so boring, Nikolya! It's tedious, there's nothing to do, I'm depressed . . . I don't even know what there is to do . . .

TRILETSKY takes her by the hand.

ANNA PETROVNA. You're taking my pulse? I'm all right . . .

TRILETSKY. No, I'm not taking your pulse . . . I'm going to plant a sloppy kiss . . .

Kisses her hand.

Kissing her hand is like falling into a downy pillow. What do you wash your hands with to make them so white? Wonderful hands! I've really got to kiss them again.

Kisses her hand.

Feel like a game of chess?

ANNA PETROVNA. Go ahead . . .

Looks at the clock.

A quarter past twelve . . . I suppose our guests must be famished . . .

TRILETSKY (*sets up the chess board*). Highly likely. Speaking for myself, I'm ravenous.

ANNA PETROVNA. I wasn't referring to you . . . You're always hungry, although you never stop eating . . .

Sits down at the chessboard.

Your move . . . Made a move already . . . You should think first and then make your move . . . I'm moving here . . . You're always hungry . . .

TRILETSKY. So that's your move . . . All right, ma'am . . . I am hungry, ma'am . . . Will we be having dinner soon?

ANNA PETROVNA. I don't think so . . . To celebrate our return home, the cook got soused and now he's flat on his back. We'll have lunch eventually. Seriously, Nikolay Ivanych, when will you be full? Eat, eat, eat . . . you never stop eating! It's really horrible! Such a little man and such a big stomach!

TRILETSKY. Oh yes! Remarkable!

ANNA PETROVNA. You barge into my room and without a by-your-leave eat half a pie! As if you didn't know it wasn't my pie? You're a pig, dovie! Your move!

TRILETSKY. I didn't know. I only knew that it would go bad on you if I didn't eat it. That's your move? Might work, ma'am . . . And this is mine . . . If I do eat a lot, it means I'm healthy, and if I'm healthy, don't give me a hard time . . . *Mens sans in corpore sano.*[2]

Why think? Make your move, my dear little lady, without thinking . . . (*Sings.*) "I have a tale to tell, to tell . . ."[3]

ANNA PETROVNA. Be quiet . . . You're keeping me from thinking.

TRILETSKY. What a shame that a woman as intelligent as yourself never gives a thought to gastronomy. A man who doesn't know how to eat is a monster . . . A moral monster! . . . Because . . . Excuse me, excuse me! You can't make that move! What? Where are you going? Well, that's another story. Because taste bears the same relation to nature as hearing and sight, I mean it's one of the five senses, which taken as a whole belong to the realm, my good woman, of psychology. Psychology!

ANNA PETROVNA. I do believe you're planning to be witty . . . Don't be witty, my dear! I'm sick and tired of it, and besides it's not in your line . . . Have you noticed that I never laugh when you're being witty? I do believe it's high time you noticed it . . .

TRILETSKY. Your move, *votre excellence*! . . .[4] Protect your knight. You don't laugh because you don't get the joke . . . That's right, ma'am . . .

ANNA PETROVNA. What are you gawking at? It's your move! What do you think? Will your "one and only" come here today or not?

TRILETSKY. She promised to come. Gave her word.

---

2 Latin: a healthy mind in a healthy body.

3 First lines of a ballad by K. Frantz, "The Dart," popular in Russia in the 1870s and early 1880s.

4 French: your excellency. As the widow of a general, Anna Petrovna is entitled to her husband's form of address.

ANNA PETROVNA. In that case it's high time she was here. It's one o'clock . . . You . . . forgive me for the bluntness of the question . . . Are you and she "just friends" or is it serious?

TRILETSKY. Meaning?

ANNA PETROVNA. Be frank, Nikolay Ivanych! I'm not asking as a gossip, but as a good friend . . . What's Miss Grekova to you and you to her? Frankly and without being witty, please . . . Well? Tell me the truth, I'm asking as a good friend . . .

TRILETSKY. What is she to me and I to her? So far I don't know, ma'am . . .

ANNA PETROVNA. At the very least . . .

TRILETSKY. I drop in on her, chat with her, bore her silly, put her dear mama to the expense of making coffee and . . . that's all. Your move. I drop by, I ought to tell you, every other day, and sometimes every day, I walk down shady lanes . . . I talk to her about my stuff, she talks to me about her stuff, then she takes me by this button and flicks lint off my collar . . . I'm constantly covered in lint.[5]

ANNA PETROVNA. Well?

TRILETSKY. Well, nothing . . . Just what it is I find attractive about her is hard to define. Whether it's boredom or love or something else, I can't figure out . . . I know that when dinner's over she bores me stiff . . . It has incidentally come to my attention that I bore her as well . . .

ANNA PETROVNA. Love, in other words?

TRILETSKY (*shrugs his shoulders*). Quite possibly. What do you think, do I love her or not?

ANNA PETROVNA. Isn't that sweet! You should know better than I . . .

TRILETSKY. Uh-oh . . . you really don't understand me! . . . Your move!

ANNA PETROVNA. I'm moving. I *don't* understand, Nikolya! It's not easy for a woman to understand the way you're behaving in this sort of relationship . . .

Pause.

---

5 Presumably from bandages.

TRILETSKY. She's a good girl.

ANNA PETROVNA. I like her. Got her wits about her . . . Only here's the thing, my friend . . . Don't get her involved in any hanky-panky! . . . None of that sort of thing . . . That's your besetting sin . . . You hang around and hang around, talk arrant nonsense, make promises, spread rumors and then you call the whole thing off . . . I'd be awfully sorry . . . What is she up to these days? . . .

TRILETSKY. Reading.

ANNA PETROVNA. And studying chemistry?

They laugh.

TRILETSKY. I suppose so.

ANNA PETROVNA. A marvelous creature . . . Careful! You knocked over that piece with your sleeve! I like her with that pointy little nose of hers! She might make quite a good scientist . . .

TRILETSKY. She can't figure out what she wants to do, poor girl!

ANNA PETROVNA. Tell you what, Nikolay . . . Ask Mariya Yefimovna to come over and see me some time . . . I'll find out what she's like . . . Now, I won't act as a marriage broker, I'll just . . . You and I will get a taste of her quality, and we'll either let her go about her business or take her on approval . . . Whichever way it turns out . . .

Pause.

I think of you as a babe in arms, fickle as the wind, and that's why I'm interfering in your affairs. Your move. Here's my advice. Either drop her entirely or else marry her . . . Only do marry her, and . . . nothing else! If, to your great surprise, you want to marry her, please think it over first . . . Please examine her from every angle, not superficially, give it some thought, turn it over in your mind, discuss it, so you won't have cause for tears later on . . . You hear me?

TRILETSKY. How can I help it . . . I'm all ears.

ANNA PETROVNA. I know you. You do everything without a second thought and you'll get married without a second thought. A woman has only to crook her finger, and you're ready to go the whole hog. You should consult with your closest friends . . . Yes . . . You can't rely on your own stupid head . . . (*Raps on the table*.) That's what your head's made of! (*Whistles*.) The wind whistles through it, my good man! It's packed with brains, but not an ounce of sense . . .

TRILETSKY. Whistles like a farmhand! Wonderful woman!

Pause.

She won't come here for a visit.

ANNA PETROVNA. Why not?

TRILETSKY. Because Platonov hangs around here . . . She can't stand him after those stunts he's pulled. The man's convinced that she's a fool, imbedded the idea in his shaggy head, and now there's no way in hell to shake it loose! For some reason he thinks it's his responsibility to give fools a hard time, play all sorts of tricks on them . . . Your move! . . . But what kind of a fool is she? As if he understands people!

ANNA PETROVNA. Hogwash. We won't let him do anything out of line. Tell her that she's got nothing to be afraid of. But what's taking Platonov so long? He should have been here long ago . . . (*Looks at the clock*.) It's bad manners on his part. We haven't seen one another for six months.

TRILETSKY. When I drove over here, the shutters on the school-house were closed tight. I suppose he's still asleep. What a scoundrel the fellow is! I haven't seen him for a long time either.

ANNA PETROVNA. Is he well?

TRILETSKY. He's always well. Alive and kicking!

Enter GLAGOLYEV SR. and VOINITSEV.

SCENE II

The same, GLAGOLYEV SR. and VOINITSEV.

GLAGOLYEV SR. (*entering*). That's the way it used to be, my dear Sergey Pavlovich. In that respect we, the setting suns, are better off and happier than you, the rising suns. Man, as you see, wasn't the loser, and woman was the winner.

They sit down.

Let's sit down, besides I'm worn out . . . We loved women like the most chivalrous of knights, put our faith in them, worshiped them, because we regarded them as the paragon of humanity . . . For a woman is the paragon of humanity, Sergey Pavlovich!

ANNA PETROVNA. Why are you cheating?

TRILETSKY. Who's cheating?

ANNA PETROVNA. And who put that pawn here?

TRILETSKY. Why, you put it there yourself!

ANNA PETROVNA. Oh, right . . . *Pardon* . . .

TRILETSKY. You're darn right *pardon*.

GLAGOLYEV SR. We had friends as well . . . In our day friendship wasn't so simple-minded and so superficial. In our day there were clubs, liberal literary circles[6] . . . For our friends, among other things, we were expected to go through fire.

VOINITSEV (*yawns*). Those were the days!

TRILETSKY. And in these horrid days of ours it's the firemen who go through fire for their friends.

ANNA PETROVNA. Don't be silly, Nikolya!

Pause.

GLAGOLYEV SR. Last winter at the Moscow opera I saw a young man burst into tears under the influence of good music . . . Isn't that a fine thing?

VOINITSEV. I'd say it's a very fine thing.

GLAGOLYEV SR. That's what I think. But why, do tell me, please, when they noticed it, did the little ladies sitting nearby and their male companions smirk at him? What were they smirking at? And when he realized that these good people were watching him weep, he started to slouch in his seat, blush, planted a crooked grin on his face and then left the theater . . .

---

6 Literally, *arzamasy*. Arzamas, named after a provincial town, was a group of Russian noblemen, men of letters, and army officers who gathered together ca. 1815–1840, for literary and political discussions; they supported Romanticism against more conservative movements.

In our day we weren't ashamed of honest tears and we didn't make fun of them . . .

TRILETSKY (*to Anna Petrovna*). I wish this sack of saccharine would die of melancholy! I can't stand it! He gives me an earache!

ANNA PETROVNA. Sssh . . .

GLAGOLYEV SR. We were much happier than you are. In our day people who appreciated music did not leave the theater, but sat through the opera to the end . . . You're yawning, Sergey Pavlovich . . . I've been imposing on you . . .

VOINITSEV. No . . . But come to the point, Porfiry Semyonych! It's high time . . .

GLAGOLYEV SR. Well, sir . . . And so on and so forth . . . Now the point I'm trying to make to you is that in our day there were people who could love and hate, and consequently, feel indignation and contempt . . .

VOINITSEV. Fine, and in our day there aren't any, is that it?

GLAGOLYEV SR. I don't think there are.

> *VOINITSEV gets up and goes to the window.*

The deficit of such people is responsible for our present state of decline . . .

> *Pause.*

VOINITSEV. Not proven, Porfiry Semyonych!

ANNA PETROVNA. I can't stand it! He reeks so badly of that unbearable cheap cologne[7] that I'm starting to feel faint. (*Coughs.*) Move back a bit!

TRILETSKY (*moves back*). She's losing and it's all the fault of my poor cologne. Wonderful woman!

VOINITSEV. It's wrong, Porfiry Semyonych, to cast aspersions on a person based only on conjecture and a partiality for the youth of days gone by!

GLAGOLYEV SR. It may be I'm mistaken.

VOINITSEV. May be . . . In this case there's no room for "may be" . . . Your accusation is no laughing matter!

---

7 Literally, the same patchouli that Gaev complains about; see *The Cherry Orchard*, note 23.

GLAGOLYEV SR. (*laughs*). But . . . you're starting to get angry, my dear man . . . Hm . . . All this proves is that there's no chivalry in you, you don't know how to treat the views of an adversary with the proper respect.

VOINITSEV. The only thing it proves is that I do know how to get indignant.

GLAGOLYEV SR. Of course, I don't mean everyone . . . There are exceptions, Sergey Pavlovich!

VOINITSEV. Of course . . . (*Bows.*) I thank you most humbly for the little concession! The whole charm of your approach lies in such concessions. But what if you ran into some simple-minded person, who didn't know you, and who actually believed you knew what you were talking about? You'd end up convincing him that we, I mean, myself, Nikolay Ivanych, my *maman* and more or less every young person is incapable of feeling indignation and contempt . . .

GLAGOLYEV SR. But . . . you just . . . I didn't say . . .

ANNA PETROVNA. I want to listen to Porfiry Semyonych. Let's call this off! Enough.

TRILETSKY. No, no . . . Play and listen at the same time!

ANNA PETROVNA. Enough. (*Gets up.*) I'm fed up with it. We'll finish the game later.

TRILETSKY. When I'm losing, she sits glued to her spot, but as soon as I start to win, it turns out she longs to listen to Porfiry Semyonych! (*To Glagolyev.*) And who's asking you to talk? You're only in the way! (*To Anna Petrovna.*) Please sit back down and carry on, otherwise I'll assume that you lost!

ANNA PETROVNA. Go ahead! (*Sits facing Glagolyev.*)

SCENE III

The same and VENGEROVICH SR.

VENGEROVICH SR. (*enters*). It's hot! This heat reminds a Yid like me of Palestine. (*Sits at the piano and runs his fingers over the keys.*) I'm told it's very hot there!

TRILETSKY (*gets up*). We'll make a note of it. (*Takes a notebook out of his pocket.*) We'll make a note of it, my good woman! (*Makes a note.*) The general's lady . . . the general's lady three rubles . . . With what's owing—ten rubles! Uh-oh! When shall I have the honor of receiving that sum?

GLAGOLYEV SR. Eh, my friends, my friends! You didn't know the past! You'd be singing a different tune . . . You'd understand . . . (*Sighs.*) You just can't understand!

VOINITSEV. Literature and history are more to be trusted, I think . . . We didn't know the past, Porfiry Semyonych, but we feel it . . . Very often this is where we feel it the most . . . (*Slaps himself on the back of the neck.*) You're the one who doesn't know or feel the present.

TRILETSKY. Would you like me to put it on your tab, *votre excellence*, or are you ready to pay up now?

ANNA PETROVNA. Stop it! You're not letting me listen!

TRILETSKY. And why should you listen to them? They'll go on talking till nightfall!

ANNA PETROVNA. Serzhel, give this maniac ten rubles!

VOINITSEV. Ten? (*Takes out his billfold.*) Let's change the subject, Porfiry Semyonovich . . .

GLAGOLYEV SR. Let's, if you don't care for it.

VOINITSEV. I don't mind listening to you, but I do mind listening to what sounds like defamation of character . . . (*Gives Triletsky ten rubles.*)

TRILETSKY. *Merci.* (*Claps Vengerovich on the shoulder.*) That's how you've got to live in this world! Sit a defenseless woman down at the chessboard and clean her out of a ten-spot without a twinge of conscience. How about it? Praiseworthy behavior?

VENGEROVICH SR. Praiseworthy behavior. Doctor, you're a real Jerusalem gentleman!

ANNA PETROVNA. Stop it, Triletsky! (*To Glagolyev.*) So a woman is the paragon of humanity, Porfiry Semyonovich?

GLAGOLYEV SR. The paragon.

ANNA PETROVNA. Hm . . . Evidently, you are a great ladies' man, Porfiry Semyonovich!

GLAGOLYEV SR. Yes, I do love the ladies. I worship them, Anna Petrovna. I see in them almost everything I love: heart, and . . .

ANNA PETROVNA. You adore them . . . And are they worthy of your adoration?

GLAGOLYEV SR. They are.

ANNA PETROVNA. You're sure about that? Firmly convinced or only talking yourself into thinking that way?

> *TRILETSKY takes the violin and draws the bow along it.*

GLAGOLYEV SR. Firmly convinced. I only need to know one of you to be convinced of it . . .

ANNA PETROVNA. Seriously? You've got a funny way of looking at things.

VOINITSEV. He's a romantic.

GLAGOLYEV SR. Maybe . . . What of it? Romanticism is not entirely a bad thing. You've discarded romanticism . . . That's all right, but I'm afraid you discarded something else along with it . . .

ANNA PETROVNA. Don't start a debate, my friend. I don't know how to make a logical argument. Whether we discarded it or not, in any case we've become more intelligent, thank God! Aren't we more intelligent, Porfiry Semyonych? And that's the main thing . . . (*Laughs.*) So long as there are intelligent people and they keep growing more intelligent, the rest will take care of itself . . .[8] Ah! stop that scraping, Nikolay Ivanych! Put the violin away!

TRILETSKY (*hangs up the violin*). Nice instrument.

GLAGOLYEV SR. Platonov once put it very neatly . . . He said, we have become more intelligent about women, and to become more intelligent about women means trampling ourselves and women in the mire . . .

TRILETSKY (*roars with laughter*). I suppose it was his saint's day[9] . . . He'd had a bit too much . . .

ANNA PETROVNA. What did he say? (*Laughs.*) Yes, sometimes he likes to come out with snide remarks like that . . . But he probably said it for effect

---

8 Vershinin is to repeat this argument in *Three Sisters*.

9 See *Three Sisters*, note 7.

. . . By the way, while we're on the subject . . . What sort of a man, in your view, is our Platonov? A hero or an anti-hero?

GLAGOLYEV SR. How can I put this? Platonov, as I see it, is the finest exponent of modern infirmity of purpose . . . He is the hero of the best, still, unfortunately, unwritten, modern novel . . . (*Laughs.*) By infirmity of purpose I mean the current state of our society: the Russian novelist experiences this infirmity. He has turned up a blind alley, he's lost, he doesn't know what to focus on, he doesn't understand . . . Indeed it's no easy task to understand gentlemen like these! (*Indicates Voinitsev.*) The novels are impossibly bad, stilted, trivial . . . and no wonder! Everything is extremely tentative, unintelligible . . . Everything is so utterly confused, muddled . . . And the exponent of this infirmity of purpose, in my opinion, is our highly intelligent Platonov. Is he well?

ANNA PETROVNA. I'm told he is.

Pause.

A remarkable man . . .

GLAGOLYEV SR. Yes . . . It's a mistake to underestimate him. I dropped in on him a few times last winter and will never forget those few hours which I had the good fortune to spend with him.

ANNA PETROVNA (*looks at the clock*). It's high time he was here. Sergey, did you send for him?

VOINITSEV. Twice.

ANNA PETROVNA. You're all talking nonsense, gentlemen. Triletsky, run and send Yakov to fetch him!

TRILETSKY (*stretching*). Shall I tell them to set the table?

ANNA PETROVNA. I'll do it myself.

TRILETSKY (*goes and at the door bumps into Bugrov*). Chugging like a locomotive, it's the grocery man! (*Slaps him on the stomach and exits.*)

SCENE IV

ANNA PETROVNA, GLAGOLYEV SR., VENGEROVICH
SR., VOINITSEV, and BUGROV.

BUGROV (*entering*). Oof! This terrible heat! About to rain, looks like.

VOINITSEV. You came through the garden?

BUGROV. I did, sir . . .

VOINITSEV. Is *Sophie* there?

BUGROV. Who's *Sophie*?

VOINITSEV. My wife, Sofya Yegorovna![10]

VENGEROVICH SR. I'll just go and . . . (*Exits into the garden.*)

SCENE V

ANNA PETROVNA, GLAGOLYEV SR., VOINITSEV,
BUGROV, PLATONOV, and SASHA
(in Russian folk costume).[11]

PLATONOV (*in the doorway, to Sasha*). Please! After you, young woman! (*Enters behind Sasha.*) Well, we didn't stay at home after all! Make your curtsey, Sasha! Good afternoon, your excellency! (*Walks over to Anna Petrovna, kisses one hand and then the other.*)

ANNA PETROVNA. You cruel, discourteous creature . . . How could you make us wait so long? Don't you know how impatient I am? Dear Aleksandra Ivanovna . . . (*Exchanges kisses with Sasha.*)[12]

PLATONOV. So we didn't stay at home after all! Hallelujah, gentlemen! For six months we haven't seen a parquet floor, or easy chairs, or high ceilings, or even the decent people beneath them . . . All winter we hibernated in our den like bears, and only today have we crawled out into broad daylight! This is for Sergey Pavlovich! (*Exchanges kisses with Voinitsev.*)

VOINITSEV. And you've got taller, and put on weight and . . . who the hell knows what else . . . Aleksandra Ivanovna! Good Lord, you've put on weight! (*Shakes Sasha's hand.*) Are you well? You've got prettier and plumper!

---

10 The rest of the page of the manuscript is missing.

11 In Southern Russia, this would consist of a blouse (*rubakha*) worn under an ankle-high, paneled skirt (*ponyova*) and apron (*perednik*), all heavily embroidered. It might also include a beaded, horned cap (*kichka*), which hid the hair of married women.

12 The old Russian greeting was an embrace and an exchange of three kisses on the cheeks.

PLATONOV (*shakes Glagolyev's hand*). Porfiry Semyonovich ... Very pleased to see you ...

ANNA PETROVNA. How are you? How are you getting on, Aleksandra Ivanovna? Please take seats, my friends! Tell us about yourselves ... Sit down!

PLATONOV (*roars with laughter*). Sergey Pavlovich! Is that you? Lord! What's happened to the long hair, the charming little blouse, and that sweet tenor voice? Come on, say something!

VOINITSEV. I'm a blithering idiot. (*Laughs.*)

PLATONOV. A basso, a basso profundo! Well? Let's take a load off ... Move over, Porfiry Semyonych! I'm sitting down. (*Sits.*) Sit down, ladies and gentlemen! Phew ... It's hot ... So, Sasha! Can you smell it?

He sits down.

SASHA. I smell it.

PLATONOV. It smells of human flesh. What a marvelous aroma! I feel as if we haven't seen one another for ages. Damn last winter, it dragged on forever! Look, there's my armchair! You recognize it, Sasha? Six months ago I was ensconced in it day and night, threshing out the eternal verities with the general's lady and gambling away your shiny ten-kopek coins ... It's hot ...

ANNA PETROVNA. I was getting tired of waiting for you, I was losing patience ... Are you all right?

PLATONOV. Quite well ... I have to tell you, your excellency, that you have got plumper and a smidgeon prettier ... Today it's so hot, and muggy ... I'm already beginning to miss the cold.

ANNA PETROVNA. How monstrously fat these two have gotten! Such a happy tribe! How's life treating you, Mikhail Vasilich?

PLATONOV. Lousy as usual ... All winter I slept and didn't see the sky for six months. Drank, ate, slept, read adventure stories[13] aloud to my wife ... Lousy!

---

13 By Thomas Mayne Reid, English novelist (1818–1883), who wrote adventure stories for boys, set in the most exotic places on the globe.

SASHA. Life treated us well, only it was boring, naturally . . .

PLATONOV. Not just boring, but extremely boring, my darling. I missed you all terribly . . . Now you're a sight for sore eyes! To see you, Anna Petrovna, after a long, extra-tedious period of decentpeoplelessness and rottenpeopleitude, this is really an unpardonable luxury!

ANNA PETROVNA. Have a cigarette for that! (*Gives him a cigarette.*)

PLATONOV. *Merci.*

Lights up.

SASHA. You got here yesterday?

ANNA PETROVNA. At ten o'clock.

PLATONOV. At eleven I saw the lights on over here, but was afraid to drop by. I expect you were exhausted.

SASHA whispers in Platonov's ear.

PLATONOV. Ah, damn it! (*Slaps himself on the forehead.*) What a memory! Why didn't you say something before? Sergey Pavlovich!

VOINITSEV. What?

PLATONOV. And he didn't say a word either! Got married and didn't say a word! (*Gets up.*) I forgot, and they don't say a word.

SASHA. I forgot too, while he was talking away . . . Congratulations, Sergey Pavlovich! I wish you . . . all the best, all the best!

PLATONOV. I am honored to . . . (*Bows.*) Best wishes and much love, my dear man! You've performed a miracle, Sergey Pavlovich! I never expected such a grave and brave move on your part! So swift and so speedy! Who could have expected such a heresy from you?

VOINITSEV. That's the kind of fellow I am! Both swift and speedy! (*Roars with laughter.*) I didn't expect such a heresy on my part. It all came together in a flash, old man. I fell in love and I got married!

PLATONOV. Not a winter has gone by without your "falling in love," but this winter you got married as well, adding a critic to your team, as our parish priest says. A wife is the harshest, most fault-finding of critics! You're in for it if she's stupid! Have you found a little job?

VOINITSEV. They're offering me a job at the prep school, but I don't know what will come of it. I don't see myself in a prep school! The pay is low, and on the whole . . .

PLATONOV. Going to take it?

VOINITSEV. So far I really don't know. Probably not . . .

PLATONOV. Hm . . . Which means you'll loaf around. Hasn't it been three years since you graduated from the university?

VOINITSEV. Yes.

PLATONOV. You see . . . (*Sighs.*) There's nobody to give you a good hiding! Have to tell your wife to do it . . . Loafing for three whole years! Eh?

ANNA PETROVNA. It's too hot now to discuss important matters . . . I feel like yawning. What kept you so long, Aleksandra Ivanovna?

SASHA. We had no time . . . Misha had to fix the bird-cage, and I had to go to church . . . The cage was broken, and we couldn't leave our nightingale like that.

GLAGOLYEV SR. But why go to church today? Is it some holiday?

SASHA. No . . . I went to order a mass from Father Konstantin. Today is the memorial of Misha's father's death, and somehow it's awkward not to have prayers said . . . So I had a requiem sung . . .

Pause.

GLAGOLYEV SR. How long has it been since your father passed away, Mikhail Vasilich?

PLATONOV. About three, four years . . .

SASHA. Three years and eight months.

GLAGOLYEV SR. You don't say so? Goodness me! How time flies! Three years and eight months! Can it be that long since our last meeting? (*Sighs.*) The last time he and I met was at Ivanovka, both on the same jury . . . And something happened which was perfectly characteristic of the deceased . . . I remember they were trying a certain wretched, alcoholic government surveyor for bribery and corruption and (*laughs*) we acquitted him . . . Vasily Andreich, the deceased, insisted on it . . . He insisted for three hours straight, made all sorts of arguments, got hot under the collar . . . "I won't convict him," he shouts, "until you swear an oath that you yourselves never take bribes!" Illogical, but . . . there was nothing to be done with him! He wore us down dreadfully with his tolerance . . . We had with us the late General Voinitsev, your husband, Anna Petrovna . . . Another man of the same stripe.

ANNA PETROVNA. He wouldn't have been for acquittal . . .

GLAGOLYEV SR. Right, he insisted on conviction . . . I remember them both, red-faced, fuming, truculent . . . The peasants sided with the general, but we gentry sided with Vasily Andreich . . . We carried the day, of course . . . (*Laughs.*) Your father challenged the general to a duel, the general called him . . . forgive me, a sonuvabitch . . . Great fun! Later on we got them drunk and they made up . . . There's nothing easier than to get Russians to make up . . . A kind fellow your father, he had a kind heart . . .

PLATONOV. Not kind, but sloppy . . .

GLAGOLYEV SR. He was a great man in his way . . . I respected him. We were on the most excellent terms!

PLATONOV. Well, look, I can't sing his praises like that. We had a falling-out, when I still didn't have a hair on my chin, and for the last three years we were bitter enemies. I did not respect him, he considered me to be good for nothing, and . . . we were both right. I do not like the man! I do not like the fact that he died in his bed. He died the way honest men die. He was a sonuvabitch and at the same time refused to admit it—terribly characteristic of the Russian scoundrel!

GLAGOLYEV SR. *De mortuis aut bene, aut nihil,*[14] Mikhail Vasilich!

PLATONOV. No . . . That's a Latin heresy. The way I see it: *de omnibus aut nihil, aut veritas.*[15] But *veritas* is better than *nihil,* it's more instructive, at any rate . . . I insist that you don't have to make excuses for the dead . . .

Enter IVAN IVANOVICH.

---

14 Latin: Speak well of the dead, or say nothing. This is garbled by Shamraev in *The Seagull.*

15 Latin: Speak the truth of everything, or say nothing.

SCENE VI

The same and IVAN IVANOVICH.

IVAN IVANOVICH (*enters*). Ta-ran-ta-ra . . . My son-in-law and my daughter! Luminaries from the constellation of Colonel Triletsky! Good afternoon, my dears! A Krupp gun[16] salute! My friends, this heat! Mishenka, my dear boy . . .

PLATONOV (*gets up*). Greetings . . . Colonel! (*Embraces him.*) How's your health?

IVAN IVANOVICH. Never better . . . The Lord is patient and doesn't punish me. Sashenka . . . (*Kisses Sasha on the head.*) Haven't set eyes on you for ever so long . . . How's your health, Sashenka?

SASHA. Good . . . You're all right?

IVAN IVANOVICH (*sits next to Sasha*). I'm always healthy. Never been sick a day in my life . . . It's been so long since I've seen you! Every day I intend to visit you, see my grandson and carp about the whole wide world with my son-in-law, but I can never make up my mind to do it . . . Too busy, my angel! Day before yesterday I wanted to drive over, wanted to show you my new double-barrel shotgun, Mishenka, but the district police chief detained me and I had to sit down to a game of cards . . . It's a wonderful double-barrel! Anglish make, buckshot range of five hundred feet . . . Is my grandson well?

SASHA. He is, and sends his regards . . .

IVAN IVANOVICH. Does he really know how to send regards?

VOINITSEV. You have to take it figuratively.

IVAN IVANOVICH. All right, all right . . . Figuratively . . . Tell him, Sashurka, to grow up fast. I'll take him hunting with me . . . I've already got a little double-barrel ready for him . . . I'll make a huntsman of him, so that I can leave him my hunting gear . . .

ANNA PETROVNA. Our Ivan Ivanych is a sweetheart! He and I shall go shooting quail on St. Peter's day.[17]

---

16 Innovative ordnance with a sliding breech mechanism, developed in the German factories of Alfred Krupp.

17 On the Orthodox calendar, June 29.

IVAN IVANOVICH. Ho-ho! Anna Petrovna, we shall mount an expedition against the snipe. We shall mount a polar expedition to Devil's Swamp . . .

ANNA PETROVNA. We'll try out your double-barrel . . .

IVAN IVANOVICH. We shall indeed. Diana[18] the divine! (*Kisses her hand.*) You remember last year, my dear? Ha, ha! I love your kind of person, goddamit! I don't care for the faint-hearted! Why, she's a women's emancipation movement all by herself! Get a whiff of her lovely shoulder, and it's scented with gunpowder. It smells of Hannibals and Hamilcars![19] A military governor, quite the military governor! Give her a pair of epaulettes, and the world will be at her feet! Let's go! And take Sasha with us! We'll take everybody! We'll show them what a warrior's blood is like, Diana the divine, your excellency, Alexandra the Great!

PLATONOV. Had a drop already, colonel?

IVAN IVANOVICH. Naturally . . . *Sans doute* . . .[20]

PLATONOV. So that accounts for all the blather . . .

IVAN IVANOVICH. I got here, my dear chum, around eight o'clock . . . You were all still asleep . . . I got here, and cooled my heels . . . I look, she comes out . . . laughs . . . A bottle of Madeira we opened. Diana drank three little glasses, and I had the rest . . .

ANNA PETROVNA. You don't have to tell them about it!

TRILETSKY runs in.

SCENE VII

The same and TRILETSKY.

TRILETSKY. Welcome, nearest and dearest!

---

18 Diana, the Roman goddess of hunting, equivalent of the Greek Artemis.

19 Hannibal (247–182 B.C.), Carthaginian general, who led the forces against Rome in the Second Punic War. His father, Hamilcar Barcas (d. 228 B.C.), was a commander-in-chief of the Carthaginians in the First Punic War.

20 French: probably, no doubt.

PLATONOV. Ah-ah-ah . . . The quack personal physician to her Excellency! *Argentum nitricum . . . aquae destillatae . . .*[21] Delighted to see you, my dear fellow! He's healthy, sleek, glistening, and aromatic!

TRILETSKY (*kisses Sasha's head*). Your Mikhail's damn well bulked up! An ox, an honest-to-God ox!

SASHA. Faugh, what a stench of cologne! Are you well?

TRILETSKY. Fit as a fiddle. Nice of you to show up. (*Sits down.*) How's business, *Michel*?

PLATONOV. What business?

TRILETSKY. Yours, naturally.

PLATONOV. Mine? Who knows what that may be! It would take a long time in the telling, pal, and be of no interest. Where did you get such a chic haircut? A handsome coiffure! Did it cost a ruble?

TRILETSKY. I don't let barbers get near it . . . I've got some ladies for that, and I don't pay ladies for haircuts in rubles . . . (*Eats fruit-flavored jelly beans.*) Dear old pal, what I . . .

PLATONOV. About to be witty? That's a no-no . . . Don't take the trouble! Spare us, please.

SCENE VIII

The same, PETRIN, and VENGEROVICH SR.

PETRIN enters with a newspaper and sits down.
VENGEROVICH SR. sits in the corner.

TRILETSKY (*to Ivan Ivanovich*). If you have tears, prepare to shed them now, my progenitor!

IVAN IVANOVICH. Why should I shed tears?

TRILETSKY. Well, for instance, for joy . . . Look upon me! I am thy son! . . . (*Points at Sasha.*) She is thy daughter! (*Points at Platonov.*) That youth is thy son-in-law! The daughter alone is worth a tidy sum! She is a pearl of

---

21 Latin: silver nitrate; distilled water.

great price, daddy dearest! Thou alone couldst have engendered such an enchanting daughter! And what about the son-in-law?

IVAN IVANOVICH. Why should I shed tears over that, my son? There's no need for tears.

TRILETSKY. And what about the son-in-law? Oh . . . that son-in-law! You couldn't find another like him if you searched the wide world over! Honest, noble, big-hearted, just! And your grandson? He's the double-damnedest little boy! Waves his hands, reaches out like this and won't stop squealing: "Grampa! grampa! Where's grampa? Let me at him, the cut-throat, let me at his whiskers!"

IVAN IVANOVICH (*looks in his pocket for a handkerchief*). Why should I shed tears? Well, God be praised . . . (*Weeps.*) There's no call for tears.

TRILETSKY. Shedding tears, colonel?

IVAN IVANOVICH. No . . . What for? Well, praise the Lord! . . . So what?

PLATONOV. Stop it, Nikolay!

TRILETSKY (*gets up and sits down next to Bugrov*). The atmospheric temperature is a hot one today, Timofey Gordeich!

BUGROV. That's a fact. It's as hot as the top bench in a steam bath. The temperature's up in the nineties, I can't deny it.

TRILETSKY. What can this mean? Why is it so hot, Timofey Gordeich?

BUGROV. You know that better than me.

TRILETSKY. I don't know. I majored in medicine.

BUGROV. Well, the way I see it, sir, the reason it's so hot is that you and me would have a good laugh if it was cold in June.

Laughter.

TRILETSKY. I see, sir . . . Now I understand . . . What's the best thing for grass, Timofey Gordeich, climate or atmosphere?

BUGROV. They're both all right, Nikolay Ivanych, only you need a little rain for the wheat . . . What's the sense of a climate if there ain't no rain? Without rain it ain't worth a plug nickle.

TRILETSKY. I see . . . That's so true . . . Your lips, I cannot deny, give utterance to the purest wisdom . . . And what's your opinion, Mr. Grocery Man, concerning everything else?

BUGROV (*laughs*). Don't have none.

TRILETSKY. Q.E.D. You are the most intelligent of men, Timofey Gordeich! Well, now, what would you say to an astronomic anomaly that would make Anna Petrovna give us something to eat? Huh?

ANNA PETROVNA. Wait a while, Triletsky! Everyone else is waiting, so you can wait too!

TRILETSKY. She doesn't know our appetites! She doesn't know how much you and I, but especially I and you, want a drink! And we shall eat and drink gloriously, Timofey Gordeich! In the first place . . . In the first place . . . (*Whispers in Bugrov's ear.*) Not bad? And that's just the booze . . . *Crematum simplex . . .*[22] Whatever your heart desires: consumption on and off the premises . . . Caviar, sturgeon, salmon, sardines . . . Next a six- or seven-layer pie . . . That high! Filled with every conceivable wonder of flora and fauna from the Old and New Testaments . . . The sooner the better . . . Starving to death, Timofey Gordeich? Be honest . . .

SASHA (*to Triletsky*). You don't so much want to eat as to make a fuss! You don't like it when people sit quietly!

TRILETSKY. I don't like it when people keel over with hunger, my chubby little cherub!

PLATONOV. If you're being witty now, Nikolay Ivanych, why aren't people laughing?

ANNA PETROVNA. Ah, I'm sick and tired of him! So sick and tired of him! His impertinence is overstepping the bounds! It's terrible! Well, just you wait, you nasty man! I'll give you something to eat! (*Exits.*)

TRILETSKY. About time too.

SCENE IX

The same, without ANNA PETROVNA.

PLATONOV. Although I wouldn't object . . . What time is it? I'm hungry too.

---

22 Latin: a simple product.

VOINITSEV. Where did my wife go, gentlemen? Platonov still hasn't met her . . . They have to get acquainted. (*Gets up.*) I'll go and look for her. She's so fond of the garden that she can't leave it.

PLATONOV. By the way, Sergey Pavlovich . . . I'd prefer you not to introduce me to your wife . . . I'd like to know if she recognizes me or not? I was once slightly acquainted with her and . . .

VOINITSEV. Acquainted with her? Sonya?

PLATONOV. A long time ago . . . When I was still a student, I think. Please make no introductions, and don't say anything, don't tell her anything about me.

VOINITSEV. All right. The man knows everybody! And when does he have time to make acquaintances? (*Exits into the garden.*)

TRILETSKY. That was quite a leading article I inserted in the *Russian Courier*,[23] gentlemen! Have you read it? Did you read it, Abram Abramych?

VENGEROVICH SR. I did.

TRILETSKY. Am I right, a remarkable article? You there, you, Abram Abramych, I made out to be a real man-eater! What I wrote about you would put all of Europe in a panic!

PETRIN (*roars with laughter*). So that was who it was about?! So that's who V is! Well then, who is B?

BUGROV (*laughs*). That's me, sir. (*Mops his forehead.*) Let's forget about it!

VENGEROVICH SR. So what! It's most commendable. If I knew how to write, I would definitely write for the papers. In the first place, they pay cash for it, and in the second, for some reason people who write are assumed to be highly intelligent. Only it wasn't you, Doctor, who wrote that article. It was by Porfiry Semyonych.

GLAGOLYEV SR. How did you find that out?

VENGEROVICH SR. I know it.

GLAGOLYEV SR. Strange . . . I did write it, that's true, but how did you manage to find out?

---

23 *Russky kuryor*, a Moscow daily newspaper in circulation from 1879 to 1891.

VENGEROVICH SR. One can find out anything if only one wants to. You sent it as a registered letter, well, the clerk at our post office has a good memory. That's all . . . And there's no guesswork involved. My Jewish cunning has nothing to do with it . . . (*Laughs.*) Don't be afraid, I won't take revenge.

GLAGOLYEV SR. I'm not afraid, but . . . I do find it strange!

GREKOVA enters.

SCENE X

The same and GREKOVA.

TRILETSKY (*leaps up*). Mariya Yefimovna! Well, this is nice! What a surprise!

GREKOVA (*gives him her hand*). Good afternoon, Nikolay Ivanych! (*Nods her head to the rest.*) Good afternoon, gentlemen!

TRILETSKY (*takes her cape*). I'll take your little cape . . . Alive and well? Good afternoon again! (*Kisses her hand.*) Are you well?

GREKOVA. As always . . . (*Embarrassed, sits on the first chair she finds.*) Is Anna Petrovna at home?

TRILETSKY. She is. (*Sits beside her.*)

GLAGOLYEV SR. Good afternoon, Mariya Yefimovna!

IVAN IVANOVICH. Is this Mariya Yefimovna? I barely recognized her! (*Walks over to Grekova and kisses her hand.*) I'm pleased to meet you . . . Most pleased . . .

GREKOVA. Good afternoon, Ivan Ivanych! (*Coughs.*) It's awfully hot . . . Don't kiss my hand, please . . . It makes me feel awkward . . . I don't like it . . .

PLATONOV (*walks over to Grekova*). I'm pleased to convey my regards! . . . (*Tries to kiss her hand.*) How are you? May I take your hand?

GREKOVA (*withdrawing her hand*). Don't . . .

PLATONOV. Why not? I'm unworthy?

GREKOVA. I don't know whether you're worthy or not, but . . . you can't mean it?

PLATONOV. Can't mean it? How do you know if I mean it or not?

GREKOVA. You wouldn't have started to kiss my hand, if I hadn't said that I didn't like hand-kissing . . . For the most part you like to do whatever I don't like . . .

PLATONOV. Already jumping to conclusions!

TRILETSKY (*to Platonov*). Go away!

PLATONOV. Right this minute . . . How is your essence of bedbugs, Mariya Yefimovna?

GREKOVA. What essence?

PLATONOV. I heard that you are extracting ether from bedbugs . . . You want to make a contribution to science . . . An excellent idea!

GREKOVA. You're always joking . . .

TRILETSKY. Yes, he's always joking . . . So, you came after all, Mariya Yefimovna . . . How is your *maman*?

PLATONOV. What a pink little rosebud you are! How overheated you are!

GREKOVA (*gets up*). Why do you keep saying these things to me?

PLATONOV. I'm just making conversation . . . I haven't had a talk with you for a long time. Why get angry? When are you going to stop getting angry with me?

GREKOVA. I've noticed that you don't feel at ease, whenever you see me . . . I don't know how I'm interfering with you, but . . . I shall try to make life easy for you and avoid you as much as possible . . . If Nikolay Ivanych hadn't given me his word of honor that you wouldn't be here, I wouldn't have come . . . (*To Triletsky.*) Shame on you for lying!

PLATONOV. Shame on you for lying, Nikolay! (*To Grekova.*) You're getting ready to cry . . . Go ahead and cry! Tears are occasionally a relief . . .

> GREKOVA *quickly goes to the door, where she runs into*
> ANNA PETROVNA.

SCENE XI

The same and ANNA PETROVNA.

TRILETSKY (*to Platonov*). It's stupid . . . stupid! Do you understand? Stupid! Do it again and . . . we're enemies!

PLATONOV. What's it got to do with you?

TRILETSKY. Stupid! You don't know what you're doing!

GLAGOLYEV SR. It's cruel, Mikhail Vasilich!

ANNA PETROVNA. Mariya Yefimovna! I'm delighted! (*Shakes Grekova's hand.*) Delighted . . . You so rarely come to call on me . . . You've come, and I love you for that . . . Let's sit down . . .

They sit down.

Delighted . . . Thanks to Nikolay Ivanovich . . . He worked hard to pry you loose from your little village . . .

TRILETSKY (*to Platonov*). And what if, let's say, I love her?

PLATONOV. Love her . . . Be my guest!

TRILETSKY. You don't know what you're saying!

ANNA PETROVNA. How are you, my dear?

GREKOVA. Well, thank you.

ANNA PETROVNA. You're exhausted . . . (*Looks her in the face.*) It must be hard to drive fourteen miles when you're not used to it . . .

GREKOVA. No . . . (*Put a handkerchief to her eyes and weeps.*)

ANNA PETROVNA. What's wrong, Mariya Yefimovna?

Pause.

GREKOVA. No . . .

TRILETSKY paces up and down the stage.

GLAGOLYEV SR. (*to Platonov*). You have to apologize, Mikhail Vasilich!

PLATONOV. For what?

GLAGOLYEV SR. You have to ask?! You were cruel . . .

SASHA (*walks over to Platonov*). Apologize, or else I'm going! . . . Apologize!

ANNA PETROVNA. I would usually burst into tears after a trip . . . One's nerves are so on edge! . . .

GLAGOLYEV SR. Finally . . . I insist on it! It's bad manners! I didn't expect it of you!

SASHA. Apologize, I'm telling you! You shameless creature!

ANNA PETROVNA. I understand. (*Looks at Platonov.*) He's already had time to . . . Forgive me, Mariya Yefimovna. I forgot to have a word with this . . . this . . . It's my fault.

PLATONOV (*walks over to Grekova*). Mariya Yefimovna!

GREKOVA (*raises her head*). What can I do for you?

PLATONOV. I apologize . . . I publicly beg your pardon . . . I am consumed with shame in fifty different bones! . . . Give me your hand . . . I swear on my honor that I mean it . . . (*Takes her hand.*) Let's make peace . . . No more sniveling . . . Friends? (*Kisses her hand.*)

GREKOVA. Friends. (*Covers her face with her handkerchief and runs off.*)

TRILETSKY goes after her.

SCENE XII

The same, less GREKOVA and TRILETSKY.

ANNA PETROVNA. I never thought that you would go that far . . . You!

GLAGOLYEV SR. Take it easy, Mikhail Vasilyevich, for heaven's sake take it easy!

PLATONOV. That's enough . . . (*Sits on the sofa.*) Forget about her . . . I did something stupid in talking to her, but stupidity doesn't deserve all this discussion . . .

ANNA PETROVNA. Why did Triletsky have to run after her? Few women enjoy being seen in tears.

GLAGOLYEV SR. I respect this sensitivity in women . . . You really didn't say . . . anything in particular to her, I think, but . . . A mere hint, one little word . . .

ANNA PETROVNA. It's wrong, Mikhail Vasilich, wrong.

PLATONOV. I apologized, Anna Petrovna.

> Enter VOINITSEV, SOFYA YEGOROVNA, and
> VENGEROVICH JR.

SCENE XIII

> The same, VOINITSEV, SOFYA YEGOROVNA,
> VENGEROVICH JR., and then TRILETSKY.

VOINITSEV (*runs in*). She's coming, she's coming! (*Sings.*) She's coming!

> VENGEROVICH JR. stops in the doorway, and crosses his arms
> over his chest.

ANNA PETROVNA. At last *Sophie*'s had enough of this unbearable heat! Please come in!

PLATONOV (*aside*). Sonya! Good God Almighty, how she's changed!

SOFYA YEGOROVNA. I was so busy chatting with Monsieur Vengerovich that I completely forgot about the heat . . . (*Sits on the sofa, a good yard's distance from Platonov.*) I'm thrilled by our garden, Sergey.

GLAGOLYEV SR. (*sits beside Sofya Yegorovna.*) Sergey Pavlovich!

VOINITSEV. What can I do for you?

GLAGOLYEV SR. Sofya Yegorovna, my dearest friend, gave me her word that you'll all come and visit me on Thursday.

PLATONOV (*aside*). She looked at me!

VOINITSEV. We shall keep that word. The whole gang will come over to your place . . .

TRILETSKY (*enters*). Oh women, women! as Shakespeare said,[24] but he got it wrong. He should have said: Ouch, you women, women!

ANNA PETROVNA. Where's Mariya Yefimovna?

TRILETSKY. I took her into the garden. Let her walk off her aggravation!

---

24 A reference to Hamlet's "O frailty, thy name is woman!"

GLAGOLYEV SR. You've never once been to my place, Sofya Yegorovna! I hope you'll like it there . . . The garden is better than yours, the river is deep, the horsies are good ones . . .

Pause.

ANNA PETROVNA. Silence . . . A fool has been born.

Laughter.

SOFYA YEGOROVNA (*quietly to Glagolyev, nodding at Platonov*). Who is that man? The one who's sitting beside me!

GLAGOLYEV SR. (*laughs*). That's our schoolmaster . . . I don't know his last name . . .

BUGROV (*to Glagolyev*). Tell me please, Nikolay Ivanych, can you cure all sorts of diseases or only some sorts?

TRILETSKY. All sorts.

BUGROV. Even anthrax?

TRILETSKY. Even anthrax.

BUGROV. So if a mad dog bit me, you could deal with it?

TRILETSKY. Did a mad dog bite you? (*Moves away from him.*)

BUGROV (*nonplussed*). God forbid! What do you mean, Nikolay Ivanych! Christ protect us!

Laughter.

ANNA PETROVNA. How do we get to your place, Porfiry Semyonych? By way of Yusnovka?

GLAGOLYEV SR. No . . . You'd be going in a circle if you drive by way of Yusnovka. Drive straight to Platonovka. I practically live in Platonovka, only a mile and a half away.

SOFYA YEGOROVNA. I know that Platonovka. Does it still exist?

GLAGOLYEV SR. How else . . .

SOFYA YEGOROVNA. I once knew the landowner there, Platonov. Sergey, do you know where that Platonov is now?

PLATONOV (*aside*). She should ask me where he is.

VOINITSEV. I think I do . . . You don't remember his first name? (*Laughs.*)

PLATONOV. I knew him once as well. His name, I think, is Mikhail Vasilich.

Laughter.

SOFYA YEGOROVNA. Yes, yes . . . His name is Mikhail Vasilich. When I knew him, he was still a student, almost a boy . . . You're laughing, gentlemen . . . But I really don't see anything funny about what I said . . .

ANNA PETROVNA (*roars with laughter and points to Platonov*). Well, recognize him at last or else he'll explode with the suspense!

PLATONOV gets to his feet.

SOFYA YEGOROVNA (*gets to her feet and looks at Platonov*). Yes . . . it is him. Why don't you say something, Mikhail Vasilich? . . . Is it . . . really you?

PLATONOV. You don't recognize me, Sofya Yegorovna? No wonder! Four and a half years have gone by, almost five, and my last five years were worse than rats for chewing up a human face . . .

SOFYA YEGOROVNA (*gives him her hand*). Only now I'm beginning to recognize you. How you've changed!

VOINITSEV (*escorts Sasha to Sofya Yegorovna*). And let me introduce his wife! . . . Aleksandra Ivanovna, the sister of one of our wittiest people — Nikolay Ivanych!

SOFYA YEGOROVNA (*gives Sasha her hand*). Pleased to meet you. (*Sits.*) You're already married! . . . A long time? Still, five years . . .

ANNA PETROVNA. Attaboy, Platonov! He never goes anywhere, but he knows everybody. *Sophie*, I commend him as a friend of ours!

PLATONOV. This magnificent commendation gives me the right to ask you, Sofya Yegorovna, how are you in general? How's your health?

SOFYA YEGOROVNA. I'm all right in general, but my health is rather poor. And how are you? What are you doing these days?

PLATONOV. Fate has toyed with me in a way I never could have predicted in the days when you regarded me as a second Byron,[25] and I saw myself as a

---

25 George Gordon, Lord Byron, English poet and lover (1788–1824), the paragon of the Romantic rebel, an influence on Pushkin and Lermontov.

future Minister of Special Affairs and a Christopher Columbus. I'm a school teacher, Sofya Yegorovna, and that's all.

SOFYA YEGOROVNA. You?

PLATONOV. Yes, me . . .

Pause.

I suppose it does seem a bit odd . . .

SOFYA YEGOROVNA. Incredible! Why . . . Why not something more?

PLATONOV. One sentence wouldn't be enough, Sofya Yegorovna, to answer your question . . .

Pause.

SOFYA YEGOROVNA. You didn't even graduate from the university?

PLATONOV. No. I dropped out.

SOFYA YEGOROVNA. Hm . . . All the same, that doesn't prevent your being a somebody, does it?

PLATONOV. Sorry . . . I don't understand your question . . .

SOFYA YEGOROVNA. I didn't express myself clearly. It doesn't stand in the way of your being a person . . . I mean, someone who works for a cause . . . for instance, at least, freedom, women's emancipation . . . It doesn't stand in the way of your being the spokesman for a cause?[26]

TRILETSKY (*aside*). What a load of rubbish!

PLATONOV (*aside*). Here we go! Hm . . . (*To her.*) How can I put it? It probably doesn't stand in my way, but . . . what way is there to stand in? (*Laughs.*) Nothing can stand in my way . . . I am an immovable rock. Immovable rocks are created to stand in the way all on their own . . .

Enter SHCHERBUK.

SCENE XIV

The same and SHCHERBUK.

SHCHERBUK (*in the doorway*). Don't give the horses any oats: they pulled very badly!

---

26 Sofya Yegorovna's ideals are those of the Russian university student of the period, devoted to the cause of freedom and progress, which she wishes to see propagated in elementary schools.

ANNA PETROVNA. Hoorah! My gentleman friend is here!

EVERYONE. Pavel Petrovich!

SHCHERBUK (*silently kisses the hands of Anna Petrovna and Sasha, then bows to the men, each one individually, and makes a bow all 'round*). My friends! Tell me, unworthy individual that I am, where is that singular female, whom my soul yearns to behold! I suspect and believe that this singular female is she! (*Points to Sofya Yegorovna.*) Anna Petrovna, may I ask you to introduce me to her, so that she learns what sort of man I am!

ANNA PETROVNA (*links arms with him and leads him to Sofya Yegorovna*). Retired Guards Cornet Pavel Petrovich Shcherbuk!

SHCHERBUK. And what about my qualities?

ANNA PETROVNA. Oh yes . . . Our friend, neighbor, dance partner, guest, and creditor.

SHCHERBUK. Indeed! Closest friend of His Excellency the late General! Under his command I would capture the fortresses, known by the name of the ladies' polonaise.[27] (*Bows.*) May I take your hand, ma'am!

SOFYA YEGOROVNA (*extends her hand and then withdraws it*). Very kind of you, but . . . it isn't necessary.

SHCHERBUK. Offense taken, ma'am . . . Your husband I held in my arms, when he was still toddling under the table . . . I bear a mark from him which I shall carry to my grave. (*Opens his mouth.*) In here! Missing tooth! See it?

Laughter.

I held him in my arms, and Seryozhenka, with a pistol he happened to be fooling around with, delivered a reprimand to my teeth. Heh, heh, heh . . . The scalawag! Dear lady, whose name I have not the honor of knowing, keep him in line! Your beauty reminds me of a certain picture . . . Only the little nose is different . . . Won't you give me your hand?

PETRIN takes a seat next to Vengerovich Sr. and reads the paper aloud to him.

---

27 Shcherbuk means that the General taught him to lead the quadrille figure known as the ladies' polonaise.

SOFYA YEGOROVNA (*extends her hand*). If you insist . . .

SHCHERBUK (*kisses her hand*). *Merci* to you! (*To Platonov.*) Are you well, Mishenka? What a fine young fellow you've grown to be! (*Sits down.*) I knew you back in the days when you still gazed at God's green earth in bewilderment . . . And you keep growing and growing . . . Phooey![28] evil eye begone! Well done! What a good-looking fellow! Now why don't you join the army, Cupid?[29]

PLATONOV. Weak chest, Pavel Petrovich!

SHCHERBUK (*points at Triletsky*). *He* told you that? Believe him, that empty vessel, and you'll soon be losing your head!

TRILETSKY. Please don't be abusive, Pavel Petrovich.

SHCHERBUK. He treated my lumbago . . . Don't eat this, don't eat that, don't sleep on the floor . . . Well, he didn't cure it. So I ask him: "Why did you take my money, and not cure me?" So he says: "It's an either-or situation," he says, "either I cure you or I take your money." How do you like that sort of fellow?

TRILETSKY. Why are you lying, Beelzebub Bucephalovich?[30] How much money did you give me, may I ask? Try to remember! I paid you six visits and got only a ruble, and a torn one at that . . . I wanted to give it to a beggar and the beggar wouldn't take it. "It's all tore up," he says, "ain't no serial number!"

SHCHERBUK. He came by six times not because I was sick, but because my tenant's daughter is a *kek shows*.[31]

TRILETSKY. Platonov, you're sitting next to him . . . Bop him one on his bald spot for me! Do me a favor!

SHCHERBUK. Leave me alone! That's enough! Do not rouse the sleeping lion! You've got a lot to learn. (*To Platonov.*) And your father was a fine fellow too! He and I and the colonel were great friends. Quite the practical

---

28 He spits to avert the evil eye attracted by his praise.

29 Roman god of love, son of Venus, equivalent to the Greek Eros.

30 Beelzebub is a demon. Bucephalos was the charger of Alexander the Great. The joking name is a roundabout way of saying that Shcherbuk is a malicious horse's ass.

31 Bad French: *quelque chose*, in this context, quite an eyeful.

joker he was! Nowadays you won't find three such mischief-makers as we were . . . Ehhh. Those times are gone forever . . . (*To Petrin.*) Gerasya! Show some fear of God! We're conversing here, and you're reading aloud! Show some manners!

PETRIN *goes on reading.*

SASHA (*nudges Ivan Ivanovich's shoulder*). Papa! Papa, don't fall asleep here! Shame on you!

IVAN IVANOVICH *wakes up and a minute later falls asleep again.*

SHCHERBUK. No . . . I can't talk! . . . (*Gets up.*) Listen to him . . . He's reading! . . .

PETRIN (*gets up and walks over to Platonov*). What did you say, sir?

PLATONOV. Absolutely nothing . . .

PETRIN. No, you said something, sir . . . You said something about Petrin . . .

PLATONOV. You were dreaming, I suppose . . .

PETRIN. Are you criticizing, sir?

PLATONOV. I didn't say anything! I assure you that you dreamed it up!

PETRIN. You can say whatever you like . . . Petrin . . . Petrin . . . What about Petrin? (*Stuffs the paper into his pocket.*) Petrin, maybe, studied at the university, got a degree in law, maybe . . . Are you aware of that? . . . My law degree will be part of me until my dying day . . . So that's how it is, sir. A senior civil servant . . . Are you aware of that? And I have lived longer than you. Six decades, thank God, I have endured.

PLATONOV. Pleased to hear it, but . . . what's the point of all this?

PETROV. Live as long as I have, dear heart, and you'll find out! Living a life is no joke! Life takes a bite out of you . . .

PLATONOV (*shrugs*). Honestly, I don't know what you're getting at, Gerasim Kuzmich . . . I don't understand you . . . You started talking about yourself, and made a transition from yourself to life . . . What do you and life have in common?

PETRIN. When life breaks you down, shakes you up, when you start to be wary of young people . . . Life, my good sir . . . What is life? Here's what it is, sir! When a man is born, he walks down one of three roads in life, for there are no other paths: you go to the right—wolves will devour you, you go to the left—you will devour the wolves, you go straight ahead—you will devour yourself.

PLATONOV. Do tell . . . Hm . . . You came to this conclusion by a scientific method, by experience?

PETRIN. By experience.

PLATONOV. By experience . . . (*Laughs.*) With due respect, Gerasim Kuzmich, tell it to the judge, not to me . . . On the whole I'd advise you not to talk to me about higher matters . . . It makes me laugh and, honest to God, I don't believe it. I don't believe in your senile, home-spun wisdom! I don't believe, friends of my father, I deeply, ever so sincerely don't believe in your simple-minded speeches about profound topics, or in anything your minds can come up with.

PETRIN. Indeed, sir . . . Really . . . You can make anything out of a young tree: a cottage and a ship and anything you like . . . but one that's old, stout and tall is good for damn all . . .

PLATONOV. I'm not talking about old men in general; I'm talking about my father's friends.

GLAGOLYEV SR. I was also a friend of your father, Mikhail Vasilich!

PLATONOV. He had no end of friends . . . Once upon a time, the whole yard would be packed with carriages and gigs.

GLAGOLYEV SR. No . . . So that means you don't believe in me either? (*Roars with laughter.*)

PLATONOV. Hm . . . How can I put this? . . . Even in you, Porfiry Semyonych, I believe very little.

GLAGOLYEV SR. Is that so? (*Extends his hand.*) Thank you, my dear boy, for your frankness! Your frankness makes you even more appealing.

PLATONOV. You're a good sort . . . I even respect you profoundly, but . . . but . . .

GLAGOLYEV SR. Please, go on and say it!

PLATONOV. But . . . but one has to be only too gullible to believe in those characters from Fonvizin's comedies, those mealy-mouthed do-gooders and sickly-sweet lovers who spend their lives rubbing elbows with total swine and riffraff,[32] and those petty tyrants who are venerated because they do neither good nor evil. Don't be angry, please!

ANNA PETROVNA. I don't care for this sort of conversation, especially when it's Platonov doing the talking . . . It always ends badly. Mikhail Vasilich, let me introduce you to our new acquaintance! (*Indicates Vengerovich Jr.*) Isak Abramovich Vengerovich, a university student . . .

PLATONOV. Ah . . . (*Gets up and goes to Vengerovich Jr.*) Pleased to meet you! Delighted. (*Extends his hand.*) I'd give a great deal nowadays to have the right to be called a student again . . .

Pause.

I'm holding out my hand . . . Take mine or give me yours . . .

VENGEROVICH JR. I won't do either . . .

PLATONOV. What?

VENGEROVICH JR. I won't give you my hand.

PLATONOV. A riddle . . . Why not, sir?

ANNA PETROVNA (*aside*). What the hell!

VENGEROVICH JR. Because I have my reasons . . . I despise such persons as you!

PLATONOV. Bully for you . . . (*Looks him over.*) I would tell you that makes me feel awfully good, except that it would tickle your vanity, which has to be safeguarded for what comes next . . .

Pause.

You look down on me like a giant gazing on a pygmy. Could it be you are in fact a giant?

VENGEROVICH JR. I'm an honest man and not a vulgarian.

---

32 Literally, "the stolid Starodums and saccharine Milonovs, who ate cabbage soup all their lives from the same bowl as the Skotinins and the Prostakovs." Characters in the comedy *The Minor* (1782), by Denis Fonvizin (1745–1792): Starodum (Oldsense), the prosy raisonneur; Milonov (Charmer), the sentimental love interest; the Skotinins (Beastlys) and Prostakovs (Simpletons), the crude and rapacious serf owners.

PLATONOV. For which I congratulate you . . . It would be pretty strange for a young student to be a dishonest man . . . None of us is questioning your honesty . . . Won't you give me your hand, young man?

VENGEROVICH JR. I don't dole out charity.

TRILETSKY goes "Boo."

PLATONOV. You don't? That's your business . . . I was referring to courtesy, not charity . . . You despise me that intensely?

VENGEROVICH JR. As much as a man can, who wholeheartedly hates vulgarity, servility, buffoonery . . .

PLATONOV (*sighs*). It's been a long time since I've heard a speech like that . . . "And a mem'ry of home rings out in the songs of the coachman!" . . .[33] I too was once an expert at tossing such bouquets . . . Only, unfortunately, this is all rhetoric . . . Charming rhetoric, but mere rhetoric . . . If only there were a smidgeon of sincerity . . . False notes jar terribly on an unpracticed ear . . .

VENGEROVICH JR. Shouldn't we put an end to this talk?

PLATONOV. What for? They're listening to us so avidly, and besides we haven't had time to get sick of one another . . . Let's keep talking in the same vein . . .

VASILY runs in, followed by OSIP.

SCENE XV

The same and OSIP.

OSIP (*enters*). Ahem . . . I have the honor and pleasure of wishing Your Excellency well on her arrival . . .

Pause.

I wish you all that you wish God to grant you.

Laughter.

PLATONOV. Whom do I see?! The devil's bosom buddy! The terror of the countryside! The most hair-raising of mortals!

---

33 A line from Pushkin's poem "The Winter Road" (1826).

ANNA PETROVNA. What have you got to say for yourself! You're not wanted here! Why did you come?

OSIP. To wish you well.

ANNA PETROVNA. A lot I need that! Clear out of here!

PLATONOV. Are you the one who, in darkest night and light of day, strikes fearsome terror into the hearts of men? I haven't seen you for ages, manslaughterer, the six sixty-six prophesied by the Apocalypse![34] Well, my friend? Expatiate on something! Lend your ears to Osip the great!

OSIP (bows). On your arrival, Your Excellency! Sergey Pavlych! On your lawful marriage! God grant that everything . . . that when it comes to family you get the best . . . of everything! God grant it!

VOINITSEV. Thank you! (To Sofya Yegorovna.) Here, Sophie, may I introduce the Voinitsev bogeyman!

ANNA PETROVNA. Don't detain him, Platonov! Let him go! I'm angry with him. (To Osip.) Tell them in the kitchen to give you something to eat . . . Look at those animal-like eyes! Did you steal a lot of our wood last winter?

OSIP (laughs). Three or four little trees . . .

Laughter.

ANNA PETROVNA (laughs). You're lying, it's a lot more! And he's even got a watch-chain! Tell me! Is it a gold watch-chain? Would you tell me what time it is?

OSIP (looks at the clock on the wall). Twenty-two minutes past one . . . May I kiss your little hand!

ANNA PETROVNA (extends her hand to him). There, kiss it . . .

OSIP (kisses her hand). Most grateful to Your Excellency for your kind indulgence! (Bows.) Why are you holding on to me, Mikhail Vasilich?

PLATONOV. I'm afraid that you're going to leave. I love you, my dear fellow! What a strapping youth, double damn you! What was the bright idea, wiseguy, in coming here?

---

34 "The number of the beast; for it is the number of a man; and his number is Six hundred three-score and six." The Revelation of John the Divine, 13:18.

OSIP. I was chasing that fool, that Vasily, and wound up in here by accident.

PLATONOV. A clever man chases a fool, and not the other way round! I am honored, gentlemen, to make an introduction! A most interesting specimen! One of the most interesting bloodthirsty beasts of prey in the zoological museum of today! (*Turns Osip around in all directions.*) Known to each and every one as Osip, horse thief, freeloader, homicide, and thief. Born in Voinitsevka, committed robbery and murder in Voinitsevka, and lost and gone forever in that same Voinitsevka!

Laughter.

OSIP (*laughs*). You're a wonderful man, Mikhail Vasilich!

TRILETSKY (*inspects Osip*). What's your occupation, my good man?

OSIP. Stealing.

TRILETSKY. Hm . . . A pleasant occupation . . . But what a cynic you are!

OSIP. What does cynic mean?

TRILETSKY. Cynic is a Greek word, which, translated into your language, means: a swine who wants the whole world to know he is a swine.

PLATONOV. He's smiling, ye gods! What a smile! And that face, what a face! There's two tons of iron in that face! You've have a hard time breaking it on a stone! (*Walks him over to the mirror.*) Look at that, you monstrosity! See it? Doesn't it surprise you?

OSIP. Just an ordinary man! Not so much as that . . .

PLATONOV. Is that right? And not a paladin? Not Ilya Muromets?[35] (*Claps him on the shoulder.*) O courageous, unconquered Russian! What sense do we make compared to thee? Petty little creatures, parasites, we huddle in our corner, we don't know where we belong . . . We should be thy companions, we need a wilderness with champions, paladins with heads that weigh a ton, hissing and whistling. Could you have bumped off Nightingale the Bandit?[36] Eh?

---

35 One of the paladins or *bogatyrs* of Russian epic, the son of a peasant who roamed through Kievan Rus in the reign of Vladimir (980–1015), protecting it from giants and enemies. Heroes of these legendary times were supposed to be of enormous size and matchless strength.

36 Nightingale (*Solovey*) the Bandit, hero of Russian folk poetry, a sort of Robin Hood.

OSIP. Who can tell!

PLATONOV. You would have bumped him off! After all, you're strong enough! Those aren't muscles, but steel cables! Which reminds me, why aren't you on a chain gang?[37]

ANNA PETROVNA. Cut it short, Platonov! Honestly, you make me sick and tired.

PLATONOV. You've been in jail at least once, Osip?

OSIP. On occasion . . . I'm there every winter.

PLATONOV. That's the way it should be . . . It's cold in the forest—go to jail. But why aren't you on a chain gang?

OSIP. I don't know . . . Let me go, Mikhail Vasilich!

PLATONOV. Aren't you of this world? Are you beyond time and space? Are you beyond customs and laws?

OSIP. Excuse me, sir . . . What it says in the law is, you only get sent to Siberia when they prove a case against you or catch you in the commission of a crime . . . Everybody knows, let's say, that I'm, let's say, a thief and a robber (*laughs*), but not everybody can prove it . . . Hm . . . Nowadays folks ain't got no gumption, they're stupid, no brains, I mean . . . Scared of everything . . . So they're scared to testify . . . They could have got me exiled, but they ain't got the hang of the law . . . Everything puts 'em in a panic . . . Folks nowadays are jackasses, long story short . . . They'd rather be trying something on the sly, ganging up on you . . . Lowdown, no-good folks . . . Ignorant . . . And it's no shame if folks like that get hurt . . .

PLATONOV. What cogent reasoning from a scoundrel! Arrived at his own conclusions, the repulsive brute! And on a theoretical basis at that . . . (*Sighs.*) The foul things that are still possible in Russia! . . .

OSIP. I ain't the only one to figure it out, Mikhail Vasilich! Nowadays everybody figures like that. Take, for instance, Abram Abramych there . . .

PLATONOV. Yes, he's yet another outlaw . . . Everybody knows it, and nobody testifies.

---

37 For the most serious crimes, criminals in tsarist Russia were exiled to prison colonies in Siberia; they were made to walk there, chained together.

VENGEROVICH SR. I suggest you leave me in peace . . .

PLATONOV. There's no point in bringing him up . . . You two are the same; the only difference is that he's smarter than you and happy as the day is long. Besides . . . he can't be called names to his face, but you can. Two peas in a pod, but . . . Sixty taverns, my friend, sixty taverns, and you haven't got sixty kopeks!

VENGEROVICH SR. Sixty-three taverns.

PLATONOV. In a year's time he'll have seventy-three . . . He's a public bene-factor, gives charity dinners, is widely respected, everyone doffs his cap to him, whereas you . . . you're a great man, but . . . pal, you don't know how to lead your life! You don't know how to lead your life, you public enemy!

VENGEROVICH SR. You're letting your imagination run away with you, Mikhail Vasilich! (*Gets up and sits on a different chair.*)

PLATONOV. He's got more lightning rods to protect his head . . . He'll live peaceably for as many years as he's lived already, if not more, and he'll die . . . he'll die even more peaceably!

ANNA PETROVNA. Stop it, Platonov!

VOINITSEV. Take it easy, Mikhail Vasilich! Osip, get out of here! Your pres-ence is only aggravating the Platonovian instincts.

VENGEROVICH SR. He wants to chase me out of here, but he won't succeed!

PLATONOV. I will succeed! If I don't succeed, I'll leave myself!

ANNA PETROVNA. Platonov, won't you give over? Stop speechifying, and tell me plainly: are you going to give over or not?

SASHA. Shut up, for heaven's sake! (*Quietly.*) It's indecent! You're embarrass-ing me!

PLATONOV (*to Osip*). Beat it! My cordial wishes for your speediest departure!

OSIP. Marya Petrovna's got a parrot that calls everybody and their dog fools, and when it gets an eyeful of a vulture or Abram Abramych, it screeches: "Damn you!" (*Roars with laughter.*) Good-bye, sir! (*Exits.*)

SCENE XVI

The same, less OSIP.

VENGEROVICH SR. Of all people, you're the last one, young man, to venture to lecture me on morality and certainly not in that way. I am a citizen and, to tell the truth, a useful citizen . . . I'm a father, and who are you? Who are you, young man? Excuse me, a show-off, a landowner who's frittered away his estate, who has assumed a sacred duty, to which he has not the slighest qualification, being a depraved individual . . .

PLATONOV. A citizen . . . If you're a citizen, then it is a very dirty word! A four-letter word!

ANNA PETROVNA. He won't give over! Platonov, why are you poisoning the day for us with your preaching? Why do you have to talk out of turn? And who gave you the right?

TRILETSKY. How can one live in peace with these most righteous and honorable of men . . . They meddle in everything, make everything their business, poke their noses in everything . . .

GLAGOLYEV SR. They started, gentlemen, with Are you well? and end with Please drop dead . . .

ANNA PETROVNA. Bear in mind, Platonov, that "if guests start name-calling, the hostess starts bawling . . ."

VOINITSEV. That is correct, and from this moment on let there be a general hush . . . Peace, harmony, and silence!

VENGEROVICH SR. He won't give me a moment's peace! What did I ever do to him? He's a fraud!

VOINITSEV. Hush . . .

TRILETSKY. Let them call each other names! All the more fun for us.

Pause.

PLATONOV. When you take a hard look and give it serious thought, you could faint! . . . And what's worst of all is that anyone who is the least bit honest, sensible, keeps his mouth shut, silent as the tomb, and only stares . . . Everyone stares at him in fear, everyone kowtows to this obese, gilded upstart, everyone is in debt to him up to their eyebrows! Honor's gone down the drain!

ANNA PETROVNA. Calm down, Platonov! This is last year's story all over again, and I won't stand for it!

PLATONOV (*drinks some water*). All right. (*Sits down.*)

VENGEROVICH SR. All right.

Pause.

SHCHERBUK. I am a martyr, my friends, a martyr!

ANNA PETROVNA. Now what?

SHCHERBUK. Woe is me, my friends! Better lie in your grave than live with a shrewish wife! We had another blow-up! She almost killed me a week ago with that devil of hers, that red-headed Don Juan.[38] I was asleep in the yard under the apple tree, I was savoring my dreams, and poring over visions of the past with envy . . . (*Sighs.*) All of a sudden . . . all of a sudden it's as if someone's bopping me on the head! Good Lord! The end, I think, has come! An earthquake, warring elements, a flood, a rain of fire . . . I open my eyes, and there stands Rusty . . . Rusty attacks me by my flank, and wallops that contingent with all his might, and then drops me on the ground! Then that wild woman jumped on me . . . Grabbed me by my innocent beard (*grabs himself by the beard*), and that was no picnic! (*Slaps his bald spot.*) They nearly killed me . . . I thought I'd kick the bucket . . .

ANNA PETROVNA. You're exaggerating, Pavel Petrovich . . .

SHCHERBUK. She's an old hag, older than anything on this earth, uglier than sin, and yet she's . . . in love! Oh, you witch! And this suits Rusty fine . . . It's my money he's after, and not her love . . .

YAKOV enters and hands Anna Petrovna a calling card.

VOINITSKY. Who is it?

ANNA PETROVNA. Stop, Pavel Petrovich! (*Reads.*) "*Comte Glagolief.*" What's all this formality for? Please, show him in! (*To Glagolyev Sr.*) Your son, Porfiry Semyonych!

GLAGOLYEV SR. My son? Out of the blue? He's abroad!

Enter GLAGOLYEV JR.

---

38 The great seducer was familiar to Russians from both Mozart's *Don Giovanni*, frequently produced on the operatic stage, and Pushkin's rarely staged but much read verse tragedy *The Stone Guest* (1830).

The same and GLAGOLYEV JR.

ANNA PETROVNA. Kirill Porfirich! How kind of you!

GLAGOLYEV SR. (*stands up*). Kirill, you're . . . here? (*Sits down.*)

GLAGOLYEV JR. Good afternoon, *mesdames*! Platonov, Vengerovich, Trilet-sky! . . . So that crackpot Platonov's here . . . Greetings, regards, and respects! It's awfully hot in Russia . . . Straight from Paris! Straight as an arrow from the land of the French! Phew . . . You don't believe it? Word of honor as a gentleman! Only dropped off my trunk at home . . . Well, that Paris, ladies and gentleman! There's a city for you!

VOINITSEV. Take a seat, Frenchie!

GLAGOLYEV JR. No, no, no . . . I didn't come as a guest, but just . . . I just have to see my father . . . (*To his father.*) Listen, why are you doing this?

GLAGOLYEV SR. Doing what?

GLAGOLYEV JR. You want to pick a fight? Why didn't you send me any money, when I asked for it, eh?

GLAGOLYEV SR. We'll discuss it at home.

GLAGOLYEV JR. Why didn't you send me any money? Are you making fun of me? Is everything a joke to you? Are you joking? Gentlemen, how can one live abroad without money?

ANNA PETROVNA. How did you find life in Paris? Do sit down, Kirill Porfirych!

GLAGOLYEV JR. Thanks to him I've come back with nothing but a tooth-brush! I sent him thirty-five telegrams from Paris! Why didn't you send me any money, I'm asking you! Are you blushing? Are you ashamed?

TRILETSKY. Don't shout, please, your lordship! If you do shout, I shall send your calling card to the examining magistrate and have you legally charged with misappropriating the title of count which does not belong to you! It's indecent!

GLAGOLYEV SR. Don't, Kirill, there'll be a scandal! I assumed that six thou-sand would be enough. Calm down!

GLAGOLYEV JR. Give me money, and I'll go away again! Give it right now! Right now give it! I'll go! Give it this minute! I'm in a hurry!

ANNA PETROVNA. Where are you off to in such a hurry? You've got time! Tell us about your travels instead . . .

YAKOV (*enters*). Luncheon is served!

ANNA PETROVNA. Really? In that case, ladies and gentlemen, let's go and eat!

TRILETSKY. Eat! Hurra-a-ah! (*With one hand he seizes Sasha's hand and with the other Glagolyev Jr.'s and starts to run.*)

SASHA. Let go! Let go, you holy terror! I can go by myself!

GLAGOLYEV JR. Let go of me! What is this boorishness? I don't care for jokes. (*Tears himself away.*)

SASHA and TRILETSKY run out.

ANNA PETROVNA (*takes Glagolyev Jr. by the arm*). Let's go, Parisian! There's no point in fuming over nothing! Abram Abramych, Timofey Gordeich . . . Please! (*Exits with Glagolyev Jr.*)

BUGROV (*gets up and stretches*). Takes so long for lunch to show up around here, you can't stop drooling. (*Exits.*)

PLATONOV (*gives Sofya Yegorovna his hand*). May I? What a look of wonder in your eyes! For you this world is undiscovered territory! This world (*in an undertone*) of fools, Sofya Yegorovna, arrant, obtuse, hopeless fools . . . (*Exits with Sofya Yegorovna.*)

VENGEROVICH SR. (*to his son*). Now you've seen him?

VENGEROVICH JR. He is a most original villain! (*Exits with his father.*)

VOINITSEV (*nudges Ivan Ivanovich*). Ivan Ivanych! Ivan Ivanych! Lunch!

IVAN IVANOVICH (*leaps up*). Huh? Somebody?

VOINITSEV. Nobody . . . Let's go have lunch!

IVAN IVANOVICH. Very good, my dear fellow!

SCENE XVIII

PETRIN and GLAGOLYEV SR.

PETRIN. You're willing to do it?

GLAGOLYEV SR. I'm not against it . . . I've already told you!

PETRIN. Darling boy . . . You definitely want to get married?

GLAGOLYEV SR. I don't know, old pal. Is she still willing?

PETRIN. She is! Goddamn me, but she is!

GLAGOLYEV SR. Who knows? It isn't right to think about . . . "Another's heart is a shadowy part." Why are you so concerned?

PETRIN. Who else should I be concerned about, darling boy? You're a good man, she's a wonderful woman . . . You want me to put in a word with her?

GLAGOLYEV SR. I'll put in my own word. You keep still in the meantime and . . . if possible, please, don't get involved! I know how to marry myself off. (*Exits.*)

PETRIN (*alone*). I wish he did! Saints in heaven, put yourselves in my shoes! . . . If the general's lady marries him, I'm a rich man! My I.O.U.s will be paid, saints in heaven! I've even lost my appetite at this joyous prospect. The servants of God, Anna and Porfiry, be joined in holy matrimony, or, rather, Porfiry and Anna . . .

Enter ANNA PETROVNA.

SCENE XIX

PETRIN and ANNA PETROVNA.

ANNA PETROVNA. Why haven't you gone in to lunch?

PETRIN. Dear lady, Anna Petrovna, may I drop a hint to you?

ANNA PETROVNA. Drop it, but do it quickly, please . . . I've got no time . . .

PETRIN. Hm . . . Could you let me have a little bit of money, dear lady?

ANNA PETROVNA. You call that a hint? That is far from a hint. How much do you need? One ruble, two?

PETRIN. Make a dent in your I.O.U.s. I'm fed up staring at those I.O.U.s . . . I.O.U.s are nothing but delusions, a nebulous dream. They say: you own something! But in fact it turns out you own nothing!

ANNA PETROVNA. Are you still on about that sixteen thousand? Aren't you ashamed? Doesn't it make your skin crawl every time you beg for that loan? Isn't it disgraceful? What do you, an old bachelor, need with such ill-gotten gains?

PETRIN. I need them because they're mine, dear lady.

ANNA PETROVNA. You finagled those I.O.U.s out of my husband, when he wasn't sober, was ill . . . Do you remember?

PETRIN. What if I did, dear lady? In any case they are I.O.U.s, which means that they require repayment in cash. Money loves to be accounted for.

ANNA PETROVNA. All right, all right . . . That's enough. I don't have any money and never shall have for your sort! Beat it, sue me! Ech, you and your law degree! You're going to die any day now, after all, so what's the point of cheating people? You crank!

PETRIN. May I drop a hint, dear lady?

ANNA PETROVNA. You may not. (*Goes to the door.*) Go and work your gums!

PETRIN. If I may, dear lady! Dearest cousin, just one little minute! Do you like Porfiry?

ANNA PETROVNA. What's this about? What business is it of yours, you shyster?

PETRIN. What business? (*Slaps his chest.*) And who, may I ask, was the best friend of the late major-general? Who closed his eyes on his deathbed?

ANNA PETROVNA. You, you, you! And said what a good boy am I!

PETRIN. I shall go and drink to the repose of his soul . . . (*Sighs.*) And to your health! Proud and arrogant, madam! Pride goeth before a fall . . . (*Exits.*)

Enter PLATONOV.

SCENE XX

ANNA PETROVNA and PLATONOV.

PLATONOV. How damned conceited can you get! You throw him out, and he sits there, as if nothing had happened . . . That is truly boorish, profiteering conceit! Penny for your thoughts, Excellency?

ANNA PETROVNA. Have you calmed down?

PLATONOV. I've calmed down . . . But let's not get angry . . . (*Kisses her hand.*) Anybody, our dear general's lady, has the right to throw every last one of them out of your house . . .

ANNA PETROVNA. How delighted I'd be, insufferable Mikhail Vasilich, to throw out all these guests! . . . But here's the problem: the honor you speechified about on my behalf today is digestible only in theory, and not in practice. Neither I nor your eloquence has the right to throw them out. After all, they're all our benefactors, our creditors . . . I only have to look cross-eyed at them—and tomorrow we will be off this estate . . . It's either estate or honor, you see . . . I pick estate . . . Take this, dear windbag, any way you like, but if you don't want me to depart these beautiful precincts, then stop reminding me about honor and don't disturb my geese . . .[39] They're calling me . . . Today after dinner we'll go for a drive . . . Don't you dare leave! (*Claps him on the shoulder.*) We'll live it up! Let's go and eat! (*Exits.*)

PLATONOV (*after a pause*). All the same I will kick them out . . . I'll kick all of them out! . . . It's stupid, tactless, but . . . I'll kick them out . . . I promised myself to have nothing to do with that herd of swine, but what can you do? Character is something innate, and lack of character is even more so . . .

Enter VENGEROVICH JR.

SCENE XXI

PLATONOV and VENGEROVICH JR.

VENGEROVICH JR. Listen, Mister Schoolmaster, I would advise you to keep off my father.

---

39 Reference to a fable by Ivan Krylov (1768–1844), the La Fontaine of Russia. A flock of geese, devoid of any personal worth, boasts of its ancestors who saved Rome. The moral goes, "'Twould not be hard to make my moral yet more clear, / But that means vexing geese, I fear!"

PLATONOV. *Merci* for the advice.

VENGEROVICH JR. I'm not joking. My father has a great many friends and so could easily have your job. I'm warning you.

PLATONOV. A big-hearted youngster! What's your name?

VENGEROVICH JR. Isaak.

PLATONOV. In other words, Abram begat Isaac. Thank you, big-hearted youngster! In your turn, be so kind as to convey to your dear papa that I wish that he and his great many friends drop dead! Go and have something to eat, otherwise they'll gobble all of it up without you, youngster!

VENGEROVICH JR. (*shrugs and goes to the door*). Strange, if it weren't so stupid . . . (*Stops.*) Do you assume that I am angry with you because you won't leave my father in peace? Not at all. I'm studying you, I'm not angry . . . I'm studying you as an example of the modern Chatsky[40] and . . . I understand you! If you had been a cheerful sort, if you hadn't been bored with being bone idle, then, believe me, you wouldn't be picking on my father. You, Mister Chatsky, are not seeking truth, but amusing yourself, having fun at others' expense . . . You haven't got any menials around these days, but you have to take it out on somebody! So you take it out on all and sundry . . .

PLATONOV (*laughs*). Honest to God, that's great! Why, you know, you've got the slightest glimmer of an imagination . . .

VENGEROVICH JR. The extraordinary thing is the revolting circumstance that you never pick a quarrel with my father one on one, *tête-à-tête*; you select the drawing-room for your amusements, where the fools can behold you in all your glory! Oh, what a ham!

PLATONOV. I'd like to have a talk with you ten years from now, even five . . . What shape will you be in then? Will you have the same impassive tone of voice, those flashing eyes? Actually, you'll deteriorate a bit, youngster! Are your studies coming along all right? . . . I see by your face that they aren't . . . You're deteriorating! Anyway, go and eat! I won't bandy words with you any more. I don't like the dirty look on your face . . .

---

40 Protagonist of Aleksandr Griboedov's classic comedy *Woe from Wit*, an "angry young man" and critic of Russian high society, the odd man out who both rejects and is rejected by his peers.

VENGEROVICH JR. (*laughs*). An aesthete. (*Goes to the door.*) Better a face with a dirty look on it than one that's asking to be slapped.

PLATONOV. Yes, it is better . . . But . . . go and eat!

VENGEROVICH JR. We are not on speaking terms . . . Don't forget that, please . . . (*Exits.*)

PLATONOV (*alone*). A youngster who doesn't know a lot, thinks a lot, and talks a lot behind your back. (*Looks through the doorway to the dining room.*) And Sofya's in there. Looking in all directions . . . She's looking for me with her velvety eyes. What a pretty creature she is! How much beauty there is in her face! Her hair hasn't changed! The same color, the same style . . . The many times I managed to kiss that hair! Wonderful memories that head of hair brings back to me . . .

Pause.

Has the time come when I have to settle for memories?

Pause.

Memory is a very good thing, but . . . can it be that for me . . . the end has come? Ugh, God forbid, God forbid! Death is preferable . . . I have to live . . . Keep on living . . . I'm still young!

Enter VOINITSEV.

S C E N E   X X I I

PLATONOV and VOINITSEV and then TRILETSKY.

VOINITSEV (*enters and wipes his mouth with a napkin*). Let's go and drink to *Sophie*'s health, there's no reason to hide! . . . What's wrong?

PLATONOV. I've been looking at and admiring your bride . . . A splendid young lady!

VOINITSEV laughs.

PLATONOV. You're a lucky bastard!

VOINITSEV. Yes . . . I admit it . . . I am lucky. Not exactly lucky, from the point of view of . . . I can't say that I'm completely . . . But generally speaking very lucky!

PLATONOV (*looks through the doorway to the dining room*). I've known her a long time, Sergey Pavlovich! I know her like the palm of my hand. How pretty she is now, but how much prettier she was then! It's a shame you didn't know her in those days! How pretty she is!

VOINITSEV. Yes.

PLATONOV. Those eyes?!

VOINITSEV. And the hair?!

PLATONOV. She was a wonderful girl! (*Laughs.*) As for my Sasha, my Avdotya, Matryona, Pelageya[41] . . . She's sitting over there! You can just see her behind that decanter of vodka! Touchy, excitable, upset by my behavior! Tormenting herself, poor thing, with the idea that now everyone condemns and hates me because I insulted Vengerovich!

VOINITSEV. Forgive the bluntness of the question . . . Are you happy with her?

PLATONOV. Family, pal . . . Take that away from me and I think I'd be a complete goner . . . Hearth and home! You'll live and learn. Only it's a shame you didn't raise more hell, then you'd have a better idea of what a family is worth. I wouldn't sell my Sasha for a million. We get along better than you can imagine . . . She's brainless, and I'm worthless . . .

TRILETSKY enters.

(*To Triletsky.*) Full up?

TRILETSKY. To the max. (*Slaps himself on the stomach.*) Solid as a rock! Let's go, my fine feathered friends, and have a drink . . . Gentlemen, we should toast the arrival of the hosts . . . Eh, pals . . . (*Embraces the two of them.*) So let's have a drink! Eh! (*Stretches.*) Eh! This human life of ours! Blessed the man who heeds not the counsel of the unrighteous . . . (*Stretches.*) My fine feathered friends! You swindlers . . .

PLATONOV. Visited your patients today?

TRILETSKY. That's for later . . . Or here's what, *Michel* . . . I tell you once and for all. Stop bothering me! You and your sermons make me sick to my stomach! Be a lover of mankind! Recognize that I am a brick wall and you

---

41 The names of peasant girls. Platonov is emphasizing Sasha's earthbound lack of sophistication.

are a pea-shooter! Or if you absolutely must, if your tongue starts itching, then write down whatever you have to say. I'll learn it by heart! Or, worst case scenario, you can even read your sermon to me at an appointed hour. I'll give you one hour a day . . . From four to five in the afternoon, for instance . . . Are you willing? I'll even pay you a ruble for that hour. (*Stretches.*) All day long, all day long . . .

PLATONOV (*to Voinitsev*). Explain to me, please, the meaning of that ad you put in the *Intelligencer*? Are things really that bad?

VOINITSEV. No, don't worry! (*Laughs.*) It's a little business deal . . . There'll be an auction, and Glagolyev will buy our estate. Porfiry Semyonych will free us from the bank, and we'll pay him, not the bank, the interest. It was his bright idea.

PLATONOV. I don't understand. What's in it for him? He's not donating it to you, is he? I don't understand this sort of donation, and you hardly . . . need it.

VOINITSEV. No . . . Actually, I don't quite understand it myself . . . Ask *maman*, she'll explain it . . . I just know that after the sale the estate will remain ours and that we'll be paying off Glagolyev. *Maman* will immediately give him her five thousand as a down payment. Anyway, it's not as easy to do business with the bank as it is with him. Ugh, I'm so fed up with that bank! Triletsky isn't as fed up with you as I'm fed up with that bank! Let's forget about business! (*Takes Platonov by the arm.*) Let's go and drink to good feelings, my friends! Nikolay Ivanych! Let's go, pal! (*Takes Triletsky by the arm.*) Let's drink to our good relations, friends! Let fate take everything I own! All these business deals be damned! So long as the people I love are alive and well, you and my Sonya and my stepmother! My life is bound up in you! Let's go!

PLATONOV. I'm coming. I'll drink to it all and I suppose I'll drink it all! It's a long time since I've been drunk, and I'd like to get drunk.

ANNA PETROVNA (*in the doorway*). O friendship, 'tis of thee! A lovely troika! (*Drinks.*) "Shall I harness to the troika swift . . ."

TRILETSKY. "Chestnut steeds . . ." Let's start on the cognac, boys!

ANNA PETROVNA (*in the doorway*). Go on and eat, you scroungers! It's all gone cold!

PLATONOV. Ugh, O friendship, 'tis of thee! I was always lucky in love, but never lucky in friendship. I am afraid, gentlemen, that you may come to grief on account of my friendship! Let's drink to the prosperous outcome of all friendships, ours included! May it end as calmly and gradually as it began! (*They exit into the dining room.*)

End of Act One

ACT TWO

TABLEAU ONE

The garden. Downstage a flowerbed with a little path around it. In the middle of the flowerbed a statue. On the statue's head a lampion. Benches, chairs, little tables. At right the façade of the house. Porch steps. The windows are open. From the windows waft laughter, talk, the sounds of a piano and violin (a quadrille, waltzes, and so on). Upstage of the garden a Chinese gazebo, adorned with lanterns. Over the entrance to the gazebo a monogram with the letters "S. V." Behind the gazebo a game of skittles is being played; we can hear the balls rolling and exclamations of "Five down! Four to go!" etc. The garden and the house are lit up. Guests and servants scurry about the garden. VASILY and YAKOV (in black tailcoats, drunk) are hanging lanterns and lighting lampions.

SCENE I

BUGROV and TRILETSKY (in a peaked cap with a cockade).

TRILETSKY (*enters from the house, arm in arm with Bugrov*). Come on, Timofey Gordeich! What's it cost you to let me have it? After all, it's only a loan I'm asking for!

BUGROV. Honest to goodness, I can't, sir! Please don't be offended, Nikolay Ivanych!

TRILETSKY. You can, Timofey Gordeich! You can do anything! You can buy the whole universe and buy it back again, only you don't want to! It's a loan I'm asking for, isn't it! Do you understand, you crackpot! Word of honor, I won't pay it back!

BUGROV. You see, sir, you see, sir? You've blurted out I won't get repaid!

TRILETSKY. I see nothing! All I see is your heartlessness. Let me have it, great man! You won't? Let me have it, I tell you! I'm pleading, you've got me imploring you! Can you really be so heartless? Where is your heart?

BUGROV (*sighs*). Eh-heh-heh, Nikolay Ivanych! When it comes to treating patients, you don't treat 'em, but you do take your fee . . .

TRILETSKY. You said it! (*Sighs.*) You're right.

BUGROV (*pulls out his wallet*). And the way you're always sneering . . . The least little thing, and it's: ha, ha, ha! How can you? You really shouldn't . . . Maybe we're uneducated, but even so we're Christians, same as you, friend bookworm . . . If I'm talking foolish, then you should set me to rights and not laugh at me . . . All right then. We're of peasant stock, rough and ready, we got thick hides, don't ask too much of us, make allowances . . . (*Opens his wallet.*) This is the last time, Nikolay Ivanych! (*Counts.*) One . . . six . . . twelve . . .

TRILETSKY (*looks into the wallet*). Good Lord! And they keep saying Russians have no money! Where did you get all that?

BUGROV. Fifty . . . (*Hands him the money.*) The last time.

TRILETSKY. And what's that banknote? Hand it over too. It's peeking at me so winsomely! (*Takes the money.*) Let me have that note too!

BUGROV (*gives it to him*). Take it, sir! You're awfully greedy, Nikolay Ivanych!

TRILETSKY. And all in one-ruble notes, all one-ruble notes . . . You been begging with a tin cup or what? Would you be passing me counterfeit money?

BUGROV. Please give 'em back, if they're counterfeit!

TRILETSKY. I would give them back, if you needed them . . . *Merci*, Timofey Gordeich! I hope you put on lots more weight and get a medal. Tell me, please, Timofey Gordeich, why do you lead such an abnormal life? You drink a lot, talk in a bass voice, sweat, don't sleep when you should . . . For instance, why aren't you sleeping now? You're a hot-blooded fellow, sulky, touchy, grocery, for you it should be early to bed! You've got more veins than other people. How can you kill yourself this way?

BUGROV. Huh?

TRILETSKY. You and your huh! Anyway, don't be afraid . . . I'm joking . . . It's too soon for you to die . . . Go on living! Have you got lots of money, Timofey Gordeich?

BUGROV. Enough to last our lifetime.

TRILETSKY. You're a good, clever fellow, Timofey Gordeich, but a terrific crook! Excuse me . . . I speak as a friend . . . We are friends, aren't we? A terrific crook! How come you're buying up Voinitsev's I.O.U.s? How come you're lending him money?

BUGROV. This business is past your understanding, Nikolay Ivanych!

TRILETSKY. You and Vengerovich want to get your hands on the General's lady's mines? The General's lady, you figure, will take pity on her stepson, won't let him go bankrupt, and will give you her mines? You're a great man, but a crook! A swindler!

BUGROV. Tell you what, Nikolay Ivanych, sir . . . I'm going to take a little nap somewhere near the gazebo, and when they start serving supper, you wake me up.

TRILETSKY. Splendid! Get some sleep.

BUGROV (*goes*). And if they don't serve supper, wake me up at half past ten! (*Exits to the gazebo.*)

SCENE II

TRILETSKY and then VOINITSEV.

TRILETSKY (*inspects the money*). Smells of peasant . . . He's been robbing people blind, the scum! What can I do with it? (*To Vasily and Yakov.*) Hey, you hired hands! Vasily, call Yakov over here. Yakov, call Vasily over here! Crawl over here! Step lively!

YAKOV and VASILY walk over to Triletsky.

They're in tailcoats! Ah, what the hell! You're the spittin' image of your betters! (*Gives Yakov a ruble.*) Here's a ruble for you! (*To Vasily.*) Here's a ruble for you! That's because you've got long noses.

YAKOV and **VASILY** (*bow*). Much obliged, Nikolay Ivanych!

TRILETSKY. What's wrong with you, you Slav slaves, wobbly on your legs? Drunk? Drunk as owls, the pair of you? You'll catch it from the General's lady, if she finds out! She'll smack your ugly kissers! (*Gives them each another ruble.*) Here's another ruble for you! That's because your name is Yakov and his is Vasily, and not the other way 'round. Take a bow!

> YAKOV and VASILY bow.

Very good! And here's another ruble for each of you because my name is Nikolay Ivanych, and not Ivan Nikolaevich! (*Gives them more.*) Take a bow! That's it! Make sure you don't spend it on drink! Or I'll prescribe you bitter medicine! You are the spittin' image of your betters! Go and light the lanterns! March! I've had enough of you!

> YAKOV and VASILY walk away. VOINITSEV crosses the stage.

(*To Voinitsev.*) Here's three rubles for you!

> VOINITSEV takes the money, automatically puts it in his pocket
> and walks far upstage.

You might say thank you!

> IVAN IVANOVICH and SASHA enter from the house.

SCENE III

TRILETSKY, IVAN IVANOVICH, and SASHA.

SASHA (*entering*). My God! When will it all end? And why hast Thou punished me this way? This one's drunk, Nikolay's drunk, so is Misha . . . At least have some fear of God, you shameless creatures, even if you don't care what people think! Everybody's staring at you! How, how can I show my face, when everyone's pointing a finger at you!

IVAN IVANOVICH. That's wrong, that's wrong! Hold on . . . You've got me confused . . . Hold on . . .

SASHA. It's impossible to take you to a respectable house. You've barely walked in the door and you're already drunk! Ooh, you're a disgrace! And an old man at that! You ought to set an example for them, and not drink with them!

IVAN IVANOVICH. Hold on, hold on . . . You've got me confused . . . What was I on about? Oh yes! And I'm not lying, Sasha girl! Believe you me! If I'd served another five years, I would've been a general! So you don't think I'd have been a general? Shame! . . . (*Roars with laughter.*) With my temperament and not be a general? With my upbringing? You haven't got a clue in that case . . . It means you haven't got a clue . . .

SASHA. Let's go! Generals don't drink like this.

IVAN IVANOVICH. When they're high-spirited, everybody drinks!! I would have been a general! And you shut up, do me a favor! Take after your mother! Yap-yap-yap . . . Good Lord, honest to God! She never let up, day and night, night and day . . . This isn't right, that isn't right . . . Yap-yap-yap . . . what was I on about? Oh yes! And you take after your late mother every which way, my teeny-weeny! All over . . . All . . . Your little eyes, and your pretty hair . . . And she waddled the same way, like a gosling . . . (*Kisses her.*) My angel! You're your late mother every which way . . . Awful how I loved that poor woman! I didn't look after her, old Fool Ivanych Merrymaker!

SASHA. That's enough out of you . . . Let's go! Seriously, papa . . . It's time you gave up drinking and making scenes. Leave it to those roughnecks . . . They're young, and besides it's out of keeping for an old man like you, honestly . . .

IVAN IVANOVICH. I obey, my dear! I understand! I won't . . . I obey . . . Yes indeed, yes indeed . . . I understand . . . What was I on about?

TRILETSKY (*to Ivan Ivanovich*). For you, your honor, a hundred kopeks! (*Gives him a ruble.*)

IVAN IVANOVICH. All right, sir . . . I'll take it, my son! *Merci* . . . I wouldn't take it from a stranger, but I'll always take from my son . . . I'll take it and rejoice . . . I don't like strangers' bank accounts, my dear children. God help me, I really don't like 'em! Honest, children! Your father's honest! Not once in my life have I robbed either the nation or my household! And all I had to do was stick the tip of a finger in a certain place, and I would have been rich and famous!

TRILETSKY. Praiseworthy, but there's no need to boast, Father!

IVAN IVANOVICH. I'm not boasting, Nikolay! I'm teaching you, my children! I'm instructing . . . We've got to answer for you before the Lord!

TRILETSKY. Where are you off to?

IVAN IVANOVICH. Home. I'm driving this buzzing bee home . . . Take me home, take me home . . . She made me promise . . . So I'll drive her home. She's afraid on her own . . . I'll drive her home, and come back again.

TRILETSKY. Naturally, come back. (*To Sasha.*) Should I give some to you too? This is for you, and this is for you! A three-spot! A three-spot for you!

SASHA. Add another two while you're at it. I'll buy Misha some summer trousers, otherwise he'll only have one pair. And there's nothing worse than having only one! When they're in the wash, he has to wear the heavyweight ones . . .

TRILETSKY. I wouldn't give him anything, summer or heavyweight, if it were up to me: he can walk around you-know-how! But what's to be done with you? Here, take another two! (*Gives her money.*)

IVAN IVANOVICH. What was I on about? Oh yes . . . Now I remember . . . All right . . . I served on the general staff, my children . . . I fought the foeman with my wits, spilled Turkish blood[42] with my brains . . . Never had any use for cold steel, no, no use at all . . . All right . . .

SASHA. Why are we standing around? It's high time. Good-bye, Kolya! Let's go, papa!

IVAN IVANOVICH. Hold on! Shut up, for Christ's sake! Cheep-cheep-cheep . . . It's like an aviary! This is how you should live, my children! Honorably, nobly, irreproachably . . . All right, all right . . . I got the Vladimir third class . . .[43]

SASHA. That's enough out of you, papa! Let's go!

TRILETSKY. We know, without the speechifying, what sort of man you are . . . Go on, drive her home!

---

42 An attempted invasion of Turkey in 1853 failed and led to the Crimean War (1853–1855), which, despite the bravery of its soldiers, Russia lost through the incompetence of its bureaucracy and serious fraud by contractors.

43 Vladimir third class, one of the medals bestowed on military and civilians for service to the state.

IVAN IVANOVICH. You are the cleverest fellow, Nikolay! A regular Pirogov![44]

TRILETSKY. Go on, go on . . .

IVAN IVANOVICH. What was I on about? Oh yes . . . I met Pirogov . . . Once when I was in Kiev[45] . . . All right, all right . . . The cleverest fellow . . . Not standoffish . . . Now I'm going . . . Let's go, Sashurka! I've got weak, children . . . Ready for the last rites . . . Ugh, Lord, forgive us sinners! We have sinned, we have sinned . . . All right, all right . . . I'm a sinner, dear children! Now I serve Mammon, and when I was young I didn't pray to God. Nobody drove a harder bargain than me . . . Materialism! Stuff and Craft![46] Ah, Lord . . . All right . . . Pray, dear children, that I don't die! Have you gone already, Sashurochka? Where are you? That's where you are . . . Let's go . . .

> *ANNA PETROVNA looks out a window.*

TRILETSKY. And won't budge from the spot . . . Poor guy's let his tongue run away with him . . . Well, go on! Don't go by the mill, the dogs will nip at you.

SASHA. Kolya, you've got his cap on . . . Give it to him or he'll catch cold . . .

TRILETSKY (*takes off the cap and puts it on his father*). Forward march, old fella! Left face . . . march!

IVAN IVANOVICH. Le-e-ft face! All right, all right . . . You're right, Nikolay! God knows you're right! And Mikhailo, my son-in-law, is right! A free-thinker, but right! I'm going, I'm going . . . (*They go.*) Let's go, Sasha . . . You going? Let me carry you!

SASHA. More of your nonsense!

IVAN IVANOVICH. Let me carry you! I always carried your mother . . . Used to carry her, though I'd be weaving back and forth . . . Once the two of us came tumbling down a hill . . . Only burst out laughing, the love, didn't get angry at all . . . Let me carry you!

---

44 Nikolay Ivanovich Pirogov (1810–1881), a Russian surgeon and anatomist, famous for a style of amputation carried out on the battlefield.

45 Capital of the Ukraine.

46 Mispronunciation of the German *Stoff und Kraft*, Matter and Strength, the title of a book of popular science (1855) by Ludwig Büchner, so successful it remained in print until 1902. Karl Marx condemned it as materialist philistinism.

SASHA. Don't make things up . . . Put your cap on straight. (*Straightens his cap.*) You're still a splendid fellow to us!

IVAN IVANOVICH. All right, all right . . .

They exit. Enter PETRIN and SHCHERBUK.

S C E N E   I V

TRILETSKY, PETRIN, and SHCHERBUK.

PETRIN (*comes out of the house arm in arm with Shcherbuk*). Put down fifty thousand in front of me, and I'll steal it . . . Word of honor, I'll steal it . . . Just so long as nobody catches me . . . I'll steal it . . . Put it down in front of you, and you'd steal it.

SHCHERBUK. I wouldn't steal it, Gerasya! No!

PETRIN. Put down a ruble, and I'll steal the ruble! Honest to goodness! Feh, feh! Who wants your honesty? An honest man is a stupid man . . .

SHCHERBUK. I'm a stupid man . . . Let me be a stupid man . . .

TRILETSKY. Here's a ruble for each of you, elders of the tribe! (*Gives each of them a ruble.*)

PETRIN (*takes the money*). Let's have it . . .

SHCHERBUK (*roars with laughter and takes the money*). *Merci*, Mister Doctor!

TRILETSKY. Bubbling over with the bubbly, respected gents?

PETRIN. A bit . . .

TRILETSKY. And here's another ruble for each of you for a mass for your souls! You're sinners, right? Take it! What you deserve is a turd apiece, but seeing it's a party . . . I'm feeling generous, damn it all!

ANNA PETROVNA (*out the window*). Triletsky, give me a ruble too! (*Hides.*)

TRILETSKY. You get not one ruble, but five rubles, Major-General Widow! Right away! (*Exits into the house.*)

PETRIN (*looks at the window*). So the fairy is in hiding?

SHCHERBUK (*looks at the window*). She's in hiding.

PETRIN. Can't stand her! A bad woman! Too much pride . . . A woman ought to be modest, respectful . . . (*Shakes his head.*) Seen Glagolyev? There's another tailor's dummy! He sits in one spot, like a mushroom, keeps his mouth shut and bugs his eyes! Is that the way to woo the ladies?

SHCHERBUK. He'll get married!

PETRIN. When will he get married? In a hundred years? Thank you kindly! In a hundred years I don't need it.

SHCHERBUK. He doesn't have to get married, Gerasya, he's an old man . . . He should marry, if he absolutely has to, some little dimwit . . . And he's not right for her . . . She's young, high-spirited, a European lady, educated . . .

PETRIN. If only he would get married! I mean I want this so much I can't find the words! After all, they got literally nothing from the death of the late General, may he rest in peace! She's got the mines, but Vengerovich has been angling for them . . . How can I contend with Vengerovich? What can I get for their I.O.U.s now? If I call them in now, how much will I get?

SHCHERBUK. Nihil.[47]

PETRIN. But if she marries Glagolyev, then I know what I'll get . . . I'll call in the I.O.U.s right away, force the sale of their property . . . No chance she'll let her stepson be ruined, she'll pay up! Eh-yeh-ugh! Come true, my dreams! Sixteen thousand, Pavochka!

SHCHERBUK. Three thousand of them mine . . . My battle-axe demands that I get it back . . . How can I get it? I don't know how to get it . . . They're not peasants . . . They're friends . . . Let her come here herself and get it . . . Let's go, Gerasya, to the servants' quarters!

PETRIN. What for?

SHCHERBUK. To whisper ballads to the lady's polonaise . . .

PETRIN. Is Dunyasha in the servants' quarters?

SHCHERBUK. She is. (*They go.*) It's more fun there . . . (*Sings.*) "Ah, unhappy is my lot, for no more do I dwell there!"

---

47 Latin: nothing.

PETRIN. Tick-tock, tick-tock . . . (*Shouts.*) Yes, sir! (*Sings.*) "The new year merrily we'll greet in true friends' company . . ."

They exit.

SCENE V

VOINITSEV and SOFYA YEGOROVNA enter from the garden upstage.

VOINITSEV. What are you thinking about?

SOFYA YEGOROVNA. I really don't know . . .

VOINITSEV. You spurn my help . . . Aren't I in a position to help you? What are these secrets, *Sophie?* Secrets from your husband . . . Hm . . .

They sit down.

SOFYA YEGOROVNA. What secrets? I don't know myself what's going on inside me . . . Don't torture yourself for no reason, Sergey! Don't pay any attention to my moods . . .

Pause.

Let's get away from here, Sergey!

VOINITSEV. From here?

SOFYA YEGOROVNA. Yes.

VOINITSEV. What for?

SOFYA YEGOROVNA. I want to . . . Let's go abroad. Shall we?

VOINITSEV. If you want to . . . But what for?

SOFYA YEGOROVNA. It's nice here, healthy, fun, but I just can't . . . Everything's going along nicely, happily, only . . . we have to leave. You gave your word not to ask questions.

VOINITSEV. We'll leave tomorrow . . . Tomorrow we won't be here any more! (*Kisses her hand.*) You're bored here! That's understandable! I understand you! It's a hell of an environment! Petrins, Shcherbuks . . .

SOFYA YEGOROVNA. It's not their fault . . . Leave them out of it.

Pause.

VOINITSEV. Why is it you women always get so broody? What's there to brood about? (*Kisses his wife's cheek.*) Enough! Cheer up! Live as long as you're alive! Why not give your brooding the brush-off, as Platonov would say? Aha! Platonov's just the thing! Why don't you talk to him more often? He's not a shallow person, badly educated, or overly boring! Have a heart-to-heart with him, get it off your chest! He'll soon cure you of your brooding! Talk to mama more often, and Triletsky . . . (*Laughs.*) Have a good talk, and don't look down your nose at them! You still haven't figured out these people . . . I commend them to you because these people are my kind of people. I love them. You'll love them too when you get to know them better.

ANNA PETROVNA (*out the window*). Sergey! Sergey! Who's there? Call Sergey Pavlovich!

VOINITSEV. What can I do for you?

ANNA PETROVNA. There you are! Let me have a minute!

VOINITSEV. Right away! (*To Sofya Yegorovna.*) We'll leave tomorrow, if you don't change your mind. (*Goes into the house.*)

SOFYA YEGOROVNA (*after a pause*). This is getting to be a real problem! I already go whole days without thinking about my husband, ignoring his presence, paying no attention to what he says . . . He's starting to get on my nerves . . . What am I to do? (*Thinks.*) It's dreadful! We haven't been married very long and already . . . And all because of that . . . Platonov! I haven't the strength, the character, nothing that could help me resist that man! He persecutes me all day long, tracks me down, his sharp eyes don't let me alone for a moment . . . It's dreadful . . . and stupid, after all! I haven't even got the strength to answer for myself! If he were to make a move, anything might happen!

SCENE VI

SOFYA YEGOROVNA and PLATONOV.

PLATONOV comes out of the house.

SOFYA YEGOROVNA. Here he comes! His eyes are roaming, looking for someone! Whom is he looking for? From his way of walking I can see whom he's after! How despicable of him not to leave me alone for a moment!

PLATONOV. It's hot! Shouldn't be drinking . . . (*On seeing Sofya Yegorovna.*) You here, Sofya Yegorovna? All on your lonesome? (*Laughs.*)

SOFYA YEGOROVNA. Yes.

PLATONOV. Avoiding the mortals.

SOFYA YEGOROVNA. There's no reason for me to avoid them. They don't bother me or get in my way.

PLATONOV. Really? (*Sits beside her.*) May I? But if you aren't avoiding people, why, Sofya Yegorovna, are you avoiding me? What for? Excuse me, let me finish! I've very glad that I can finally have a word with you. You avoid me, pass me by, don't look at me . . . Why is this? Are you being funny or serious?

SOFYA YEGOROVNA. I wasn't intending to avoid you! Where did you get that idea?

PLATONOV. At first your attitude seemed to be friendly toward me, you favored me with your kind attention, and now you don't even want to see me! I go into one room—you go into another, I walk into the garden—you walk out of the garden, I start to talk to you, you clam up or say some flat, mopey "yes" and walk away . . . Our relationship has changed into a kind of misunderstanding . . . Is it my fault? Am I repulsive? (*Gets up.*) I don't feel at fault in any way. Please be so kind right now as to spare me this boarding-school-miss, stupid situation! I don't intend to put up with it any longer!

SOFYA YEGOROVNA. I admit I . . . do avoid you a bit . . . If I'd known that you found it unpleasant, I would have behaved differently . . .

PLATONOV. You do avoid me? (*Sits down.*) You admit it? But . . . what for, what's the point?

SOFYA YEGOROVNA. Don't shout, I mean . . . don't talk so loudly! I hope you're not going to scold me. I don't like it when people shout at me. I am not avoiding you as a person, but talks with you . . . As a person you are, so far as I know, a good man . . . Everyone here loves you, respects you, some even admire you, consider it an honor to converse with you . . .

PLATONOV. Oh come on . . .

SOFYA YEGOROVNA. When I first came here, right after our first talk, I became one of your fans myself, but, Mikhail Vasilich, I was unlucky, luck definitely did not come my way . . . You soon became almost unbearable to me . . . I can't put it less harshly, forgive me . . . Almost every day you talked to me about how you loved me once, how I loved you, and so on . . . A student loved a girl, a girl loved a student . . . the story is too old and ordinary for anyone to talk about it so much and for either of us to invest any special significance in it . . . That's not the point, though . . . The point is that when you talked to me about the past, you . . . you talked as if you were asking for something, as if back then, in the past, you had failed to obtain something that you wanted to have now . . . Every day your tone was monotonously the same, and every day it struck me that you were hinting at some sort of obligation laid on the two of us by our common past . . . And then it struck me that you are attaching too much significance . . . or, to put it more plainly, exaggerating our relationship as close friends! You stare so strangely, get carried away, shout, grab my hand, and follow me around . . . As if you were spying on me! What is it for? . . . In short, you won't leave me alone . . . What is this surveillance all about? What am I to you? Honestly, one might think you were lying in wait for the right moment, which would somehow serve your purposes . . .

Pause.

PLATONOV. Is that all? (*Gets up.*) *Merci* for your candor! (*Goes to the door.*)

SOFYA YEGOROVNA. Are you angry? (*Gets up.*) Wait, Mikhail Vasilich! Why take offense? I didn't mean . . .

PLATONOV (*stops*). Eh you!

Pause.

So it turns out that you are not sick and tired of me, but that you're scared, a coward . . . Are you a coward, Sofya Yegorovna? (*Walks up to her.*)

SOFYA YEGOROVNA. Stop, Platonov! You're a liar! I was not scared and I don't intend to be scared!

PLATONOV. Where's your will power, where's the force of your well-regulated mind, if every slightly above-average man who comes along can pose a threat to your Sergey Pavlovich! I used to hang around here long before you showed up, but I talked to you, because I took you to be an intelligent woman who might understand! What deeply entrenched depravity! Nevertheless . . . Sorry, I got carried away . . . I have no right to say that to you . . . Forgive me for my bad manners . . .

SOFYA YEGOROVNA. No one gave you the right to say such things! Just because people listen to you, it doesn't follow that you have the right to say whatever comes into your head! Get away from me!

PLATONOV (*roars with laughter*). People are persecuting you?! Following you around, grabbing you by the hand? They want to abduct you, poor creature, from your husband?! Platonov is in love with you, the eccentric Platonov?! What happiness! Bliss! Why, what bonbons to feed our petty vanity, such as no candy store ever offered! Ridiculous . . . Gorging on sweets is out of character for a progressive woman! (*Exits into the house.*)

SOFYA YEGOROVNA. You're rude and impertinent, Platonov! You've gone crazy! (*Follows him and stops in the doorway.*) It's horrid! Why did he say all that? He wanted to confuse me . . . No, I won't put up with it . . . I will go and tell him . . . (*Exits into the house.*)

S C E N E   V I I

OSIP, YAKOV, and VASILY.

OSIP (*enters*). Five down! Six to go! What the hell are they up to! Would have had better luck playing cards with 'em . . . Ten rubles a game . . . Whist or poker . . . (*To Yakov.*) How're ya, Yasha! That fella . . . u-u-uh . . . Vengerovich here?

YAKOV. He's here.

OSIP. Go and call 'im! But call 'im on the quiet! Tell 'im that there's a big deal on . . .

YAKOV. Sure. (*Exits into the house.*)

OSIP (*breaks off a lantern, puts it out and sticks it in his pocket*). Last year I was in town at Darya Ivanovna's, the fence who runs a barroom with girls on tap, played cards . . . Three kopeks was the lowest stakes . . . But the forfeits came to two rubles . . . Won eight rubles . . . (*Breaks off another lantern.*) A hot time in the old town!

VASILY. Them lanterns ain't hung up for you! Why tear 'em down?

OSIP. Why, I didn't see you there! How're ya, jackass! How you getting on? (*Walks over to him.*) How's business?

Pause.

Oh you swayback! Oh you pig's nursemaid! (*Takes off Vasily's cap.*) You're a funny guy! Honest to God, real funny! Have you got even an ounce o' brains? (*Throws the cap on to a tree.*) Slap my face because I'm a menace to society!

VASILY. Let somebody else slap it for you, I'm not going to hit you!

OSIP. But will you kill me? No, if you're smart, you won't gang up to kill me, but do it yourself! Spit in my face because I'm a menace to society!

VASILY. I won't spit. Why don't you leave me alone?

OSIP. You won't spit? Afraid of me, is that it? Get down on your knees before me!

Pause.

Well? Kneel down! Who'm I talking to? The wall or flesh-and-blood?

Pause.

Who'm I talking to?

VASILY (*kneeling down*). This is wrong of you, Osip Ivanych!

OSIP. Ashamed to kneel? I like that a lot . . . A gent in a tailcoat, and on his knees in front of a robber . . . Well, now shout hurray at the top of your lungs . . . How about it?

Enter VENGEROVICH SR.

S C E N E   V I I I

OSIP and VENGEROVICH SR.

VENGEROVICH SR. (*enters from the house*). Who is calling for me here?

OSIP (*quickly removes his cap*). Me, sir, your highandmightiness.

VASILY gets up, sits on the bench, and weeps.

VENGEROVICH SR. What do you want?

OSIP. You pleased to look in at the barroom and ask for me, so I came!

VENGEROVICH SR. Oh yes . . . But . . . couldn't you at least pick another spot?

OSIP. For decent people, Your Excellency, any spot will do!

VENGEROVICH SR. I need you more or less . . . Let's get away from here . . . Over to that bench!

They go to the bench far upstage.

Stand somewhat farther off, as if you weren't talking to me . . . That's it! The tavern-keeper Lev Solomonych sent you?

OSIP. Just so.

VENGEROVICH SR. No point to it . . . I didn't want *you*, but . . . what's to be done? You're hopeless. It isn't right to do business with you . . . You're such a bad man . . .

OSIP. Very bad! Worse than anyone on earth.

VENGEROVICH SR. Not so loud! The amount of money I've made over to you, it's dreadful, but you act as if my money were a pebble or some other piece of trash . . . You take liberties, you steal . . . You're turning away? You don't like the truth? Truth dazzles your eyes?

OSIP. It does, but not your kind, Your Excellency! You asked me here just to read me a lecture?

VENGEROVICH SR. Not so loud . . . You know . . . Platonov?

OSIP. Yes, the schoolteacher. Why wouldn't I know 'im?

VENGEROVICH SR. Yes, the schoolteacher. A teacher, who only teaches how to insult people and nothing more. How much would you charge to disable that teacher?

OSIP. What do you mean disable?

VENGEROVICH SR. Not kill, but disable . . . It doesn't do to kill people . . . What's the point of killing them? Murder is something that . . . Disable means beating him up so that he'll remember it all his life long . . .

OSIP. That can be done, sir . . .

VENGEROVICH SR. Break some of his bones, disfigure his face . . . What'll you charge? Shhh . . . Someone's coming . . . Let's go someplace farther off . . .

> *They walk far upstage . . . Enter from the house*
> *PLATONOV and GREKOVA.*

SCENE IX

VENGEROVICH SR. and OSIP (upstage),
PLATONOV and GREKOVA.

PLATONOV (*laughs*). What, what? How's that? (*Roars with laughter.*) How's that? I didn't catch that . . .

GREKOVA. You didn't catch it? Is that so? I can repeat it . . . I can express myself even more rudely . . . You won't be offended, of course . . . You're so used to all sorts of rudeness that my words will hardly come as a surprise . . .

PLATONOV. Speak out, speak out, my beauty!

GREKOVA. I am not a beauty. Anyone who thinks I'm a beauty has no taste . . . Frankly—I'm not beautiful, am I? What do you think?

PLATONOV. I'll tell you later. Now you speak out!

GREKOVA. Then listen here . . . You are either an above-average man or else . . . a scoundrel, one or the other.

> *PLATONOV roars with laughter.*

You're laughing . . . Actually, it is funny . . . (*Bursts out laughing.*)

PLATONOV (*roars with laughter*). She said it! Bully for the little fool! Well, I'll be! (*Takes her round the waist.*)

GREKOVA (*sits down*). However, let me . . .

PLATONOV. She's just the same as other people! She philosophizes, practices chemistry, and the remarks she comes up with! Who'd have thought it of her, the wallflower! (*Kisses her.*) Very pretty little, crack-brained rascal . . .

GREKOVA. Do let me . . . What is this? I . . . I didn't say . . . (*Gets up and sits down again.*) Why are you kissing me? I'm quite . . .

PLATONOV. She spoke and bowled me over! Let's say something, says she, and startle him! Let him see how clever I am! (*Kisses her.*) She's confused . . . she's confused . . . Looks around stupidly . . . Ah, ah . . .

GREKOVA. You . . . you love me? Yes? . . . Yes?

PLATONOV (*squeaks*). And you love me?

GREKOVA. If . . . if . . . then . . . yes . . . (*Weeps.*) You do love me? Otherwise you shouldn't act this way . . . You do love me?

PLATONOV. Not a smidge, my precious! I don't love little fools, being a sinful man! I do love one fool, but there's nothing to be done about that . . . Oh! She's turned pale! Her eyes are shooting sparks! You'll find out who you're dealing with, says she! . . .

GREKOVA (*rises*). Are you making fun of me or what?

PLATONOV. Who knows, there may be a slap in the offing . . .

GREKOVA. I am proud . . . I don't mean to soil my hands . . . I told you, my dear sir, that you are either an above-average man or a scoundrel, now I tell you that you are an above-average scoundrel! I despise you! (*Exits into the house.*) I won't break into tears now . . . I'm glad that I've found out at last the sort of creature you are . . .

Enter TRILETSKY.

SCENE X

The same and TRILETSKY (in a top hat).

TRILETSKY (*enters*). The cranes are crying! Where did they drop in from? (*Looks aloft.*) So early . . .

GREKOVA. Nikolay Ivanych, if you respect me . . . even the slightest bit, break off relations with that man! (*Points at Platonov.*)

TRILETSKY (*laughs*). For pity's sake! He is my most respected in-law!

GREKOVA. And friend?

TRILETSKY. And friend.

GREKOVA. I don't envy you. And I don't think I envy him either. You're a kind man, but . . . that facetious tone . . . There are times when your jokes make me sick . . . No offense meant, but . . . I've been insulted, and you . . . make jokes! (*Weeps.*) I've been insulted . . . But, nevertheless, I will not burst into tears . . . I am proud. Be on good terms with this man, love him, admire his intelligence, fear him . . . You all think he's like Hamlet . . . Well, admire him! It's nothing to do with me . . . I don't need anything from you . . . Crack jokes with him, as much as you like, that . . . scoundrel! (*Exits into the house.*)

TRILETSKY (*after a pause*). Got all that, pal?

PLATONOV. Not a clue . . .

TRILETSKY. It's about time, Mikhail Vasilich, in all honor, in all conscience you left her alone. It's really disgraceful . . . Such an intelligent, such a big man, and you get involved in this damned stuff . . . That's why people call you a scoundrel . . .

Pause.

I can't actually tear myself in half so that one half respects you and the other stays on friendly terms with a girl who's called you a scoundrel . . .

PLATONOV. Don't respect me, and you won't have to tear yourself in half.

TRILETSKY. I can't help but respect you! You don't know yourself what you're saying!

PLATONOV. That means there's only one thing left: don't be on friendly terms with her. I don't understand you, Nikolay! What good can an intelligent man like you see in that little fool?

TRILETSKY. Hm . . . The General's lady often scolds me for not being enough of a gentleman and points you out as a model gentleman . . . The way I see it, that scolding should be entirely directed at you, the model. Everyone, and especially you, is shouting from every rooftop that I'm in love with her, you laugh, tease, suspect, spy . . .

PLATONOV. Can you be a bit more explicit . . .

TRILETSKY. I think I am being perfectly explicit . . . And at the same time you can in all conscience call her a little fool, a piece of trash to my face . . . You're no gentleman! Gentlemen know that people in love have a certain vanity . . . She is not a fool, buddy boy! She is not a fool! She is an innocent victim, that's what! There are moments, my friend, when you need somebody to hate, somebody to sink your teeth into, somebody to play your dirty tricks on . . . Why not try it on her? She's perfect! Weak, defenseless, looks up to you with such gullible confidence . . . I understand it all very well . . . (*Gets up.*) Let's go get a drink!

OSIP (*to Vengerovich*). If you don't let me have the rest afterward, I'll steal hundreds more. Never you fear!

VENGEROVICH SR. (*to Osip*). Not so loud! Once you've beaten him up, don't forget to say: "With the tavern-keeper's compliments!" Ssh . . . Go away! (*Goes towards the house.*)

OSIP exits.

TRILETSKY. What the hell, Abram Abramych! (*To Vengerovich.*) Are you ill, Abram Abramych?

VENGEROVICH SR. Not at all . . . Thank God, I'm well.

TRILETSKY. What a pity! And I'm in such need of money! Can you believe it? Ready to cut my throat, as the saying goes . . .

VENGEROVICH SR. Consequently, Doctor, do your words imply that you need patients with throats to cut? (*Laughs.*)

TRILETSKY. A clever riposte! A bit heavy-handed, but still clever! Ha-ha-ha and encore ha-ha-ha! Laugh, Platonov! Lend me something, my dear man, if you can!

VENGEROVICH SR. You already owe me a great deal, Doctor!

TRILETSKY. Why bring that up? Common knowledge, isn't it? Just how much do I owe you?

VENGEROVICH SR. Nearly . . . All right . . . Two hundred and forty-five rubles, I believe.

TRILETSKY. Give, great man! Oblige me, and I'll oblige you one of these days! Be ever so kind, generous, and daring! The most daring of Jews is the one who lends money without a receipt! Be the most daring of Jews!

VENGEROVICH SR. Hm . . . Jews . . . Always Jews and more Jews . . . I assure you, gentlemen, that in all my life I've never seen a Russian who would lend money without a receipt, and I assure you that nowhere is it practiced so widely as by underhanded Jewry! . . . May God strike me dead, if I'm lying! (*Sighs.*) There are many, a great many things you young people could learn to your success and advantage from us Jews, and particularly from old Jews . . . A very great many things . . . (*Pulls his wallet out of his pocket.*) A person lends you money with enthusiasm, with pleasure, and you . . . love to laugh and make jokes . . . That's no good, gentlemen! I'm an old man . . . I have got children . . . Think of me as a lowlife, but treat me like a human being . . . That's what your studies at the university were all about . . .

TRILETSKY. Well said, Abram Abramych my friend!

VENGEROVICH SR. It's no good, gentleman, it's bad . . . A person might think that there was no difference between you, educated people, and my employees . . . And no one is permitted to call me his friend . . . How much do you want? It's very bad, young people . . . How much do you want?

TRILETSKY. How much will you let me have . . .

Pause.

VENGEROVICH SR. I'll let you have . . . I can give you . . . five hundred rubles . . . (*Gives him the money.*)

TRILETSKY. Splendid! (*Takes the money.*) Great man!

VENGEROVICH SR. You've got my hat, Doctor!

TRILETSKY. Yours, is it? Hm . . . (*Takes off the hat.*) Here, take it . . . Why don't you have it cleaned? After all, it doesn't cost much! What's the Yiddish for top hat?

VENGEROVICH SR. Whatever you like. (*Puts on the top hat.*)

TRILETSKY. That top hat suits you, it's in character. A baron, a regular baron![48] Why don't you buy yourself a title?

VENGEROVICH SR. I don't know anything about that! Leave me alone, please!

---

48 In nineteenth-century Europe, baron was the lowest order of nobility, often conferred on successful financiers from obscure backgrounds who had done service to the state. The Jewish Baron Rothschild was the paradigm.

TRILETSKY. You're a great man! Why aren't people willing to understand you?

VENGEROVICH SR. Why don't people leave a man in peace, you ought to say! (*Exits into the house.*)

SCENE XI

PLATONOV and TRILETSKY.

PLATONOV. How come you took that money from him?

TRILETSKY. Just did . . . (*Sits down.*)

PLATONOV. What do you mean: just did?

TRILETSKY. I took it, end of story! Are you sorry for him or something?

PLATONOV. That's not the point, chum!

TRILETSKY. Then what is?

PLATONOV. You don't know?

TRILETSKY. I don't know.

PLATONOV. Liar, you do know!

Pause.

I could have been smitten with a great love for you, my darling, if for at least one week, at least one day you had lived according to some rules, even the flimsiest ones! For characters like you, rules are as necessary as daily bread . . .

Pause.

TRILETSKY. I don't know about that . . . It's not up to you and me, pal, to reinvent our flesh! It's not up to us to repress it . . . I knew this when you and I were still in high school getting flunked in Latin . . . Let's cut the pointless chatter . . . Or may the roof of our mouths cleave to our tongues![49]

Pause.

---

49 Triletsky misquotes Psalm 137:6.

The other day, pal o' mine, I was visiting a certain lady I know, looking at the portraits of "Contemporary Movers and Shakers" and reading their biographies. And what do you think, dear fellow? Why, neither of us was among them, no! Couldn't find us, no matter how hard I tried! *Lasciate,* Mikhail Vasilich, *ogni speranza!*[50] —as the Italians say. I could not find you or me among the contemporary movers and shakers and—imagine! I couldn't care less! Now Sofya Yegorovna is not like that . . . she does care . . .

PLATONOV. What's Sofya Yegorovna got to do with this?

TRILETSKY. She's miffed not to be amongst the "Contemporary Movers and Shakers" . . . She imagines all she has to do is lift her little finger—the terrestrial globe will gasp in amazement, humanity will fling up its cap in delight . . . She imagines . . . Hm . . . Not one intellectual novel contains as much twaddle as she does . . . And actually she's not worth a red cent. Ice! Stone! A statue! It makes me feel like walking up to her and scraping a chip of plaster off her nose . . . The least little thing . . . instant hysterics, raising her voice, deep sighs . . . Not an ounce of grit in her . . . A clever doll . . . She regards me with contempt, considers me a waste of time . . . Just what makes her Seryozhenka better than you or I? Tell me what? His only virtues are that he doesn't drink vodka, thinks lofty thoughts and without a twinge of conscience describes himself as a man of the future. However, judge not lest ye be judged . . . (*Gets up.*) Let's go get a drink!

PLATONOV. I'm not coming. I suffocate in there.

TRILETSKY. I'll go on my own. (*Stretches.*) By the way, what does that monogram S. and V. mean? Is it Sofya Voinitseva or Sergey Voinitsev? Whom did our philologist intend to honor by those initials, himself or his spouse?

PLATONOV. It occurs to me that those initials signify: "Salve Vengerovich!"[51] On his money merrily we roll along.

TRILETSKY. Right . . . What's up with the general's lady today? She bursts out laughing, groans, goes around kissing everybody . . . As if she were in love . . .

---

50 Italian: Abandon all hope—the motto over the portal to Hell, according to Dante (*Divine Comedy*, Canto 3).

51 Latin: Hail Vengerovich.

PLATONOV. Who is there for her to fall in love with? Herself? Don't you believe in her laughter. It's impossible to believe in the laughter of a clever woman who never weeps: she laughs out loud whenever she wants to cry. Though our general's lady doesn't want to cry, but to shoot herself . . . You can see it in her eyes . . .

TRILETSKY. Women don't shoot themselves, they take poison . . . But let's not talk philosophy . . . Whenever I talk philosophy, I make up a pack of lies . . . A wonderful female that general's lady of ours! Ordinarily I think awfully dirty thoughts whenever I look at a woman, but she is the only woman off whom my unbridled fantasies bounce like pebbles off a wall. The only one . . . When I look into her no-nonsense face, I start to believe in Platonic love. You coming?

PLATONOV. No.

TRILETSKY. I'll go by myself . . . I'll have a drink with the parish priest . . . (*Goes and in the doorway bumps into Glagolyev Jr.*) Ah! His lordship, the do-it-yourself count! Here's three rubles for you! (*Shoves three rubles into his hand and exits.*)

SCENE XII

PLATONOV and GLAGOLYEV JR.

GLAGOLYEV JR. Curious personality! Right out of the blue: here's three rubles for you! (*Shouts.*) I can give you three rubles myself! Hm . . . What an idiot! (*To Platonov.*) I'm genuinely appalled by his stupidity. (*Laughs.*) Monstrously stupid!

PLATONOV. Why aren't you dancing, dancing-boy?

GLAGOLYEV JR. Dancing? Here? With whom, might I ask? (*Sits beside him.*)

PLATONOV. So there's no one here?

GLAGOLYEV JR. Nothing but stereotypes! They're all stereotypes, wherever you look! Those snouts, acquiline noses, airs and graces . . . And the ladies? (*Roars with laughter.*) What the hell do you call them! At such gatherings I always prefer the refreshments to the dancing.

Pause.

Here in Russia, however, the air is so stale! So dank, suffocating . . . I can't stand Russia! . . . Ignorance, stench . . . Brrr . . . What a difference . . . You ever been to Paris?

PLATONOV. Never.

GLAGOLYEV JR. Pity. Even so, you've still got time to visit it. When you do go there, let me know. I shall reveal all the secrets of Paris to you. I shall give you three hundred letters of introduction, and put three hundred of the chic-est French tarts at your disposal . . .

PLATONOV. Thank you, I've got a full plate. Tell me, is it true what they're saying, that your father wants to buy Platonovka?

GLAGOLYEV JR. I don't know if it's true. I keep myself aloof from business matters . . . But have you noticed how *mon père*[52] is courting your general's lady? (*Roars with laughter.*) There's yet another stereotype! The old goat wants to get married! As thick as a plank! Though your general's lady is *charmante*! Not bad at all!

Pause.

She's quite a darling, quite a darling . . . And her figure?! Naughty, naughty! (*Claps Platonov on the shoulder.*) Lucky devil! Does she lace herself up? Lace herself up really tight?

PLATONOV. I don't know . . . I'm not present when she gets dressed . . .

GLAGOLYEV JR. But I was told . . . Then you're not . . .

PLATONOV. You're the idiot, Count!

GLAGOLYEV JR. But I was joking . . . Why get angry? What a crackpot you are, really! (*Quietly.*) Is it true what they say, that sometimes she loves money to the point of blacking out?

PLATONOV. You'll have to ask her about that yourself. I don't know.

GLAGOLYEV JR. Ask her myself? (*Roars with laughter.*) What an idea! Platonov! What are you saying?!

PLATONOV (*sits on another bench*). You really are an expert at boring people stiff!

---

52 French: my father.

GLAGOLYEV JR. (*roars with laughter*). But what if I did ask her myself? And yet, why not ask her?

PLATONOV. Stands to reason . . . (*Aside.*) Just ask her . . . She'll box your stupid ears for you! (*To him.*) Ask her!

GLAGOLYEV JR. (*leaps up*). I swear it's a great idea! Damn and blast! I shall ask, Platonov, and I give you my word of honor that she'll be mine! I feel it in my bones! I'll ask her right away! I'll make a bet that she'll be mine! (*Runs into the house and in the doorway bumps into Anna Petrovna and Triletsky.*) Mille pardons, madame![53] (*Bows and scrapes and exits into the house.*)

PLATONOV sits back in his old place.

S C E N E   X I I I

PLATONOV, ANNA PETROVNA, and TRILETSKY.

TRILETSKY (*on the porch steps*). There he sits, our great sage and philosopher! He sits on the alert, impatient to pounce on his prey: whom shall he read a lecture to before bedtime?

ANNA PETROVNA. Not a nibble, Mikhail Vasilich!

TRILETSKY. That's bad! Not taking the bait today for some reason! Poor moralist! I feel sorry for you, Platonov! However, I am drunk and . . . however, the deacon is waiting for me! Good-bye! (*Exits.*)

ANNA PETROVNA (*goes to Platonov*). Why are you sitting here?

PLATONOV. It's suffocating inside the house, and this lovely sky is better than your ceiling whitewashed by peasant women!

ANNA PETROVNA (*sits down*). Isn't it splendid weather! Pure air, cool, a starry sky, and the moon! I'm sorry that it isn't possible for our class to sleep outside in the open air. When I was a little girl, I always spent the night in the garden in summer.

Pause.

Is that a new necktie?

---

53 French: a thousand pardons, madam.

PLATONOV. It is.

Pause.

ANNA PETROVNA. I've been in rather an odd mood today . . . Today I like everything . . . I'm having fun! Now tell me something, Platonov! Why do you keep silent? I came out here precisely to hear you talk . . . That's just like you!

PLATONOV. Talk about what?

ANNA PETROVNA. Tell me something a bit novel, a bit nice, a bit spicy . . . Today you're so very clever, so very good-looking . . . Honestly, I think that I'm more in love with you today than ever . . . You're such a darling today! And not such a trouble-maker!

PLATONOV. And today you are such a beauty . . . But then you always are a beauty!

ANNA PETROVNA. Are we friends, Platonov?

PLATONOV. In all likelihood . . . Probably we are friends . . . What else can you call it but friendship?

ANNA PETROVNA. In any case, friends, right?

PLATONOV. I would even declare, great friends . . . I'm extremely used to you and attached . . . It would take a long time to break myself of the habit of you . . .

ANNA PETROVNA. Great friends?

PLATONOV. Why all these niggling questions? Cut it out, dear lady! Friends . . . friends . . . Just like an old maid . . .

ANNA PETROVNA. All right . . . We are friends, and you do know that a friendship between a man and a woman is only one step away from love, my dear sir?

PLATONOV. So that's it! (*Laughs.*) Why are you bringing that up? You and I are never going to stroll down the road to perdition, no matter how far we stray . . .

ANNA PETROVNA. Love as the road to perdition . . . What a metaphor! Your wife's not listening now! *Pardon*, if I'm getting too familiar . . . For heaven's sake, *Michel*, it just popped out! Why shouldn't we stroll down that road?

Are we human or not? Love is a good thing . . . What's there to blush about?

PLATONOV (*stares fixedly at her*). You, I see, are either having your charming joke or else you want . . . to make a deal . . . Let's go and dance a waltz!

ANNA PETROVNA. You don't know how to dance! I have to have a proper talk with you . . . It's about time . . . (*Looks around.*) Make an effort, *mon cher*, to listen and not spout philosophy!

PLATONOV. Let's go and kick up our heels, Anna Petrovna!

ANNA PETROVNA. Let's sit farther off . . . Come over here! (*Sits on a different bench.*) Only I don't know how to begin . . . You're such an awkward and tricky piece of humanity . . .

PLATONOV. Shouldn't I begin, Anna Petrovna?

ANNA PETROVNA. You talk nothing but stuff and nonsense, Platonov, when you begin! Well, I'll be! He's embarrassed! That'll be the day! (*Claps Platonov on the shoulder.*) Misha's a joker! Well, go on and talk, talk . . . Only keep it short . . .

PLATONOV. I will be brief . . . All I have to say is: why bother?

Pause.

Word of honor, it isn't worth it, Anna Petrovna!

ANNA PETROVNA. Why not? Now you listen to me . . . You don't understand me . . . If you had been unattached, I would have become your wife without a second thought, my rank and title would have been yours to have and to hold forever, but as it is . . . . Well? Is silence a token of assent? So, how about it?

Pause.

Listen here, Platonov, in cases like this it is indecent to keep silent!

PLATONOV (*leaps up*). Let's forget this conversation, Anna Petrovna! Come on, for God's sake, let's act as if it had never happened! It never was!

ANNA PETROVNA (*shrugs*). Strange man! Why ever not?

PLATONOV. Because I respect you! I respect my respect for you so much that giving it up would be harder for me than dropping dead! My friend, I am a free man, I am not averse to having a good time, I am not opposed to relations with women, not even opposed to passionate romances, but . . . to have a tawdry little affair with you, to make you the subject of my idle thoughts, you, an intelligent, beautiful, independent woman?! No! That's too much! You'd better banish me to the ends of the earth! To spend a month stupidly, then another, and then . . . to part with a blush?!

ANNA PETROVNA. The subject is love!

PLATONOV. And what if I don't love you? I do love you as a good, intelligent, kind-hearted woman . . . I love you desperately, madly! I would give my life for you, if you wanted it! I love you as a woman — as a human being! Does every kind of love have to be mixed up with one particular kind of love? My love for you is a thousand times more precious than the one you've got in mind! . . .

ANNA PETROVNA (*gets up*). Go, my dear, and take a nap! When you wake up, we'll talk about it . . .

PLATONOV. Let's forget this conversation . . . (*Kisses her hand.*) Let's be friends, but let's not play tricks on one another: our relationship deserves a better fate! . . . And besides, after all, I am . . . even if only a little bit, married! Let's drop this conversation! Let everything be as it was before!

ANNA PETROVNA. Go on, my dear, go on! Married . . . Do you really love me? Then why do you bring up your wife? March! Later we'll talk, in an hour or two . . . Now you're having a fit of lying . . .

PLATONOV. I don't know how to lie to you . . . (*Quietly, in her ear.*) If I did know how to lie to you, I would have been your lover a long time ago . . .

ANNA PETROVNA (*sharply*). Get out of here!

PLATONOV. You're lying, you're not angry . . . It's only make-believe . . . (*Exits into the house.*)

ANNA PETROVNA. The man's a crackpot! (*Sits down.*) He doesn't have the slightest idea what he's saying . . . "To mix up every kind of love with one specific kind of love . . ." What nonsense! Like a male novelist writing about his love for a female novelist . . .

Pause.

Insufferable man! You and I will be nattering away like this till Judgment Day! If I can't take you honorably, I'll take you by force . . . This very day!

It's high time we both gave up this stupid waiting game . . . I'm fed up . . . I'll take you by force . . . Who's that coming? Glagolyev . . . looking for me . . .

Enter GLAGOLYEV SR.

SCENE XIV

ANNA PETROVNA and GLAGOLYEV SR.

GLAGOLYEV SR. It's boring! These people talk about things I heard years ago: they think things that I thought about when I was a child . . . It's all old, there's nothing new . . . I'll have a word with her and then go.

ANNA PETROVNA. What are you mumbling about, Porfiry Semyonych? May I know?

GLAGOLYEV SR. You're here? (*Comes to her.*) I'm scolding myself for being unwanted here . . .

ANNA PETROVNA. Because you're not like us? That's enough of that! People can get used to cockroaches, so you can get used to our sort! Come sit next to me, let's have a talk!

GLAGOLYEV SR. (*sits beside her*). I've been looking for you, Anna Petrovna! I have something I have to talk to you about . . .

ANNA PETROVNA. Well, go ahead and talk . . .

GLAGOLYEV SR. I'd like to discuss something with you . . . I'd like to know the answer to my . . . letter . . .

ANNA PETROVNA. Hm . . . What is it you want of me, Porfiry Semyonych?

GLAGOLYEV SR. I, as you know, renounce . . . any conjugal rights . . . Those rights aren't for me! I need a friend, a clever housekeeper . . . I have a paradise, but it contains no . . . angels.

ANNA PETROVNA (*aside*). Whatever he says, it's a lump of sugar! (*To him.*) I often wonder what I would do in paradise—I'm a human being, not an angel—if I got into it?

GLAGOLYEV SR. How can you know what you will do in paradise, if you don't know what you will do tomorrow? A good person will always find something to do, on earth or in heaven . . .

ANNA PETROVNA. That's all very pretty, but will my life with you be worth my while? It's rather peculiar, Porfiry Semyonych! Excuse me, Porfiry Semyonych, but your proposal strikes me as very peculiar . . . Why do you want to get married? What use can a friend in a skirt be to you? It's none of my business, excuse me . . . but it's gone this far, I'll finish my thought. If I were your age, had as much money, intelligence, and sense of fair play as you do, I would never go after anything in this world except the general welfare . . . I mean, if I may put it this way, I would never go after anything except the satisfaction of loving my fellow man . . .

GLAGOLYEV SR. I don't know how to fight for people's welfare . . . For that you need a will of iron and knowhow, but God hasn't bestowed them on me! I was born only to love great deeds and perform a lot of cheap, worthless ones . . . Only to love! Come to me!

ANNA PETROVNA. No. Not another word on this subject . . . Do not take my refusal to be of any vital significance . . . Vanity, my friend! If we could possess everything that we love, there would be no room left . . . for our possessions . . . Which means, people aren't behaving entirely without intelligence and affection when they turn you down . . . (*Laughs out loud.*) There's some philosophy for your dessert! What's all that noise? Do you hear? I'll bet it's Platonov making trouble . . . What a temperament!

Enter GREKOVA and TRILETSKY.

SCENE XV

ANNA PETROVNA, GLAGOLYEV SR., GREKOVA, and TRILETSKY.

GREKOVA (*entering*). This is the meanest insult imaginable! (*Weeps.*) The meanest! Only someone truly corrupt could see it and keep still!

TRILETSKY. I believe you, I believe you, but what's my part in all this? What's it got to do with me? Am I supposed to club him on the head, is that it?

GREKOVA. You should club him on the head, if there's nothing else to do! Get away from me! I, I, a woman, would not keep still, if someone had insulted you to my face so vilely, so shamelessly and undeservedly!

TRILETSKY. But actually I did . . . Please be reasonable! . . . What did I do wrong? . . .

GREKOVA. You're a coward, that's what you are! Get away from me and back to your revolting refreshments! Good-bye! Be so kind as not to visit me any more! We don't need one another . . . Good-bye!

TRILETSKY. Good-bye, as if I care, good-bye! I'm fed up with all of this, it's become infinitely sickening! Tears, tears . . . Ah, my God! My head's swimming . . . *coenurus cerebralis!*[54] Oh dear oh dear oh dear . . . (*Waves his hand in dismissal and exits.*)

GREKOVA. *Coenurus cerebralis* . . . (*Starts to leave.*) Another insult . . . What for? What did I do?

ANNA PETROVNA (*walks over to her*). Mariya Yefimovna . . . I won't keep you . . . I would leave here myself if I were you . . . (*Kisses her.*) Don't cry, my pet . . . Most women were created to put up with all sorts of nastiness from men . . .

GREKOVA. Well, *I* wasn't . . . I'll get him . . . fired! He won't be a teacher here any more! He hasn't got the right to be a teacher! Tomorrow I'll go to the superintendent of public schools . . .

ANNA PETROVNA. That's enough of that . . . In a day or two I'll pay you a visit, and together we'll sit in judgment on Platonov, but until then calm down . . . Stop crying . . . You shall have satisfaction . . . Don't be angry with Triletsky, my pet . . . He didn't stand up for you because he's too kind and gentle, and people like that aren't capable of standing up . . . What did he do to you?

GREKOVA. In front of everybody he kissed me . . . called me a fool and . . . and . . . shoved me up against the table . . . Don't think he can get away with that with impunity! Either he's a madman or else . . . I'll show him! (*Exits.*)

ANNA PETROVNA (*follows her*). Good-bye! See you soon! (*To Yakov.*) Yakov! Get Mariya Yefimovna's carriage! Ah, Platonov, Platonov . . . He'll go on making trouble until he gets into trouble himself . . .

GLAGOLYEV SR. A beautiful girl! Our gracious Mikhail Vasilich doesn't like her . . . Insults her . . .

---

54 Latin: a brain wave.

ANNA PETROVNA. For no good reason! Today he'll insult her, tomorrow he'll apologize . . . That's the blue blood in him talking!

Enter GLAGOLYEV JR.

S C E N E   X V I

The same and GLAGOLYEV JR.

GLAGOLYEV JR. (*aside*). With her! With her again! What the hell is going on, after all? (*Looks point-blank at his father.*)

GLAGOLYEV SR. (*after a pause*). What do you want?

GLAGOLYEV JR. You're sitting here, and people are looking for you! Go on, people are calling for you!

GLAGOLYEV SR. Who's calling for me?

GLAGOLYEV JR. People!

GLAGOLYEV SR. I assume it's people . . . (*Gets up.*) As you like, but I won't give up on you, Anna Petrovna! Chances are you'll be talking out of the other side of your mouth once you get to know me! I'll be seeing you . . . (*Exits into the house.*)

S C E N E   X V I I

ANNA PETROVNA and GLAGOLYEV JR.

GLAGOLYEV JR. (*sitting beside her*). The old goat! The jackass! No one is calling for him! I put one over on him!

ANNA PETROVNA. When you learn to be more clever, you will curse yourself for the way you treat your father!

GLAGOLYEV JR. You must be joking . . . Here's why I came out here . . . Two words . . . Yes or no?

ANNA PETROVNA. Meaning?

GLAGOLYEV JR. (*laughs*). As if you don't understand? Yes or no?

ANNA PETROVNA. I have no idea what you mean!

GLAGOLYEV JR. You will in a minute . . . A flash of gold is great at giving people ideas . . . If it's "yes," then wouldn't you like, generalissimo of my heart, to creep into my pocket and pull out my billfold with Daddy's money in it? . . . (*Holds out his side pocket.*)

ANNA PETROVNA. That's frank . . . Clever people actually get slapped for that kind of talk!

GLAGOLYEV JR. From an attractive woman even a slap can be attractive . . . First she slaps you, and then a little later she says "yes" . . .

ANNA PETROVNA (*gets up*). Pick up your cap and clear out of here this very second!

GLAGOLYEV JR. (*gets up*). Where to?

ANNA PETROVNA. Wherever you like! Clear out and never dare show your face here again!

GLAGOLYEV JR. Phoo . . . What's there to get angry about? I will not leave, Anna Petrovna!

ANNA PETROVNA. Well then, I'll give orders to have you turned out! (*Exits into the house.*)

GLAGOLYEV JR. What a temper you've got. After all I didn't say anything so very, specially . . . What did I say? There's no need to lose your temper . . . (*Exits following her.*)

SCENE XVIII

PLATONOV and SOFYA YEGOROVNA enter from the house.

PLATONOV. Even now at the school I'm stuck in a job which really isn't my sort of thing, but ought to belong to a real teacher . . . So that's how things have been since we split up! . . . (*Sits down.*) Putting aside what I've done to other people, what good have I done to myself? What seeds have I planted, nurtured, and cultivated in myself? . . . And now! Ech! Things are ghastly and hideous . . . It's outrageous! Evil is bubbling all around me, polluting the earth, swallowing up my brothers in Christ and my fellow Russians, while I just sit with my arms at my sides, as if I'd been doing hard labor; I sit, I stare, I keep my mouth shut . . . I'm twenty-seven, at thirty I'll be the same—I don't foresee any changes!—later on obesity and torpor, obtuseness, complete indifference to anything that isn't of the flesh, and then death!! A wasted life! My hair starts to stand on end, whenever I think about that death!

Pause.

How am I to rise above this, Sofya Yegorovna?

Pause.

You don't say anything, you don't know . . . Well, how could you? Sofya Yegorovna, I'm not feeling sorry for myself! To hell with this fellow, with my ego! But what's happened to you? Where is your pure heart, your sincerity, sense of fair play, your boldness? Where is your health? What have you done with it? Sofya Yegorovna! To idle away whole years, to make other people work for you, to feast your eyes on other people's sufferings and yet look them square in the face—that's what I call depravity!

SOFYA YEGOROVNA gets up.

(*Sits her down again.*) This is my last word, just hold on! What turned you into such an affected, languid, mealy-mouthed creature? Who taught you to lie? And the way you used to be! Excuse me! I'll let you go right away! Let me speak! You were so good, Sofya Yegorovna, so great! Dearest, Sofya Yegorovna, maybe you could still rise above it, it's not too late! Think about it! Gather all your strength and rise above it, for heaven's sake! (*Grasps her by the hand.*) My dearest, tell me frankly, for the sake of what we've shared in the past, what compelled you to marry that man? What lured you into that marriage?

SOFYA YEGOROVNA. He's a fine man . . .

PLATONOV. Don't say what you don't believe!

SOFYA YEGOROVNA (*gets up*). He's my husband, and I must ask you . . .

PLATONOV. Let him be whatever he wants, but I'm telling the truth! Sit down! (*Sits her down.*) Why didn't you pick out a hard-working man, a man who was suffering? Why didn't you pick out anybody except that pygmy, bogged down in debts and idleness? . . .

SOFYA YEGOROVNA. Leave me alone! Stop shouting! Someone's coming . . .

GUESTS pass by.

PLATONOV. The hell with them! Let everybody hear! (*Quietly.*) Forgive me for my crudeness . . . But I did love you! I loved you more than anything in the world, and that's why you are dear to me now . . . I so loved this hair, these arms, this face . . . Why do you powder your face, Sofya Yegorovna? Stop doing it! Ech! If someone else had come your way, you would quickly have risen above this, but now you'll just sink deeper into the mud! Poor creature . . . Wretch though I am, if I had the strength, I'd tear both of us out of this morass by the roots . . .

Pause.

Life! Why don't we live the way we could?!

SOFYA YEGOROVNA (*gets up and hides her face in her hands*). Leave me alone!

A noise inside the house.

Get away from me! (*Walks toward the house.*)

PLATONOV (*follows her*). Take your hands away from your face! That's right! You aren't leaving? Surely not? Let's be friends, *Sophie*! You can't be leaving? We'll have another talk? All right?

Inside the house louder noise and running down stairs.

SOFYA YEGOROVNA. All right.

PLATONOV. Let's be friends, my dearest . . . Why should we be enemies? Let me . . . Just a few words more . . .

VOINITSEV runs in from the house, followed by GUESTS.

S C E N E   X I X

*The same, VOINITSEV and GUESTS, then ANNA
PETROVNA and TRILETSKY.*

VOINITSEV (*running in*). Ah . . . There they are, the leading characters! Let's go set off the fireworks! (*Shouts.*) Yakov, to the river, march! (*To Sofya Yegorovna.*) Changed your mind, *Sophie*?

PLATONOV. She's not going, she's staying here . . .

VOINITSEV. Really? In that case hurray! Your hand, Mikhail Vasilich! (*Squeezes Platonov's hand.*) I always trusted your powers of persuasion! Let's go set off the fireworks! (*Goes with the guests upstage into the garden.*)

PLATONOV (*after a pause*). Yes, that's how things are, Sofya Yegorovna . . . Hm . . .

VOINITSEV'S VOICE. *Maman*, where are you? Platonov!

PLATONOV. I guess I'll go over there too, damn it . . . (*Shouts.*) Sergey Pavlovich, wait, don't set them off without me! Send Yakov to me, pal, for the balloon! (*Runs into the garden.*)

ANNA PETROVNA (*runs out of the house*). Wait, all of you! Sergey, wait, not everybody's here yet! Shoot off the cannon in the meantime! (*To Sofya.*) Come along, *Sophie*! Why so down in the mouth?

PLATONOV'S VOICE. Over here, my little lady! We'll strike up the old song, and not start a new one!

ANNA PETROVNA. I'm coming, *moan share*![55] (*Runs out.*)

PLATONOV'S VOICE. Who's coming with me in the boat? Sofya Yegorovna, don't you want to come on the river with me?

SOFYA YEGOROVNA. To go or not to go? (*Thinks.*)

TRILETSKY (*enters*). Hey! Where are you? (*Sings.*) I'm coming, I'm coming! (*He stares fixedly at Sofya Yegorovna.*)

SOFYA YEGOROVNA. What do you want?

TRILETSKY. Nothing, ma'am . . .

SOFYA YEGOROVNA. Well, then get away from here! I'm not in the mood today to converse or listen . . .

TRILETSKY. I know, I know . . .

Pause.

For some reason I have this awful desire to run a finger down your forehead: what is it made of? A burning desire! . . . Not to insult you, but just . . . to put my mind at ease . . .

---

55 Mispronunciation of French *mon cher*, my dear.

SOFYA YEGOROVNA. Clown! (*Turns away.*) You're not a comedian, but a clown, a buffoon!

TRILETSKY. Yes . . . A clown . . . My clowning earns me my grub from the general's lady . . . Yes indeed, ma'am . . . And pocket money . . . And when they're fed up with me, they'll kick me off the premises in disgrace. It's the truth I'm telling, isn't it, ma'am? However, I'm not the only one saying it . . . Even you said it, when you chose to call on Glagolyev, that freemason of our times . . .

SOFYA YEGOROVNA. All right, all right . . . I'm glad you've heard about it . . . Now, you see, it means I am able to tell the difference between clowns and true wits! If you were an actor, you would be the favorite of the gallery, but the expensive seats would hiss you . . . I hiss you.

TRILETSKY. The witticism is successful to a supernatural degree . . . Praiseworthy . . . I am honored to make my bow! (*Bows.*) Till our next pleasant meeting! I would go on bandying words with you, but . . . I'm tongue-tied, struck dumb! (*Goes upstage to the garden.*)

SOFYA YEGOROVNA (*stamps her foot*). The scoundrel! He has no idea of my opinion of him! Trivial little man!

PLATONOV'S VOICE. Who'll come on the river with me?

SOFYA YEGOROVNA. Oh, well . . . Whatever will be will be! (*Shouts.*) I'm coming! (*Runs off.*)

SCENE XX

GLAGOLYEV SR. and GLAGOLYEV JR. enter from the house.

GLAGOLYEV SR. That's a lie! That's a lie, you vicious little brat!

GLAGOLYEV JR. Don't be silly! What's my motive for lying? Ask her yourself, if you don't believe me! As soon as you left, on that very same bench I whispered a few words to her, put my arms around her, planted a juicy one on her . . . At first she asked for three thousand, well, uh, I got her to lower it to a thousand! So give me a thousand rubles!

GLAGOLYEV SR. Kirill, a woman's honor is at stake! Don't besmirch that honor, she is sacred! Keep quiet!

GLAGOLYEV JR. I swear on *my* honor! You don't believe me? I swear by all that's holy! Give me the thousand rubles! I'll bring her the thousand right now . . .

GLAGOLYEV SR. This is horrible . . . You're lying! She was joking with you, with a fool!

GLAGOLYEV JR. But . . . I put my arms around her, I tell you! What's so surprising about that? All women are like that nowadays! Don't believe in their innocence! I know them! And you wanted to get married again! (*Roars with laughter.*)

GLAGOLYEV SR. For God's sake, Kirill! Do you know the meaning of slander?

GLAGOLYEV JR. Give me a thousand rubles! I'll hand them over to her before your very eyes! On this very bench I held her in my arms, kissed her, and made her lower her price . . . I swear! What more do you need? That's why I chased you away, so that I could bargain with her! He doesn't believe that I'm able to win over a woman! Offer her two thousand, and she's yours! I know women, pal!

GLAGOLYEV SR. (*pulls his billfold out of his pocket and throws it on the ground*). Take it!

GLAGOLYEV JR. *picks up the billfold and counts the money.*

VOINITSEV'S VOICE. I'm going to begin! *Maman*, fire! Triletsky, climb on to the gazebo! Who stepped on that box? You!

TRILETSKY'S VOICE. I'm climbing, damn it all! (*Roars with laughter.*) Who is that? Bugrov's been squashed! I stepped on Bugrov's head! Where're the matches?

GLAGOLYEV JR. (*aside*). I am avenged! (*Shouts.*) Hoo-oo-ray! (*Runs out.*)

TRILETSKY. Who's howling out there? Give it to him in the neck!

VOINITSEV'S VOICE. Shall we begin?

GLAGOLYEV SR. (*clutches his head*). My God! The depravity! The iniquity! I worshiped her! Forgive her, Lord! (*Sits on a bench and hides his face in his hands.*)

VOINITSEV'S VOICE. Who took the fuse? *Maman*, aren't you ashamed of yourself? Where's my fuse, the one that was lying here?

ANNA PETROVNA'S VOICE. Here it is, scatterbrain!

GLAGOLYEV SR. *tumbles off the bench.*

ANNA PETROVNA'S VOICE. You! Who are you! Don't hang around here! (*Shouts.*) Hand it over! Hand it over!

SOFYA YEGOROVNA *runs in.*

SCENE XXI

SOFYA YEGOROVNA (*alone*).

SOFYA YEGOROVNA (*pale, with her hair in disarray*). I can't! It's too much, beyond my strength! (*Clutches her breast.*) My ruin or . . . happiness! It's stifling here! . . . He will either ruin me, or . . . be the harbinger of a new life! I welcome, I bless . . . you . . . new life! I've come to a decision!

VOINITSEV'S VOICE (*shouts*). Watch out!

Fireworks.

TABLEAU TWO

A forest. A railroad cutting. At the start of the cutting, on the left side a schoolhouse. Alongside the cutting, which disappears into the distance, stretches a railroad track, which takes a right turn near the school. A row of telegraph poles. Night.

SCENE I

SASHA (*sits in an open window*) and OSIP (*with a rifle on his back, stands in front of the window*).

OSIP. How did it happen? Couldn't be simpler . . . I'm walking along a ravine, not far from here, I see her standing in a little gully: she's tucked up her dress and with a burdock leaf she's scooping up water from a stream. Scoops and drinks, scoops and drinks, and then wets her head . . . I slide down, walk close up and stare at her . . . She pays me no mind: fool, it's like, you're a peasant, it's like, why should I give you a second thought?

"Ma'am," says I, "your excellency, I figure you want a drink of nice cold water?" — "And what business is it of yours," says she. "Go back where you came from!" That's what she says and don't look at me . . . I got bashful . . . Shame came all over me, and I was embarrassed that I'm of the peasant persuasion . . . "Why are you looking at me, nitwit? Never seen people before," says she, "or what?" And she looked me through and through . . . "Or do you like what you see," says she. — "I like it like crazy," says I. "Someone like you, your excellency, a noble, refined critter, what a beauty . . . A woman more beautiful than you," says I, "I never seen in all my born days . . . Our village beauty Manka, the constable's daughter," says I, "next to you looks like a horse, a camel . . . You got so much refinement! If I could kiss you," says I, "I think I'd drop down dead." She bursts out laughing . . . "Is that so," says she. "Kiss me, if you feel like it!" When I heard them words a fire ran through me. I walked up to her, took her nice as you please by her pretty shoulder and kissed her hard as I could right here, on this here spot, on the cheek and neck in one go . . .

SASHA (*laughs out loud*). And what'd she do?

OSIP. "Well, now," says she, "clear off! Wash yourself more often," says she, "and don't forget your fingernails!" So away I went.

SASHA. She's bold as brass! (*Gives Osip a plate of cabbage soup.*) Here, eat this! Sit somewhere!

OSIP. I'm no great lord, so I'll stand . . . Thank you very much for your loving kindness, Aleksandra Ivanovna! I'll pay you back for your caring one of these days . . .

SASHA. Take off your cap . . . You shouldn't eat with your cap on. And say grace when you eat!

OSIP (*takes off his cap*). It's a long time since I observed them religious things . . . (*Eats.*) And ever since then it's like I been off my head . . . Would you believe it? I don't eat, don't sleep . . . She's always there before my eyes . . . Used to be I'd close my eyes, and there she stands . . . Such tenderness came over me that I like to strung myself up! With mooning over her I almost did drown myself, I wanted to shoot the General . . . And when she became a widow, I began running all sorts of errands . . . I shot partridges for her, snared quail, painted her gazebo all the colors of the rainbow . . . Once I even brought her a live wolf . . . Did her all sorts of pleasures . . . Used to be, she'd give an order, I'd carry it out . . . If she'd ordered me to eat my head, I'd eat my head . . . Tender feelings . . . You can't do nothing about 'em . . .

SASHA. Yes . . . When I fell in love with Mikhail Vasilich and still didn't know that he loved me, I mooned about horribly too . . . Many's the time I prayed God for death, sinner that I am . . .

OSIP. There you see, ma'am . . . Feelings like that . . . (*Drinks from the plate.*) Might there be any more of that soup? (*Hands back the plate.*)

SASHA (*exits and half a minute later reappears in the window with a small saucepan*). There's no soup, but would you like some potatoes? Fried in goose fat . . .

OSIP. *Merci* . . . (*Takes the saucepan and eats.*) Something awful the way I put that soup away! And so I'd walk up and down, up and down, like a crazy man . . . I mean 'cause of what I was saying, Aleksandra Ivanovna . . . I'd walk up and down, up and down . . . Last year after Holy Week[56] I bring her a hare . . . "Here if you please," says I, "your excellency . . . Brought you this cross-eyed little critter!" She took it in her hands, stroked it and asks me: "Is it true what folks are saying, Osip, that you're a robber?" — "The Gospel truth," says I. "Folks don't say things like that just to hear theirselves talk . . ." I went and told her everything . . . — "You got to reform," says she. "Go on a pilgrimage," says she, "go on foot to Kiev. From Kiev to Moscow, from Moscow to Trinity Monastery, from Trinity Monastery to New Jerusalem, and then home again. Go and in a year you'll be a new man." I put on a beggar's rags, slung a knapsack on my back, and walked to Kiev . . . Nothing doing! I was reformed, but only halfway . . . Those spuds hit the spot! Outside Kharkov[57] I linked up with a swell gang traveling my way, drank up my money, got in a fight and came back here. Even lost my patchport . . . [58]

Pause.

Now she won't take nothing from me . . . She's angry . . .

---

56 The week between Palm Sunday and Easter.

57 Trinity Monastery was located in Zagorsk, north of Moscow. New Jerusalem was a monastery in the Zvenigorod district of Moscow guberniya, founded in 1636. Kharkov is the university town in Ukraine which, in Chekhov, usually stands for provincial boredom.

58 Russians required identity papers when traveling internally. The mispronunciation "patchport" comes from Gogol's *Dead Souls*.

SASHA. Why don't you go to church, Osip?

OSIP. I'd go, but then . . . Folks would start laughing . . . "Looky," they'll say, "he's come to make a confession!" Besides, it's dangerous to go near a church in the daytime. Lots of people there—they'll kill ya.

SASHA. Well, then, why do you do harm to poor people?

OSIP. And why not harm them? That's no concern o' yours, Aleksandra Ivanovna! Don't trouble your head over the rough stuff. It's nothing you got to understand. Besides, don't Mikhail Vasilich do harm to people?

SASHA. No one! If he does harm someone, it's unintentionally, accidentally. He's a good man!

OSIP. I admit I respect him more than anybody else . . . The General's kid, Sergey Pavlych, is a stupid guy, no brains; your brother's got no brains either, even if he is a doctor, but Mikhail Vasilich's sharp, got lots of knowhow! Has he got a rank in the civil service?

SASHA. Of course! He's a registrar, junior grade![59]

OSIP. That so?

Pause.

Good for him! So he's got a rank . . . Hm . . . Good for him! Only there ain't much charity in him . . . For him everybody's a fool, for him everybody's a flunky . . . How can you act that way? If I was a good man, I wouldn't act like that . . . I would be kind to the worst flunkies, fools, and crooks . . . They're the most miserable of folks, mark my words! You got to feel sorry for them . . . There ain't much goodness in him, not much . . . He ain't proud, he's chummy with all sorts, but not a lick o' goodness . . . It's nothing you got to worry your head about . . . Thank you kindly! I could eat spuds like that till my dying day . . . (*Hands over the saucepan.*) Thanks . . .

SASHA. Don't mention it.

OSIP (*sighs*). You're a wonderful woman, Aleksandra Ivanovna! How come you feed me all the time? Is there even a drop of womanly bitchiness in

59 The fourteenth and lowest rank in the bureaucratic hierarchy. As a public-school teacher, Platonov has to belong to the civil service.

you, Aleksandra Ivanovna? (*Laughs.*) Religious! (*Laughs.*) First time I seen the likes of you . . . Saint Aleksandra, pray God for us sinners! (*Bows.*) Oh be joyful, Saint Aleksandra!

SASHA. Mikhail Vasilich is coming.

OSIP. You're fibbing . . . At this very moment he's with the young mistress talking about tender feelings . . . A good-looking man you've got there! If he wanted, the whole female sex would be after him . . . And such a sweet-talker . . . (*Laughs.*) Keeps playing up to the general's lady . . . She'll send him packing, she don't care how good-looking he is . . . He'd like to, maybe, but she . . .

SASHA. You're starting to make uncalled-for remarks . . . I don't like it . . . Get going!

OSIP. I'll go right now . . . You should have been in bed long ago . . . I suppose you're waiting up for your husband?

SASHA. Yes . . .

OSIP. A good wife! Platonov, I figure, musta took ten years searching for such a wife, with candles and detectives . . . Found her somewheres . . . (*Bows.*) Good-bye, Aleksandra Ivanovna! Good night!

SASHA (*yawns*). Get going!

OSIP. I'm going . . . (*Goes.*) I'm going home . . . My home is where the floor is the earth, the ceiling is the sky, and nobody knows where the walls and roof are . . . Anybody cursed by God lives in this home . . . It's vast, but there's nowhere to lay your head . . . The only good thing is you don't have to pay the county propitty taxes on it . . . (*Stops.*) Good night, Aleksandra Ivanovna! Please pay me a visit! In the forest! Ask for Osip, every bird and lizard knows who I am! Look there at how that little stump is glowing! Like a dead man riz up from his grave . . . And there's another! My mother told me that under a stump that's glowing there's a sinner buried, and the stump glows so that folks'll pray for him . . . There'll be a stump glowing over me . . . I'm a sinner too . . . And there's a third! A heap of sinners in this world! (*Exits and whistles for a couple of minutes.*)

SCENE II

SASHA *(alone).*

SASHA *(comes out of the school with a candle and a book).* How long Misha's been away . . . *(Sits down.)* I hope he won't damage his health . . . These open-air parties always make a person sick . . . Besides, I want to go to bed . . . Where did I leave off? *(Reads.)* "It is high time, at long last, to proclaim once more those great, eternal ideals of humanity, those immortal principles of freedom which were the guiding stars of our fathers and which we betrayed, to our dismay." What does that mean? *(Thinks.)* I don't understand . . . Why don't they write so that everyone can understand? What's next . . . Mmm . . . I'll skip the preface . . . *(Reads.)* "Sacher Masoch"[60] . . . What a funny name! . . . Masoch . . . I suppose he's not Russian . . . What's next . . . Misha insists I read it, so I've got to read it . . . *(Yawns and reads.)* "One merry winter's evening" . . . Well, this can be skipped . . . A description . . . *(Turns over the pages and reads.)* "It was hard to decide who was playing which instrument . . . Powerful, majestic tones of an organ played by a firm male hand suddenly shifted to a delicate flute as if sounded by magnificent female lips and finally died away . . . " Shhh . . . Someone's coming . . . *(Pause.)* Those are Misha's footsteps . . . *(Blows out the candle.)* At last . . . *(Gets up and shouts.)* Hey! One, two, one, two! Left, right, left, right! Left! left!

Enter PLATONOV.

SCENE III

SASHA and PLATONOV.

PLATONOV *(entering).* To spite you: right! right! Actually, my dear, neither right nor left! A drunken man knows neither right nor left: he knows forward, backward, sideways, and down . . .

SASHA. Please come here, my little drunkard, sit over here! Let me show you how to step sideways and down! Sit down! *(Throws her arms round Platonov's neck.)*

---

60 Although Leopold Ritter von Sacher-Masoch (1835–1895) is best known for lending his name to the concept of "masochism," he also wrote works of social criticism, including the one Sasha is reading: *Ideals of Our Time*, translated into Russian in 1877. Chekhov knew his play *These Slavs of Ours* (*Unsere Sclaven*). Sacher-Masoch's attempt to describe the sexual instinct without moralizing may be what leads Platonov to recommend him to his wife.

PLATONOV. Let's sit . . . (*Sits.*) Why aren't you asleep, you infusoria?[61]

SASHA. I don't feel like it . . . (*Sits beside him.*) They kept you late!

PLATONOV. Yes, late . . . . Has the passenger train gone by yet?

SASHA. Not yet. The freight train went by about an hour ago.

PLATONOV. Which means, it isn't two o'clock yet. Have you been back a long time?

SASHA. I've been home since ten . . . When I got back, Kolka was screaming to beat the band . . . I left without saying good-bye, I hope they forgive me . . . Was there dancing after I left?

PLATONOV. There was dancing, and there was a supper, and there were scandalous scenes . . . Among other things . . . did you know? Did it happen while you were there? Old man Glagolyev had a stroke!

SASHA. What are you saying?!

PLATONOV. Yes . . . Your brother let his blood and intoned a requiem mass . . .

SASHA. How did it happen? What came over him? He seemed healthy by the look of him . . .

PLATONOV. A mild stroke . . . Mild luckily for him and unluckily for his little jackass, whom he stupidly dignifies by the name of son . . . They drove him home . . . Can't have a party without a scandal! Such is our fate, I suppose!

SASHA. I can imagine how frightened Anna Petrovna and Sofya Yegorovna must have been! How gorgeous that Sofya Yegorovna is! I rarely see such pretty women . . . There's something special about her . . .

Pause.

PLATONOV. Ugh! Stupid, despicable . . .

SASHA. What?

PLATONOV. What have I done?! (*Covers his face with his hands.*) Shameful!

---

61 A protozoa found in decaying animal or vegetable matter. Platonov is calling Sasha a tiny creature that battens on his rotting flesh. "Maggot" might serve as a substitute.

SASHA. What did you do?

PLATONOV. What did I do? Nothing nice! When have I ever done anything I wasn't ashamed of afterwards?

SASHA (*aside*). He's drunk, poor dear! (*To him.*) Let's go to bed!

PLATONOV. I was more despicable than ever! Where's your self-respect after that! What's worse than to be devoid of self respect! My God! There's nothing about me anyone could count on, nothing anyone could respect and love!

Pause.

Although you love me . . . I don't understand! Evidently you've found something in me that can be loved? You love me?

SASHA. What a question! How could I not love you?

PLATONOV. I know, but tell me specifically the good thing that you love me for! Point out the good thing that you love about me!

SASHA. Hm . . . What do I love you for? How cranky you are today, Misha! How can I help but love you, since you're my husband?

PLATONOV. You love me only because I'm your husband?

SASHA. I don't understand you.

PLATONOV. You don't understand? (*Laughs.*) Oh, you, my perfect little fool! Why aren't you a fly? With your brains you could be the smartest fly in the world of flies! (*Kisses her on the forehead.*) What would happen to you if you did understand me, if you lost your lovely ignorance! Would you be so happy a woman, if you and your pristine little mind could realize that there is nothing lovable about me? Don't understand, my treasure, don't get informed, if you want to love me! (*Kisses her hand.*) My ownliest one! And I am happy basking in the warmth of your ignorance! I have a family, like other people . . . I have a family . . .

SASHA (*laughs*). Crackpot!

PLATONOV. You're my treasure! My dear little, stupid little country girl! Shouldn't have you as a wife, but keep you on the table under glass! And how did you and I manage to bring Nikolka into God's green world? You shouldn't be giving birth to Nikolkas, but shaping toy soldiers out of cookie-dough, my better half!

SASHA. You're talking nonsense, Misha!

PLATONOV. God forbid you ever understand! Do not understand! Let the world be square so ships sail off the edge![62] Where would we find faithful wives, if it weren't for women like you, Sasha? (*Tries to kiss her.*)

SASHA (*won't let him*). Get out of here! (*Angrily.*) Why did you marry me, if I'm such a fool! You should have found yourself a clever woman! I didn't force you!

PLATONOV (*roars with laughter*). So you know how to get angry? Ah, what the hell! Why, this is a genuine discovery in the field of . . . Which field? A genuine discovery, my darling! So you know how to get angry? You're not joking?

SASHA (*gets up*). Go to bed, pal! If you didn't drink, you wouldn't be making discoveries! Drunkard! And a schoolteacher at that! You're not a teacher, but a piggy-wig! Get to bed! (*Slaps him on the back and exits into the schoolhouse.*)

SCENE IV

PLATONOV (alone).

PLATONOV. Am I actually drunk? That can't be, I didn't drink that much . . . And yet, my head's not quite normal . . .

Pause.

And when I talked to Sofya, was I . . . drunk? (*Thinks.*) No, I wasn't! I was not, unfortunately, good grief! I was not! My damned sobriety! (*Leaps up.*) How has her wretched husband done me any harm? Why did I sling such mud at him in her hearing? Don't forgive me for this, conscience of mine! I babbled away to her like a little kid, struck poses, played scenes, boasted . . . (*Mimics himself.*) "Why didn't you marry a hard-working man, a man who's suffering?" Why should she marry a hard-working man, a man who's suffering? Why, you lunatic, did you say things you didn't believe? Ah! . . . She believed them . . . She listened to the ravings of an idiot and looked down at her feet! Went all limp, the wretched woman, melted . . . How stu-

---

62 Literally, "let the world stand on whales and the whales on pitchforks," a medieval Russian belief.

pid all this is, how despicable, absurd! It's perfectly revolting . . . (*Laughs.*) A self-centered bully! They used to poke fun at our merchants for being self-centered bullies, laugh them to scorn[63] . . . It was laughter through tears and tears through laughter . . . Who laughs at me? When? Ridiculous! He doesn't take bribes, doesn't steal, doesn't beat his wife, thinks decent thoughts, but . . . he's a scoundrel! A ridiculous scoundrel! An above-average scoundrel! . . .

Pause.

I have to leave here . . . I'll ask the school inspector for another post . . . I'll write to town today . . .

Enter VENGEROVICH JR.

SCENE V

PLATONOV and VENGEROVICH JR.

VENGEROVICH JR. (*entering*). Hm . . . The schoolhouse, in which that half-baked sage sleeps on forever . . . Is he doing his usual sleeping or his usual bickering? (*On seeing Platonov.*) There he is, hollow, yet reverberant . . . Neither sleeping nor bickering . . . An abnormal state of affairs . . . (*To him.*) Still up?

PLATONOV. As you see! Why stop here? Let me wish you a good night!

VENGEROVICH JR. I'll be going right away. You're bound by the spell of solitude? (*Looks around.*) You feel yourself a lord of creation? On such a splendid night . . .

PLATONOV. On your way home?

VENGEROVICH JR. Yes . . . Father took the carriage, and I am compelled to make my way on foot. Enjoying yourself? But then isn't it pleasant—don't you agree?—to drink champagne and under its influence have the nerve for self-scrutiny! May I sit beside you?

PLATONOV. You may.

---

63 A reference to the plays of Aleksandr Ostrovsky, which depicted the typical Russian merchant as a *samodur*, a term that conflates "homegrown tyrant" with "complacent fool."

VENGEROVICH JR. Thank you. (*Sits down.*) I like to say thank you for every-thing. How sweet to sit here, here on these steps, and feel yourself monarch of all you survey! Where is your girlfriend, Platonov? After all, amid this rustling, this whispering of nature, the singing and chirping of grasshop-pers, the only thing missing is lovers' prattle to turn it all into paradise! This coy, flirtatious breeze lacks only the warm breath of a charming creature to make your cheeks flush with happiness! The whispering of Mother Nature lacks words of love . . . A woman!! You stare at me in amazement . . . Ha, ha! Am I not speaking my native tongue? True, it isn't native to me . . . Once I've sobered up, I'll blush more than once at such words . . . Still, why shouldn't I spout poetry? Hm . . . Who's stopping me?

PLATONOV. Nobody.

VENGEROVICH JR. Or, perhaps, this language of the gods is out of keeping with my status, my looks? Is my face unpoetic?

PLATONOV. It is unpoetic . . .

VENGEROVICH JR. Unpoetic . . . Hm . . . Delighted. We Jews do not have poetic features. Nature played us a dirty trick, didn't endow us Jews with poetic features! We are usually judged by our faces and on the grounds that we have certain features, they deny us any poetic feelings . . . They say that Jews are not poets.

PLATONOV. Who says that?

VENGEROVICH JR. Everybody says it . . . But, after all, it's dirty slander!

PLATONOV. Stop equivocating! Who says it?

VENGEROVICH JR. Everybody says it, but in fact we have a great many gen-uine poets, not Pushkins, not Lermontovs,[64] but still the genuine article! Auerbach, Heine, Goethe . . .[65]

PLATONOV. Goethe's German.

VENGEROVICH JR. Jewish!

------

64 Aleksandr Sergeevich Pushkin (1799–1837) and Mikhail Yurevich Lermontov (1814–1841) are considered Russia's greatest lyric poets.

65 Berthold Auerbach (1812–1882), prolific German writer on Judaism and freedom of religion; Heinrich Heine (1797–1856), Germany's greatest lyric poet; and Johann Wolfgang von Goethe (1749–1832), the towering figure of German literature and culture.

PLATONOV. German!

VENGEROVICH JR. Jewish! I know what I'm talking about!

PLATONOV. And I know what I'm talking about, but have it your way! It's hard to win an argument with a half-educated Jew.

VENGEROVICH JR. Very hard . . .

Pause.

But even if there were no poets! Big deal! We have poets—fine, we don't have poets—even better! A poet, regarded as a man of feeling, is in most cases a parasite, an egotist . . . Did Goethe, as a poet, ever give a crust of bread to a single German proletarian?

PLATONOV. That's stale! That's enough of that, youngster! He didn't take a crust of bread away from a German proletarian! That's the important thing . . . Besides, better to be a poet than nothing! A million times better! Anyway, let's not talk . . . Never mind the crust of bread, about which you haven't the slightest clue, and poets, whom your shriveled-up soul doesn't understand, and me, whom you will not leave in peace!

VENGEROVICH JR. I will not, I will not trouble your great heart, you effervescent fellow! . . . I will not pull the cozy coverlet off you . . . Sleep on!

Pause.

Just look at that sky! Yes . . . It's nice here, peaceful, nothing but trees . . . None of those smug, self-satisfied faces . . . Yes . . . The trees are whispering but not to me . . . And the moon doesn't gaze upon me as affably as she does on Platonov here . . . She's trying to freeze me with a look . . . You, and I'm quoting, are not one of us . . . Get out of here, out of paradise, back to your grubby Yid place of business . . . Although that's rot . . . I'm rambling . . . that's enough! . . .

PLATONOV. Enough . . . Go on, youngster, go home! The longer you sit here, the more you run off at the mouth . . . And this running off at the mouth will make you blush later on, as you've said yourself! Go on!

VENGEROVICH JR. I want to run off at the mouth! (*Laughs.*) Now I'm a poet!

PLATONOV. No man is a poet who is ashamed of being young! You are experiencing youth, so be young! Ridiculous, stupid, perhaps, but still human!

VENGEROVICH JR. All right . . . What stupidity! You are one big crackpot, Platonov! You are all crackpots around here . . . You should have lived in the time of Noah . . . And the general's lady is a crackpot, and Voinitsev is a crackpot . . . By the way, the general's lady isn't bad from the physical standpoint . . . What sharp eyes she's got! What dainty fingers she's got! . . . Not bad, when you take her to pieces . . . Breast, neck . . .

Pause.

Why not? Am I your inferior or what? At least once in my life! If thoughts have such a powerful attractive effect on my . . . spinal cord, what bliss would inflame me body and soul if she were to appear right now between those trees and beckon me with her diaphanous fingers! . . . Don't look at me like that . . . I'm being a fool now, a little boy . . . And yet, who dares forbid me at least once in my life to be a fool? On scientific grounds I'd like to be a fool right now, and happy the way you are . . . I'm happy too . . . Whose business is it? Hm . . .

PLATONOV. But . . . (*Looks closely at Vengerovich's watch-chain.*)

VENGEROVICH JR. Anyway, personal happiness is selfish!

PLATONOV. Oh yes! Personal happiness is selfish, and personal unhappiness is virtuous! You really are full of crap! What a chain! What wonderful trinkets! How it shines!

VENGEROVICH JR. Taken a fancy to this chain?! (*Laughs.*) You're attracted by this pinchbeck, this glitter . . . (*Shakes his head.*) Just when you're preaching to me almost in verse, you can get turned on by gold! Take the chain! Throw it away! (*Tears off his chain and throws it aside.*)

PLATONOV. What a pompous jingle-jangle! The sound alone lets you know it's heavy!

VENGEROVICH JR. The gold is heavy in more than weight! You're lucky that you can sit on these filthy steps! Here you don't suffer the full heaviness of this filthy gold! Oh, for me these are golden shackles, golden fetters!

PLATONOV. Fetters which don't last forever! Our fathers knew how to drink them away!

VENGEROVICH JR. How many wretches, how many starvelings, how many drunkards there are under the sun! When, at long last, will the millions who sow in abundance and have nothing to eat cease to starve! When, I ask you? Platonov, why don't you answer me?

PLATONOV. Leave me out of it! Do me a favor! I don't like bells that go on ringing for no rhyme or reason! Excuse me, but leave me out of it! I want to go to bed!

VENGEROVICH JR. I'm a bell? Hm . . . More likely you're the bell . . .

PLATONOV. I'm a bell and you're a bell, only the difference is I ring myself, and you're rung by other people . . . Good night! (*Gets up.*)

VENGEROVICH JR. Good night!

Inside the school a clock strikes two.

It's two o'clock already . . . One should have been asleep all this time, but I'm not asleep . . . Insomnia, champagne, excitement . . . An abnormal life, responsible for the breakdown of one's organism . . . (*Gets up.*) I think I'm getting an ache in my chest . . . Good night! I won't give you my hand and I'm proud of it. You have no right to shake my hand . . .

PLATONOV. How stupid! As if I cared.

VENGEROVICH JR. I hope that our talk and my . . . running off at the mouth were heard by no one but ourselves and will stay that way . . . (*Goes far upstage and comes back again.*)

PLATONOV. What do you want now?

VENGEROVICH JR. My chain was somewhere around here . . .

PLATONOV. There it is, your chain! (*Tosses the chain with his foot.*) Didn't forget it after all! Listen here, do me a favor, donate this chain to someone I know who is in the ranks of those who sow in abundance but have nothing to eat! This chain will feed him and his family for a whole year! . . . May I present it to him?

VENGEROVICH JR. No . . . I'd be happy to give it to you, but, word of honor, I can't! It's a gift, a keepsake . . .

PLATONOV. Yes, yes . . . Clear out of here!

VENGEROVICH JR. (*picks up the chain*). Leave me alone, please! (*Goes back upstage, exhausted, sits down on the railroad track, and hides his face in his hands.*)

PLATONOV. The vulgarity! To be young and yet not to be a guiding light! What profound depravity! (*Sits down.*) It's disgusting when we run into people who give us a glimpse of our own shameless past! I was once a bit like him . . . Ugh!

Horse's hoofbeats are heard.

SCENE VI

PLATONOV and ANNA PETROVNA (enters in a riding-habit, holding a hunting crop).

PLATONOV. Madam General!

ANNA PETROVNA. How am I to see him? Should I knock? (*On seeing Platonov.*) You're here? How a propos! I knew that you weren't asleep yet . . . Besides, how can one sleep at a time like this? God gave us the winter for sleeping . . . Good evening, you brute of a man! (*Holds out her hand.*) Well? What're you waiting for? Your hand!

PLATONOV holds out his hand.

ANNA PETROVNA. You're not drunk?

PLATONOV. Who the hell knows! I'm either sober, or as drunk as the most confirmed alcoholic . . . And what's come over you? Chose to take a walk to keep your weight down, most respected somnambula?

ANNA PETROVNA (*sits beside him*). N-yes-sir . . .

Pause.

Yes, sir, dearest Mikhail Vasilich! (*Sings.*) "All this gladness, all this torment . . ."[66] (*Roars with laughter.*) What big, wondering eyes! That's enough, don't be afraid, dear friend!

PLATONOV. I'm not afraid . . . for myself at any rate . . .

Pause.

You, I see, have made up your mind to do something silly . . .

ANNA PETROVNA. In my old age . . .

---

66 From the chorus of the "gypsy" ballad "In a fatal hour."

PLATONOV. Old women have an excuse . . . They're senile . . . But what kind of old woman are you? You're as young as summer in June. Your life is ahead of you.

ANNA PETROVNA. I need life now, and not ahead of me . . . And I am young, Platonov, dreadfully young! I feel . . . My youth is running alongside me like a wind! Diabolically young . . . It's cold!

Pause.

PLATONOV (*leaps up*). I don't want to understand or guess or assume . . . I don't want any of it! Go away! Call me an ignoramus and leave me! I'm begging you! Hm . . . How come you're looking at me that way? You should . . . you should give it some thought!

ANNA PETROVNA. I've already given it some thought . . .

PLATONOV. You give it some more thought, you proud, intelligent, beautiful woman! Why, what motive has brought you here?! Ah! . . .

ANNA PETROVNA. I wasn't brought here, I rode over, my dear!

PLATONOV. With such a mind, such beauty, youth . . . you come to me? My eyes, my ears are deceiving me. . She came to conquer, to capture the fortress! I'm no fortress! It wasn't for conquests that you came here . . . I'm weak, terribly weak! Understand that!

ANNA PETROVNA (*gets up and walks over to him*). Running yourself down is worse than pride . . . What's it to be, *Michel*? Doesn't this have to end somehow? You agree yourself, that . . .

PLATONOV. I won't end it, because I never started it!

ANNA PETROVNA. Eh . . . despicable sophistry! And aren't you ashamed to tell lies? On such a night, under such a sky . . . and you tell lies? Lying is for autumn, if you must, in the mud, in the slush, but not now, not here . . . You're being overheard, you're being watched . . . Look up there, you crackpot!

Pause.

Up there the stars are twinkling that you are lying . . . Enough, my dear! Be as nice as all outdoors! Don't spoil this stillness with your own petty ego . . . Chase away your demons! (*Embraces him with one arm.*) There's no one I could ever have loved as I love you! No woman you could ever have loved as you love me . . . Let's take for ourselves nothing but this love, and all the rest, which tortures you so, let others worry about . . . (*Kisses him.*) Let's take for ourselves nothing but this love . . .

PLATONOV. Odysseus deserved to have the sirens sing to him, but I'm not King Odysseus, siren![67] (*Embraces her.*) If only I could make you happy! How lovely you are! But I won't make you happy! I'll make you what I've made all the other women who threw themselves at me . . . I'll make you unhappy!

ANNA PETROVNA. What a high opinion you have of yourself! Are you really so dangerous, Don Juan? (*Roars with laughter.*) How good-looking you are in the moonlight! Magnificent!

PLATONOV. I know myself! The only romances with happy endings are the ones I'm not in . . .

ANNA PETROVNA. Let's sit down . . . Over here . . . (*They sit on the railroad tracks.*) What else do you have to say, philosopher?

PLATONOV. If I were an honest man, I would leave you . . . I had a foreboding of this today, I foresaw it . . . Why didn't I, scoundrel that I am, go away?

ANNA PETROVNA. Chase away your demons, *Michel!* Don't poison yourself . . . After all, it's a woman who came to you, not a beast . . . A glum face, tears in his eyes . . . Pooh! If you don't like this, I shall leave . . . Want me to? I'll leave, and everything will stay just as it was before . . . Shall I? (*Roars with laughter.*) Nincompoop! Take, snatch, grab! . . . What more do you want? Smoke me to the end like a cigarette, stub me out, cut me up into little pieces . . . Be a man! (*Pushes him around.*) Funny fellow!

PLATONOV. But are you really mine? Are you really meant for me? (*Kisses her hands.*) Go to somebody else, my dear . . . Go to a man who deserves you . . .

ANNA PETROVNA. Ah . . . Will you stop talking rubbish! After all, it's a very simple matter: a woman has come to you, who loves you and whom you

---

67 On his travels home to Ithaca from the Trojan War, Odysseus was menaced by the sirens, sea creatures who sang men to their doom. *Odyssey*, Book XII.

love . . . The weather is superb . . . What could be simpler? What's the point of all this philosophy, politics? Are you trying to put on an act?

PLATONOV. Hm . . . (*Gets up.*) What if you came here to trifle with me, lead me down the garden path, put one over on me? . . . What then? I'm not available for part-time jobs . . . I won't let myself be toyed with! You won't be able to pay me off with pennies, as you've paid off scores of others! . . . I'm too expensive for short-term affairs . . . (*Clutches his head.*) To respect, to love you and at the same time . . . the triviality, vulgarity, a philistine, plebeian game!

ANNA PETROVNA (*walks up to him*). You love me, respect me, then why are you, you restless soul, haggling with me, talking this filth to me? Why all these "if"s? I love you . . . I told you, and you know yourself that I love you . . . What more do you want? Serenity is what I want . . . (*Puts her head on his chest.*) Serenity . . . Understand me at last, Platonov! I want to rest . . . To forget, and not need anything else . . . You don't know . . . You don't know how oppressive my life is, and I . . . want to live!

PLATONOV. But I'm not able to provide serenity!

ANNA PETROVNA. Just try and stop philosophizing! . . . Live! Everything lives, everything moves . . . Life is all around . . . Let us live too! Tomorrow solve the problems but today, tonight, live, live . . . Live, *Michel*!

Pause.

Actually, why am I warbling away to you? (*Roars with laughter.*) Tell me, please! I'm singing, while he's giving me a hard time.

PLATONOV (*grasps her by the hand*). Listen . . . For the last time . . . As a man of honor I'm telling you . . . Go away! For the last time! Go away!

ANNA PETROVNA. You mean it? (*Roars with laughter.*) You're not joking? . . . You're being silly, pal! Now I'll never leave you! (*Throws her arms around his neck.*) You hear? For the last time I'm telling you: I won't let you go! Come what may, no matter what! Even if you destroy me, even if you ruin yourself, I'll have you! Live! Tra-ta-ta-ta . . . ra-ra-ra . . . Why tear yourself away, you crackpot? You're mine! Now preach your philosophy!

PLATONOV. Once more . . . As a man of honor . . .

ANNA PETROVNA. If I can't get you honorably, I'll take you by force . . . Love me, if you do love me, but don't behave like a fool! Tra-ta-ta-ta . . . "The bells peal out in victory . . ."[68] You're mine, you're mine! (*Tosses a black kerchief over his head.*) You're mine!

PLATONOV. Yours? (*Laughs.*) You shallow woman! You aren't doing yourself any good . . . There'll be tears, after all! I won't be your husband, because you weren't meant for me and I won't let myself be toyed with . . . We'll see who'll toy with whom . . . We'll see . . . You'll be in tears . . . Let's go, shall we?

ANNA PETROVNA (*roars with laughter*). Allons![69] (*Takes him by the arm.*) Wait . . . Someone's coming. Let's stand behind that tree a while . . . (*Hides behind the tree.*) Someone in a frockcoat, not a peasant . . . Why don't you write editorials for the newspapers? You'd be great at it . . . No fooling.

Enter TRILETSKY.

SCENE VII

The same and TRILETSKY.

TRILETSKY (*walks toward the school and knocks on the window*). Sasha! Little sister! Sashurka!

SASHA (*opens the window*). Who's there? Is that you, Kolya? What'd you want?

TRILETSKY. You're not in bed yet? Let me spend the night, dear heart!

SASHA. Make yourself at home . . .

TRILETSKY. You can put me in the classroom . . . But for pity's sake don't let Misha find out that I'm sleeping over: he and his philosophy won't let me get a wink! My head's swimming something awful . . . I'm seeing double . . . I stand in front of one window, but it looks as though there's two: which should I crawl through? Call an inquest! Good thing I'm not married! If I were married, I'd think I was a bigamist . . . I'm seeing double! You've got two heads on two necks! By the way, incidentally . . . Over by that felled

---

68 A misquoted line from G. R. Derzhavin's poem "Chorus for a quadrille," written in 1791 to celebrate the taking of Izmail and set to music by O. A. Kozlovsky.

69 French: let's go!

oak, the one by the river—you know it?—I blew my nose, ladybird, and forty rubles dropped out of my handkerchief . . . Pick them up, dear heart, first thing tomorrow . . . Finders keepers.

SASHA. As soon as day breaks the carpenters will pick them up . . . What a careless person you are, Kolya! Ah, yes! I almost forgot . . . The shop-keeper's wife came by and asked urgently that you go to her place as soon as possible . . . Her husband suddenly took ill . . . Some sort of stroke . . . Go quickly!

TRILETSKY. Bless and blast him! I'm not up to it . . . I've got shooting pains in my own head, and my belly . . . (*Crawls through the window.*) Please step aside . . .

SASHA. Hurry and climb in! You've caught your foot on me . . . (*Shuts the window.*)

PLATONOV. Who the hell's coming now!

ANNA PETROVNA. Wait.

PLATONOV. Let go of me. I'll step out, if I want to! Who is it?

ANNA PETROVNA. Petrin and Shcherbuk.

> Enter PETRIN and SHCHERBUK, *without their frockcoats,*
> *staggering. The former is wearing a black tophat,*
> *the latter a gray one.*

SCENE VIII

VENGEROVICH JR. (upstage), PLATONOV, ANNA PETROVNA, PETRIN, and SHCHERBUK.

PETRIN. *Vivat*, Petrin, bachelor of laws! Hooray! Where's the road? Where've we got to? What is this? (*Roars with laughter.*) This, Pavochka, is the Public School System! This is where they teach fools to forget God and swindle people! That's where we've wound up . . . Hm . . . So, sir . . . Here, pal, is where that . . . what's his name, damn it?—Platoshka lives, a civilized man . . . Pava, where's Platoshka? Give me your opinion, don't be shy! Singing a duet with the General's lady? Ugh, Lord, Thy will be done . . . (*Shouts.*) Glagolyev is a fool! She told him to take a hike, and he went and had a stroke!

SHCHERBUK. I want to go home, Gerasya . . . I want to go to bed, like crazy! They can all go to hell, the lot of 'em!

PETRIN. And where are our frockcoats, Pava? We'll go spend the night at the stationmaster's, but we've got no frockcoats . . . (*Roars with laughter.*) Did those hussies take 'em off us? Ah, you, lover boy, lover boy! . . . The hussies made off with the frockcoats . . . (*Sighs.*) Eh, Pava, Pavochka . . . You had any sham-pane? I guess you're drunk now? And whose were you drinking? You were drinking what's mine . . . You were drinking what's mine, and eating what's mine . . . That gown on the general's lady is mine, the stockings on Seryozhka are mine . . . all mine! I've given them everything! Down to the wobbly heels on my worn-out boots . . . I've given them everything, squandered everything on them, and what have I got to show for it? Ask me, what have I got to show? An up-yours and a snub . . . Yes . . . The footman at the table passes me by and tries to jostle me with his elbow, she herself treats me like a swine . . .

PLATONOV. I've had enough of this!

ANNA PETROVNA. Hold on . . . They'll be leaving right away! What a beast that Petrin is! The way he lies! And that old dishrag believes him . . .

PETRIN. That kike gets more respect . . . A kike at the head of the table, and us down at the end . . . And why? Because the kike gives 'em more money . . . And on his brow are etched the fatal words: to be sold at public auction!

SHCHERBUK. That's from Nekrasov[70] . . . They say Nekrasov's dead . . .

PETRIN. All right then! Not another kopek! You hear? Not a kopek! Let the old man spin in fury in his grave . . . Let 'im take it out on . . . the gravediggers! Over and done with! I'll call in the I.O.U.s! Tomorrow! I'll shove your nose in the muck, you ingrate!

SHCHERBUK. She's a count, a baron! She's got a general's face! While I'm . . . a Kalmuck[71] and nothing more . . . Let me worship Dunyasha . . .

---

70 Nikolay Alekseevich Nekrasov (1821–1878), Russian lyric poet, devoted to radical reform of the social structure; Petrin is paraphrasing a line from the poem "The Beggar Girl and the Fashion Plate." Nekrasov also makes an appearance in *The Wood Goblin*, Act Four, *The Seagull*, Act One, and *The Cherry Orchard*, Act Two.

71 A Mongolian living on the Caspian sea. Ethnic Russians held them in contempt for their flat faces.

What a bumpy road! There should be a surfaced road here with telegraph poles . . . with harness-bells . . . Jingle, jingle, jingle . . .

They exit.

SCENE IX

The same less PETRIN and SHCHERBUK.

ANNA PETROVNA (*comes out from behind the tree*). Have they gone?

PLATONOV. They've gone . . .

ANNA PETROVNA (*takes him by the shoulders*). Shall we wend our way?

PLATONOV. Let's go! I'll go, but if you had any idea how little I want to go! . . . I'm not going to you, but to the devil, who is hammering on the back of my skull: go on, go on! So understand this! If my conscience won't accept your love, it's only because I'm absolutely certain that you are making an irreparable mistake . . .

SASHA (*in the window*). Misha, Misha! Where are you?

PLATONOV. Damn it!

SASHA (*in the window*). Ah . . . I see you . . . Who's that with you? (*Bursts out laughing.*) Anna Petrovna! I barely recognized you! You're so black! What are you wearing? Good evening!

ANNA PETROVNA. Good evening, Aleksandra Ivanovna!

SASHA. You're in a riding habit? Been out for a canter, I suppose? What a wonderful idea! It's such a nice night! Let's you and I go too, Misha!

ANNA PETROVNA. I've had enough of it, Aleksandra Ivanovna . . . I'm going home now . . .

SASHA. In that case, of course . . . Come inside, Misha! . . . I really don't know what to do! Kolya's feeling bad . . .

PLATONOV. Which Kolya?

SASHA. My brother Nikolay . . . He had an awful lot to drink, I guess . . . Please come in! You pay us a visit too, Anna Petrovna! I'll run down to the cellar and get some cream . . . We'll each have a glass . . . The cream's nice and cold!

ANNA PETROVNA. Thank you . . . I'm going home now . . . (*To Platonov.*) Go ahead . . . I'll wait . . .

SASHA. I'd be running down to the cellar anyway . . . Go on, Misha! (*Disappears.*)

PLATONOV. I completely forgot that she existed . . . She trusts me, that one, trusts me like?! Go on . . . I'll put her to bed and come over . . .

ANNA PETROVNA. Quick as you can . . .

PLATONOV. Almost had a scene! Good-bye for now . . . (*Exits into the schoolhouse.*)

S C E N E   X

ANNA PETROVNA, VENGEROVICH JR., and then OSIP.

ANNA PETROVNA. What a shock . . . I'd completely forgot that she existed too . . . .

Pause.

It's cruel . . . Still, it's not the first time he's cheated on her, poor girl! Oh dear, oh dear . . . One sin drives out the other! Nobody but God will know! Not the first time . . . All this hole-in-corner business! Now I've got to wait till he puts her to bed! . . . A full hour will crawl by, if not more . . .

VENGEROVICH JR. (*moves to her*). Anna Petrovna . . . (*Falls on his knees before her.*) Anna Petrovna . . . (*Seizes her hand.*) Anna!

ANNA PETROVNA. Who's that? Who're you? (*Stoops down to him.*) Who is it? You, Isak Abramych? Is it you? What's wrong with you?

VENGEROVICH JR. Anna! (*Kisses her hand.*)

ANNA PETROVNA. Go away! It isn't nice! You're a grown man!

VENGEROVICH JR. Anna!

ANNA PETROVNA. I've had it with your clawing at me! Get out of here! (*Shoves him by the shoulder.*)

VENGEROVICH JR. (*sprawls on the ground*). Ugh! It's stupid . . . stupid!

OSIP (*enters*). Comedians! That wouldn't happen to be you, your excellency? (*Bows.*) What brings you to our neck o' the woods?

ANNA PETROVNA. Is that you, Osip? Greetings! Were you prying? Spying? (*Takes him by the chin.*) Saw it all?

OSIP. All.

ANNA PETROVNA. Then how come you're so pale? Eh? (*Laughs.*) You in love with me, Osip?

OSIP. If you say so . . .

ANNA PETROVNA. In love?

OSIP. I can't figure you out . . . (*Weeps.*) I thought you were a saint . . . If you had ordered me to jump in the fire, I'd've jumped in the fire . . .

ANNA PETROVNA. Then why didn't you walk to Kiev?

OSIP. What do I care about Kiev? I thought *you* were a saint . . . For me there were no saints except you . . .

ANNA PETROVNA. That'll do, you nitwit . . . Bring me some more little hares . . . I am accepting gifts again . . . Good-bye for now . . . Come to me tomorrow, and I'll give you some money: you can take the train to Kiev . . . You going? Good-bye . . . Don't you dare lay a finger on Platonov on my land! You hear me?

OSIP. I don't take orders from you any more . . .

ANNA PETROVNA. You don't say so, goodness me! You don't insist that I enter a nunnery? As if it's his business! . . . Well, well . . . He's crying . . . Are you a little boy or what? That'll do . . . When he's about to come to me, fire a shot! . . .

OSIP. At him?

ANNA PETROVNA. No, in the air . . . Good-bye, Osip! A loud shot! Will you fire it?

OSIP. I will.

ANNA PETROVNA. There's a clever boy . . .

OSIP. Only he won't go to you . . . He's with his wife now.

ANNA PETROVNA. That's just talk . . . Good-bye, cutthroat! (*Runs out.*)

SCENE XI

OSIP and VENGEROVICH JR.

OSIP (*flings his cap on the ground and weeps*). It's over! It's all over, and the hell with it!

VENGEROVICH JR (*on the ground*). What is he saying?

OSIP. I saw all that stuff, I heard it! My eyes popped out of my head, somebody was pounding a great big hammer in my ears! I heard it all! How can I keep from killing him, when I want to tear him to shreds, crush 'im . . . . (*Sits on the embankment with his back to the schoolhouse.*) Got to kill him . . .

VENGEROVICH JR. What's he saying? Kill whom?

SCENE XII

The same, PLATONOV and TRILETSKY.

PLATONOV (*pushes Triletsky out of the school*). Get out! Please head for the shopkeeper's right this minute! March!

TRILETSKY (*stretches*). I'd rather you rousted me out with a big stick tomorrow than wake me up today!

PLATONOV. You're a scoundrel, Nikolay, a scoundrel! You understand?

TRILETSKY. What can you do? Doesn't that mean that's how God made me?

PLATONOV. And what if the shopkeeper's already dead?

TRILETSKY. If he's dead, then let him rest in peace, and if he's still carrying on the struggle for existence, there's no point in you saying these awful things . . . I will not go to the shopkeeper's! I want to get some sleep!

PLATONOV. You will go, you pig! You will go! (*Pushes him.*) I won't let you sleep! What's wrong with you, in fact? What are you making of yourself? Why don't you do something? What's the point of spending all your money on food, wasting the best days of your life and loafing around?

TRILETSKY. You're a pest . . . What right have you got, pal . . . a regular chigger!

PLATONOV. What kind of creature are you, please let me know? This is awful! What are you living for? Why don't you study science? Why don't you keep up your scientific education? Science, why don't you study it, animal?

TRILETSKY. We shall discuss this interesting subject some time when I'm not sleepy, but for now let me sleep . . . (*Scratches himself.*) What the hell! If it's not one thing, it's another: "get out of bed, you skunk!" Hm . . . Code of ethics . . . Damn them all, those codes of ethics!

PLATONOV. What God do you serve, you strange creature? What kind of man are you? No, we'll never be of any use! No, not us!

TRILETSKY. Listen, Mikhail Vasilich, who gave you the right to lay your chilly big bear paws on another person's heart? Your tactlessness is beyond belief, pal!

PLATONOV. Nothing will come of us, except weeds out of the earth! We're a lost tribe! We're not worth a tinker's dam! (*Weeps.*) Not one single person to gladden my eyes! It's all so vulgar, filthy, shabby . . . Go away, Nikolay! Go on!

TRILETSKY (*shrugs*). You're crying?

Pause.

I'll go to the shopkeeper! You hear me? I'm on my way!

PLATONOV. Do what you like!

TRILETSKY. I'm on my way! Here I go . . .

PLATONOV (*stamps his feet*). Get out, go away!

TRILETSKY. Fine . . . Go to bed and sleep, *Michel*! It's not worth getting excited about! Good-bye! (*Starts to go and stops.*) Just one word in parting . . . Advise all preachers, yourself included, that the preacher should practice what he preaches . . . If you can't rejoice in the sight of yourself, don't ask me to gladden your eyes, which, incidentally, are very attractive in the moonlight! They shine in your head like little shards of green glass . . . And another thing . . . There's no point in talking to you . . . You should get a sound thrashing, have your bones broken, I should turn my back on you forever over that girl . . . Somebody should give you the talking-to you've never had in all your born days! But . . . I'm not up to it! Duels are not my thing! Lucky for you! . . .

Pause.

Good-bye. (*Exits.*)

PLATONOV, VENGEROVICH JR., and OSIP.

PLATONOV (*clutches his head*). I'm not the only one like this, they're all like this! All of them! Where are the real people, my God? What am I thinking! Don't go to her! She isn't yours! She's somebody's else property! You'll ruin her life, corrupt her forever! Go away from here! No! I will go to her, I will live here, I will get drunk, act like a heathen . . . Lechers, fools, drunkards . . . Nothing but drunkards! A stupid mother breeds with a drunken father! Father . . . mother! Father . . . O, I hope your bones are spinning in your graves, for the way you drunkenly and stupidly messed up my life!

Pause.

No . . . What was I saying? God forgive me . . . Rest in peace . . . (*Stumbles over Vengerovich lying on the ground.*) Who's that?

VENGEROVICH JR. (*gets to his knees*). A wild, hideous, disgraceful night!

PLATONOV. Aha? . . . Go and write down this wild night in your idiotic diary with ink from your father's conscience! Get out of here!

VENGEROVICH JR. Yes . . . I will make a note of it! (*Exits.*)

PLATONOV. What was he doing here? Eavesdropping? (*To Osip.*) Who're you? Why are you here, my loose cannon? Eavesdropping too? Get out of here! Or wait . . . Go after Vengerovich and take away his chain!

OSIP (*gets up*). What chain?

PLATONOV. There's a gold watch-chain dangling across his chest! Go after him and take it! Step lively! (*Stamps his feet.*) Quick, or you won't catch up to him! He's running now to the village like a madman!

OSIP. And you're off to the General's lady?

PLATONOV. Hurry up, scoundrel! Don't beat him up, just take the chain! Go on! What are you standing here for? Run!

OSIP runs out.

(*After a pause.*) To go . . . Or not to go? (*Sighs.*) Go . . . I'll go and strike up that long, basically boring, ghastly song . . . I used to think I was clad in impenetrable armor! And what happens? A woman says one word, and a storm starts brewing inside me . . . Most people go distracted over world crises, but for me it's a woman! My whole life—it's a woman! Caesar had his Rubicon,[72] I have a woman . . . A vacuous skirt-chaser! It wouldn't be so pitiful if I didn't fight it, but I do fight it! Weak, weak to the nth degree!

SASHA (*in the window*). Misha, are you there?

PLATONOV. Yes, my poor treasure!

SASHA. Come inside!

PLATONOV. No, Sasha! I want to stay in the fresh air. My head is splitting. Go to sleep, my angel!

SASHA. Good night! (*Closes the window.*)

PLATONOV. It's tough to cheat on someone who believes in you unconditionally! I'm in a sweat and flushed . . . I'll go! (*Starts to go.*)

KATYA and YAKOV come to meet him.

SCENE XIV

PLATONOV, KATYA, and YAKOV.

KATYA (*to Yakov*). Wait here . . . I'll only be a minute . . . I'm just getting a book . . . Don't leave, mind you! (*Goes to meet Platonov.*)

PLATONOV (*on seeing Katya*). You? What do you want?

KATYA (*alarmed*). Ah . . . there you are, sir! I have to see you.

PLATONOV. Is that you, Katya? All of 'em from the mistresses to the maids inclusive, all night owls! What's up with you?

KATYA (*quietly*). The mistress sent you a letter.

PLATONOV. What?

KATYA. The mistress sent you a letter!

PLATONOV. Are you raving? What mistress?

KATYA (*more quietly*). Sofya Yegorovna . . .

---

72 A river in northern Italy, once the border between Cisalpine Gaul and Italy. By crossing the Rubicon in 49 B.C., Julius Caesar began a civil war; so the phrase "crossing the Rubicon" has come to mean "taking a decisive step."

PLATONOV. What? Are you crazy? Take a cold shower! Get out of here!

KATYA (*gives him the letter*). Here it is!

PLATONOV (*snatches the letter*). A letter . . . a letter . . . What sort of letter? Couldn't you have brought it tomorrow? (*Unseals it.*) How am I supposed to read it?

KATYA. The lady'd like a reply real soon . . .

PLATONOV (*lights a match*). The devil brought the bunch of you here! (*Reads.*) "Am taking first step. Come, let's take it together. Am reborn. Come and take me. Yours." What the hell . . . It's some sort of telegram! "Will wait till four in gazebo near four pillars. My drunken husband out hunting with young Glagolyev. All yours S." That's all I needed! My God! That's all I needed! (*To Katya.*) What're you looking at?

KATYA. How can I help looking, since I got eyes?

PLATONOV. Gouge out your eyes! This letter's for me?

KATYA. You, sir . . .

PLATONOV. Liar! Get out of here!

KATYA. Very good, sir.

Exits with YAKOV.

SCENE XV

PLATONOV (alone).

PLATONOV (*after a pause*). There they are, the consequences . . . You've landed in it for good! You've corrupted a woman, a living creature, just like that, for no good reason, no need at all . . . Damn my tongue! It's led to this . . . What to do now? Come on, smart guy, think up something! Curse yourself now, tear out your hair . . . (*Thinks.*) Go away! I'll go away right now and never dare show my face here until doomsday! March away from here to the four corners of the earth, and bend to the iron rod of necessity and hard work! Better a life of hardship than one with this in the background!

Pause.

I'll go away . . . But . . . could it be that Sofya actually loves me? Really? (*Laughs.*) What for? How obscure and strange everything is in this world!

Pause.

Strange . . . Could it be that this beautiful, marmorial woman with the wonderful hair is capable of falling in love with a penniless crackpot? Can she love me? Unlikely! (*Lights a match and peruses the letter.*) Yes . . . Me? Sofya? (*Roars with laughter.*) She loves me? (*Clutches his chest.*) Happiness! This is real happiness! This is my happiness! It's a new life, with new characters, new scenery! I'll go! March to the gazebo near the four pillars! Wait for me, my Sofya! You were mine and will be again! (*Starts to go and stops.*) I won't go! (*Walks back.*) Tear apart my family? (*Shouts.*) Sasha, I'm coming in! Open up! (*Clutches his head.*) I won't go, I won't go . . . I won't go!

Pause.

I will go! (*Starts to go.*) Go, destroy, trample, defile . . . (*Runs into Voinitsev and Glagolyev Jr.*)

SCENE XVI

PLATONOV, VOINITSEV, and GLAGOLYEV JR.

VOINITSEV and GLAGOLYEV JR. have rifles over
their shoulders.

VOINITSEV. There he is! There he is! (*Embraces Platonov.*) So? A-hunting we shall go!

PLATONOV. No . . . Wait a bit!

VOINITSEV. Why tear yourself away, friend? (*Roars with laughter.*) Drunk, I'm drunk! For the first time in my life I'm drunk! My God, I'm so happy! My friend! (*Embraces Platonov.*) Shall we go? She sent me away . . . Asked me to shoot some game for her . . .

GLAGOLYEV JR. Let's get going! It's already light . . .

VOINITSEV. Did you hear what we're planning? How's this for a brilliant idea? We're thinking of putting on *Hamlet*! Word of honor! We'll put on such a show they won't know what the hell hit 'em! (*Roars with laughter.*) You're so pale . . . Are you drunk too?

PLATONOV. Leave me alone . . . I'm drunk.

VOINITSEV. Hold on . . . It's my idea! Tomorrow we'll start painting the sets! I'm Hamlet, *Sophie* is Ophelia, you are Claudius, Triletsky is Horatio . . . I'm so happy! And contented! Shakespeare, *Sophie*, you and *maman*! What more do I need! Except for some Glinka.[73] That's all I need! I'm Hamlet . . .

> And to this villain,
> Forgetting shame as woman, wife and mother,
> How could you yield yourself! . . .[74]

(*Roars with laughter.*) How's that for a Hamlet?

PLATONOV (*tears himself away and starts to run*). You bastard! (*Runs out.*)

VOINITSEV. Toodle-oo! He's drunk! In a major way! (*Roars with laughter.*) How do y'like that friend of ours?

GLAGOLYEV JR. Stewed to the gills . . . Let's go!

VOINITSEV. Let's go . . . "And were you my friend, perchance[75] . . . Ophelia! O nymph, in thy orisons be all my sins remember'd!"

They leave.

The sound of a passing train is heard.

SCENE XVII

OSIP and then SASHA.

OSIP (*runs in with the watch chain*). Where is he? (*Looks around.*) Where is he? He's gone? He's not here? (*Whistles.*) Mikhail Vasilich! Mikhail Vasilich! Hey!

---

73 Mikhail Ivanovich Glinka (1804–1857), Russian composer, who wrote the first national Russian operas, *A Life for the Tsar* (1836) and *Ruslan and Lyudmila* (1841).

74 Voinitsev is quoting from a Russian translation that corresponds only roughly to Shakespeare's "Could you on this mountain leave to feed, / And batten on this moor?" (Act III, scene 4). Or else "O shame! where is thy blush! Rebellious hell, / If thou canst mutine in a matron's bones, / To flaming youth let virtue be as wax, / And melt in her own fire."

75 Possibly a paraphrase of "Give me that man that is not passion's slave. . . ." The "nymph" line is misquoted by Lopakhin in Act Two of *The Cherry Orchard*.

Pause.

No? (*Runs over to the window and knocks on it.*) Mikhail Vasilich! Mikhail Vasilich! (*Breaks the glass.*)

SASHA (*in the window*). Who's there?

OSIP. Call Mikhail Vasilich! Quick!

SASHA. What's happened? He's not home!

OSIP (*shouts*). No? Went to the General's lady, I guess! The General's lady was here and summoned him to her! All is lost, Aleksandra Ivanovna! He's gone to the General's lady, damn him!

SASHA. Liar!

OSIP. As God is my judge, to the General's lady! I heard and saw it all! They were hugging over there, kissing . . .

SASHA. Liar!

OSIP. May my father, may my mother never get into heaven if I'm lying! To the General's lady! Left his wife! Chase him, Aleskandra Ivanovna! No, no . . . All is lost! And now you're unhappy! (*Takes the rifle from his shoulder.*) She gave me one last order, and I'll carry it out for one last time! (*Shoots into the air.*) Let her meet him! (*Throws the rifle on the ground.*) I'll cut his throat, Aleksandra Ivanovna! (*Leaps over the embankment and sits on the stump.*) Don't worry, Aleksandra Ivanovna . . . don't worry . . . I'll cut his throat . . . Never fear . . .

Lights appear.

SASHA (*enters in a nightgown, with her hair undone*). He left . . . He cheated on me . . . (*Sobs.*) I'm lost . . . Kill me, Lord, after this . . .

A train whistle.

I'll throw myself under the locomotive . . . I don't want to live . . . (*Lies on the tracks.*) He cheated on me . . . Kill me, mother of God!

Pause.

Forgive me, Lord . . . Forgive me, Lord . . . (*Screams.*) Kolya! (*Gets to her knees.*) My son! Save me! Save me! Here comes the train! . . . Save me!

OSIP comes galloping up to Sasha.

(*Falls on to the tracks.*) Ah . . .

OSIP (*picks her up and carries her into the schoolhouse*). I'll cut his throat . . . Don't you worry!

The train comes through.

End of Act Two

ACT THREE

A room in the schoolhouse. Doors right and left. A cupboard with crockery, a chest of drawers, an old upright piano, chairs, a sofa upholstered in oilcloth, a guitar, etc. Total chaos.

SCENE I

SOFYA YEGOROVNA and PLATONOV.

PLATONOV is asleep on the sofa. His face is covered with a straw hat.

SOFYA YEGOROVNA (*rouses Platonov*). Platonov! Mikhail Vasilich! (*Shakes him.*) Wake up! Michel! (*Takes the hat off his face.*) How can you put such a filthy hat on your face? Feh, what a slob, an unholy mess! Lost his shirt-studs, sleeps with his chest bare, unwashed, in a dirty night-shirt . . . *Michel!* I'm talking to you! Get up!

PLATONOV. Huh?

SOFYA YEGOROVNA. Wake up!

PLATONOV. Later . . . Fine . . .

SOFYA YEGOROVNA. That's enough of that! Will you please get up!

PLATONOV. Who's that? (*Gets up.*) Is that you, Sofya?

SOFYA YEGOROVNA (*holds her watch before his eyes*). Take a look!

PLATONOV. Fine . . . (*Lies down again.*)

SOFYA YEGOROVNA. Platonov!

PLATONOV. Well, what'd you want? (*Gets up.*) Well?

SOFYA YEGOROVNA. Look at the time!

PLATONOV. So what? Sofya, there you go again with your whims and caprices!

SOFYA YEGOROVNA. Yes, here I go again with my whims and caprices, Mikhail Vasilich! Please look at the time! What time is it now?

PLATONOV. Half past seven.

SOFYA YEGOROVNA. Half past seven . . . So you've forgot the agenda?

PLATONOV. What agenda? Express yourself more clearly, Sofya! I'm in no mood today for jokes or solving moronic riddles!

SOFYA YEGOROVNA. What agenda? So you have forgot? What's wrong with you? Your eyes are red, you're all rumpled . . . Are you sick?

Pause.

The agenda: for both of us to be at the cabin at six o'clock . . . You forgot? Six o'clock has come and gone . . .

PLATONOV. Anything else?

SOFYA YEGOROVNA (*sits next to him*). Aren't you ashamed? Why didn't you come? You gave your word of honor . . .

PLATONOV. I would have kept my word, if I hadn't fallen asleep . . . Didn't you see I was asleep? So why are you pestering me?

SOFYA YEGOROVNA (*shakes her head*). What an unreliable person you are! Why are you scowling at me? Unreliable in regard to me, at least . . . Think about it . . . Have you ever once shown up on time at our rendezvous? How many times have you failed to keep your word of honor to me?

PLATONOV. Pleased to hear it!

SOFYA YEGOROVNA. It's not clever, Platonov, it's disgraceful! Why do you stop being noble, intelligent, being yourself, whenever I'm with you? What's the point of this low-class behavior, unworthy of the man responsible for the salvation of my inner life? When I'm around you act like some kind of freak . . . No affectionate glance, or tender remark, not a single word of love! I come to you—and you reek of wine, you're dressed appallingly, your hair uncombed, your answers are rude and irrelevant . . .

PLATONOV (*leaps up and paces up and down the stage*). And she's off!

SOFYA YEGOROVNA. Are you drunk?

PLATONOV. What do you care?

SOFYA YEGOROVNA. That's so charming! (*Weeps.*)

PLATONOV. Women!

SOFYA YEGOROVNA. Don't talk to me about women! A thousand times a day you talk to me about them! I'm sick and tired of it! (*Gets up.*) What are you doing to me? Do you want to be the death of me? I'm sick because of you! Day and night my chest aches thanks to your good graces! Don't you see it? Don't you want to know about it? You hate me! If you loved me, you wouldn't dare treat me this way! I'm not some kind of simple village wench for you, some uncouth, coarse soul! I won't allow any . . . (*Sits down.*) For heaven's sake! (*Weeps.*)

PLATONOV. That's enough!

SOFYA YEGOROVNA. Why are you killing me? It's barely three weeks since that night, and I'm already thin as a rake! Where is the happiness you promised me? When is this treatment going to end? Think about it, you clever, noble, honorable man! Think about it, Platonov, before it's too late! Think about it right now . . . Sit down on this chair, clear your mind and think about one thing only: what are you doing to me?

PLATONOV. I'm not able to think.

Pause.

You think about it yourself! (*Walks over to her.*) You think about it! I deprived you of your family, your happy ending, your future . . . What for? To what end? I robbed you, like your worst enemy! What can I give you? How can I repay you for your sacrifices? This illicit affair spells your unhappiness, your downfall, your ruin! (*Sits down.*)

SOFYA YEGOROVNA. I've become intimate with him, and he dares call our relationship an illicit affair!

PLATONOV. Oh dear . . . Now is not the time to nitpick every word! You've got your view of that relationship, I've got mine . . . I ruined you, that's all there is to it! And not just you . . . Wait till you hear the tune your husband sings when he finds out!

SOFYA YEGOROVNA. You're afraid that he'll make life unpleasant for you?

PLATONOV. That's not what I'm afraid of . . . I'm afraid that we might be the death of him . . .

SOFYA YEGOROVNA. Then why, you craven coward, did you come to me, if you knew that we might be the death of him?

PLATONOV. Please, don't be so . . . over-emotional! You don't impress me with those chest tones . . . And why did you . . . Anyway . . . (*waves his hand in dismissal*) talking to you always ends up in a flood of tears . . .

SOFYA YEGOROVNA. Yes, yes . . . I never used to weep until I became intimate with you! Be afraid, tremble! He knows already!

PLATONOV. What?

SOFYA YEGOROVNA. He knows already!

PLATONOV (*sits up*). He does?!

SOFYA YEGOROVNA. He . . . This morning I talked things over with him . . .

PLATONOV. Jokes . . .

SOFYA YEGOROVNA. You've turned pale? You should be hated, not loved! I've gone crazy . . . I don't know why . . . why do I love you? He knows already! (*Plucks him by the sleeve.*) So tremble, tremble! He knows everything! I swear to you on my honor that he knows everything! Tremble!

PLATONOV. That's impossible . . . It can't be possible!

Pause.

SOFYA YEGOROVNA. He knows everything . . . Didn't it have to be done sooner or later?

PLATONOV. Why are *you* trembling? How did you explain it to him? What did you say?

SOFYA YEGOROVNA. I explained to him that I had already . . . that I cannot . . .

PLATONOV. What'd he do?

SOFYA YEGOROVNA. He was like you . . . He panicked! And how insufferable your face looks at this moment!

PLATONOV. What did he say?

SOFYA YEGOROVNA. At first he thought I was joking, but when I had convinced him of the contrary, he turned pale, began to stagger, began to cry, began to grovel on his knees . . . He wore the exact same disgusting expression that you have now!

PLATONOV. What have you done, you foul creature?! (*Clutches his head.*) You've killed him! And you can, and you dare say this so coolly and calmly? You've killed him! Did you . . . mention my name?

SOFYA YEGOROVNA. Yes . . . How else?

PLATONOV. What'd he do?

SOFYA YEGOROVNA (*leaps up*). You should be ashamed, at long last, Platonov! You don't know what you're saying! The way you see it, I suppose, there was no cause to tell him anything?

PLATONOV. There wasn't! (*Lies on the sofa face down.*)

SOFYA YEGOROVNA. You're a man of honor, what are you saying?

PLATONOV. It would have been more honorable not to say anything than to kill him! We've killed him! He started crying, groveled on his knees . . . Ah! (*Leaps up.*) Unhappy man! If it hadn't been for you, he would never have found out about our relationship so long as he lived!

SOFYA YEGOROVNA. I was obliged to have it out with him! I'm an honest woman!

PLATONOV. You know what you did by having it out? You've separated from your husband forever!

SOFYA YEGOROVNA. Yes, forever . . . How else? Platonov, you're starting to talk like a . . . louse!

PLATONOV. Forever . . . What will become of you when we break up? And we're going to break up any minute now! You'll be the first to see your mistake! You'll be the first to open your eyes and walk out on me! (*Waves his hand in dismissal.*) Anyhow . . . do whatever you want, Sofya! You're more honest and more intelligent than I am, take charge of this whole tiresome mess! You deal with it! Resurrect me if you can, put me back on my feet! Only hurry up, for God's sake, or else I'll go out of my mind!

SOFYA YEGOROVNA. Tomorrow we'll go away from here.

PLATONOV. Yes, yes, we'll go away . . . Only hurry up!

SOFYA YEGOROVNA. I have to get you away from here . . . I wrote to my mother about you. We'll stay with her . . .

PLATONOV. Wherever you like! . . . You deal with it any way you can!

SOFYA YEGOROVNA. *Michel*! This really is a new life . . . Understand this! . . . Listen to me, *Michel*! Let everything be the way I see it! I have a clearer head than you do! Believe me, my dear! I will put you back on your feet! I'll take you where there is more light, where there's none of this muck, this dust, indolence, this filthy nightshirt . . . I'll make a man of you . . . I shall make you happy! Do understand . . . I'll make a worker of you! We shall be real people, *Michel*! We shall eat the bread we earn, we shall run with sweat, we shall develop callouses . . . (*Puts her head on his chest.*) I shall work . . .

PLATONOV. Where will you work? There are women a lot different from you, a lot stronger, and even so they roll around like bales of hay, with nothing to do! You don't know how to work, besides what'll you work at? In our present situation, Sonya, it would be more use to analyze things clearly, and not console oneself with illusions . . . However, you know best!

SOFYA YEGOROVNA. You'll see! There are women who are a lot different from me, but I am stronger than they are . . . Believe me, *Michel*! I shall light your way! You resurrected me, and all my life I shall be grateful . . . Shall we leave tomorrow? Really? I'll go and start packing for the trip right now . . . You pack too . . . And come to the cabin at ten o'clock and bring your things . . . Will you come?

PLATONOV. I will.

SOFYA YEGOROVNA. Give me your word of honor that you will come!

PLATONOV. Ah-ah-ah . . . I just said so!

SOFYA YEGOROVNA. Give me your word of honor!

PLATONOV. Word of honor . . . Swear to God! . . . We'll go!

SOFYA YEGOROVNA (*laughs*). I believe you, I do! Come even earlier . . . I'll be ready before ten o'clock . . . And we'll ride away tonight! We'll start to live, *Michel*! You don't understand your own happiness, you silly man!

This really is our happiness, our life! . . . Tomorrow you will be another man, a fresh one, a new one! We shall breathe new air, new blood will flow in our veins . . . (*Laughs out loud.*) Off with you, decrepit man! Here's my hand! Squeeze it hard! (*Offers her hand.*)

PLATONOV kisses her hand.

SOFYA YEGOROVNA. Be sure to come, you big clumsy oaf! I shall be wait-ing . . . Don't brood . . . Good-bye for now! It won't take long to pack! . . . (*Kisses him.*)

PLATONOV. Good-bye . . . Was that eleven or ten?

SOFYA YEGOROVNA. Ten . . . Come even earlier! Good-bye! Dress more respectably for the trip . . . (*Laughs.*) I've got a little money . . . We'll have supper on the way . . . Good-bye! I'll go and pack . . . Be happy! I'll be waiting at ten o'clock! (*Runs out.*)

SCENE II

PLATONOV *(alone).*

PLATONOV (*after a pause.*) The same old tune . . . I've heard it a million times . . .

Pause.

I'll write letters to him and Sasha . . . Let them have a good cry, forgive and forget! . . . Good-bye, Voinitsevka! Good-bye, all! Sasha and the General's lady . . . (*Opens the cupboard.*) Tomorrow I'll be a new man . . . Brand spanking new! What'll I put my shirts in? I haven't got a suitcase . . . (*Pours wine.*) Good-bye, schoolhouse! (*Drinks.*) Good-bye, my little brats! Your wicked, but soft-hearted Mikhail Vasilich is disappearing! Did I just have a drink? What for? I won't drink any more . . . This is the last time . . . I'll sit down and write to Sasha . . . (*Lies down on the sofa.*) Sofya sincerely believes . . . Blessed are the believers! . . . Laugh, General's lady! And the General's lady actually will have a good laugh! She'll die laughing! . . . Yes! I think there was a letter from her . . . Where is it? (*Gets a letter from the windowsill.*) The hundredth letter, if not the two-hundredth since that crazy night . . . (*Reads.*) "Platonov, since you have not answered my letters, you are a tactless, cruel, stupid ignoramus! If you ignore this letter too, and do not pay me a visit, then, come what may, I shall pay you a visit, damn you! I have been waiting all day. It's stupid, Platonov! Someone might think you were ashamed of that night. Let's forget it, if that's the case! Sergey and Sofya are behaving abominably—the honeymoon, sticky with wild honey, is over. And all because a certain silver-tongued little dunderhead doesn't visit them. You are the little dunderhead. See you soon!"

Pause.

What handwriting! Precise, bold . . . Commas, periods, perfect spelling— everything in its place . . . A woman who can write correctly is a rare phenomenon . . .

Enter MARKO.

I'll have to write her a letter, otherwise she'll come here, heaven help us . . . (*On seeing Marko.*) A phenomenon . . .

SCENE III

PLATONOV and MARKO.

PLATONOV. Please come in! Who are you looking for? (*Gets up.*)

MARKO. Your honor . . . (*Pulls a summons out of his satchel.*) A little summons for your grace . . .

PLATONOV. Ah . . . How nice. What kind of summons? Who sent you?

MARKO. Ivan Andreich, the justice of the peace, sir . . .

PLATONOV. Hm . . . the justice? What does he want with me? Hand it over! (*Takes the summons.*) I don't understand . . . An invitation to a christening or what? Fertile as a fruit fly, the old sinner! (*Reads.*) "In his status as defendant charged with an offense against Mariya Yefimovna, daughter of state councillor Grekov." (*Roars with laughter.*) Why, I'll be damned! Bravo! I'll be damned! Bravo, essence of bedbug! When will the case come to trial? Day after tomorrow? I'll be there, I'll be there . . . Tell them I'll be there, old-timer . . . A clever girl, honest to God, a clever girl! Attagirl! Should have done it a long time ago!

MARKO. Please affix your signature, sir!

PLATONOV. My signature? Happy to . . . Pal, you look an awful lot like a wounded duck!

MARKO. Not at all, sir . . .

PLATONOV (*sits at the table*). What do you look like then?

MARKO. I look like God's image, sir . . .

PLATONOV. If you say so . . . Served under Tsar Nicholas?[76]

MARKO. Right you are . . . After the Sebastopol campaign[77] I was retired. Active duty over, I spent four years in the infirmary . . . A non-com . . . I was in the artillery, sir . . .

PLATONOV. If you say so . . . Were the cannons any good?

MARKO. Nothin' special . . . Round bore . . .

PLATONOV. Got a pencil?

MARKO. I do, sir . . . I received this summons there and there. Name and surname.

PLATONOV (*rises*). Take it. I signed five times. What's your justice of the peace like? Gambles?

MARKO. Right you are.

PLATONOV. From five P.M. to five A.M.?

MARKO. Right you are.

PLATONOV. Gambled away his chain of office yet?

MARKO. Not yet, sir.

PLATONOV. Tell him . . . Actually, don't tell him anything . . . Naturally, he doesn't pay his card debts . . . He plays cards, the idiot, runs up debts, and has a whole litter of children . . . She really is a clever girl, honest to God! Never expected this, definitely never expected this! Who are the witnesses? Who else is getting a subpoena?

---

76 Nicholas I (1796–1855), an absolutist monarch, militarized all Russia and instituted the reactionary "Holy Alliance"; he waged wars against Persia, Turkey, Polish insurgents, and, finally, in the Crimean War, against England and France as well.

77 Sebastopol, a port city on the Black Sea, played a major role in the Crimean War (1853–1856); after a siege of one year, later described by Lev Tolstoy, it fell to the enemy.

MARKO (*riffles through the summonses and reads*). "Doctor Nikolay Ivanych Triletsky, sir" . . .

PLATONOV. Triletsky? (*Roars with laughter.*) They're putting on a comedy! Who else?

MARKO (*reads*). "Mister Kirill Porfirich Glagolyev, sir, Mister Alfons Ivanych Shrifter, his honor Retired Guards Cornet Maksim Yegorych Aleutov, sir, the son of Actual State Councilor High-school Student Mister Ivan Talié, Degree Candidate of St. Petersburg Neversity . . . ."

PLATONOV. Is it written down "Neversity?"

MARKO. Not at all, sir . . .

PLATONOV. Then why did you read it that way?

MARKO. Out of ignorance, sir . . . (*Reads.*) " . . . uni . . . uni . . . neversity Mister Sergey Pavlych . . . Pavlovich Voinitsev, the wife of degree candidate of St. Petersburg uni . . . neversity Mrs. Sofya Yegorovna Voinitseva, Student of Kharkov University Mister Isak Abramych Vengerovich." That's all, sir!

PLATONOV. Hm . . . It's the day after tomorrow, but tomorrow I have to go away . . . What a pity. I can imagine what the trial would be like . . . Hm . . . What a nuisance! I would have enjoyed it . . . (*Walks around the stage.*) A nuisance!

MARKO. How's about a tip from your honor . . .

PLATONOV. Huh?

MARKO. A tip to buy tea[78] . . . A good five miles I walked, sir . . .

PLATONOV. A tip? Skip it . . . Though, what am I saying? All right, my dear fellow! I won't give you a tip to buy tea, but I'll give you some tea instead . . . It'll be a better deal for me, and more likely to keep you sober . . . (*Takes a tea canister out of the cupboard.*) Come over here . . . It's good, strong tea . . . Maybe not forty-proof, but strong . . . What shall I put it in?

MARKO (*holds out his pocket*). Pour it in here, sir . . .

---

78 The Russian for tip is *na chay*, literally, for tea, but it is assumed that the recipient will spend it on something stronger.

PLATONOV. Right in your pocket? Won't it stink?

MARKO. Pour it in, sir, pour it in, sir . . . Don't worry about it . . .

PLATONOV (*pours in the tea*). Enough?

MARKO. Thank you kindly . . .

PLATONOV. What an old duffer you are . . . I like you old vets! . . . You've got heart! . . . But even your bunch sometimes turns up some holy terrors . . .

MARKO. It takes all kinds, sir . . . Only the Lord is without sin . . . Cheers!

PLATONOV. Hold on . . . Just a minute . . . (*Sits and writes on the summons.*) "I kissed you that time, because . . . because I was annoyed and didn't know what I was after, now, though, I would kiss you like a holy relic. I acted despicably to you, I admit. I am despicable to everybody. In court, unfortunately, we will not meet. Tomorrow I go away forever. Be happy and at least do me justice! Don't forgive me!" (*To Marko.*) You know where Miss Grekova lives?

MARKO. I know, sir. About nine miles from here, if you cross the river at the ford, sir.

PLATONOV. That's right . . . At Zhilkovo . . . Take her this letter, and you'll get a three-spot. Give it right to the lady herself . . . No reply is expected . . . If she gives it back, don't take it . . . Deliver it today . . . Right away . . . Deliver it, and then hand out your subpoenas. (*Walks up and down the stage.*)

MARKO. I understand.

PLATONOV. What else? Oh, yes! Tell everybody that I asked Grekova's pardon and she refused.

MARKO. I understand. Cheers!

PLATONOV. Good-bye, friend! Look after yourself!

MARKO exits.

SCENE IV

PLATONOV (alone).

PLATONOV. Which means, I've settled my account with Grekova . . . She'll blacken my name through the whole district . . . Just what I deserve . . .

First time in my life a woman's punished me . . . (*Lies on the sofa.*) You do them dirt, and they throw themselves into your arms . . . Sofya, for instance . . . (*Covers his face with a handkerchief.*) I was free as the wind, and I just lie here and dream . . . Love . . . *Amo, amas, amat* . . .[79] Got all involved . . . Ruined her, and flattered my vanity . . . (*Sighs.*) Those poor Voinitsevs! What about Sasha? Poor little kid! How will she go on living without me? She'll pine away, she'll die . . . She walked out, learned the truth, walked out with our child, without a single word . . . Walked out right after that night. If I could only say good-bye to her . . .

ANNA PETROVNA (*in the window*). May I come in? Hey! Is there anybody there?

PLATONOV. Anna Petrovna! (*Leaps up.*) The General's lady! What am I to tell her! Why has she come here, I wonder? (*Tidies himself up.*)

ANNA PETROVNA (*in the window*). May I come in? I'm coming in! You hear me?

PLATONOV. She's here! What excuse have I got not to let her in? (*Combs his hair.*) How can I show her the door? I'll have a drink, before she comes in . . . (*Quickly opens the cupboard.*) And why the hell . . . I don't understand! (*Has a quick drink.*) It's all right if she doesn't know about this, but what if she does? I'll go red in the face . . .

SCENE V

PLATONOV and ANNA PETROVNA.

ANNA PETROVNA enters.

PLATONOV slowly shuts up the cupboard.

ANNA PETROVNA. My respects! Good to see you!

PLATONOV. It won't shut . . .

Pause.

ANNA PETROVNA. You there! Good afternoon!

---

79 Latin: I love, thou lovest, he loves . . . One of the first declensions learned in a Latin class; see *Three Sisters*, note 57.

PLATONOV. Ah . . . Is that you, Anna Petrovna? *Pardon,* I didn't notice . . . Only it won't shut . . . That's odd . . . (*Drops the key and picks it up again.*)

ANNA PETROVNA. Come over here to me! Leave the cupboard alone! Leave it!

PLATONOV (*walks over to her*). Good afternoon . . .

ANNA PETROVNA. Why won't you look at me?

PLATONOV. I'm ashamed. (*Kisses her hand.*)

ANNA PETROVNA. Ashamed of what?

PLATONOV. Everything . . .

ANNA PETROVNA. Hm . . . Have you been seducing somebody?

PLATONOV. Yes, sort of . . .

ANNA PETROVNA. Let's hear it for Platonov! Who is she?

PLATONOV. I won't say . . .

ANNA PETROVNA. Let's sit down . . .

They sit on the sofa.

We'll find out, young man, we'll find out . . . Why be ashamed on my account? After all, I'm an old acquaintance of your sinful soul . . .

PLATONOV. Don't ask, Anna Petrovna! I'm in no mood today to attend my own cross-examination. Talk if you feel like it, but don't ask any questions.

ANNA PETROVNA. All right. Did you get the letters?

PLATONOV. Yes.

ANNA PETROVNA. Then why didn't you show up?

PLATONOV. I can't take this.

ANNA PETROVNA. Why can't you?

PLATONOV. I can't.

ANNA PETROVNA. Pouting?

PLATONOV. No. What should I be pouting for? Don't ask questions, for heaven's sake!

ANNA PETROVNA. Please give me an answer, Mikhail Vasilich! Sit down and behave! Why haven't you been to see us for the last three weeks?

PLATONOV. I was sick.

ANNA PETROVNA. That's a lie!

PLATONOV. It's a lie. Don't ask questions, Anna Petrovna!

ANNA PETROVNA. How you reek of drink! Platonov, what's the meaning of all this? What's wrong with you? Do you know what you look like? Your eyes are red, your face is bestial . . . You're filthy, the room is covered in filth . . . Look around, what's the reason for all this mess? What's wrong with you? Have you been drinking?

PLATONOV. I've been drinking abominably!

ANNA PETROVNA. Hm . . . Same story as last year . . . Last year you seduced somebody and went around like a wet hen until the fall, same as now . . . Don Juan and a craven coward rolled into one. Don't you dare drink!

PLATONOV. I won't . . .

ANNA PETROVNA. Word of honor? Still, why plague you with words of honor? (*Gets up.*) Where is your wine?

PLATONOV indicates the cupboard.

It's disgraceful, Misha, to be so chicken-hearted! Where is your strength of character? (*Unlocks the cupboard.*) And the disorder in this cupboard! Aleksandra Ivanovna's going to give it to you, when she gets back! Do you want your wife to come back?

PLATONOV. I want only one thing: don't ask questions and don't stare me in the face!

ANNA PETROVNA. Which bottle has wine in it?

PLATONOV. All of 'em.

ANNA PETROVNA. All five? Ah you drunkard, you drunkard! There's a whole bar-room in this cupboard of yours! Aleksandra Ivanovna had better get back here fast . . . You'll explain it to her somehow . . . I'm not a very formidable rival . . . I can make a deal . . . It's not my intention to split you up . . . (*Drinks from a bottle.*) This wine's tasty . . . Come on, let's have a little drink! Shall we? Let's have one drink and then give up drinking forever!

PLATONOV goes to the cupboard.

Hold the glass! (*Pours wine.*) Bottoms up! I won't pour you any more.

PLATONOV drinks.

And now I'll drink too . . . (*Pours.*) To the health of bad men! (*Drinks.*) You're a bad man! It's good wine! You've got taste . . . (*Hands him the bottle.*) Take it! Bring it over here! (*Goes to the window.*) Kiss your tasty wine good-bye! (*Looks out the window.*) It's a pity to pour it out . . . Let's have another drink, eh? Shall we?

PLATONOV. As you like . . .

ANNA PETROVNA (*pours*). Drink up . . . Quick!

PLATONOV (*drinks*). Your health! God give you joy!

ANNA PETROVNA (*pours and drinks*). Did you miss me? Let's sit down . . . Put down the bottle for now . . .

They sit down.

Miss me?

PLATONOV. Every moment.

ANNA PETROVNA. How come you didn't show up?

PLATONOV. Don't ask questions! I won't tell you anything not because I'm keeping secrets from you, but because I'm taking pity on your ears! I'm a lost soul, an utterly lost soul, my dear! Pangs of conscience, anguish, depression . . . agony, in short! You've come, and I feel easier.

ANNA PETROVNA. You've lost weight, lost your looks . . . I can't stand these romantic heroes! What are you making yourself out to be, Platonov? Playing the hero of some novel? Depression, anguish, conflicting passions, love with prefaces . . . Phoo! Behave like a human being! Live, you silly man, the way real people live! What, are you such an archangel that you can't live, breathe, or sit like a mere mortal?

PLATONOV. That's easy for you to say . . . What am I supposed to do?

ANNA PETROVNA. A person is alive, I mean a man is alive and doesn't know what he's supposed to do! Most peculiar! What is he to do? If you like, I'll answer your question as best I can, even though it doesn't deserve an answer, being a pointless question!

PLATONOV. You won't have an answer . . .

ANNA PETROVNA. In the first place, live like a human being, I mean, don't drink, don't lie around, wash more often, and come to my house, and in the second place, be content with what you've got . . . You're acting like a fool, my good sir! As if this pretense of teaching weren't enough? (*Gets up.*) Come to my house right now!

PLATONOV. How's that? (*Gets up.*) Come to your place? No, no . . .

ANNA PETROVNA. Let's go! You'll see people, talk a little, listen a little, quarrel a little . . .

PLATONOV. No, no . . . And don't make it an order!

ANNA PETROVNA. Why not?

PLATONOV. I cannot, and that's all!

ANNA PETROVNA. You can! Put on your hat! Let's go!

PLATONOV. I cannot, Anna Petrovna! Not for anything! I won't set foot outside the house!

ANNA PETROVNA. You can! (*Puts his hat on him.*) You're being silly, Platonov, old pal, you're being silly! (*Takes him by the arm.*) Well? One, two! . . . Go on, Platonov! Forward, march!

Pause.

How about it, *Michel*! Come on!

PLATONOV. I can't!

ANNA PETROVNA. You're as stubborn as a young bull! Start marching! Well? One, two . . . *Michel*, darling, dearest, sweetie . . .

PLATONOV (*tears himself away*). I won't go, Anna Petrovna!

ANNA PETROVNA. Let's take a walk around the schoolhouse!

PLATONOV. Why keep pestering me? Haven't I told you that I won't go! I want to stay at home, so let me do what I want!

Pause.

I won't go!

ANNA PETROVNA. Hm . . . How about this, Platonov . . . I'll lend you some money, and you can leave here for someplace else for a month or two . . .

PLATONOV. Where?

ANNA PETROVNA. Moscow, Petersburg . . . Will you go? Take a trip, *Michel*! It's imperative that you make a change! Travel around, look at people, go to the theater, get refreshed, make a change . . . I'll give you money, letters . . . Would you like me to go with you? Would you? Let's take a trip, let's have fun . . . We'll come back here renewed and resplendent . . .

PLATONOV. It's a wonderful idea, but, unfortunately, it won't work . . . I am leaving here tomorrow, Anna Petrovna, but not with you!

ANNA PETROVNA. As you like . . . Where are you going?

PLATONOV. I'm just going . . .

Pause.

I am leaving here forever . . .

ANNA PETROVNA. Hogwash . . . (*Drinks from the bottle.*) Nonsense!

PLATONOV. It's not hogwash, my dear! I'm going! Forever!

ANNA PETROVNA. But what for, you peculiar man?

PLATONOV. Don't ask questions! Honest to God, forever! I'm leaving and . . . Good-bye, that's what! Don't ask! You won't pry anything out of me now . . .

ANNA PETROVNA. Nonsense!

PLATONOV. Today is the last time we'll see one another . . . I'm cutting out forever . . . (*Takes her by the hands and then by the shoulders.*) Forget the idiot, the jackass, the bastard and the scoundrel Platonov! He will vanish into thin air, fade into the background . . . We shall meet again, perhaps, dozens of years from now, when we will both be in a position to chuckle and shed senile tears over these days but now . . . the hell with them! (*Kisses her hand.*)

ANNA PETROVNA. Drink up! (*Pours him wine.*) There's nothing wrong in a drunkard spouting nonsense . . .

PLATONOV (*drinks it up*). I won't get drunk . . . I will remember, mother o' mine, my good fairy! . . . I shall never forget! Laugh, you cultured, clear-minded woman! Tomorrow I'll run away from here, I'll run from myself, I don't know where, I'll run to a new life! I know only too well what this new life will be like!

ANNA PETROVNA. That's all very pretty, but what has come over you?

PLATONOV. What? I . . . Later you'll find out all about it! My friend, when you are horrified by my behavior, don't curse me! Remember that I'm all but punished already . . . Parting with you forever is worse than punishment . . . What are you smiling at? Believe me! Word of honor, believe me! My heart is so bitter, so putrid and vile, that I'd be glad to smother myself!

ANNA PETROVNA (*through tears*). I don't think you'd be capable of anything horrible . . . Will you write to me at least?

PLATONOV. I don't dare write to you, besides you won't care to read my letters! Absolutely forever . . . good-bye!

ANNA PETROVNA. Hm . . . You'll be lost without me, Platonov! (*Rubs her forehead.*) I'm just the tiniest bit tipsy . . . Let's go together!

PLATONOV. No . . . Tomorrow you'll know it all and . . . (*Turns away from the window.*)

ANNA PETROVNA. Do you need money?

PLATONOV. No . . .

ANNA PETROVNA. So . . . I can't help?

PLATONOV. I don't know. Send me a card photo of you today . . . (*Turns around.*) Go away, Anna Petrovna, or I don't know what the hell I might do! I'll start sobbing, beat myself up and . . . Go away! There's no way to keep me here! I'm talking to you in plain Russian! What are you waiting for! I have to go, is that so hard to understand! Why do you look at me like that? What's the point of making such a face?

ANNA PETROVNA. Good-bye . . . (*Offers her hand.*) We shall meet again . . .

PLATONOV. No . . . (*Kisses her hand.*) We mustn't . . . Go away, my nearest and dearest . . . (*Kisses her hand.*) Good-bye . . . Leave me . . . (*Covers his face with her hand.*)

ANNA PETROVNA. You've gone soft on me, dear heart . . . Well? Let go of my hand . . . Good-bye! Let's have one for the road, shall we? (*Pours.*) Drink up! Happy journey, and happiness at journey's end!

PLATONOV drinks.

What if you were to stay, Platonov? Eh? (*Pours and drinks.*) We'd have a rare old time . . . Where's the crime in that? Can such things be in Voinitsevka?

Pause.

One more, to drown our sorrows?

PLATONOV. Sure.

ANNA PETROVNA (*pours*). Drink, my darling . . . Eh, damn it all to hell!

PLATONOV (*drinks*). Be happy! Live your life . . . You can get on without me . . .

ANNA PETROVNA. Let's drink if we're drinking . . . (*Pours.*) If you drink you die, and if you don't drink you die, so it's better to die drinking . . . (*Drinks.*) I'm a drunkard, Platonov . . . Eh? Have another? Don't have to, though . . . We'll get tongue-tied, and how will we talk then? (*Sits down.*) There's nothing worse than being a cultured woman . . . A cultured woman with nothing to do . . . What's the meaning of me, what's the point of my life?

Pause.

Unintentionally immoral . . . I'm an immoral woman, Platonov . . . (*Roars with laughter.*) Eh? And I love you, maybe, because I'm immoral . . . (*Rubs her forehead.*) So I'll be a lost soul too . . . My sort are always lost souls . . . I should have been some kind of professor, headmaster . . . If I had been a diplomat, I'd have screwed up the whole world good and proper . . . A cultured woman . . . with nothing to do. Useless, in other words . . . Horses, cows, and dogs are useful, but you are useless, a superfluous woman . . . Huh? Why don't you say something?

PLATONOV. Both of us are in a bad way . . .

ANNA PETROVNA. If I had only had children . . . Do you like children? (*Gets up.*) Do stay, darling! Won't you stay? We would have such a good life! . . . Have fun, be friends . . . You're leaving, but what about me? After all, I'd like to settle down . . . *Michel*! I have to settle down! I want to be . . . a wife, a mother . . .

Pause.

Say something! Speak! Will you stay? After all . . . after all, you do love me, you crackpot? You love me?

PLATONOV (*looks out the window*). I'll kill myself, if I stay.

ANNA PETROVNA. You love me, don't you?

PLATONOV. Who doesn't love you?

ANNA PETROVNA. You love me, I love you, what more do you need? You're losing your mind, I suppose . . . What more do you need? Why didn't you come to me that night?

Pause.

Will you stay?

PLATONOV. Go away, for heaven's sake! You're tormenting me!

ANNA PETROVNA (*offers her hand*). Well . . . in that case . . . I wish you all the best . . .

PLATONOV. Do go away, or I'll tell you all about it, and if I tell you, I'll kill myself!

ANNA PETROVNA. I offer my hand . . . Don't you see it? I'll pop over here for a minute tonight . . .

PLATONOV. Don't! I'll come to you to say good-bye! I'll come to your place myself . . . I won't come for any reason! You won't see me again, and I won't see you! You really don't want to see me! You'll turn against me forever! A new life . . . (*Embraces and kisses her.*) For the last time . . . (*Shoves her out the door.*) Good-bye! Go and be happy! (*Bolts the door shut.*)

ANNA PETROVNA (*behind the door*). I swear to God we'll meet again!

PLATONOV. No! Good-bye! (*Puts his fingers in his ears.*) I'm not listening! Shut up and go away! I'm stopping my ears!

ANNA PETROVNA. I'm going! I'll send over Sergey and give you my word that you won't go, but if you do, it'll be with me! Good-bye!

Pause.

SCENE VI

PLATONOV (alone).

PLATONOV. Has she gone? (*Goes to the door and listens.*) She's gone . . . But maybe she hasn't gone? (*Opens the door.*) After all, she's a devil . . . (*Looks behind the door.*) She's gone . . . (*Lies on the sofa.*) Good-bye, charming woman! . . . (*Sighs.*) And I'll never see her again . . . She's gone . . . She might have stayed another five minutes . . .

Pause.

It wouldn't have been so bad! I'll ask Sofya to put off the trip another couple of weeks, and go away with the General's lady! Right . . . Two weeks— that's all! Sofya will agree to that . . . She can stay with her mother in the meantime . . . I'll ask her . . . eh? While I'm away with the General's lady, Sofya can have a bit of a rest . . . recover her strength, I mean . . . After all, I won't be gone for an eternity!

Knock at the door.

I'll go! That's settled! Splendid . . .

Knock.

Who's knocking? The General's lady? Who's there?

Knock.

Is that you? (*Gets up.*) I won't let you in! (*Goes to the door.*) Is she there?

Knock.

She's giggling, sounds like . . . (*Laughs.*) She *is* there . . . Have to let her in. . . . (*Opens the door.*) Ah!

Enter OSIP.

SCENE VII

PLATONOV and OSIP.

PLATONOV. What's going on? That you, Satan? What's brought you here?

OSIP. Good afternoon, Mikhail Vasilich!

PLATONOV. What have you got to say for yourself? To what and to whom am I obliged for a visit from such an important personage? Tell me quickly and then go to hell!

OSIP. I'll take a seat . . . (*Sits down.*)

PLATONOV. Be so kind!

Pause.

Are you your old self, Osip? What's wrong with you? Your face is inscribed with all ten plagues of Egypt![80] What's happened to you? You're pale, thin, gaunt . . . Are you sick?

OSIP. You got plagues inscribed on your face too . . . What's happened to you? I got all hell riding my tail, but what about you?

PLATONOV. Me? I don't know anything about hell . . . I'm riding my own tail . . . (*Touches Osip on the shoulder.*) Skin and bones!

OSIP. Where's your extra pounds? Sick, Mikhail Vasilich? Result of good behavior?

PLATONOV (*sits beside him*). Why did you come?

OSIP. To say good-bye . . .

PLATONOV. Are you really going away?

OSIP. I'm not going away, you are.

PLATONOV. How about that! How do you know?

OSIP. Why wouldn't I know?

PLATONOV. I'm not going away, pal, not I. You've come on a fool's errand.

OSIP. You *are* going away, sir . . .

PLATONOV. And you know it all, and it's all your business . . . You, Osip, are a witch. I am going away, my dear fellow. You're right.

OSIP. There, you see, that means I know. I even know where you're going!

---

80 The ten plagues visited on the Egyptians by God to persuade them to let the Hebrews go. See Exodus 7–10.

PLATONOV. Is that so? You're really something . . . Even I don't know. An authority, quite the authority! Well, tell me, where am I off to?

OSIP. Would you like to know?

PLATONOV. For heaven's sake! This is fascinating! Where am I off to?

OSIP. The next world.

PLATONOV. Quite a distance!

Pause.

A riddle. Are you the one who's going to send me there?

OSIP. Right you are. I brought you the ticket.

PLATONOV. Most kind of you! . . . Hm . . . In other words, you've come here to kill me?

OSIP. Right you are . . .

PLATONOV (*mimics him*). Right you are . . . What impudence, damn it! He's come to dispatch me to the next world . . . Hm . . . You planning to kill me on your own behalf or did someone commission it?

OSIP (*shows a twenty-five ruble note*). That's it . . . Vengerovich gave me this so I'd cripple your grace! (*Tears up the money.*)

PLATONOV. Aha . . . The older Vengerovich?

OSIP. The man himself . . .

PLATONOV. Then why did you tear up the money? Want to show how big-hearted you are, or what?

OSIP. I don't know how to show I'm big-hearted, but I tore up the money so you wouldn't be thinking in the next world that I killed you for money.

PLATONOV *gets up and walks up and down the stage.*

Are you afraid, Mikhail Vasilich? Scared? (*Laughs.*) Run away, shout! I'm not standing by the door, I'm not holding the door: there's a way out. Go and call folks, tell 'em that Osip's come to kill you! For he has come to kill you . . . Don't you believe me?

Pause.

PLATONOV (*walks over to Osip and looks at him*). Wonderful.

Pause.

What are you smiling for? Idiot! (*Hits him on the arm.*) Stop smiling! I'm talking to you! Shut up! I'll see you hanged! I'll smash you to a pulp, cut-throat! (*Quickly walks away from him.*) And yet . . . Don't get me angry . . . I mustn't get angry . . . It makes me sick.

OSIP. Slap my face because I'm a menace to society!

PLATONOV. As much as you please! (*Walks over to Osip and slaps him.*) What? Staggering? Just wait, see how you'll start to stagger, when a hundred cudgels are drumming on your empty head! You remember how pock-marked Filka died?

OSIP. A dog dies a dog's death.

PLATONOV. V-v-v . . . what a disgusting creature you are! I could mangle you, villain! Why do you do them harm, you despicable soul, like a disease, like a wildfire? What have they done to you? V-v-v . . . Bastard!! (*Hits him on the cheek.*) Filth! I'll take you and . . . I'll take you . . . (*Quickly walks away from Osip.*) Get out!

OSIP. Spit in my face because I'm a menace to society!

PLATONOV. Spit's too good for you!

OSIP (*gets up*). So you dare to talk like that?

PLATONOV. Get out of here, before I grind you into the mud!

OSIP. You wouldn't dare! You're a menace to society too!

PLATONOV. You're bandying words with me again? (*Walks up to him.*) You came to kill me, I believe? Well! Kill me! Here I am! Kill me now!

OSIP. I respected you, Mister Platonov, I took you to be somebody important! But now . . . It's a shame to kill you, but I got to . . . You're the real menace . . . Why did the young lady come by here today?

PLATONOV (*shakes him by the chest*). Kill me! Come on and kill me!

OSIP. And why did the General's lady come by here afterwards? That mean you're cheating on the General's lady? And where's your wife? Which of them three is the one that matters most? And you're not a menace to society after that? (*Quickly trips him up and falls on top of him on the floor.*)

PLATONOV. Get off me! I'll kill you, you won't kill me! I'm stronger than you!

They wrestle.

Careful!

OSIP. You turn over on your stomach! Don't twist my arm! It's not my arm's fault for anything, so why twist it? There you go again! When you're in the next world, give General Voinitsev my sincerest regards!

PLATONOV. Let go!

OSIP (*pulls a knife out of his belt*). Careful! All the same I'll kill you! And you're so strong! Somebody important! Don't feel like dying? Then hands off what don't belong to you!

PLATONOV (*shouts*). My arm! Wait, wait . . . My arm!

OSIP. Don't feel like dying? You're gonna be in the kingdom of heaven any minute now . . .

PLATONOV. Only don't stab me in the back, you ironclad animal, stab me in the chest! My arm! Let go, Osip! A wife, a son . . . Is this a dagger that I see before me? O cursèd spite![81]

SASHA runs in.

SCENE VII

The same and SASHA.

SASHA (*runs in*). What's going on? (*Shrieks.*) Misha! (*Runs to the wrestlers and falls on them.*) What are you doing?

OSIP. Who's that? Aleksandra Ivanovna? (*Jumps up.*) Let him live! (*To Sasha.*) Here's a jackknife for you! (*Hands over the knife.*) I won't cut his throat with you standing by . . . Let him live! I'll cut his throat later! He won't get away! (*Leaps through the window.*)

PLATONOV (*after a pause*). What a devil . . . Greetings, Sasha! That is you, isn't it? (*Groans.*)

---

81 Quotations from *Macbeth* and *Hamlet*. Platonov still doesn't take Osip seriously.

SASHA. He hasn't hurt you? Can you get up? Hurry up!

PLATONOV. I don't know . . . That creature's made out of cast iron . . . Give me your hand! (*Gets up.*) Don't be afraid, my dearest . . . I'm still in one piece. He only roughed me up a little . . .

SASHA. What a nasty man he is! Didn't I tell you not to go near him!

PLATONOV. Where's the sofa? What are you looking at? Your faithless one is still alive! Don't you see that? (*Lies on the sofa.*) Thanks for coming, otherwise you'd be a widow, and I'd be deceased!

SASHA. Lie on a cushion! (*Puts a cushion under his head.*) That's right! (*Sits at his feet.*) Does it hurt anywhere?

Pause.

Why have you closed your eyes?

PLATONOV. No, no . . . I just . . . So you've come back, Sasha? You've come back, my treasure? (*Kisses her hand.*)

SASHA. Our Kolya's taken sick!

PLATONOV. What's wrong with him?

SASHA. A sort of cough, temperature, a rash . . . Two nights now he hasn't slept and screams . . . Doesn't drink, doesn't eat . . . (*Weeps.*) He's come down with something, Misha! I'm afraid for him! . . . I'm so afraid! And I had a bad dream . . .

PLATONOV. Why doesn't your darling brother take a look? After all, he's a doctor!

SASHA. Him? Is there any sympathy in him? Four days ago he dropped by for a minute, turned on his heel, and left. I've told him about Kolya's illness, but he pinches his cheeks and yawns . . . Called me a fool . . .

PLATONOV. There's another nincompoop! He'll yawn himself silly one of these days! And he'll walk out on himself, when he falls ill!

SASHA. What's to be done?

PLATONOV. Hope against hope . . . You living with your father now?

SASHA. Yes.

PLATONOV. What's he do?

SASHA. Nothing. Walks up and down his room, smokes his pipe, and makes plans to come over and see you. I showed up at his house all upset, so he figured out that I . . . that you and I . . . What's to be done about Kolya?

PLATONOV. Don't worry, Sasha!

SASHA. How can I not worry? If he dies, God forbid, what will become of us then?

PLATONOV. Yes . . . Pray God He doesn't take our little boy from us! Why punish you? For marrying a good-for-nothing?

Pause.

Sasha, take care of my little midget! Take care of him for me, and I swear to you by all that's holy that I'll make a man of him! His every move will be your delight! After all, he's a Platonov too, poor thing! Only he ought to change his name . . . As a man I'm petty, insignificant, but as a father I shall be great! Don't fear for his prospects! Ugh, my arm! (*Groans.*) My arm hurts . . . That cutthroat pummeled it hard . . . What's wrong with it? (*Examines his arm.*) It's red . . . Well, the hell with it! That's how it is, Sasha . . . . Your son will make you happy! You're laughing . . . Laugh, my precious! But now you're crying? What's there to cry about? Hm . . . Don't cry, Sasha! (*Embraces her head.*) She's come back . . . But why did you leave me? Don't cry, little squirrel! Why these tears? After all, I love you, little girl! . . . I love you so much! Great is my guilt, but what can you do? You've got to forgive me . . . There, there . . .

SASHA. Is your affair over?

PLATONOV. Affair? What kind of word is that, you little philistine?

SASHA. Isn't it over?

PLATONOV. How can I put it? It's not exactly an affair, but a sort of hideous hodgepodge . . . Don't let this hodgepodge get to you! If it isn't over, it soon . . . will be!

SASHA. But when?

PLATONOV. We can only imagine that it'll be soon! Soon we'll start living again, Sasha, in the old way! The hell with all the new stuff! I'm all worn out, used up . . . Don't put any more stock in the durability of this liaison than I do myself! It won't last . . . She will be the first to cool off and the first to react to this liaison with laughter and remorse. Sofya's no partner for me. The things that get her excited are things that were stale for me long ago; with tears of tenderness she looks at things I can't look at without laughing . . . She's no fit partner for me . . .

Pause.

Believe me! Sofya won't be your rival much longer . . . Sasha, what's come over you?

SASHA gets up and staggers.

(*Rises.*) Sasha!

SASHA. You . . . you're with Sofya, and not with the General's lady?

PLATONOV. First time you've heard this?

SASHA. Sofya? . . . Vile . . . sordid . . .

PLATONOV. What's wrong with you? You're pale, staggering . . . (*Groans.*) Don't torture me at least, Sasha! My arm hurts, while you keep on . . . Is this really . . . news to you? You're hearing it for the first time? Then why did you go away that night? Wasn't it on account of Sofya?

SASHA. The General's lady is to be expected, but another man's wife? Sordid, sinful . . . I didn't expect this sort of dirty doings from you! God will punish you, you shameless man! (*Goes to the door.*)

PLATONOV (*after a pause*). You're outraged? But where are you off to?

SASHA (*stops in the doorway*). May God grant happiness . . .

PLATONOV. To whom?

SASHA. To you, sir, and Sofya Yegorovna.

PLATONOV. She's been reading idiotic novels. Sasha! I'm not "sir" to you: we've got a little boy, and I . . . after all, I am your husband! And in the second place, I don't need happiness! . . . Stop, Sasha! Now you're going away . . . And, I suppose, forever?

SASHA. I can't take this! Ugh, my God, my God . . .

PLATONOV. You can't take it?

SASHA. My God . . . And is it really true? (*Puts her hands to her temples and squats down.*) I . . . I don't know what to do . . .

PLATONOV. You can't take it? (*Walks over to her.*) It's up to you . . . . Although I wish you'd stay! What's the bawling for, you little silly?

Pause.

Eh, Sasha, Sasha . . . Great is my guilt, but is there really no way to forgive me?

SASHA. Have you forgiven yourself?

PLATONOV. A philosophical question! (*Kisses her on the head.*) I wish you'd stay . . . I'm really sorry! Really when you're away there's vodka, filth, Osips . . . I'm sick to death of it! Stay as a sick-nurse, not a wife! You're a funny bunch, you women! You're funny, Sasha! If you can feed that villain Osip, if you never stop fussing over dogs and cats, if you stay up half the night reading the doxology for your so-called enemies, what difference does it make if you toss a crust to your misbehaving but apologetic husband? Why you do act like an executioner? Stay, Sasha! (*Embraces her.*) I can't be without a nanny! I'm a villain, I seduced another man's wife, I'm Sofya's lover, maybe even the lover of the General's lady, I'm a polygamist, a major felon when it comes to family . . . Be outraged, be indignant! But who will love you the way I love you? Who will appreciate such a dear little country girl the way I appreciate her? Who will you cook a meal for, whose soup will you oversalt? You'd be doing the right thing if you left me . . . Justice demands it, but . . . (*lifts her up*) who will pick you up like this? Can you exist, my precious, apart from me?

SASHA. I can't take it! Let me go! I'm ruined! You're joking, while I'm ruined! (*Tears herself away.*) Don't you realize that this is no joke? Good-bye! I cannot live with you! Now everyone will regard you as a despicable person! How will that make me feel?! (*Sobs.*)

PLATONOV. Have it your own way! (*Kisses her on the head and lies on the sofa.*) I understand . . .

SASHA. You wrecked our family . . . We had a happy, peaceful life . . . There was no one in the world happier than me . . . (*Sits down.*) What have you done, Misha? (*Gets up.*) What have you done? There's no turning back now . . . I am ruined . . . (*Sobs.*)

PLATONOV. Then go already!

SASHA. Good-bye! You won't see me again! Don't come to see us . . . Father will bring Kolya to visit you . . . God will forgive you, as I forgive you! You've destroyed our life!

PLATONOV. You gone yet?

SASHA. I'm gone . . . Fine . . . (*Looks at Platonov for a moment and leaves.*)

SCENE IX

PLATONOV (alone) and then VOINITSEV.

PLATONOV. And here's the man who's starting a new life! It hurts!! I'm losing everyone . . . I'm going crazy! My God! Sasha, a little mosquito, a bedbug—and she dares, even she . . . the might of something holy gives her the right to throw stones at me! Damned circumstances! (*Lies on the sofa.*)

VOINITSEV enters and stops in the doorway.

(*After a pause.*) Is this the epilogue or only another farce?

(*On seeing Voinitsev, closes his eyes and snores softly.*)

VOINITSEV (*walks over to Platonov*). Platonov!

Pause.

You're not asleep . . . I can see it in your face . . . (*Sits beside him.*) I wouldn't have thought . . . it was possible to sleep . . .

PLATONOV sits up.

(*Rises and looks out the window.*) You've killed me . . . Did you know that?

Pause.

Thank you . . . What about me? Never mind . . . Let it be. In other words, this is how it's supposed to be . . . (*Weeps.*)

PLATONOV rises and slowly goes to another corner of the room.

Just once fate conferred a gift on me and . . . it's been taken away! They weren't enough for him, his brains, his good looks, his big heart . . . He had to have my happiness as well! He took it away . . . How about me? What about me? I'm nothing . . . That's it . . . A morbid, dim-witted mind, effeminate, sentimental, not overly talented . . . With a tendency to idleness, mysticism, superstition . . . You've polished off a friend!

PLATONOV. Get out of here!

VOINITSEV. Right away . . . I came to challenge you to a duel, but now that I'm here I start whining . . . I'm going.

Pause.

So I've lost her once and for all?

PLATONOV. Yes.

VOINITSEV (*whistles*). That's it . . . Stands to reason . . .

PLATONOV. Get out of here! I'm begging you! Get out!

VOINITSEV. Right away . . . What's there for me to do here? (*Goes to the door.*) There's nothing for me to do here . . .

Pause.

Give her back to me, Platonov! Have a heart! After all, she's mine! Platonov! You're so happy! Save me, dear fellow! How about it? Give her back! (*Sobs.*) After all, she's mine! Mine! You understand?

PLATONOV (*goes to the sofa*). Go away . . . I'll shoot myself . . . I swear on my honor!

VOINITSEV. You don't have to . . . Never mind! (*Waves his hand in dismissal and exits.*)

PLATONOV (*clutches his head*). Oh wretched, pitiful man! My God! Damn this god-forsaken head of mine! (*Sobs.*) Stay away from people, you rat! I've been a jinx for people, people have been a jinx for me! Stay away from people! They beat you up and beat you up, and can't manage to beat you down! Under every chair, under every splinter lurks a murderer, who stares you in the face, and wants to kill you! Beat me to death! (*Beats himself on the chest.*) Beat me, before I beat myself to death! (*Runs to the door.*) Don't beat me on the chest! My chest is already ripped wide open! (*Shouts.*) Sasha! Sasha, for the love of God! (*Opens the door.*)

Enter GLAGOLYEV SR.

SCENE X

PLATONOV, GLAGOLYEV SR., and then GLAGOLYEV JR.

GLAGOLYEV SR. (*enters muffled up with a crutch*). You home, Mikhail Vasilich? Pleased to see you . . . I've disturbed you . . . But I won't keep you, I'll go at once . . . We'll put just one question to you. You answer it, and I'll go. What's wrong with you, Mikhail Vasilich? You're pale, shaky, trembling . . . What's come over you?

PLATONOV. What's come over me? Ah? I'm drunk, I suppose, or . . . I'm going out of my mind! I'm drunk . . . drunk . . . My head's spinning . . .

GLAGOLYEV SR. (*aside*). I'll ask. "What a sober fellow keeps inside, a drunken one will never hide." (*To him.*) The question is an odd one, perhaps even a stupid one, but, for heaven's sake, answer me, Mikhail Vasilich! My question is for me one of life and death! I shall accept your answer, because I know you to be the most honorable of men . . . Even if my questions strike you as odd, absurd, silly, and even, perhaps, insulting, for heaven's sake . . . make me an answer! I find myself in a peculiar situation! A lady we both know . . . You know her well . . . I considered her the peak of human perfection . . . Anna Petrovna Voinitseva . . . (*Supports Platonov.*) Don't fall down, for heaven's sake!

PLATONOV. Go away! I always considered you . . . sir, to be an old fool!

GLAGOLYEV SR. You're her friend, you know her like the palm of your hand . . . Either people have defamed her to me, or else . . . they've opened my eyes . . . Is she an honest woman, Mikhail Vasilich? She . . . she . . . Does she have the right to be the wife of an honest man?

Pause.

I don't know how to formulate my question . . . Understand me, for heaven's sake! They told me that she . . .

PLATONOV. Everything's vulgar, vile, filthy on this earth! Everything's . . . vulgar . . . vile . . . (*Falls senseless on to Glagolyev and tumbles to the floor.*)

GLAGOLYEV JR. (*enters*). What are you hanging around here for? I don't intend to wait!

GLAGOLYEV SR. Everything's vulgar, filthy, vile . . . Everything, which means, including her . . .

GLAGOLYEV JR. (*looks at Platonov*). Father, what's going on with Platonov?

GLAGOLYEV SR. Revoltingly drunk . . . Yes, vulgar, filthy . . . A profound, inexorable, stinging truth!

Pause.

Let's go to Paris!

GLAGOLYEV JR. What? To Pa . . . To Paris? Why should you go to Paris? (*Bursts out laughing.*)

GLAGOLYEV SR. To roll in the mud the way this fellow's rolling in it! (*Points to Platonov.*)

GLAGOLYEV JR. To roll in the mud . . . in Paris?!

GLAGOLYEV SR. Let's look for happiness in another line of work! Enough! I'm fed up with acting a comedy for myself, hoodwinking myself with ideals! No more faith or love! No more decent people! Let's go!

GLAGOLYEV JR. To Paris?

GLAGOLYEV SR. Yes . . . If we're going to sin, let's sin in a foreign country, not our native land! Until we're rotting in our graves, let's live like other people! Be my instructor, son! Let's go to Paris!

GLAGOLYEV JR. Now that's sweet, father! You taught me to read, and I'll teach you to live! Let's go!

They exit.

End of Act Three

ACT FOUR

The study of the late General Voinitsev. Two doors. Antique furniture, Persian carpets, flowers. The walls are hung with rifles, pistols, daggers (Caucasian workmanship), and so on. Family portraits. Busts of Krylov, Pushkin, and Gogol.[82] *A whatnot with stuffed birds. A bookcase filled with books. On the bookcase cigarette holders, little boxes, sticks, gun barrels, and so on. A writing desk, littered with papers, portraits, statuettes, and firearms. Morning.*

SCENE I

SOFYA YEGOROVNA and KATYA enter.

SOFYA YEGOROVNA. Don't get so excited! Talk sense!

---

82 A constellation of Russian literary geniuses: besides the poet Pushkin, Ivan Krylov (1768–1844), the great fabulist, and Nikolay Gogol (1809–1852), the great comic prose writer and dramatist.

KATYA. Something bad's going on, madam! Doors and windows all wide open, inside everything upside-down, smashed up . . . The door's torn off its hinges . . . Something bad happened, madam! That's why one of our hens crowed like a cock!

SOFYA YEGOROVNA. What do you think it was?

KATYA. I don't think about it, madam. What can I think? I only know something happened . . . Either Mikhail Vasilich went far away, or else he laid hands on himself . . . The gent, madam, has a passionate nature! I've known him for two years now . . .

SOFYA YEGOROVNA. No . . . Were you in the village?

KATYA. Yes, ma'am . . . Nowhere to be found . . . Four hours or so I walked around . . .

SOFYA YEGOROVNA (*sits down*). What's to be done? What's to be done?

Pause.

You're sure that he's nowhere around here? Sure?

KATYA. I don't know, madam . . . Something bad has happened . . . That's why my heart's aching! Give it up, madam! After all, it's a sin! (*Weeps.*) I feel sorry for the master Sergey Pavlovich . . . He was such a good-looker, and now what's he like? All worn out these last two days, the darling, running around like a wild man. A good master gone to the dogs . . . I feel sorry for Mikhail Vasilich too . . . There was a time he was a real cut-up, there was a time you couldn't get away from his jokes, and now he looks like death warmed over . . . Give it up, madam!

SOFYA YEGOROVNA. Give what up?

KATYA. Love. What's the sense in it? Nothing but shame. And I feel sorry for you too. What are you like now? You've lost weight, don't drink, don't eat, don't sleep, all you do is cough . . .

SOFYA YEGOROVNA. Go out again, Katya! Maybe he's back at the school . . .

KATYA. Right away . . .

Pause.

You should get some sleep.

SOFYA YEGOROVNA. Go out again, Katya! Have you gone?

KATYA (*aside*). You don't come of peasant stock! (*Sharply, tearfully.*) Where am I to go, madam?

SOFYA YEGOROVNA. I want to get some sleep. I didn't sleep all night long. Don't shout so loudly! Get out of here!

KATYA. Yes, ma'am . . . There's no reason to eat your heart out this way! . . . You should go to your room and lie down! (*Exits.*)

SCENE II

SOFYA YEGOROVNA *and then* VOINITSEV.

SOFYA YEGOROVNA. It's horrible! Yesterday he gave his word of honor he'd show up at the cabin at ten o'clock and he didn't . . . I waited for him till dawn . . . So much for word of honor! So much for love, so much for our eloping! . . . He doesn't love me!

VOINITSEV (*enters*). I'm going to bed . . . Maybe I'll get some sleep . . . (*On seeing Sofya Yegorovna.*) You . . . in my room? In my study?

SOFYA YEGOROVNA. Is that where I am? (*Looks around.*) Yes . . . But I came in inadvertently, without even noticing . . . (*Goes to the door.*)

VOINITSEV. Just a minute!

SOFYA YEGOROVNA (*stops*). Well?

VOINITSEV. Please, let me have a few minutes of your time . . . Can you stay here for a few minutes?

SOFYA YEGOROVNA. Talk! You have something you want to say?

VOINITSEV. Yes . . .

Pause.

The time is past when we were not strangers to one another in this room . . .

SOFYA YEGOROVNA. It is past.

VOINITSEV. Forgive me, though, I was starting to get carried away. You're leaving?

SOFYA YEGOROVNA. Yes.

VOINITSEV. Hm . . . Soon?

SOFYA YEGOROVNA. Today.

VOINITSEV. With him?

SOFYA YEGOROVNA. Yes.

VOINITSEV. I wish you happiness!

Pause.

A firm foundation for happiness! Flesh run amok and another person's heartbreak . . . Another person's heartbreak always contributes to somebody's happiness! However, that's stale . . . People would rather hear a new lie than an old truth . . . Never mind! Live as best you can!

SOFYA YEGOROVNA. You wanted to say something . . .

VOINITSEV. Does it sound as if I'm silent? All right then . . . Here's what I wanted to say . . . I want to be completely candid with you, not beholden to you, and therefore I ask you to forgive my behavior yesterday . . . Last night I was rude to you, crude, malicious . . . Forgive me, please . . . Will you forgive me?

SOFYA YEGOROVNA. I forgive you. (*Makes to leave.*)

VOINITSEV. Wait a second, wait, that's not all! I have something more to say. (*Sighs.*) I'm going mad, *Sophie*! I haven't got the strength to bear this dreadful blow . . . I'm mad, and yet I quite understand . . . Amidst the fog spreading in my brain, amidst the mass of something gray, leaden, heavy, there glints a little glimmer of light, which enables me to understand it all . . . If that little glimmer goes out on me too, well then, that means . . . I'm utterly lost. I quite understand . . .

Pause.

Here I stand in my own study; in this study once occupied by my father, Major-General Voinitsev of His Majesty's retinue, knight of St. George, a great and glorious man! People only saw what was wrong with him . . . They saw the way he beat and trampled, but how he was beaten and trampled, nobody wanted to see . . . (*Points at Sofya Yegorovna.*) Here is my ex-wife . . .

SOFYA YEGOROVNA tries to leave.

VOINITSEV. Wait a second! Let me finish! I'm talking like an idiot, but listen to me! After all, it's for the last time!

SOFYA YEGOROVNA. You've said it all before . . . What more can you say? We have to separate . . . What more is there to say? Are you trying to prove that I am doing you wrong? Don't bother! I know what to think of myself . . .

VOINITSEV. What can I say? Ugh, Sofya, Sofya! You know nothing! Nothing, otherwise you wouldn't look down your nose at me like that! The things that are going on inside me are horrible! (*Gets on his knees before her.*) What are you doing, *Sophie?* Where are you driving the two of us? For heaven's sake, be merciful! I'm dying and losing my mind! Stay with me! I will forget all about it, I've already forgiven all of it . . . I'll be your slave, I'll love you . . . I will, in a way I haven't loved before! I'll make you happy! You'll be happy with me, like a goddess! He won't make you happy! You'll ruin both yourself and him! You'll be the ruin of Platonov, Sofya! . . . I know you can't be forced to be kind, but do stay! You'll be happy again, you won't look as pale as a corpse, so miserable! I'll be a man again, I'll be able to face you again . . . Platonov! That's pie in the sky, but . . . do stay! Let's turn back the clock, before it's too late! Platonov will agree . . . I know him . . . He doesn't love you, but just . . . you gave yourself to him, and he took you . . . (*Rises.*) Are you crying?

SOFYA YEGOROVNA (*rises*). Don't assume these tears have anything to do with you! Perhaps, Platonov will agree . . . Let him agree! (*Sharply.*) You're all such vulgar people! Where is Platonov?

VOINITSEV. I don't know where he is.

SOFYA YEGOROVNA. Stop pestering me! Leave me alone! I hate you! Get out of here! Where's Platonov? Vulgar people . . . Where is he? I do hate you!

VOINITSEV. What for?

SOFYA YEGOROVNA. Where is he?

VOINITSEV. I gave him money, and he promised me he'd go away. If he kept his promise, it means he's gone away.

SOFYA YEGOROVNA. You bought him off? Are you lying?

VOINITSEV. I paid him a thousand rubles, and he gave you up. Although that's a lie! It's all lies! Don't believe me, for heaven's sake! Alive and well, that damned Platonov! Go and get him, smother him in kisses! . . . I didn't buy him off! And how can you . . . he be happy? For this is my wife, my Sofya . . . What does it all mean? And even now I don't believe it! Are you and he on Platonic terms? It hasn't gone as far as . . . the main event?

SOFYA YEGOROVNA. I'm his wife, mistress, whatever you like! (*Tries to leave.*) What's the point in keeping me here? I haven't the time to listen to all this . . .

VOINITSEV. Wait a bit, Sofya! You're his mistress? Whatever do you mean? You talk so shamelessly! (*Grabs her by the arm.*) How could you? How could you?

Enter ANNA PETROVNA.

SOFYA YEGOROVNA. Leave me alone! (*Exits.*)

SCENE III

VOINITSEV and ANNA PETROVNA.

ANNA PETROVNA enters and looks out the window.

VOINITSEV (*waves his hand in dismissal*). It's all over!

Pause.

What's going on out there?

ANNA PETROVNA. Osip's been killed by the peasants.

VOINITSEV. Already?

ANNA PETROVNA. Yes . . . Near the well . . . Do you see it? There he is!

VOINITSEV (*looks out the window*). So what? It serves him right.

ANNA PETROVNA. Have you heard the news, sonny boy? They're saying Platonov has vanished somewhere and . . . Read the letter?

VOINITSEV. I have.

ANNA PETROVNA. Bye-bye estate! How do you like that? Bingo . . . The Lord gaveth, and the Lord tooketh away . . . There's your famous financial wheeling and dealing for you! And all because we put our trust in Glagolyev . . . He promised to buy the estate, and didn't even go to the auction . . .

The servant girl says that he's gone to Paris . . . Pulled one over on us, the bastard, in his old age! If it hadn't been for him, you and I could have paid off the interest fine and dandy and could have gone on living here . . . (*Sighs.*) In this world you mustn't trust your enemies, or your friends, for that matter!

VOINITSEV. Yes, you mustn't trust your friends!

ANNA PETROVNA. Well, landed gentry? What will you do now? Where will you go? The Lord gaveth to your ancestors, but tooketh away from you . . . You've got nothing left . . .

VOINITSEV. It doesn't matter to me.

ANNA PETROVNA. No, it does matter. How are you going to eat? Let's sit down . . . (*Sits down.*) How gloomy you are . . . What's to be done? It's a shame we've got to abandon the cozy little nest, but what can you do, love? You can't turn back . . . That's how it's got to be, I suppose . . . Be a clever boy, Serzhel! The first thing is to be calm and collected.

VOINITSEV. Don't pay any attention to me, *maman*! Why bother about me? You can hardly sit still yourself . . . First console yourself, and then come and console me.

ANNA PETROVNA. Well . . . Womenfolk don't matter . . . Womenfolk are always in the background . . . The first thing is to be calm and collected! You've lost what was yours, but the important thing is not what used to be but what lies ahead. You've got your whole life ahead of you, a good, hard-working, man's life! What's there to grieve about? You'll go into a prep school or a high school, you'll start working . . . I think you're a fine fellow. A philologist, well meaning, never been involved in anything shady, you've got convictions, demure, a married man . . . If you want to, you'll go far! I think you're a clever boy! Only you mustn't quarrel with your wife . . . You no sooner got married when you started quarreling . . . Why don't you tell me about it, Serzhel? Your heart is aching, but you keep it quiet . . . What's going on between the two of you?

VOINITSEV. Nothing's going on, it's already gone on.

ANNA PETROVNA. What then? Or maybe it's a secret?

VOINITSEV (*sighs*). A terrible misfortune has befallen our house, mamma Anyuta! Why haven't I told you before now? I don't know. I kept hoping against hope, and besides I was ashamed to say anything . . . I only learned about it myself yesterday morning . . . And I couldn't care less about the estate!

ANNA PETROVNA (*laughs*). How alarming! Has she lost her temper or something?

VOINITSEV. You laugh! Just wait, you'll wipe that smile off your face!

Pause.

She has betrayed me . . . I'm honored to introduce myself: a cuckold!

ANNA PETROVNA. Don't be silly, Sergey?! What silly fantasies! To say such monstrous things and without a second thought! You're incredible! Sometimes you talk such drivel it simply makes my ears droop! A cuckold . . . You don't even know the meaning of the word . . .

VOINITSEV. I do know, *maman*! Not in theory, but I already know it in practice!

ANNA PETROVNA. Don't insult your wife, you crackpot! Ah . . .

VOINITSEV. I swear to God!

Pause.

ANNA PETROVNA. This is strange . . . What you're saying is impossible. You're spreading slander! Impossible! Here, in Voinitsevka?

VOINITSEV. Yes, here, in your damned Voinitsevka!

ANNA PETROVNA. Hm . . . And who here, in our damned Voinitsevka, would come up with the impossible idea of planting horns on your aristocratic head? Absolutely nobody! Young Glagolyev, perhaps? Not likely. Glagolyev has stopped coming here . . . There's no one suitable for your *Sophie* here. Your jealousy is ridiculous, my dear!

VOINITSEV. Platonov!

ANNA PETROVNA. What about Platonov?

VOINITSEV. He's the one.

ANNA PETROVNA (*jumps up*). You can talk nonsense, but the sort of nonsense you're talking now, listen here . . . What drivel!! You should know when to stop! It's inexcusably ridiculous!

VOINITSEV. Ask her, go and ask him yourself, if you don't believe me! I didn't want to believe it and I still don't want to believe it, but she is leaving today, deserting me! I have to believe it! And he's going with her! Can't you see me going around, gaping at all the world like a drowned kitten! I'm ruined!

ANNA PETROVNA. It can't be that, Sergey! It's a figment of your puerile imagination! Believe me! There's nothing to it!

VOINITSEV. Believe *me*, she is leaving today! Believe that over the last two days she has said over and over again that she is his mistress! She said it herself! What has happened may be impossible to believe, but against your will and for all your skill you have to believe it!

ANNA PETROVNA. I remember, I remember . . . Now I understand what's going on . . . Get me a chair, Sergey! No, never mind . . . So that's what's going on! Hm . . . Hold on, hold on, let me remember it in order . . .

Pause.

Enter BUGROV.

SCENE IV

ANNA PETROVNA, VOINITSEV, and BUGROV.

BUGROV (*enters*). Good morning, sir and ma'am! A happy Sunday, sir and ma'am! Live and be well, sir and ma'am!

ANNA PETROVNA. Yes-yes-yes . . . It's horrible . . .

BUGROV. There's a touch of rain, but it's hot . . . (*Mops his brow.*) Fff . . . Steam rises off you, walking or riding . . . Are you all right, sir and ma'am?

Pause.

I dropped by here in person seeing as how yesterday the auction took place, as you know . . . And besides this, you know, it's a little bit (*laughs*) of a ticklish situation and offensive to you, of course, so I . . . don't want you to hold it against me, if you don't mind! I'm not the one who bought the estate! Abram Abramych bought it, only in my name . . .

VOINITSEV (*rings forcefully*). To hell with the lot of 'em . . .

BUGROV. Quite so, sir . . . You mustn't think it, sir . . . Wasn't me, sir . . . Consequently, only in my name, accordingly! (*Sits down.*)

YAKOV enters.

VOINITSEV (*to Yakov*). How many times have I asked you lowlifes, bastards (*coughs*), good-for-nothings, not to let anybody in without announcing them! A good hiding's in store for all of you, you swine! (*Tosses the bell under the table.*) Get out of here! Bastards . . . (*Paces up and down the stage.*)

YAKOV shrugs and exits.

BUGROV (*coughs*). In my name only, sir . . . Abram Abramych asked me to convey that you can live here to your heart's content, even till Christmas . . . There'll be a few little alterations, but they won't inconvenience you, sir . . . And if it happens they do, you can move into the servants' quarters . . . Plenty of rooms, and it's warm, sir . . . He also asked me to inquire, sir, if you wouldn't like to sell me, that is in my name, the mines? The mines belong to you, ma'am, Anna Petrovna . . . Wouldn't you like to sell them to us at this time? We'll pay a good price . . .

ANNA PETROVNA. No . . . I won't sell a single mine to any of you devils! What are you offering? A penny? You know what you can do with that penny!

BUGROV. Abram Abramych also asked me to convey that in case if it ain't to your liking, Anna Petrovna, to sell him your mines minus what's owed by Sergey Pavlich and the late general Pavel Ivanych, then he will call in the I.O.U.s . . . And so will I, ma'am . . . Hee-hee, ma'am . . . Friendship is one thing, you know, but money's something else . . . Business is business! It's a hell of a deal. I, that is . . . bought your I.O.U.s from Petrin. .

VOINITSEV. I won't allow anyone to speculate on my stepmother's property! It's her property, not mine! . . .

BUGROV. The lady, perhaps, will feel sorry for you . . .

VOINITSEV. I haven't got the time to discuss it with you! Good grief . . . (*Waves his hand in dismissal.*) Do whatever you want!

ANNA PETROVNA. Leave us alone, Timofey Gordeich! Excuse us . . . Please go away!

BUGROV. Of course, ma'am . . . (*Gets up.*) Please don't trouble yourselves . . . You can live here at least till Christmas. Tomorrow or day after I'll drop by, ma'am. Keep well, ma'am! (*Exits.*)

ANNA PETROVNA. Tomorrow we leave this place! Yes, now I remember . . . Platonov . . . So that's it, that's what he is running away from!

VOINITSEV. Let them do whatever they want! Let them take it all! I no longer have a wife, I don't need anything else! No wife, *maman*!

ANNA PETROVNA. Yes, you no longer have a wife . . . But what did he see in that wishy-washy Sofya? What did he see in that slip of a girl? What could he see in her? How indiscriminate these stupid men are! They're capable of being attracted by any sl . . . And where were you while this was going on, Mr. Loving Husband? Where were your eyes? Crybaby! Whimpering while somebody made off with his wife right under his nose! And you call this a man! You're a baby! They marry you off, baby boys, fools, only to be laughingstocks, what jackasses! You're both of you totally useless, you and your Platonov! What a wretched mess!

VOINITSEV. Nothing will help now, and neither will scolding. She's not mine any more, and he's not yours. What more is there to say? Leave me alone, *maman*! You can't bear my stupid face!

ANNA PETROVNA. But what's to be done? We have to do something! We have to save them!

VOINITSEV. Save whom? The only person who needs saving is me . . . They're happy for the time being . . . (*Sighs.*)

ANNA PETROVNA. There you go being reasonable! They're the ones, not you, who have to be saved! Platonov doesn't love her! Don't you know that? He seduced her, the way you once seduced that stupid German girl! He doesn't love her! I assure you! What did she say to you? Why don't you talk?

VOINITSEV. She said that she is his mistress.

ANNA PETROVNA. She's his fool, and not his mistress! Shut up! Maybe this can still be fixed . . . Platonov is capable of turning a mere kiss or a squeeze of the hand into a big deal . . . Things haven't got to the main event with them yet! I'm sure of it . . .

VOINITSEV. They have!

ANNA PETROVNA. You don't understand a thing.

Enter GREKOVA.

SCENE V

VOINITSEV, ANNA PETROVNA, and GREKOVA.

GREKOVA (*enters*). So there you are! Good morning! (*Offers her hand to Anna Petrovna.*) Good morning, Sergey Pavlovich! Forgive me, please, I believe I'm disturbing you . . . An inopportune guest is worse than . . . worse than . . . How does the saying go? Worse than a wild Indian, that's it . . . I'll only stay one little minute . . . You just can't imagine! (*Laughs.*) I've something to show you right away, Anna Petrovna . . . Forgive me, Sergey Pavlovich, we'll have to keep it a secret . . . (*Leads Anna Petrovna aside.*) Forgive me . . . (*Hands her a note.*) I received this yesterday . . . Read it!

ANNA PETROVNA (*peruses the note*). Ah . . .

GREKOVA. Did you know, I had him served with a writ . . . (*Lays her head on Anna's breast.*) Send for him, Anna Petrovna! Have him come here!

ANNA PETROVNA. What do you want to see him for?

GREKOVA. I want to see the look on his face now . . . What's he look like now? Send for him! Please do! I want to say a few words to him . . . You don't know what I've done! What I've done! Don't listen, Sergey Pavlovich! (*In a whisper.*) I went to the superintendent . . . They are transferring Mikhail Vasilich to another job at my request . . . What have I done! (*Weeps.*) Send for him! . . . Who knew that he would write this letter! Ah, if only I had known! My God . . . I'm in pain!

ANNA PETROVNA. Go into the library, my dear! I'll come to you right away, then we'll talk about it . . . I have to speak with Sergey Pavlovich in private . . .

GREKOVA. The library? All right . . . But you'll send for him? What kind of look is on his face after this letter? Have you read it? Let me hide it! (*Hides the letter.*) My dear, darling . . . I beg of you! I'll go . . . but you'll send for him! Don't listen, Sergey Pavlovich! Let's talk in German, Anna Petrovna! *Schicken Sie, meine Liebe!*[83]

ANNA PETROVNA. All right . . . Just get going!

GREKOVA. All right . . . (*Quickly kisses her.*) Don't be angry with me, my dear! I . . . I'm in agony! You can't imagine! I'm leaving, Sergey Pavlovich! You can go on with your discussion! (*Exits.*)

ANNA PETROVNA. I'm going to get this sorted out right now . . . Stop fretting! Maybe there's a way to patch up your family life . . . Dreadful state of affairs! Who could have expected it! I'll talk things over with Sofya right now! I'll put her to a proper interrogation . . . You're wrong and you're acting silly . . . And yet, no! (*Covers her face with her hands.*) No, no . . .

VOINITSEV. No! I'm not wrong!

ANNA PETROVNA. Anyway, I'll talk things over with her . . . And I'll go and talk things over with him . . .

VOINITSEV. Go and talk! But it's no use! (*Sits behind the desk.*) Let's get out of here! There's no hope! And no little straws to grasp at . . .

ANNA PETROVNA. I'll sort this all out right now . . . And you sit there bawling! Go to bed, you great big man! Where's Sofya?

VOINITSEV. In her room, I suppose . . .

ANNA PETROVNA exits.

SCENE VI

VOINITSEV and then PLATONOV.

VOINITSEV. The depths of despair! How long is this going to drag on? Tomorrow and the day after tomorrow, a week, a month, a year . . . This torment will never end! I should shoot myself.

PLATONOV (*enters with his arm in a sling*). There he sits . . . Crying, looks like . . .

Pause.

---

83 German: Send for him, my dear.

Peace be unto your soul, my poor friend! (*Walks over to Voinitsev.*) For heaven's sake, listen to me! I didn't come to defend my actions . . . It's not for either of us to judge me . . . I came to make a request not on my behalf, but on yours . . . I ask you as a brother . . . Hate, despise me, think what you like about me, but do not . . . kill yourself! I'm not talking about revolvers, but . . . just in general . . . Your health is poor . . . Grief will do you in . . . I won't go on living! I'll kill myself, don't kill yourself! You want me to die? Want me to stop living?

Pause.

VOINITSEV. I don't want anything.

Enter ANNA PETROVNA.

S C E N E   V I I

VOINITSEV, PLATONOV, and ANNA PETROVNA.

ANNA PETROVNA. He's here? (*Slowly walks over to Platonov.*) Platonov, is it true?

PLATONOV. It's true.

ANNA PETROVNA. He still dares . . . dares to say it so calmly! It's true . . . You rotten creature, didn't you know that this is rotten, despicable?

PLATONOV. Rotten creature . . . Can't you show a little more courtesy? I knew nothing! All I knew and still do know of this business is that I never wished on him a thousandth part of what he's going through now!

ANNA PETROVNA. Nevertheless, it shouldn't keep you, a friend, from knowing that a friend's wife should not and cannot be a friend's plaything! (*Shouts.*) You don't love her! You were simply bored!

VOINITSEV. Ask him, *maman*, why he's come here?

ANNA PETROVNA. Rotten! It's rotten to play with people! They are the same flesh and blood as you, you extremely clever man!

VOINITSEV (*jumps up*). He actually came here! The impertinence! Why did you show up here? I know why you showed up, but you won't dazzle and impress us with your fine-sounding phrases!

PLATONOV. Who do you mean by "us"?

VOINITSEV. Now I know what all those fine-sounding phrases are worth! Leave me in peace! If you came here to expiate your guilt with flowery verbiage, you should know that magniloquent speeches do not expiate guilt!

PLATONOV. If magniloquent speeches do not expiate guilt, then shouting and spitefulness do not establish it, although, as I recall, didn't I say that I would shoot myself?

VOINITSEV. You won't expiate your guilt that way! Not by words which I no longer believe! I despise your words! That is how a Russian expiates his guilt! (*He points to the window.*)

PLATONOV. What's out there?

VOINITSEV. Out by the well lies a man who has expiated his guilt!

PLATONOV. So I saw . . . Then why are *you* speechifying, Sergey Pavlovich? After all, I thought you were overwhelmed with grief . . . You wallow in grief and at the same time you ham it up? To what should this be attributed: insincerity or . . . stupidity?

VOINITSEV (*sits down*). *Maman*, ask him why he came here?

ANNA PETROVNA. Platonov, what brings you here?

PLATONOV. Ask me yourself, why bother *maman*? You've lost everything! Your wife's walked out on you—and you've lost everything, there's nothing left! *Sophie*, as beautiful as a day in May, is an ideal, which eclipses all other ideals! Without a woman a man is like a steam engine without steam! Your life is over, the steam's evaporated! You've lost everything! Honor, and human dignity, and birth and breeding, everything! The end has come!

VOINITSEV. I am not listening. You can leave me out of it!

PLATONOV. Naturally. Don't insult me, Voinitsev! I didn't come here to be insulted! Your misery doesn't give you the right to sling mud at me! I'm a human being, and you should treat me like a human being. You're unhappy, but you and your unhappiness cannot compare with the sufferings I've undergone since you left! It was a horrible night, Voinitsev, after you left! I swear to you humanitarians that your unhappiness isn't worth one iota of my pain!

ANNA PETROVNA. That may very well be, but who cares about your night, your pain!

PLATONOV. So *you* don't care?

ANNA PETROVNA. I assure you that we do not care!

PLATONOV. Really? Stop lying, Anna Petrovna! (*Sighs.*) But perhaps you're right to see it that way . . . Perhaps . . . But then where am I to find real people? Whom can I go to? (*Hides his face in his hands.*) Where are there real people? They don't understand . . . Don't understand! Who does understand? Fools, sadists, heartless wretches . . .

VOINITSEV. No, I do understand you! I did understand! It's out of character, my dear sir, my erstwhile friend, this tugging at our heartstrings! I understand you! You're a crafty bastard! That's what you are!

PLATONOV. I forgive you, you idiot, for that remark! Hold your tongue, don't say any more! (*To Anna Petrovna.*) What are you hanging around here for, you thrill seeker? Curious? It's none of your business! We don't need witnesses!

ANNA PETROVNA. And it's none of your business, either! You can . . . withdraw! The effrontery of the man! To bespatter, besmirch, and bestrew us with dirt, and then drop in and complain about his pain! What a diplomat! However . . . forgive me! If you don't want to hear any more of this, then leave! Do us a favor!

VOINITSEV (*jumps up*). What more does he want of me, I don't understand! What do you want, what do you expect from me? I don't understand?

PLATONOV. I can see that you don't understand . . . It's a wise man who takes his sorrows not to other people, but to the bottle . . . Wise as can be! (*Goes to the door.*) I am sorry that I spoke to you, stooped to your level . . . It was stupid of me to consider you decent people . . . You're all the same . . . savages, coarse, uncouth yokels . . . (*Slams the door and exits.*)

ANNA PETROVNA (*wrings her hands*). How nasty . . . Please catch up with him this minute and tell him . . . Tell him that . . .

VOINITSEV. What can I tell him?

ANNA PETROVNA. You'll find something to tell him . . . Something. Hurry, Serzhel! I implore you! He came here with good intentions! You should have understood him, but you were cruel to him. Hurry, my dearest!

VOINITSEV. I cannot! Leave me alone!

ANNA PETROVNA. But, after all, he's not the only one to blame! Serzhel, we're all to blame! We all have passions, we're all weak . . . Hurry! Say something conciliatory! Show him that you are a man! For heaven's sake! . . . Well, how about it! Well! Hurry!

VOINITSEV. I'm losing my mind . . .

ANNA PETROVNA. Lose your mind, but don't you dare insult people! Ah . . . but hurry up, for heaven's sake! (*Weeps.*) Sergey!

VOINITSEV. Leave me alone, *maman!*

ANNA PETROVNA. I'll go myself . . . Why shouldn't I run myself? I'll do it . . .

PLATONOV (*enters*). Ow! (*Sits on the sofa.*)

VOINITSEV gets up.

ANNA PETROVNA (*aside*). What's wrong with him?

Pause.

PLATONOV. My arm hurts . . . I'm as hungry as a starving dog . . . I'm cold . . . Shivering with fever . . . I'm sick! Can't you see that I'm sick! I'm losing my life! What do you want from me? What are you after? Isn't that damned night enough for you?

VOINITSEV (*walks over to Platonov*). Mikhail Vasilich, let's forgive one another . . . I . . . But you understand my position . . . Let's part properly . . .

Pause.

I forgive you . . . Word of honor, I forgive you! And if you could forget it all, I would be as happy as ever! Let's leave one another in peace!

PLATONOV. Yes.

Pause.

No, I'm falling apart . . . The engine has broken down. I'm awfully sleepy, my eyelids stick together, but I'm unable to sleep . . . I sue for peace, I beg your pardon, I'm guilty, I'll be still . . . Do whatever you like, and think whatever you choose . . .

VOINITSEV walks away from Platonov and sits at the desk.

PLATONOV. I won't leave this place, even if you set fire to the house! Anyone who finds my presence distasteful can leave the room . . . (*Tries to lie down.*) Give me something warm . . . Not to eat, to cover myself with . . . I won't go home . . . It's raining outside . . . I'll lie here.

ANNA PETROVNA (*walks over to Platonov*). Do go home, Mikhail Vasilich! I'll come and bring you whatever you need. (*Touches him on the shoulder.*) Go on! Go home!

PLATONOV. Anyone who finds my presence distasteful can leave the room . . . Let me have a drink of water! I want a drink.

ANNA PETROVNA hands him the carafe.

(*Drinks from the carafe.*) I'm sick . . . Very sick, my good woman!

ANNA PETROVNA. Go home! . . . (*Places a hand on his forehead.*) Your head is hot . . . Go home. I'll send for Triletsky.

PLATONOV (*quietly*). It's bad, Your Excellency! Bad . . . Bad . . .

ANNA PETROVNA. And what about me? Go away! I beg of you! You've got to go away no matter what! You hear me?

Enter SOFYA YEGOROVNA.

SCENE VIII

The same and SOFYA YEGOROVNA.

SOFYA YEGOROVNA (*enters*). Be so kind as to take back your money! What's the point of this generosity? I already told you, I believe . . . (*On seeing Platonov.*) You . . . here? Why are you here?

Pause.

That's peculiar . . . What are you doing here?

PLATONOV. Talking to me?

SOFYA YEGOROVNA. Yes, you!

ANNA PETROVNA. Let's go, Sergey! (*Exits and a minute later reenters on tiptoe and sits in a corner.*)

PLATONOV. It's all over, Sofya!

SOFYA YEGOROVNA. Is that right?

PLATONOV. Yes, that's right . . . We'll talk about it later.

SOFYA YEGOROVNA. Mikhail Vasilich! What do you mean by . . . all?

PLATONOV. I don't need anything, love or hate, just leave me in peace! I beg of you . . . And I don't even want to talk . . . What we've had is good enough for me . . . For pity's sake . . .

SOFYA YEGOROVNA. What is he saying?

PLATONOV. I'm saying I've had enough. I don't need a new life. And there's nowhere to go with the old one . . . I don't need anything!

SOFYA YEGOROVNA (*shrugs her shoulders*). I don't understand . . .

PLATONOV. You don't understand? Our liaison is over, that's what!

SOFYA YEGOROVNA. You're not going to go away, is that it?

PLATONOV. There's no need to turn pale, Sofya . . . I mean Sofya Yegorovna![84]

SOFYA YEGOROVNA. You're worming out of it?

PLATONOV. Looks like it . . .

SOFYA YEGOROVNA. You bastard! (*Weeps.*)

PLATONOV. I know . . . I've heard it a thousand times . . . We should talk about it later and . . . in private.

SOFYA YEGOROVNA sobs.

You should go to your room! The most pointless thing about unhappiness is tears . . . It was meant to happen and it happened . . . Nature has her laws, and our life . . . has its logic . . . It happened quite logically . . .

Pause.

SOFYA YEGOROVNA (*sobs*). What's this got to do with me? What does it matter to me, to my life, which you took from me, that you lost interest? What's this got to do with me? Don't you love me any more?

PLATONOV. You'll console yourself somehow . . . At least, for instance, won't you let this affair be a lesson to you for the future?

---

84 To call her solely by her first name implies intimacy. To use both first name and patronymic is more formal.

SOFYA YEGOROVNA. Not a lesson, but a ruination! You dare to say this? It's despicable!

PLATONOV. What are you crying for? I find this all so . . . revolting! (*Shouts.*) I'm sick!

SOFYA YEGOROVNA. He swore, he begged, he began it first, and now he's come here! I disgust you? You only wanted me for two weeks? I hate you! I can't look at you! Get out of here! (*Sobs more violently.*)

ANNA PETROVNA. Platonov!

PLATONOV. Huh?

ANNA PETROVNA. Get out of here!

PLATONOV gets up and slowly goes to the door.

SOFYA YEGOROVNA. Wait . . . Don't leave! Do you . . . mean it? Maybe, you're not sober . . . Sit down a while and think it over! (*Clutches him by the shoulder.*)

PLATONOV. I've already sat and thought. Wash your hands of me, Sofya Yegorovna! I'm not the man for you! I've been rotting for so long, my soul's turned into a skeleton so long ago there's no rebirth possible for me! Better bury me at a distance, so I won't pollute the air! Believe me one last time!

SOFYA YEGOROVNA (*wrings her hands*). What am I to do now? What am I to do? Teach me! After all, I'm dying! I won't survive this vileness! I won't survive another five minutes! I'll kill myself . . . (*Sits in an armchair that stands in a corner.*) What are you doing to me? (*Goes into hysterics.*)

VOINITSEV (*walks over to Sofya Yegorovna*). Sophie!

ANNA PETROVNA. God knows what's going on! Calm down, Sophie! Get her some water, Sergey!

VOINITSEV. Sophie! Don't kill yourself . . . Stop it! (*To Platonov.*) What are you waiting around here for, Mikhail Vasilich? Get going, for heaven's sake!

ANNA PETROVNA. That'll do, Sophie, that'll do! That's enough!

PLATONOV (*walks over to Sofya Yegorovna*). What's this for? Dear, dear . . . (*Quickly walks away.*) Idiocy!

SOFYA YEGOROVNA. Get away from me! All of you! I don't need your help! (*To Anna Petrovna.*) Get away! I hate you! I know who I can thank for all of this! You won't get away with it!

ANNA PETROVNA. Ssh . . . It's not right to start name calling.

SOFYA YEGOROVNA. If it hadn't been for your corrupting influence over him, he wouldn't have destroyed me! (*Sobs.*) Get away! (*To Voinitsev.*) And you . . . you go away too!

> VOINITSEV *walks away, sits at the desk, and puts his head in his hands.*

ANNA PETROVNA (*to Platonov*). Go away from here, I tell you! You're being wonderfully idiotic today! What more do you want?

PLATONOV (*covers his ears*). Where am I to go? I'm frozen stiff . . . (*Goes to the door.*) The sooner I go to hell the better . . .

> Enter TRILETSKY.

SCENE IX

The same and TRILETSKY.

TRILETSKY (*in the doorway*). I'll give you such an announcing your own mother won't recognize you!

YAKOV'S VOICE. The master ordered it . . .

TRILETSKY. Go and kiss your master you-know-where! He's as big a blockhead as you are! (*Enters.*) Don't tell me he's not here? (*Falls on to the sofa.*) Dreadful! This . . . this . . . this . . . (*Jumps up.*) Ugh! (*To Platonov.*) The tragedy is reaching its climax, tragedian! Its climax, sir!

PLATONOV. Whad'you want?

TRILETSKY. What are you doing around here? Where have you been hanging out, wretch? Aren't you ashamed, how could you? Spouting philosophy here? Delivering sermons?

PLATONOV. Talk like a human being, Nikolay! Whad'you want?

TRILETSKY. It's inhuman! (*Sits and hides his face in his hands.*) A disaster, what a disaster! Who would have expected it?

PLATONOV. What's happened?

TRILETSKY. What's happened? You really don't know? Do you care at all? Have you got the time?

ANNA PETROVNA. Nikolay Ivanych!

PLATONOV. Is it Sasha or what? Speak, Nikolay! That's all I need! What's wrong with her?

TRILETSKY. She poisoned herself with sulphur matches!

PLATONOV. What are you saying?

TRILETSKY (*shouts*). She poisoned herself with sulphur matches![85] (*Jumps up.*) Here, read! Read! (*Puts a note in front of his face.*) Read, philosopher!

PLATONOV (*reads*). "It's a sin to pray for suicides, but pray for me. I've taken my life because I'm ill. Misha, love Kolya and my brother, the way I love you. Take care of father. Live according to the law. Kolya, God bless you, as I bless you with a mother's blessing. Forgive a sinful woman. The key to Misha's chest of drawers is in my wool dress" . . . My precious! A sinful woman! Her a sinful woman! That's all I needed! (*Clutches his head.*) She took poison . . .

Pause.

She took poison . . . Where is she? Listen! I'll go to her! (*Tears off his sling.*) I . . . I'll revive her!

TRILETSKY (*lies face down on the sofa*). Before reviving her, you shouldn't have killed her!

PLATONOV. Killed . . . Why, you lunatic, did you say . . . that word? Do you think I killed her? Do you . . . do you think I wanted her death? (*Weeps.*) She took poison . . . That's all I needed, to be crushed beneath a wheel, like a dog! If this is a punishment, then . . . (*shakes his fist*) it's a cruel, immoral punishment! No, this is more than I can handle! Much more! What's it for? Let's say I'm a sinner, a miserable wretch . . . but all the same I'm still alive!

---

85 The method was to steep the matches in water to release the sulphur in their tips, and then drink the water.

Pause.

Look at me now, all of you! Look! Do you like what you see?

TRILETSKY (*leaps up*). Yes, yes, yes . . . Now let's have a good cry . . . By the way, your eyes are in a perpetual state of damp . . . You should get a good hiding! Put on your cap! Let's go! Husband! Loving husband! Destroyed a woman for no reason at all, no reason at all! Brought her to that point! And these folks are entertaining him here! They like him! An eccentric fellow, an interesting subject, with an expression of mournful nobility in his face! And traces of former good looks! Let's get going! You'll see what you've done, conversation piece, eccentric!

PLATONOV. No words . . . no words . . . I don't need words!

TRILETSKY. It's lucky for you, you butcher, that I stopped by your house before daybreak! Why, what would have happened, if I hadn't stopped by, if I hadn't come in the nick of time? She would have died! Do you understand this or don't you? Ordinarily you understand everything, except the most ordinary things! Oh, I would have given it to you then! I wouldn't have stood and gazed at your pathetic facial expressions! If only you had wagged your damned tongue less and listened more, this disaster wouldn't have occurred! I wouldn't trade her for ten such clever fellows as you! Let's go!

VOINITSEV. Stop shouting! Ah . . . I'm so sick and tired of all of you . . .

TRILETSKY. Let's go!

PLATONOV. Hold on . . . So she . . . isn't dead, you're saying?

TRILETSKY. Would you like her to be dead?

PLATONOV (*shrieks*). She isn't dead! I can't understand how . . . She isn't dead? (*Embraces Triletsky.*) She's alive? (*Roars with laughter.*) Alive!

ANNA PETROVNA. I don't understand! . . . Triletsky, please talk sense! Today for some reason they're all exceptionally stupid! What's the meaning of this letter?

TRILETSKY. She did write this letter . . . If it hadn't been for me, she would have had time to die . . . And now she's awfully sick! I don't know whether her system can take it . . . Oh, just let her die, and then . . . Get away from me, please!

PLATONOV. You gave me such a fright! My God! She's still alive! Which means, you didn't let her die? My dear fellow! (*Kisses Triletsky.*) Dear man! (*Roars with laughter.*) I didn't believe in medicine, but now I even believe in you! How is she now? Weak? Ailing? But we'll get her on her feet!

TRILETSKY. Will she pull through?

PLATONOV. She will! If she can't, I'll do it for her! Why didn't you say straight out that she's alive? Anna Petrovna! Dear lady! A glass of cold water, and I'm happy! Forgive me, ladies and gentlemen, all of you! Anna Petrovna! I'm losing my mind! . . . (*Kisses Anna Petrovna's hand.*) Sasha's alive . . . Water, water . . . my dear lady!

> ANNA PETROVNA *exits with the empty carafe and a minute later reenters with water.*

(*To Triletsky.*) Let's go to her! On her feet, on her feet! Ransack all medicine from Hippocrates[86] to Triletsky! We'll turn it all inside-out! Who should be living on this earth if not her? Let's go! But no . . . wait a bit! My head's spinning . . . . I'm awfully sick . . . Hold on . . . (*Sits on the sofa.*) I'll rest and then we'll go . . . She's very weak?

TRILETSKY. Very . . . He's overjoyed! What he's overjoyed about I don't understand!

ANNA PETROVNA. I was frightened too. You should have spoken more clearly! Drink this! (*Gives Platonov some water.*)

PLATONOV (*drinks greedily*). Thank you, kind lady! I'm a villain, a deep-dyed villain! (*To Triletsky.*) Sit beside me! (*Triletsky sits.*) You're exhausted too . . . Thank you, friend. Did she take a lot?

TRILETSKY. Enough to send her to the next world.

PLATONOV. What a girl . . . Well, thank God. My arm hurts . . . Let me have another drink. I'm awfully sick myself, Nikolay! Can hardly keep my wits about me . . . Look how I'm about to fall over . . . I suppose I've got a temperature. Toy soldiers in calico uniforms and pointy little caps keep flashing before my eyes . . . Yellow and green all around . . . Prescribe me some *chinini sulphurici* . . .[87]

---

86 Greek physician (480–377 B.C.), whose oath is still administered to doctors of medicine.

87 Correctly, *chininum sulphuricum*, sulphate of quinine, an alkaloid found in cinchona bark, used in treating malaria. Later in life, Chekhov named his dachshund Quinine.

TRILETSKY. I should prescribe you a good hundred lashes!

PLATONOV (*roars with laughter*). Joker, joker . . . Sometimes I do laugh at your witticisms. Are you my brother-in-law or my wife's brother? My God, how sick I am! You can't imagine how sick I am!

TRILETSKY takes his pulse.

ANNA PETROVNA (*quietly to Triletsky*). Take him away, Nikolay Ivanych! I'll come to see you myself today, I'll have a word with Aleksandra Ivanovna. What was she thinking of to scare us like that? Is she in danger?

TRILETSKY. It's hard to say as yet. She didn't manage to poison herself, but on the whole . . . she's in a bad way.

PLATONOV. What did you give her?

TRILETSKY. What was appropriate. (*Gets up.*) Let's go!

PLATONOV. And what did you give the General's lady just now?

TRILETSKY. You're delirious . . . Let's go!

PLATONOV. Let's go . . . (*Gets up.*) Sergey Pavlovich! Let it go! (*Sits down.*) Let it go! What are you so down in the mouth about? As if they'd stolen the sun from the earth! And yet there was a time he studied philosophy! Be a Socrates![88] Eh? Sergey Pavlovich! (*Quietly.*) However, I myself don't know what to say . . .

TRILETSKY (*puts his hand on Platonov's head*). You had to get sick on top of everything else! Although to purge your conscience a little sickness wouldn't hurt!

ANNA PETROVNA. Platonov, go, for heaven's sake! Send to town for other doctors . . . A second opinion wouldn't hurt . . . Actually, I'll send for them myself, don't worry about it . . . Comfort Aleksandra Ivanovna!

PLATONOV. Anna Petrovna, there's a baby grand crawling down your bosom! Ridiculous! (*Laughs.*) Ridiculous! Sit down, Nikolay, and play something on it! . . . (*Roars with laughter.*) Ridiculous! I'm sick, Nikolay . . . I'm speaking seriously . . . No kidding . . . Let's go!

Enter IVAN IVANOVICH.

---

88 The Greek philosopher Socrates (470–399 B.C.) remained impassive in the face of his death at the hands of the Athenian state.

SCENE X

The same and IVAN IVANOVICH.

IVAN IVANOVICH (*unkempt, in a dressing gown*). My Sasha! (*Weeps.*)

TRILETSKY. All we needed was you and your tears! Get out of here! Why've you come a-running?

IVAN IVANOVICH. She's dying! She wants the last rites! I'm scared, I'm scared . . . Ugh, I'm so scared! (*Walks over to Platonov.*) Mishenka! I implore you in the name of God and all His saints! Dear, clever, handsome, honorable man! Go and tell her that you love her! Give up all these lousy love affairs! I implore you on bended knee! She's really dying! She's my only daughter . . . my only one! If she dies . . . I'll drop dead before the priest can get there! You tell her that you love her, you admit she's your wife! Calm her down, for Christ's sake! Mishenka! Lying can be a way to salvation . . . God will see that you are righteous, but lie to save your nearest and dearest! Let's go, do me the favor! You'll grant this favor to me, an old man, for Christ's sake! A hundredfold will the Lord reward you! I'm all a-tremble, I'm a-tremble with fear!

PLATONOV. Already had time to hit the bottle, Colonel? (*Laughs.*) We'll cure Sasha and have a drink together! Ah, how I want a drink!

IVAN IVANOVICH. Let's go, most noble . . . most just! You say two words to her, and she'll be saved! Drugs are no use, when it's the mental psychiatrics that're suffering!

TRILETSKY. Come out of here, Father, for just a minute! (*Takes his father by the arm.*) Who told you that she's dying? Where did you get that idea? She's quite out of danger! You wait in that room. We'll go with him to see her right away. You should be ashamed to barge into somebody else's house like this!

IVAN IVANOVICH (*to Anna Petrovna*). You did a bad thing, Diana! God won't forgive you! He's a young man, inexperienced . . .

TRILETSKY (*shoves him into the next room*). Wait in there! (*To Platonov.*) Are you ready to go?

PLATONOV. I'm awfully sick . . . I'm sick, Nikolay!

TRILETSKY. Are you ready to go, I'm asking you, yes or no?

PLATONOV (*gets up*). Not so many words . . . What can I do so my mouth won't be so dry? Let's go . . . I think I came here without a cap . . . (*Sits down.*) Look for my cap!

SOFYA YEGOROVNA. He should have foreseen this. I gave myself to him, without a second thought . . . I knew that I was killing my husband, but I . . . for his sake I stopped at nothing! (*Rises and walks over to Platonov.*) What have you done to me? (*Sobs.*)

TRILETSKY (*clutches his head*). Call an inquest! (*Walks up and down the stage.*)

ANNA PETROVNA. Calm down, *Sophie!* It's not the time . . . He's sick.

SOFYA YEGOROVNA. Is it possible, is it humane to turn a human life into a joke this way? (*Sits next to Platonov.*) After all my whole life is ruined now . . . I'm no longer alive . . . Save me, Platonov! It's not too late! Platonov, it's not too late!

Pause.

ANNA PETROVNA (*weeps*). Sophie . . . What do you want? There'll be a time for this . . . What can he say to you now? Didn't you hear . . . didn't you hear?

SOFYA YEGOROVNA. Platonov . . . I beg of you one more time . . . (*Sobs.*) No?

PLATONOV *moves away from her.*

Never mind . . . That's all right . . . (*Falls to her knees.*) Platonov!

ANNA PETROVNA. This is going too far, *Sophie!* Don't you dare do this! Nobody's worth . . . kneeling to . . . (*Raises her up and seats her.*) You are . . . a woman!

SOFYA YEGOROVNA (*sobs*). Tell him . . . Explain . . .

ANNA PETROVNA. Summon up all your strength of character . . . You have to be . . . firm . . . You're a woman! There . . . that's enough! Go to your room!

Pause.

Go on, go to bed . . . (*To Triletsky.*) Nikolay Ivanovich! What's to be done?

TRILETSKY. You'd better ask dear little Mishenka about that! (*Walks up and down the stage.*)

ANNA PETROVNA. Put her to bed! Sergey! Nikolay Ivanovich! Please help me, at last!

    VOINITSEV rises and walks over to Sofya Yegorovna.

TRILETSKY. Let's take her there. I'll have to give her a sedative.

ANNA PETROVNA. At this moment I could take chloroform myself . . . (*To Triletsky.*) Be a man, Sergey! Don't you lose your head at least! I don't feel any better than you, but even so . . . I'm standing on my two feet . . . Let's go, *Sophie*! What a day this turned out to be . . .

    They lead out SOFYA YEGOROVNA.

Brace up, Serzhel! Let's behave like real people!

VOINITSEV. I'll make an effort, *maman*. I'll take heart . . .

TRILETSKY. Don't fret, Sergey old pal! One way or another we'll pull you through! You're not the first, and you won't be the last!

VOINITSEV. I'll make an effort . . . Yes, I'll make an effort . . .

    They leave.

S C E N E X I

PLATONOV, then GREKOVA.

PLATONOV (*alone*). A cigarette, Nikolay, and some water! (*Looks around.*) They're not here? I'd better leave . . .

    Pause.

I've destroyed, snuffed out weak women, who weren't to blame for anything . . . It wouldn't have been so pathetic, if I'd killed them some other way, driven by monstrous passions, sort of Spanish style, but I killed them just like that . . . any stupid old way, Russian style . . . (*Waves his hand in front of his eyes.*) *Mouches volantes* . . .[89] Little clouds . . . I suppose I'm getting delirious . . . Crushed, squashed, flattened . . . When was the last

---

89 French: flying blister-flies.

time I put up a bold front? (*Hides his face in his hands.*) Shame, stinging shame . . . I'm sick with shame! (*Gets up.*) I was hungry, cold, worn out, dead beat, a phony in everything I did, when I came to this house . . . They gave me a warm corner, clothed me, lavished affection on me . . . Quite a nice payback I've given them! But then I'm sick . . . I feel bad . . . I should kill myself . . . (*Walks over to the desk.*) Take your pick, there's a whole arsenal . . . (*Picks up a revolver.*) Hamlet was afraid to dream . . . I'm afraid to . . . live! What's next if I go on living? Shame would devour me . . . (*Puts the revolver to his temple.*) *Finita la commedia!*[90] One less learnèd pig! Christ, forgive me my sins!

Pause.

Well? Instant death, in other words . . . Hurt, arm, as much as you like now . . .

Pause.

Not up to it!! (*Puts the pistol on the desk.*) I want to live . . . (*Sits on the sofa.*) I want to live . . . (*GREKOVA enters.*) Should have some water . . . Where is Triletsky? (*On seeing Grekova.*) Who's that? Ha, ha, ha . . . (*Laughs.*) My worst enemy . . . Shall we go to court tomorrow?

Pause.

GREKOVA. But, naturally, after that letter we are no longer enemies.

PLATONOV. It doesn't matter. Any water?

GREKOVA. You want water? What's wrong with you?

PLATONOV. I'm sick . . . I'm about to have a temperature . . . I liked it. Clever. But it would have been even cleverer, if you had stayed away from me entirely . . . I wanted to shoot myself . . . (*Laughs.*) Didn't manage it . . . Instinct . . . Your mind goes one way, your nature another . . . Sharp eyes! Are you a clever girl? (*Kisses her hand.*) Your hand's cold . . . Listen . . . You want to help me out?

GREKOVA. Yes, yes, yes . . .

PLATONOV. Take me to your place! I'm sick, I want a drink, I'm in horrible, unbearable pain! I want to sleep, but there's nowhere to lie down . . . Even

---

90 Italian: the comedy is over! Chekhov also puts it in Astrov's mouth in *Uncle Vanya*.

if I've only got a shed, just a corner, water and . . . a bit of quinine. For pity's sake! (*Holds out his hand.*)

GREKOVA. Let's go! I'll be glad to! . . . You can live with me, as long as you like . . . You still don't know what I've done! Let's go!

PLATONOV. *Merci*, clever little girl . . . A cigarette, water, and a bed! Is it raining out?

GREKOVA. It is.

PLATONOV. We'll have to drive through the rain . . . We won't go to court. Peace! (*Looks at her.*) Am I delirious?

GREKOVA. Just a bit. Let's go! My carriage is covered.

PLATONOV. A pretty little thing . . . What are you blushing for? I won't touch. I'll kiss your cold little hand . . . (*Kisses her hand and draws her to him.*)

GREKOVA (*sits on his lap*). No . . . It isn't proper . . . (*Gets up.*) Let's go . . . Your face looks so strange . . . Let go of my hand!

PLATONOV. I'm sick. (*Gets up.*) Let's go . . . On the cheek . . . (*Kisses her on the cheek.*) Without any ulterior motives. I can't . . . Anyway, what nonsense. Let's go, Marya Yefimovna! And, for pity's sake, as fast as you can! I wanted to shoot myself with that . . . that revolver over there . . . On the cheek . . . (*Kisses her on the cheek.*) I'm delirious, but I see your face . . . I love all people! All of 'em! I even love you . . . . People were for me the most precious thing of all . . . I didn't mean to offend anybody, but I offended them all . . . All of 'em . . . (*Kisses her hand.*)

GREKOVA. I understood it all . . . I understand your situation . . . *Sophie* . . . right?

PLATONOV. *Sophie*, Zizi, Mimi, Masha . . . Lots of you . . . I love 'em all . . . When I was at the university, I used to go to Theatre Square[91] and sweet-talk the fallen women . . . Most people go to the theater, and I go to the square . . . I bought out Raisa . . . I collected three hundred smackers from the students and bought out another girl . . . Shall I show you her letters?

GREKOVA. What's come over you?

---

91 A square in central Moscow, bounded by the Bolshoy and Maly theaters.

PLATONOV. You think I've lost my mind? No, it's just how it is . . . Delirious raving . . . Ask Triletsky . . . (*Takes her by the shoulder.*) And everybody loves me . . . Everybody! You insult 'em, every now and then, but they . . . love you . . . Grekova, for instance, I insulted her, shoved her up against a table, and she . . . loves me. You, though, are that Grekova . . . Sorry . . .

GREKOVA. Where does it hurt?

PLATONOV. Platonov hurts. Do you really love me? Love me? Frankly . . . I don't want anything . . . Now just you tell me, do you love me?

GREKOVA. Yes . . . (*Lays her head on his chest. .*) Yes . . .

PLATONOV (*kisses her on the head*). Everybody loves me . . . When I get better, I'll seduce you . . . First the sweet talk, and then I'll seduce you . . .

GREKOVA. It doesn't matter . . . I don't want anything else . . . You're the only . . . man for me. I don't want to know any others! Do what you want with me . . . You . . . you're the only man for me! (*Weeps.*)

PLATONOV. I understand why Oedipus the King gouged out his eyes.[92] I'm so vile and I recognize how vile I am so profoundly! Get away from me! It's not worth it . . . I'm sick. (*Extricates himself.*) I'll leave right now . . . Forgive me, Mariya Yefimovna! I'm losing my mind! Where's Triletsky?

Enter SOFYA YEGOROVNA.

SCENE XII

The same and SOFYA YEGOROVNA.

SOFYA YEGOROVNA walks over to the desk and rummages through it.

GREKOVA (*grabs Platonov by the hand*). Ssh . . .

Pause.

SOFYA YEGOROVNA picks up a revolver, fires at Platonov, and misses.

(*Stands between Platonov and Sofya Yegorovna.*) What are you doing? (*Shouts.*) Get in here! Get in here quickly!

---

92 In Sophocles' tragedy, Oedipus blinds himself when he becomes aware that he has murdered his father and wed his mother.

SOFYA YEGOROVNA. Let me at him . . . (*Runs around Grekova and shoots Platonov in the chest, point-blank.*)

PLATONOV. Hold on, hold on . . . What's going on? (*Falls.*)

ANNA PETROVNA, IVAN IVANOVICH, TRILETSKY, and VOINITSEV run in.

S C E N E   X I I I

The same, ANNA PETROVNA, IVAN IVANOVICH, TRILETSKY, VOINITSEV, then the servants and MARKO.

ANNA PETROVNA (*pulls the revolver away from Sofya Yegorovna and tosses it on the sofa*). Platonov! (*Bends over Platonov.*)

VOINITSEV covers his face and turns to the door.

TRILETSKY (*bends over Platonov and hurriedly unbuttons his frockcoat. Pause.*) Mikhail Vasilich! Can you hear me?

Pause.

ANNA PETROVNA. For heaven's sake, Platonov! *Michel . . . Michel!* Hurry, Triletsky . . .

TRILETSKY (*shouts*). Water!

GREKOVA (*hands him the carafe*). Save him! You must save him! (*Paces up and down the stage.*)

TRILETSKY drinks the water and tosses the carafe aside.

IVAN IVANOVICH (*clutches his head*). Now didn't I say that I'd drop dead? Well I'm dropping dead! Watch me drop dead! (*Falls to his knees.*) Almighty God! I'm dropping dead . . . Watch me drop dead . . .

YAKOV, VASILY, KATYA, and the COOK run in.

MARKO (*enters*). From the Justice of the Peace, sir . . .

Pause.

ANNA PETROVNA. Platonov!

PLATONOV raises himself and runs his eyes over them all.

Platonov . . . It's nothing . . . Have some water!

PLATONOV (*points to Marko*). Give him a three-spot! (*Falls and dies.*)

ANNA PETROVNA. Brace up, Sergey! All this shall pass. Nikolay Ivanovich . . . All this shall pass . . . Brace up . . .

KATYA (*bows at the feet of Anna Petrovna*). It's all my fault! I brought the note! The money tempted me, madam! Forgive me, a miserable creature!

ANNA PETROVNA. Be strong . . . Why lose our heads? He's only a bit . . . He'll get over it . . .

TRILETSKY (*shouts*). He's dead!

ANNA PETROVNA. No, no . . .

GREKOVA sits at the desk, stares at the slip of paper and weeps bitterly.

IVAN IVANOVICH. May he rest in peace . . . Dropped dead . . . Dropped dead . . .

TRILETSKY. Life's a kopek! Good-bye, Mishka! You've lost your kopek! What are you staring at? He shot himself! The party's over! (*Weeps.*) Who am I going to drink with at your wake now? Oh, the fools! They couldn't protect Platonov! (*Rises.*) Father, go tell Sasha that she can die now! (*Swaying, he walks over to Voinitsev.*) What about you? Hey! (*Embraces Voinitsev.*) Platoshka's dead! (*Sobs.*)

VOINITSEV. What's to be done, Nikolay?

TRILETSKY. Bury the dead and repair the living!

ANNA PETROVNA (*slowly rises and goes to Sofya Yegorovna*). Calm down, Sophie! (*Sobs.*) What have you done? But . . . but . . . calm down! (*To Triletsky.*) Don't say anything to Aleksandra Ivanovna, Nikolay Ivanych! I'll tell her myself! (*Goes to Platonov and falls to her knees before him.*) Platonov! My life! I don't believe it! I don't believe it! Are you really dead? (*Takes him by the hand.*) My life!

TRILETSKY. Get to work, Seryozha! Let's help your wife, and then . . .

VOINITSEV. Yes, yes, yes . . . (*Goes to Sofya Yegorovna.*)

IVAN IVANOVICH. The Lord has forsaken us . . . For our sins . . . For my sins . . . Why did you sin, you old clown? Killed God's creatures, got drunk, talked dirty, sat in judgment . . . The Lord lost patience and struck you down.

End of Act Four

VARIANTS TO

Untitled Play

These come from an earlier autograph manuscript of the play.

page 6 / *After*: **SHCHERBUK — VEROCHKA**, 40 ⎤
                                                    ⎬ *his daughters*
                   LIZOCHKA, 25 ⎦

ACT ONE

page 9 / *After*: you never stop eating! — Let's take this morning, for instance . . . I was watching you and was amazed . . . Two glasses of tea, then a huge slice of beef, five eggs, two cups of coffee, about ten slices of toast . . .

page 9 / After: *in corpore sano*[1] — as my teacher used to say, and he spoke the truth, if you don't take into consideration the fact that his healthy ox's head held a very feeble brain . . .

page 9 / *After*: That's right, ma'am . . . — But you've got a Lenten face on today . . . You should smear it with butter . . .
ANNA PETROVNA. That's flat, Nikolay Ivanych, very flat! Nothing funny about it, my charmer!
TRILETSKY. Never mind, ma'am . . .

Pause.

---

1 Latin: in a healthy body.

page 10 / *After*: down shady lanes — I bicker with her.

page 11 / *After*: Got her wits about her . . . — Not like our stupid little girls . . .

page 11 / *After*: I suppose so. — I don't understand it myself. I wish someone would help . . .

page 11 / *After*: A marvelous creature . . . — She's frittering away her whole life in one place, living out her years along with all these antediluvian, bird-brained Katechkas, Lizochkas, Matryoshas, who . . . who can't hold a candle to her! Damn it, it's offensive!

page 11 / *After*: **ANNA PETROVNA.** — No . . . what a tone! This is the first time I've heard you go on like this. This is very nice . . . So your little honey knows how to get a rise out of you!

page 11 / *After*: Whichever way it turns out . . . — We'll get married, Kolichka!

page 11 / *After*: affairs. — And besides you're a close friend . . .

page 12 / *After*: *Pause.* —

ANNA PETROVNA. If, contrary to expectation you don't want to get married, but play around, have a little fun, then . . . don't you dare touch her! You hear me? I'll curse you out, I'll make your life a misery, I'll come to hate you! You should stick to your Katyas, Lizas, and Matyoshas. I'll find it out, if there's anything like that . . .

TRILETSKY. All right . . .

page 12 / *After*: Platonov hangs around here. — and your Platonov is no more than a pig.

page 12 / *After*: still asleep. — Nowadays he sleeps more than he lives.

page 13 / *Before*: We had friends as well — I'm not saying that we were perfect.
Pause.

page 13 / *After*: literary circles — with real people running them

page 13 / *After*: Don't be silly, Nikolya! — And would you go through fire for your enemies, Porfiry Semyonovich?

page 14 / *After*: no laughing matter! — It's annoying, honest to God! You come up with things for an outdoors party, you write a beautiful Demosthenic speech,[2] you contribute to some newsrag, and you make a fuss all over again . . .

page 15 / *After*: concession! — Lucky for us that we know that your concessions make a total hash of your arguments! . . . You're always making concessions . . .

page 15 / *After*: I didn't say . . . —

VOINITSEV (*laughs*). Lucky for us that you don't have the strength, my dear fellow, lucky for us that you are not called to punish and instruct those who don't know how to be indignant and to despise! Lucky for you, as well! One should proceed from words to deeds, but your deeds would be a rude mistake . . . You would wreak havoc, despite the fact that you are the finest, kindest of men . . . First one should verify by deeds, feel, see, and only then speak . . .

page 16 / *After*: in this world! — *Zoy mus man leben oyf der velt, mayn liber porits!*[3]

page 17 / *After*: Nice instrument. — (*Sings.*)

> *Et j'frotte, frotte,*
> *Et allez donc*
> *Vient un monde*
> *A la maison . . .*[4]

page 18 / *After*: to spend with him. —

TRILETSKY. Why don't you like him, Abram Abramych? Why don't you care for the poor fellow?

VENGEROVICH SR. Who told you that I don't care for him? He's a splendid young man . . . But then again, I don't like him because he's so fault-finding, hotheaded . . . But then again you don't like him either, it's not just me!

page 19 / *Before*: You cruel, discourteous creature — What are you on about?

page 21 / *After*: my darling. — Don't be a guitar, you'd die of boredom.

---

2 Demosthenes (383–322 B.C.), Greek orator, was famous for his political speeches against Philip of Macedon.

3 Yiddish: So must one live in this world, my dear sir!

4 French: And I rub, rub, / And look there / Some company's come / To the house.

page 21 / *After: Merci. —*

ANNA PETROVNA. Is your little boy well?

                 They light cigarettes.

SASHA. He is. He's already starting to walk . . .

page 21 / *After:* Got married and didn't say a word! — I would have reminded him, if we weren't such bears!

page 21 / *After:* all the best, all the best! — Later I'll tell you of what!

page 21 / *After:* she's stupid! —

VOINITSEV. Yes'm, Aleksandra Ivanovna! I've settled down, as you see, and become a solid citizen. And all because I got married . . .

SASHA. That's only natural that's the reason.

VOINITSEV. I've had it, I think to myself, with loafing around on my own, I'll do what Aleksandra Ivanovna suggests. I'll go and get married, I think! So I made up my mind . . .

SASHA. And you did the right thing, Sergey Pavlovich! Now you're going to be happy. Now you'll live the right way, you'll learn about the very best aspect of life!

VOINITSEV. I always confided my secrets to you and I'll go on confiding them, Aleksandra Ivanovna! Happy up to my eyebrows! I feel as if I'm in not seventh, but forty-seventh heaven! And I'm so glad that I did something to please you I can't find the words! I didn't always please you in the past, but now I see that I've pleased you.

PLATONOV. Well, there's no better way to please her than to get married. She's crazy about weddings!

SASHA. I don't love weddings, I love order. The way I see it, when the time comes to get married, you get married. Loafing around with nothing to do is sinful and far from clever. You've pleased me a lot, Sergey Pavlovich! Thank you!

page 22 / *After:* three whole years! Eh? — To graduate from the university and kill time! I don't understand you, gentlemen! I definitely do not understand you! What are you waiting for?

VOINITSEV. I don't have to work at a prep school! I'm not starving to death, I don't feel any special calling for the teaching profession, I'm not going to die any time soon . . . What's the rush? (*Laughs.*) Let's not talk about it.

ANNA PETROVNA. Anyone who doesn't mind loafing for three years, of course, is going to have no trouble loafing for ten or even twenty . . . But let's change the subject.

page 23 / *Replace*: I do not like the fact . . . Russian scoundrel!

with: It's painful to remember, dear Porfiry Semyonych! His illness, death,
creditors, the sale of the estate . . . and to all this add in our enmity . . . It's
horrible! . . . His death was bestial, inhuman . . . The man died as only a
man could die who was a lecher to the marrow of his bones, rich in his lifetime, a beggar at his death, a man with a defective mind and an unbearable temper . . . I had the misfortune to be present at his demise: he lost his
temper, cursed and swore, wept, roared with laughter . . . He contorted his
face, he balled his fists and looked around for his flunkies' ugly mugs . . .
From his eyes flowed the champagne, once drunk by him and his parasites
on the money of those who wore rags and ate mush . . . I made an effort to
get him to make a confession . . . I was supposed to begin my talk in a pious
tone, I remember . . . I reminded him of those he had flogged, insulted,
raped, I reminded him of the Sebastopol campaign,[5] when he, along with
other patriots, shamelessly robbed his nation . . . And I reminded him of
something else . . . And he stared me in such amazement! He was surprised, burst out laughing . . . What crap, and I quote, are you spouting! To
be a hard-bitten scoundrel and at the same time not to want to admit it—
that's the terrible characteristic of the Russian scoundrel!

page 23 / *After*: excuses for the dead . . . — I'm sitting at his bedside . . . It's
stuffy, dark all around . . . All around poverty after wealth, dirty, untidy,
everything flung about over . . . Playing cards scattered underfoot, whisky
bottles rolling around . . . A drunken orderly snoring in the hall . . . He's
making faces . . . A depression chokes me, a horrible depression, never in
my life will I forget that depression! It all starts to make me sick, turns my
hair gray . . . Here they are on my temples, those gray hairs . . . Remarkable
those gray hairs! I often see them on my contemporaries! . . . The ideas that
wandered through my mind! If I had known then how to write down those
thoughts and could read them to you now, you would say that life is disgusting to very last detail. And he turned gray too after he died . . . He turned
gray from viciousness . . . "We're beggars now, Mishka," he says, "we're
dying! . . . And where are my friends now, what's become of them? Where
are they? Where now are those highnesses, excellencies, honors, whose presence once made the glasses tremble, the tables turn pale and the flies run for
cover? Where? The quality don't want beggars, not them, don't want dying
men, but rich and depraved idiots!" So he says, and gnashes his teeth . . .

5　See *Untitled Play*, note 42.

page 24 / *After*: Never been sick a day in my life . . . — My heart once ached on account of the female sex, but that ailment doesn't need cough drops and drugs . . .

page 24 / *After*: a wonderful double-barrel! — Damned if there's a better one!

page 26 / *After*: Spare us, please. —
TRILETSKY. And your wife's got so plump! (*Looks at Sasha through his fist.*) Short and stout . . . In a year's time she'll be round as a ball.
SASHA. When are you going to stop talking nonsense!
TRILETSKY. Never . . . You're getting fat, sister! My congratulations! (*To Platonov.*) You must be feeding her well. Which means you're a honest man! Is your Kolka all right? (*Gets up and sits next to Ivan Ivanovich.*)
SASHA. He is.
       Enter PETRIN and VENGEROVICH SR.

page 26 / *Before*: If you have tears, — It's a long time since I've seen him. I suppose he's become quite big for a little boy.

page 28 / *After*: In the first place . . . — I have beheld the groceries, and therefore I can inform you . . .

page 29 / *After*: have time to make acquaintances? — I won't tell her anything, but I don't think she knows yet that we're are being visited by a certain Platonov . . . If she does, she will probably recognize you.

page 30 / *After*: I do find it strange! —
PLATONOV. I don't see anything strange about it. It would have been strange, if it were someone besides Abram Abramych who crawls into other people's purses and other people's envelopes . . . He's a specialist at that sort of thing.
       SASHA tugs Platonov by the sleeve.
GLAGOLYEV SR. I'm not saying that . . . But . . . don't get involved, Mikhail Vasilich!
VENGEROVICH SR. I may be a swindler, but I tend to take offense when someone qualifies me by the name swindler . . . Therefore I ask . . .
PLATONOV. Don't ask, please! I understand you . . .
VENGEROVICH SR. Excellent, then. Since we understand one another, we will not stoop to behaving foolishly. Let us not insult one another for no rhyme or reason . . .

page 30 / *After*: at home? — From this day forth I shall believe you!

GLAGOLYEV SR. Good afternoon, Mariya Yefimovna!

GREKOVA. You didn't believe me before?

TRILETSKY. How can I put it? Sometimes I believed you, sometimes I didn't. I don't usually believe women much.

GLAGOLYEV SR. (*laughs*). Nikolay Ivanovich can't help making compliments! Good afternoon, Mariya Yefimovna!

page 31 / *After*: Already jumping to conclusions! — Oh you women!

page 34 / *After*: She's coming! —

VENGEROVICH JR. (*entering*). Don't forget that Auerbach is a Jew, Heine is a Jew . . .

SOFYA YEGOROVNA. That doesn't mean much to the masses . . . It may have a certain meaning for me, but hardly for the masses . . . If someone other than me is to believe you, you need something more persuasive . . .

page 35 / *After the stage direction: Laughter.* —

GLAGOLYEV SR. Or a quiet angel flew by.

PLATONOV. A quiet angel has no business here.

page 37 / *After*: to answer your question . . . —

TRILETSKY (*to Bugrov*). A wonderful fellow, that Platonov! Look at him: a marquis, the most authentic marquis, and a schoolteacher, just everything. Believe then in *suum cuique!*[6]

GLAGOLYEV SR. That remark was made in a tone suggesting there is something disgraceful, humiliating about teaching . . . If our most kind Mikhail Vasilich made a blunder, it is only that, in starting out life and picking a career, he lost sight of the fact that in society one must present a handsome exterior, but this blunder from Mikhail Vasilich's point of view is, so far as I know, not a blunder.

PLATONOV. I didn't pick out my career and didn't make a blunder. I never picked out anything and never made anything.

page 37 / *After*: stand in the way all on their own . . . — However, don't you scowl so hard, Sofya Yegorovna! I'm not a complete waste of time. I have an excellent hobby. My hobby consists in not spoiling my baby boy, playing the guitar and constantly cursing the moment when I came up with

6 Latin: in full, *Suum cuique pulcrum,* Everyone thinks his own is most beautiful.

the insane, homicidal idea of leaving the university, leaving what I now so love . . .

page 38 / *After*: ladies' polonaise. — I made conquests, I turned men into cuckolds, but now I'm retired.

page 39 / *After*: no serial number!" — What do you still have to drag your loins in here for?

page 40 / *After*: I suppose . . . — (*To Sofya Yegorovna*.) There, as you see . . . A fascinating tribe!

page 40 / *After*: you start to be wary of young people . . . —

SHCHERBUK (*out the window*). They're here? They're here to hoist their own father on a pike? To show off their disobedience? In green dresses, the idiots, they've tarted themselves up! Look, Christian folk! Lizards! (*Whistles*.) Green as grass! Shshsh . . .

VEROCHKA (*offstage*). Papa dear, you can talk dirty at home . . .

ANNA PETROVNA. Who's that? Your daughters, Pavel Petrovich? Why don't they come in? (*Out the window*.) Good afternoon! Come in, we'll say our hellos inside!

VEROCHKA (*offstage*). Is the doctor here, Your Excellency?

ANNA PETROVNA. The doctor won't pick on you. Come inside!

VEROCHKA (*offstage*). And is Mister Platonov there?

ANNA PETROVNA. I promise you they won't pick on you.

Laughter.

SHCHERBUK. They're here! They might as well have brought their mother too!

SCENE XV
The same, VEROCHKA, and LIZOCHKA.
Enter, make curtsies and sit at the piano.

TRILETSKY. Ah, ah! (*Hides his face behind a handkerchief*.) Ah! Whom do I see?

Laughter.

For shame! For shame! I'm so embarrassed! There are unmarried women here!

SHCHERBUK sprawls in an armchair and gazes disdainfully at
his daughters.

VEROCHKA. Best wishes on your lawful marriage, your excellency!

ANNA PETROVNA. Not me, but Sergey Pavlovich . . .

VOINITSEV. Thank you very, very much! How are you?

VEROCHKA. *Merci* . . . Your Excellency, I . . . Mama dear sends you her regards . . .

ANNA PETROVNA. *Merci* . . . (*To Triletsky.*) Stop it!

SHCHERBUK. My eyes are dazzled! What beauties! They came to show off their manners . . . Parlay voo fransay? Vui! Non!

PLATONOV. Why are you in hiding, Nikolay?

TRILETSKY. Lizaveta Pavlovna is here . . . Ah! I'm so embarrassed . . .

LIZOCHKA. Mama dear sent you her regards, Your Excellency.

ANNA PETROVNA. Thank you. (*To Triletsky.*) Stop it!

SHCHERBUK (*winks at Triletsky*). Aren't they the pretty things! They should obey their father!

ANNA PETROVNA. Pay no attention, Vera Pavlovna, or you, Yelizaveta Pavlovna, to that laughter. The doctor is always laughing and mostly for no good reason. Mister Platonov is the same.

PLATONOV. I have no idea of laughing.

ANNA PETROVNA. Pay no attention . . . Remember the fable: "Once friends went for a walk one night . . ."? Remember?

VEROCHKA. I don't remember, Your Excellency.

Huge laugh.

SHCHERBUK (*applauds*). A regular philistine! They do not understand decorum and propriety! That's what comes of not showing respect to your father, you slags!

VEROCHKA. Papa dear, you can talk dirty at home . . .

SHCHERBUK (*turns his back on her*). There are no paternal feelings in my breast! I had a few but they're gone! Begone!

TRILETSKY (*hugs himself in glee*). Oof! This is just to my taste! (*Embraces Shcherbuk.*) Great Beelzebub Bucephalovich! Great man!

page 41 / *After*: my father's friends. —

SHCHERBUK. Little beauties, little cuties . . . They're here! Their mother doesn't keep them at home!

ANNA PETROVNA. Pavel Petrovich! (*Shakes her head.*)

page 42 / *After*: Don't be angry, please! — What value can I put on your good words, your noble appearance, your kindly smiles, endearments, how can I put any faith in them, if I know that you, his friends, were incapable and, perhaps, even too lazy to protect my father from thousands of follies, and if I know that you haven't got the strength to grab me by the scruff of my neck and pull me out of the quicksand?

page 43 / *After*: You don't? . . . — It's not for you to talk about charity . . . Take a look: everyone's surprised and affected. Around here it's usually boldness or stupidity that raises eyebrows.

page 43 /   S C E N E   X V I
                    The same, VASILY, and OSIP.

VASILY (*runs in*). Sergey Pavlych! Mistress!

OSIP (*chases Vasily and slams the door*). Slap my face because I'm a menace to society! (*Stops in bewilderment.*)

VASILY. He's tortured me to death . . . He pummeled my whole back with his fists . . . There's no escape . . .

OSIP. He flew in here! . . . They've already arrived . . . (*Laughs.*) Honest to God, it's an accident. I was chasing him, and wound up in here . . . (*Starts to withdraw.*) An accident . . .

ANNA PETROVNA. What new stupidity is this?

PLATONOV. Ah . . . Whom do I see!? The devil's bosom buddy! Hold on, hold on! (*Grasps Osip by the shoulder.*) Hold on, my dear fellow.

ANNA PETROVNA (*to Vasily*). Put Yakov in your place and retire to the kitchen to wipe your feet! (*To Platonov.*) Let him go, Mikhail Vasilich! (*To Osip.*) Greetings, Osip, and clear out!

VASILY. Massacred my whole back . . . Been feeding his face since first thing in the morning . . . Damned fellow can't get enough to eat!

                    Laughter.

ANNA PETROVNA. You'll tell us later! Get out!

VASILY. Yes, ma'am. (*Exits.*)

page 44 / *After*: give you something to eat . . . — You ought get a shave as well, your physiugly face looks like a cactus . . . You ask Yakov for a shave . . .

page 48 / *After*: And who gave you the right? — (*Whispers in Verochka's ear.*) *VEROCHKA sits at the piano and loudly plays a waltz.*

page 48 / *After*: Honor's gone down the drain! — Where is it? It's got old, worn out, turned into a hollow sound used to describe something obsolete . . .

page 49 / *After*: All of a sudden . . . —

VEROCHKA. Why are you telling this, Papa dear?

SHCHERBUK. Begone, Medusa![7]

---

7 In Greek mythology, a Gorgon whose hideous face and glaring eyes could turn men to stone.

page 49 / *After*: not her love . . . — For amours he goes (*points at Lizochka*) to her! He's turned her into a she-idiot. She used to be a submissive daughter, but he's spoiled her . . .

page 50 / *After*: There's a city for you! — A house twenty stories high!

page 51 / *After*: hopeless fools . . . — Stop being surprised! Be surprised by the staying power of your clever, luminous family.

page 51 / *After*: (*Exits with Sofya Yegorovna.*) —
VEROCHKA *and* LIZOCHKA *exit into the garden.*

page 53 / *After*: You crank! — Go and yawn!

page 53 / *After*: What business is it of yours, you shyster? — What's it got to do with you as a matter of fact! Don't you think I can take myself and get married? Why don't you mind your own business?

page 55 / *After*: A big-hearted youngster! — Now I shall be careful!

page 56 / *After*: (*Looks through the doorway to the dining room.*) — They're eating as if there's no tomorrow! Triletsky is gulping down sardines like a shark . . . Voinitsev isn't eating, but stares wide-eyed at his wife. Lucky dog! He loves her the way Adam loved his Eve! He'd be ready to eat candle-wax if it would make her happy . . . He's having a wonderful time! Soon it will pass and never come again.

page 56 / *After*: kiss that hair! — *stage direction: Pause.*

page 56 / *After*: that head of hair brings back to me . . . — It's past, it's gone, it's sunk as if drowned, as if it had never been! Ech . . . human happiness! Just enough to smear on your lips . . . There, pal, get a whiff of it just once, and you'll remember all your life long what it smells like!

page 56 / *After*: a very good thing — a glorious, lawful, even if tormenting, thing, even if it is sometimes like envy . . .

page 57 / *Replace*: **PLATONOV** (*looks through the doorway to the dining room*).
with: **PLATONOV**. Only there's one annoying thing . . . Still, why be so skeptical? What I wanted to say about rapid transit . . . Oh the hell with it! Enjoy yourselves! There's no point in getting ahead of ourselves . . . We can and should live happily with it . . . (*Looks through the dining-room door.*) Not an ordinary woman . . . Not like my Sashka . . .
Pause.

page 57 / *After*: let's have a drink! —

VOINITSEV (*nods at Triletsky*). Have you heard? "If people are there, he'll pull up a chair!" He's been courting Grekova! Have you noticed?

TRILETSKY. Save it for later. Say, are we going to get drunk today or not?

page 57 / *After*: and your sermons make me sick to my stomach! — Leave me alone, do me a favor!

page 58 / *After*: All day long, all day long . . . — Honestly, I'm soon going to prescribe you to my patients for chronic diseases, as sweat-producing and sleep-inducing.

page 58 / *After*: All day long . . . —

PLATONOV. Shut up!

page 59 / *After*: grief on account of my friendship — the way that my former friend but present enemy once came to grief, master of pharmacy Frantz Zakharovich Shriftbaum!

ACT TWO

T A B L E A U   O N E

page 60 / *After*: only you don't want to! — You've got such a clever mind, such as you never had before!

page 61 / *After*: General's lady's mines? — You're a con man, a con man!

page 63 / *Replace*: I didn't look after her, old Fool Ivanych Merry-maker!
with: The Lord took her away! Forgive me. Forgive me, Sasha! I didn't look after your mother . . . I didn't look after her, old Fool Ivanych Merry-maker! I hastened her death!

page 63 / *After*: I understand! — From this minute on not a drop! You give the orders, and the ghost of your mother is on your side . . .

page 63 / *After*: All right, sir . . . — But, young man, aren't you the son of Colonel Triletsky?

TRILETSKY. So it seems, I am, sir!

IVAN IVANOVICH. In that case I'll take it! (*Roars with laughter.*)

page 63 / *After*: rich and famous! — During the war I had thousands, hundreds of thousands in my hands, and didn't take the slightest kopek from the Russian Empire . . . I was content with nothing but my pay . . .

page 64 / *After*: I got the Vladimir third class . . . — Not second, second would have a star on it . . . Third . . . Here it is . . . Around my neck . . . Can you see it, Sasha? There it is . . . This is the Anna, this is the Stanislav, this is the Anna third class with crossed swords . . . This is for the Rumanian campaign . . . And here for no particular reason is the Persian Lion and Sun . . . Medals . . . One for life-saving . . . A silver one . . . In '63, I pulled the wife of the regimental doctor out of the water by her hair . . . The military George . . . I got another one for Sebastopol, on the very day you were born, Nikolay . . . During the war I was sent to supreme command three times . . . — "Been in the service long, Triletsky?" — "Thirty-one years, your imperial highness!" — "Stand easy. Go with God! My regards!" God will provide, my children . . . He's already provided for my son-in-law . . . Over and done with! The grave, requiem mass . . . Your old man is falling apart, has fallen apart . . .

page 65 / *After*: when I was young — I played Pechorin and Bazarov

page 65 / *After*: L-e-eft face! — Forward ma . . . arch!

page 66 / *After*: All right, all right . . . — Hello and good-bye!

page 66 / *After*: I'm feeling generous, damn it all! — Here's another little ruble for the two of you, because the two of you put together aren't worth the two-hundredth part of this little ruble!

page 67 / *After*: he's an old man . . . — What for? Still on about her?

page 67 / *After*: some little dimwit . . . — What's she need a husband for? Camouflage? A Potiphar[8] who's never around? Never fear, she's not marrying him for love, if she does marry him. Tempted by his riches.

page 68 / *After*: What are you thinking about? — You don't want to understand the wretched situation I'm in! I'm suffering, *Sophie*! Your frigid *yes* and *no* are an utter calamity for me! You never laugh, you never smile, you

---

8 In the Old Testament, the wife of Potiphar, the Pharaoh's butler, tried to seduce his slave Joseph and, when he resisted, accused him of rape. See *Genesis* 39.

never say a word, with something constantly on your mind . . . This thing you're thinking about, which gives me no peace, no place, tears my soul to pieces . . .

page 68 / *After*: my moods — but forgive me for the *yes* and *no*.

page 70 / *Before*: There's no reason — I am not avoiding people, Mikhail Vasilich!

page 70 / *After*: have a word with you — when you're alone, when you have only a perceptibly small, not great, desire to get away from me

page 70 / *After*: repulsive? — After all, listen, to feel oneself a pariah, whom people run away from, is not very pleasant, it's insulting, depressing!

page 71 / *After*: (*Walks up to her*). — Can you think that if I wanted to undermine the welfare of your Sergey Pavlovich, to make off with you now in my arms, I would start by using a weapon that for me is holier than any on earth? No, respected Sofya Yegorovna, I'm not strewing my pearls for the right to possess you, and if you become necessary to me, I shall take you for what you're worth!

page 71 / *After*: to your Sergey Pavlovich! — Hold on, be quiet! Let me finish! You've seen my desire to let you know that I didn't complete my acquisition at that time, that I have some claims . . . You saw and . . . got scared? Your wretched family was against it! You have no right to despise me!

page 72 / *After*: eight rubles . . . — And played cards, lost two bottles of Lafitte . . .

page 74 / *After*: Worse than anyone on earth. — You looking for good people, Abram Abramych?

page 80 / *Before*: I could have smitten with a great love — There are people, my boy, who don't smoke cigarettes, don't talk nonsense to womenfolk, don't put on boots without previously checking to see if there are boot trees in them . . . Boot trees or rules, they're everything for them . . . And they'll set off for the next world according to some legal statute . . . They're arid, pedantic, constantly fussing over themselves and their rules.

page 80 / *After*: to our tongues! —
PLATONOV. Stupid . . . You spout the most hopeless poppycock . . . To talk that way you don't have to have attended medical school for five years.

TRILETSKY. "Medical schools," my grandfather Brigadier Triletsky wrote to his posterity, "are nothing but self-indulgence and perplexity for the upper classes. Among the ancient Hellenes and Romans of the Empire physicians were slaves, and astrologers superstitious swindlers, and a slavish nature has absolutely nothing to do with your blue blood! For your noble blue blood is such that however powerfully you strive to be a slave, you never will be, for a lord cannot be a boor, and a boor cannot be a lord." A clever brain, you must admit, my grandfather!

PLATONOV. But don't you cut off legs? Don't you provide ointments for rashes?

TRILETSKY. The other day . . .

page 81 / *Replace*: Couldn't find us . . . she does care . . .

with: However, I won't grieve . . . My mind is fully made up on that point . . . No slavish hope will creep in . . . I'm very calm . . . I'm not Sofya Yegorovna!

page 81 / *Before*: She's miffed — She has hopes . . .

page 81 / *After*: She imagines . . . Hm . . . — I don't love her, being a sinful man. I find it depressing. From her head to her heels a bookworm, crammed with those lofty matters, concepts, high ideals, sublime, damn it, truth, faith, lack of faith, spontaneous impulses . . .

page 81 / *After*: Let's go get a drink! — That doesn't require honor or knowledge or duty or anything sublime, but no one has a right to forbid it either. Am I right? Let's go, pal!

page 81 / *After*: On his money merrily we roll along . . . — These easygoing Voinitsevs surprise me not a little! Fireworks cost twenty-five smackers, champagne a hundred smackers, wine, vodka also go for a hundred . . . That's three hundred rubles, all told, for this pernicious party. Three hundred rubles! And they probably borrowed five hundred from Vengerovich . . . Three hundred they've squandered today, and with the other two hundred Sergey will order a bicycle or buy his wife a little watch . . .

TRILETSKY. They're organizing an amateur theatrical.

PLATONOV. Do tell! The scenery will cost about a hundred and fifty smackers . . . And up to their eyebrows in debt . . . Starting with the General's lady's chess games with Vengerovich! As God is my judge! And there's some kind of underhanded deal being cooked up about the estate . . . It's annoying and pathetic, especially since you consider them to be intelligent people!

page 82 / *After*: (*Roars with laughter*). — Pockmarks and chalk instead of powder . . .

page 83 / *After*: stench — and raggedy leggings instead of a scarf

page 83 / *After*: get married! — Well I shall thwart his eagerness to get married!

page 83 / *After*: You're the idiot, Count! — It's incredibly depressing to talk to you!

page 87 / *After*: Insufferable man! — After all he knows that I love him, that *he* loves me, he can't breathe without me . . . Oh, no, you don't! He has to play his little games, he has to put on his acts, has to flirt with his tongue! Plays with my respect like a musician on a violin! He doesn't like to look at things simply, but has to have a preface to them . . . Oh, no, you don't! Don't try it on me!

page 89 / *After*: rather peculiar, Porfiry Semyonych! — You need my spiritual goodness, as you write in your letter, but what do you know about my spiritual goodness?

page 89 / *Before*: But actually I did . . . If only you would act for yourself . . .

page 92 / *After*: That's frank — Oh, you idiot, you idiot!

page 92 / *After*: (*Sits down.*) — It's become hideously obscured, my golden age is gone forever! I turned it into filthy nonsense . . . I buried it all in the grave, except this body . . .

page 93 / *Before*: How am I to rise above — My talents must be deeply hidden, they're stuck in the quicksand . . . Either I haven't unearthed them over the course of a lifetime or I'm stuck in it myself . . .
                              Pause.

page 93 / *After*: I'm not feeling sorry for myself! — I'm reaching the point when I must come to the definite conclusion that I am an irremediably ruined man!

page 93 / *After*: to lie? — Who gave you the right to prattle all day long on my behalf about labor, suffering, freedom, if you do nothing for them and intend to do nothing?

T A B L E A U　T W O

page 100 / *After*: prayed God for death, sinner that I am . . . — But, Osip, imagine my joy, when one day he walks over to me and says all of a sudden: "Little girl, would you like to be my wife?" Imagine my joy . . . In my joy I quite lost all sense of shame and threw my arms around his neck . . .

page 107 / *After*: despicable, absurd! — Why did I kiss her down by the river? There's got to be a reason I didn't pass up that pleasure. (*Sits down.*) Kiss her, you dunce: it's a pretty face! She even offered her cheek! Aaah . . .
　　　　　　　　　　　　　　Pause.
I've got to get away from here . . . It's over!

page 107 / *After*: perfectly revolting . . . — The General's lady seemed like a peasant wench, Sofya a stupid old maid, I . . . What about Grekova?

page 107 / *After*: When? — They start to laugh through bloody tears . . .

page 107 / *After*: self-scrutiny! — When I'm drunk, I soar aloft and build towers of Babylon!

page 108 / *After*: monarch of all you survey! — Nature, Thou art mine! Thou art for me!

page 109 / *Before*: Just look at that sky! — On such a night, however, as this, it's all right to be a bit of a poet . . .

page 109 / *After*: Just look at that sky! Yes . . . — Happy the man who can breathe this air! Yes . . . In my bosom there is such warmth, such expansiveness . . . Isn't this a poetic feeling, after all?

page 109 / *After*: ashamed of being young! — who blushes at emotions, which old age remembers with pleasure! Enough of setting up obstacles to what now constitutes your true strength! Do not alienate your youth! Do not violate its nature! You will be accursed! Woe to the man who was not and will not be young!

page 110 / *After*: Am I your inferior or what? — At least once in my life I should give free rein to my flesh . . . Sometimes rejuvenation works in conjunction with stupidity . . .

page 111 / *Before*: Leave me out of it! — . . . And when, my dear sir, will you and your dear papa stop opening taverns? And when will I stop being the most fervent customer at your taverns? When will the Vengeroviches dis-appear and stop eating the hard-earned bread of the Platonovs? When? Let's shut up, my dear fellow . . . Or here's what . . .

page 111 / Replace: (Goes far upstage and comes back again.)
with: (Goes far upstage.)

PLATONOV. Poor fellow! So much contradiction, so much unnecessary crap, insufferably old-fashioned pedantry in this poor little body! Ech! They should give me back my youth again! I could show him . . . And sits and moans! There's nothing to be done with him! He has to tell the world, that personal happiness is egoism! That's the only thing he's got to do! What inexcusable impoverishment! His tongue and another man's words . . . No more! No more of other people's words and other people's brains!

VENGEROVICH JR. walks back.

page 112 / After: Ugh! — Youth, youth! . . . On one hand, a healthy body, a lively brain, total honesty, boldness, love of freedom, light and greatness, and, on the other, contempt for hard work, desperate phrase-making, foul language, licentiousness, boasting . . . On one hand, Shakespeare and Goethe, and on the other money, career, and whoring! What about arts and sciences? (Laughs.) Poor orphans! Neither called nor chosen! It's high time to file them in the archives or lock them up in a home for illegitimate children . . . (Roars with laughter.) A hundred million people with heads, brains and — a handful of scholars, some fifty artists and not a single writer! That's an awful lot! Neither called nor chosen! Have fun, kind people! Arts and sciences is hard work, it's the triumph of ideas over muscles, it's an evangelical life . . . and what is life to us? Without living we still know how to die!

Pause.

It's horrible!

page 113 / Replace: PLATONOV (leaps up).
with: PLATONOV. What do you want from me? (Leaps up.) What do you want from me?

page 113 / After: I rode over, my dear! — (Laughs out loud.)

page 114 / Before: But are you really mine? — Do I really know what makes your eyes shine so brightly? You want happiness, you expect the triumph of youth, passions, ardor . . . Courageous and honorable words of love . . .

page 116 / *Replace*: No fooling.

with: Would you like me to introduce you to the editor of our local paper? I'm
  acquainted with him . . . No fooling . . . Oh you . . . Oh you, my darling
  big bass drum! Oh you . . .

page 117 / *Replace*: carpenters
with: janitors

page 118 / *After*: you ingrate! —

PLATONOV (*walks up to him*). Get out of here!

PETRIN. Huh?

PLATONOV. Clear out of here!

PETRIN. Why get angry? No need to get angry, sweetheart! Where's the road?
  There it is, the road! (*Shouts.*) Where's the road? There's the roadoden-
  dron! Good-bye, Mister Platonov! Did you hear, sweetheart, the way I
  cursed her out?

PLATONOV. I heard.

PETRIN. Don't you dare . . . tell her! I was joshing. Pava and I . . .

PLATONOV. All right . . . Go away! By the way, Gerasim Kuzmich . . . If I
  ever see you at the Voinitsevs' again, if I hear just one word about that sixteen thousand, you old crook, then . . . I'll throw you out the window!

PETRIN. I understand, young man! Take my arm, Pavochka! You're the only
  friend I have left . . .

> *They start to go.*

You'll throw me out, your arms are too short! I'll call in the I.O.U.s, and a
  certain somebody will be out of a school job! I'll get you fired! We don't
  need your ideas! We don't need all these ideas and hocus-pocus! We need
  teachers, not Spinozas and Martin Zadeks![9] I'll denounce you and get you
  fired! Honest to God, I'll get you fired! We know all about his ideas, Pavochka! I'll drag him through the mud! I'll write a letter to the district police
  chief right away . . .

PLATONOV. And what will you scribble?

PETRIN (*shouts*). That'll do, sir! That'll do! We understand!

> *They start to go.*

PLATONOV. That'll do, but remember that you were educated at Moscow
  University, that by the stupidest of fates you call yourself a cultured Rus-

---

9 A comic juxtaposition of the seventeenth-century Dutch philosopher and a contemporary Russian news commentator.

sian! Don't be crass, because your crassness is sullying not only you but the reputation of cultured Russians!

PETRIN. All right! Sing, nightingale!

PLATONOV. Leave slander and denunciations to those who don't value that wretched reputation! I won't say anything else! Sober up and mark my words!

page 119 / *Replace*: but if you had any idea . . . an irreparable mistake . . .

with: It's not me going to your place, but my weak body . . . I would have thrown you over, if it hadn't been for this, this ill-behaved body!

ANNA PETROVNA. How loathsome! . . . (*Strikes Platonov with her riding-crop.*) Talk, talk, but mind what you're saying! (*Walks away from Platonov.*) You want to go, go, you don't want to — the hell with it! I'm not about to beg you! That's going too far!

PLATONOV. But . . . It's too late to be insulted! (*Walks behind her and takes her by the arm.*)

                    ANNA PETROVNA *tears away her arm.*

PLATONOV. It doesn't matter, after all . . . I'll go . . . Now you've unleashed the devil in me . . . Are you turning away? It's too late to be insulted! We're now both stuck in the same situation and no matter how much we offend one another's dignity, we cannot separate . . . We're weak! Don't be insulted, woman! (*Embraces her.*) I don't mean to insult you! I wanted to express myself more graphically . . . I'd kill myself rather than insult you . . . You're everything to me! Even when you're sinning I think you're great!

page 121 / *Replace*: Good-bye

with: Zheh voo saloo![10]

page 124 / *Replace*: What am I thinking!

with: Where is their strength, their reason? What a one I am! My soul weeps, but some kind of cursed power, some kind of demon holds me back, shoves with all his might . . .

page 124 / *After*: I will make a note of it! — Filth . . . filth! I'll make a note and show it to anyone I want to corrupt!

page 128 / *After*: (*Runs out.*)

ECHO. You bastard . . . turd . . . turd . . .

---

10 Bad pronunciation of the French, *Je vous salue!*, So long!

ACT THREE

page 132 / *After*: for your sacrifices? — Ugh, Sofya, Sofya . . . those sacrifices of yours . . . dreadful! . . . your ruin!

page 134 / *After*: of this whole tiresome mess! — I'm a lunatic! I don't know what I'm to say and to do!

page 136 / *After the stage direction*: Pause. — And we will forget him, and he will forget us . . . Time will do its work . . .

page 136 / *After*: and the General's lady . . . — Today I am still yours, but tomorrow . . . What will things be like tomorrow?

page 136 / *After*: (*Lies down on the sofa.*) — Tomorrow I'll be a new man . . . Interesting!

page 136 / *After*: ignoramus! — What power keeps you at home?

page 137 / *Replace*: Sergey and Sofya are behaving
with: Sergey and Sofya have both suddenly come down with a fit of bickering and are behaving

page 137 / *After*: You are the little dunderhead. — You're a very great fool, Mishenka!

page 137 / *After the stage direction*: Pause. — A general's lady to end all general's ladies!

page 138 / *After*: like God's image, sir . . . — A Christian, I've served God and Tsar faithful and true for twenty-five years, sir . . .
Pause
I swore an oath faithful and true on the Holy Bible . . .

page 140 / *After*: like a holy relic. — You'll impose a fine. It's about time I was taught a good lesson. Don't forgive me, don't forgive me for any reason, even though I humbly beg your forgiveness . . .

page 141 / *After*: a woman's punished me . . . — It's about time, they've been pampering me for far too long . . .

page 141 / *Before*: I was free — Another day or so left, I'd be going to trial . . . Triletsky would make a speech to the point. Grekova would cry her eyes out at the trial . . . After the trial peace and drunkenness, of course . . . Ech! . . .

page 141 / *After*: poor Voinitsevs! — Your friend and eccentric Platonov cost you dear . . . When will *you* sic the law on me? . . .

page 142 / *After*: Everything . . . — Especially about the things you'll learn about in the not too distant future and which . . . I would ask you not to mention, if you know them already . . .

page 146 / *After*: and the scoundrel Platonov — don't look for him when he disappears, don't ask about him

page 146 / *After*: fade into the background . . . — Until the time when the name Platonov will be only a hollow sound for you, until he is obscured in your memory by a dense fog, until the time when we will never meet again!

page 148 / *After*: I'm a drunkard, Platonov . . . — When my General was alive, I drank an awful lot . . . Drank, drank, drank . . . And I shall go on drinking!

page 149 / *After*: and I won't see you! — I'm a goner!

page 149 / *After*: A new life . . . Get angry, don't get angry, but . . .

page 156 / *After*: I'll make a man of him! — I shall show him the way, I shall teach him how to redeem my sinful life and the life of my fathers! Day and night I shall sanctify him . . .

page 156 / *After*: your delight! — Nikolay Mikhailov Platonov will go far!

page 156 / *After*: You're laughing . . . — I've tickled your maternal vanity . . .

page 158 / *After*: I'm really sorry! — I'll stay with you . . .

page 159 / *After*: My God! — (*Bites the pillow.*)

page 159 / *Replace*: (*Lies on the sofa.*)
with: (*Looks out the window.*)

page 159 / *Replace*: VOINITSEV *enters and stops in the doorway.* . . . can't manage to beat you down!
with: She's getting in the cart.

Pause.

After all this is my wife, my family, warmth . . . Where is she going? What will become of it? Incredible! (*Shouts.*) Help her get in! What are you looking at? (*Quietly.*) She's covered her face with a kerchief and is looking over here out of the corner of her eye . . . She's driven off . . . How will it all end, I should like to know? What more is to come? It's dreadful! (*Shouts.*) He's here!?

Pause.

He's here . . . Where's he going? Here. No, no, not here . . . Why is he coming to me? (*Quickly lies down.*) He's taking a walk . . . This is his usual time for taking a walk . . . Are you trembling? Aaaah . . . (*Lends an ear.*) Anyway, I'd better get ready . . . I'll face him boldly and ask no quarter . . . I'll let him call me names, cover me with abuse . . . Footsteps? His? Hm . . . I'm sleeping, I'm sleeping . . . (*Covers his face.*) He's coming . . . What a pity the door isn't locked.

VOINITSEV appears in a window.

PLATONOV. He walked up to the window . . . Maybe it isn't him!

VOINITSEV (*in the window*). He isn't here? Strolling somewhere in the forest, dreaming about happiness and convincing the whole universe of how right he is? (*Leans over the windowsill.*) Your happiness doesn't belong to you! What's to be done? (*Thinks.*) I'll go inside and write him a challenge to a duel . . . He prides himself on his chivalrous actions, now let him come and fight! I'll offer him satisfaction . . . I won't give her up to him without a fight, I won't, even if all rights, opinions and convictions put together took her away from me! Whether he's right or not — has nothing to do with me! I can't discuss it! I'm suffering and . . . I want revenge! That's what! I've gone crazy!

PLATONOV coughs slightly.

VOINITSEV (*on seeing Platonov*). Is that him? He's asleep . . . Wouldn't you know . . . He can sleep! If the rat felt even a tenth part of the humiliation inflicted on me, he wouldn't sleep! (*Looks around.*) Right now . . . For the first time in my life I feel hatred and . . . I'll kill. Right now . . . Right now . . . (*Raises a dagger.*)

PLATONOV (*jumps up*). Get back!

VOINITSEV quickly leaps back out of the window and hides.

S C E N E   X
PLATONOV (alone).

I beg of you! For heaven's sake! What are you doing? Get back! I'll kill myself, if my death is what you're after! (*Stamps his feet.*) Get away! O wretched, pathetic man! . . . Is that him? Vanished? (*Slaps himself on the head.*) He was trying to kill me! He, Sergey Voinitsev, a cultured, honorable, noble, loving man! It's smashed, cracked everything that I believed in, that I loved! The head God gave me is cursed! I've brought this sensitive soul to the point of murder! I did it! I was disastrous for people, people were disastrous for me! (*Sobs.*) Keep away from people!

page 159 / *After*: not overly talented . . . — How will I end? It's common knowledge . . . If I don't die of consumption, I'll end by becoming a mystic.

page 160 / *Replace*: (*whistles*)
with: (*sobs*)

page 160 / *After*: Stands to reason . . . — (*Sobs.*) Damn you.

page 160 / *After*: I'll go at once . . . — *stage direction: Pause.*

page 161 / *After*: filthy . . . — (*Weeps.*)

ACT FOUR

page 162 / *Before*: **SOFYA YEGOROVNA.** Don't get so excited! —
KATYA. He ain't nowheres, mistress!
SOFYA YEGOROVNA. Where did you look for him?
KATYA. Everywheres, everywheres I could . . . At the schoolhouse I poked my nose in every corner. Doors and windows all broke in, but he ain't there . . . I even went down cellar . . . A carpenter was sitting by the cellar, I asked him whether he seen him . . . and he says I ain't seen 'im. I thought if I go through the woods . . .
SOFYA YEGOROVNA. Did you stop by the priest's?
KATYA. I sure did . . . The holy father says that they ain't seen Mikhail Vasilich a whole week . . . Went by the deacon's . . . Went by Aleksey Makarych the clerk's, and he don't know . . . I figured the gent might be taking a hike in the woods . . . so I went through the woods . . . I looked and looked . . .

page 163 / *After*: Go out again, Katya! — Go back to the holy father, to that carpenter . . .

page 164 / *After*: He doesn't love me! — All right! He doesn't love me . . . Otherwise he wouldn't torture me this way . . . Maybe the school inspec-

tor called him to town for some reason . . . No, no . . . He didn't come yesterday, doesn't come today . . . (*Gets up.*)

page 166 / *After*: look down your nose at me like that! — My mind can't grasp
it! It's horrible to remember! You know what happened yesterday? Yesterday I almost killed Platonov! I almost cut his throat! If he hadn't woken up,
I would have killed him! I crept over to him with a knife, like a highway
robber, to a sleeping, unarmed man!

SOFYA YEGOROVNA. When?

VOINITSEV. Last night! He saw me!

SOFYA YEGOROVNA (*sits and covers her face*). What happened?

VOINITSEV. I wanted to kill him because he stole my wife! I didn't want to
let him have you without a fight! If he hadn't woke up, I would have killed
him outright with that damned dagger!

page 166 / *After*: Where is he? — Did he get scared of your knife and run
away? He can't have run away!

page 166 / *Before*: Where is he? — You were willing to kill him when he was
asleep, why didn't you kill him when he woke up? Stab him in the back?
A man awake is more dangerous than a man asleep?

page 173 / *After*: Good morning, Sergey Pavlovich! — Ah, you can't imagine!

page 174 / *After*: I'm not wrong! — (*Slaps himself on the forehead.*)

page 174 / *After*: I should shoot myself. — (*Sobs.*)
Pause.

page 175 / *Replace*: do not . . . kill yourself! . . . Grief will do you in . . .
with: but don't sully your hands with a crime . . . Are you the one to be killed?
You? A bitter insult! God will see that I believe in your unhappiness and
that it makes me no less unhappy than you! Why be the cause of another
crime? You want revenge? Hm . . . But revenge is stupid, isn't it, as stupid
as a savage! What would become of you if you succeeded in . . . a murder?
You . . . you would be ruined! In any case murder is the lowest ebb of all
human vulgarity! Now, let's assume, I did something despicable . . . Why
should you defile yourself, yourself, for that?
Pause.

Nothing to say? Hm . . . You don't understand me . . . In any case, if your
thirst for revenge is that great, if the desire for vengeance has got the upper
hand over your human dignity, if grief has disabled your reason because
you always were a reasonable man, then tell me . . .

page 175 / *Replace*: **VOINITSEV.** I don't want anything.

with: **VOINITSEV.** I want you to.

PLATONOV. Fine. I'll shoot myself. I'll shoot myself with pleasure. (*Claps him on the shoulder.*) Cultivated people aren't worth a good goddam . . . It's no great honor to live with such gee . . . gentlemen . . .

page 176 / *After*: bother *maman?* — I came to a cultivated, humane opponent of capital punishment to advise him and ask him not to kill . . . Ech! The lower you stoop, the further you have to turn away your face!

page 176 / *After*: The end has come! — Now a person can creep in with a knife, a person can put a bullet through his brain, insult a man, insult all holy feeling!

page 176 / *Replace*: since you left!

with: you jumped through the window! If you had seen me that night, you with your thirst for revenge would have had a gullet full of it!

page 177 / *Before*: I am sorry that I spoke to you — The hell—with you!

page 177 / *Replace*: **ANNA PETROVNA** (*wrings her hands*).

with: **ANNA PETROVNA** (*runs over to Voinitsev*). Serzhel . . . What is he . . . what was he referring to? You were with him yesterday?

                    Pause.

Speak! Don't torment me, speak!

VOINITSEV. There's no need . . .

ANNA PETROVNA (*shakes him by the shoulders*). Speak! What happened?

VOINITSEV. Spare me . . . You at least should have some compassion!

ANNA PETROVNA. Speak!

                    Pause.

VOINITSEV. I wanted to kill him . . . I crept in to him with a knife . . . If he hadn't woke up . . . He was asleep . . .

ANNA PETROVNA. Aah . . . Now I get it . . . And after that you dared to call *him* a bastard? Fine! What'll become of this, what'll become of this . . . (*Wrings her hands.*)

page 178 / *After*: insult people! — To creep up on a sleeping man with a knife and then . . . then to call him a bastard, and kick him out! . . . You're not worth this man's tiniest finger, you little brat!

page 179 / *After*: Go on! — God grant we shall make peace somehow . . .

page 180 / *After*: I don't need anything! — I'm worn out, Sofya, honest to God, I'm worn out! There's a lot of you, but I'm on my own . . . Take pity on me, please!

page 180 / *After*: that's what! — I can't drag on any farther . . . What's been is enough for me . . .

page 180 / *After*: Looks like it . . . — Now I'm ready for anything, if only to find some peace and quiet for my poor body.

page 181 / *Replace*: God knows what's going on!
with: **ANNA PETROVNA** (*walks over to Sofya*).

page 182 / *After*: how could you? — (*Weeps.*)

page 183 / *Replace: Pause.*
with: She actually tried to poison herself . . . Didn't have the little bit of strength to shift the great big grief on to her narrow shoulders. Her feelings as a mother didn't stop her . . .
>
> *Pause.*

And it's all my fault!

page 190 / *After*: Hamlet was afraid to dream . . . — I guess he didn't go to high school . . .

page 190 / *After*: my sins! — Forgive me, idea! All the same I really . . .

page 190 / *After*: I want to live . . . — This everlasting hide! It's been bruised, flayed, bartered, made into boots, those boots have worn out, but it still wants to go on living . . .

page 192 / *After*: Ask Triletsky . . . — He gave Sasha an antidote and saved her . . .

page 194 / *After*: No, no . . . — (*Screams and falls on Platonov.*)

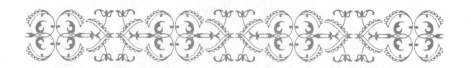

ALONG THE HIGHWAY

*C*hekhov wrote this "dramatic étude"—which he privately referred to as a "little nonsense for the stage"—in autumn 1884. The piece was based on his short story, "Autumn," which had appeared the previous year. Story and play share the same locale, Uncle Tikhon's tavern, and the same basic premise: To pay for another shot of vodka, a nobleman on the skids gives the tavernkeeper a locket with the portrait of his unfaithful but still beloved wife. A peasant who used to be in his service recognizes the gentleman and relates his tale of woe.

Adapting this for the stage, Chekhov conscientiously enlarged his canvas. The anonymous "company of cabmen and pilgrims" is differentiated into the pilgrims Nazarovna and Yefimovna, the religious itinerant Savva, and the factory worker Fedya. The important new astringent in the dramatic blend is the ruffian Yegor Merik, who had also suffered an unhappy love affair in the past. Unfortunately, Chekhov felt that his prose sketch was too static as it stood, and so he had recourse to a violent climax. The gentleman's wife, by the unlikeliest of coincidences, takes shelter in the pothouse and is almost killed by the delirious Merik. The story had ended with the author's rhetorical question, "Spring, where art thou?" The play concludes with Merik's overwrought exclamation, "My heart is breaking! My wretched heart is breaking! Take pity on me, Christian folk!"

The mitigating factor are speeches of the transients, especially the workman Fedya, dreaming of perfect cities and free arable land in the East. These, along with the religious quotations of the pilgrims, function like the lyrical metaphors in Gogol, providing a contrast, albeit a Utopian one, to the squalor depicted on the stage.

The play was submitted to the censor, an unavoidable step if it was to be performed on a public stage. This particular censor, a Baltic German named E. I. Kaiser von Nilckheim, indignantly underlined the word "lord" (*barin*) every time it appeared in the manuscript, and, in his unfavorable report, commented that "among all the vagrants and transients come to the pothouse to get warm and spend the night, there appears a decayed *gentleman* (*dvoryanin*) who *begs the barman to give him a drink on credit. . . .* This gloomy and squalid play, in my opinion, cannot be passed for production." Kaiser von Nilckheim thus has the dubious distinction of being the first of a long string of critics to complain that Chekhov's plays are gloomy.

The play was not published until 1914, ten years after Chekhov's death, when a production was mounted at the Malakhov Theatre in Moscow. Reviewers varied in their assessments from ecstatic—one of them saw Fedya as an archetype of Lopakhin in *The Cherry Orchard*—to, mostly, hostile. Used to the lyrical qualities of Chekhov's mature works, they were taken aback by the raw melodrama of *Along the Highway*.

ALONG THE HIGHWAY

На большой дороге

A Dramatic Sketch in One Act

CHARACTERS

TIKHON YEVSTIGNEEV, *keeper of a wayside tavern*

SEMYON SERGEEVICH BORTSOV, *a ruined landowner*

MARIYA YEGOROVNA, *his wife*

SAVVA, *an old wandering penitent*

NAZAROVNA
— *female pilgrims*
YEFIMOVNA

FEDYA, *an itinerant factory worker*

YEGOR MERIK, *a tramp*

KUZMA, *a vagrant*

A POSTAL COURIER

Mariya Yegorovna's **COACHMAN**

PILGRIMS, DROVERS, VAGRANTS, *etc.*

The action takes place in one of the southern Russian provinces.

The stage represents Tikhon's tavern. At right the bar and shelves of bottles. Upstage a door, leading outside. Above it on the outside hangs a red oil lantern. The floor and benches along the wall are completely packed with pilgrims and vagrants. Many of them are sleeping sitting up, for want of room. Very late at night. As the curtain rises thunder is heard and lightning flashes in the doorway.

SCENE I

*TIKHON is behind the bar. On one of the benches, FEDYA is
sprawling, quietly playing the concertina. Near him sits
BORTSOV, dressed in threadbare summer clothes. On the floor
near the benches SAVVA, NAZAROVNA, and YEFIMOVNA
have found places.*

YEFIMOVNA (*to Nazarovna*). Give the old-timer a poke, dearie! Looks as if he's bound for glory.

NAZAROVNA (*pulling an edge of the fustian coat off Savva's face*). God-fearin' man, hey, god-fearin' man! Ye alive, or be ye dyin'?

SAVVA. Why should I be dyin'? I'm alive, dearie. (*Raises himself on one elbow.*) Cover up my legs, ye poor old thing! There ye go. More to the right. There ye go, dearie. God keep ye.

NAZAROVNA (*covering Savva's legs*). Sleep, my old dear.

SAVVA. Sleep, d'ye say? If I got the patience to put up with this torture, sleep's the last thing I need, dearie. A sinner don't deserve to be left in peace. What's that noise, sister?

NAZAROVNA. God's own thunder. The wind's howling, and the rain's pelting down cats and dogs. The droplets're hitting the roof and the winders like dried peas.

Thunder.

Bless us, bless us, bless us . . .

FEDYA. Thundering and hooting and making a racket . . . and no end in sight! Whoosh . . . like a whole forest rustling . . . Whoosh . . . The wind's howling like a dog . . . (*Huddles up.*) It's cold! My clothes is soppin' wet, you could take 'n' wring 'em out, that door's wide open . . . (*Plays quietly.*) My squeeze-box is soaked, good Christians, it's outa music, otherwise I'd pump you out a concert that would knock your socks off! Wonderful! A quartrill, if you want, or a polka, let's say . . . or some Russian pop tune . . . we can do it all. In town, when I shined shoes at the Grand Otel, the money was peanuts, but when it came to handling the squeeze-box I had all the notes down pat. And I know guitar too.

VOICE FROM THE CORNER. You fool, don't talk foolish.

FEDYA. So says the fool.

Pause.

NAZAROVNA (*to Savva*). Old man, right now you should be lying in the warm, warming your poor leg.

Pause.

Old man! God-fearin' man! (*Nudges Savva.*) Hey, you fixing to die?

FEDYA. You should have a little spot of vodka, gramps. You have a drink, and it'll light a fire in your belly, light a fire, and take your mind off things. Have a drink!

NAZAROVNA. Leave off that blasphemiousness, young fella! Mebbe the old man's going to glory and repenting his sins, and you with your smart talk and your squeeze-box . . . Stop that music! You shameless thing!

FEDYA. And why are you nagging at him? He may be at death's door, but you . . . with yer old women's blather . . . 'Cause he's a righteous man, he can't chew you out, so you're tickled pink, dee-lighted you got somebody gotta listen to you, you fool . . . Sleep, gramps, don't listen! Let 'em blab on, just you pay 'em no mind. A woman's tongue is the devil's broom, it sweeps good sense and wisdom out of the room. Pay 'em no mind . . . (*Clasps his hands in distress.*) You're all skin and bones, pal! This is scary! Just like he was a dead skellington! Not a breath o' life in him! Hey, you fixing to drop dead?

SAVVA. Why should I drop dead? God forbid, good people, I should die before my time . . . I'll go through a bit of a bad spell, and then I'll git up again with God's help . . . The Mother o' God won't let me drop dead in foreign parts . . . I'll die at home . . .

FEDYA. You come a far piece?

SAVVA. Vologda's my home.[1] Vologda itself . . . a small tradesman from them parts . . .

FEDYA. And where's this Vologda?

TIKHON. Other side of Moscow . . . Province of . . .

---

1 Capital of the Vologda Guberniya in northern Russia, noted for its cathedral and cluster of ancient buildings.

FEDYA. My, my, my . . . You come a far piece, whiskers! All that way on foot?

SAVVA. On foot, laddie. Been to St. Tikhon's, and now I'm on my way to the Holy Mountains . . .[2] From the Holy Mountains, if it's God's will, to Odesta . . . From there, folks say, you can get a cheap fare to Jerusalem. S'posed to be twenty-one rubles . . .

FEDYA. So you been to Moscow?

SAVVA. I'll say! nigh on to five times . . .

FEDYA. Nice sort of town? (*Starts to smoke.*) Worth the trip?

SAVVA. Plenty o' shrines, laddie . . . Where there's plenty o' shrines, it's nice all over . . .

BORTSOV (*steps up to the bar and Tikhon*). I'll ask you once more! For Christ's sake let me have one!

FEDYA. The main thing about a town is it should be clean . . . If it's dusty, then water it down, if it's muddy, mop it up. There should be tall buildings . . . a the-ayter, policemen . . . cab drivers, the kind that . . . I've lived in towns myself, so I know all about it.

BORTSOV. One little shot . . . just a short one. Put it on my tab! Let me have it!

TIKHON. Oh, sure.

BORTSOV. I'm begging you! Have a heart!

TIKHON. Go away!

BORTSOV. You don't understand me . . . Understand, you ignoramus, if there's an ounce of brains in your thick peasant's skull, I'm not the one begging you, it's, to use your own vulgar way of speaking, my guts begging! My disease begging! Can't you understand!

TIKHON. There's nothing to understand . . . Get out of here!

BORTSOV. In fact, if I don't get a drink right away, understand, if I don't satisfy this craving, I might do something violent. I'm capable of doing God

---

2 St. Tikhon of Zadonsk (1724–1783), a famous Russian monk, preacher, and devotional author, gave his name to a monastery in the northern Voronezh province. The Holy Mountains are a monastery in Kharkov in the Ukraine.

knows what! You've seen in this tavern of yours, you lout, plenty of drunks in your time, and you still can't figure out what makes them tick? They're sick! Chain 'em up, beat 'em, stab 'em, but let 'em have vodka! Now, I'm pleading most humbly! Have a heart! I'm stooping to your level! My God, the way I'm stooping!

TIKHON. Let's see your money, then you'll get vodka . . .

BORTSOV. Where am I supposed to get money? It's all drunk up! Every last bit of it! What am I supposed to give you? All I've got left is my overcoat, but I can't give you that . . . It covers my naked body. You want my cap? (*Takes off his cap and hands it to Tikhon.*)

TIKHON (*inspects the cap*). Hm . . . There are caps and then there are caps . . . Full of holes like a sieve.

FEDYA (*laughs*). A gentleman's cap! Walk down the street in it and tip it to all the mamzelles. Top o' the morning, good day to yez! How you doing?

TIKHON (*hands back the cap to Bortsov*). Wouldn't have it as a gift. Piece of crap.

BORTSOV. You don't like it? In that case, put it on my tab! On my way back from town I'll bring you your five kopeks! Then you can choke on your five kopeks! You can choke! I hope they stick in your craw! (*Coughs.*) I hate you!

TIKHON (*banging his fist on the bar*). What are you pestering me for? What kind of a man are you? What kind of a crook? What're you doing here?

BORTSOV. I want a drink! No, I don't want it, my disease wants it! Understand!

TIKHON. Don't make me lose my temper! Or you'll be on the other side of the door double quick.

BORTSOV. What am I to do? (*Walks away from the bar.*) What am I to do? (*Becomes rapt in thought.*)

YEFIMOVNA. It's the foul fiend tormenting you. Never you mind him, sir. The father o' lies is whispering in yer ear: "Drink! drink!" Just you say to him: "I won't drink! I won't drink!" He'll leave you be!

FEDYA. That skull o' yours, I'll bet, is going bam-bam-bam . . . and your belly's rumbling! (*Roars with laughter.*) You're a funny one, yer honor! Just you lay down and get some sleep! No point flapping around this joint like a scarecrow! This ain't no corn field!

BORTSOV (*viciously*). Shut up! Nobody asked you anything, you jackass!

FEDYA. You talk and talk and make no sense! We know your sort! There's plenty of your sort shambling along the highway here! Talking o' jackasses, when I wallop you one upside your head, you'll howl worse'n the storm wind. Jackass yourself! Piece of shit!

Pause.

Son of a bitch!

NAZAROVNA. Mebbe the holy old man's saying his prayers and giving up his soul to God, while these roughnecks is beating each other up and using all sorts of bad language . . . Shameless creatures!

FEDYA. And you, you sawed-off stump, you're hanging out in a barroom, so stop sniveling! In a barroom there's barroom manners.

BORTSOV. What am I to do? What's there to do? How can I make him under-tand? What greater eloquence do I need? (*To Tikhon.*) The blood's clotting in my chest! Good old Tikhon! (*Weeps.*) Good old Tikhon!

SAVVA (*groans*). There's shooting pains in my leg, like a bullet o' fire . . . Sister pilgrim, honey!

YEFIMOVNA. What is it, dearie?

SAVVA. Who's crying?

YEFIMOVNA. The gent.

SAVVA. Ask the gent to shed a tear for me so's I'll get to die in Vologda. Tear-ful prayers work wonders.

BORTSOV. I'm not praying, granddad! These are not tears! They're my life's blood! They've squeezed my heart and the lifeblood's run out. (*Sits down at Savva's feet.*) My life's blood! But how can you grasp that! Your primitive mind, granddad, can't grasp that. You people are living in the dark ages!

SAVVA. And where's them with the light?

BORTSOV. Enlightened people do exist, granddad . . . They would under-stand!

SAVVA. They do, they do, my son . . . The saints was enlightened . . . They understand all kinds of troubles . . . You wouldn't have to tell 'em, they'd understand . . . They'd look in your eyes—and understand . . . And you've such a comfort once they understand, it's like there never was no trouble— it's gone as if by magic!

FEDYA. So you seen any saints?

SAVVA. It comes to pass, young fella . . . There's all kinds of folks in this world. There be sinners, and there be servants o' God.

BORTSOV. I'm not following any of this . . . (*Gets up quickly.*) A conversation ought to be comprehensible, but am *I* making any sense right now? All I've got is instinct, thirst! (*Quickly walks over to the bar.*) Tikhon, take my overcoat! Understand me? (*About to take off his coat.*) The overcoat . . .

TIKHON. And what's under the overcoat? (*Looks at Bortsov beneath the overcoat.*) A naked body? Don't take it off, I don't want it . . . I'm not going to take a sin on my soul.

Enter MERIK.

SCENE II

The same and MERIK.

BORTSOV. Fine, I'll take the sin on myself! All right?

MERIK (*silently removes his fustian coat and stands in his tight, sleeveless jacket. He has an axe in his belt*). Some folks feel the cold, but the bear and the man with no family ties is always hot. I'm sweating like a pig! (*Puts his axe on the floor and takes off his sleeveless jacket.*) Whiles you're pulling one foot outa the mud, you're pouring sweat by the bucket. You get that foot out, then the other's stuck in the mud.

YEFIMOVNA. That's so . . . Sonny-boy, is it still coming down so hard?

MERIK (*after a glance at Yefimovna*). I don't have no truck with womenfolk.

Pause.

BORTSOV (*to Tikhon*). I'll take the sin on myself! Did you hear me or not?

TIKHON. I don't want to hear, leave me alone!

MERIK. It's dark, like somebody smeared the sky with tar. Can't see yer nose before yer face. And the rain whips ya in the kisser, like one of yer snowstorms . . . (*Bundles his clothes and his axe in his arms.*)

FEDYA. Fine times for our pal the robber: even beasts of prey take cover, but it's Christmas for you jokers.

MERIK. What man said those words?

FEDYA. Looky over here . . . don't s'pose they jest slipped out.

MERIK. We'll make a note o' that . . . (*Walks over to Tikhon.*) Evening, fat face! Doncha know me?

TIKHON. If you expect me to know every drunk who comes off the highway, I figure I'd need a dozen eyeballs in my head.

MERIK. Jest you take a good look . . .

Pause.

TIKHON. Well, I do know ya, dern it all! I knowed ya by yer eyes! (*Gives him his hand.*) Andrey Polikarpov?

MERIK. I was Andrey Polikarpov, but now, seems as how I'm Yegor Merik.

TIKHON. Why's that?

MERIK. Whatever label God sends, that's my moniker. Two months now I been Merik . . .

Pause.

Rrr . . . Thunder on, I ain't scared! (*Looks around.*) No bloodhounds here?

TIKHON. What dy'a mean bloodhounds! Mostly bugs and mosquitoes . . . A squishy bunch . . . These days the bloodhounds are prolly snoozing in their feather-beds . . . (*Loudly.*) Good Christians, keep an eye on your pockets and your duds, if you care about 'em! This here's a bad man! He'll rob ya!

MERIK. Well, let 'em look to their money, if they got any, but when it comes to clothes, I won't touch 'em. There's nowhere to fence 'em.

TIKHON. Where in tarnation are you heading?

MERIK. Kuban River.[3]

---

3 A river in the Trans-Caucasian part of the Russian Empire; the region around it was proverbial for its rich lands and fertility.

TIKHON. No kidding!

FEDYA. Kuban? Honest to God? (*Raises himself up a bit.*) That's a glorious place! A kind o' land, pals, you wouldn't see if you dreamed three years running! Wide open spaces! They say there's all the most of birds, wild game, all kinds o' animals and—oh, Lordy! The grass grows all year round, the folks are salt o' the earth, more land than they know what to do with! The gov'ment, they say . . . this soldier fella was telling me the other day . . . will give three hundred acres a head. Good times, dammit!

MERIK. Good times . . . Good times walks behind yer back . . . Where ya can't see 'em . . . If you can bite yer own elbow, you'll see good times . . . Nothin' but stupidity . . . (*Looks at the benches and the people.*) Looks like a chain gang . . . Greetings, you huddled masses!

YEFIMOVNA (*to Merik*). You got the evil eye! . . . The foul fiend's inside you, my lad . . . Don't you look at us.

MERIK. Greetings, you huddled masses!

YEFIMOVNA. Turn away! (*Shoves Savva.*) Savvushka, a wicked man's got his eye on us! He'll harm us, dearie! (*To Merik.*) Turn away, I said, you viper!

SAVVA. He won't touch you, sister, he won't touch you . . . God won't let him.

MERIK. Greetings, good Christians! (*Shrugs his shoulders.*) Not a word! I don't s'pose ye're sleeping, you clumsy louts! Why don't you say something?

YEFIMOVNA. Turn away those eyes! And turn away from your hellish pride!

MERIK. Shut up, you old bag! It wasn't hellish pride but affection and a kind word I wanted to bestow on your bitter fate! You look like flies clustered together 'gainst the cold—so, I felt sorry for ya, I wanted to speak a kind word, ease your misery, and you turn your snouts away! So what? Who needs it! (*Walks over to Fedya.*) And where would you be from?

FEDYA. Around here, the Khamonev factory town. The brickworks.

MERIK. Get the hell up!

FEDYA (*raising himself a bit*). What?

MERIK. Get up! Get up and out, I'm gonna bunk there . . .

FEDYA. Izat so . . . So it's your spot, is it?

MERIK. It's mine. Go lay on the ground!

FEDYA. Move along, you tramp . . . You don't scare me.

MERIK. A wiseguy . . . Go on, clear out, no backtalk! Or you'll be sorry, you stupid man!

TIKHON (*to Fedya*). Don't talk back to him, lad! Let it go!

FEDYA. What right have you got to it? Bugs out his big fish eyes at me and thinks I'll get skeered! (*Collects his gear in his arms, goes and makes a bed on the floor.*) Devil! (*Lies down and covers up his head.*)

MERIK (*makes up a bed on the bench*). I don't figure you ever seen a devil if you call me one. Devils ain't like me. (*Lies down and puts his axe beside him.*) Go to bed, little axe, little brother . . . Let me tuck in your shaft.

TIKHON. Where'd you get the axe?

MERIK Stole it . . . Stole it, and now I'm stuck with it like a kid with a broken toy: it's a shame to throw it away and I got nowheres to keep it. Like a wife you can't stand . . . Yeah . . . (*Covers himself up.*) Devils, pal, ain't like me.

FEDYA (*sticking his head out from under the covers*). What are they like?

MERIK. They're like steam, breath . . . Blow like this (*he blows air*), that's what they're like. No way to see 'em.

VOICE FROM THE CORNER. If you sit under a harrow, you'll see 'em sure enough.

MERIK. I sat under one, never seen 'em . . . Old women tell lies and so do stupid peasants . . . You ain't gonna see a devil or a wood goblin or a ghost . . . Our eyes ain't made so's we can see everything . . . When I was a kid, I used to go to the forest at night on purpose to see a wood goblin . . . Used to be I'd shout and shout for a ha'nt, I'd call on the wood goblin and wouldn't blink an eye, but never seen none. I'd go to the graveyard at night, tried to see ghosts—the old women tell lies. All kinds of animals I seen, but anything spooky—nor hide nor hair! Our eyes ain't the right kind. . . .

VOICE FROM THE CORNER. Don't say that, it so happens you do see 'em . . . In our village a peasant was gutting a wild boar . . . He's ripping out the tripes, when one pops out of them!

SAVVA (*raising himself a bit*). Young fellas, don't talk about the foul fiend! It's a sin, my dears!

MERIK. Aaah . . . the gray beard! The skellington! (*Laughs.*) Ain't no need to go to the graveyard, we got our own ghosts crawling out from under the floorboards to read us the riot act . . . A sin . . . It ain't yer place with your stupid notions to preach to folks! Ye're a benighted lot, ignoramuses . . . (*Lights up a pipe.*) My father was a peasant and he used to love to preach too. One time he steals a sack of apples from the village priest at night, brings it to us and preaches: "Watch out, you kids, don't gobble up them apples before Transfiguration Day, 'cause it's a sin." . . . Just like you . . . You mustn't talk about the devil, but you can act like the devil . . . For example, just you take this old bag . . . (*Points at Yefimovna.*) She seen me as the Antichrist, but I'll bet in her time she's sold her soul to . . . the devil at least five times for womenfolk's hanky-panky.

YEFIMOVNA. Pfoo, pfoo, pfoo![4] . . . May the power of the Cross protect us! (*Hides her face in her hands.*) Savvushka!

TIKHON. Why are you scaring us? Make you happy!

> *The door bangs in the wind.*

Jesus Christ! . . . That's what I call a wind!

MERIK (*stretches*). Ech, I should show you how strong I am!

> *The door bangs in the wind.*

Test my strength against this here wind! It can't rip the door off, but, gimme the chance, I'd tear up this whole barroom by the roots! (*Stands up and lies down again.*) It gets you down!

NAZAROVNA. Say a prayer, you heathen! What are you raving about?

YEFIMOVNA. Don't rile him, dern him! He's looking at us again! (*To Merik.*) Don't look at us, you wicked man! Them eyes, them eyes, like Satan's at morning mass!

SAVVA. Let 'im look, godly sisters! Say a prayer, the eye won't harm you . . .

BORTSOV. No, I can't stand it! It's more than I can bear! (*Walks over to the bar.*) Listen, Tikhon, I'm asking you for the last time . . . Just half a shot!

---

4 Indicates that she spits three times to avert the evil eye.

TIKHON (*shakes his head no*). Money!

BORTSOV. My God, haven't I told you already! It's all drunk up! Where am I supposed to get any? Would it ruin you if you gave me a drop of vodka on credit? A shot of vodka costs you a penny, but it will save me from agony! I'm in agony! I'm not faking it, it's agony! Understand!

TIKHON. Go tell it to the judge, not me . . . Go on, beg outside with good Christians, let them treat you outa Christian charity if they want, but all I give outa Christian charity is bread.

BORTSOV. You'd take from them, the poor creatures, but I . . . excuse me! I haven't got it in me to rob them! It's not in me! Understand? (*Slams his fist on the bar.*) Not in me!

Pause.

Hm . . . Hold on a bit . . . (*Turns to the pilgrims.*) That's not a bad idea, good Christians! Sacrifice a mere five kopeks! My guts are pleading! I'm sick!

FEDYA. Looky there, make a sacrifice . . . Swindler . . . Wouldja like a little water?

BORTSOV. How low I've sunk! How low I've sunk! Never mind! Never mind about me! I was joking!

MERIK. Don't go begging to him, sir . . . He's a notorious tightwad . . . Hold on, I got five kopeks rattling around somewheres . . . Let's us both have a drink . . . fifty-fifty . . . (*Rummages in his pockets.*) Hell . . . it was stuck in there somewheres . . . Coulda sworn something was jingling in my pocket the other day . . . No, nothin' . . . Nothin', pal! Just your luck!

Pause.

BORTSOV. I have got to have a drink, otherwise I'll commit a crime or kill myself . . . What am I to do, my God! (*Looks out the doorway.*) Should I leave? Go off into that darkness, wherever my feet take me . . .

MERIK. How about it, godly sisters, why don't you preach to him? And you, Tikhon, how come you don't throw him out? He ain't paid for his night's lodging, after all. Throw 'im out, right on his ear! Ech, folks is cruel nowadays. Ain't got no soft hearts and kindliness in 'em . . . Folks is mean! A man's drowning, and they shout at him: "Drown faster, we ain't got time to watch, it's a workday!" And as for throwing him a rope, don't make me laugh . . . A rope costs money.

SAVVA. Judge not, good man!

MERIK. Shut up, you old wolf! You're vicious folks! Child killers! Dealers in souls! (*To Tikhon.*) Come here and take off my boots! Step lively!

TIKHON. Hey, he's gone hog wild! (*Laughs.*) Reg'lar bogeyman!

MERIK. Git over here, I said! Step lively!

Pause.

You hear me or not? Am I talking to the wall? (*Gets up.*)

TIKHON. All right . . . that'll do!

MERIK. I want you, you mule-skinner, to pull off my boots, the boots of a beggar tramp!

TIKHON. All right . . . don't fly off the handle! Come on, have a little drink . . . Come and drink!

MERIK. Folks, what do I want? For him to treat me to vodka or take off my boots? Did I say it wrong, didn't you hear me? (*To Tikhon.*) Mebbe you didn't catch my drift? I'll wait just one minute, then I figure you'll catch it.

Something of a stir among the pilgrims and vagrants. They get up and stare at Tikhon and Merik. Silent suspense.

TIKHON. The foul fiend brought you here! (*Comes out from behind the bar.*) Some fine gentleman made an entrance! Well, let's have 'em, or what? (*Pulls off Merik's boots.*) Spawn of Cain . . .

MERIK. That's it. Line 'em up neat . . . That's it . . . Get out!

TIKHON (*having taken off the boots, goes behind the bar*). Think you're pretty smart! Get smart with me again, and you'll fly out of this joint on the double! Right! (*To Bortsov, who is approaching.*) You again?

BORTSOV. Well, you see, I might let you have some gold . . . Listen here, if you like, I'll give you . . .

TIKHON. Why are you shaking like that? Talk sense!

BORTSOV. Even though it's vile and base on my part, what am I to do? I'm resolved to do this dirty deed, since I'm not in my right mind . . . I'd be acquitted by any court . . . Take it, but only on one condition: give it back to me afterwards, when I return from town. I give it to you before witnesses . . . Ladies and gentlemen, please serve as witnesses! (*Takes a gold locket out of his bosom.*) Here it is . . . I ought to remove the portrait, but there's nowhere for me to put it; I'm all wet! . . . Well, take it with the portrait! Only, look here . . . you sort of . . . shouldn't graze the face with your fingers . . . I beg of you . . . I was rude to you, my dear man . . . stupid, but you'll forgive me and . . . don't put your fingers on it . . . Don't cast your eyes upon the face . . . (*Gives Tikhon the locket.*)

TIKHON (*inspects the locket*). A stolen watch . . . Well, all right, have a drink . . . (*Pours out the vodka.*) Guzzle that down.

BORTSOV. Only those fingers of yours . . . don't sort of . . . (*Drinks slowly, with convulsive pauses.*)

TIKHON (*opens the locket*). Hm . . . A fine lady! . . . Where'd you pick up something like that?

MERIK. Show us! (*Gets up and walks over to the bar.*) Let's have a look!

TIKHON (*pushes his hand away*). Where'd you crawl in from? Hands off while you're looking.

FEDYA (*rises and walk over to Tikhon*). Lemme look too!

Pilgrims and vagrants walk over to the bar from all directions.

A group.

MERIK (*firmly holds in his hands Tikhon's hand with the locket and silently stares at the portrait.*)

Pause.

A beautiful she-devil! A real lady . . .

FEDYA. A real lady . . . Them cheeks, eyes . . . Pull away your hand, I can't see! Hair down to her waist . . . Real life-like! You'd think she was talking . . .

Pause.

MERIK. For a weak man that's the first step to ruination. Get a woman like that round your neck and . . . (*waves his hand in dismissal*) and—you're done for!

We can hear KUZMA's voice: "Who-o-oa . . . Stop, my hearties!"

Enter KUZMA.

SCENE III

The same and KUZMA.

KUZMA (*enters*). "Here on the road a tavern's nigh, Don't walk past it, don't drive by." You can drive past your dear old dad in broad daylight, and take no notice of 'im, but you can see a tavern in the dark from a hundred miles off. Clear a space, God-fearing folk! Hey, barkeep! (*Slams his fist on the bar.*) A glass of real Madeira! Make it snappy!

FEDYA. Lookit you, in a hell of a rush!

TIKHON. Stop waving your arms around! You'll get caught on something!

KUZMA. Why'd God give 'em to us except to wave around. Melting, are you, my little sugar cubes, sheltering in your auntie's hen house! Rain got you skeered, my delicate blossoms! (*Drinks.*)

YEFIMOVNA. You'd be skeered too, good man, if you was caught on the road on a night like this. Nowadays, thank God, we're blessed with lots o' villages and farms along the way, there's somewheres to git out of the wet, but times past, the Lord save us from the way it used to be! Seventy miles you'd tramp and don't even talk about a village or a farm, no sign of even a wood chip. So you'd spend the night on the bare ground . . .

KUZMA. So how long you been suff'ring in this world, old woman?

YEFIMOVNA. Going on eighty, dearie.

KUZMA. Going on eighty! Soon you'll be old as Methusaleh. (*Looks at Bortsov.*) And what sort of stewed fruit have we got here? (*Stares straight at Bortsov.*) A gent!

BORTSOV *recognizes Kuzma and, in his embarrassment, goes to
a corner and sits down on the bench.*

Semyon Sergeich! Is that you or ain't it? Huh? How'd you wind up in this joint? This ain't no place for you!

BORTSOV. Be quiet!

MERIK (*to Kuzma*). Who is he?

KUZMA. A miserable wretch! (*Nervously paces along the bar.*) Huh? In a cheap tavern, for pity's sake! In rags! Drunk! This has really got me spooked, pals ... Really got me spooked ... (*Speaks to Merik in an undertone.*) That's our master ... owner of our estate, Semyon Sergeich, Mister Bortsov ... I can't believe my eyes! Wouldja lookit the state he's in now? There you have it ... drink'll lay you that low ... Fill it up, you! (*Drinks.*) I'm from his village, Bortsovka, maybe you heard of it, about a hundred and fifty miles from these parts, in Yegorov district. His father owned serfs ... What a shame!

MERIK. Rich was he?

KUZMA. A big man ...

MERIK. Played fast and loose with the old man's propitty?

KUZMA. No, it was fate, old pal ... He was a big-time gent, rich, sober ... (*To Tikhon.*) I bet you seen him yourself, once upon a time, driving past the tavern to town. Real classy horses, smart and trim, a carriage on springs—top of the line! He kept five troikas, believe me brother ... About five years ago, I remember, he's crossing by the Mikishkin ferry and instead of five kopeks he tosses 'em a ruble ... "Got no time," he says, "to wait for change ..." How 'bout that!

MERIK. I s'pose he lost his mind.

KUZMA. Looks like he's still got his wits about him ... It's all 'cause of gutlessness! And easy living! Mainly, boys, it was on account of a skirt ... He fell in love, poor boob, with a woman from town, and figured she was the prettiest thing in all the world ... Hunt an eagle and bring home a crow. A girl from a good family ... Not 'zactly a slut or like that, but sort of ... flighty ... Her tail going—wag! wag! Her eyes going—squint! squint! And never stops laughing, never ever! Not a brain in her head ... Gents go for that kind of thing, figure it's cute, but our folks down home would kick her out the door ... Anyhow ... he falls in love and—now he's done for, the gent is doomed! He starts carrying on with her, one thing leads to another, tea and sugar, and so on ... boating all night long, and playing the piano ...

BORTSOV. Don't tell them, Kuzma! What's the point? Is my life any business of theirs?

KUZMA. Excuse me, your lordship, I've spoke my piece . . . I told 'em and that's all they'll get . . . I spoke my piece because you got me spooked . . . I was really spooked! Fill 'er up, boy! (*Drinks.*)

MERIK (*in an undertone*). And did she love him back?

KUZMA (*in an undertone, which gradually shifts into his usual tone of voice*). You kidding? The master ain't no nobody . . . Not fall in love, when there's a couple of thousand acres and money that ain't chicken feed . . . And him so respectable, highfalutin and sober . . . And on good terms with the big shots, like this here . . . takes their hand . . . (*takes Merik by the hand*) "how do and fare thee well, thank you kindly" . . . Anyhow, this one time it's night and I'm crossing the master's garden . . . that garden, pal, wow! Went on for miles . . . I'm walking quiet as you please, and then I sees the two of 'em sitting on a bench and kissing (*makes the sound of kissing*) one another. He kisses her once, twice, she, the snake, kisses him a couple o' times . . . He takes her little white hand, and she's all—flares up! and squeezes up, squeezes up against him so she can . . . "I love you, Senya," she says . . . And Senya, like a soul in torment, walks around and brags about how happy he is, being as how he's so gutless . . . A ruble here, a ruble there . . . Gave me money for a horse. Forgave everyone's debts, he's so dee-lighted . . .

BORTSOV. Ah . . . What's the point of telling that story? These people have no sympathy . . . It's painful, after all!

KUZMA. Just speaking my piece, sir! They're asking! Why not tell 'em a little bit? All right, I won't, if it makes you angry . . . I won't . . . To hell with 'em . . .

The harness bells on a mail coach are heard.

FEDYA. Don't yell it, just nice and quiet . . .

KUZMA. I am saying it nice and quiet . . . He don't like it, so nothing doing . . . And there's no more to tell. They got married—and that's that . . . All over. Pour out a glass for big-hearted Kuzma! (*Drinks.*) I don't hold with drunkenness! At the very minute when the ladies and gents is sitting down to the banquet after the wedding, she ups and runs away in a carriage . . . (*In a whisper.*) Hurries off to town to some shyster lawyer, her lover boy . . . Eh? How 'bout that? The very exact minute! Yessir . . . killing's too good for her!

MERIK (*thoughtfully*). Right . . . So what happened next?

KUZMA. He went nuts . . . Look, you can see, he started by hitting the bottle and wound up, like they say, bashing the whole brewery . . . First it was bottles, then it was barrels . . . And all that time he's in love with her. Look at 'im: he still loves her! I figure he's walking back to town now just to get an eyeful of her . . . He'll get a good look and—come back again . . .

The mail coach drives up to the tavern. The POSTAL COURIER enters and drinks.

TIKHON. The mail's behind schedule!

The POSTAL COURIER silently pays up and exits. The mail coach departs with a jingling of harness bells.

A VOICE FROM THE CORNER. In this foul weather robbing a mail coach'd be a piece of cake!

MERIK. I've lived on earth thirty-five years and never yet robbed a mail coach.

Pause.

Now it's gone and it's too late . . . Too late . . .

KUZMA. Planning to get a taste of prison life?

MERIK. Stealing don't guarantee a taste. Big deal, prison! (*Sharply.*) What next?

KUZMA. You mean about that poor boob?

MERIK. Who else?

KUZMA. The next thing, pals, which led to his downfall is his brother-in-law, his sister's husband . . . He gets the bright idea of vouching for this brother-in-law to a savings and loan . . . thirty thousand or so . . . The brother-in-law is a brother-outlaw . . . you know how it goes, the crook's got his eyes on the prize, so he behaves like a skunk . . . Takes the money, but can't be bothered to pay it back . . . So our boss has to pay the whole thirty thousand. (*Sighs.*) A fool and his money are soon parted. The wife's got kids by her shyster, and the brother-in-law buys an estate near Poltava,[5] while our

---

5 Town in the Ukraine, southwest of Kharkov, noted for its fairs.

guy, like a jerk, goes from one bar-room to another belly-aching to us peasants: "I've lost faith, pals! There ain't nobody I trust no more!" Gutlessness! Every fella's got his own troubles, some snake's eating his heart out, but does that mean you crawl into a bottle? For example, take our village elder[6] now. That wife of his carries on with the schoolteacher in broad daylight, spends her husband's money on booze, and the elder goes around with a big grin on his face . . . Only thing is he's lost a lot o' weight . . .

TIKHON (*sighs*). God grants each man the strength he needs . . .

KUZMA. There's all kinds of strength, true enough . . . Well? What do I owe you? (*Pays up.*) Take my heart's blood! Good-bye, boys! I wish you good night, and sweet dreams! I'm off, it's time . . . I'm driving the midwife from the infirmary to the boss's wife . . . I figure the poor woman's sick and tired of waiting, drenched to the skin . . . (*Runs out.*)

TIKHON (*after a pause*). Hey, you! What's yer name? Sad sack, have a drink! (*Pours it out.*)

BORTSOV (*hesitantly walks over to the bar and drinks*). So I suppose I owe you for two drinks now.

TIKHON. Who said anything about owing? Drink—that's all I said! Drown your sorrows!

FEDYA. Have a drink on me too, sir! Ech! (*Tosses a five-kopek coin on the bar.*) Drink—and you'll die, don't drink—and you'll die too! You can get along without vodka, but with vodka, honest to God, you loosen up more! When there's vodka, you forget your troubles . . . Bottoms up!

BORTSOV. Whew! It's strong!

MERIK. Hand it over! (*Takes the locket from Tikhon and examines the portrait.*) Hm . . . Ran away right after the wedding . . . What would you call 'er?

VOICE FROM THE CORNER. Pour him out another little glass, Tisha. Let 'im have one on me!

MERIK (*forcefully slams the locket on the floor*). Damn the bitch! (*Quickly goes to his place and lies down with his face to the wall.*)

---

6 Peasant communities chose a *starshina*, or head man, from among themselves to settle disputes and maintain law and order.

Consternation.

BORTSOV. What was that? What's going on? (*Picks up the locket.*) How dare you, you brute? What gives you the right? (*Tearfully.*) You want me to kill you? Huh? Peasant! Ignoramus!

TIKHON. That'll do, sir, temper, temper. . . . It ain't made o' glass, it won't break . . . Have another drink, then go to sleep . . . (*Pours it out.*) I've had an earful of the bunch of you, it's high time I closed up shop. (*Goes and bolts the door to the outside.*)

BORTSOV (*drinks*). How dare he? What an idiot! (*To Merik.*) You understand? You're an idiot, you jackass!

SAVVA. Good boys! Dear sirs! Set a watch over your mouths and keep the doors of your lips![7] What good is all this racket? Let folks sleep!

TIKHON. Go to bed, go to bed . . . That's enough outa you! (*Goes behind the bar and locks the cashbox.*)

FEDYA. About time! (*Lies down.*) Sweet dreams, pals!

MERIK (*gets up and spreads his sheepskin coat on the bench*). Come on, sir, lie down here!

TIKHON. Where're you gonna sleep?

MERIK. Wherever I can . . . The floor will do . . . (*Spreads his fustian coat on the floor.*) It don't matter to me. (*Puts his axe beside him.*) For him sleeping on the floor'd be hell . . . He's used to silk and cotton batting . . .

TIKHON (*to Bortsov*). Lay down, your worship! That's enough staring at that pitcher! (*Puts out the candle.*) Throw it away!

BORTSOV (*staggering*). Where am I to lie down?

TIKHON. In the tramp's place! You hear, he's letting you have it!

BORTSOV (*walks over to the proffered place*). But I'm sort of . . . wee bit drunk . . . This . . . what's it? I'm supposed to lie there? Huh?

TIKHON. Right there, right there, don't worry, lay down . . . (*Stretches out on the bar.*)

---

7 Paraphrase of Psalm 141, verse 3: "Set a watch, O Lord, before my mouth; and keep the doors of my lips."

BORTSOV (*lies down*). I'm . . . drunk . . . Everything's spinning round . . . (*Opens the locket.*) Do you have a candle end?

Pause.

You're a strange girl, Masha . . . You stare at me from the frame and laugh . . . (*Laughs.*) Drunk! Should you be laughing at a drunkard? You mind your own *p*s and *q*s, as the comedian says in that play,[8] and . . . love the drunkard a little.

FEDYA. The way that wind is blowing! Spooky!

BORTSOV (*laughs*). What a girl . . . How can you whirl around like that? Can't get hold of you!

MERIK. He's raving. Started looking at that pitcher again. (*Laughs.*) That beats the band! Eddicated gents has dreamed up all kinds of machines and medicines, but there still ain't a guy smart enough to come up with a cure for the female sex . . . They're aiming to cure all diseases, but it never occurs to them that more folks is ruined by womanfolk than by diseases . . . Sneaky, greedy, never let up, not a brain in their heads . . . The mother-in-law picks on the new bride, the bride works hard to put one over on her husband . . . And there's no end to it . . .

TIKHON. Womenfolk have run him ragged, he's an unholy mess.

MERIK. It ain't just me . . . For ages and ages, ever since the world began, people been in a sorry state . . . It's no wonder and no accident that in fairy tales and folksongs the devil and the female are on the same side . . . No accident! There's more than a grain o' truth in that . . .

Pause.

There's that gent making a fool of himself, but what about me going screwy and turning tramp, walking out on my folks?

FEDYA. Womenfolk?

MERIK. Just the same as the gent there . . . I went around like a soul in torment, under a spell, bragged about how happy I was . . . like I was on fire

---

8 Literally, "as Shchastlivtsev says." A comic actor, whose name means Happy, a central character in Aleksandr Ostrovsky's play *The Forest*. The line does not appear in the text but was an actor's improvisation that became traditional in the last scene.

night and day, but the time came when my eyes was opened . . . It weren't love, nothing but a con game . . .

FEDYA. So what'd you do to her?

MERIK. None of yer business . . .

Pause.

I killed her, that what you think? My arms is too short . . . What I did weren't to kill her, but to . . . feel sorry for her . . . Go on and live and be . . . happy! Only don't let me set eyes on you, let me forget you, you snake in the grass!

Knocking at the door.

TIKHON. Who the hell is that . . . Who's there?

Knocking.

Who's knocking? (*Gets up and go to the door.*) Who's knocking? Move along, we're closed!

VOICE BEHIND THE DOOR. Let us in, Tikhon, for pity's sake! A spring's busted in the carriage! Help us out, be a father to us! I'll patch it up with a bit o' rope, and then one way or another we'll get where we're going . . .

TIKHON. Who're you driving?

VOICE BEHIND THE DOOR. Driving a lady from town to Varsonofeevo . . . There's only three miles left to go . . . Help us out, for pity's sake!

TIKHON. Go ahead and tell the lady that for ten rubles you'll get your rope and we'll fix your spring . . .

VOICE BEHIND THE DOOR. You gone crazy or what? Ten rubles! You're a mad dog! Taking advantage of folks in trouble!

TIKHON. You know best . . . Take it or leave it . . .

VOICE BEHIND THE DOOR. Well, all right, hold on . . .

Pause.

The lady said: Go ahead.

TIKHON. A very warm welcome to you! (*Opens the door and lets the COACHMAN in.*)

The same and the COACHMAN.

COACHMAN. Evening, good Christians! Well, let's have the bit o' rope! Hurry up! Boys, who's gonna lend a hand? There's a tip in it!

TIKHON. Never mind about tips . . . Let 'em snooze, the two of us can handle it.

COACHMAN. Oof, I'm all done in! Cold, mud, wet to the bone . . . One more thing, friend . . . You got a little room here, so's the lady can warm up? The carriage is broke down on one side, no way she can go on sitting in it . . .

TIKHON. Now she wants a room too? Let her warm up in here, if she's froze . . . We'll make some space. (*Walks over to Bortsov and clears off a place beside him.*) Get up, you lot, get up! You can spawl on the floor for an hour, whiles a lady gets warm. (*To Bortsov.*) Get up, your honor! Have a seat! (*BORTSOV raises himself a bit.*) Here's a spot for you.

The COACHMAN exits.

FEDYA. So now we got visitors, dern her hide! Now we won't get to sleep till it's light!

TIKHON. Sorry I didn't ask for fifteen rubles . . . She'd have give it . . . (*Stands in front of the door expectantly.*) You mind yer manners, you lot . . . None of yer backtalk . . .

Enter MARIYA YEGOROVNA followed by the COACHMAN.

S C E N E   V

The same and MARIYA YEGOROVNA.

TIKHON (*bowing*). A very warm welcome to you, your ladyship! Ours is just a humble peasant hut, a hangout for spiders. But there's no call to be finicky!

MARIYA YEGOROVNA. I can't see a thing here . . . Where am I to go?

TIKHON. This way, your ladyship! (*Leads her to a place nearby Bortsov.*) This way, if you'll be so kind! (*Blows on the place.*) A separate room I ain't got, sorry, but don't you fret, ma'am: the folks here is nice and quiet . . .

MARIYA YEGOROVNA (*sits next to Bortsov*). How dreadfully close it is in here! At least open the door a bit!

TIKHON. Right away, ma'am! (*Runs and opens the door to the outside.*)

MERIK. Folks is freezin', but they got to keep the door wide open! (*Gets up and slams the door shut.*) Who's she to give orders 'round here? (*Lies down.*)

TIKHON. Sorry, your ladyship, we got this here idjit . . . a kind of halfwit . . . But don't you be skeered, he's harmless . . . Only, excuse me, ma'am, I can't fix it for ten rubles . . . Fifteen rubles, if you like . . .

MARIYA YEGOROVNA. Very well, only be quick about it!

TIKHON. Right this minute . . . We'll just be a second . . . (*Fishes out a rope from under the bar.*) Right this minute . . .

Pause.

BORTSOV (*takes a look at Mariya Yegorovna*). Marie . . . Masha . . .

MARIYA YEGOROVNA (*staring at Bortsov*). What now?

BORTSOV. Marie . . . Is that you? Where did you come from?

MARIYA YEGOROVNA, recognizing Bortsov, cries out and leaps to the middle of the tavern.

(*Goes to her.*) Marie, it is I . . . I! (*Roars with laughter.*) My wife! Marie! Where in the world am I? People, let's have lights!

MARIYA YEGOROVNA. Get away from me! You're lying, it isn't you! Impossible! (*Hides her face in her hands.*) It's a lie, nonsense!

BORTSOV. That voice, those gestures . . . Marie, it is I! Wait a minute and I'll stop . . . being drunk . . . My head's spinning . . . My God! Hold on, hold on . . . I can't figure it out. (*Shouts.*) My wife! (*Falls at her feet and sobs.*)

A group forms around the couple.

MARIYA YEGOROVNA. Will you get away from me! (*To the Coachman.*) Denis, let's go! I cannot stay here another minute!

MERIK (*jumps up and stares fixedly in her face*). The pitcher! (*Seizes her by the arm.*) It's her her own self! Hey, folks! It's the gent's wife!

MARIYA YEGOROVNA. Get away from me, you clodhopper! (*Tries to tear her arm away from him.*) Denis, what are staring at? (*DENIS and TIKHON run over to her and grab Merik by the arms.*) This is a den of thieves! Let go of my arm! I'm not afraid of you! . . . Get away!

MERIK. Take it easy, I'll let you go right now . . . Just let me speak my piece to you . . . Speak my piece so's you understand . . . Take it easy . . . (*Turns to Tikhon and Denis.*) Git off me, you lugs, let go o' me! I ain't letting her go till I speak my piece! Take it easy . . . right now. (*Beats his fists against his forehead.*) No, God ain't give me the brains! I can't come up with the right words!

MARIYA YEGOROVNA (*tears away her arm*). Go away, you! You're all drunk . . . Let's go, Denis! (*About to walk to the door.*)

MERIK (*stands in her way*). Hey, you should at least take a look at him! You should at least treat him to one kind word. For Christ's sake!

MARIYA YEGOROVNA. Get this . . . halfwit . . . away from me.

MERIK. Then the hell with you, you goddam bitch! (*Swings his axe.*)

> *Terrible commotion. Everyone leaps up noisily and shouts in horror. SAVVA stands between Merik and Mariya Yegorovna . . . DENIS forcefully shoves Merik aside and carries his mistress out of the tavern. After this everyone stands around like blocks of wood. Prolonged pause.*

BORTSOV (*grasps at the air with his hands*). Marie . . . Where are you, Marie!

NAZAROVNA. My God, my God . . . You've tore my heart to shreds, you murderers! There's a curse on this night!

MERIK (*dropping the arm holding the axe*). Did I kill her or not? . . .

TIKHON. Thanks be to God, you saved your neck . . .

MERIK. I didn't kill 'er, I guess . . . (*Staggering, he goes to his bedding.*) Fate didn't want me to die over a stolen axe . . . (*Falls on the bedding and sobs.*) My heart is breaking! My wretched heart is breaking! Take pity on me, good Christians!

Curtain

COLLABORATION

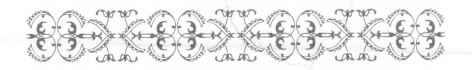

THE POWER OF HYPNOTISM

Сила гипнотизма

Joke in One Act

by An. Chekhov and Iv. Shcheglov[1]

On A. P. Chekhov's first trip to Petersburg, he and I used to sit up long past midnight at Palkin's inn. . . . Our discussion of serious topics shifted to merry themes, and A. P., among other things, improvised, in character, a whole short vaudeville, which was called "The Power of Hypnotism."

A certain dark-eyed little widow has turned the heads of two of her admirers: a fat major with a superb majorial moustache and a youth with no moustache at all, a pharmacist's assistant. Both rivals,—military and civilian,—are crazy about her and ready to make any sacrifice for the sake of her flashing eyes, which possess a certain special, hypnotic power. The cruel little widow explains to the amorous major that she has nothing against his proposal and that the only obstacle to their kissing as man and wife is the major's bushy moustache. And wishing to test the demonic power of her eyes, the little widow uses them to hypnotize the major, which she does so successfully that the major silently makes for the door and hurries straight out of the parlor to the nearest barber . . . The widow also makes the young pharmacist do something stupid. And, because the little widow has "a third" in reserve, as a result, both admirers end up dupes.

---

1 Ivan Leontyevich Leontyev (1856–1911), an army captain, who in the early 1880s embarked on a promising career as a playwright and novelist under the name Ivan Shcheglov. He was an expert at depicting the rising bourgeoisie, and his novel *Suburban Husband* (*Dachny muzh*) added a phrase to the language. His career petered out in the mid-1890s. This translation is based on the text in Shcheglov's *Zhizn vverkh nogami. Iumoristicheskie ocherki i parodii* (*A Topsy-turvy Life. Humorous sketches and parodies*) (St. Petersburg, 1911).

I recall that the last scene, that is the major's appearance without his moustache, made us both laugh a lot.

"You understand," Chekhov said to me, "I'd like to write this playlet in the tone of the most outrageous farce . . . For instance, the amorous druggist secretly pours a love potion of his own devising into the little widow's coffee . . . Or, for instance, a messenger appears with a letter—and the messenger suddenly turns out to be not a messenger at all, but the little widow's sweetheart in disguise. Something along those lines! . . ."

Then Chekhov left for Moscow and gradually forgot about the vaudeville he'd thought up. When I questioned him about the playlet, he begged off, claiming he lacked the proper "mood for a vaudeville." Then he rapidly wrote a full-length play (*Ivanov*) and the vaudeville was put off to some indefinite time. In his later letters A. P. never brought up *The Power of Hypnotism*, and invited me to visit him in the summer so that we could write a full-length funny comedy together. This plan was not destined to be realized, however, and only after Chekhov's death did it occur to me to carry out the projected collaboration in a different way: to complete from memory, following the words and hints of A. P., *The Power of Hypnotism*.

Although the text in the reconstructed *Power of Hypnotism* is entirely mine, the whole scenario and outlines of the characters planned by Chekhov were drawn too boldly for there to be any need to deviate from them.

Only the "major" (a rank that has vanished nowadays) I promoted to a "colonel," and "the fake messenger" was turned into a genuine fiancé, to use him in the denouement of the vaudeville.

Iv. Shcheglov

St. Petersburg
July 1910

THE POWER OF HYPNOTISM

Joke in One Act

CHARACTERS [2]

YULIYA ADAMOVNA KRASNUSHKINA, *an interesting little widow*

SHIPUNOV, *a colonel in the reserves*

LEDENTSOV, *a young pharmacist's assistant*

A MESSENGER

> *The action takes place in the summer, at a country cottage.*

I

KRASNUSHKINA, SHIPUNOV, and LEDENTSOV.

*KRASNUSHKINA is sitting on a bench under a linden tree.
On either side of her, on their knees, SHIPUNOV
and LEDENTSOV.*

SHIPUNOV. I love you! . . .

LEDENTSOV. So do I!! . . .

SHIPUNOV. Oh, Yuliya . . . be mine!

LEDENTSOV. And mine! . . . Oh!! (*clutches at his heart. SHIPUNOV casts his rival a scornful, envious glance.*)

SHIPUNOV (*resolutely*). Just one word: *yes* or *no*?

LEDENTSOV (*irresolutely*). One word . . . just: no or yes? (*Suspenseful pause.*)

KRASNUSHKINA (*her eyes twinkling enigmatically*). Both yes . . . and no! . . .

> *SHIPUNOV and LEDENTSOV exchange glances of perplexity
> and incomprehension.*

---

2 All the names are jokes and might be rendered into Dickensian English as Julia Blushington, Col. Fizzgig, and Mr. Coffdrop.

SHIPUNOV. How come: neither yes nor no?

LEDENTSOV. Well, how come?

KRASNUSHKINA (*flirtatiously*). Oh, just . . . because! . . .

> SHIPUNOV and LEDENTSOV get up from their knees
> in disappointment.

SHIPUNOV. I must confess, it's rather strange . . .

LEDENTSOV. Hm . . . it's strange, I must confess . . . (*Slaps himself on the forehead.*) There's probably some secret involved!

SHIPUNOV. Women always have the same secret: if it's not one man or another, it means that there is . . . a third!

KRASNUSHKINA (*her eyes twinkling enigmatically*). Perhaps . . .

SHIPUNOV. What did I say!

LEDENTSOV. So did I! . . .

SHIPUNOV (*exploding*). No, I said it, not *you*!

LEDENTSOV. Why: *you*, and not *me*?

SHIPUNOV. Because . . . I am not *you*!

LEDENTSOV (*getting excited*). But *you* . . . are not *me*!

SHIPUNOV. And I'm proud that . . . *I am* not *you*!

LEDENTSOV. And I'm proud that . . . *you are* not *me*!!

SHIPUNOV. Well, that's for sure—you hernia truss . . .

LEDENTSOV (*shouts*). Repeat what you just said? . . .

SHIPUNOV (*shouts*). Hernia truss! . . . Pepsin! Aspirin! Saccharine!

LEDENTSOV. Hold me back . . . or else I won't be held responsible for my actions!! (*Offstage a dog barks.*)

KRASNUSHKINA (*interposes her parasol, so that it serves as a barrier, separating them*). Gentlemen, have you gone crazy? You are in my summer cottage, in my presence . . . and all of a sudden you're practically dueling! (*Shoots a languorous, hypnotic glance at them. The rivals calm down and droop their heads guiltily. Pause.*) After all, put yourself in my place: I let the servant girl go to the market, I'm here all alone, I have no husband . . . I might . . . well, I might be sick with fright, if something like this were to recur!!

SHIPUNOV (*leaning toward Krasnushkina, in an undertone*). Put yourself in my place as well: I cannot declare my feelings in the presence of some disinfectant . . .

LEDENTSOV (*having overheard this last word shouts:*) Yuliya Adamovna . . . I will not be held responsible for my actions!! (*Offstage a dog barks.*)

KRASNUSHKINA (*to Shipunov*). That's Nero calling for his bath . . . (*To Ledentsov.*) Monsieur Ledentsov . . . you really must calm down! . . . Go to the kitchen, take Nero and walk him over to the pond . . .

LEDENTSOV. How can I take him, I'd like to know, when he's almost the size of a bear! Yesterday, when I took him for a swim, he grabbed on to my left foot . . .

KRASNUSHKINA. You're afraid of such trifles and dare, after that, to talk about love! (*Hypnotizes him.*) You will go . . . and give him a bath!!

> LEDENTSOV *exits across the balcony. Offstage a dog barks*
> *again and LEDENTSOV cries out. Pause.*

I I

KRASNUSHKINA and SHIPUNOV.

KRASNUSHKINA. I got back from my swim in such a dreamy mood, and then suddenly out of the blue—the two of you with your declarations . . . and such Hispanic passions . . . Horrors! . . . And how many times has my doctor warned me that any talk of love on an empty stomach is extremely harmful . . . Because of you, I still haven't had my coffee . . . (*Goes to the balcony, sits down at the table and drinks her coffee.*) Well, sir, I shall drink my coffee, and you may declare your feelings . . .

SHIPUNOV (*stands gloomily, in a picturesque pose, near the balcony*). To speak for myself, I have but a single feeling: I cannot live without you!

KRASNUSHKINA. And how did you manage to live before?

SHIPUNOV. How can you call that living: it was like a kind of bachelor decadentalism . . .

KRASNUSHKINA. So you want to get married? . . .

SHIPUNOV. I don't want to, but I'm burning with desire!

KRASNUSHKINA. And it has to be . . . me?

SHIPUNOV. Other women do not exist for me!!

KRASNUSHKINA (*evasively*). You are forgetting, Colonel, that every woman has her foibles and whims . . .

SHIPUNOV (*gallantly twirls his magnificent moustache*). Damn it all, there is no sacrifice I would not make for the woman I adore! . . .

KRASNUSHKINA. Why should I believe you? . . .

SHIPUNOV. Because a mere glance from your eyes is a law for me! I swear by the horns of Satan that whatever you demand of me . . . will be instantly performed!!

KRASNUSHKINA. Even if I were to demand . . . (*Stares at his moustache and smiles enigmatically.*)

SHIPUNOV. You do not finish your sentence . . . is something troubling you??

KRASNUSHKINA. Indeed, I am troubled by the prospect of our marriage. I will be your wife, and you will be my husband . . . and then you'll want to kiss me! . . .

SHIPUNOV. What's wrong with that? Naturally, once I am your husband . . . I shall want to kiss your splendid lips!

KRASNUSHKINA. But that's absolutely out of the question . . .

SHIPUNOV. Why is it out of the question?

KRASNUSHKINA. Because my splendid lips . . . cannot abide a big moustache . . . Fie, it prickles so unpleasantly!

SHIPUNOV (*puzzled*). What do you mean?

KRASNUSHKINA (*hypnotizes him*). The meaning is quite simple: if you love me . . . you will shave it off . . .

SHIPUNOV. I'm ready for anything, by the horns of Satan—but not my moustache! . . . For pity's sake, Pushkin himself sang of the hussar's moustache:

... He began to twirl his long moustache ...

And besides there is a circular from the War Department concerning moustaches ... A moustache is, in a manner of speaking, government issue!!

KRASNUSHKINA. Well, in other words, you don't love me ... Good-bye! (*Turns away.*)

SHIPUNOV. I ... don't love you? Why, I can't sleep nights because of you; I've given up my club, cards, the races ... I'm literally going out of my mind with love!! ...

KRASNUSHKINA. If that's the case, then what's keeping you ... from spending half an hour at the barbershop? ... (*Hypnotizes him.*) Snip-snip ... and you will get a definite answer ...

SHIPUNOV (*wavering*). A definite one ...

KRASNUSHKINA. I just said so. (*Gets up, walks over to him and hypnotizes him powerfully.*) Go ... and be shaved! ...

SHIPUNOV (*under a hypnotic spell, moves backward to the gate*). I go ... and shall be shaved ... Oh, those eyes! I swear by the horns of Satan it's beyond human power to withstand that gaze!! I go, ma'am ... (*Clicks his spurs.*)

KRASNUSHKINA. Go ... and I promise you something ... you least expect!

SHIPUNOV (*completely stupefied*). You promise something? ... Oh, I'm going, I'm going!! ... (*Exits.*)

III

KRASNUSHKINA (alone) and then LEDENTSOV.

KRASNUSHKINA. Well, that's one shown the door—now to make short work of the other one ... (*A dog barks offstage.*) There he is ... There's really is something ... magnetic ... about my eyes! ... Many people have remarked on it from a distance. Only there's never been a suitable occasion to try out their power ... (*Takes out a hand mirror and smartens herself up. LEDENTSOV appears on the balcony, limping on his right foot. Taking advantage of Krasnushkina having her back to him, he pulls out of his pocket a packet of powder and hastily sprinkles the powder into Krasnushkina's cup.*)

LEDENTSOV (*resolutely*). I'll commit a crime, and she shall be *mine*!!

KRASNUSHKINA (*sees it all in her hand-mirror*). What is he doing? He sprinkled something in my coffee . . . What a lunatic! . . . (*Quickly turns around and almost bumps into Ledentsov.*) What were you doing out there . . . on the balcony? You were sprinkling something into my coffee! . . . Well, confess: did you sprinkle, sprinkle?? . . .

LEDENTSOV (*falling to his knees*). Forgive me, but I . . . this . . . wanted to . . . I mean I turned to the last resort! . . .

KRASNUSHKINA. What is the last resort?

LEDENTSOV (*on his knees*). The resort that stimulates love! . . . My own invention in the form of a powder . . . I've just petitioned the Health Department for a patent . . . it's called "amoroso furioso"!! . . .

KRASNUSHKINA. Get up . . . I forgive you! . . . Love excuses a great many things . . . But promise me never to pour in any more "amoroso"!

LEDENTSOV. Why get up! I would rather die at your feet!!

KRASNUSHKINA. Get up . . . and get out! You're always in a hurry to die . . .

LEDENTSOV. How can I leave you . . . before I receive a definite answer?

KRASNUSHKINA. You will get a definite answer in half an hour: it can't be done earlier . . . On the other hand I promise you *something* (*correcting herself*), something you least expect! . . .

LEDENTSOV. You promise . . . something? Oh! . . . (*Clutches at his heart.*)

KRASNUSHKINA. Yes, but on one condition: you tidy yourself up a bit first . . . The way you look now you'd better not appear before me!

LEDENTSOV (*looking himself over*). What doesn't look right? What's untidy about me?

KRASNUSHKINA. Both what's in your head . . . and on your head! . . . It's your long hair (*tousles his hair*). Isn't this really unsightly? It's quite out of keeping for a suitor . . . And besides, I can't stand long hair . . . you understand, I can't stand it!!.

LEDENTSOV. But excuse me, Yuliya Adamovna, I am a poet, aren't I? . . . After all, it's inconceivable: a poet . . . and no long hair! . . .

KRASNUSHKINA. You . . . a poet! Since when?

LEDENTSOV. Since six o'clock this morning! Yesterday when you gave me a violet from your bouquet, I could not sleep all night from bliss, and towards morning I composed verses devoted entirely to you . . . (*declaims with strong emotion*).

> In the twilight of life, so wretched and gritty,
> You made me smell sweet with your violet pretty . . .
> I came back to life—no longer a vagrant,
> I soared in the air amidst odors so fragrant! . . .
> I soared!! . . .

KRASNUSHKINA. *Merci*, the verses are very charming . . . But all the same it shouldn't keep you from dropping by the barbershop! . . .

LEDENTSOV (*depressed*). Which means, I've got to be . . . shorn!

KRASNUSHKINA. If I say so, that's what it means . . . What sort of love is it that cannot make even an empty sacrifice! (*Hypnotizes him.*) Why don't you have it done? . . .

LEDENTSOV. Does it have to be close-cropped,—I mean, like a hedgehog?

KRASNUSHKINA. Definitely "like a hedgehog" . . . I can't imagine my husband-to-be as anything but a hedgehog! . . .

LEDENTSOV. In that case . . . I shall have it done!

KRASNUSHKINA. It's about time. (*Hypnotizes him.*) Snip-snip . . . and no one will recognize you! . . .

LEDENTSOV (*under the hypnotic spell*). Snip-snip . . . and no one will recognize me!! (*Sends a kiss through the air.*) I evacuate! . . . I evaporate! . . . (*Exits.*)

I V

KRASNUSHKINA (alone).

KRASNUSHKINA. It looks as if I've gone rather far with my "summer flirtations"! . . . If Boris doesn't show up today, I really don't know how I'm going to get myself out of this . . . Judging by his letter, he was supposed to be back from his cruise last night . . . Boris darling, come back quickly! (*Stops pensively by the balcony.*) Ah, it's really my fault that things have turned out this way! Being alone in a cottage is so boring that you're glad for any chance acquaintance . . . And besides it's so interesting: to try out the power of my feminine charms on men! . . . Just last winter a gypsy fortune teller predicted that I would cause all sorts of trouble with my eyes . . . Yes, and then she predicted . . . (*Laughs.*) Well, what nonsense! . . . That I should beware . . . "of meeting a red-headed messenger" . . . Apparently, if I meet a red-headed messenger, all my powers will suddenly disappear . . . And here's the problem: now I'm afraid of all red-headed messengers!! (*She suddenly screams, on seeing a tall messenger with a big red beard coming through the gate. The messenger, despite the summer weather, is wearing a long overcoat with a turned-up collar, with a satchel over his shoulder.*)

V

KRASNUSHKINA and MESSENGER (BORIS in disguise).

BORIS (*in a feigned hoarse voice*). Does Yuliya Adamovna Krasnushkina live here?

KRASNUSHKINA (*upset*). Krasnushkina . . . that's me!

BORIS. Here's a telegram for you, ma'am . . . (*Hands her a telegram and jealously looks on.*)

KRASNUSHKINA. God forbid there's been an accident! (*With trembling hands she tears open the envelope.*) "Arriving today. Your Boris"—(*excited*). He's coming! He's coming! At last . . . Oh, how happy I am!! (*Rummages in her purse.*) Here's a half-ruble tip . . . drink to the health of Boris! (*The messenger bows low.*) Lord, how happy I am! . . . If it weren't for that red beard, I think I might kiss him in my delight! . . .

BORIS. Well, in that case . . . we can take off the beard! (*Pulls off the beard and the cap. Before Krasnushkina stands a young officer in a naval uniform. A cry of joy.*)

KRASNUSHKINA. Boris . . . is it you?

BORIS. Why, of course . . . (*A prolonged kiss.*)

KRASNUSHKINA (*helping him out of his overcoat and satchel*). Well, what's the reason for the mystification? Are you trying to test my love? . . . (*BORIS cheerfully nods assent.*) Naughty boy! How can you doubt my feelings for even a moment!! And, finally, how can you . . . try a woman's patience so long? Furthermore . . .

BORIS. It hasn't been so long. We arrived at Cronstadt only this morning . . . and I took a torpedo boat straight to here! I lingered only five minutes to change my clothes . . . From early morning, as the saying goes, not a morsel has passed my lips. And there's coffee, right on cue! That's just what I need . . . (*Goes to the balcony and pours coffee into the cup, into which the love powder has been sprinkled.*)

KRASNUSHKINA (*tragically*). Boris . . . do not drink! . . .

BORIS. What do you mean: "Do not drink"? That's very kind of you . . .

KRASNUSHKINA (*agitated*). What I meant to say was "Do drink!" . . . I'm so excited by your unexpected arrival . . . (*To herself.*) God knows what he sprinkled in it! However, if it stimulates love . . . let it be!!

BORIS (*drinks*). The coffee's delicious, but awfully sweet . . . (*Raises the cup.*) "I drink to the health of Boris!" (*Laughs*).

KRASNUSHKINA. And how about the "fifty-kopek piece"? . . .

BORIS. Well, forgive me: we won't give back the "fifty-kopek piece" for anything! I'll have it made into a charm for my watch chain and will wear it as the dearest memento . . . (*Finishing his coffee.*) I don't know what's come over me? . . . I have never loved so madly! . . . Oh Yuliya, love is setting my blood on fire!! (*Speeds from the balcony and enfolds Krasnushkina in an ardent embrace.*) I feel like smothering you today in my embrace!!! . . .

KRASNUSHKINA (*dismayed*). Love . . . embrace . . . But when do we get married? . . .

BORIS. Married . . . why not right now! . . .

KRASNUSHKINA. Right now . . . is impossible! What about tomorrow morning . . .

BORIS. Till tomorrow is much too long! This evening is better!

KRASNUSHKINA. I really don't know . . . I have to make some arrangements . . .

BORIS. No you don't. The simpler the better. Wouldn't a wedding party create delays? . . .

KRASNUSHKINA. I don't think so! . . . I have tamed two best men . . . with that very aim in mind . . .

BORIS (*jealously*). Who are they?

KRASNUSHKINA. One is a colonel, and the other . . . Well, speak of the devil . . . (*Far upstage SHIPUNOV and LEDENTSOV appear: the former has shaved off his moustache, and the latter has his head shorn; both look rather crestfallen.—KRASNUSHKINA cannot keep from laughing.*)

BORIS. What's so funny?

KRASNUSHKINA. Ah, they're hilarious! I'll tell you all about it later . . . For now hide behind the tree! . . . (*Boris shrugs and hides behind the garden bench, back of the linden tree.*)

V I

The same, SHIPUNOV, and LEDENTSOV.

SHIPUNOV (*stepping forward*). Here I am!

LEDENTSOV (*appearing behind Shipunov*). Here we are!! . . .

SHIPUNOV. You promised me something . . . if I fufilled your wish . . . Alas! (*Points to his shaven upper lip.*)

LEDENTSOV. And you also promised me, if I . . . (*Points to his smooth-shaven pate.*) Alack and alas!!

SHIPUNOV. Hm . . . I'd be curious to know: where exactly is this mysterious something?

LEDENTSOV. That's just it:—where is it?? . . .

KRASNUSHKINA (*mixed up*). He . . . I mean it . . . it is here! (*Waves to Boris.*) Mister *something* . . . please come over here! . . . (*BORIS comes out of hiding.*) May I introduce you to: Baron Frank . . . Boris Nikolaevich . . . my *husband-to-be!* (*To him.*) And these . . . are the *best men-to-be* . . . Shipunov and Ledentsov! (*Shipunov and Ledentsov are dumbfounded.*) I hope, gentlemen, you will not refuse us the kindness of being our best men?? . . . (*Affectionately embraces Boris.—LEDENTSOV, unable to support the sight, falls with a groan on to the chest of Shipunov.*)

Curtain

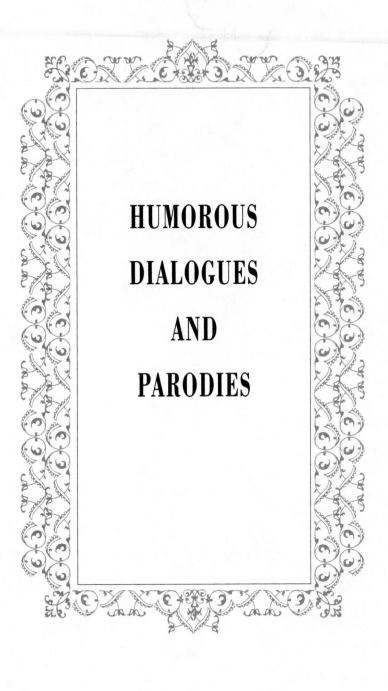

HUMOROUS

DIALOGUES

AND

PARODIES

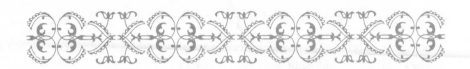

*A*s a medical student in Moscow, Chekhov was drawn into the world of journalism through his brothers, Aleksandr, a writer, and Nikolay, an artist. Through their agency, he began to compose cartoon captions for the humor journal *The Alarm Clock* in 1879, and gradually started writing comic squibs that were not dependent on illustration. Between 1880 and 1887 he contributed jokes, monologues, dialogues, anecdotes, parodies, and short stories to magazines in both Moscow and St. Petersburg, using a host of pen names, among them Antosha Chekhonte, The Doctor Who's Lost His Patients, The Man without a Spleen, The Spleen without a Man, and My Brother's Brother.

These first steps in writing dialogue are heavily derivative of the Russian comic traditions. Significantly, his earliest playlet, *The Fool, or The Retired Captain*, resembles matchmaker scenes in Gogol and Ostrovsky, even though its conclusion is more scabrous than anything to be found in them. The two-part *Honorable Townsfolk* recalls Saltykov-Shchedrin's satires of provincial life. Others are simply extended gags.

Chekhov's journalism entailed much theater attendance, for in the early 1880s he wrote what amounted to a behind-the-scenes gossip column with occasional reviews. This activity led in turn to an acquaintance with actors and managers. Growing familiarity bred contempt but could not efface his fascination with the stage.

One of the prime butts of Chekhov's ridicule was Mikhail Valentinovich Lentovsky, who enjoyed considerable success running the Hermitage Pleasure Garden and an operetta theater, the Bouffe, although his New Theatre, devoted to legitimate drama, foundered. After he was declared bankrupt, the merchant class, to whose taste he catered, enabled him to make a fresh start, and in 1886 he founded the Skomorokh (Minstrel) Theatre. Plays of Gogol and Ostrovsky and even *Hamlet* could be found there, but the bulk of the repertory was made up of farces, melodramas, and fairy extravaganzas. His productions abounded in pyrotechnical displays, explosions, fires, collapsing bridges, and all the impedimenta of sensationalism.

Nikolay Chekhov worked for Lentovsky as a scene painter, allowing the brothers entry to green rooms and dressing-rooms, and although Anton himself kept up good relations with the manager, he fired hilarious sallies at the mixtures of fustian and lycopodium powder that reigned at Lentovsky's theater. Chekhov pooh-poohed the stage's claim to be an educational force, a means of uplifting the people. For him, the chasm between the theater's aspirations and the tawdriness of its personnel was too patent to assume society would be edified by playgoing. He was also bemused by the pretensions of dramatists. His "dramatic sketch" *The Sudden Death of a Steed,* which mocks playwriting dilettantes, offers such a rich piece of nonsense that it was later staged by Moscow's rollicking cabaret The Bat (known in the West as the Chauve-Souris) before the First World War.

THE FOOL, OR THE RETIRED CAPTAIN[1]

Дура, или Капитан в отставке

(A Scenelet from an Unproduced Vaudeville)

The marrying season. RETIRED CAPTAIN SOUSOV[2] (sits on an oilcloth-covered divan, both hands clasped, pressing one leg against his body. He rocks back and forth while he talks.) THE MATCHMAKER LUKINISHNA[3] (an obese old woman with a stupid but kindly face) is placed to one side on a stool. Her face bears an expression of aversion, mingled with wonder. In profile she looks like a snail, full face like a black spider. She speaks obsequiously and hiccups after every word.

CAPTAIN. Still, if you look at this from a point of view, then Ivan Nikolaevich acted very practically. He did the right thing in getting married. You may be a professor or a genius, but if you're not married, you aren't worth a red cent. You've got no civil rights or social standing . . . Anyone who isn't married can have no real weight in society . . . Just take me for example . . . I'm a man of the educated classes, a home-owner, with money . . . There's my rank as well . . . and a medal, but what good am I? Who am I, if you look at me from a point of view? A loner . . . A kind of synonym and nothing more (*thinks about it*). Everyone's married, everyone's got kids, only I . . . like in that ballad . . . (*sings a sorrowful ballad in a tenor voice*). That's what my life is like . . . If only I had even some shop-soiled bride!

LUKINISHNA. Why shop-soiled? For you, dearie, a shop-soiled one won't do. With your nobleness and all your, pardon the expression, virtues you could marry anybody, and with money . . .

CAPTAIN. I don't need money. I won't stoop to do such a dirty deed as marry for money. I have my own money and I don't want to eat my wife's bread, she should eat mine. If you pick a poor girl, she will have feelings, be understanding . . . I'm not so selfish that for self-interest I'd . . .

---

1 Published in *Splinters* (*Oskolki*) 38 (September 17, 1883), p. 5.

2 A double-punning name: *Sous* = Sauce, and *So-usy* = With a moustache.

3 Literally, the daughter of Luke, but with hints of *lukavy*, cunning, and *luk*, onion.

LUKINISHNA. That's the truth, dearie . . . A poor creature will be more beautiful than a rich girl . . .

CAPTAIN. And I don't need beauty, either. What good is it? You don't drink water from a face. Beauty should be not in one's person, but in one's soul . . . What I want is goodness, meekness, a sort of innocence . . . I want my wife to respect me, worship me . . .

LUKINISHNA. Hm . . . How could she not worship you, if you are her lawful husband? Ain't she got no eddication or what?

CAPTAIN. Hold on, don't interrupt. I don't need education either. Nowadays you can't do without education, of course, but there are all sorts of educations. Granted, if your wife's got French and German and different lingoes it's very nice: but what's the good of it, if she doesn't know how to, say, sew on your buttons? I'm of the educated class, welcome everywhere, I can talk to Prince Kanitelin[4] the way I'm talking to you now, but my nature is a simple one. I need a simple girl. I don't need brains. The man should have all the brains, but a female creature can get on without brains.

LUKINISHNA. You're so right, dearie. Nowdays even the papers write about the brainy ones that they won't do at all.

CAPTAIN. A fool will love and worship and appreciate my status as a man. She will walk in fear. Whereas a brainy one will eat your bread but won't appreciate whose bread it is. Go find me a fool . . . Hear me aright: a fool. Have you got anything like that in stock?

LUKINISHNA. I got all sorts in stock (*gives it some thought*). Which one's for you? Lots of fools, because even the brainy ones are fools . . . Each of these fools has got her own brains . . . You want a full-fledged fool? (*Thinks.*) I got this one fool of a girl, but I don't know if you'd like her . . . Of merchant stock she comes and with a dowry of about five thousand . . . Personally it's not that she's not beautiful, but just—neither this nor that . . . a bit scrawny, a bit scraggly . . . Affectionate, refined . . . Loads of loving kindness! She'd give the shirt off her back if anybody asked . . . Oh, and meek . . . Her mother could yank her around by the hair, and you wouldn't hear a peep out of her—not a blessed word! And she minds her parents, she can be took to church, and when it comes to keeping house . . . But as to what's

---

4 Joke name from *kanitel*, blather, hot air.

up here (*puts a finger to her forehead*) . . . Don't blame me, sinner that I am, for speaking my mind, but, to tell you the God's honest truth: she ain't got none! A fool . . . She's quiet, quiet, like a murder victim quiet . . . She sits, nice and quiet, then suddenly out of the blue—up she jumps! Just like you'd scalded her with boiling water. Springs off her chair, like she was scorched, and then the yammering begins . . . She yammers and yammers . . . With no end in sight she yammers . . . Those parents of hers are fools, and the food's no good, and don't talk to her like that. And they've found nobody she can live with and it's like they was tormenting the life out of her . . . "You," she says, "can't understand me . . . " The gal's a fool! The merchant Kashalotov[5] made a match with her—and she turned him down! Laughed in his face, that's what . . . A rich merchant, handsome, aligant, like a cute young officer laddy. Or else, sometimes, she'll take up some stupid little book, go in the pantry and start reading . . .

CAPTAIN. No, that fool doesn't suit my specifications . . . Find another one (*gets up and looks at his watch*). For now *bon sure*.[6] Time for me to go . . . I'll go my bachelor's way . . .

LUKINISHNA. Go, dearie! Happy hunting! (*Gets up.*) On Saturday night I'll drop in concerning a bride (*goes to the door*) . . . Well, now as to that . . . would you be needing a little female companionship along your bachelor's way?

A. *Chekhonte*

---

5 Joke name from *kashalot*, sperm whale.

6 Mispronunciation of *bon jour*, French for "good day."

A YOUNG MAN[1]

Молодой человек

At a table, covered with impressive inkblots, sits
PRAVDOLYUBOV. Before him stands UPRYAMOV,[2] a young
man with a facetious expression on his face.

PRAVDOLYUBOV (*with tears in his eyes*). Young man! I have children of my own . . . I have a heart . . . I understand . . . which is why this pains me so. I assure you, as a man of honor, that denying this will only do you harm. Tell me frankly, where were you going just now?

UPRYAMOV. To . . . to the editorial offices of a humor magazine.

PRAVDOLYUBOV. Hm . . . You're a humorist, I suppose? (*Shakes his head reproachfully*.) You should be ashamed! So young and yet so depraved . . . What's that you're holding?

UPRYAMOV. Manuscripts.

PRAVDOLYUBOV. Hand them over! (*Takes them and looks them over*.) Now, sir . . . let's have a look . . . What's this one?

UPRYAMOV. Subjects for editorial cartoons.

PRAVDOLYUBOV (*is bursting with indignation, but, quickly mastering his feelings, calms down and becomes impartial, process-server–style*). What's this drawing?

UPRYAMOV. You see, it's the drawing of a man. He is standing with one foot in Russia and the other in Austria. He is doing magic tricks. "Gentlemen," he is saying. "A ruble moves from my right pocket to my left and turns into 65 kopeks!" As a companion-piece to this drawing there's another. You see, here's the credit ruble with little hands and feet. He keeps falling down over and over, and there's a German running after him and clipping him with a scissors . . . Did you get it? This one's a tavern . . . This is our press, and this press . . . And here are settlers in a birch forest; there are children

---

1 First published in *Splinters* (*Oskolki*) 5 (February 4, 1884), p. 5. Moscow readers were surprised that it passed the censorship.

2 Joke names: Pravdolyubov = Lover of Truth; Upryamov = Upright.

too, begging for gruel . . . A special kind of gruel, as you must be aware . . . Here's a drawing of a lackey . . .

PRAVOLYUBOV. And who is this in the mousetrap?

UPRAYMOV. That's Privy Counselor Rossitsky; the trap is baited with government-issue pork . . .

PRAVOLYUBOV (*smacking his lips at the word "pork"*). A privy counselor . . . (*Blushes for humanity.*) So young and yet so depraved . . . Are you aware, my goosir, that a privy counselor is the equivalent of a lieutenant general in the army? How can you fail to understand that? What crude lack of understanding, what profanity! (*Sighs.*) What am I to do with you now? What? (*Grows pensive, but soon a personal feeling transcends his sense of duty, and the prey slips from his grasp.*) I cannot look at you, pathetic, unhappy young man! You disgust me, you are pitiful! Get out of here! May my scorn serve as your punishment!

UPRYAMOV, *not at all contrite, with an ambiguous smile, sets off for the editorial offices.*

UNCLEAN TRAGEDIANS AND LEPROUS PLAYWRIGHTS[1]

Нечистые трагики и прокаженные драматурги

A Horribly-Dreadfully-Excitingly-Desperate Trrragedy

by My Brother's Brother

Lots of acts, even more scenes

CHARACTERS

MIKH. VAL. LENTOVSKY,[2] *man and impresario*

TARNOVSKY, *a harrowing man; on a first-name basis with devils, whales, and crocodiles; pulse 225, temperature 109.4°*

THE AUDIENCE, *a lady amiable in every respect; eats whatever is put in front of her*

CHARLES XII, *King of Sweden;*[3] *the manners of a fireman*

THE BARONESS, *a brunette with a modicum of talent; does not turn down insignificant roles*

GENERAL EHRENSWERD, *a frightfully big man with the voice of a mastodon*

DELAGARDI, *an ordinary man; plays the role with the free-and-easy manner of . . . a prompter*

---

1 A parody of K. Tarnovsky's adaptation from a German melodrama, *The Clean and the Leprous,* which opened at Lentovsky's New Dramatic Theatre in Moscow on January 15, 1884. First published in *The Alarm-clock (Budilnik)* 4 (1884), pp. 50–51.

2 Mikhail Valentinovich Lentovsky (1843–1906), actor and manager, important in promoting Russian music-hall and operetta. Chekhov liked him personally but regularly made fun of his crowd-pleasing productions.

3 The action takes place in Sweden; the role of the king was played by V. L. Forkatti.

STELLA, *the impresario's sister*[4]

BURL, *a man brought in on Svobodin's[5] shoulders.*

HANSEN[6]

OTHERS

EPILOGUE.*

The crater of a volcano. At a desk, covered in blood, sits TARNOVSKY; instead of a head, a skull sits on his shoulders; sulphur blazes in his mouth; out of his nostrils leap sneering green imps. He dips his pen not in an inkwell but in the lava that witches are stirring. It's horrifying. Flying through the air are the shudders that run up and down your spine. Far upstage shivery shakes are hanging on red-hot hooks. Thunder and lightning. The calendar of Aleksey Suvorin[7] (the county secretary) is lying right there as stoic as a process-server, as it predicts the collision of the earth with the sun, the destruction of the universe, and the price rise in pharmaceutical drugs. Chaos, horror, terror . . . The reader's fancy can provide the rest.

TARNOVSKY (*gnawing his pen*). How am I to write this sort of thing, currrse it! I can't come up with anything! There's already been a *Trip to the Moon* . . . there's been a *Vagabond*, too[8] . . . (*Drinks boiling oil.*) Have to come up with something else . . . something that'll make the merchant's wives

*I wanted to put down "Prologue," but the editor says that the more improbable the better. Whatever he wants! (*Typesetter's note.*)

---

4 Lentovsky's sister, A. V. Lentovskaya-Ryuban, was an actress in his company.

5 Pavel Mikhailovich Svobodin (Koznenko, 1850–1892) was an actor in the company in the 1883–1884 season and played the simpleton Burl. His performance as Count Shabelsky in *Ivanov* in 1889 so pleased Chekhov that they became good friends.

6 I. Hansen (b.1841), the theater's balletmaster, played the mute role of Axel.

7 Aleksey Sergeevich Suvorin (1834–1912), journalist and publisher, had risen from peasant origins to become a millionaire and influence monger in the conservative camp; he and Chekhov were good friends until they took different sides in the Dreyfus Affair. His publishing house issued calendars and almanacs, among other things.

8 Lentovsky had presented successful productions of the Offenbach operetta (based on Jules Verne) *A Trip to the Moon* (1878), and a melodrama called *The Forest Vagabond* (based on the French melodrama *Les Pirates de la Savane*) in 1884.

across the river dream of devils three days running . . . (*Rubs his cranium.*) Hm . . . Bestir yourselves, great brains! (*He thinks: thunder and lightning; the volley of a thousand cannons is heard, performed according to a design by Mr. Shekhtel;*[9] *out of the cracks crawl a dragon, vampires, and serpents; into the crater falls a great steamer trunk, out of which pops Lentovsky, clad in a big poster.*)

LENTOVSKY. Greetings, Tarnovsky!

TARNOVSKY

WITCHES   — (*together*). All hail, my liege!

OTHERS

LENTOVSKY. Well then? Is the play ready, currrse it! (*Waves a cudgel.*)

TARNOVSKY. No, no way, Mikhail Valentinovich. I think, y'see, I sit and I come up with nothing. You have tasked me with too hard a task! You want my play to freeze the audience's blood, an earthquake to take place in the hearts of the merchant's wives from across the river, my monologues to make the lamps go out . . . But don't you agree that such a thing is beyond the powers of even so great a dramatist as Tarnovsky! (*He is embarrassed at having praised himself.*)

LENTOVSKY. Rrrubbish, currrse it! More gunpowder, Bengal lights, highfalutin monologues—and it's done! For the sake of the costumes, cursssse it, set it in the highest society . . . Betrayal . . . Prison . . . The prisoner's beloved is forcibly married to the villain . . . In the villain's role we'll cast Pisaryov[10] . . . Next, an escape from prison . . . gunshots . . . I won't spare the gunpowder . . . Next, a baby, whose noble origins will be disclosed only in the sequel . . . And at the very end more gunshots, another fire, and the triumph of virtue . . . In short, concoct something hackneyed, the way the Rocamboles and Counts of Monte-Cristo[11] concoct things . . . (*Thunder, lightning, hoarfrost, dew. The volcano erupts. LENTOVSKY is expelled.*)

---

9 Frants Osipovich Shekhtel (1859–1926), an architect, who later designed the Moscow Art Theatre building and the Chekhov library in Taganrog.

10 Modest Ivanovich Pisaryov (1844–1905), an excellent realistic actor, who later created the role of Dorn in *The Seagull* in 1896.

11 Rocambole is a romantic burglar in adventure novels by Ponson de Terrail; the Count of Monte Cristo is the protagonist of Dumas *père's* novel of the same name. Chekhov later made an abridgment of it for Suvorin.

ACT ONE

The AUDIENCE, USHERS, HANSEN, and others.

USHERS (*helping the audience members off with their fur coats*). A tip, an't please your worship! (*Not getting a tip, they grab the audience members by the tails of their coats.*) O, black ingratitude!!! (*Are ashamed for humanity.*)

ONE OF THE AUDIENCE. What, is Lentovsky recovered?

USHER. Started fighting again, which means he's recovered![12]

HANSEN (*dressing in his dressing room*). I'll amaze them! I'll show them! All the papers will start talking!

(*The action continues, but the reader is impatient; he is thirsting for Act Two, and therefore — curtain!*)

ACT TWO

The court of Charles XII. Behind his back, VALTS[13] is swallowing swords and red-hot coals. Thunder and lightning.

CHARLES XII and his courtiers.

CHARLES (*strides across the stage and rolls his eyes*). Delagardi! You have betrayed the fatherland! Hand over your sword to the captain and be so good as to march into prison!

DELAGARDI (*utters a few heartfelt words and exits*).

CHARLES. Tarnovsky! In your heart-rending play you have made me live through an extra ten years! Be so good as to head for prison! (*To the*

---

12 After recovering from an illness, Lentovsky had been hauled into court and sentenced to a month's house arrest for disturbing the peace through his production of *Frol Skobeev.*

13 Konstantin Fyodorovich Valts (1846–1929), scene designer and chief stagehand of the Moscow Imperial Theatres, a specialist in spectacular stage effects. He was blamed by the newspapers for the collapse of the stage at the Bolshoy Theatre during a ballet in 1883.

Baroness.) You love Delagardi and have a baby by him. In the interests of the plot I'm not supposed to know about that incident and am supposed to marry you off to a man you don't love. Marry General Ehrenswerd.

BARONESS (*marrying the General*). Ah!

GENERAL EHRENSWERD. I'll make it hot for 'em! (*Is appointed warden of the prison, where Delagardi and Tarnovsky are incarcerated.*)

CHARLES. Well, now I'm free right up to the fifth act. I'll go to my dressing room!

ACTS THREE AND FOUR

STELLA (*plays all right, as usual*). Count, I love you!

YOUNG COUNT. And I love you, Stella, but I implore you in the name of love, tell me, why the hell did Tarnovsky get me mixed up in this godawful mess? What does he want from me? What's my relationship to this plot?

BURL. Why, it was all Sprut's doing! Thanks to him I wound up in the army. He beat me, dogged me, bit me . . . and my name's not Burl if he wasn't the one who wrote this play! He's capable of anything just to make things hot for me!

STELLA (*having found out her parentage*). I'm going to father to set him free! (*On the way to the prison she meets Hansen. HANSEN performs an entrechat.*)

BURL. Thanks to Sprut I wound up in the army and am taking part in this play. Probably, it's Sprut, just to make it hot for me, who made this Hansen trip the light fantastic! Well, just you wait! (*The boards collapse. The stage caves in. HANSEN performs a leap that causes all the old maids present to feel faint.*)

ACTS FIVE AND SIX

STELLA (*meets her dear papa in prison and with him comes up with a plan of escape*). I'll save you, father! But how can it done so that

Tarnovsky won't escape with us? If he escapes from prison, he'll write a new melodrama!

GENERAL EHRENSWERD (*tortures the Baroness and the incarcerated*). Because I'm the villain, I'm not supposed to resemble a human being at all! (*Eats raw meat.*)

DELAGARDI and **STELLA** (*escape from prison*).

EVERYONE. Hold 'em! Catch 'em!

DELAGARDI. Be that as it may, we'll escape all the same and stay in one piece! (*Gunshot.*) Spit on it! (*Falls dead.*) And spit on this too! The author kills, but also resurrects! (*CHARLES comes out of the dressing room and orders the virtuous to triumph over vice. General rejoicing. The moon smiles, and so do the stars.*)

AUDIENCE (*pointing out TARNOVSKY to Burl*). There he is, there's Sprut! Catch him!

BURL (*strangles Tarnovsky. TARNOVSKY falls dead, but immediately leaps up again. Thunder, lightning, hoarfrost, the murder of Coverley,*[14] *a great migration of peoples, shipwreck and the tying up of all the loose ends.*)

LENTOVSKY. And yet I am not satisfied! (*Is swallowed up.*)

---

14 *The Murder of Coverley* was a sensational melodrama in which a train runs across the stage; Lentovsky had produced it in 1883.

AN IDEAL EXAMINATION[1]

Идеальный экзамен

(A Short Answer to All Long Questions)

Conditio sine qua non:[2] a very learned teacher and a very clever pupil. The former is malicious and persistent, the latter is invulnerable. Just as an ideal fire brigade should arrive half an hour before the fire, so an ideal student has answers ready half an hour before the question. For brevity's sake and to avoid a large fee,* I've put the gist in dramatic form.

TEACHER. You have just said that earth can be represented as a ball. But you forget that it contains high mountains, deep valleys, Moscow carriage ways, which prevent it from being round!

PUPIL. They no more prevent it from being round than do little indentations on an orange or pimples on a face.

TEACHER. And what does face mean?

PUPIL. The face is the mirror of the soul, and can get smashed as easily as any other mirror.

TEACHER. And what does mirror mean?

PUPIL. A mirror is a piece of furniture on which a woman hangs her weapons ten times a day. A mirror is a woman's experimental laboratory.

TEACHER (*sarcastically*). Goodness me, aren't you clever! (*After a moment's thought.*) Now I'm going to ask you a certain question . . . (*Quickly.*) What is life?

PUPIL. Life is a fee paid not to authors but to their works.

TEACHER. And how large is that fee?

PUPIL. It is equal to the fee which bad editors pay for very bad translations.

*I don't understand what this is for! *Author.*

---

1 Published in *Splinters* (*Oskolki*) 24 (June 16, 1884), pp. 277–280.

2 Latin, the indispensable condition.

TEACHER. Well, sir . . . Now, can you tell me something about railroads?

PUPIL (*rapidly and distinctly*).The railroad, in the general acceptance of that word, is the name of an instrument which serves to transport fortunes, let blood and provide persons of low income powerful sensations. It consists properly of the rails and the railroad regulations. The latter are the following. Railroad stations are subject to hygiene inspections equivalent to those of slaughter-houses, the railroad to those of cemeteries: With a view to preserving the cleanliness of the air both of them must be kept at a respectable distance from residential areas. An individual, transported by the railroad, will be referred to as the passenger, but once he has arrived at his place of destination, he will be renamed the deceased. In case a man, on his way to visit his auntie in Tambov or his cousin in Saratov, is reluctant to submit to the will of the Fates and join his ancestors, he must state his reluctance, but no later than six months after the crash. Those wishing to write a will shall receive pen and ink from the chief conductor for a set fee. In case of a collision, derailment and the like, the passengers are obligated to keep silent and hug the ground. In case two trains collide, a third must not get involved . . .

TEACHER. That'll do, hold on . . . Now then, what is justice?

PUPIL. Justice is the railroad fines, hung up on the inside wall of every carriage: for a broken window two rubles, for a torn curtain three rubles, for slashed upholstery on the seat five rubles, for breakage of one's own person in case of a crash the passenger will not be fined.

TEACHER. Who cleans the Moscow streets?

PUPIL. Rain.

TEACHER. And who gets paid for it?

PUPIL. (Name a river.)

TEACHER. Well now . . . And what can you tell me about the horse-drawn railroad?

PUPIL. The horse-drawn tramway or, to put it more simply, the horse-and-equine-drawn transit system, consists of an inside, an outside, and the transit system regulations. The inside costs five kopeks, the outside three kopeks, the transit system regulations nothing. The first was given to mankind for the most comfortable contemplation of the conductors' morals, the second for peeping in the morning into second-floor windows with low necklines, the third to be obeyed. These rules are as follows. The horse-drawn tram does not exist for the public, but the public for the horse-drawn tram. On the conductor's entrance into the carriage the public must smile pleasantly. Movement forward, movement backward, and absolute stillness are synonymous. Speed is equal in negative proportion to size, now and then zero, and on major holidays one and a half miles per hour. If a car should be derailed, the passenger pays nothing.

TEACHER. Tell me, please, what is the reason that two cars on meeting one another ring a bell and what's the reason the ticket-collectors tear off corners of the tickets?

PUPIL. They both constitute a trade secret of the inventors.

TEACHER. Which writer do you like the most?

PUPIL. The one who knows how to end a sentence with a period at the right moment.

TEACHER. Makes sense . . . But do you know who is responsible for the exaggerations, which are plaguing the reader at this very moment?

PUPIL. That constitutes a trade secret of the editorial board . . . However, just for you, I can probably . . . If you like, I'll reveal that secret to you . . . (*In a whisper*). These exaggerations were committed in his old age by

A. Chekhonte

"CHAOS-VILE IN ROME"[1]

"Кавардак в Риме"

A Comic Oddity in Three Acts, Five Scenes, with a Prologue and
Two Flops.

CHARACTERS

COUNT FALCONI,[2] *a very fat man*

COUNTESS, *his nervous wife*

LUNA, *a planet pleasant in every respect*[3]

ARTHUR,[4] *an artist-ventriloquist, who drinks with his belly*

HESSE, *an artist. You are requested not to confuse him with the
match manufacturer and matchbox satirist Hesse*[5]

THE ORPHAN GIRL, *in red stockings. Innocent and virtuous, but
not so much as to prevent her from adopting
masculine garb*

LENTOVSKY, *with a pair of scissors. Disappointed.*

THE BOX OFFICE, *an old maid*

SOLID PROFITS

SLIM PROFITS ┤ *her children*

*Drummers, fakirs, nuns, frogs, a papier-mâché bull, a superfluous
artist, thousands of hopes, wicked fairies, and so on.*

---

1 Published in *The Alarm-clock* (*Budilnik*) 38 (October 1884), p. 457. A parody of *Carnival in
Rome*, a comic opera in three acts with music by Johann Strauss, words by J. Braun, translation by
A. M. de-Ribas, produced at Lentovsky's Theatre, Moscow, September 22, 1884.

2 Played by the actor Bogdanov.

3 A phrase from Gogol's *Dead Souls*, where a lady of society is described as "pleasant in every
respect."

4 Played by Leonov.

5 A. Hesse owned a match factory in Ruza and printed jokes on his matchboxes.

PROLOGUE

It begins with an apotheosis from designs by Shekhtel:[6] *THE BOX OFFICE, pale, emaciated, holds in her arms her starving son SLIM PROFITS, and with a prayer stares at the audience. LENTOVSKY pulls out a dagger, trying to kill SLIM PROFITS, but cannot succeed, for the dagger is blunt. Picture. Bengal lights, groans . . . A vampire flies across the stage.*

LENTOVSKY. I'll kill you, oh detested babe! Ivan, bring me another knife! (*IVAN, who looks like Andrássy,*[7] *brings him a knife, but this time a WICKED FAIRY descends.*)

WICKED FAIRY (*whispers to Lentovsky*). Put on "Chaos-Vile in Rome" and it's in the bag: Slim Profits will perish.

LENTOVSKY (*slaps himself on the forehead*). Why didn't I think of it sooner! Grigory Aleksandrovich, put on "Chaos-Vile in Rome!" (*ARBENIN's*[8] *voice is heard: "Splendid!"*) With a prrrocession, damn it! (*Falls asleep in sweet hopes.*)

ACT ONE

ORPHAN GIRL (*sits on a tiny rock*). I am in love with Arthur . . . I can tell you nothing more. I myself am small, my voice is a small one, my role is a small one, but if I speak at great length, on the other hand you have ears and patience. Nothing's happened to little me, but just you wait, Tamarin[9] is going to treat you to such a long, wordy bit! Don't scowl like that again! (*Turns sour.*)

LUNA. Hmm! (*Yawns and frowns.*)

---

6 See *Unclean Tragedians and Leprous Playwrights*, note 9.

7 Count D. Andrássy (1823–1890), Hungarian statesman and Austro-Hungarian minister of foreign affairs (1871–1879).

8 Grigory Aleksandrovich Arbenin, the stage manager of the theater, was responsible for most of the translations of plays in its repertory.

9 The actor Tamarin played the role of the pseudo-artist Raphaeli.

RAPHAELI-TAMARIN (*enters*). I now shall tell you . . . The matter, you see, is this . . . (*Takes a deep breath and begins a long monologue. Twice he sits down, five times he drips sweat, but finally he gets hoarse and, feeling ante-humous death throes in his throat, looks imploringly at Lentovsky.*)

LENTOVSKY (*taking the scissors*). Already we've got to make cuts.

LUNA (*frowning*). Should we scram? Judging by the first act, nothing but misery will come of this operetta.

RAPHAELI (*buys a picture of Arthur from the Orphan Girl for a thousand rubles*). We'll pass it off as my picture.

FALCONI (*enters with the Countess*). I'm not needed in the first act, neither is my lady-wife, but nevertheless, by the will of the author allow us to show ourselves . . . My lady is a treacherous sort. Please love and pity us . . . If it's not funny, forgive us.

COUNTESS (*betrays her husband*). Woe to the wife of a jealous husband! (*Betrays her husband.*)

HESSE. I'm not needed on stage, but meanwhile I stand here . . . What do I do with my arms?

Not knowing where to put his arms, he walks.

ORPHAN GIRL (*having taken money from Raphaeli, goes to Rome to Arthur, with whom she is in love. For some unknown reason she disguises herself in male garb. Everyone follows her to Rome.*)

LUNA. How deadly boring . . . Should I go into eclipse? (*An eclipse of the moon begins.*)

ACTS TWO AND THREE

COUNTESS (*betrays her husband*). Arthur sweetie-pie . . . .

ORPHAN GIRL. I shall visit Arthur as a pupil. (*Visits and grows sour. She is presented with a wreath as a honorable degree.*)

ARTHUR. I am in love with the countess, but I don't need that kind of love. I want to love quietly, platonically . . .

COUNTESS (*betrays her husband*). What a pretty little fellow (*catches sight of the Orphan Girl*). I'll give him a kiss! (*Betrays her husband and Arthur.*)

ARTHUR. I am outraged!

ORPHAN GIRL (*changes her clothes for women's garb*). I am a woman! (*Exits following Arthur, who has suddenly fallen in love with her.*)

AUDIENCE. Is that all? Hm . . .

OPERETTA (*vanishing*). How many various varieties have vanished on this very spot!

LENTOVSKY (*grabbing the vanishing Operetta by the scruff of her neck*). Oh no, stop! (*Begins to cut her up with his scissors.*)[10] Stop, my dear girl . . . We'll just trim you down a bit . . . (*Finished with his cutting, he stares hard at her.*) Only ruined her, damn it.

OPERETTA. What will be, shall be. (*Vanishes.*)

EPILOGUE

Apotheosis. LENTOVSKY on his knees. A GOOD FAIRY, defending THE BOX OFFICE with her baby, stands before him in the pose of an advocate . . . The prospect reveals new operettas and HEAVY PROFITS.

---

10 By the fourth performance, Lentovsky had already made cuts in the performance.

A MOUTH AS BIG AS ALL OUTDOORS[1]

Язык до Киева доведет

> Whither, sweetheart, art thou fled?
> Where am I to seek thee?
> *Folksong*

1. Take off your cap! It's not permitted here!

2. It's not a cap, it's a top hat!

1. It doesn't matter, sir!

2. No, it does matter, sir . . . You can buy a cap for fifty kopeks, but try and find a top hat for that!

1. Cap or hat . . . all the same. ..

2 (*taking off his hat*). You ought to express yourself more clearly . . . (*Imitating.*) Cap, cap . . .

1. Please stop this talking. You're preventing other people from hearing!

2. You're the one who keeps talking and preventing them, not me. I am silent, my friend . . . And I would have been dead silent, if you hadn't been a-bothering me.

1. Sssh . . .

2. Don't you shush me . . . (*After a silence.*) I can shush myself . . . And you don't have to bug your eyes at me . . . You don't scare me . . . I've seen your sort before . . .

2's **Wife.** Oh stop it! That'll do!

2. What's he pestering me for? What did I do to him? Anything? Why is he on my case? Or maybe you'd like me to complain to the policeman on duty.

1. Later, later . . . Keep quiet.

---

1 Published in *Splinters* (*Oskolki*) 44 (November 3, 1884), pp. 5–6. The Russian title is from the proverbial "He's got a tongue that stretches as far as Kiev."

2. Aha, now you're scared! Just what I thought . . . Won't put your money where your mouth is.

Among the audience. Sssh . . .

2. Even the audience has noticed . . . Pretends to be for law and order, but behaves disorderly himself . . . (*Smiles sarcastically.*) Even got medals on his chest . . . a saber . . . People, take a look!

1 goes out after a moment.

2. He got embarrassed, left . . . Probably still got a shred of conscience left, if words can embarrass him . . . If he'd gone on talking, I might have said something uncalled for. I know how to deal with that sort of gent!

2's Wife. Shut up, the audience is looking!

2. Let 'em look . . . . I've paid my own good money, nobody else's . . . And if I got something to say, don't get me riled . . . That guy left . . . that guy himself, so I'll keep quiet now . . . If no one's bothering me, why should I keep on talking? There's no cause to keep on talking . . . I understand . . . (*Applauds.*) Encore! Encore!

1, 3, 4, 5, and 6 (*literally rising out of the ground*). If you please! Get out, sir!

2. Where's that coming from? (*Turning pale.*) What's this supposed to mean?

1, 3, 4, 5, and 6. For pity's sake, sir! (*Seize 2 under the arms.*) Don't drag your feet . . . If you please, sir! (*They drag him along.*)

2. You pay your own good money and all of a sudden . . . this sort of thing . . . (*Gets carried away.*)

Among the audience. They've got rid of the bum!

The Man without a Spleen

HONORABLE TOWNSFOLK[1]

Господа Обыватели

A Play in Two Acts

ACT ONE

The Town Council. In session.

CITY MANAGER (*after smacking his lips and slowly digging into his ear*). On this matter, gentlemen, will you please attend to the opinion of Fire Chief Semyon Vavilych, who is a specialist in this sort of thing? Let him explain, and then we'll deliberate on it!

FIRE CHIEF. This is the way I figure it . . . (*Blows his nose into a checkered handkerchief.*) The ten thousand allotted to the fire department may be a lot of money, but . . . (*passes a hand over his bald spot*) it only looks that way. It isn't money so much as a dream, a mirage. Of course, ten thousand will get you a fire brigade, but what kind? Just a joke! Don't you see . . . The most important object in human life is a look-out tower for fires, and any scientist will tell you the same thing. Now our municipal lookout tower is, to put it categorically, quite unsuitable, because it's low. The buildings are tall (*he lifts up his arms*), they hem in the lookout tower on all sides, and it's not only a fire you can't see, but, God forbid, the sky. The firemen are my responsibility, firemen, but is it their fault that they can't see it? Next, as to horses and concerning water casks . . . (*Unbuttons his waistcoat, exhales, and proceeds with his speech in the same spirit.*)

COUNCILMEN (*unanimously*). Add another two thousand to the estimate!

The CITY MANAGER takes a momentary pause to expel the journalists from the council chamber.

FIRE CHIEF. Very good, sir. Now, perhaps, you will decide that the lookout tower should be raised six feet . . . Very good. But if you look at it from the

1 Published in *Splinters* (*Oskolki*) 50 (December 15, 1884), p. 4.

viewpoint and in the sense that the governmental interests of, so to speak, society are involved, then I have to note, honorable councilmen, that if a contractor is hired to handle this, then I have to point out that this will cost the town twice as much, because the contractor will look out for his own interests, and not society's. If it were to be built in an economic way, in no particular hurry, if bricks, say, cost fifty rubles a thousand and were carted by the fire horses and if (*turns his eyes to the ceiling, as if mentally calculating*) and if fifteen beams, forty-five feet long and ten inches wide . . . (*Calculates.*)

COUNCILMEN (*voting in the majority*). Entrust the rebuilding of the watchtower to Semyon Vavilych, for which purpose at the earliest opportunity assign a thousand five hundred and twenty-three rubles forty-four kopeks!

FIRE CHIEF'S WIFE (*sitting amongst the public, whispers to the lady next to her*). I don't know why my Senya is making such a fuss! With his health to get involved in rebuilding? Then too, it's ridiculous—all day long up to your eyebrows in workmen! He'll earn a pittance for the repairs, five hundred rubles or so, but he'll ruin a thousand rubles' worth of his health. His good nature is killing him, the fool!

FIRE CHIEF. Very good, sir. Now let's talk about the working staff. Of course, as, you might say, an interested party (*embarrassed*), I can only remark that I . . . I really don't care . . . I'm no longer a young man, I'm ill, I could die any day now. The doctor said that I've got hardening of the intestines and if I don't look after my health, then my veins will burst and I'll die before the priest gets there . . .

WHISPER IN THE PUBLIC. Live like a dog, die like a dog.

FIRE CHIEF. But I'm not concerned about myself. I have lived my life, thank God. I need nothing . . . Only I'm surprised and . . . and even offended . . . (*Waves his hand in hopelessness.*) You work for a mere salary, honorably, blamelessly . . . no rest day or night, no concern for your health and . . . and you wonder what it's all for? Why am I getting involved? What's my interest? I'm not discussing myself, but in general . . . No one else would live on such pay . . . A drunkard might take on a job like this, but a businesslike man of substance would rather starve to death than get involved with horses and firemen for such a salary . . . (*Shrugs his shoulders.*) What's my interest? If foreigners were to see us, the way we're set up, I think we'd get raked over the coals in the all the European newspapers. In Western

Europe, take at least Paris, for instance, on every street there's a lookout tower and every year they give the fire chief a bonus based on a percentage of his annual salary. A person can work in a place like that!

COUNCILMEN. Give Semyon Vavilych for his many long years of service a bonus of two hundred rubles!

FIRE CHIEF'S WIFE (*whispers to the lady next to her*). It's a good thing he asked . . . Clever fellow. The other day we were at Father Archpriest's, lost a hundred rubles to him at poker[2] and now, don't you know, we're in a bad way! (*Yawns.*) Ah, such a bad way! It should be time to go home and have some tea.

ACT TWO

The scene is at the lookout tower. WATCHMEN.

SENTRY ON THE LOOKOUT TOWER (*shouts down*). Hey! There's a fire at the lumber yard! Sound the alarm!

LOWER SENTRY. You spotted it just now? People have been running around for half an hour, and you, you freak, suddenly get a glimmer of it now? (*Sententiously.*) Set a fool high or low—it makes no difference (*sounds the alarm*).

Within three minutes, in a window of his apartment which is opposite the lookout tower, the FIRE CHIEF appears, in a state of undress and with sleepy eyes.

FIRE CHIEF. Where's the fire, Denis?

LOWER SENTRY (*comes to attention and salutes*). At the lumberyard, yer washup!

FIRE CHIEF (*shakes his head*). God save us! The wind is blowing, there's such a dry spell . . . (*Waves his hand.*) God preserve us! Nothing good ever comes of these calamities! . . . (*Rubs his hand over his face.*) Tell you what, Denis . . . Tell them, my good friend, to harness the horses and drive over

---

2 Poker for profit was forbidden by law.

there, and right away I'll . . . I'll show up in a little while . . . Have to get dressed, one thing and another . . .

LOWER SENTRY. There's no one to go, yer washup! They've all gorn away, only Andrey's home.

FIRE CHIEF (*alarmed*). Where are they, the bastards?

LOWER SENTRY. Makar was nailing on new soles, now he's taking the boots to the subbubs, to the deacon. Mikhail, yer washup, you your own self were pleased to send to sell the oats . . . Yegor's took the fire horses down to the river to your sister-in-law's farm manager. Nikita's plastered.

FIRE CHIEF. What about Aleksey?

LOWER SENTRY. Aleksey went to catch crayfish, because you was pleased to order him to a while back, you said you've having a dinner party tomorrow.

FIRE CHIEF (*shaking his head in contempt*). I ask you, how are you to work with people like this! Ignorance, illiteracy . . . drunkenness . . . If foreigners were to see this, you'd be raked over the coals in the European newspapers! There, take Paris at least, the fire brigade is always riding through the streets, running over people: whether there's a fire or not, merrily they roll along! A fire's broken out at the lumber yard, a real danger, but not one of them is at home, it's like . . . devils mash 'em flat! No, we're a far cry from Europe! (*Turns his face back to the room, tenderly.*) Mashenka, get out my uniform!

A. Chekhonte

AT THE SICKBED[1]

У постели больного

*At the sickbed stand DOCTORS POPOV and
MILLER, arguing:*

POPOV. I confess I don't hold much with conservative methods.

MILLER. Colleague, this has got nothing to do with being conservative. You go on about professions of faith and having no faith, orthodoxies or heterodoxies . . . I'm talking about diet, which ought to be changed *in concreto* . . .[2]

PATIENT. Ugh! (*Gets out of bed with effort, goes to the door, and timidly peers into the next room*). These days even walls have ears, after all.

POPOV. He's complaining that his chest is constricted . . . it's suffocating him . . . stifling him . . . Don't treat him without a powerful stimulant . . .

The PATIENT groans and timidly peers out the window.

MILLER. But before you give him a stimulant, I would ask you to pay some attention to his general state of health . . .

PATIENT (*turning pale*). Ah, gentlemen, don't talk so loudly! I'm a family man . . . a civil servant . . . There are people walking outside the windows . . . I have a maid-servant . . . Ah! (*Waves his hand hopelessly.*)

The Man without a Spleen

---

1 Published in *Splinters* (*Oskolki*) 48 (December 1, 1884), p. 6.

2 Latin, definitively.

THE CASE OF THE YEAR 1884[1]

(From Our Correspondent)

Дело о 1884 годе

(от нашего корреспондента)

Today is now the sixth day at N. courthouse of the trial of the secular year 1884, accused of dereliction of duty. The court is perceptibly weary. The accused weeps and now and then whispers to its defense lawyer. This very day there began the examination of the material evidence ... When, at the request of the public prosecutor, *The Citizen*[2] was read aloud and an issue of *The Ray* appeared with a portrait of Okreits,[3] the public was excluded from the courtroom, so that the subjects mentioned might not lead them into temptation . . . After this the pleas began on both sides.

"Please, your —nor," the defense attorney concluded his speech, "enter into the record that the whole time I was speaking the Public Prosecutor coughed, blew his nose and thumped the water bottle . . . "

PRESIDENT OF THE COURT. Accused, your last word!

THE ACCUSED (*weeps*). I would like to say something, although it is pointless, if you've already made up your mind to rake me over the coals. I am accused, in the first place, of inertia—the fact that I've done nothing, that in my time the economic situation did not improve, the exchange rate hasn't risen, manufacturing is stuck in the mud and so on . . . That is not my fault . . . Remember that when I was appointed to the post of new year, I found, . . . (*Tells in detail what he found.*)

PRESIDENT. This has nothing to do with the case! Please speak to the matter at hand!

THE ACCUSED (*panicking*). Yes, sir, your —nor! The Public Prosectuor accuses me of wasting my time on trivia, of twiddling my thumbs . . . True,

---

1 Published in *Fragments* (*Oskolki*) 1 (January 5, 1884), p. 6.

2 A conservative paper published by V. I. Meshchersky.

3 *The Ray*, a weekly illustrated magazine, bore a portrait of its anti-Semitic publisher, S. S. Okreits, on its cover. Chekhov considered Okreits to be on the lowest rung of the literary ladder.

during my existence on earth I have done nothing sensible. A new form of label for bottles was put on sale, rags were patched, fools were made to pray to God, and they bashed their foreheads against the ground . . .

PRESIDENT. Accused, if you refer to individuals, I shall bar you from speaking.

ACCUSED. What am I to say then? (*After a moment's thought.*) Fine, I'll move to the press . . . They say that all the newspapers are vacuous, dull, that the press only insults people behind their backs, that talented people are literally shoved under water . . . What can I do about it, if . . .

PRESIDENT. Bailiff! Remove the accused from the courtroom!

On the accused being led from the courtroom, the jury was presented with the questionnaire.

The court pronounced sentence: the secular year 1884, after being deprived of all civil rights, is to be exiled and deported to Lethe[4] forever.

The Man without a Spleen

---

4 The river of oblivion that flowed through the ancient Greek underworld.

A DRAMA[1]

Драма

CHARACTERS

POPPA DEAR, *who has 11 eligible daughters*

A YOUNG MAN

COAT-TAILS

YOUNG MAN (*enters Poppa Dear's study after waving his hand in desperation and saying, "The hell with it! you can only die once!"*). Ivan Ivanych! Permit me to ask for the hand in marriage of your youngest daughter Varvara!

POPPA DEAR (*casting down his eyes and with false modesty*). I'd be delighted, but . . . she's still so young . . . so inexperienced . . . And besides . . . you want to deprive me . . . of my solace . . . (*wipes away tears*) . . . the support of my old age . . .

YOUNG MAN (*quickly*). In that case . . . I dare not insist . . . (*Bows and starts to go.*)

POPPA DEAR (*strenuously retaining him by the coat-tails*). Hold on! A pleasure! Happy to oblige! My benefactor!

COAT-TAILS (*pitifully*). Rrrripppp . . .

The Man without a Spleen

---

1 Published in *The Cricket* (*Sverchok*) 37 (September 25, 1886), pp. 4–5. Chekhov rewrote it in narrative form in 1887.

BEFORE THE ECLIPSE[1]

Перед затмением

(Excerpt from a Fairy Musical)

The SUN and the MOON are beyond the horizon, drinking tea.

SUN (*pensively*). M-yes, my dear fellow . . . Please accept twenty-five rubles, but more I cannot manage.

MOON. Believe me, in all conscience, your radiance, it's worth much more to you. Please bear in mind: the honorable astronomers are desirous that the eclipse begin in the Kingdom of Poland at 5 o'clock in the morning and end in Upper Udinsk at 12, consequently I have to take part in the ceremony at seven, sir . . . If you offer me five smackers an hour, it'll be cheap at the price, sir. (*Snatches the train on a scudding cloud and blows his nose in it.*) Please don't be stingy, your radiance. I'll set you up such obscurity that even the lawyers will get jealous. You'll get complete satisfaction, sir . . .

SUN (*after a pause*). It's funny that you should be haggling . . . You forget that I invited you to take part in a ceremony which has a universal character, so that this eclipse could win you popularity . . .

MOON (*with a sigh and bitterly*). We know what that sort of popularity means, your radiance! "The moon hid behind the clouds" and that's all. Nothing but defamation of character . . . (*Drinks.*) Or else: "On the spire of the steeple shone the midnight moon." And again: "The moon swims through the dark night skies . . ."[2] Never in my life have I swum, your radiance, why such an insult?

SUN. M-yes, actually the press's treatment of you is, to say the least, peculiar . . . But be patient, my friend . . . The time will come, and history will appreciate you . . .

---

1 First published in *The Alarm Clock (Budilnik)* 31 (August 9, 1887), pp. 3–4.

2 The first quotation is from a gypsy ballad; the second is from a popular folksong based on the poem "The Prisoner" by F. N. Glinka; the third is from the "Tiger Cub Waltz," with words and music by M. Shilovsky.

On earth the sewage-disposal carts rumble on by; both planets
clutch tight to the clouds and hold their noses.

MOON. Don't take a breath . . . The way they do things on earth, what can you say! A worthless planet! (*Drinks.*) And I'll never forget so long as I live how Mister Pushkin cursed me. "That stupid moon in that stupid sky above the horizon . . ."[3]

SUN. Of course, it's offensive, but all the same, pal, it's publicity! I think Johann Hoff[4] would have paid a bundle to have Pushkin single him out for abuse . . . Publicity is a great thing. Just you wait till there's an eclipse and they'll start talking about you.

MOON. No, *ahtenday*[5] a bit, your radiance! If anyone gets famous from this eclipse, it'll be you and you alone. They don't know that you can't do without me any more than without arms . . . Who else would you hide behind if not me? If you were to hire a lawyer, you'd have to pay through the nose—two thousand, at least. Whereas, have it your own way, I don't ask more than thirty.

SUN (*pensively*). Well, all right, only see that you don't ask for a tip later on. Have a drink! (*Pours.*) I hope that you will put some effort into it . . .

MOON. Don't you worry . . . The eclipse will be first rate, in all conscience, sir . . . From the very creation of world I've been producing moonlight and never had any complaints . . . Everything will be honest and aboveboard. May I please have an advance . . .

SUN (*giving him an advance*). I hear the water wagons starting out . . . It's time for me to rise . . . Well, I think I'll schedule the eclipse for August 7, in the morning . . . That's plenty of time for you to be ready . . . You'll conceal me so that the eclipse will be the fullest possible . . .

MOON. And on what area would you like the shadow to fall?

SUN (*pensively*). It would be nice to swan around Western Europe, but they hardly appreciate our efforts there . . . The local diplomats consider themselves specialists when it comes to keeping things dark, and therefore it's

---

3 A quotation from Pushkin's poetical novel *Yevgeny Onegin*, chapter 3, verse v.

4 Hoff was court purveyor of extractive essences (beer, candy, chocolate). He advertised widely.

5 Bad French, wait.

hard to surprise them . . . Consequently, there's always Russia . . . Even the astronomers want it that way. Well, sir, drop the shadow over Moscow, but do it cleverly. Try hard to make sure the eclipse delivers a message. Obscure only the northern part of Moscow, and leave the southern one alone . . . Let Zamoskvorechye, which lies in the southern part, see the way we ignore it . . . The kingdom of darkness![6]

MOON. Very good, your radiance.

SUN. And besides the merchants don't understand eclipses . . . Many of them have come back from Nizhny[7] and still haven't slept off their binges, and their wives are imagining devil knows what . . . Well, sir, we shall lightly touch Klin, Zavidy, in general the places where astronomers gather, then to Kazan and so forth. I'm still thinking about it . . . (*Pause.*)

MOON. Your radiance, tell me, in all conscience, why the deuce did you dream up this eclipse?

SUN. Well, you see . . . but I hope this will remain between us . . . I invented the eclipse in order to revive my popularity . . . Of late I've noticed a certain indifference in the public . . . For some reason they haven't been talking much about either of us and haven't paid attention to my light. I've even heard that the sun has grown old, that it's absurd, that it would be easy to get on without it . . . Many have even foresworn me in print . . . I think that the eclipse will compel everybody to talk about me. That's one thing. Secondly, humanity is bored to death and fed up to the eyebrows . . . It wants a diversion . . . You know, when a merchant's wife gets fed up with jam and apricot leather, she starts to gorge on oatmeal; so, when humanity is fed up with daylight, it needs to treat itself to an eclipse . . . However, it's time for me to rise . . . The lads of Hunter's Row[8] are already heading for the market. Good-bye.

MOON. Just one more word, your radiance . . . (*Timidly.*) While the eclipse is on, you should abstain from this sort of thing . . . (*Points to the beer*

---

6 Zamoskvorechye (literally, "across the river") was the district in Moscow where the merchants lived. Their portrayal by the dramatist Ostrovsky as backward petty despots led the critic Dobrolyubov to refer to that world as "the kingdom of darkness."

7 Nizhny Novgorod, site of an important annual fair.

8 *Okhotny ryad*, a major shopping street in Moscow.

bottle.) It'll barely be one o'clock and you'll be half seas over, and things are likely to get awkward.

SUN. Yes, I will have to abstain . . . (*After a moment's consideration.*) However, if anything goes wrong, I won't drink in moderation, but . . . we'll cover the sky with clouds, and no one will see us . . . Anyway, good-bye, it's time to go . . . (*He rises—alas!—covered by clouds and mist.*)

MOON. Grievous are our sins! (*Lies down and covers himself with a cloud; in a minute we can hear snoring.*)

A. Ch.

A STATEMENT MADE ON COMPULSION[1]

Вынужденное заявление

In 1876, July 7, at 8:30 P.M., I wrote a play. If my adversaries wish to know its contents, here it is. I submit it to the verdict of society and the press.

THE SUDDEN DEATH OF A STEED,
OR
THE MAGNANIMITY OF THE
RUSSIAN PEOPLE!

Скоропостижная конская смерть, или Великодушие русского народа!

A Dramatic Sketch in One Act

CHARACTERS

LYUBVIN,[2] *a young man*

COUNTESS FINIKOVA, *his mistress*

COUNT FINIKOV, *her husband*

NIL YEGOROV, *cabman no. 13326*

The action takes place in broad daylight on Nevsky Prospect.

---

1 First published in *New Times* (*Novoe vremya*) 4721 (April 22, 1888). "In those far-distant years Chekhov's joke produced a terrific uproar among the minor dramatists" (N. M. Yezhov, *Historical Messenger* [*Istorichesky vestnik*] 139, 2 [1915]).

2 Joke names: Lyubvin suggests "lover-boy," and Finikov "date palms."

ACT ONE

*The COUNTESS and LYUBVIN are riding in
NIL YEGOROV's cab.*

LYUBVIN (*embracing her*). Oh, how I love you! And yet I won't feel easy, until we reach the station and are sitting in the railway carriage. I have a feeling that your blackguard of a husband is in hot pursuit of us at this very moment. I'm shaking in my shoes. (*To Nil.*) Drive faster, you devil!

COUNTESS. Faster, driver! Give her a taste of the whip! You don't know how to drive, you son of a barnyard fowl!

NIL (*lashing the horse*). Gee-up! Gee-up, you plague! The lady and gent'll give us a tip.

COUNTESS (*shouts*). Give it to her! Give it to her! Make it hot for this piece of trash or we'll miss the train!

LYUBVIN (*embracing her and aroused by her unearthly beauty*). Oh, my dearest! Soon, soon the hour will come when you shall belong wholly to me, and no longer to your husband! (*Looking around, in horror.*) Your husband is following us! I can see him! Driver, drive on! Faster, you blackguard, with a hundred devils on your collar.

COUNTESS. Give it to him in the neck! Hold on, I'll do it myself with my parasol . . . (*Thwacks Nil.*)

NIL (*whipping with all his might*). Giddyap! Giddyap! Stir your stumps, you pain-in-the-neck!

The exhausted horse drops and expires.

LYUBVIN. The horse has dropped dead! Oh, horrors! He's catching up to us!

NIL. Oh my aching head, how am I going to make a living now? (*Falls on the corpse of his beloved horse and sobs.*)

ACT TWO

The same and the COUNT.

COUNT. You'd run away from me?! Stop! (*Seizes his wife by her hand.*) Treacherous woman! Didn't I love you? Didn't I provide for you?

LYUBVIN (*faintheartedly*). I'm going to make tracks! (*Runs away to the noise of a gathering crowd.*)

COUNT (*to Nil*). Driver! The death of your horse has saved my hearth and home from desecration. Had it not suddenly expired, I should not have caught up with the fugitives. Here's a hundred rubles for you!

NIL (*magnanimously*). Noble count! I do not need your money! For me a sufficient reward is the awareness that the death of my beloved horse has served to protect hearths and homes! (*The delighted crowd lifts him up.*)

Curtain

On February 30, 1886, this play of mine was performed on the shores of Lake Baikal by amateur actors. At that time I was inscribed as a member of the Society of Dramatic Writers[3] and received from the treasurer A. A. Maikov an appropriate fee.

Therefore, being a member of the aforementioned Society and having the rights appertaining to this vocation, on behalf of our faction I urgently demand that, first, the chairman, treasurer, secretary, and committee publicly ask my forgiveness; 2, that all the aforementioned officials be blackballed and replaced by members of our faction; 3, that twenty-five thousand of the annual budget of the Society be annually assigned to purchasing tickets to the Hamburg lottery and that every win be divided amongst all the members equally; 4, that at general and extraordinary meetings of the Society military

---

3 The Society for Russian Dramatic Authors and Opera Composers had been founded in 1874 to protect their rights in a theater world that played fast and loose with scripts and scores. Chekhov was a member of the Society from November 16, 1887; he regarded it primarily as a "commercial institution," whose collection of royalties for writers superseded all its other functions.

music be played and decent refreshments be served; 5, because all the income of the Society goes to the benefit of the only thirty members whose plays are running in the provinces, and because the remaining three hundred members don't get a penny, because their plays are running nowhere, then with a view to fairness and equality the higher authorities are to be petitioned to forbid those thirty members from putting on their plays and thereby destroying the balance, so necessary for the normal course of events.

In conclusion I consider it necessary to warn that if a negative answer is given to any one of the aforesaid points, I shall be compelled to resign as a member of the Society.

Member of the Society of Dramatic Writers and Opera Composers

Akaky Tarantulov

From the editors. By inserting this statement by the respected member of the Society of Dramatic Writers and Opera Composers, we flatter ourselves with the hope that it will evoke the fullest sympathy at least from the half of the worthy members of this Society, whose merits are as great as those of Mr. Akaky Tarantulov. Russian drama is precisely that important type of poetry, in which the Akaky Tarantulovs can acquire everlasting fame from the chilly Finnish crags to the flaming backstage, from the awe-inspiring Kremlin to the blather of the general sessions of the Society of Dramatic Writers and Opera Composers . . .

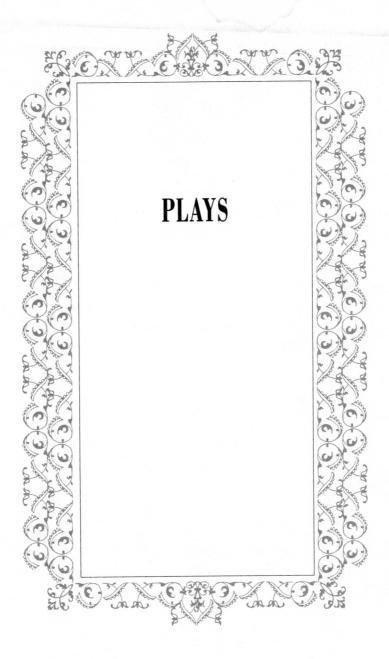

PLAYS

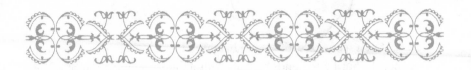

SWAN SONG (CALCHAS)

*C*hekhov based *Calchas* (late 1886 or early 1887) on a short story of the same name and, he boasted, knocked it off in an hour and five minutes. As with *The Evils of Tobacco*, it was meant as a "dramatic étude" for a popular comic actor, Vladimir Davydov. "It should play 15 to 20 minutes," Chekhov suggested. "As a rule little things are much better to write than big ones: they're less pretentious, but still successful . . . what more does anyone need?" (letter to M. V. Kiselyov, January 14, 1887). Davydov performed it at Korsh's Theatre on February 19, 1888, but put in so many ad-libs about great actors of the past that Chekhov could barely recognize his text. Later he made some slight emendations, which he submitted to the censorship in hopes of a performance at a state theater, and changed the title to *Swan Song*. "A long title, bittersweet, but I can't think up another, though I thought a long time" (to Aleksandr Lensky, October 26, 1888). (It is seven syllables in Russian: *Lebedinaya pesna.*)

Svetlovidov—which means "of bright aspect," a *nom de théâtre*—began life as an army officer, like one of Tolstoy's heroes, but lost caste by going on the stage. Even there, his career has been one of decline, from tragedian to buffo. He has been playing Calchas, the wily old oracle-monger in Offenbach's comic opera *La Belle Hélène*, a secondary part chosen for his benefit performance, no doubt because the popular operetta would fill the house. So, throughout this play, Svetlovidov's declamations from *King Lear*, *Othello*, and *Hamlet* are continually undercut by his ludicrous appearance.

Although the play draws heavily on Dumas' *Kean* to allow a skilled character actor a field day, it still encompasses a particularly Chekhovian theme—coming to terms with life. Svetlovidov, in the course of fifteen minutes, passes from self-pity as a ruined tragedian to self-contempt as a hammy clown to self-acceptance as an attendant lord, like T. S. Eliot's Prufrock, who can "swell a progress, start a scene or two." At the height of his delusion, he spouts Lear's storm speech; but by the end, he exits with a pettish repudiation of society from Griboedov's classic comedy *Woe from Wit*. This diminuendo suggests a small-scale enlightenment, a compressed version of the awareness that tragic heroes take five acts to achieve.

SWAN SONG

(Calchas)

Лебединая песня (Калхас)

A Dramatic Study in One Act

CHARACTERS

VASILY VASILYICH SVETLOVIDOV,[1] *a comic actor, an old man of sixty-eight*

NIKITA IVANYCH, *a prompter, an old man*

The action takes place on the stage of a provincial theater, at night, after the performance.

The empty stage of an ordinary provincial theater. At right, a row of unpainted, badly jerry-built doors, leading to the dressing rooms; the left- and upstage areas are cluttered with junk. Center stage is an overturned stool. — Night. Darkness.

1

SVETLOVIDOV in the costume of Calchas,[2] *holding a candle, enters from his dressing room and bursts into laughter.*

SVETLOVIDOV. Here's a how-de-do! A fine state of affairs. I fell asleep in my dressing room! The show ended ages ago, everyone's left the theater, and I'm sawing wood as neat as you please. Ah, you old fool, old fool! You old hound! So, looks like, you got so sploshified you fell asleep sitting up! Clever boy! Pin a medal on you, sweetheart. (*Shouts.*) Yegorka! Yegorka, what the hell! Petrushka! They're asleep, damn and blast 'em, hell's bells!

---

1 Svetlovidov is evidently a stage name, "Radiant of countenance," a sharp contrast to the actor's woebegone mien.

2 The wily old oracle monger in Offenbach's comic opera *La Belle Hélène*. The costume included a long-haired wig, a comical chiton, and a garland.

Yegorka! (*Picks up the stool, sits on it and puts the candle on the floor.*) Can't hear a sound . . . Naught but the answering echo . . . Yegorka and Petrushka got a three-ruble note from me today to keep an eye on things— and now you can't find them with bloodhounds . . . They've gone out, I suppose, the so-and-so's, and locked up the theater . . . (*Twists his head around.*) Am I drunk! Oof! The wines and spirits I downed today to celebrate my benefit performance,[3] my God! My whole body reeks of it, and a regiment's pitched camp in my mouth . . . Disgusting . . .

Pause.

Stupid . . . The old nitwit got drunk and doesn't even know what he's supposed to be celebrating . . . Oof, good God! My back aches, and my skull's splitting, and I'm all over chills, and my soul is as cold and dark as a dungeon. Even if you don't care about your health, you might at least show some pity to your old age, Mister Funny Man . . .

Pause.

Old age . . . However much you try to give it the slip, however much you bluster or play the fool, your life's been lived . . . sixty-eight years gone bye-bye, my dear sir! You won't get them back . . . The cup's been drained, and there's only the tiniest drop left at the very bottom . . . Just the lees and the dregs . . . That's how it goes . . . That's the way things go, Vasya my boy . . . Like it or not, it's time to rehearse the role of a dead man. Old lady Death is just around the corner . . . (*Stares out.*) Even though I've been on stage for forty-five years, I think this is the first time I've seen the theater by night . . . Yes, the very first time . . . This is most peculiar, blast it . . . (*Walks down to the footlights.*) Can't see a thing . . . Well, the prompter's box is just visible . . . there's that stage-box with an initial on it, a music stand . . . and beyond that—darkness! A black, bottomless pit, like a grave, where Death herself is lurking . . . Brr! . . . It's cold! A draft's coming from the auditorium, like down a chimney flue . . . Couldn't wish for a better spot for calling up ghosts! Spooky, damn it . . . Gives me the creeps . . . (*Shouts.*) Yegorka! Petrushka! Where are you, you devils? Lord, why did I have to mention the foul fiend? For heaven's sake, give up bad language, give up drinking, after all you're an old man, it's time to die . . . When people are sixty-eight, they go to morning mass, prepare for death, while you

---

3 Dedicated to a specific performer, who was usually allowed to pick the plays and receive the takings on that occasion.

... O Lord! Cursing, drunk as a skunk, this ridiculous costume ... What a sight! I'd better go change my clothes right now ... Spooky! If I really have to spend all night here, I may drop dead with fright ... (*Goes to his dressing room.*)

> *Meanwhile from the dressing room farthest upstage appears*
> *NIKITA IVANYCH in a white dressing gown.*

2

SVETLOVIDOV and NIKITA IVANYCH.

SVETLOVIDOV (*on seeing Nikita Ivanych, cries out in horror and recoils*). Who are you? What's going on? What do you want? (*Stamps his feet.*) Who are you?

NIKITA IVANYCH. It's me, sir!

SVETLOVIDOV. Who are you?

NIKITA IVANYCH (*slowly draws near him*). It's me, sir ... The prompter, Nikita Ivanych ... Vasil Vasilych, it's me, sir! ...

SVETLOVIDOV (*collapses in exhaustion on to the stool, breathes hard and trembles all over*). My God! Who is it? Is that you ... you, Nikitushka? Wh ... why are you here?

NIKITA IVANYCH. I sleep over in the dressing rooms, sir. Only, please do me a favor, don't tell Aleksey Fomich, sir ... I've nowhere else to spend the night, it's the God's own truth.

SVETLOVIDOV. You, Nikitushka ... My God, my God! I got sixteen curtain calls, three wreaths, and lots of other things ... Everyone was so excited, but not a soul bothered to wake up a drunken old man and take him home ... I am an old man, Nikitushka ... I'm sixty-eight years of age ... I'm sick! My feeble soul is weary ... (*Falls into the prompter's arms and weeps.*) Don't go, Nikitushka ... Old, impotent, at death's door ... It's terrible, terrible! ...

NIKITA IVANYCH (*tenderly and respectfully*). It's time you went home, Vasil Vasilych, sir!

SVETLOVIDOV. I won't go! I have no home,—no, no, no!

NIKITA IVANYCH. Good Lord! Has the gent forgotten where he lives?

SVETLOVIDOV. I won't go there, I won't! I'm all alone there . . . there's nobody at my place, Nikitushka, no family, no old woman, no children . . . Solitary as the wind across the plains . . . I'll die, and there'll be nobody to remember . . . I'm terrified to be left alone . . . No one to warm me, to show me any affection, to tuck a drunken man into bed . . . Who cares for me? Who needs me? Who loves me? Nobody loves me, Nikitushka!

NIKITA IVANYCH (*through tears*). The public loves you, Vasil Vasilych!

SVETLVIDOV. The public has gone home, it's fast asleep and forgot about its funny man! No, nobody needs me, nobody loves me . . . I've got no wife, no children . . .

NIKITA IVANYCH. Well then, you've got nothing to worry about . . .

SVETLOVIDOV. After all, I'm a human being, I'm alive, blood courses through my veins, not water. I'm a gentleman, Nikitushka, of noble birth . . . Before I fell into this pit, I served in the army, in the artillery . . . What a lad I was, handsome, upright, dashing, passionate! God, where did it all go? Nikitushka, and what an actor I was then, eh? (*Rising, leans for support on the prompter's arm.*) Where did it all go, where is it, the time? My God! Just now I was staring into this pit—and remembered everything, every-thing! This pit has swallowed up forty-five years of my life, and what a life, Nikitushka! I stare into the pit now and see it all down to the last detail, plain as the nose on your face. To be young and enthusiastic, confident, impassioned, to love women! Women, Nikitushka!

NIKITA IVANYCH. It's time you were in bed, Vasil Vasilych, sir.

SVETLOVIDOV. When I was a young actor, when I was just beginning to get the hang of it, I remember—a woman fell in love with me for my acting . . . Refined, straight as a poplar tree, young, innocent, pure and sultry as a sunrise in summer! Those blue eyes of hers, her wonderful smile could dis-pel the darkest night. Ocean waves break against stones, but against the waves of her hair cliffs, ice floes, snowdrifts could break! I remember, I was standing before her, as I stand before you now . . . She was more beautiful than ever, she gazed upon me so that I shall never forget that gaze even in my grave . . . The caress, the velvet touch, the deep emotions, the radiance of youth! Intoxicated, happy, I fall to my knees before her, I ask her to seal my happiness . . . (*Goes on in a faltering voice.*) But she . . . she says: give up the theater! Give-up-the-the-ay-ter! . . . You understand? She could love an actor, but be his wife—never! I remember, that very day I went on stage and . . . The role was a vulgar one, a buffoon . . . I went on stage and felt as if I saw the light . . . Then I understood that this is not a sacred art, it's all a baneful illusion, I am a slave, a plaything of someone else's leisure time, comic relief, a clown! Then I knew what the public means! From that time on I put no stock in applause or wreathes or accolades . . . Yes, Nikitushka! It applauds me, lays out a ruble for my photograph but I am an outsider, in its eyes I am practically a whore! . . . To flatter its vanity, it makes my acquaintance, but won't stoop to let me marry its sister, its daughter . . . I put no stock in it! (*Drops on to the stool.*) I put no stock in anything!

NIKITA IVANYCH. You look a fright, Vasil Vasilych! You even gave me the willies . . . Let's go home, do the right thing!

SVETLOVIDOV. Then I saw the light . . . and that light cost me dear, Nikitushka! After that incident I started . . . after that young woman . . . I started to go on the skids for no reason at all, my life of no earthly use, not a thought for the morrow . . . Played low comedy parts, smart-alecks, clowned it up, corrupted people's minds, and yet what an artist I had been once, what a talent! I buried my talent, cheapened it and garbled my lines, lost my sense of who I was . . . This black pit sucked me in and gulped me down! I didn't used to feel it before, but today . . . when I woke up, I looked around and there were sixty-eight years behind me. Only now do I see how old I am! The party's over! (*Sobs.*) The party's over!

NIKITA IVANYCH. Vasil Vasilich! My dear man, dear heart . . . Now, now, calm down . . . Good Lord! (*Shouts.*) Petrushka! Yegorka!

SVETLOVIDOV. And yet the talent, the power! You cannot imagine the eloquence, the wealth of emotions and grace, the variety of expression . . . (*slaps himself on the chest*) in this breast! It makes me choke up! . . . Listen, old man . . . hold on, let me catch my breath . . . Here's a bit from *Godunov:*[4]

---

4 Pushkin's blank-verse historical chronicle *Boris Godunov* (1824/5). This is a quotation from the soliloquy of the Pretender Dmitry, referring to the Polish noblewoman from whom he is trying to win support.

The ghost of Ivan the Dread called me forth,
Named me Dmitry from the grave.
Then did the people rally to my cause
And doom Boris to die my victim.
I am Tsarévich. 'Tis enough. Shame 'twere
To stoop before a proud princess of Poland!

Not bad, eh? (*Energetically.*) Wait, here's something from *King Lear.* You get the picture, black sky, rain, thunder—rrr! . . . lightning—zhzhzh! . . . streaking all across the sky, and then:

Blow, winds, and crack your cheeks! rage! blow!
You cataracts and hurricanoes, spout
Till you have drench'd our steeples, drown'd the cocks!
Your sulphurous and thought-executing fires,
Vaunt couriers to oak-cleaving thunderbolts,
Singe my white head! And thou, all-shaking thunder,
Strike flat the thick rotundity o' the world!
Crack nature's moulds, all germens spill at once
That make ingrateful man![5]

(*Impatiently.*) Quick, the fool's line! (*Stamps his feet.*) Feed me the fool's line, quick! I'm in a hurry.

NIKITA IVANYCH (*playing the Fool*). "O nuncle, court holy-water in a dry house is better than this rain-water out o' door. Good nuncle, in, and ask thy daughters' blessing; here's a night pities neither wise man nor fool."

SVETLOVIDOV.

"Rumble thy bellyful! Spit, fire! spout, rain!
Nor rain, wind, thunder, fire, are my daughters:
I tax not you, you elements, with unkindness;
I never gave you kingdom, called you children."

That's power! That's talent! That's an artist! Something else . . . the sort of thing to bring back the good old days . . . Let's have a bit . . . (*utters a peal of happy laughter*) from *Hamlet*! Here, I'll start . . . What shall it be? Ah, got it . . . (*Playing Hamlet.*) "O! the recorders: let me see one." "Why do you go about as if you would drive me into a toil?"

---

5 Lear on the heath in Act III, scene 2 of Shakespeare's tragedy.

NIKITA. "O! my lord, if my duty be too bold, my love is too unmannerly."

SVETLOVIDOV. "I do not understand that. Will you play upon this pipe?"

NIKITA. "My Lord, I cannot."

SVETLOVIDOV. "I pray you."

NIKITA. "Believe me, I cannot."

SVETLOVIDOV. "I do beseech you."

NIKITA. "I know no touch of it, my lord."

SVETLOVIDOV. "'Tis as easy as lying; govern these vantages with your finger and thumb, give it breath with your mouth, and it will discourse most eloquent music."

NIKITA. "I have not the skill."

SVETLOVIDOV. "Why, look you now, how unworthy a thing you make of me. You would play upon me; you would seem to know my stops; you would pluck out the heart of my mystery. Do you think I am easier to be played on than a pipe? Call me what instrument you will, though you can fret me, you cannot play upon me."[6] (*Roars with laughter.*) Bravo! Encore! Bravo! Old age can go to hell! There's no such thing as old age, it's all nonsense, rubbish! Strength is gushing through all my veins like a fountain,— there's youth, vigor, life! Where there's talent, Nikitushka, old age ceases to exist! Have I gone crazy, Nikitushka? Am I out of my mind? Wait, let me get in the mood . . . O, Lord, my God! Now, listen, how tender and subtle, how musical! Ssh . . . Hush!

> Quiet is the Ukrainian night.
> A limpid sky, the stars shine bright.
> The air's unwilling to cast off
> Its drowsiness. The silvered leaves
> Quiver lightly on the poplar trees . . .[7]

The sound of doors opening.

What's that?

---

6 *Hamlet*, Act IV, scene 2.

7 From Pushkin's dramatic poem *Poltava*.

NIKITA IVANYCH. I guess it's Petrushka and Yegorka on their way back . . . That's talent, Vasil Vasilich! That's talent!

SVETLOVIDOV (*shouts, turning to the direction of the noise*). Over here, my fine feathered friends! (*To Nikita Ivanych.*) Let's go change our clothes . . . Old age ceases to exist, it's all nonsense, rubbish . . . (*Laughs merrily.*) What are you weeping for? My dear imbecile, what are you snivelling about? Ey, that's no good! That's no good at all! There, there, old man, that's enough of that! Why look at me like that? There, there . . . (*Embraces him through tears.*) You musn't cry . . . Where there's art, where there's talent, old age or loneliness or illness cease to exist, and even death half . . . (*Weeps.*) No, Nikitushka, our party's over . . . What kind of a talent am I? A squeezed lemon, a dripping icicle, a rusty nail, and you are an old theater rat, a prompter . . . Let's go!

They start to go.

What kind of talent am I? In serious plays I'm useful only in Fortinbras's retinue[8] . . . and I'm even too old for that now . . . Yes . . . You remember that bit from *Othello*, Nikitushka?

> Farewell the tranquil mind; farewell content!
> Farewell the plumèd troop and the big wars
> That make ambition virtue! O, farewell!
> Farewell the neighing steed, and the shrill trump,
> The spirit-stirring drum, the ear-piercing fife,
> The royal banner, and all quality,
> Pride, pomp, and circumstance of glorious war![9]

NIKITA IVANYCH. Talent! Talent!

SVETLOVIDOV. And this one:

> I'll out of Moscow straight! My visits here are ended!
> I'll fly and not look back! Where no ill tongues disparage,

---

8 When Fortinbras, Prince of Norway, makes his entrance in the last scene of *Hamlet*, he is accompanied by a retinue of soldiers. Compare T. S. Eliot's J. Alfred Prufrock: "To swell a scene . . ."

9 The end of Othello's monologue in Act III, scene 3.

I'll seek a refuge for my feelings much offended!
My carriage here! My carriage![10]

Exits with NIKITA IVANYCH.

Slow Curtain

VARIANTS TO

Swan Song (Calchas)

Variants from the anthology *The Season* (S), the censor's copy (C), the lithographed script (L), the journal *Performer* (P), and the anthology *Plays* (Pl).

page 307 / *Replace: old man*
with: *old man with a long, gray beard* (S, C, L, P)

page 307 / *Replace: cluttered with junk*
with: *cluttered with all sorts of theatrical junk* (S)

page 308 / *Replace:* Disgusting . . . Oof, good God!
with: Eh, why do you have to drink, you old nincompoop! Why do you have
   to! (S)

page 308 / *Replace:* your life's been lived . . . left at the very bottom
with: you're already fifty-eight — bye-bye! This life — my respects, is over! The
   cup's been drained and almost nothing's left (S)

page 308 / *Replace:* sixty-eight years
with: fifty-eight years (S, C, L, P)

page 308 / *Replace:* forty-five years
with: thirty-five years (S, C, L, P)

---

10 Svetlovidov's final quotation is from a comedy, Griboedov's classic verse satire *Woe from Wit*.
These are the last lines of the protagonist Chatsky, who has become completely disillusioned with
Moscow society.

page 308 / *Replace:* A black, bottomless pit, like a grave

with: A black, bottomless pit, a gaping maw, from which darkness and cold stare out . . .

Pause.

Infinitely deep and empty, like a grave. (S)

page 308 / *After:* calling up ghosts! — *stage direction: The bell for matins is heard.* (S)

page 310 / *Replace:* Those blue eyes of hers . . . could dispel the darkest night.

with: I did not see her as a human being, as a woman . . . In my eyes she was the sun, whose beauty one could not withstand (S)

page 310 / *After:* snowdrifts could break! —

NIKITA IVANYCH. Vasil Vasilich, honest to God, it's time to go to bed! Vasil Vasilich! (*Waves his hand in dismissal.*) What a nuisance you are! (S)

page 311 / *Replace:* Then I understood . . . a clown!

with: I didn't give up the stage, but my eyes were opened and I understood a good deal . . . I understood that I am a slave, a plaything of someone else's leisure time, comic relief, a clown! I began to understand that this is not sacred art, it's all a baneful deception. (S)

page 311 / *After:* Yegorka! — Is there anyone there? God, the candle's going out! (S)

page 314 / *Replace:* Farewell the tranquil mind . . . the circumstance of glorious war!

with: Had it pleas'd Heaven,
       To try me with Affliction, had they rain'd
       All kinds of sores, and shames on my bare head:
       Steep'd me in poverty to the very lips,
       Given to captivity me and my utmost hopes.

page 314 / *After:* glorious war! —

       And O you mortal engines, whose rude throats
       Th'immortal Jove's dread clamors counterfeit,
       Farewell: Othello's occupation's gone. (C, L, P)

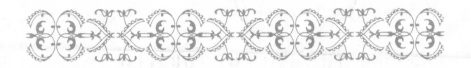

THE EVILS OF TOBACCO, FIRST VERSION

*O*riginally, Chekhov intended this as a monologue for the talented though alcoholic comedian Gradov-Sokolov, but he believed that, by dashing it off in two and a half hours in February 1886, he had spoiled it. "I consigned it to the devil, and to the Petersburg gazette," where it appeared, signed "A. Chekhonte." He made some revisions when the piece was republished in his collection *Motley Tales* later that year, raising the emotional tone, with a reader, rather than a spectator, in mind. One of his literary friends, A. S. Lazarev (Gruzinsky) considered it inferior to the other stories in the collection and twitted Chekhov for including it. Chekhov defended it, but the criticism may have stuck, for he returned to the monologue throughout the rest of his career, emending it until it reached the shape in which it is ordinarily reprinted today.

The mockery in the early versions is directed at amateur lecturers on science who seek to edify the common man. These educational efforts had become popular in the 1880s, when, owing to governmental repression, political action to improve society was made virtually impossible. Here the speaker, bearing the caricatural name of Markel Nyukhin, whose English equivalent might be Marcellus Snuffle, reveals not only his incompetence but the tawdriness of his family life. The Latin jargon and pompous gestures serve only to act as a cover-up for an existence as impoverished spiritually as it is materially. At this point, Chekhov seems unsympathetic to the butt of his jokes, but over time he would develop a more nuanced attitude to Nyukhin.

THE EVILS OF TOBACCO

О вреде табака

Scene-monologue

C A S T

MARKEL IVANYCH NYUKHIN,[1] *the husband of his wife, who runs a music school and a girls' board-ing school*

The stage represents the speaker's platform of a provincial club.

NYUKHIN (*enters pompously, bows, adjusts his waistcoat, and begins ceremoniously*). Ahem, ahem . . . gracious ladies and gentlemen! Someone suggested to my wife that on behalf of charity I should deliver a lecture on a popular topic. True scholarship is modest and not fond of making public appearances, but in view of the worthy cause my wife agreed—and here I am before you. I'm no professor and a stranger to academic degrees, but it's no secret to any of you that I . . . that I . . . (*hems and haws and quickly glances at a scrap of paper he pulls out of his waistcoat pocket*) . . . that I, for a good thirty years now, unceasingly, at the cost of my own health and the good things in life, have been working on questions of a scientific bent and have even published occasional scientific articles in a local organ of the press . . . Just the other week, they published my article on "The Evils of Domestic Animals,"[2] under the pseudonym "Faust." For the subject of my lecture today I have chosen the evils visited on humanity by the use of tobacco. Of course, it's difficult in one mere lecture to exhaust the full importance of the subject, but I shall try to be concise and confine myself to the major points . . . First of all I hasten to express my reservations. In most cases, popularization is an evil in itself . . . It inspires in society a sense of superior knowledge, an attempt at the cheap application of learning and indifference to serious, strictly scientific work . . . I am a foe of pop-

---

1 A joke name, from *nyukhat*, to take snuff, to sniffle. Markel is the Russian form of Marcellus.

2 When Chekhov republished this in his collection *Motley Tales*, he changed the title of the lecture to "The Evils of Teaism and Coffeeism on the Organism."

ularization and in this regard I part company with a great many famous scientists, as, for instance, Vogt and (*glances at his paper*) Moleshott.[3] Only last year, I sent to the famous scientific colleagues I have named a letter in which I set forth my views on popularization, but got no answer from them, probably because I had taken the precaution of sending my letters by ordinary post and not special delivery . . . As a foe of popularization, I shall be strictly scientific, I suggest that you, my listeners, prepare to be deeply sensible of the full importance of the subject and attend to my current lecture with due seriousness . . . The frivolous person, the person who's put off by the dryness of a strictly scientific lecture doesn't have to listen and can leave! . . . (*Makes a pompous gesture and adjusts his waistcoat.*) And now I shall begin . . . As I begin my lecture I ought to preface my remarks with an historical sketch of the first discovery of tobacco and the association of ideas which led humanity to poison itself with this exotic toxin, but given the shortness of time, I have to begin with the most essential thing . . . Please pay attention . . . I especially solicit the attention of the medical professionals assembled here, who can glean a good deal of useful information from my lecture, because tobacco, besides its deleterious effects, can be also used as medicine. So, on February 10th, 1871, it was prescribed to my wife as a kind of enema. (*Glances at his paper.*) Tobacco is an organic substance. It is extracted from the plant *Nicotiana Tabacum*, a member of the *Solaneae* family. It grows in America. Its chief component is comprised of the horrible, destructive toxin nicotine, which, in my opinion, is none other than a nitrous volatile alkaloid ammonia, in which every particle of hydrogen is replaced by a three-atom radical, known to science by the name of nicotillene . . . Chemically it consists of ten atoms of carbon, fourteen atoms of hydrogen and . . . two . . . atoms . . . of nitrogen . . . (*Gasps and clutches at his chest, while dropping the scrap of paper.*) Air! (*To keep from falling and maintain his balance, he plies his arms and legs.*) Ugh! Let me catch my breath . . . Hold on . . . Just a minute . . . . I'll overcome this attack by sheer willpower . . . (*Beats his chest with his fist.*) Enough! Oof! (*A momentary pause, during which Nyukhin walks back and forth along the stage and catches his breath.*) For quite some time now . . . I've been suffering from attacks of asphyxia . . . asthma . . . My first seizure began on August 13th 1869, . . . the very day

3 Paul Friedrich Immanuel Vogt (1844–1885), German chemist, and Jacob Moleshott (1822–1893), Dutch medical writer, authorities whom Chekhov would have studied as a young medical student.

when my wife gave birth to my sixth daughter, Veronika . . . My wife has exactly ten daughters in all . . . of sons nary a one, which delights my wife because sons in a girls' boarding school would be unseemly from a number of angles . . . In the whole boarding school there's only one man and that's me . . . But the highly respectable, well-thought-of families, who have confided the fate of their children to my wife, can put their minds at ease where I am concerned . . . Thanks to my wife's discretion the young ladies regard me not so much as a member of an opposite sex, but as a dress-maker's dummy, suitable for use in instruction in that type of highest civic order, which is denominated a family . . . However . . . considering the shortness of time, we will not digress from the subject of the lecture . . . Now, where had I stopped? Oof! The asthma attack interrupted me at the most interesting point. Still, no cloud but has a silver lining. For me and for you, particularly for those medical professionals gathered here, this attack may serve as the most splendid of lessons. In nature there are no effects without causes . . . Let us seek out the causes of my latest seizure . . . (*Applies a finger to his forehead and thinks.*) Got it! The unique remedy for asthma is to refrain from stimulating and heavy food, but, before coming here for the lecture, I over-indulged myself. I have to mention that today at my wife's boarding school we had pancakes. Instead of a dinner of roast meat, every pupil was served two pancakes apiece. I am my wife's husband, and therefore I do not think it my place to praise that noble individual, but I swear to you that nowhere do they serve such sensible, hygienic, and effi-cacious meals as at my wife's boarding school. I can personally testify to this, because at my wife's boarding school I have the honor to be in charge of the housekeeping department. I buy the provisions, supervise the ser-vants, every night turn over the accounts to my wife, stitch the composition books, concoct insecticides, purify the air by means of an atomizer, count the linen, make sure that one toothbrush is not used by more than five pupils, and that no more than ten girls dry themselves on a single towel. Today it fell to my duties to dole out flour and butter to the cook in such quantity as strictly corresponded with the number of pupils. I had to be present in the kitchen the whole time and keep watch. It's impossible to trust the servants. Many's the time, thanks to the sloppiness and careless-ness of cooks and washerwomen, I have failed to earn my wife's trust! I left the kitchen without permission, the servant-girl took advantage of this and as a result I aroused my benefactress's legitimate wrath. True, I bore my punishment wih due humility, but the loss, incurred by my inattentive-

ness, could in no way be recompensed. And so, today they made pancakes.
I ought to mention that the pancakes were intended only for the pupils.
For the members of my wife's family they were preparing a roast, for which
purpose a shank of veal had been kept in the cellar since Friday of the previous week. My wife and I came to the conclusion that if we did not roast
that shank today, it would go bad by tomorrow. But to proceed. When the
pancakes had been cooked and counted out, my wife came into the
kitchen to say that five of the pupils were being punished for misconduct
and were therefore deprived of pancakes. What are we supposed to do with
them? Serve them to our daughters? But my wife forbids our daughters to
eat doughy foods . . . (*Sighs and shakes his head.*) Oh loving heart! Angel
of kindness! She decided that I should eat five of the ten pancakes.[4] I ate
them, after drinking a preliminary shot of vodka. Now the cause of my
seizure is revealed. *Da ist Hund begraben!*[5] And yet . . . (*Looks at his watch.*)
I have strayed a bit from my subject. Let us proceed . . . And so, nicotine
chemically consists of . . . of . . . (*Nervously fumbles in his pocket and looks
around for his scrap of paper.*) I suggest that you memorize this formula . . .
A chemical formula is a guiding light . . . (*When he sees the paper, he drops
a handkerchief over it.*) When it comes to formulas, I am pedantic and
implacable. The pupil has to have the formula memorized as firmly as her
own name. (*Picks up the paper along with the handkerchief.*) I forgot to tell
you that at my wife's boarding school, besides doing the housekeeping, I'm
also charged with teaching mathematics, physics, chemistry, geography,
history, and object lessons. In addition to these studies, my wife's boarding
school offers the French, German, and English languages, literature, Holy
Scripture, needlework, music, dancing, and etiquette. A curriculum, please
note, much broader than that of any high school. The meals and amenities are ideal! And all this at the lowest of prices! Full-course pupils pay
three hundred rubles, half-course pupils two hundred, day pupils a hundred. For dancing, music and drawing there are separate terms, arranged
with my wife . . . A wonderful boarding school! It is located on the corner
of Breadloaf Street and Five Dog Lane, in the house of the widow of Staff
Captain Mamashyochkina.[6] To discuss terms my wife can be at home at

---

4 In *Motley Tales,* this is replaced by "She said, 'Eat the pancakes yourself, Markesha!'"

5 Bad German for "That's where the dog is buried" or "That's the root of the matter."

6 A joke name suggesting "mommy's cheek."

any time, and the school's curriculum can be purchased from the doorman for 50 kopeks a copy. (*Glances at his paper.*) And so, I urge you to memorize the formula! Nicotine is chemically composed of ten atoms of carbon, fourteen atoms of hydrogen, and two of nitrogen. It resembles a colorless liquid with an ammoniac odor. (*Pulls a snuffbox out of his pocket and takes a pinch.*) It is a component of tobacco along with tobaccic and nicotinic acids, which have a distinctly perceptible odor of camphor. (*Sneezes.*) Setting aside nicotillene and (*sneezes*) nicotianin, let us turn our attention to nicotine. (*Scratches his nose.*) That's funny? For us, personally speaking, what is important is the spontaneous action of nicotine (*looks in his snuffbox*) on the nervous system and the muscles of the digestive tract. Oh, Lord! They've put something in it again! (*Sneezes.*) Well, what am I going to do with these nasty, lowdown little brats? Yesterday they put face powder in my snuffbox, and today something acrid, stinking. (*Sneezes and scratches his nose.*) It really is vile, foul! Please forgive me, but this powder is raising merry hell in my nose! Brrr! . . . Nasty, vicious monsters! You may deduce from such behavior flaws in the strict discipline at my wife's boarding school! No, gracious ladies and gentlemen, the school is not to blame! You are to blame! Society is to blame! The family must be hand in glove with my wife's school, but instead it only demoralizes the child. (*Sneezes.*) My wife's family has been hand in glove with my wife's school and, believe me, not one of my wife's daughters would indulge in such behavior towards a senior instructor . . . But let's forget about this! (*Sneezes.*) Let's forget it . . . Nicotine puts the stomach and the kidneys into a condition of tetanus! (*Pause.*) However, I notice smiles on several faces. Obviously, not all my listeners have sufficiently and fully appreciated the high seriousness of the subject which concerns us. There are even some who find it possible to laugh, when truths, consecrated by exact science, are uttered to them from the podium! . . . (*Sighs.*) I impute this laughter to a defective education . . . One must not laugh at what is great, beautiful, sacred . . . Woe to the man who laughs! My wife's daughters never laugh. They are well educated, and I can die happy.[7] (*Sneezes.*) My wife has nine daughters. The eldest of them, Anna, is twenty-seven, the youngest is seventeen. Everything in nature that is beautiful, pure, sublime . . . great . . . deeply moral is brought together in those nine young, innocent creatures. So far not a sin-

---

7 In *Motley Tales* this is replaced by "Of course, I dare not offer you reproof, but . . . I always say to my wife's daughters, 'Children, do not laugh at that which transcends laughter!'"

gle one of them is married, but, just by looking at them, one could guarantee that they would make the most splendid wives.[8] (*Sighs.*) However, how difficult it is nowadays to get married![9] (*Shakes his head.*) Ah, young people! young people! With your obstinacy, your material propensities you deprive yourself of one of the supreme pleasures, the pleasure of family life! . . . If you only knew how lovely that life is! I have lived with my wife for thirty-three years, and I can say they were the best years of my life. They have flown by like one happy moment. (*Weeps.*) How often have I grieved her with my failings! Poor woman! I may have taken my punishment humbly, but how badly I incurred her wrath! (*Pause.*) And I do not understand why my wife's daughters are taking so long in getting married! Probably because no men ever get to see them.[10] But you young men should take a look. Who knows? Maybe, one of the nine will be to your liking. Of course my wife can't throw parties, but . . . I can confide to you a secret (*comes down to the footlights*), my daughters can be seen on major holidays at their auntie's, Natalya Semyonovna.[11] There'll be refreshments.[12] But owing to shortness of time we shall not stray from the subject. We had stopped at tetanus. However (*looks at his watch*) until the next time! (*Exits.*)

---

8 In *Motley Tales* this is replaced by "Forgive me for this agitation and this quaver in my voice; you see before you the happiest of fathers!"

9 In *Motley Tales* this is followed by "Awfully difficult! It's easier to borrow money on a third mortgage than to find a husband for even one of your daughters!"

10 In *Motley Tales* this is replaced by "My wife's daughters are taking so long getting married because they're shy and because no men ever get to see them."

11 In *Motley Tales* this is followed by "Zavertyukhina, the one who suffers from rheumatism and collects old coins." (A joke name meaning "all wrapped up.")

12 In *Motley Tales* this is followed by "And when my wife isn't around, you might get a bit of . . ."

IVANOV, FIRST VERSION

*C*hekhov wrote *Ivanhov*, his first work to be staged, at the prompting of the theatrical impresario Korsh and in the wake of the creative gust that had produced the important transitional story "The Steppe." He dashed off the play in under two weeks in October 1887, pleased with its "unhackneyed subject" and its lack of longueurs. He defined his own originality this way: "Modern dramatists start their plays exclusively with angels, cads, and buffoons—try and find those elements anywhere in Russia! Sure, you'll find them, but not in such extreme forms as dramatists require. I wanted to do something original; I didn't hatch out a single villain, a single angel (though I couldn't refrain from buffoons). I didn't accuse anyone. I didn't acquit anyone" (to his brother Aleksandr, October 24, 1887).

Ivanov was first played at Korsh's Theatre in Moscow on November 19, 1887, for the benefit of Nikolay Svetlov, who created the role of Borkin; it enjoyed a mixed success. The actors' praise and the audience's plaudits made Chekhov euphoric, and he wrote to Aleksandr, "You can't imagine what's happened! From that meaningless little turd that is my playlet . . . there's been a hell of a development . . . in his 32 years in the theater the prompter had never seen anything like it." He triumphantly signed himself, "Schiller Shakespearovich Goethe" (November 24, 1887). But his younger brother Mikhail recalled the event differently: "The success of the performance was uneven; some hissed, others, the majority, applauded and called for the author, but in general *Ivanov* was misunderstood, and for a long time afterward the newspapers were explicating the personality of the character of its leading hero." The impressionable playwright gradually came to the conclusion that the audience had welcomed Ivanov himself as a distillation of the *Zeitgeist*. His mooning and moaning, his fits of self-castigation summed up for the generation of the 1880s its own pusillanimous torpor during the "dark decade," a period of political repression and social inaction. Ivanov's death provided a kind of vicarious expiation.

That was not what Chekhov had in mind. Superficially, Ivanov, his name the Russian equivalent of "Jones," seemed another common- or garden-variety "superfluous man": "a university graduate, in no way remarkable; a somewhat excitable, ardent nature, strongly inclined to honorable and straightforward enthusiasm, like most educated gentry" was how Chekhov described him. His past was nobler than his present: his projects for serving the people — rational farming, higher education — have evaporated. Chekhov, however, wanted to avoid idealizing this disillusionment, by then a stale treatment, to an examination by the character himself of the reasons for his empty life and contemptible behavior. Ivanov was to suffer through his own awareness of wasted potential and vestigial honor. A basic dramatic problem was to keep the audience from romanticizing Ivanov's pessimism, and, at the same time, to keep Ivanov from looking like the immoralist that Doctor Lvov makes him out to be.

The stage portrayal of this complex inner turmoil was tricky for an inexperienced playwright, trying to employ age-old strategies of dramatic carpentry to contain a rich psychological subject. Basically, the "plot" might have come from a typical society melodrama: a scoundrel abandons his exploited wife in hopes of repairing his fortunes by wedding a young heiress. This sensational story line is how Ivanov's actions look to outsiders such as Lvov.

The play's lifeblood is gossip. In the first act, we hear of slanderous rumors about Ivanov, but no one takes them seriously. In the second act, the school for scandal is in session at Lebedev's home, but the gossipmongers are so caricatured that again their power to harm is discounted. Ivanov is now associated with Borkin's shady machinations, however. In Act Three, Lebedev still refuses to believe the tattle, though he warns Ivanov about it. Aided by Lvov, the rumors reach Anna's ears, provoking her confrontation with her husband and her collapse. In the play's first version, this theme continued into Act Four, with even Lebedev harboring doubts about Anna's death. Ivanov, publicly charged with villainy by the Doctor, dies of a heart attack "because," said Chekhov, "he can't endure the outrageous insult" (to Aleksandr, November 20, 1887). This was to turn the play into a tract about provincial narrow-mindedness, and, indeed, many of the critics described Ivanov as the honorable but vacillating victim of scandalmongers.

After friends in St. Petersburg assured him that the character drawing was solid, and that, contrary to what some critics said, the play was not immoral, Chekhov decided on minor revisions. He realized that the final heart attack posed a problem for an actor while it undermined the real causes of Ivanov's destruction. With a new ending, a monologue to clarify Ivanov's state of mind, and some minimal rearrangement, it would be suitable for submission to the Imperial Alexandra Theatre in St. Petersburg. "Now my Mr. Ivanov will be much better understood. The ending doesn't quite satisfy me (except for the gunshot, it's all flabby), but I am comforted by the fact that it's still in an unfinished form" (to Suvorin, December 19, 1888).

IVANOV

Иванов

Comedy in Four Acts and Five Tableaux

FIRST VERSION

C H A R A C T E R S

IVANOV, NIKOLAY ALEKSEEVICH, *Permanent member of the Council for Peasant Affairs*[1]

ANNA PETROVNA, *his wife, born Sarra Abramson*[2]

SHABELSKY, MATVEY SEMYONOVICH, *Count, his maternal uncle*

LEBEDEV, PAVEL KIRILLYCH, *Chairman of the Rural Board*[3]

ZINAIDA SAVISHNA, *his wife*

SASHA, *the Lebedevs' daughter, 20*

LVOV, YEVGENY KONSTANTINOVICH, *a young country doctor*[4]

---

1 A district committee to supervise self-governing peasant communes; its members might include the district police chief, a justice of the peace, and a "permanent member," a salaried official appointed by the government on the nomination of the Rural Board. The "permanent member" was highly responsible for the control of rural institutions.

2 As a converted Jew, Sarra had to take a Christian saint's name and patronymic.

3 *Zemstvo,* an elective council created in 1864 to administer minor regional economic, educational and sanitary matters; its elected members included both landowners and peasants. Throughout the 1880s, a period of political repression, the *zemstvos* worked sluggishly.

4 "Good grief, all one had to do was pronounce these words for a Russian intellectual, a university student, a coed to make a respectful face. Once a country doctor came on stage, the audience's sympathy was enlisted, he was the 'shining light,' the 'social idealist,' he has the right to be the 'positive' character in the play.

"And suddenly this hero . . . is left alone and says: 'What the hell! It's bad enough *they don't pay me for my visits* . . . etc.' So: one stroke, just one lie, and the mask is off" (V. I. Nemirovich-Danchenko, *Out of the Past* [1938]). See end of Act One.

BABAKINA, MARFA YEGOROVNA, *a young widow, landowner,*
daughter of a rich merchant

KOSYKH, DMITRY NIKITICH, *a tax collector*

BORKIN, MIKHAIL MIKHAILOVICH, *a distant relative of Ivanov*
and manager of his estate

DUDKIN, *the son of a rich factory owner*

AVDOTYA NAZAROVNA, *an old woman of no fixed profession*

YEGORUSHKA, *a poor relation of the Lebedevs*

FIRST GUEST

SECOND GUEST

PYOTR, *Ivanov's manservant*

GAVRILA, *the Lebedevs' manservant*

GUESTS *of both sexes, manservants*

The action takes place in one of the districts[5] of Central Russia.

ACT ONE

*A garden on Ivanov's estate. Left, the façade of a house with a
veranda. One of the windows is open. In front of the veranda is a
broad, semi-circular expanse, with paths leading straight ahead
and to the left, to the garden. At the right, little garden settees and
tables. A lamp is lit on one of the latter. Evening is drawing on. At
the rise of the curtain one can hear a duet for piano and cello
being practiced in the house.*

---

5 *Guberniya*, a provincial region administered by a governor and divided into counties (*uyezdy*).

I

IVANOV and BORKIN.

IVANOV is sitting at a table, reading a book.

BORKIN, wearing heavy boots and carrying a rifle, appears at the bottom of the garden; he is tipsy; after he spots Ivanov, he tiptoes up to him and, when he has come alongside him, aims the gun in his face.

IVANOV (*on seeing Borkin, shudders and jumps up*). Misha, God knows what . . . you scared me . . . I'm jittery enough as it is, but you keep playing these stupid jokes . . . (*Sits.*) He scared me, so he's pleased with himself . . .

BORKIN (*roars with laughter*). Right, right . . . sorry, sorry. (*Sits beside him.*) I won't do it any more, no more . . . (*Takes off his vizored cap.*) It's hot. Would you believe, sweetheart, I've covered over ten miles in something like three hours . . . I've knocked myself out, had a hell of a time . . . Just feel my heart, the way it's pounding . . .

IVANOV (*reading*). Fine, later . . .

BORKIN. No, feel it right now. (*Takes his hand and puts it on his chest.*) You hear it? Boom-boom-boom-boom-boom-boom-boom. That means I've got heart trouble. Any minute I could keel over and die. Say, would you be sorry if I died?

IVANOV. I'm reading . . . later . . .

BORKIN. No, seriously, would you be sorry if I suddenly up and died? Nikolay Alekseevich, would you be sorry if I died? . . .

IVANOV. Stop pestering me!

BORKIN. Dear boy, tell me, would you be sorry?

IVANOV. I'm sorry that you reek of vodka. It's disgusting, Misha.

BORKIN (*laughs*). I really reek? I can't believe it . . . Actually, I can believe it. At Plesniki I ran into the coroner, and the two of us, I must admit, knocked back about eight drinks apiece. Fundamentally, drinking is very bad for your health. Tell me, is it really bad? Huh? Is it bad for you?

IVANOV. This is unbearable, for the last time . . . Get it through your head, Misha, that this teasing . . .

BORKIN. Right, right . . . sorry, sorry! . . . Take it easy, sit down . . . (*Gets up and walks away.*) Incredible people, you're not even allowed to talk. (*Comes back.*) Oh, yes! I almost forgot . . . Let's have it, eighty-two rubles! . . .

IVANOV. What eighty-two rubles?

BORKIN. To pay the workmen tomorrow.

IVANOV. I haven't got it.

BORKIN. Thank you very kindly! (*Mimics him.*) I haven't got it . . . After all, don't the workmen have to be paid? Don't they?

IVANOV. I don't know. I haven't got anything today. Wait till the first of the month when I get my salary.[6]

BORKIN. Just try and have a conversation with characters like this! . . . The workmen aren't coming for their money on the first of the month, but tomorrow morning!

IVANOV. What am I supposed to do about it now? Go on, saw me in half, nag at me . . . And where you did you pick up this revolting habit of pestering me whenever I'm reading, writing or . . .

BORKIN. What I'm asking you is: do the workmen get paid or not? Eh, what's the use of talking to you! . . . (*Waves his hand in dismissal.*) Landowners too, the hell with 'em, lords of creation . . . Experimental farming methods . . . Nearly three hundred acres of land and not a penny in their pocket . . . It's like a wine cellar without a corkscrew. I'll go and sell the carriage horses tomorrow! Yes sir! . . . I sold the oats while they were still standing in the field, tomorrow I'll go and sell the rye. (*Strides up and down the stage.*) You think I'll wait for an invitation? Do you? Well, no sir, you're not dealing with that sort of person . . .

I I

The same, SHABELSKY (offstage), and ANNA PETROVNA.

SHABELSKY's voice from the window: "It's impossible to play with you . . . You've no more ear than a gefilte fish, and your touch is a disgrace . . . A Semitic, guttural touch, you can smell the garlic in it a mile off."

---

6 His government salary as Permanent Member of the Council for Peasant Affairs.

ANNA PETROVNA (*appears in the open window*). Who was talking out here just now? Was it you, Misha? Why are you stamping around like that?

BORKIN. Talk to your *Nicolas-voilà*[7] and it'd get you stamping too . . .

ANNA PETROVNA. Listen, Misha, have them bring some hay to the croquet lawn. I want to turn somersaults . . .

BORKIN (*waves his hand in dismissal*). Leave me alone, please . . .

ANNA PETROVNA (*laughs*). Really, what a tone to take . . . That tone of voice doesn't suit a chubby little cherub like you at all, Misha. If you want women to love you, never get angry with them and don't act self-important . . . (*To her husband.*) Nikolay, let's turn somersaults now and forever! . . .

IVANOV. Anyuta, it's bad for you to stand in an open window. Go in, please . . . (*Shouts.*) Uncle, shut the window!

The window is shut.

BORKIN. Don't forget, day after tomorrow, the interest has to be paid to Lebedev.

IVANOV. I remember. I'll be at Lebedev's today and I'll ask them to postpone it . . . (*Looks at his watch.*)

BORKIN. When are you going over there?

IVANOV. Right now . . .

BORKIN (*quickly*). Hold on, hold on! isn't today, I think, Shurochka's birthday? . . . Well, well, well, well . . . And me forgetting all about it . . . What a memory, eh? (*Skips.*) I'll go, I'll go . . . (*Sings.*) I'll go . . . I'll go for a swim, chew some paper, take three drops of ammonia[8] and it's off to a fresh start. . . . Darling, Nikolay Alekseevich, sweetie-pie, love of my life, you're always a nervous wreck, no kidding, you're whining, constantly melancholeric,[9] and yet you and I, no kidding, could get a hell of a lot of things done

---

7 An in-joke for the play's first audiences. *Nicolas-voilà* (French: It's Nick in the nick o' time!) was a tagline from a song in a musical farce popularized by the actor Davydov, who created the role of Ivanov.

8 Chewing perfumed paper to sweeten the breath, and taking ammonia to cure a hangover.

9 Russian: *merlekhlyundiya*, Chekhov's joking version of *melancholy*, which he picked up from medical school slang. Masha repeats it in *Three Sisters*.

together! I'm ready to do anything for you . . . You want me to marry Marfusha Babakina for your sake? Marfutka's so much crap, damn it, but
should I marry her? Half the dowry is yours . . . I mean, not half, but all of
it . . . Take all of it! . . .

IVANOV. If you're going to talk rot . . .

BORKIN. No, seriously, no kidding, you want me to marry Marfusha? Go
fifty-fifty on the dowry . . . But why am I talking to you? As if you understood me? (*Mimics him.*) "If you're going to talk rot." You're a good man,
an intelligent man, but you haven't got an ounce of, what d'y'call it, you
know, get up and go. If only you'd do things in a big way, raise a little hell
. . . You're a neurotic, a crybaby, but if you were a normal man, you could
make a million in a year's time . . . For instance, if I had 2,300 rubles right
now, in two weeks I'd have twenty thousand. You don't believe me? You
think I'm talking nonsense? No, it's not nonsense . . . Just give me 2,300
rubles, and in a week I'll show you twenty thousand. On the other side of
the river Ovsyanov is selling a strip of land, just across from us, for 2,300
rubles. If we buy that strip, we'll own both sides of the riverbank. And if we
own both sides, you understand, we have the right to dam the river . . . Am
I right? We could put up a mill, and as soon as we announce that we want
to build a dam, everyone who lives downstream will kick up a fuss, and
right away we go *kommen Sie hier,*[10] if you don't want a dam, pay up. Get
it? Zarev's factory will pay us five thousand, Korolkov three thousand, the
monastery will pay five thousand . . .

IVANOV. It's all hocus-pocus, Misha . . . If you want us to stay friends, keep it
to yourself.

BORKIN (*sits at the table*). Of course! . . . I knew it! You won't do anything
yourself, and you tie my hands . . .

I I I

The same, SHABELSKY, and LVOV.

SHABELSKY (*coming out of the house with Lvov*). Doctors are just like
lawyers, the sole difference being, lawyers only rob you, while doctors rob
you *and* kill you . . . Present company excepted. (*Sits on a little settee.*)

---

10 German: Come here.

Quacks, charlatans . . . Perhaps in some Utopia you can come across an exception to the general rule, but . . . over the course of a lifetime I've squandered about twenty thousand and never met a single doctor, who didn't strike me as a barefaced impostor . . .

BORKIN (*to Ivanov*). Yes, you won't do anything yourself and you tie my hands. That's why we don't have any money . . .

SHABELSKY. I repeat, present company excepted . . . There may be exceptions, although, even so . . . (*Yawns.*)

IVANOV (*closing the book*). Doctor, what have you got to say?

LVOV (*with a glance at the window*). The same thing I said this morning: she has to go to the Crimea at once. (*Walks up and down the stage.*)

SHABELSKY (*bursts out laughing*). The Crimea! . . . Why don't you and I, Misha, hang out a shingle as medicos? It's so easy . . . A woman sneezes or coughs because she's bored, some Madame Angot or Ophelia,[11] quick, take a scrap of paper and prescribe along scientific principles: first, a young doctor, then a trip to the Crimea, in the Crimea a strapping Tatar, on the way back a private compartment with someone who's gambled away all his money but a cute little dandy all the same . . .

IVANOV (*to the Count*). Ah, stop pestering, you pest! (*To Lvov.*) To go to the Crimea you need money. Suppose I find it, she definitely refuses to take the trip . . .

LVOV. Yes, she does . . .

Pause.

BORKIN. Say, Doctor, is Anna Petrovna really so seriously ill that she has to go to the Crimea? . . .

LVOV (*with a glance at the window*). Yes, tuberculosis . . .

BORKIN. Psss . . . that's no good . . . For some time now I've noticed from her face that she wasn't long for this world.

---

11 Shabelsky cites literary heroines at random. Madame Angot, a French market-woman of the French Directoire period, renowned for her salty speech, is a character in Charles Lecocq's comic opera *La Fille de Madame Angot* (1872), which Chekhov may have seen in Moscow in 1878. Ophelia is Polonius's daughter, once loved by Hamlet.

LVOV. But . . . don't talk so loudly . . . you can be heard in the house . . .

Pause.

BORKIN (*sighing*). This life of ours . . . Human life is like a posy, growing gloriously in a meadow, a goat comes along, eats it, end of posy . . . (*Sings.*) "Would you know my soul's unrest . . ."[12]

SHABELSKY. Nonsense, nonsense, and more nonsense! . . . (*Yawns.*) Nonsense and monkeyshines . . .

Pause.

BORKIN. Well, gentlemen, I keep trying to teach Nikolay Alekseevich how to make money. I've let him in on one wonderful idea, but my pollen, as usual, has fallen on barren ground . . . You can't hammer anything into him . . . Look at him: what's he like? Melancholy, spleen, tedium, depression, heartache . . .

SHABELSKY (*rises and stretches*). You're a brilliant thinker, you come up with something for everyone, you teach everyone how to live, but you've never taught me a single thing . . . Teach me, Mr. Know-it-all, show me a way to get ahead . . .

BORKIN (*rises*). I'm going for a swim . . . Good-bye, gentlemen . . . (*To the Count.*) You've got twenty ways to get ahead . . . If I were in your shoes, I'd make about twenty thousand in a week. (*Going.*)

SHABELSKY (*goes after him*). What's the gimmick? Come on, teach me . . .

BORKIN. There's nothing to teach. It's very easy . . . (*Returns.*) Nikolay Alekseevich, give me a ruble!

IVANOV silently gives him the money.

Merci! (*To the Count.*) You've still got a handful of aces.

SHABELSKY (*going after him*). Well, what are they? (*Stretches.*)

BORKIN. In your shoes, in a week I'd make about thirty thousand, if not more.

Exits with the Count.

---

12 Chekhov later puts this song in the mouth of Yepikhodov in *The Cherry Orchard.*

IVANOV (*after a pause.*) Pointless people,[13] pointless talk, the pressing need to answer stupid questions, Doctor, it's all wearied me to the point of illness. I've become irritable, touchy, impatient, so petty that I don't know what I am any more. Whole days at a time my head aches, I can't sleep, ringing in my ears . . . And there's absolutely nowhere to escape to . . . Absolutely nowhere . . .

LVOV. Nikolay Alekseevich, I have to have a serious talk with you.

IVANOV. Talk away.

LVOV. It's concerning Anna Petrovna. (*Sits.*) She won't consent to go to the Crimea, but she might if you went with her . . .

IVANOV (*after thinking about it*). If we were to go together, we'd need money. Besides, they certainly wouldn't give me a leave of absence. I've already taken one leave this year . . .

LVOV. Let's assume that's true. Now, moving on. The most important treatment for tuberculosis is absolute peace and quiet, and your wife doesn't have a moment's peace. She's constantly upset by the way you treat her. Excuse me, I'm concerned and I'll speak bluntly. Your behavior is killing her.

Pause.

Nikolay Alekseevich, give me some cause to think better of you!

IVANOV. It's all true, true . . . I'm probably terribly to blame, but my mind's messed up, my soul is mired in a kind of indolence, and I can't seem to understand myself. I don't understand other people or myself. (*With a glance at the window.*) They can hear us, let's go, let's take a walk.

Gets up.

My dear friend, I should tell you the story from the very beginning. But it's long and so complicated that I wouldn't finish before morning.

They walk.

Anyuta is a remarkable, an exceptional woman . . . For my sake she converted to my religion, cast off her father and mother, turned her back on

---

13 *Lishnye lyudi*, usually translated as "superfluous men," a technical term in Russian culture, popularized by Ivan Turgenev: well-born, well-educated members of society who fail to contribute anything to it. Ivanov applies the term to himself in Act Two.

wealth, and if I'd demanded another hundred sacrifices, she would have made them, without blinking an eye. Well, sir, there nothing at all remarkable about me and I made no sacrifices at all. Though it's a long story . . . The whole gist of it, dear Doctor (*hesitates*), is . . . to make a long story short, I married when I was passionately in love and swore love everlasting, but . . . five years have gone by, she's still in love with me, while I . . . (*Splays his hands in a gesture of futility.*) Now you're going to tell me that she'll die soon, but I don't feel any love or pity, just a sort of void, weariness . . . Anyone looking at me from the outside would probably think this is awful; I don't understand myself what's going on inside me . . .

They go off down a garden path.

I V

SHABELSKY, then ANNA PETROVNA.

SHABELSKY (*enters, roaring with laughter*). Honest to God, he's not a crook, he's a visionary, a virtuoso! Ought to put up a monument to him. He's a thorough blend of modern pus in all its variety: lawyer, doctor, speculator, accountant. (*Sits on a low step of the veranda.*) And yet he seems never to have gone to school anywhere, that's what's amazing . . . What a brilliant criminal he probably would have been, if he'd picked up a bit of culture, the liberal arts! "In a week," he says, "you could have twenty thousand. You've got a handful of aces," he says, "your title as Count." (*Roars with laughter.*) "Any girl with a dowry would marry you" . . .

ANNA PETROVNA opens the window and looks down.

"Want me to make a match between you and Marfusha?" he says. *Qui est-ce que c'est* Marfusha?[14] Ah, that . . . Balabalkina creature . . . Babakalkina . . . the one that looks like a washerwoman and blows her nose like a cab driver . . . .

ANNA PETROVNA. Is that you, Count?

SHABELSKY. What's that?

ANNA PETROVNA laughs.

(*In a Jewish accent.*) Vot you should leffing at?

---

14 Broken French: Who on earth is this Marfusha?

ANNA PETROVNA. I was remembering a certain saying of yours. Remember, you said it at dinner? A thief unchastised, a horse . . . How did it go?

SHABELSKY. A kike baptized, a thief unchastised, a horse hospitalized are not to be prized.

ANNA PETROVNA (*laughs*). You can't even make a simple play on words without malice. You're a malicious person . . . (*Seriously.*) Joking aside, Count, you are very malicious. Living with you is depressing and terrifying. You're always grumbling, grousing, you think everyone's a scoundrel and a villain. Tell me, Count, frankly: have you ever said anything nice about anyone?

SHABELSKY. What sort of cross-examination is this!

ANNA PETROVNA. You and I have been living together under the same roof for five years now, and never once have I heard you speak of people neutrally, without sarcasm or sneering. What harm have people done you? (*Coughs.*) Do you think you're better than everyone else?

SHABELSKY. I certainly don't think that. I'm the same blackguard and swine in man's clothing[15] as everyone else. *Mauvais ton*, an old has-been. I always have a bad word for myself too. Who am I? What am I? I was rich, independent, somewhat happy, and now . . . a parasite, a freeloader, a dislocated buffoon . . . If I get indignant, if I express disdain, people laugh in my face; if I laugh, they shake their heads at me sadly and say: the old man's off his rocker . . . Most of the time, though, they don't listen to me, take no notice of me . . .

ANNA PETROVNA (*calmly*). Screeching again . . .

SHABELSKY. Who's screeching?

ANNA PETROVNA. The owl. It screeches every evening.

SHABELSKY. Let it screech. Things can't get worse than they already are. (*Stretches.*) Ah, my dearest Sarra, just let me win one or two hundred thousand, and then watch me kick up my heels! . . . You wouldn't see me for dust. I'd run away from this dump, from freeloading, and I wouldn't set foot here till doomsday . . .

ANNA PETROVNA. And just what would you do if you won?

---

15 Literally, swine in a skullcap. Both this phrase and *mauvais ton* (bad form) are allusions to a letter defaming the town's officials in the last act of Gogol's comedy *The Inspector General* (1836).

SHABELSKY (*after a moment's thought*). I? First of all I'd go to Moscow and listen to gypsy music. Then . . . then I'd scamper off to Paris. I'd rent an apartment, attend the embassy church . . .

ANNA PETROVNA. What else?

SHABELSKY. I'd spend whole days sitting by my wife's grave, lost in thought. I would sit at her grave like that till I kicked the bucket. My wife is buried in Paris . . .

Pause.

ANNA PETROVNA. That's awfully depressing. Shall we play another duet or something?

SHABELSKY. All right. Get out the music.

ANNA PETROVNA exits.

V

SHABELSKY, IVANOV, and LVOV.

IVANOV (*appearing on the path with Lvov*). Dear friend, you got your degree only last year, you're still young and vigorous, but I'm thirty-five. I have the right to give you advice. Don't marry Jewish girls or neurotics or intellectuals, but pick out something ordinary, drab, without flashy colors or extraneous sounds. Generally speaking, match your life to a standard pattern. The grayer and more monotonous the background, the better. My dear man, don't wage war singlehandedly against thousands, don't tilt at windmills, don't run headlong into walls . . . God forbid you go in for any experimental farming methods, alternative schools, impassioned speeches . . . Shut yourself up in your shell and go about your petty, God-given business. That's more comfortable, more authentic, more healthy. Whereas the life I've led,—what a bore! Ah, what a bore! . . . So many mistakes, injustices, so much absurdity . . . (*On seeing the Count, annoyed.*) You're always spinning around in front of us, uncle, you never let me have a moment's privacy!

SHABELSKY (*in a tearful voice*). Damn it all, there's no place for me anywhere. (*Jumps up and goes into the house.*)

IVANOV (*shouts after him*). There, I'm sorry, I'm sorry. (*To Lvov.*) Why did I have to insult him? No, I'm definitely going to pieces. Got to get a grip on myself. Got to . . .

LVOV (*overwrought*). Nikolay Alekseevich, I've been listening to you and . . . and, excuse me, I'll speak frankly, no beating about the bush. Your voice, your intonations, let alone your words, are so full of heartless egotism, such cold cruelty . . . A person near and dear to you is perishing because she is near to you, her days are numbered, while you . . . you cannot love, you take walks, hand out advice, strike poses . . . I cannot find a way to express it, I haven't got the gift of gab, but . . . but I find you deeply repugnant! . . .

IVANOV. Could be, could be . . . A third party might have a clearer picture . . . It's quite possible that you do understand me . . . I'm probably very, very much at fault . . . (*Lends an ear.*) I think the horses have been brought round. I have to go and change . . . (*He walks to the house and stops.*) Doctor, you don't like me and you don't conceal the fact. It does your heart credit . . . (*Exits into the house.*)

LVOV (*alone*). This damned temper of mine . . . Again I missed my chance and didn't talk to him the way I should . . . I can't talk to him coolly and calmly! No sooner do I open my mouth and say a single word, when something here (*points to his chest*) starts to choke up, goes in reverse, and my tongue cleaves to the roof of my mouth . . . I hate this Tartuffe,[16] this puffed-up swindler, most heartily . . . Now he's going out . . . His unhappy wife's one pleasure is his being near her; she breathes through him, pleads with him to spend at least one night with her, and he . . . he cannot . . . For him, you see, the house is stifling and claustrophobic. If he spent even one night at home, he'd put a bullet through his brain from sheer ennui! Poor fellow . . . he needs wide open spaces, so he can perpetrate some more underhanded acts . . . Oh, I know why you ride over to those Lebedevs every night! I know!

V I

LVOV, IVANOV (in a hat and overcoat), SHABELSKY, and
ANNA PETROVNA.

SHABELSKY (*coming out of the house with Ivanov and Anna Petrovna*). Really, *Nicolas*, this is inhuman! You go out every night by yourself, and leave us all on our own. Bored stiff, we go to bed at eight o'clock. This is an abomination, not life! How come you can go out and we can't? How come?

---

16 The religious hypocrite in Molière's comedy *Tartuffe, or The Imposter* (1664–1667).

ANNA PETROVNA. Count, leave him alone! Let him go, let him . . .

IVANOV (*to his wife*). Well, where would you, a sick woman, go? You're sick and you mustn't go out of doors after sundown . . . Ask the doctor here. You're not a child, Anyuta, you have to be sensible . . . (*To the Count.*) And why should *you* go out?

SHABELSKY. I'd go to blue blazes, I'd crawl down a crocodile's gullet rather than stay here. I'm bored . . . I'm petrified with boredom . . . Everybody's sick and tired of me . . . You leave me at home so she won't be bored on her own, and I've nagged her to death, chewed her to pieces!

ANNA PETROVNA. Leave him alone, Count, leave him! Let him go if it gives him pleasure.

IVANOV. Anya, why take that tone? You know I don't go there for pleasure! I have to discuss the terms of the loan.

ANNA PETROVNA. I don't understand why you feel the need to make excuses? Go ahead! Who's keeping you here?

IVANOV. Friends, let's not devour one another! Is this absolutely necessary?

SHABELSKY (*in a tearful voice*). *Nicolas*, dear boy, do please take me with you! I'll get an eyeful of those crooks and idiots and, maybe, have some fun! Honestly, I haven't been anywhere since Easter . . .

IVANOV (*annoyed*). All right, let's go! I'm sick and tired of the lot of you!

SHABELSKY. Really? Well, *merci, merci* . . . (*Merrily takes him by the arm and leads him aside.*) May I wear your straw hat?

IVANOV. You may, only hurry up, for pity's sake!

The COUNT runs into the house.

You have to be reasonable, Anya. Get better and then we'll go out, but for now you need your rest . . . Well, good-bye . . . . (*Walks over to his wife and kisses her on the head.*) I'll be back by one . . .

ANNA PETROVNA (*leads him down to the footlights*). Kolya . . . (*Laughs.*) What if you stayed home? We could turn somersaults in the hay the way we used to . . . we could have supper together, read . . . The grouch and I have practiced lots of duets for you . . .

Pause

Stay home, we'll have a laugh . . . (*Laughs and weeps.*) Or, Kolya, how does it go? The flowers return every spring, but joy never does?[17] Am I right? Well, go on, go on . . .

IVANOV. I . . . I'll be back soon . . . (*Goes, stops and thinks.*) No, I can't! . . . (*He exits.*)

ANNA PETROVNA. Go on . . . (*Sits at the table.*)

LVOV (*paces up and down the stage*). Anna Petrovna, make yourself a rule: as soon as the clock strikes six, you have to go to your room and not come out until morning. The evening damp is bad for your health . . .

ANNA PETROVNA. Your wish is my command, sir . . .

LVOV. What's "your wish is my command, sir" supposed to mean! I'm talking seriously.

ANNA PETROVNA. Then try to talk unseriously. (*Coughs.*)

LVOV. There, you see, you're coughing already . . .

V I I

LVOV, ANNA PETROVNA, and SHABELSKY.

SHABELSKY (*comes out of the house in a hat and overcoat*). Where is he? (*Goes quickly, stops in front of Anna Petrovna and makes a face.*) Gevalt . . . Vay iss mir . . . Pekh . . . Gevalt . . .[18] Excusink me, pliss! (*Bursts out laughing and makes a rapid exit.*)

LVOV. Buffoon . . .

Pause. The distant strains of a concertina are heard.

ANNA PETROVNA (*stretches*). How boring . . . Out there the coachmen and the cooks are having a dance, while I . . . I'm like some thing that's been discarded . . . Yevgeny Konstantinovich, why are you pacing back and forth? Come over here, sit down! . . .

LVOV. I can't sit down . . .

---

17 A quotation from a folksong.

18 Yiddish: alas . . . woe is me . . . bad luck . . .

Pause.

ANNA PETROVNA. Doctor, are your father and mother still alive?

LVOV. My father's dead, my mother's alive.

ANNA PETROVNA. Do you miss your mother?

LVOV. I've no time to miss anyone.

ANNA PETROVNA (*laughs*). The flowers return every spring, but joy never does. Who quoted that line to me? God help my memory . . . I think Nikolay quoted it. (*Lends an ear.*) The owl is screeching again!

LVOV. Then let it screech . . .

Pause.

ANNA PETROVNA. Doctor, I'm beginning to think that Fate has dealt me a losing hand. Most people, who may be no better than I am, lead happy lives and never pay for their happiness, why am I the only one to pay at such a cost? Why am I being charged such high interest? . . . What did you say?

LVOV. I didn't say anything.

ANNA PETROVNA. And I'm starting to wonder so much at the unfairness of people: why don't they reciprocate love for love, why do they pay back truth with lies? (*Shrugs her shoulders.*) Doctor, you're not a family man, so you can't understand a lot of this . . .

LVOV. You wonder . . . (*He sits beside her.*) No, I wonder, wonder at you! . . . Now, explain, spell it out for me, for heaven's sake, how could you, an intelligent, honorable, almost saintly woman, have let yourself be so brazenly tricked and dragged into this nest of screech owls? Why are you here? What do you have in common with this cold, heartless—but let's leave your husband out of it! . . . what do you have in common with this vacuous, vulgar milieu? Oh, good God in heaven . . . This constantly grumbling, decrepit, insane count, this creepy super-swindler Misha, with that repulsive look on his face . . . Explain to me, what are you doing here? How did you end up here?

ANNA PETROVNA (*laughs*). That's exactly the way he used to talk . . . Word for word . . . But his eyes are bigger, and when he used to talk about something with enthusiasm, they'd be like glowing coals . . . Keep talking, keep talking . . .

LVOV (*rises and waves his hand in dismissal*). What am I supposed to talk about? Please go inside . . .

ANNA PETROVNA. You say that Nikolay's this and that, six of one, half of a dozen of the other. How do you know this? Can you really analyze a person in six months' time? Doctor, he's a remarkable man, and I'm sorry that you didn't get to know him two or three years ago. Now he's depressed, taciturn, doesn't do anything, but in the past . . . Such splendor! . . . I fell in love with him at first sight. (*Laughs.*) One glimpse of him and I was caught in the mousetrap, snap! . . . He said: let's go . . . I cut myself off from everything, you know, the way people snip off withered leaves with a scissors, and I went . . .

> Pause.

And now it's different . . . Now he goes to the Lebedevs, to be entertained by other women, while I . . . I sit in the garden and listen to the owl screeching . . .

> The WATCHMAN taps.[19]

Doctor, don't you have any brothers?

LVOV. No.

> ANNA PETROVNA sobs.

Well, what is it now, what's wrong with you?

ANNA PETROVNA (*rises*). I can't help it, Doctor, I'm going to go over there . . .

LVOV. Over where? . . .

ANNA PETROVNA. Where he is . . . I'll drive over there . . . Have them harness the horses . . . (*Runs to the house.*)

LVOV. You can't possibly go . . .

ANNA PETROVNA. Leave me alone, it's none of your business . . . I can't stand it, I shall go . . . Have them bring the horses . . . (*Runs into the house.*)

---

19 On Russian country estates watchmen would make the rounds, tapping on a board to warn intruders of their presence. Also see *The Seagull*, Act Four, and *Uncle Vanya*, Act Two.

LVOV. No, I definitely refuse to practice under such conditions . . . It's not bad enough that they don't pay me a penny, but they also turn my feelings inside-out! . . . No, I refuse, enough is enough! . . . (*Goes into the house.*)

Curtain

ACT TWO

A reception room in the Lebedevs' house. At right, an entry directly into the garden, doors right and left. Antique, expensive furniture. A chandelier, candelabrums, and pictures, all under dustcovers.[20] *To the left of the door a sofa, in front of it a round table with a large lamp, armchairs beside it, on the downstage side of the table against the wall three armchairs in a row. At right an upright piano, with a fiddle lying on it; chairs on either side of it. Upstage, near the entry to the veranda an unfolded card table.*

I

ZINAIDA SAVISHNA, DUDKIN, FIRST GUEST, SECOND GUEST, KOSYKH, AVDOTYA NAZAROVNA, YEGORUSHKA, GAVRILA, MAID-SERVANT, TWO OLD LADY GUESTS, YOUNG LADIES, *and* BABAKINA.

ZINAIDA SAVISHNA *is sitting on the sofa; on both sides of her in armchairs are the old lady guests; across from her on straight chairs sit* DUDKIN, FIRST GUEST, *and five or six young ladies. At the card table* KOSYKH, AVDOTYA NAZAROVNA, YEGORUSHKA, *and two guests are seated, playing cards.*[21] GAVRILA *is standing by the door at right. The* MAID-SERVANT *is handing round a tray of sweetmeats. Guests circulate from the garden to the door at right and back again.* BABAKINA *enters through the door at right and heads for Zinaida Savishna.*

---

20 Furniture in manor houses was kept under dustcovers when a room was unused or the family was away. It is a sign of Zinaida Savishna's niggardliness that it should remain covered during a party.

21 The game being played is whist (Russian, *vint*), closely related to bridge. Each player holds thirteen cards.

ZINAIDA SAVISHNA (*delighted*). Sweetheart, Marfa Yegorovna . . .

BABAKINA. How are you, Zinaida Savishna . . . I'm honored to congratulate you on your birthday girl . . .

They exchange kisses.

God bless . . .

ZINAIDA SAVISHNA. Thank you, sweetheart, I'm pleased to see you . . . Well, how are you feeling?

BABAKINA. Thanks ever so for asking. (*Sits next to the sofa.*) How are you, young people!

DUDKIN and FIRST GUEST rise and bow.

FIRST GUEST (*laughs*). Young people . . . Are you so old?

BABAKINA (*sighing*). What would we be doing among the youngsters?

FIRST GUEST (*laughs respectfully*). For heaven's sake, how can you . . .

DUDKIN. You may be what's called a widow, but you could give a nine-point handicap to any young woman . . .

GAVRILA serves Babakina tea.

ZINAIDA SAVISHNA (*to Gavrila*). Why are you serving it like that? You should bring some preserves . . . gooseberry or something . . .

BABAKINA. Don't go to the trouble, thanks ever so . . .

Pause.

DUDKIN Did you come by way of Mushkino, Marfa Yegorovna? . . .

BABAKINA. No, Zamishche. The road's better there . . .

DUDKIN. True enough, ma'am . . .

KOSYKH. Two spades . . .

YEGORUSHKA. Pass.

AVDOTYA NAZAROVNA. Pass.

SECOND GUEST. Pass.

BABAKINA. Lottery tickets, Zinaida Savishna sweetheart, have gone right through the roof again.[22] Have you ever heard of such a thing: the first drawing already costs two hundred and seventy, and the second well nigh two hundred and fifty . . . Never heard of anything like it . . .

ZINAIDA SAVISHNA (*sighs*). It's all very well for those who've got a lot of them . . .

BABAKINA. Don't you think so, sweetheart; they may cost a lot, but they make an unprofitable investment for your capital. The insurance alone will be the death of you.

ZINAIDA SAVISHNA. That's so, but all the same, my dear, you go on hoping . . . (*Sighs.*) God is merciful . . .

DUDKIN. At the present time, if you consider it from a point of view, wherever you invest your money, there's no profit in it. Gilt-edged securities are nothing but a pain, but on the other hand unloading 'em—I wouldn't go that far: it sounds like you're whistling in the dark. The way I see it, if a person's got money, the very best thing for him would be buy a revolver, fire it and rest in peace . . . There's why money nowadays is nothing but a headache . . .

BABAKINA (*sighs*). That's so true!

FIRST GUEST (*to the young lady beside him.*) A man walks up up to another man and sees—there's a dog sitting there. (*Laughs.*) So he asks, "What's your dog's name?" And the other man says, "Liqueurs." (*Roars with laughter.*) Liqueurs . . . Get it? Like-yours . . . (*Embarrassed.*)

DUDKIN. At our warehouse in town we've got a dog, his name is Fake-fur . . .

BABAKINA. What?

DUDKIN. Fake-fur.

> Faint laughter. ZINAIDA SAVISHNA gets up and goes out the
> door at right. A prolonged silence.

YEGORUSHKA. Two diamonds.

---

22 Russians of limited means made a run on the 5-percent interest-bearing lottery tickets issued by the stock exchange in 1864 and 1866; in 1887, the price was raised and stabilized at a hundred rubles a ticket.

AVDOTYA NAZAROVNA. Pass.

SECOND GUEST. Pass.

KOSYKH. Pass.

I I

The same, ZINAIDA SAVISHNA, and LEBEDEV.

ZINAIDA SAVISHNA (*entering from the door right with Lebedev, quietly*). Why are you planted out there? What a prima donna! Sit with the guests . . . (*Sits in her former place.*)

LEBEDEV (*going to the armchair farthest at left, yawns*). Ugh, forgive us sinners . . . (*On seeing Babakina.*) Good Lord, our pot of jam is sitting here! . . . Our Turkish delight! . . . (*Greets her.*) How is your most precious little self?

BABAKINA. Thanks ever so.

LEBEDEV. Well, God be praised, God be praised . . . (*Sits in an armchair.*) Well, well . . . Gavrila!

> GAVRILA *serves him a shot of vodka and a glass of water; he drinks the vodka and chases it down with water.*

DUDKIN. Your very good health! . . .

LEBEDEV. What do you mean, good health? I haven't croaked yet, and I'm thankful for that. (*To his wife.*) Zyuzyushka, where's our birthday girl?

KOSYKH (*tearfully*). Tell me, for heaven's sake: well, how come we didn't take a single trick? (*Leaps up.*) Well, then why did we lose, damn it all to hell!

AVDOTYA NAZAROVNA (*leaps up, angrily*). Because, my good man, if you don't know how to play, don't sit in . . . Since when are you entitled to lead somebody else's suit? That's how you got stuck with that pickled ace of yours . . .

> *They both run out from behind the table.*

KOSYKH (*in a tearful voice*). If I may, my friends . . . I was holding diamonds: ace, king, queen, jack, and eight low cards, ace of spades and one, you understand, one lousy little heart, and she, for some damn reason, couldn't call a little slam! . . . I bid no trumps . . .

AVDOTYA NAZARONA (*interrupting*). I'm the one who bid no trumps! You bid: two no trumps . . .[23]

KOSYKH. This is a disgrace! . . . If I may . . . you had . . . I had . . . you had . . . (*To Lebedev.*) Now you be the judge, Pavel Kirillych . . . I was holding diamonds: ace, king, queen, jack, and eight low cards . . .

LEBEDEV (*covers up his ears*). Stop, do me a favor . . . stop . . .

AVDOTYA NAZAROVNA (*shouts*). I was the one who bid: no trumps!

KOSYKH (*fiercely*). Call me a villain and an outcast if I ever sit down to play with that old barracuda again! (*Quickly heads for the veranda, but stops at the card table; to Yegorushka.*) Did you keep count? What did you write down? Hold on . . . thirty-eight times eight . . . is . . . eighty-eight . . . Oh, the hell with it! . . . (*Exits into the garden.*)

> SECOND GUEST *follows him out,* YEGORUSHKA *remains at the table.*

AVDOTYA NAZAROVNA. Oof . . . He's got me all overheated . . . . Stickleback . . . Barracuda yourself! . . .

BABAKINA. Well, now you've gone and lost your temper, granny . . .

AVDOTYA NAZAROVNA (*on seeing Babakina, throws up her hands*). My honey-bun, my beauty! . . . She's here, and, blind as a biddy, I didn't see her . . . Sweetie-pie . . . (*Kisses her on the shoulder and sits beside her.*) What a treat! Let me take a good look at you, my snow-white swan! Poo, poo, poo . . . evil eye begone! . . .[24]

LEBEDEV. Well, now she's wound up . . . You'd better find her a bride-groom . . .

AVDOTYA NAZAROVNA. And I will! I won't go quiet to my grave, with all my sins on my head, until I get her married and your Sanichka too! I won't go quiet . . . (*Deep sigh.*) Only there now, where are you to find bridegrooms

---

23 To lead is to play the first card or play one's suit. A trick are the four cards played in each round. A slam is obtaining all thirteen tricks in one hand. A trump is the last card dealt out—the turn-up. To call for a trump is to signal one's partner to lead trumps.

24 Since compliments might attract envy and, hence, the evil eye, bad luck was averted by spitting three times over one's shoulder.

nowadays? There they sit, these bridegrooms of ours, as crestfallen as drenched roosters! . . .

DUDKIN. Because no one's paying us any attention . . .

I I I

The same and SASHA.

SASHA enters from the garden and quietly goes to her father.

ZINAIDA SAVISHNA. Sashenka, don't you see that Marfa Yegorovna is here?

SASHA. Sorry. (*Goes to Babakina and greets her.*)

BABAKINA. You're getting to be quite standoffish, Sanichka, quite standoff-ish . . . haven't paid me a single visit.

Exchanges kisses.

Congratulations, sweetheart . . .

SASHA. Thank you. (*Sits next to her father.*)

LEBEDEV. Yes, Avdotya Nazarovna, it's hard to find bridegrooms nowadays. Not just bridegrooms—you can't get a passable best man. The young people these days, no offense meant, have, God bless 'em, an off-taste, like leftovers reheated . . . Can't dance or talk or have a serious drink with 'em . . .

AVDOTYA NAZAROVNA. Well, drinking's one thing they know all about, just let 'em at it . . .

LEBEDEV. There's no great trick to drinking, even a horse knows how to drink . . . No, I'm talking serious drinking! . . . In our time, used to be, you'd get worn out at lectures all day long, and as soon as it was dark, you'd go straight to wherever a fire was blazing and spin like a top till dawn came up . . . And you'd dance, and flirt with the young ladies, and that took knowhow. (*Flicks himself on the throat.*)[25] Used to be, you'd blather and philosophize till your jaw came unhinged . . . But nowadays . . . (*Waves his hand in dismissal.*) I don't understand . . . They're wishy-washy, neither

---

25 A gesture meaning "Let's get drunk."

this nor that. In the whole district there's only one decent fellow, and he's married (*sighs*) and it looks like he's starting to go crazy too . . .

BABAKINA. Who's that?

LEBEDEV. Nikolasha Ivanov.

BABAKINA. Yes, he's a good man (*makes a face*), only so unhappy! . . .

ZINAIDA SAVISHNA. You said it, sweetheart, how can he be happy! (*Sighs.*) What a mistake he made, poor thing! He married his kike bitch[26] and figured, poor thing, that her father and mother would heap mountains of gold on her, but it came out quite the opposite . . . From the time she converted, her father and mother wouldn't have anything to do with her, cursed her . . . Not a penny did he get out of them. He's sorry for it now, but it's too late . . .

SASHA. Mama, that's not true . . .

BABAKINA (*heatedly*). Shurochka, why isn't it true? After all, everybody knows it. If it weren't for gain, why else would he marry the kike bitch? Aren't there plenty of Russian girls? He miscalculated, sweetheart, miscalculated . . . (*Vigorously.*) Lord, and now doesn't he make it hot for her, the slut! . . . Simply laughable . . . He'll come home from somewhere and right away he goes: "Your father and mother cheated me! Get out of my house!" And where can she go? Father and mother won't take her in, she could become a housemaid, but she wasn't brought up to work . . . So he rags on her and rags on her, until the Count stands up for her. If it weren't for the Count, he would have done her in long ago . . .

AVDOTYA NAZAROVNA. Besides that, sometimes he locks her up in the cellar with "Eat your garlic, you so-and-so"[27] . . . She eats it and eats it, till she starts to stink from the inside out.

Laughter.

SASHA. Papa, that's got to be another lie!

LEBEDEV. Well, so what? Let 'em gossip if it keeps 'em healthy . . . (*Shouts.*) Gavrila!

---

26 Zinaida Savishna uses the abusive term *zhidovka* (female kike or yid).

27 Anti-Semitic prejudice held that garlic was a favorite food of Jews and that they stank of it.

GAVRILA *serves him vodka and water.*

ZINAIDA SAVISHNA. So that's why he's ruined, poor thing. His business, sweetheart, has quite fallen off . . . If Borkin weren't looking after the estate, there wouldn't be anything for him and his kike bitch to eat. (*Sighs.*) As for us, sweetheart, the way we've suffered on account of him! . . . Suffered so much that only God can tell! Would you believe, my dear, for three years now, he's owed us nine thousand . . .

BABAKINA (*horrified*). Nine thousand!

ZINAIDA SAVISHNA. Yes . . . It was that hubby dear of mine who arranged to lend it to him . . . He can't tell the difference between someone you can lend to and someone you can't . . . The principal I've given up on already, may it rest in peace, but I wish he'd pay the interest on time . . .

SASHA (*heatedly*). Mama, you've told us about this a thousand times already.

ZINAIDA SAVISHNA. What's got into you? Why are you standing up for him?

SASHA (*rises*). But how can you have the heart to say such things about an honest, decent man who never did you any harm? Why, what has he done to you?

ZINAIDA SAVISHNA (*sneering*). Decent and honest man . . .

FIRST GUEST (*sincerely*). Aleksandra Pavlovna, I assure you that you're quite mistaken . . . How is he honest? (*Gets up.*) Do you call that honesty? Two years ago, during the cattle epidemic, he bought livestock, insured the cattle . . .

ZINAIDA SAVISHNA (*interrupting*). He insured the cattle, infected them with cow-pox and collected the insurance money. Honesty . . .

FIRST GUEST. Everyone knows it perfectly well . . .

SASHA. It's not true, it a lie. Nobody bought cattle and infected them, it's only Borkin who concocted that scheme and bragged about it all over the place. When Ivanov found out about it, Borkin had to beg his forgiveness for two weeks running. Ivanov's only fault is that he has a weak and generous nature and doesn't have the heart to kick Borkin out . . .

FIRST GUEST. A weak nature . . . (*Laughs.*) Aleksandra Pavlovna, honest to God, open your eyes . . .

ZINAIDA SAVISHNA. You should be ashamed to stand up for him . . .

SASHA. I'm sorry that I got involved in this conversation . . . (*Walks quickly to the door at right.*)

LEBEDEV. Shura's a hothead! . . . (*Laughs.*) The girl's a powder-keg . . .

FIRST GUEST (*stands in her path*). Aleksandra Pavlovna, honest to God, I won't go on! . . . Sorry . . . word of honor, I won't do it any more! . . .

ZINAIDA SAVISHNA. At least in front of the guests, Sashenka, don't display your temper.

SASHA (*in a quavering voice*). All his life he's worked for others; everything he had has been filched and pilfered from him; because of his generous projects anyone who wanted could make a fortune out of him . . . Never in his life has he defiled himself with lies, scheming, not once have I heard that he spoke ill of anyone . . . and what's the result? Wherever you go, all you hear is: Ivanov, Ivanov, Ivanov . . . as if there were no other topic of conversation.

LEBEDEV. Hot head . . . That'll do . . . .

SASHA. Yes, he's made mistakes, but every mistake made by such people as he is worth twenty times our good deeds . . . If you could only . . . (*Looks around and sees Ivanov and Shabelsky.*)

I V

The same, IVANOV, and SHABELSKY.

SHABELSKY (*entering with Ivanov from the door at right*). Who's speechifying around here? You, Shurochka! (*Roars with laughter and shakes her hand.*) Congratulations, my angel. May God postpone your death and make sure you're not reincarnated . . .

ZINAIDA SAVISHNA (*gleefully*). Nikolay Alekseevich . . . Count! . . .

LEBEDEV. Bah . . . Who do I see . . . Count! . . . (*Goes to meet him.*)

SHABELSKY (*on seeing Zinaida Savishna and Babakina, extends his arms in their direction*). Two gold-mines on one sofa! A sight for sore eyes . . . (*Greets them; to Zinaida Savishna.*) How are you, Zyuzyushka. (*To Babakina.*) How are you, my little puff-ball . . .

ZINAIDA SAVISHNA. I'm so pleased. You're such an infrequent guest here, Count! (*Shouts.*) Gavrila, tea . . . Please, take a seat . . . (*Gets up, exits through the door right, and immediately returns, with an extremely preoccupied look.*)

> *SASHA sits in her former seat. IVANOV, after silently exchanging greetings with everyone, sits beside her. The YOUNG LADIES like a flock of geese pass back and forth to the veranda.*

LEBEDEV (*to Shabelsky*). Where've you turned up from out of the blue? What wild horses have dragged you here? This is a surprise, or I'll be damned . . . (*Kisses him.*) Count, you're a real cutthroat . . . Respectable people don't behave this way . . . (*Takes him by the arm down to the footlights.*) Why haven't you visited us? Angry or something?

SHABELSKY. How am I supposed to visit you? Flying on a broomstick? I haven't got horses of my own, and Nikolay won't take me with him, makes me stay with the kike so she won't get bored. Send your own horses for me, and then I'll pay you a visit . . .

LEBEDEV (*waves his hand in dismissal*). Oh sure . . . Zyuzyushka would rather drop dead than use the horses. Old pal, dear man, you really are dearer and sweeter to me than all the rest of them! Of all the old-timers, you and I are the only ones left! "In you I love my bygone suff'rings, In you I love my wasted youth . . ."[28] Joking aside, I could almost weep. (*Kisses the Count.*)

SHABELSKY. Cut it out, cut it out! You smell like a wine cellar . . .

LEBEDEV. Dear heart, you can't imagine how bored I am without my friends! Ready to hang myself from tedium . . . (*Quietly.*) Zyuzyushka and her money-lending have driven away all the respectable people, there's only Zulus left . . . these Dudkins, Budkins . . . Here, have some tea . . .

> *GAVRILA serves the Count tea.*

ZINAIDA SAVISHNA (*walks over to the Count; worried, to Gavrila*). Well, how are you serving it? You should bring some preserves . . . Gooseberry or something . . .

---

28 Lines from Lermontov's poem "No, 'tis not thee I love so warmly" (1841), which was set to music by at least three composers.

SHABELSKY (*roars with laughter; to Ivanov*). There, didn't I tell you? (*To Lebedev.*) I made a bet with him on the way that, as soon as we got here, Zyuzyushka would immediately offer us gooseberry preserves . . .

ZINAIDA SAVISHNA. Count, you're still the same scoffer . . . (*Sits on the sofa.*)

LEBEDEV. Twenty kegs they made of it, how else can you get rid of the stuff?

SHABELSKY (*sitting in an armchair next to the table*). Still saving up, Zyuzyushka? Well now, are you a millionaire yet, eh?

ZINAIDA SAVISHNA (*with a deep sigh*). Yes, if you judge by appearances, nobody's richer than we are, but where's the money coming from? Nothing but talk . . .

SHABELSKY. Well, yes, yes! . . . we know! . . . "We know how badly you play checkers"[29] . . . (*To Lebedev.*) Pasha, tell me on your honor, have you saved up a million? . . .

LEBEDEV. For heaven's sake, I don't know, you'd better ask Zyuzyushka . . .

SHABELSKY (*to Babakina*). And my pudgy little puff-ball is soon going to have a little million! . . . Good grief, she's getting prettier and plumper not by the day, but by the hour! . . . That's what it means to have lots of dough . . .

BABAKINA. Thanks ever so, your highness, only I don't like being made fun of.

SHABELSKY. My dearest gold-mine, how am I making fun of you? It's simply a cry from the heart, a spontaneous overflow of feelings that finds issue at my lips . . . I love you and Zyuzyushka infinitely . . . (*Merrily.*) Excitement! . . . Ecstasy . . . I can't gaze on either one of you indifferently . . .

ZINAIDA SAVISHNA. You're just the same as ever. (*To Yegorushka.*) Yegorushka, put out the candles! Why do you let them burn for no reason, if you're not playing?

YEGORUSHKA *is startled; puts out the candles and sits down.*

(*To Ivanov.*) Nikolay Alekseevich, how is your lady wife getting on?

---

29 A line from Gogol's *Dead Souls*: the blustering Nozdryov says it to Chichikov, when they are playing checkers for a stake of the former's dead serfs.

IVANOV. Badly. Today the doctor definitely confirmed that she has tuberculosis . . .

ZINAIDA SAVISHNA. You don't say so? What a pity! . . . (*Sighs.*) We're all so fond of her . . .

SHABELSKY. Hogwash, hogwash, hogwash! . . . It's not tuberculosis, just medical quackery, hocus-pocus. Æsculapius[30] wants to hang around, so he comes up with tuberculosis. Luckily the husband's not the jealous type . . .

    IVANOV makes a gesture of impatience.

As for Sarra herself, she's a Semite. I don't trust a single one of her words or movements . . . Excusink me pliss, oy vay iss mir . . . Go ahead and kill me, but I don't trust her . . . Forgive me, *Nicolas*, but . . . after all . . . I'm not saying anything particularly bad . . . In my opinion, if Sarra took ill, it means she's schemed up a *gescheft*,[31] but I don't believe she's going to die: that's a *gesheft* too . . .

LEBEDEV (*to Shabelsky*). You're an incredible character, Matvey . . . You put on this misanthrope act and show it off like a retarded kid with a new toy. You're as human as anyone else, but once you start talking, it's as if your tongue were spewing poison or you had a hacking cough . . . Yes, honest to God! . . .

SHABELSKY. What am I supposed to do, be lovey-dovey with swindlers and scoundrels, I suppose? . . .

LEBEDEV. Just where do you see swindlers and scoundrels?

SHABELSKY. Present company excepted, of course, but . . .

LEBEDEV. There's that "but" of yours . . . This is all an act . . .

SHABELSKY. An act . . . You're lucky you don't have any sort of worldview.

LEBEDEV. Why should I have a worldview? . . . I sit, expecting to drop dead any minute—that's my worldview. You and I, my boy, haven't got time to concoct worldviews . . . That's how it goes . . . (*Shouts.*) Gavrila! . . .

SHABELSKY. You've Gavrila-ed it up enough already . . . Look how red your nose has got! . . .

---

30 Ancient Greek god of medicine; in this Latin form, a fanciful term for a physician.

31 Yiddish: business deal, with the connotation of swindle.

LEBEDEV (*drinks*). Never mind, dear heart . . . I'm not going to get married today . . .

V

The same and BORKIN.

BORKIN, *dressed foppishly, holding a package, skipping and humming, enters from the door at right. A murmur of approval.*

        YOUNG LADIES. Mikhail Mikhailovich . . .

Together   **LEBEDEV.** *Michel Michelich!* . . . Do my ears deceive me . . .

        SHABELSKY. The life of the party! . . .

BORKIN. Here I am again . . . (*Runs over to Sasha.*) Noble signorina, I make so bold as to congratulate the universe on the birth of such a marvelous blossom as yourself . . . As a token of my delight, I venture to present you (*hands over the package*) with fireworks and Bengal lights[32] of my own making. May they light up the night just as you brighten the shadows of this kingdom of darkness! . . . (*Theatrical bow.*)

SASHA. Thank you . . .

LEBEDEV (*roars with laughter, to Ivanov*). Why don't you fire this Judas?

BORKIN (*to Lebedev*). Pavel Kirillich . . . (*To Ivanov.*) My patron . . . (*Sings.*) *Nicolas-voilà*, ho-hi-ho! (*Goes round to everyone.*) The most respected Zinaida Savishna . . . The most divine Marfa Yegorovna . . . The most venerable Avdotya Nazarovna . . . The most highnessy Count . . .

SHABELSKY (*roars with laughter*). The life of the party . . . Hardly in the door and the mood's lifted . . . Have you noticed?

ZINAIDA SAVISHNA, BABAKINA, *and the COUNT get up from behind the table and converse standing up. TWO OLD LADIES leave.*

BORKIN. Oof . . . I'm worn out . . . I think I've greeted everyone. Well, what's new, ladies and gentlemen? Nothing special, that hits you over the head? (*Vigorously to Zinaida Savishna.*) Ah, listen, mamma dear . . . As I'm riding over here just now . . . (*To Gavrila.*) Let me have some tea, Gavrusha,

---

32 Fireworks used for signaling.

only no gooseberry preserves. (*To Zinaida Savishna.*) As I'm riding over here just now, peasants on the riverbank were stripping bark from your willow bushes. Why don't you lease out your willow bushes?

LEBEDEV (*roaring with laughter, to Ivanov*). Why don't you fire this Judas?

ZINAIDA SAVISHNA (*alarmed*). Why, that's perfectly true, it never crossed my mind!

BORKIN (*does calesthenics with his arms*). I can't sit still . . . Mamma dear, anything special we can turn our hand to? Marfa Yegorovna, I'm in good form . . . I'm in tiptop shape. (*Sings.*) "Once again I stand before you . . ."[33]

ZINAIDA SAVISHNA. Organize something, otherwise we'll die of boredom.

BORKIN. Ladies and gentlemen, why these long faces? They're sitting around like jurymen in a box . . . Let's come up with something . . . What would you enjoy? truth or dare, jump-rope, tag, dancing?

YOUNG LADIES (*clap their hands*). Dancing, dancing . . . . (*They run into the garden.*)

BORKIN. I'm all set . . . Dudkin, start dancing! . . . (*Moves armchairs to the wall.*) Yegorushka, where are you? Tune up the fiddle . . .

> YEGORUSHKA *shudders and goes to the piano. BORKIN sits at the piano and hits an A. YEGORUSHKA tunes the fiddle.*

IVANOV (*to Lebedev*). I have a request, Pasha. The day after tomorrow is when my note falls due, and I've got no way to pay the interest. Is there any way to offer an extension or add the interest to the principal?

LEBEDEV (*alarmed*). My dear boy, it's no affair of mine . . . Talk it over with Zyuzyushka, but I . . . I know nothing about it . . .

IVANOV (*rubs his forehead*). This is agony! . . .

SASHA. What's wrong with you?

IVANOV. I feel repulsive today.

SASHA. I can see that by your face . . . Let's go into the drawing-room . . .

> IVANOV *and* SASHA *go out the door at right.*

---

33 The opening line of a gypsy ballad based on a poem by V. I. Krasov. Chekhov also puts this song into the mouth of Dr. Dorn in *The Seagull.*

BORKIN (*shouts*). The music's about to start . . .

DUDKIN invites Babakina.

BABAKINA. No, it would be sinful if I danced today. My husband died on this very day . . .

> *BORKIN and YEGORUSHKA play the polka "À propos Faust";*
> *the COUNT puts his hands over his ears and goes out on the*
> *veranda. He is followed by AVDOTYA NAZAROVNA. It is*
> *evident from Dudkin's movements that he is trying to convince*
> *Babakina of something. The young ladies ask the First Guest to*
> *dance, but he refuses. DUDKIN waves his hand in dismissal and*
> *goes out into the garden.*

BORKIN (*looking around*). Ladies and gentlemen, what's going on? (*Stops playing*). Why aren't you dancing?

YOUNG LADIES. We've got no partners . . .

BORKIN (*gets up*). Which means we're not going to get anywhere . . . In that case let's go let off some fireworks or something . . .

YOUNG LADIES (*clap their hands*). Fireworks, fireworks . . . (*They run into the garden.*)

BORKIN (*takes the package and offers his hand to Babakina*). Zheh voo pree . . .[34] (*Shouts.*) Ladies and gentleman, to the garden . . . (*Exits.*)

Everyone exits, except LEBEDEV and ZINAIDA SAVISHNA.

ZINAIDA SAVISHNA. That's my idea of a young man. The minute he arrives, everyone cheers up. (*Turns down the big lamp.*) Since they're all in the garden, there's no need to leave lights burning. (*Puts out the candles.*)

LEBEDEV (*following her*). Zyuzyushka, we have to give the guests something to eat . . .

ZINAIDA SAVISHNA. Look at all these candles . . . no wonder people think we're rich. (*Puts them out.*)

LEBEDEV (*following her*). Zyuzyushka, for heaven's sake, you should give people something to eat . . . . They're young, they must be starving by now, poor things . . . Zyuzyushka . . .

---

34 Mispronunciation of "je vous prie," "please."

ZINAIDA SAVISHNA. The Count didn't finish his tea. A waste of perfectly good sugar. I'll put it aside and give it to Matryona to drink. (*Takes the glass and goes out the door at left.*)

LEBEDEV. Drat! . . . (*He goes into the garden.*)

V I

IVANOV and SASHA.

SASHA (*entering with Ivanov from the door at right*). Everyone's gone into the garden . . .

IVANOV. That's the way things are, Shurochka. I don't do anything or think about anything, and I'm exhausted, body and soul . . . Day and night my conscience bothers me, I feel that I'm deeply at fault, but where that fault lies, I can't figure out . . . And then there's my wife's illness, lack of money, the constant grumbling, gossip, noise . . . My home has become loathsome to me, living in it is worse than torture. (*He looks around.*) I don't know what's come over me, I tell you frankly, Shurochka, what's become unbearable for me is the company of my wife, who loves me . . . and such filthy, selfish thoughts creep into my head, which I couldn't even conceive of before . . .

Pause.

It's nasty . . . I'm pestering you with my tedium, Shurochka, forgive me, but I can forget only at those moments when I'm talking to you, my friend . . . Around you I'm like a dog barking at the sun. Shurochka, I've known you since the time you were born, I've always loved you, spoiled you . . . I would give a great deal to have a daughter like you right now . . .

SASHA (*joking, through tears*). Nikolay Alekseevich, let's run away to America . . .

IVANOV. I feel too listless to cross that threshold, and you come up with America . . .

They walk to the entry to the garden.

Well now, Shura, is it hard to go on living? I see, I see it all . . . This air doesn't suit you . . .

VII

The same and ZINAIDA SAVISHNA.

ZINAIDA SAVISHNA comes out of the door at left.

IVANOV. Sorry, Shurochka, I'll catch up with you . . .

SASHA exits into the garden.

Zinaida Savishna, forgive me, I've come here with a request . . .

ZINAIDA SAVISHNA. What's the matter, Nikolay Alekseevich?

IVANOV (*hesitates*). The fact is, you see, the day after tomorrow is the date my note falls due. I'd be very much obliged if you could offer an extension or let me add the interest to the principal. At the moment I have absolutely no money . . .

ZINAIDA SAVISHNA (*alarmed*). Nikolay Alekseevich, how can this be? What kind of a system is this? No, don't even think of such a thing, for heaven's sake, don't torment an unhappy woman like me . . .

IVANOV. Sorry, sorry . . . (*Goes into the garden.*)

ZINAIDA SAVISHNA. Pooh, good heavens, how he upset me! . . . I'm trembling all over . . . trembling . . . (*Goes out the door at right.*)

VIII

KOSYKH.

KOSYKH (*enters at the door left and crosses the stage*). I was holding spades: ace, king, queen, jack, eight low spades, ace, and one . . . one puny little heart and she, damn her to hell, can't call one little slam . . . (*Exits through door at right.*)

IX

DUDKIN and AVDOTYA NAZAROVNA.

AVDOTYA NAZAROVNA (*enters from the garden with Dudkin*). How I'd like to tear her to shreds, the tightwad . . . how I'd like to tear her to shreds . . . Is this a joke, I'm sitting here from five o'clock, she could at least offer me a little rusty herring . . . What a house . . . What entertainment . . .

DUDKIN. Hold on, we'll worm some schnapps out of Yegorushka. I'll have a drink, old girl, and then—off home! Oh, the hell with it all! . . . With the boredom and the hunger you could howl like a wolf . . . And I don't need any of your brides . . . How the hell can a man think of love if he hasn't had a nip since lunch? . . .

AVDOTYA NAZAROVNA. It's not Sashenka's fault . . . It's all her mother's doing . . .

DUDKIN. Why are you making a match between me and Sashenka? Blanc-mange, lefaucheux-grand-merci[35] and all that sort of cleverness . . . I'm a positive fellow with a temper . . . Give me something substantial . . .

AVDOTYA NAZAROVNA. We'll go, have a look around, or something . . .

DUDKIN Ssh! . . . Nice and quiet . . . Marfutka would have been just the ticket, but the problem is she's a flibberty-gibbet . . . I dropped in on her last night, and her house was chockful of all sorts of actors . . .

They go out through the door at left.

X

ANNA PETROVNA and LVOV enter through the door at right.

LVOV. Why, I ask you, did we have to come here?

ANNA PETROVNA. Never mind, they'll be glad we came . . . Nobody here. They must be in the garden . . . Let's go into the garden.

They go into the garden.

X I

AVDOTYA NAZAROVNA and DUDKIN.

DUDKIN (*entering from the door at left*). It's not in the dining room, so I bet it's somewhere in the pantry. We've got to worm it out of Yegorushka. Let's go through the drawing-room.

AVDOTYA NAZAROVNA. How I'd like to tear her to shreds! . . .

They go out through the door at right.

---

35 French: custard, spider, thanks a lot.

X I I

BABAKINA, BORKIN, and SHABELSKY.

BABAKINA and BORKIN run in from the garden, laughing;
behind them, laughing and rubbing his hands,
minces SHABELSKY.

BABAKINA. Such boredom! (*Roars with laughter.*) Such boredom! . . . They all walk and sit around as if they'd swallowed a poker. All my bones are numb with boredom. (*Skips about.*) Have to limber up!

BORKIN takes her round the waist and kisses her on the cheek.

SHABELSKY (*roars with laughter and snaps his fingers*). I'll be damned! (*Wheezes.*) In a manner of speaking . . .

BABAKINA. Let go, take your hands away, you shameless creature, or else God knows what the Count will think! Leave me alone . . .

BORKIN. Love of my life, red carbuncle of my heart! . . . (*Kisses her.*) Lend me 2,300 rubles! . . .

BABAKINA. N-O—no . . . Anything else, but when it comes to money—thanks ever so . . . No, no, no . . . Ah, take your hands off me . . .

SHABELSKY (*minces near them*). Little puff-ball . . . She has her charms . . .

BORKIN (*seriously*). That's enough . . . Let's talk business . . . Let's consider things objectively, in a businesslike way. Answer me straight, without equivocation or hocus-pocus: yes or no? Listen to me! (*Points to the Count.*) He needs money, a minimal income of three thousand a year. You need a husband. Want to be a countess?

SHABELSKY (*roars with laughter*). A wonderful cynic!

BORKIN. Want to be a countess? Yes or no?

BABAKINA (*upset*). You're making this up, Misha, honestly . . . And people don't do business this way, off the cuff like this . . . If the Count cares to, he can himself or . . . or I don't know how this suddenly, all at once . . .

BORKIN. Now, now . . . don't confuse the issue . . . It's a business deal . . . Yes or no?

SHABELSKY (*laughing and rubbing his hands*). Actually, how about it? Damn it, should I really commit this dirty deed myself? Eh? Little puff-ball . . . . (*Kisses Babakina on the cheek.*) Superb . . . A tasty little pickle . . .

BABAKINA. Leave off, leave off, you've quite upset me . . . Go away, go away . . . No, don't go away . . .

BORKIN. Quickly . . . Yes or no? Time's running out . . .

BABAKINA. You know what, Count? You . . . you drive over to my place on a visit for two or three days . . . We'll have fun there, not like here . . . Drive over tomorrow . . . (*To Borkin.*) No, you were joking, weren't you?

BORKIN (*angrily*). Now who'd start joking about serious business?

BABAKINA. Leave off, leave off . . . Ah, I feel faint . . . I feel faint . . . A countess . . . I feel faint . . . I'm falling . . .

> BORKIN *and the* COUNT, *laughing, take her by the arms and, kissing her on the cheeks, lead her out the door at right.*

XIII

IVANOV, SASHA, then ANNA PETROVNA.

IVANOV and SASHA run in from the garden.

IVANOV (*clutching his head, in horror*). It can't be! Don't, don't, Shurochka! . . . Ah, don't!

SASHA (*passionately*). I love you madly . . . Without you there's no meaning to my life, no happiness and joy . . . For me, you're everything . . .

IVANOV. What for, what for, my God, I don't understand a thing . . . Shurochka, don't do this! . .

SASHA. In my childhood you were my only joy, I loved you and your soul, like myself, and now your form incessantly fills my thoughts day and night and keeps me from living. I love you, Nikolay Alekseevich . . . With you anywhere to the ends of the earth, wherever you want, even the grave, only, for God's sake, soon, otherwise I'll suffocate . . .

IVANOV (*bursts into peals of happy laughter*). What is this? Does this mean starting life over from the beginning? Shurochka, does it? . . . Happiness is mine for the taking! (*Draws her to him.*) My youth, my prime . . .

ANNA PETROVNA enters from the garden and, on seeing her husband and Sasha, stops as if rooted to the spot.

Does it mean coming to life? Does it? Back to an active role again?

Kiss. After they kiss, IVANOV and SASHA look around and see Anna Petrovna.

(*In horror.*) Sarra!

Curtain

ACT THREE

Ivanov's study. Desk, covered with an unruly sprawl of papers, books, official letters, knickknacks, revolvers; alongside the papers, a lamp, a carafe of vodka, a plate of herring, pieces of bread and pickled gherkins. On the wall regional maps, pictures, shotguns, pistols, sickles, riding crops, and so on. It is midday.

I

SHABELSKY, LEBEDEV, BORKIN, and PYOTR.

SHABELSKY and LEBEDEV are sitting on either side of the desk. BORKIN is center stage astride a chair. PYOTR is standing by the door.

LEBEDEV. France has a clear and well-defined policy . . . The French know what they want. They need to give the Krauts a good thrashing and that'll be that, while Germany, my boy, is singing a very different tune. Germany has plenty of other irons in the fire besides France . . .

SHABELSKY. Hogwash! . . . In my opinion, the Germans are cowards and so are the French . . . They give each other the finger behind their backs. Believe me, it won't go beyond giving each other the finger. They won't fight.[36]

---

36 In 1887, Germany's militarism provoked a strain in its relations with France, and war nearly broke out three times in the course of that year.

BORKIN. The way I see it, why fight? What's the point of all these arms buildups, conferences, defense budgets? You know what I'd do? I'd get together all the dogs in the whole nation, infect them with a good dose of Pasteur's rabies[37] and let 'em loose behind enemy lines. All the combatants would be raving mad within a month.

SHABELSKY bursts out laughing.

LEBEDEV (*laughs*). That head may not look all that large, but it swarms with big ideas, countless multitudes of 'em, like fishes in the sea.

SHABELSKY. A virtuoso . . . every day he gives birth to a thousand projects, snatches the stars from the sky, but all to no avail . . . He's never got a penny in his pocket . . .

LEBEDEV. Art for art's sake.

BORKIN. I'm not toiling for myself, but for others, for love of humanity.

LEBEDEV. God bless you, you're good for a laugh, *Michel Michelich* . . . (*Stops laughing.*) Well, gentlemen, "only warlike talk is heard, but as for vodka, not a word."[38] *Repetatur!* . . .[39]

Rises and walks over to the vodka.

(*Fills three shot glasses.*) Our good health . . .

They drink and take a snack.

A little bit of herring, my dears, the appetizer of all appetizers . . .

SHABELSKY. Well, no, gherkin's better . . . Learned men have been pondering from the dawn of time and never come up with anything cleverer than a pickled gherkin. (*To Pyotr.*) Pyotr, go and get more gherkins and tell 'em in the kitchen to bake four onion tarts. And see that they're hot . . .

PYOTR exits.

LEBEDEV. Another good thing to eat with vodka is caviar. Only how? Got to use your head . . . Take a quarter pound of pressed caviar, two bulbs of

---

37 Louis Pasteur, the French bacteriologist (1822–1895) was in the news; his Institut Pasteur, whose aim was to treat hydrophobia by inoculation, opened in Paris in 1888.

38 A line from Denis Davydov's *Songs of an Old Hussar* (1817), the poetic diary of a versifying army officer.

39 Latin: Do it again!

green onion, olive oil, mix it all up and, you know, like this . . . a little lemon juice on top . . . To die for! . . . You could go crazy from the smell alone . . . (*Energetically.*) Have you ever eaten caviar made from saffron milkcap mushrooms?

SHABELSKY. No . . .

LEBEDEV. Hm . . . Mince your pickled saffron milkcaps finely, finely, till they're like caviar or, you know what I mean, buckwheat groats . . . Put in onion, olive oil . . . a bit of pepper, vinegar . . . (*Kisses his fingers.*) What a combination . . .

BORKIN. Another nice thing to chase down vodka is fried smelts. Only you've got to know how to fry them. You've got to gut them, then roll them in fine bread crumbs and fry them crisp, so they crunch between your teeth . . . cru-cru-cru . . .

SHABELSKY. Yesterday at Babakina's there was a good appetizer—button mushrooms.

LEBEDEV. No kidding . . .

SHABELSKY. Only prepared some special way. You know, with onion, bay leaf, all sorts of spices. As soon as they took the lid off the saucepan, it gave off a vapor, an aroma . . . sheer rapture . . .

LEBEDEV. How about it? *Repetatur*, gentlemen!

They drink.

Our health . . . (*Looks at his watch.*) I don't think I can wait till Nikolasha shows up. It's time for me to go. At Babakina's, you say, they served mushrooms, but you have yet to see a mushroom at our place. Would you like to tell me, Count, why the hell you spend so much time at Marfutka's?

SHABELSKY (*nods at Borkin*). That one, he wants to marry me off to her . . .

LEBEDEV. Marry? . . . How old are you?

SHABELSKY. Sixty-two . . .

LEBEDEV. Just the age for getting married, and Marfutka's the ideal mate for you.

BORKIN. It's got nothing to do with Marfutka, but with Marfutka's coin of the realm.

LEBEDEV. Which is what you're after: Marfutka's coin of the realm . . . You want some green cheese from the moon as well?

BORKIN. As soon as the man's married, he'll line his *empochers*,[40] then you'll see green cheese. You'll be drooling for it . . .

SHABELSKY. Bless my soul, he's really serious. This genius is convinced that I'm obeying his orders and getting married . . .

BORKIN. How else? Didn't you already agree to it?

SHABELSKY. You're out of your mind . . . When did I agree to it? Psss . . .

BORKIN. Thank you . . . Thank you very much! So this means you're going to let me down? One minute he's getting married, the next he's not . . . who the hell can tell the difference, and I've already given my word of honor! So you're not getting married?

SHABELSKY (*shrugs his shoulders*). He's serious . . . A wonderful fellow!

BORKIN (*exasperated*). In that case, what was the point of getting a respectable woman all hot and bothered? She's frantic to be a countess, can't sleep, can't eat . . . . Is that a laughing matter? . . . Is that the decent thing to do?

SHABELSKY (*snaps his fingers*). What then, what if I actually do commit this dirty deed all by myself? Eh? For spite? I'll go and commit the dirty deed. Word of honor . . . Might be fun! . . .

I I

The same and LVOV.

LEBEDEV. Our regards to Æsculapius . . . (*Gives Lvov his hand and sings.*) "Doctor, save me, my dear fellow, thoughts of death turn me quite yellow . . ."[41]

LVOV. Nikolay Alekseevich still isn't here?

LEBEDEV. Well, no, I've been waiting for him for over an hour . . .

LVOV impatiently paces up and down the stage.

Dear boy, how is Anna Petrovna?

---

40 Bad French: pockets.

41 Paraphrase of a line from "The Doctor Serenade" by W. Ch. Dawinhof (words by A. M. Ushakova).

LVOV. In a bad way . . .

LEBEDEV (*sighs*). May I go and convey my respects?

LVOV. No, please, don't. I think she's sleeping . . .

Pause.

LEBEDEV. An attractive woman, a splendid woman . . . (*Sighs.*) On Shu-rochka's birthday, when she fainted at our place, I stared into her face and that's when I realized that she hasn't long to live, poor thing. I can't under-stand why she took a turn for the worse just then. I run in, lo and behold: she's white as a sheet, lying on the floor, Nikolasha is kneeling beside her, white as well, Shurochka's all in tears. The whole of the next week, Shurochka and I went around in a daze . . .

SHABELSKY (*to Lvov*). Tell me, my respected apostle of science, which sci-entist discovered that the most salutary thing for chest ailments is private visits from a young physician? It's a great discovery, truly great . . . How would you classify it: as allopathy or homeopathy?[42]

> LVOV *is about to reply, but makes a scornful gesture and exits.*

If looks could kill . . . .

LEBEDEV. You're giving your tongue a workout . . . Why did you insult him?

SHABELSKY (*irritated*). And why does he lie to me? Tuberculosis, no hope, she's dying . . . He's lying . . . I can't stand it . . .

LEBEDEV. What makes you think he's lying?

SHABELSKY (*rises and walks around*). I cannot abide the thought that a liv-ing human being suddenly, for no reason at all, can up and die. Let's change the subject . . .

I I I

LEBEDEV, SHABELSKY, BORKIN, and KOSYKH.

KOSYKH (*runs in, panting*). Is Nikolay Alekseevich at home? Good after-noon! (*Quickly shakes everyone's hand.*) At home?

---

42 Allopathy is curing a disease by inducing a different kind of disease; homeopathy is treating a dis-ease by minute doses of drugs that would induce disease-like symptoms in a healthy person.

BORKIN. He is not . . .

KOSYKH (*sits and jumps up*). In that case, good-bye . . . (*Drinks a glass of vodka and has a quick bite.*) I'll move on . . . Business . . . I'm exhausted . . . I can barely stand on my feet . . .

LEBEDEV. What wind has blown you here?

KOSYKH. I've been at Barabanov's. We were playing whist all night long and only just finished . . . I lost every last thing . . . That Barabanov plays like a shoemaker! (*In a tearful voice.*) Just you listen: I was holding hearts the whole time . . . (*Turns to Borkin, who jumps away from him.*) He leads diamonds, I go hearts again, he goes diamonds . . . Well, not one trick . . . (*To Lebedev.*) We try to take four clubs . . . I've got an ace, queen and four more clubs, ace, ten, and three more spades . . .

LEBEDEV (*covers his ears*). Spare me, spare me, for Christ's sake, spare me!

KOSYKH (*to the Count*). You know what I mean: ace, queen, and four more clubs, ace, ten, three more spades . . .

SHABELSKY (*pushing him away with his hands*). Go away, I don't want to hear it . . .

KOSYKH. And suddenly, of all the bad luck: the ace of spades was trumped first round.

SHABELSKY (*grabs a revolver off the desk*). Get out of here or I'll shoot!

KOSYKH (*waves his hand in dismissal*). What the hell . . . Can't a man even talk to people? It's like living in Australia: no common interests, no solidarity . . . Every man lives on his own . . . Anyway, I've got to go . . . it's time. (*Takes his cap.*) Time is money . . . (*Gives Lebedev his hand.*) Pass! . . .

Laughter.

LEBEDEV. You've played cards, dear heart, to the point that you say pass instead of good-bye . . .

KOSYKH *leaves and bumps into Avdotya Nazarovna in
the doorway.*

I V

SHABELSKY, LEBEDEV, BORKIN, and AVDOTYA NAZAROVNA.

AVDOTYA NAZAROVNA (*cries out*). Blast you, you've knocked me off my feet!

EVERYONE. Ah-ah-ah! . . . The unavoidable! . . .

AVDOTYA NAZAROVNA. Here they are, I've been looking for them all over the house. Good afternoon, my fine feathered friends, greetings, greetings . . . (*Greets them.*) I've been through all the rooms, but there's that doctor, enough to drive you crazy, bugging out those beady eyes of his, with his "What do you want? Get out of here . . . You'll disturb the patient," he says. As if it was that easy . . .

LEBEDEV. What's she doing here?

AVDOTYA NAZAROVNA. Business, my good sir! (*To the Count.*) Business on your behalf, your grace. (*Bows.*) I was told to give you my regards and ask after your health . . . (*Sings.*)

> Short is the time the flower doth in the garden grow,
> Short is the time Matvey his love doth woo.

And she, my baby-doll, told me to say that if you don't come this evening, she will cry her little eyes out. "So," she says, "my dear, take him aside and whisper secretly in his ear." But why secretly? We're all friends here. And in a case like this, we're not robbing the henhouse, it's by law and by love, by mutual agreement . . . Never, for all my sins, do I touch a drop, but in a case like this I'll have a drink . . .

LEBEDEV. And so will I . . . (*Pours.*) And you, you old crow, you're still going strong. I've known you for well nigh thirty years and you've always been old . . .

AVDOTYA NAZAROVNA. I've lost count of the years . . . Two husbands I've buried, I would have taken a third, but nobody'll have you without a dowry. Eight children I've had, more or less . . . (*Takes a glass.*) Well, God grant we've embarked on a successful venture, God grant it ends in success . . . May they live long and prosper, and may we behold them and rejoice. May they abide in harmony and love. (*Drinks.*) Pretty strong vodka . . .

SHABELSKY (*roaring with laughter, to Lebedev*). But, do you realize, the strangest thing of all is that they take it seriously, as if I . . . Wonderful . . . (*Rises.*) Or else, actually, Pasha, should I commit this dirty deed on my own? For spite . . . new tricks for an old dog, as they say . . . Eh, Pasha? No kidding . . .

LEBEDEV. You're talking drivel, Count. Our concern, yours and mine, my boy, is to be mindful of our deaths, for Marfutka and her coin of the realm have passed you by long ago . . . Our time is over . . .

SHABELSKY. No, I will do the deed. Word of honor, I'll do the deed . . .

Enter IVANOV and LVOV.

V

The same, IVANOV, and LVOV.

LVOV. Please grant me just five minutes.

LEBEDEV. Nikolasha . . . (*Goes to meet Ivanov and kisses him.*) Good afternoon, my dear friend . . . I've been waiting for you a whole hour . . .

AVDOTYA NAZAROVNA (*bows*). Good afternoon, my dear sir! . . .

IVANOV (*bitterly*). Gentlemen, once again you've turned my study into a barroom! . . . I've asked each and every one of you a thousand times not to do it . . . (*Walks over to the desk.*) There, look, you've spilled vodka on the papers . . . crumbs . . . pickles . . . it's really disgusting! . . .

LEBEDEV. Sorry, Nikolasha, sorry . . . Forgive us. You and I, dear friend, have some very important business to talk over . . . .

BORKIN. So do I.

LVOV. Nikolay Alekseevich, may I have a word with you?

IVANOV (*points to Lebedev*). He's the one who needs me. Wait, you're next . . . (*To Lebedev.*) What's on your mind?

LEBEDEV. Gentlemen, I'd like to speak in private . . . Please . . .

The COUNT, laughing and making faces, exits with AVDOTYA NAZAROVNA, followed by BORKIN, then LVOV.

IVANOV. Pasha, you can drink as much as you like, it's your funeral, but please don't let my uncle drink.[43] He never drank at my house before . . . It's bad for him.

LEBEDEV (*alarmed*). My dear boy, I didn't know . . . I didn't even notice . . .

IVANOV. God forbid, but if that old baby should die, you're not the one who'll feel bad, I am . . . What do you want?

Pause.

LEBEDEV. You see, my dear friend . . . I don't know how to begin, so that it doesn't sound so heartless . . . Nikolasha, I'm embarrassed, I'm blushing, my tongue's twisted, but, dear boy, put yourself in my place, bear in mind that I'm a man under orders, a flunky, a doormat . . . Do forgive me . . . Uneasy lies the head that fears a gown . . .[44]

IVANOV. What do you mean?

LEBEDEV. The wife sent me . . . Do me a favor, be a friend, pay her the interest! You wouldn't believe how she's nagged, worn me down, tortured the life out of me . . . Get her off your back, for heaven's sake! . . .

IVANOV. Pasha, you know I haven't got any money right now . . .

LEBEDEV. I know, I know, but what am I to do? She won't wait. If she sues you for defaulting, how can Shurochka and I look you in the face again?

IVANOV. I'm embarrassed myself. Pasha, I'd be glad if the earth swallowed me up, but . . . but where am I get it? Teach me, where? The only thing left is to wait for autumn when I can sell the wheat . . .

LEBEDEV (*shouts*). She won't wait!

Pause.

IVANOV. Your position is an unpleasant one, a delicate one, but mine's even worse. (*Walks and thinks.*) And one can't come up with anything . . . There's nothing left to sell . . .

LEBEDEV. You should ride over to Mühlbach, ask him . . . After all, he owes you sixteen thousand . . .

43 Sonya repeats this line to Astrov in *Uncle Vanya*, Act Two.

44 In Russian, Lebedev twists the proverb "A shriven head escapes the axe" (A fault confessed is half redressed) to "A shriven head gets a work-over by the wife though it may escape the axe."

IVANOV waves his hand in hopeless dismissal.

Here's how it is, Nikolasha . . . I know you'll start swearing, but . . . respect an old boozehound! Between friends . . . Regard me as a friend . . . You and I are both students, liberals . . . Mutual ideas and interests . . . Both alumni of Moscow U. . . . Alma mater . . . (*Takes his wallet out of his pocket.*) I've got some money stashed away, not a soul at home knows about it. Take a loan . . . (*Takes out money and puts it on the desk.*) Pocket your pride, and take it for friendship's sake . . . I'd take it from you, word of honor . . .

IVANOV (*walks around*). It doesn't matter . . . at the moment I've no pride left. I even think if you were to slap my face, I wouldn't say a word.

LEBEDEV. There it is on the desk. One thousand one hundred. You ride over there today and hand it to her in person. "There you are," say, "Zinaida Savishna, I hope it chokes you!" Only look, don't give any clue that you borrowed it from me, God forbid . . .

Pause.

Your heart is aching?

IVANOV waves his hand in dismissal.

Yes, business . . . . (*Sighs.*) A time of grief and sorrow has come to you. A man, my good friend, is like a samovar. It doesn't always stand in a shady spot on the shelf, but sometimes it's heated with burning coals: psh . . . psh . . . That simile isn't worth a damn, well, let someone smarter come up with a better one . . . (*Sighs.*) Misery hardens the heart. I don't feel sorry for you, Nikolasha, you'll land on your feet, the pain will lessen but I'm offended, my boy, and annoyed by other people . . . Do me a favor, tell me what's the reason for all this gossip? There's so much gossip circulating about you in the district, my boy, watch out, our friend the district attorney might pay you a visit . . . You're a murderer and a blood-sucker and a thief and a traitor . . .

IVANOV. It's all rubbish, now I've got a headache.

LEBEDEV. All because you think too much.

IVANOV. I don't think at all.

LEBEDEV. Well, Nikolasha, don't you give a damn about all that and come and see us. Shurochka's fond of you, she understands and appreciates you.

She's a decent, good person, Nikolasha. Nothing like her mother and father, but I guess some young fellow came passing by . . . I look at her sometimes, pal, and I can't believe that a bottle-nosed drunkard like me has such a treasure. Drop by, talk to her about clever things and—it'll cheer you up. She's an honest, sincere person.

Pause.

IVANOV. Pasha, dear man, leave me alone . . .

LEBEDEV. I understand, I understand . . . (*Hastily looks at his watch.*) I understand. (*Kisses Ivanov.*) Good-bye . . . I still have to go to the dedication of a school.[45] (*Goes to the door and stops.*) A clever girl . . . Yesterday Shurochka and I started talking about the gossip. (*Laughs.*) And she blurted out an aphorism: "Papa dear," she says, "glowworms glow in the dark only to make it easier for night birds to see them and eat them, and good people exist so that there can be slander and gossip." How do you like that? A genius, a George Sand . . .[46] I thought only Borkin had great ideas in his head, but now it turns out . . . I'm going, I'm going . . . (*Exits.*)

VI

IVANOV, then LVOV.

IVANOV (*alone*). I'll sign the papers and I'll take my gun and go out for a walk . . . To clear my head of this nastiness . . . (*Fastidiously hunched over, he takes a snack and some bread off the little table.*)

LVOV (*enters*). I've got to have it out with you, Nikolay Alekseevich . . .

IVANOV (*taking the carafe of vodka*). If we were to have it out every day, Doctor, we'd be too debilitated for anything else.

LVOV. Will you be so good as to listen to me?

IVANOV. I listen to you every day and so far I can't understand a thing: what do you personally want from me?

---

45 Elementary schools fell under the jurisdiction of the Rural Board, of which Lebedev is chairman.

46 The pseudonym of Aurore Dudevant (1804–1876), whose overwrought and liberal-minded romantic novels were highly popular in Russia: Turgenev called her "one of our saints," Belinsky "a modern Joan of Arc."

LVOV. I speak clearly and firmly, and the only person who could fail to understand me is one without a heart.

IVANOV. My wife is facing death — that I know; I have unpardonably wronged her — that I also know; you're a decent, upright man — I know that too! What more do you want?

LVOV. I am outraged by human cruelty . . . A woman is dying. She has a father and mother whom she loves and would like to see before she dies; they know perfectly well that she will die soon and that she goes on loving them, but, damn their cruelty, they evidently want Jehovah to see how steadfast they are in their religion; they still go on cursing her . . . You, the man for whom she sacrificed everything, her religion and her parents' home and her peace of mind, in the most blatant manner and with the most blatant intentions you head over to those Lebedevs every day . . .

IVANOV. Oh, I haven't been there for two weeks now . . .

LVOV (*not listening to him*). People such as you have to be spoken to bluntly, with no beating around the bush, and if you don't like what I have to say, then don't listen! I'm used to calling things by their rightful names . . . You need this death in order to carry out new feats of valor, all right, but can't you at least wait? If you were to let her die in the natural scheme of things, without stabbing her with your barefaced cynicism, would the Lebedevs and their dowry disappear? Not now, but in a year or two, you, a wonderful Tartuffe, will manage to turn a young girl's head and make off with her dowry just the same as now . . . Why are you in such a hurry? Why do you need your wife to die now, and not in a month or a year's time?

IVANOV. This is excruciating . . . Doctor, you're a really bad physician if you suppose that a man can control himself forever. It's taking the most appalling will-power not to reply to your insults.

LVOV. That's enough, who are you trying to fool? Drop the mask.

IVANOV. Clever man, think of this: in your opinion, nothing's easier than understanding me . . . Right? I married Anna to get a big dowry . . . I didn't get the dowry, I missed the mark, and now I'm driving her to her grave, in order to marry another woman and get that dowry . . . Right? How simple and uncomplicated . . . A man is such a simple and unsophisticated machine . . . No, Doctor, each of us has far more cogs, screws, and valves in him than to enable us to judge one another on first impressions or a few outward signs. I don't understand you, you don't understand me, we don't understand one another. You may be an excellent general practitioner and still have no understanding of people. Don't be so smug and look at it my way.

LVOV. Do you really think that you're so unfathomable, that I am so brainless that I can't tell the difference between disgraceful behavior and decent behavior?

IVANOV. Obviously, you and I will never find common ground . . . For the last time I ask you, and, please answer without more ado, what do you personally want from me? What do you hope to achieve? (*Annoyed.*) And whom have I the honor of addressing: the Counsel for my prosecution or my wife's physician? . . .

LVOV. I am a physician, and, as a physician, I demand that you change your way of life . . . It is killing Anna Petrovna!

IVANOV. But what am I to do? What? If you understand me better than I understand myself, then tell me in no uncertain terms: what am I to do?

LVOV. At least, don't act so openly.

IVANOV. Oh, my God! Do you really understand yourself? (*Drinks water.*) Leave me alone. I'm a thousand times at fault, I'll answer for it before God, but no one has entitled you to torture me on a daily basis . . .

LVOV. And who has entitled you to insult my truth-telling, by insulting my person? You have worn me down and poisoned my mind. Until I wound up in this district, I could deal with the fact that stupid, inane, self-deluded people existed, but I never believed there were criminal types who consciously, deliberately used their intelligence to do evil . . . I respected and loved people, but once I came in contact with you . . .

SASHA enters in a riding habit.

VII

The same and SASHA.

LVOV (*on seeing Sasha*). Now, I hope, we understand one another perfectly well . . . (*Shrugs his shoulders and exits.*)

IVANOV (*alarmed*). Shura, is that you . . .

SASHA. Yes, it is . . . Weren't you expecting me? Why haven't you been to see us for so long?

IVANOV (*looking around*). Shura, for God's sake, this is inconsiderate . . . Your coming here might have a dreadful effect on my wife . . .

SASHA. I'll go right away . . . I was worried: are you all right? Why haven't you been to see us for so long?

IVANOV. Go away, for God's sake . . . we cannot meet so long as . . . so long as . . . well, you understand me . . . (*Delicately pushes her to the door.*)

SASHA. Just tell me one thing: are you all right?

IVANOV. No, I've been tormenting myself, people torment me nonstop . . . I'm at the end of my rope and, if it were not for thoughts of you, I would long ago have blown my brains out. You see, I'm trembling . . . Shurochka, for God's sake, take me away from here as soon as possible . . . (*Presses his head against her shoulder.*) Let me have some rest and forget myself for only a moment . . .

SASHA. Soon, soon, Nikolay . . . Don't lose heart, it's disgraceful . . .

VIII

IVANOV, SASHA, and PYOTR.

PYOTR brings in the tarts on a piece of paper and puts them on the desk.

IVANOV (*starting*). Who? what? (*On seeing Pyotr.*) What do you want?

PYOTR. Tarts, the Count ordered 'em . . .

IVANOV. Get out of here . . .

PYOTR exits.

SASHA. I promise you, my dearest . . . here is my hand: good days will come, and you shall be happy. Be brave, look at how courageous and happy I am . . . (*Weeps.*)

IVANOV. It's as if we want her to die . . . How unwholesome this is, how abnormal . . . I'm so much at fault . . .

SASHA (*in horror*). Nikolay, who wants her to die? Let her live, even for a hundred years . . . And how are you at fault? Is it your fault that you fell out of love with her, that fate is driving her to death? Is it your fault that you love me? Think well of it . . . look (*weeps*) . . . look circumstances straight in the face, be brave . . . It's not your fault and it's not mine, it's circumstance . . .

IVANOV. Be brave . . . a time will come . . . fell in love . . . fell out of love—these are all platitudes. Hackneyed phrases, which are no help at all.

SASHA. I talk the way everybody does and I don't know how else to talk . . .

IVANOV. And our whole love affair is a trite platitude . . . "He was downhearted and had lost his bearings . . . She showed up, strong and bold in spirit, and offered him a helping hand." . . . It's all right and appropriate for novels, but in life . . . it's not right, it's not right . . . Look, you love me, my own, you've lent me a helping hand, and I'm still pathetic and helpless, just as I was before . . .

I X

The same and BORKIN.

BORKIN (*looks in at the door*). Nikolay Alekseevich, may I? (*On seeing Sasha.*) Sorry, I didn't see . . . (*Enters.*) Bonjour . . . (*Bows.*)

SASHA (*embarrassed*). How do you do . . .

BORKIN. You've got plumper, prettier . . .

SASHA (*to Ivanov*). I'm leaving now, Nikolay Alekseevich . . . I'm leaving . . . (*Exits.*)

BORKIN. A vision of loveliness . . . I came about prose, and ran into poetry . . . (*Sings.*) "Thou didst appear, like a bird flown towards the light . . ."[47]

> IVANOV *paces up and down the stage in agitation.*

(*Sits.*) There's something about her, *Nicolas* . . . a certain something that other women haven't got . . . Am I right? Something special . . . fantastical . . . (*Sighs.*) Actually, the richest eligible girl in the whole district, but her dear mama is such a sourpuss that no one wants to make a match. When

---

47 From E. S. Shashina's ballad "Three Words" (text by O. P. Pavlova).

she dies everything will go to Shurochka, but until she dies she'll give ten thousand or so, a curling iron and a flat iron, and even then she'll make you beg for it on your knees. (*Rummages in his pockets.*) Let's smoke a *de-los-majoros*.[48] Care for one? (*Offers his cigar case.*) They're not bad . . . Quite smokeworthy.

IVANOV (*walks over to Borkin, choked with rage*). Don't set foot in my house another minute! . . . Not another minute! . . .

> BORKIN *rises a bit and drops the cigar.*

Not another minute . . .

BORKIN. *Nicolas*, what does this mean? What are you angry about?

IVANOV. What about? Where did you get those cigars? Do you think I don't know where you take the old man every day and what for . . .

BORKIN (*shrugs his shoulders*). What's it got to do with you?

IVANOV. You're such a crook . . . Your vulgar schemes, which you broadcast through the whole district, have made me a dishonest man in people's eyes . . . We've got nothing in common, and I ask you to leave my home this very minute . . . (*Walks quickly.*)

BORKIN. I know that you're saying all this out of irritation, and therefore I won't be angry with you. Insult me as much as you like . . . (*Picks up the cigar.*) It's time you gave up this melancholy act . . . You're no schoolboy . . .

IVANOV. What did I tell you? (*Trembling.*) Are you playing games with me?

> *Enter ANNA PETROVNA.*

X

The same and ANNA PETROVNA.

BORKIN. Well, look, Anna Petrovna's here . . . I'm going. (*Exits.*)

> IVANOV *stops beside the desk and stands, his head bowed.*

---

48 Spanish: correctly *de los majores*, of the best.

ANNA PETROVNA (*after a pause*). Why did she come here just now?

Pause.

I'm asking you: why did she come here?

IVANOV. Don't question me, Anyuta . . .

Pause.

I'm much at fault . . . Think up whatever punishment you want, I'll bear it, but . . . don't question me . . . I haven't got the strength to talk . . .

ANNA PETROVNA (*angrily raps a finger on the desk*). Why was she here?

Pause.

Ah, so that's what you're like! Now I understand you. Finally I see what sort of man you are. Dishonorable, vile . . . You remember, you came and lied to me, saying you loved me . . . I believed it and left father, mother, religion and followed you . . . You lied to me about truth, goodness, your honorable intentions, I believed every word . . .

IVANOV. Anyuta, I never lied to you . . .

ANNA PETROVNA. I lived with you for five years, I broke down and sickened at the idea that I'd renounced my faith, but I loved you and never left you for a single minute . . . You were my idol . . . And now what? All this time you've been deceiving me in the most shameless manner . . . .

IVANOV. Anyuta, don't make things up . . . I was mistaken, yes . . . but I've never lied in my life . . . You don't dare reproach me for that . . .

ANNA PETROVNA. Now it's all come out . . . You married me and thought my father and mother would forgive me, give me money . . . That's what you thought.

IVANOV. Oh my God! Anyuta, to try my patience like this . . . (*Weeps.*)

ANNA PETROVNA. Be quiet . . . When you realized there was no money, you came up with a new game . . . Now I remember it all and I understand . . . (*Weeps.*) You never loved me and were never faithful to me. Never!

IVANOV. Sarra, that's a lie! . . . Say what you want, but don't insult me with lies . . .

ANNA PETROVNA. You always lied to me . . . Dishonorable, vile man . . . You owe Lebedev money, and now, in order to squirm out of your debt, you want to turn his daughter's head, deceive her the way you did me . . . Isn't that so?

IVANOV (*choking*). Shut up, for God's sake! . . . I can't answer for myself . . . I'm choking with rage, and I . . . I'm liable to insult you . . .

ANNA PETROVNA. You always were a shameless deceiver, and not just of me . . . You pinned all those underhanded actions on Borkin, but now I know whose they really are . . .

IVANOV. Sarra, shut up, get out, or else I'll say something I'll regret . . . It's all I can do to keep from calling you something horrible, humiliating . . . (*Shouts.*) Shut up, you kike bitch!

ANNA PETROVNA. I will not shut up . . . Too long you've been deceiving me, for me to be able to keep silent . . .

IVANOV. So you won't shut up? (*Struggles with himself.*) For God's sake . . .

ANNA PETROVNA. Now go and cheat the Lebedev girl . . .

IVANOV. Then know that you . . . will die soon . . . The doctor told me that you'll die soon . . .

ANNA PETROVNA (*sits down, her voice faltering*). When did he say that?

Pause.

IVANOV (*clutching his head*). It's all my fault! God, it's all my fault! . . . (*Sobs.*)

XI

The same and LVOV.

LVOV (*enters and, on seeing Anna Petrovna, quickly heads for her*). What's going on? (*Examines her face. To Ivanov.*) What were you doing just now?

IVANOV. God, it's all my fault! . . . all my fault! . . .

LVOV. Anna Petrovna, Anna Petrovna, what's wrong with you? (*To Ivanov.*) Wait! I swear to you on the honor which you do not possess, you shall pay for her! . . . I'll unmask you . . . I'll show you! . . .

IVANOV. It's all my fault, all my fault . . .

Curtain

Nearly a year goes by between Acts Three and Four.

ACT FOUR

TABLEAU ONE

A small room in the Lebedevs' house. Simple, antique furnishings.
Doors at right and left.

I

DUDKIN and KOSYKH.

Both in dress-coats with nosegays in their lapels; they stand near
the door at left and hurriedly smoke hand-rolled cigarettes.

KOSYKH (*gleefully*). Yesterday I called a little slam in clubs, and took a grand slam . . . Only again that Barabanov spoiled the whole shebang for me . . . We play . . . I bid: no trumps. He goes pass . . . Clubs . . . He goes pass . . . I go two clubs . . . three clubs . . . he goes pass, and imagine . . . can you imagine, I call a slam, and he doesn't show his ace. If he'd shown his ace, I could have called a grand slam in no-trumps . . .

DUDKIN. Hold on, a carriage is drawing up. It's the best man, I suppose. (*Looks out the window.*) No . . . (*Looks at his watch.*) But it's high time he got here . . .

KOSYKH. Yes, the bride's been dressed for a long time now . . .

DUDKIN. Eh, pal, if I were the bridegroom (*whistles*), I would have done a deal . . . Right this very minute, right now, when the bride is already dressed and ready to go to church, I'd show up here and put the screws on Zyuzyushka: hand over a hundred thousand, or I won't get married . . . Hand it over . . .

KOSYKH. But she wouldn't hand it over . . .

DUDKIN. She would . . . When everything's all set at the church and people are waiting, she would . . . But now Ivanov isn't getting a red cent. She didn't even give him the five thousand . . .

KOSYKH. On the other hand, when she dies, he'll get it all.

DUDKIN. Oh sure, wait for her to die . . . Before she croaks, she'll bury it in the ground. All these hags are the same. I had a lousy uncle like that, just before he died he chewed up all his interest-bearing bonds and swallowed them. As God is my judge . . . The doctor pays his visit, there he lies with a belly out to here—wow . . . Ivanov thinks that now they'll lay it on 'im: "take it all, my dear man . . ." That'll be the day . . . He was a wash-out with the Jew bitch, had to eat crow, and the same thing'll happen here . . . The man's got no luck . . . No luck at all . . . Might just as well lay down and die . . . After all, he's a smart guy, a wheeler-dealer, a con man, knows his politics backwards and forwards, but look—fate was against him . . . Lady Luck never smiled . . .

I I

The same and BABAKINA.

BABAKINA (*overdressed, pompously crosses the stage between Dudkin and Kosykh; they both laugh up their sleeves; she looks round*). Idiot . . .

   DUDKIN touches her waist with his finger and roars with laughter.

Peasant . . . (*Exits.*)

   DUDKIN and KOSYKH burst out laughing.

KOSYKH (*roaring with laughter*). The dame's gone off her rocker . . . Until she started angling for a title, she made a lot of sense, but now that she has hopes of being a countess, you can't come near her. Used to be, you'd fill a sack with cognac and liqueurs, drop by her place for a few days and paint the town red . . . a regular music-hall, but nowadays you mustn't lay a finger on her . . . (*Mimics her.*) Peasant!

DUDKIN. Listen, she's going to be a countess . . .

KOSYKH. Sure she is . . . the Count is laughing at her, stringing her along, believe you me. He just likes to chat her up and get supper free, gratis and for nothing. For a whole year now he's been leading her around by the nose. But, pal, why should I feel sorry for Marfutka—a skinflint! a regular skinflint! . . . Mishka Borkin and the Count are fluttering round her, prancing and dancing every which way, so she'll give them money: but not a penny! . . . Last year all Mishka got from her for his matchmaking was

two hundred paper rubles, and Ivanov immediately sent them back to her
. . . So Mishka wound up empty-handed, went to all that trouble and nothing to show for it.

I I I

The same, LEBEDEV, and SASHA (dressed in white.)

LEBEDEV (*entering, with Sasha*). Let's talk in here. (*To Dudkin and Kosykh.*)
Go into the other room, you Zulus, and join the young ladies. We have to
talk in private.

DUDKIN (*as he passes Sasha, snaps his fingers in ecstasy*). Pretty as a picture! . . . *Fine champagne!* . . .

LEBEDEV. Pass by, caveman, pass by . . .

KOSYKH and DUDKIN leave.

Sit down, Shurochka . . . that's right . . . (*Sits and looks round.*) Listen carefully and with due respect. Here's the thing: your mother insisted that I
inform you of the following . . . (*Blows his nose.*) Since the groom's best
man hasn't shown up yet and we still haven't said the benediction over you,
to avoid misunderstandings and any potential arguments later on, you've got
to know once and for all that we . . . I mean, not we, but your mother . . .

SASHA. Papa, could you cut it short?

LEBEDEV. You've got to know that you have been granted a dowry of fifteen
thousand silver rubles in banknotes. That's that . . . see that there are no
arguments later on! Hold on . . . be quiet. That's only for starters, here
comes the main course. You've been granted a dowry of fifteen thousand,
but, in view of the fact that Nikolay Alekseevich owes your mother nine
thousand, a deduction is being made from your dowry in the amount of the
debt, and, that way, you'll only get six thousand. *Vous comprenez?*[49] You've
got to know this so that there won't be any arguments later on. Hold on, I
haven't finished. Five hundred were set aside for the wedding; but because
the wedding is at the bridegroom's expense, that five hundred will be
deducted from the six thousand. Which leaves, you see, five thousand five
hundred, which you will receive after the ceremony, moreover, your gen-

---

49 French: you understand?

erous mother will not use the occasion to pass off on you coupons that fall due ten years from now or shares in the Skopin bank.[50]

SASHA. Why are you telling me this?

LEBEDEV. Your mother insisted.

SASHA (*rises*). Papa, if you had the slightest respect for me or yourself, you wouldn't let yourself talk to me this way. (*Angrily.*) Do I need your dowry . . . I didn't ask for it then and don't ask for it now . . . Do leave me alone, don't humiliate my ears with your cheese-paring! . . .

LEBEDEV. I'm not talking about the dowry, but your mother . . .

SASHA. I've told you a hundred times that I won't take a penny . . . But we will pay back the debt we owe you. We'll borrow the money somewhere and repay you. Leave me in peace.

LEBEDEV. What are you taking it out on me for? In Gogol's play the two rats at least sniffed around first, and only then went away.[51]

SASHA. Leave me in peace . . .

LEBEDEV (*flaring up*). Fooey . . . The way you're all carrying on, I'll end up sticking a knife in myself or cutting somebody else's throat! . . . That one sets up a fearful howl all the livelong day, nagging, pestering, pinching pennies, while this one, an intelligent, humane, damn it all, emancipated woman, can't understand her own father . . . I'm humiliating her ears . . . Well, before coming here to insult your ears, out there (*points to the door*) I was being cut up into little pieces, drawn and quartered . . . (*Walks around in perturbation.*) She can't understand . . . (*Mimics.*) I won't take a penny . . . Oh no, she wanted to be different . . . What are you and your husband going to live on?

SASHA. Our own income, he's not a beggar . . .

LEBEDEV (*waves his hand in dismissal*). That one nags, this one philosophizes, there's no way to say a word to Nikolay: another very clever fellow

---

50 A bank in the southern county town of Skopin in Ryazan failed in 1884 and was a topic of conversation for years. Chekhov reported on the Moscow trial of the bank's president and head cashier.

51 At the start of Gogol's comedy *The Inspector General*, the worried Mayor tells of a dream in which two rats of "exceptional size" came, sniffed around, and then went away again.

. . . You've got my head swimming, you've mixed me all up . . . oh, you! (*Goes to the door and stops.*) I don't like it. I don't like anything about you!

SASHA. What don't you like?

LEBEDEV. I don't like any of it . . . any of it . . .

SASHA. Any of what?

LEBEDEV. So now I'm supposed to pull up a chair and start telling you a story. I don't like anything about it . . . And I don't want to be at your wedding . . . (*Walks over to Sasha, affectionately.*) You'll forgive me, Shurochka . . . Maybe your getting married is clever, honorable, uplifting, highly principled, but something about it isn't right . . . isn't right . . . isn't right . . . It isn't like other marriages. You're young, fresh, pure as a pane of glass, beautiful, whereas he's a widower, thirty-five years old . . . worn to a shadow, to a nub . . . . Listen, in another five years he'll have wrinkles and a bald spot . . . (*Kisses his daughter.*) Shurochka, forgive me, but something smells rotten . . . There's already a lot of talk . . . About how Sarra died at his place, then suddenly for some reason he wanted to marry you . . .

SASHA. He's your friend, papa . . .

LEBEDEV. Friend or not, all the same something, do you understand, is not quite right . . . (*Vigorously.*) Anyway, I'm being an old biddy, an old biddy . . . I'm as biddified as an old hoop-skirt . . . Don't listen to me . . . . Don't listen to anybody . . .

I V

The same and ZINAIDA SAVISHNA.

ZINAIDA SAVISHNA (*enters, dressed in a new gown, her head bound in a wet towel*). Turns out the groom's best man has arrived. We have to go to the benediction . . .[52] (*Weeps.*)

SASHA (*pleading*). Mamma!

LEBEDEV. Zyuzyushka, it's high time you turned off the waterworks! . . . For heaven's sake, for a whole year now you've been, excuse the expression, blubbering.

---

52 In Russian Orthodox wedding ceremonies, the benediction is given before the church ceremony takes place.

Pause.

You reek of vinegar, like a salad . . .

SASHA (*pleading*). Mamma!

ZINAIDA SAVISHNA. If you don't need a mother, (*weeps*) if you manage without obeying your mother, then . . . what do you need me for? You have my blessing, I'll satisfy you that way, you have my blessing . . .

LEBEDEV. Zyuzyushka, you should be joyful . . .

ZINAIDA SAVISHNA (*taking the handkerchief from her face, no longer weeping*). What's there to be joyful about? He's marrying her for the dowry and so as not to pay off his debt, and you are overjoyed . . . (*Weeps.*) Our only daughter, and God alone knows how she . . . If, according to you, he's an honest, commonsensical man, he should have paid off the debt before he proposed to her . . .

LEBEDEV (*to Sasha*). Be quiet, be quiet, swear off the stuff . . . Drink tea, pal, till your dying day . . . It won't be long now . . .

V

The same and IVANOV.

IVANOV, wearing a tailcoat, enters in evident agitation.

Together

LEBEDEV (*alarmed*). What's up! Where did you come from?

SASHA. Why are you here?

IVANOV. Sorry, friends, let me talk to Sasha alone . . .

LEBEDEV. It isn't proper to drop in on the bride before the ceremony. You should have been at the church a long time ago . . .

IVANOV. Pasha, please . . . .

*LEBEDEV, shrugging his shoulders, exits with
ZINAIDA SAVISHNA.*

SASHA. What's wrong with you?

IVANOV (*upset*). Shurochka, my angel.

SASHA. You're over-excited . . . What's happened?

IVANOV. My happiness, my darling, listen to me . . . Forget that you love me, focus all your attention on me and listen . . .

SASHA. Nikolay, don't frighten me . . . what is it?

IVANOV. Just now as I was getting dressed for the ceremony, I looked at myself in the mirror and the hair at my temples . . . was gray . . . Shurochka, we mustn't! Before it's too late, we mustn't, we mustn't! . . . (*Clutches at his head.*) We musn't! . . . Run out on me . . . (*Ardently.*) You're young, pure, you've got your life ahead of you, while I . . . gray at the temples, broken down, this sense of guilt, my past . . . We're no match . . . I'm no match for you! . . .

SASHA (*sternly*). Nikolay . . . how can you call this affection? . . . They've been waiting for you at the church a long time, and you rush over here to whine. None of this is new, I've already heard it and I'm sick and tired of it . . . Go to the church, don't keep people waiting.

IVANOV (*takes her hands*). I love you too much, you are too dear to me for me to dare stand in your way. I won't make you happy . . . I swear to God, I won't! . . . While it's not too late, call it off. It'll be the honorable and intelligent thing to do. I'll go home right now, and you can explain to your folks that there won't be any wedding . . . Tell them anything . . . (*Walks around in agitation.*) My God, my God, I sense, Shurochka, that you don't understand me . . . I'm old, my day is done, I'm covered in rust . . . the vigor of my life is spent forever, there's no future, my memories are gloomy ones . . . A feeling of guilt grows in me with every passing hour, chokes me . . . Doubts, forebodings . . . Something is going to happen . . . Shurochka, something going to happen . . . The dark clouds are gathering—I feel it.

SASHA (*restraining him by the hand*). Kolya, you're talking like a child . . . Calm down . . . You're heartsick and weary . . . Your heart has taken control over your healthy and powerful mind, but don't let it do what it wants, and exert your intelligence. Just consider: where are the clouds? What are you guilty of? And what do you want? You've run over here to tell me that you're old; perhaps, but then I'm no infant . . . And besides, what's old age got to do with it? If your dear head were suddenly covered with gray hairs, I would love you more than ever, because I know what made them gray . . . (*Weeps.*) Hold on, I'll be all right . . . (*Wipes away the tears.*)

IVANOV. Talk on, talk on . . .

SASHA. A feeling of guilt is wearing you out . . . Everyone, except father, tells me nothing but bad things about you. Yesterday I got an anonymous letter, warning me . . .

IVANOV. The doctor wrote it, the doctor . . . That man is persecuting me . . .

SASHA. It doesn't matter who wrote it . . . Everyone speaks ill of you, but I don't know another man who could be more honorable, more magnanimous and more sublime than you . . . In short, I love you, and where there is love there can be no wavering or niggling . . . I will be your wife and I want to be . . . It is decided and there can be no more arguments. I love you and will go with you wherever you want, beneath whatever clouds you like . . . Whatever may happen to you, wherever fate may drive you, I will be with you forever and wherever. I cannot understand my life any other way . . .

IVANOV (*walks around*). Yes, yes, Shurochka, yes . . . Actually, I'm talking drivel . . . I've infected myself with a psychosis, I've been tormenting myself and persecuting you with my tedium . . . In fact, I've got to become normal and soon . . . it's a matter of getting busy and living the way everyone does . . . Too many pointless ideas have built up in my mind . . . There's nothing unusual, wonderful, in my marrying you, but my paranoia is turning it into a major event, an apotheosis . . . Everything's normal and good . . . So, Shurochka, I'll be going . . .

SASHA. Go, and we'll be there presently . . .

IVANOV (*kisses her*). Forgive me, you must be sick and tired of me . . . Today we'll get married, and tomorrow down to business . . . (*Laughs.*) My splendor, my philosopher. I'm boasting about being old, while you, it would appear, have an older brain than mine by ten years . . . (*Stops laughing.*) Seriously, Shurochka, we are the same as all other people, and we will be as happy as everyone else . . . And if we're at fault, that will also be the same as everyone else . . .

SASHA. Go, go, it's time . . .

IVANOV. I'm going, I'm going . . . (*Laughs.*) How clumsy I am, what a child I am still, nothing but a dishrag . . . (*Goes to the door and bumps into Lebedev.*)

V I

IVANOV, SASHA, and LEBEDEV.

LEBEDEV. Come here, come over here . . . (*Takes Ivanov by the hand and leads him down to the footlights.*) Now look me straight in the eyes, look . . . (*Silently stares him in the eyes for a long time.*) Well, Christ be with you . . . (*Embraces him.*) Be happy and forgive me, my dear boy, for my evil thoughts . . . (*To Sasha.*) Shurochka, of course he's still young . . . Look at him, isn't that what you called a he-man? A real fighting man . . . Come over here, Shurka . . . (*Sternly.*) Come on . . .

SASHA *walks over to him.*

(*Takes Ivanov and Sasha by the hands, looks around.*) Listen, the way mother wants it, God bless her: give them no money, they don't need it. Shurka, you say that you (*mimics*) "don't need a penny." Principles, altruism, Schopenhauer[53] . . . It's all nonsense, and here's what I've got to say . . . (*Takes a deep breath.*) I've got a secret ten thousand stashed in the bank . . . (*looks around*), not a dog in this house knows about it . . . It's Granny's . . . (*Releasing their hands.*) Steal it! . . .

IVANOV. Good-bye . . . (*Laughs merrily and exits.*)

SASHA *follows him.*

LEBEDEV. Gavrila! . . . (*Exits and shouts through the doorway.*) Gavrila! . . .

V I I

DUDKIN and KOSYKH.

Both run in and quickly start to smoke.

KOSYKH. We've still got time for a quick smoke.

DUDKIN. He showed up to put the squeeze on them for the dowry . . . (*Excited.*) Attaboy . . . Honest to God, attaboy . . . Attaboy . . .

53　The German philosopher Arthur Schopenhauer (1788–1860) was lodged in the popular imagination as a paragon of systematic pessimism.

TABLEAU TWO

A drawing-room in the Lebedevs' house. Velvet furniture, an
antique bronze, family portraits. An upright piano, on it a violin,
a cello beside it. Lots of lights. A door left. At right a wide doorway
to a reception room, from which a bright light emanates. Back
and forth from the doors left and right scurry footmen with dishes,
platters, bottles, and so forth. At the rise of the curtain shouts are
heard from the reception room: "Bitter, bitter, sweeten it up . . ."[54]

I

AVDOTYA NAZAROVNA, KOSYKH, and DUDKIN come out
of the reception room with wineglasses.

A VOICE FROM THE RECEPTION ROOM: "To the health of the
groom's men . . ."

Music backstage plays a fanfare. Cries of "hoorah" and the sound
of chairs being pulled back.

AVDOTYA NAZAROVNA. What a sweet couple I hitched up . . . Lovey-dovey,
you could send 'em off to Moscow for show. He's handsome, well built,
educated, refined, dead sober, and Sashenka's a little angel, a little flower,
a little sweetie-pie . . . You won't find another match like that one . . .

In the reception room shouts of "hoorah."

KOSYKH

    (together). Hoo-ra-ah-ah . . .

DUDKIN

AVDOTYA NAZAROVNA (sings).

    Don't sit, Sashenka, don't sit still,
    Open the window, look out from the sill:
    Does the sun shine down in the yard from on high?
    Does my Kolyushka on his horse ride by?[55]

---

54 At traditional Russian weddings, the cry "Bitter! Bitter!" is meant for the bride and groom to kiss
and thus "sweeten things up."

55 A folksong connected with the wedding ritual, sung by the bridesmaids to the bride the day
before the ceremony, at the bridal shower.

That's how it is . . . I've been kicking up my heels, sinner that I am . . . There's nuthin' I can't do . . .

DUDKIN wants to say something, but cannot.

KOSYKH. It makes you jealous when you see other people's happiness . . . Avdotya Nazarovna, do me a favor, match me up with a bride . . . A bachelor's single life has gotten so repulsive that at home I walk from room to room and stare at the air vents . . . You hang around and hang around, and, before you know how the hell it happened, your life's gone by.

AVDOTYA IVANOVNA. How long have I've been saying I could marry you off in a minute . . .

KOSYKH. It's another story when you're married . . . You sit at home . . . it's warm . . . the lamp's lit, there's some sort of a kind of wife walking around . . . Honest to God, she walks around you, while you sit at the table with friends and play whist . . . You say: no trumps . . . pass . . . clubs . . . pass . . . hearts . . . pass . . . two hearts . . . pass. And finally a slam in hearts . . . It's all pass, pass, pass . . .

DUDKIN touches Avdotya Nazarovna's waist and clacks his tongue.

AVDOTYA NAZAROVNA. Why, you're so sozzled you think I'm some sweet young thing . . . Oh dear, the way people forget themselves in other people's houses. You can't make your tongue work, just like you was struck with paralysis.

A VOICE FROM THE RECEPTION ROOM. "To the health of Sergey Afanasyevich and Mariya Danilovna . . ."

The music plays a fanfare. Hoorah.

(She goes into the reception room and sings.)

> Pretty, pretty, mamma dear,
> Better than them all,
> And then he hung his little head
> Lower than them all.

She exits.

DUDKIN. Raisa Sergeevna, let's go . . .

KOSYKH. What makes you think I'm Raisa Sergeevna . . .

DUDKIN. I don't give a damn . . . let's go . . . give the footman two bits, I haven't got any change . . . (*Shouts.*) Grigory, hand it over . . .

KOSYKH. What are you yelling for? Who's this Grigory? (*Lights up a cigarette.*)

DUDKIN. I don't give a damn, let's go . . . Let's live it up . . . (*Shouts.*) Grigory, hand it over . . .

I I

The same and BORKIN (in a dresscoat with a nosegay).

BORKIN (*runs out of the reception room, out of breath*). How come they aren't serving champagne? (*To a footman.*) Serve some more champagne, and step lively . . .

FOOTMAN. There is no more champagne . . .

BORKIN. What the hell kind of system is this . . . Five bottles for a hundred people . . . It's an outrage.

> *KOSYKH walks over to the cello and pulls the bow across the strings.*

What kind of wine *is* left?

FOOTMAN. Table wine, sparkling wine . . .

BORKIN. At forty kopeks a bottle? (*To Kosykh.*) Ah, will you stop scraping away, please . . . (*To the footman.*) Well then, bring me some sparkling table wine, only step lively . . . Oof, I'm wrecked . . . I must have made a good twenty toasts at least . . . (*To Dudkin and Kosykh.*) Here goes, now we'll make a toast to the Count and Babakina as groom and bride. Listen, gents: shout hooray as loud as you can. Later on I'll explain this idea I got. So we'll have to have a drink to the idea . . . Let's go . . . (*Links arms with Kosykh and exits into the reception room with him.*)

DUDKIN (*follows him*). Semyon Nikolaevich . . . First let's have a drink at the buffet, and then in general . . .

The music plays a march from Boccaccio,[56] *cries of "Stop the music." The music is cut off.*

A VOICE FROM THE RECEPTION ROOM: *"To the health of the bride's auntie Margarita Savishna . . ."*

Fanfare.

I I I

SHABELSKY *and* LEBEDEV.

LEBEDEV (*entering from the reception room, with the Count*). Don't make trouble, please, give up all this malice or you'll simply get stomach ulcers, or maybe you think that you're actually Mephistopheles.[57] It's true . . . Put a fuse in your mouth, light it and breathe fire at people . . .

SHABELSKY. No, seriously, I want to commit something so low-down, so vulgar that not only I, but everyone will be nauseated. And I will commit it. Word of honor, I will . . . I've already told Borkin to announce my engagement today. (*Laughs.*) It'll be low-down, but it matches the times and the people. Everybody's a lowlife, so I'll be a lowlife too . . .

LEBEDEV. I'm fed up with you . . . Listen, Matvey, keep talking like that and they'll throw you in the, excuse the expression, booby hatch.

SHABELSKY. And why should a booby hatch be any worse than an escape hatch or a nuthatch? Do me a favor, throw me in there right now . . . You'd be doing me a favor . . .

LEBEDEV. You know what, my boy? Take your hat and go home . . . There's a wedding going on here, everybody's celebrating, while you caw . . . caw . . . like a crow. God be with you . . .

SHABELSKY. A wedding . . . everybody's celebrating . . . Something idiotical, barbaric . . . There's music, noise, drunkenness, just as if any Tom, Dick or Harry[58] was getting married. Up to now I considered you and Niko-

---

56 From Act I of the operetta by Franz von Suppé (1879).

57 The diabolical tempter and naysayer in Goethe's *Faust* and Gounod's opera of it: "the Spirit which denies."

58 In the original, "Tit Titych's wedding." Tit Titych Bruskin is a merchant in Ostrovsky's comedy *Your Binge, My Hangover* (1856).

lay to be men of culture, but today I see that you are both as *mauvais ton* as Zyuzyushka and Marfutka. This isn't a wedding, but a barroom.

LEBEDEV. A barroom, but it wasn't me that made it a barroom nor was it Nikolasha. It's customary . . . there's a custom—shout yourself hoarse, sing at the top of your lungs, and customs, my boy, are just like laws. *Mores leges imitantur*[59]—that's something else I remember from university. Let's not you and I try to change people.

> *SHABELSKY leans on the piano and sobs.*

Good grief . . . Matvey . . . Count . . . What's wrong with you? Dear heart, my dear fellow . . . my angel . . . Have I offended you? Well, forgive me, old hound that I am . . . Forgive a drunkard . . . Have some water . . .

SHABELSKY. Don't want any. (*Raises his head.*)

LEBEDEV. What are you crying for?

SHABELSKY. No reason, just because . . .

LEBEDEV. No, Matvey, don't lie . . . what for? What's the reason?

SHABELSKY. I just caught a glimpse of that cello and . . . and I remembered the little kike girl . . . .

LEBEDEV. Oh boy, what a time you picked to remember . . . May she rest in peace, bless her, but this is no time for reminiscing . . .

SHABELSKY. We would play duets together . . . A wonderful, superb woman . . . (*Leans on the piano.*)

> *VOICE FROM THE RECEPTION ROOM: "To the health of the ladies . . ."*
>
> *Fanfare and hooray.*

They're all vulgar little, petty little, insignificant little, untalented little creatures . . . I'm a grouch; like a coquette, I put on God knows what kind of airs, I don't believe a single word I say, but you have to agree, Pasha, everyone is trivial, insignificant, appallingly vulgar. I'm ready to love

---

59 Latin: Customs are the result of laws.

mankind before I die, but after all they're not humans, but subhumans, microcephali,[60] filth, soot . . .

LEBEDEV. Subhumans . . . It's all on account of stupidity, Matvey . . . They are stupid, but just you wait—their children will be intelligent . . . If the children aren't intelligent, wait for the grandchildren, it can't happen all at once . . . It'll take centuries . . .

SHABELSKY. Pasha, when the sun shines, it's cheerful even in a graveyard . . . when there's hope, then it's good even to be old . . . But I haven't got a hope, not one single one . . .

LEBEDEV. Yes, you're really in a bad way . . . You've got no children, no money, no occupation . . . Well, that's the way it goes, fate doesn't care a damn for you . . .

> *The music plays a waltz for half a minute, during which time*
> *LEBEDEV and SHABELSKY look as if they're talking to*
> *one another.*

SHABELSKY. We'll settle up in the next world. I'll go to Paris and take a look at my wife's grave. In my lifetime I've given away plenty, I squandered half my fortune, and therefore I have the right to ask. Besides, I'm asking it from a friend.

LEBEDEV (*dismayed*). Dear heart, I haven't got a penny . . . Word of honor, *omnia mea mecum porto.*[61] I live off my wife's groceries, no salary of my own. I did have a secret ten thousand stashed away, but this very day I promised it to Shurochka. (*Vigorously.*) Hold on, stop whining . . . Eureka[62] . . . I'll put in a word with Nikolay, and you'll be in Paris . . . Off to Paris . . . We'll deal you three thousand out of the ten. Four . . . You can travel around all year long, and then you'll come home and, who knows, you might have a grand-nephew . . . Ow . . . ow . . . Word of honor . . .

---

60 The scientific term for "pinheads," persons born with smaller than normal skulls.

61 Latin: I carry all I have on me.

62 Greek: I have found it! Attributed to Archimedes (ca. 287–212 B.C.), when he discovered the law of specific gravity.

I V

The same and IVANOV.

IVANOV (*entering from the reception room*). Uncle, are you here? My dear man, I'm smiling and laughing like the most good-natured of mortals . . . (*Laughs.*) I beg you most cordially to be merry, you smile too . . . Don't poison our merriment by looking down in the mouth. Take Pasha by the right arm, me by the left and we'll go have a drink to your health. I'm more happy and contented than I've been for a long time. Everything is fine, normal . . . wonderful . . . I've had a glass of champagne (*laughs*) and I think the whole world is spinning around with my happiness . . . (*Alarmed*). Matvey, have you been crying?

SHABELSKY. Yes . . .

IVANOV. What for?

SHABELSKY. I was remembering her . . . Sarra . . .

Pause.

IVANOV. Thank you for remembering her . . . She was a beautiful, exceptional woman . . . There are few women like her, Matvey . . .

LEBEDEV. She was attractive. It's true . . .

Pause.

IVANOV (*to the Count*). Do you remember that word I flung at her in the heat of the moment, when she came into my study? My God, we can remember it now calmly, but at the time I almost died of horror. I didn't sleep a wink for five whole days, didn't eat a single crumb, but after all she forgave me . . . She forgave me everything when she died. And I feel that even now she's looking down on us with her bright eyes and forgives us. She's sleeping in her grave now; we're alive, music is playing around us, and a time will come when we shall die, and people will say of us: now he's sleeping in the grave . . . I like this natural order and I like nature itself. (*Laughs.*) Everything is extraordinarily appealing to me today . . . Pasha, you are the most honest of men . . . I don't need to drink any more, but you, gentlemen, go and have a drink . . .

LEBEDEV. Count, a little cognac? Eh? What'll you have?

SHABELSKY. I don't care.

IVANOV. I won't drink myself, but I like to see other people drink. (*Taps his forehead.*) When you're happy, you're happy, but these last few days I've been so enervated that I thought I'd faint . . . A sort of whimper ran through my whole body . . . (*Laughs.*) Let's go.

V

The same and BORKIN.

BORKIN (*entering from the reception room*). Boy, where are you? They're looking for you. (*On seeing Ivanov.*) Ah . . . Go in quickly, they're calling for you . . . Although, wait just a minute, *Nicolas*, I have to let you in on a wonderful idea. For this idea, gents, you all, no matter how many you are, ought to pay at least a thousand rubles . . . Listen, *Nicolas*: let's you, me, Zinaida Savishna and Babakina, all of us, go shares in opening a stud farm . . . Are you willing?

LEBEDEV. Well . . . whist has turned this lad's wits.

IVANOV (*laughs*). Misha, you're a clever, capable fellow . . . I sincerely wish you well. Let bygones be bygones.

BORKIN (*moved*). Nikolay Alekseevich, you're a good man . . . I love you and am obliged to you for a great deal. Let's drink as brothers! . . .

IVANOV. That's not necessary, Misha, it's all nonsense . . . What matters is, be an honest, good man . . . Let bygones be bygones . . . You're at fault, I'm at fault, but we won't go into that. We are all people—human beings, all sinners, guilty in the sight of God. The only person who isn't sinful and is strong is someone with no red blood and no heart.

LEBEDEV (*to Ivanov*). Today you're talking like a German pastor. Drop this sermonizing . . . If we're going to drink, let's drink, but don't waste valuable time. Let's go, count . . . (*He links arms with the Count and Ivanov.*) Forward . . . (*Drinks.*) Let's the three of us polish off a bottle right now . . .

BORKIN (*barring their way*). Gents, I'm not joking about this stud farm . . . This is serious business . . . First of all, it's a money-making operation, and, second, it's needed . . . It'll turn a profit sooner than you think . . . First of all, there are lots of ponds, second, incredible watering holes, third, land for a farm.

V I

The same and BABAKINA.

BABAKINA (*enters from the reception room*). Now where is my escort? Count, how dare you leave me alone? There's no one for me to clink glasses with . . . Ooh, you're a disgrace! (*Strikes the Count on the arm with her fan.*)

SHABELSKY (*squeamishly*). Leave me alone . . . get away from me . . .

SHABELSKY, LEBEDEV, and IVANOV go into the
reception room.

BABAKINA (*dumbfounded*). What's going on? What right has he to do that? Thanks ever so much . . .

BORKIN. Marfunchik, I'll drop by tomorrow, we'll have a serious talk and come to terms . . . (*Breathing hard.*) In the initial phase we'll need quite a bit of money. If every shareholder invests about two thousand to start with, that'll be more than enough . . .

BABAKINA. How dare he? I treated him with affection, refinement, like a lady, and he goes—get away from me . . . What's going on? Is he off his rocker or what?

BORKIN (*impatiently*). Ah, that's not the point . . . He doesn't want to get married, the hell with him . . . There are things more important than being a count or getting married. Just think, Marfunchik; in the whole district we've only got one stud farm, and that one's about to be sold at auction. A terrible dearth of good horses is felt. If we go into business on a broad scale, we can order two or three good stallions . . .

BABAKINA (*angrily*). Stop it, quit it . . .

BORKIN. Just please let me hammer it home . . . (*Passionately.*) To do this we need no more than two or three thousand, that's all, and in five to ten years we'll make a fortune . . . First of all, lots of ponds, second, watering holes, third . . .

BABAKINA (*weeps*). All year long he'd come by three times a week, drink, eat, drive my horses around, and now, when his nephew is getting married to a rich girl, I'm not needed any more. Thanks ever so . . . Maybe I didn't give him any money, but after all I'm not a millionaire . . .

BORKIN (*clasping his hands*). I'm talking business to her, and she's raving . . . Wonderful people . . . Try and do business with people like this . . . Those guys refuse to listen, this one's raving like a loon . . . My friends, it's high time you cast off your indolence, apathy, you've got to get down to business! . . . How can you fail to notice that we're being ruined by indifferentism![63]

BABAKINA (*spitefully, through her tears*). Stop! . . . I'll scratch his eyes out! . . . Nobody's going to set foot in my house again . . . Not one of these scoundrels better dare poke his nose in! . . . (*Weeps.*)

BORKIN. Which means, my idea is going to go bust and the deal will fall through. (*Bitterly.*) Thank you, madam . . . I'm much obliged to you . . . You've got money for frippery and Madeira, but you won't spare a penny on a solid, profitable business deal . . . You bow down before the golden calf, Mammon . . .

BABAKINA tries to leave.

(*Takes her by the hand, which she yanks away; resolutely.*) Well, Marfa Yegorovna, in that case I've got another idea . . . Marfochka, if you begrudge two thousand, then let me make you a proposal . . . I am making you a proposal . . .

BABAKINA (*spitefully and surprised*). What?

BORKIN. I offer you my hand and heart. I love you passionately, madly. From the first time I saw you, I understood the meaning of my life . . . To love you and not to possess you is torture . . . the Spanish Inquisition . . .

BABAKINA. No, no, no, no . . .

BORKIN. True, I have enjoyed reciprocity in the fullest sense, but this did not satisfy me. I want legal wedlock, so I may belong to you forever . . . (*Takes her round the waist.*) I love and I suffer . . . Oh thou, who in thy grief complains in vain to God, o man . . .[64] What more can I tell you? Let's get hitched, and that's that . . . You've got plenty of money, it's nothing to do with you personally, I'm a businesslike, stable fellow . . . besides I'm in love . . .

BABAKINA. But after all, you . . . are always joking . . . You proposed last year too, and the next day you showed up and took it back.

---

63 The same unusual word that Medvedenko uses at the beginning of *The Seagull.*

64 A quotation from an ode by Lomonosov based on the Book of Job, which Khlestakov also quotes in Gogol's *Inspector General* in a similar courting scene.

BORKIN. Word of honor, it's no joke . . . Here I am on my knees. (*Gets on his knees.*) I love you to the point of madness . . .

A FOOTMAN *passes by.*

BABAKINA (*cries out*). Ah . . . the footman saw us . . .

BORKIN. Let everybody see us . . . I'll explain it all right away. (*Gets up.*)

BABAKINA. Only, Misha, I'm not going to give you a lot of money . . .

BORKIN. We'll see about that, we'll see . . . (*Kisses her.*) Marfunchik, my big-bassdrumchik . . . Let's start living . . . We'll have such racehorses that the winnings alone'll make me a fortune.

BABAKINA (*shouts*). Don't crumple my dress, my dress . . . It cost two hundred rubles . . .

V I I

BABAKINA, BORKIN, and AVDOTYA NAZAROVNA.

AVDOTYA NAZAROVNA (*comes out of the reception room and, on seeing the couple kissing, screams*). Ah . . .

BORKIN. Avdotya Nazarovna, greetings . . . The bridegroom and the bride . . . I'm getting married . . . (*He and Babakina go to the door to the reception room.*) Has she gone nuts? I say I'm getting married! . . . (*Kisses Babakina.*) There . . . now I don't need any shareholders, I can open the stud farm myself . . .

AVDOTYA NAZAROVNA. My sweetie-pie, my beauty . . . I wish you joy!

BORKIN. Wait, make way . . . (*Exits with Babakina into the reception room.*)

AVDOTYA NAZAROVNA (*following them, shouts*). Just take a look, good people, what a match I've made! . . . Take a look . . . (*Exits.*)

V I I I

LVOV (alone).

LVOV (*enters from the door at left; looks at his watch*). I'm a little late, but then they're probably all drunk, they won't notice . . . (*Goes to the door at right and his hands shake in agitation.*) The main thing is not to get excited . . .

(*Looks through the doorway.*) He's sitting next to her, smiling . . . He's cheated, robbed and smiles at his victim . . . (*Shrinks with agitation.*) The main thing is not to get excited . . . He sits happy, healthy, merry, and unpunished. There you have it, the triumph of virtue and truth . . . He didn't manage to rob one wife, so he tortured her and drove her to her grave . . . Now he's found another girl . . . He'll play the hypocrite with this one too, until he cleans her out and, once he's done that, lays her where poor Sarra is lying . . . The same old mercenary story . . .

VOICE FROM THE RECEPTION ROOM: *"To the health of*
all the guests . . ."

Fanfare and cheers.

He'll live beautifully to a ripe old age, and die with a clear conscience . . . No, I'll strip you bare, I'll tear the mask off you . . . You won't smile that way at me . . . When everybody learns what kind of bird you are, that'll wipe the grin off your face . . . (*Nervously buttons up his frock coat.*) I'm a decent person, and it's my duty to open people's eyes . . . (*Nervously clears his throat.*) I'll do my duty and tomorrow clear out of this damned district . . . (*Loudly.*) Nikolay Alekseevich Ivanov, I declare in the hearing of everyone present, that you are a bastard!

An uproar in the reception room.

I X

LVOV, IVANOV, SHABELSKY, LEBEDEV, BORKIN,
KOSYKH, then SASHA.

IVANOV. Why? why? Tell me: why? (*Enervated, he drops on to a sofa.*)

EVERYONE. Why?

LEBEDEV (*to Lvov*). Explain, for Christ's sake, why did you insult him? (*Clutches his head and walks around in agitation.*)

SHABELSKY (*to Ivanov*). Nicolas, Nicolas, for heaven's sake . . . Don't pay any attention . . . Rise above it . . .

BORKIN. My good sir . . . this is an outrage . . . I challenge you to a duel . . .

LVOV. Mister Borkin, I consider it degrading to talk to you, let alone fight you . . . But Mister Ivanov may receive satisfaction at any time, if he so desires.

SASHA (*enters from the reception room, staggers*). Why? Why did you insult him? Gentlemen, please, make him tell me . . . why?

LVOV. Aleksandra Pavlovna, I did not insult him without sufficient reason. I came here as a decent person to open your eyes, and I beg you to hear me out. I will tell all . . .

SASHA. What can you tell? what secrets do you know? That he drove his first wife to the grave? That's what everybody says. That he married me for the dowry and to keep from paying his debt to my mother? That's common knowledge in the whole neighborhood as well. Ah, these cruel, petty, insignificant people . . . (*To her husband.*) Nikolay, let's get out of here . . . (*Takes him by the arm.*)

LEBEDEV (*to Lvov*). I, as the host in my own house . . . as the father of my son-in-law . . . I mean, daughter, my good sir . . .

SASHA *screams loudly and drops on to her husband . . .*

Everyone runs over to Ivanov.

Holy saints, he's dead . . . water . . . a doctor . . .

SHABELSKY (*weeping*). Nicolas! Nicolas!

EVERYONE. Water, a doctor, he's dead . . .

Curtain

VARIANTS TO

Ivanov, First Version

Variants in the censor's copy for the performance at Korsh's Theatre in 1887.

ACT ONE

page 338 / *Replace*: **SHABELSKY** (*after a moment's thought*). I? First of all I'd go to Moscow and listen to gypsy music.
with: **SHABELSKY.** I? (*after a moment's thought*). First of all I'd go to Moscow, listen to gypsy music.

page 341 / *Replace*: (*comes out of the house in a hat and overcoat*)
with: (*comes quickly out of the house in a hat and overcoat*)

ACT TWO

page 352 / *After*: spoke ill of anyone . . . — Honorable, big-hearted, trustworthy, malleable as wax . . .

page 360 / *Before*: What's the matter — *the stage direction*: (*affectionately*)

ACT THREE

page 369 / *Before*: And suddenly, of all the bad luck — *the stage direction*: (*to the Count.*)

ACT FOUR

TABLEAU ONE

page 386 / *After*: *in a wet towel* — *limply.*

TABLEAU TWO

page 399 / *After*: we'll make a fortune . . . — It's a profitable deal and won't make us break a sweat.

page 401 / *After*: (*Exits*. — *Fanfare and cheers.*

page 402 / *After*: out of this damned district . . . — Well, it's high time . . .

The following changes were made in the 1888 revision for the production at the Alexandra Theatre in St. Petersburg, and are taken from the censor's copy.

ACT TWO

page 359 / *Replace*: Scenes VI and X
with:

V I

SASHA (*entering through the door at right with Ivanov*). Let's go into the garden . . . It's stuffy here.

IVANOV. Here's how things stand, Shurochka. I do nothing and think about nothing, and am weary in body and soul and brain . . . Day and night my conscience aches, I feel that I am profoundly at fault, but precisely where my fault lies, I do not understand . . . On top of that there's my wife's illness, lack of money, constant squabbling, gossip, noise . . . My house has become repulsive to me, and living in it is for me worse than torture . . . I don't know, Shurochka, what's come over me, but I tell you frankly, what's become unbearable is the company of my wife, who loves me . . . and such foul selfish thoughts creep into my head, which I couldn't even conceive of before . . .

Pause.

Vile and nasty . . . I'm pestering everyone with my tedium, Shurochka, forgive me, but I only can forget it for a moment while I'm talking to you, my friend . . . When I'm with you I'm like a dog barking at the bright sun. Shurochka, I've known you since you were born, I've always loved you, spoiled you . . . I would give a great deal to have a daughter like you right now . . .

SASHA (*joking through tears*). Nikolay Alekseevich, let's run away to America . . .

IVANOV. I feel too listless to cross this threshold, and you come up with America . . .

They walk to the entry to the garden.

Well, now, Shura, is it hard to go on living? I see, I see it all . . . This air doesn't suit you . . .

page 361 /   X

ANNA PETROVNA and LVOV enter from the door at right.

LVOV. Now why, I ask you, have we come here?

ANNA PETROVNA. Never mind, they'll be glad we came. There's no one here . . . I suppose, they're in the garden . . . Let's go into the garden . . .

They go into the garden.

ACT THREE

page 376 / *Replace*: Scene VII
with:

VII

IVANOV and SASHA.

IVANOV (*alarmed*). Shura, is that you?

SASHA. Yes, it is . . . Didn't you expect me? Why haven't you been to see us for so long?

IVANOV. Shura, for god's sake, this is indiscreet . . . Your coming here might have a dreadful effect on my wife . . .

SASHA. She won't see me . . . I came by the back door . . . I'll leave right away . . . I'm worried: are you all right? Why haven't you been to see us for so long?

IVANOV. My wife is offended enough without this, she's dying, and you come here . . . Shura, Shura! It's inconsiderate and . . . and inhuman!

SASHA. What's that got to do with me? You haven't been by for two weeks, don't answer my letters . . . I'm in agonies. It seemed to me that you were suffering unbearably here, ill, dead . . . Not a single night did I sleep a wink . . . I'll go right away. At least tell me: are you all right?

IVANOV. No . . . I've been tormenting myself, people torment me nonstop . . . I am simply at the end of my rope. You see, I'm trembling all over. And now on top of it you . . . Why did you come?

SASHA. Nikolay, this is cowardly!

IVANOV. It's as if we wish her death . . . How unwholesome this is, how abnormal! Shura, I'm so much at fault, so much at fault!

SASHA. Who wants her to die? What's the point of those dreadful words? Let her live another hundred years and may God grant she live even longer . . . But how are you at fault? Is it really your fault that you fell out of love with her? Is it your fault that you love me? Think nice thoughts . . .

IVANOV. I'm thinking . . .

SASHA. It's not your fault, it's the force of circumstance. Be brave . . . I promise you, my dear, here's my hand on it, good days will come and you will be happy.

IVANOV. Be brave . . . a time will come . . . in love, out of love—these are all platitudes. Hackneyed phrases, which are no help at all.

SASHA. I talk the way everybody does and I don't know how else to talk.

IVANOV. And this whole love affair of ours is commonplace, trite . . . "He was downhearted and had lost his bearings . . . She showed up, strong and bold in spirit, and offered him a helping hand. ." It's all right and appropriate only for novels, but in life—it's not right, not right . . . It's not what's needed . . . So you love me, my girl, you've lent a helping hand, and all the same I'm pathetic and helpless . . . And you yourself? You've set out with the goal of salvation, resurrection, doing a deed of valor, but look at yourself: you're trembling, pale, your eyes are filled with tears . . . No, Shura, you and I make bad heroes!

SASHA. You mean to go on like this today, I see . . . Goodbye! Listen to me: I love you and I'll follow you wherever you wish, even to Siberia, beneath whatever clouds you like . . . I'm ready to die for you. Whatever may happen to you, wherever fate may drive you, I shall be with you forever and wherever . . .

IVANOV. Yes, yes, yes . . . Talk, talk . . . (*Presses his face to her shoulder.*) I've been tormenting you, tormenting myself. Shurochka, in the name of all that's holy, take me away from here as soon as possible . . . Let me rest and forget myself for only a moment . . .

First revised version of the end of Act Three.

X

The same and LVOV.

LVOV (*enters and, on seeing Anna Petrovna, quickly addresses himself to her*). What's going on? (*Examines her face, to Ivanov.*) What's been going on with you just now?

IVANOV. God, It's all my fault! . . . all my fault!

LVOV. Anna Petrovna, what's wrong with you? (*To Ivanov.*) Just you wait! I swear by the honor which you do not possess, you shall pay for her! I'll put you through hell . . . I'll show you! . . .

IVANOV. It's all my fault, all my fault . . .

Curtain

ACT FOUR

VII

The same and IVANOV.

IVANOV enters; he is in a tailcoat and gloves; in evident agitation.

LEBEDEV. That's all we needed! What's going on! What are you doing here?

SASHA. Why are you here?

IVANOV. Sorry, friends, let me talk with Sasha in private . . .

LEBEDEV. It isn't proper for the groom to visit the bride. You should have been at the church a long time ago!

IVANOV. Sasha, I beg you . . .

> *LEBEDEV, shrugging his shoulders, ZINAIDA SAVISHNA,
> SHABELSKY, and BABAKINA leave.*

SASHA. What's wrong with you?

IVANOV (*getting excited*). Shurochka, my angel . . .

SASHA. You're over-excited . . . What's happened?

IVANOV. My happiness, my darling, listen to me . . . Forget that you love me, focus all your attention on me and listen . . .

SASHA. Nikolay, don't frighten me, what's wrong?

IVANOV. Just now as I was getting dressed for the ceremony, I looked at myself in the mirror, and my temples were . . . gray . . . Shurochka, we mustn't . . . Before it's too late, we mustn't . . . we musn't! (*Clasps her head.*) We mustn't! . . . Call it off! . . . (*Ardently.*) You're young, beautiful, pure, you have your whole life ahead of you, while I . . . gray at the temples, a broken-down wreck, this sense of guilt, the past . . . We're no match! . . . I'm no match for you!

SASHA (*sternly*). None of this is new, I've heard it all before, and I'm sick and tired of it . . . Go to the church, don't keep people waiting! . . .

IVANOV (*takes her hands*). I love you too much and you're too dear to me for
me to dare stand in your way. I won't make you happy . . . I swear to God,
I won't! . . . While it's not too late, call it off. It'll be the honorable and
intelligent thing to do. I'll go home right now, and you can explain to your
folks that there won't be any wedding . . . Tell them anything . . . (*Walks
around in agitation.*) My God, my God, I sense Shurochka, that you, don't
understand me . . . I'm old, my day is done, I'm covered in rust . . . the
vigor of my life is spent forever, there's no future, my memories are gloomy
ones. A feeling of guilt grows in me with every passing hour, chokes me . . .
Doubts, forebodings . . . Something is going to happen . . . Shurochka,
something is going to happen! The dark clouds are gathering, I feel it.

SASHA. What do you want then?

IVANOV. This very minute, without delay, call it off. Well? Make up your
mind. I beg you, I implore you . . . I see by your eyes you're wavering,
you're afraid to speak the truth. Understand, my dear, inexperienced girl:
what's speaking in you is not love, but the obstinacy of an honorable
nature. You set out with the goal, come what may, of resurrecting the
human being in me, saving me; you flattered yourself that you were performing a deed of valor . . . yes, yes, yes, don't deny it! Now you're ready to
give it up, but a false feeling prevents you. Don't ruin yourself! My joy,
listen to the man who loves you more than life itself! Well? Do you agree?
Do you?

Pause.

SASHA. If that's what you want, then please: let's put our wedding off a year.

IVANOV. No, no, right away . . . This very minute! Shurochka, I won't go, I
won't leave you in peace, until you call it off . . . Well? Do you agree? Tell
me! I'm dying with impatience . . . Do you?

Pause.

Do you?

SASHA nods her head.

You were even smiling with relief. (*Breathes easily.*) What a weight off my
shoulders . . . You're free, and now I'm free. You've taken a ten-ton weight
off my conscience.

Pause.

And so she called it off . . . If you hadn't agreed, this is what I would have . . . (*Pulls a revolver out of his pocket.*) I brought it along on purpose . . . (*Hides the revolver.*) It was easier for me to kill myself than to ruin your life . . . She called it off . . . Right? . . . I'm going home . . . I've got weak . . . And I'm ashamed and humiliated and . . . I feel myself to be pathetic . . . Which door should I leave by?

Pause.

Why are you silent? Dumbfounded. Yes . . . Don't you see, what a fuss . . . There's something I wanted to say just now and I forgot . . . (*Covers his face with his hands.*) I'm so ashamed!

SASHA. Good-bye, Nikolay Alekseevich. Forgive me! (*Goes to the door.*)

VIII

The same and LEBEDEV.

LEBEDEV (*running into Sasha in the doorway*). Wait, wait . . . I'll say two words. (*Takes Sasha and Ivanov by the hands, glancing around.*) Listen . . . This is what mother wants, God bless her. She's not giving any money and there's no need to. Shura, you say that you don't need a dowry. Principles, altruism, Schopenhauer . . . It's all nonsense, but here's what I've got to say to you. I've got ten thousand in a secret bank account (*glancing around*), not a dog in the house knows about it . . . It's Granny's . . . . Grab it! Only a condition is better than money: give Matvey three thousand or so.

SASHA. Let go! (*Pulls away her hand and, swaying a bit, exits.*)

LEBEDEV. What's the meaning of that dream?

IVANOV. There won't be a wedding, Pasha. It's over.

LEBEDEV. How's that again?

IVANOV. Tell the guests. There won't be a wedding. I asked her to call it off.

LEBEDEV. Is this philosophy or in truth?

IVANOV. The truth. I've leaving right now.

Pause.

My God, my God!

LEBEDEV. I don't understand a thing. In other words, I have to go and explain to the guests that there won't be a wedding. Is that right or what?

Pause.

God be your judge, Nikolasha, it's not for me to judge you, but excuse me, we're no longer friends. God bless you, wherever you go. We don't understand one another. Get out!

IVANOV. I should like, Pasha, that now God send me some kind of dreadful calamity—a disease, hunger, prison, disgrace . . . something of the kind. I can hardly stand on my feet, I'm exhausted . . . Another minute and I think I'll collapse. Where's Matvey? Let him take me home. And I love your Sasha, love her awfully . . . Now I love Sarra too. Poor woman! You remember that thing I called her, in the heat of the moment, when she came into my study? Then I nearly died of horror. For five days I didn't get a moment's sleep, didn't eat a single crumb. And after all she forgave me; forgave me everything when she died!

The GUESTS gather in the reception room.

I X

The same and SHABELSKY.

SHABELSKY (*enters*). Forgive me, Pavel, I won't come to the wedding. I'm going home. My spirits are low. Good-bye.

IVANOV. Wait. Matvey, let's go together. If only God would have sent me a disease or poverty . . . I think I would have come to life then.

VOICES IN THE RECEPTION ROOM: "The best man has arrived!"

LEBEDEV (*in a whisper, angrily*). Tell the guests yourself, I don't know how. How can I tell them! What shall I tell them? Gentlemen, for God's sake!

X

The same, BORKIN, and then LVOV.

BORKIN (*enters with a bouquet; he is in a tailcoat and with a best man's boutonniere*). Oof! Where is he? (*To Ivanov.*) Why did you come here? They've been waiting for you in the church a long time, and here you are spouting philosophy. What a comedian! Honest to God, a comedian! After all, you're not supposed to ride with the bride, but separately with me, and then I come back here to escort the bride to church. How can you possibly not know that! Positively a comedian!

LEBEDEV. Well, what shall I say? What words? Dying is easier . . . (*Pulls Ivanov by the arm.*) What are you standing there for? Go away! At least get out of our sight!

LVOV (*enters, to Ivanov*). Ah, there you are. (*Loudly.*) Nikolay Alekseevich Ivanov, I declare in the hearing of everyone that you are a bastard!

General confusion.

IVANOV (*clutching his head*). Why? Why? Tell me, why?

SHABELSKY (*to Ivanov*). *Nicolas! Nicolas*, for God's sake . . . Don't pay any attention. Rise above it.

BORKIN (*to Lvov*). My dear sir, this is an outrage! I challenge you to a duel.

LVOV. Mister Borkin, I consider it degrading not only to fight, but even to talk to you. Whereas Mister Ivanov, if he so desires, may receive satisfaction at any time.

SHABELSKY. Dear sir, I'll fight you!

IVANOV. Allow me, gentlemen. Let me speak. (*Shaking his head.*) I'm now capable of speaking and I know how to speak like a human being. His insult nearly killed me, but after all it's not his fault! Put yourself in his shoes! Isn't it ridiculous? He's known me for over two years, but there wasn't a single minute when he could understand what sort of man I am. For two years he conscientiously analyzed me, suffered, didn't give himself or me or my wife a moment's peace, and all the same I remain a riddle and a conundrum. I was not understood by my wife or my friends or my enemies or Sasha or these guests. Am I honorable or base? intelligent or stupid? healthy or psychotic? do I love or do I hate? No one knew, and everyone got lost guessing. Truth is as clear and simple as God's daylight, any little kid could understand it, but even intelligent people didn't understand me. Which means that there is no truth in me. Ah, how I understand myself now, how absurd I am to myself! How indignantly I responded to that "bastard"! (*Roars with laughter.*) Yes, I was honorable, bold, ardent, indefatigable, did the work of three men, knew how to get indignant, weep, love, hate, but to the point that I only wore myself out. Yes, I loved people, loved a woman, as none of you could, but my love lasted only two or three years, until my indolent soul wore out, until it began to seem to me that love is rubbish, that affection is cloying, that songs and passionate speeches are vulgar and stale. I was quick to get enthusiastic, shouldered burdens beyond my strength, but quickly grew weak, lost heart and from a hero turned into a pitiful coward. Now I'm thirty-five, I've accomplished less than a sparrow, but already I'm debilitated, exhausted, my insignificant achievements and sacrifices have crushed me; no faith, all passion spent, I am disappointed, sick. For what reason? My pretentions were heroic, but my strength was that of a worm. No discipline, no iron in my blood, no will-power. I'm pathetic, insignificant, and destructive as a moth. Woe to those people who respect and love such as I, put them on a pedestal, worship them, excuse them, sympathize! Unhappy those women who, instead of loving brave, magnanimous, strong, healthy, handsome men, love cowardly, feeble, whining, puny men! My younger self, the original Ivanov has begun to speak in me! I despise and hate myself. Don't look at me: I'm ashamed! Don't look! . . . Or are you waiting until I finish my speech? O, I know what to do with myself! There's good reason that I keep trembling with anger and hatred for myself. Just you wait, right now! (*Pulls out the revolver.*) Here I go! (*Shoots himself.*)

Curtain

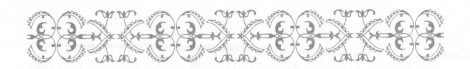

THE BEAR

As usual, Chekhov's earliest reference to his work-in-progress was offhandedly negative: "Having nothing better to do, I wrote a vapid little French-style vaudevillette (*vodevilchik*) entitled *The Bear* (letter to I. L. Leontyev-Shcheglov, February 22, 1888). No sooner had it appeared in print than Chekhov's friends insisted that he submit it to the dramatic censor and recommended the perfect actors to play it. The censor was not amused, disturbed by the "more than strange plot" and "the coarseness and indecency of the tone of the whole play," and forbade its production. He was overruled, however, by a superior in the bureaucracy, who, by suppressing a few lines, rendered it suitable for the public. The play had its premiere at Korsh's Theatre in Moscow on October 28, 1888, with the clever ingenue Nataliya Rybchinskaya as Popova and Chekhov's boyhood friend Nikolay Solovtsov as Smirnov. Solovtsov, a tall, ungainly fellow with a stentorian voice, had probably been in Chekhov's mind for the role of the bear as he wrote it.

The Bear was, from the start, a runaway success: the audience roared with laughter and interrupted the dialogue with applause, and the newspaper praised it to the skies. Theaters all over Russia added it to their repertories and the best Russian actors clamored to play in it. In Chekhov's lifetime it brought in regular royalties, and it has been constantly revived on both professional and amateur stages all over the world ever since.

The plot updates Petronius's ancient Roman tale of the Widow of Ephesus, which Christopher Fry later turned into the one-act play *A Phoenix Too Frequent.* That ribald fable tells of a widow whose grief for a dead husband melts under the ardor of the soldier guarding the corpse of a crucified criminal. She eventually colludes with him to replace the body stolen during their lovemaking with her own deceased spouse. Chekhov substitutes for the corpse the carriage horse Toby, as a token of the widow's transference of affection.

The Bear's comedy derives from the characters' lack of self-knowledge. The widow Popova fancies herself inconsolably bereaved, a fugitive from the world, while Smirnov takes himself to be a misogynist to the core. They both are *alazons* in the classic sense: figures made ludicrous by pretending to be more than they actually are. If the languishing Popova is based on the Petronian source, Smirnov is a descendant of Molière's Alceste, professing a hatred of society's hypocrisy but succumbing to a woman who exemplifies that society. The two poseurs come in conflict, and the roles reverse: the inconsolable relict snatches up a pistol and, like any case-hardened bully, insists on a duel, while the gruff woman-hater finds himself incapable of facing down his female opponent. (It was the improbable duel that most outraged the censors.) It is in the cards that the dimpled widow and the brute in muddy boots will fall into one another's arms by the final curtain.

Nevertheless, the comedy is also grounded in the harsh facts of Russian rural life: lack of money. Like *Ivanov*, the play begins with a landowner having to pay the interest on a loan and not having the money to do so. Smirnov's boorishness is prompted as much by his desperate fear at losing his estate by defaulting on his mortgage as Ivanov's funk is by his inability to pay his workmen or his creditors. This financial stress will remain a constant in Chekhov's plays, motivating the basic action of *Uncle Vanya* and culminating in the overriding themes of lending and loss in *The Cherry Orchard*.

THE BEAR

Медведь

A Joke in One Act

(dedicated to N. N. Solovtsov)[1]

CHARACTERS

YELENA IVANOVNA POPOVA, *a young widow with dimples in her cheeks, a landowner*

GRIGORY STEPANOVICH SMIRNOV,[2] *a middle-aged landowner*

LUKA, *Popova's man-servant, an old fellow*

A drawing-room in Popova's manor house.

I

POPOVA (in deep mourning, her eyes fixed on a portrait photograph) and LUKA.

LUKA. This won't do, mistress . . . You're running yourself down is all . . . The housemaid and the cook are out picking berries, every living thing rejoices, even the tabby cat, she knows how to have fun, running around outside, tracking dicky birds, while you sit inside the livelong day, like in a nunnery, and don't have no fun. Honest to goodness! Just figure, a year's gone by now, and you ain't set foot outside the house!

POPOVA. And I never shall . . . What for? My life is already over. He lies in the grave, I've buried myself within these four walls . . . We're both dead.

---

1 Nikolay Nikolaevich Solovtsov (Fyodorov, 1857–1902), a schoolmate of Chekhov's in Taganrog, who became an actor at the Alexandra Theatre in St. Petersburg 1882 to 1883, and was actor and director at Korsh's Theatre in Moscow from 1887 to 1889. He staged Chekhov's play *The Wood Goblin* at Abramova's Theatre in 1889–1890.

2 An ironic name, from *smirny* (peaceful, serene).

LUKA. There you go again! And I shouldn't listen, honestly. Nikolay Mikhailovich is dead, that's how it is with him, it's God's will, rest in peace . . . You
done your bit of grieving—and that's that, time to get on with your life.
Can't go on weeping and wearing black for the next hundred years. In my
time my old woman died on me too . . . So what? I grieved a bit, I cried off
and on for a month, and then I was over her, but if I was to weep and wail
a whole lifetime, it'd be more than the old girl was worth. (*Sighs.*) You've
neglected all the neighbors . . . You don't go visiting yourself, and you
don't invite nobody here. We're living, if you don't mind my saying so, like
spiders,—we never see the light of day. The footmen's liveries have been
et up by mice . . . It'd be a different matter if there wasn't no decent people, but after all the county's packed with ladies and gents . . . In Ryblovo
there's a regiment posted, officers like sugar plums, you can't get your fill
of looking at 'em! And in camp not a Friday goes by without a ball and, just
figure, every day the brass band plays music . . . Eh, mistress dearie! Young,
beautiful, the picture of health—all you need is to live and enjoy yourself
. . . Beauty's not a gift that lasts forever, y' know! Ten years from now or so,
you'll be in the mood for preening and dazzling the officer gents, but it'll
be too late.

POPOVA (*resolutely*). I beg you never to talk to me about that sort of thing!
You know, from the day Nikolay Mikhailovich died, life has lost all meaning for me. It may look to you as if I'm alive, but looks are deceiving! I have
taken an oath not to remove my mourning until I'm laid in my grave, nor
to see the light of day . . . Do you hear me? Let his spirit see how much I
love him . . . Yes, I know, you're well aware that he was nothing but unjust
to me, cruel and . . . and even unfaithful, but I shall be faithful to the day
I die and show him that I know how to love. There, from the other side of
the grave, he will see that I am just as I was before he died . . .

LUKA. Better'n this kind o' talk, you should take a turn in the garden, or else
have 'em hitch up Toby or Paladin and pay a call on the neighbors . . .

POPOVA. Oh! . . . (*Weeps.*)

LUKA. Mistress! . . . Dear lady! . . . What's wrong? God bless you!

POPOVA. He was so fond of Toby! He always rode him over to the Korcha-
gins and the Vlasovs. He sat a horse so wonderfully well! Such a graceful
expression when he tugged at the reins with all his might! Remember?
Toby, Toby! Tell them to give him an extra portion of oats.

LUKA. Yes, ma'am!

The doorbell rings insistently.

POPOVA (*startled*). Who's that? Tell them I am in to nobody!

LUKA. Yes indeed, ma'am! (*Exits.*)

I I

POPOVA (alone).

POPOVA (*looking at the photograph*). You see, *Nicolas,* how I know how to love and forgive . . . My love will flicker out when I do, when my poor heart ceases to beat. (*Laughs, through tears.*) And aren't you ashamed? I'm a good girl, a faithful little wife, I've locked myself up in a fortress and will be true to you to the day I die, while you . . . aren't you ashamed, you chubby thing? You cheated on me, made scenes, left me on my own for whole weeks at a time . . .

I I I

POPOVA and LUKA.

LUKA (*enters, anxiously*). Mistress, there's somebody asking for you. Wants to see you . . .

POPOVA. But didn't you tell him that I am in to nobody since the death of my husband?

LUKA. I told 'im, but he don't want to listen, he says it's very urgent business.

POPOVA. I am *in—to—no—bo—dy!*

LUKA. I told him, but . . . some kind o' maniac . . . he cusses and shoves right into the room . . . he's there in the dining room right now . . .

POPOVA (*irritated*). All right, show him in . . . How uncouth!

LUKA exits.

How tiresome these people are! What do they want from me? Why do they have to disturb my serenity? (*Sighs.*) No, it's obvious, I really shall have to get me to a nunnery . . . (*Musing.*) Yes, a nunnery . . .

IV

POPOVA, LUKA, and SMIRNOV.

SMIRNOV (*entering, to Luka*). Numbskull, you're too fond of hearing yourself talk . . . Jackass! (*On seeing Popova, with dignity.*) Madam, may I introduce myself: retired lieutenant of artillery, landowner Grigory Stepanovich Smirnov! Forced to disturb you on the most urgent business . . .

POPOVA (*not offering her hand*). What can I do for you?

SMIRNOV. Your late husband, whom I had the honor to know, left two I.O.U.s owing me twelve hundred rubles. Because tomorrow my interest payment to the bank[3] falls due, I would ask you, madam, to repay me the money today.

POPOVA. Twelve hundred . . . But what was my husband in debt to you for?

SMIRNOV. He bought oats from me.

POPOVA (*sighing, to Luka*). Now don't you forget, Luka, to tell them to give Toby an extra portion of oats.

LUKA exits.

(*To Smirnov.*) If Nikolay Mikhailovich still owes you money, why, it stands to reason, I shall pay; but, please forgive me, I have no cash on hand today. The day after tomorrow my foreman will be back from town, and I'll ask him to pay you what's owing, but in the meantime I cannot comply with your request . . . Besides, today is exactly seven months since my husband died, and the way I'm feeling now I am completely indisposed to deal with financial matters.

SMIRNOV. And the way I'm feeling now if I don't pay the interest tomorrow, I'll be up the creek good and proper. They'll foreclose on my estate!

POPOVA. The day after tomorrow you'll get your money.

SMIRNOV. I don't need the money the day after tomorrow, I need it now.

POPOVA. Excuse me, I cannot pay you today.

SMIRNOV. And I cannot wait until the day after tomorrow.

---

3 The Gentry Land Bank, established by the government in the 1880s to offer financial assistance to impecunious landowners.

POPOVA. What's to be done, if I don't have it at the moment!

SMIRNOV. In other words, you can't pay up?

POPOVA. I cannot . . .

SMIRNOV. Hmm! . . . Is that your last word?

POPOVA. Yes, my very last.

SMIRNOV. Your last! Positively?

POPOVA. Positively.

SMIRNOV. Thank you very much indeed. We'll just make a memo of that, shall we? (*Shrugs his shoulders.*) And people expect me to be cool, calm, and collected! Just now on the road I ran into the tax collector and he asks: "Why are you always losing your temper, Grigory Stepanovich?" Well, for pity's sake, how can I keep from losing my temper? I need money like crazy . . . I rode out yesterday morning almost at dawn, dropped in on everyone who owes me money, and not a single one of them paid me! I'm dog-tired, spent the night in some godforsaken hole—in a kike tavern[4] next to a keg of vodka . . . Finally I show up here, forty miles from home, I hope to get something, and they greet me with "the way I'm feeling now!" How can I keep from losing my temper?

POPOVA. I believe my words were clear: when the foreman returns from town, you'll get it.

SMIRNOV. I didn't come to the foreman, but to you! What the blue blazes, pardon the expression, do I need with your foreman!

POPOVA. Forgive me, my dear sir, I am not accustomed to that peculiar expression and that tone of voice. I will not listen to you any more. (*Exits quickly.*)

V

SMIRNOV (alone).

SMIRNOV. Say pretty please! "The way I'm feeling now . . ." Seven months ago her husband died! But do I have to pay the interest or don't I? I ask you:

---

4 In Western Russia, many rural inns were run by Jews, and a standard anti-Semitic joke was that they were flea-infested clip joints. A "kike tavern" was a figure of speech for "chaos, bedlam."

do I have pay the interest or don't I? So, you had a husband die on you, there's some way you're feeling now, and the rest of the double-talk . . . the foreman's gone off somewhere, damn him to hell, but what do you expect me to do? Fly away from my creditors in a hot-air balloon or what? Or run off and bash my skull against the wall? I ride over to Gruzdyov's—he's not at home. Yaroshevich is in hiding, I have a fatal falling-out with Kuritsyn and almost throw him out a window, Mazutov[5] has got the trots, and this one has a way she's feeling. Not one of the lousy deadbeats will pay up! And all because I've been too indulgent to them, I'm a soft touch, a pushover, a sissy! I'm too delicate with them! Well, just you wait! You'll learn who I am! I won't let you pull anything over on me, damn it! I'll stay here, I'll stick around until she pays up! Brr! . . . I'm really angry today, really angry! Anger is making the thews in my thighs quiver, I have to catch my breath . . . Fooey, my God, I'm even coming over faint! (*Shouts.*) You there!

V I

SMIRNOV and LUKA.

LUKA (*enters*). What's wrong?

SMIRNOV. Get me some kvas[6] or water!

LUKA exits.

No, what kind of logic is that! A man needs money like crazy, he's on the verge of hanging himself, and she won't pay because, don't you see, she's indisposed to deal with financial matters! . . . Honest-to-God weaker-sex logic, all her brains are in her bustle! That's why I never liked, still do not like to talk to women. For me it's easier to sit on a keg of gunpowder than talk to a woman. Brr! . . . I've got goosebumps crawling up and down my skin—that's how much that petticoat has enraged me! All I need is to see in the distance some "weaker vessel" and my calves start to cramp with anger. It makes you want to call for help.

---

5 Joke names: Gruzdyov, from *gruzd*, a kind of mushroom; Kuritsyn, from *kuritsa*, hen; Mazutov, from *mazut*, fuel oil.

6 A refreshing drink of low alcohol content, made from fermented black bread and malt, much preferred to beer by the peasantry. Lopakhin orders it in Act One of *The Cherry Orchard*.

VII

SMIRNOV and LUKA.

LUKA (*enters and serves water*). The mistress is sick and won't see anyone.

SMIRNOV. Get out!

LUKA exits.

Sick and won't see anyone! Then don't, don't see me . . . I'll sit in this spot here until you hand over the money. You can be sick for a week, and I'll sit here for a week . . . You can be sick for a year—and I'll stay a year . . . I'll have what's due me, my fair lady! You don't get to me with your mourning weeds and dimples on your cheeks . . . We know the meaning of those dimples! (*Shouts out the window.*) Semyon, unhitch the horses! We'll be here for a while! I'm sticking around! Tell 'em in the stable to give the horses oats! Again, you swine, you've got the left trace-horse[7] tangled up in the reins! (*Mimics him.*) "It makes no never mind . . ." I'll give you no never mind! (*Walks aways from the window.*) Disgusting . . . the heat's unbearable, nobody pays what they owe, I got no sleep last night, and now this petticoat in mourning with the way she's feeling now . . . My head aches . . . Should I have some vodka or what? I suppose a drink'll be all right . . . (*Shouts.*) You there!

LUKA (*enters*). What d'you want?

SMIRNOV. Get me a glass of vodka!

LUKA exits.

Oof! (*Sits and looks around.*) Got to admit, I'm a pretty picture! Covered with dust, boots muddy, haven't washed, or combed my hair, straw on my vest . . . I'll bet the little lady took me for a highway robber. (*Yawns.*) It is a bit uncouth to show up in a drawing-room looking like this, well, never mind . . . I'm not here as a guest, but as a bill collector, there's no rules of etiquette for bill collectors . . .

LUKA (*enters and serves vodka*). You're taking a lot of liberties, sir . . .

SMIRNOV (*angrily*). What?

LUKA. I . . . I didn't mean . . . I strictly . . .

---

7 See *Uncle Vanya*, note 59.

SMIRNOV. Who do you think you're talking to? Hold your tongue!

LUKA (*aside*). Jumped right down my throat, the monster . . . Why the hell did he have to show up?

LUKA exits.

SMIRNOV. Oh, I really am angry. So angry that, I think I could grind the whole world into dust . . . I'm even feeling faint . . . (*Shouts.*) You there!

VIII

POPOVA and SMIRNOV.

POPOVA (*enters, averting her eyes*). Dear sir, during my lengthy isolation I have grown unaccustomed to the human voice and I cannot bear shouting. I earnestly beg you not to disturb my peace!

SMIRNOV. Pay me my money and I'll go.

POPOVA. I told you in plain Russian: I don't have any loose cash at the moment, wait until the day after tomorrow.

SMIRNOV. I also had the honor of telling you in plain Russian: I don't need the money the day after tomorrow, but today. If you don't pay me today, then tomorrow I shall have to hang myself.

POPOVA. But what am I supposed to do, if I haven't got any money? How very peculiar!

SMIRNOV. So you won't pay me right this minute? No?

POPOVA. I can't . . .

SMIRNOV. In that case I shall stay sitting here until I get it . . . (*Sits.*) The day after tomorrow you'll pay up? Wonderful! I shall sit until the day after tomorrow just like this. Look, see how I'm sitting . . . (*Jumps up.*) I ask you: do I have to pay the interest tomorrow or not? . . . Or do you think I'm joking?

POPOVA. Dear sir, I ask you not to shout! This isn't a stable!

SMIRNOV. My question was not is this a stable, but do I need to pay the interest tomorrow or not?

POPOVA. You don't know how to behave in the presence of a lady!

SMIRNOV. Yes, ma'am, I do know how to behave in the presence of a lady!

POPOVA. No, you don't! You are an ill-mannered, boorish fellow! Respectable people don't talk to ladies this way!

SMIRNOV. Ah, this is wonderful! How would you like me to talk to you? In French or something? (*Maliciously, lisping.*) *Madame*, shay voo pree[8] . . . I'm absolutely delighted that you won't pay me my money . . . Ah, *pardon*, that I'm disturbing you! Isn't the weather lovely today! And how that mourning becomes you! (*Bowing and scraping.*)

POPOVA. That's not witty, it's rude.

SMIRNOV (*mimics her*). That's not witty, it's rude! I don't know how to behave in the presence of a lady! Madam, in my lifetime I've seen more women than you've had hot dinners! Three times I fought a duel with firearms over a woman, I've walked out on a dozen women and ten have walked out on me! Yes, ma'am! There was a time when I played the fool, got all sticky-sentimental, talked the sweet-talk, laid on the soft-soap, clicked my heels . . . I loved, suffered, bayed at the moon, went spineless, melted, turned hot and cold . . . I loved passionately, madly, you-name-it-ly, damn it, squawked like a parrot about women's rights, spent half my fortune on hearts and flowers, but now—thanks but no thanks! You won't lead me down the garden path again! Enough is enough! Black eyes, flashing eyes,[9] crimson lips, dimpled cheeks, the moon, low whispers, heavy breathing—for all this, madam, I now don't give a tinker's dam! Present company excepted, but all women, great and small, are phonies, show-offs, gossips, trouble-makers, liars to the marrow of their bones, vain, fussy, ruthless, their reasoning is a disgrace, and as for what's in here (*slaps his forehead*), forgive my frankness, a sparrow could give ten points to any thinker in petticoats! You gaze at some romantic creature: muslin, moonshine, a demi-goddess, a million raptures, but take a peep into her soul—a common- or garden-variety crocodile! (*Grabs the back of a chair, the chair creaks and breaks.*) But the most outrageous thing of all is that this crocodile for some reason imagines that its masterpiece, its prerogative and monopoly is the tender passion! Damn it all to hell, hang me upside-down on this nail—does a woman really know how to love anyone other than a lapdog? In love she only knows how to whimper and snivel! While a man suffers and sacrifices, all of her love is

---

8 Mispronunciation of French, *je vous prie*, "I beg you."

9 *Dark eyes, flashing eyes*, the first words of "Ochi chyornye," a well-known Russian folksong.

expressed only in swishing the train on her dress and trying to lead him more firmly by the nose. You have the misfortune to be a woman, you probably know what a woman's like from your own nature. Tell me on your honor: have you ever in your life seen a woman be sincere, faithful and constant? You have not! Faithfulness, constancy,—that's only for old bags and freaks! You'll sooner run into a cat with horns or a white blackbird than a constant woman!

POPOVA. I beg your pardon, but, in your opinion, just who is faithful and constant in love? Not the man?

SMIRNOV. Yes, ma'am, the man!

POPOVA. The man! (*Malicious laugh.*) The man is faithful and constant in love! Do tell, now there's news! (*Heatedly.*) What right have you to say that! Men faithful and constant! If it comes to that, let me tell you that of all the men I've known and still know, the very best was my late husband . . . I loved him passionately, with every fiber of my being, as only a young, intelligent woman can love: I gave him my youth, happiness, life, my fortune, breathed through him, worshiped him like an idolator, and . . . and—then what? This best of men cheated me in the most shameless manner on every occasion! After his death I found in his desk a whole drawer full of love letters, and during his lifetime—horrible to remember!—he would leave me alone for weeks at a time, make advances to other women before my very eyes and betrayed me, squandered my money, ridiculed my feelings . . . And, despite all that, I loved him and was faithful to him . . . What's more, now that he's dead, I am still faithful and constant to him. I have buried myself for ever within these four walls, and until my dying day I shall not remove this mourning . . .

SMIRNOV (*a spiteful laugh*). Mourning! . . . I don't understand who you take me for? Don't I know perfectly well why you wear that black masquerade outfit and have buried yourself within these four walls? Of course I do! It's so mysterious, so romantic! Some young cadet or bob-tailed poet will be walking by the estate, he'll peer into the window and think: "Here lives the mysterious Tamara,[10] who for love of her husband has buried herself within four walls." We know these tricks!

---

10 Russian literature knows several Tamaras: a famous queen of Georgia (1184–1213); a Georgian Lorelei or wandering spirit in Lermontov's poem "Tamara"; and the Georgian maiden who flees to a nunnery to avoid the Demon's love, in Anton Rubinstein's opera from Lermontov, *The Demon* (1871).

POPOVA (*flaring up*). What? How dare you say such things to me!

SMIRNOV. You've buried yourself alive, but look, you haven't forgot to powder your face!

POPOVA. How dare you talk to me that way?

SMIRNOV. Please don't raise your voice to me, I'm not your foreman! Allow me to call things by their rightful names. I'm not a woman and I'm used to expressing opinions straight out! So be so kind as not to raise your voice!

POPOVA. I'm not raising my voice, you're raising your voice! Be so kind as to leave me in peace!

SMIRNOV. Pay me the money and I'll go.

POPOVA. I haven't got any money!

SMIRNOV. No, ma'am, hand it over!

POPOVA. Just out of spite, you won't get a kopek! You can leave me in peace!

SMIRNOV. I don't have the pleasure of being either your spouse or your fiancé, so please don't make scenes for my benefit. (*Sits.*) I don't care for it.

POPOVA (*panting with anger*). You sat down!

SMIRNOV. I sat down.

POPOVA. I insist that you leave!

SMIRNOV. Hand over the money . . . (*Aside.*) Ah, I am really angry! Really angry!

POPOVA. I do not choose to have a conversation with smart-alecks! Please clear out of here!

Pause.

You aren't going? No?

SMIRNOV. No.

POPOVA. No?

SMIRNOV. No!

POPOVA. Very well then! (*Rings.*)

IX

The same and LUKA.

POPOVA. Luka, escort this gentleman out!

LUKA (*walks over to Smirnov*). Sir, please leave when you're asked! There's nothing doing here . . .

SMIRNOV (*leaping up*). Shut up! Who do you think you're talking to? I'll toss you like a salad!

LUKA (*grabs his heart*). Heavenly fathers! . . . Saints alive! . . . (*Falls into an armchair.*) Oh, I feel faint, faint! I can't catch my breath!

POPOVA. Where's Dasha? Dasha! (*Shouts.*) Dasha! Pelageya! Dasha! (*Rings.*)

LUKA. Ugh! They've all gone out to pick berries . . . There's no one in the house . . . Faint! Water!

POPOVA. Will you please clear out of here!

SMIRNOV. Would you care to be a little more polite?

POPOVA (*clenching her fists and stamping her feet*). You peasant! You unlicked bear! Upstart! Monster!

SMIRNOV. What? What did you say?

POPOVA. I said that you're a bear, a monster!

SMIRNOV (*taking a step*). Excuse me, what right have you got to insult me?

POPOVA. Yes, I am insulting you . . . well, so what? You think I'm afraid of you?

SMIRNOV. And do you think because you're a member of the weaker sex, you have the right to insult people with impunity? Really? I challenge you to a duel!

LUKA. Saints in heaven! . . . Holy saints! . . . Water!

SMIRNOV. We'll settle this with firearms!

POPOVA. Just because you've got fists like hams and bellow like a bull, you think I'm afraid of you? Huh? You're such an upstart!

SMIRNOV. I challenge you to a duel! I brook no insults and therefore I'll overlook the fact that you are a woman, a frail creature!

POPOVA (*trying to shout over him*). You bear! You bear! You bear!

SMIRNOV. It's high time we rid ourselves of the prejudice that only men have to pay for insults! Equal rights are equal rights, damn it all! I challenge you to a duel!

POPOVA. You want to settle it with firearms? As you like!

SMIRNOV. This very minute!

POPOVA. This very minute! My husband left some pistols behind . . . I'll bring them here at once . . . (*Hurriedly goes and returns.*) I shall take great pleasure in pumping a bullet into your thick skull! You can go to hell! (*Exits.*)

SMIRNOV. I'll smoke her like a side of bacon! I'm no snotnose kid, no sentimental puppy, female frailty has no effect on me!

LUKA. Dear, kind master! . . . (*Gets on his knees.*) Do me the favor, pity me, an old man, clear out of here! You've skeered me to death, and now you're fixing to shoot up the place!

SMIRNOV (*not listening to him*). Shooting at one's fellow human, that's what I call equality, women's rights! That puts both sexes on an equal footing! I will plug her on principle! But can you call her a woman? (*Mimics.*) "Damn you to hell . . . I'll pump a bullet into your thick skull"? What's that all about? She got flushed, her eyes blazed . . . She accepted my challenge! Honest to God, it's the first time in my life I've ever seen . . .

LUKA. For heaven's sake, go away! I'll have prayers said for you forever!

SMIRNOV. Now that's a woman! That's something I can understand! An honest-to-God woman! Not a sourpuss, not a limp rag, but flames, gunpowder, a rocket! I'm almost sorry I'll have to kill her!

LUKA (*weeps*). Master . . . my dear sir, go away!

SMIRNOV. I actually like her! I really do. Even if she didn't have dimples in her cheeks, I'd like her! Even willing to forgive her the debt . . . and my anger's gone . . . Wonderful woman!

X

The same and POPOVA.

POPOVA (*enters with pistols*). Here they are, the pistols . . . But, before we fight, you will be so kind as to show me how to shoot . . . Never in my life have I held a pistol in my hands.

LUKA. Save us, Lord, and be merciful . . . I'll go see if I can find the gardener and the coachman . . . How did this disaster land on our head . . . (*Exits.*)

SMIRNOV (*glancing at the pistols*). You see, there are different types of pistol . . . There are special dueling pistols, the Mortimer, with percussion caps. What you've got here are revolvers of the Smith and Wesson make, triple action with an extractor, battlefield accuracy . . . Splendid pistols . . . Cost at least ninety rubles the brace . . . You have to hold a pistol like this . . . (*Aside.*) Her eyes, her eyes! An incendiary woman!

POPOVA. This way?

SMIRNOV. Yes, that way . . . Whereupon you raise the cocking piece . . . then take aim like so . . . Head back a bit ! Extend your arm, in the appropriate manner . . . That's it . . . Then with this finger squeeze this doodad here—and that's all there is to it . . . Only rule number one is: keep a cool head and take your time aiming . . . Try not to let your hand shake.

POPOVA. Fine . . . It's not convenient to shoot inside, let's go into the garden.

SMIRNOV. Let's go. Only I warn you that I shall fire into the air.

POPOVA. Of all the nerve! Why?

SMIRNOV. Because . . . because . . . It's my business, that's why!

POPOVA. You're chickening out? Are you? Ah-ah-ah-ah! No, sir, no worming out of it! Please follow me! I won't rest until I've blown a hole in your head . . . that very head I hate so much! Are you chickening out?

SMIRNOV. Yes, I am.

POPOVA. That's a lie! Why don't you want to fight?

SMIRNOV. Because . . . because I . . . like you.

POPOVA (*malicious laugh*). He likes me! He dares to say that he likes me! (*Points to the door.*) You may go.

SMIRNOV (*silently puts down the revolver, takes his cape, and goes; near the door he stops, for half a minute both look silently at one another; then he says, irresolutely crossing to Popova*). Listen here . . . Are you still angry? . . . I'm damnably infuriated as well, but, don't you understand . . . How can I put this . . . The fact is, you see, the way the story goes, speaking for myself . . . (*Shouts.*) Well, is it really my fault that I like you? (*Grabs the back of a chair, the chair creaks and breaks.*) What the hell sort of breakaway furniture have you got! I like you! Understand? I . . . I am practically in love!

POPOVA. Get away from me—I hate you!

SMIRNOV. God, what a woman! Never in my life have I seen anything like her! I'm done for! I'm destroyed! I'm caught in the mousetrap like a mouse!

POPOVA. Get out of here, or I'll shoot!

SMIRNOV. Go ahead and shoot! You cannot understand what bliss it would be to die beneath the gaze of those wonderful eyes, to die from a gunshot fired by that small, velvety, dainty hand . . . I've gone out of my mind! Think it over, come to a decision right now, because once I leave this place, we shall never meet again! Come to a decision . . . I'm a gentleman, a respectable fellow, I have an income of ten thousand a year . . . if you toss a coin in the air, I can shoot a bullet through it . . . My horses are superb . . . Will you be my wife?

POPOVA (*outraged, brandishes the revolver*). Shoot! Twenty paces!

SMIRNOV. I've gone out of my mind . . . I don't understand a thing . . . (*Shouts.*) You there, water!

POPOVA (*shouts*). Twenty paces!

SMIRNOV. I've gone out of my mind, I've fallen in love like a little kid, like a fool! (*Grasps her by the arm, she shrieks in pain.*) I love you! (*Gets on his knees.*) I love as I have never loved before! Twenty women I've walked out on, ten have walked out on me, but not one of them did I love the way I love you . . . I've gone all touchy-feely, I've turned to sugar, I'm limp as a dishrag . . . I'm kneeling like a fool and offering you my hand . . . It's a shame, a disgrace! It's five years since I've been in love, I swore never again, and all of a sudden I'm head over heels, out of character like a long peg in a short hole![11] I offer you my hand. Yes or no? You don't want to? You don't have to! (*Gets up and quickly goes to the door.*)

---

11 Chekhov uses the phallic image *ogloblya v chuzhoy kuzov*, a long shaft in someone else's wagon.

POPOVA. Hold on . . .

SMIRNOV (*stops*). Well?

POPOVA. Never mind, you can go . . . Although, hold on . . . No, go, go away! I hate you! Or no . . . Don't go! Ah, if you'd had any idea how really angry I am, really angry ! (*Throws the revolver on the table.*) My fingers are swollen from that awful thing . . . (*Tears her handkerchief in rage.*) Why are you standing there? Clear out of here!

SMIRNOV. Good-bye.

POPOVA. Yes, yes, go away! . . . (*Shouts.*) Where are you off to? Hold on . . . Go on, though. Oh, I'm really angry! Don't come over here, don't come over here!

SMIRNOV (*crossing to her*). I'm really angry at myself! I fell in love like a schoolboy, got on my knees . . . Goosebumps are creeping up and down my skin . . . (*Rudely.*) I love you! I need to fall in love with you like I need a hole in the head! Tomorrow I've got to pay the interest, haymaking's begun, while you're here . . . (*Takes her round the waist.*) I'll never forgive myself . . .

POPOVA. Get away! Hands off! I . . . hate you! Twenty pa-paces!

A protracted kiss.

X I

The same, LUKA with an axe, the GARDENER with a rake, the COACHMAN with a pitchfork, and WORKMEN with staves.

LUKA (*on seeing the kissing couple*). Saints preserve us!

Pause.

POPOVA (*with downcast eyes*). Luka, tell the stable boys that Toby gets no oats today.

Curtain

VARIANTS TO

The Bear

Lines come from publication in the newspaper *New Times* (*Novoe Vremya*) (NT), the censor's copy (Cens.), the lithographed script (Lith.), the periodicals *Performer* (*Artist*) (P), and *Alarm-clock* (*Budilnik*) (AC).

page 423 / *After*: as a guest . . . — for god's sake . . . (NT, Cens., Lith., AC)

page 424 / *After*: really am angry — devil take me quite! How can I not get angry? (NT)

page 425 / *After*: have walked out on me — and now I know perfectly well how to behave with them. (NT, Cens, Lith., P, AC)

page 425 / *After*: fussy — mischievous as kittens, cowardly as rabbits (NT)

page 427 / *After*: you won't get a kopek! — you'll get it a year from now! (NT, Cens., Lith., P, AC)

page 427 / *After*: (*Rings.*) — *Enter LUKA.* (NT, Cens., Lith., AC)

page 428 / *After*: an upstart! — A crude dullard! (NT)

page 429 / *After*: like a side of bacon! — There won't be a wet patch left on her! (NT)

page 431 / *After*: a shame, a disgrace! — I feel myself now in such a nasty situation you can't imagine! (NT, Cens., Lith., P, AB)

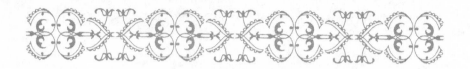

THE PROPOSAL

A vulgarish and boringish vaudevillette, but suitable for the provinces" was how Chekhov disparaged *The Proposal*, even as he asked friends to intercede with the censors on its behalf. Inspired by the success of *The Bear*, he was anxious to get his next farce on the boards. It had its first production at the theater at the Imperial residence at Tsarskoe Selo on August 9, 1889, with a cast of Pavel Svobodin (who had created Shabelsky) as Lomov, Mariya Ilinskaya as Nataliya, and the popular fat comedian Varlamov as Chubukov. It was greeted with unbroken laughter, not least from Tsar Alexander III, who congratulated the actors. *The Proposal* shared *The Bear*'s fate as a favorite curtain-raiser and benefit play in the provinces for years.

The Proposal is the first of Chekhov's farces to employ the device of thwarted expectation of what the title announces. Just as the characters in *The Wedding* and *The Celebration* fail to pull off the intended ceremonies, so the offer of marriage in this play is continually postponed and eventually eliminated. Botched proposals are a Chekhovian speciality. The cross-purposes of the "imaginary invalid" Lomov, incongruously decked out in tails and gloves, and Nataliya, in her apron, mount to a boisterous, breathless pitch. Chekhov understood how to accelerate the basic misapprehensions into a barrage of insults, and, after building to a climax, how to reinvigorate the action by introducing a fresh contretemps (which he may have learned from Turgenev's one-act *Luncheon with the Marshal of Nobility*). Later, the final interview of Tusenbach and Irina in *Three Sisters* and Lopakhin's failure to propose to Varya in *The Cherry Orchard* will show Chekhov modulating the tone to one of shattered hopes and mutually conflicting illusions.

THE PROPOSAL

Предложение

A Joke in One Act

C H A R A C T E R S

STEPAN STEPANOVICH CHUBUKOV,[1] *a landowner*

NATALIYA STEPANOVNA, *his daughter, 25*

IVAN VASILYEVICH LOMOV,[2] *Chubukov's neighbor, a healthy, well-fed, but very hypochrondriacal landowner*

The action takes place on Chubukov's estate.

A parlor in Chubukov's house.

I

CHUBUKOV and LOMOV (enters wearing a tailcoat and white gloves).

CHUBUKOV (*going to meet him*). Darling boy, look who it is! Ivan Vasilyevich! Absolutely delighted! (*Shakes his hand.*) This is what I call a pleasant surprise, laddy . . . How are you?

LOMOV. Well, thank you kindly. And how are *you* getting on?

CHUBUKOV. We plug along in a modest sort of way, my cherub, all the better for your asking and so on. Have a seat, please do . . . The thing of it is, it's wrong to neglect your neighbors, laddy. Darling boy, why are you in formal dress? A tailcoat, gloves, and so on. You headed anywhere in particular, my trusty friend?

LOMOV. No, I'm only calling on you, respected Stepan Stepanych.

---

1 From *chubuk*, a long-stemmed pipe of Turkish origin.

2 From *lom*, a shard, scrap, bit of waste.

CHUBUKOV. Then why the tailcoat, the elegance!

LOMOV. Well, you see, here's what it's about. (*Takes him by the arm.*) I have come, respected Stepan Stepanych, to trouble you with a certain question. More than once now I have had the honor of calling on your assistance, and you have always, in a manner of speaking . . . but, excuse me, I'm getting excited. I'll take a sip of water, respected Stepan Stepanych. (*Drinks water.*)

CHUBUKOV (*aside*). He's here to ask for money! He won't get it! (*To him.*) What's the matter, my beauty?

LOMOV. Well, you see, Respect Stepanych . . . sorry, Stepan Respectych . . . I mean, I'm awfully excited, as you may have noticed . . . In short, you're the only one who can assist me, although, of course, I don't deserve it in any way and . . . and I don't have the right to count on your support . . .

CHUBUKOV. Ah, stop beating around the bush, laddy! Spit it out! Well?

LOMOV. Right away . . . this very minute. The fact is, I have come here to ask for the hand of your daughter Nataliya Stepanovna.

CHUBUKOV (*overjoyed*). Darling boy! Ivan Vasilyevich! Say that again—did I hear it right?

LOMOV. I have the honor to ask . . .

CHUBUKOV (*interrupting*). My darling boy . . . I am delighted and so on . . . The thing of it is and so forth. (*Embraces and kisses him.*) I've wanted this for a long time. It's always been my wish. (*Sheds a tear.*) And I've always been fond of you, my cherub, like my own son. God grant you both wisdom and love and so on, and I've really wanted . . . Why am I standing around like a lunkhead? I'm dazed with delight, quite dazed! Oof, with all my heart . . . I'll go and call Natasha and that sort of thing.

LOMOV (*deeply moved*). Respected Stepan Stepanych, what do you think, can I count on her consent?

CHUBUKOV. The thing of it is, a good-looking fellow like you and . . . how can she not consent! She loves you like a cat loves catnip, I'll wager, and so on . . . Be right back! (*Exits.*)

I I

LOMOV (alone).

LOMOV. It's cold . . . I'm trembling all over, as if I were about to take an exam. The main thing is to make up your mind. If you think about it too long, and hesitate, talk it over a lot and wait for the perfect woman or true love, then you'll never get married . . . Brrr! . . . It's cold! Nataliya Stepanovna is an excellent housekeeper, passable looking, educated . . . what more do I need? However, there goes a ringing in my ears with all this excitement. (*Drinks water.*) And I've really got to get married . . . First of all, I'm already thirty-five—what they call a critical age. Second of all, I need an orderly, well-regulated life . . . I've got heart trouble, constant palpitations, I'm touchy and always flying off the handle . . . Right now, look, my lips are quivering and my right eyelid's starting to flicker . . . But the most awful thing is when I go to sleep. No sooner do I get in bed and start to doze off, when suddenly something starts in my left side—a twitch! and it moves to my shoulders and head . . . I leap out of bed like a lunatic, pace the floor a bit and lie down again, but no sooner do I start to doze off, when there it is in my side again—that twitch! And so it goes twenty times over . . .

I I I

NATALIYA STEPANOVNA and LOMOV.

NATALIYA STEPANOVNA (*enters*). Oh, for heaven's sake! It's only you, and Papa was saying: go inside, there's a dealer come about the merchandise. Good morning, Ivan Vasilyevich!

LOMOV. Good morning, respected Nataliya Stepanovna!

NATALIYA STEPANOVNA. Excuse me, I'm in an apron and housedress . . . We've been shelling peas for drying. Why has it been so long since your last visit? Please sit down . . .

They sit down.

Would you like some breakfast?

LOMOV. No thank you, I've already eaten . . .

NATALIYA STEPANOVNA. Go ahead and smoke . . . Here are the matches . . . Splendid weather, but yesterday it rained so hard that none of the farmhands did a lick of work all day. How much hay have you mown? Can you imagine, I was a greedy little pig and mowed the whole field, and now I've got second thoughts, I'm afraid my hay might rot. It would have been better to wait. But what's this? I do believe you're wearing a tailcoat! That's a new one! You going to a dance or what? By the way, you're looking good . . . Honestly, why are you all dolled up?

LOMOV (*excited*). Well, you see, respected Nataliya Stepanovna . . . The fact is that I've made up my mind to ask you to hear me out . . . Of course, you must be wondering and even angry, but I . . . (*Aside.*) It's awfully cold!

NATALIYA STEPANOVNA. What's this about?

Pause.

Well?

LOMOV. I shall endeavor to be brief. As you know, respected Nataliya Stepanovna, it's been a long time now, since we were children, in fact, that I've had the honor of knowing your family. My late auntie and her husband, who, as I expect you know, bequeathed me my land, always had the deepest regard for your daddy and your late mamma. The Lomov clan and the Chubukov clan have always been on the friendliest and, one might even say, familial footing. Besides, as I expect you know, my land is closely adjacent to yours. If you will don't mind recalling, my Bullock Fields are bounded by your grove of birch trees.

NATALIYA STEPANOVNA. Sorry to interrupt you. You said "my Bullock Fields" . . . Are they actually yours?

LOMOV. They're mine, ma'am . . .

NATALIYA STEPANOVNA. Well, is that so! The Bullock Fields are ours, not yours!

LOMOV. No, ma'am, they're mine, respected Nataliya Stepanovna.

NATALIYA STEPANOVNA. That's news to me. How do you figure they're yours?

LOMOV. How do I figure? I'm talking about the Bullock Fields that form a wedge between your birch grove and Stinkhole Swamp.

NATALIYA STEPANOVNA. That's right, yes, yes . . . They're ours . . .

LOMOV. No, you're mistaken, respected Nataliya Stepanovna—they're mine.

NATALIYA STEPANOVNA. Come to your senses, Ivan Vasilyevich! Since when have they been yours?

LOMOV. Since when? As long as I can remember, they've always been ours.

NATALIYA STEPANOVNA. Now, that's really going too far!

LOMOV. You can see it in the deeds, respected Nataliya Stepanovna. Bullock Fields were once in dispute—that's true; but now everybody knows that they're mine. And there's no point arguing about it. If you don't mind, my auntie's granny made over those Fields without limit of time or payment for the use of your daddy's granddaddy's peasants, so that they would bake bricks for her. Our daddy's granddaddy's peasants had had the use of the Fields rent-free for some forty years and were used to considering them their own, so later when circumstances altered . . .[3]

NATALIYA STEPANOVNA. It's not at all the way you're telling it! Both my granddaddy and my great-granddaddy assumed that their land ran up to Stinkhole Swamp—which means, Bullock Fields are ours. What's there to argue about?—I don't understand. It's really annoying!

LOMOV. I can show it to you in the deeds, Nataliya Stepanovna!

NATALIYA STEPANOVNA. No, you must be joking or putting me on . . . What a surprise! We've owned the land for nigh on to three hundred years, and all of a sudden somebody points out to you that it's not your land! Ivan Vasilyevich, forgive me, but I can't believe my own ears . . . It's not that I care so much about the Fields. They're barely a dozen acres or so, and they're worth maybe three hundred rubles, but it's the unfairness of the thing that upsets me. Say what you will, but I cannot put up with unfairness.

LOMOV. Hear me out, for pity's sake! Your daddy's granddaddy's peasants, as I've already had the honor to tell you, baked bricks for my auntie's granny. Auntie's granny, eager to do something nice for them . . .

NATALIYA STEPANOVNA. Granddaddy, granny, auntie . . . I can't make head or tail of this! They're our Fields, and that's that.

---

3 Lomov uses the euphemistic term *polozhenie,* or situation, referring to the Imperial decree of 1861, emancipating the serfs but not endowing them with land.

LOMOV. Mine, ma'am!

NATALIYA STEPANOVNA. Ours! You can show me proofs for two days running, you can put on a dozen tailcoats, but they're ours, ours, ours! . . . I won't take what's yours and I won't give up what's mine . . . Say whatever you like!

LOMOV. I don't need Bullock Fields, Nataliya Stepanovna, but it's the principle of the thing. If you like, then, please, I'll give them to you.

NATALIYA STEPANOVNA. I can give them to you myself, they're mine! . . . This is all very peculiar, to put it mildly, Ivan Vasilyevich! Up to now we considered you a good neighbor, a friend, last year we lent you our threshing machine, and that's why we couldn't finish threshing our own wheat until November, and now you treat us as if we were gypsies. You make us a present of our own land. Excuse me but this is not neighborly behavior! To my way of thinking, it's downright impertinence, if you don't mind my saying so . . .

LOMOV. In other words, I'm supposed to be appropriating what's yours? Madam, I have never grabbed other people's land and won't allow anyone to accuse me of such a thing . . . (*Quickly goes to the carafe and drinks water.*) Bullock Fields are mine!

NATALIYA STEPANOVNA. That's a lie, they're ours!

LOMOV. Mine!

NATALIYA STEPANOVNA. That's a lie! I'll prove it to you! This very day I'll send men with scythes to those Fields!

LOMOV. What, ma'am?

NATALIYA STEPANOVNA. This very day my men will be mowing it down!

LOMOV. I'll toss 'em out on their ear!

NATALIYA STEPANOVNA. You wouldn't dare!

LOMOV (*clutches at his heart*). Bullock Fields are mine! Understand? Mine!

NATALIYA STEPANOVNA. Stop shouting, please! You can shout and talk yourself hoarse with anger in your own home, but please get a grip on yourself while you're here!

LOMOV. Madam, if it were not for my appalling, agonizing palpitations, if the veins were not throbbing in my temples, I would speak to you in quite a different tone! (*Shouts.*) Bullock Fields are mine!

NATALIYA STEPANOVNA. Ours!

LOMOV. Mine!

NATALIYA STEPANOVNA. Ours!

LOMOV. Mine!

I V

The same and CHUBUKOV.

CHUBUKOV (*entering*). What's going on? What's all this shouting for?

NATALIYA STEPANOVNA. Papa, please explain to this gentleman who owns Bullock Fields: us or him?

CHUBUKOV (*to him*). The Fields're ours, my chick!

LOMOV. For pity's sake, Stepan Stepanych, how do you figure they're yours? You of all people should have some sense! My auntie's granny handed over the Fields on a temporary, rent-free basis for the use of your granddaddy's peasants. The peasants used the land for forty years and got to thinking of it as their own, so when circumstances altered . . .

CHUBUKOV. Excuse me, my valued friend . . . You're forgetting that the peasants paid your granddaddy nothing and so on, precisely because the Fields were in dispute at the time and so forth . . . And now every whipper-snapper knows perfectly well that they are ours. In other words, you haven't seen the surveyor's map!

LOMOV. But I'll prove to you that they're mine!

CHUBUKOV. You won't prove it, my dearest boy.

LOMOV. No, I will prove it!

CHUBUKOV. Laddy, why shout like that? Shouting certainly doesn't prove anything. I don't want what's yours and I'm not inclined to give up what's mine. On what grounds? If it comes to that, my dear, dear boy, if you're inclined to dispute the Fields and so on, I'd rather turn them over to the farmers than to you. So there!

LOMOV. I don't understand! What right have you got to give away other people's property?

CHUBUKOV. Permit me to know whether I have the right or not. The thing of it is, young man, that I'm not used to being spoken to in that tone of voice and so on. I am twice your age, young man, and I request you to speak to me without losing your head and so forth.

LOMOV. No, you simply take me for a fool and laugh at me! You're calling my land your land and even expect me to be calm and collected and talk to you like a human being! Good neighbors don't behave this way, Stepan Stepanych! You're not a neighbor, but a land grabber!

CHUBUKOV. What's that, sir? What did you say?

NATALIYA STEPANOVNA. Papa, send the men out with scythes to the Fields right away!

CHUBUKOV (to Lomov). What did you just say, my good sir?

NATALIYA STEPANOVNA. Bullock Fields are ours, and I won't give them up, I won't, I won't!

LOMOV. We'll see about that! I'll prove in court that they're mine!

CHUBUKOV. In court! Go ahead and take it to court, my good sir, and so forth! Go ahead! I know you, the thing of it is, you've just been waiting for a chance to sue us and so on ... A litigious character! Every member of your family has been lawsuit crazy! Every last one!

LOMOV. Please refrain from insulting my family! Every member of the Lomov clan has been honorable and not a single one has been tried for embezzlement like your beloved uncle!

CHUBUKOV. But every member of your Lomov clan has been crazy as a loon!

NATALIYA STEPANOVNA. Every one, every one, every one!

CHUBUKOV. Your grandfather drank like a fish, and that young auntie of yours, you know the one, Nastasiya Mikhailovna, ran off with an architect and so on ...

LOMOV. And your mother was lopsided. (Clutches at his heart.) There's a twitching in my side ... A hammering in my head ... Holy saints! ... Water!

CHUBUKOV. Well, your father cheated at cards and ate like a slob!

NATALIYA STEPANOVNA. And your auntie's a scandal-monger, to put it mildly!

LOMOV. My left leg's paralyzed . . . Well, you're a bunch of schemers . . . Ugh, my heart! . . . And it's no secret to anyone that just before the elections you bri . . . There're spots before my eyes . . . Where's my hat?

NATALIYA STEPANOVNA. How contemptible! How dishonorable! How nasty!

CHUBUKOV. Well, you personally, the thing of it is, are a spiteful, two-faced and underhanded individual! Yessiree!

LOMOV. There's my hat . . . My heart . . . Where's the way out? Where's the door? Ugh! . . . I think I'm dying . . . My foot's dragging . . . (*Goes to the door.*)

CHUBUKOV (*following him*). And never set those feet in my house again!

NATALIYA STEPANOVNA. Take us to court! Then we'll see!

LOMOV staggers out.

V

CHUBUKOV and NATALIYA STEPANOVNA.

CHUBUKOV. The hell with him! (*Walks around in agitation.*)

NATALIYA STEPANOVNA. How do you like that stinker? After that try and believe in good neighbors!

CHUBUKOV. The bastard! The overstuffed dummy!

NATALIYA STEPANOVNA. What a crackpot! Appropriates somebody else's land and then dares to brag about it.

CHUBUKOV. And this hobgoblin, this, thing of it is, thing that goes bump in the night has the unmitigated gall to propose marriage and so forth! How about that? A marriage proposal!

NATALIYA STEPANOVNA. What's that about a marriage proposal?

CHUBUKOV. I'll say! He drove over here to propose to you.

NATALIYA STEPANOVNA. To propose? To me? Why didn't you tell me this before?

CHUBUKOV. That's why he got himself all dolled up in a tailcoat! Like a frankfurter in a tight casing! The puny runt!

NATALIYA STEPANOVNA. To me? Propose! Ah! (*Drops into an armchair and moans.*) Bring 'im back! Bring 'im back! Ah! Bring 'im back!

CHUBUKOV. Bring who back?

NATALIYA STEPANOVNA. Quick, quick! I feel faint! Bring 'im back! (*Goes into hysterics.*)

CHUBUKOV. What's the matter? (*Clutches his head.*) What a miserable wretch I am! I should shoot myself! I should hang myself! They're torturing me to death!

NATALIYA STEPANOVNA. I'm dying! Bring 'im back!

CHUBUKOV. Phooey! Right away. Stop bawling! (*Runs out.*)

NATALIYA STEPANOVNA (*alone, moans*). What have we done? Bring 'im back! Bring 'im back!

CHUBUKOV (*runs back in*). He's coming right away and so on, damn him! Oof! Talk to him yourself, the thing of it is I don't want to . . .

NATALIYA STEPANOVNA (*moans*). Bring 'im back!

CHUBUKOV (*shouts*). He's on his way, I tell you. "Oh, Lord, a heavy burden this, Be father to a grown-up miss . . ."[4] I'll cut my throat! I'll definitely cut my throat! We've cursed the man, heckled him, kicked him out, and it's all because of you . . . you!

NATALIYA STEPANOVNA. No . . . you!

CHUBUKOV. So now the thing of it is it's my fault!

LOMOV appears in the doorway.

Well, you talk to him! (*Exits.*)

---

4 A direct quotation from A. S. Griboedov's satiric comedy *Woe from Wit* (Act I, scene 10).

V I

NATALIYA STEPANOVNA and LOMOV.

LOMOV (*enters, utterly exhausted*). The most awful palpitations . . . My leg's numb . . . my side is throbbing . . .

NATALIYA STEPANOVNA. Excuse me, we got a bit carried away, Ivan Vasilyevich . . . Now I remember: Bullock Fields are in fact yours.

LOMOV. My heart's pounding horribly . . . The Fields are mine . . . There are spots before both my eyes . . .

NATALIYA STEPANOVNA. The fields are yours, yours . . . Do sit down . . .

They sit down.

We were wrong . . .

LOMOV. I insist on the principle of the thing . . . I don't care about the land, but I do care about the principle . . .

NATALIYA STEPANOVNA. The principle, exactly . . . Let's have a little talk about something else.

LOMOV. Especially since I've got proof. My auntie's granny made over to your daddy's granddaddy's peasants . . .

NATALIYA STEPANOVNA. All right, all right, that's enough of that . . . (*Aside.*) I don't know how to begin . . . (*To him.*) Planning to go hunting soon?

LOMOV. For grouse, respected Nataliya Stepanovna, I think I'll start when the harvest's over. Oh, did you hear? Imagine my bad luck! My Dasher, whom you are good enough to know, has gone lame.

NATALIYA STEPANOVNA. What a shame! How did it happen?

LOMOV. I don't know. I suppose he dislocated something or some other dogs bit him . . . (*Sighs.*) My very best dog, not to mention what he cost me! I actually paid Mironov one hundred twenty-five rubles for him.

NATALIYA STEPANOVNA. You paid too much, Ivan Vasilyevich!

LOMOV. To my way of thinking, it was pretty cheap. He's a wonderful dog.

NATALIYA STEPANOVNA. Papa paid eighty-five rubles for his Splasher, and, after all, Splasher is far superior to your Dasher!

LOMOV. Splasher superior to Dasher! What are you talking about! (*Laughs.*)
Splasher superior to Dasher!

NATALIYA STEPANOVNA. Of course, he's superior! It's true, Splasher is still
a pup, he's not matured yet, but judging by his paws and his carriage you
won't find his better at Volchanetsky's.[5]

LOMOV. Excuse me, Nataliya Stepanovna, but actually you're forgetting that
he's got an underslung jaw, and a dog with an underslung jaw can't get a
good grip.

NATALIYA STEPANOVNA. An underslung jaw? That's the first time I've
heard that!

LOMOV. I assure you, the lower jawbone is shorter than the upper.

NATALIYA STEPANOVNA. Did you measure it?

LOMOV. I did. He'll be all right as far as tracking goes, of course, but when it
comes to retrieving, he can hardly . . .

NATALIYA STEPANOVNA. In the first place, our Splasher is pedigreed, a
thoroughbred greyhound, sired by Buckle-down and Chiseler, but as for
that rust-colored mutt of yours there's no point in talking about blood-lines
. . . And besides he's old and hideous as a swaybacked nag.

LOMOV. He may be old, but I wouldn't take five of your Splashers for him
. . . You must be kidding? Dasher is a dog, whereas Splasher . . . it's ridiculous even to argue about it . . . Things like your Splasher you can find at
any kennel—common as dirt. Twenty-five rubles would be asking too
much.

NATALIYA STEPANOVNA. Ivan Vasilyevich, you are possessed today by a
certain demon of contradiction. First you decide that the Fields belong to
you, next you think that Dasher is superior to Splasher. I don't like it when
a man doesn't say what's on his mind. After all, you know perfectly well that
Splasher is a hundred times better than your . . . that stupid Dasher. Why
do you have to contradict?

LOMOV. I see, Nataliya Stepanovna, that you take me for either a blind man
or a fool. Why can't you get it through your head that your Splasher has an
underslung jaw!

---

5 A well-known breeder.

NATALIYA STEPANOVNA. That isn't true.

LOMOV. His jaw is underslung!

NATALIYA STEPANOVNA (*shouts*). That isn't true!

LOMOV. What are you yelling for, madam?

NATALIYA STEPANOVNA. Why do you talk such rubbish? This is really aggravating! It's high time you put your Dasher to sleep, and yet you go on comparing him with Splasher!

LOMOV. Excuse me, I can't prolong this argument. I have palpitations.

NATALIYA STEPANOVNA. I've noticed that the hunters who argue the most are the ones who know the least.

LOMOV. Madam, I implore you to be quiet . . . My heart is pounding away . . . (*Shouts*). Be quiet!

NATALIYA STEPANOVNA. I will not be quiet until you admit that Splasher is a hundred times better than your Dasher!

LOMOV. A hundred times worse! He should drop dead, your Splasher! Temples . . . eyes . . . shoulder . . .

NATALIYA STEPANOVNA. Well, your stupid Dasher doesn't have to *drop* dead, because he's already dead on his feet!

LOMOV (*weeps*). Will you be quiet! I'm having a heart attack!

NATALIYA STEPANOVNA. I will not be quiet!

VIII

The same and CHUBUKOV.

CHUBUKOV (*enters*). What's going on now?

NATALIYA STEPANOVNA. Papa, tell me honestly, in all conscience: which dog is better—our Splasher or his Dasher?

LOMOV. Stepan Stepanovich, I entreat you, just tell me one thing: does your Splasher have an underslung jaw or not? Yes or no?

CHUBUKOV. And what if he does? A lot of difference that makes! On the other hand there's no better dog in the district and so on.

LOMOV. But isn't my Dasher actually better? In all honesty?

CHUBUKOV. Don't get overexcited, my dear friend . . . Allow me . . . Your Dasher, the thing of it is, has his good points . . . He's pedigreed, his paws are firm, his haunches ride high, and so forth. But that dog, if you must know, my beauty, has two fundamental flaws: he's old and his bite's too short.

LOMOV. Excuse me, I have palpitations . . . Let's look at the facts . . . Please remember that on Maruskin Meadows my Dasher was coursing neck and neck with the Count's Smasher, while your Splasher was lagging a whole half-mile behind.

CHUBUKOV. He was lagging behind, because the Count's master of hounds struck him with his whip.

LOMOV. For good reason. The rest of the dogs are chasing the fox, while Splasher starts to worry a sheep.

CHUBUKOV. That's not true, sir! . . . Laddy, I'm a hot-tempered fellow, and, the thing of it is, I suggest that you drop this argument. He struck him because everyone gets jealous when he looks at another man's dog . . . Yessiree! They're all haters! And you, my good sir, are not blameless! The thing of it is, the minute you spot any man's dog that's better than your Dasher, you start in right away with a kind of . . . sort of . . . and so forth . . . I remember it all, indeed I do!

LOMOV. And so do I!

CHUBUKOV (*mimicking*). And so do I . . . And just what do you remember?

LOMOV. Palpitations . . . My leg's gone numb . . . . I can't bear it.

NATALIYA STEPANOVNA (*mimicking*). Palpitations . . . What sort of a hunter are you? You ought to be lying in a warm corner of the kitchen, swatting spiders, not chasing the fox! Palpitations . . .

CHUBUKOV. Truth be told, what sort of hunter *are* you? With your palpitations, the thing of it is, you should stay at home, and not jolt up and down in a saddle. It would be a fine thing if you actually did some hunting, but you only ride in order to start arguments and mess with other people's dogs and so on. I'm a hot-tempered fellow, we'll change the subject. The thing of it is, though, you're no hunter!

LOMOV. And you *are*? You ride only to suck up to the Count and spin your schemes . . . My heart! . . . You're a schemer!

CHUBUKOV. What's that, sir? I'm a schemer! (*Shouts.*) Shut your mouth!

LOMOV. Schemer!

CHUBUKOV. Spoiled brat! Puppy!

LOMOV. Old buzzard! Hypocritical fraud!

CHUBUKOV. Shut up, or I'll shoot you with a uncleaned gun like a partridge! You pipsqueak!

LOMOV. Everybody knows that—ugh, my heart!—that you beat your late wife . . . Leg . . . temples . . . Spots . . . I'm falling, falling! . . .

CHUBUKOV. And your housekeeper leads you around by the nose!

LOMOV. Look, look, look . . . my heart's fit to burst! My shoulder's come detached . . . Where's my shoulder? . . . I'm dying! (*Drops into an armchair.*) Doctor! (*Faints.*)

CHUBUKOV. Spoiled brat! Mamma's boy! Pipsqueak! I feel faint! (*Drinks water.*) I feel faint!

NATALIYA STEPANOVNA. What kind of a hunter are you? You don't even know how to sit on a horse! (*To her father.*) Papa! What's wrong with him? Papa! Look, papa! (*Yelps.*) Ivan Vasilyevich! He's dead!

CHUBUKOV. I feel faint . . . I'm gasping for breath! . . . Air! . . .

NATALIYA STEPANOVNA. He's dead! (*Tugs at Lomov's sleeve.*) Ivan Vasilich! Ivan Vasilich! What have we done? He's dead! (*Drops into an armchair.*) Get a doctor, get a doctor! (*Goes into hysterics.*)

CHUBUKOV. Oof! . . . What's going on? What's wrong with you?

NATALIYA STEPANOVNA (*moans*). He's dead! . . . dead!

CHUBUKOV. Who's dead? (*After a glance at Lomov.*) As a matter of fact he is dead! Good Lord! Water! Call a doctor! (*Lifts a glass to Lomov's lips.*) Drink this! . . . No, he's not drinking . . . Which means, the thing of it is, he's dead . . . I'm the most miserable man on earth! Why didn't I put a bullet in my brain? Why haven't I shot myself before now? What am I waiting for? Give me a knife! Give me a pistol!

LOMOV stirs.

He's reviving, I think . . . Drink some water! . . . That's right . . .

LOMOV. Spots . . . mist . . . Where am I?

CHUBUKOV. Get married right away—and then you can go to hell! She's consented! (*Uniting Lomov's and his daughter's hands.*) She's consented and so forth. My blessings on you and so on. Only leave me in peace!

LOMOV. Huh? What? (*Getting up a bit.*) How's that?

CHUBUKOV. She's consented! So? Kiss one another and . . . to hell with you!

NATALIYA STEPANOVNA (*moans*). He's alive . . . Yes, yes, I consent . . .

CHUBUKOV. Kiss one another!

LOMOV. Huh? How's that? (*Exchanges kisses with Nataliya Stepanovna.*) Very nice . . . Excuse me, what's this all about? Ah, yes, I get it . . . Heart . . . spots . . . I'm happy, Nataliya Stepanovna . . . (*Kisses her hand.*) My leg's gone numb . . .

NATALIYA STEPANOVNA. I . . . I'm happy too . . .

CHUBUKOV. There's a weight off . . . Oof!

NATALIYA STEPANOVNA. But . . . all the same, now you've got to agree: Dasher is not as good as Splasher.

LOMOV. Better!

NATALIYA STEPANOVNA. Worse!

CHUBUKOV. Now, domestic bliss is off to a running start! Champagne!

LOMOV. Better!

NATALIYA STEPANOVNA. Worse! Worse! Worse!

CHUBUKOV (*trying to shout over them*). Champagne! Champagne!

Curtain

VARIANTS TO

The Proposal

The variants come from the censor's copy (C), the lithographed publication (L), the newspaper *New Times* (NT), the journal *The Performer* (P), and the collection *Plays* (Pl).

page 439 / *After*: It's not at all the way you're telling it! — The peasants have nothing to do with it. (C, L)

page 441 / *After*: or him? — **LOMOV.** Yes, yes, whose are the Fields? (C, L, P)

page 442 / *Before*: What did you just say, my good sir? — Shut up! (C, L)

page 442 / *Before*: Bullock fields are ours — I won't shut up! (C, L)

page 442 / *After*: Go ahead! —
NATALIYA STEPANOVNA. Even if there are a hundred, two hundred courts, I won't let you, I won't let you, I won't let you!
CHUBUKOV. Shut up! (*To Lomov.*) (C, L)

page 443 / *After*: Yessiree! — **NATALIYA STEPANOVNA.** Good neighbors don't behave this way! (C, L)

page 443 / *After*: Then we'll see! — I'll send the men with scythes this very minute! (C, L)

page 444 / *After*: No . . . you! — You're uneducated and crude! If it hadn't been for you, he wouldn't have left! (C, P)

page 444 / *After*: the thing of it is it's my fault! — Well, hold on a bit, my dear girl, and so on: when I shoot myself or hang myself, you'll know it's all your fault! Yours! You drove me to it! (C, L)

page 445 / *After*: about something else. — Did you go to the fair in Nikitovka? (C, L)

page 445 / *After*: that's enough of that . . . — Let's forget it.
Pause.
LOMOV. Not that I care about the Fields, let 'em go, but it's the principle of the thing . . .

NATALIYA STEPANOVNA. All right, all right . . . (C, L)

page 447 / *After*: or his Dasher? — CHUBUKOV. Are you arguing again? Again? I can't stand this! (C, L)

page 448 / *After*: has his good points . . . — NATALIYA STEPANOVNA. Absolutely none!

CHUBUKOV. He's pedigreed . . . (C, L)

page 448 / *After*: That's not true, sir! . . . — The master of hounds is a drunken ignoramus, and that's why he hit him. (C, L)

page 449 / *After*: Puppy! — A walking medicine chest!

page 449 / *After*: Hypocritical fraud! — I know you through and through!

page 449 / *After*: You pipsqueak! —

NATALIYA STEPANOVNA. Splasher is a million times better than Dasher! Bullock Fields are ours! So there!

CHUBUKOV. Bullock Fields are ours! (C, L)

page 450 / *After*: NATALIYA STEPANOVNA. Worse! —

LOMOV. Better!

NATALIYA STEPANOVNA. Worse! (C, L, NT, P)

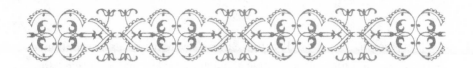

IVANOV, FINAL VERSION

The acceptance of *Ivanov* at the Alexandra Theatre made revisions all the more urgent. Chekhov's friend, the millionaire publisher Aleksey Suvorin, kept advising him to beef up the character of Sasha, especially now that the star actress Mariya Savina was to play her. So Chekhov added Sasha to the attackers in Act Four, and had Ivanov taking active measures in his own defense. Moreover, Suvorin insisted on misreading the central protagonist, which constrained Chekhov to write long expository speeches, explanations, confessions, and acts of contrition to counter preconceptions of heroism and villainy. He gave his hero a long monologue about dreams of becoming the young Ivanov once more. "If Ivanov turns out looking like a cad or a superfluous man, and the doctor is a great man . . . then, obviously, my play won't come off, and there can be no talk of a production" (to Suvorin, December 30, 1888). (See Variants to First Version.)

Doctor Lvov also needed revising. In traditional drama, doctors were *raisonneurs*, whose sagacious moralizing clued the audience into the way to think about the characters. Lvov, however, does not heal breaches; he creates them through his purblind and self-righteous assumptions. In this respect, he much resembles Gregers Werle in Ibsen's *The Wild Duck*, who, in his quixotic attempt to strip away illusions, destroys the lives of those around him. Chekhov's task was to make sure that Lvov did not come across either as an objective spokesman or a fatuous prig. As he wrote to Suvorin, "Such persons are necessary, and for the most part sympathetic. To draw them as caricatures, even in the interests of the stage, is dishonorable and serves no purpose" (December 30, 1888).

Rehearsals for the Petersburg production went badly, despite a strong cast, and Chekhov was dissatisfied with the comic actor Vladimir Davydov, who played the lead in a monotonous style to indicate seriousness. Even though the opening night was a huge success, Chekhov sneaked away, regarding the

ovation as a binge that would later give him a severe hangover. He continued
to revise *Ivanov*, dropping one comic character, Dudkin, and, in general, ton-
ing down the farcical elements. Chekhov intended to "sum up everything
that's been written so far about whining and languishing people, and in my
Ivanov put an end to such writing" (to Suvorin, January 7, 1889). A third version appeared in 1889, with more explanations between Lvov and Anna, and
the removal of Ivanov's monologue in the last act. Even then, Chekhov was
not content and kept tinkering with it until 1901.

Chekhov never managed to eliminate the mannerisms of boulevard drama
that vitiated the subtlety of his concept. The Act Two curtain, with a consump-
tive wife intruding on her husband in the arms of another woman, is effective
claptrap; at least we are spared the fainting that is described in the next act.
Scenes of vituperation rise, in the best melodrama manner, to one consummate insult. "Kike bitch," Ivanov screams at Anna in his ugliest moment; "Bastard" (or "Cad," "Bounder"—*podlets* is too dated to be translated easily) is
the summation of Lvov's contempt for Ivanov. Chekhov was to handle the
slanging-match between Arkadina and Treplyov in *The Seagull* more dexter-
ously. Even the final suicide is, as the critic Aleksandr Kugel opined, "a sacrifice made by Chekhov's soul to the god of theatrical gimmickry," literally
ending the play with a bang. It may have been copied directly from Luka
Antropov's popular comedy-melodrama *Will-o'-the-Wisps* (1873).

For a modern audience, the anti-Semitic slurs are a problem. The Jews
were the largest and most persecuted minority in the Russian Empire, offi-
cially segregated into an area of Western and Southern Russia known as the
Pale of Settlement. Seen as aliens, they were severely limited as to education
and profession, as well as residence, heavily taxed, and often subjected to
the periodic massacres known as pogroms. Although Chekhov privately used
the slighting term *zhid* ("Yid," "kike") without thinking twice about it, at a
time when anti-Semitism was public policy, his tolerance and lack of prejudice were exceptional. His fiction is filled with admirable or sympathetic Jewish characters. Two years before he wrote *Ivanov*, he may have proposed
marriage to Yevdokiya Éfros, a Jew who refused to convert to Russian Orthodoxy. Later on, her husband, the lawyer Yefim Konovitser, became one of
many Jews on friendly terms with Chekhov, among them the painter Isaak
Levitan. In 1898, Chekhov broke with his close friend and associate Suvorin
because the publisher's newspapers supported the anti-Semitic faction in the
Dreyfus affair.

Anna is a familiar literary type, the noble, self-sacrificing Jewess descended from *Ivanhoe*'s Rebecca of York, who, in nineteenth-century fiction, drama, and opera, is nobler than her "race" and usually dies or converts for love of a Christian. Ivanov is shown married to a Jew as a token of his quixotic social idealism. It is akin to a white South African marrying a Zulu woman in protest against apartheid. The revulsion Ivanov feels for Anna is part and parcel of his general loss of ideals. The comedown from his once noble if unrealistic stance to his present moral torpor is revealed at the end of Act Three when he insults her.

Within the conventional framework, a Chekhovian sense of atmospherics is beginning to emerge. He knew well the resonance that derived from a properly chosen setting, and structured the play to alternate between private and public life. We first see Ivanov alone, seated in a natural surrounding against the background of his house. He is outside it, because it represents to him a suffocating prison to be escaped. The primal image of an isolated Ivanov is almost immediately shattered by Borkin with his gun. The unused firearm of the opening will be recalled in the gunshot that ends the play.

As if to exacerbate the incursions into his privacy, Ivanov flees to a more peopled spot, the party at the Lebedevs'. But there the guests are already yawning at the very boredom he hoped to avoid. Act Two begins in a crowd of people, some so anonymous as to be designated merely as First Guest, Second Guest, etc. Even before Ivanov and Shabelsky appear, their lives are trotted out as slander and conjecture; Ivanov's innermost motives are distorted, and his most intimate action here, the embrace of Sasha, is intruded upon by the worst possible witness, his wife.

Act Three returns to Ivanov's study, which ought to be his sanctum, but is, as the stage direction makes clear, a jumble, a visual metaphor for the disorder of his existence. His papers, presumably the products of his brain and the instruments of his labor, lie cheek by jowl with food and drink, consumed by others who expatiate on gastronomy. Coming as it does after Anna's melodramatic discovery, this interlude strikes the note of triviality and neutralizes what might otherwise be overly theatrical. It is Chekhov's way of cooling overheated actions by pairing them with the banal. Ivanov himself seems aware of this, for he resents the intrusion of his workaday friends on his moping. Their commentary reduces his soul searching to cheap and obvious motives.

"It's like living in Australia," says Kosykh, evoking the provincial barbarity where vast expanses stretch between estates, and yet privacy is impossible. The last act interweaves public and private worlds as the wedding party prepares for benediction before going to church. The event could not be more conspicuous, despite the personal nature of the conjugal bond, and the characters have difficulty finding a quiet corner in which to unburden their minds. Ivanov's entrance is regarded as a tactless invasion, a bridegroom seeing the bride before the ceremony, and his self-destruction is enacted before a crowd of horrified onlookers.

IVANOV

Иванов

Drama in Four Acts

FINAL VERSION

[Bracketed footnote numerals refer to footnotes in *Ivanov*, First Version.]

CHARACTERS

IVANOV, NIKOLAY ALEKSEEVICH, *Permanent member of the Council for Peasant Affairs*[1]

ANNA PETROVNA, *his wife, born Sarra Abramson*[2]

SHABELSKY, MATVEY SEMYONOVICH, *Count, his maternal uncle*

LEBEDEV, PAVEL KIRILLYCH, *Chairman of the Rural Board*[3]

ZINAIDA SAVISHNA, *his wife*

SASHA, *the Lebedevs' daughter, 20*

LVOV, YEVGENY KONSTANTINOVICH, *a young country doctor*[4]

BABAKINA, MARFA YEGOROVNA, *a young widow, landowner, daughter of a rich merchant*

KOSYKH, DMITRY NIKITICH, *a tax collector*

BORKIN, MIKHAIL MIKHAILOVICH, *a distant relative of Ivanov and manager of his estate*

AVDOTYA NAZAROVNA, *an old woman of no fixed profession*

YEGORUSHKA, *a poor relation of the Lebedevs*

FIRST GUEST

SECOND GUEST

THIRD GUEST

FOURTH GUEST

PYOTR, *Ivanov's manservant*

GAVRILA, *the Lebedevs' manservant*

GUESTS *of both sexes*

MANSERVANTS

The action takes place in one of the districts[5] *of Central Russia.*

ACT ONE

A garden on Ivanov's estate. Left, the façade of a house with a veranda. One of the windows is open. In front of the veranda is a broad, semicircular expanse, with paths leading straight ahead and to the left, to the garden. At the right, little garden settees and tables. A lamp is lit on one of the latter. Evening is drawing on. At the rise of the curtain one can hear a duet for piano and cello being practiced in the house.

I

IVANOV and BORKIN.

IVANOV is sitting at a table, reading a book. BORKIN, wearing heavy boots and carrying a rifle, appears at the bottom of the garden; he is tipsy; after he spots Ivanov, he tiptoes up to him and, when he has come alongside him, aims the gun in his face.

IVANOV (*on seeing Borkin, shudders and jumps up*). Misha, God knows what . . . you scared me . . . I'm jittery enough as it is, but you keep playing these stupid jokes . . . (*Sits.*) He scared me, so he's pleased with himself . . .

BORKIN (*roars with laughter*). Right, right . . . sorry, sorry. (*Sits beside him.*) I won't do it any more, no more . . . (*Takes off his vizored cap.*) It's hot. Would you believe, sweetheart, I've covered over ten miles in something like three hours . . . I've knocked myself out . . . Just feel my heart, the way it's pounding . . .

IVANOV (*reading*). Fine, later . . .

BORKIN. No, feel it right now. (*Takes his hand and puts it on his chest.*) You hear it? Boom-boom-boom-boom-boom-boom-boom. That means I've got heart trouble. Any minute I could keel over and die. Say, would you be sorry if I died?

IVANOV. I'm reading . . . later . . .

BORKIN. No, seriously, would you be sorry if I suddenly up and died? Nikolay Alekseevich, would you be sorry if I died?

IVANOV. Stop pestering me!

BORKIN. Dear boy, tell me, would you be sorry?

IVANOV. I'm sorry that you reek of vodka. It's disgusting, Misha.

BORKIN (*laughs*). I really reek? I can't believe it . . . Actually, I can believe it. At Plesniki I ran into the coroner, and the two of us, I must admit, knocked back about eight drinks a piece. Fundamentally, drinking is very bad for your health. Tell me, is it really bad for a person's health? Is it bad for you?

IVANOV. This is unbearable, for the last time . . . Get it through your head, Misha, that this teasing . . .

BORKIN. Right, right . . . sorry, sorry! . . . Take it easy, sit down . . . (*Gets up and walks away.*) Incredible people, you're not even allowed to talk. (*Comes back.*) Oh, yes! I almost forgot . . . Let's have it, eighty-two rubles! . . .

IVANOV. What eighty-two rubles?

BORKIN. To pay the workmen tomorrow.

IVANOV. I haven't got it.

BORKIN. Thank you very kindly! (*Mimics him.*) I haven't got it . . . After all, don't the workmen have to be paid? Don't they?

IVANOV. I don't know. I haven't got anything today. Wait till the first of the month when I get my salary.[6]

BORKIN. Just try and have a conversation with characters like this! . . . The workmen aren't coming for their money on the first of the month, but tomorrow morning!

IVANOV. What am I supposed to do about it now? Go on, saw me in half, nag at me . . . And where you did you pick up this revolting habit of pestering me whenever I'm reading, writing or . . .

BORKIN. What I'm asking you is: do the workmen get paid or not? Eh, what's the use of talking to you! . . . (*Waves his hand in dismissal.*) Landowners too, the hell with 'em, lords of creation . . . Experimental farming methods . . . Nearly three hundred acres of land and not a penny in their pocket . . . It's like a wine cellar without a corkscrew. I'll go and sell the carriage-horses tomorrow! Yes, sir! . . . I sold the oats while they were still standing in the field, tomorrow I'll go and sell the rye. (*Strides up and down the stage.*) You think I'll wait for an invitation? Do you? Well, no sir, you're not dealing with that sort of person . . .

I I

The same, SHABELSKY (offstage), and ANNA PETROVNA.

SHABELSKY's voice from the window: "It's impossible to play with you . . . You've no more ear than a gefilte fish, and your touch is a disgrace."

ANNA PETROVNA (*appears in the open window*). Who was talking out here just now? Was it you, Misha? Why are you stamping around like that?

BORKIN. Talk to your *Nicolas-voilà*[7] and it'd get you stamping too.

ANNA PETROVNA. Listen, Misha, have them bring some hay to the croquet lawn.

BORKIN (*waves his hand in dismissal*). Leave me alone, please . . .

ANNA PETROVNA. Really, what a tone to take . . . That tone of voice doesn't suit you at all. If you want women to love you, never get angry with them and don't act self-important . . . (*To her husband.*) Nikolay, let's turn somersaults in the hay! . . .

IVANOV. Anyuta, it's bad for your health to stand in an open window. Go in, please . . . (*Shouts.*) Uncle, shut the window!

The window is shut.

BORKIN. Don't forget, day after tomorrow, the interest has to be paid to Lebedev.

IVANOV. I remember. I'll be at Lebedev's today and I'll ask them to postpone it . . . (*Looks at his watch.*)

BORKIN. When are you going over there?

IVANOV. Right now.

BORKIN (*quickly*). Hold on, hold on! isn't today, I think, Shurochka's birthday? . . . Well, well, well, well . . . And me forgetting all about it . . . What a memory, eh? (*Skips.*) I'll go, I'll go . . . (*Sings.*) I'll go . . . I'll go for a swim, chew some paper, take three drops of ammonia,[8] and it's off to a fresh start . . . Darling, Nikolay Alekseevich, sweetie-pie, love of my life, you're always a nervous wreck, no kidding, you're whining, constantly melancholeric,[9] and yet you and I, no kidding, could get a hell of a lot of things done together! I'm ready to do anything for you . . . You want me to marry Marfusha Babakina for your sake? Half the dowry is yours . . . I mean, not half, but all of it, take all of it! . . .

IVANOV. If you're going to talk rot . . .

BORKIN. No, seriously, no kidding, you want me to marry Marfusha? Go fifty-fifty in the dowry . . . But why am I talking to you? As if you understood me? (*Mimics him.*) "If you're going to talk rot." You're a good man, an intelligent man, but you haven't got an ounce of, what d'y'call it, you know, get up and go. If only you'd do things in a big way, raise a little hell . . . You're a neurotic, a crybaby, but if you were a normal man, you could make a million in a year's time. For instance, if I had two thousand three hundred rubles right now, in two weeks I'd have twenty thousand. You don't believe me? You think I'm talking nonsense? No, it's not nonsense . . . Just give me two thousand three hundred rubles, and in a week I'll show you twenty thousand. On the other side of the river Ovsyanov is selling a strip of land, just across from us, for two thousand three hundred rubles. If we buy that strip, we'll own both sides of the riverbank. And if we own both sides, you understand, we have the right to dam the river. Get it? We could put up a mill, and as soon as we announce that we want to build a dam, everyone who lives downstream will kick up a fuss, and right away we go *kommen Sie hier,*[10] if you don't want a dam, pay up. Get it? Zarev's factory will pay us five thousand, Korolkov three thousand, the monastery will pay five thousand . . .

IVANOV. It's all hocus-pocus, Misha . . . If you want us to stay friends, keep it to yourself.

BORKIN (*sits at the table*). Of course! . . . I knew it! You won't do anything yourself, and you tie my hands . . .

I I I

The same, SHABELSKY, and LVOV.

SHABELSKY (*coming out of the house with Lvov*). Doctors are just like lawyers, the sole difference being, lawyers only rob you, while doctors rob you *and* kill you . . . Present company excepted. (*Sits on a little settee.*) Quacks, charlatans . . . Perhaps in some Utopia you can come across an exception to the general rule, but . . . over the course of a lifetime I've squandered about twenty thousand and never met a single doctor who didn't strike me as a barefaced impostor.

BORKIN (*to Ivanov*). Yes, you won't do anything yourself and you tie my hands. That's why we don't have any money . . .

SHABELSKY. I repeat, present company excepted . . . There may be exceptions, although, even so . . . (*Yawns.*)

IVANOV (*closing the book*). Doctor, what have you got to say?

LVOV (*with a glance at the window*). The same thing I said this morning: she has to go to the Crimea at once. (*Walks up and down the stage.*)

SHABELSKY (*bursts out laughing*). The Crimea! . . . Why don't you and I, Misha, hang out a shingle as medicos? It's so easy . . . A woman sneezes or coughs because she's bored, some Madame Angot or Ophelia,[11] quick, take a scrap of paper and prescribe along scientific principles: first, a young doctor, then a trip to the Crimea, in the Crimea a strapping Tatar . . .

IVANOV (*to the Count*). Ah, stop pestering, you pest! (*To Lvov.*) To go to the Crimea you need money. Suppose I find it, she definitely refuses to take the trip . . .

LVOV. Yes, she does.

Pause.

BORKIN. Say, Doctor, is Anna Petrovna really so seriously ill that she has to go to the Crimea?

LVOV (*with a glance at the window*). Yes, tuberculosis.

BORKIN. Psss! . . . that's no good . . . For some time now I've noticed from her face that she wasn't long for this world.

LVOV. But . . . don't talk so loudly . . . you can be heard in the house . . .

Pause.

BORKIN (*sighing*). This life of ours . . . Human life is like a posy, growing gloriously in a meadow, a goat comes along, eats it, end of posy . . .

SHABELSKY. Nonsense, nonsense and more nonsense! . . . (*Yawns.*) Nonsense and monkey shines.

Pause.

BORKIN. Well, gentlemen, I keep trying to teach Nikolay Alekseevich how to make money. I've let him in on one wonderful idea, but my pollen, as usual, has fallen on barren ground. You can't hammer anything into him . . . Look at him: melancholy, spleen, tedium, depression, heartache . . .

SHABELSKY (*rises and stretches*). You're a brilliant thinker, you come up with something for everyone, you teach everyone how to live, but you've never taught me a single thing . . . Teach me, Mr. Know-it-all, show me the way to get ahead . . .

BORKIN (*rises*). I'm going for a swim . . . Good-bye, gentlemen . . . (*To the Count.*) You've got twenty ways to get ahead . . . If I were in your shoes, I'd make about twenty thousand in a week. (*Going.*)

SHABELSKY (*goes after him*). What's the gimmick? Come on, teach me.

BORKIN. There's nothing to teach. It's very easy . . . (*Returns.*) Nikolay Alekseevich, give me a ruble!

IVANOV silently gives him the money.

Merci! (*To the Count.*) You've still got a handful of aces.

SHABELSKY (*going after him*). Well, what are they?

BORKIN. In your shoes, in a week I'd make about thirty thousand, if not more. (*Exits with the Count.*)

IVANOV (*after a pause.*) Pointless people,[13] pointless talk, the pressing need to answer stupid questions, Doctor, it's all wearied me to the point of illness. I've become irritable, touchy, impatient, so petty that I don't know what I am any more. Whole days at a time my head aches, I can't sleep, ringing in my ears . . . And there's absolutely nowhere to escape to . . . Absolutely nowhere . . .

LVOV. Nikolay Alekseevich, I have to have a serious talk with you.

IVANOV. Talk away.

LVOV. It's concerning Anna Petrovna. (*Sits.*) She won't consent to go to the Crimea, but she might if you went with her.

IVANOV (*after thinking about it*). If we were to go together, we'd need money. Besides, they certainly wouldn't give me a leave of absence. I've already taken one leave this year . . .

LVOV. Let's assume that's true. Now, moving on. The most important treatment for tuberculosis is absolute peace and quiet, and your wife doesn't have a moment's peace. She's constantly upset by the way you treat her. Excuse me, I'm concerned and I'll speak bluntly. Your behavior is killing her.

Pause.

Nikolay Alekseevich, give me some cause to think better of you!

IVANOV. It's all true, true . . . I'm probably terribly to blame, but my mind's messed up, my soul is mired in a kind of indolence, and I can't seem to understand myself. I don't understand other people or myself. (*With a glance at the window.*) They can hear us, let's go, let's take a walk.

Gets up.

My dear friend, I should tell you the story from the very beginning. But it's long and so complicated that I wouldn't finish before morning.

They walk.

Anyuta is a remarkable, an exceptional woman . . . For my sake she converted to my religion, cast off her father and mother, turned her back on wealth, and if I'd demanded another hundred sacrifices, she would have made them, without blinking an eye. Well, sir, there nothing at all remarkable about me and I made no sacrifices at all. Though it's a long story . . .

The whole gist of it, dear Doctor (*hesitates*), is . . . to make a long story short, I married when I was passionately in love and swore love everlasting, but . . . five years have gone by, she's still in love with me, while I . . . (*Splays his hands in a gesture of futility.*) Now you're going to tell me that she'll die soon, but I don't feel any love or pity, just a sort of void, weariness. Anyone looking at me from the outside would probably think this is awful; I don't understand myself what's going on inside me . . .

They go off down a garden path.

I V

SHABELSKY, *then* ANNA PETROVNA.

SHABELSKY (*enters, roaring with laughter*). Honest to God, he's not a crook, he's a visionary, a virtuoso! Ought to put up a monument to him. He's a thorough blend of modern pus in all its variety: lawyer, doctor, speculator, accountant. (*Sits on a low step of the veranda.*) And yet he seems never to have gone to school anywhere, that's what's amazing . . . What a brilliant criminal he probably would have been, if he'd picked up a bit of culture, the liberal arts! "In a week," he says, "you could have twenty thousand. You've got a handful of aces," he says, "your title as Count." (*Roars with laughter.*) "Any girl with a dowry would marry you" . . .

ANNA PETROVNA opens the window and looks down.

"Want me to make a match between you and Marfusha?" he says. *Qui est ce que c'est* Marfusha?[14] Ah, that Balabalkina creature . . . Babakalkina . . . the one that looks like a washerwoman.

ANNA PETROVNA. Is that you, Count?

SHABELSKY. What's that?

ANNA PETROVNA laughs.

(*In a Jewish accent.*) Vot you should leffing at?

ANNA PETROVNA. I was remembering a certain saying of yours. Remember, you said it at dinner? A thief unchastised, a horse . . . How did it go?

SHABELSKY. A kike baptized, a thief unchastised, a horse hospitalized are not to be prized.

ANNA PETROVNA (*laughs*). You can't even make a simple play on words without malice. You're a malicious person. (*Seriously.*) Joking aside, Count, you are very malicious. Living with you is depressing and terrifying. You're always grumbling, grousing, you think everyone's a scoundrel and a villain. Tell me, Count, frankly: have you ever said anything nice about anyone?

SHABELSKY. What sort of cross-examination is this!

ANNA PETROVNA. You and I have been living together under the same roof for five years now, and never once have I heard you speak of people neutrally, without sarcasm or sneering. What harm have people done you? Do you think you're better than everyone else?

SHABELSKY. I certainly don't think that. I'm the same blackguard and swine in man's clothing[15] as everyone else. *Mauvais ton*, an old has-been. I always have a bad word for myself too. Who am I? What am I? I was rich, independent, somewhat happy, and now . . . a parasite, a freeloader, a dislocated buffoon. If I get indignant, if I express disdain, people laugh in my face; if I laugh, they shake their heads at me sadly and say: the old man's off his rocker . . . Most of the time, though, they don't listen to me, take no notice of me . . .

ANNA PETROVNA (*calmly*). Screeching again . . .

SHABELSKY. Who's screeching?

ANNA PETROVNA. The owl. It screeches every evening.

SHABELSKY. Let it screech. Things can't get worse than they already are. (*Stretches.*) Ah, my dearest Sarra, just let me win one or two hundred thousand, and then watch me kick up my heels! . . . You wouldn't see me for dust. I'd run away from this dump, from freeloading, and I wouldn't set foot here till doomsday . . .

ANNA PETROVNA. And just what would you do if you won?

SHABELSKY (*after a moment's thought*). First of all I'd go to Moscow and listen to gypsy music. Then . . . then I'd scamper off to Paris. I'd rent an apartment, attend the Russian church . . .

ANNA PETROVNA. What else?

SHABELSKY. I'd spend whole days sitting by my wife's grave, lost in thought. I would sit at her grave like that till I kicked the bucket.

Pause.

ANNA PETROVNA. That's awfully depressing. Shall we play another duet or something?

SHABELSKY. All right. Get out the music.

ANNA PETROVNA exits.

V

SHABELSKY, IVANOV, and LVOV.

IVANOV (*appearing on the path with Lvov*). Dear friend, you got your degree only last year, you're still young and vigorous, but I'm thirty-five. I have the right to give you advice. Don't marry Jewish girls or neurotics or intellectuals, but pick out something ordinary, drab, without flashy colors or extraneous sounds. Generally speaking, match your life to a standard pattern. The grayer and more monotonous the background, the better. My dear man, don't wage war singlehandedly against thousands, don't tilt at windmills, don't run headlong into walls . . . God forbid you go in for any experimental farming methods, alternative schools, impassioned speeches . . . Shut yourself up in your shell and go about your petty, God-given business. That's more comfortable, more authentic, more healthy. Whereas the life I've led, what a bore! Ah, what a bore! . . . So many mistakes, injustices, so much absurdity . . .[1] (*On seeing the Count, annoyed.*) You're always spinning around in front of us, uncle, you never let me have a moment's privacy!

SHABELSKY (*in a tearful voice*). Damn it all, there's no place for me anywhere. (*Jumps up and goes into the house.*)

IVANOV (*shouts after him*). There, I'm sorry, I'm sorry. (*To Lvov.*) Why did I have to insult him? No, I'm definitely going to pieces. Got to get a grip on myself. Got to . . .

LVOV (*overwrought*). Nikolay Alekseevich, I've been listening to you and . . . and, excuse me, I'll speak frankly, no beating about the bush. Your voice, your intonations, let alone your words, are so full of heartless egotism, such

---

1 "What my Ivanov says to Doctor Lvov is said by a worn-out, haggard man; on the contrary, a man must constantly if not crawl out, then peep out of his shell, and he must grapple with ideas all his life, otherwise it's not a life, but an existence" (Chekhov to his brother Mikhail, March 5, 1901).

cold cruelty . . . A person near and dear to you is perishing because she is near to you, her days are numbered, while you . . . you cannot love, you take walks, hand out advice, strike poses . . . I cannot find a way to express it, I haven't got the gift of gab, but . . . but I find you deeply repugnant! . . .

IVANOV. Could be, could be . . . A third party might have a clearer picture . . . It's quite possible that you do understand me . . . I'm probably very, very much at fault . . . (*Lends an ear.*) I think the horses have been brought round. I have to go and change . . . (*He walks to the house and stops.*) Doctor, you don't like me and you don't conceal the fact. It does your heart credit. (*Exits into the house.*)

LVOV (*alone*). This damned temper of mine . . . Again I missed my chance and didn't talk to him the way I should . . . I can't talk to him coolly and calmly! No sooner do I open my mouth and say a single word, when something here (*points to his chest*) starts to choke up, goes in reverse, and my tongue cleaves to the roof of my mouth. I hate this Tartuffe,[16] this puffed-up swindler, most heartily . . . Now he's going out . . . His unhappy wife's one pleasure is his being near her, she breathes through him, pleads with him to spend at least one night with her, and he . . . he cannot . . . For him, you see, the house is stifling and claustrophobic. If he spent even one night at home, he'd put a bullet through his brain from sheer ennui! Poor fellow . . . he needs wide open spaces, so he can perpetrate some more underhanded acts . . . Oh, I know why you ride over to those Lebedevs every night! I know!

V I

*LVOV, IVANOV (in a hat and overcoat), SHABELSKY, and
ANNA PETROVNA.*

SHABELSKY (*coming out of the house with Ivanov and Anna Petrovna*). Really, *Nicolas*, this is inhuman! You go out every night by yourself, and leave us all on our own. Bored stiff, we go to bed at eight o'clock. This is an abomination, not life! How come you can go out and we can't? How come?

ANNA PETROVNA. Count, leave him alone! Let him go, let him . . .

IVANOV (*to his wife*). Well, where would you, a sick woman, go? You're sick and you mustn't go out of doors after sundown . . . Ask the doctor here.

You're not a child, Anyuta, you have to be sensible . . . (*To the Count.*) And why should *you* go out?

SHABELSKY. I'd go to blue blazes, I'd crawl down a crocodile's gullet rather than stay here. I'm bored! I'm petrified with boredom! Everybody's sick and tired of me. You leave me at home so she won't be bored on her own, and I've nagged her to death, chewed her to pieces!

ANNA PETROVNA. Leave him alone, Count, leave him! Let him go if it gives him pleasure.

IVANOV. Anya, why take that tone? You know I don't go there for pleasure! I have to discuss the terms of the loan.

ANNA PETROVNA. I don't understand why you feel the need to make excuses? Go ahead! Who's keeping you here?

IVANOV. Friends, let's not devour one another! Is this absolutely necessary?

SHABELSKY (*in a tearful voice*). Nicolas, dear boy, do please take me with you! I'll get an eyeful of those crooks and idiots and, maybe, have some fun. Honestly, I haven't been anywhere since Easter!

IVANOV (*annoyed*). All right, let's go! I'm sick and tired of the lot of you!

SHABELSKY. Really? Well, *merci, merci* . . . (*Merrily takes him by the arm and leads him aside.*) May I wear your straw hat?

IVANOV. You may, only hurry up, for pity's sake!

The COUNT runs into the house.

How sick and tired I am of the lot of you! But what am I saying, my friends? Anya, I'm speaking to you in an impossible tone. This is something new for me. Well, good-bye, Anya, I'll be back by one.

ANNA PETROVNA. Kolya, darling, do stay home!

IVANOV (*excited*). My sweetest, my dearest, unhappy woman, for pity's sake don't keep me from going out at night. It's cruel, unfair on my part, but let me commit this injustice! The house weighs on me like lead! As soon as the sun goes down my mind starts to be poisoned by tedium. Such tedium! Don't ask why it's like that. I don't know myself. I swear to the God we believe in, I don't know! I'm gloomy here, and when you go to the Lebedevs, it's even worse there; you come back from there, it's still gloomy here, and so it goes all night long . . . It's totally hopeless! . . .

ANNA PETROVNA. Kolya . . . then you should stay here! We'll talk about things, the way we used to . . . We'll have some supper together, we'll read . . . The grouch and I practiced lots of duets for you . . . (*Embraces him.*) Do stay!

Pause.

I don't understand you. This has been going on all year long. Why have you changed?

IVANOV. I don't know, I don't know . . .

ANNA PETROVNA. And why don't you want me to go out with you in the evenings?

IVANOV. If you must know, then, I suppose I can tell you. It's rather cruel to talk this way, but it's best to get it out . . . When I'm tormented by tedium, I . . . I start to stop loving you. At times like that I run away from you. In short, I have to get out of the house.

ANNA PETROVNA. Tedium? I understand, I understand . . . You know what, Kolya? You should try, as you used to, to sing, laugh, lose your temper . . . Stay here, we'll laugh, have some homemade cordial, and we'll chase away your tedium in a minute. Would you like me to sing something? Or we'll go, sit in your study, in the shadows, the way we used to, and you can tell me about your tedium . . . Your eyes are filled with such pain! I'll gaze into them and cry, and we'll both feel better. . . . (*Laughs and cries.*) Or, Kolya, how does it go? The flowers return every spring, but joy never does?[17] Am I right? Well, go on, go on . . .

IVANOV. Pray to God for me, Anya! (*He goes, stops and thinks.*) No, I can't. (*He exits.*)

ANNA PETROVNA. Go on . . . (*Sits at the table.*)

LVOV (*paces up and down the stage*). Anna Petrovna, make yourself a rule: as soon as the clock strikes six, you have to go to your room and not come out until morning. The evening damp is bad for your health.

ANNA PETROVNA. Your wish is my command, sir.

LVOV. What's "your wish is my command, sir" supposed to mean! I'm talking seriously.

ANNA PETROVNA. But I don't want to be serious. (*Coughs.*)

LVOV. There, you see, you're coughing already . . .

VII

LVOV, ANNA PETROVNA, and SHABELSKY.

SHABELSKY (*comes out of the house in hat and overcoat*). Where's Nikolay? Have the horses been brought round? (*Goes quickly and kisses Anna Petrovna's hand.*) Good night, lovely lady! (*Makes a face.*) Gevalt![18] Excusink me, pliss! (*Rapid exit.*)

LVOV. Buffoon!

> *Pause; the distant strains of a concertina are heard.*

ANNA PETROVNA. How boring! . . . Out there the coachmen and the cooks are having a dance, while I . . . I'm like some thing that's been discarded . . . Yevgeny Konstantinovich, why are you pacing back and forth? Come over here, sit down! . . .

LVOV. I can't sit down.

> *Pause.*

ANNA PETROVNA. They're playing "The Goldfinch" in the kitchen. (*Sings.*) "Goldfinch, goldfinch, where have you been? Drinking vodka on the hills so green?"

> *Pause.*

Doctor, are your father and mother still alive?

LVOV. My father's dead, my mother's alive.

ANNA PETROVNA. Do you miss your mother?

LVOV. I've no time to miss anyone.

ANNA PETROVNA (*laughs*). The flowers return every spring, but joy never does. Who quoted that line to me? God help my memory . . . I think Nikolay quoted it. (*Lends an ear.*) The owl is screeching again!

LVOV. Then let it screech.

ANNA PETROVNA. Doctor, I'm beginning to think that Fate has dealt me a
losing hand. Most people, who may be no better than I am, lead happy
lives and never pay for their happiness. But I have paid for everything,
absolutely everything! . . . And at such a cost! Why am I being charged
such high interest? . . . My dear man, you're always so solicitous of me,
you're so tactful, you're afraid to tell me the truth, but you think I don't
know what sort of illness I have? I know all too well. Still, it's boring to talk
about . . . (*In a Jewish accent.*) Excusink me, pliss! Do you know how to tell
funny stories?

LVOV. I don't.

ANNA PETROVNA. Nikolay knows how. And I'm starting to wonder so much
at the unfairness of people: why don't they reciprocate love for love, why
do they pay back truth with lies? Tell me: how long will my father and
mother go on hating me? They live nearly forty miles from here, but I can
feel their hatred, night and day, even in my dreams. And what can you prescribe to make sense of Nikolay's tedium? He says he stops loving me only
in the evenings, when he's gnawed by tedium. I can understand that and
put up with it, but imagine if he's fallen out of love with me completely!
Of course, that's impossible, but what if all of a sudden? No, no, I mustn't
even think about it. (*Sings.*) "Goldfinch, goldfinch, where have you
been?" (*Shudders.*) The horrible thoughts I have! . . . Doctor, you're not a
family man, so you can't understand a lot of this . . .

LVOV. You wonder . . . (*He sits beside her.*) No, I wonder, wonder at you! Now,
explain, spell it out for me, how could you, an intelligent, honorable, almost
saintly woman, have let yourself be so brazenly tricked and dragged into
this nest of screech owls? Why are you here? What do you have in common with this cold, heartless . . . but let's leave your husband out of it! —
what do you have in common with this vacuous, vulgar milieu? Oh, good
God in heaven! . . . this constantly grumbling, decrepit, insane count, this
creepy super-swindler Misha, making his vile faces . . . Explain to me, what
are you doing here? How did you end up here?

ANNA PETROVNA (*laughs*). That's exactly the way he used to talk . . . Word
for word . . . But his eyes are bigger, and when he used to talk about something with enthusiasm, they'd be like glowing coals . . . Keep talking, keep
talking!

LVOV (*rises and waves his hand in dismissal*). What am I supposed to talk about? Please go inside . . .

ANNA PETROVNA. You say that Nikolay's this and that, six of one, half of a dozen of the other. How do you know this? Can you really analyze a person in six months' time? Doctor, he's a remarkable man, and I'm sorry that you didn't get to know him two or three years ago. Now he's depressed, taciturn, doens't do anything, but in the past . . . Such splendor! . . . I fell in love with him at first sight. (*Laughs.*) One glimpse of him and I was caught in the mousetrap, snap! He said: let's go . . . I cut myself off from everything, you know, the way people snip off withered leaves with a scissors, and I went . . .

Pause.

And now it's different . . . Now he goes to the Lebedevs, to be entertained by other women, while I . . . sit in the garden and listen to the owl screeching. . . .

The WATCHMAN *taps.*[19]

Doctor, don't you have any brothers?

LVOV. No.

ANNA PETROVNA *sobs.*

Well, what is it now? What's wrong with you?

ANNA PETROVNA (*rises*). I can't help it, Doctor, I'm going to go over there . . .

LVOV. Over where?

ANNA PETROVNA. Where he is . . . I'll drive over there . . . Have them harness the horses . . . (*Runs into the house.*)

LVOV. No, I definitely refuse to practice under such conditions! It's not bad enough that they don't pay me a penny, but they also turn my feelings inside-out! . . . No, I refuse! Enough is enough! . . . (*Goes into the house.*)

Curtain

ACT TWO

A reception room in the Lebedevs' house; there is an entry directly into the garden; doors right and left. Antique, expensive furniture. A chandelier, candelabrums, and pictures, all under dustcovers.[20]

I

ZINAIDA SAVISHNA, FIRST GUEST, SECOND GUEST, THIRD GUEST, KOSYKH, AVDOTYA NAZAROVNA, YEGORUSHKA, GAVRILA, MAID-SERVANT, OLD LADY GUESTS, YOUNG LADIES, and BABAKINA.

ZINAIDA SAVISHNA is sitting on a sofa. On both sides of her in armchairs are OLD LADY GUESTS; on straight chairs the YOUNG PEOPLE. In the distance, near the entry to the garden, people are playing cards;[21] *among the players: KOSYKH, AVDOTYA NAZAROVNA, and YEGORUSHKA. GAVRILA is standing by the door at right; the MAID-SERVANT is handing round a tray of sweetmeats. Throughout the whole act guests circulate from the garden to the door at right and back again. BABAKINA enters through the door at right and heads for Zinaida Savishna.*

ZINAIDA SAVISHNA (*delighted*). Sweetheart, Marfa Yegorovna . . .

BABAKINA. How are you, Zinaida Savishna! I'm honored to congratulate you on your birthday girl . . .

They exchange kisses.

God bless . . .

ZINAIDA SAVISHNA. Thank you, sweetheart, I'm pleased to see you . . . Well, how are you feeling?

BABAKINA. Thanks ever so for asking. (*Sits next to the sofa.*) How are you, young people!

The GUESTS rise and bow.

FIRST GUEST (*laughs*). Young people . . . Are you so old?

BABAKINA (*sighing*). What would we be doing among the youngsters?

FIRST GUEST (*laughs respectfully*). For heaven's sake, how can you . . . You may be what's called a widow, but you could give a nine-point handicap to any young woman.

GAVRILA serves Babakina from a teatray.

ZINAIDA SAVISHNA (*to Gavrila*). Why are you serving it like that? You should bring some preserves. Gooseberry or something . . .

BABAKINA. Don't go to the trouble, thanks ever so . . .

Pause.

FIRST GUEST. Did you come by way of Mushkino, Marfa Yegorovna? . . .

BABAKINA. No, Zamishche. The road's better there.

FIRST GUEST. True enough, ma'am.

KOSYKH. Two spades.

YEGORUSHKA. Pass.

AVDOTYA NAZAROVNA. Pass.

SECOND GUEST. Pass.

BABAKINA. Lottery tickets, Zinaida Savishna sweetheart, have gone right through the roof again.[22] Have you ever heard of such a thing: the first drawing already costs two hundred and seventy, and the second well nigh two hundred and fifty . . . Never heard of anything like it . . .

ZINAIDA SAVISHNA (*sighs*). It's all very well for those who've got a lot of them . . .

BABAKINA. Don't you think so, sweetheart; they may cost a lot, but they make an unprofitable investment for your capital. The insurance alone will be the death of you.

ZINAIDA SAVISHNA. That's so, but all the same, my dear, you go on hoping . . . (*Sighs.*) God is merciful . . .

THIRD GUEST. The way I see it, *mesdames*, I consider that at the present time it's very unprofitable to have capital at all. Gilt-edged securities may earn very small dividends, but putting money in circulation is extremely risky. As I understand it, *mesdames*, the man who has capital at the present time is in a more precarious situation than the man who, *mesdames* . . .

BABAKINA (*sighs*). That's so true!

The FIRST GUEST yawns.

How can a person yawn in the presence of ladies!

FIRST GUEST. *Pardon, mesdames,* it was an accident.

ZINAIDA SAVISHNA gets up and exits through the door at right; a prolonged silence.

YEGORUSHKA. Two diamonds.

AVDOTYA NAZAROVNA. Pass.

SECOND GUEST. Pass.

KOSYKH. Pass.

BABAKINA (*aside*). Good Lord, it's so boring, you could drop dead!

I I

The same, ZINAIDA SAVISHNA, and LEBEDEV.

ZINAIDA SAVISHNA (*entering from the door right with Lebedev, quietly*). Why are you planted out there? What a prima donna! Sit with the guests. (*Sits in her former place.*)

LEBEDEV (*yawns*). Ugh, forgive us sinners! (*On seeing Babakina.*) Good Lord, our pot of jam is sitting here! Our Turkish delight! (*Greets her.*) How is your most precious little self?

BABAKINA. Thanks ever so.

LEBEDEV. Well, hallelujah! . . . Hallelujah! (*Sits in an armchair.*) Well, well . . . Gavrila!

GAVRILA serves him a shot of vodka and a glass of water. He drinks the vodka and chases it down with water.

FIRST GUEST. Your very good health! . . .

LEBEDEV. What do you mean, good health! . . . I haven't croaked yet, and I'm thankful for that. (*To his wife.*) Zyuzyushka, where's our birthday girl?

KOSYKH (*tearfully*). Tell me, for heaven's sake: well, how come we didn't take a single trick? (*Leaps up.*) Well, then why did we lose, damn it all to hell!

AVDOTYA NAZAROVNA (*leaps up, angrily*). Because, my good man, if you don't know how to play, don't sit in. Since when are you entitled to lead somebody else's suit? That's how you got stuck with that pickled ace of yours!

They both run out from behind the table.

KOSYKH (*in a tearful voice*). If I may, my friends . . . I was holding diamonds: ace, king, queen, jack and eight low cards, ace of spades, and one, you understand, one lousy little heart, and she, for some damn reason, couldn't call a little slam! . . . I bid no trumps . . .

AVDOTYA NAZAROVNA (*interrupting*). I'm the one who bid no trumps! You bid: two no trumps . . .[23]

KOSYKH. This is a disgrace! . . . If I may . . . you had . . . I had . . . you had . . . (*To Lebedev.*) Now you be the judge, Pavel Kirillych . . . I was holding diamonds: ace, king, queen, jack, and eight low cards . . .

LEBEDEV (*covers up his ears*). Stop, do me a favor . . . stop . . .

AVDOTYA NAZAROVNA (*shouts*). I was the one who bid: no trumps!

KOSYKH (*fiercely*). Call me a villain and an outcast if I ever sit down to play with that old barracuda again! (*Quickly exits into the garden.*)

*The SECOND GUEST follows him out; YEGORUSHKA
remains at the table.*

AVDOTYA NAZAROVNA. Oof! . . . He's got me all overheated. . . . Stickle-back! . . . Barracuda yourself!

BABAKINA. Well, now you've gone and lost your temper, Granny!

AVDOTYA NAZAROVNA (*on seeing Babakina, throws up her hands*). My honey-bun, my beauty! . . . She's here, and, blind as a biddy, I didn't see her . . . Sweetie-pie . . . (*Kisses her on the shoulder and sits beside her.*) What a treat! Let me take a good look at you, my snow-white swan! Poo, poo, poo . . . evil eye begone![24]

LEBEDEV. Well, now she's wound up . . . You'd better find her a bride-groom . . .

AVDOTYA NAZAROVNA. And I will! I won't go quiet to my grave, with all my sins on my head, until I get her married and your Sanichka too! I won't go quiet . . . (*Deep sigh.*) Only there now, where are you to find bridegrooms nowadays? There they sit, these bridegrooms of ours, as crestfallen as drenched roosters! . . .

THIRD GUEST. An extremely feeble simile. The way I look at it, *mesdames*, if young people nowadays prefer a celibate life, the guilty party is, so to speak, social conditions . . .

LEBEDEV. Now, now! . . . no philosophizing! . . . I don't care for it! . . .

I I I

The same and SASHA.

SASHA (*enters and goes up to her father*). Such splendid weather, and you're sitting in here, ladies and gentlemen, in this stuffy air.

ZINAIDA SAVISHNA. Sashenka, don't you see that Marfa Yegorovna is here?

SASHA. Sorry. (*Goes to Babakina and greets her.*)

BABAKINA. You're getting to be quite standoffish, Sanichka, quite stand-offish, haven't paid me a single visit. (*Exchanges kisses.*) Congratulations, sweetheart . . .

SASHA. Thank you. (*Sits next to her father.*)

LEBEDEV. Yes, Avdotya Nazarovna, it's hard to find bridegrooms nowadays. Not just bridegrooms—you can't get a passable best man. The young people these days, no offense meant, have, God bless them, an off-taste, like leftovers reheated . . . Can't dance or talk or have a serious drink with 'em . . .

AVDOTYA NAZAROVNA. Well, drinking's one thing they know all about, just let 'em at it . . .

LEBEDEV. There's no great trick to drinking, even a horse knows how to drink . . . No, I'm talking serious drinking! . . . In our time, used to be, you'd get worn out at lectures all day long, and as soon as it was dark, you'd go straight to wherever a fire was blazing and spin like a top till dawn came up . . . And you'd dance, and flirt with the young ladies, and that took knowhow. (*Flicks himself on the throat.*)[25] Used to be, you'd blather and philosophize till your jaw came unhinged . . . But nowadays . . . (*Waves his hand in dismissal.*) I don't understand . . . They're wishy-washy, neither this nor that. In the whole district there's only one decent fellow, and he's married (*sighs*), and it looks like he's starting to go crazy, too . . .

BABAKINA. Who's that?

LEBEDEV. Nikolasha Ivanov.

BABAKINA. Yes, he's a good man (*makes a face*), only so unhappy! . . .

ZINAIDA SAVISHNA. You said it, sweetheart, how can he be happy! (*Sighs.*) What a mistake he made, poor thing! He married his kike bitch[26] and figured, poor thing, that her father and mother would heap mountains of gold on her, but it came out quite the opposite . . . From the time she converted, her father and mother wouldn't have anything to do with her, cursed her . . . Not a penny did he get out of them. He's sorry for it now, but it's too late . . .

SASHA. Mama, that's not true.

BABAKINA (*heatedly*). Shurochka, why isn't it true? After all, everybody knows it. If it weren't for gain, why else would he marry a Jew girl? Aren't there plenty of Russian girls? He miscalculated, sweetheart, miscalculated . . . (*Vigorously.*) Lord, and now doesn't he make it hot for her! Simply laughable. He'll come home from somewhere and right away he goes: "Your father and mother cheated me! Get out of my house!" And where can she go? Father and mother won't take her in, she could become a housemaid, but she wasn't brought up to work . . . So he rags on her and rags on her, until the Count stands up for her. If it weren't for the Count, he would have done her in long ago . . .

AVDOTYA NAZAROVNA. Besides that, sometimes he locks her up in the cellar with "Eat your garlic, you so-and-so" . . . She eats it and eats it, till she starts to stink from the inside out.

Laughter.

SASHA. Papa, that's got to be another lie!

LEBEDEV. Well, so what? Let 'em gossip if it keeps 'em healthy . . . (*Shouts.*) Gavrila!

GAVRILA serves him vodka and water.

ZINAIDA SAVISHNA. So that's why he's ruined, poor thing. His business, sweetheart, has quite fallen off . . . If Borkin weren't looking after the estate, there wouldn't be anything for him and his kike bitch to eat. (*Sighs.*) As for us, sweetheart, the way we've suffered on account of him! . . . Suffered so much that only God can tell! Would you believe, my dear, for three years now, he's owed us nine thousand!

BABAKINA (*horrified*). Nine thousand!

ZINAIDA SAVISHNA. Yes . . . It was that hubby dear of mine who arranged to lend it to him. He can't tell the difference between someone you can lend to and someone you can't. The principal I've given up on already, may it rest in peace, but I wish he'd pay the interest on time.

SASHA (*heatedly*). Mama, you've told us about this a thousand times already!

ZINAIDA SAVISHNA. What's got into you? Why are you standing up for him?

SASHA (*rises*). But how can you have the heart to say such things about a man who never did you any harm? Why, what has he done to you?

THIRD GUEST. Aleksandra Pavlovna, if I may put in a word or two! I respect Nikolay Alekseich and always considered it an honor to know him, but, *entre nous*, he strikes me as a confidence trickster.

SASHA. Well, bully for you, if that's how he strikes you.

THIRD GUEST. In evidence I proffer the following item, which was related to me by his attaché or, so to speak, cicerone[2] Borkin. Two years ago, during the cattle epidemic, he bought livestock, insured them . . .

ZINAIDA SAVISHNA. Yes, yes, yes! I remember that incident. I've heard about it too.

THIRD GUEST. Insured them, mind you, then infected them with cow-pox and collected the insurance money.

SASHA. Ah, that's all nonsense! Nonsense! Nobody bought cattle and infected them! Borkin himself concocted that scheme and bragged about it all over

---

2 Italian: a guide who shows antiquities. The pretentious Third Guest is misusing foreign words.

the place. When Ivanov found out about it, Borkin had to beg his forgiveness for two weeks running. Ivanov's only fault is that he's a soft touch and doesn't have the heart to kick Borkin out, his fault is that he trusts people too much! Everything he had has been filched and pilfered from him; because of his generous projects anyone who wanted could make a fortune out of him.

LEBEDEV. Shura's a hothead! That'll do!

SASHA. Why do they talk such nonsense about him? Ah, all this is boring, so boring! Ivanov, Ivanov, Ivanov—there's no other topic of conversation. (*Goes to the door and returns.*) I'm amazed. (*To the young people.*) I am truly amazed at your patience, gentlemen! Aren't you bored just sitting here this way? The very air is condensing with ennui! Say something, entertain the young ladies, show signs of life! Well, if all you can talk about is Ivanov, then laugh, sing, dance, something . . .

LEBEDEV (*laughs*). Tell 'em off, tell 'em off good and proper.

SASHA. Well, listen, just do me this favor! If you don't want to talk, laugh, sing, if that's all a bore, I beg you, I implore you, at least once in your life, out of curiosity, just as a surprise or a practical joke, gather your strength and suddenly think up something witty, brilliant, at least say something outrageous or obscene, so long as it's funny and original! Or suddenly come up with something infinitesmal, barely perceptible, but the tiniest bit like an achievement, so that the ladies, at least once in their lives, might look at you and go "Aah!" Listen, you want to please the ladies, don't you, then why don't you make an effort to please them? Ah, gentlemen! You're all wrong, wrong, wrong! . . . One look at you and the flies drop dead and the lamps go black with soot. Wrong, wrong! . . . I've told you a thousand times and I'll go on telling you, that you're all wrong, wrong, wrong! . . .

I V

The same, IVANOV, and SHABELSKY.

SHABELSKY (*entering with Ivanov from the door at right*). Who's speechifying around here? You, Shurochka! (*Roars with laughter and shakes her hand.*) Congratulations, my angel, may God postpone your death and make sure you're not reincarnated . . .

ZINAIDA SAVISHNA (*gleefully*). Nikolay Alekseevich, Count! . . .

LEBEDEV. Bah! Who do I see . . . Count! (*Goes to meet him.*)

SHABELSKY (*on seeing Zinaida Savishna and Babakina, extends his arms in their direction*). Two gold-mines on one sofa! A sight for sore eyes! (*Greets them; to Zinaida Savishna.*) How are you, Zyuzyushka! (*To Babakina.*) How are you, my little puff-ball! . . .

ZINAIDA SAVISHNA. I'm so pleased. You're such an infrequent guest here, Count! (*Shouts.*) Gavrila, tea! Please, take a seat! (*Gets up, exits through the door right and immediately returns, with an extremely preoccupied look.*)

> SASHA *sits in her former seat.* IVANOV *silently exchanges greetings with everyone.*

LEBEDEV (*to Shabelsky*). Where've you turned up from out of the blue? What wild horses have dragged you here? This is a surprise, or I'll be damned . . . (*Kisses him.*) Count, you're a real cutthroat! Respectable people don't behave this way! (*Takes him by the arm down to the footlights.*) Why haven't you visited us? Angry or something?

SHABELSKY. How am I supposed to visit you? Flying on a broomstick? I haven't got horses of my own, and Nikolay won't take me with him, makes me stay with Sarra so she won't get bored. Send your own horses for me, and then I'll pay you a visit . . .

LEBEDEV (*waves his hand in dismissal*). Oh sure! . . . Zyuzyushka would rather drop dead than use the horses. Old pal, dear man, you really are dearer and sweeter to me than all the rest of them! Of all the old-timers, you and I are the only ones left! "In you I love my bygone suff'rings, In you I love my wasted youth."[28] Joking aside, I could almost weep. (*Kisses the Count.*)

SHABELSKY. Cut it out, cut it out! You smell like a wine cellar . . .

LEBEDEV. Dear heart, you can't imagine how bored I am without my friends! Ready to hang myself from tedium . . . (*Quietly.*) Zyuzyushka and her money-lending have driven away all the respectable people, there's only Zulus left . . . these Dudkins,[3] Budkins . . . Here, have some tea.

> GAVRILA *serves the Count tea.*

---

3 Dudkin (Mr. Bagpipe), "son of a rich factory-owner," was a character in the first version of *Ivanov*. Chekhov cut Dudkin from the script in the interests of a more serious play, and divided his lines between First and Third Guests.

ZINAIDA SAVISHNA (*worried, to Gavrila*). Well, how are you serving it? You should bring some preserves . . . Gooseberry or something . . .

SHABELSKY (*roars with laughter; to Ivanov*). There, didn't I tell you? (*To Lebedev.*) I made a bet with him on the way that, as soon as we got here, Zyuzyushka would immediately offer us gooseberry preserves . . .

ZINAIDA SAVISHNA. Count, you're still the same scoffer . . . (*Sits.*)

LEBEDEV. Twenty kegs they made of it, how else can you get rid of the stuff?

SHABELSKY (*sitting beside the table*). Still saving up, Zyuzyushka? Well now, are you a millionaire yet, eh?

ZINAIDA SAVISHNA (*with a sigh*). Yes, if you judge by appearances, nobody's richer than we are, but where's the money coming from? Nothing but talk . . .

SHABELSKY. Well, yes, yes! . . . we know! . . . "We know how badly you play checkers"[29] . . . (*To Lebedev.*) Pasha, tell me on your honor, have you saved up a million?

LEBEDEV. For heaven's sake, I don't know. You'd better ask Zyuzyushka . . .

SHABELSKY (*to Babakina*). And my pudgy little puff-ball is soon going to have a little million! Good grief, she's getting prettier and plumper not by the day, but by the hour! That's what it means to have lots of dough . . .

BABAKINA. Thanks ever so, your highness, only I don't like being made fun of.

SHABELSKY. My dearest gold-mine, how am I making fun of you? It's simply a cry from the heart, a spontaneous overflow of feelings that finds issue at my lips . . . I love you and Zyuzyushka infinitely . . . (*Merrily.*) Excitement! . . . Ecstasy! I can't gaze on either one of you indifferently . . .

ZINAIDA SAVISHNA. You're just the same as ever. (*To Yegorushka.*) Yegorushka, put out the candles! Why do you let them burn for no reason, if you're not playing?

YEGORUSHKA *is startled; puts out the candles and sits down.*

(*To Ivanov.*) Nikolay Alekseevich, how is your lady wife getting on?

IVANOV. Badly. Today the doctor definitely confirmed that she has tuberculosis . . .

ZINAIDA SAVISHNA. You don't say so? What a pity! . . . (*Sighs.*) We're all so fond of her.

SHABELSKY. Hogwash! . . . It's not tuberculosis, just medical quackery, hocus-pocus. Æsculapius[30] wants to hang around, so he comes up with tuberculosis. Luckily the husband's not the jealous type. (*IVANOV makes a gesture of impatience.*) As for Sarra herself, I don't trust a single one of her words or movements. In my whole life I've never trusted doctor or lawyers or women. Hogwash, quackery, and hocus-pocus!

LEBEDEV (*to Shabelsky*). You're an incredible character, Matvey! . . . You put on this misanthrope act and show it off like a retarded kid with a new toy. You're as human as anyone else, but once you start talking, it's as if your tongue were spewing poison or you had a hacking cough . . . Yes, honest to God!

SHABELSKY. What am I supposed to do, be lovey-dovey with swindlers and scoundrels, I suppose?

LEBEDEV. Just where do you see swindlers and scoundrels?

SHABELSKY. Present company excepted, of course, but . . .

LEBEDEV. There's that "but" of yours . . . This is all an act.

SHABELSKY. An act . . . You're lucky you don't have any sort of world view.

LEBEDEV. Why should I have a world view? I sit, expecting to drop dead any minute. That's my world view. You and I, my boy, haven't got time to concoct world views. That's how it goes . . . (*Shouts.*) Gavrila!

SHABELSKY. You've Gavrila-ed it up enough already . . . Look how red your nose has got! . . .

LEBEDEV (*drinks*). Never mind, dear heart . . . I'm not going to get married today.

ZINAIDA SAVISHNA. It's been a long time since Dr. Lvov paid us a call. He's quite forgotten us.

SASHA. My pet peeve. A sense of decency on two legs. He can't ask for some water or smoke a cigarette without showing off his exceptional decency. Walking or talking, it's tattooed on his forehead: I am a decent person! It's boring to have him around.

SHABELSKY. Narrow-minded, straitlaced sawbones! (*Mocks him.*) "Clear the way for precious honest toil!" He squawks at every step like a parrot, and thinks he's actually a second Dobrolyubov.[4] Anyone who doesn't squawk is a low-life. His views are wonderful in their profundity. If a peasant is well-off and lives like a human being, that means he's a low-life, money-grubbing exploiter.[5] I wear a velvet jacket, and a valet helps me dress—I'm a low-life too and a slave owner.[6] So decent, so decent that decency is oozing from every pore! He can't find a place good enough for him. He's got me scared . . . Honest to God! . . . Look at him sideways, out of a sense of duty he'll punch you in the snoot or call you a low-life.

IVANOV. He has been awfully hard to take, but all the same I like him, there's something sincere about him.

SHABELSKY. A pretty sort of sincerity! Last night he walks up to me and out of the blue: "Count, I find you deeply repugnant!" Thank you very kindly! And it's not done simply, but tendentiously: his voice quavers, and his eyes blaze, and his knees knock together . . . To hell with his stilted sincerity! So he thinks I'm repulsive, nasty, that's natural enough . . . So do I, but why say it to my face! I may be a trashy person, but, after all, be that as it may, I've got gray hairs . . . Untalented, insensitive decency!

LEBEDEV. Well, well, well! . . . I guess you've been young once yourself and can understand.

SHABELSKY. Yes, I was young and foolish, in my time I played Chatsky,[7] unmasking villains and swindlers, but never in my life did I call a thief a thief to his face or mention the rope in the hanged man's house. I was well bred. But this dim-witted sawbones of ours would feel he had reached the pinnacle of his mission, seventh heaven, if fate gave him the chance, in the name of principles and humane ideals, to bash me in the snoot in public or hit me below the belt.

---

4 Nikolay Aleksandrovich Dobrolyubov (1836–1861), liberal critic and journalist, who had a great influence over Russian youth in the 1860s. His article ("The Kingdom of Darkness") on Ostrovsky's plays suggested that Russia was in thrall to conservative, domestic tyranny; the term crops up in Borkin's compliments in the next scene.

5 *Kulak*, literally, fist, applied to sharp-dealing, tight-fisted tradesmen and rich peasants.

6 Since the serfs were not emancipated until 1861, Shabelsky probably had owned serfs in his youth.

7 Chatsky is the leading character in Griboedov's comedy *Woe from Wit* (1821–1823), a young gentleman returned from abroad who is disgusted by the hypocrisy of Moscow society. The society, in turn, decides, on the basis of his anti-social behavior, that he is mad.

LEBEDEV. All young people have their quirks. I had an uncle who was a follower of Hegel[8] . . . he used to invite a houseful of guests, get drunk, stand
on a chair and go: "You're ignoramuses! You're going to Hell! A new dawn
awaits!" Blah-blah, blah-blah, blah-blah . . . He'd keep telling them off . . .

SASHA. What did the guests do?

LEBEDEV. Nothing . . . They'd listen and go on drinking. Once, though, I
challenged him to a duel . . . My own uncle. All on account of Francis
Bacon.[9] I remember I was sitting, God help my memory, just the way
Matvey is, and my uncle and the late Gerasim Nilych were standing over
there, roughly where Nikolasha is . . . Well, sir, Gerasim Nilych asks me,
dear friend, a question . . .

V

The same and BORKIN.

*BORKIN, dressed foppishly, holding a package, skipping and
humming, enters from the door at right. A murmur of approval.*

YOUNG LADIES. Mikhail Mikhailovich!

Together — LEBEDEV. *Michel Michelich!* Do my ears deceive me . . .

SHABELSKY. The life of the party!

BORKIN. Here I am again! (*Runs over to Sasha.*) Noble signorina, I make so
bold as to congratulate the universe on the birth of such a marvelous blossom as yourself . . . As a token of my delight, I venture to present you
(*hands over the package*) with fireworks and Bengal lights[32] of my own
making. May they light up the night just as you brighten the shadows of
this kingdom of darkness. (*Theatrical bow.*)

SASHA. Thank you.

LEBEDEV (*roars with laughter, to Ivanov*). Why don't you fire this Judas?

BORKIN (*to Lebedev*). Pavel Kirillich! (*To Ivanov.*) My patron . . . (*Sings.*)
Nicolas-voilà, ho-hi-ho! (*Goes round to everyone.*) The most respected

8 A follower of the German philosopher G. W. F. Hegel (1770–1831), whose systematic dialectics
rejected irrationality.

9 Francis Bacon (1561–1626), empirical philosopher and natural scientist, who insisted on facts.
Bacon's experiential approach is at the farthest pole from Hegel's abstractions.

Zinaida Savishna . . . The most divine Marfa Yegorovna . . . The most venerable Avdotya Nazarovna. The most highnessy Count . . .

SHABELSKY (*roars with laughter*). The life of the party . . . Hardly in the door and the mood's lifted. Have you noticed?

BORKIN. Oof, I'm worn out . . . I think I've greeted everyone. Well, what's new, ladies and gentlemen? Nothing special, that hits you over the head? (*Vigorously to Zinaida Savishna.*) Ah, listen, mamma dear . . . As I'm riding over here just now . . . (*To Gavrila.*) Let me have some tea, Gavrusha, only no gooseberry preserves! (*To Zinaida Savishna.*) As I'm riding over here just now, peasants on the riverbank were stripping bark from your willow bushes. Why don't you lease out your willow bushes?

LEBEDEV (*to Ivanov*). Why don't you fire this Judas?

ZINAIDA SAVISHNA (*alarmed*). Why, that's perfectly true, it never crossed my mind!

BORKIN (*does calisthenics with his arms*). I can't sit still . . . Mamma dear, anything special we can turn our hand to? Marfa Yegorovna, I'm in good form . . . I'm in tiptop shape. (*Sings.*) "Once again I stand before you . . ."[33]

ZINAIDA SAVISHNA. Organize something, otherwise we'll die of boredom.

BORKIN. Ladies and gentlemen, why these long faces? They're sitting around like jurymen in a box! . . . Let's come up with something. What would you enjoy? Truth or dare, jump-rope, tag, dancing, fireworks? . . .

YOUNG LADIES (*clap their hands*). Fireworks, fireworks! (*They run into the garden.*)

SASHA (*to Ivanov*). Why are you so boring today?

IVANOV. My head aches, Shurochka, and I'm bored . . .

SASHA. Let's go into the drawing-room.

> *They go out the door at right; everyone goes into the garden,*
> *except ZINAIDA SAVISHNA and LEBEDEV.*

ZINAIDA SAVISHNA. That's my idea of a young man: the minute he arrives, everyone cheers up. (*Turns down the big lamp.*) Since they're all in the garden, there's no need to leave lights burning. (*Puts out the candles.*)

LEBEDEV (*following her*). Zyuzyushka, we have to give the guests something to eat . . .

ZINAIDA SAVISHNA. Look at all these candles . . . no wonder people think we're rich. (*Puts them out.*)

LEBEDEV (*following her*). Zyuzyushka, for heaven's sake, you should give people something to eat . . . They're young, they must be starving by now, poor things . . . Zyuzyushka . . .

ZINAIDA SAVISHNA. The Count didn't finish his tea. A waste of perfectly good sugar.

LEBEDEV. Drat! . . . (*They go into the garden.*)

V I

IVANOV and SASHA.

SASHA (*entering with Ivanov from the door at right*). Everyone's gone into the garden.

IVANOV. That's the way things are, Shurochka. I used to work a lot and think a lot, and never get tired; now I don't do anything or think about anything, and I'm exhausted, body and soul. Day and night my conscience bothers me, I feel that I'm deeply at fault, but where that fault lies, I can't figure out. And then there's my wife's illness, lack of money, the constant grumbling, gossip, pointless talk, that stupid Borkin . . . My home has become loathsome to me, living in it is worse than torture. I tell you frankly, Shurochka, something else that's become unbearable for me is the company of my wife, who loves me. You are an old friend and you won't mind if I'm frank. I came to your place to have some fun, but I'm bored here too, and my home pulls me back again. Forgive me, I'll leave right away, nice and quietly.

SASHA. Nikolay Alekseevich, I understand you. You're unhappy because you're lonely. You need someone close to you to love you and understand you. Only love can reinvigorate you.

IVANOV. Well, is that so, Shurochka! All we need is for an old dead duck like me to embark on a new love affair! God keep me from such a disaster! No, Miss Know-it-all, it's got nothing to do with love affairs. I tell you, as God

is my judge, I'll put up with all of it: the tedium and neurosis and penni-
lessness and loss of my wife and premature old age and loneliness, but
what I will not put up with, will not endure is making a mockery of myself.
I am dying of shame to think that I, a strong, healthy man, have turned into
a Hamlet or a Manfred,[10] or a pointless person . . . what the hell is going
on! Some pathetic types are flattered when you call them Hamlets or
pointless, but for me it's a disgrace. It wounds my pride, shame overwhelms
me, and I suffer . . .

SASHA (*joking, through tears*). Nikolay Alekseevich, run away with me to
America.

IVANOV. I feel too listless to cross that threshold, and you come up with
America . . . (*They walk to the entry to the garden.*) Actually, Shura, it must
be hard for you to go on living here! When I look at the people around you,
it terrifies me: which of them will you marry? The only hope is for some
passing lieutenant or university student to abduct you and elope . . .

VII

The same and ZINAIDA SAVISHNA.

*ZINAIDA SAVISHNA comes out of the door at left with a jar
of preserves.*

IVANOV. Sorry, Shurochka, I'll catch up with you . . .

SASHA exits into the garden.

Zinaida Savishna, forgive me, I've come here with a request . . .

ZINAIDA SAVISHNA. What's the matter, Nikolay Alekseevich?

IVANOV (*hesitates*). The fact is, you see, the day after tomorrow is the date my
note falls due. I'd be very much obliged if you could offer an extension or
let me add the interest to the principal. At the moment I have absolutely
no money . . .

---

10 Manfred, the hero of Lord Byron's eponymous poem, a romantic outlaw who, with the help of
magic, controls the spirits of nature. The poem greatly influenced Pushkin and Lermontov.

ZINAIDA SAVISHNA (*alarmed*). Nikolay Alekseevich, how can this be? What kind of a system is this? No, don't even think of such a thing, for heaven's sake, don't torment an unhappy woman like me . . .

IVANOV. Sorry, sorry . . . (*Goes into the garden.*)

ZINAIDA SAVISHNA. Pooh, good heavens, how he upset me! . . . I'm trembling all over . . . trembling . . . (*Goes out the door at right.*)

V I I I

KOSYKH.

KOSYKH (*enters at the door left and crosses the stage*). I was holding spades: ace, king, queen, jack, eight low spades, ace, and one . . . one puny little heart and she, damn her to hell, can't call one little slam! (*Exits through door at right.*)

I X

AVDOTYA NAZAROVNA and FIRST GUEST.

AVDOTYA NAZAROVNA (*enters from the garden with First Guest*). How I'd like to tear her to shreds, the tightwad . . . how I'd like to tear her to shreds! Is this a joke, I'm sitting here from five o'clock, she could at least offer me a little rusty herring . . . What a house! . . . What entertainment! . . .

FIRST GUEST. It's so boring, you could simply bang your head against the wall! What people, God have mercy! . . . The boredom and hunger could make you howl like a wolf and start gnawing on people . . .

AVDOTYA NAZAROVNA. How I could tear her to shreds, sinner that I am!

FIRST GUEST. I'll have a drink, old girl, and then—off home! And I don't need any of your brides. How the hell can a man think of love if he hasn't had a nip since lunch?

AVDOTYA NAZAROVNA. We'll go, have a look around, or something . . .

FIRST GUEST. Ssh! . . . Nice and quiet! I think there's some schnapps in the dining room, in the sideboard. We'll worm it out of Yegorushka . . . Ssh!

They go out through the door at left.

X

ANNA PETROVNA and LVOV (enter through the door
at right.)

ANNA PETROVNA. Never mind, they'll be delighted. Nobody here. They must be in the garden.

LVOV. Now, why, I ask you, did you bring me here to these vultures? It's no place for you and me. Decent people shouldn't have anything to do with such surroundings!

ANNA PETROVNA. Listen, Mr. Decent Person! It isn't nice to escort a lady and the whole way talk about nothing but your decency! It may be decent but, to put it mildly, it's boring. Never talk to women about your own virtues. Let them find them out for themselves. My Nikolay, when he was your age, did nothing but sing songs and tell shaggy dog stories when women were around, and yet they all knew what sort of a man he was.

LVOV. Oh, don't talk to me about your Nikolay, I understand him only too well!

ANNA PETROVNA. You're a good man, but you don't understand a thing. Let's go into the garden. He never made comments like: "I'm a decent person! I'm stifling in these surroundings! Vultures! An owl's nest! Crocodiles!" He left the menagerie alone, and when he did occasionally get upset, the only thing I'd hear from him would be: "Ah, how unjust I was today!" or "Anyuta, I feel sorry for that fellow!" That's how he used to be, but you . . .

They go out.

XI

AVDOTYA NAZAROVNA and FIRST GUEST.

FIRST GUEST (*entering from the door at left*). It's not in the dining room, so I bet it's somewhere in the pantry. We've got to worm it out of Yegorushka. Let's go through the drawing-room.

AVDOTYA NAZAROVNA. How I'd like to tear her to shreds! . . .

They go out through the door at right.

XII

BABAKINA, BORKIN, and SHABELSKY.

BABAKINA and BORKIN run in from the garden, laughing; behind
them, laughing and rubbing his hands, minces SHABELSKY.

BABAKINA. Such boredom! (*Roars with laughter.*) Such boredom! They all
walk and sit around as if they'd swallowed a poker! All my bones are numb
with boredom. (*Skips about.*) Have to limber up!

BORKIN takes her round the waist and kisses her on the cheek.

SHABELSKY (*roars with laughter and snaps his fingers*). I'll be damned!
(*Wheezes.*) In a manner of speaking . . .

BABAKINA. Let go, take your hands away, you shameless creature, or else
God knows what the Count will think! Leave me alone!

BORKIN. Love of my life, red carbuncle of my heart! . . . (*Kisses her.*) Lend
me two thousand three hundred rubles! . . .

BABAKINA. N-O—no. . Anything else, but when it comes to money—thanks
ever so . . . No, no, no! . . . Ah, take your hands off me!

SHABELSKY (*minces near them*). Little puff-ball . . . She has her charms . . .

BORKIN (*seriously*). That's enough. Let's talk business. Let's consider things
objectively, in a business-like way. Answer me straight, without equivocation or hocus-pocus: yes or no? Listen to me! (*Points to the Count.*) He
needs money, a minimal income of three thousand a year. You need a husband. Want to be a countess?

SHABELSKY (*roars with laughter*). A wonderful cynic!

BORKIN. Want to be a countess? Yes or no?

BABAKINA (*upset*). You're making this up, Misha, honestly . . . And people
don't do business this way, off the cuff like this . . . If the Count cares to,
he can himself or . . . or I don't know how this suddenly, all at once . . .

BORKIN. Now, now, don't confuse the issue! It's a business deal . . . Yes or no?

SHABELSKY (*laughing and rubbing his hands*). Actually, how about it? Damn
it, should I really commit this dirty deed myself? Eh? Little puff-ball. . . .
(*Kisses Babakina on the cheek.*) Superb! . . . A tasty little pickle! . . .

BABAKINA. Leave off, leave off, you've quite upset me . . . Go away, go away!
. . . No, don't go away!

BORKIN. Quickly! Yes or no! Time's running out . . .

BABAKINA. You know what, Count? You drive over to my place on a visit for two or three days . . . We'll have fun there, not like here . . . Drive over tomorrow . . . (*To Borkin.*) No, you were joking, weren't you?

BORKIN (*angrily*). Now who'd start joking about serious business?

BABAKINA. Leave off, leave off . . . Ah, I feel faint! I feel faint! A countess . . . I feel faint! . . . I'm falling . . .

> BORKIN *and the* COUNT, *laughing, take her by the arms and, kissing her on the cheeks, lead her out the door at right.*

XIII

IVANOV, SASHA, then ANNA PETROVNA.

IVANOV and SASHA run in from the garden.

IVANOV (*clutching his head in despair*). It can't be! Don't, don't, Shurochka! . . . Ah, don't!

SASHA (*passionately*). I love you madly . . . Without you there's no meaning to my life, no happiness and joy! For me, you're everything . . .

IVANOV. What for, what for! My God, I don't understand a thing . . . Shurochka, don't do this!

SASHA. In my childhood you were my only joy; I loved you and your soul, like myself, and now . . . I love you, Nikolay Alekseevich . . . With you anywhere to the ends of the earth, wherever you want, even the grave, only, for God's sake, soon, otherwise I'll suffocate . . .

IVANOV (*bursts into peals of happy laughter*). What is this? Does this mean starting life over from the beginning? Shurochka, does it? . . . Happiness is mine for the taking! (*Draws her to him.*) My youth, my prime . . .

> ANNA PETROVNA *enters from the garden and, on seeing her husband and* SASHA, *stops as if rooted to the spot.*

Does it mean coming to life? Does it? Back to an active role again?

> *Kiss. After they kiss,* IVANOV *and* SASHA *look around and see Anna Petrovna.*

(*In horror.*) Sarra!

Curtain

ACT THREE

Ivanov's study. Desk, covered with an unruly sprawl of papers, books, official letters, knickknacks, revolvers; alongside the papers, a lamp, a carafe of vodka, a plate of herring, pieces of bread, and pickled gherkins. On the wall regional maps, pictures, shotguns, pistols, sickles, riding crops, and so on. It is midday.

I

SHABELSKY, LEBEDEV, BORKIN, and PYOTR.

SHABELSKY and LEBEDEV are sitting on either side of the desk. BORKIN is center stage astride a chair. PYOTR is standing by the door.

LEBEDEV. France has a clear and well-defined policy . . . The French know what they want. They need to give the Krauts a good thrashing and that'll be that, while Germany, my boy, is singing a very different tune. Germany has plenty of other irons in the fire besides France . . .

SHABELSKY. Hogwash! . . . In my opinion, the Germans are cowards and so are the French . . . They give each other the finger behind their backs. Believe me, it won't go beyond giving each other the finger. They won't fight.[36]

BORKIN. The way I see it, why fight? What's the point of all these arms buildups, conferences, defense budgets? You know what I'd do? I'd get together all the dogs in the whole nation, infect them with a good dose of Pasteur's rabies[37] and let 'em loose behind enemy lines. All the combatants would be raving mad within a month.

LEBEDEV (*laughs*). That head may not look all that large, but it swarms with big ideas, countless multitudes of 'em, like fishes in the sea.

SHABELSKY. A virtuoso!

LEBEDEV. God bless you, you're good for a laugh, *Michel Michelich!* (*Stops laughing.*) Well, gentlemen, "only warlike talk is heard, but as for vodka, not a word."[38] *Repetatur!*[39] (*Fills three shot-glasses.*) Our good health!

They drink and take a snack.

A little bit of herring, the appetizer of all appetizers.

SHABELSKY. Well, no, gherkin's better . . . Learned men have been pondering from the dawn of time and never come up with anything cleverer than a pickled gherkin. (*To Pyotr.*) Pyotr, go and get more gherkins and tell 'em in the kitchen to bake four onion tarts. And see that they're hot.

PYOTR exits.

LEBEDEV. Another good thing to eat with vodka is caviar. Only how? Got to use your head . . . Take a quarter pound of pressed caviar, two bulbs of green onion, olive oil, mix it all up and, you know, like this . . . a little lemon juice on top . . . To die for! You could go crazy from the smell alone.

BORKIN. Another nice thing to chase down vodka is fried smelts. Only you've got to know how to fry them. You've got to gut them, then roll them in fine breadcrumbs and fry them crisp, so they crunch between your teeth . . . cru-cru-cru . . .

SHABELSKY. Yesterday at Babakina's there was a good appetizer—button mushrooms.

LEBEDEV. No kidding . . .

SHABELSKY. Only prepared some special way. You know, with onion, bay leaf, all sorts of spices. As soon as they took the lid off the saucepan, it gave off a vapor, an aroma . . . sheer rapture.

LEBEDEV. How about it? *Repetatur*, gentlemen!

They drink.

Our health. (*Looks at his watch.*) I don't think I can wait till Nikolasha shows up. It's time for me to go. At Bababkina's, you say, they served mushrooms, but you have yet to see a mushroom at our place. Would you like to tell me, Count, why the hell you spend so much time at Marfutka's?

SHABELSKY (*nods at Borkin*). That one, he wants to marry me off to her . . .

LEBEDEV. Marry? . . . How old are you?

SHABELSKY. Sixty-two.

LEBEDEV. Just the age for getting married. And Marfutka's the ideal mate for you.

BORKIN. It's got nothing to do with Marfutka, but with Marfutka's coin of the realm.

LEBEDEV. Which is what you're after: Marfutka's coin of the realm . . . You want some green cheese from the moon as well?

BORKIN. As soon as the man's married, he'll line his *poches*,[40] then you'll see green cheese. You'll be drooling for it.

SHABELSKY. Bless my soul, he's really serious. This genius is convinced that I'm obeying his orders and getting married . . .

BORKIN. How else? Didn't you already agree to it?

SHABELSKY. You're out of your mind . . . When did I agree to it? Pss . . .

BORKIN. Thank you . . . Thank you very much! So this means you're going to let me down? One minute he's getting married, the next he's not . . . who the hell can tell the difference, and I've already given my word of honor! So you're not getting married?

SHABELSKY (*shrugs his shoulders*). He's serious . . . A wonderful fellow!

BORKIN (*exasperated*). In that case, what was the point of getting a respectable woman all hot and bothered? She's frantic to be a countess, can't sleep, can't eat. . . . Is that a laughing matter? . . . Is that the decent thing to do?

SHABELSKY (*snaps his fingers*). What then, what if I actually do commit this dirty deed all by myself? Eh? For spite? I'll go and commit the dirty deed. Word of honor . . . Might be fun!

Enter LVOV.

I I

The same and LVOV.

LEBEDEV. Our regards to Æsculapius . . . (*Gives Lvov his hand and sings.*) "Doctor, save me, my dear fellow, thoughts of death turn me quite yellow . . ."[41]

LVOV. Nikolay Alekseevich still isn't here?

LEBEDEV. Well, no, I've been waiting for him for over an hour.

LVOV impatiently paces up and down the stage.

Dear boy, how is Anna Petrovna?

LVOV. In a bad way.

LEBEDEV (*sighs*). May I go and convey my respects?

LVOV. No, please, don't. I think she's sleeping . . .

Pause.

LEBEDEV. An attractive woman, a splendid woman . . . (*Sighs.*) On Shurochka's birthday, when she fainted at our place, I stared into her face and that's when I realized that she hasn't long to live, poor thing. I can't understand why she took a turn for the worse just then. I run in, lo and behold: she's white as a sheet, lying on the floor, Nikolasha is kneeling beside her, white as well, Shurochka's all in tears. The whole of the next week, Shurochka and I went around in a daze.

SHABELSKY (*to Lvov*). Tell me, my respected apostle of science, which scientist discovered that the most salutary thing for chest ailments is private visits from a young physician? It's a great discovery! Truly great! How would you classify it: as allopathy or homeopathy?[42]

LVOV is about to reply, but makes a scornful gesture and exits.

If looks could kill. . . .

LEBEDEV. You're giving your tongue a workout! Why did you insult him?

SHABELSKY (*irritated*). And why does he lie to me? Tuberculosis, no hope, she's dying . . . He's lying! I can't stand it!

LEBEDEV. What makes you think he's lying?

SHABELSKY (*rises and walks around*). I cannot abide the thought that a living human being suddenly, for no reason at all, can up and die. Let's change the subject!

I I I

LEBEDEV, SHABELSKY, BORKIN, and KOSYKH.

KOSYKH (*runs in, panting*). Is Nikolay Alekseevich at home? Good afternoon! (*Quickly shakes everyone's hand.*) At home?

BORKIN. He is not.

KOSYKH (*sits and jumps up*). In that case, good-bye! (*Drinks a glass of vodka and has a quick bite.*) I'll move on . . . Business . . . I'm exhausted . . . I can barely stand on my feet . . .

LEBEDEV. What wind has blown you here?

KOSYKH. I've been at Barabanov's. We were playing whist all night long and only just finished . . . I lost every last thing . . . That Barabanov plays like a shoemaker! (*In a tearful voice.*) Just you listen: I was holding hearts the whole time . . . (*Turns to Borkin, who jumps away from him.*) He leads diamonds, I go hearts again, he goes diamonds . . . Well, not one trick. (*To Lebedev.*) We try to take four clubs. I've got an ace, queen, and four more clubs, ace, ten, and three more spades . . .

LEBEDEV (*covers his ears*). Spare me, spare me, for Christ's sake, spare me!

KOSYKH (*to the Count*). You know what I mean: ace, queen, and four more clubs, ace, ten, three more spades . . .

SHABELSKY (*pushing him away with his hands*). Go away, I don't want to hear it!

KOSYKH. And suddenly, of all the bad luck: the ace of spades was trumped first round.

SHABELSKY (*grabs a revolver off the desk*). Get out of here or I'll shoot!

KOSYKH (*waves his hand in dismissal*). What the hell . . . Can't a man even talk to people? It's like living in Australia: no common interests, no solidarity . . . Every man lives on his own . . . Anyway, I've got to go . . . it's time. (*Takes his cap.*) Time is money . . . (*Gives Lebedev his hand.*) Pass! . . .

Laughter.

KOSYKH leaves and bumps into Avdotya Nazarovna in
the doorway.

I V

SHABELSKY, LEBEDEV, BORKIN, and AVDOTYA
NAZAROVNA.

AVDOTYA NAZAROVNA (*cries out*). Blast you, you've knocked me off my feet!

EVERYONE. Ah-ah-ah! . . . The unavoidable! . . .

AVDOTYA NAZAROVNA. Here they are, I've been looking for them all over the house. Good afternoon, my fine feathered friends, greetings, greetings . . . (*Greets them.*)

LEBEDEV. What's she doing here?

AVDOTYA NAZAROVNA. Business, my good sir! (*To the Count.*) Business on your behalf, your grace. (*Bows.*) I was told to give you my regards and ask after your health . . . And she, my baby-doll, told me to say that if you don't come this evening, she will cry her little eyes out. "So," she says, "my dear, take him aside and whisper secretly in his ear." But why secretly? We're all friends here. And in a case like this, we're not robbing the henhouse, it's by law and by love, by mutual agreement. Never, for all my sins, do I touch a drop, but in a case like this I'll have a drink!

LEBEDEV. And so will I. (*Pours.*) And you, you old crow, you're still going strong. I've known you for well nigh thirty years and you've always been old . . .

AVDOTYA NAZAROVNA. I've lost count of the years . . . Two husbands I've buried, I would have taken a third, but nobody'll have you without a dowry. Eight children I've had, more or less . . . (*Takes a glass.*) Well, God grant we've embarked on a successful venture, God grant it ends in success! May they live long and prosper, and may we behold them and rejoice! May they abide in harmony and love . . . (*Drinks.*) Pretty strong vodka!

SHABELSKY (*roaring with laughter, to Lebedev*). But, do you realize, the strangest thing of all is that they take it seriously, as if I . . . Wonderful! (*Rises.*) Or else, actually, Pasha, should I commit this dirty deed on my own? For spite . . . new tricks for an old dog, as they say! Eh, Pasha? No kidding . . .

LEBEDEV. You're talking drivel, Count. Our concern, yours and mine, my boy, is to be mindful of our deaths, for Marfutka and her coin of the realm have passed you by long ago . . . Our time is over.

SHABELSKY. No, I will do the deed! Word of honor, I'll do the deed!

Enter IVANOV and LVOV.

V

The same, IVANOV, and LVOV.

LVOV. Please grant me just five minutes.

LEBEDEV. Nikolasha! (*Goes to meet Ivanov and kisses him.*) Good afternoon, my dear friend . . . I've been waiting for you a whole hour.

AVDOTYA NAZAROVNA (*bows*). Good afternoon, my dear sir!

IVANOV (*bitterly*). Gentlemen, once again you've turned my study into a bar-room! . . . I've asked each and every one of you a thousand times not to do it . . . (*Walks over to the desk.*) There, look, you've spilled vodka on the papers . . . crumbs . . . pickles . . . it's really disgusting!

LEBEDEV. Sorry, Nikolasha, sorry . . . Forgive us. You and I, dear friend, have some very important business to talk over. . . .

BORKIN. So do I.

LVOV. Nikolay Alekseevich, may I have a word with you?

IVANOV (*points to Lebedev*). He's the one who needs me. Wait, you're next . . . (*To Lebedev.*) What's on your mind?

LEBEDEV. Gentlemen, I'd like to speak in private. Please . . .

The COUNT exits with AVDOTYA NAZAROVNA, followed by BORKIN, then LVOV.

IVANOV. Pasha, you can drink as much as you like, it's your funeral, but please don't let my uncle drink.[43] He never drank at my house before. It's bad for him.

LEBEDEV (*alarmed*). My dear boy, I didn't know . . . I didn't even notice . . .

IVANOV. God forbid, but if that old baby should die, you're not the one who'll feel bad, I am . . . What do you want?. . . .

LEBEDEV. You see, my dear friend. I don't know how to begin, so that it doesn't sound so heartless . . . Nikolasha, I'm embarrassed, I'm blushing, my tongue's twisted, but, dear boy, put yourself in my place, bear in mind that I'm a man under orders, a flunky, a doormat . . . Do forgive me . . .

IVANOV. What do you mean?

LEBEDEV. The wife sent me . . . Do me a favor, be a friend, pay her the interest! You wouldn't believe how she's nagged, worn me down, tortured the life out of me! Get her off your back, for heaven's sake! . . .

IVANOV. Pasha, you know I haven't got any money right now.

LEBEDEV. I know, I know, but what am I to do? She won't wait. If she sues you for defaulting, how can Shurochka and I look you in the face again?

IVANOV. I'm embarrassed myself. Pasha, I'd be glad if the earth swallowed me up, but . . . but where am I get it? Teach me, where? The only thing left is to wait for autumn when I can sell the wheat.

LEBEDEV (*shouts*). She won't wait!

Pause.

IVANOV. Your position is an unpleasant one, a delicate one, but mine's even worse. (*Walks and thinks.*) And one can't come up with anything . . . There's nothing left to sell . . .

LEBEDEV. You should ride over to Mühlbach, ask him, after all he owes you sixteen thousand.

IVANOV waves his hand in hopeless dismissal.

Here's how it is, Nikolasha . . . I know you'll start swearing, but . . . respect an old boozehound! Between friends . . . Regard me as a friend . . . You and I are both students, liberals . . . Mutual ideas and interests . . . Both alumni of Moscow U. . . . Alma mater . . . (*Takes out his wallet.*) I've got some money stashed away, not a soul at home knows about it. Take a loan . . . (*Takes out money and puts it on the desk.*) Pocket your pride, and take it for friendship's sake . . . I'd take it from you, word of honor . . .

Pause.

There it is on the desk: one thousand one hundred. You ride over there today and hand it to her in person. "There you are," say, "Zinaida Savishna, I hope it chokes you!" Only don't give any clue that you borrowed it from me, God forbid! Otherwise I'll never hear the end of it from Gooseberry Preserves! (*Stares into Ivanov's face.*) There, there, don't be like that! (*Quickly takes the money off the desk and puts it in his pocket.*) Don't! I was joking . . . Forgive me, for Christ's sake!

Pause.

Your heart is aching?

IVANOV waves his hand in dismissal.

Yes, business. . . . (*Sighs.*) A time of grief and sorrow has come to you. A man, my good friend, is like a samovar. It doesn't always stand in a shady spot on the shelf, but sometimes it's heated with burning coals: psh . . . psh! That simile isn't worth a damn, well, let someone smarter come up with a better one . . . (*Sighs.*) Misery hardens the heart. I don't feel sorry for you, Nikolasha, you'll land on your feet, the pain will lessen but I'm offended, my boy, and annoyed by other people . . . Do me a favor, tell me what's the reason for all this gossip? There's so much gossip circulating about you in the district, my boy, watch out, our friend the district attorney might pay you a visit . . . You're a murderer and a blood-sucker and a thief and a traitor . . .

IVANOV. It's all rubbish, now I've got a headache.

LEBEDEV. All because you think too much.

IVANOV. I don't think at all.

LEBEDEV. Well, Nikolasha, don't you give a damn about all that and come and see us. Shurochka's fond of you, she understands and appreciates you. She's a decent, good person, Nikolasha. Nothing like her mother and father, but I guess some young fellow came passing by . . . I look at her sometimes, pal, and I can't believe that a bottle-nosed drunkard like me has such a treasure. Drop by, talk to her about clever things and—it'll cheer you up. She's an honest, sincere person . . .

Pause.

IVANOV. Pasha, dear man, leave me alone . . .

LEBEDEV. I understand, I understand . . . (*Hastily looks at his watch.*) I understand. (*Kisses Ivanov.*) Good-bye. I still have to go to the dedication of a school.[45] (*Goes to the door and stops.*) A clever girl . . . Yesterday Shurochka and I started talking about the gossip. (*Laughs.*) And she blurted out an aphorism: "Papa dear," she says, "glowworms glow in the dark only to make it easier for night birds to see them and eat them, and good people exist so that there can be slander and gossip." How do you like that? A genius, a George Sand![46]

IVANOV. Pasha! (*Stops him.*) What's wrong with me?

LEBEDEV. I've been meaning to ask you about that, yes, but I confess I was too shy. I don't know, pal! On the one hand, I had the impression that you've been suffering all kinds of bad luck, on the other hand, I know that you're not that sort of fellow, that you . . . You wouldn't let trouble get you down. It's something else, Nikolasha, but what it is—I don't understand.

IVANOV. I don't understand either. The way I see it, it's either . . . although, no!

Pause.

You see, here's what I was about to say. I used to have a workman, Semyon, you remember him. Once, at threshing time, he wanted to show off his strength to the farm girls, hoisted two sacks of rye on to his back and got a hernia. He died soon after. The way I see it, I've got my own personal hernia. High school, university, then farming, district schools, projects . . . I didn't believe the same things as other people, I didn't marry like other people, I'd get enthused, I'd take risks, I'd throw away money, as you well know, right, left and center, I was happy and miserable like no one else in the whole district. Those were all my sacks of rye, Pasha . . . I hoisted a load on my back, and my back caved in. At the age of twenty we're all heroes, we take it all on, can do it all, and by thirty we're already worn out, good for nothing at all. How else can you explain this lassitude? But, maybe I'm wrong . . . Wrong, wrong! . . . God bless you, Pasha, you must be sick and tired of me.

LEBEDEV (*briskly*). You know what? Your surroundings, my boy, have got you down!

IVANOV. That's stupid, Pasha, and stale. Get out!

LEBEDEV. It really is stupid. Now I can see for myself it's stupid. I'm going, I'm going! . . . (*Exits.*)

V I

IVANOV, then LVOV.

IVANOV. No-good, pathetic, insignificant, that's the kind of man I am. You have to be an equally pathetic, broken-down, flabby-faced drunk, like Pasha, to go on loving and respecting me. How I despise myself, my God! How profoundly I hate my voice, my walk, my hands, my clothes, my thoughts. Well, isn't this ridiculous, isn't this offensive? Barely a year's gone by since I was healthy and strong, I was hale and hearty, indefatigable, impassioned, worked with these very hands, talked so that even ignoramuses were moved to tears, was capable of weeping when I saw misery, feel outraged when I encountered evil. I knew the meaning of inspiration, I knew the splendor and poetry of quiet nights, when from dusk to dawn you sit at your desk or beguile your mind with dreams. I had faith, I gazed into the future as into the eyes of a loving mother . . . And now, oh, my God! I'm weary, I have no faith, I waste days and nights in idleness. They don't obey me, brains or hands or feet. The estate goes to rack and ruin, the forests topple beneath the axe. (*Weeps.*) My land stares at me like an orphan. I have no expectations, no compassion for anything, my mind quakes in fear of the day to come . . . And this business with Sarra? I swore everlasting love, I promised happiness, I opened before her eyes a future she had never dreamed of. She believed in it. For the past five years all I could see was how she was flickering out under the weight of her sacrifices, how she was growing exhausted struggling with her conscience, but, God knows, not a single black look at me or word of reproach . . . And then what? I fell out of love with her . . . How? Why? What for? I don't understand. Here she is suffering, her days are numbered, while I, like the lowest of cowards, run away from her pale face, sunken chest, imploring eyes . . . Shameful, shameful!

Pause.

Sasha, a mere girl, is affected by my misfortunes. She declares her love for me, almost an old man, and I get intoxicated, forget about everything in this world, enchanted as if by music, and I shout: "A new life! Happiness!" But the next day I believe as little in this life and happiness as I do in fairies . . . What's wrong with me? What abyss am I pushing myself into? What is the source of this debility of mine? What has become of my nerves? My sick wife has only to wound my vanity or a servant-girl get something wrong, or a gun misfire, and I turn rude, nasty, a different person entirely . . .

Pause.

I don't understand, I don't understand, I don't understand! I simply feel like blowing my brains out! . . .

LVOV (*enters*). I've got to have it out with you, Nikolay Alekseevich!

IVANOV. If we were to have it out every day, Doctor, we'd be too debilitated for anything else.

LVOV. Will you be so good as to listen to me?

IVANOV. I listen to you every day and so far I can't understand a thing: what do you personally want from me?

LVOV. I speak clearly and firmly, and the only person who could fail to understand me is one without a heart.

IVANOV. My wife is facing death, that I know; I have unpardonably wronged her, that I also know; you're a decent, upright man, I know that too! What more do you want?

LVOV. I am outraged by human cruelty . . . A woman is dying. She has a father and mother whom she loves and would like to see before she dies; they know perfectly well that she will die soon and that she goes on loving them, but, damn their cruelty, they evidently want Jehovah to see how steadfast they are in their religion; they still go on cursing her! You, the man for whom she sacrificed everything—her religion and her parents' home and her peace of mind,—in the most blatant manner and with the most blatant intentions you head over to those Lebedevs every day!

IVANOV. Oh, I haven't been there for two weeks now . . .

LVOV (*not listening to him*). People such as you have to be spoken to bluntly, with no beating around the bush, and if you don't like what I have to say, then don't listen! I'm used to calling things by their rightful names . . . You need this death in order to carry out new feats of valor, all right, but can't you at least wait? If you were to let her die in the natural scheme of things, without stabbing her with your barefaced cynicism, would the Lebedevs and their dowry disappear? Not now, but in a year or two, you, a wonderful Tartuffe, will manage to turn a young girl's head and make off with her dowry just the same as now . . . Why are you in such a hurry? Why do you need your wife to die now, and not in a month or a year's time?

IVANOV. This is excruciating . . . Doctor, you're a really bad physician if you suppose that a man can control himself forever. It's taking the most appalling willpower not to reply to your insults.

LVOV. That's enough, who are you trying to fool? Drop the mask.

IVANOV. Clever man, think of this: in your opinion, nothing's easier than understanding me! Right? I married Anna to get a big dowry . . . I didn't get the dowry, I missed the mark, and now I'm driving her to her grave, in order to marry another woman and get that dowry . . . Right? How simple and uncomplicated . . . A man is such a simple and unsophisticated machine . . . No, Doctor, each of us has far more cogs, screws and valves in him than to enable us to judge one another on first impressions or a few outward signs. I don't understand you, you don't understand me, we don't understand one another. You may be an excellent general practitioner— and still have no understanding of people. Don't be so smug and look at it my way.

LVOV. Do you really think that you're so unfathomable, that I am so brainless that I can't tell the difference between disgraceful behavior and decent behavior?

IVANOV. Obviously, you and I will never find common ground . . . For the last time I ask you, and, please answer without more ado, what do you personally want from me? What do you hope to achieve? (*Annoyed.*) And whom have I the honor of addressing: the Counsel for my prosecution or my wife's physician?

LVOV. I am a physician, and, as a physician, I demand that you change your way of life . . . It is killing Anna Petrovna!

IVANOV. But what am I to do? What? If you understand me better than I understand myself, then tell me in no uncertain terms: what am I to do?

LVOV. At least, don't act so openly.

IVANOV. Oh, my God! Do you really understand yourself? (*Drinks water.*) Leave me alone. I'm a thousand times at fault, I'll answer for it before God, but no one has entitled you to torture me on a daily basis . . .

LVOV. And who has entitled you to insult my truth-telling, by insulting my person? You have worn me down and poisoned my mind. Until I wound up in this district, I could deal with the fact that stupid, inane, self-deluded people existed, but I never believed there were criminal types who consciously, deliberately used their intelligence to do evil . . . I respected and loved people, but once I came in contact with you . . .

IVANOV. I've heard this before!

LVOV. Have you indeed? (*On seeing SASHA enter; she is in a riding habit.*) Now, I hope, we understand one another perfectly well! (*Shrugs his shoulders and exits.*)

V I I

IVANOV and SASHA.

IVANOV (*alarmed*). Shura, is that you?

SASHA. Yes, it is. Good afternoon. Weren't you expecting me? Why haven't you been to see us for so long?

IVANOV. Shura, for God's sake, this is inconsiderate! Your coming here might have a dreadful effect on my wife.

SASHA. She won't see me. I came in the back way. I'll go right away. I was worried: are you all right? Why haven't you been to see us for so long?

IVANOV. My wife's upset even without this, she's almost dying, and you ride over here. Shura, Shura, this is frivolous and inhuman!

SASHA. What am I supposed to do? You haven't been to see us for two weeks, don't answer letters. I was in agony. I imagined you suffering here unbearably, ill, dead. I didn't get a single night's sleep . . . I'll go right away . . . At least tell me, are you well?

IVANOV. No, I've been tormenting myself, people torment me nonstop . . . I'm at the end of my rope! And now you too! This is so sick, so abnormal! Shura, so much of this is my fault, my fault!

SASHA. You really do like to say horrible, heartbreaking things! Your fault? Really? Your fault? Well, then, tell me: how so?

IVANOV. I don't know, I don't know . . .

SASHA. That's no answer. Every sinner ought to know how he's sinned. Have you printed counterfeit money or something?

IVANOV. That's not funny.

SASHA. Your fault you fell out of love with your wife? That may be, but a man isn't master of his feelings, you didn't want to fall out of love. Your fault that she saw us in a loving embrace? No, you didn't want her to see . . .

IVANOV (*interrupting*). Et cetera, et cetera . . . Fell in love, fell out of love, no master of my feelings,—these are all clichés, platitudes, they're no help . . .

SASHA. It's tiresome to talk to you. (*Looks at a picture.*) How well that dog is painted! Is it done from life?

IVANOV. From life. And our whole love affair is a trite cliché: he was downhearted and had lost his bearings. She showed up, strong and bold in spirit, and offered him a helping hand. It's beautiful, but it resembles truth only in novels, not in life. . . .

SASHA. It's the same in life.

IVANOV. I see you have a sophisticated knowledge of life! My whining inspires you with reverent awe, you imagine you've discovered a second Hamlet in me, but, so far as I'm concerned, this psychosis of mine, and all its symptoms, can serve only as rich material for comedy and nothing else! People should burst out laughing, split their sides at my affectations, but for you—it's a cry for help! Come to my rescue, do a valiant deed! Ah, I really am hard on myself today! I feel that today's nervous tension will come to a head somehow . . . Either I'll break something or . . .

SASHA. That's right, that's right, that's just what you need. Break something, smash or scream. You're angry with me, I've done something stupid, by deciding to come here. Well, then take it out on me, bawl me out, stamp your feet. Well? Start losing your temper . . .

Pause.

Well?

IVANOV. Silly girl.

SASHA. Excellent! I do believe we're smiling! Be good, deign to smile once more!

IVANOV (*laughs*). I've noticed: whenever you try to rescue me and teach me to see sense, common sense, you get a look on your face that's naive, incredibly naive, and your eyes open wide, as if you were staring at a comet. Hold still, your shoulder's covered with dust. (*Wipes the dust off her shoulder.*) A naive man is a fool. But you women manage to be naive so that it comes across as charming and wholesome and affectionate and not so foolish as it might seem. How do you pull that off? When a man is healthy, strong and cheerful, you ignore him, but as soon as he starts sliding downhill and bemoaning his fate, you cling to him. Is it really worse to be the wife of a strong, courageous man, than to be the nursemaid of some sniveling loser?

SASHA. Much worse!

IVANOV. Why is that? (*Laughs loudly.*) Darwin[11] didn't know about that, or else he would have given you hell! You're undermining the human race. Thanks to you soon earth will breed nothing but bellyachers and psychopaths.

SASHA. Men just don't get it. Every girl prefers a loser to a success, because every girl is attracted by active love . . . Don't you get it? Active. Men are involved in business and so they shove love far into the background. Talk to his wife, walk around the garden with her, pass the time pleasantly, weep at her grave — that's all. But for us love is life itself. I love you, that means that I dream about how I'll cure you of tedium, how I'll go with you to the ends of the earth . . . You're in the clouds, I'm in the clouds; you're in the dumps, I'm in the dumps. For instance, for me it would be a great joy to stay up nights copying out your papers or to keep watch all night so that no one wakes you, or to walk with you a hundred miles on foot. I remember, three years ago, at threshing time, you once dropped in on us all covered in dust, sunburnt, exhausted, and asked for a drink. I brought you a glass, and you were already stretched out on the sofa, dead to the world. You slept in our house for half a day, and the whole time I stood outside the door and made sure that no one came in. And it made me feel so good! The harder the work, the greater the love, I mean, you understand, the more deeply felt it is.

IVANOV. Active love . . . Hm . . . It's an aberration, a young girl's fancies, or, maybe, that's how things ought to be . . . (*Shrugs his shoulders.*) Who the hell knows! (*Cheerfully.*) Shura, word of honor, I am a respectable man! . . . Judge for yourself: I have always loved to philosophize, but never in my life have I said: "our women are depraved" or "a woman's taken the road to perdition." For heaven's sake, I was only grateful and nothing more! Nothing more! My little girl, my pretty, what fun you are! While I, what a ridiculous numbskull! I upset good Christians, bemoan my fate for days on end. (*Laughs.*) Boo-hoo! boo-hoo! (*Quickly walks away from her.*) But go away, Sasha! We've been forgetting . . .

---

11 The English scientist Charles Darwin (1809–1882) argued that in natural selection the female of a species chooses for reproduction the strongest or most capable male.

SASHA. Yes, it's time to go. Good-bye! I'm afraid that your decent doctor out of a sense of duty will report to Anna Petrovna that I'm here. Listen to me: go to your wife right now and sit, sit, sit . . . If you have to sit for a year, sit for a year. Ten years—sit ten years. Do your duty. And grieve, and ask her forgiveness, and weep—that's how it ought to be. But the main thing is, don't neglect business.

IVANOV. I've got that old feeling, as if I've been gorging on toadstools. All over again!

SASHA. Well, God bless you! You can stop thinking about me! In two weeks or so you'll drop me a line, and I'll be grateful for it. And I'll write to you . . .

BORKIN looks in at the door.

V I I I

The same and BORKIN.

BORKIN. Nikolay Alekseevich, may I? (*On seeing Sasha.*) Sorry, I didn't see . . . (*Enters.*) Bonjour! (*Bows.*)

SASHA (*embarrassed*). How do you do . . .

BORKIN. You've got plumper, prettier . . .

SASHA (*to Ivanov*). I'm leaving now, Nikolay Alekseevich . . . I'm leaving. (*Exits.*)

BORKIN. A vision of loveliness! I came about prose, and ran into poetry . . . (*Sings.*) "Thou didst appear, like a bird flown towards the light . . ."[47]

IVANOV paces up and down the stage in agitation.

(*Sits.*) There's something about her, *Nicolas*, a certain something that other women haven't got. Am I right? Something special . . . fantastical . . . (*Sighs.*) Actually, the richest eligible girl in the whole district, but her dear mama is such a sourpuss that no one wants to make a match. When she dies everything will go to Shurochka, but until she dies she'll give ten thousand or so, a curling iron and a flat iron, and even then she'll make you beg for it on your knees. (*Rummages in his pockets.*) Let's smoke a *de-los-majoros*.[48] Care for one? (*Offers his cigar case.*) They're not bad . . . Quite smokeworthy.

IVANOV (*walks over to Borkin, choked with rage*). Don't set foot in my house another minute! Not another minute!

BORKIN *rises a bit and drops the cigar.*

Not another minute!

BORKIN. *Nicolas,* what does this mean? What are you angry about?

IVANOV. What about? Where did you get those cigars? Do you think I don't know where you take the old man every day and what for?

BORKIN (*shrugs his shoulders*). What's it got to do with you?

IVANOV. You're such a crook! Your vulgar schemes, which you broadcast through the whole district, have made me a dishonest man in people's eyes! We've got nothing in common, and I ask you to leave my home this very minute! (*Walks quickly.*)

BORKIN. I know that you're saying all this out of irritation, and therefore I won't be angry with you. Insult me as much as you like . . . (*Picks up the cigar.*) It's time you gave up this melancholy routine. You're no schoolboy . . .

IVANOV. What did I tell you? (*Trembling.*) Are you playing games with me?

Enter ANNA PETROVNA.

I X

The same and ANNA PETROVNA.

BORKIN. Well, look, Anna Petrovna's here . . . I'm going. (*Exits.*)

IVANOV stops beside the desk and stands, his head bowed.

ANNA PETROVNA (*after a pause*). Why did she come here just now?

Pause.

I'm asking you: why did she come here?

IVANOV. Don't question me, Anyuta . . .

Pause.

I'm much at fault. Think up whatever punishment you want, I'll bear it, but . . . don't question me . . . I haven't got the strength to talk.

ANNA PETROVNA (*angrily*). Why was she here?

Pause.

Ah, so that's what you're like! Now I understand you. Finally I see what sort of man you are. Dishonorable, vile . . . You remember, you came and lied to me, saying you loved me . . . I believed it and left father, mother, religion and followed you . . . You lied to me about truth, goodness, your honorable intentions, I believed every word . . .

IVANOV. Anyuta, I never lied to you . . .

ANNA PETROVNA. I lived with you for five years, I broke down and sickened at the idea that I'd renounced my faith, but I loved you and never left you for a single minute . . . You were my idol . . . and now what? All this time you've been deceiving me in the most shameless manner . . .

IVANOV. Anyuta, don't tell falsehoods. I was mistaken, yes, but I've never lied in my life . . . You don't dare reproach me for that . . .

ANNA PETROVNA. Now it's all come out . . . You married me and thought my father and mother would forgive me, give me money . . . That's what you thought.

IVANOV. Oh my God! Anyuta, to try my patience like this! (*Weeps.*)

ANNA PETROVNA. Be quiet! When you realized there was no money, you came up with a new game . . . Now I remember it all and I understand. (*Weeps.*) You never loved me and were never faithful to me . . . Never!

IVANOV. Sarra, that's a lie! . . . Say what you want, but don't insult me with lies . . .

ANNA PETROVNA. Dishonorable, vile man . . . You owe Lebedev money, and now, in order to squirm out of your debt, you want to turn his daughter's head, deceive her the way you did me. Is that a falsehood?

IVANOV (*choking*). Shut up, for God's sake! I can't answer for myself . . . I'm choking with rage, and I . . . I'm liable to insult you . . .

ANNA PETROVNA. You always were a shameless deceiver, and not just of me . . . You pinned all those underhanded actions on Borkin, but now I know whose they really are . . .

IVANOV. Sarra, shut up, get out, or else I'll say something I'll regret! It's all I can do to keep from calling you something horrible, humiliating . . . (*Shouts.*) Shut up, you kike bitch!

ANNA PETROVNA. I will not shut up . . . Too long you've been deceiving me, for me to be able to keep silent . . .

IVANOV. So you won't shut up? (*Struggles with himself.*) For God's sake . . .

ANNA PETROVNA. Now go and cheat the Lebedev girl . . .

IVANOV. Then know that you . . . will die soon . . . The doctor told me that you'll die soon . . .

ANNA PETROVNA (*sits down, her voice faltering*). When did he say that?

Pause.

IVANOV (*clutching his head*). It's all my fault! God, it's all my fault! (*Sobs.*)

Curtain

Nearly a year goes by between Acts Three and Four.

ACT FOUR

One of the drawing-rooms in the Lebedevs' house. In front an arch separating the drawing-room from a reception room, doors at right and left. An antique bronze, family portraits. Decorations for a party. An upright piano, on it a violin, a cello beside it. Throughout the whole act, guests walk through the reception room, dressed for a ball.

I

LVOV.

LVOV (*enters, looks at his watch.*) Five o'clock. I suppose the benediction[52] will begin any time now . . . They'll give the benediction and drive off to the wedding. There you have it, the triumph of virtue and truth! He didn't manage to rob Sarra, so he tortured her to death and drove her to her grave, now he's found another girl. He'll play the hypocrite with this one too, until he cleans her out and, once he's done that, lays her where poor Sarra is lying. The same old mercenary story . . .

Pause.

In seventh heaven, a happy man, he'll live beautifully to a ripe old age, and die with a clear conscience. No, I'll strip you bare! When I rip that damned mask off you and everyone learns what kind of bird you are, I'll make you fly down from seventh heaven into such a pit the foul fiend himself won't be able to yank you out of it! I'm a decent person, it's my job to step forward and make the blind to see. I'll do my duty and tomorrow clear out of this damned district! (*Thoughtfully.*) But how can I go about it? Spelling it out to the Lebedevs is a waste of time. Challenge him to a duel? Make a scene? My God, I'm as flustered as a little kid and I've completely lost the ability to analyze the situation. How do I do it? A duel?

I I

LVOV and KOSYKH.

KOSYKH (*enters, gleefully to Lvov*). Yesterday I called a little slam in clubs, and took a grand slam. Only again that Barabanov spoiled the whole she-bang for me! We play. I bid: no trumps. He goes pass. Two no trumps. He goes pass. I go two diamonds . . . three clubs . . . and imagine, can you imagine: I call a slam, and he doesn't show his ace. If he'd shown his ace, the bastard, I could have called a grand slam in no-trumps.

LVOV. Excuse me, I don't play cards, and so I can't share your enthusiasm. Will the benediction be soon?

KOSYKH. I guess so, soon. They're trying to bring Zyuzyushka round. She's wailing like a banshee, she's upset over the dowry.

LVOV. And not over her daughter?

KOSYKH. Dowry. And she's ticked off. If he gets married, it means he doesn't have to pay back the debt. You can't very well sue your son-in-law for defaulting.

III

The same and BABAKINA.

BABAKINA (*overdressed, pompously crosses the stage between Lvov and Kosykh; the latter bursts out laughing up his sleeve; she looks round*). Idiot!

KOSYKH *touches her waist with his finger and roars with laughter.*

Peasant! (*Exits.*)

KOSYKH (*roaring with laughter*). The dame's gone off her rocker! Until she started angling for a title, she was a dame like any dame, but now you can't come near her. (*Mimics her.*) Peasant!

LVOV (*upset*). Listen, tell me truly, what do you think of Ivanov?

KOSYKH. A waste of time. He plays like a shoemaker. Last year, during Lent, there was this thing. We sit down to play: me, the Count, Borkin and him. It's my deal . . .

LVOV (*interrupting*). Is he a good man?

KOSYKH. What, him? A rogue male! A chiseler like nobody's business. He and the Count are two of a kind. They've got a knack for sniffing out where dirty work is to be done. Came to a dead end with the Jew girl, had to eat crow, but now he's worming his way into Zyuzyushka's strongboxes. I'll bet, or may I be triply damned, in a year's time he'll have Zyuzyushka on the streets. He'll do it to Zyuzyushka, and the Count'll do it to Babakina. They'll snatch the cash and live happily ever after, getting richer and richer. Doctor, why are you so palé today? You look a fright.

LVOV. Never mind, that's how it is. I had too much to drink yesterday.

IV

The same, LEBEDEV, and SASHA.

LEBEDEV (*entering, with Sasha*). Let's talk in here. (*To Lvov and Kosykh.*) Go into the other room, you Zulus, and join the young ladies. We have to talk in private.

KOSYKH (*as he passes Sasha, snaps his finger in ecstasy*). Pretty as a picture! The Queen of Trumps!

LEBEDEV. Pass by, caveman, pass by!

LVOV and KOSYKH leave.

Sit down, Shurochka, that's right . . . (*Sits and looks round.*) Listen carefully and with due respect. Here's the thing: your mother insisted that I inform you of the following . . . You understand? I'm not talking on my own behalf, but your mother insisted.

SASHA. Papa, cut it short!

LEBEDEV. You have been granted a dowry of fifteen thousand silver rubles. That's that . . . See that there are no arguments later on! Hold on, be quiet! That's only for starters, here comes the main course. You've been granted fifteen thousand, but, since Nikolay Alekseevich owes your mother nine thousand, a deduction is being made from your dowry . . . Well now, ma'am, after that, in addition . . .

SASHA. Why are you telling me this?

LEBEDEV. Your mother insisted!

SASHA. Leave me alone! If you had the slightest respect for me or yourself, you wouldn't let yourself talk to me this way. Do I need your dowry! I didn't ask for it then and don't ask for it now!

LEBEDEV. What are you taking it out on me for? In Gogol's play the two rats at least sniffed around first, and only then went away,[51] while you, my emancipated lady, don't bother sniffing around, you just take it out on me!

SASHA. Do leave me alone, don't humiliate my ears with your nickle-and-diming!

LEBEDEV (*flaring up*). Fooey! The way you're all carrying on, I'll end up sticking a knife in myself or cutting somebody else's throat! That one sets up a fearful howl all the livelong day, nagging, pestering, pinching pennies, while this one, an intelligent, humane, damn it all, emancipated woman, can't understand her own father! I'm humiliating her ears! Well, before coming here to insult your ears, out there (*points to the door*) I was being cut up into little pieces, drawn and quartered. She can't understand! The two of you have got my head swimming, you've mixed me all up . . . oh, you! (*Goes to the door and stops.*) I don't like it. I don't like anything about you!

SASHA. What don't you like?

LEBEDEV. I don't like any of it! Any of it!

SASHA. Any of what?

LEBEDEV. So now I'm supposed to pull up a chair and start telling you a story. I don't like anything about it, and I don't want to be at your wedding! (*Walks over to Sasha, affectionately.*) You'll forgive me, Shurochka, maybe your getting married is clever, honorable, uplifting, highly principled, but something about it isn't right, it isn't right! It isn't like other marriages. You're young, fresh, pure as a pane of glass, beautiful, whereas he's a widower, worn to a shadow, to a nub. And I can't figure him out, God bless him. (*Kisses his daughter.*) Shurochka, forgive me, but something smells rotten. There's already a lot of talk. About how Sarra died at his place, then suddenly for some reason he wanted to marry you . . . (*Vigorously.*) Anyway, I'm being an old biddy, an old biddy. I'm as biddified as an old hoopskirt . . . Don't listen to me. Don't listen to anybody but yourself.

SASHA. Papa, I feel myself that it's wrong . . . Wrong, wrong, wrong. If only you knew how hard it is for me! Unbearable! It's awkward and painful to me to confess this. Papa, darling, snap me out of this, for God's sake . . . teach me what to do.

LEBEDEV. Such as what? What?

SASHA. I'm more frightened than ever! (*Looks around.*) I feel as if I don't understand him and never will. The whole time we were engaged, not once did he smile, not once did he look directly into my eyes. Constant complaints, remorse over something, hints at some vague fault, trembling . . . I got tired of it. There are even moments when I feel as if I . . . I don't love him as intensely as I should. And when he rides over here or talks to me, I start to get bored. What does all this mean, Papa dear? It's terrifying!

LEBEDEV. My little dove, my only child, listen to your old father. Call it off!

SASHA (*alarmed*). What do you mean, what do you mean?

LEBEDEV. Honestly, Shurochka. There'll be a scandal, the whole district will start wagging their tongues, but, after all, it's better to live through a scandal than destroy your whole life.

SASHA. Don't say that, don't say that, Papa! I won't listen to you. One must fight off these gloomy thoughts. He's a good, unhappy, misunderstood man; I will love him, I will understand him, I will set him on his feet. I will carry out my mission. It's settled!

LEBEDEV. That's not a mission, it's a psychosis.

SASHA. That's enough. I confessed to you something I didn't want to confess even to myself. Don't tell anyone. Let's forget it.

LEBEDEV. I don't understand a thing. Either I've got obtuse in my old age or you all have become so very clever, but, even if you cut my throat, I still don't understand a thing.

V

The same and SHABELSKY.

SHABELSKY (*entering*). To hell with everybody, myself included! It's exasperating!

LEBEDEV. What's got into you?

SHABELSKY. No, seriously, come what may, I'll have to pull off something on my own so low-down, so vulgar that not only I, but everyone will be nauseated. And I will do the dirty deed. Word of honor. I've already told Borkin to announce my engagement today. (*Laughs.*) Everyone's a low-life, so I'll be a low-life too.

LEBEDEV. I'm fed up with you! Listen, Matvey, keep talking like that and they'll throw you in the, excuse the expression, booby hatch.

SHABELSKY. And why should a booby hatch be any worse than an escape hatch or a nuthatch? Do me a favor, throw me in there right now. You'd be doing me a favor. They're all such petty little, insignificant little, untalented little creatures, I'm a contemptible creature myself, I don't believe a word I say . . .

LEBEDEV. You know what, my boy? Put a fuse in your mouth, light it and breathe fire at people. Or better yet: here's your hat, there's the door. There's a wedding going on here, everybody's celebrating, while you caw-caw like a crow. Yes, honestly. . . .

SHABELSKY leans on the piano and sobs.

Good grief! . . . Matvey! . . . Count! . . . What's wrong with you? Dear heart, my love . . . my angel . . . Have I offended you? Well, forgive me, old hound that I am . . . Forgive a drunkard . . . Have some water . . .

SHABELSKY. Don't want any. (*Raises his head.*)

LEBEDEV. What are you crying for?

SHABELSKY. No reason, just because . . .

LEBEDEV. No, Matvey, don't lie . . . what for? What's the reason?

SHABELSKY. I caught a glimpse of that cello and . . . and I remembered the little Jew-girl. . . .

LEBEDEV. Oh boy, what a time you picked to remember! May she rest in peace, bless her, but this is no time for reminiscing . . .

SHABELSKY. We would play duets together . . . A wonderful, superb woman!

SASHA sobs.

LEBEDEV. What, you too? Will you stop it? Lord, they're both bawling, while I . . . I . . . At least get out of here, the guests will see!

SHABELSKY. Pasha, when the sun shines, it's cheerful even in a graveyard. When there's hope, then it's good even to be old. But I haven't got a hope, not one single one!

LEBEDEV. Yes, you're really in a bad way . . . You've got no children, no money, no occupation . . . Well, that's the way it goes. (*To Sasha.*) But what's *your* problem?

SHABELSKY. Pasha, give me some money. We'll settle up in the next world. I'll go to Paris, I'll take a look at my wife's grave. In my lifetime I've given away plenty, I squandered half my fortune, and so I've got the right to ask. Besides, I'm asking it from a friend . . .

LEBEDEV (*dismayed*). Dear heart, I haven't got a penny! But, all right, all right! I mean, I'm not promising, but you understand . . . fine, fine! (*Aside.*) They've tortured me to death!

V I

The same, BABAKINA, and then ZINAIDA SAVISHNA.

BABAKINA (*enters*). Now where is my escort? Count, how dare you leave me alone? Ooh, you're a disgrace! (*Strikes the Count on the arm with her fan.*)

SHABELSKY (*squeamishly*). Leave me alone! I hate you!

BABAKINA (*dumbfounded*). What . . . Huh? . . .

SHABELSKY. Please get away from me.

BABAKINA (*drops into an armchair*). Ah! (*Weeps.*)

ZINAIDA SAVISHNA (*enters, weeping*). Someone's arrived . . . I think it's the best man. It's time for the benediction . . . (*Sobs.*)

SASHA (*pleading*). Mamma!

LEBEDEV. Now they've all started blubbering! A quartet! Will you please turn off the waterworks! Matvey! . . . Marfa Yegorovna! . . . Look, now I . . . I've started crying . . . (*Weeps.*) Good grief!

ZINAIDA SAVISHNA. If you don't need a mother, if you're disobedient . . . then do whatever you like, you have my blessing . . .

Enter IVANOV; he is wearing a tailcoat and gloves.

V I I

The same and IVANOV.

LEBEDEV. That's all we need! What's up!

SASHA. Why are you here?

IVANOV. Sorry, ladies and gentlemen, let me talk to Sasha alone.

LEBEDEV. It isn't proper for the groom to drop in on the bride! It's time for you to be at the church!

IVANOV. Pasha, please. . . .

LEBEDEV shrugs his shoulders; he, ZINAIDA SAVISHNA, the COUNT, and BABAKINA leave.

V I I I

IVANOV and SASHA.

SASHA (*sternly*). What do you want?

IVANOV. I'm choking with spite, but I can speak calmly. Listen. Just now I was getting dressed for the ceremony, I looked at myself in the mirror and the hair at my temples . . . was gray. Shura, we mustn't! Shura, while it's not too late, we should call off this mindless farce . . . You're young, pure, you've got your life ahead of you, while I . . .

SASHA. None of this is new, I've already heard it a thousand times and I'm sick and tired of it! Go to the church, don't keep people waiting.

IVANOV. I'll go home right now, and you can explain to your folks that there won't be any wedding. Tell them anything. It's time we came to our senses. I was playing Hamlet, and you the high-minded damsel—we've had enough of it.

SASHA (*flaring up*). What sort of tone is this? I'm not listening.

IVANOV. But I'm speaking and I'll go on speaking.

SASHA. Why did you come here? Your whining is becoming ridiculous.

IVANOV. No, I have stopped whining! Ridiculous? Yes, I am ridiculous. And if I could make myself a thousand times more ridiculous and get the whole world to laugh, I'd do it! I stared at myself in the mirror—and it was as if a bullet shot me in my conscience! I laughed at myself and nearly went out of my mind with shame. (*Laughs.*) Melancholy! Justifiable tedium! Unreasoning grief! The only thing I left out is writing poetry. To whine, to bemoan my fate, to drive everyone to distraction, to proclaim that the zest in life has been squandered forever, that I've got rusty, outlived myself, that I've given in to faintheartedness and am stuck up to my ears in this foul melancholia,—to proclaim this, when the sun is shining brightly, when even the ants are hauling their loads and pleased with themselves,—thanks but no thanks! To see how some consider you a charlatan, others pity you, yet others stretch out a helping hand, a fourth group—the worst of all—heed your groans, regard you as a second Mohammed, and wait for you to preach them a new religion any minute now. No, thank God, I still have pride and conscience! On the way over here, I laughed at myself, and I felt as if I need the birds to laugh at me, the trees to laugh . . .

SASHA. This isn't spite, but insanity!

IVANOV. You think so? No, I'm not insane. Now I see things in their true light, and my mind is as clear as your conscience. We love each other, but our wedding cannot be! I can rant and rave and mope as much as I please, but I have no right to ruin other people! With my whining I poisoned the last year of my wife's life. While you've been my fiancée, you've lost the ability to laugh and aged five years. Your father, for whom everything in life was clear, thanks to me can't understand people any more. If I go to a gathering, a party, a hunt, wherever I go I bring along boredom, depression, dissatisfaction. Hold on, don't interrupt! I'm being impetuous, frantic, but, excuse me, spite chokes me, and I cannot speak any other way. I never used to lie, never used to run down life, but, ever since I became a grumbler, involuntarily, without noticing it myself, I do run it down, rail at fate, complain, and everyone who hears me is infected with a distaste for life and also starts running it down! And what a tone! As if I were doing Nature a favor by living. Who the hell do I think I am!

SASHA. Hold on . . . What you've just said means that you're fed up with whining and it's time to begin a new life! . . . That's wonderful! . . .

IVANOV. I don't see anything wonderful about it. And what's this new life? I'm a hopeless goner! It's time we both understood that. New life!

SASHA. Nikolay, come to your senses! What makes you think you're a goner? What is this cynicism? No, I don't want to talk or listen . . . Go to the church!

IVANOV. A goner!

SASHA. Don't shout that way, the guests will hear!

IVANOV. If a reasonably intelligent, educated, and healthy man for no apparent reason starts to bemoan his fate and go downhill, then he's already on the skids without a brake, and there's no escape for him! Well, where's my escape? To what? I can't drink—wine gives me a headache; I don't know how to write bad poetry, I can't romanticize my feeblemindedness and treat it as something sublime. Debility is debility, weakness is weakness— I have no other names for them. I'm a goner, a goner—and it's not worth discussing! (*Look around.*) They might interrupt us. Listen. If you love me, help me. Right this minute, call it off without delay! Quick . . .

SASHA. Oh, Nikolay, if you only knew how you've worn me out! How you've broken my heart! You're a good, intelligent man, so judge: well, can you set these tasks? Every single day, there's a task, each one more difficult than the last . . . I wanted love to be active, not agonizing.

IVANOV. And when you become my wife, the tasks will be even more complex. Call it off! Understand, it's not love speaking through you, but the obstinacy of an honest nature. You set yourself the goal, come what may, of resurrecting the man in me, rescuing me, you flattered yourself that you would do a deed of valor . . . Now you're ready to retreat, but you're prevented by a false feeling. Don't you see!

SASHA. What strange, savage logic you use! Well, can I call it off? How can I call it off? You don't have a mother, sisters, friends . . . You're a wreck, your estate's been plundered, the people around you speak ill of you . . .

IVANOV. I did something stupid coming here. I should have done what I intended . . .

Enter LEBEDEV.

I X

The same and LEBEDEV.

SASHA (*runs to meet her father*). Papa, for God's sake, he ran over here like a madman and is torturing me! He insists that I call it off, he doesn't want to ruin me. Tell him that I want no part of his magnanimity! I know what I'm doing.

LEBEDEV. I can't figure this out . . . What magnanimity?

IVANOV. There will be no wedding!

SASHA. There will! Papa, tell him there will be a wedding!

LEBEDEV. Hold on, hold on! . . . Why don't you want there to be a wedding?

IVANOV. I've explained why to her, but she refuses to understand.

LEBEDEV. No, don't explain it to her, but to me, and explain it so that I can understand! Ah, Nikolay Alekseevich! God be your judge! You've filled our lives with so much murk and gloom I feel as if I'm living in a chamber of horrors: no matter where I look, I don't understand a thing . . . It's sheer agony . . . Well, what do you ask me, an old man, to do with you? Challenge you to a duel or what?

IVANOV. No duels are called for. All that's called for is to have a brain in one's head and understand plain Russian.

SASHA (*walks up and down the stage in agitation*). This is horrible, horrible! Just like a child!

LEBEDEV. There's nothing left but to throw up your hands and that's it. Listen, Nikolay. In your opinion, everything you're doing is clever, subtle, in accordance with all the rules of psychology, but in my opinion, it's a scandal and a disaster. Listen to me, an old man, one last time! Here's what I have to say to you: calm your mind! Look at things simply, the way everybody else does! In this world everything is simple. The ceiling is white, boots are black, sugar is sweet. You love Sasha, she loves you. If you love her, stick around, if you don't, go away, we won't hold any grudges. This is simple enough, isn't it! You're both healthy, intelligent, moral, and well fed, thank God, and clothed . . . What more do you need? No money? Big deal! Money doesn't bring happiness . . . Of course, I understand . . . your estate is mortgaged, you've got nothing to pay the interest with, but I'm a father, I understand . . . Mother can do as she likes, God bless her; she won't give money—who needs it? Shurochka says you don't need the dowry. Principles, Schopenhauer[53] . . . It's all nonsense . . . I've got ten thousand stashed in the bank . . . (*Looks around.*) Not a dog in this house knows about it . . . It's Granny's . . . It's for the two of you . . . Take it, only one condition with the money: give Matvey two thousand or so . . .

GUESTS *gather in the reception room.*

IVANOV. Pasha, this conversation is going nowhere. I act as my conscience dictates.

SASHA. And I act as *my* conscience dictates. You can say what you like, I won't let you go. Papa, the benediction right now! I'm going to get Mamma . . . (*Exits.*)

X

IVANOV and LEBEDEV.

LEBEDEV. I don't understand a thing . . .

IVANOV. Listen, you poor old soul . . . To explain to you who I am—decent or contemptible, sane or psychopath, I won't even begin. I couldn't get it through your thick skull. I was young, overenthusiastic, sincere, reasonably intelligent; I loved, hated and had beliefs different from everyone else's, I worked and hoped for ten men, tilted at windmills, banged my head against walls; without calculating my strength, or reasoning, or knowing life, I hoisted a load on my back, which immediately snapped my spine and strained my sinews; I rushed to consume my one and only youth, I got drunk, got enthused, worked hard; knew no moderation. And tell me: could it be any other way? After all, there aren't many of us and there's plenty of work to be done, plenty! God, what plenty! And here's how life, my adversary, takes its cruel revenge! I wore myself out! Thirty years and the hangover has already set in, I'm old, I already go around in a dressing gown.[12] With a heavy head and an indolent mind, worn out, overtaxed, broken, faithless, loveless, aimless, like a shadow, loitering around people, I don't know: who am I, why am I alive, what do I want? And I've started thinking that love is absurd, caresses are cloying, there's no meaning to hard work, songs and impassioned speeches are vulgar and stale. And wherever I go I bring along tedium, cold boredom, dissatisfaction, distaste for life . . . I'm a hopeless goner! Before you stands a man of thirty-five who's always exhausted, disenchanted, crushed by the insignificance of what he's accomplished; he's burning up with shame, scoffs at his own weakness . . . Oh, how pride mutinies within me, how fury chokes me! (*Swaying.*) Look how I've worn myself out! I'm even staggering . . . I've got weak. Where's Matvey? Let him take me home.

VOICES IN THE RECEPTION ROOM: *"The best man's here!"*

X I

The same, SHABELSKY, BORKIN, and then LVOV and SASHA.

SHABELSKY (*entering*). In somebody else's shabby dress coat . . . with no gloves . . . and for that reason all those sneering looks, stupid jokes, vulgar smiles . . . Disgusting pygmies!

BORKIN (*enters quickly with a bouquet; he's in a tailcoat with a best-man's favor in his buttonhole*). Oof! Where is he? (*To Ivanov.*) They've been wait-

---

12 A reference to Oblomov, the protagonist of Goncharov's eponymous novel of 1859, an indolent landowner who spends his days in a dressing gown, lolling on a sofa, incapable of making a decision.

ing for you at the church for a long time and here you are talking philosophy. What a comedian! Honest to God, a comedian! After all, you're not
supposed to ride with the bride, but separately with me, then I drive back
from the church and pick up the bride. Can't you even get that right? Positively a comedian!

LVOV (*enters, to Ivanov*). Ah, you're here? (*Loudly.*) Nikolay Alekseevich Ivanov,
I declare in the hearing of everyone, that you are a bastard!

IVANOV (*coldly*). Thank you kindly.

General consternation.

BORKIN (*to Lvov*). My good sir, this is an outrage! I challenge you to a duel!

LVOV. Mister Borkin, I consider it degrading to talk to you, let alone fight
you! But Mister Ivanov may receive satisfaction, if he so desires.

SHABELSKY. Dear sir, I'll fight with you!

SASHA (*to Lvov*). Why? Why did you insult him? Gentlemen, please, make
him tell me: why?

LVOV. Aleksandra Pavlovna, I did not insult him without sufficient reason. I
came here as a decent person to open your eyes, and I beg you to hear me
out.

SASHA. What can you say? That you're a decent person? The whole world
knows that! You'd better tell me out of your clear conscience: do you
understand what you've done or don't you? You came in here just now, Mr.
Decent Person, and flung a horrible insult at him, which nearly killed me;
in the past, when you dogged him like a shadow, and kept him from living,
you were convinced that you were doing your duty, that you are a decent
person. You meddled in his private life, badmouthed him and ran him
down wherever you could, peppered me and all my friends with anonymous letters,—and all the time you thought you were being a decent person. With the idea that it's decent, you, a doctor, didn't even spare his sick
wife or give her a moment's peace with your suspicions. And whatever
viciousness, whatever nasty act of cruelty you commit, you'll go on thinking that you are an exceptionally decent and progressive person!

IVANOV (*laughing*). This isn't a wedding, it's a debating society! Bravo, bravo!

SASHA (*to Lvov*). So think about that now; do you understand what you've done or don't you? Narrow-minded, heartless people! (*Takes Ivanov by the arm.*) Let's get out of here, Nikolay! Father, let's go!

IVANOV. Where are we to go? Hold on, I'll put an end to this right now! Youth has re-awakened in me, the original Ivanov has found his voice! (*He pulls out a revolver.*)

SASHA (*screams*). I know what he wants to do! Nikolay, for heaven's sake!

IVANOV. I've been on the skids too long, now it's time to call a halt! Time to know when you've worn out your welcome! Step aside! Thank you, Sasha!

SASHA (*cries out*). Nikolay, for heaven's sake! Stop him!

IVANOV. Leave me alone!

> *He runs off to the side and shoots himself.*

Curtain

VARIANTS TO

Ivanov, Final Version

Variants from the censor's copy of 1889, the journal *Northern Herald (Severny Vestnik)*, and *Plays* (1897).

ACT ONE

page 462 / *Replace*: first, a young doctor, then a trip to the Crimea, in the Crimea a strapping Tatar . . .
with: first a young doctor, then a trip to the Crimea, in the Crimea a strapping Tatar, on the way back a private train compartment with some dandy, who has lost all his money but is sweet . . . (Censor 1889)

ACT TWO

page 476 / *Replace*: *The FIRST GUEST yawns.*

with: **FIRST GUEST** (*to the young lady beside him*). What, ma'am?

YOUNG LADY. Tell me a story.

FIRST GUEST. What am I supposed to tell you?

YOUNG LADY. Well, something funny.

FIRST GUEST. Funny? (*After a moment's thought.*) A man came up to another man and sees—there's a dog sitting there, you understand. (*Laughs.*) So he asks, "What's your dog's name?" And the other man says, "Liqueurs." (*Roars with laughter.*) Liqueurs . . . Get it? Like-yours . . .

YOUNG LADY. Like?

FIRST GUEST. Liqueurs.

YOUNG LADY. There's nothing funny about that.

THIRD GUEST. That's an old joke . . . (*Yawns.*) (Censor 1889)

page 477 / *Replace*: (*Quickly exits into the garden.*)

with: (*Quickly exits to the terrace and stops near the card table. To Yegorushka.*) How much did you put down? What did you put down? Wait . . . thirty-eight multiplied by eight . . . makes . . . eight times eight . . . Ah, the hell with it! . . . (*Goes into the garden.*) (Censor 1889)

page 485 / *After*: I'm a low-life too and a slave owner. — Nikolay doesn't stay home nights—he's a low-life too: it means he tortures his wife so as to put her in her grave and marry a rich woman. (Censor 1889)

page 488 / *After*: A waste of perfectly good sugar. — I'll take it away, and let Matryona finish it. (Censor 1889)

·ACT THREE

page 494 / *Replace*: A virtuoso!

with: A virtuoso . . . every day he generates thousands of projects, tears the stars out of the sky, but never makes a profit . . . He never has a penny in his pocket . . .

LEBEDEV. Art for art's sake . . . (Censor 1889; *Northern Herald*)

page 498 / *After the stage direction: Laughter.* —
LEBEDEV. Why, he's so addicted to card playing, the dear heart, that instead of good-bye he says pass . . . (Censor 1889; *Northern Herald*)

page 499 / *After: (Greets them.)* — I went through all the rooms, and there's that doctor, like he's been eating loco-weed, he bugged his eyes at me, and—"What'ya want? Get outta here . . . You'll give the patient a turn," he says . . . As if it's that easy . . . (Censor 1889)

page 502 / *After: a George Sand!* — I thought only Borkin had great ideas in his head, but now it seems . . . I'm going, I'm going . . . (*Exits.*) (Censor 1889)

page 503 / *After:* farming, district schools, projects, — speeches, cheese-making that failed, a stud farm, magazine articles, plenty of mistakes . . . (Censor 1889])

page 503 / *Replace:* At the age of twenty . . . how else can you explain this lassitude?
with: All us Russians at twenty and twenty-five don't get excited in moderation, we plunge into the fire and mindlessly squander our strength, and nature punishes us for this cruelly: at thirty we're already old and worn out. (Censor 1889; *Northern Herald*)

page 504 / *After:* brains or hands or feet — as if it weren't Ivanov inside me, but an old, sick horse . . . (Censor 1889)

page 507 / *After:* Have you indeed? — Well, if it's come to that, then know that I love your wife! I love her as intensely as I hate you! That's my right and that's my privilege! When I first saw her torment, my heart couldn't stand it and . . . (Censor 1889; *Northern Herald*)

page 508 / *After:* do a valiant deed! — The distinguishing feature of young Russian women is always the fact that they can't tell the difference between a good painting and a caricature. (Censor 1889)

page 509 / *After:* but bellyachers and psychopaths — Ah, my little crackpot! What are you laughing at? You're too young to teach me and save me. Little crackpot!
SASHA. If you don't mind, what a thing to say! Really, this won't do at all!
IVANOV. You are, my little crackpot!

SASHA. Can we do without the sarcasm?

IVANOV (*shaking his head*). We cannot!

SASHA. All right then! We know how to punish you. How about getting a move on! (*Shoves his shoulder, then pulls him by the arm with all her might.*) Move! Lord, what a heavy lummox! Get a move on, Oblomov!

IVANOV. No, I won't stir from this spot. The likes of you, dear girl, won't get me to budge. You can try with all your might and even send for your dear mamma to help! No, madam, it takes far more strength. A whole houseful of widows and a girl's boarding school won't move me from this spot.

SASHA. Oof, I'm out of breath . . . I wish you were an empty vessel!

IVANOV. There now, you shameless hussy, that'll teach you to save people! Oh you . . . dark-eyed thing! (Censor 1889; *Northern Herald*)

page 509 / *After*: Nothing more! — Eh, feed me to the wolves, if only I could fumigate the sniveling brat out of myself, I might be a real man! Watch out, here comes the train! (*Chases Sasha.*) Choo-choo!

SASHA (*jumps on to the sofa*). Get away, get away, get away!

IVANOV. Oh frailty, thy name is woman! (*Roars with laughter.*) (Censor 1889; *Northern Herald*)

page 509 / *After*: what a ridiculous numbskull! — You know, in the reeds along the Dnieper there nests a certain bird—a grayish, very sullen, pitiful little thing, and it's called a bittern. It sits all day in the reeds, dolefully going: boo-hoo! boo-hoo! Like a cow locked up in a barn. That's what I'm like. I sit by myself in the reeds and (Censor 1889)

ACT FOUR

page 516 / *After*: I'm not talking on my own behalf, but your mother insisted. — Listen. Since the best man hasn't got here yet and since we still haven't spoken the benediction over you, to avoid any misunderstanding, you should know once and for all that we . . . I mean not we, but your mother . . . (Censor 1889)

page 522 / *After*: wherever I go I bring along boredom, depression, dissatisfaction — My life has become loathsome to me, but that alone does not give me the right to leach the color out of other people's lives. (Censor 1889)

page 522 / *After*: I have no other names for them — So wherein lies my salvation? Tell me, in love? That's an old gimmick! Love is that extra stab in the back; it complicates spiritual uplift, it adds a new tedium to tedium. Winning two hundred thousand? The same thing. Stimulating and uplifting my spirit can be achieved only by heaven itself, but the stimulation is followed by the hangover, and my spirit falls even lower than before. You must understand this and not hide from yourself! Our old friend, depression, has only one salvation, and, unfortunately, we are too intelligent for that salvation. (Censor 1889; *Northern Herald*; *Plays*)

page 523 / *After*: You don't have a mother, sisters, friends . . . — Alone, alone, like an orphan. Whom shall I throw you at? (Censor 1889; *Northern Herald*; *Plays*)

page 523 / *After*: I should have done what I intended . . . — This is all I wanted . . . (*Shows a revolver and hides it again.*) It's easier to kill myself than to ruin your life. But I thought that you would listen to common sense and . . .

SASHA. Hand over the revolver!

IVANOV. I won't.

SASHA. Hand it over, I tell you!

IVANOV. Sasha, I have too much love for you and too much anger for small talk. I'm asking you to call it off! It's a final demand in the name of fairness, humane feeling! (Censor 1889)

page 525 / *Replace*: I was young . . . fury chokes me!

with: I'll ask you only about one thing. If once in your life you encountered a young man, ardent, sincere, no fool, and you see that he loves, hates and believes not as everyone else does, works and hopes for ten, makes an unusual marriage, tilts at windmills, bangs his head against the wall, if you see how he has hoisted a load which snaps his spine and strains his sinews, then say to him: don't hasten to squander your strength on youth alone, preserve it for your whole life; get drunk, get excited, work, but be temperate, otherwise fate will punish you cruelly! At thirty you will already have a hangover and you will be old. With a heavy head, with an indolent soul, worn out, broken down, without faith, without love, without a goal, like a shadow, you will loiter amidst people and not know: who are you? why are you alive? what do you want? And it will seem to you that love is rubbish, affection cloying, that there's no sense in hard work, that songs and passionate speeches are vulgar and stale. And wherever you go, everywhere you will bring with you longing, cold boredom, dissatisfaction, revulsion to life, and there will be no salvation for you. Ruined irrevocably! You'll say, how before you there stood a man of thirty-five already impotent, disappointed, crushed by his insignificant accomplishment, how he burned with shame in your eyes, was mocked for his weakness, how pride was aroused in him, and how stupidly he ended up! How this raving choked him! (Censor 1889; *Northern Herald*)

page 526 / *After*: Positively a comedian! —

SASHA. It doesn't matter, we'll all go together right now. (*Takes Ivanov by the arm.*) Let's go!

IVANOV. An energetic individual! (*Laughs.*) I'm marrying a drill sergeant . . . (Censor 1889)

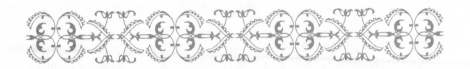

TATYANA REPINA

atyana Repina is an anomaly among Chekhov's one-acts. It can be understood only in relationship to another play by someone else. In 1889, Aleksey Suvorin wrote a "comedy," founded on an actual occurrence: the suicide, eight years earlier, of the young actress and operetta singer Yevlaliya Kadmina. Jilted by her lover, she poisoned herself and came on stage to die in the last act of Ostrovsky's *Vasilisa Melentyeva*, whose heroine also succumbs to poisoning. Kadmina perished in gruesome torments before the eyes of a Kharkov audience, and so won posthumous notoriety. Chekhov considered her an "extraordinary celebrity" and even collected her photograph.

Suvorin's *Tatyana Repina* follows the facts fairly closely. Repina, a high-spirited and talented provincial actress, is thrown over by her lover, who hopes to repair his ruined fortunes by marrying an heiress. Deeply hurt, publicly insulted by a gross Jewish banker, seeing nothing to live for, Tatyana takes poison before going on stage and dies performing the last act of Ostrovsky's play as her friends look on aghast. From a modern standpoint, Chekhov's enthusiasm for Suvorin's sensation drama is hard to comprehend; yet he was lavish in his praise and offered copious advice in his letters. He predicted a success that came to pass in both capitals, and got embroiled in the Moscow rehearsals as an intercessor between actors and author, while Suvorin was busy helping to stage Chekhov's *Ivanov* in Petersburg.

Chekhov's one-act is therefore a kind of private joke, the "what happens after the curtain goes down" that St. John Hankin perfected in his *Dramatic Sequels*. Chekhov hypothesizes an epidemic of suicides following in the wake of Repina's desperate act, and depicts the marriage taking place between the dead actress's lover and his rich fiancée. The hieratic formality of the Orthodox wedding ceremony authentically reproduced, with interpolations of trivial remarks by the bystanders, provides the structure. The counterpoint between the sonorous Church Slavonic with its portentous vows and the mundane chitchat of the wedding party produces a sour and sardonic effect. Eventually, the church choirs have to compete with a worldly chorus of "Voices," which begins to spread the news of the suicide epidemic, passing along fragments of gossip. In this antiphony, female neurotics are reproved for being copycats while the choristers intone "Lord, have mercy" and "Amen."

Suvorin's *Tatyana Repina* is interesting in foreshadowing *The Seagull*. Chekhov's favorite character in Suvorin's play was the journalist Adashev, who denigrates his profession as a man of letters in a manner that Chekhov replicated in the Trigorin-Nina interview in *Seagull*.[1] It is Adashev, a *raison-neur*, who tells Tatyana, after she has, unbeknownst to him, taken the poison, his opinion that suicide is cowardice.

> Here in Russia suicide has really become something contagious. There's no shortage of gunpowder for good people. Children run for the revolver when they get low grades, grown-ups on account of trifles . . . They fall out of love— a bullet to the brain. Their vanity's been wounded, they aren't appreciated— they shoot themselves. What's become of strength of character?[2]

Chekhov picks up this notion and carries it to its logical conclusion in his afterpiece, but he also deals with it in his later works. Treplyov's two suicide attempts in *Seagull* and Uncle Vanya's pilfering morphine must be viewed in this light. After *Ivanov*, Chekhov treated suicide as an act of weakness in its refusal to cope with life's demands.

Chekhov's *Tatyana Repina*, a pastiche rather than a parody, is most intriguing as an experiment in polyphonic structure; in miniature, it practices the intricate interweaving of melodramatic pathos and diurnal crassness that was to become the trademark of Chekhov's major plays. Not just the suicides, but the mismatched marriages, failed careers, and dashed hopes that will, in the last plays, be jumbled amid meals, card games, and dirty galoshes are foreshadowed here.

NOTES

1 Nina overhearing Trigorin in the dining room in the last act ("He's here too . . . Why, yes . . . Never mind . . . Yes") may be an echo of Tatyana's overhearing her lover singing at his bachelor supper ("Is he there? Wait . . . Yes, yes, that's his voice . . . *l'amour qui nous* . . . He is there, he is . . . [*Listens intently.*]).

2 A. S. Suvorin, *Tatyana Repina, komediya v chetyrakh deistvyakh* (St. Petersburg: A. Suvorin, 1889), Act IV, scene 3.

TATYANA REPINA

Татьяна Репина

A Drama in One Act

(Dedicated to A. S. Suvorin)

Translator's note: Except for the clergy, the main characters derive from Suvorin's *Tatyana Repina*. Sabinin, an impecunious landowner, had been Tatyana's lover, but jilted her for a rich woman, Vera Olenina. The Jewish banker David Sonnenstein had made the match in order to profit from the sale of Sabinin's estate. The journalist Adashev was a close friend of Tatyana's, Matveev the manager of the theatrical troupe she starred in, and Kokoshkina a comic chatterbox. Kotelnikov was a skirt-chasing landowner, and Patronnikov a lawyer.

CHARACTERS

OLENINA

KOKOSHKINA

MATVEEV

SONNENSTEIN

SABININ

KOTELNIKOV

KOKOSHKIN

PATRONNIKOV

VOLGIN, *a young officer*

A UNIVERSITY STUDENT

A YOUNG LADY

FR. IVAN, *the archpriest of the cathedral, an old man of 70*

FR. NIKOLAY ⎤
⎟ *young priests*
FR. ALEKSEY ⎦

DEACON

SACRISTAN

KUZMA, *the church caretaker*

LADY IN BLACK

THE DEPUTY DISTRICT ATTORNEY

ACTORS AND ACTRESSES

> *Between six and seven o'clock in the evening. A cathedral church.
> All the hanging lamps and candle stands are lit. The royal gates*[1]
> *of the altar screen are open. Two choirs, the diocesan and the
> cathedral, are singing. The church is packed with people. It is
> dark and stuffy. A marriage ceremony is being solemnized.
> SABININ and OLENINA are getting married. Among the first
> group of groom's men are KOTELNIKOV and Officer VOLGIN,
> among the second his brother, a UNIVERSITY STUDENT, and
> the DEPUTY DISTRICT ATTORNEY. All the local
> intelligentsia. Elegant attire. The ceremony is being performed by
> FR. IVAN in a discolored kamelaukion,*[2] *shaggy FR. NIKOLAY
> in a skullcap, and a very young FR. ALEKSEY in dark glasses;
> behind and somewhat to the left of FR. Ivan is a tall, thin
> DEACON with a book. In the crowd the local theatrical troupe
> with MATVEEV at their head.*

FR. IVAN (*reads*). Remember too, O Lord, the parents who reared them: for the prayers of the parents secure the foundations of the house. Remember, O Lord our God, Thy servants who are in attendance and are gathered here to rejoice. Remember, O Lord our God, Thy servant Pyotr and Thy handmaid Vera and bless them. Bestow upon them fruit of the womb, children and children's children, bonds of harmony in body and soul; raise

---

1 In Russian Orthodox churches, the raised chancel on the eastern side is reserved for clergy and choristers. The iconostasis, a screen of painted icons, richly carved frames, and eternal lamps, separates the choir from the sanctuary. The central doors in the iconostasis are called the *tsarskie vrata*, or royal gates, and may be used only by priests.

2 The high hat of violet velvet, characteristic of Greek Orthodox clergy.

them up, like unto the cedars of Lebanon, like unto the well-tended vine. Bestow upon them corn from the sheaves, that having all things in sufficiency, they may thrive in all works that are good and pleasing unto Thee; and may they behold the sons of their sons, like unto a newly planted olive grove, around their table; and may they shine before Thee, like unto the heavenly bodies, that they be good and pleasing unto Thee, our Lord. And with Thee be the power and the glory, the honor and the devotion to Thine eternal father and Thy life-endowing spirit, now and forever, world without end.

DIOCESAN CHOIR (*sings*). Amen.

PATRONNIKOV. It's stuffy! What's that medal 'round your neck, David Solomonovich?

SONNENSTEIN. It's Belgian. And why are there so many people here? Who let 'em in? Oof! It's like a steam bath!

PATRONNIKOV. The police are worth crap.

DEACON. Let us pray to the Lord!

CATHEDRAL CHOIR (*sings*). O Lord, be merciful.

FR. NIKOLAY (*reads*). O Holy God, Who didst create man out of dust and mould his wife from his rib and yoked her to him to be his helpmeet, for it was pleasing to Thy majesty that man be not alone on earth; and even now, O Lord, do Thou stretch forth Thine own hand from Thy holy dwelling place and conjoin this Thy servant Pyotr and this Thy handmaid Vera, for by Thee is wife bestowed on husband. Yoke them together in bonds of harmony, crown them in one flesh, bestow on them fruit of the womb, the boon of children and children's children. For Thine is the might, and Thine is the kingdom, and the power, and the glory, Father and Son and Holy Spirit, now and forever, world without end.

CATHEDRAL CHOIR (*sings*). Amen.

YOUNG LADY (*to Sonnenstein*). Now they're going to put the crowns on them. Look, look!

FR. IVAN (*takes a crown from the analogion[3] and turning his face to Sabinin*). The servant of God Pyotr is crowned for the handmaid of God Vera in the

---

3 Church Slavonic, the lectern in Greek Orthodox churches.

name of the Father and the Son and the Holy Spirit, amen. (*Hands the crown to Kotelnikov.*)

IN THE CROWD. The best man's the exact same height as the groom. Not very attractive. Who is he?
—That's Kotelnikov. The officer's not very attractive either. Lord, let the lady through! You can't get through here, *madame.*

FR. IVAN (*turning to Olenina*). The handmaid of God Vera is crowned for the servant of God Pyotr in the name of the Father and the Son and the Holy Spirit. (*Hands the crown to the student.*)

KOTELNIKOV. The crowns are heavy. My arm's already fallen asleep.

VOLGIN. Never mind, I'll be taking over for you soon. Who's that stinking of cheap perfume, I'd like to know?

DEPUTY DISTRICT ATTORNEY. It's coming from Kotelnikov.

KOTELNIKOV. That's a lie.

VOLGIN. Ssh!

FR. IVAN. O Lord our God, may they be crowned with honor and glory! O Lord our God, may they be crowned with honor and glory! O Lord our God, may they be crowned with honor and glory!

KOKOSHKINA (*to her husband*). Doesn't Vera look pretty today? I can't take my eyes off her. And she isn't nervous at all.

KOKOSHKIN. She's an old hand at this. After all, she's getting married for the second time.

KOKOSHKINA. Yes, that's true. (*Sighs.*) I wish her joy with all my soul! She has such a kind heart!

SACRISTAN (*walking out into the middle of the church*). The Prokimenon[4] chapter eight. Thou settest a crown of pure gold on his head; He asked life of Thee, and Thou gavest it him.

DIOCESAN CHOIR (*sings*). Thou settest on his head . . .

PATRONNIKOV. I'd like a smoke.

---

4 A verse from the Psalms, sung before the Gospels and the Acts of the Apostles are read. In the Western Bible, this is from Psalm 21.

SACRISTAN. A reading from the Apostle Paul.[5]

DEACON. Let us hearken!

SACRISTAN (*intoning in a low bass*). Brethren, give thanks always for all things unto God and the Father in the name of our Lord Jesus Christ; submitting yourselves one to another in the fear of God. Wives, submit yourselves unto your own husbands, as unto the Lord. For the husband is the head of the wife, even as Christ is the head of the church; and he is the savior of the body. Therefore as the church is subject unto Christ, so let wives be to their husbands in everything . . .

SABININ (*to Kotelnikov*). You're crushing my head with the crown.

KOTELNIKOV. You're imagining it. I'm holding the crown a good six inches away from your head.

SABININ. I'm telling you, you're crushing me!

SACRISTAN. Husbands, love your wives, even as Christ also loved the church, and gave Himself for it; that He might sanctify and cleanse it with the washing of water by the word, that He might present it to Himself a glorious church, having neither spot, nor wrinkle, nor any such thing; but that it should be holy and without blemish.

VOLGIN. That's a good bass voice . . . (*To Kotelnikov.*) You want me to take over for you?

KOTELNIKOV. I'm not tired yet.

SACRISTAN. So ought men to love their wives as their own bodies. He that loveth his wife loveth himself. For no man ever yet hated his own flesh; but nourisheth and cherisheth it, even as the Lord the church, for we are members of His body, of His flesh and of His bones. For this reason shall a man leave his father and mother . . .

SABININ. Hold the crown higher. You're crushing me.

KOTELNIKOV. Don't be silly!

SACRISTAN. . . . and shall be joined unto his wife, and they two shall be one flesh . . .

---

5 Epistles to the Ephesians 5:20–33.

KOKOSHKIN. The Governor's here.

KOKOSHKINA. Where do you see him?

KOKOSHKIN. He's standing over near the choir on the right, next to Altukhov. He's incognito.

KOKOSHKINA. I see 'im, I see 'im. He's talking to Mashenka Hansen. He's got a crush on her.

SACRISTAN. This is a great mystery: but I speak concerning Christ and the church. Nevertheless, let every one of you in particular love his wife even as himself, and the wife see that she reverence her husband!

CATHEDRAL CHOIR (*sings*). Hallelujah, hallelujah, hallelujah . . .

IN THE CROWD. You hear that, Nataliya Sergeevna? The wife should reverence her husband.
　—Leave me out of it!

Laughter.

　—Ssh! People, it's impolite!

SACRISTAN. Ask for wisdom, let us hear the Holy Gospel!

FR. IVAN. Peace be with you!

DIOCESAN CHOIR (*sings*). And with Thy Spirit!

IN THE CROWD. The Acts of the Apostles, the Gospels . . . how long this all takes! It's high time they left our soul in peace.
　—It's impossible to breathe. I'm leaving.
　—Don't go. Wait, it'll be over soon.

FR. IVAN. A reading from the Holy Gospel of St. John![6]

DEACON. Let us hearken.

FR. IVAN (*removes his kamelaukion*). And the third day there was a marriage in Cana of Galilee; and the mother of Jesus was there; and both Jesus was called, and his disciples, to the marriage. And when they wanted wine, the mother of Jesus saith unto him, They have no wine. Jesus saith unto her, Woman, what have I to do with thee? mine hour is not yet come . . .

---

6 John 2:1–11.

SABININ (*to Kotelnikov*). Will it be over soon?

KOTELNIKOV. I don't know, I'm an ignoramus about this stuff. I suppose it'll be soon.

VOLGIN. The procession is still to come.

FR. IVAN. His mother saith unto the servants, Whatsoever he saith unto you, do it. And there were set there six waterpots of stone, after the manner of the purifying of the Jews, containing two or three firkins apiece. Jesus saith unto them, Fill the waterpots with water. And they filled them up to the brim. And he saith unto them, Draw out now, and bear unto the governor of the feast . . .

A groan is heard.

VOLGIN. *Kes keh say?*[7] Did somebody get trampled or what?

IN THE CROWD. Sssh! Quiet!

Groan.

FR. IVAN. . . . and they bare it. When the ruler of the feast had tasted the water that was made into wine, and knew not whence it was: (but the servants which drew the water knew;) the governor of the feast called for the bridegroom, and saith unto him . . .

SABININ (*to Kotelnikov*). Who's groaning now?

KOTELNIKOV (*staring into the crowd*). Something's moving . . . Some lady in black . . . I suppose she fainted . . . They're taking her away . . .

SABININ (*staring*). Hold it higher, the crown . . .

FR. IVAN. . . . every man at the beginning doth set forth good wine; and when men have well drunk, then that which is worse; but thou hast kept the good wine until now. This beginning of miracles did Jesus in Cana of Galilee, and manifested forth His glory; and His disciples believed on Him—

IN THE CROWD. I can't understand why they let hysterics in here!

DIOCESAN CHOIR. Glory unto Thee, O Lord, glory unto Thee!

PATRONNIKOV. Stop humming like a bee, David Solomonovich. And don't turn your back on the altar. It's not right.

---

7 Mispronunciation of *Qu'est-ce que c'est*, French, what is it?

SONNENSTEIN. It's that young lady who's humming like a bee, not me . . . heh, heh, heh.

SACRISTAN. Let all of us say with all our soul and with all our mind . . .

CATHEDRAL CHOIR (*sings*). Lord, have mercy . . .

DEACON. Lord Almighty, God our Father, we pray, hear us and be merciful.

IN THE CROWD. Ssh! Quiet!
—But I'm the one being pushed!

CHOIR (*sings*). O Lord, have mercy!

IN THE CROWD. Ssh! Quiet!
—Who fainted?

DEACON. Have mercy on us, God, in Thy great loving kindness, we pray Thee, hear us and be merciful.

CHOIR (*sings*). O Lord, have mercy. (*Three times.*)

DEACON. Let us also pray for our most devout, most autocratic Great Sovereign our Emperor Aleksandr Aleksandrovich of all the Russias, for his power, victory, well-being, peace, health, his salvation, and may our Lord God help and succor him in all things and humble beneath his feet all his foes and adversaries.

CHOIR (*sings three times*). O Lord, have mercy.

A groan. Movement in the crowd.

KOKOSHKINA. What's going on? (*To the lady beside her.*) This is impossible, darling. They might at least open the doors . . . You could die from the heat.

IN THE CROWD. They're taking her out, but she won't let them . . . Who is she? Ssh!

DEACON. Let us also pray for his consort, the most devout sovereign lady, the Empress Mariya Fyodorovna . . .

CHOIR (*sings*). Lord, have mercy.

DEACON. Let us also pray for his heir, the true believer lord, tsarevich and Grand Duke Nikolay Aleksandrovich and all the imperial household.

CHOIR (*sings*). Lord, have mercy!

SABININ. Oh, my God . . .

OLENINA. What?

DEACON. Let us also pray for the most holy official Synod and our most reverend lord Theophilus, Bishop of Hither and Yon, and all our brothers in Christ.

CHOIR (*sings*). Lord, have mercy.

IN THE CROWD. Yesterday at the Hotel Europa some other woman poisoned herself.
  —Yes. They say, some doctor's wife.
  —How come, do you know?

DEACON. Let us also pray for all their Christ-loving host . . .

CHOIR (*sings*). Lord, have mercy.

VOLGIN. It sounds like somebody's crying . . . The public is really behaving indecently here.

DEACON. Let us also pray for our brethren, priests, and holy monks, and all our brothers in Christ.

CHOIR (*sings*). Lord, have mercy.

MATVEEV. The choirs are in splendid voice today.

COMIC ACTOR. Wish we had a few of those, Zakhar Ilyich!

MATVEEV. Is that all you want, jerkface!

Laughter.

  Ssh!

DEACON. Let us also pray for the grace, life, peace, health, salvation to the devoted servants of God Pyotr and Vera.

CHOIR (*sings*). O Lord, have mercy!

DEACON. Let us also pray for the blessed . . .

IN THE CROWD. Yes, some doctor's wife . . . at the hotel . . .

DEACON. . . . and never to be forgotten, most holy orthodox patriarchs . . .

IN THE CROWD. That's the fourth one to pull a Tatyana Repina and poison herself. Try and explain these poisonings to me, my good man!
—A psychosis. Nothing else.
—Are they copycats, do you think?

DEACON. . . . and the devout tsars and true believing tsarinas, and the founders of this holy temple, and all the fathers and brothers who have gone before us . . .

IN THE CROWD. Suicide is contagious . . .
—The number of these female psychopaths that are turning up, it's horrible!
—Ssh! Will you stop moving around!

DEACON. . . . Orthodox folk who lie here and everywhere.

IN THE CROWD. Stop yelling, please.

A groan.

CHOIR (*sings*). O Lord, have mercy!

IN THE CROWD. Repina poisoned the air with her suicide. All the young ladies have caught the contagion and gone crazy thinking they've been abused.
—Even the air in the church is poisoned. Can you feel the tension?

DEACON. Let us also pray for those who bring fruit and do good in this holy and reverend temple, for those who labor in the sweat of their brows, those who await Thy grace and compassion . . .

CHOIR (*sings*). O Lord, have mercy . . .

FR. IVAN. For a merciful God art Thou and one That loves mankind and to Thee we offer up glory, in the name of the Father and the Son and the Holy Spirit, now and forever, world without end.

CHOIR (*sings*). Amen.

SABININ. Kotelnikov!

KOTELNIKOV. What?

SABININ. Nothing . . . Oh my God . . . Tatyana Repina's here . . . She's here . . .

KOTELNIKOV. Have you gone out of your mind?

SABININ. The lady in black . . . that's her. I recognized her . . . I saw . . .

KOTELNIKOV. There's no resemblance . . . She's just a brunette too and that's all.

DEACON. Let us pray to the Lord!

KOTELNIKOV. Stop whispering to me, it's indecent. You're being watched . . .

SABININ. For heaven's sake . . . I can hardly stand on my feet. It is her.

A groan.

CHOIR. O Lord, have mercy!

IN THE CROWD. Quiet! Ssh! People, who's shoving at the back? Ssh!
    —They've taken her behind a pillar . . .
    —I can't move anywhere what with all the ladies . . . They should stay at home!

SOMEONE (*shouts*). Quiet!

FR. IVAN (*reads*). O Lord our God, in Thy redemptive care, as in Cana of Galilee . . . (*Casts a glance at the public.*) What people, honestly . . . (*Reads.*) . . . Thou didst show marriage to be honorable by Thy presence . . . (*Raising his voice.*) Please be more quiet! You are preventing us from performing the sacrament! Don't walk around the church, don't engage in conversation, and don't make noise, just stand quietly and pray to God. That's right. You should be God-fearing. (*Reads.*) Our Lord God, in Thy redemptive care, as in Cana of Galilee, Thou didst show marriage to be honorable by Thy presence, do Thou now Thyself keep Thy servants Pyotr and Vera, whom Thou hast already been pleased to conjoin with one another, in peace and concord, consecrate their marriage also, watch that their bed be undefiled, vouchsafe that their cohabitation be blameless and bestow on them a venerable old age, with a pure heart, keeping Thy commandments. For Thou art our God, the God of mercy and salvation, we offer up glory to Thee, with Thine eternal father, and with Thine all-holy and good and life-endowing spirit, now and forever, world without end.

DIOCESAN CHOIR (*sings*). Amen.

SABININ (*to Kotelnikov*). Did they go and tell the police not to let anybody in . . .

KOTELNIKOV. Who else can they let in? The church is packed to the rafters. Shut up . . . stop whispering.

SABININ. She . . . Tatyana's here.

KOTELNIKOV. You're raving. She's lying in her grave.

DEACON. Succor us, save us, have mercy on us and preserve us, God, by Thy grace abounding!

CATHEDRAL CHOIR (*sings*). Lord, have mercy.

DEACON. That all the day may be perfect, holy, peaceful, and without sin we pray the Lord . . .

CATHEDRAL CHOIR (*sings*). Grant it, O Lord.

DEACON. For an angel of peace, a true preceptor, a preserver of our souls and bodies we pray the Lord.

CHOIR (*sings*). Grant it, O Lord.

IN THE CROWD. This deacon never ends . . . First it's Lord have mercy, then it's grant it O Lord.
—I'm sick and tired of standing.

DEACON. Forgiveness and respite of our sins and trespasses we pray the Lord.

CHOIR (*sings*). Grant it, O Lord!

DEACON. Goodness and prosperity to our souls and peace to the world we pray the Lord.

IN THE CROWD. They're starting to make noise again! Hey, people!

CHOIR (*sings*). Grant it, O Lord!

OLENINA. Pyotr, you're trembling all over and breathing hard . . . Are you feeling faint?

SABININ. The lady in black . . . she . . . It's all our fault . . .

OLENINA. What lady?

A groan.

SABININ. Repina is groaning . . . I'll be brave, I'll be brave . . . Kotelnikov is crushing my head with that crown . . . Never mind, never mind . . .

DEACON. That the remaining days of our life end in peace and repentance, we pray to the Lord.

CHOIR. Grant it, O Lord.

KOKOSHKIN. Vera's as pale as death. Look, I think there are tears in her eyes. And he, he . . . look!

KOKOSHKINA. I already told her that the public would behave badly! I don't understand why she decided to get married here. She should have gone to the country.

DEACON. A Christian end to our life, without sickness, without shame, in peace and with a clear conscience on the Day of Judgment, we pray to Christ.

CHOIR (*sings*). Grant it, O Lord!

KOKOSHKINA. We ought to ask Father Ivan to speed things up. She looks awful.

VOLGIN. Allow me, I'll change places with you! (*Changes places with Kotelnikov.*)

DEACON. Having prayed for the unity of the faith and communion of the Holy Spirit both for ourselves and for each other, we dedicate our whole lives to Christ!

CHOIR (*sings*). To Thee, O Lord!

SABININ. Be brave, Vera, like me . . . Yes . . . Anyway, the service will be over soon. We'll go away at once . . . It's her . . .

VOLGIN. Ssh!

FR. IVAN. And vouchsafe us, Master, boldly and with impunity to dare to call upon Thee, our heavenly father God, and make utterance!

DIOCESAN CHOIR (*sings*). Our Father, Which art in heaven, hallowed be Thy name, Thy kingdom come . . .

MATVEEV (*to the actors*). Make a little room, kids, I want to kneel down. (*Kneels and bows to the ground.*) Thy will be done, on earth as it is in heaven. Give us this day our daily bread and forgive us our trespasses . . .

DIOCESAN CHOIR. . . . Thy will be done, as it is in heaven . . . in heaven . . . our daily bread . . . daily!

MATVEEV. Remember, O Lord, Thy deceased handmaid Tatyana, and forgive her her sins both of commission and omission, and forgive us and have mercy upon us . . . (*Getting up.*) It's hot!

DIOCESAN CHOIR. . . . give us this day and forgive . . . forgive us our trespasses . . . as we forgive those who trespass against us . . . our . . .

IN THE CROWD. Well, they're really dragging out the notes!

DIOCESAN CHOIR. . . . and lead us not . . . us . . . us! into temptation, but deliver us from e-e-e-vil!

KOTELNIKOV (*to the Deputy District Attorney*). The groom's got ants in his pants. Look at how he's trembling!

DEPUTY DISTRICT ATTORNEY. What's come over him?

KOTELNIKOV. The lady in black who just had hysterics he thinks is Tatyana. He's hallucinating.

FR. IVAN. For thine is the kingdom and the power and the glory, Father, Son, and Holy Spirit, now and forever, world without end.

CHOIR. Amen.

DEPUTY DISTRICT ATTORNEY. Watch out that he doesn't pull some kind of stunt!

KOTELNIKOV. He'll kee-eep it together! He's not that sort!

DEPUTY DISTRICT ATTORNEY. Yes, he's been through the wringer.

FR. IVAN. Peace be unto you.

CHOIR. And to Thy spirit.

DEACON. Bow your heads before the Lord!

CHOIR. Before Thee, O Lord!

IN THE CROWD. I think they'll have the procession now. Sssh!
   —Was there an inquest on the doctor's wife?
   —Not yet. They say her husband ran out on her. But after all Sabinin ran out on Repina! Didn't he?
   —Yes indeed . . .
   —I remember the inquest on Repina . . .

DEACON. Pray to the Lord!

CHOIR. O Lord, have mercy!

FR. IVAN (*reads*). God, who by Thy might createst all things and upholdest the universe and adornest the crown of all things created by Thee, bless this common cup provided for the communion of the couple conjoined in matrimony with the blessing of Thy spirit. For blessèd is Thy name and glorified Thy kingdom, now and forever, world without end. (*Gives Sabinin and Olenina a sip of wine.*)

CHOIR. Amen.

DEPUTY DISTRICT ATTORNEY. Look out, he's about to faint.

KOTELNIKOV. He's a tough customer. He'll hold up.

IN THE CROWD. Don't split up, people. We'll all leave together. Is Zipunov here?
—He's around somewhere. Just have to block the carriage and hiss for five minutes or so.

FR. IVAN. Please give me your hands. (*Binds the hands of Sabinin and Olenina with a handkerchief.*) Not too tight?

DEPUTY DISTRICT ATTORNEY (*to the student*). Give me the crown, young man, and you carry her train.

DIOCESAN CHOIR (*sings*). Rejoice, Esais, the virgin is with child . . .

> FR. IVAN *walks around the analogion; followed by the YOUNG COUPLE and the GROOM'S MEN.*

IN THE CROWD. That student's got tangled up in her train.

DIOCESAN CHOIR. . . . and bringeth forth a son, Emmanuel, God and man; the Orient is His name . . .

SABININ (*to Volgin*). Is it over?

DIOCESAN CHOIR. . . . whom magnifying we call the Virgin blest.

> FR. IVAN *walks around the lectern a second time.*

CATHEDRAL CHOIR (*sings*). Holy martyrs, who suffered mightily for our salvation and are crowned, pray to the Lord our God to have mercy on our souls.

FR. IVAN (*goes around for the third time and intones*). . . . our so-ouls.

SABININ. My God, this goes on forever.

DIOCESAN CHOIR (*sings*). Glory unto Thee, Christ our God, apostle's praise and martyrs' joy, who preached the consubstantial Trinity.

OFFICER IN THE CROWD (*to Kotelnikov*). Warn Sabinin that the high-school boys and university students are planning to hiss him in the street.

KOTELNIKOV. Thank you. (*To the Deputy District Attorney.*) Honestly, how long does this stuff go on! This service will never be over!

DEPUTY DISTRICT ATTORNEY. Now *your* hands are starting to tremble . . . What a lot of lightweights you all are!

KOTELNIKOV. I can't get Repina out of my mind. I keep imagining Sabinin singing and her crying.

FR. IVAN (*taking the crown from Volgin, to Sabinin*). Be thou magnified, O bridegroom, as Abraham, and blessed as Isaac, and increased as Jacob, walking in peace and working in righteousness the commandments of God!

YOUNG ACTOR. What beautiful lines to have to speak to a bastard like that!

MATVEEV. God doesn't play favorites.

FR. IVAN (*taking the crown from the Deputy District Attorney, to Olenina*). And thou, O bride, be thou magnified as Sarah, and gladdened as Rebecca, and do thou increase like unto Rachel, rejoicing in thine own husband, fulfilling the conditions of the law; for so it is well pleasing unto God.

IN THE CROWD (*a powerful movement towards the exit*).
  —Quiet, people! It isn't over yet!
  —Ssh! Stop shoving!

DEACON. Let us pray to the Lord!

CHOIR. Lord, be merciful!

FR. ALEKSEY (*reads, having taken off his dark glasses*). God, our God, Who wast present at Cana of Galilee and didst bless the marriage there, bless these thy servants, who by Thy providence are conjoined in the community of marriage; bless their incomings and outgoings, prosper their lives with good things, accept their crowns into Thy kingdom, immaculate and undefiled, and deliver them from evil, world without end.

CHOIR (*sings*). Amen.

OLENINA (*to her brother*). Tell them to give me a chair. I feel faint.

UNIVERSITY STUDENT. It'll be over right away. (*To the Deputy District Attorney.*) Vera feels faint!

DEPUTY DISTRICT ATTORNEY. Vera Aleksandrovna, it'll be over right away! In a minute . . . Be patient, my dear!

OLENINA (*to her brother*). Pyotr isn't listening to me . . . It's as if he's in a stupor . . . My God, my God . . . (*To Sabinin.*) Pyotr!

FR. IVAN. Peace be unto you!

CHOIR. And to Thy spirit!

DEACON. Bow your heads before the Lord.

FR. IVAN (*to Sabinin and Olenina*). Father, Son, and Holy Spirit, the all-holy and consubstantial and life-endowing Trinity, one divinity and kingdom bless you, and grant you long life, children and children's children, steadfastness in life and faith, and prosper you with all the good things of this earth! And consider you worthy to receive the promised salvation, through the intercession of the holy Mother of God and all the saints, amen! (*To Olenina, with a smile.*) You may kiss your husband.

VOLGIN (*to Sabinin*). What are you standing there for? Kiss her!

The YOUNG COUPLE exchange kisses.

FR. IVAN. Congratulations! God bless you . . .

KOKOSHKIN (*goes to Olenina*). My dear, my darling . . . I'm so glad! Congratulations!

KOKOSHKINA (*to Sabinin*). Congratulations, now that you're spliced! . . . Well, no need to be so pale now, the rigmarole's over . . .

DEACON. In Thy wisdom!

Congratulations.

CHOIR (*sings*). More honorable than the cherubim and incomparably more glorious than the seraphim, who immaculate gave birth to God from the word, his most pure Mother we extol thee. In the name of the Lord, bless us, O Fa-a-ather!

The people throng out of the church; KUZMA puts out the
candles in the standing candelabrums.

FR. IVAN. As by Thy presence in Cana of Galilee Thou showed marriage to be honorable, may Christ our true God, praised by the prayers of His immaculate mother, by the holy, glorious, and praiseworthy apostles, by the holy and divinely appointed kings and peers of the apostles, Constantine and Helen, by the holy great martyr Procopius and all the saints, have mercy upon us and save us, for Thou art good and the lover of mankind.

CHOIR. Amen. O Lord, have mercy, O Lord, have mercy, O Lo-o-ord, have me-e-er-cy!

LADIES (*to Vera*). Congratulations, my dear . . . Live a hundred years . . . (*Kisses.*)

SONNENSTEIN. *Madame* Sabinin, you are, so to speak, how can I put this in plain Russian . . .

DIOCESAN CHOIR. Many, ma-a-any years!! Many years . . .

SABININ. *Pardon*, Vera! (*Takes Kotelnikov by the arm and quickly leads him aside; trembling and panting.*) Let's go to the cemetery right now!

KOTELNIKOV. Have you gone crazy! It's night now! What do you want to do there?

SABININ. For heaven's sake, let's go! Please . . .

KOTELNIKOV. You have to drive home with your bride! Lunatic!

SABININ. I was wishing they'd all go to hell, damn it all a thousand times over! I . . . I'm going! Have to order a requiem mass . . . Anyway, I'm losing my mind . . . I was almost dead . . . Ah, Kotelnikov, Kotelnikov!

KOTELNIKOV. Let's go, let's go . . . (*Leads him back to the bride.*)

A minute later a piercing whistle is heard from the street. Little by
little the people leave the church. Only the DEACON and
KUZMA remain.

KUZMA (*puts out the hanging lamps*). A heap of folks, that was . . .

DEACON. M-yes . . . A rich wedding. (*Puts on a fur coat.*) Those people live it up.

KUZMA. No point to it. All for nothing.

DEACON. How so?

KUZMA. This here wedding . . . Every day we marry 'em, christen 'em, and bury 'em, and there ain't no point to any of it.

DEACON. And what would *you* do if you had your way?

KUZMA. Nothing . . . Just the same . . . Ain't no point to it. And they sing, and burn incense, and preach, but God ain't listening. Forty years I been working here, and not once did it happen that God listened . . . Whether God's there at all I don't know . . . All for nothing . . .

DEACON. M-yes . . . (*Puts on his galoshes.*) Start philosophizing and you'll get your brains in a spin.[8] (*Walks in squeaky galoshes.*) Good-bye. (*Exits.*)

KUZMA (*alone*). Today lunchtime we buried a gentleman, just now we had a wedding, tomorrow morning there'll be a christening. And there's no end to it. Who needs it? Nobody . . . So, all for nothing.

A groan is heard.

From the altar enter FR. IVAN and shaggy FR. ALEKSEY[9] in dark glasses.

FR. IVAN. And he pocketed a decent dowry too, I suppose . . .

FR. ALEKSEY. No doubt about it.

FR. IVAN. This life of ours, just look at it! Once I made a match, got married, and got a dowry, but that's all forgotten in the whirligig of time. (*Shouts.*) Kuzma, why have you doused all the lights? I'll be falling down in the dark.

KUZMA. I thought you'd already left.

FR. IVAN. How about it, Father Aleksey? Shall we go to my place and have some tea?

---

8 Paraphrase of a line in Griboedov's satiric comedy *Woe from Wit*; Famusov says, "If for philosophizing you go in, right away your brain starts to spin" (Act II, scene 1).

9 Chekhov seems to have forgot that he earlier distinguished Fr. Nikolay as the shaggy one.

FR. ALEKSEY. No, thank you kindly, Father Archpriest. I've got no time. I've got another report to write.

FR. IVAN. Well, you know best.

LADY IN BLACK (*comes out from behind a pillar, staggering*). Who's there? Take me away . . . take me away . . .

FR. IVAN. What's that? Who's there? (*Frightened.*) What are you after, good woman?

FR. ALEKSEY. Lord, forgive us sinners . . .

LADY IN BLACK. Take me away . . . take me away . . . (*Groans.*) I'm the sister of Officer Ivanov . . . his sister.

FR. IVAN. Why are you here?

LADY IN BLACK. I've poisoned myself . . . out of hate . . . He abused me . . . Why is he happy? My God . . . (*Shouts.*) Save me, save me! (*Sinks to the floor.*) Everyone should take poison . . . everyone! There's no justice . . .

FR. ALEKSEY (*horrified*). What blasphemy! God, what blasphemy!

LADY IN BLACK. Out of hatred . . . Everyone should take poison . . . (*Groans and rolls on the floor.*) She's in her grave, while he . . . he . . . Insult a woman and you insult God . . . A woman is destroyed . . .

FR. ALEKSEY. What blasphemy to religion! (*Clasps his hands.*) What blasphemy to life!

LADY IN BLACK (*tears at what she is wearing and shouts*). Save me! Save me! Save me! . . .

Curtain

and all the rest I leave to A. S. Suvorin's imagination.

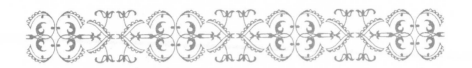

AN INVOLUNTARY TRAGEDIAN

*C*hekhov had promised the comic actor Konstantin Varlamov an acting vehicle and turned to his story *One of Many* (1887) about a paterfamilias who must spend his time shunting back and forth between the dacha where his loved ones are summering and the town, where he carries out their innumerable commissions. For the sake of the stage, Chekhov altered the list of errands, deleting from the items to be purchased "a child's coffin" and expunging racy remarks that could pass in print but would never get past the dramatic censor. Varlamov did not in fact appear in the play, so the first actor to create the harried family man was the far less famous M. I. Bibikov, at an amateur perfomance at the Petersburg German Club on October 1, 1889. Basically, *Tragedian* is a straightforward comic monologue, with the officious friend acting as "feed" or straight man.

The allusion to Molière in the original title—*A Tragedian in Spite of Himself*—alerts one to the extreme contradictions of the protagonist. Molière dealt in paradoxical natures: the imaginary invalid, the learned ladies, the bourgeois aristocrat, or the misanthrope, originally subtitled "the grouch in love" (*l'atrabilaire amoureux*). Described as "the father of a family," Tolkachov is a characteristic hero of a Chekhov farce, being a man on the edge of a nervous breakdown. He begins the play by calling for a pistol to commit suicide and ends it by quoting *Othello*, demanding the blood of his interlocutor. Between these two extremes, the banal situation he describes comes less from the world of tragedy than from that of existential absurdity His multifarious errands compel him to live in a muddle of inanimate objects. "For instance, do you put the heavy brass mortar and pestle in with the glass lampshade or the carbolic acid with the tea? How do you pack the bottles of beer with the bicycle?" This surrealistic mélange, followed by a hyperbolic comparison of married life to the Israelites' labor in the Egyptian brickyards or the Spanish Inquisition, creates an impression of an ordinary middle-class existence as Bosch's hell. Although firmly in the Gogol tradition, Chekhov is here halfway to Jarry and Ionesco.

AN INVOLUNTARY TRAGEDIAN
(FROM THE LIFE OF VACATIONERS)

Трагик поневоле
(Из дачной Жизни)

A Joke in One Act

CHARACTERS [1]

IVAN IVANOVICH TOLKACHOV, *the father of a family*

ALEKSEY ALEKSEEVICH MURASHKIN, *his friend*

The action takes place in Petersburg, in Murashkin's apartment.

Murashkin's study. Well-upholstered furniture—MURASHKIN is sitting at a writing desk. Enter TOLKACHOV, holding a glass globe for a lamp, a toy bicycle, three hatboxes, a large bundle of clothing, a shopping bag filled with bottled beer, and lots of little parcels. He has a dazed look in his eyes and drops on to the sofa in exhaustion.

MURASHKIN. Good afternoon, Ivan Ivanych! Delighted to see you! What have you been up to?

TOLKACHOV (*breathing hard*). My good friend, dear heart . . . I've come to you with a request . . . Please . . . lend me a revolver until tomorrow. Be a friend!

MURASHKIN. What'll you do with a revolver?

TOLKACHOV. I need it . . . Ugh, good grief! . . . Let me have some water . . . Quick, water! . . . I need it . . . Tonight I have to drive through a dark forest, so you see, I . . . in case of emergency. Lend it to me, do me a favor!

MURASHKIN. Uh-oh, you're lying, Ivan Ivanych! What the deuce do you mean dark forest? More likely, you're up to something? I can see by your face that you're up to no good! What's the matter with you? Do you feel ill?

---

1 Suggestive comic names: Murashkin from *murashka*, ant, and Tolkachov from *tolkach*, go-getter.

TOLKACHOV. Hold on, let me catch my breath . . . Oof, good grief! I'm dog tired. There's this feeling running all through my body and my brain-pan that I've been made into shish kebab. I can't stand another minute of it. Be a friend, don't ask questions, don't go into details . . . lend me a revolver! For pity's sake!

MURASHKIN. That's enough of that! Ivan Ivanych, why so down in the mouth? You're the father of a family, a senior civil servant! You should be ashamed!

TOLKACHOV. What kind of father of a family? I'm a martyr! I'm a beast of burden, a peon, a slave, a contemptible worm, who goes on hoping against hope and puts off taking his own life! I'm a doormat, a numbskull, an idiot! Why do I go on living? What's it for? (*Leaps up.*) Go on, tell me, what am I living for? What's the point of this neverending series of moral and physical torments? I can understand being a martyr to an idea, sure! but to be a martyr to who the hell knows what, lady's petticoats and lampshades, no!—thank you kindly! No, no, no! I've had enough! Enough!

MURASHKIN. Stop shouting, the neighbors will hear!

TOLKACHOV. Let the neighbors hear, I don't care! If you don't lend me a revolver, somebody else will, I'm no longer among the living! It's a done deal!

MURASHKIN. Take it easy, you tore off my button. Try to be calm and collected. I still don't understand what's so bad about your life?

TOLKACHOV. What's bad? You ask: what's bad? Just let me tell you! Just let me! I'll spill my guts to you and maybe it'll take a load off my chest. Let's sit down. Now, listen to this . . . Ugh, good grief, I'm winded! . . . Let's take as an example this very day, today. Shall we? As you know, from ten to four I have to make a noise at the office. Overheated, stale air, flies, and the most utter, my dear pal, chaos. My secretary's away on leave, Khrapov's[2] gone off to get married, the office small fry are obsessed with summer rentals, love affairs, and amateur theatricals. They're all so drowsy, worn out, haggard, you can't get a word of sense out of them . . . The secretary's duties are being performed out by a creature who's deaf in the left ear and in love; the general public is bonkers, hustling and bustling in and out, losing their tem-

---

2 Comic name from *khrap*, snore.

pers, making threats,—it's such bedlam you want to shout "Help." A total
zoo, all hell broke loose. And the work itself is diabolical: the same old same
old, the same old same old, inquiries, reports, inquiries, reports,—as monotonous as the tide ebbing and flowing. You understand, it's simply enough
to make your eyes pop out of your skull. Let me have some water . . . You
leave the daily grind broken, worn to a frazzle, you should be eating dinner and falling into bed, but no!—remember you've rented a place in the
country, which means you're a slave, a piece of crap, a loofah, an icicle,
and it's your job to run around, like a headless chicken, filling orders. The
folks at our country place have a sweet little habit: if a vacationer goes to
town, then, every vacationing twerp, not to mention his wife, has the power
and right to foist a heap of errands on him. The wife demands that I stop
by the dressmaker's and bawl her out because she made the bodice too loose
but the shoulders too narrow; Sonichka has a pair of shoes to be exchanged,
my wife's sister wants twenty kopeks' worth of crimson silk for a pattern and
seven feet of ribbon . . . Wait a minute, I can read it to you. (*Pulls a list out
of his pocket and reads it.*) Globe for lamp; one pound ham sausage; five
kopeks' worth of cloves and cinnamon; castor oil for Misha; ten pounds
granulated sugar; get from home the brass mortar and pestle for the sugar;
carbolic acid, insect powder, ten kopeks' worth of face powder; twenty bottles of beer; smelling-salts and a corset for Mme. Chanceau, size eighty-two
. . . oof! and get from home Misha's fall overcoat and galoshes. That's the
order of my wife and family. Now for the errands for my beloved friends
and neighbors, may they rot in hell. The Vlasins are throwing a nameday
party for their Volodya tomorrow, I've got to buy him a bicycle; Lieutenant-
Colonel Vikhrin's[3] wife is in an interesting condition, so I'm obliged to drop
in on the midwife every day and ask her to pay a call. And so on, and so on.
There are five lists in my pockets and my handkerchief is all in knots. So,
old pal, in the interval between work and the train you run around town
like a dog with its tongue hanging out,—on the run, on the run, and cursing your life. From the department store to the pharmacy, from the pharmacy to the dressmaker, from the dressmaker to the butcher, and then back
to the pharmacy. One place you trip over yourself, another place you lose
your money, in a third place you forget to pay and they chase you down
making a scene, in the fourth place you step on a lady's train . . . phooey!
All this heavy exercise drives you frantic and makes you such a wreck that

---

3 Comic name from *vikhr*, whirlwind.

all night long your bones ache and you dream of crocodiles. Well, sir, your errands are run, everything's bought, now how are you supposed to pack up this whole kit and kaboodle? For instance, do you put the heavy brass mortar and pestle in with the glass lampshade or the carbolic acid with the tea? How do you pack the bottles of beer with the bicycle? It's slaving in the brick yards of Egypt, a brain teaser, a riddle! No matter how much you wrack your brains and try to be clever, you always end up smashing and spilling something, and at the station and on the train you'll be standing, your arms spreadeagled, your legs bowed, holding a package under your chin, covered with shopping, cardboard boxes and the rest of the crap. Then the train pulls out, passengers start to dump your things all over the place: your stuff is occupying other people's seats. They yell, they call the conductor, they threaten to have you thrown off, and what can I do? I stand there and bug out my eyes, like a whipped mule. Now for the next installment. I get back to my cottage. There you should have a nice drink for all these righteous labors, a bite to eat and a bit of a snooze — am I right? — but it is not to be. My darling wifie has seen to that for quite some time. You've hardly had a spoonful of soup, when she pounces wham! on yours truly and it's — wouldn't you like to go out to an amateur theatrical or a dance social? You can't say no. You're a husband and the word "husband" translated into vacation language means a dumb pack-animal, which you can travel on and load with as heavy a burden as you like, with no fear of interference from the Society for the Prevention of Cruelty to Animals. So you go and gape at Scandal in a Respectable Family or some other stupid farce,[4] you applaud on your wife's command while you're drooping, drooping, drooping, and expect every minute you'll have a stroke right on the spot. At the social you watch the dancers and collect partners for the wife, and if there aren't enough partners, then you yourself have got to dance the quadrille. You're dancing with Miss Two-Left-Feet, smiling like an idiot, and thinking all the while, "How long, O Lord?" You get home after midnight from the theater or the dance, and you're no longer a man, you're a bag of bones, ready for the scrap heap. But now at last you've reached the finish line: you strip off your things and get into bed. It's wonderful, you close your eyes and doze off . . . It's all so lovely, so poetic: it's nice and warm, don't you know, and the kids aren't screaming in the next room, and the wife isn't there, and your conscience is clear — what more could you ask for. You're

4 In the original, Motnya, a farce by K. A. Tarnovsky. Scandal in a Respectable Family was also a farce, this one by N. I. Kulikov. Chekhov had seen both as a schoolboy in Taganrog.

about to fall asleep—and suddenly . . . suddenly you hear: bzzzz! . . . Mosquitoes! (*Leaps up.*) Mosquitoes, damn, blast and anathematize them, mosquitoes! (*Shakes his fists.*) Mosquitoes! It's the Plagues of Egypt,[5] the Spanish Inquisition! Bzzz! It buzzes so pathetically, so mournfully, you'd think they're begging your pardon, but once the bastards take a bite out of you, you're up scratching for an hour. So you smoke, and you squash them, and you put your head under the covers—no escape! At the bitter end you spit in disgust and surrender to be torn to pieces: dig in, damn you! You barely have time to get used to the mosquitoes when there's a new plague of Egypt: in the living room your wife begins to practice her ballads with her tenors. They sleep all day, and at night they rehearse amateur concerts. Oh, my God! A tenor is a torment far worse than mosquitoes. (*Sings.*) "Say not that her youth was wasted . . ." "Once again I stand bewitched before thee . . ."[6] Oh, the ba-a-stards! They've destroyed me, body and soul! To drown them out just a bit, I've got this trick: I tap my finger on my forehead next to my ear. So I'm tapping away till around four in the morning, when they finally take their leave. Ugh, let me have some more water, pal . . . I'm done in . . . Well, sir, you've had no sleep, you get up at six and it's— forward march to the station to catch the train. You run, for fear you'll miss it, through the mud, fog, cold, brr! Then you get to town, and the whole merry-go-round starts over again. That's how it goes, pal. My life, I assure you, stinks, I wouldn't wish a life like this on my worst enemy. Can you imagine, it's undermined my health! Shortness of breath, heartburn, shattered nerves, indigestion, spots before my eyes . . . Believe you me, I've turned into a mental case . . . (*Looks around.*) This is just between us . . . I plan to consult an eminent specialist in psychosis.[7] A hell of a mood comes over you at times, pal. So in those moments of aggravation and craziness, when the mosquitoes bite or the tenors sing, suddenly your eyesight blurs, suddenly you jump up, run around the house like a maniac, shouting: "I crave blood! Blood!"[8] In fact, at times like those you do want to stick a knife

---

5 The Ten Plagues that God visited upon the Egyptians to compel them to release the Hebrews from slavery and let them go (Exodus 7–10).

6 "Say not that her youth," a ballad based on a poem by N. A. Nekrasov ("A heavy cross fell to her lot," 1855) and set to music by many composers. "Once again," the opening of a "gypsy" ballad from a lyric by V. I. Krasov. Chekhov cites them frequently in his plays.

7 In the original, Cechott and Merzheevsky. O. A. Chechott (b. 1842) and I. P. Merzheevsky (1838–1908) were well-known St. Petersburg psychiatrists.

8 From Shakespeare's *Othello* (Act III, scene 3): "Blood, O Iago, blood!"

in somebody or bash his head in with a chair. That's what summer rentals can do to you! And nobody's sorry for you, nobody sympathizes, it's as if that's the way it's supposed to be. People even laugh. But you understand, I'm a living creature, I want to go on living! This isn't a farce, it's a tragedy! Listen, if you won't let me have a revolver, then at least show some sympathy!

MURASHKIN. I do sympathize.

TOLKACHOV. I can see the way you sympathize . . . Good-bye. I'm off to get some sardines and salami . . . there's still the tooth powder, and then to the station.

MURASHKIN. Where's the cottage you're renting?

TOLKACHOV. On Dead Man's Creek.

MURASHKIN (*delighted*). Really? Listen, do you know a woman who's renting there, Olga Pavlovna Finberg?

TOLKACHOV. I do. In fact she's a friend of ours.

MURASHKIN. Is that so? Well, what a coincidence! It's so convenient, it would be so kind of you . . .

TOLKACHOV. What are you getting at?

MURASHKIN. Dear old pal, could you run me a little errand? Be a friend! Now, promise me that you'll do it?

TOLKACHOV. What is it?

MURASHKIN. A friend in need is a friend indeed! For my sake, my dear man. First of all, convey my regards to Olga Pavlovna and tell her that I'm alive and well, and kiss her hand. Second, bring her a little something. She asked me to buy her a portable sewing machine, and there's no one to deliver it to her . . . Bring it, dear boy! And, while you're at it, bring along this canary in a cage . . . only very carefully, otherwise the door will break off . . . Why are you looking at me like that?

TOLKACHOV. A sewing machine . . . a canary in a cage . . . Tweety birds and dicky birds . . .

MURASHKIN. Ivan Ivanovich, what's wrong with you? Why are you turning so red?

TOLKACHOV (*stamping his feet*). Hand over the sewing machine! Where's the cage? Now you pile yourself on top! Devour a man! Tear him to pieces! Finish him off! (*Clenching his fists.*) I must have blood! Blood! Blood!

MURASHKIN. You've gone out of your mind!

TOLKACHOV (*bearing down on him*). I must have blood! Blood!

MURASHKIN (*terrified*). He's gone out of his mind! (*Shouts.*) Petrushka! Mariya! Where are you? Somebody, help!

TOLKACHOV (*chasing him around the room*). I must have blood! Blood!

Curtain

VARIANT TO

An Involuntary Tragedian

The variant comes from the censor's copy (C), Bazarov's published edition (B), and the lithographed script (L).

page 558 / *After*: buy him a bicycle; — The Kuritsyns' baby died, and I have to get a child's coffin. (C, B, L)

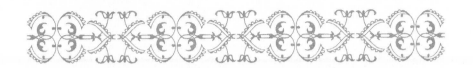

THE WEDDING

$\mathcal{C}$hekhov characterized *The Wedding* as a "play in one act," thus distinguishing it from his one-act comedies called "jokes" (*shutki*). It differs, too, in being based on real experiences and individuals from Chekhov's past. The Greek confectioner Dymba was modeled on a clerk in his father's grocery store in Taganrog; the flirtatious midwife he had met when serving as best man at a wedding in 1887. Between 1885 and 1886, Chekhov had lived in a Moscow flat beneath the quarters of a caterer who rented out rooms for weddings and balls. At times, he seemed obsessed with nuptial ceremonials, which are the subject of many of his stories written in the 1880s. This play was first performed at the Art and Literary Society at the Moscow Hunt Club on November 28, 1900, as part of a Chekhov evening. Lev Tolstoy, who was present, laughed till he cried.

The Wedding masterfully displays the dissolution of social convention. Every pretense kept up by one character is demolished by another. No one's secrets are safe. Over the course of the play, we discover that the groom has married the bride for the sake of a paltry dowry, which has yet to be paid; that the bride is herself totally insensitive to her situation; that her parents are the most narrow and parsimonious of philistines; and that the guests bear no particular goodwill to the newlyweds. The play revolves around one principal deception: to dress out the banquet, a "General," that is, a high-ranking official, a V.I.P., is required as guest of honor. The bride's mother has charged a friend with this task; he has pocketed the money and brought a deaf naval captain. The mother discovers the swindle and turns the old man out without further ado. At that moment, the farcical tone of the play alters. The old captain, disabused and stripped of any consideration, can only gasp in horror, "How disgusting! How revolting!" After the old man's exit, the guests and hosts revert to their squabbling. The moment of genuine feeling has made no dent in their thick hides.

Again, Chekhov employed the comic device of the gap between reality and the characters' aspirations. Hoping to sound refined, they mangle French and mispronounce polysyllabic words. Zmeyukina, a midwife whose profession is of the earthiest, constantly demands "atmosphere" and delicate feelings. In anticipation of Solyony in *Three Sisters*, she quotes the romantic poet Lermontov. The father of the bride invariably dismisses anything unfamiliar with contempt, branding it "monkeyshines." The main oration of the evening is delivered by a Greek who butchers the Russian language. Yet when a native Russian speaker rises to address the guests, it is the retired Captain, whose naval lingo is every bit as incomprehensible. Assuming that he is entertaining the company, the old salt bores the guests into stupor and then mutiny.

A sense of inhumanity hangs over the entire action, with no character ever making true contact with another. A deeply etched caricature in the style of Daumier or Goya, *The Wedding* subjects the lower-middle class to merciless derision. And in the process, Chekhov casts a shadow over that stalwart family value, the institution of holy matrimony.

THE WEDDING

Свадьба

A Play in One Act

CAST [1]

Yevdokim Zakharovich ZHIGALOV, *civil servant, retired*

NASTASYA TIMOFEEVNA, *his wife*

DASHENKA, *their daughter*

Epaminond Maksimovich APLOMBOV, *her bridegroom*

Fyodor Yakovlevich REVUNOV-KARAULOV, *naval captain, 2nd class, retired*

Andrey Andreevich NYUNIN, *an insurance agent*

Anna Martynovna ZMEYUKINA, *a midwife, 30, in a bright crimson dress*

Ivan Mikhailovich YAT, *a telegraph operator*

Kharlampi Spiridonovich DYMBA, *a Greek caterer*

Dmitry Stepanovich MOZGOVOY, *sailor in the Volunteer Fleet* [2]

GROOM'S MEN, [3] **BRIDESMAIDS, WAITERS, ETC.**

---

1 Most of the names are puns or plays on Russian words. *Zhigalov* recalls *zhigalo*, ringleader, bellwether; *zhigalka*, horse-fly, tallow candle; and *zhiga*, invective. *Aplombov* seems to come from the French *aplomb*, self-confidence; *Nyunin*, from *nyuni*, slavering lips; *nyunit*, to moan and groan; *nyunya*, whining child, cry-baby; *Zmeyukina* from *zmey*, dragon, *zmeya*, snake. *Yat*, the name of a letter in the Cyrillic alphabet, sounded like є but written otherwise, thus providing a trap for schoolchildren and clerks (it was abolished in the spelling reforms of 1917). *Mozgovoy*, from *mozg*, brain; spinal cord, bone marrow. Revunov-*Karaulov*, one who cries for help (*karaul*).

2 Founded during the Russo-Turkish War (1877–1878); its three ships were later ordered to the Pacific to transport prisoners to Vladivostok and the island of Sakhalin.

3 In Russian Orthodox wedding ceremonies, both the bride and the groom have attendants, who hold the crowns over their heads and accompany them in the procession.

A brightly lit reception room. A large table, laid for supper.
Tailcoated waiters are fussing around the table. Offstage, a band
is playing the last figure of a quadrille.

ZMEYUKINA, YAT, *and* BEST MAN *cross the stage.*

ZMEYUKINA. No, no, no!

YAT (*following her*). Take pity on me! Take pity on me!

ZMEYUKINA. No, no, no!

BEST MAN (*chasing after them*). You can't do this, people! Where are you off to? What about the "gran rawn"? "Gran rawn, seel voo playt!"[4]

They leave. Enter NASTASYA TIMOFEEVNA
and APLOMBOV.

NASTASYA TIMOFEEVNA. Why are you pestering me with this silly talk, you'd better go dance.

APLOMBOV. I'm no Spinoza to spin around with my legs bent into a pretzel.[5] I'm a respectable person, with good references, and I derive no amusement from such idle pursuits. But this isn't about dancing. Excuse me, *maman*, but I can't figure out why you act the way you do. For instance, in addition to some indispensable domestic articles, you promised to give me, along with your daughter, two lottery tickets. Where are they?

NASTASYA TIMOFEEVNA. I've got such a splitting headache . . . It must be this awful weather . . . we're in for a thaw!

APLOMBOV. Don't try to hoodwink me. Today I found out you put those tickets in pawn. Pardon me, *maman*, but the only people who act like that are swindlers. I'm not complaining out of selfishness—I don't need your lottery tickets, but it's the principle of the thing, and I won't have anybody putting anything over on me. I've procured your daughter's happiness, but if you don't hand over those tickets today, I'll make your daughter's life a living hell. On my honor as a gentleman!

---

4 Mispronounced French, *Grand rond, s'il vous plaît*. A "grand rond" is a round dance, a figure in a quadrille.

5 The Dutch philosopher Benedictus Spinoza (1632–1677) is confused here with the dancer Leone Espinosa (1825–1903), who worked at the Moscow Bolshoy Theatre from 1869 to 1872.

NASTASYA TIMOFEEVNA (*glancing at the table and counting the place settings*). One, two, three, four, five . . .

A WAITER. The chef wants to know how you'd like the ice cream served: with rum, Madeira, or on its own?

APLOMBOV. Rum. And tell your boss there's not enough wine. Tell him to serve more "Ho Soturn."[6] (*To Nastasya Timofeevna.*) Likewise you promised, and it was fully agreed upon, that there'd be a General at this supper party. Well, where is he, I'd like to know?

NASTASYA TIMOFEEVNA. This, my dear, is not *my* fault.

APLOMBOV. Whose then?

NASTASYA TIMOFEEVNA. It's Andrey Andreevich's fault . . . Yesterday he went and promised to bring the most genuine General. (*Sighs.*) Must not have run across one anywheres, or he would have brought him . . . Does that mean we're stingy? For our darling daughter we wouldn't stint a thing. You want a General, you'll get a General . . .

APLOMBOV. And besides that . . . Everyone, you included, *maman*, knows that before I'd proposed to Dashenka, that telegraph operator Yat was going out with her. Why did you invite him? Didn't you realize it would get on my nerves?

NASTAYA TIMOFEEVNA. Ooh, what's your name?—Epaminond Maksimych, you've not been married a full day yet, and already you've tortured both me and Dashenka to death with your blather. What'll it be like after a year? You're such a pest, ooh, a pest.

APLOMBOV. You don't like hearing the truth? Aha? Thought so. Then behave like a decent person. That's all I ask of you: behave like a decent person!

Couples dancing the grand rond cross the room from one door to the other. The first couple is the BEST MAN and DASHENKA, the last YAT and ZMEYUKINA. These last two fall behind and remain in the room.

ZHIGALOV and DYMBA enter and walk up to the table.

---

6 Mispronunciation of Haut Sauternes, a sweet white dessert wine. Drinking it before the meal is another sign of gaucherie.

BEST MAN (*shouting*). Promenade! M'sewers, promenade! (*Offstage.*) Promenade!

The couples go off.

YAT (*to Zmeyukina*). Take pity on me! Take pity, fascinating Anna Martynovna!

ZMEYUKINA. Aah, what's wrong with you . . . I already told you, I'm not in voice today.

YAT. Sing something, I implore you! Just one single note! Take pity on me! Just one note!

ZMEYUKINA. You're driving me crazy . . . (*She sits and waves her fan.*)

YAT. No, you're simply heartless! That so cruel a creature, pardon the expression, should have so spectacular a voice, spectacular! With a voice like that, excuse the expression, you shouldn't be a midwife, but a singer in concert halls with an audience! For instance, the divine way you handle those trills . . . like this. (*He croons.*) "I loved you once, but ever loved in vain . . ." Spectacular!

ZMEYUKINA (*croons*). "I loved you, and that love might still perhaps . . ."[7] Is that it?

YAT. That's the very thing! Spectacular!

ZMEYUKINA. No, I'm not in voice today. Here—fan a breeze my way . . . It's so hot. (*To Aplombov.*) Epaminond Maksimych, why so melancholy? Is that the way a bridegroom should behave? Aren't you ashamed of yourself, you naughty man? Well, a penny for your thoughts?

APLOMBOV. Marriage is a serious step! You've got to consider everything in depth and in detail.

ZMEYUKINA. You're all such naughty cynics! Just being around you smothers me . . . I need atmosphere! You hear! I need atmosphere! (*She croons.*)

YAT. Spectacular! Spectacular!

---

7 The 1829 poem by Aleksandr Pushkin (1799–1837)—"I loved you once, perhaps I love still . . . / Love has not fully died out in my heart . . ."—was set to music by many composers, including Alyabiev, Bulakhov, Varlamov, and Gurilev, etc.

ZMEYUKINA. Fan me, keep fanning, or I think my heart'll burst. Tell me, please, why do I feel so smothered?

YAT. It's because you're sweating, ma'am . . .

ZMEYUKINA. Phooey, don't be so vulgar! Don't you dare use such expressions!

YAT. Sorry! Of course, you're accustomed, pardon the expression, to aristocratic society and . . .

ZMEYUKINA. Aah, leave me alone! I need poetry, excitement! Fan me, fan me . . .

ZHIGALOV (*to Dymba*). Shall we have another? (*Pours.*) There's always time for a drink. The main thing, Kharlampy Spiridonych, don't neglect your business. Drink up, but keep a clear head . . . Though if you want a little nip, why not have a little nip? Always time for a little nip . . . Your health! (*They drink.*) Say, have you got any tigers in Greece!

DYMBA. We got.

ZHIGALOV. How about lions?

DYMBA. And lions we got. In Russia is notting, in Greece is all ting.[8] Dere I got fodder and oncle and brodders, but here is notting.

ZHIGALOV. Hmm . . . any whales in Greece?

DYMBA. All ting we got.

NASTASYA TIMOFEEVNA (*to her husband*). Why are you eating and drinking any old way? It's time we all sat down. Don't stick your fork in the lobsters . . . That's there for the General. He may show up yet . . .

ZHIGALOV. Have you got lobsters in Greece?

DYMBA. We got . . . All ting we got dere.

ZHIGALOV. Hmm . . . have you got senior civil servants too?

ZMEYUKINA. I can imagine what a wonderful atmosphere there is in Greece!

ZHIGALOV. And I'll bet a lot of monkeyshines as well. Greeks are just like Armenians or gypsies. Can't sell you a sponge or a goldfish without trying to put one over on you. Shall we have another?

---

8 In Russian, Dymba not only makes mistakes in grammar but cannot pronounce the sound *ch*.

NASTASYA TIMOFEEVNA. Why keep drinking any old way? It's time to sit down. Almost midnight! . . .

ZHIGALOV. If it's sitting you want, sitting you'll get. Ladies and gentlemen, please be so kind! Do me the favor! (*He shouts.*) Supper's on! Young people!

NASTASYA TIMOFEEVNA. Dear guests! Be so kind! Take your seats!

ZMEYUKINA (*sitting at the table*). I need poetry! "But he, the rebel, seeks the storm, as if a storm could offer peace."[9] I need a storm!

YAT (*aside*). Wonderful woman! I'm in love! Head over heels in love!

> Enter DASHENKA, MOZGOVOY, BEST MAN, GROOM'S
> MEN, MAIDS OF HONOR, etc. Everyone sits noisily at the
> table. A moment's pause, the band plays a march.

MOZGOVOY (*rising*). Ladies and gentlemen! I'm supposed to say the following . . . We've got all sorts of toasts and speeches lined up. So let's not beat around the bush, but start right in! Ladies and gentlemen, I propose a toast to the newlyweds!

> The band plays a fanfare. Cheers. Clinking glasses.

MOZGOVOY. It's bitter![10] Sweeten it up!

EVERYONE. It's bitter! Sweeten it up!

> APLOMBOV and DASHENKA kiss.

YAT. Spectacular! Spectacular! I must remark, ladies and gentlemen, and give credit where credit's due, that this room and the whole affair is magnificent! First-rate, enchanting! But do you know the one thing missing for absolute perfection? Electric lighting, pardon the expression! Every country has already installed electric lighting, and only Russia lags behind.

ZHIGALOV (*weightily*). Electricity . . . Hm . . . Well, in my opinion, electric light is just a lot of monkeyshines . . . They shovel in a little coal and think they've pulled the wool over your eyes! No, pal, if you're going to light us up, don't give us coal, but something with body to it, something special

---

9 Quotation from the poem "The Sail" ("Parus," 1832) by Mikhail Lermontov, which Chekhov also quotes in the last act of *Three Sisters.*

10 The idea is that the young couple must kiss to "sweeten things up."

that a man can sink his teeth into! Give us fire—got me?—fire, which comes from nature, not your imagination!

YAT. If you'd ever seen what an electric battery's made out of, maybe you'd change your mind.

ZHIGALOV. But I don't want to see it. Monkeyshines. They're swindling the common man . . . Squeezing the last drop out of him . . . We know their kind . . . As for you, young man, why stick up for monkeyshines, better have a drink and fill the glasses. That's the thing to do!

APLOMBOV. I'm in complete agreement, Dad. What's the point of trotting out these highbrow conversations? Personally I've got nothing against discussing any kind of invention in a scientific context, but is this the proper time! (*To Dashenka.*) What's your opinion, "ma chair"?[11]

DASHENKA. The gentleman's just trying to show off his eddication, talking about what nobody understands.

NASTASYA TIMOFEEVNA. We've lived all our life without education, thank God, and this is the third daughter we've married off to a good man. If, according to you, we're so uneducated, why come here? Go back to your educated friends!

YAT. Nastasya Timofeevna, I've always respected your family, so if I bring up the electric light, it doesn't mean I'm showing off. I'll even have a drink. I've always wished Darya Yevdokimovna a good husband from the bottom of my heart. Nowadays, Nastasya Timofeevna, it's not easy to find a good husband. These days everyone's getting married for what he can make off it, for the money . . .

APLOMBOV. That's an insinuation!

YAT (*backing off*). No insinuations intended . . . I wasn't talking about present company . . . I just . . . generally speaking . . . For heaven's sake! Everybody knows you're marrying for love . . . The dowry's skimpy enough.

NASTASYA TIMOFEEVNA. No, it is *not* skimpy! You open your mouth, young sir, and pay no mind to what comes out. Besides the thousand rubles cash money, we're giving three ladies' coats, a bed, and all the furniture. Just try and dig up such a dowry anywheres else!

---

11 *Ma chère*, French, my dear.

YAT. I didn't mean . . . Certainly, furniture's a fine thing and . . . so are coats, of course, but I was concerned about this gentleman's taking offense at my insinuations.

NASTASYA TIMOFEEVNA. Then don't make any. Out of consideration for your parents we invited you to this wedding, and you make all kinds of remarks. If you knew that Epaminond Maksimych was marrying for money, why didn't you say something earlier? (*Tearfully.*) I reared her, nursed her, cared for her . . . she was her mother's pride and joy, my little girl . . .

APLOMBOV. So you believe him? Thank you ever so much! Most grateful to you! (*To Yat.*) As for you, Mr. Yat, although you're a friend of mine, I won't have you acting so discourteously in other people's houses! I'll thank you to clear out!

YAT. How's that again?

APLOMBOV. If only you were the same kind of gentleman what I am! In a word, please clear out of here!

The band plays a fanfare.

GROOM'S MEN (*to Aplombov*). Let it alone! Calm down! Hey, cut it out! Sit down! Take it easy!

YAT. I didn't do a thing . . . I just . . . I certainly don't understand why . . . As you like, I'll go . . . Only first pay me back the five rubles you borrowed last year for a quilted, pardon the expression, waistcoat. I'll have one more drink, and then . . . I'll go, only first you pay me what you owe me.

GROOM'S MEN. Hey, come on, come on! That's enough! Is it worth arguing over nothing?

BEST MAN (*shouts*). To the health of the bride's parents, Yevdokim Zakharych and Nastasya Timofeevna!

The band plays a fanfare. Cheers.

ZHIGALOV (*moved, bows in all directions*). I thank you! Dear guests! I'm most grateful to you for remembering us and showing up, and not being stand-offish! . . . Now don't think that this is a lot of hooey or monkeyshines on my part, for it's strictly from the heart! From the very bottom of my heart! Nothing's too good for decent people! My humble thanks! (*Exchange of kisses.*)

DASHENKA (*to her mother*). Mummy dear, why are you crying? I'm so happy!

APLOMBOV. *Maman's* upset at the imminent parting. But I suggest that she'd better remember what we were talking about before.

YAT. Don't cry, Nastasya Timofeevna! Don't you realize what human tears are? A sign of feebleminded psychiatrics, that's all!

ZHIGALOV. Have you got mushrooms in Greece?

DYMBA. We got. All ting we got dere.

ZHIGALOV. Well, I bet you haven't got the creamy ones.

DYMBA. Krim we got. All ting we got.

MOZGOVOY. Kharlampy Spiridonych, it's your turn to make a speech! Ladies and gentlemen, let him make a speech!

EVERYONE (*to Dymba*). Speech! Speech! Your turn!

DYMBA. Pliss? Not to understanding . . . How is what?

ZMEYUKINA. No, no! Don't you dare turn us down! It's your turn! Stand up!

DYMBA (*rises, bashful*). I talk sometings . . . Is Russia and is Griss. Now in Russia is such a pipples, and in Griss is such a pipples . . . And pipples on ocean is sailing *karávia*, in Russian means sheeps, but on land is all sorts which is railroad trains. I understanding good . . . We Griks, you Russians, and I not needing nottings . . . I can talk also dis . . . Is Russia and is Griss.

NYUNIN enters.

NYUNIN. Wait a minute, ladies and gentlemen, stop eating! Hold on! Nastasya Timofeevna, step over here a minute! (*Takes Nastasya Timofeevna aside; out of breath.*) Listen . . . The General's on his way . . . I finally got hold of one . . . Had a perfectly awful time of it . . . The General's genuine, highly respectable, old, must be about eighty, then again maybe ninety . . . .

NASTASYA TIMOFEEVNA. When will he get here?

NYUNIN. Any minute now. You're going to thank me for the rest of your life. Not a general, but a rose garden, a Napoleon![12] Not an ordinary foot sol-

---

12 In the original, Boulanger. Georges Ernest Jean Marie Boulanger (1837–1891), French Minister of War from 1886 to 1887, an ambitious and reactionary troublemaker, who preached revenge against the Prussians.

dier, not infantry, but navy! In rank he's a captain second class, but in their lingo, the navy's, that's the same as a Major-General or in the civil service an actual State Councilor. Absolutely the same. Even higher.

NASTASYA TIMOFEEVNA. You're not trying to finagle me, are you, Andryusha sweetie?

NYUNIN. What's that, you think I'm a four-flusher? Don't you worry!

NASTASYA TIMOFEEVNA (*sighing*). I wouldn't want to throw our money down the drain, Andryusha sweetie . . .

NYUNIN. Don't you worry! He's not just a General, but an oil painting! (*Raising his voice.*) I says to him, "You've quite forgotten us," I says, "Your Excellency! It's not nice, Your Excellency, to forget your old friends! Nastasya Timofeevna," I says, "thinks very highly of you!" (*Goes to the table and sits down.*) Then he says, "Excuse me, my friend, how can I go when I don't know the groom?"—"Oh, that's enough of that, Your Excellency, don't stand on ceremony! The groom," I says, "is a splendid fellow, wears his heart on his sleeve. Works," I says, "as an appraiser in a pawnshop, but don't think, Your Excellency, that he's some kind of puny little runt or a shifty conman either. Nowadays," I says, "even highborn ladies work in pawnshops." He claps me on the shoulder, we each smoke a panatela, and now he's on his way . . . Wait a bit, ladies and gentlemen, stop eating . . .

APLOMBOV. But when will he get here?

NYUNIN. Any minute now. When I left him, he was putting on his galoshes. Hold on, ladies and gentlemen, don't eat.

APLOMBOV. Then you'd better tell them to play a march . . .

NYUNIN (*shouts*). Hey, musicians! A march!

The band plays a march for a minute.

WAITER (*announcing*). Mister Revunov-Karaulov.

*ZHIGALOV, NASTASYA TIMOFEEVNA, and NYUNIN run
to meet him.*

Enter REVUNOV-KARAULOV.

NASTASYA TIMOFEEVNA (*bowing*). Make yourself at home, Your Excellency! Pleased to meet you!

REVUNOV. Pleasure's all mine!

ZHIGALOV. We're just plain, simple, ordinary people, Your Excellency, but don't suppose that for our part we'd go in for any monkeyshines. We put great stock in decent folks, nothing's too good for 'em. Make yourself at home!

REVUNOV. Pleasure's all mine, delighted!

NYUNIN. May I introduce, Your Excellency! The bridegroom, Epaminond Maksimych Aplombov, and his newly born . . . I mean, his newly wedded wife! Ivan Mikhailych Yat, who works in the telegraph office! A foreigner of Greek persuasion in the catering line, Kharlampy Spiridonych Dymba! Osip Lukich Babelmandebsky! Et cetera, et cetera . . . All the rest are no account. Take a seat, Your Excellency!

REVUNOV. Pleasure's all mine! Excuse me, ladies and gentlemen. I'd like to have a word with Andryusha. (*Takes Nyunin aside.*) I'm a little confused, my boy . . . Why do you call me Your Excellency? For I'm no General, after all! Captain second class — that's even lower than a colonel.

NYUNIN (*speaks in his ear as if he were deaf*). I know, Fyodor Yakovlevich, but please allow us to call you Your Excellency! This here family, y'see, is very old-fashioned, they respect their elders and love to kowtow to people of rank . . .

REVUNOV. Oh, if that's the way things are, all right . . . (*Going to the table.*) Pleasure's all mine!

NASTASYA TIMOFEEVNA. Take a seat, Your Excellency! Be so kind! Eat a little something, Your Excellency! Only forgive us, you must be used to delicacies and we only got plain fare!

REVUNOV (*not having heard*). How's that, ma'am? I see . . . Yes'm. (*Pause.*) Yes'm . . . In the olden times people always lived simply and were contented. I'm a man of rank, but even so I live simply . . . Today, Andryusha comes to me and asks me here to the wedding. "How can I go," I ask, "when I don't know 'em? It's awkward!" But he says, "They're simple people, old-fashioned, enjoy entertaining guests . . ." Well, of course, if that's the way things are . . . why not? Happy to oblige. At home, all by my lonesome, it's boring, but if my presence at the wedding can give anybody pleasure, then, I say, let's do 'em a favor . . .

ZHIGALOV. You mean, it was from the heart, Your Excellency? I look up to you! I myself am a simple man, without any monkeyshines, and I look up to others like me. Have a bite, Your Excellency!

APLOMBOV. Have you been in retirement long, Your Excellency?

REVUNOV. Huh? Yes, yes . . . that's right . . . Very true. Yessir . . . . but excuse me, what have we here? The herring's bitter . . . and so's the bread. Have to sweeten it up!

EVERYONE. Bitter! Bitter! Sweeten it up!

APLOMBOV and DASHENKA kiss.

REVUNOV. Heh, heh, heh . . . Your health.

Pause.

Yessir . . . in the olden days everything was simple and everybody was contented . . . I love simplicity . . . I'm an old man, you know, went into retirement in eighteen hundred and sixty-five . . . I'm seventy-two . . . Yes, indeed. Even so, in the old days, they liked to put on the dog every once in a while, but . . . (*Noticing Mozgovoy.*) You there . . . a sailor, are you?

MOZOGOY. Aye, aye, sir.

REVUNOV. Aha . . . Aye . . . Yes . . . Serving in the navy was always tough. A man had to keep his wits about him and rack his brains. The slightest little word had its own special meaning, so to speak! For instance, "Topmen aloft to the foresail and mainsail yards!" What does that mean? Never fear, your sailor gets the drift! Heh, heh. It's as tricky as that arithmetic of yours!

NYUNIN. To the health of His Excellency Fyodor Yakovlevich Revunov-Karaulov!

The band plays a fanfare. Cheers.

YAT. Now, Your Excellency, you've been good enough to mention how hard it is serving in the navy. But you think telegraphy's any easier? These days, Your Excellency, nobody's employed on the telegraph unless he can read and write French and German. But the toughest thing we're up against is sending telegrams. Awfully hard! Just listen to this. (*Taps his fork on the table, in imitation of sending a telegram in Morse code.*)

REVUNOV. What does it mean?

YAT. It means: "I respect you, Your Excellency, for your loving kindness." You think that's easy? Here's some more . . . (*Taps.*)

REVUNOV. Make it louder . . . I can't hear . . .

YAT. And that means: "Madam, how happy I am to hold you in my embrace!"

REVUNOV. What's all this about a madam? Yes . . . (*To Mozgovoy.*) Look here, suppose you're running before a full breeze and have to . . . have to set your top-gallants and royals! Then you've got to give the command, "Crosstrees aloft to the shrouds, the top-gallants and royals . . ." And while they're casting loose the sails on the yards, below they're manning the top-gallant and royal sheets, halyards and braces . . .[13]

BEST MAN (*rising*). My dear ladies and kind gentle . . .

REVUNOV (*interrupting*). Yessiree . . . No end of different commands . . . Aye, aye . . . "In on the top-gallant and royal sheets! Haul taut the halyards!" Pretty good, eh? But what's it all mean, what's the sense of it? Why, very simple. They haul, y'see, the top-gallant and royal sheets and lift off the halyards . . . all together! Next they square the royal sheets and royal halyards as they hoist, and meanwhile, keeping a weather-eye out, they ease off the braces from those sails, so that when, as a result, the sheets are taut and all the halyards run right up, then the top-gallants and royals are drawing and the yards are braced according to the way the wind's blowing . . .

NYUNIN (*to Revunov*). Fyodor Yakovlevich, our hostess requests you talk about something else. The guests can't make head or tail of this, so they're bored . . .

REVUNOV. What? Who's bored? (*To Mozgovoy.*) Young fellow! Now then, suppose your craft lies close-hauled on the starboard tack under full sail and you've got to wear ship. What command must you give? Why, look here: pipe all hands on deck, wear ship! . . . Heh, heh . . .

NYUNIN. Fyodor Yakovlevich, that's enough! Have something to eat.

REVUNOV. As soon as they're all on deck, the command is given at once: "Stand by to wear ship!" Ech, what a life! You give the commands, and

---

13 In his memoirs, Chekhov's brother Mikhail reported that in 1883 Chekhov had inherited a book from the late F. F. Popudolgo, *Commands for the Most Important Naval Maneuvers*, which "provided him material for the role of Revunov-Karaulov."

then you watch the sailors running to their posts like lightning, and they unfurl the top-gallants and the braces. And then you can't hold back and you shout, "Well done, my hearties!" (*Chokes and coughs.*)

BEST MAN (*rushes to take advantage of the consequent pause*). On this day of days, so to speak, when we are all gathered together to honor our beloved . . .

REVUNOV (*interrupting*). Yessiree! And, y'see, you've got to remember all that! For instance: let fly the foresheet, the mainsheet! . . .

BEST MAN (*offended*). Why does he keep interrupting? We'll never get through a single speech at this rate!

NASTASYA TIMOFEEVNA. We're ignorant folk, Your Excellency, we can't make head or tail of this, so you'd better talk about something that's more use . . .

REVUNOV (*not hearing*). I've already eaten, thanks. You did say: goose? No thanks . . . Aye . . . I was recalling the olden days . . . Those were jolly times, young fellow! You sail the seas, not a care to your name, and . . . (*His voice a-tremble.*) remember the excitement when they had to tack about! What seaman doesn't catch fire at the memory of that maneuver?! Why, as soon as the command rings out: Pipe all hands on deck, ready about—you'd think an electric spark was running through the lot of 'em. From the admiral down to the lowliest deckhand—every heart is beating faster . . .

ZMEYUKINA. Boring! Boring!

General murmur.

REVUNOV (*not hearing*). No thanks, I've eaten. (*Carried away.*) They all stand at the ready, and fix their eyes on the first mate . . . "Haul taut the foretop and main braces on the starboard and the mizzentop braces and counterbraces on the port side!" commands the first mate. It's all carried out in an instant . . . "Let fly the foresheet, the jib sheet . . . Hard a'starboard!" (*Rises.*) The craft comes up with the wind, and finally the sails start flapping about. First mate: "The braces, look alive to the braces," and his own eyes are fixed to the main topsail, and when at last even that sail starts to flap, I mean, the moment when the craft comes about, the command rings out like thunder: "Let go the main top bowline, pay out the braces!" Then everything flies, snaps—all hell breaks loose!—it's all carried out with nary a hitch. We've managed to bring her about!

NASTASYA TIMOFEEVNA (*boiling over*). A general, but with no manners . . . You ought to be ashamed at your time of life! It's unreal, stop!

REVUNOV. A veal chop? No, I haven't had one . . . Thanks.

NASTASYA TIMOFEEVNA (*loudly*). I said, you should be ashamed at your time of life! A general, but with no manners!

NYUNIN (*embarrassed*). Ladies and gentlemen, look here . . . what's the difference? Honestly . . .

REVUNOV. In the first place, I'm not a general, I'm a captain second class, which is equivalent in the military ranking to a lieutenant-colonel.

NASTASYA TIMOFEEVNA. If you're no general, then why did you take the money? We didn't pay you good money so you could act like a hooligan!

REVUNOV (*bewildered*). What money?

NASTASYA TIMOFEEVNA. You know what money. You got twenty-five rubles from Andrey Andreevich, no questions asked . . . (*To Nyunin.*) As for you, Andryusha sweetie, you're a disgrace! I didn't ask you to hire this sort of thing!

NYUNIN. Come on . . . cut it out! What's the difference?

REVUNOV. Hired? . . . Paid? . . . What is this?

APLOMBOV. Excuse me, just a second . . . you did receive twenty-five rubles from Andrey Andreevich, didn't you?

REVUNOV. What twenty-five rubles? (*Realizing.*) So that's it! Now I understand it all . . . How disgusting! How disgusting!

APLOMBOV. You did take the money, didn't you?

REVUNOV. I never took any money! Get away from me! (*Moves away from the table.*) How disgusting! How revolting! To insult an old man this way, a navy man, an officer who's seen active duty! . . . If you were respectable people, I could challenge someone to a duel, but now what can I do? (*In despair.*) Where's the door? How do I get out? Waiter, show me the way out! Waiter![14] (*Going out.*) How revolting! How disgusting! (*Exits.*)

---

14 In Russian, *chelovek* can mean both "human being, person" and "waiter." The Captain can be heard to appeal to his fellow men to deliver him from this inhuman herd.

NASTASYA TIMOFEEVNA. Andryusha sweetie, where's the twenty-five rubles?

NYUNIN. Why bother discussing such trifles? Big deal! Everyone else is enjoying himself, but who the hell knows what you're on about . . . (*Shouts.*) To the health of the happy couple! Band, play a march! Band!

The band plays a march.

NYUNIN. To the newlyweds' health!

ZMEYUKINA. I'm suffocating! I need atmosphere! I start to suffocate whenever I'm near you.

YAT (*in ecstasy*). Spectacular woman! Spectacular!

Noise.

BEST MAN (*trying to make himself heard*). My good friends! On this day of days, so to speak . . .

Curtain

VARIANTS TO

The Wedding

Lines come from the two surviving manuscript copies.

page 567 / *After*: Does that mean we're stingy? — Do me a favor, at least a whole regiment.

page 567 / *After*: You want a General, you'll get a General — We'll provide it all . . . And if not, then it means Andrey Andreich didn't find a suitable one. It should be time to sit down to supper . . . Twelve o'clock.

page 567 / *After*: Didn't you realize it would get on my nerves? —
NASTASYA TIMOFEEVNA. We didn't invite him, dearie. He came on his own.
APLOMBOV. He'd better not make a scene or else he'll learn from me what it's like to come uninvited.

page 568 / *After*: M'sewers, promenade! — Donay mwa toozhoor!

page 569 / *After*: have you got senior civil servants too? —

YAT. Why, I'll bet that in Greece there aren't such beautiful parties of the female sex as certain individuals . . .

page 570 / *Replace*: Wonderful woman! I'm in love! Head over heels in love!
with: A midwife, no looks to speak of, but give her the once-over, what manners! Right away an obvious aristocrat!

page 571 / *After*: Squeezing the last drop out of him — They should all be hanged.

page 573 / *After*: A sign of feebleminded psychiatrics, that's all! —

MOZGOVOY (*rising*). Ladies and gentlemen! Allow me to say the following. Anna Martynovna is in arrears! When we played forfeits, it fell out that she had to kiss the man who was the most dark-haired of them all. The most dark-haired of us all was Lapkin, but he got embarrassed and left. Now Anna Martynovna really has to pick out another dark-haired man and do what needs to be done . . .

EVERYONE. Yes, yes . . . Of course, of course!

ZMEYUKINA. How silly! Leave off!

MOZGOVOY. Who is the darkest of us all?

BEST MAN. Kharlampy Spiridonych!

EVERYONE. Yes, yes! Please, Kharlampy Spiridonych!

ZMEYUKINA. I don't want to kiss! (*Hides her face behind a napkin.*)

YAT. No-o, ma'am, no-o, ma'am, Anna Martynovna, please don't be evasive . . . Have a heart, ma'am!

DYMBA (*confused*). Why is what? I notting . . .

ZMEYUKINA. Really, I don't even understand . . . It's even strange . . . (*Aside.*) He's so handsome! Such eyes!

YAT (*rubbing his hands*). No-o, no-o! You have to!

A *fanfare.*

ZMEYUKINA. Now what? If that was the forfeit that fell to me, then if you please, but . . . it's even extravagantly . . .

Exchanges kisses with Dymba. The kiss is prolonged. DYMBA,
whose lips were stuck to Zmeyukina's, staggers back and keeps his
balance with his arms.

YAT (*anxious*). That's very long! Enough! All right!

EVERYONE (*anxious*). Enough!

DYMBA (*tearing himself away from Zmeyukina*). Oof! Why is what? This is
  who . . . I not understanding.

YAT

⎤

— *together.* She's faint! Water! Faint!

MOZGOVOY ⎦

YAT (*giving Zmeyukina water, aside*). Right away it's obvious she's an aristocrat! (*To her.*) Calm down! I implore you . . . That's right . . . She's opened
  her eyes . . . (*Aside.*) Quite the aristocrat!

ZMEYUKINA (*coming to herself*). Where am I? In what atmosphere am I?
  Where is he? (*To Dymba.*) You demon! You have set me afire with your kiss!

DYMBA (*confused*). Why is what? I notting . . .

page 573 / *After*: in Russia is such a pipples, and in Griss is such a pipples . . .
  — Is good! So is what?

page 574 / *After*: not infantry, but navy! — I controlled the seas and commanded the storms.

page 575 / *After*: Be so kind! — (*Aside.*) But what a scrawny, what a shop-
  soiled! Not even any epaulets . . . Well, at least there are lots of medals! (*To
  him.*)

page 576 / *Replace*: Yes . . . Serving in the navy was always tough . . . Never
  fear, your sailor gets the drift!

with: I guess it's all newfangled nowadays, not the way it was with us . . . It
  wasn't all peaches and cream, cushy . . . However, the naval service was
  always a tough one. It had nothing to do with the infantry, or, let's say, the
  cavalry . . . There's no brainwork to the infantry . . . There even a peasant
  can figure out what's what . . . You know it yourself: left-right, left-right, or
  form fours, or right turn! But what you and I were up against, young man,
  no sir! You're joking! You and I have to think things out and cudgel our
  brains. The least little word has, so to speak, its secret . . . eh . . . conundrum! For example: topmen to the shrouds, fore- and mainsails! . . . What
  does that mean? Why, it means that whoever's assigned to look after the
  topsails, has to find himself without fail at that time at the top, otherwise
  you have to give the order: cross-treemen to the shrouds! There's another
  meaning as well . . .

page 578 / *Replace*: (*not hearing*) . . . I was recalling the olden days . . .

with: You don't understand because these are . . . terms! Of course! But the
  young man understands. Yes . . . I was reminiscing about old times with
  him . . .

page 578 / *Replace*: (*not hearing*). No thanks, I've eaten . . . We've managed
   to bring her about!

with: (*sobbing*). Then they raise the jib-halyards, brace the main topsail and
   others, at the afore-mentioned, close-haul the sail, and then they dash to
   the location of fore and main tack, haul the sheets and haul in the bowline
   . . . I'm cry . . . I'm crying . . . So happy . . .

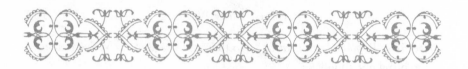

THE WOOD GOBLIN

*I*n 1888, even before he had finished work on *Ivanov*, Chekhov suggested to Aleksey Suvorin that they collaborate on a comedy. He drew up a list of characters, episodes, and a distribution of assignments. Suvorin soon dropped out, and Chekhov reworked the play into *The Wood Goblin* in spring 1889. On May 14, 1889, Chekhov wrote Suvorin:

> The play turned out boring, pieced together like a mosaic . . . nowhere in the whole play is there a single lackey or peripheral comic character or little widow. There are eight characters in all and only three of them are episodic. As a rule I tried to avoid superfluity, and I think I have succeeded.

What Chekhov saw as a structural flaw, the play's mosaic-like quality, would become a characteristic element of his playwriting in the future.

The Wood Goblin was read by the committee that passed on plays for the Petersburg state theaters. Its devastating and unanimous decision was to reject it as a "beautiful dramatized novella," as Chekhov confided to the actor Nikolay Pavel Svobodin (October 25, 1889). However, the play was solicited by Chekhov's boyhood friend Solovtsov, who had left Korsh's theater to start a new one in Moscow with the heiress Mariya Abramova. So *The Wood Goblin*, with a hastily rewritten fourth act, was first presented at Abramova's private theater on December 27, 1889, in a very weak production. The role of the beautiful Yelena was taken by the corpulent Mariya Glebova, and, as Chekhov's younger brother remembered, "to the romantic lead, the actor Roschin-Insarov, making a declaration of love to her was positively incongruous: he called her beautiful, yet he could not get his arms around her to embrace her. Then the glow of the forest fire was such that it aroused laughter."[1] Dissatisfied, Chekhov withdrew the play, which had been received with indifference.

His dissatisfaction related, however, more to the play's internal imperfections than to its faulty staging. The problem with *The Wood Goblin* is that it tries very hard to make a positive statement. It had been preceded by the novella "A Dismal Story," whose central characters, a played-out scientist and his ward, a despairing actress, have reached an impasse in life. No way out of the sterility that confronts them seems possible. Critics had been dwelling on Chekhov's pessimism and it was beginning to get under his skin. He was drawn to the popular teachings of Tolstoy, centered around the passive resistance to evil and ascetic way of life, but he was unable to give himself wholly to any doctrine. Still, he experimented with these fashionable beliefs in his new play.

In *The Wood Goblin*, Chekhov subscribes to the Tolstoyan notion of universal love as a means of unraveling the Gordian knot of social problems. The cast of characters he had drawn up for Suvorin had included two Tolstoyan characters: Anuchin, an old man whose public repentance made him the happiest person in the district, and the pilgrim Fedosy, a plain-speaking and optimistic lay brother of the Mount Athos monastery. All that survives of these characters in *The Wood Goblin* is a last-act speech of Orlovsky Sr., who relates his midlife crisis and regeneration.

Baldly put, the speech in which Dr. Khrushchov, the "Wood Goblin," complains that people must treat one another as human beings, without preconceptions and labels, formulates the play's ideology. The happy ending Chekhov boasted of comes about as the characters discover this idea for themselves. The couples who had been divided by mutual distrust now link up, and stand on the brink of a new life full of truth.

In the first version of *The Wood Goblin*, this was not entirely clear, and Chekhov worked hard to remove similarities to *Ivanov*. He radically changed the character of Zheltukhin, originally portrayed as a slogan-spouting liberal, prone to quoting the protest poetry of Nikolay Nekrasov. In the produced version, the characters are evenly divided between the self-centered rationalists (Uncle *Georges*, his mother, Zheltukhin, the Professor, and Sofiya before her reformation) and the pure in heart, who avoid self-analysis and are spontaneous in their reactions (the Orlovskys, Yulya, Dyadin). Chekhov changed the denouement to point this up. Originally, the Professor was to undergo a change of heart, see the error of his ways, and forgive Yelena, while Fyodor, who had abducted her, would be chastened by news of his father's death. Instead, the absurd Dyadin is made to make off with Yelena, and Orlovsky Sr. does not die of shock. Now it is Fyodor who undergoes a sudden and unconvincing conversion to simplicity, while the Professor remains obtuse to the end.

"I filled the comedy with good, healthy people, half sympathetic, and a happy ending. The general tone is entirely lyrical," Chekhov wrote to Pleshcheev, on September 30, 1889. This is a play of conversion, but without overt religious references or a confessional tone. The most important new element in his playwriting is the suppression of a prominent hero in favor of a closely interrelated group. The ties that bind the characters in this neighborhood are more intricate than those in *Ivanov*.

Khrushchov the Wood Goblin lends his name to the play, not because he is the pivotal figure, but because his epiphany in the last act is the summation of the play's meaning. In Chekhov's later plays, a monologue such as his about the need for heroes in Russia would be alloyed by some ironic flaw in the character. Here it is meant to be taken as read. The critic Aleksandr Chudakov notes that Khrushchov is perhaps the first hero in Russian drama "whose purpose in life is the preservation of nature,"[2] but, unlike Astrov, his counterpart in *Uncle Vanya*, his concern with conservation is not, by itself, a redeeming trait. Merit is not achieved by saving forests or serving science or by any practical activity; pure morality in human relations is of higher value. The crucial turning point for Khrushchov is finding Voinitsky's diary, which shows him how badly the Wood Goblin had misjudged his fellows. The device is clumsy, a relic of the well-made play, but Chekhov needed it to trigger Khrushchov's about-face, his awakening when he casts off his suspicions of others.

Both *Platonov* and *Ivanov* had centered upon somewhat outstanding individuals corroded by their own cynicism and self-doubt. In *The Wood Goblin*, those qualities recur in Voinitsky, who, riddled with irony, finds the less complicated natures of Fyodor and Khrushchov appealing. Incapable of change, he has to commit suicide, to leave the stage clear for the reversals of the last act.

Despite the pleas of enthusiasts, Chekhov refused to have the play reprinted. "I hate that play and am trying to forget it," he wrote to A. I. Urusov, on April 16, 1900. But the ideology, if too blatantly expressed, was to abide. Chekhov's later plays continue to attribute greater importance to honesty in human relations than to any doctrinaire or programmatic prescriptions for society.

NOTES

1 M. P. Chekhov, *Vokrug Chekhova* (Moscow: Moskovsky rabochy, 1980), p. 152.

2 A. P. Chudakov, *Chekhov's Poetics*, tr. F. J. Cruise and D. Dragt (Ann Arbor: Ardis, 1983), p. 210.

THE WOOD GOBLIN[1]

Леший

A Comedy in Four Acts

CHARACTERS

ALEKSANDR VLADIMIROVICH SEREBRYAKOV, *a retired professor*

YELENA ANDREEVNA, *his wife, 27*

SOFYA ALEKSANDROVNA (SONYA), *his daughter by his first wife, 20*

MARIYA VASILYEVNA VOINITSKAYA, *the widow of a senior civil servant, mother of the professor's first wife*

YEGOR PETROVICH VOINITSKY, *her son*

LEONID STEPANOVICH ZHELTUKHIN, *a very rich man who studied technology at the university but never earned a degree*

YULIYA STEPANOVNA (YULYA), *his sister, 18*

IVAN IVANOVICH ORLOVSKY, *a landowner*

FYODOR IVANOVICH, *his son*

MIKHAIL LVOVICH KHRUSHCHOV, *landowner, who has a medical degree*

ILYA ILYICH DYADIN

---

1 Dr. Khrushchov's nickname, "Leshy," makes too diabolic an impression when translated as "Wood Demon." The mischievous sprite that the ancient Slavs and their posterity believed inhabited the forests is closer to Puck or Robin Goodfellow, in his fondness for leading travelers astray and imitating the sounds of various animals. In Chekhov's day, Russians said *"leshy vozmi"* as a mild expletive, the way an Englishman might say "Deuce take it."

VASILY, *Zheltukhin's servant*

SEMYON, *a workman at the mill*

ACT ONE

*The garden on Zheltukhin's estate. A house with a terrace; on the
veranda in front of the house are two tables: a large one, set for
lunch, and another smaller one with appetizers.
A little after two o'clock.*

I

ZHELTUKHIN and YULYA enter from the house.

YULYA. You'd better put on that nice gray suit. This one doesn't suit you.

ZHELTUKHIN. It doesn't matter. Trivia.

YULYA. Lyonechka, why are you so grumpy? How can you behave like this
on your birthday? You're being a naughty boy! . . . (*Lays her head on his
breast.*)

ZHELTUKHIN. A little less affection, please!

YULYA (*through tears*). Lyonechka!

ZHELTUKHIN. Instead of these curdled kisses, all these loving glances and
watch stands[2] made out of little shoes, which are no damned use to me,
you should do what I asked you to! How come you didn't write to the Serebryakovs?

YULYA. Lyonechka, I did write!

ZHELTUKHIN. Which one did you write to?

YULYA. Sonechka. I asked her to be sure and come by today, to be sure to
come at one. Cross my heart, I did write!

---

2 A small case that keeps a watch upright on a table, so its face can be seen.

ZHELTUKHIN. But it's already past two and they aren't here . . . Oh well, if that's the way they want it! I'll have to give it up, nothing'll come of it . . . Except humiliation, a sense of grievance and nothing more . . . She pays me no attention. I'm not good-looking, I'm uninteresting, there's nothing romantic about me, and if she did marry me, it would only be out of self-interest . . . for the money! . . .

YULYA. Not good-looking . . . You have no idea what you look like.

ZHELTUKHIN. Oh sure, as if I were blind! My beard grows out of here, out of my neck, not like other people's . . . A moustache, who the hell knows what kind . . . a nose . . .

YULYA. Why are you pressing down on your cheek?

ZHELTUKHIN. There's that pain under my eye again.

YULYA. Yes, it is a little bit swollen. Let me kiss it and it'll go away.

ZHELTUKHIN. Don't be stupid!

Enter ORLOVSKY, and VOINITSKY.

I I

The same, ORLOVSKY, and VOINITSKY.

ORLOVSKY. Lovey, when are we going to eat? It's past two already!

YULYA. Godfather dear, the Serebryakovs aren't here yet!

ORLOVSKY. How long are we supposed to wait for them? I want to eat, honey bunch. And so does Yegor Petrovich here.

ZHELTUKHIN (*to Voinitsky*). Are your folks going to show up?

VOINITSKY. When I left the house, Yelena Andreevna was getting dressed.

ZHELTUKHIN. In other words, they're sure to show up?

VOINITSKY. Sure is impossible to say. Our V.I.P. may suddenly come down with gout[3] or some other whim—and then they'll stay home.

---

3 A periodic painful swelling in the lower joints, owing to the accumulation of uric acid; often a result of rich diet, heavy drinking, and a sedentary life.

ZHELTUKHIN. In that case, let's eat. What's the point of waiting? (*Shouts.*) Ilya Ilyich! Sergey Nikodimych!

DYADIN and a few other GUESTS enter.

III

The same, DYADIN, and GUESTS.

ZHELTUKHIN. Please start on the appetizers. Please do. (*Near the appetizers.*) The Serebryakovs haven't come, Fyodor Ivanych isn't here, neither is the Wood Goblin . . . They've abandoned us!

YULYA. Godfather dear, would you like some vodka?

ORLOVSKY. Just a tiny drop. That's it . . . That'll be enough.

DYADIN (*tying a napkin around his neck*). What a wonderful manager you are, Yuliya Stepanovna! Whether I'm driving across your fields or walking in the shade of your orchard, or contemplating this table, everywhere I see the sovereign power of your magic little hands.[4] Your good health!

YULYA. I've got my hands full, Ilya Ilyich! Yesterday, for instance, Nazarka didn't drive the turkey chicks into the henhouse, they spent the night in the dewy grass, and today five of the chicks dropped dead.

DYADIN. That shouldn't happen. The turkey is a delicate fowl.

VOINITSKY (*to Dyadin*). Waffles, cut me a slice of that ham!

DYADIN. With particular pleasure. It's a beautiful ham. One of the wonders of the Arabian Nights. (*Cuts a slice.*) I am slicing it for you, Zhorzhenka, according to all the laws of art. Beethoven and Shakespeare couldn't slice it like this. Only the knife's a little dull. (*Hones the knife on another knife.*)

ZHELTUKHIN (*shuddering*). Vvvv! . . . Stop that, Waffles! I can't stand it!

ORLOVSKY. Tell us about it, Yegor Petrovich. What's going on at your place?

VOINITSKY. Nothing's going on.

ORLOVSKY. Anything new?

---

4 This may be one of Chekhov's sly parodies of Pushkin's famous lyric "Whether I walk the noisy streets."

VOINITSKY. Nothing. It's all old. The way it was last year is the way it is now. As usual, I talk a lot and do very little. My old magpie of a *maman* goes on babbling about women's rights; one eye peers into the grave, while the other pores over her high-minded pamphlets, looking for the dawn of a new life.

ORLOVSKY. What about Sasha?

VOINITSKY. The Professor, unfortunately, still hasn't been nibbled away by the moths. From morn to darkest night he sits alone in the study and writes. "With straining brain and furrowed brow, We write for nights and days, Yet all our poetry somehow Can never meet with praise."[5] I feel sorry for the paper! Sonechka reads high-minded pamphlets as she always did and keeps a very high-minded diary.

ORLOVSKY. What a darling, what a dear . . .

VOINITSKY. With my powers of observation I ought to be writing a novel. The subject is begging to be put down on paper. A retired professor, a pedantic old fossil, a guppy with a terminal degree . . . Gout, rheumatism, migraine, liver complaints and all sorts of stuff. As jealous as Othello.[6] Living reluctantly on his first wife's estate, because he can't afford to live in town. Endlessly griping about his bad luck, although as a matter of fact he's incredibly lucky.

ORLOVSKY. Come now!

VOINITSKY. Of course he is! Just think about the luck he's had! Let's put aside the fact that the son of a humble sexton, a seminary student on a tuition scholarship, acquired academic degrees and chairs, the title Your Excellency, married the daughter of a senator,[7] and so on. That's not what matters, though. Check this out. For precisely twenty-five years the man reads and writes about art, although he understands absolutely nothing about art. For twenty-five years he chews over other people's ideas about realism, nat-

---

5 Quotation from the satirical poem "At Second Hand" (*Chuzhoy tolk,* 1794) by Ivan Dimitriev (1760–1837). The poem, which mocks the rhetorical form of the ode, was one of the standard texts of the pre-Pushkin era.

6 Shakespeare's Moorish general was known on the Russian stage chiefly through the touring performances of the Italian tragedians Tomasso Salvini and Ernesto Rossi.

7 If Yelena Andreevna's father is a senator, he outranks a general in the military, which means the Professor "married up."

uralism, and the rest of that rubbish; for twenty-five years he reads and writes about stuff that intelligent people have known for ages and fools couldn't care less about—which means, for twenty-five years he's been pouring the contents of one empty bottle into another emptier bottle. And add to that, what success! What celebrity! What for? Why? What right has he got?

ORLOVSKY (*laughs loudly*). Envy, envy!

VOINITSKY. Yes, envy! Look at his success with women! Not even Don Juan enjoyed such unqualified success! His first wife, my sister, a beautiful, gentle creature, pure as that blue sky overhead, noble, open-hearted, with more admirers than he had students, loved him as only pure angels can love beings as pure and beautiful as themselves. My mother, his mother-in-law, adores him to this day, and to this day he inspires her with awe and reverence. His second wife, a woman with looks, brains—you've seen her—married him when he was an old man, made him a gift of her youth, beauty, independence, her brilliance . . . What for? Why? And such a talent, a fine musician! It's wonderful the way she plays the piano!

ORLOVSKY. A talented family one and all. An exceptional family.

ZHELTUKHIN. Yes, Sofya Aleksandrovna, for instance, has a magnificent voice. A wonderful soprano! I never heard anything like it in Petersburg. Though, you know, it's a little forced in the higher octave. Such a pity! The higher octave for me! That higher octave! Ah, if she had that octave, I'll wager my head, she'd be able to produce . . . something wonderful, believe you me . . . Sorry, gentlemen, I've got to have a word with Yulya . . . (*Takes Yulya aside.*) Send someone on horseback to them. Send a note to say that if they can't come now, they might at least drop in for dinner. (*More quietly.*) But don't act like a fool, don't embarrass me, write it in good Russian . . . Drop has only one p . . . (*Aloud and tenderly.*) Please, my dear.

YULYA. All right . . . (*Exits.*)

DYADIN. They say that the professor's lady wife, Yelena Andreevna, whose acquaintance I have not the honor of enjoying, is distinguished not only by spiritual beauty, but by physical beauty as well.

ORLOVSKY. Yes, she's a splendid young lady.

ZHELTUKHIN. She's faithful to the professor?

VOINITSKY. Sorry to say she is.

ZHELTUKHIN. Why sorry?

VOINITSKY. Because this faithfulness is phony from start to finish. It's all sound and no sense. To cheat on an old husband you can't stand—that's immoral; to try and stifle the vestiges of youth and vital feeling in your-self—that's not immoral. Where the hell is the sense in that?

DYADIN (*in a plaintive voice*). Zhorzhenka, I don't like it when you say things like that. Why, now, honestly . . . I'm even trembling . . . Gentlemen, I don't possess any talent or flowery eloquence, but allow me to declare without magniloquent phrases as my conscience dictates . . . Gentlemen, anybody who cheats on a wife or husband is, I mean, a disloyal person, someone who might even betray his country!

VOINITSKY. Turn off the waterworks![8]

DYADIN. Excuse me, Zhorzhenka . . . Ivan Ivanych, Lyonechka, my dear friends, consider the mutability of my fate. It is no secret, it is not veiled by the shadows of obscurity,[9] that my wife ran away with the man she loved the day after our wedding on account of my unprepossessing looks . . .

VOINITSKY. And was quite right to do so.

DYADIN. Excuse me, gentlemen! In the aftermath of that event I have not shirked my duty . . . I love her to this day, and I'm faithful to her, I help any way I can, and I have bequeathed my estate to the kiddies she bore to the man she loved. I have not shirked my duty and I'm proud of it. I'm proud! Happiness was denied me, but what I did have left was my pride. What about her? Her youth has flown now, her beauty, subject to the laws of nature, has faded, the man she loved has passed away, may he rest in peace . . . What does she have left? (*Sits down.*) I mean this seriously, and you laugh.

ORLOVSKY. You're a kindly man, you have a heart of gold, but your talk is so prolix and the way you wave your arms around . . .

> *FYODOR IVANOVICH comes out of the house; he is wearing a sleeveless overcoat of fine cloth and high boots; his chest is covered*

---

8 From the "Thoughts and Aphorisms" of the poet Kozma Prutkov, a fictional creation of A. K. Tolstoy and the brothers Zhemchuznikov, "published" between 1854 and 1863. One of his synthetic aphorisms is "If you have waterworks, turn them off; give the waterworks a rest too."

9 One of Chekhov's favorite flowery phrases, later put into the mouth of Lopakhin in *The Cherry Orchard*.

*with decorations, medals, and a massive gold chain with
pendants; expensive rings on his fingers.*

IV

The same and FYODOR IVANOVICH.

FYODOR IVANOVICH. Greetings, lads!

ORLOVSKY (*gleefully*). Fedyusha my dear, sonny boy!

FYODOR IVANOVICH (*to Zheltukhin*). Happy birthday . . . grow up to be big and strong . . . (*Exchanges greetings with everyone.*) Progenitor! Waffles, greetings! I wish you a hearty appetite, and good digestion.

ZHELTUKHIN. Where had you got to? You shouldn't be so late.

FYODOR IVANOVICH. It's hot! Got to have some vodka.

ORLOVSKY (*admiring him*). My dear boy, that's a magnificent beard you've got . . . Gentlemen, isn't he a beauty? Look him over: is that a beauty?

FYODOR IVANOVICH. Here's to the birthday boy! (*Drinks.*) The Serebryakovs aren't here?

ZHELTUKHIN. They didn't come.

FYODOR IVANOVICH. Hm . . . And where's Yulya?

ZHELTUKHIN. I don't know what's holding her up in there. It's time to bring in the meat pie. I'll call her right away. (*Exits.*)

ORLOVSKY. Our Lyonechka, the birthday boy, is a bit out of sorts today. Sulky.

VOINITSKY. He's just a swine.

ORLOVSKY. His nerves are on edge, there's nothing you can do about it . . .

VOINITSKY. Too much vanity, hence the nerves. If he were standing here and you said that this herring is good, he would immediately take offense: why didn't you praise *him*. Pretty much a waste of time and space. But here he comes.

Enter YULYA and ZHELTUKHIN.

V

The same, ZHELTUKHIN, and YULYA.

YULYA. Good afternoon, Fedenka! (*Exchanges kisses with Fyodor Ivanovich.*) Have a bite, my dear . . . (*To Ivan Ivanovich.*) Look, godfather, here's the gift I gave Lyonechka today! (*Displays a little shoe to be used as a watch stand.*)

ORLOVSKY. My darlin', my little girl, a tiny shoe! That's quite something . . .

YULYA. The gold thread alone cost eight and a half rubles. Look at the edging: tiny little pearls, tiny little pearls, tiny little pearls . . . And these are letters: Leonid Zheltukhin. And here in silk thread: "A gift to the one I love . . ."

DYADIN. Please let me have a look at it! Fascinating!

FYODOR IVANOVICH. Drop it . . . that's enough of that! Yulya, have them serve the champagne!

YULYA. Fedenka, that's for tonight!

FYODOR IVANOVICH. Well, why wait—for tonight! Bring it now! Or else I'm leaving. Word of honor, I'm leaving. Where do you keep it? I'll go get it myself.

YULYA. You're always interfering with my housekeeping, Fedya. (*To Vasily.*) Vasily, here's the key! The champagne's in the storeroom, you know, in the corner by the sack of raisins, in a basket. Only see to it you don't break anything.

FYODOR IVANOVICH. Vasily, three bottles!

YULYA. They'll never make a good manager out of you, Fedenka . . . (*Serves everyone pie.*) Have some more, gentlemen . . . Dinner won't be for a while yet, not until half-past five . . . They'll never make anything of you, Fedenka . . . You're incorrigible.

FYODOR IVANOVICH. Look, she's taken up lecturing!

VOINITSKY. I think someone just drove up . . . Did you hear?

ZHELTUKHIN. Yes . . . It's the Serebryakovs . . . At last!

VASILY. The Serebryakov family has arrived!

YULYA (*cries out*). Sonechka! (*Runs out.*)

VOINITSKY (*sings*). Let's go and meet them, let's go and meet them . . . (*Exits.*)

FYODOR IVANOVICH. Look at the way they're rejoicing!

ZHELTUKHIN. The tactlessness of some people! He's sleeping with the professor's lady and can't conceal it.

FYODOR IVANOVICH. Who is?

ZHELTUKHIN. That *Georges.* The way he lavished praise on her just now, before you came, was practically indecent.

FYODOR IVANOVICH. How do you know he's sleeping with her?

ZHELTUKHIN. You think I'm blind? . . . Besides, it's the talk of the whole district . . .

FYODOR IVANOVICH. Nonsense. So far nobody is sleeping with her, but I soon shall soon be . . . Understand? *I* shall!

V I

The same; SEREBRYAKOV, MARIYA VASILYEVNA,
VOINITSKY arm in arm with YELENA ANDREEVNA,
SONYA, and YULYA enter.

YULYA (*kissing Sonya*). My dearest! My dearest!

ORLOVSKY (*going to meet them*). Sasha, greetings, my dear fellow, greetings, my boy! (*Exchanges kisses with the Professor.*) Are you well? Shall we thank God?

SEREBRYAKOV. How about you, neighbor? You're the same as ever—bravely done! Most pleased to see you. Been here long?

ORLOVSKY. Got here on Friday. (*To Marlya Vasilyevna.*) Marya Vasilyevna! How are you getting on, Your Excellency? (*Kisses her hand.*)

MARIYA VASILYEVNA. My dear . . . (*Kisses him on the head.*)

SONYA. Godfather dear!

ORLOVSKY. Sonechka, dear heart! (*Kisses her.*) My little dove, my little canary . . .

SONYA. Your face is just as kind, sentimental, sweet as ever . . .

ORLOVSKY. And you've got taller and prettier and all grown up, dear heart . . .

SONYA. Well, how are you, generally speaking? Are you well?

ORLOVSKY. Frightfully well!

SONYA. Good for you, godfather! (*To Fyodor Ivanovich.*) And I was ignoring the elephant in the room.[10] (*Exchanges kisses with him.*) Sunburned, bristly . . . a regular spider!

YULYA. Dearest!

ORLOVSKY (*to Serebryakov*). How's life treating you, neighbor?

SEREBRYAKOV. All right . . . And you?

ORLOVSKY. What could be wrong with me? I'm living it up! I turned my estate over to my son, married off my daughters to good people, and now I'm the freest man going. I know how to have a good time!

DYADIN (*to Serebryakov*). Your Excellency, you chose to be a bit late. The temperature of the pie has gone down considerably. May I introduce myself: Ilya Ilyich Dyadin, or, as some people very wittily express it on account of my pockmarked face, Waffles.

SEREBRYAKOV. Pleased to meet you.

DYADIN. *Madame! Mademoiselle!* (*Bows to Yelena Andreevna and Sonya*). These are all friends of mine, Your Excellency. Once I possessed a large fortune, but owing to domestic vicissitudes, or, as the expression goes in intellectual circles, for reasons over which the editor has no control, I had to relinquish my share to my brother, who, on a certain unhappy occasion, was short seventy thousand rubles of government money. My profession is the exploitation of the tempestuous elements. I make the stormy waves turn the wheel of a mill, which I rent from my friend the Wood Goblin.

VOINITSKY. Waffles, turn off the waterworks!

DYADIN. I shall always pay my reverent respects (*bows down to the ground*) to the luminaries of science, who adorn our national horizon. Forgive me the

---

10 From Ivan Krylov's fable "The Sight-seer" (1814): a curiosity seeker is so distracted with minor phenomena that he ends up saying, "I noticed not the elephant at all."

audacious dream of paying your excellency a visit and beguiling my heart with a colloquy about the latest scientific findings.

SEREBRYAKOV. Please do come. I shall be delighted.

SONYA. Now, do tell us, godfather . . . Where did you spend the winter? Where did you disappear to?

ORLOVSKY. I was in Gmunden, I was in Paris, Nice, London, dear heart . . .

SONYA. That's wonderful! You lucky man!

ORLOVSKY. Come with me in the fall! Would you like to?

SONYA (*sings*). "Tempt me not, it dare not be . . ."[11]

FYODOR IVANOVICH. Don't sing after lunch, or else your husband's wife will be a fool.

DYADIN. Now, it would be interesting to observe this table *à vol d'oiseau.*[12] What a fascinating nosegay! A combination of grace, beauty, profound learning, swee . . .

FYODOR IVANOVICH. What a fascinating tongue! What the hell is this? You sound as if somebody were shaving your back with a carpenter's plane . . .

Laughter.

ORLOVSKY (*to Sonya*). And you, dear heart, are still not married . . .

VOINITSKY. For pity's sake, who's she supposed to marry? Humboldt is dead, Edison's in America, Lassalle's dead too[13] . . . The other day I found her diary on the table: this big! I open it up and read: "No, I shall never fall in love . . . Love is the egocentric attraction of my *self* to an object of the opposite sex . . ." And who the hell knows what else is in it? "Transcendentally, the culminating point of the integral principle" . . . phooey! And where did you go to school?

---

11 From Evgeny Baratynsky's elegy "Dissuasion" (1821), set to music as a duet by Glinka and many other composers.

12 French: a bird's-eye view.

13 These names are shorthand for different types of genius: Baron Alexander von Humboldt (1769–1859), German naturalist and traveler who explored Russian Asia in 1829; Thomas Alva Edison (1847–1931), who patented over a thousand inventions; and Ferdinand Lassalle (1825–1864), German Socialist who promoted political power for workers.

SONYA. Leave it to others to be ironical, you shouldn't, Uncle *Georges* . . .

VOINITSKY. What are you getting angry about?

SONYA. If you say another word, one of us will have to go home. You or I . . .

ORLOVSKY (*laughs loudly*). Why, what a temper!

VOINITSKY. Yes, a temper, I grant you that . . . (*To Sonya.*) Well, your little paw! Give me your little paw! (*Kisses her hand.*) Peace and harmony . . . I won't do it again.

V I I

The same and KHRUSHCHOV.

KHRUSHCHOV (*coming out of the house*). Why aren't I a painter? What a wonderful composition!

ORLOVSKY (*gleefully*). Misha! My dear little godson!

KHRUSHCHOV. Many happy returns to the birthday boy! Greeting, Yulechka, how pretty you look today! Godfather! (*Exchanges kisses with Orlovsky.*) Sofya Aleksandrovna . . . (*Greets everyone.*)

ZHELTUKHIN. Well, how can a person be so late? Where were you?

KHRUSHCHOV. With a patient.

YULYA. The pie's gone cold long ago.

KHRUSHCHOV. Never mind, Yulechka, I'll eat it cold. Where should I sit?

SONYA. Sit down here . . . (*Offers him the place beside her.*)

KHRUSHCHOV. The weather's splendid today, and I've got a hell of an appetite . . . Hold on, I'll have some vodka . . . (*Drinks.*) To the birthday boy! I'll try this little pie . . . Yulechka, kiss this pie, it'll make it tastier . . .

She kisses it.

Merci. How are you getting on, godfather? I haven't seen you for a long time.

ORLOVSKY. Yes, we haven't met for quite a while. I was abroad, you see.

KHRUSHCHOV. I heard, I heard . . . I envied you. Fyodor, how about you?

FYODOR IVANOVICH. I'm all right, your good wishes are our bulwark never-failing . . .

KHRUSHCHOV. How's business?

FYODOR IVANOVICH. I can't complain. We earn a living. Only, pal, there's too much back and forth. Wears me down. From here to the Caucasus, from the Caucasus back here, from here back to the Caucasus—and it never ends, you're on the go like a maniac. After all, I've got two estates there!

KHRUSHCHOV. I know.

FYODOR IVANOVICH. I spend my time advertising for settlers and all I attract is tarantulas and scorpions. My business is going all right for the most part, but as for "down, down, ye surging passions"[14]—it's the same old story.

KHRUSHCHOV. In love, of course?

FYODOR IVANOVICH. On which account, Wood Goblin, I need a drink. (*Drinks.*) Ladies and gentlemen, never fall in love with married women! Word of honor, it's better to be wounded in the shoulder and shot in the leg, like your humble servant, than love a married woman . . . So much trouble it's simply . . .

SONYA. Hopeless?

FYODOR IVANOVICH. What a word to use! Hopeless . . . There's nothing hopeless under the sun. Hopeless, unrequited love, oohing and aahing— that's just self-indulgence. You only have only to apply willpower . . . If I will my gun not to misfire, it won't. If I will a young lady to love me, she'll love me. Just like that, Sonya old pal. And once I've got my eye on a woman, I think it'll be easier for her to fly to the moon than get away from me.

SONYA. Aren't you a terror . . .

FYODOR IVANOVICH. You won't get away from me, no! I wouldn't have to say a dozen words to her, before she's in my power . . . Yes . . . I only have to say to her: "Madam, every time you look out a window, you must

---

14 From Glinka's ballad based on a poem of Nikolay Kukolnik, "Doubt" (1838).

remember me. I will it." Which means, she'll remember me a thousand times a day. That's not all, I bombard her with letters on a daily basis.

YELENA ANDREEVNA. Letters are an unreliable medium. She may receive them but not read them.

FYODOR IVANOVICH. You think so? Hm . . . I've lived on this earth thirty-five years, and have never yet met the phenomenal woman who has the fortitude not to open a letter.

ORLOVSKY (*admiring him*). How do you like that? My sonny boy, my beauty! I was just the same. Down to the last detail! Only I didn't go to war, just drank vodka and wasted money—terrible way to carry on!

FYODOR IVANOVICH. I do love her, Misha, seriously, excruciatingly . . . She only has to say the word and I would give her all I've got . . . I'd carry her off to my place in the Caucasus, the mountains, we would live in clover . . . Yelena Andreevna, I would protect her, like a faithful hound, and I'd treat her like in that song our marshal of nobility[15] sings, "And thou shalt be queen of the world, my love for all eternity."[16] Ech, she doesn't know the happiness she's missing!

KHRUSHCHOV. Who is this lucky creature?

FYODOR IVANOVICH. A little knowledge is a dangerous thing . . . But that's enough about that. Now let's have a song from a different opera. I remember, about ten years ago—Lyonya was still in high school at the time—we were celebrating his birthday just as we are now. I was riding home from here, and at my right hand sat Sonya, and at my left Yulka, and both were clinging to my beard. Gentlemen, let's drink to the health of the friends of my youth, Sonya and Yulya!

DYADIN (*laughs loudly*). This is fascinating! This is fascinating!

FYODOR IVANOVICH. Once when the war was over[17] I was getting drunk with a Turkish pasha in Trebizond . . . He starts asking me . . .

DYADIN (*interrupting*). Gentlemen, let's drink a toast to distinguished relations! *Vivat* friendship! Long may it thrive!

---

15 A deputy elected by the local and district assemblies of nobles, to represent them in dealings with the government. They were often chosen for their social rather than their political skills.

16 Sung by the Demon in Rubinstein's opera *The Demon*, based on the poem by Lermontov.

17 The Russo-Turkish war of 1877–1878.

FYODOR IVANOVICH. Stop, stop, stop! Sonya, please pay attention! I'm going to make a wager, damn my eyes! I am putting three hundred rubles down on the table! After lunch let's play a round of croquet, and I bet I'll make it through all the hoops and back in one go.

SONYA. I'd accept, only I haven't got three hundred rubles.

FYODOR IVANOVICH. If you lose, you'll sing to me forty times.

SONYA. It's a deal.

DYADIN. This is fascinating! This is fascinating!

YELENA ANDREEVNA (*looking at the sky*). What kind of bird just flew by?

ZHELTUKHIN. It's a hawk.

FYODOR IVANOVICH. Ladies and gentlemen, to the health of the hawk!

> SONYA *bursts out laughing.*

ORLOVSKY. Well, our girl's off and running now! What's got into you?

> KHRUSHCHOV *bursts out laughing.*

And what's come over you?

MARIYA VASILYEVNA. Sophie, that's indecorous!

KHRUSHCHOV. Ugh, sorry, my friends . . . I'll be over it right away, right away . . .

ORLOVSKY. That's what you call idle laughter.

VOINITSKY. Just point a finger at the two of them, and they'll burst out laughing. Sonya! (*Shows her a finger.*) Here, look . . .

KHRUSHCHOV. That's enough! (*Looks at his watch.*) Well, Mikhail was a jolly old soul, he called for his food and called for his bowl, and now his time is up. It's time to go.

SONYA. Where are you off to?

KHRUSHCHOV. To see a patient. My medical practice is as distasteful as a shrewish wife, or a long winter . . .

SEREBRYAKOV. Excuse me, and yet medicine is your profession, your vocation, so to speak . . .

VOINITSKY (*ironically*). He's got another vocation. He excavates peat from his land.

SEREBRYAKOV. What?

VOINITSKY. Peat. Some engineer figured it out, black on white, that his land contains seven hundred and twenty thousand rubles' worth of peat. No joke.

KHRUSHCHOV. I don't excavate peat for profit.

VOINITSKY. What do you excavate it for then?

KHRUSHCHOV. So you won't cut down trees.

VOINITSKY. Why shouldn't I cut them down? To hear you talk, forests exist only so that lads and lassies can play "peek-a-boo" among the trees.

KHRUSHCHOV. I never said that.

VOINITSKY. And everything I've been honored to hear from you so far in defense of forests is old, irrelevant, and tendentious. Excuse me, please. I'm not criticizing without good reason, I practically know your speeches for the defense by heart . . . For instance . . . (*Raising his voice and gesticulating, as if imitating Khrushchov.*) O, my friends, you destroy the forests, but they beautify the land, they teach people to understand beauty and inspire them with a sense of grandeur. Forests alleviate a harsh climate. In lands where the climate is mild, less energy is spent on the struggle with nature and therefore human beings there are milder and more delicate; there people are beautiful, athletic, very sensitive, their speech is refined, their movements graceful. There art and sciences flourish, their philosophy is not gloomy, their attitude to women is full of exquisite chivalry. And so on and so forth . . . Which is all very charming, but not convincing, so allow me to go on stoking my stoves with logs and building my sheds out of wood.

KHRUSHCHOV. Chop down forests when it's absolutely necessary, but why destroy them? All the Russian forests are toppling beneath the axe, the habitats of birds and beasts are dwindling, tens of thousands of trees are perishing, rivers are running shallow and drying up, gorgeous natural scenery is disappearing irretrievably, and all because lazy human beings can't be bothered to bend down and pick up fuel from the earth. A person has to be an unreasoning barbarian (*pointing at the trees*) to destroy what cannot be re-created. Human beings are endowed with reason and creative faculties in order to enhance what is given to them, but so far they have not created but destroyed. Forests are ever fewer and fewer, rivers dry up, wildlife is wiped out, the climate is spoiled, and every day the earth grows more impoverished and ugly. You stare at me sarcastically, and everything I say strikes you as old and frivolous, but when I walk through the peasants' forests that I have saved from being chopped down, or when I hear the wind rustling in my stand of saplings, planted by my own hands, I realize that the climate is to some slight degree in my control, and if, a thousand years from now, humanity is happy, then even I will be partially responsible. When I plant a birch tree, and then see how it grows green and sways in the wind, my soul swells with pride at the awareness that I am helping God create an organism.

FYODOR IVANOVICH (*interrupting*). Your health, Wood Goblin!

VOINITSKY. That's all very well, but if you were to consider the matter not from a pulp-fiction viewpoint, but from a scientific one, then . . .

SONYA. Uncle *Georges*, you're talking through your hat. Be quiet!

KHRUSHCHOV. As a matter of fact, Yegor Petrovich, let's not talk about this. Please.

VOINITSKY. As you like.

MARIYA VASILYEVNA. Ah!

SONYA. What's the matter, Granny?

MARIYA VASILYEVNA (*to Serebryakov*). I forgot to tell you, Aleksandr . . . I must be losing my memory . . . today I got a letter from Kharkov from Pavel Alekseevich . . . He sent his regards . . .

SEREBRYAKOV. Thank you, delighted.

MARIYA VASILYEVNA. He sent his new pamphlet and asked me to show it you.

SEREBRYAKOV. Interesting?

MARIYA VASILYEVNA. Interesting, but rather peculiar. He opposes the very thing he was defending seven years ago. It's very, very typical of our times. Never have people betrayed their convictions as frivolously as they do now. It's appalling!

VOINITSKY. It's not at all appalling. Have some carp, *maman.*

MARIYA VASILYEVNA. But I want to talk!

VOINITSKY. For fifty years now we've been talking about influences and factions, it's high time we stopped.

MARIYA VASILYEVNA. For some reason you don't like to listen when I talk. Pardon me, *Georges,* but this last year you have changed so much that I utterly fail to recognize you . . . You used to be a man of steadfast convictions, a shining light . . .

VOINITSKY. Oh yes! I was a shining light but no one ever basked in my rays. May I leave the table? I was a shining light . . . Don't rub salt in my wounds! Now I'm forty-seven. Before last year I was the same as you, deliberately trying to cloud my vision with all these abstractions and book learning to keep from seeing real life—and I thought I was doing the right thing. And now, if you only knew, what a big idiot I feel myself to be for having wasted my time so stupidly when I could have had everything that's withheld from me now by my old age!

SEREBRYAKOV. Hold on! *Georges,* you seem to be blaming your former convictions for something . . .

SONYA. That's enough, Papa! It's boring!

SEREBRYAKOV. Hold on. You are indeed blaming your former convictions for something. But they aren't to blame, *you* are. You have forgotten that convictions without deeds are a dead letter. One must take action.[18]

VOINITSKY. Take action? Not everyone is capable of being a perpetual-motion writing machine.

SEREBRYAKOV. What do you mean by that?

VOINITSKY. Nothing. Let's change the subject. We're not at home.

MARIYA VASILYEVNA. I really am losing my memory . . . . I forgot to remind you, Aleksandr, to take your drops before lunch. I brought them along, but I forgot to remind you . . .

SEREBRYAKOV. You needn't have.

---

18 *Nado delo delat,* "one must do something," "be active," "be committed," "get involved." A motto of liberalism in the 1860s, it does *not* mean "One must work."

MARIYA VASILYEVNA. But after all you're a sick man, Aleksandr! You're a very sick man!

SEREBRYAKOV. Why shout it from the housetops? Old, sick, old, sick . . . that's all I ever hear! (*To Zheltukhin.*) Leonid Stepanych, may I leave the table and go inside? It's rather hot here and the mosquitoes are ferocious.

ZHELTUKHIN. Please do. Lunch is over.

SEREBRYAKOV. Thank you. (*Exits into the house, followed by Marya Vasilyevna.*)

YULYA (*to her brother*). See to the professor! It's impolite!

ZHELTUKHIN (*to her*). The hell with him! (*Exits.*)

DYADIN. Yulya Stepanovna, may I thank you from the bottom of my heart. (*Kisses her hand.*)

YULYA. Don't mention it, Ilya Ilyich! You've eaten so little . . .

They thank her.

Don't mention it, gentlemen! You all ate so little!

FYODOR IVANOVICH. Well, gents, what shall we do now? Let's go right now to the croquet lawn and settle our wager . . . and after that?

YULYA. After that we'll have dinner.

FYODOR IVANOVICH. And after that?

KHRUSHCHOV. After that you can all come to my place. In the evening we'll organize a fishing party on the lake.

FYODOR IVANOVICH. Excellent.

DYADIN. Fascinating.

SONYA. Let me get this straight, gentlemen . . . In other words, right now we're going to the croquet lawn to settle the wager . . . Then we'll have an early dinner with Yulya and about seven we'll drive over to the Woo . . . I mean, to Mikhail Lvovich's. Wonderful. Let's go, Yulechka, and get the balls. (*She and YULYA exit into the house.*)

FYODOR IVANOVICH. Vasily, bring the wine to the croquet lawn! We'll drink to the health of the winner. Well, my old progenitor, let's take part in this noble game.

ORLOVSKY. Wait, my own dear boy, I have to sit with the professor for about five minutes, otherwise it would seem impolite. One has to observe etiquette. Meanwhile, play my ball, and I'll be there soon . . . (*Exits into the house.*)

DYADIN. I shall go at once and listen to the most learned Aleksandr Vladimirovich. I anticipate a sublime pleasure, whi . . .

VOINITSKY. I'm sick to death of you, Waffles. Go on.

DYADIN. I'm going, sir. (*Exits into the house.*)

FYODOR IVANOVICH (*going into the garden, sings*). "And thou shalt be queen of the world, my love for all eternity . . ."(*Exits.*)

KHRUSHCHOV. I'm going to slip away nice and quiet. (*To Voinitsky.*) Yegor Petrovich, I sincerely entreat you, let's never talk about forests or medicine again. I don't know why, but when you launch into that sort of talk, for the rest of the day I feel as if I've been eating my dinner out of a rusty pot. My respects! (*Exits.*)

V I I I

YELENA ANDREEVNA and VOINITSKY.

VOINITSKY. A narrow-minded fellow. Everyone is entitled to talk nonsense, but I don't like it when they talk it with deep feeling.

YELENA ANDREEVNA. Well, *Georges*, you behaved impossibly again! You had to provoke Mariya Vasilyevna and Aleksandr with talk about perpetual motion! It's all so petty!

VOINITSKY. And what if I hate him?

YELENA ANDREEVNA. There's no point in hating Aleksandr, he's the same as anybody else . . .

SONYA and YULYA cross into the garden with the croquet balls and mallets.

VOINITSKY. If you could see your face, your movements . . . What an indolent life you lead! Ah, the indolence of it!

YELENA ANDREEVNA. Ah, indolent and boring as well!

Pause.

Everyone insults my husband to my face, unconstrained by my presence. Everyone throws me sympathetic glances: unhappy creature, she's got an old husband! Everybody, even very respectable people, want me to leave Aleksandr . . . This concern for me, all these compassionate glances and sighs of pity come down to one thing. It's what the Wood Goblin was saying just now, you all recklessly chop down forests, and soon nothing will be left on earth. That's just how you recklessly destroy a human being, and soon, thanks to you, there won't be any loyalty or purity or capacity for self-sacrifice left on earth. Why can't you look at a decent woman with indifference if she isn't yours? Because—that Wood Goblin's right—inside all of you there lurks a demon of destruction. You have no pity for forests or birds or women or one another . . .

VOINITSKY. I don't like this philosophizing!

YELENA ANDREEVNA. Tell that Fyodor Ivanych that I'm fed up with his impertinence. It's beginning to be sickening. To look me in the face and tell me in front of everybody about his love for some married woman— wonderfully witty!

Voices in the garden: "Bravo! Bravo!"

And yet, how nice that Wood Goblin is! He stops by our place rather often, but I'm inhibited and haven't once had a proper chat with him, haven't shown him much affection. He probably thinks that I'm ill tempered and stuck-up. No doubt, *Georges*, that's why we're such friends, you and I, we're both exasperating, tiresome people! Exasperating! Don't look at me that way, I don't like it.

VOINITSKY. How else can I look at you if I love you? You're my happiness, life, my youth! . . . I know, my chances of reciprocity are practically nil, but I don't want anything, just let me look at you, hear your voice . . .

I X

The same and SEREBRYAKOV.

SEREBRYAKOV (*at the window*). Lenochka, where are you?

YELENA ANDREEVNA. Here.

SEREBRYAKOV. Come and sit with us a bit, my dear . . . (*Disappears.*)

YELENA ANDREEVNA exits into the house.

VOINITSKY (*following her*). Let me talk about my love, don't drive me away, and that alone will be my greatest joy.

Curtain

ACT TWO

Dining room in Serebryakov's house. A sideboard, and a dining table in the middle of the room. Past one o'clock at night. We can hear the watchman tapping in the garden.[19]

I

SEREBRYAKOV (*sits in an armchair before an open window and drowses*) *and YELENA ANDREEVNA* (*sits beside him and drowses too*).

SEREBRYAKOV (*waking*). Who's there? Sonya, you?

YELENA ANDREEVNA. I'm here . . .

SEREBRYAKOV. You, Lenochka . . . The pain's unbearable!

YELENA ANDREEVNA. Your lap rug's fallen on the floor . . . (*Wraps up his legs.*) Aleksandr, I'll close the window.

SEREBRYAKOV. No, I'm suffocating . . . I just now started to doze off and dreamed that my left leg belonged to somebody else . . . I woke up with the agonizing pain. No, it isn't gout, more like rheumatism. What's the time now?

YELENA ANDREEVNA. Twenty past one.

Pause.

SEREBRYAKOV. In the morning see if we've got a Batyushkov[20] in the library. I think we have him.

---

19 See *Ivanov*, First Version, note 19.

20 Konstantin Nikolaevich Batyushkov (1781–1855), Russian Romantic poet, an immediate forerunner of Pushkin, and author of the best anacreontic verse in Russian. Evidently the Professor wants to read about wine, woman, and song.

YELENA ANDREEVNA. Huh? . . .

SEREBRYAKOV. Look for Batyushkov's works in the morning. I seem to remember we had a copy. But why am I finding it so hard to breathe?

YELENA ANDREEVNA. You were tired. Second night without sleep.

SEREBRYAKOV. They say that Turgenev had gout that developed into *angina pectoris*.[21] I'm afraid I may have it too. Wretched, repulsive old age. Damn it to hell. When I got old, I began to disgust myself. Yes, and all the rest of you, I daresay, are disgusted to look at me.

YELENA ANDREEVNA. You talk about your old age as if it was our fault you're old.

SEREBRYAKOV. You're the first one to be disgusted by me.

YELENA ANDREEVNA. This is tiresome! (*She moves away and sits at a distance.*)

SEREBRYAKOV. Of course, you're in the right. I'm no fool and I understand. You're young, healthy, beautiful, enjoy life, while I'm an old man, practically a corpse. That's it, isn't it? Have I got it right? And, of course, it was stupid of me to live this long. But wait a while, I'll soon liberate you all. I can't manage to hang on much longer.

YELENA ANDREEVNA. Sasha, I'm worn out . . . If I've earned any reward for these sleepless nights, all I ask of you is: be quiet! For God's sake be quiet. That's all I ask.

SEREBRYAKOV. It turns out that thanks to me you're all worn out, bored, wasting your youth, I'm the only one enjoying life and having a good time. Oh, yes, of course!

YELENA ANDREEVNA. Do be quiet! You've run me ragged!

SEREBRYAKOV. I've run all of you ragged . . . Of course.

YELENA ANDREEVNA (*weeping*). This is unbearable! Say it, what do you want from me?

---

21 Latin for "a frog on the chest." Severe chest pain caused by deficient oxygenation of the heart muscles. The novelist Ivan Turgenev (1818–1883), who had suffered from gout, actually died of spinal cancer.

SEREBRYAKOV. Not a thing.

YELENA ANDREEVNA. Well then, be quiet; I beg of you.

SEREBRYAKOV. Funny, isn't it: let *Georges* start talking or that old she-idiot Mariya Vasilyevna—and nothing happens, everyone listens, but let me say just one word, watch how they all start feeling sorry for themselves. Even my voice is disgusting. Well, suppose I am disgusting, I'm selfish, I'm a tyrant, but surely in my old age haven't I got a right to be selfish? Surely I've earned it? I had a hard life. Ivan Ivanych and I were students together. Ask him. He kicked up his heels, consorted with gypsy girls, looked after me, and all the while I lived in a cheap, squalid room in a boarding house, worked night and day like an ox, starved and fretted because I was living off of somebody else. Later I was in Heidelberg and never saw Heidelberg; I was in Paris and never saw Paris: the whole time I sat indoors and worked. Once I got my chair, I devoted my whole life to the service of learning, as the saying goes, faithfully and honestly as I'm doing even now. Surely, I ask you, I've earned the right to a peaceful old age, to have people show me some consideration?

YELENA ANDREEVNA. No one is disputing your rights.

The window rattles in the wind.

The wind's rising, I'll close the window. (*Closes it.*) It'll rain presently. No one is disputing your rights.

Pause. The WATCHMAN *in the garden taps and sings a song.*

SEREBRYAKOV. To labor all one's life in the cause of learning, to grow accustomed to one's study, to the lecture hall, to esteemed colleagues and suddenly, with no rhyme or reason, to find oneself in this mausoleum, to spend every day seeing stupid people, listening to trivial chitchat . . . I want to live, I love success, I love celebrity, fame, and here it's like being in exile. Every minute yearning for the past, watching the successes of others, fearing death . . . I can't do it! I haven't got the strength! And on top of that they won't forgive me my old age!

YELENA ANDREEVNA. Wait, be patient: in five or six years I too shall be old.

Enter SONYA.

I I

The same and SONYA.

SONYA. I don't know why the doctor is taking so long. I told Stepan that if he couldn't find the district doctor[22] to go and get the Wood Goblin.

SEREBRYAKOV. What do I care about your Wood Goblin? He understands as much about medicine as I do about astronomy.

SONYA. Just for your gout we can't send for a whole medical school.

SEREBRYAKOV. I won't even give that maniac[23] the time of day.

SONYA. Have it your way. (*Sits.*) It's all the same to me.

SEREBRYAKOV. What's the time now?

YELENA ANDREEVNA. Nearly two.

SEREBRYAKOV. It's stifling . . . Sonya, get me the drops from the table!

SONYA. Right away. (*Gives him the drops.*)

SEREBRYAKOV (*aggravated*). Ah, not those! A person can't ask for a thing!

SONYA. Please don't be crotchety. Some people may care for it, but don't try it on me, if you'll be so kind. I do not like it.

SEREBRYAKOV. This girl has an impossible temper. What are you getting angry for?

SONYA. And why do you go on whining so miserably? For pity's sake, someone would think you actually were miserable. There are few people on this earth as lucky as you are.

SEREBRYAKOV. Yes, of course! I'm very, very lucky!

SONYA. Naturally, you're lucky . . . And if you do have gout, you know perfectly well that the attack will be gone by morning. What's there to moan about? What self-importance!

Enter VOINITSKY in dressing gown, holding a candle.

---

22 The official physician appointed by the *zemstvo* or rural board, like Dr. Lvov in *Ivanov*. Khrushchov practices as a sideline.

23 In the original, *yurodivy*, a holy fool, feebleminded beggars considered to be touched by God and hence licensed to speak the truth.

I I I

The same and VOINITSKY.

VOINITSKY. Clear out now! *Hélène* and Sonya, go to bed. I've come to take over for you.

SEREBRYAKOV (*terrified*). No, no, don't leave me with him! No! He'll talk me blue in the face!

VOINITSKY. But they've got to get some rest! This is the second night they've had no sleep.

SEREBRYAKOV. Let them go to bed, but you go away too. Thank you. I implore you. For the sake of our former friendship, don't protest. We'll talk later.

VOINITSKY. Our *former* friendship . . . I admit this is news to me.

YELENA ANDREEVNA. Be quiet, *Georges.*

SEREBRYAKOV. My dear, don't leave me alone with him! He'll talk me blue in the face!

VOINITSKY. This is starting to get ridiculous.

> KHRUSHCHOV's *voice offstage: "They're in the dining room?*
> *This way? Please have them see to my horse!"*

The doctor's come.

I V

The same and KHRUSHCHOV.

KHRUSHCHOV. How do you like this weather? The rain kept on my tail, and I barely got away from it. Good evening. (*Exchanges greetings.*)

SEREBRYAKOV. Excuse us for troubling you. I didn't ask for this at all.

KHRUSHCHOV. There, there, it doesn't matter! But what have you been getting up to, Aleksandr Vladimirovich? Aren't you ashamed to be under the weather? Dear, dear, that's naughty! What's the matter with you?

SEREBRYAKOV. Why do doctors always talk in that condescending tone of voice?

KHRUSHCHOV (*laughs*). Well, you shouldn't be so observant. (*Gently.*) Let's go to bed. You're not comfortable here. In bed you'll be warmer and more peaceful. Let's go . . . I'll examine you there and . . . and everything will be all right.

YELENA ANDREEVNA. Listen to him, Sasha, go on.

KHRUSHCHOV. If it hurts you to walk, we'll carry you there in this armchair.

SEREBRYAKOV. Never mind, I can do it . . . I can walk . . . (*Gets up.*) Only they've troubled you for nothing.

> *KHRUSHCHOV and SONYA take him under the arms.*

Besides, I'm not a great believer in . . . pharmaceuticals. Why are you escorting me? I can do it myself. (*Exits with KHRUSHCHOV and SONYA.*)

V

YELENA ANDREEVNA and VOINITSKY.

YELENA ANDREEVNA. I've worried myself sick over him. Can hardly stand on my feet.

VOINITSKY. He makes you sick and I make me sick. This is the third night now I haven't slept.

YELENA ANDREEVNA. There's something oppressive about this house. Your mother hates everything except her pamphlets and the Professor; the Professor is irritable, won't trust me, is afraid of you; Sonya's nasty to her father, nasty to me and won't talk to me; you hate my husband and openly despise your mother; I'm a nuisance, irritable and today some twenty times I was ready to burst into tears . . . In short, it's all-out war. I keep asking myself, what's the point of this war, what's it for?

VOINITSKY. Let's drop the philosophizing!

YELENA ANDREEVNA. There's something oppressive about this house. *Georges*, you're an educated, intelligent man, I should think you'd understand that the world is being destroyed not by criminals, not by fires, but by underhanded hatred, enmity between decent people, all this petty bickering, which goes unnoticed by those who refer to our house as a haven for highbrows. Help me to bring everyone together! I haven't got the strength to do it on my own.

VOINITSKY. First bring the two of us together! My darling . . . (*Clutches her hand.*)

YELENA ANDREEVNA. Stop it! (*Extricates her hand.*) Go away!

VOINITSKY. Any moment now the rain will end, and everything in nature will be refreshed and breathe easy. I'll be the only thing not refreshed by the storm. Day and night, like an incubus, the idea chokes me that my life has been wasted irretrievably. I've got no past, it's been stupidly squandered on trivialities, and the present is horrible in its absurdity. Here, take my life and my love; what am I to do with them? My better feelings are fading away for no reason at all, like a sunbeam trapped at the bottom of a mineshaft, and I'm fading along with them . . .

YELENA ANDREEVNA. Whenever you talk to me about your love, it's as if I go numb and don't know what to say. Forgive me, there's nothing I can say to you. (*About to go.*) Good-night!

VOINITSKY (*blocks her path*). And if only you had any idea how I suffer at the thought that right beside me in this house another life is fading away — yours! What are you waiting for? What damned philosophizing stands in your way? Face the fact that the highest morality does not consist of clapping your youth in irons and trying to stifle your zest for life . . .

YELENA ANDREEVNA (*stares fixedly at him*). Georges, you're drunk!

VOINITSKY. Could be, could be . . .

YELENA ANDREEVNA. Is Fyodor Ivanovich in your room?

VOINITSKY. He's spending the night in my room. Could be, could be. Anything could be!

YELENA ANDREEVNA. So you were drinking heavily today? What for?

VOINITSKY. It makes me feel alive somehow . . . Don't stop me, *Hélène*!

YELENA ANDREEVNA. You never used to drink and you never used to talk as much as you do now. Go to bed! You're boring me. And tell your friend Fyodor Ivanych that he doesn't stop pestering me, I shall take measures. Go on!

VOINITSKY (*clutching her hand*). My darling . . . wonderful woman!

Enter KHRUSHCHOV.

V I

The same and KHRUSHCHOV.

KHRUSHCHOV. Yelena Andreevna, Aleksandr Vladimirovich is asking for you.

YELENA ANDREEVNA (*extricating her hand from Voinitsky*). Right away!
(*Exits.*)

KHRUSHCHOV (*to Voinitsky*). There's nothing sacred to you! You and the
dear lady who just left should bear in mind that her husband was once
the husband of your sister and that a young girl is living with you under
the same roof! Your affair is already the talk of the whole district. What a
disgrace! (*Goes out to his patient.*)

VOINITSKY (*alone*). She left . . .

Pause.

Ten years ago I met her at my poor sister's. Then she was seventeen and I
was thirty-seven. Why didn't I fall in love with her then and propose to her?
After all it could have been! And now she'd be my wife . . . Yes . . . Now
both of us would be awakened by the storm; she'd be frightened by the
thunder and I'd hold her in my arms and whisper, "Don't be afraid, I'm
here." Oh, marvelous thoughts, wonderful, it makes me laugh . . . but, my
God, the thoughts are snarled up in my head . . . Why am I old? Why
doesn't she understand me? Her speechifying, indolent morality, indolent
drivel about destroying the world—it's profoundly hateful to me . . .

Pause.

Why was I born so nasty? How I envy that bad boy Fyodor or that idiotic
Wood Goblin! They're spontaneous, sincere idiots . . . They don't suffer
this damned, poisonous irony . . .

Enter FYODOR IVANOVICH, wrapped in a blanket.

V I I

VOINITSKY and FYODOR IVANOVICH.

FYODOR IVANOVICH (*in the doorway*). You alone here? No ladies?
(*Enters.*) The storm woke me up. An impressive little downpour. What's
the time now?

VOINITSKY. How the hell should I know!

FYODOR IVANOVICH. Could have sworn I heard the voice of Yelena Andreevna.

VOINITSKY. She was here a moment ago.

FYODOR IVANOVICH. Magnificent woman! (*Spots the medicine bottles on the table.*) What's all this? Peppermint drops? (*Tastes.*) Yes indeed, a magnificent woman . . . Is the Professor sick or what?

VOINITSKY. Sick.

FYODOR IVANOVICH. I don't understand that kind of existence. They say that the ancient Greeks would fling feeble and sickly children off Mont Blanc into an abyss. His sort should be flung in too!

VOINITSKY (*irritated*). Not Mont Blanc, but the Tarpeian rock.[24] What crass ignorance! . . .

FYODOR IVANOVICH. Well, one rock's much like any other . . . as if I gave a good goddam? Why are you so mopey today? Feel sorry for the Professor or what?

VOINITSKY. Leave me alone.

Pause.

FYODOR IVANOVICH. Or else, maybe, in love with the Professor's lady? Huh? That's it! It could happen . . . sigh . . . only watch out: if the gossip going round the district has only one hundredth of a particle of truth in it and I find out about it, don't bother pleading for mercy, I'll fling you off the Tarpeian rock . . .

VOINITSKY. She's my friend.

FYODOR IVANOVICH. Already?

VOINITSKY. What's that mean — "already"?

FYODOR IVANOVICH. A woman can be a man's friend only in the following sequence: first, an acquaintance, next, a mistress, and thereafter a friend.

VOINITSKY. A vulgar philosophy.

FYODOR IVANOVICH. On which account we've got to have a drink. Let's go, I think I've still got some Chartreuse left. Let's have a drink. And when

---

24 They're both wrong: the ancient Romans threw condemned criminals off the Tarpeian rock.

it's light, we'll head over to my place. Want to go for a rod? I've got a book-keeper, Luka, who never says "ride," always says, "rod."[25] Terrible crook. So, want to go for a rod? (*Seeing SONYA enter.*) Heavens to Betsy, 'scuse me, I'm not wearing a tie. (*Runs out.*)

V I I I

VOINITSKY *and* SONYA.

SONYA. So, Uncle *Georges*, you and Fedka were drinking champagne again and riding around in the troika. Birds of a feather flock together. Well, he's been an incorrigible, natural-born playboy for quite some time, but are you? At your age it doesn't suit you at all.

VOINITSKY. Age has nothing to do with it. When life has no reality, people live on illusions. After all it's better than nothing.

SONYA. All our hay is mown; Gerasim told me today that everything's rotting in the rain, and you're obsessed with illusions. (*Alarmed.*) Uncle, there are tears in your eyes!

VOINITSKY. What tears? Nothing of the sort . . . don't be silly . . . Just now the way you looked at me like your poor mother. My precious . . . (*Avidly kisses her hands and face.*) My dear sister . . . my darling sister . . . Where is she now? If only she knew! Ah, if only she knew!

SONYA. What? Uncle, knew what?

VOINITSKY. Oppressive, wrong . . . Never mind . . .

Enter KHRUSHCHOV.

Later . . . Never mind . . . I'm going . . . (*Goes.*)

I X

SONYA *and* KHRUSHCHOV.

KHRUSHCHOV. Your daddy absolutely refuses to obey orders. I tell him it's gout, and he says it's rheumatism; I ask him to lie down, he sits up. (*Takes his peaked cap.*) Nerves.

---

25 In Russian, the wordplay is on *idet*, "let's go, let's pay a visit," and *idyot*, which sounds like *idiot*, "imbecile," a joke Chekhov often used privately, especially in letters to his brother Aleksandr.

SONYA. He's spoiled. Put your cap away. Wait until the rain is over. Would you like a bite to eat?

KHRUSHCHOV. Yes, I suppose so.

SONYA. I love midnight snacks. I think there's something in the sideboard. (*Rummaging in the sideboard.*) Does he really need a doctor? What he needs is a dozen ladies sitting beside him, staring into his eyes and moaning, "Professor!" Here, have some cheese . . .

KHRUSHCHOV. You shouldn't talk about your own father like that. I agree, he's a difficult case, but if you compare him with the rest, all those Uncle *Georges*es and Ivan Ivanychs aren't worth his little finger.

SONYA. Here's a bottle of something. I'm not referring to my father, but to the great man. I love my father, but great men with their Byzantine ceremonials have me bored to tears.

They sit down.

What a downpour!

Lightning.

Look!

KHRUSHCHOV. The storm's passing over, we'll only catch the tail-end of it.

SONYA (*pouring*). Have a drink.

KHRUSHCHOV. Long life to you. (*Drinks.*)

SONYA. Are you angry with us for rousting you out at night?

KHRUSHCHOV. On the contrary. If you hadn't, I would be asleep now, and seeing you in the flesh is far more pleasant than dreaming about you.

SONYA. Then how come you look so angry?

KHRUSHCHOV. Because I am angry. There's nobody around, so a man can speak frankly. How pleased I'd be, Sofya Aleksandrovna, to take you away from here this minute. I cannot breathe this air of yours, and I think that it's poisoning you. Your father, all wrapped up in his gout and his books and reluctant to recognize anything else, that Uncle *Georges* with his biliousness, lastly your stepmother . . .

SONYA. What about my stepmother?

KHRUSHCHOV. There are no words to express it . . . there simply aren't! My lovely girl, there's a lot I don't understand about people. Everything about a human being ought to be beautiful: face, dress, soul, ideas . . . Often I'll see a beautiful face and a dress to match that make my head swim with ecstasy, but the soul and the ideas—good God! A handsome exterior may sometimes conceal a soul so black that no bleach can whiten it . . . Forgive me, I'm getting carried away . . . You really are infinitely dear to me . . .

SONYA (*drops a knife*). I dropped it . . .

KHRUSHCHOV (*picks it up*). Never mind . . .

Pause.

Sometimes, when you walk through a forest on a dark night, if all the time in the distance there's a glimmer of light, you don't mind the fatigue or the dark or the prickly branches hitting you in the face. I work from morn to darkest night, winter and summer, knowing no rest, I contend with people who don't understand me, at times I suffer unbearably . . . but I've finally found my glimmer of light. I won't boast that I love you more than anything else in the world. Love for me is not the be-all and end-all in life . . . it is my reward! My good one, my glorious one, there is no higher reward for someone who works, struggles, suffers . . .

SONYA (*excited*). Sorry . . . Just one question, Mikhail Lvovich.

KHRUSHCHOV. What? Ask it quickly . . .

SONYA. Don't you see . . . you often drop in on us, and sometimes I drop in on you with my folks. Admit that that makes you feel guilty . . .

KHRUSHCHOV. For what?

SONYA. What I mean is, your democratic feelings are offended by the fact that we're your close acquaintances. I went to a private girls' school. Yelena Andreevna is an aristocrat, we dress fashionably, and you're a democrat . . .

KHRUSHCHOV. So that's it . . . that's it . . . let's not talk about it! Now is not the time!

SONYA. What matters is that you dig peat with your own hands, you plant trees . . . it's rather peculiar. In other words, you're a populist . . .[26]

---

26 *Narodnik*, member of a revolutionary movement, following the teachings of Aleksandr Herzen and Mikhail Bakunin, which, in the "crazy summer" of 1873, sent young people into the country to educate the peasants.

KHRUSHCHOV. A democrat, a populist . . . Sofya Aleksandrovna, can you say that seriously and even with a quaver in your voice?

SONYA. Yes, yes, seriously, a thousand times seriously.

KHRUSHCHOV. No, no, no . . .

SONYA. I assure you and swear by whatever you like that if I had, say, a sister and you fell in love with her and proposed to her, you would never forgive yourself for it, and you'd be ashamed to look in the faces of your district doctors and female physicians, ashamed that you had fallen in love with a boarding school miss, a prim and proper young lady who never majored in anything and dresses in the latest fashions. I know this perfectly well . . . I see in your eyes that it's true! In a word, to cut a long story short, these forests of yours, the peat, the embroidered peasant blouses—they're all a pose, an affectation, a lie and nothing more.

KHRUSHCHOV. What's this for? My child, why are you insulting me? Anyhow, I am an imbecile. It serves me right: don't stick your nose in where it's not wanted! Good-bye! (*Goes to the door.*)

SONYA. Good-bye . . . I was harsh, please forgive me.

KHRUSHCHOV (*returning*). If you only knew how oppressive and stifling it is here! An environment in which everyone sidles up to a man, peers at him out of the corner of their eye and pigeonholes as him as a populist, a psychopath, a windbag—anything at all other than a human being! "Oh, that one," they'll say, "he's a psychopath!"—and be delighted. "That one's a windbag!"—and they're as pleased as if they'd discovered America! And when they don't understand me and don't know what label to stick on my brow, they say, "He's peculiar, really peculiar!" You're not yet twenty, but already you're old and no-nonsense like your father and Uncle *Georges*, and I wouldn't be at all surprised if you invited me over to treat your gout. That's no way to live! Whoever I am, look me straight in the eye and identify me first as a human being, otherwise you'll never be at peace in your dealings with people. Good-bye! And mark my words, with those shrewd, suspicious eyes of yours, you'll never fall in love!

SONYA. That isn't true!

KHRUSHCHOV. It is!

SONYA. It isn't true! Just to spite you . . . I am in love! I am in love, and it pains me, pains me! Leave me alone! Go away, I entreat you . . . don't visit our house . . . don't visit us . . .

KHRUSHCHOV. I am honored to take my leave! (*Exits.*)

SONYA (*alone*). He flew into a rage . . . God forbid I ever have a temper like that man's!

Pause.

He speaks beautifully, but how can I be sure that it isn't just hot air? He's constantly thinking and talking about his forests, he plants trees . . . That's all very well, but it could be that it's a psychosis . . . (*Covers her face with her hands.*) I don't understand a thing! (*Weeps.*) He studied medicine, but he doesn't spend any time practicing medicine . . . It's all so peculiar, peculiar . . . Lord, help me to figure this out!

Enter YELENA ANDREEVNA.

X

SONYA and YELENA ANDREEVNA.

YELENA ANDREEVNA (*opens a window*). The storm has passed! What lovely air!

Pause.

Where's the Wood Goblin?

SONYA. Gone.

Pause.

YELENA ANDREEVNA. *Sophie!*

SONYA. What?

YELENA ANDREEVNA. Are you going to go on sulking at me? We haven't done one another any harm. Why do we have to be enemies? Enough is enough . . .

SONYA. I wanted to myself . . . (*Embraces her.*) My dear!

YELENA ANDREEVNA. Splendid . . .

Both are agitated.

SONYA. Is Papa in bed?

YELENA ANDREEVNA. No, he's sitting in the parlor . . . We don't talk to one another for months on end and God knows why . . . (*Notices the table.*) What's this?

SONYA. The Wood Goblin had some supper.

YELENA ANDREEVNA. And there's some wine . . . Let's pledge one another as sisters.[27]

SONYA. Let's.

YELENA ANDREEVNA. Out of the same glass . . . (*Pours.*) That's better. Well, here goes—friends?

SONYA. Friends.[28]

They drink and kiss.

For a long time now I've wanted to make it up, but somehow I was embarrassed . . . (*Weeps.*)

YELENA ANDREEVNA. What are you crying for?

SONYA. No reason, it's the way I am.

YELENA ANDREEVNA. Well, never mind, never mind . . . (*Weeps.*) You little crackpot, now you've got me crying!

Pause.

You're angry with me because you think I married your father for ulterior motives . . . If you'll believe an oath, I'll swear to you, I married him for love. I was attracted to him as a scholar and a celebrity. The love was unreal, artificial, but at the time I thought it was real. It's not my fault. But from the day we got married you've gone on punishing me with your shrewd, suspicious eyes.

SONYA. Well, truce, truce! We'll forget. That's the second time today I've heard that I've got shrewd, suspicious eyes.

---

27 In the original, she uses the German word *Bruderschaft*, "brotherhood" or "fellowship." They are pledging, arms linked, out of one glass, like fraternity brothers.

28 Literally, *na ty*, meaning their relationship will now be on a "thou" basis, rather than the formal "you."

YELENA ANDREEVNA. You mustn't look at people that way. It doesn't suit you. You must trust everyone, otherwise life becomes unliveable.

SONYA. The burnt child fears the fire. I've been disappointed so many times.

YELENA ANDREEVNA. By whom? Your father is a good, honorable man, a hard worker. Today you scolded him for being lucky. If he really has been lucky, his involvement in his work would prevent him from noticing how lucky he is. I have done no intentional wrong to your father or you. Your uncle *Georges* is a very kind, honorable, but unhappy, discontented man . . . Then who is it you don't trust?

SONYA. Tell me truthfully, friend to friend . . . Are you happy?

YELENA ANDREEVNA. No.

SONYA. One more question. Tell me frankly, would you like to have a young husband?

YELENA ANDREEVNA. What a little girl you are still . . . Of course I would! (*Laughs.*) Go on, ask me something else, ask me . . .

SONYA. Do you like the Wood Goblin?

YELENA ANDREEVNA. Yes, very much.

SONYA (*laughs*). I must look funny . . . don't I? Now he's gone, but I keep hearing his voice and footsteps, and I look out the dark window—and his face appears to me. Let me say what's on my mind . . . But I can't say it out loud, I'm embarrassed. Let's go to my room, we'll talk there. Do you think I'm being silly? Admit it . . . Is he a good man?

YELENA ANDREEVNA. Very, very.

SONYA. It all seems so peculiar, his forests, the peat . . . I don't understand.

YELENA ANDREEVNA. Are forests really the point? Darling, what you have to understand is, he's got talent![29] Do you know the meaning of talent? Daring, an uncluttered mind, breadth of vision . . . he plants a tree or digs a ton of peat—and already he's planning ahead, what the result will be in a thousand years, he's already imagining the happiness of mankind. Peo-

---

[29] "Talent" is one of Chekhov's favorite words of praise, equivalent almost to "genius." His characters name it as a positive quality when they are unable to specify someone's virtues. The opposite, "untalented," is extremely negative.

ple like that are rare, and one must love them. God bless you. You're both pure, daring, honest . . . He's a bit unbalanced, you're sensible, intelligent . . . You'll complement one another wonderfully . . . (*Gets up.*) But mine is a dreary walk-on part . . . In the field of music and in my husband's house, in any of life's dramas—no matter where, in short, I've only had a walk-on part. Personally speaking, Sonya, when you think about it, I'm probably very, very unhappy! (*Walks nervously around the stage.*) No happiness for me in this world. No! Why are you laughing?

SONYA (*laughs, covering her face*). I'm so happy! How happy I am!

YELENA ANDREEVNA (*wringing her hands*). As a matter of fact, how unhappy I am!

SONYA. I'm happy . . . happy.

YELENA ANDREEVNA. I'd like to play the piano . . . I want to play something right now . . .

SONYA. Do play. (*Embraces her.*) I can't sleep . . . Play.

YELENA ANDREEVNA. Presently. Your father isn't asleep. When he's ill, music irritates him. Go and ask. If he doesn't object, I'll play . . . go on . . .

SONYA. Right this minute. (*Exits.*)

In the garden the WATCHMAN is tapping.

YELENA ANDREEVNA. It's been a long time since I played. I'll play and weep, weep like a fool . . . (*Out the window.*) Is that you tapping, Yefim?

Voice of the WATCHMAN: Uh-huh!

Don't tap, the master's not well.

Voice of the WATCHMAN: "I'll go right now! (Whistles under his breath.) Blacky! Laddy! Blacky!" [30]

Pause.

SONYA (*returning*). The answer's no!

Curtain

---

30 *Zhuchka*, from *zhuk*, beetle, a common name for a black dog.

ACT THREE

*The drawing-room in Serebryakov's house. Three doors: right, left
and center. Daytime. We can hear Yelena Andreevna offstage
playing on the piano Lensky's aria preceding the duel in
Yevgeny Onegin.*[31]

I

*ORLOVSKY, VOINITSKY, and FYODOR IVANOVICH
(the last in Circassian costume with a fur shako in his hand).*

VOINITSKY (*listening to the music*). That's Yelena Andreevna playing . . . My favorite piece . . .

The offstage music fades away.

Yes . . . a fine piece . . . I don't think it's ever been so boring around here as it is now . . .

FYODOR IVANOVICH. You have no idea what real boredom is, my boy. When I was a volunteer in Serbia, that's what I call boredom! Hot, muggy, dirty, head splitting with a hangover . . . Captain Kashkinazi was with me . . . Ran out of conversation ages ago, nowhere to go, nothing to do, don't feel like drinking—sickening, get me, you simply want to stick your head in a noose! We sit, like vipers, glaring at one another . . . He glares at me, and I glare at him . . . I glare at him, and he glares at me . . . We glare at one another and don't know why . . . Another hour, get me, goes by, and we go on glaring. Suddenly out of the blue he jumps up, grabs his saber and goes for me . . . What d'ye think of that! . . . Of course, I immediately—he's about to kill me!—draw my saber, and we go at it hot and heavy: chik-chak, chik-chak, chik-chak . . . They had a hard time pulling us apart. I was all right afterward, but Captain Kashkinazi goes around with a scar on his cheek to this very day. That how fed up to the gills people can get sometimes . . .

---

31 The young poet Lensky sings this aria in Chaikovsky's opera *Yevgeny Onegin* (based on Pushkin's verse novel), just before he is killed in a duel.

ORLOVSKY. Yes, it happens.

Enter SONYA.

I I

The same and SONYA.

SONYA (*aside*). I don't know what to do with myself . . . (*Walks and laughs.*)

ORLOVSKY. Pussycat, where are you off to? Sit with us.

SONYA. Fedya, come over here . . . (*She leads Fyodor Ivanovich aside.*) Come over here . . .

FYODOR IVANOVICH. What's got into you? Why is do you look so radiant?

SONYA. Fedya, give me your word you'll do what I ask!

FYODOR IVANOVICH. Well?

SONYA. Ride over . . . to the Wood Goblin.

FYODOR IVANOVICH. What for?

SONYA. No reason . . . just ride over . . . Ask him how come he hasn't been here for so long . . . Two weeks now.

FYODOR IVANOVICH. She's blushing! For shame! Gentlemen, Sonya is in love!

EVERYONE. For shame! For shame!

SONYA covers her face and runs away.

FYODOR IVANOVICH. She slinks around from room to room like a shadow and doesn't know what to do with herself. She's in love with the Wood Goblin.

ORLOVSKY. A splendid little girl . . . I love her. I had hoped, Fedyusha, that you would marry her—you couldn't find a better bride, oh well, I suppose it's God's will . . . But how nice and pleasant it would have been for me! I'd drive over to your place, and you'd have a young wife, a hearth and home, the little samovar would be boiling away . . .

FYODOR IVANOVICH. That's not my cup of tea. If I ever did have a bee in my bonnet about getting married, I'd probably marry Yulya. She's small, at least, and you should always pick the lesser of two evils. And she's a good housekeeper too . . . (*Slaps his forehead.*) I've got an idea!

ORLOVSKY. What's the matter?

FYODOR IVANOVICH. Let's have some champagne!

VOINITSKY. It's too early, besides it's hot . . . Wait a while . . .

ORLOVSKY (*admiring*). My sonny boy, my beauty . . . He wants champagne, the dear boy!

Enter YELENA ANDREEVNA.

III

The same and YELENA ANDREEVNA.

YELENA ANDREEVNA walks across the stage.

VOINITSKY. Wonder at her: she can't walk, without tottering from sheer indolence. Very charming! Very!

YELENA ANDREEVNA. Stop it, *Georges*. It's boring enough without your buzzing around.

VOINITSKY (*blocking her path*). A talent, an artist! Well, do you look like an artist? An apathetic, Oblomov-like[32] sluggard . . . So very virtuous that, forgive me, it makes me sick to look at you.

YELENA ANDREEVNA. Then don't look . . . Leave me alone . . .

VOINITSKY. Why are you mooning about? (*Vigorously.*) Come, my dear, show how clever you are! The blood of water nymphs courses through your veins, be a water nymph!

YELENA ANDREEVNA. Give over!

VOINITSKY. Satisfy your desires at least once in your life, fall in love as fast as you can, head over heels, with some water sprite . . .[33]

---

32 The title character of Goncharov's novel, synonymous with sloth, indolence, lack of energy, negligence, and apathy.

33 A water nymph or *rusalka* is not a mermaid; although she is dangerous and sexy, she is also undead, usually the spirit of a drowned girl. A water sprite or *vodovoy* is more benign, the aquatic equivalent of a wood sprite or *leshy*.

FYODOR IVANOVICH. Plop! take a nosedive into a whirlpool, so that Herr Professor and the rest of us throw up our hands in amazement!

VOINITSKY. A water nymph, eh? Love while the loving is good![34]

YELENA ANDREEVNA. And what do you know about it? As if I weren't aware without your help how I should live, if I had my way! I would fly like an uncaged bird away from you all, from your drowsy expressions, boring, idle chatter, forget that you even exist, and then no one would dare teach me lessons. But I have no will of my own. I'm a coward, inhibited, and I go on thinking that if I were unfaithful, all wives would take an example from me and leave their husbands, God would punish me and my conscience would torment me, otherwise I'd show you what a free life is all about! (*Exits.*)

ORLOVSKY. A darling, a beauty . . .

VOINITSKY. I think I'm about to despise that woman! Inhibited as a young virgin, but philosophizes like an old deacon, a paragon of virtue! Sour grapes! Curdled cream!

ORLOVSKY. That'll do, that'll do . . . Where's the professor now?

VOINITSKY. In his study. Writing.

ORLOVSKY. He sent me a letter to come here on some business natter. Do you know what the business is?

VOINITSKY. He has no business. He writes drivel, moans and groans and oozes envy, that's all.

> *ZHELTUKHIN and YULYA enter from the door at right.*

I V

The same, ZHELTUKHIN, and YULYA.

ZHELTUKHIN. Good afternoon, gentlemen! (*Exchanges greetings.*)

YULYA. Good afternoon, godfather dear! (*Exchanges kisses.*) Good afternoon, Fedenka. (*Exchanges kisses.*) Good afternoon, Yegor Petrovich! (*Exchanges kisses.*)

---

34 From Nikolay Nekrasov's nature poem "The Green Sound" (1862). In the earlier version of the play, Zheltukhin quotes it at length in the last act. See Variants.

ZHELTUKHIN. Is Aleksandr Vladimirovich in?

ORLOVSKY. He is. He's in his study.

ZHELTUKHIN. I have to see him. He wrote me about some business deal . . . (*Exits.*)

YULYA. Yegor Petrovich, did you get the buckwheat yesterday you sent that note about?

VOINITSKY. Thank you, I did. How much do we owe you? We had a delivery of something else from you last spring, I don't remember what . . . We'll have to settle up. I can't stand disorderly accounts and postponed payments.

YULYA. Last spring we delivered sixty-four bushels of rye, Yegor Petrovich, two heifers, a bull-calf, and your farmhands sent for some butter.

VOINITSKY. How much do we owe you?

YULYA. How can I tell you? I can't say without an abacus.

VOINITSKY. I'll get an abacus right away, if that's what you need . . . (*Exits and immediately returns with an abacus.*)

ORLOVSKY. Sweetie-pie, how's your brother-man?

YULYA. Fine, thank God. Godfather dear, where did you buy that necktie?

ORLOVSKY. In town, at Kirpichyov's.

YULYA. It's handsome. I'll have to buy Lyonechka one just like it.

VOINITSKY. Here's the abacus you wanted.

> *YULYA sits down and clicks the beads on the abacus.*

ORLOVSKY. What a housekeeper God bestowed on Lyonya! A mere dot of a thing, invisible to the naked eye, but look how she works! Just look!

FYODOR IVANOVICH. Yes, while he just walks around pressing his cheek. The loafer . . .

ORLOVSKY. My cape-ricious darling . . . You know, she really does wear a cape. Last Friday I was walking around the bazaar, and she was over near the wagons in a cape . . .

YULYA. You've mixed me all up.

VOINITSKY. Let's go somewhere else, gentlemen. The reception room or somewhere. I'm sick and tired of this place . . . (*Yawns.*)

ORLOVSKY. The reception room it is . . . I couldn't care less.

They go out through the door at left.

YULYA (*alone, after a pause*). Fedya dressed up like a Chechen[35] . . . That's what happens when parents don't raise them properly . . . There's no better-looking man in all the district, intelligent, rich, and good for absolutely nothing . . . A perfect fool . . . (*Clicks beads on the abacus.*)

Enter SONYA.

V

YULYA and SONYA.

SONYA. You're here, Yulechka? I didn't know . . .

YULYA (*exchanges kisses*). My dear!

SONYA. What are you doing here? Accounts? What a good housekeeper you are, it even makes me jealous . . . Yulechka, why aren't you married?

YULYA. Well . . . They sent a matchmaker to me, but I turned them down. They can't match me up with a decent suitor! (*Sighs.*) No!

SONYA. Why not?

YULYA. I'm an uneducated girl. I was just in my second year in high school, when they took me out!

SONYA. Why did they take you out, Yulechka?

YULYA. For incompetence.

SONYA laughs.

Why are you laughing, Sonechka?

---

35 The Chechens are fiercely independent, Islamic natives of the eastern Caucasus, occupying west Daghestan. They fought desperately against Russian aggression in the eighteenth and nineteenth centuries until their chieftain, Shamyl, surrendered in 1859, when many of them fled to the mountains or to Armenia.

SONYA. Something odd is going through my mind . . . Yulechka, I'm so happy today, so happy, that this happiness is beginning to bore me . . . I don't know what to do with myself . . . Well, let's talk about something else, let's . . . Were you ever in love?

YULYA nods her head Yes.

Really? Is he interesting?

YULYA whispers in her ear.

Who? Fyodor Ivanych?

YULYA (*nods her head yes*). What about you?

SONYA. I am too . . . only not with Fyodor Ivanych. (*Laughs.*) Well, tell me more.

YULYA. For a long time now I've needed to talk to you, Sonechka.

SONYA. Please do.

YULYA. I want to explain something. You see . . . I've always felt a spiritual bond with you . . . I'm friends with lots of girls, but you're the best of them all . . . If you were to say, "Yulechka, give me ten horses or, say, two hundred sheep," I'd do it with pleasure . . . I would refuse you nothing . . .

SONYA. What's making you embarrassed, Yulechka?

YULYA. I'm ashamed . . . I . . . I feel a spiritual bond with you . . . you're the best of them all . . . not proud . . . What a pretty little cotton print you're got on!

SONYA. We'll talk about the print later . . . Go on . . .

YULYA (*getting excited*). I don't know the clever way to put this . . . May I suggest that you . . . make me happy . . . I mean . . . I mean . . . I mean . . . by marrying Lyonechka. (*Hides her face.*)

SONYA (*getting up*). Let's not talk about it, Yulechka . . . We mustn't, we mustn't . . .

Enter YELENA ANDREEVNA.

V I

The same and YELENA ANDREEVNA.

YELENA ANDREEVNA. There's absolutely nowhere to go to. Both Orlovskys and *Georges* are strolling around the house, and wherever you go, they're always there. It's getting to be simply tiresome. What do they want? They should take a drive somewhere.

YULYA (*through tears*). Good afternoon, Yelena Andreevna! (*Wants to exchange kisses.*)

YELENA ANDREEVNA. Good afternoon, Yulechka. Excuse me, I'm not very fond of kissing. Sonya, what is your father doing?

Pause.

Sonya, why don't you answer me? I asked you: what is your father doing?

Pause.

Sonya, how come you won't answer me?

SONYA. You want to know? Come over here please . . . (*Leads her somewhat aside.*) If you like, I'll tell you . . . My heart feels too pure today for me to speak to you while I go on concealing things. Here, take this! (*Hands her a letter.*) I found this in the garden. Yulechka, let's go! (*Exits with YULYA out the door at left.*)

V I I

YELENA ANDREEVNA, then FYODOR IVANOVICH.

YELENA ANDREEVNA (*alone*). What is this? A letter from *Georges* to me! Why is that my fault? Oh, how cruel, how brazen . . . Her heart is so pure that she cannot talk to me . . . My God, what an insult . . . My head is spinning, I'm going to faint . . .

FYODOR IVANOVICH (*enters through the door at left and walks across the stage*). Why do you always act startled whenever you see me?

Pause.

Hm . . . (*Takes the letter from her hands and tears it to shreds.*) Forget about it. You must think only of me.

YELENA ANDREEVNA. What's the meaning of this?

FYODOR IVANOVICH. The meaning is that once I've made up my mind about a woman, she won't get out of my clutches.

YELENA ANDREEVNA. No, the meaning is that you're idiotic and impertinent.

FYODOR IVANOVICH. At seven-thirty this evening you must be at the bottom of the garden by the little bridge, waiting for me . . . Well, ma'am? That's all I have to say to you . . . And so, angel mine, until seven-thirty. (*Wants to take her by the hand.*)

YELENA ANDREEVNA slaps his face.

Forcefully expressed . . .

YELENA ANDREEVNA. Get out of here!

FYODOR IVANOVICH. At your service, ma'am . . . (*Goes and returns.*) I am touched . . . Let us reason together calmly. You see . . . I've experienced everything in this world, I've even eaten goldfish soup a couple of times . . . But I haven't yet gone up in a balloon or even once run off with the wives of learned professors . . .

YELENA ANDREEVNA. Get out . . .

FYODOR IVANOVICH. I'll go in a minute . . . I've experienced everything . . . And that's made me so impertinent, that I simply don't know what to do with myself. I mean I'm telling you all of this so that if you ever need a friend or a faithful dog, then call on me . . . I'm touched . . .

YELENA ANDREEVNA. I don't need any dogs . . . Get out.

FYODOR IVANOVICH. At your service . . . (*Deeply moved.*) Nevertheless, and all the same, I'm touched . . . I am definitely touched . . . Yes . . . (*Hesitantly exits.*)

YELENA ANDREEVNA (*alone*). My head is splitting . . . Every night I have bad dreams and a premonition of something horrible . . . Yet how despicable this is! These young people were born and raised together, they're on a first-name basis with each another, they're always kissing: they should live in peace and harmony, but they look as if they're about to sink their teeth into one another . . . The Wood Goblin is saving the forests, but who is there to save the people? (*Goes to the door at left, but, on seeing ZHEL-TUKHIN and YULYA coming to meet her, exits through the central door.*)

V I I I

ZHELTUKHIN and YULYA.

YULYA. How unlucky we are, Lyonechka, ah, how unlucky!

ZHELTUKHIN. Who gave you permission to talk to her about me? A free-lance matchmaker, you unspeakable female! You've spoiled it all for me! She'll think that I don't know how to speak for myself, and . . . and it's so lower-class! I've said a thousand times that we should leave it alone. Nothing but humiliation and all this innuendo, bad behavior, vulgarity . . . The old man has probably figured out that I'm in love with her, and is already taking advantage of my feelings! He wants me to buy this estate from him.

YULYA. How much is he asking?

ZHELTUKHIN. Ssh! . . . Someone's coming . . .

> *Enter from the door at left SEREBRYAKOV, ORLOVSKY, and MARIYA VASILYEVNA, who is reading a pamphlet along the way.*

I X

The same, SEREBRYAKOV, ORLOVSKY, and MAIYA VASILYEVNA.

ORLOVSKY. I'm not in the best of health either, my dear boy. Why, for two days now my head's been aching and my whole body tingles . . .

SEREBRYAKOV. Where are the others? I do not like this house. Just like a labyrinth. Twenty-six enormous rooms, everyone scatters, and you can never find anyone. (*Rings.*) Request Yegor Petrovich and Yelena Andreevna to come here!

ZHELTUKHIN. Yulya, you've got nothing to do, go and find Yegor Petrovich and Yelena Andreevna.

> *YULYA exits.*

SEREBRYAKOV. Ill health one might be reconciled to, if the worse came to the worst, but what I cannot stomach is my state of mind at present. I have the feeling that I'm already dead or have dropped off the earth on to some alien planet.

ORLOVSKY. It depends on how you look at it . . .

MARIYA VASILYEVNA (*reading*). Give me a pencil . . . Another contradiction! I have to jot it down.

ORLOVSKY. Please take this one, Your Excellency! (*Hands her a pencil and kisses her hand.*)

Enter VOINITSKY.

X

The same, VOINITSKY, then YELENA ANDREEVNA.

VOINITSKY. You're asking for me?

SEREBRYAKOV. Yes, *Georges.*

VOINITSKY. What do you want from me, sir?[36]

SEREBRYAKOV. Sir? . . . Why are you getting angry?

Pause.

If I've offended you in any way, then please forgive me . . .

VOINITSKY. Drop that tone . . . Let's get down to business . . . What do you want?

Enter YELENA ANDREEVNA.

SEREBRYAKOV. And here's Lenochka . . . Please take your seats, ladies and gentlemen.

Pause.

I have invited you here, my friends, to inform you that we are about to be visited by an Inspector General.[37] However, joking aside. The matter is a serious one. Ladies and gentlemen, I have convened you in order to solicit your aid and advice and, knowing your customary civility, I trust to receive them. I am a man of learning, a bookworm, and have ever been a stranger

---

36 In the original, Voinitsky uses the formal "you," *vy*, whereas the Professor addresses him with the informal *ty*.

37 The famous opening line of the Mayor in Gogol's classic comedy *The Inspector General*, Act I, scene 1, to the officials who have gathered in his house. A cliché joke of pedagogues.

to practical life. I cannot do without the counsel of informed individuals, and so I ask you, Ivan Ivanych, and you, Leonid Stepanych, and you, *Georges* . . . What it comes down to is *manet omnes una nox*,[38] that is, we are all mortal in the sight of God; I am old, ill and therefore deem it appropriate to regulate my material concerns insofar as they relate to my family. My life is over now, it's not myself I'm thinking of, but I have a young wife, an unmarried daughter . . . To go on living in the country I find impossible.

YELENA ANDREEVNA. It's all the same to me.

SEREBRYAKOV. We were not made for country life. To live in town on those funds which we earn from this estate is equally impossible. The day before yesterday I sold the forest for four thousand rubles, but that is an extraordinary measure which could not be taken advantage of annually. We must seek out measures which will guarantee us a regular, more or less fixed amount of income. I have thought of one such measure and I have the honor to submit it for your discussion. Leaving aside the details, I set it forth in its general outlines. Our estate yields on average no more than two percent. I propose to sell it. If we turn the money thus acquired into interest-bearing securities, we shall receive from four to five percent. I think there may even be a surplus of a few thousand, which will enable us to buy a small cottage in Finland . . .[39]

VOINITSKY. Hold on, my ears seem to be deceiving me. Repeat what you just said . . .

SEREBRYAKOV. Turn the money into interest-bearing securities and with the surplus left over buy a cottage in Finland . . .

VOINITSKY. Not Finland . . . You said something else.

SEREBRYAKOV. I propose to sell the estate.

VOINITSKY. There, that's it . . . You'll sell the estate . . . Splendid, good thinking . . . And where do you propose I go with my old mother?

SEREBRYAKOV. All that will be discussed in due time . . . Not everything at once . . .

---

38 Latin: "The same night awaits us all," from Horace's *Odes*, Book 1, ode 28.

39 Since Finland was part of the Russian Empire, its rural areas within easy reach of St. Petersburg were dotted with summer cottages and villas. The Professor is trying to find a cheap way of returning to the scene of his celebrity.

VOINITSKY. Hold on . . . Obviously, up to now I didn't have a grain of common sense. Up to now I was stupid enough to think that this estate belongs to Sonya. My late father bought this estate as a dowry for my sister. Up to now I was naive, I didn't interpret the laws like a heathen, and I thought the estate passed from my sister to Sonya.

SEREBRYAKOV. Yes, the estate belongs to Sonya. Who disputes it? Without Sonya's consent I will not resolve to sell it. Besides, I'm proposing to do this on Sonya's behalf.

VOINITSKY. This is incomprehensible, incomprehensible! Either I've gone out of my mind, or . . . or . . .

MARIYA VASILYEVNA. *Georges*, don't contradict the Professor. He knows better than we what is right and what is wrong.

VOINITSKY. No, give me some water . . . (*Drinks water.*) Say what it is you want! What do you want!

SEREBRYAKOV. I don't understand why you're getting so worked up, *Georges*? I don't say my project is ideal. If everyone finds it infeasible, I shall not insist.

> Enter DYADIN; *he is wearing a tailcoat, white gloves, and a wide-brimmed top hat.*

X I

The same and DYADIN.

DYADIN. I have the honor to wish you good day. I beg your pardon for daring to intrude without being announced. Sorry, but I crave your indulgence, because there wasn't a single domestic in your front hall.

SEREBRYAKOV (*at a loss*). Delighted . . . Do please . . .

DYADIN (*bowing and scraping*). Your Excellency! Mesdames! My intrusion on your premises has a dual purpose. Firstly, I've come here to pay a visit and pay my reverential respects, secondly, to invite you all, if the weather permits, to make an excursion to my domain. I reside in the watermill, which I rent from our mutual friend the Wood Goblin. It is a secluded, poetical corner of the earth, where by night you can hear the water nymphs splashing, and by day . . .

VOINITSKY. Hold on, Waffles, we're talking business . . . Wait, later . . . (*To Serebryakov.*) You go ahead and ask *him*. This estate was bought from his uncle.

SEREBRYAKOV. Ah, why should I ask him? What for?

VOINITSKY. This estate was bought at that time for ninety-five thousand! Father paid only seventy down, so there was a mortgage of twenty-five thousand left. Now listen . . . This estate would not be free and clear if I hadn't relinquished an inheritance in favor of my sister, whom I loved devoutly. Moreover, for ten years I worked like an ox and paid off the whole debt.

ORLOVSKY. What do you want then, my dear boy?

VOINITSKY. The estate is clear of debt and not in a mess thanks only to my personal efforts. And now, when I'm growing old, they want to throw me out of here on my ear!

SEREBRYAKOV. I can't understand what you're driving at!

VOINITSKY. For twenty-five years I ran this estate, worked hard, sent you money like the most conscientious bookkeeper, and in all that time not once did you thank me! The whole time, both in my youth and now, you paid me a salary of five hundred rubles a year—a pittance!—and not once did you have the decency to raise it by even one ruble!

SEREBRYAKOV. *Georges*, how was I to know! I'm not a man of business and I have no head for such things. You could have raised it yourself as much as you liked!

VOINITSKY. Why didn't I steal? Why don't you all despise me because I didn't steal? That would have been the thing to do! and now I wouldn't be a pauper!

MARIYA VASILYEVNA (*sternly*). *Georges!*

DYADIN (*getting upset*). Zhorzhenka, you mustn't, you mustn't . . . I'm all a-tremble . . . Why spoil good relations? (*Kisses him.*) You mustn't . . .

VOINITSKY. For twenty-five years I and my mother here, like moles, sat between these four walls . . . All our thoughts and feelings concerned no one but you. Days we talked about you, about your work, took pride in you, uttered your name with reverence; nights we wasted reading periodicals and books, which I now deeply despise!

DYADIN. You mustn't. Zhorzhenka, you mustn't . . . I can't take it . . .

SEREBRYAKOV. I don't understand, what do you want?

VOINITSKY. To us you were a creature of a higher order, and we learned your articles by heart . . . But now my eyes have been opened! I see it all! You write about art, but not one thing do you understand about art! All your work, which I loved, isn't worth a tinker's dam!

SEREBRYAKOV. My friends! Try and calm him down, once and for all! I'm going!

YELENA ANDREEVNA. *Georges*, I insist that you keep quiet! You hear me?

VOINITSKY. I won't keep quiet! (*Blocking Serebryakov's path.*) Stop, I haven't finished! You ruined my life! I haven't lived, I haven't lived! Thanks to your charity I blighted, destroyed the best years of my life! You are my deadliest enemy!

DYADIN. I can't take it . . . can't take it . . . I'm going to another room. (*Exits in extreme consternation into the room at right.*)

SEREBRYAKOV. What do you want from me? And what right do you have to take such a tone with me? A nobody! If the estate is yours, then take it, I have no use for it!

ZHELTUKHIN (*aside*). Well, now they've stirred up a hornet's nest! I'm going! (*Exits.*)

YELENA ANDREEVNA. If you don't keep quiet, I'm leaving this hellhole this very minute! (*Screams.*) I can't take any more of this!

VOINITSKY. My life is wasted! I'm talented, intelligent, daring . . . If I had had a normal life, I might have evolved into a Schopenhauer, a Dostoevsky[40] . . . My tongue's running away with me! I'm losing my mind . . . Mommy, I'm desperate! Mommy!

MARIYA VASILYEVNA. Do as the Professor says!

VOINITSKY. Mommy! What am I to do? Don't, don't say anything! I know what I have to do! (*To Serebryakov.*) You're going to remember me! (*Exits through the center door.*)

---

40 Arthur Schopenhauer, German philosopher (1788–1860), apostle of pessimism, and Fyodor Mikhailovich Dostoevsky, Russian novelist (1821–1881), apostle of salvation through Slavic Christianity.

MARIYA VASILYEVNA goes after him.

SEREBRYAKOV. Ladies and gentlemen, what is all this, I mean really? Get that madman away from me!

ORLOVSKY. Never mind, never mind, Sasha, let his temper cool down a bit. Don't get so excited.

SEREBRYAKOV. I cannot live under the same roof with him! He lives right there (*indicates the center door*), practically on top of me . . . Move him into the village, to the servant's quarters, or I'll move, but to stay in the same house with him is out of the question . . .

YELENA ANDREEVNA (*to her husband*). If there is a repeat of anything like this, I shall leave!

SEREBRYAKOV. Oh, please, don't try and scare me!

YELENA ANDREEVNA. I'm not trying to scare you, but you have all apparently conspired to make my life a living hell . . . I'm going . . .

SEREBRYAKOV. Everyone knows perfectly well that you are young, I am old, and that you're doing me a great favor living here . . .

YELENA ANDREEVNA. Keep going, keep going . . .

ORLOVSKY. There, there, there . . . My friends . . .

KHRUSHCHOV enters hurriedly.

X I I

The same and KHRUSHCHOV.

KHRUSHCHOV (*agitated*). I'm delighted to find you at home, Aleksandr Vladimirovich . . . Forgive me, I may have come at a bad time and am disturbing you . . . But that's not the point. Good afternoon . . .

SEREBRYAKOV. What can I do for you?

KHRUSHCHOV. Excuse me, I'm overexcited—it's because I just rode over here so quickly . . . Aleksandr Vladimirovich, I heard that the day before yesterday you sold your forest to Kuznetsov for timber. If that's true, and not mere gossip, then I beg you not to do it.

YELENA ANDREEVNA. Mikhail Lvovich, my husband is not disposed to talk business at the moment. Let's go into the garden.

KHRUSHCHOV. But I have talk to him right now!

YELENA ANDREEVNA. You know best . . . I've done all I can . . . (*Exits.*)

KHRUSHCHOV. Let me ride over to Kuznetsov and tell him that you've reconsidered . . . All right? May I? To fell a thousand trees, to destroy them for the sake of a few thousand, for pay for women's fripperies, caprices, luxuries . . . To destroy so that future generations will curse our barbarity! If you, a learned, famous man, make up your mind to such cruelty, what are other people, far inferior to you, to do? This is really horrible!

ORLOVSKY. Misha, put it off to later!

SEREBRYAKOV. Let's go, Ivan Ivanovich, there'll be no end to this.

KHRUSHCHOV (*blocks Serebryakov's path*). In that case, tell you what, Professor . . . Wait, in three months I'll put the money together and buy it from you myself.

ORLOVSKY. Excuse me, Misha, but this is rather peculiar . . . Well, you are, let's say, a man of ideals . . . we humbly thank you for that, we bow down to you (*bows*), but why make such a fuss![41]

KHRUSHCHOV (*flaring up*). Everybody's darling godfather! There are a lot of good-natured people on this earth, and that always struck me as suspicious! They're good-natured because they couldn't care less!

ORLOVSKY. So you've come here to quarrel, my dear boy . . . That's not nice! An ideal is an ideal, but, lad, you've got to have something else as well . . . (*Points to his heart.*) Without this, my dear boy, all your forests and peat aren't worth a tinker's dam . . . Don't be offended, but you're still green, oof, are you ever green!

SEREBRYAKOV (*sharply*). And next time be so good as not to come in unannounced, and please spare me your psychotic stunts! You all wanted to try my patience, and you succeeded . . . Please leave me alone! All these forests of yours, the peat I consider to be delirium and psychosis—there, that's my opinion! Let's go, Ivan Ivanovich! (*He exits.*)

---

41 Literally, "why break chairs?," a quotation from the first act of Gogol's *Inspector General*, when the Mayor is complaining about an overzealous schoolteacher.

ORLOVSKY (*following him*). That's going too far, Sasha . . . Why be so cutting? (*Exits.*)

KHRUSHCHOV (*alone, after a pause*). Delirium, psychosis . . . Which means, in the opinion of a famous scholar and professor, I'm insane . . . I submit to Your Excellency's authority and shall now go home and shave my head. No, the earth which still supports you is insane!

He goes quickly to the door at right; enter from the door at left SONYA, who had been eavesdropping in the doorway throughout all of Scene XII.

XIII

KHRUSHCHOV and SONYA.

SONYA (*runs after him*). Wait . . . I heard it all . . . Go on talking . . . Say something right away or else I won't be able to keep it in and I'll start talking!

KHRUSHCHOV. Sofya Aleksandrovna, I have already had my say. I pleaded with your father to spare the forest, I was in the right, but he insulted me, called me insane . . . I am insane!

SONYA. That's enough, that's enough . . .

KHRUSHCHOV. Yes, the sane are the ones who disguise themselves as learned men to conceal their hearts of stone and pass off their callousness as profound wisdom! The sane are the ones who marry old men so they can cheat on them in broad daylight, so they can buy themselves stylish, elegant gowns with money made by felling forests!

SONYA. Listen to me, please listen . . . (*Seizes his hand.*) Let me tell you . . .

KHRUSHCHOV. Let's stop this. Let's put an end to it. I mean nothing to you, your opinion of me I know already and there's nothing left for me to do here. Good-bye. I'm sorry that the only memory I shall retain of our close acquaintance, which I so cherished, is of your father's gout and your debating points about my democratic tendencies . . . But I'm not the one to blame . . . Not I . . .

SONYA weeps, hides her faces and quickly exits out the door at left.

I was careless enough to fall in love here, let it be a lesson to me! Away from this dungeon!

He heads for the door at right; enter at the left
YELENA ANDREEVNA.

XIV

KHRUSHCHOV *and* YELENA ANDREEVNA.

YELENA ANDREEVNA. Are you still here? Wait . . . Just now Ivan Ivanovich told me that my husband was rude to you . . . Forgive him, he is irritable today and did not understand you . . . As for me, my heart is on your side, Mikhail Lvovich! Believe in the sincerity of my respect, I sympathize, I'm moved, and allow me to offer you my friendship out of a pure heart! (*Extends her hands.*)

KHRUSHCHOV (*in disgust*). Get away from me . . . I despise your friendship! (*Exits.*)

YELENA ANDREEVNA (*alone, moans*). What for? What for?

A shot offstage.

XV

YELENA ANDREEVNA, MARIYA VASILYEVNA, *then* SONYA, SEREBRYAKOV, ORLOVSKY, *and* ZHELTUKHIN.

MARIYA VASILYEVNA staggers out the central door, screams, and falls unconscious.

SONYA enters and runs out the central door.

SEREBRYAKOV

ORLOVSKY   What is it?

ZHELTUKHIN

SONYA's screams are heard; she returns and cries out: "Uncle Georges has shot himself!" She, ORLOVSKY, SEREBRYAKOV, and ZHELTUKHIN run out the central door.

YELENA ANDREEVNA (*moans*). What for? What for?

DYADIN appears in the doorway at right.

XVI

YELENA ANDREEVNA, MARIYA VASILYEVNA,
and DYADIN.

DYADIN (*in the doorway*). What's going on?

YELENA ANDREEVNA (*to him*). Take me away from here! Throw me down a mineshaft, kill me, but I cannot stay here. Quickly, for pity's sake! (*Exits with DYADIN.*)

Curtain

ACT FOUR

A forest and the house by the mill, which Dyadin rents
from Khrushchov.

I

YELENA ANDREEVNA and DYADIN are sitting on a bench
beneath a window.

YELENA ANDREEVNA. Ilya Ilyich, dovey, tomorrow please drive over to the post office again.

DYADIN. Absolutely.

YELENA ANDREEVNA. I shall wait another three days. If my brother hasn't answered my letter by then, I'll borrow some money from you and go to Moscow myself. I can't live with you here at the mill forever.

DYADIN. You're quite right . . .

Pause.

It's not my place to teach you, my deeply respected lady, but all your letters, telegrams, which I take to the post office every day—they are all, forgive me, labors lost. Whatever answer your brother may send, sooner or later you have to go back to your husband.

YELENA ANDREEVNA. I won't go back . . . We have to look at it rationally, Ilya Ilyich. I don't love my husband. The young people I did love were unfair to me from start to finish. Why should I go back there? You'll say— duty . . . I know that perfectly well, but, I repeat, we have to look at it rationally . . .

Pause.

DYADIN. Quite right, ma'am . . . The greatest of Russian poets, Lomonosov,[42] ran away from the district of Archangel to seek his fortune in Moscow. Of course, that was noble on his part . . . But why did *you* run away? After all, your happiness, no matter how rational you may be, is, to put it bluntly, nowhere to be found . . . It is ordained that the canary bird sit in a cage and gaze at the happiness of others, yes, and sit there for all its life long.

YELENA ANDREEVNA. But maybe I'm not a canary, but an uncaged sparrow!

DYADIN. Oho! A bird is identified by its flight pattern, most respected lady . . . These past two weeks any other lady would have had plenty of time to visit a dozen towns and leave everybody in her dust, but you chose to run only as far as the mill, and even here you've been eating your heart out . . . No, where's there to go? You shall live with me for a little while longer, your feelings will simmer down, and you'll go back to your husband. (*Hearkening.*) Someone's driving up in a carriage. (*Gets up.*)

YELENA ANDREEVNA. I shall go.

DYADIN. I dare not impose my presence on you any further . . . I'll go to my room in the mill and have a little nap . . . This morning I got up earlier than Aurora.

YELENA ANDREEVNA. When you wake up, come and we'll take tea together. (*Goes into the house.*)

DYADIN (*alone*). If I lived in a cultural center, they would draw a caricature of me in a magazine with a hilarious satirical caption. Goodness me, at my advanced age and with my unprepossessing appearance, I've carried off the young wife of a famous professor! It's fascinating! (*Exits.*)

---

42 A joke. Most Russians would consider Pushkin, rather than the neoclassic and derivative Mikhail Lomonosov (1711–1765), to be the greatest Russian poet.

I I

SEMYON (carries buckets) and YULYA (enters).

YULYA. Good afternoon, Semyon, God save you! Is Ilya Ilyich at home?

SEMYON. He is. He went to the mill.

YULYA. Go and fetch him.

SEMYON. Right away. (*Exits.*)

YULYA (*alone*). He's sleeping, I suppose . . . (*Sits on the little bench beneath the widow and sighs deeply.*) Some people sleep, others enjoy themselves, but I spend my days on the go, on the go . . . God won't let me die. (*Sighs even more deeply.*) Lord, how can people be as foolish as that Waffles! I was driving past his barn just now, and a little black piglet ran out the door . . . If those pigs start rooting in other people's grain sacks, he'll be hearing about it . . .

Enter DYADIN.

I I I

YULYA and DYADIN.

DYADIN (*putting on a frockcoat*). Is it you, Yulya Stepanovna? Sorry, I'm in a state of undress . . . I was about to drop into the arms of Morpheus.

YULYA. Good afternoon.

DYADIN. Forgive me for not inviting you inside . . . My house is in a bit of a mess and so on . . . If you like, please come to the mill . . .

YULYA. I'll just sit here. This is why I've dropped in on you, Ilya Ilyich. Lyonechka and the Professor, for some recreation, want to have a picnic here at your mill today, a tea party . . .

DYADIN. Extremely gratified.

YULYA. I came ahead of them . . . They'll be here soon. Please arrange for a table to be set up, oh, and a samovar, of course . . . Have Senka get the baskets of food out of my carriage.

DYADIN. Can do.

Pause.

What's it like now? How are things over there?

YULYA. Bad, Ilya Ilyich . . . Believe you me, it's made me sick with worry. You know, of course, that the Professor and Sonya are living with us now?

DYADIN. I know.

YULYA. After Yegor Petrovich did himself in, they couldn't live in his house. They're afraid. By day there's no problem, but when night falls, they all gather in one room and sit there until dawn. They're all terrified. They're afraid that Yegor Petrovich is haunting the dark corners . . .

DYADIN. Superstition . . . And do they mention Yelena Andreevna?

YULYA. Of course, they mention her.

> *Pause.*

She cleared out!

DYADIN. Yes, a subject that deserves treatment by a painter of shipwrecks and tempests . . .[43] She up and cleared out.

YULYA. And now nobody knows where . . . Maybe she went away, but maybe, in her desperation . . .

DYADIN. God is merciful, Yuliya Stepanovna! Everything will turn out for the best.

> *Enter KHRUSHCHOV with a portfolio and a case with drawing implements.*

I V

The same and KHRUSHCHOV.

KHRUSHCHOV. Hey! Anybody here? Semyon!

DYADIN. Look over here!

KHRUSHCHOV. Ah! . . . Good afternoon, Yulechka!

YULYA. Good afternoon, Mikhail Lvovich.

---

43 In the original, "worthy of the brush of Aivazovsky." Ivan Konstantinovich Aivazovsky (1817–1900), Russian painter famous for his seascapes, particularly storms and naval battles, whom Chekhov had met in Feodosiya on the Black Sea in 1888.

KHRUSHCHOV. I've dropped by your place again, Ilya Ilyich, to get some work done. Sitting at home's no good. Tell them to set up my table under this tree as they did yesterday, oh and tell them to get two lamps ready. It's getting dark already . . .

DYADIN. At your service, your honor. (*Exits.*)

KHRUSHCHOV. How are you getting on, Yulechka?

YULYA. We're getting on.

KHRUSHCHOV. Hm . . . And what's your Lyonechka doing?

YULYA. Sits at home . . . Always with Sonechka . . .

KHRUSHCHOV. I'll bet!

Pause.

He ought to marry her.

YULYA. Is that so? (*Sighs.*) God grant it! He's a cultured, well-born man, she's from a good family too . . . I always wished for it . . .

KHRUSHCHOV. She's a fool . . .

YULYA. Now, don't say that.

KHRUSHCHOV. And your Lyonechka is as bright as a button too . . . Generally speaking, your whole crowd is the pick of the litter. The best and the brightest!

YULYA. I suppose you haven't had dinner today.

KHRUSHCHOV. Why do you think that?

YULYA. You're so ill tempered.

Enter DYADIN and SEMYON; they are carrying a small table.

V

The same, DYADIN, and SEMYON.

DYADIN. You know a sure thing when you see it. You picked a beautiful spot for your work. It's an oasis! A genuine oasis! Imagine that you're surrounded by palm trees, Yulechka is a gentle gazelle, you're a lion, I'm a tiger.

KHRUSHCHOV. You're a decent enough fellow, a sensitive soul, Ilya Ilyich, but why do you act this way? These sickly sweet words, the way you shuffle your feet, jerk your shoulders . . . If a stranger caught sight of you, he'd think you're not a man but some other damned thing! . . . It's annoying . . .

DYADIN. Which means, it was so ordained at my birth . . . Fatal predestination.

KHRUSHCHOV. There you go again, fatal predestination. Drop all that. (*Pinning a diagram to the table.*) I'm going to spend the night here.

DYADIN. I am extremely pleased . . . Now you're angry, Misha, but my heart's filled with indescribable joy! As if a dicky-bird were sitting in my breast, warbling a little ditty.

KHRUSHCHOV. O be joyful.

Pause.

You've got a dicky-bird in your breast, and I've got a toad in mine. A million things have gone wrong! Shimansky sold his forest for timber . . . That's one! Yelena Andreevna ran away from her husband, and now nobody knows where she is. That's two! I feel with every passing day that I'm becoming more stupid, more picayune, and more untalented . . . That's three! Yesterday I wanted to tell you, but I couldn't, I didn't have the courage. You may congratulate me. The late Yegor Petrovich left behind a diary. This diary first got into Ivan Ivanych's hands, I was with him and I've read it over about a dozen times . . .

YULYA. Our folks read it too.

KHRUSHCHOV. *Georges's* affair with Yelena Andreevna, which reverberated through the whole district, turns out to be a vulgar, filthy slander . . . I believed that slander and defamed him along with the others, hated, despised, insulted him.

DYADIN. Of course, that was wrong.

KHRUSHCHOV. The first person whom I believed was your brother, Yulechka! I'm a fine one too! I believed your brother, whom I don't respect, but I didn't believe the woman who was sacrificing herself before my very eyes. I was more eager to believe evil than good, I couldn't see past my own nose. And this means that I am as common as everybody else.

DYADIN (*to Yulya*). Let's go to the mill, my girl. Let the bad-tempered fellow work here, while you and I have some fun. Let's go . . . Get on with your work, Mishenka. (*He and YULYA exit.*)

KHRUSHCHOV (*alone; mixes colors in a saucer*). One night I saw him press his face to her hand. In his diary he has described that night in detail, described how I came by there, what I said to him. He's put down my words and calls me a stupid, narrow-minded fellow.

Pause.

It's too dark . . . Should be lighter . . . She never loved me . . . I made a blot . . . (*Scrapes the paper with a knife.*) Even if I admit there may be some truth to it, still it doesn't do to think about it . . . It began stupidly, it ended stupidly . . .

SEMYON and WORKMEN bring in a big table.

What are you doing? What's this for?

SEMYON. Ilya Ilyich told us to. Company's coming from the Zheltukhins' for tea.

KHRUSHCHOV. Thank you kindly. That means, I've got to leave off work . . . I'll pack up and go home.

Enter ZHELTUKHIN arm in arm with SONYA.

V I

KHRUSHCHOV, ZHELTUKHIN, and SONYA.

ZHELTUKHIN (*sings*). "Reluctant to this mournful shore an unknown power doth me draw . . ."[44]

KHRUSHCHOV. Who's that? Ah! (*Hastens to pack up his drawing implements in their case.*)

---

44 The Prince's cavatina from Dargomyzhsky's opera *The Rusalka* (Act I, scene 2); in its source, Pushkin's dramatic fragment, the Prince's words open the last scene. Chekhov is suggesting that, by hiding at the mill, Yelena had become a kind of water nymph.

ZHELTUKHIN. Just one more question, *Sophie* dear . . . Do you remember on my birthday you had lunch at our place? You've got to admit that that time you burst out laughing at the way I looked.

SONYA. That's enough of that, Leonid Stepanych. How can you say a thing like that? I burst out laughing at nothing in particular.

ZHELTUKHIN (*on seeing Khrushchov*). Ah, look who it is! You're here too? Afternoon.

KHRUSHCHOV. Afternoon.

ZHELTUKHIN. Working? Wonderful . . . Where's Waffles?

KHRUSHCHOV. Over there . . .

ZHELTUKHIN. Where's over there?

KHRUSHCHOV. I think I've made it clear. Over there, in the mill.

ZHELTUKHIN. I'll go and get him. (*Walks, singing.*) "Reluctant to this mournful shore . . ." (*Exits.*)

SONYA. Good afternoon . . .

KHRUSHCHOV. Good afternoon.

> *Pause.*

SONYA. What are you drawing?

KHRUSHCHOV. Nothing special . . . it's of no interest.

SONYA. Is it a chart?

KHRUSHCHOV. No, it's a diagram of the forests in our district. I've mapped them out.

> *Pause.*

The green color indicates the places where there were forests in our grandfathers' day and earlier; the light green is where forests have been felled in the last twenty-five years, well, and the light blue is where forests are still intact . . . Yes . . .

> *Pause.*

Well, what about you? Happy?

SONYA. Now, Mikhail Lvovich, is not the time to think about happiness.

KHRUSHCHOV. What else is there to think about?

SONYA. Our sorrow came about only because we were thinking too much about our happiness . . .

KHRUSHCHOV. If you say so, ma'am.

Pause.

SONYA. Every cloud has its silver lining. Sorrow has taught me. We have to forget about our own happiness, Mikhail Lvovich, and think only about other people's happiness. Our whole life has to be made up of sacrifices.

KHRUSHCHOV. Well, yes . . .

Pause.

Marya Vasilyevna had a son who shot himself and she still keeps on looking for contradictions in her silly pamphlets. A disaster struck you, and you play games with your vanity; you try to pervert your life and think you're making a sacrifice . . . Nobody's got any heart . . . Neither of us . . . It's all going wrong, everything's falling to rack and ruin . . . I shall leave now and not get in the way of you and Zheltukhin . . . What are you crying about? I didn't mean to do that.

SONYA. Never mind, never mind . . . (*Wipes her eyes.*)

Enter YULYA, DYADIN, and ZHELTUKHIN.

VII

The same, YULYA, DYADIN, ZHELTUKHIN, then
SEREBYAKOV and ORLOVSKY.

SEREBRYAKOV's voice: "Yoo-hoo! Where are you, my friends?"

SONYA (*shouts*). Papa, over here!

DYADIN. They're bringing the samovar! Fascinating! (*He and YULYA fuss with things on the table.*)

Enter SEREBRYAKOV and ORLOVSKY.

SONYA. Over here, Papa!

SEREBRYAKOV. I see, I see . . .

ZHELTUKHIN (*loudly*). Gentlemen, I call this session to order! Waffles, uncork the cordial!

KHRUSHCHOV (*to Serebryakov*). Professor, let's forget everything that passed between us! (*Extends his hand.*) I beg your pardon . . .

SEREBRYAKOV. Thank you. Most delighted. You should forgive me as well. The day after that episode when I tried to contemplate all that had occurred and recalled our interchange, I felt very uncomfortable . . . Let us be friends. (*Takes him by the arm and goes to the table.*)

ORLOVSKY. Should have done it a long time ago, my dear boy. A bad peace is better than a good quarrel.

DYADIN. Your Excellency, I'm glad that you have chosen to pay a visit to my oasis. Indescribably delighted!

SEREBRYAKOV. Thank you, my good man. It is beautiful here indeed. A veritable oasis.

ORLOVSKY. So you're a nature lover, Sasha?

SEREBRYAKOV. Quite so.

Pause.

Let us not be silent, gentlemen, let us speak. In our situation that's by far the best thing. One must look misfortune in the face boldly and directly. I can look at it more bravely than any of you, and that is because I am more unhappy than any of you.

YULYA. Gentlemen, I don't provide any sugar; drink it with jam.[45]

DYADIN (*bustling around among the guests*). I'm so pleased, I'm so pleased!

SEREBRYAKOV. Recently, Mikhail Lvovich, I have experienced so much and done so much thinking that I believe I could write a whole treatise on the art of living. We live and learn all our lives, but it is the misfortunes that instruct us.

DYADIN. Let the dead past bury the dead. God is merciful, all's well that ends well.

---

45 Part of Yulya's economy: refined sugar, which has to be bought, is more expensive than fruit jam, which can be made on the estate.

SONYA *gives a start.*

ZHELTUKHIN. What made you start?

SONYA. Someone was shouting.

DYADIN. It's the peasants down by the river catching crayfish.

Pause.

ZHELTUKHIN. Gentlemen, after all we did come to an agreement to spend this evening as if nothing had happened . . . Honestly, there's a kind of tension . . .

DYADIN. Your Excellency, I cherish for learning not just reverence, but even a kindred feeling. My brother Grigory Ilyich's wife's brother, maybe you deign to know him, Konstantin Gavrilych Novosyolov,[46] had a master's degree in comparative literature.

SEREBRYAKOV. I didn't know him, but I know of him.

Pause.

YULYA. Yesterday was exactly two weeks since Yegor Petrovich died.

KHRUSHCHOV. Yulechka, let's not talk about that.

SEREBRYAKOV. Be brave, be brave!

Pause.

ZHELTUKHIN. All the same you can feel a kind of tension . . .

SEREBRYAKOV. Nature abhors a vacuum. She has deprived me of two close friends, and, in order to fill the gap, she has sent me new friends. I drink to your health, Leonid Stepanovich!

ZHELTUKHIN. Thank you, my dear Aleksandr Vladimirovich! In my turn let me drink to your fruitful academic activities.

> If wisdom and virtue's seeds you sow
> The Russian people are bound to show
> Always their heartfelt thanks![47]

---

46 A joke name, meaning "Recent Settler."

47 From Nekrasov's poem "To the Sowers" (1876).

SEREBRYAKOV. I treasure your compliment. I cordially look forward to the time when our friendly relations will evolve into something more familial.

Enter FYODOR IVANOVICH.

VIII

The same and FYODOR IVANOVICH.

FYODOR IVANOVICH. Here's where it is! A picnic!

ORLOVSKY. My sonny boy . . . my beauty!

FYODOR IVANOVICH. Good afternoon. (*Exchanges kisses with Sonya and Yulya.*)

ORLOVSKY. We've haven't seen you for a whole two weeks. Where were you? What kept you so long?

FYODOR IVANOVICH. I just rode over to Lyonya's place, where they told me you were here, so I rode over here.

ORLOVSKY. Where have you been hanging out?

FYODOR IVANOVICH. I haven't slept for three nights . . . Yesterday, father, I lost five thousand at cards. I was drinking and playing cards, and rode back and forth to town five separate times. Went on a bender.

ORLOVSKY. Attaboy! You're probably a little tipsy now?

FYODOR IVANOVICH. Sober as a judge. Yulka, tea! Only with lemon, nice and sour . . . And how do you like that *Georges*, huh? Out of the blue ups and blows his brains out! And the thing he picked to do it with too: a Lefoché! He couldn't use a Smith and Wesson![48]

KHRUSHCHOV. Shut up, you swine!

FYODOR IVANOVICH. A swine, but a purebred one! (*Strokes his beard.*) The beard alone is worth a pretty penny . . . So I'm a swine and a fool and scum, but I merely have to will it—and a loving bride will drop in my lap. Sonya, marry me! (*To Khrushchov.*) However, I'm sorry . . . *Pardon* . . .

KHRUSHCHOV. Stop playing the fool.

---

48 Different brands of revolver. Fyodor, as a military man, would prefer the Smith & Wesson, which was standard issue for the Russian army, to a French make.

YULYA. You're a lost cause, Fedenka! In the whole district there's no bigger drunkard and spendthrift than you. It makes me sorry just to look at you. A reprobate sinner—the wrath of God!

FYODOR IVANOVICH. Well, now she's started bellyaching again! Come on, sit next to me . . . That's it. I'll come and stay with you for a couple of weeks . . . I need a rest. (*Kisses her.*)

YULYA. You should be ashamed with people around. You should be a comfort to your father in his old age, but you only disgrace him. A stupid way to live, that's all there is to it.

FYODOR IVANOVICH. I'll give up the drink! *Basta!* (*Pours himself a drink.*) Is this plum cordial or cherry?

YULYA. Stop drinking, no drinks.

FYODOR IVANOVICH. One little glass is all right. (*Drinks.*) Wood Goblin, I'll give you a pair of horses and a rifle. I'm going to live with Yulya . . . I'll stay with her for a couple of weeks.

KHRUSHCHOV. A stay in a disciplinary battalion would do you more good.

YULYA. Tea, drink tea!

DYADIN. Have some cookies with it, Fedenka.

ORLOVSKY (*to Serebryakov*). Sasha, old pal, for forty years I led exactly the same kind of life as my Fyodor. Once, dear boy, I started counting up: how many women had I made unhappy in my time? I counted and counted, got as far as seventy and gave it up. Well, sir, as soon as I reached the age of forty, suddenly, Sasha, old pal, something came over me. A desolation, I didn't know what to do with myself, in short, my spirits sank, and that was that. I did one thing after another, I'd read books, I'd work, I'd travel— nothing helped! Well, sir, my dear boy, I was paying a call on a now deceased neighbor of mine, his Most Serene Highness Prince Dmitry Pavlovich. We had a snack, then we had dinner . . . After dinner, to keep from napping, we arranged for target shooting in the courtyard. Scads and scads of people gathered round. Our Waffles was there too.

DYADIN. I was, I was . . . I remember.

ORLOVSKY. The desolation I was feeling—you understand—good Lord! I couldn't bear it. Suddenly, tears welled up in my eyes, I started to sway and

I began to shout to the whole courtyard, at the top of my lungs:" My friends, good people, forgive me for Christ's sake!" And at that very minute my heart grew pure, loving, warm, and from that time on, my dear boy, in all the district there's no happier man than I am. And you should do the same thing.

SEREBRYAKOV. Do what?

A glow appears in the sky.

ORLOVSKY. The same as I did. You have to give in, to capitulate.

SEREBRYAKOV. A little sample of our homegrown philosophy. You advise me to ask for forgiveness. What for? Other people should be asking forgiveness of me!

SONYA. Papa, after all, *we're* the ones at fault!

SEREBRYAKOV. Really? Gentlemen, obviously, at the moment you have in mind my relationship with my wife. Do you really believe that I am at fault? This is almost laughable, gentlemen. She shirked her duty, deserted me at a critical moment in my life . . .

KHRUSHCHOV. Aleksandr Vladimirovich, listen to me . . . For twenty-five years you've been a professor and served learning, I plant forests and practice medicine, but what's the point, who's it all for, if we don't show mercy to the ones we're working for? We say that we serve people, and at the same time we are inhumanly destroying each another. For instance, did you or I do anything to save *Georges*? Where is your wife, whom we all insulted? Where is your peace of mind, where is your daughter's peace of mind? It's all wrecked, destroyed, it's all gone to rack and ruin. Gentlemen, you call me a Wood Goblin, but after all I'm not the only one, there's a wood goblin lurking in all of you, you are all wandering through a dark wood and groping your way through life. Of intelligence, understanding, and feeling we have only just enough to spoil our own lives and other people's.

YELENA ANDREEVNA enters from the house and sits on the bench beneath the window.

I X

The same and YELENA ANDREEVNA.

KHRUSHCHOV. I considered myself to be a humane man of ideals and yet I never forgave people the slightest error, believed slanders, gossiped with the rest, and when, for example, your wife trustingly offered me her friendship, I blurted out from the heights of my grandeur: "Get away from me! I despise your friendship!" That's the sort of man I am. There's a wood goblin lurking in me, I'm petty, average, blind, but you, Professor, are no great champion either! And meanwhile throughout the district, women take me to be a hero, a man of progress, while you are famous all over Russia. But if people like me are seriously taken to be heroes, and people like you are seriously famous, it means we're in sore need of real people and anybody can be passed off as a somebody, there are no real heroes, no geniuses, no people who could lead us out of this dark wood, could put to rights the mess we make, no real champions, who might genuinely deserve an honorable fame . . .

SEREBRYAKOV. Excuse me . . . I did not come here to engage in a polemic with you and defend my right to be famous.

ZHELTUKHIN. Generally speaking, Misha, let's change the subject.

KHRUSHCHOV. I'll be done in a minute and go away. Yes, I'm petty, but you, Professor, are no champion! *Georges* was petty, the cleverest thing he could come up with was blowing his brains out. Everyone's petty! As to the women . . .

YELENA ANDREEVNA (*interrupting*). As to the women, they are no better. (*Comes to the table.*) Yelena Andreevna left her husband, and do you think she did anything sensible with her freedom? Don't worry . . . She will come back . . . (*Sits down at the table.*) And I have come back . . .

General consternation.

DYADIN (*roars with laughter*). This is fascinating! Gentlemen, don't blame me, let me put in a word or two! Your Excellency, it is I who abducted your wife just as once a certain Paris did Helen! I did it! Although there are no pockmarked Parises, but, friend Horatio, there are more things in heaven and earth than are dreamt of in your philosophy![49]

KHRUSHCHOV. I don't understand a thing . . . Is that you, Yelena Andreevna?

YELENA ANDREEVNA. I've been staying with Ilya Ilyich the last two weeks . . . Why are you all looking at me like that? Well, good afternoon . . . I was

---

49 Dyadin is alluding to two of Chekhov's favorite works, Offenbach's comic opera *La Belle Hélène* (1864) and Shakespeare's tragedy *Hamlet*. The mixture is characteristic.

sitting by the window and heard it all. (*Embraces Sonya.*) Let's be reconciled. How are you, my dear little girl . . . Peace and harmony!

DYADIN (*rubbing his hands*). This is fascinating!

YELENA ANDREEVNA (*to Khrushchov*). Mikhail Lvovich. (*Gives him her hand.*) Let the dead past bury its dead. Good afternoon, Fyodor Ivanych . . . Yulechka . . .

ORLOVSKY. My dear boy, our professor's lady is glorious, a beauty . . . She has come back, returned to us once more . . .

YELENA ANDREEVNA. I missed you all so much. Afternoon, Aleksandr! (*Extends her hand to her husband, but he turns away.*) Aleksandr!

SEREBRYAKOV. You shirked your duty.

YELENA ANDREEVNA. Aleksandr!

SEREBRYAKOV. I won't deny that I'm very glad to see you and I'm ready to talk to you, but not here, at home . . . (*Walks away from the table.*)

ORLOVSKY. Sasha!

Pause.

YELENA ANDREEVNA. So . . . Which means, Aleksandr, our problem has a very easy solution: none at all. Well, if that's how it has to be! I'm a walk-on part, my happiness is like a canary's, a woman's happiness . . . To be a stay-at-home all my life, eat, drink, sleep, and listen every day to people talk about their gout, their rights, their just deserts. Why are you all hanging your heads, as if you're embarrassed? Let's have a swig of that cordial, shall we? Ech!

DYADIN. It'll all turn out all right, things'll work out, we'll all live happily ever after.

FYODOR IVANOVICH (*walks over to Serebryakov, excited*). Aleksandr Vladimirovich, I'm touched . . . I beg you, caress your wife, say at least one kind word to her, and, on the word of a gentleman, I'll be your faithful friend for life, I'll give you my best team of horses.

SEREBRYAKOV. Thank you, but, excuse me, I don't understand you . . .

FYODOR IVANOVICH. Hm . . . you don't understand . . . Once I was on my way home from hunting, lo and behold—on a tree there sits a screech owl.

I send him a blast of buckshot! He goes on sitting . . . I send a number nine cartridge . . . He goes on sitting . . . Nothing gets through to him. He goes on sitting and just blinks his eyes.

SEREBRYAKOV. To what are you referring?

FYODOR IVANOVICH. To the screech owl. (*Returns to the table.*)

ORLOVSKY (*hearkening*). Excuse me, gentlemen . . . Quiet . . . I think there's an alarm bell ringing somewhere . . .

FYODOR IVANOVICH (*who has seen the glow*). Oy-oy-oy! Look at the sky! What a glow!

ORLOVSKY. Good heavens, we're sitting here and we'll miss it!

DYADIN. Neat.

FYODOR IVANOVICH. My, my, my! That's what I call fireworks! It's near Alekseevskoe.

KHRUSHCHOV. No, Alekseevskoe would be more to the right . . . More likely it's at Novo-Petrovskoe.

YULYA. How awful! I'm afraid of fires!

KHRUSHCHOV. It's definitely Novo-Petrovskoe.

DYADIN (*shouts*). Semyon, run to the dam, and find out where the fire is coming from. Maybe you can see it!

SEMYON (*shouts*). It's the Telibeev forest on fire.

DYADIN. What?

SEMYON. The Telibeev forest!

DYADIN. The forest . . .

Prolonged pause.

KHRUSHCHOV. I have to go there . . . to the fire. Good-bye . . . Excuse me, I was brusque—it's because I've never felt so depressed as today . . . My heart is heavy . . . But that's not a problem . . . One has to be a man and stand firmly on one's own feet. I won't shoot myself and throw myself under the mill wheel . . . I may not be a hero, but I shall become one! I shall grow eagle's wings, and neither this glow nor the devil himself will frighten me! Let the forests burn—I shall plant new ones! If one woman fails to love me, I shall love another woman! (*Exits quickly.*)

YELENA ANDREEVNA. What a fine fellow!

ORLOVSKY. Yes . . . "If one woman fails to love me,—I shall love another woman." What's that supposed to mean?

SONYA. Take me away from here . . . I want to go home . . .

SEREBRYAKOV. Yes, it's high time we went. The damp here is impossible. My lap rug and my overcoat are somewhere . . .

ZHELTUKHIN. The lap rug's in the carriage, and the overcoat's here. (*Hands him the overcoat.*)

SONYA (*powerfully agitated*). Take me away from here . . . Take me away . . .

ZHELTUKHIN. I'm at your service . . .

SONYA. No, I'll go with my godfather. Take me with you, godfather dear . . .

ORLOVSKY. Let's go, my dear girl, let's go. (*Helps her to put on her things.*)

ZHELTUKHIN (*aside*). Damn it all . . . Nothing but bad behavior and humiliation.

> *FYODOR IVANOVICH and YULYA pack the dishes and*
> *napkins into the basket.*

SEREBRYAKOV. The heel of my left foot is aching . . . Rheumatism, I suppose . . . I won't sleep all night again.

YELENA ANDREEVNA (*buttoning up her husband's overcoat*). Dear Ilya Ilyich, bring my hat and my cape from the house!

DYADIN. Right this minute! (*Exits into the house and returns with the hat and the cape.*)

ORLOVSKY. The glow, my dear girl, has terrified you. Don't be afraid, it's dying down. The fire is being put out . . .

YULYA. There's half a jar of sour-cherry jam left . . . Well, let Ilya Ilyich finish it off. (*To her brother.*) Lyonochka, take the basket.

YELENA ANDREEVNA. I'm ready. (*To her husband.*) Well, take me, statue of the Commendatore,[50] and let's go to hell together in your twenty-six melancholy rooms! That's all I'm good for!

SEREBRYAKOV. Statue of the Commendatore . . . I ought to laugh at that metaphor, but the pain in my foot prevents me. (*To everyone.*) Good-bye, my friends! Thank you for your hospitality and the pleasant company . . . A magnificent evening, excellent tea—it's all very nice, but, excuse me, there's something of yours that I cannot accept—this homegrown philosophy of yours and your views on life. One must take action, gentlemen. Your way is impossible! One must take action . . . Yes, indeed . . . Good-bye. (*Exits with his wife.*)

FYODOR IVANOVICH. Let's go, cape-able lady! (*To his father.*) Good-bye, progenitor! (*Exits with YULYA.*)

ZHELTUKHIN (*with the basket, following him*). This basket is heavy, damn it . . . I can't stand these picnics. (*Exits and shouts offstage.*) Aleksey, drive up!

X

ORLOVSKY, SONYA, and DYADIN.

ORLOVSKY (*to Sonya*). Well, why are you still sitting? Let's go, sweetie-pie . . . (*Exits with Sonya.*)

DYADIN (*aside*). And nobody said good-bye to me . . . It's fascinating! (*Puts out the candles.*)

ORLOVSKY (*to Sonya*). What's wrong with you?

SONYA. I can't go, godfather dear . . . I haven't got the strength! I'm in despair, godfather dear . . . I'm in despair! It's unbearably hard!

ORLOVSKY (*anxious*). What is it? My dear girl, my beauty . . .

SONYA. Let's stay . . . Let's remain here a while.

ORLOVSKY. First it's take me home, then it's stay here . . . I can't figure you out . . .

---

50 At the end of Mozart's opera *Don Giovanni*, the statue of Dona Anna's father, the Commendatore whom Don Juan had slain, comes to life and drags the Don to hell.

SONYA. This is where I lost my happiness today . . . I can't . . . Ah, godfather dear, why aren't I dead! (*Embraces him.*) Ah, if only you knew, if only you knew!

ORLOVSKY. Take a sip of water . . . Let's sit for a while . . . come on . . .

DYADIN. What's the matter? Sofya Aleksandrovna, dearie . . . I can't, I'm all a-tremble . . . (*Tearfully.*) I can't look at this . . . My dear little child . . .

SONYA. Ilya Ilyich, my dear, take me to the fire! I implore you!

ORLOVSKY. Why do you have to be at the fire? What are you going to do there?

SONYA. I implore you, take me or I'll go there on my own. I'm in despair . . . Godfather dear, it's hard for me, unbearably hard. Take me to the fire.

KHRUSHCHOV enters hurriedly.

X I

The same and KHRUSHCHOV.

KHRUSHCHOV (*shouts*). Ilya Ilyich!

DYADIN. Over here! What's up with you?

KHRUSHCHOV. I can't get there on foot, lend me a horse.

SONYA (*on recognizing Khrushchov, joyously cries out*). Mikhail Lvovich! (*Goes to him.*) Go on, godfather dear, I have to talk to him. (*To Khrushchov.*) Mikhail Lvovich, you said that you will love another woman . . . (*To Orlovsky.*) Go on, godfather dear . . . (*To Khrushchov.*) I am another woman now . . . I want nothing but the truth . . . Nothing, nothing but the truth! I love, love you . . . love . . .

ORLOVSKY. So that's what that song and dance was all about. (*Roars with laughter.*)

DYADIN. It's fascinating!

SONYA (*to Orlovsky*). Go away, godfather dear. (*To Khrushchov.*) Yes, yes, only the truth and nothing more . . . Talk to me, talk . . . I have told you everything . . .

KHRUSHCHOV (*embracing her*). My dove!

SONYA. Don't go away, godfather dear . . . When you declared your love to me, I was breathless with joy the whole time, but I was shackled by prejudices; I was prevented from telling you my true feelings by the same thing that now prevents my father from smiling at Yelena. Now I'm free . . .

ORLOVSKY (*roars with laughter*). They're singing in tune, at last! Scrambled on to the shore! I am pleased to congratulate you. (*Bowing low.*) Ah, you, naughty, naughty! Wasting time chasing one another's tails!

DYADIN (*embracing Khrushchov*). Mishenka, dovie, I'm delighted! Mishenka!

ORLOVSKY (*embracing and kissing Sonya*). Darling, my little canary bird . . . My little god-daughter . . .

SONYA *bursts out laughing.*

Well, there she goes again!

KHRUSHCHOV. Excuse me, I can't come to my senses . . . Let me talk to her a while . . . Don't stand in our way . . . Please, leave us . . .

FYODOR IVANOVICH *and* YULYA *enter.*

XII

The same, FYODOR IVANOVICH, *and* YULYA.

YULYA. But after all, Fedenka, you never stop talking nonsense! You never stop talking nonsense!

ORLOVSKY. Sssh! Quiet, kiddies! Here comes my buccaneer. Let's hide, my friends, quick! Please!

ORLOVSKY, DYADIN, KHRUSHCHOV, *and* SONYA *hide.*

FYODOR IVANOVICH. I left my whip and gloves here.

YULYA. You never stop talking nonsense!

FYODOR IVANOVICH. All right, I'm talking nonsense . . . What of it? I don't want to ride to your place right now . . . Let's go for a walk, and then we'll have something to eat.

YULYA. You are a true pain in the neck! Sheer torture! (*Claps her hands.*) Why, what a fool that Waffles is! The table still hasn't been cleared! Someone could steal the samovar . . . Ah, Waffles, Waffles, you may be old, but you've got fewer brains than a baby!

DYADIN (*aside*). Thank you kindly.

YULYA. As we came by, there was someone laughing here . . .

FYODOR IVANOVICH. It's the peasant women going for a swim . . . (*Picks up a glove.*) Here's somebody's glove . . . Sonya's . . . Today Sonya was bitten by a bug. In love with the Wood Goblin. She's smitten with him up to her eyebrows, but he, the blockhead, doesn't see it.

YULYA (*angrily*). Where are we going then?

FYODOR IVANOVICH. To the dam . . . Let's go for a walk . . . There's no prettier spot in the whole district . . . Beautiful!

ORLOVSKY (*aside*). My sonny-boy, a good-looker, with that bushy beard . . .

YULYA. I just heard a voice.

FYODOR IVANOVICH. "Nature's wonderful works, where the wood goblin lurks, and the water nymphs perch in the branches . . ."[51] That's it to a T, uncle! (*Claps her on the shoulder.*)

YULYA. I'm not your uncle.

FYODOR IVANOVICH. Let us reason in peace. Listen, Yulechka. I've gone through hell and high water . . . I'm already thirty-five, and I have no vocation, except as a lieutenant in the Serbian military and a noncom in the Russian reserves. I dangle between heaven and earth . . . I have to change my way of life, and you know . . . you understand, now I've got this notion in my head that if I do get married, my whole life will be turned around . . . Marry me, eh? It might as well be you as anyone else . . .

YULYA (*embarrassed*). Hm . . . well, you see . . . you've got to reform first, Fedenka.

FYODOR IVANOVICH. Come on, don't haggle like a gypsy! A straight answer!

YULYA. I'm ashamed . . . (*Looking around.*) Hold on, someone might come in or overhear us . . . I think Waffles is looking out the window.

FYODOR IVANOVICH. Nobody's there.

YULYA (*flings herself around his neck*). Fedenka!

---

51 Misquoted from Pushkin's verse fable *Ruslan and Lyudmila*.

SONYA *bursts out laughing;* ORLOVSKY, DYADIN, *and*
KHRUSHCHOV *laugh loudly, clap their hands, and shout:*
"Bravo! Bravo!"

FYODOR IVANOVICH. Phew! Scared the stuffing out of me! Where did you
pop up from?

SONYA. Yulechka, congratulations! Me too, me too!

Laughter, kisses, noise.

DYADIN. This is fascinating! This is fascinating!

Curtain

VARIANTS TO

The Wood Goblin

From the censor's manuscript.

ACT ONE

page 588 / *After*: (*Lays her head on his breast*) — I'll go and bring you back a
gift. I'll go and get it.

page 589 / *After*: if that's the way they want it! — (*Annoyed.*)

page 590 / *After*: Sergey Nikodimych! — Vasily, call in the guests!

page 590 / *Replace*: Please do. (*Near the appetizers.*)
with: Sit down, gentlemen, please. Many are called but few are chosen.

page 590 / *After*: That shouldn't happen. The turkey is a delicate fowl. —
YULYA. Of course, they're not geese. Geese take no work, but with turkeys
you have keep a sharp lookout.

page 590 / *After*: Stop that, Waffles! I can't stand it! —

YULYA. Eat, gentlemen, don't stand on ceremony. Be so kind! Godfather dear, eat something! Let me serve you this tiny little sardine!

ORLOVSKY. Thank you, my girl, I'll eat it.

page 591 / *After*: What a darling, what a dear . . . —

VOINITSKY. Time and again it's a quarrel over the professor. They stop talking to one another and they snarl at one another, like mice in a sack of groats. Sometimes Sonichka doesn't call her Yelena Andreevna, but "that woman" or "a certain person," and the professor pretends not to notice it.

ORLOVSKY. That's peculiar.

page 591 / *Before*: Just think about the luck he's had! — I don't know another man that lucky!

page 592 / *After*: you've seen her — young, charming, poetical, gracious —

page 592 / *Replace*: at least drop in for dinner . . . All right . . . (*Exits.*)
with: at least stop by for dinner . . . Please.

YULYA. All right. (*Exits.*)

ZHELTUKHIN (*comes back to the table*). I owe you an apology, Ivan Ivanovich. Last Sunday you celebrated a school opening, but I couldn't come, word of honor. All day long my shoulder was aching. Thank you, my dear fellow, sincerely. (*Extends his hand.*)

ORLOVSKY. What for?

ZHELTUKHIN. What for?

> If wisdom and virtue's seeds you sow
> The Russian people are bound to show
> Always their heartfelt thanks.

ORLOVSKY. Well, look at that! Dear boy, you don't suppose I built the school? That was my daughter.

page 593 / *Replace*: I'm even trembling . . . anybody who cheats on a wife or husband
with: I'm even trembling . . . (*Gets up.*) I don't possess the gift of eloquence and talent, but allow me to speak my conscience without high-flown phrases. A spouse may be young, beautiful, let's assume, but, gentlemen, youth and beauty will pass, while duty remains for all eternity. Anybody who cheats on a wife or husband—

page 593 / *After*: you wave your arms around . . . —

DYADIN. Hm . . . I'm sorry, sir! Gentlemen, let me ask your pardon for my outward appearance!

VOINITSKY. Now you're getting angry. What a crank! Speak Russian and not Chinese, and then we won't laugh at you.

page 594 / *After*: Greetings, lads! — (*In a different voice.*) Your healt' we wish vla . . . vla . . . vla

page 594 / *Before*: It's hot! — (*Sits down.*)

page 595 / *Replace*: Scenes V, VI, and VII *with*:

V

The same, ZHELTUKHIN, and YULYA.

VOINITSKY. So, Ivan Ivanovich, you say that you like the Wood Goblin a lot. Yes, I agree, he's a fine, sympathetic individual.

YULYA. Greetings, Fedenka! (*Exchanges kisses.*)

FYODOR IVANOVICH. Greetings to the birthday boy.

VOINITSKY. I really, really like that Wood Goblin. Such a far-seeing, open mind . . .

ZHELTUKHIN. Misha Khrushchov? Oh sure! Upright, honorable, quite the convivial chap. But do you know . . . he's a friend of mine, I'm very fond of him, but there are moments when I can't stomach him. There's something about him . . . I cannot put it into words, but something rather repellent. Pay close attention when he's standing near you in profile, there's a certain strange expression on his face . . . a blend of satyr and Mephistopheles. In short, you'll understand what I mean.

VOINITSKY. I do understand.

YULYA. Look, godfather, here's the gift I gave Lyonechka today! (*Displays a little shoe to serve as a watch stand.*)

ORLOVSKY. My darlin', my little girl, a tiny shoe! That's quite something . . .

YULYA. The gold thread alone cost eight and a half rubles. Look at the edging: tiny little pearls, tiny little pearls, tiny little pearls . . . And these are letters: Leonid Zheltukhin. And here in silk: "A gift to the one I love . . ."

DYADIN. Please let me have a look at it! Fascinating! A person endowed with a rich imagination might fancy that you stole this tiny shoe from the foot of an airy fairy.

FYODOR IVANOVICH. Drop it . . . that's enough of that! Yulya, have them serve champagne!

YULYA. Fedenka, that's for tonight!

FYODOR IVANOVICH. Well, why wait—for tonight! Bring it now! Or else I'm leaving. Word of honor, I'm leaving. Where do you keep it? I'll go get it myself.

YULYA. You're always making a mess of the housekeeping, Fedya. (*To Vasily.*) Vasily, here's the key! The champagne's in the storeroom, you know, in the corner by the sack of raisins, in a basket. Only make sure you don't break anything.

FYODOR IVANOVICH. Vasily, three bottles!

YULYA. They'll never make a good housekeeper out of you, Fedenka . . . You always make a mess. (*Serves everyone pie.*) There's chicken to come, carp and artichokes. Have some more, gentlemen . . . Dinner won't be for a while yet, not until six . . .

VOINITSKY. I think someone just drove up . . . Did you hear?

ZHELTUKHIN. Yes . . . It's the Serebryakovs . . . Finally!

VASILY. The Serebryakov family has arrived!

YULYA (*cries out*). Sonichka! (*Runs out.*)

VOINITSKY (*sings*). Let's go and meet them, let's go and meet them . . . (*Exits.*)

FYODOR IVANOVICH. Look at the way they're rejoicing!

ZHELTUKHIN. The way *Georges* is rejoicing in particular! The tactlessness of some people! He sleeps with the Professor's lady and cannot hide it. The way he lavished praise on her just now, before you came, was practically indecent.

FYODOR IVANOVICH. How do you know he's sleeping with her?

ZHELTUKHIN. It's the talk of the whole district, my dear fellow . . .

FYODOR IVANOVICH. How about I go and stop your district's gullet with this mustard-pot.

V I

The same, SEREBRYAKOV, MARIYA VASILYEVNA,
VOINITSKY arm in arm with YELENA ANDREEVNA,
SONYA, and YULYA (enter).

YULYA (*kissing Sonya*). My dearest! My dearest!

ORLOVSKY (*going to meet them*). Sasha, greetings, my dear fellow, greetings, my boy! (*Exchanges kisses with the Professor.*) Are you well? Shall we thank God?

SEREBRYAKOV. How about you, neighbor? You're the same as ever, bravely done! Very pleased to see you. Been here long?

ORLOVSKY. Got here on Friday. Mariya Vasilyevna! How are you getting on, Your Excellency? (*Kisses her hand.*)

MARIYA VASILYEVNA. My dear . . . (*Kisses him on the head.*)

SONYA. Godfather dear!

ORLOVSKY. Sonechka! Dear heart! (*Kisses her.*) My little dove, my little canary . . .

SONYA. Your face is just as kind, sentimental, sweet as ever . . .

ORLOVSKY. And you've got taller and prettier and all grown up, dear heart . . .

SONYA. Well, how are you in general? Are you well?

ORLOVSKY. Frightfully well!

SONYA. Good for you, godfather! Ah, what a magnificent pie!

YULYA. Dearest!

FYODOR IVANOVICH (*to Sonya*). Aren't you going to say hello to me? (*Exchanges kisses with her.*)

SONYA. And I didn't even notice the elephant in the room. Sunburned, bristly . . . a regular spider! Fedya, if you care for me, quick, smear me some caviar.

ORLOVSKY (*to Serebryakov*). How are you getting on, neighbor? I expect you're writing all the time?

SEREBRYAKOV. Yes, just a bit. That's the routine I'm in: I work at my desk from morn to night. It's a habit. How are you?

ORLOVSKY. What should be wrong with me? I'm alive! I turned my estate over to my son, married off my daughters to good people, and now I'm the freest man going. I know how to have a good time!

DYADIN (*to Serebryakov*). Your Excellency, you were pleased to be a bit late. The temperature of the pie has gone down considerably. May I introduce myself: Ilya Ilyich Dyadin, or, as some people very wittily express it on account of my pockmarked face, Waffles.

SEREBRYAKOV. Pleased to meet you.

DYADIN. *Madame! Mademoiselle!* (*Bows to Yelena Andreevna and Sonya*). Everyone here is a friend of mine, Your Excellency. Once I possessed a large fortune, but, owing to domestic vicissitudes, or, as the expression is in intellectual circles, for reasons over which the editor has no control, I had to give up my share to my own brother, who, on a certain unhappy occasion, was in arrears of seventy thousand rubles of government money. My profession: the exploitation of the tempestuous elements. Of my previous grandeur all that is left are my friends and a love of virtue. I make the stormy waves turn the wheel of a mill, which I rent from my friend the Wood Goblin.

VOINITSKY. Waffles, turn off the waterworks!

DYADIN. I shall always pay my reverent respects to the luminaries of science, who adorn our national horizon. Forgive me the audacity of dreaming of paying Your Excellency a visit and charming my heart with a colloquy about the latest scientific findings.

SEREBRYAKOV. Please do come. I shall be delighted.

SONYA. Now, do tell us, godfather . . . Where did you spend the winter? Where did you disappear to?

ORLOVSKY. I was in Gmunden, I was in Paris, Nice, London, dear heart . . .

SONYA. You lucky man! It must be nice to have lots of money. You just pick up and go.

DYADIN. Beg pardon, *mademoiselle*. I take the liberty of rephrasing your happy thought in this way: it must be nice not to need money. Not every millionaire leads a jolly life and not every beggar is downcast. The man who does not need money is nature's nobleman.

SONYA. But what if you don't have any money?

DYADIN. An extremely subtle observation! I am defeated. (*Roars with laughter.*) I am defeated! Bravo, *mademoiselle*!

SONYA *laughs into her napkin.*

Now, it would be interesting to observe this table *à vol d'oiseau*. What a fascinating nosegay! A combination of grace, beauty, profound learning, swee . . .

FYODOR IVANOVICH (*interrupting him*). What a fascinating tongue! What the hell is this? You talk as if somebody were shaving your back with a carpenter's plane . . . "Your piehole fill and your tongue keep still."

SEREBRYAKOV (*eats*). "Your piehole fill and your tongue keep still." I recall a minor episode involving that proverb. A certain professor—I don't believe I need to name names—when I was in Petersburg, invited me to his home for lunch. On the appointed day I arrived at his summer cottage and among others ran into the late Sergey Mikhailovich Solovyov. We were early and so the host, in order to keep us busy, began to talk to us about persons who had come down in life. He talked at great length and bored us frightfully. I thought he'd never end. When they served the pie, Sergey Mikhailovich took a piece and said, "Your piehole fill and your tongue keep still." Of course he said it automatically, with any ulterior motive, but the host took him at his word and shut up. It all turned a bit awkward.

MARIYA VASILYEVNA (*bursts out laughing*). I can imagine . . .

SEREBRYAKOV. Later we laughed long and hard.

VOINITSKY (*aside*). Yes, very funny!

Pause.

SONYA. When you were away, godfather dear, the whole winter was so boring it was simply awful.

ORLOVSKY. It's your own fault. Why don't you visit your neighbors?

SONYA. I did visit Yulechka, but as for the rest—no, thank you very much! God forbid. Boredom is preferable to our neighbors.

ORLOVSKY. Why is that?

SONYA. Spare me. Not a single ordinary person, they all deserve to be put in a museum. Populists in embroidered peasant blouses, country doctors, like Bazarov.[1]

ORLOVSKY. You've no cause to think that way.

SONYA. Followers of Tolstoy, who, when they pay you a visit, insist on coming through the back door . . . no, spare me, for pity's sake! And the poseurs in town get on my nerves too . . .

ORLOVSKY. You've got too much imagination! How come you don't write serial stories for the papers?

VOINITSKY. She writes a diary. A really thick one! It's resolved all the issues.

ORLOVSKY. Dear heart, you should fall in love and get married.

VOINITSKY. For pity's sake, who's she supposed to marry. Humboldt is dead, Edison's in America, Lassalle's dead too . . .

SONYA. Leave it to others to be ironical, but you shouldn't, Uncle *Georges* . . .

VOINITSKY. What are you getting angry for?

SONYA. If you say another word, one of us will have to go home. You or I . . .

ORLOVSKY (*roars with laughter*). Why, what a temper!

VOINITSKY. Yes, a temper, I grant you that . . . (*To Sonya.*) Well, your little paw! Give me your little paw! (*Kisses her hand.*) Peace and harmony . . . I won't do it again.

V I I

The same and KHRUSHCHOV.

KHRUSHCHOV (*coming out of the house*). Why am I not an artist? What a wonderful composition.

ORLOVSKY (*gleefully*). Misha! My dear little godson!

---

1 A leading character in Turgenev's *Fathers and Sons* (1862), a cynical "Nihilist," taken to be a caricature of the radicals of the time, until the critic Pisaryov cited Bazarov as the prototype of the progressive democrat.

FYODOR IVANOVICH. The wood goblin!

KHRUSHCHOV. Many happy returns to the birthday boy! Greeting, Yulechka, how pretty you look today! Godfather! (*Exchanges kisses with Orlovsky*). Sofya Aleksandrovna . . . (*Greets everyone.*)

ZHELTUKHIN. Well, how can a person be so late? Where were you?

KHRUSHCHOV. With a patient.

YULYA. The pie's gone cold long ago.

KHRUSHCHOV. Never mind, Yulechka, I'll eat it cold. Where should I sit?

SONYA. Sit down here . . . (*Offers him the place beside her.*)

KHRUSHCHOV. The weather's splendid today. And that little pie is throwing me a mouth-watering glance! I'll eat it up right now . . . (*Drinks vodka.*) To the birthday boy! I'll taste this little pie . . . Yulechka, kiss this pie. It'll make it tastier . . .

> *She kisses it.*

Merci. How are you getting on, godfather? I haven't seen you for a long time.

ORLOVSKY. Yes, we haven't met for quite a while. I was abroad, you see.

KHRUSHCHOV. I heard, I heard . . . I envied you. Fyodor, how about you?

FYODOR IVANOVICH. I'm all right.

KHRUSHCHOV. How's your business?

FYODOR IVANOVICH. I can't complain. Only, there's too much back and forth. Wears me down . . . From here to the Caucasus, from the Caucasus back here, from here back to the Caucasus—and it never ends. You're on the go like a maniac. After all I've got two estates there!

KHRUSHCHOV. I know.

FYODOR IVANOVICH. I'm working at finding settlers and all I attract is tarantulas and scorpions. The business is going well in general, but as to "down, down, ye surging passions"—it's the same old story.

KHRUSHCHOV. In love, of course?

FYODOR IVANOVICH. On which account, I need a drink. (*Drinks.*) Ladies and gentlemen, never fall in love with married women! Word of honor, it's better to be wounded in the shoulder and shot in the leg, like your most humble servant, than love a married woman . . . So much trouble it's simply . . .

SONYA. Hopeless?

FYODOR IVANOVICH. Don't be ridiculous! Hopeless . . . If a man seriously wanted to make a catch, he could catch anything at all! Hopeless, unrequited love, oohing and aahing—that's just self-indulgence. If I will my gun not to misfire, it won't. I can't recall any time it misfired. Just like that, Sonya, old pal. And once I have my eye on a woman, I think it'll be easier for her to fly to the moon than get away from me. You won't get away from me, no! I wouldn't have to say three sentences to her, before she's in my power. Yes. I only have to say to her: "Madam, every time you look out a certain window, you must remember me. I will it." Which means, she'll remember me a thousand times a day. That's not all, I bombard her every day with letters.

YELENA ANDREEVNA. Letters are an unreliable medium. She may receive them but not read them.

FYODOR IVANOVICH. You think so? Hm . . . I've lived on this earth thirty-five years, and somehow haven't met with such phenomenal women as have the fortitude not to open a letter.

ORLOVSKY (*admiring him*). How do you like that? My sonny boy! I was just the same, down to the last detail! Only I didn't go to war, just drank vodka and wasted money—dreadful business!

FYODOR IVANOVICH. I do love her, Misha, seriously. If she only made the wish, I would give her everything: my freedom, my strength, my money. I'd carry her off to my place in the Caucasus, the mountains, we would live in clover . . . Yelena Andreevna, I would protect her, like a loyal hound, and for me she would be, like our marshal of nobility sings, "And thou shalt be queen of the world, my love for all eternity." Ech, she doesn't know the happiness she's missing!

KHRUSHCHOV. Who is this happy creature?

FYODOR IVANOVICH. A little knowledge is a dangerous thing . . . But enough about this. Now let's have a song from a different opera. I remember, about ten years ago—Lyonya was still in high school at the time—we were celebrating his birthday just as we are now. I was riding home from here, and at my right hand sat Sonya, and on my left Yulka, and both were holding on to my beard. Gentlemen, let's drink to the health of the friends of my youth, Sonya and Yulya!

DYADIN (*laughs loudly*). This is fascinating! This is fascinating!

FYODOR IVANOVICH. Once when the war was over I was getting drunk with a Turkish pasha in Trebizond . . . He starts asking me . . .

DYADIN (*interrupting*). Gentlemen, let's drink a toast to distinguished relations! *Vivat* friendship! Long may it live!

FYODOR IVANOVICH. Stop, stop, stop! Sonya, please pay attention! I'm going to make a wager! I am putting three hundred rubles down on the table! After lunch let's go play croquet, and I'll bet that I'll get through all the hoops and back in one go.

SONYA. I accept. Only I haven't got three hundred rubles.

FYODOR IVANOVICH. If you lose, you'll sing to me forty times.

SONYA. Agreed.

DYADIN. This is fascinating! This is fascinating!

ZHELTUKHIN (*getting up*). Ladies and gentlemen, if we're going to drink, let's drink to better days, better people, to ideals!

> *SONYA bursts out laughing.*

ORLOVSKY. Well, our girl's gone off now! What's come over you?

> *KHRUSHCHOV bursts out laughing.*

And what's wrong with you?

MARIYA VASILYEVNA. Sophie, that's indecorous!

KHRUSHCHOV. Ugh, sorry, my friends . . . I'll be done right away . . . right away . . . .

ZHELTUKHIN. You found something funny about my toast . . .

KHRUSHCHOV. Not at all. Word of honor, no. Absolutely no reason at all.

VOINITSKY. Just show the two of them a finger, and they'll burst out laughing. Sonya! (*Shows her a finger.*) Here, look . . .

KHRUSHCHOV. That's enough! (*Looks at his watch.*) Well, Mikhail was a jolly old soul, he called for his food and called for his bowl, and now his time is up. It's time to go.

SONYA. Where are you off to?

KHRUSHCHOV. To a patient. My medical practice is as distasteful as a shrewish wife, or a long winter . . .

SEREBRYAKOV. Excuse me, and yet medicine is your profession, your vocation, so to speak . . .

VOINITSKY (*ironically*). He's got another vocation. He excavates peat on his land.

SEREBRYAKOV. What?

VOINITSKY. Peat. Some engineer figured it out, like two times two, that his land contains seven hundred and twenty thousand rubles worth of peat. No joke.

KHRUSHCHOV. I don't excavate peat for profit.

VOINITSKY. What do you excavate it for then?

KHRUSHCHOV. I like that question . . . What do I excavate it for? For tooth powder! (*Annoyed.*) All the Russian forests are toppling beneath the axe, the habitats of birds and beasts are dwindling, tens of thousands of trees are perishing, rivers are running shallow and drying up, gorgeous natural scenery is disappearing irretrievably, and all because lazy human beings can't be bothered to bend down and pick up fuel from the earth. I don't see anything to laugh about in that.

VOINITSKY. I'm not laughing. Where'd you get that idea?

KHRUSHCHOV. You destroy the forests, but they beautify the land, they teach people to understand beauty, their grandeur inspires us with a sense of grandeur. Forests alleviate a harsh climate. Where the climate is mild, less energy is spent on the struggle with nature and therefore human beings there are milder and more delicate. In countries where the climate is mild, the people are beautiful, athletic, very sensitive, their speech is refined, their movements graceful. There art and sciences flourish, their philosophy is not gloomy, their attitude to women is full of exquisite chivalry. You stare at me sarcastically, and everything I say strikes you as old and frivolous, but when I walk through the peasants' forests that I have saved from being chopped down, or when I hear the wind rustling in my stand of saplings, planted by my own hands, I realize that the climate is to some slight degree in my control, and if, a thousand years from now, humanity is happy, then even I will be partially responsible. When I plant a birch tree, and then see how it grows green and sways in the wind, my soul swells with pride at the awareness that I am helping God create an organism.

FYODOR IVANOVICH. Your health, Wood Goblin!

KHRUSHCHOV. A person has to be an unreasoning barbarian and have no fear of God to burn up this beauty in his stove, to destroy what we cannot create. Human beings are endowed with reason and creative faculties in order to enhance what is given to them but so far they have not created but destroyed. Forests are ever fewer and fewer, rivers dry up, wildlife is wiped out, the climate is spoiled, and every day the earth grows more impoverished and ugly.

VOINITSKY. Which is all very charming, but where, my dear fellow, did you get the idea that climates become milder because of forests? If you were to consider the matter not from a pulp-fiction point of view, but from a scientific one, you'd say quite the opposite . . .

KHRUSHCHOV. If you think things would be better without forests, then why are you sitting still and not destroying what's left? Yegor Petrovich, you know what? Let's not talk about this.

VOINITSKY. As you like.

MARIYA VASILYEVNA. Ah!

SONYA. What's the matter, Granny?

MARIYA VASILYEVNA (*to Serebryakov*). I beg your pardon, Aleksandr . . . I forgot to tell you . . . I must be losing my memory . . . today I got a letter from Kharkov from Pavel Alekseevich . . . He sent his regards . . .

SEREBRYAKOV. Thank you, delighted.

MARIYA VASILYEVNA. He sent his new pamphlet and asked me to show it you.

SEREBRYAKOV. Interesting?

MARIYA VASILYEVNA. Interesting, but rather peculiar. He opposes the very thing he was defending seven years ago. It's very, very typical of our times. Never have people betrayed their convictions as frivolously as they do now.

ZHELTUKHIN. No ideals!

MARIYA VASILYEVNA. Somehow the pieces on the board have been moved around, and it's positively difficult to figure out nowadays who belongs to which faction and where their sympathies lie. It's appalling!

VOINITSKY. It's not at all appalling. Have some carp, *maman*.

MARIYA VASILYEVNA. But I want to talk!

VOINITSKY. For fifty years now we've been talking about sympathies and factions, it's high time we stopped.

MARIYA VASILYEVNA. For some reason you don't like to listen when I talk. Pardon me, *Georges*, but this last year you have changed so much that I utterly fail to recognize you . . . You used to be a man of steadfast convictions, a shining light . . .

VOINITSKY. Oh yes! I was a shining light but no one ever basked in my rays. May I leave the table? I was a shining light . . . Don't rub salt in my wounds! Now I'm forty-seven. Before last year I was the same as you, deliberately trying to cloud my vision with all these abstractions to keep from seeing real life—and I thought I was doing the right thing. I never fell in love, wasn't loved, had no family, didn't drink wine, didn't enjoy myself, because I was trying to consider all that as vulgar! And now, if you only knew how I hate myself for having wasted my time so stupidly when I could have had everything that's withheld from me now by my old age! I've wasted my life stupidly, and the awareness of that is gnawing at my heart now.

SEREBRYAKOV. Hold on . . . *Georges*, you seem to be blaming your former convictions for something . . .

SONYA. That's enough, Papa! It's boring!

SEREBRYAKOV. Hold on . . . You are indeed blaming your former convictions for something. But they aren't to blame, *you* are. You have forgotten that convictions without deeds are a dead letter. One must take action.

VOINITSKY. Take action? Not everyone is capable of being a perpetual-motion writing machine.

SEREBRYAKOV. What do you mean by that?

VOINITSKY. Nothing. Let's change the subject. We're not at home.

MARIYA VASILYEVNA. I really am losing my memory . . . . I forgot to remind you, Aleksandr, to take your drops before lunch. I brought them along, but I forgot to remind you . . .

SEREBRYAKOV. You needn't have.

MARIYA VASILYEVNA. But after all you're a sick man, Aleksandr! You're a very sick man!

SEREBRYAKOV. Why shout it from the rooftops? Old, sick, old, sick . . . that's all I ever hear! (*To Zheltukhin.*) Leonid Stepanych, may I leave the table and go inside? It's rather hot here and the mosquitoes are ferocious.

ZHELTUKHIN. Please be so kind. Lunch is over.

SEREBRYAKOV. Thank you. (*Exits into the house, followed by MARIYA VASILYEVNA.*)

YULYA (*to her brother*). Go after the Professor! It's impolite!

ZHELTUKHIN (*to her*). The hell with him! (*Exits.*)

DYADIN. Yuliya Stepanovna, may I thank you from the bottom of my heart. (*Kisses her hand.*)

YULYA. Don't mention it, Ilya Ilyich! You've eaten so little . . .

They thank her.

Don't mention it, gentlemen! You all ate so little!

FYODOR IVANOVICH. Well, gents, what shall we do now? Let's go right now to the croquet lawn and settle our wager . . . and after that?

YULYA. After that we'll have dinner.

FYODOR IVANOVICH. And after that?

KHRUSHCHOV. After that you can all come to my place. In the evening we'll arrange a fishing party on the lake.

FYODOR IVANOVICH. Excellent.

DYADIN. Fascinating.

KHRUSHCHOV. It's really nice at my place, gentlemen! You sit at home in the evening or at night you go out on the lake in a boat; the sky is reflected in the water so that there's one sky full of stars over head, and another down below under the boat. Two skies, two moons . . . It's awe-inspiring!

SONYA. Let me get this straight, gentlemen. That means, right now we're going to the croquet lawn to settle the wager . . . Then we'll have an early dinner with Yulya and about seven we'll drive over to the Woo . . . I mean, to Mikhail Lvovich's. Wonderful. Let's go, Yulechka, and get the balls.

She and YULYA exit into the house.

FYODOR IVANOVICH. Vasily, bring the wine to the croquet lawn! We'll drink to the health of the winner. Well, my old progenitor, let's take part in this noble game.

ORLOVSKY. Wait, my own dear boy, I have to sit with the Professor for about five minutes, otherwise it would be impolite. One has to observe etiquette. Meanwhile play my ball, and I'll be there soon . . . (*Exits into the house.*)

DYADIN. I shall go at once and listen to the most learned Aleksandr Vladimirovich. I anticipate a sublime pleasure, whi . . .

VOINITSKY. I'm sick to death of you, Waffles. Go on.

DYADIN. I'm going, sir. (*Exits into the house.*)

FYODOR IVANOVICH (*going into the garden, sings*). "And thou shalt be queen of the world, my love for all eternity . . ."(*Exits.*)

KHRUSHCHOV. I'm going to leave nice and quietly. (*To Voinitsky.*) Yegor Petrovich, I beg you most sincerely, let's never talk about forests or medicine again. I don't know why, but when you launch into that sort of talk, all day long I have the feeling I've eaten my dinner out of a rusty pot. My respects!

YELENA ANDREEVNA. Sorry . . . Just now you invited everyone to your home . . . Am I included?

KHRUSHCHOV (*embarrassed*). I mean . . . Of course, of course! I'd be very pleased. However it's going on four o'clock . . . My respects . . . (*Exits.*)

page 608 / *After*: life, my youth! . . . — Love for you has made me a different man . . .

ACT TWO

page 623 / *Before*: You're angry with me — Let's talk frankly, like friends.

ACT THREE

page 626 / *Replace*: Yes . . . a fine piece . . . it's ever been so boring around here as it is now . . .

with: I don't think it's ever been so boring around here, you walk from room to room, you sit, you stand, as if waiting for something.

ORLOVSKY. But I like it, my dear boy. You sit, you stand, your shoulder itches, you scratch it, and time passes by.

VOINITSKY. As if waiting for something . . . And what are you waiting for? You look back, all your life's been filled with boredom, you look at the present, more boredom.

page 627 / *Replace*: If I ever did have a bee in my bonnet . . . Let's have some champagne!

with: VOINITSKY. He has to have chik-chak, chik-chak.

ORLOVSKY. A beautiful girl . . .

FYODOR IVANOVICH. She slinks like a shadow, from room to room and can't find a place for herself. She's in love with the Wood Goblin.

VOINITSKY. Well, isn't she the lucky girl.

FYODOR IVANOVICH. Why not? He's a good fellow.

ORLOVSKY. Amen to that! May God help them . . . If people are good, you've got to act in a way that makes them even better. We ought to make the Wood Goblin some kind of gift. Fedya, you should send him a team of horses, or something . . .

FYODOR IVANOVICH. All right. Remind me when we get home. A team of horses and maybe I could add a gun. (*Stretches*.) Oof! Gentlemen, let's have some champagne, shall we?

page 629 / *Replace*:

YELENA ANDREEVNA. And what do you know about it? . . .

ORLOVSKY. A darling, a beauty . . .

with: YELENA ANDREEVNA. Don't tempt me, you devil! (*Exits*.)

page 629 / *Replace*: Sour grapes! Curdled cream!

with: If you don't want to live, then go to a desert, to a convent, die at last, but why hoodwink people, why under the guise of virtue pass off something that is downright criminal? After all, isn't it criminal to cripple one's youth, after all . . .

page 630 / *After*: Fine, thank God. — Only his neck hurts a bit.

page 631 / *Replace*: ORLOVSKY. The reception room it is . . . I couldn't care less.

with: FYODOR IVANOVICH. Let's go.

page 631 / *Replace*: YULYA (*alone, after a pause*.) . . . (*Clicks beads on the abacus*.)

with: **YULYA** (*alone*). First I have to . . . Two calves at three fifty a piece. I could charge three a piece for them . . . (*Clicks.*) A bullock . . . well, ten . . . (*Clicks.*) For yesterday's barley thirty-two rubles. Eighty gallons of oil at twenty-three kopeks . . . Three times eight is twenty-four . . . four, carry the two, one times three is three . . . Hm . . . for the oil, that makes four rubles fourteen kopeks. (*Clicks.*) I can knock off the fourteen kopeks.

page 631 / *Replace*: They can't match me up with a decent suitor!

with: You know, when you've got such a good, clever, exceptional brother, somehow you don't want to marry any Tom, Dick, or Harry. After all, they can't match me up with a decent suitor!

page 632 / *After*: spiritual bond with you . . . — We've been friends.

page 632 / *After*: What's making you embarrassed, Yulechka? — Is it a secret or what?

page 633 / *Replace*: Scene VII
with:

V I I

YELENA ANDREEVNA, then FYODOR IVANOVICH.

YELENA ANDREEVNA (*alone*). What is this? A letter from *Georges* to me! Why is that my fault? Oh, how cruel, how shameless. Her heart is so pure that she cannot talk to me . . . My God, what an insult . . . My God, my head is spinning, I'm going to faint . . .

FYODOR IVANOVICH (*enters through the door at left and walks across the stage*). Why do you all give a start when you see me?

Pause.

Hm . . . (*Takes the letter from her hands and tears it to shreds.*) Drop all this . . . You must think only of me . . . (*Exits through the door at right.*)

YELENA ANDREEVNA (*alone*). What did he just say? What did he do? Talking about windows again? That damned man embarrasses me, I'm afraid of him, but yet Sonya's heart is so pure that she cannot talk to me . . . (*Weeps.*) I should get out of this maelstrom—out into the fields and walk day and night so that I see nothing, hear nothing, think nothing . . . (*Goes to the door at left, but, on seeing ZHELTUKHIN and YULYA coming to meet her, exits through the central door.*)

page 635 / *Replace*: Scene IX
with:

I X

The same, SEREBRYAKOV, ORLOVSKY, and
MARIYA VASILYEVNA.

ORLOVSKY. I'm not in the best of health either, my dear boy. Why, for two days now my head's been aching and my whole body tingles . . . (*Blows into the palm of his hand.*) And my breath is hot.

SEREBRYAKOV. Where are the others? I do not like this house. Just like a labyrinth. Twenty-six enormous rooms, everyone scatters, and you can never find anyone. (*Rings.*) Request Yegor Petrovich and Yelena Andreevna to come here!

ZHELTUKHIN. Yulya, you've got nothing to do, go and find Yegor Petrovich and Yelena Andreevna.

YULYA exits.

SEREBRYAKOV. Ill health one might be reconciled to, if the worse came to the worst, but what I cannot stomach is my state of mind at the present time. I have the feeling that I'm already dead or have dropped off the earth on to some alien planet.

ZHELTUKHIN. I've got exactly the same feeling. Here in Russia the only people who live well are the rich peasants and the heroes of Shchedrin's novels.[2] And I wouldn't be at all surprised if you and I starved to death or . . . or well, generally speaking . . .

ORLOVSKY. It depends on how you look at it. That might be so. But this is the way I understand your mood, Sasha. Before you retired, before you wound up here, you were happy, content with yourself and others, you didn't feel old or sick, but as soon as you wound up here against your will, everything went contrary for you: you don't like the people, you don't like yourself, the set-up here is alien to you, so you feel sick and old . . . In that case, of course, you're bound to feel a turmoil in your soul . . .

SEREBRYAKOV. Yes, I do feel it.

ORLOVSKY. And when there's turmoil in your soul, you can't help yourself with words or tears or any kind of idea. Sasha, old pal, for forty years I led exactly the same kind of life as my Fyodor. I went on benders, and tossed money around, and when it came to the fair sex I was nobody's fool either. The other day I was asking him: "Fedya, tell me honestly, how many women have you made unhappy in your time?" He thought a bit and says,

---

2 Mikhail Saltykov-Shchedrin (1826–1889), a writer influenced by French socialism and Russian populism; his novels were satirical indictments of Russian life.

"I don't remember. Around sixty, but maybe it's seventy. You can't recall them all." That's how many I had too. Well sir, as soon I reached the age of forty, suddenly, Sasha, old pal, something came over me. A desolation, I didn't know what to do with myself, I wept, didn't want to see people, even considered shooting myself—in short, turmoil, and that's that. What's to be done then? I did one thing after another, I'd read books, I'd work, I'd travel—nothing helped! Well, sir, old pal o' mine, now you'll ask: what saved me? A trifle. I was paying a call on a now deceased neighbor of mine, his Most Serene Highness Prince Dmitry Pavlovich. We had a snack, then we had dinner . . . After dinner, to keep from napping, we arranged for target shooting in the courtyard. Scads and scads of people gathered round: the gentry, and peasants, and sportsmen, and even our Waffles. The desolation I was feeling, you understand—good Lord! I couldn't bear it. Suddenly, tears welled up in my eyes, I started to sway and began to shout to the whole courtyard, at the top of my lungs: "My friends, good people, forgive me for Christ's sake!" And at that very minute my heart grew pure, loving, warm, and from that time on, my dear boy, in all the district there's no happier man than I am. And you should do the same thing.

SEREBRYAKOV. Ivan Ivanych, you're an intelligent man! Why should I ask for forgiveness? It's an absurd, homegrown philosophy! Other people should be asking my forgiveness! (*To Zheltukhin.*) Tell me please, are there any ordinary, normal people around here? Every last one is a deep thinker or a philosopher. Out of the blue, he starts to think thoughts. One for no reason at all asks forgiveness, another raves about those forests . . . No, gentlemen, one must take action! One can't go on like this. One must take action.

MARIYA VASILYEVNA (*reading*). Give me a pencil . . . Another contradiction! I have to jot it down.

ORLOVSKY. Please take this one, Your Excellency! (*Hands her a pencil and kisses her hand.*)

ZHELTUKHIN (*sighing*). We won't be taking action around here any time soon. The time's not ripe, Aleksandr Vladimirovich. Much too early. The all-prevailing ignorance allied with the inertia of the ruling classes, moreover . . .

ORLOVSKY. Anyway I've got headache and . . . and . . . my face is flushed . . .

SEREBRYAKOV. Excuse me, I'm detaining you . . .

ORLOVSKY. Not at all, I just need to shake it off . . .

Enter VOINITSKY.

page 637 / *Replace*: To live in town . . . impossible.

with: The means we currently have at our disposal is insufficient for urban living. To live in town on the income from the estate is impossible.

page 638 / *After*: excursion — an expedition, so to speak,

page 639 / *After*: This estate was bought from his uncle — Waffles, how much
did my father pay for this estate?

page 639 / *Replace*: For twenty-five years . . . sat between these four walls

with: Hold on, let me have my say at least once in my life. Twenty-five [*sic*] I
and she, my mother, sat like moles between these four walls

page 640 / *Replace*: I'm going to another room . . . I can't take any more
of this!

with: Excuse me . . . (*Exits in powerful excitement.*)

YELENA ANDREEVNA. *Georges*, I insist that you keep quiet!

SEREBRYAKOV. What do you want from me?

page 641 / *Replace*: Move him into the village . . . There, there, there . . . My
friends

with: If he needs to, let him move to the servant's quarters, to the village, but
I cannot remain with him. I shall go! I shall go!

YELENA ANDREEVNA. Aleksandr, I'm worn out. If you truly consider him
to be deranged, I beg of you, don't respond to his insults. Otherwise this
war will never end. I'm begging you . . .

ZHELTUKHIN. I have been an involuntry witness to this dismaying scene
and therefore I ask your permission to intervene. Today I'll have a word
with him and act so that he will ask your forgiveness.

YELENA ANDREEVNA. No, there no need for forgiveness! I'm afraid of
these forgivenesses . . .

page 641 / *Replace*: Scene XII
with:

X I I

The same and KHRUSHCHOV.

KHRUSHCHOV (*agitated*). I'm delighted to find you at home, Aleksandr
Vladimirovich . . . Forgive me, I may have come at a bad time and am dis-
turbing you . . . But that's not the point. Sorry, I haven't said hello . . .
Good afternoon, Godfather.

SEREBRYAKOV. What can I do for you?

KHRUSHCHOV. Excuse me, I'm over-excited—it's because I just rode over here so quickly . . . Aleksandr Vladimirovich, I heard that the day before yesterday you sold your forest to Kuznetsov for timber. If that's true, and not mere gossip, then I beg you, for heaven's sake, not to do it.

SEREBRYAKOV. Forgive me, I don't understand you and . . . and I am not disposed to understand.

KHRUSHCHOV. Let me ride over to Kuznetsov and tell him that you've reconsidered! All right? May I? I implore, I entreat you by all you hold sacred! (*Weeps.*) To fell thousands of trees, to destroy them for the sake of a few thousand, to pay for women's fripperies, caprices, luxuries . . . To destroy so that future generations will curse our barbarity! If you, a learned, famous man, make up your mind to such cruelty, what are other people, far inferior to you, to do? This is really horrible!

ZHELTUKHIN. Misha, put it off to later . . . Aleksandr Vladimirovich isn't disposed . . .

KHRUSHCHOV (*to Serebryakov*). You turn away from me . . . If, after imploring you like a beggar, I am, in your opinion, wrong, then prove it to me . . . You're a professor, a celebrity, rich in knowledge and long in life—I'll believe you! Prove it to me!

SEREBRYAKOV. Let's go, Ivan Ivanych, there'll be no end to this.

KHRUSHCHOV (*blocks Serebryakov's path*). In that case, tell you what, Professor . . . Wait, in three months I'll put the money together and buy it from you myself . . . Ivan Ivanovich, Godfather, at least you'll stand up for me! At least say something, anything!

ORLOVSKY. The man's a crackpot! What can I say?

KHRUSHCHOV (*flaring up*). Of course, what is there to say? Keep quiet and do nothing! Eh, Godfather, there are a lot of good-natured people on this earth, and that always struck me as suspicious! They're good-natured because they're couldn't care less!

YELENA ANDREEVNA (*to her husband*). Aleksandr, listen to Mikhail Lvovich!

KHRUSHCHOV. You may go, Professor, wherever you like, I won't detain you. I am not ashamed for having just humiliated myself and even wept in front of you. You and Ivan Ivanych aren't ashamed either, which means everything is working out just fine, for which I congratulate you! My respects!

SEREBRYAKOV (*sharply*). And next time be so good as not to come in unannounced, and please spare me your psychotic stunts! You all wanted to try my patience, and you succeeded . . . Please leave me alone! All these forests of yours, the peat I consider to be delirium and psychosis—there, that's my opinion! Let's go, Ivan Ivanovich!

YELENA ANDREEVNA (*follows him*). Aleksandr, that's going too far!

She, SEREBRYAKOV, and ORLOVSKY exit.

KHRUSHCHOV (*alone, after a pause*). Delirium, psychosis . . . Which means, in the opinion of a famous scholar and professor, I'm insane . . . I submit to Your Excellency's authority and shall now go home and shave my head. No, the earth which still supports you is insane!

He goes quickly to the door at right; enter from the door at left SONYA, who had been eavesdropping in the doorway throughout all of Scene XII.

page 643 / *After*: heard it all — . . . Here's a handkerchief, dry your tears . . . I shall keep this handkerchief as a souvenir . . .

page 644 / *Replace*: Just now Ivan Ivanovich told me . . . in the sincerity of my respect

with: I was a witness to it all . . . My soul belongs to you! Believe in the sincerity of my respect for you

page 644 / *After*: Get away for me . . . — begone!

page 644 / *Replace*: Scenes XV and XVI
with:

X V

YELENA ANDREEVNA, MARYA VASILYEVNA, then SONYA, SEREBRYAKOV, ORLOVSKY, and ZHELTUKHIN. MARYA VASILYEVNA staggers out of the central door, screams and falls unconscious.

SONYA enters and runs out the central door.

SEREBRYAKOV
ORLOVSKY　　　　⎫ What is it?
ZHELTUKHIN

SONYA's screams are heard; she returns and cries out: "Uncle Georges has shot himself!" She, ORLOVSKY, SEREBRYAKOV, and ZHELTUKHIN run out the central door.

YELENA ANDREEVNA (*moans*). What for? What for?

FYODOR IVANOVICH appears in the door at right.

XVI

YELENA ANDREEVNA, MARYA VASILYEVNA, and
FYODOR IVANOVICH.

FYODOR IVANOVICH (*in the doorway*). What's going on?

YELENA ANDREEVNA (*to him*). Take me away from here! Throw me down a mineshaft! Kill me, abuse me! . . . . (*Falls into his arms.*)

FYODOR IVANOVICH (*bursts into forced laughter, imitating an operatic Mephistopheles*). Ha, ha, ha! (*An octave lower.*) Ha, ha, ha!

Curtain

Early version of Act Four.

ACT FOUR

A forest and the house by the mill, which Dyadin rents
from Khrushchov.

I

SEMYON (carries a bucket), YULYA, then DYADIN.

YULYA (*entering*). Good afternoon, Semyon, God save you! Is Ilya Ilyich at home?

SEMYON. He is. He's sleeping in the mill.

YULYA. Go and wake him.

SEMYON. Right away. (*Exits.*)

YULYA (*alone; sits on the litle bench beneath the window and sighs deeply.*). Ugh! Some people sleep, others enjoy themselves, but I spend my days on the go, on the go . . . I think I'm the unhappiest person on earth. God won't let me die. (*Sighs even more deeply.*) Lord, how can there be such foolish people as that Waffles! I was driving just now past his barn, and a little black piglet ran out the door . . . If those pigs start rooting in other people's grain sacks, he'll be hearing about it . . .

Enter DYADIN, putting on his frockcoat.

DYADIN. Is it you, Yuliya Stepanovna? Sorry, I'm in a state of undress . . . After dinner I dropped off in the arms of Morpheus.[3]

---

3 A roundabout way of saying "asleep"; Morpheus was the Greek god of dreams.

YULYA. Good afternoon, Ilya Ilyich.

DYADIN. Forgive me for not inviting you inside . . . My house is in a bit of a mess and so on . . . If you like, please come to the mill . . .

YULYA. I'll just sit here. Ilya Ilyich, what's the matter with you? Why do you mix up my sacks?

DYADIN. What you do mean by that remark?

YULYA. Our sacks are bought at Kharlamov's, and they're marked with the letter X, but you sent us ones with a V on them.

DYADIN. *Ce sont des* trivia. It's of no importance. They can be changed at any moment in time.

YULYA. Then please change them. Here's why I've dropped in on you, Ilya Ilyich. Lyonechka and the Professor, for some recreation, want to have a picnic here at your mill today, a tea party . . .

DYADIN. Extremely gratified.

YULYA. I came ahead of them. They'll be here soon. Please arrange for a table to be set up, oh and a samovar, of course . . . Have Senka get the baskets of food out of my carriage.

DYADIN. Can do.

Pause.

What's it like now? How are things over there?

YULYA. Bad, Ilya Ilyich. Such a pack of troubles you can't imagine. You know, of course, that the Professor and Sonya are living with us now? After Yegor Petrovich laid hands on himself, they got afraid to live in his house. The Professor is so done in, keeps losing weight, and stays mute, mute, mute . . . Sonichka, poor thing, keeps crying, and you can't pry a word out of her. By day there's no problem, but when night falls, they all gather in one room and sit there until dawn. They're all terrified. They're afraid that Yegor Petrovich is haunting the dark corners . . .

DYADIN. Superstition. I don't believe in ghosts, or even spiritualism. And do they mention Yelena Andreevna?

YULYA. Of course, they mention her. She ran off with Fedinka, didn't she! Did you hear?

DYADIN. Yes, a subject that deserves treatment by a painter of shipwrecks and tempests . . . She up and cleared out. (*Laughs.*) What a story! All the servants in the courtyard and the *paysans* in the countryside saw how he drove her away in his calèche. With one arm he's holding her in an unconscious state, and with the other he's lashing the horses with all his might, like Phoebus,[4] borne aloft in a chariot. And for all that he only did five miles. He halted not far from here, in the Count's woods, near old lady Yakunchikha's cabin, and went to get Yelena Andreevna a drink of water. While he went for the water, she was in such a state. He came back, and there wasn't a trace of her. He goes all over the place—nowhere to be found! And what do you think? In his wrath, seeing that his Don Juanesque scheme had not succeeded, he broke in Yakunchikha's door, all the windows, smashed the crockery and gave Yakunchikha herself a couple of black eyes. It's fascinating!

YULYA. So she's lost now. Nobody knows where . . . Maybe she went away, but maybe, in her desperation . . . all sorts of things might happen!

DYADIN. God is merciful, Yuliya Stepanovna! Everything will turn out for the best. I must confess, my heart is so full of bliss, so full of bliss! I am so boundlessly happy that, without recourse to fancy phrases, I can express it to you in the words of a certain poet . . .

YULYA (*interrupting him*). Why are you that way?

DYADIN. I don't know . . . I mean I don't have the right to explain it to you! I don't have the right, although I'm ablaze with impatience . . .

> *Enter KHRUSHCHOV with a portfolio and a case with drawing implements.*

I I

The same and KHRUSHCHOV.

KHRUSHCHOV. Hey! Anybody here? Semyon!

DYADIN. Look over here!

KHRUSHCHOV. Ah! . . . Good afternoon, Yulichka!

---

4 The Greek sun god, an avatar of Apollo, whose drive across the heavens accounted for the daylight hours.

YULYA. Good afternoon, Mikhail Lvovich.

KHRUSHCHOV. I've dropped by your place again, Ilya Ilyich, to get some work done. Sitting at home's no good. Tell them to set up my table under this tree as they did yesterday, oh, and tell them to get two lamps ready. It's getting dark already . . .

DYADIN (*goes*). Fine. At your service, your honor.

KHRUSHCHOV. There's a little box in there with my thumbtacks and a saucer. Don't forget!

DYADIN. I know! (*Exits.*)

KHRUSHCHOV. How are you getting on, Yulechka?

YULYA. We're getting on.

Pause.

Mikhail Lvovich, in your tree nursery how much are the pyramindal poplars?

KHRUSHCHOV. Not pyramindal, but pyramidal.

YULYA. That's what I said, pyramindal . . . How much?

KHRUSHCHOV. You'll come by, you'll pick some out . . . It'd be obvious there, we'll figure it out. Are the Serebryakovs living with you?

YULYA. Yes.

KHRUSHCHOV. Which means, your Lyonichka is spending all day at home . . . I'll bet he's happy.

YULYA. He sits at home. Always with Sonichka . . . Goes for walks with her, reads her poetry. All the same it's easier for her . . . And the way he reads, Mikhail Lvovich! Yesterday I even wept.

Enter DYADIN and SEMYON; they are carrying a small table.

III

The same, DYADIN, and SEMYON.

DYADIN. You know a sure thing when you see it. You picked a beautiful spot for your work. It's an oasis! A genuine oasis! Imagine that you're surrounded by palm trees, Yulichka is a gentle gazelle, you're a lion, I'm a tiger.

KHRUSHCHOV. You're a decent enough fellow, a sensitive soul, Ilya Ilyich, but why do you act this way? These sickly sweet words, the way you shuffle your feet, jerk your shoulders . . . If a stranger caught sight of you, he'd think you're not a man but some other damned thing! . . . It's annoying . . .

DYADIN. Which means, it was so ordained at my birth . . . Fatal predestination.

KHRUSHCHOV. There you go again, fatal predestination. Drop all that. (*Pinning a diagram to the table*.) I'm going to spend the night here.

DYADIN. I am extremely pleased . . . Now you're angry, Misha, while my heart's filled with indescribable joy! As if a dicky-bird were sitting in my breast, warbling a little ditty.

KHRUSHCHOV. O be joyful.

Pause.

Your heart is rejoicing and my mine is as gloomy as can be. You've got a dicky-bird in your breast, and I've got a toad in mine. Boredom, grief, my conscience is nagging at me—I even want to burst into tears. A million things are going wrong! Shimansky sold his forest for timber . . . That's one! Ivan Ivanych is mortally ill; he's got typhus and they think it'll be complicated by inflammation of the lungs. That's two! Yelena Andreevna ran away with that blockhead Fyodor, and now nobody knows where she is. That's three! She either ran away somewhere, or else threw herself in the water, took poison—take your pick, whatever you please. But the main thing, the most awful thing of all, the thing that torments me the most is that I cannot sit at home alone and I fear the darkness. Yesterday I wanted to tell you, but I couldn't, I didn't have the courage. You know what? The late Yegor Petrovich left behind a diary, and this diary makes it clear as day that we've all been nasty slanderers! This diary first got into Ivan Ivanych's hands; I stopped by to treat him and I've read it over about a dozen times . . .

YULYA. Our folks read it too.

KHRUSHCHOV. *Georges*'s affair with Yelena Andreevna, which reverberated through the whole district, turns out to be a vulgar, filthy slander. I believed that slander and defamed him along with the others, hated, despised, insulted him . . . Why are you silent? Why don't you say something?

DYADIN. Mishenka, I swear to you by God Almighty and by my eternal salvation, Yelena Andreevna is the most splendid of women! Meek, high-minded, righteous, sensitive, and with such a heart that, in my foolishness,

I have no words to express it. (*Weeps.*) Mishenka! Believe me! When I was favored with the honor of making her closer acquaintance, my heart was filled with ineffable bliss. It's pleasant to see physical beauty close up, but infinitely more pleasant to see spiritual beauty.

KHRUSHCHOV. The first person whom I believed was your brother, Yulichka! I'm a fine one too! He was the first to tell me about it! That's a bad man you've got there! What did he deceive me for?

YULYA weeps.

DYADIN. Mishenka, you mustn't, you mustn't . . . Ssh! . . . Don't insult her.

KHRUSHCHOV. What's there to cry about? Tears won't help.

DYADIN (*to Yulya*). Let's go to the mill, my girl. Let the bad-tempered fellow work here, while you and I take some exercise. Let's go . . . Get on with your work, Mishenka!

KHRUSHCHOV (*alone; mixes colors in a saucer*). One night I saw him pressing his face to her hand. In his diary he has described that night in detail, described how I came by there, what I said to him . . . He's put down my words and calls me a stupid, narrow-minded fellow.

Pause.

It's too dark . . . Should be lighter . . . And further on he abuses Sonya because she fell in love with me. Rest in peace, you poor fool, but your close observation betrayed you there: she never loved me . . . My hands are trembling like a drunkard's . . . I made a blot . . . (*Scrapes the paper with a knife.*) Even if I grant there may be some truth in it, all the same it doesn't do to think about it . . . It began stupidly, it ended stupidly . . . And I basically did the right thing when I burned her photograph yesterday . . . Yes . . . Otherwise I would . . .

SEMYON and WORKMEN bring in a big table.

What are you doing? What's this for?

SEMYON. Ilya Ilyich told us to. Company's coming from the Zheltukhins' for tea.

KHRUSHCHOV. Thank you kindly. That means, I've got to stop caring about work . . . I'll pack it up and go home.

Enter ZHELTUKHIN arm in arm with SONYA.

I V

KHRUSHCHOV, ZHELTUKHIN, and SONYA.

ZHELTUKHIN (*sings*). "Reluctant to this mournful shore an unknown power doth me draw . . ."

KHRUSHCHOV. Who's that? Ah! (*Hastens to pack up his drawing implements in their case.*)

ZHELTUKHIN. I risk tiring you out, Sofya Aleksandrovna. Just one last question. Do you remember on my birthday you had lunch at our place? You've got to admit that at that time you roared with laughter at my toast.

SONYA. I broke out laughing for no particular reason. You don't have to be so unforgiving with me, Leonid Stepanych.

ZHELTUKHIN (*on seeing Khrushchov*). Ah, you're here too? Afternoon.

KHRUSHCHOV. Afternoon.

ZHELTUKHIN. Working? Wonderful . . . Where's Waffles?

KHRUSHCHOV. Over there . . . in the mill.

ZHELTUKHIN. I'll go and get him. (*Walks, singing.*) "Reluctant to this mournful shore . . ." (*Exits.*)

SONYA. Good afternoon . . .

KHRUSHCHOV. Good afternoon.

Pause.

SONYA. What are you drawing?

KHRUSHCHOV. Nothing special . . . it's of no interest.

SONYA. Is it a map?

KHRUSHCHOV. No, it's a diagram of the forests in our district. I've mapped them out.

Pause.

The green color indicates the places where there were forests in our grandfathers' day and earlier; the light green is where forests have been felled in the last twenty-five years, well, and the light blue is where forests are still intact. There's twice as much light green as light blue.

Pause.

I want to make a map of the whole province . . .

Pause.

Well, what about you? Happy? Sorry, it's a ridiculous question; I didn't ask it the right way . . .

SONYA. Now, Mikhail Lvovich, is not the time to think about happiness.

KHRUSHCHOV. What else is there to think about?

SONYA. Our sorrow came about only because we were thinking too much about our happiness.

KHRUSHCHOV. Sorry.

SONYA. Every cloud has its silver lining. Sorrow has taught me, and now I understand how I went astray . . . We have to forget about our happiness, Mikhail Lvovich, and every moment think only about other people's happiness. Our whole life has to be made up of sacrifices.

KHRUSHCHOV. Well, yes, marrying Zheltukhin . . .

Pause.

Mariya Vasilyevna had a son who shot himself and she still keeps on looking for contradictions in her pamphlets. A disaster befell you, and you solace your vanity with ideas about some kind of sacrifices . . . Nobody's got any heart . . . Neither you nor I . . . Things are going wrong, it's all falling to rack and ruin . . . I'm going to leave now . . .

SONYA. They're coming here, and I'm crying . . .

Enter YULYA, DYADIN, and ZHELTUKHIN.

V

The same, YULYA, DYADIN, ZHELTUKHIN,
then SEREBRYAKOV.

SEREBRYAKOV's voice: "Yoo-hoo! Where are you, my friends?"

SONYA (*shouts*). Papa, over here! (*Quickly dries her eyes.*)

DYADIN. They're bringing the samovar! Fascinating! (*He and YULYA fuss with things on the table.*)

Enter SEREBRYAKOV; with him the HOUSEKEEPER with
a basket.

SONYA. Over here, Papa!

SEREBRYAKOV. I see, I see . . .

ZHELTUKHIN (*loudly*). Gentlemen, I call this session to order! Uncork the cordial!

KHRUSHCHOV (*to Serebryakov*). Professor, let's forget everything that passed between us! (*Extends his hand.*) I beg your pardon. Believe in my sincerity!

SEREBRYAKOV. Thank you. Most delighted. You should forgive me as well. The day after that episode when I tried to contemplate all that had occurred and recalled our interchange, I was horrified by my cruelty. Let us be friends. (*Takes him by the arm and goes to the table.*)

DYADIN. Your excellency, I'm glad that you have chosen to pay a visit to my oasis . . . Very, very pleased!

SEREBRYAKOV. Thank you. Sit down, my friends. (*Sits at the table.*) It is beautiful here indeed. A veritable oasis. Let us not be silent, my friends, let us talk. In our situation that's by far the best thing. We are responsible for our own misfortunes, let us bear them cheerfully. I can look at them more cheerfully than the rest of you, and that is because I am more to blame than the rest of you.

YULYA. Gentlemen, I don't provide any sugar; drink it with jam.

DYADIN (*bustling around among the guests*). I'm so pleased, I'm so pleased! A little bit of cordial! Mishenka, have a little sweet roll!

SEREBRYAKOV. Recently, Mikhail Lvovich, I have experienced so much and done so much thinking that I believe I could write a whole treatise on the art of living. I repeat, the day after that event I was horrified by my cruelty; I was surprised how little I had seen and understood before and at the same time how much I had talked. Now it strikes me as strange that I never to talked to my wife about anything except my gout and my rights, but at the time I thought that what was needed . . . (*His voice quavering with tears.*) Of course, it's all my fault . . . I won't even mention *Georges*, who, if only . . .

ZHELTUKHIN. Aleksandr Vladimirovich, we promised each other not to talk about that today. You've forgotten our agreement.

DYADIN. Let the dead past bury the dead. God is merciful, all's well that ends well. Away with melancholy! Let us drink tea with jam, with sugar, with a little bit of lemon and a little bit of cordial, while Lenichka himself will recite a bit of poetry.

SEREBRYAKOV. As a matter of fact, Leonid Stepanych, do recite something. You recite beautifully.

ZHELTUKHIN. What shall I recite for you?

SEREBRYAKOV. Something inoffensive . . . You've got a large supply.

ZHELTUKHIN. As you wish, sir . . . (*After a moment's thought.*) Here's a bit of Nekrasov, something in your line, Misha . . .

> The Green Sound hums its way along,[5]
> The Sound of Green, the Sound of Spring!
> Like spilt milk,
> The cherry orchards stand,
> Ever so quietly they hum:
> Warmed by the heat of the sun,
> The cheerful pinewood
> Forests hum;
> And close at hand, with new green
> The pale-leafed face
> And little white birch tree
> With a green braid
> Sough the new song!
> The lowly reed hums,
> The stately maple hums . . .
> They hum in a new way,
> A new way, a springtime way . . .
> The Green Sound hums its way along,
> The Sound of Green, the Sound of Spring!
> The savage thought grows weak,
> The knife falls from the hand,
> And I keep hearing but one song

5 Nekrasov's "The Green Sound" had become a rallying cry for progressive Russian youth in the 1870s, thanks to its platform recitation by the acress Mariya Yermolova.

—In the forest, in the meadow:
"Love, when the loving is good.
Be patient, when patience is called for,
Bid farewell, when farewell's to be said,
And—God be thy judge!"

SONYA shudders.

ZHELTUKHIN. What made you shudder like that?

SONYA. Someone was shouting.

DYADIN. It's the peasants down by the river catching crayfish.

Pause.

SEREBRYAKOV. How is Ivan Ivanych's health?

KHRUSHCHOV. Bad.

Pause.

ZHELTUKHIN. Gentlemen, after all we did make an agreement to spend this evening as if nothing had happened . . . Honestly, there's a kind of tension . . .

DYADIN. Your Excellency, I cherish for learning not just reverence, but even a kindred feeling. My brother Grigory Ilyich's wife's brother, maybe you deign to know him, Konstantin Gavrilych Novosyolov, had a master's degree in comparative literature.

SEREBRYAKOV. I didn't know him, but I know of him.

Pause.

SONYA. Yesterday was exactly fifteen days since Uncle *Georges* died.

ZHELTUKHIN. Sofya Aleksandrovna, the agreement!

SONYA. Sorry.

YULYA weeps.

ZHELTUKHIN. What's come over you?

YULYA. Lyonichka said it first.

ZHELTUKHIN. What did I say?

YULYA. You did, you did!

KHRUSHCHOV. Yulichka, let's not talk about it! I implore you!

SEREBRYAKOV. Cheer up, cheer up, cheer up! Even though the doctor's forbidden it, all the same, I'll have a little cordial. Follow my example, my friends! (*Drinks.*)

Pause.

ZHELTUKHIN. All the same, you can feel a kind of tension . . . Ladies and gentleman, more life, more noise! (*Raps with his knife.*) The chairman has the floor!

SEREBRYAKOV. A psychological wrinkle. What strange desires people sometimes have! For some reason I'd very much like someone to insult me grossly or I'd like to fall ill . . . Obviously, my soul, I mean my psyche, is in need of a powerful reaction.

Pause.

KHRUSHCHOV jumps up abruptly.

ZHELTUKHIN. What's wrong?

KHRUSHCHOV (*agitated*). My God, I can't stand it, I haven't got the strength to put up with it any more! It makes me sick to my stomach! A villain, a shameless slanderer! At a difficult moment in her life she held out her arms to me and offered me her friendship, and I said to her: "Get away from me! I despise your friendship!" Just like everyone else, like a common slave, I insulted her, slandered her, hated her! Despise me, hate me, point your fingers at me . . .

DYADIN (*anxiously*). Mishenka, you mustn't . . . (*Kisses him.*) You mustn't . . .

KHRUSHCHOV. Aleksandr Vladimirovich, for twenty-five years you were a professor and served learning, I plant forests, but what's the point, who's it for, if we have no heart, we give each other no quarter, but destroy each other? Could you and I have done anything to save *Georges*? Where is your wife, whom I so inhumanly insulted? Where is our peace, where is my love? Everything's been destroyed, wrecked, it's all gone to rack and ruin! It's all destroyed! Everyone run and shout . . .

SONYA and YULYA leap up. Total confusion.

DYADIN. Dear boy, Mishenka, calm down . . .

KHRUSHCHOV. It's horrible! Horrible! It's all destroyed!

YULYA (*embraces and kisses him*). Mikhail Lvovich, darling, precious . . .

SEREBRYAKOV. Give him some water.

KHRUSHCHOV. Forgive me, friends, I lost my self-control . . . I can't endure this tension. Now I've got it off my chest. Sit down . . . Calm down.

ZHELTUKHIN. That's enough! *Basta!*

DYADIN. Ladies and gentlemen, I swear that everything will come out all right. I don't have the right to explain it to you, but . . . but, in short, God is merciful.

SONYA. Papa, it's already getting dark. Let's go home.

SEREBRYAKOV. No, let's sit a while longer, my dear child. I can't stand the walls at home. The later we go home, the better.

Enter FYODOR IVANOVICH.

V I

The same and FYODOR IVANOVICH.

SONYA (*alarmed*). Uncle *Georges!*

KHRUSHCHOV. Where do you see him? That's enough!

SONYA. There he is!

KHRUSHCHOV. Where? That's Fyodor . . . Friends, the best thing to do is keep still, don't answer questions . . . Professor, pay him no attention.

SEREBRYAKOV. I have nothing against him. Let him be.

KHRUSHCHOV. Ssh!

FYODOR IVANOVICH (*walking over to the table*). Greetings! In the lap of nature? An amusing story. Afternoon, Wood Goblin!

Pause.

Why don't you give me your hand?

KHRUSHCHOV (*extending his hand*). Here, take it . . .

FYODOR IVANOVICH (*sits down*). Is that you, Professor? Sorry, I didn't recognize you. Too much rich living.

Pause.

It's a lucky thing you're here, Professor. I have to have a serious talk with you. These are all our friends, so I imagine we can speak frankly. Here's what it's all about. Sooner or later I'll find Yelena Andreevna and marry her. Give her a divorce. I'll pay you whatever you like . . .

KHRUSHCHOV. Ssh . . .

FYODOR IVANOVICH. However, does it sound as if I'm asking for the moon? Let's discuss things calmly. (*To Zheltukhin.*) Lyonya, I rode over to your place in person. When I found out you were having a picnic, I hastened, as you see, to visit a friend. Why didn't you invite me to the picnic?

ZHELTUKHIN. A peculiar question. How can I invite you? In the first place, I didn't know where you were, in the second place, this idea, I mean the idea of a picnic, struck us just this afternoon. I didn't have the time . . . Besides, given the situation . . .

FYODOR IVANOVICH. You're not very astute. Answer me: why didn't you invite me to this picnic?

ZHELTUKHIN. Let's change the subject.

FYODOR IVANOVICH. Hm . . . My friend, I've experienced everything in this world. Except for flying in hot-air balloons, and I still haven't challenged you to a duel even once. The balloons are unlikely, but a duel is an imminent possibility.

KHRUSHCHOV (*shouts*). Get out of here, you impudent fellow!

FYODOR IVANOVICH. Hush, hush! I'm a bundle of nerves.

KHRUSHCHOV. Get out of here!

FYODOR IVANOVICH. Let's discuss things calmly. What I mean is this: first I'll fight you, Lyonya, and then you, Wood Goblin . . .

KHRUSHCHOV. What's going on here, at last? Don't be afraid, Yulichka! Sofya Aleksandrovna, sit down! (*To Fyodor Ivanovich.*) Come with me and we'll talk it over!

TRIFON enters rapidly, goes to the house, and raps on
the window.

V I I

The same and TRIFON.

DYADIN. Who is that? What do you want?

TRIFON. Is that you, Ilya Ilyich?

DYADIN. What do you want?

TRIFON. Good afternoon. Greetings to your honor. Regards from Lyudmila Ivanovna and she wants me to inform you that today at dinner Ivan Ivanych passed away.

FYODOR IVANOVICH. Father!? My God . . . Who's that? That you, Trifon?

TRIFON. That's right, sir . . .

FYODOR IVANOVICH. When did this happen?

TRIFON. Today at dinner.

FYODOR IVANOVICH. My God . . . I haven't been home for a week . . . Father . . . Poor soul . . . Let's go, Trifon . . . Hurry . . . (*In a faltering voice.*) Excuse me, friends . . . Professor, I still have something to talk to you about . . . I can't remember . . . You're a friend of my father . . . No, that's not it . . . Here it is: your wife is a saint . . . (*Exits with TRIFON.*)

YULYA (*after a pause*). Poor Godfather!

SEREBRYAKOV. Let's go home, Sonya. It's time now.

SONYA. No, Papa, I can't now. Let's all sit here. That was the last straw . . . Nothing more can happen now . . . Nothing . . .

Pause.

KHRUSHCHOV. How depressing, how tense it all is! Lyonya, say something, sing, recite, or something! Recite!

ZHELTUKHIN. What should I recite?

Pause.

We hear someone in the house playing Lensky's aria from
Yevgeny Onegin.

KHRUSHCHOV. What's that? That's Yelena Andreevna playing. Where did she come from? Where is she? What does this mean?

DYADIN. It's fascinating! She's here, here in my house! From the Count's woods she ran here and has been living with me for two weeks now. Misha, what bliss! (*Shouts.*) Yelena Andreevna, please come out here! No more hiding!

SONYA. Listen to what she's playing! It's her favorite aria.

KHRUSHCHOV. Where is she? (*Runs into the house.*)

SEREBRYAKOV. I don't understand a thing . . . not a thing.

DYADIN (*rubbing his hands*). Right away, right away . . . We've come to the end!

> *Enter from the house YELENA ANDREEVNA, followed by KHRUSHCHOV.*

I X

> *The same, YELENA ANDREEVNA, and KHRUSHCHOV.*

KHRUSHCHOV. Just one word! Only one word! Don't be cruel as I was, but forgive me, I implore you!

YELENA ANDREEVNA. I heard it all. (*Kisses him on the head.*) That's enough. Let's be friends. Afternoon, Aleksandr! Afternoon, Sonya!

SONYA (*rushes to throw her arms around her neck*). Lenochka!

> *They all surround Yelena Andreevna. Kisses all around.*

YELENA ANDREEVNA. All these days I was brooding and thinking as much as you were. You forgave me, I forgave you, and we've all become better people. Let us live a new way—a springtime way. Let's go home. I was bored and missed you.

DYADIN. This is fascinating!

KHRUSHCHOV. How light my heart is now! There's nothing wrong, it's dee-lightful!

SEREBRYAKOV. Let's go, Lenochka . . . Now the walls will seem charming to me.

YELENA ANDREEVNA. I was sitting at the window and heard it all. My poor friends! Well, let's hurry and go! (*Takes her husband by the arm.*) Let's let bygones by bygones . . . Mikhail Lvovich, come and see us!

KHRUSHCHOV. I'm at your service.

YULYA (*to her brother*). You should ask for forgiveness too.

ZHELTUKHIN. I can't stand this sourness! This sickly sweetness . . . Let's go home, it's getting damp . . . (*Coughs.*)

YELENA ANDREEVNA. Sonya's laughing . . . Laugh, my dear! I'll laugh too. That's how it ought to be . . . Let's go, Aleksandr! (*She and her husband exit.*)

ZHELTUKHIN. Let's go! (*He and his sister exit; he shouts from offstage*). Aleksey, the carriage!

KHRUSHCHOV (*to Sonya*). When one's mind is clear, one's eyes are clear! I see it all. Let's go, my darling! (*Embraces her and they exit.*)

DYADIN (*alone*). And they all forgot about me! This is fascinating! This is fascinating!

Curtain

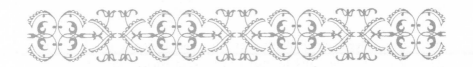

THE CELEBRATION

*I*n 1891, private commercial banks were a relatively new feature in Russian life. The State bank itself dated back only to the reforms of 1866. The financial institution in Chekhov's farce is about to celebrate its fifteenth birthday, on which occasion the bank manager Shipuchin will receive a testimonial from grateful shareholders. While he prepares a speech of thanks and his clerk Khirin is, with an ill will, crunching numbers for the thank-you speech, they are interrupted, first by Shipuchin's giddy and garrulous wife, and then by old Mrs. Merchutkina, nagging on behalf of her civil-servant husband. The more the women talk, the more the men are driven to distraction. The deputation arrives with its scroll and silver loving-cup to behold a vision of chaos: the manager's wife fainting on the sofa, the old lady collapsing in the arms of a babbling Shipuchin, and Khirin threatening the females with murder.

The peculiar position of *The Celebration* lies halfway between the failed experiment of *The Wood Goblin* and Chekhov's transitional play *The Seagull*. Founded on a published short story, "A Defenseless Creature" (1887), it was written in December 1891 but not performed until a Chekhov evening at the Moscow Hunt Club in 1900. By the time *The Celebration* reached the stage, Chekhov was already known to the public as the author of *The Seagull, Uncle Vanya,* and *Three Sisters.* Many were upset by what seemed a throwback to comic anarchy. *The Moscow News* referred to it as a "strange play" that ends with "the bank manager making an insulting gesture at his bookkeeper, while the latter tears books and files to pieces, tossing the ravaged pieces in the manager's face." Chekhov later rewrote this finale into the Gogolian tableau that greets the astonished delegation of shareholders.

The first St. Petersburg production, on the stage of the Alexandra Theatre in May 1903, was even more questionably received. Although the audience was dying with laughter at the antics of the elephantine Varlamov as Khirin and the hilarious comedienne Levkeeva as Merchutkina, certain critics wondered at the crude vulgarity of it all, and speculated about whether such a piece had a place in a national theater. They could not reconcile its extravagant comedy with the Chekhov they had come to expect.

There is a savagery to *The Celebration* that exceeds even the contumely of *The Wedding*. Each member of the comic quartet is despicable: both women are portrayed as idiotic chatterboxes, the clerk is a crabbed misogynist, and the bank manager is an ineffectual fussbudget. The setting enforces hypocrisy. As Shipuchin says, "at home I can be a slob, a low brow, and indulge my bad habits, but here everything has to be on a grand scale. This is a bank!" The impending ceremony imposes a temporal pressure that propels the mounting hysteria. The result is a hilarious clash of monomanias, not at all what the textbooks call a "Chekhovian mood."

THE CELEBRATION

Юбилей

A Joke in One Act

C H A R A C T E R S [1]

SHIPUCHIN, ANDREY ANDREEVICH, *Chairman of the Board of the —— Mutual Credit Society, a middle-aged man, with a monocle*

TATYANA ALEKSEEVNA, *his wife, 25*

KHIRIN, KUZMA NIKOLAEVICH, *the bank's bookkeeper, an old man*

MERCHUTKINA, NASTASYA FYODOROVNA, *an old woman in a baggy overcoat*

SHAREHOLDERS OF THE BANK

EMPLOYEES OF THE BANK

The action takes place at the —— Mutual Credit Bank.

The office of the Chairman of the Board. A door at left, leading to the bank's boardroom. Two desks. Pretentious furnishings displaying refined taste: velvet armchairs, flowers, statues, carpets, a telephone. —Midday.

KHIRIN alone; he is wearing felt boots.[2]

KHIRIN (*shouts through the door*). Have the pharmacy send over fifteen kopeks' worth of valerian drops[3] and tell them to bring fresh water to the

---

1 The names are suggestive: Shipuchin from *shipat*, to fizzle or sputter; Khirin from *khirit*, to be sickly or to decay; and Merchutkina from *mertsat*, to flicker, *mertsalka*, nightlight.

2 *Valenki* are lower-class indoor footwear, the equivalent of Khirin wearing mukluks or fuzzy house-slippers at the office.

3 See *The Seagull*, note 46.

Chairman's office! I have to tell you a hundred times! (*Goes to the desk.*) They'll be the death of me with their tormenting. I've been writing for four days straight without a wink of sleep; from morning to night I'm here writing, and I'm home only from night to morning. (*Coughs.*) And on top of that there's an inflammation running through my whole body. Chills, fever, coughing jags, my legs ache and swimming before my eyes there's something like . . . exclamation points. (*Sits.*) That fancy-pants of ours, that skunk, the Chairman of the Board, is going to make a speech to our general assembly today: "Our bank now and in the future." A silver-tongued orator,[4] take my word for it . . . (*Writes.*) Two . . . one . . . one . . . six . . . zero . . . seven . . . Then, six . . . zero . . . one . . . six . . . He wants to pull the wool over their eyes, while I sit here and slave for him like a convict! . . . All he's put in this speech is hearts and flowers, not one hard figure, so I have to spend the livelong day clicking the abacus, damn his soul to hell! . . . (*Clicks bead on the abacus.*) I can't stand it! (*Writes.*) Which means, one . . . three . . . seven . . . two . . . one . . . zero . . . He promised to reward my hard work. If everything comes off successfully today and he manages to hoodwink his audience, he's promised me a gold medal and a bonus of three hundred . . . We shall see. (*Writes.*) Well, if my labors go unrewarded, pal, don't be surprised if . . . I've got an explosive temper . . . Pal, when I fly off the handle, I'm liable to do something violent . . . Believe you me!

Offstage noise and applause. SHIPUCHIN's voice: "Thank you! Thank you! I'm very moved!" Enter SHIPUCHIN. He is wearing white tie and tails; he is holding an album that has just been presented to him.

SHIPUCHIN (*standing in the doorway and addressing the boardroom*). This gift of yours, my dear co-workers, I shall cherish until my dying day as a memento of the happiest hours of my life! Yes, my dear sirs! I thank you once again! (*Blows a kiss and goes to Khirin.*) My dear fellow, my most respected Kuzma Nikolaich!

The whole time he is on stage employees occasionally come in with papers for him to sign and then leave.

KHIRIN (*rising*). I'm honored to congratulate you on the fifteenth anniversary of our bank and wish that . . .

---

4 In the original, Gambetta. The French politician Léon Gambetta (1838–1882) was famous as a public speaker.

SHIPUCHIN (*shakes his hand energetically*). Thank you, my dear man! Thank you! On this very special day, in view of the celebration, I propose that we exchange kisses! . . .

They exchange kisses.

Delighted, delighted! Thank you for your work . . . for everything, thanks for everything! If, during the time I have been Chairman of the Board of this bank, I have accomplished anything of use, I am first and foremost obliged to my co-workers. (*Sighs.*) Yes, dear fellow, fifteen years! Fifteen years, or my name's not Shipuchin! (*Brightly.*) Well, how's my speech coming? Any progress?

KHIRIN. Yes. There's still about five pages to go.

SHIPUCHIN. That's fine. In other words, it'll be ready by three o'clock?

KHIRIN. If nobody gets in the way, I can finish it. There's only a trifling amount left to do.

SHIPUCHIN. Splendid. Splendid, or my name's not Shipuchin! The general assembly begins at four. Please, my dear fellow. Let me have the first half, I'll give it a once-over . . . Let me have it now . . . (*Takes the speech.*) I invest enormous hopes in this speech . . . It is my *profession de foi*,[5] or, to put it more clearly, my display of fireworks . . . Fireworks, or my name's not Shipuchin! (*Sits and reads the speech to himself.*) I'm worn out, though, damnably worn out . . . Last night I had an attack of gout, all morning I've been hustling and bustling and running around, then this excitement, ovations, all this commotion . . . I'm worn out!

KHIRIN (*writes*). Two . . . zero . . . zero . . . three . . . nine . . . two . . . zero . . . The numbers are turning green before my eyes . . . Three . . . one . . . six . . . four . . . one . . . five . . . (*Clicks the beads on the abacus.*)

SHIPUCHIN. Something else unpleasant . . . This morning your wife came to me and complained about you again. She said that last night you chased her and your sister-in-law with a knife. Kuzma Nikolaich, what way is that to behave? Ay-ay!

KHIRIN (*sternly*). In view of the celebration, Andrey Andreich, may I make a request. Please, at least out of respect for my hard labor in this penitentiary, don't get involved in my home life. Please don't!

---

5 French: my credo.

SHIPUCHIN (*sighs*). You have an impossible temper, Kuzma Nikolaich! You're a splendid fellow, highly respectable, but with women you behave like some kind of Jack the Ripper.[6] Honestly. What I don't understand is why you hate them so much?

KHIRIN. And what I don't understand is: why you love them so much?

Pause.

SHIPUCHIN. The employees just presented me with an album, and the shareholders of the bank, so I've heard, want to present me with a testimonial and a silver loving cup . . . (*Toying with his monocle.*) Lovely, or my name's not Shipuchin! It's not a meaningless gesture . . . To uphold the reputation of the bank one needs some pomp and circumstance, damn it! You're part of the team, so of course you know what's going on . . . I composed the testimonial myself, I also bought the silver loving cup myself . . . Why, the binder for the testimonial cost forty-five rubles, but you can't do without it. It would never have crossed their minds. (*Looks around.*) What a set of furniture! What interior décor! They do say that I'm too fussy, that all I want is for the door knobs to be polished, the employees to wear tasteful neckties, yes, and for there to be a stately doorman at the entrance. Well, no, my good sirs. Doorknobs and a stately doorman are not mere baubles. A man may be as much of a slob as he likes at home, eat and sleep like a hog, take too much to drink . . .

KHIRIN. Please, I beg you, no insinuations!

SHIPUCHIN. Ah, no one's making insinuations! What an impossible temper you have . . . I'm only saying: at home I can be a slob, a lowbrow, and indulge my bad habits, but here everything has to be on a grand scale. This is a bank! Here every little detail has to make an impression, in a manner of speaking, and present a solemn appearance. (*Picks up a piece of paper from the floor and tosses it into the fireplace.*) My great achievement is precisely my upholding the reputation of the bank! . . . The main thing is tone! The main thing, or my name's not Shipuchin. (*After a glance at Khirin.*) My dear man, the deputation of shareholders might come in at any moment, and you're wearing felt boots, that muffler . . . some jacket

---

6 The London murderer and mutilator of prostitutes was frequently discussed in Russian newspapers in 1890.

of an uncivilized color . . . You should put on tails, or, at least a black frockcoat . . .

KHIRIN. I consider my health more precious than your bank shareholders. I've got inflammation all through my body.

SHIPUCHIN (*getting excited*). But you must agree that this is a mess! You're spoiling the effect of the ensemble!

KHIRIN. When the deputation arrives, I can always hide. It's no big problem . . . (*Writes.*) Seven . . . one . . . seven . . . two . . . five . . . zero. I'm no fan of messes myself! You would have done better not to invite ladies to the celebratory banquet today . . .

SHIPUCHIN. What piffle . . .

KHIRIN. I know, you've let them in today so you'll have a full house, and it'll look chic, but, listen, they'll spoil the whole thing for you. They lead to nothing but stress and mess.

SHIPUCHIN. On the contrary, the company of females is uplifting!

KHIRIN. Yes . . . Your wife is supposed to be well-bred, but last Wednesday she blurted out something that had me in a dither for the next two days. Suddenly in the presence of bystanders she asks: "Is it true that for our bank my husband bought shares in the Trashko-Pashko bank, and now they've gone down on the stock exchange? Oh, my husband is so worried!" This in front of bystanders! And why you confide in her I can't understand! You want them to bring you up on criminal charges?

SHIPUCHIN. Now, that'll do, that'll do! For a celebration this is all far too depressing. By the way, you've reminded me. (*Looks at his watch.*) My wifie is supposed to be here any minute. Actually, I should have driven to the station to meet her, poor dear, but there's no time and . . . and I was worn out. To tell the truth, I'm put out with her! I mean, I'm not put out, but I would prefer if she stayed another little day or two at her mother's. She insists that I spend the whole evening with her, today, when they've been planning a little postprandial excursion . . .[7] (*Shudders.*) There now, I've started to get a nervous twitch. My nerves are so frayed that I think the

---

7 All-male testimonial banquets and school reunions often ended with a trip to a brothel.

least little trifle is enough to make me burst into tears! No, I have to be firm, or my name's not Shipuchin.

Enter TATYANA ALEKSEEVNA in a mackintosh,[8] *with a traveling handbag on a strap across her shoulder.*

SHIPUCHIN. Bah! Speak of the devil!

TATYANA ALEKSEEVNA. My dear! (*Runs to her husband, a protracted kiss.*)

SHIPUCHIN. Why, we were just talking about you! . . . (*Looks at his watch.*)

TATYANA ALEKSEEVNA (*panting*). Were you bored without me? Are you well? I haven't even been home yet, I came straight from the station. I've got so much to tell you about, so much . . . I can't wait . . . I won't take off my things, I'll only be a minute. (*To Khirin.*) How are you, Kuzma Nikolaich! (*To her husband.*) Is everything all right at home?

SHIPUCHIN. Everything. Why, you've got plumper and prettier this past week . . . Well, how was the trip?

TATYANA ALEKSEEVNA. Wonderful. Mamma and Katya send you their regards. Vasily Andreich told me to give you a kiss. (*Kisses him.*) Auntie sent you a pot of jam, and everyone's annoyed that you don't write. Zina told me to give you a kiss. (*Kisses him.*) Oh, if you only knew the things that went on! The things that went on! I'm even terrified to tell you! Ah, the things that went on! But I can tell from your eyes that you're not pleased to see me!

SHIPUCHIN. On the contrary . . . My dearest . . . (*Kisses her.*)

KHIRIN coughs angrily.

TATYANA ALEKSEEVNA (*sighs*). Oh, poor Katya, poor Katya! I feel so sorry for her, so sorry!

SHIPUCHIN. We're having the celebration today, my dearest, at any moment a deputation of the bank's shareholders might show up, and you're not dressed.

TATYANA ALEKSEEVNA. That's right, the celebration! Congratulations, gentlemen . . . I wish you . . . That means, today is the assembly, the ban-

---

8 A woman's waterproof cape.

quet . . . I love it. But you remember, that lovely testimonial, which you took so much trouble to compose for the shareholders? Will they be reading it to you today?

KHIRIN coughs angrily.

SHIPUCHIN (*embarrassed*). My dear, people don't talk about such things . . . Really, you ought to go home.

TATYANA ALEKSEEVNA. Right away, right away. It'll take a minute to tell you about it and then I'll go. I'll start the whole story right from the beginning. Well now . . . After you left me off, remember, I sat next to that stout lady and started reading. I never try to make conversation on a train. I went on reading for three stations and not a single word to anybody . . . Well, night came on, and you know, all these gloomy thoughts came with them! Across from me sat a young man, quite proper, not bad at all, dark-haired . . . Well, we started talking . . . A sailor dropped in, then some student or other . . . (*Laughs.*) I told them I wasn't married . . . The way they paid court to me! We chattered away till midnight, the dark-haired one told awfully funny stories, and the sailor kept singing. My chest began to hurt from laughing. And when the sailor—oh, those sailors!—when the sailor happened to find out my name is Tatyana, you know what he sang? (*Sings in a bass voice.*) "Onegin, this I cannot hide, Tatyana's my love, she is my bride! . . ."[9] (*Laughs loudly.*)

KHIRIN coughs angrily .

SHIPUCHIN. However, Tatyana, we're disturbing Kuzma Nikolaich. Go home, my dear . . . Later . . .

TATYANA ALEKSEEVNA. Never mind, never mind, let him listen, this is very interesting. I'll be done in a minute. At the station Seryozha came for me. Some other young man turned up there, a tax collector, I believe . . . Quite acceptable, good-looking little fellow, especially his eyes . . . Seryozha introduced him, and all three of us drove off . . . The weather was wonderful . . .

Offstage voices: "You can't! You can't! What do you want?"
Enter MERCHUTKINA.

---

9 Prince Gremin's aria in Pyotr Ilyich Chaikovsky's 1879 opera *Yevgeny Onegin* (Act III, scene 1).

MERCHUTKINA (*in the doorway, waving someone away*). What are you grabbing at? I never! I have to talk to him myself! . . . (*Enters. To Shipuchin.*) I have the honor, Your Excellency . . . Wife of a county clerk, Nastasya Fyodorovna Merchutkina, sir.

SHIPUCHIN. How can I help you?

MERCHUTKINA. If you don't mind, Your Excellency, my husband, county clerk Merchutkin, was ailing for five months, and while he was home in bed getting better, they fired him for no reason at all, Your Excellency, and when I went to get his salary, they'd, if you don't mind, gone and deducted from his salary twenty-four rubles thirty-six kopeks. What for? I ask. "Well," says they, "he borrowed from the mutual-aid fund and other people vouched for him." How could that be? Could he borrow anythin' without my consent? It's impossible, Your Excellency! I'm a poor woman, I only keep body and soul together by taking in lodgers . . . I'm weak, defenseless . . . I put up with everybody's insults and never hear a kind word from a soul.

SHIPUCHIN. If I may . . . (*Takes her petition from her and reads it standing up.*)

TATYANA ALEKSEEVNA (*to Khirin*). But I should begin at the beginning . . . Suddenly last week I got a letter from Mamma. She writes that my sister Katya was proposed to by a certain Grendilevsky. A good-looking, unpretentious young man, but without any means and no fixed occupation. And to make it worse, can you imagine, Katya was attracted to him. What was there to do? Mamma writes that I should come without delay and bring my influence to bear on Katya . . .

KHIRIN (*severely*). If you don't mind, you've put me out! You—Mamma and Katya, and now I'm put out and totally confused.

TATYANA ALEKSEEVNA. As if it makes any difference! You listen when a lady's talking to you! Why are you so touchy today? In love? (*Laughs.*)

SHIPUCHIN (*to Merchutkina*). If I may, though, what is this all about? I don't understand . . .

TATYANA ALEKSEEVNA. In love? Aha? He's blushing!

SHIPUCHIN (*to his wife*). Tanyusha, my dear, step into the boardroom for a minute. I'll be there right away.

TATYANA ALEKSEEVNA. All right. (*Exits.*)

SHIPUCHIN. I don't understand any of this. Apparently, madam, you have come to the wrong place. Your request has absolutely nothing to do with us. You should take care to apply to the department where your husband worked.

MERCHUTKINA. My good sir, I've already been to five different places, they won't even accept my petition anywheres. I was losing my mind, but thanks to my son-in-law Boris Matveich, I got the bright idea to come to you. "Ma dear," says he, "you appeal to Mister Shipuchin: he's got pull, that gent can do anything . . ." Help me, Your Excellency!

SHIPUCHIN. Mrs. Merchutkina, we can do nothing for you. You understand: your husband, so far as I can tell, worked in the medical division of the War Office, whereas our institution is entirely private, mercantile, we're a bank. How can you fail to understand this?

MERCHUTKINA. Your Excellency, to prove my husband was sick, I got a doctor's certificate. Here it is, Your Excellency . . .

SHIPUCHIN (*annoyed*). Lovely, I believe you, but, I repeat, this has nothing to do with us.

Offstage TATYANA ALEKSEEVNA's *laugh; then men's laughter.*

(*After a glance at the door.*) She's keeping the employees from their work. (*To Merchutkina.*) This is bizarre, even laughable. Your husband must know where to apply, doesn't he?

MERCHUTKINA. He, Your Excellency, so far as I'm concerned, don't know a thing. All he keeps saying is: "It's none of your business! get out!" and that's all . . .

SHIPUCHIN. I repeat, madam: your husband worked in the medical division of the War Office, and this is a bank, a private, mercantile institution . . .

MERCHUTKINA. Right, right, right . . . I understand, my good sir. In that case, your excellency, make them give me at least fifteen rubles! I'll settle for not all at once.

SHIPUCHIN (*sighs*). Oof!

KHIRIN. Andrey Andreich, at this rate I'll never finish the speech!

SHIPUCHIN. Right away. (*To Merchutkina.*) I'm not getting through to you. Try and understand that to apply to us with such a request is as strange as filing for a divorce, for instance, at a pharmacy or the Assay Office.[10]

> *Knock at the door. TATYANA ALEKSEEVNA's voice: "Andrey,*
> *may I come in?"*

(*Shouts.*) Wait, my dear, just a minute! (*To Merchutkina.*) They didn't pay you in full, but what's it got to do with us? And besides, madam, we've got a celebration today, we're busy . . . and somebody might come in here at any moment . . . Excuse me . . .

MERCHUTKINA. Your Excellency, take pity on me, an orphan! I'm a weak, defenseless woman . . . They've been the death of me with their tormenting . . . What with suing my lodgers, and dealing with my husband's stuff, and running around on household chores, and besides that my son-in-law is out of work.

SHIPUCHIN. Mrs. Merchutkina, I . . . No, excuse me, I cannot talk to you! You've even got my head swimming . . . You are keeping us from work, and wasting time for no good reason . . . (*Sighs, aside.*) Here's a holy terror, or my name's not Shipuchin! (*To Khirin.*) Kuzma Nikolaich, will you please explain to Mrs. Merchutkina . . . (*Waves his hand in dismissal and exits into the boardroom.*)

KHIRIN (*walks over to Merchutkina. Sternly.*) How can I help you?

MERCHUTKINA. I'm a weak, defenseless woman . . . I may look tough, but if you take me to pieces, there's not a single healthy nerve in me! I can barely stand on my feet and I got no appetite. When I had my coffee today, I didn't get the least bit o' satisfaction from it.

KHIRIN. I'm asking you, how can I help you?

MERCHUTKINA. Make them, my good sir, give me fifteen rubles, and the rest at least in a month.

KHIRIN. But I thought you were told in plain Russian: this is a bank!

MERCHUTKINA. Right, right . . . And if necessary, I can produce a doctor's certificate.

---

10 Prior to 1896, this government office carried out all testing of gold and silver.

KHIRIN. Have you got a brain in your head or not?

MERCHUTKINA. Dearie, I'm asking for what's legally mine, that's all. I don't want nobody else's.

KHIRIN. I'm asking you, madam: have you got a brain in your head or what? Well, damn it all, I haven't got the time to chitchat with you! I'm busy. (*Points to the door.*) Please!

MERCHUTKINA (*surprised*). But what about the money? . . .

KHIRIN. In other words, you haven't got a brain in your head, here's what you've got . . . (*Taps a finger on the desk, then on his forehead.*)

MERCHUTKINA (*offended*). What? Well, never you mind, never you mind . . . Behave that way with your own wife . . . I'm a county clerk's wife . . . With me you better not!

KHIRIN (*flaring up, in an undertone*). Get out of here!

MERCHUTKINA. But, but, but . . . You better not!

KHIRIN (*in an undertone*). If you don't get out this second, I'll send for the porter! Out! (*Stamps his feet.*)

MERCHUTKINA. Never you mind, never you mind! I'm not scared o' you! We seen your sort before . . . You empty space!

KHIRIN. I don't think in all my life I've ever laid eyes on anything more repulsive . . . Oof! She's got the blood rushing to my head . . . (*Breathing heavily.*) I'll say it once more . . . Now listen! If you, you old gargoyle, don't clear out of here, I'll grind you into powder! I've got the kind of temper that can make you a cripple for the rest of your life! I might do something violent!

MERCHUTKINA. Hark, hark, the dogs do bark. You blowhard. You don't scare me. We seen your kind before.

KHIRIN (*in despair*). I can't look at her! I feel sick! I can't! (*Goes to the desk and sits.*) You've filled the bank with females, so I can't write the speech! I can't!

MERCHUTKINA. I'm not asking for what's somebody else's, just what's legally mine. Look at this shameless creature! In a workplace he sits in felt boots . . . A peasant . . .

Enter SHIPUCHIN and TATYANA ALEKSEEVNA.

TATYANA ALEKSEEVNA (*following her husband.*) Then we drove to a soiree at the Berezhnitskys'. Katya was wearing a pale blue cotton-silk dress with light lace and a low neckline . . . A hairdo piled high suits her face very nicely, so I did her hair myself . . . When she was dressed, with her hair done, she was simply bewitching!

SHIPUCHIN (*already with a migraine*). Yes, yes . . . bewitching . . . They might come in here any minute.

MERCHUTKINA. Your Excellency!

SHIPUCHIN (*depressed*). Now what? How can I help you?

MERCHUTKINA. Your excellency! . . . (*Points to Khirin.*) This here one, this one right here . . . this here one here put his finger to his forehead, and then on the desk . . . You ordered him to deal with my case, but he made fun and talked dirty. I'm a weak, defenseless woman . . .

SHIPUCHIN. All right, madam, I'll take care of it . . . I'll take measures . . . Please get out . . . later! . . . (*Aside.*) My gout's flaring up again! . . .

KHIRIN (*walks over to Shipuchin, quietly*). Andrey Andreich, let me send for the doorman, he'll throw her out in two shakes. What's going on, after all?

SHIPUCHIN (*alarmed*). No, no! She'll make an outcry, and there are lots of private apartments in this building.

MERCHUTKINA. Your Excellency!

KHIRIN (*in a whining voice*). But I have to write the speech, don't I! I haven't got the time! . . . (*Goes back to the desk.*) I can't do it!

MERCHUTKINA. Your Excellency, when will I get it? I need the money right away.

SHIPUCHIN (*aside, indignantly*). No, an ex-tra-or-din-ar-i-ly nasty female! (*To Merchutkina, blandly.*) Madam, I've already told you. This is a bank, a private, mercantile establishment . . .

MERCHUTKINA. Do me a favor, Your Excellency, be a father to me . . . If a doctor's certificate ain't enough, then I can produce a statement from the police too. Tell them to give me the money!

SHIPUCHIN (*breathing heavily*). Oof!

TATYANA ALEKSEEVNA (*to Merchutkina*). Granny, they're telling you you're in the way. How can you, really.

MERCHUTKINA. Beautiful lady, be a mother to me, there's not a soul who'll take my part. All I can manage to do is eat and drink, and now I don't get no satisfaction from coffee.

SHIPUCHIN (*faintly, to Merchutkina*). How much do you want to receive?

MERCHUTKINA. Twenty-four rubles thirty-six kopeks.

SHIPUCHIN. All right! (*Pulls twenty-five rubles out of his wallet and give them to her.*) Here's twenty-five rubles for you. Take it . . . and get out!

KHIRIN angrily coughs.

MERCHUTKINA. Thank you kindly, Your Excellency . . . (*Puts away the money.*)

TATYANA ALEKSEEVNA (*sitting beside her husband*). Anyway, it's time for me to go home . . . (*After looking at her watch.*) But I still haven't finished . . . . I'll be done in just one little minute and then I'll go . . . The things that went on! Ah, the things that went on! So, we drove to the soiree at the Berezhnitskys' . . . It was all right, it was fun, but nothing special . . . Of course, Katya's admirer Grendilevsky was there . . . Well, I had a word with Katya, I cried a bit, I worked my influence on her, and that very evening she had it out with Grendilevsky and turned him down. Well, I'm thinking, it's over and done with, all's for the best: it's calmed down mamma, it's saved Katya and now I myself am calm . . . And what do you think? Just before supper Katya and I are walking down a garden path and suddenly . . . (*Getting excited.*) And suddenly we hear a gunshot . . . No, I can't talk about this in cold blood! (*Fanning herself with her handkerchief.*)

SHIPUCHIN (*sighs*). Oof!

TATYANA ALEKSEEVNA (*weeps*). We run to the summer-house and there . . . there lies poor Grendilevsky . . . with a pistol in his hand . . .

SHIPUCHIN. No, I can't stand it! I can't stand it! (*To Merchutkina.*) What can I do for you now?

MERCHUTKINA. Your Excellency, is it possible for my husband to get his job back again?

TATYANA ALEKSEEVNA (*weeping*). He'd shot himself right in the heart . . . just there . . . Katya fainted dead away, poor thing . . . And he was awfully scared himself, he's lying there and . . . and asks us to send for a doctor. The doctor came right away and . . . and saved the wretched man . . .

MERCHUTKINA. Your Excellency, it is possible for my husband to get his job back again?

SHIPUCHIN. No, I can't stand it! (*Weeps.*) I can't stand it! (*Extends both his arms to Khirin, in despair.*) Throw her out! Throw her out, for pity's sake!

KHIRIN (*walking over to Tatyana Alekseevna*). Get out of here!

SHIPUCHIN. Not her, the one over there . . . that dreadful . . . (*points at Merchutkina*) that one there!

KHIRIN (*not understanding him, to Tatyana Alekseevna*). Get out of here! (*Stamps his feet.*) Get out now!

TATYANA ALEKSEEVNA. What? What's wrong with you? Have you gone crazy?

SHIPUCHIN. This is horrible! I'm a miserable wretch! Throw her out! Throw her out!

KHIRIN (*to Tatyana Alekseevna*). Out! I'll cripple you! I'll mangle you! I'll do something violent!

TATYANA ALEKSEEVNA (*runs away from him, he follows her*). How dare you! You're being rude! (*Cries out.*) Andrey! Save me! Andrey! (*Screams.*)

SHIPUCHIN (*runs after them*). Stop it! I implore you! Quiet! Spare me!

KHIRIN (*chasing Merchutkina*). Get out of here! Catch her! Smash her! Cut her throat!

SHIPUCHIN (*shouts*). Stop it! Will you please! I implore you!

MERCHUTKINA. Saints alive . . . saints alive! (*Screams.*) Saints alive! . . .

TATYANA ALEKSEEVNA (*shouts*). Save me! Save me! . . . Ah, ah . . . I feel faint! Faint! (*Jumps onto a chair, then falls on the sofa and groans, as if in a swoon.*)

KHIRIN (*chasing Merchutkina*). Smash her! Flog her! Cut her throat!

MERCHUTKINA. Ah, ah . . . saints alive, I'm blacking out! Ah! (*Falls unconscious into Shipuchin's arms.*)

A knock at the door and a voice offstage: "The deputation!"

SHIPUCHIN. Deputation . . . reputation . . . occupation . . .

KHIRIN (*stamps his feet*). Get out, damn it to hell! (*Rolls up his sleeves.*) Hand her over to me! I could do something violent!

> *Enter the five-man deputation; all in tailcoats. One of them is holding the testimonial in a velvet binder, another the loving cup. EMPLOYEES look on through the doorway to the boardroom. TATYANA ALEKSEEVNA is on the sofa, MERCHUTKINA in Shipuchin's arms, both moaning quietly.*

SHAREHOLDER (*reads loudly*). Highly respected and cherished Andrey Andreich! On casting a retrospective glance at the past of our financial institution and running our mind's eye over the course of its gradual development, the impression we receive is gratifying to the nth degree. True, in the early days of its existence the limited scope of its original capital, the lack of any profitable operations, as well as the vagueness of its goals gave point to Hamlet's question: "To be or not to be?," and at one time voices were even raised in favor of closing the bank. But then you put yourself at the head of our institution. Your knowhow, energy and characteristic discretion were reasons for its exceptional success and rare prosperity. The reputation of the bank . . . (*coughs*) the reputation of the bank . . .

MERCHUTKINA (*groans*). Ugh! Ugh!

TATYANA ALEKSEEVNA (*groans*). Water! Water!

SHAREHOLDER (*carries on*). Reputation . . . (*coughs*) reputation of the bank was raised by you to such a height that our institution can now compete with the best foreign institutions . . .

SHIPUCHIN. Deputation . . . reputation . . . occupation . . . "two friends went for a walk one night and business talked in the moonlight . . ."[11] "Say not that your youth was wasted, that my jealousy tormented you."[12]

SHAREHOLDER (*carries on in embarrassment*). Then, casting an objective glance at the present, highly respected and cherished Andrey Andreich, we

---

11 Opening lines of Ivan A. Krylov's fable "The Passersby and the Dogs."

12 "Gypsy Song," a ballad by Ya. F. Prigozhy to the words of a poem by Nikolay Nekrasov, "A heavy cross fell to her lot . . ." (1856). Also quoted in *The Seagull*.

... (*Lowering his voice.*) Under the circumstances we'll come back later ... We'd better come back later ...

They leave in confusion.

VARIANTS TO

The Celebration

Early version of the ending to the play (from the autograph manuscript). In this earlier version, Shipuchin is called Kistunov and Merchutkina is Shchukina.

V I I

KISTUNOV, KHIRIN, and TATYANA ALEKSEEVNA.

TATYANA ALEKSEEVNA is lying on the sofa and groaning.

KHIRIN (*after a brief pause*). What did I tell you? What did I tell you? They came, they wrecked the place, they made scenes, one got twenty-five smackers and left, and there's the other baby-doll ... (*Points at Tatyana Alekseevna.*) They outdid themselves! I told you a thousand times that you mustn't let them within shooting distance of you.

KISTUNOV. Deputation ... reputation ... Old bag, wife, felt boots ... Somebody shot himself ... "Two friends one night went for a walk and business talked." (*Rubbing his eyes.*) For two weeks I've being composing this speech for the shareholders, bought on my own account a silver loving cup, paid my own seventy-five rubles for the binder for the speech, five whole days stood in front of the mirror and rehearsed the pose ... and now what? It's all failed! All of it! I'm disgraced! Ruined! My reputation gone!

KHIRIN. And whose fault is it? Yours! Yours! You ruined the whole business!

KISTUNOV. Shut up! It's your fault, not mine!

KHIRIN. Yours! Yours!

KISTUNOV. No, yours! If it wasn't for your nasty felt boots and your damned insufferable temper, none of this would have happened! Why did you chase my wife? Why did you shout at her? How dared you?

KHIRIN. And if you weren't a coquette, and tried to throw a little less dust in their eyes . . . But, to hell with me, I don't want to work here any more! Please let me have the gold medal and three hundred bonus! Please hand them over!

KISTUNOV. You'll get nothing, you old bastard! I'll give you the finger!

KHIRIN. Is that right? . . . Then here's your report! (*Tears up the report.*) There! That's for you! I've put you in hot water! Just you wait!

KISTUNOV (*shouts*). Clear out of here! (*Rings.*) Hey, throw him out!

KHIRIN (*stamps his feet*). Out of my sight! I'm ready to do something violent! I won't answer for myself! Get away!

KISTUNOV. Get out!

With cries of "Get away! Get out!" they chase one another.

Noise. The employees rush in.

Curtain

Lines from the autograph manuscript.

page 708 / *After*: while I sit here and — do the sums and calculate the per- centages and make fair copies, and

page 710 / *After*: Pause. —
KISTUNOV. For what . . . Hm . . . Women, my dear fellow, are . . . the sort of thing . . . it's when . . . it's the aroma of life . . . But go on writing, my dear man . . . Have to make haste.
KHIRIN. There are all sorts of aromas . . .
Pause.

page 710 / *Replace*: You're part of the team, so of course you know what's going on . . . a stately doorman at the entrance.
with: Only I don't know where the ceremony of reading the speech is to take

place: at the club before the banquet or else here? I'd like it to be here, and hinted as much to them . . . (*Looks around.*) Such furniture! Neat and tidy! They may say I'm a fussbudget, that all I need is for the doorknobs to be polished, the employees to wear fashionable neckties, and a stately door-man to stand at the entrance, but look—the rest can go to hell.

page 710 / *Before*: The main thing is tone! — You have to pay attention to public opinion! It's not a bank, they say, but a government department! There, they say, it's awesome to go in! . . .

page 714 / *After*: What was there to do? — If she marries him, what will they live on? On love alone you don't get fat!

page 715 / *After*: and that's all . . . — And who has to deal with it? They're all hanging 'round my neck! Mine! (*Weeps.*)

page 716 / *After*: and besides that my son-in-law is out of work. — It's a won-der that I can eat and drink and I can barely keep body and soul together. I didn't sleep a wink all night . . .

page 717 / *Replace*: We seen your sort before
with: **KHIRIN.** Get out of here!
SHCHUKINA. We seen your sort. I'll go to the lawyer Dmitry Karlych, and you'll be out of a job. Three lodgers I've sued, and for your foul mouth I'll strip you down to your felt boots.

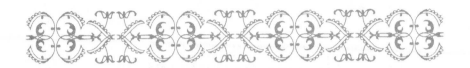

THE EVE OF THE TRIAL

$\mathcal{I}$n 1886 Chekhov published a story with this title, and he returned to it in the early 1890s to convert it into a play. In the process, he blackened the criminal record of his hero, Zaitsev, bringing him to trial not simply for bigamy and a series of beatings but for bigamy, forging his grandmother's will, and attempted murder. The scene in which Zaitsev plays mock doctor to "examine" the woman in the room next door was considerably enlarged; so was his sleazy courtship of her. Her character was altered to make her seem an experienced coquette ready to cuckold her husband. However, since the play was left unfinished, Zaitsev's farewell the next morning and his payment for his "honest labor" were never worked out, nor was the climax, the scene in court when Zaitsev is surprised to find that the Public Prosecutor is in fact the hoodwinked husband.

Why Chekhov gave it up is matter for speculation. Perhaps he realized that the seduction would be hard to get past the censor or that the necessary division into two or three scenes would defeat the comedy's economy as a curtain raiser. As it stands, *The Eve of the Trial* is close to French boulevard farce in its sexual obsessions. The tone is more insistently vulgar than in any of Chekhov's other short plays. Bedbugs, fleas, and smells are ubiquitous, a dramatic legacy from Gogol, no doubt, but emphasized here ad nauseam.

The "gags" are part of a long popular tradition. The mock doctor's examination could easily coarsen into an American burlesque sketch. The Aesopic names Gusev and Zaitsev (Goose and Hare) belong in a clown show. When Zaitsev contemplates suicide, he conducts a ventriloqual exchange with his gun. Crooning endearments to a suicide weapon is a comic device that goes back to the commedia dell'arte and the folk comedies of Ruzzante. Zaitsev is thus a provincial Russian Harlequin, amoral and appetitive, whose ruminations on self-destruction cast a satiric reflection on the suicides in Chekhov's serious works.

THE EVE OF THE TRIAL

Ночь перед судом

(Unfinished)

CHARACTERS [1]

FYODOR NIKITICH GUSEV, *a gentleman of advanced years*

ZINOCHKA, *his young wife*

ALEKSEY ALEKSEICH ZAITSEV, *passing through*

THE MASTER OF A POSTING STATION

A posting station.[2] A gloomy room with smoke-blackened walls, big sofas upholstered in oilcloth. A cast-iron stove with a stovepipe, which traverses the room.

ZAITSEV (with a suitcase), STATION MASTER (with a candle.)

ZAITSEV. That's quite a stench in this place of yours, Señor! You can't draw a breath! It stinks of sealing-wax, something sourish, bedbugs . . . Phooey!

STATION MASTER. Smells are only natural.

ZAITSEV. Tomorrow wake me up at six o'clock . . . And see that the troika is ready . . . I have to make it to town by nine.

STATION MASTER. All right . . .

ZAITSEV. What time is it now?

STATION MASTER. One-thirty . . . (*Exits.*)

---

1 Joke names: Mr. Goose and Mr. Hare.

2 Way stations set up by the government, where travelers could change horses and rest for the night. Postal couriers had first call on horses, so stays in posting stations were usually long and uncomfortable.

ZAITSEV (*taking off his fur coat and felt boots*). It's cold! You could go crazy with the cold . . . Right now I'm feeling as if somebody had plastered me over with snow, poured water on top of me, and then did a botch job of carving me out of it . . . What with these snowdrifts, this infernal blizzard, another five minutes out of doors, and I think I'd be a dead duck. I'm dead tired. And all on account of what? It would be nice if I were on my way to a rendezvous to collect a legacy, but I'm actually heading for my own destruction . . . I hate to think about it . . . Tomorrow the circuit court is in session in town, and I'm on my way there to be a defendant. I'm going to be tried for attempted bigamy, forging my grandmother's will to the tune of over three hundred rubles, and attempted murder of a billiard hustler . . . The jury'll find against me—there's no doubt about it. Here today, tomorrow night behind bars, and six months from now in the chilly wastes of Siberia . . . Brrr!

Pause.

Still, I do have a way out of that dire situation. I do! In case the jury does find against me, I'll turn to my old friend . . . A loyal, trusty friend! (*Takes a horse pistol out of his suitcase.*) Here he is! How's the boy? I traded Che-prakov[3] a couple of hounds for him. What a beauty! Just shooting yourself with him would be a kind of satisfaction . . . (*Tenderly.*) You loaded, boy? (*In a piping voice, as if answering for the pistol.*) I'm loaded . . . (*In his own voice.*) I bet you'll go off with a bang, right? A real rip-roaring ear-splitter? (*Piping.*) A real rip-roaring ear-splitter . . . (*In his own voice.*) Oh, you silly kid, gun o' my heart . . . All right, now lie down and go to sleep . . . (*Kisses the pistol and places it in the suitcase.*) As soon as I hear "Guilty as charged," then right away—bang to the brain and the sweet bye-and-bye . . . But I'm frozen as hell . . . Brrr! Got to get warm! . . . (*Does calisthenics with his arms and skips around the stove.*) Brrr!

ZINOCHKA *peeps through the doorway and immediately retires
from view.*

What was that? I thought someone just looked in at the door . . . Hm . . . Yes, someone did look in . . . In other words, I've got neighbors? (*Hearkens at the door.*) Can't hear anything . . . Not a sound . . . I suppose they're just passing through as well . . . I ought to wake them up, if they're decent peo-

---

3 Joke name from *cheprak*, saddle-cloth.

ple, sit down to a game of whist . . . A grand slam in no trumps! One way of keeping occupied, damn it . . . Even better if it's a woman. I've got to admit I like nothing better than a roadside fling. Sometimes when you're on the road you luck out with an affair like you wouldn't find in a Turgenev novel . . . I remember a case just like this once when I was riding around Samara province. I had stopped at a posting station . . . It's night, you get the picture, the cricket's chirping in the stove, silent as the grave . . . I'm sitting at the table drinking tea . . . Suddenly I hear this mysterious rustling . . . I open the door and . . .

ZINOCHKA (*behind the door*). This is an outrage! This is beyond belief! This isn't a posting station, but a madhouse! (*After a glance through the doorway, shouts.*) Station master! Station master! Where are you!

ZAITSEV (*aside*). What a beauty! (*To her.*) Madam, there is no station master. The oaf is fast asleep. What can I do for you? May I be of service?

ZINOCHKA. This is dreadful, dreadful! The bedbugs are about to eat me alive!

ZAITSEV. Really? Bedbugs? Ah . . . how dare they?

ZINOCHKA (*through tears*). In short, it is dreadful! I'm going to leave at once! Tell that scoundrel of a station master to harness the horses! The bedbugs have drained me of my blood!

ZAITSEV. Poor creature! To be so beautiful, and have to put up with this . . . No, it is beyond belief!

ZINOCHKA (*shouts*). Station master!

ZAITSEV. Madam . . . *mademoiselle* . . .

ZINOCHKA. I'm not a *mademoiselle* . . . I'm married.

ZAITSEV. All the better . . . (*Aside.*) What a sweetheart! (*To her.*) What I mean is, not having the honor to know your name, madam, and being in my own turn a well-brought-up, respectable person, I venture to put myself at your disposal . . . I can alleviate your distress . . .

ZINOCHKA. How so?

ZAITSEV. I have an excellent remedy—I always travel with flea powder . . . Allow me to offer it to you most cordially, from the bottom of my heart!

ZINOCHKA. Ah, please do!

ZAITSEV. In that case, I shall immediately . . . this very minute . . . I'll get it out of my suitcase. (*Runs to the suitcase and rummages around in it.*) What sparkling eyes, that little nose . . . We'll have an affair! I can feel it! (*Rubbing his hands.*) That's always been my luck: as soon as I hole up in some posting station, there's an affair . . . So lovely that even *my* eyes are shooting sparks . . . Here it is! (*Comes back to the door.*) Here it is, come to your rescue . . .

ZINOCHKA *holds out her hand from behind the door.*

No, allow me to go into your room and sprinkle it around . . .

ZINOCHKA. No, no . . . How can I let you into my room?

ZAITSEV. Why can't you? There's nothing more normal, especially since . . . especially since I'm a doctor, and doctors and ladies' hairdressers are always entitled to intrude into private life . . .

ZINOCHKA. You're not lying when you say you're a doctor? Honestly?

ZAITSEV. Word of honor!

ZINOCHKA. Well, if you are a doctor . . . then please do . . . Only why should I put you to any trouble? I can send my husband for it . . . Fedya! Fedya! Will you wake up, you great lummox!

GUSEV's *voice:* "Huh?"

Come in here, the doctor's been kind enough to lend us some flea powder. (*Retires from view.*)

ZAITSEV. Fedya! "This big surprise I greet with thanks!"[4] I need this Fedya like a hole in the head! Damn him! No sooner do I manage to get to know her, no sooner do I come up with the brilliant idea of saying I'm a doctor, then all of a sudden there's this Fedya . . . It's like shoving me under a cold shower . . . Try and get any flea powder from me! There's nothing lovely about her . . . No great catch, with that funny kisser . . . not one thing or the other . . . I can't stand women like that!

GUSEV (*in a dressing gown and nightcap*). Pleased to meet you, doctor . . . My wife just told me that you've got some flea powder.

---

4 A reference to the opening line of V. A. Sollogub's poetic improvisation of the 1860s, which became a catchphrase.

ZAITSEV (*rudely*). Yes I do!

GUSEV. Be so kind as to lend us a little. That insectlopedia[5] has got the better of us . . .

ZAITSEV. Take it!

GUSEV. Thank you kindly . . . Much obliged to you. So you got caught on the road by the snowstorm as well?

ZAITSEV. Yes!

GUSEV. Quite so, sir . . . Dreadful weather . . . Where are you headed?

ZAITSEV. To town.

GUSEV. We're going to town as well. Tomorrow I've got my work cut out for me in town, I have to get a good night's sleep, but that insectlopedia won't let me . . . We've got the most awful hideous scorpions . . . If it were up to me, I'd indict all these station masters for their bedbugs under Statute one hundred and twenty of the Penal Code enforced by the circuit courts in regard to unleashed animals. Much obliged to you, doctor . . . And what diseases you do specialize in?

ZAITSEV. Chest ailments and . . . and heads.

GUSEV. Quite so, sir . . . Much obliged . . . (*Exits.*)

ZAITSEV (*alone*). What a stick insect! If it were up to me, I'd douse *him* from head to foot with flea powder. I'd like to beat him at cards, the scum, and leave him holding the bag ten times running! Or even better, play him at billiards and accidentally whack him with the cue, so he'd remember me for a week . . . That blob instead a nose, little blue veins all over his face, that wart on his forehead and . . . and on top of that he dares to have a wife like her! What right has he got? It's an outrage! No, it's really nasty . . . And then people ask why I take such a gloomy view of life? Well, try and keep from being a pessimist!

GUSEV (*in the doorway*). Don't be shy, Zinochka . . . After all, he is a doctor! Don't stand on ceremony and ask him . . . There's nothing to be afraid of . . . Sherventsov was no good, but maybe this one will be . . . (*To Zaitsev.*) Excuse me, Doctor, for disturbing you . . . Please tell me why my wife has

---

5 In Russian, the pun is on *entsiklopediya* and *klop* (bedbug).

this congestion in her chest? A cough, you know . . . congests, as if, you know, something were impacted . . . Why is that?

ZAITSEV. It's a long story . . . It takes time to explain . . .

GUSEV. Then what are we waiting for? I've got the time . . . We can't sleep anyway. Give her the once-over, my dear fellow!

ZAITSEV (*aside*). I'm in a pickle for sure!

GUSEV (*shouts*). Zina! Ah, what's the matter with you, honestly . . . (*To him.*) She's shy . . . Introverted, just like me . . . Modesty's a fine thing, but why take it to extremes? To be shy with the doctor when you're ill is the worst thing for you.

ZINOCHKA (*enters*). Honestly, I'm so embarrassed . . .

GUSEV. That'll do, that'll do . . . (*To him.*) I ought to mention that she's being treated by Sherventsov. He's all right, a nice guy, sharp as a tack, knows what he's doing, but . . . who knows? I don't trust him! He doesn't have heart, no matter what you say! I can see, Doctor, that you're not in the mood, but do be so kind!

ZAITSEV. I . . . I'm not against it . . . I don't mind . . . (*Aside.*) What a predicament!

GUSEV. You examine her, and meanwhile I'll drop in on the station master and order up a little samovar . . . (*Exits.*)

ZAITSEV. Please have a seat . . .

She sits.

How old are you?

ZINOCHKA. Twenty-two.

ZAITSEV. Hm . . . A dangerous age. Let me feel your pulse! (*Takes her pulse.*) Hm . . . M-yes . . .

Pause.

What are you laughing at?

ZINOCHKA. You aren't pretending to be a doctor, are you?

ZAITSEV. Certainly not! What do you take me for? Hm . . . nothing wrong with the pulse . . . M-yes . . . And a plump, dainty little hand . . . Damn it,

I love roadside flings! You travel for miles on end and suddenly you come across this kind of . . . little hand . . . Do you like medicine?

ZINOCHKA. Yes.

ZAITSEV. Isn't that nice! Awfully nice! Let me take your pulse!

ZINOCHKA. But, but, but . . . don't get carried away!

ZAITSEV. What a lovely voice, charming eyes darting hither and yon . . . The smile alone could make you lose your mind . . . Is your husband jealous? Very? Your pulse . . . your pulse alone, and I could die happy!

ZINOCHKA. Excuse me, if I may, my dear sir . . . My dear sir! I see that you take me for some sort of . . . You are mistaken, my dear sir! I am a married woman, my husband occupies a position in society.

ZAITSEV. I know, I know, but can I help it if you are so beautiful?

ZINOCHKA. Well, I, my dear sir, shall not allow you . . . Please leave me alone, otherwise I shall have to take measures . . . My dear sir! I love and respect my husband too much to allow some passing smart-aleck to talk such smut to me . . . You're on quite the wrong track if you think that I . . . Here's my husband coming back, I think . . . Yes, yes, he's coming . . . Why don't you say something? What are you waiting for . . . Go on, go on . . . Kiss me or something!

ZAITSEV. My dearest. (*Kisses her.*) Sweetie-pie! Puggy-wuggy! (*Kisses her.*)

ZINOCHKA. But, but, but . . .

ZAITSEV. My pussy-kitten . . . (*Kisses her.*) My flibbertigibbet . . . (*When he sees GUSEV enter.*) One more question: when do you cough the most, on Tuesdays or Thursdays?

ZINOCHKA. Fridays . . .

ZAITSEV. Hm . . . Let me take your pulse!

GUSEV (*aside*). It looked as if he were kissing her . . . Exactly the same as with Sherventsov . . . I don't understand a thing about medicine . . . (*To his wife.*) Zinochka, you be serious . . . You musn't go on like this . . . You musn't neglect your health! You ought to pay close attention to what the doctor tells you. Nowadays medicine has made enormous progress! Enormous progress!

ZAITSEV. Oh, indeed! Listen, here's what I've got to say. At the moment there's nothing seriously wrong with your wife's health, but if she doesn't undergo a course of treatment, her illness may have dangerous consequences: a heart attack and inflammation of the brain . . .

GUSEV. There, you see, Zinochka! You see! The trouble I have with you . . . and I'd rather not even look at you, honestly . . .

ZAITSEV. I'm going to write a prescription . . . (*Tears a piece of paper out of the station register, sits down and writes.*) *Sic transit* . . . . two drachms . . . *Gloria mundi*[6] . . . one ounce . . . *Aquae destillatae*[7]. . two grains . . . Now you'll take these powders, three times a day.

GUSEV. In water or in wine?

ZAITSEV. In water . . .

GUSEV. Boiled?

ZAITSEV. Yes, boiled.

GUSEV. I am truly grateful to you, doctor . . .

VARIANTS TO

The Eve of the Trial

Variants come from a manuscript rough draft.

page 727 / *Before*: You loaded, boy? — My little fool, you're such a butter-ball . . .

page 728 / *After*: I've got to admit I like nothing better than a roadside fling — A little romance, a little affair, adultery . . .

page 728 / *After*: The bedbugs are about to eat me alive! — *A line starts*: It won't be the bedbugs . . .

page 731 / *After*: Introverted, just like me . . . — *A line starts*: I love virtue

---

6 Latin proverb, So passes the glory of the world.

7 Latin: distilled water.

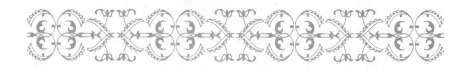

THE SEAGULL

$\mathcal{T}$he first production of *The Seagull*, at the Alexandra Theatre in St. Petersburg on October 17, 1896, has come down in theatrical legend as a classic fiasco. This is an exaggeration, however. The cast was a strong one, with Davydov, the original Ivanov, as Sorin and the luminous Vera Kommissarzhevskaya as Nina. During the scant week of rehearsals, Chekhov was in attendance, prompting the actors and correcting the director. Like most sensitive playwrights, he was dismayed by wasted time and the actors' predilection for superficial characterizations that stunted his brainchildren; but by the last rehearsals his expectations had risen.

These were dashed on opening night, for the spectators had come with expectations of their own, hoping to see their favorite comedienne Levkeeva, whose benefit performance it was. They laughed, booed, and whistled at whatever struck them as funny, from Nina's soliloquy to Treplyov's entrance with the dead gull, to the actors' ad-libs when they went up in their lines. Chekhov fled the theater, vowing never again to write for the stage. Nevertheless, the ensuing performances, with the actors more secure, played to respectful houses. Before *The Seagull* closed in November, it had become a *succès d'estime*, with Kommissarzhevskaya proclaimed as brilliant. It was successfully revived in Kiev, Taganrog, and other provincial centers, providing Chekhov with handsome royalties.

The writer Nemirovich-Danchenko, an admirer of the play, thought *The Seagull* was just the thing to rescue the flagging fortunes of his newly founded Moscow Art Theatre, whose first season was in danger of bankruptcy. Nemirovich pressed it upon his reluctant colleague Stanislavsky, who at first found the play incomprehensible and unsympathetic. Stanislavsky retired to his country estate to compose a directorial score, which he sent piecemeal to Moscow, where Nemirovich was rehearsing the actors.

Stanislavsky's fundamental approach to staging *The Seagull* differed little from his direction of historical drama. He sought in contemporary Russian life the same picturesque groupings, the same telling mannerisms, the same pregnant pauses that had enthralled audiences when he reconstructed seventeenth-century Muscovy or Renaissance Venice. Rather than inquiring into Chekhov's intentions, Stanislavsky took the play as romantic melodrama: Nina was an innocent ruined by that "scoundrelly Lovelace" Trigorin, and Treplyov was a misunderstood Byronic genius, the hero of the piece. Nor, at this stage of his development, did Stanislavsky try organically to elicit performances from the actors. Their every move, reaction, and intonation were prescribed by his score and learned by rote.

The opening night, December 17, 1898, despite off-stage jitters, was a palpable hit, insuring the theater's success, and the seagull became the Moscow Art Theatre's trademark. Chekhov was less than ecstatic. He thought that Stanislavsky misinterpreted Trigorin by making him too elegant and formal; he detested Mariya Roksanova's ladylike Nina. Whatever his misgivings, the educated, middle-class audiences took to the play precisely because, for the first time, "the way we live now" was subjected to the same careful counterfeit presentment that had hitherto been applied only to the exotic past. The spectators beheld their own tics and heard their own speech patterns meticulously copied.

Taking advantage of the outdoor settings of the early acts and the dimly lit interior at the end, Stanislavsky laid on climatic and atmospheric effects to create an overpowering mood (*nastroenie*). The method, relying on sound effects, diffused lighting, and a snail's pace, worked so well for *The Seagull* that it became standard operating procedure at the Art Theatre for Chekhov's later plays and, indeed, those of almost any author. In the last analysis, it was the pervasive mood that made *The Seagull* a hit. The young actor Meyerhold, who played Treplyov, later credited Stanislavsky with being the first to link the sound of rain on the window and morning light peeping through the shutters with the characters' behavior. "At that time this was a discovery."[1] The dramatist Leonid Andreev was to call it "panpsychism," the animation of everything in a Chekhov play from distant music to the chirp of a cricket to munching an apple, each contributing equally to the play's total effect.[2]

Chekhov's objections to the Moscow interpretation did not, however, spring from its style, but from the imbalance in meaning that Stanislavsky had induced. Although it contains what Chekhov called "a ton of love," *The Seagull* is not a soap opera about triangular relationships or a romantic dramatization of Trigorin's "subject for a short story." It is perhaps Chekhov's most personal play in its treatment of the artist's *métier*. The theme of splendors and miseries of artists is plainly struck by Medvedenko at the start, when he envi-

ously refers to Nina and Treplyov sharing in a creative endeavor. Nina picks
it up when she explains why her parents won't let her come to Sorin's estate:
"They say this place is Bohemia." Years of theater-going, reviewing, dealing
with performers and managers were distilled by Chekhov into a density of
metaphor for the artistic experience, for the contrasts between commercial-
ism and idealism, facility and aspiration, purposeless talent and diligent mediocrity. Of the central characters, one is a would-be playwright, another a
successful author; one is an acclaimed if second-rate star of the footlights,
another an aspiring actress.

Stanislavsky's black-and-white vision of the play also ran counter to Chekhov's attempt to create multiple heroes and multiple conflicts. Treplyov
seems the protagonist because the play begins with his artistic credo and his
moment of revolt, and it ends with his self-destruction. In terms of stage time,
however, he shares the limelight with many other claimants, whose ambitions
cancel out one another.

Nina, likewise, cannot be singled out as the one survivor who preserves her
ideals in spite of all. The type of the victimized young girl, abandoned by her
love and coming to a bad end, recurred in Russian literature from N. M. Karam-
zin's *Poor Liza* (1792) onward. Often, she was depicted as the ward of an old
woman who, in her cruelty or wilful egoism, promotes the girl's downfall.
Many plays of Ostrovsky and Aleksey Potekhin feature such a pair, and the
relationship is subtly handled by Turgenev in *A Month in the Country* (1850).
In *The Seagull*, the relationship is rarefied: it is Arkadina's example, rather than
her intention, that sends Nina to Moscow, maternity, and mumming.

Chekhov's early stories abound with actresses who lead erratic lives and
endure slurs and contempt for it; but Nina continues to dismiss the shoddi-
ness of the work she is given, determined to develop an inner strength, regardless of old forms or new. Should she be extolled as a shining talent to be
contrasted with Arkadina's *routinier* activity? Nina's ideas on art and fame are
jejune and couched in the bromides of cheap fiction; her inability to see Treplyov's play as other than words and speeches, her offer to eat black bread and
live in a garret for the reward of celebrity, are obtuse and juvenile. Hers are
not dreams that deserve to be realized, and there is nothing tragic in her having to reconcile them with the ordinary demands of life.

Similarly, Chekhov does not mean us to accept at face value Treplyov's
harsh verdicts on his mother and her lover. They may truckle to popular
demand, but they are crippled by self-doubt. Arkadina, barnstorming the
countryside in the Russian equivalent of *East Lynne*, is convinced that she is
performing a public service; her stage name ambivalently refers both to Arca-

dia and to a garish amusement park in St. Petersburg. Trigorin, well aware that he is falling short of his masters Tolstoy and Turgenev, still plugs away in the tradition of well-observed realism.

Treplyov and Trigorin cannot be set up as hostile antitheses; as Chudakov says, they "themselves call their basic theses into question."[3] Treplyov's desire for new forms is a more vociferous and less knowing version of Trigorin's self-deprecation. The younger writer scorns the elder as a hack, but by the play's end, he is longing to find formulas for his own writing. Arkadina may not have read her son's story and Trigorin may not have cut the pages on any story but his own; but Treplyov himself admits he has never read Trigorin's stuff, thus partaking of their casual egoism. Since both Treplyov and Trigorin contain elements of Chekhov, a more productive antithesis might be that of idealism and materialism, with Treplyov the romantic at one end and the schoolmaster Medvedenko at the other. The two men are linked by Masha, who loves the one and barely puts up with the other. Each act opens with her statement of the hopelessness of her situation. Even here, though, the antithesis is not complete: Treplyov is as hamstrung by his poverty as Medvedenko, and the teacher cherishes his own wishes to make art with a beloved object.

The literary critic Prince Mirsky pointed out that *bezdarnost* ("lack of talent") was a "characteristically Chekhovian word"[4] in its absence of positive qualities. Chekhov described talent to Suvorin as the ability "to distinguish important evidence from unimportant" (May 30, 1888). In *The Seagull*, "talent" is the touchstone by which the characters evaluate themselves and one another. Treplyov fears "he has no talent at all," but he rebukes Nina for considering him a "mediocrity, a nonentity" and points sarcastically to Trigorin as the "genuine talent." In her anger, Arkadina lashes out at her son by referring to "people with no talent but plenty of pretensions," to which he retaliates, "I'm more talented than the lot of you put together." In Act One, Arkadina encourages Nina to go on stage by saying, "You must have talent," and in the last act, Treplyov grudgingly acknowledges that "she showed some talent at screaming or dying." Trigorin complains that his public regards him as no more than "charming and talented," yet when Arkadina caresses him with "You're so talented," he succumbs to her blandishments.

The point is that "talent" exists independently of human relations and can be consummated in isolation. To be talented is not necessarily to be a superior person. As usual, Dr. Dorn sees most acutely to the heart of the matter: "You're a talented fellow," he tells Treplyov, "but without a well-defined goal . . . your talent will destroy you." Tactlessly, in Arkadina's presence, he declares, "there aren't many brilliant talents around these days . . . but the average actor has improved greatly"; sharing Chekhov's distrust of the grand gesture, he prefers a betterment of the general lot to artistic supermen. Even Nina finally realizes that fame and glamour are less important than staying power.

Treplyov's display of talent, his symbolist play located in a void where all things are extinct and the only conflicts are between the Universal Will and the Principle of Eternal Matter, may seem like parody. Chekhov, however, is careful to place the harsh criticism on the lips of Arkadina, whose taste and motives are suspect, and Nina, who is parroting actor's jargon she has heard from her. Chekhov is not ridiculing Treplyov for his espousal of a new form but for his inability to preserve the purity of his ideal: his symbolist venture is a garble of popular stage techniques incongruous with his poetic aspirations, "Curtain, downstage, upstage, and beyond that, empty space," "special effects." He seems unable to find an original play to express his nebulous ideas; his play, as Chekhov said to Suvorin of the Norwegian Bjørnson's *Beyond Human Power*, "has no meaning because the idea isn't clear. It's impossible to have one's characters perform miracles, when you yourself have no sharply defined conviction as to miracles" (June 20, 1896). In his notebooks, Chekhov stipulated, "Treplyov has no fixed goals, and that's what destroyed him. Talent destroyed him."

Chekhov, for his part, did manage to initiate his own new form in *The Seagull*, inchoate and transitional though it may be. For the first time, he did away with "French scenes," allowing each act to develop not through the entrances and exits of characters but by a concealed inner dynamic. The overall rhythm of the play is also carefully scored. As he told Suvorin, on November 21, 1895, "I wrote it forte and ended it pianissimo, contrary to all the rules of dramatic art." The forte passages occur in the first three acts, which are compressed into a week's time; then there is a lapse of two years before the pianissimo of Act Four. The characters must fill in this long gap in their own knowledge by the awkward device of asking one another what's been going on. But this is the result of Chekhov's eagerness to keep offstage what a traditional playwright would have saved for his obligatory scenes. The most intense and sensational actions—Nina's seduction and abandonment, the death of her child, Trigorin's return to Arkadina—are, like Treplyov's two suicide attempts, left to our imagination. We are allowed to see the antecedents and the consequences, but not the act itself.

The two-year hiatus between the third and fourth acts stresses the recurrent theme of memory. The past is always idyllic: Arkadina's reminiscence of life along the lakeshore, Poling's evocation of her past fling with the Doctor,

Shamraev's evocation of antediluvian actors, Sorin's rosy picture of an urban existence are the older generation's forecast of the clashing recollections of Treplyov and Nina. With wry irony, Chekhov divulges each of his characters' insensitivity or obliviousness. "It's too late," insists Dorn, when Polina tries to rekindle their earlier affair. "I don't remember," shrugs Arkadina, when her charitable behavior is recalled. "Don't remember," says Trigorin, when he is shown the gull he had stuffed in memory of his first conversation with Nina.

Another new form that Chekhov initiated in *The Seagull* is the emblematic progression of localities. The first act is set in "a portion of the park on Sorin's estate," where the path to the lake is blocked off by Treplyov's trestle stage. This particular region is remote from the main house, and Treplyov has chosen it as his private turf: the characters who make up his audience must enter his world of shadows and dampness. They spend only a brief time there, before returning to the safe norms evoked by the strains of the piano drifting into the clearing. Treplyov wants his work of art to be seen as coexistent with nature, with what Dorn calls "the spellbinding lake." Ironically, his manmade stage prevents people from walking to the lake, which his mother equates with "laughter, noise, gunshots, and one romance after another," the ordinary recreations Treplyov disdains. The most casual response to the lake comes from Trigorin, who sees it simply as a place to fish.

Act Two moves to Arkadina's territory, a house with a large veranda. The lake can now be seen in the bright sunlight, not the pallid moonshine. The surrounding verdure is a "croquet lawn," as manicured and well-kempt as Arkadina herself who keeps "up to the mark . . . my hair done *comme il faut*." Notably, Treplyov is the only member of the family circle who does not go into the house in this act. It stands for his mother's hold on life, and from its depths comes the call that keeps Trigorin on the estate.

The dining room of Act Three brings us into the house, but it is a neutral space, used for solitary meals, wound-dressing, farewells. The act is organized as a series of tête-à-têtes that are all the more intense for taking place in a somewhere no one can call his own. The last act takes place in a drawing room that Treplyov has turned into a workroom. As the act opens, preparations are being made to convert it into a sickroom. The huddling together of the dying Sorin and the artistically moribund Treplyov implies that they are both "the man who wanted" but who never got what he wanted: a wife and a literary career. Once again, Treplyov has tried to set up a space of his own, only to have it overrun by a bustling form of life that expels him to the margins. To have a moment alone with Nina, he must bar the door to the dining room with a chair; the moment he removes the impediment, the intruders fill his space, turning it into a game-room. His private act of suicide must occur elsewhere.

This final locale has a Maeterlinckian tinge, for there is a glass door, through which Nina enters, romantically draped in a *talma,* an enveloping cloak named after Napoleon's favorite tragedian. After days spent wandering around the lake, she emerges from an aperture no other character uses, to come in from "the garden," where "it's dark . . . that stage . . . stands bare and unsightly, like a skeleton, and the scene curtain flaps in the wind." Maeterlinck's dramas are full of mysterious windows and doors that serve as entries into another world, beyond which invisible forces are to be intuited and uncanny figures glimpsed. Quoting Turgenev, Nina identifies herself as a "homeless wanderer, seeking a haven." But what is "warm and cozy" to her is claustrophobic and stifling to Treplyov.

In fact, the whole estate is an enclosure for the characters' frustration. This is no Turgenevian nest of gentry, for none of the characters feels at home here. Arkadina would rather be in a hotel room learning lines; Sorin would like to be in his office, hearing street noise. Seeing his nephew withering away on the estate, he tries to pry loose some money for a trip abroad. Nina's are always flying visits, time snatched from her oppressed life elsewhere. Medvedenko is there on sufferance. Shamraev the overseer is a retired military man with no skills as a farm manager. Only Trigorin is loath to depart, because, for him, the estate provides enforced idleness. The lake's enchantment can be felt as the spell of Sleeping Beauty's castle. Everyone who sets foot there is suspended in time, frozen in place. Real life seems to go on somewhere else.

This symbolic use of environment is better integrated than the more obvious symbol of the seagull. In Ibsen's *The Wild Duck,* the title is of essential importance: all the leading characters are defined by their attitude to the bird, and it exists, unseen, as they re-create it in their private mythologies. The seagull, however, has significance for only three characters: Treplyov, who employs it as a symbol, Trigorin, who reinterprets its symbolic meaning, and Nina, who adopts and eventually repudiates the symbolism. For Treplyov, it is a means of turning art into life: feeling despised and rejected, he shoots the bird as a surrogate and, when the surrogate is in turn rejected, shoots himself. Nina had felt "lured to the lake like a gull" but will not accept Treplyov's bird imagery for his self-identification. However, when her idol Trigorin spins his yarn about a girl who lives beside a lake, happy and free as a gull, she avidly adopts the persona, even though his notion of her freedom is wholly inaccurate. The story turns out to be false, for the man who ruined the bird is not the one who ruins the girl. Nor is Nina ruined in any real sense. She starts to sign her letters to Treplyov "The Seagull" (or "A Seagull" — Russian has no definite articles); he links this with the mad miller in Pushkin's poem *The Rusalka*, who insanely thought himself a crow after his daughter, seduced and abandoned, drowned herself. Both Treplyov and Trigorin try to recast Nina as a fictional character, the conventional ruined girl who takes her own life. In the last act, however, she refuses this identity: "I'm a seagull. No, not that," spurning both Treplyov's martyr-bird and Trigorin's novelletish heroine. She survives, if only in an anti-romantic, workaday world. Ultimately, Chekhov prefers the active responsibilities contingent on accepting one's lot, even if this means a fate like Nina's.

NOTES

1 A. G. Gladkov, "Meyerhold govorit," *Novy Mir* 8 (1961): 221.

2 Leonid Andreev, "Letters on the Theatre," in *Russian Dramatic Theory from Pushkin to the Symbolists*, ed. and trans. L. Senelick (Austin: University of Texas Press, 1981), pp. 238–242.

3 A. P. Chudakov, *Chekhov's Poetics*, trans. F. J. Cruise and D. Dragt (Ann Arbor: Ardis, 1983), p. 193.

4 D. S. Mirsky, *Contemporary Russian Literature 1881–1925* (London: George Routledge and Sons, 1926), p. 88.

THE SEAGULL[1]

Чайка

A Comedy in Four Acts

C A S T

ARKADINA,[2] IRINA NIKOLAEVNA, *married name Treplyova,*
actress

TREPLYOV,[3] KONSTANTIN GAVRILOVICH, *her son, a young*
man

SORIN,[4] PYOTR NIKOLAEVICH, *her brother*

NINA MIKHAILOVNA ZARECHNAYA,[5] *a young woman, daughter*
of a wealthy landowner

SHAMRAEV, ILYA AFANASEVICH, *retired lieutenant, overseer of*
Sorin's estate

POLINA ANDREEVNA, *his wife*

MASHA, *his daughter*

TRIGORIN, BORIS ALEKSEEVICH, *a man of letters*

---

1 Why do *seagulls* hover over an inland lake on Sorin's estate? In Russian, *chaika* is simply a gull. *Sea* has the connotation of distance and freedom, quite out of keeping with this play. In English, however, *The Seagull* has gained common currency as the play's title, so I have retained it here, but refer simply to the "gull" in the text.

2 Ivan Bunin complained that Chekhov gave the women in his plays names befitting provincial actresses, but since two of the women in *The Seagull* are provincial actresses, no great harm is done. Arkadina is a stage name based on *Arcadia*, with its promise of a blissful pastoral existence (the sort of boring country life Arkadina loathes); but Arcadia was also the name of a garish amusement park in Moscow.

3 *Treplyov* hints at *trepat*, to be disorganized or feverish, *trepach*, an idle chatterbox, and *trepetat*, to quiver or palpitate.

4 *Sorin* seems to come from *sorit*, to mess things up, and is indicative of the old man's habitually rumpled state.

5 *Zarechnaya* means "across the river" and suggests Nina's dwelling on the opposite side of the lake, as well as her alien spirit in the world of Sorin's estate.

DORN, EVGENY SERGEEVICH, *a doctor of medicine*

MEDVEDENKO,[6] **SEMYON SEMYONOVICH,** *a schoolteacher*

YAKOV, *a workman*

A COOK

A HOUSEMAID

> *The action takes place on Sorin's country estate.*
> *Between Acts Three and Four two years elapse.*

ACT ONE

> *A section of the park on Sorin's estate. A wide pathway leading*
> *from the audience upstage into the park and toward a lake is*
> *blocked by a platform, hurriedly slapped together for an amateur*
> *theatrical, so that the lake is completely obscured. Bushes to the*
> *left and right of the platform. A few chairs, a small table. The sun*
> *has just gone down. On the platform, behind the lowered curtain,*
> *are YAKOV and other workmen; we can hear them coughing and*
> *hammering. MASHA and MEDVEDENKO enter left, on their*
> *way back from a walk.*

MEDVEDENKO. How come you always wear black?

MASHA. I'm in mourning for my life. I'm unhappy.

MEDVEDENKO. But how come? (*Thinking about it.*) I don't get it . . . You're healthy, and that father of yours may not be rich, but he's doing all right. My life's a lot tougher than yours. All I make is twenty-three rubles a month, not counting deductions,[7] but you don't see me in mourning.

> *They sit down.*

MASHA. It's got nothing to do with money. Even a poor person can be happy.

---

6 *Medved* means bear, and the name's ending suggests a Ukrainian origin.

7 A voluntary contribution from one's monthly salary toward an old-age pension.

MEDVEDENKO. In theory, but in reality it doesn't work that way; there's me and my mother and two sisters and my little brother, and my pay comes to twenty-three rubles. Got to buy food and drink, don't you? And tea and sugar? And tobacco? It gets you going in circles.

MASHA (*looking round at the platform*). The show will be starting soon.

MEDVEDENKO. Yes. Miss Zarechnaya is going to act in a play written by Konstantin Gavrilovich. They're in love, and today their souls will merge in an attempt to present a joint artistic creation. But my soul and yours have no mutual points of convergence. I love you, my longing for you drives me out of the house, every day I walk four miles here and four miles back and all I ever get from you is indifferentism.[8] No wonder. I've got no money and lots of dependents . . . . Who wants to marry a man who can't support himself?

MASHA. Don't be silly. (*Takes snuff.*) Your love is touching, but I can't reciprocate, that's all. (*Holding out the snuffbox to him.*) Help yourself.

MEDVEDENKO. Don't care for it. (*Pause.*)

MASHA. It's so muggy, there's bound to be a storm tonight. All you ever do is philosophize or talk about money. The way you think, there's nothing worse than being poor, but I think it's a thousand times easier to wear rags and beg in the streets than . . . Oh well, you wouldn't understand.

SORIN and TREPLYOV enter right.

SORIN (*leaning on a stick*). My boy, this country life kind of has me all—you know—and take my word for it, I'll never get used to it. I went to bed last night at ten, and this morning I woke up feeling as if my brain were glued to my skull from too much sleep, and all the rest. (*Laughs.*) And after supper I accidentally fell asleep again, and now I'm a total wreck, I have nightmares, when's all said and done . . .

TREPLYOV. You're right, you ought to be living in town. (*On seeing Masha and Medvedenko.*) Friends, when it starts you'll be called, but you're not supposed to be here now. Please go away.

SORIN (*to Masha*). Mariya Ilyinishna, would you kindly ask your dad to untie the dog, the way it howls. My sister didn't get a wink of sleep again last night.

---

8 He does not use the ordinary Russian word for indifference, *ravnodushie*, but the more exotic and pedantic *indifferentizm*.

MASHA. Talk to my father yourself, because I won't. Leave me out of it, if you don't mind. (*To Medvedenko.*) Come on!

MEDVEDENKO. Be sure and let us know when it's about to start.

They both go out.

SORIN. Which means the dog'll howl all night again. It's the same old story. I never get my way in the country. Used to be you'd take a month's vacation and come here for relaxation and all the rest, but now they pester you with all sorts of rubbish, so one day of it and you're ready to make your escape. (*Laughs.*) I've always left this place with a sense of deep satisfaction . . . Well, but now I'm retired there's nowhere to escape to, when all's said and done. Like it or not, you stay . . .

YAKOV (*to Treplyov*). Konstantin Gavrilych, we're going for a swim.

TREPLYOV. All right, but be in your places in ten minutes. (*Looks at his watch.*) It'll be starting soon.

YAKOV. Yes, sir. (*Exits.*)

TREPLYOV (*looking over the platform*). This is what I call a theater. Curtain, downstage, upstage,[9] and beyond that empty space. No scenery at all. The view opens right on to the lake and the horizon. We'll take up the curtain at eight-thirty sharp, just when the moon's rising.

SORIN. Splendid.

TREPLYOV. If Miss Zarechnaya's late, of course, the whole effect will be spoiled. It's high time she got here. Her father and stepmother watch her like hawks, and it's as hard to pry her loose from that house as if it were a prison. (*He straightens his uncle's tie.*) Your hair and beard are a mess. You should get a haircut or something.

SORIN (*smoothing out his beard*). The tragedy of my life. Even when I was young I looked like I'd gone on a bender—and all the rest. Women never found me attractive. (*Sitting.*) How come my sister's in a bad mood?

TREPLYOV. How come? She's bored. (*Sitting beside him.*) She's jealous.

---

9 In the original, "First wing, then second," referring to the wing-and-border arrangement of the nineteenth-century stage. Treplyov is displaying his familiarity with theatrical jargon.

She's already dead set against me and the performance and my play, because her novelist[10] might take a shine to Miss Zarechnaya.[11] She hasn't seen my play, but she hates it already . . .

SORIN (*laughs*). Can you imagine, honestly . . .

TREPLYOV. She's already annoyed that here on this little stage the success will belong to Miss Zarechnaya and not to her. (*After a glance at his watch.*) A case study for a psychology textbook—that's my mother. No argument she's talented, intelligent, ready to burst into tears over a novel, can rattle off reams of social protest poetry[12] by heart, has the bedside manner of an angel; but just try and praise a star like Duse[13] to her face. O ho ho! You mustn't praise anybody but her, you must write about her, rhapsodize, go into ecstasies over her brilliant acting in flashy vehicles like *Camille* or *Drugged by Life*,[14] but now that that kind of stimulant isn't available here in the country, she gets bored and spiteful, and we're all against her, it's all our fault. On top of that she's superstitious, scared of whistling in the dressing room or the number thirteen.[15]

---

10 Trigorin always uses the neutral, workmanlike word "writer" (*pisatel*) to describe himself, but Treplyov employs the more limited *belletrist*, a writer of fiction and light essays.

11 This line was excised by the censor. It was replaced by "because she isn't acting in it and Miss Zarechnaya is."

12 Literally, "can rattle off all of Nekrasov by heart"—Nikolay Alekseevich Nekrasov (1821–1878), Russian populist poet who called his inspiration the "Muse of vengeance and melancholy." His poems about the downtrodden masses, suffering peasants, and appeals for justice were popular parlor recitations at liberal gatherings in the 1880s, but Chekhov uses such recitations to indicate hypocrisy and posing in the reciter.

13 Eleonora Duse (1859–1924), the great Italian actress, who first toured Russia in 1891, where Chekhov saw her as Cleopatra. He wrote, on March 17, 1891, "I don't understand Italian, but she acted so well that I seemed to understand every word. Remarkable actress. I've never seen anything like her." Like George Bernard Shaw, he preferred her to her rival Sarah Bernhardt.

14 Arkadina's repertory consists of rather sensational, fashionably risqué dramas. *Camille* is *La Dame aux camélias* (1852), a play by Alexandre Dumas *fils*, concerning a courtesan with a heart of gold and lungs of tissue paper who gives up her love and eventually her life to advance her lover. It was first played in Russia in 1867, and later seen there during tours of Sarah Bernhardt in 1881 and 1892 and Eleonora Duse in 1892. Chekhov loathed *Drugged by Life*, a play by Boleslav Markevich, based on his novel *The Abyss*, and performed in Moscow in 1884 under the title *Olga Rantseva*. To quote Chekhov's review, "In general the play is written with a lavatory brush and stinks of obscenity." Its central character is a woman of loose morals, who, after four acts of dissipation and costume changes, dies in the fifth in an odor of sanctity. The connection to Arkadina's life and her expensive wardrobe is clear.

15 Literally, three candles on a table. This is a fatal omen, for at a Russian wake two candles were placed at the corpse's head, one at its feet. Therefore, if three lights are burning, one must be snuffed out.

And she's a tightwad. She's got seventy thousand in a bank in Odessa—I know it for a fact. But ask her for a loan and she'll go into hysterics.

SORIN. You've got it in your head that your mother doesn't like your play, so you're upset and all the rest. Take it easy, your mother adores you.

TREPLYOV (*picking the petals from a flower*). She loves me—she loves me not, she loves me—she loves me not, she loves me—she loves me not. (*Laughs.*) You see, my mother doesn't love me. Why should she! She wants to live, love, wear bright colors, but I'm twenty-five, and a constant reminder that she's not young any more. When I'm not around, she's only thirty-two; when I am, she's forty-three, and that's why she hates me. She also knows that I don't believe in the theater. She loves the theater, she thinks she's serving humanity, the sacred cause of art, but as far as I'm concerned, the modern theater is trite, riddled with clichés. When the curtain goes up on an artificially lighted room with three walls, and these great talents, acolytes of the religion of art, act out how people eat, drink, make love, walk, wear their jackets; when they take cheap, vulgar plots and cheap, vulgar speeches and try to extract a moral—not too big a moral, easy on the digestion, useful around the house; when in a thousand different ways they serve up the same old leftovers, again and again and again—I run out the exit and keep on running, the way Maupassant ran from the Eiffel Tower,[16] because it was crushing his brain beneath *its* tawdry vulgarity.

SORIN. You've got to have theater.

TREPLYOV. New forms are what we need. New forms are what we need, and if there aren't any, then we're better off with nothing. (*Looks at his watch.*) I love my mother, love her deeply; but she smokes, drinks, lives openly with that novelist,[17] her name constantly in the papers—it gets me down. Sometimes it's just my plain human ego talking; it's a shame my mother is a famous actress, because I think if she were an ordinary woman, I might be happier. Uncle, can there be a more maddening and ridiculous situation

---

16 Guy de Maupassant (1850–1893), French writer, whose works began to appear in Russian in 1894 and 1896. He died of syphilis and drugs, not modern technology. The Eiffel Tower was erected by Gustave Eiffel in 1889 for the Paris Exposition and, at 300 meters, was the highest man-made structure of the time. It was controversial, many persons of taste considering it an eyesore. Maupassant detested it as a symbol of materialism and modern vulgarity; he chose to dine at its restaurant, the only place in Paris from which one could not see the tower.

17 This last phrase was excised by the censor, and replaced by Chekhov with "but she leads a disorderly life, constantly carrying on with that novelist."

than the one I'm in: her parties will be packed with celebrities, actors and writers, and I'll be the only nobody in the room, and they put up with me just because I'm her son. Who am I? What am I? Expelled from the University in my junior year for circumstances which, as they say, were beyond the editor's control,[18] with no talent at all, and no money either, according to my passport I'm a bourgeois from Kiev.[19] My father actually is a bourgeois from Kiev, but he was also a famous actor. So when all those actors and writers at her parties used to condescend with their kind attentions, I'd feel as if their eyes were sizing up how insignificant I was—I could guess what they were thinking and I'd go through agonies of humiliation.

SORIN. While we're on the subject, tell me, please, what sort of fellow is this novelist? I can't figure him out. He never opens his mouth.[20]

TREPLYOV. Clever enough, easygoing, a bit, what's the word, taciturn. He's all right. He's not even forty, but he's jaded, jaded within an inch of his life . . . Now he only drinks beer and can love only those who are no longer young . . .[21] As for his writing, it's . . . how can I put it? Charming, talented . . . but . . . compared to Tolstoy or Zola,[22] a little Trigorin goes a long way.

SORIN. But I love authors, my boy. There was a time when I desperately wanted two things: I wanted to get married and I wanted to be an author, but I didn't manage to do either one. Yes. It would be nice to be even a second-rate author, when all's said and done . . .

TREPLYOV (*listening hard*). I hear footsteps . . . (*Embraces his uncle.*) I can't live without her . . . Even the sound of her footsteps is musical . . . I'm out

---

18 A journalistic euphemism to cover passages deleted by the censorship. It suggests that Treplyov was expelled for political activity.

19 Literally, a Kievan *meshchanin*, that is, a burgher, townsman, artisan, or small tradesman. The word bears connotations of narrow-mindedness, philistinism, and parochialism. By marrying Treplyov's father, Arkadina had come down in station. And although Kiev, the capital of Ukraine, was the seventh most populous city in Russia, to be associated with it suggests provincialism.

20 Nemirovich-Danchenko believed the character of Trigorin to be based on Chekhov's friend Ivan Potapenko, a successful novelist noted for his modesty, self-deprecation, lavish living, and appeal to women.

21 This phrase was excised by the censor and replaced by Chekhov with "already famous and jaded within an inch of his life . . ."

22 Lev Nikolaevich Tolstoy (1828–1910) was widely considered Russia's greatest author and her moral conscience. The works of Émile Zola (1840–1902) usually appeared in Russian translation shortly after their appearance in French.

of my mind with happiness. (*Quickly goes to meet* NINA ZARECHNAYA *as she enters.*) Enchantress, girl of my dreams . . .

NINA (*excited*). I'm not late . . . I'm sure I'm not late . . .

TREPLYOV (*kissing her hands*). No, no, no . . .

NINA. All day I've been on edge, I've been so worried! I was afraid Father wouldn't let me go . . . But he's just gone out with my stepmother. The sky was red, the moon's already on the rise, so I took a whip to the horses, lashed them. (*Laughs.*) But I'm glad I did. (*Squeezes Sorin's hand tightly.*)

SORIN (*laughs*). I do believe your pretty eyes have tears in them . . . Heh-heh! Mustn't do that!

NINA. You're right . . . You see the way I'm panting. In half an hour I've got to go, we must hurry. Don't, don't, for heaven's sake, don't make me late. Father doesn't know I'm here.

TREPLYOV. As a matter of fact, it is time to begin. I have to collect everybody.

SORIN. I'll go fetch 'em and all the rest. Right this minute. (*Crosses right and sings.*) "Back to France two grenadiers . . ."[23] (*Looking round.*) Once I started singing just like that, and some assistant D.A.[24] says to me, "Your Honor, that's a powerful voice you've got . . ." Then he thought a bit and added, "Powerful . . . but repulsive." (*Laughs and exits.*)

NINA. Father and his wife won't let me come here. They say this place is bohemian . . . they're afraid I might become an actress . . . But I'm drawn here to the lake, like a gull . . . My heart is filled with all of you. (*Looks around.*)

TREPLYOV. We're alone.

---

23 The opening lines of a poem by Heinrich Heine, "Die beide Grenadiere" (1822), set to music by Robert Schumann (1827). The rest of the verse goes in translation:

> They had been imprisoned in Russia.
> And when they got to a German billet,
> They hung their heads.

According to Arthur Ganz, it is ironic that "one of the great romantic evocations of the power of the will (here a will that vows to seize upon its object even from beyond the grave), [is] precisely the quality that Sorin lacks" (*Drama Survey*, Spring 1966).

24 We learn later that Sorin had been an Actual State Councillor, fourth class in the tsarist table of ranks, equivalent to a Major-General and a Rear Admiral, so he is being twitted by an underling. A person who attains this rank may be addressed as "Your Excellency."

NINA. I think there's someone over there.

TREPLYOV. No one. (*Kiss.*)

NINA. What kind of tree is that?

TREPLYOV. Elm.

NINA. How come it's so dark?

TREPLYOV. It's nightfall, things get dark. Don't leave so soon, for my sake.

NINA. Can't.

TREPLYOV. What if I ride over to your place, Nina? I'll stand all night in the garden and stare at your window.

NINA. Can't, the watchman will catch you. Trésor still isn't used to you and he'll start barking.

TREPLYOV. I love you.

NINA. Ssh . . .

TREPLYOV (*having heard footsteps*). Who's there? That you, Yakov?

YAKOV (*behind the platform*). Right.

TREPLYOV. Got the methylated spirits? And the sulphur? When the red eyes make their entrance, there has to be a smell of sulphur. (*To Nina.*) Go on, they've got it all ready for you. Are you excited?

NINA. Yes, very. Your Mama doesn't count. I'm not afraid of her, but then there's Trigorin . . . Acting with him in the audience frightens and embarrasses me . . . A famous writer . . . Is he young?

TREPLYOV. Yes.

NINA. His stories are so wonderful!

TREPLYOV (*coldly*). I wouldn't know, I haven't read them.

NINA. It isn't easy to act in your play. There are no living characters in it.

TREPLYOV. Living characters! Life should be portrayed not the way it is, and not the way it's supposed to be, but the way it appears in dreams.

NINA. There isn't much action in your play, it's like a readthrough.[25] And a play, I think, definitely ought to have love interest . . .

They both go behind the platform. Enter POLINA
ANDREEVNA and DORN.

POLINA ANDREEVNA. It's starting to get damp. Go back, put on your galoshes.

DORN. I'm overheated.

POLINA ANDREEVNA. You don't take care of yourself. It's sheer obstinacy. You're a doctor and you know perfectly well that damp air is bad for you, but you want me to suffer; you deliberately sat up all last night on the veranda . . .

DORN (*sings*). "Say not that thy youth was wasted."[26]

POLINA ANDREEVNA. You were so infatuated talking to Irina Nikolaevna . . . you didn't notice the cold. Admit you're attracted to her.

DORN. I'm fifty-five years old.

POLINA ANDREEVNA. Don't be silly, that's not old for a man. You're beautifully preserved and women still find you attractive.

DORN. Then what can I do for you?

POLINA ANDREEVNA. You're all of you ready to fall on your faces at an actress's feet. All of you!

DORN (*sings*). "Once again I stand before thee . . ."[27] If society loves actors and treats them differently from, say, shopkeepers, it's only natural. It's what's we call idealism.

POLINA ANDREEVNA. Women have always fallen in love with you and flung themselves at you. Do you call that idealism?

DORN (*shrugging*). So what? My relationships with women have always been a good thing. What they really loved was my being a first-class doctor. Ten

---

25 *Chitka*, which is theatrical slang. Nina's vocabulary has profited by listening to Arkadina.

26 A line from Nekrasov's poem "A heavy cross fell to her lot" (1856), set to music by Adolf Prigozhy.

27 In full, "stand bewitched before thee," a line from V. I. Krasov's *Stanzas* (1842), set to music by Aleksandr Alyabiev.

or fifteen years ago, remember, I was the only competent obstetrician[28] in the whole county. Not to mention, I was a man of honor.

POLINA ANDREEVNA (*seizes him by the hand*). My dearest!

DORN. Hush. They're coming.

> *Enter ARKADINA, arm in arm with SORIN; TRIGORIN,*
> *SHAMRAEV, MEDVEDENKO, and MASHA.*

SHAMRAEV. At the Poltava fair[29] in 1873 she gave a marvelous performance. Sheer delight! Wonderful acting! Would you also happen to know what's become of the comedian Chadin, Pavel Chadin? He was inimitable in *Krechinsky's Wedding,*[30] better than the great Sadovsky,[31] take my word for it, dear lady. Where is he these days?

ARKADINA. You're always asking me about these prehistoric characters. How should I know? (*Sits down.*)

SHAMRAEV (*sighs*). Good old Chadin! You don't see his like nowadays. The stage is going downhill, Irina Nikolaevna! In the old days there were mighty oaks, but now all you see are stumps.

DORN. There's not a lot of brilliant talent around these days, it's true, but the general level of acting has improved considerably.

SHAMRAEV. I can't agree with you there. Still, it's a matter of taste. *De gustibus, pluribus unum.*[32]

> *TREPLYOV enters from behind the platform.*

---

28 Dorn uses the French word *accoucheur*, an indication of his refinement.

29 Capital of the *guberniya* of the same name, located in the Ukraine; its main industry was horse trading, slaughterhouses, and machinery manufacture. Its population was largely Little Russians (the standard tsarist term for Ukrainians) and Jews. Acting companies proliferated in such towns during the fairs.

30 In the original, "as Raspluev." "Ivan Antonovich, a small but thickset man around fifty," a great comic role in Aleksandr Sukhovo-Kobylin's *Krechinsky's Wedding* (first staged 1855), the cynical henchman of the confidence-man hero.

31 Stage name of Prov Mikhailovich Yermilov (1818–1872), a famous character actor and member of the Maly Theatre troupe in Moscow from 1839 to his death. He was responsible for the growing popularity of Ostrovsky's plays. Sukhovo-Kobylin believed that Sadovsky had vulgarized the part of Raspluev, which he created.

32 In the original, *de gustibus aut bene aut nihil*, a violent yoking together of three different Latin sayings: *De gustibus non disputantur*, "there's no point arguing over taste"; *De mortuis nil nisi bene*, "Say naught but good of the dead"; and *Aut Caesar aut nihil*, "Either Caesar or nothing."

ARKADINA (*to her son*). My darling son, when are we to begin?

TREPLYOV. In a minute. Have some patience.

ARKADINA (*reciting from* Hamlet).[33] "My son, Thou turn'st mine eyes into my very soul, And there I see such black and grainéd spots As will not leave their tinct."

TREPLYOV (*reciting from* Hamlet). "Then wherefore dost thou yield to sin, seeking love in a morass of crime?" (*A bugle is blown behind the platform.*) Ladies and gentlemen, we're about to begin! Your attention, please! (*Pause.*) I'm starting. (*Thumps with a stick and speaks loudly.*) O ye venerable and ancient shades, that nocturnally hover above this lake, put us to sleep and let us dream of what will be in two hundred thousand years!

SORIN. In two hundred thousand years, nothing will be.

TREPLYOV. Then let them reveal that nothing.

ARKADINA. Let them. We're asleep already.

> *The curtain rises; the vista on to the lake is revealed; the moon is over the horizon, reflected in the water; on a large boulder* NINA ZARECHNAYA *is seated, dressed all in white.*

NINA. Humans, lions, eagles and partridges, antlered deer, geese, spiders, silent fishes that inhabit the waters, starfish and those beings invisible to the naked eye,—in short, all living things, all living things, all living things, having completed the doleful cycle, are now extinct . . . Already thousands of centuries have passed since the earth bore any living creature, and this pale moon to no avail doth light her lamp. No more does the meadow awake to the cries of cranes, and the may flies are no longer to be heard in the linden groves. Chilly, chilly, chilly. Empty, empty, empty. Ghastly, ghastly, ghastly. (*Pause.*) The bodies of living creatures have crumbled into dust, and Eternal Matter has converted them into stones, water, clouds, and all their souls are mingled into one. The universal soul—'tis I . . . in person . . . . In me are mingled the souls of Alexander the Great, and Caesar, and Shakespeare, and Napoleon, and the lowliest of leeches. In me human con-

---

33 A quotation from *Hamlet*, the closet scene, Act III, scene 3. In Nikolay Polevoy's Russian translation, Arkadina's quotation is reasonably accurate, but Treplyov's is a loose paraphrase of "making love over the nasty sty." The original image would have been too coarse for nineteenth-century playgoers and censors.

sciousness is mingled with animal instinct, and I remember everything, everything, everything, and I relive each life within myself.

Will-o'-the-wisps appear.

ARKADINA (*in a low voice*). This is something avant-garde.[34]

TREPLYOV (*entreating her reproachfully*). Mama!

NINA. I am alone. Once every hundred years I ope my lips to speak, and my voice echoes dolefully in this void, and no one hears . . . Even ye, pale fires, hear me not . . . Toward morning ye are engendered by the putrescence of the swamp, and roam till dawn, but sans thoughts, sans will, sans throbbing life. Fearing lest life spring up in you, the father of Eternal Matter, Satan, at every moment effects in you, as in stones and water, an interchange of atoms, and you transmutate incessantly. Throughout the universe there remains constant and immutable naught but spirit. (*Pause.*) Like a prisoner, flung into a deep empty pit, I know not where I am nor what awaits me. All that is revealed to me is that in the dogged, cruel struggle with Satan, the principle of material forces, it is decreed that I shall conquer, and thereafter matter and spirit shall blend in glorious harmony and the kingdom of universal will shall emerge. But this will come to pass only very gradually, over a long, long series of millennia, when the moon and the twinkling dog-star and the earth are turned to dust . . . But until that time, all will be ghastly, ghastly, ghastly . . . (*Pause; against the background of the lake two red dots appear.*) Behold, my mighty adversary, Satan, draws nigh. I see his dreadful crimson eyes . . .

ARKADINA. What a stink of sulphur. Is that necessary?

TREPLYOV. Yes.

ARKADINA (*laughs*). Of course, special effects.

TREPLYOV. Mama!

NINA. He misses human beings . . .

POLINA ANDREEVNA (*to Dorn*). You took off your hat. Put it back on, or you'll catch cold.

---

34 Literally, *chto-to dekadentskoe*, something decadent. At this time, symbolist and decadent writing, popularized by Maeterlinck, was considered the cutting edge of literary innovation in Europe, and was beginning to gain disciples in Russia.

ARKADINA. The doctor's tipping his hat to Satan, the father of eternal matter.

TREPLYOV (*flaring up, loudly*). The play's over! That's enough! Curtain!

ARKADINA. What are you angry about?

TREPLYOV. Enough! Curtain! Ring down the curtain! (*Stamping his feet.*) Curtain! (*The curtain comes down.*) I apologize! I lost sight of the fact that playwriting and playacting are only for the chosen few. I infringed the monopoly! I feel . . . I . . . (*He wants to say something more, but waves his hand dismissively and exits left.*)

ARKADINA. What's come over him?

SORIN. Irina, dear heart, you mustn't treat a young man's self-esteem that way.

ARKADINA. What did I say to him?

SORIN. You offended him.

ARKADINA. He told us beforehand that it was a joke, so I treated his play as a joke.

SORIN. Even so . . .

ARKADINA. Now it turns out that he wrote a masterpiece! Pardon me for living! The real reason he staged this production and asphyxiated us with sulphur was not to make a joke, but to give us an object-lesson . . . He wanted to teach us how to write and how to act. This is starting to get tiresome. These constant jabs at me and digs, I don't care what you say, would get on anybody's nerves! Temperamental, conceited little boy.

SORIN. He wanted to give you a treat.

ARKADINA. Really? And yet you'll notice that he didn't pick an ordinary sort of play, but forced us to listen to this avant-garde gibberish. For the sake of a joke I'm willing to listen to gibberish too, but this is all pretentiousness about new forms, a new age in art. So far as I can tell, there's no new forms in it, nothing but a nasty disposition . . .

TRIGORIN. Everyone writes the way he wants and the way he can.

ARKADINA. Let him write the way he wants and the way he can, only let him leave me in peace.

DORN. "Mighty Jove, once angry grown . . ."[35]

ARKADINA. I'm not Jove, I'm a woman. (*Lighting a cigarette.*) I'm not angry, I'm only annoyed that a young man should waste his time in such a tiresome way. I didn't mean to offend him.

MEDVEDENKO. There's no basis for distinguishing spirit from matter, because spirit itself is probably an agglomeration of material atoms. (*Eagerly, to Trigorin.*) Now, you know, somebody ought to write a play and get it produced about—our friend the schoolteacher. He leads a tough, tough life!

ARKADINA. That's all very true, but don't let's talk about plays or atoms. What a glorious night! Do you hear the singing, ladies and gentlemen?[36] (*Listening hard.*) How lovely!

POLINA ANDREEVNA. It's on the other side of the lake.

Pause.

ARKADINA (*to Trigorin*). Sit beside me. Some ten or fifteen years ago, here, on the lake, you could hear music and singing nonstop almost every night. There were six country houses along the shore. I can remember laughter, noisemaking, shooting, and one love affair after another . . . The romantic lead and idol of all six houses at that time is among us, may I present (*nods to Dorn*) Doctor Yevgeny Dorn. He's fascinating even now, but in those days he was irresistible. However, my conscience is starting to bother me. Why did I insult my poor little boy? I feel bad about it. (*Loudly.*) Kostya! My child! Kostya!

MASHA. I'll go look for him.

ARKADINA. Please do, darling.

MASHA (*crosses left*). Yoo-hoo! Konstantin! . . . Yoo-hoo! (*Exits.*)

NINA (*coming out from behind the platform*). It looks like we're not going to go on, so I can come out. Good evening! (*Exchanges kisses with Arkadina and Polina Andreevna.*)

SORIN. Bravo! Bravo!

---

35 A saying that continues "has stopped being Jove" or "is in the wrong."

36 The Moscow Art Theatre used Glinka's *Temptation*.

ARKADINA. Bravo, bravo! We loved it. With such looks, such a wonderful voice it's wrong, it's criminal to vegetate in the country. You probably have talent too. You hear me? You have an obligation to go on the stage!

NINA. Oh, that's my fondest dream! (*Sighs.*) But it will never come true.

ARKADINA. Who knows? May I introduce: Boris Trigorin.

NINA. Ah, I'm delighted . . . (*Embarrassed.*) I read all your things . . .

ARKADINA (*seating her beside her*). Don't be embarrassed, darling. He's a celebrity, but he's a simple soul. You see, he's embarrassed himself.

DORN. I suppose we can raise the curtain now, it feels spooky this way.

SHAMRAEV (*loudly*). Yakov, haul up that curtain, boy!

The curtain is raised.

NINA (*to Trigorin*). It's a strange play, isn't it?

TRIGORIN. I didn't understand a word. Still, I enjoyed watching it. Your acting was so sincere. And the scenery was gorgeous. (*Pause.*) I suppose there are a lot of fish in that lake.

NINA. Yes.

TRIGORIN. I love fishing. For me there's no greater pleasure than sitting on the bank at dusk, watching the float bob up and down.[37]

NINA. But, I should think, anyone who's enjoyed creating a work of art couldn't enjoy anything else.

ARKADINA (*laughing*). Don't talk like that. Whenever anyone compliments him, he just shrivels up.

SHAMRAEV. I remember at the Moscow Opera House once the famous Silva[38] hit low C. And at the time, as luck would have it, sitting in the gallery was the bass from our church choir, and all of a sudden, you can imagine our intense surprise, we hear from the gallery: "Bravo, Silva!"—a

---

37 Chekhov's two favorite pastimes in the country were fishing with a float—a cork attached to a weighted line that moves when a fish bites—and gathering mushrooms.

38 Although Éloi Silva, a Belgian tenor born in 1846, was a star at the Petersburg Italian opera, mainly in Meyerbeer, Chekhov has simply lifted the name and applied it to a bass.

whole octave lower . . . Something like this (*in a basso profundo*): Bravo, Silva . . . The audience was dumbfounded.

Pause.

DORN. The quiet angel just flew by.[39]

NINA. My time's up. Good-bye.

ARKADINA. Where are you off to? So early? We won't let you go.

NINA. Papa's waiting for me.

ARKADINA. That man, honestly . . . (*Exchanges kisses.*) Well, what can we do. It's a shame, a crying shame to let you go.

NINA. If you only knew how hard it is for me to leave!

ARKADINA. Somebody should see you home, you darling girl.

NINA (*alarmed*). Oh, no, no!

SORIN (*to her, imploring*). Do stay!

NINA. I can't, Pyotr Nikolaevich.

SORIN. Do stay just one more hour and all the rest. Now, how 'bout it, come on . . .

NINA (*after thinking it over, tearfully*). I can't! (*Shakes hands and exits hurriedly.*)

ARKADINA. The girl's really and truly unhappy. They say her late mother bequeathed her husband her whole huge fortune, down to the last penny, and now this child is left with nothing, because her father's already willed it to his second wife. It's outrageous.

DORN. Yes, her dear old dad is a pedigreed swine. Credit where credit's due.

SORIN (*rubbing his chilled hands*). We'd best be going too, ladies and gentlemen, it's starting to get damp. My legs ache.

ARKADINA. They must be wooden legs, they can hardly move. Well, let's go, you star-crossed old man. (*Takes him by the arm.*)

SHAMRAEV (*offering his arm to his wife*). Madame?

---

39 A common saying, used whenever a pause suddenly falls over a conversation. Chekhov uses it in his stories frequently.

SORIN. I hear that dog howling again. (*To Shamraev.*) Kindly see that he's unchained, Ilya Afanasevich.

SHAMRAEV. Can't be done, Pyotr Nikolaevich, I'm afraid robbers might break into the barn. Got my millet stored there. (*To Medvedenko, walking beside him.*) Yes, a whole octave lower: "Bravo, Silva!" Wasn't a professional singer, either, just an ordinary member of the church choir.

MEDVEDENKO. How much does an ordinary member of the church choir make?

They all go out, except DORN.

DORN (*alone*). I don't know, maybe I'm confused or I'm crazy but I liked the play. There's something in it. When that girl was talking about being lonely and then, when Satan's red eyes appeared, my hands trembled with excitement. Fresh, naive . . . Oh, I think he's coming this way. I'd like to tell him the nicest things I can.

TREPLYOV (*enters*). Nobody's here.

DORN. I am.

TREPLYOV. That Masha creature's been looking for me all over the park. Unbearable female.

DORN. Konstantin Gavrilovich, I liked your play very much. It's an unusual piece of work, and I didn't get to hear how it ends, but even so, it makes a powerful impression. You're a talented fellow, you ought to keep at it. (*TREPLYOV squeezes his hand tightly and embraces him impulsively.*) Foo, don't be so high-strung. Tears in his eyes . . . What was I saying? You took a subject from the realm of abstract ideas. That was appropriate, because a work of art definitely ought to express a great idea. The beauty of a thing lies entirely in its seriousness. You're awfully pale!

TREPLYOV. Then what you're saying is—keep at it!

DORN. Yes . . . But write about only what's important and everlasting. You know, I've lived my life with variety and discrimination; I've had it all, but if I ever got the chance to experience the spiritual uplift artists feel at the moment of creation, I think I'd relinquish my physical trappings and all that they entail, and let myself be wafted far away from earth into the empyrean.

TREPLYOV. Sorry, where's Miss Zarechnaya?

DORN. And another thing. Every work of art ought to have a clear, well-defined idea. You ought to know what you're writing for, otherwise if you travel this picturesque path without a well-defined goal, you'll go astray and your talent will destroy you.

TREPLYOV (*impatiently*). Where's Miss Zarechnaya?

DORN. She went home.

TREPLYOV (*in despair*). What am I going to do? I have to see her . . . I 've got to see her . . . I'm going . . .

MASHA enters.

DORN (*to Treplyov*). Calm down, my friend.

TREPLYOV. But I'm going anyway. I have to go.

MASHA. Come home, Konstantin Gavrilovich. Your Mama's waiting for you. She's worried.

TREPLYOV. Tell her I've gone. And will you all please leave me in peace! Stay here! Don't come after me!

DORN. Now, now, now, my dear boy . . . you musn't act this way . . . isn't nice.

TREPLYOV (*tearfully*). Good-bye, Doctor. Thanks . . . (*Exits.*)

DORN (*sighs*). Youth, youth!

MASHA. When people have nothing better to say, they go: youth, youth . . . (*Takes snuff.*)

DORN (*takes away her snuffbox and tosses it into the bushes*). That's disgusting! (*Pause.*) Sounds like music in the house. Better go in.

MASHA. Wait.

DORN. What?

MASHA. I want to tell you something else. I have to talk to someone . . . (*Getting excited.*) I don't love my father . . . but I feel close to you.[40] Why do I

---

[40] In an early draft of the play, Masha's father was revealed to be Dr. Dorn at this point. When the play was revived at the Moscow Art Theatre, Nemirovich-Danchenko advised Chekhov to eliminate this plot element:

> I said either this theme has to be developed or else entirely removed. Especially since it ends the first act. The end of a first act by its very nature has to wind up tightly the situation to be developed in the second act.

feel so intensely that we have something in common . . . Help me. Help me, or I'll do something stupid, I'll mess up my life, wreck it . . . I can't stand it any more . . .

DORN. What do you mean? Help you how?

MASHA. I'm in pain. Nobody, nobody knows how much pain I'm in. (*Lays her head on his chest, quietly.*) I love Konstantin.

DORN. They're all so high-strung! They're all so high-strung! And all this love . . . Oh, spellbinding lake! (*Tenderly.*) But what can I do, my child? What? What?

Curtain

ACT TWO

A croquet lawn. Up right, a house with a wide veranda, the lake can be seen, with the sun's rays reflected on it. Flowerbeds. Midday. Hot. To one side of the croquet lawn, in the shade of an old linden tree, ARKADINA, DORN, and MASHA are sitting on a bench. DORN has an open book on his lap.

ARKADINA (*to Masha*). Come on, let's get up. (*Both rise.*) Let's stand side by side. You're twenty-two, and I'm nearly twice that. Yevgeny Sergeich, which of us is younger?[41]

DORN. You, of course.

Chekhov said, "The audience does like it when at the end of an act a loaded gun is aimed at it."

"True enough," I replied, "but then it has to go off, and not simply be chucked away during the intermission."

It turns out that later on Chekhov repeated this remark more than a few times.

He agreed with me. The ending was revised.

(Vl. I. Nemirovich-Danchenko, *Out of the Past* [1938])

41 In Chekhov's story "Ariadne" (1895) there is a similar passage:

"I just wonder, sir, how you can live without love?" he said. "You are young, handsome, interesting, — in short, you are a fashion plate of a man, but you live like a monk. Ah, these old men of twenty-eight! I am almost ten years older than you, but which of us is the younger? Ariadne Grigoryevna, who is younger?"

"You, of course," replied Ariadne.

ARKADINA. Thank you, kind sir . . . And why? Because I work, I feel emotions, I'm constantly on the go, while you sit still in the same place; you don't live . . . And I have a rule: don't peer into the future. I never give a thought to old age or death. What will be will be.

MASHA. But I feel as if I were born ages and ages ago; I lug my life around like a dead weight, like the endless train on a gown . . . And lots of times I don't feel much like going on living. (*Sits.*) Of course, this is all silly. I have to shake myself out of it, slough it off.

DORN (*sings quietly*). "Tell her of love, flowers of mine . . ."[42]

ARKADINA. Besides, I'm as neat and tidy as an English gentleman. Darling, I keep myself up to the mark, if I say so myself, and I'm always dressed and have my hair done *comme il faut*.[43] Would I ever venture to leave the house, just step into the garden, in a smock or with my hair down? Never. The reason I'm in such good shape is because I was never sloppy, never let myself go, like some people . . . (*With her hands on her hips, strides up and down the lawn.*) There you see—light on my feet. Fit to play a girl of fifteen.

DORN. Fine and dandy, but regardless of all that I'll go on reading. (*Picks up the book.*) We'd stopped at the grain merchant and the rats.

ARKADINA. And the rats. Read away. (*Sits down.*) Actually, give it to me, I'll read it. 'S my turn. (*Takes the book and runs her eyes over it.*) And the rats . . . Here we go . . . (*Reads.*) "And, of course, for people in society to pamper novelists and lure them into their homes is as dangerous as if a grain merchant were to breed rats in his granaries. Meanwhile they go on loving them. So, when a woman has picked out the writer she wishes to captivate, she lays siege to him by means of compliments, endearments and flattering attentions . . ."[44] Well, that may be what the French do, but there's

---

42 Siébel's song in Act III, scene one, of Gounod's opera *Faust*. In Russia, quoting it meant "You're talking through your hat."

43 French, "properly, suitably."

44 From *Sur l'eau* (1888), Maupassant's diary of a Mediterranean cruise, taken to restore his shattered nerves. The passage continues:

Just like water, which, drop by drop, pierces the hardest rock, praise falls, word by word, on the sensitive heart of a man of letters. So, as soon as she sees he is tenderized, moved, won over by this constant flattery, she isolates him, she gradually cuts the connections he might have elsewhere, and insensibly accustoms him to come to her house, to enjoy himself there,

nothing of the sort in our country, we have no master plan. In Russia before a woman captivates a writer, she's usually fallen head over heels in love with him herself, take my word for it. You don't have far to look, just consider me and Trigorin.

Enter SORIN, leaning on a stick, next to NINA;
MEDVEDENKO wheels an empty armchair behind them.

SORIN (*in the tone used to coddle children*). Are we? Are we having fun? Are we happy today, when's all said and done? (*To his sister.*) We're having fun! Father and Stepmother have gone out of town, and now we're free for three whole days.

NINA (*sits beside Arkadina and embraces her*). I'm happy! Now I can be all yours.

SORIN (*sits in the armchair*). She's the prettiest little thing today.

ARKADINA. Smartly dressed, interesting . . . You're clever at that sort of thing. (*Kisses Nina.*) But we mustn't praise her too much, or we'll put a hex on her.[45] Where's Boris Alekseevich?

NINA. He's down by the swimming hole, fishing.

ARKADINA. I'm surprised he doesn't get fed up with it! (*About to go on reading.*)

NINA. What have you got there?

ARKADINA. "At Sea" by Maupassant, sweetheart. (*Reads a few lines to herself.*) Well, the rest is uninteresting and untrue. (*Closes the book.*) I feel uneasy. Tell me, what's the matter with my son? How come he's so tiresome and surly? He spends whole days on the lake, and I almost never see him.

MASHA. He's sick at heart. (*To Nina, shyly.*) Please, do recite something from his play!

NINA (*shrugs*). You want me to? It's so uninteresting!

---

to put his mind at ease there. To get him nicely acclimated to her house, she looks after him and prepares his success, puts him in the limelight, as a star, shows him, ahead of all the former habitués of the place, a marked consideration, an unequaled admiration.

45 Literally, "put the evil eye on her," presumably by arousing envy.

MASHA (*with restrained excitement*). Whenever he recites, his eyes blaze and his face turns pale. He has a beautiful, mournful voice; and the look of a poet.

SORIN's snoring is audible.

DORN. Sweet dreams!

ARKADINA. Petrusha!

SORIN. Aah?

ARKADINA. You asleep?

SORIN. Certainly not.

Pause.

ARKADINA. You don't look after yourself, and you should, brother.

SORIN. I'd be glad to look after myself, but the doctor here won't prescribe a treatment.

DORN. Treatments at age sixty!

SORIN. Even at sixty a person wants to go on living.

DORN (*vexed*). Oh yeah! Well, take a couple of aspirins.[46]

ARKADINA. I think he'd feel better if he went to a health spa.

DORN. Think so? Let him go. Then again, let him stay here.

ARKADINA. Try and figure *that* out.

DORN. There's nothing to figure out. It's perfectly clear.

Pause.

MEDVEDENKO. The best thing Pyotr Nikolaevich could do is stop smoking.

SORIN. Rubbish.

DORN. No, it's not rubbish. Alcohol and tobacco rob you of your personality. After a cigar or a shot of vodka, you're not Pyotr Nikolaevich any more,

---

46 Valerian, a mild sedative, the equivalent of aspirin (which was not widely marketed until 1899). The nervous actors of the Moscow Art Theatre, on the opening night of *The Seagull*, had dosed themselves heavily with valerian.

you're Pyotr Nikolaevich plus somebody else; your sense of self, your "ego" gets fuzzy around the edges, and you start talking about yourself in the third person—as "that other fellow."

SORIN (*laughs*). 'S all right for you to lecture me! You've lived in your lifetime, but what about me? I worked in the Department of Justice for twenty-eight years, but I still haven't lived, haven't had any experiences, when all's said and done, and, take my word for it, I've still got a lust for life. You're jaded, you don't care, and so you can be philosophical, but I want to live a little and so I drink sherry at dinner and smoke cigars and all the rest. So there and all the rest.

DORN. A man should take life seriously, but trying treatments at sixty, complaining there wasn't enough fun in your youth is, pardon me, ridiculous.

MASHA (*rises*). Time for lunch, I guess . . . (*Walks with a sluggish, unsteady gait.*) Foot fell asleep . . . (*Exits.*)

DORN. She'll go and knock down a couple of drinks before lunch.

SORIN. The poor thing's got no happiness in her life.

DORN. Piffle, Your Excellency.

SORIN. You talk like a man who's had it all.

ARKADINA. Ah, what can be more boring than this darling rural boredom! Hot, quiet, nobody lifts a finger, everybody philosophizes . . . It's nice being with you, my friends, lovely listening to you, but . . . sitting in my hotel room and learning my lines—what could be better!

NINA (*rapturously*). How wonderful! I know just what you mean.

SORIN. Of course things're better in town. You sit in your office, the doorman doesn't let anyone in without being announced, the telephone . . . cabs on every corner and all the rest . . .

DORN (*sings*). "Tell her of love, flowers of mine . . ."

Enter SHAMRAEV, followed by POLINA ANDREEVNA.

SHAMRAEV. Here's our crowd. Good morning! (*Kisses Arkadina's hand, then Nina's.*) The wife tells me you're planning to drive with her into town today. Is that right?

ARKADINA. Yes, that's our plan.

SHAMRAEV. Hm . . . That's just great, but how you do expect to get there, dear lady? Our rye is being carted today, all the hired hands are busy. And which horses will you take, may I ask?

ARKADINA. Which? How should I know which?

SORIN. We've still got the carriage horses.

SHAMRAEV (*getting excited*). Carriage horses? And where am I to get harnesses? Where am I to get harnesses? This is marvelous! This is incredible! Dear, dear lady! Forgive me, I bow down to your talent, I'm ready to give up ten years of my life for your sake, but horses I cannot give you.

ARKADINA. And what if I have to go? A fine how-do-you-do!

SHAMRAEV. Dear lady! You don't know what it means to run a farm!

ARKADINA (*flaring up*). Here we go again! In that case, I shall leave for Moscow this very day. Have them hire horses for me in town, or else I'll go to the station on foot!

SHAMRAEV (*flaring up*). In that case I tender my resignation! Go find yourself another overseer. (*Exits.*)

ARKADINA. Every summer it's the same thing, every summer I'm exposed to insults. I'll never set foot in this place again! (*Exits left, where the swimming hole is supposed to be; in a minute she can be seen crossing into the house; TRIGORIN follows her with fishing poles[47] and a pail.*)

SORIN (*flaring up*). This is a disgrace! This is who the hell knows what! This is going to make me lose my temper, when all's said and done. Bring all the horses here this very minute!

---

47 "I was rehearsing Trigorin in *The Seagull*. And Anton Pavlovich invited me himself to talk over the role. I arrived with trepidation.

"'You know,' Anton Pavlovich began, 'the fishing poles ought to be, you know, homemade, bent. He makes them himself with a penknife . . . The cigar is a good one . . . Maybe it's not a really good one, but it definitely has to have silver paper . . .'

"Then he fell silent, thought a bit and said:

"'But the main thing is the fishing-poles . . .'" (Vasily Kachalov, *Shipovnik Almanac* 23 [1914]).

Chekhov shared Trigorin's love of fishing and wrote in a letter, "To catch a perch! It's finer and sweeter than love!"

NINA (*to Polina Andreevna*). To refuse Irina Nikolaevna, a famous actress! Isn't every one of her wishes, even her whims, more important than your farming? It's just incredible!

POLINA ANDREEVNA (*in despair*). What can I do? Put yourself in my position: what can I do?

SORIN (*to Nina*). Let's go in to my sister . . . We'll all plead with her not to leave. Isn't that the thing? (*Looking in the direction of Shamraev's exit.*) Insufferable fellow! Dictator!

NINA (*helping him to rise*). Sit down, sit down . . . We'll wheel you . . . (*She and MEDVEDENKO wheel the armchair.*) Oh, this is just awful!

SORIN. Yes, yes, this is awful . . . But he won't leave, I'll talk it over with him.

They leave; only DORN and POLINA ANDREEVNA remain.

DORN. People are so predictable. Ultimately the right thing would simply be to toss your husband out on his ear, but in fact it'll end up with that old fusspot Pyotr Nikolaevich and his sister begging *him* for forgiveness. Wait and see!

POLINA ANDREEVNA. He even sent the carriage horses into the fields. And every day there are squabbles like that. If you only knew how it upsets me! It's making me ill: you see, I'm trembling . . . I can't put up with his crudeness. (*Beseeching.*) Yevgeny, dearest, light of my life, take me with you . . . Time's running out for us, we aren't young any more, now at least when our lives are over, let's stop hiding, stop lying . . . (*Pause.*)

DORN. I'm fifty-five years old, it's too late for me to change my way of life.

POLINA ANDREEVNA. I know, you're rejecting me because there are other women you're intimate with too. You can't possibly take all of them in. I understand. Forgive me, I'm getting on your nerves.

NINA appears near the house; she is plucking flowers.

DORN. No, not at all.

POLINA ANDREEVNA. I'm sick with jealousy. Of course, you're a doctor, there's no way you can avoid women. I understand . . .

DORN (*to Nina, who walks by*). How are things indoors?

NINA. Irina Nikolaevna's crying and Pyotr Nikolaevich is having an asthma attack.

DORN (*rises*). I'll go give them both some aspirin . . .

NINA (*offers him the flowers*). Please take these!

DORN. *Merci bien.* (*Goes into the house.*)

POLINA ANDREEVNA (*going with him*). What adorable little flowers! (*Near the house, in a muffled voice.*) Give me those flowers! Give me those flowers! (*Once she gets the flowers, she tears them up and throws them aside. They both go into the house.*)

NINA (*alone*). How odd to see a famous actress crying, and over such a trivial matter! And isn't it odd, a best-selling author, a favorite with the reading public, written up in all the papers, his portrait on sale, translated into foreign languages, yet he spends the whole day fishing and he's overjoyed when he catches a couple of perch. I thought that famous people were proud, inaccessible, that they despised the public and their own fame, their celebrity was a kind of revenge for blue blood and wealth being considered more respectable . . . But here they are crying, fishing, playing cards, laughing, and losing their tempers, like anybody else . . .

TREPLYOV (*enters bare-headed, carrying a rifle and a slain gull*). You're alone here?

NINA. Alone. (*TREPLYOV lays the gull at her feet.*) What does this mean?

TREPLYOV. I did something nasty, I killed this gull today. I lay it at your feet.

NINA. What's wrong with you? (*Picks up the gull and stares at it.*)

TREPLYOV (*after a pause*). I'll soon kill myself the very same way.

NINA. I don't know who you are any more.

TREPLYOV. Yes, ever since I stopped knowing who you are. You've changed toward me, your eyes are cold, my being here makes you tense.

NINA. Lately you've been so touchy, and you talk in code, symbols of some kind. And this gull is obviously a symbol too, but, forgive me, I don't understand it . . . (*Lays the gull on the bench.*) I'm too ordinary to understand you.

TREPLYOV. It started that night when my play was a stupid fiasco. Women don't forgive failure. I burned everything, everything to the last scrap of paper. If only you knew how unhappy I am! Your coolness to me is horrible, incredible, it's like waking up and seeing that the lake has suddenly dried up or sunk into the ground. You say you're too ordinary to understand me. Oh, what's there to understand? You didn't like my play, you despise my ideas, you've started thinking of me as a mediocrity, a nobody, like all the rest . . . (*Stamping his foot.*) That's something *I* understand, oh, I understand all right! There's a kind of spike stuck in my brain, damn it and damn my vanity, which sucks my blood, sucks it like a snake . . . (*Catching sight of TRIGORIN, who is walking and reading a notebook.*) There goes the real genius; he paces the ground like Hamlet, and with a book too. (*Mimicking.*) "Words, words, words . . ."[48] His sun hasn't even shone on you yet, but already you're smiling, your eyes are thawing in his rays. I won't stand in your way. (*He exits quickly.*)

TRIGORIN (*making notes in the book*). Takes snuff and drinks vodka . . . Always wears black. Courted by a schoolteacher . . .

NINA. Good afternoon, Boris Alekseevich!

TRIGORIN. Good afternoon. Circumstances have taken an unexpected turn, so it turns out we leave today. In all likelihood we'll never see one another again. And that's a pity. I don't often get the chance to meet young girls, young and interesting ones; I've long forgotten, I can't quite imagine what it must feel like to be eighteen, nineteen, and that's why in my novellas and stories the young girls are usually stilted. I really would like to be in your shoes, if just for an hour, to find out how your mind works and more or less what sort of stuff you're made of.

NINA. And I should like to be in your shoes.

TRIGORIN. What for?

NINA. To find out how it feels to be a famous, talented writer. How does fame feel? How do you realize that you're famous?

TRIGORIN. How? Nohow, I suppose. I never thought about it. (*Thinking it over.*) It's either-or: either you're exaggerating my fame or there's no real way to realize it.

---

48 *Polonius*: What do you read, my lord?

Hamlet: Words, words, words. (*Hamlet*, Act II, scene 2)

Treplyov's mention of the sun may reflect his unconscious recollection of Hamlet's earlier lines about Ophelia, that she not stand too much "i' the sun."

NINA. But what about seeing your name in the papers?

TRIGORIN. If it's praise, I feel good, and if it's a scolding, then I'm in a bad mood for a couple of days.

NINA. The world's amazing! How I envy you, if you only knew! People's fates are so different. Some people can barely crawl through their boring, obscure existence, the same as everyone else, all unhappy; still others, like you, for instance—you're one in a million—are granted a life that's interesting, brilliant, meaningful . . . You're happy . . .

TRIGORIN. Am I? (*Shrugging.*) Hm . . . You stand here talking about fame, happiness, a brilliant, interesting life,[49] but to me it sounds sweet and gooey, sorry, just like marshmallows, which I never eat. You're very young and very kind.

NINA. Your life is so beautiful!

TRIGORIN. What's so especially good about it? (*Looks at his watch.*) I ought to get some writing in now. Forgive me, I've got no time . . . (*Laughs.*) You've stepped on my pet corn, as the saying goes,[50] and now I'm starting to get upset and a little bit angry. All right, let me make a statement. Let's talk about my beautiful, brilliant life . . . Well, now, where shall we begin? (*After thinking a bit.*) Some people are obsessive compulsives, a person who thinks all the time, for instance, about the moon, well, I have my own particular moon. All the time, I'm obsessed with one compulsive thought: I have to write, I have to write, I have to . . . I've barely finished one story, when already for some reason I have to write another, then a third, after the third a fourth . . . I write nonstop, like an express train, and I can't help it. What's so beautiful and brilliant about that, I ask you? Oh, what an uncivilized way of life! I'm here talking to you, I'm getting excited, but meanwhile I never forget there's a story of mine waiting to be finished. I see that cloud over there, that looks like a grand piano. I think: have to refer to that somewhere in a story, a cloud drifted by that looked like a grand piano. I catch a whiff of heliotrope,[51] I instantly reel it in on my moustache: cloy-

---

49 Compare Chekhov's letter to M. V. Kiselyova, September 21, 1886: ". . . It's no great treat to be a great writer. First, the life is gloomy . . . Work from morn to night, and not much profit . . . The money would make a cat weep . . ."

50 An English comic phrase, from the works of the humorist Jerome K. Jerome, who was very popular in Russia.

51 *Heliotropium peruvianum*, a small blue or dark-blue flower, with a faint aroma of vanilla.

ing smell, widow's color, refer to it in describing a summer evening. I'm angling in myself and you for every phrase, every word, and I rush to lock up all these words and phrases in my literary icebox: some time or other they'll come in handy! When I finish work, I run to the theater or go fishing; should be able to relax there, forget myself, oh, no, a heavy cannonball has started rolling around in my head—a new subject, and I'm drawn back to my desk, hurry, hurry, write, write. And so it goes forever and ever and ever, and I know no peace, and I feel that I'm devouring my own life, that to give away honey to somebody out there in space I'm robbing my finest flowers of their pollen, tearing up those flowers and trampling on their roots. Wouldn't you say I'm crazy? Surely my friends and relatives don't behave as if I were sane? "What are you puttering with now?[52] What will you give us next?" The same old same old, and I start thinking that this friendly attention, praise, admiration—it's all a plot, they're humoring me like an invalid, and sometimes I'm afraid that they're just on the verge of creeping up behind me, grabbing me and clapping me into a straitjacket, like the madman in Gogol's story.[53] And years ago, the years of my youth, my best years, when I was starting out, my writing was sheer agony. A second-rate writer, especially when luck isn't with him, sees himself as clumsy, awkward, irrelevant, his nerves are shot, frayed; he can't help hanging around people connected with literature and art, unrecognized, unnoticed by anyone, afraid to look them boldly in the face, like a compulsive gambler who's run out of money. I couldn't visualize my reader, but for that very reason he loomed in my imagination as hostile, suspicious. I was afraid of the public, it terrified me, and every time a new play of mine managed to get produced,[54] I thought the dark-haired spectators disliked it, while the fair-haired spectators couldn't care less. Oh, it's awful! Excruciating![55]

NINA. I'm sorry, but surely inspiration and the creative process itself must provide sublime moments of happiness?

---

52 Rather than the verb *pisat*, to write, Chekhov uses *popisyvat*, which, as George Calderon put it, "suggests that his writing is a sort of game, something that serves to keep him out of mischief. The critic Mikhailovsky used it, in the early days, of Chekhov's compositions."

53 Poprishchin, the hero of Gogol's "Diary of a Madman," a minor bureaucrat whose frantic scribbling reveals his delusions of adequacy. He falls in love with the daughter of his bureau chief and ends up in a madhouse.

54 This reflects Chekhov's own feelings after the opening of the revised *Ivanov* in 1889.

55 Tolstoy considered this speech the only good thing in the play. Chekhov himself considered obsessional writing to be the sign of a true writer.

TRIGORIN. Yes. When I'm writing, it's nice enough. And correcting the proofs is nice too, but . . . it's barely come off the presses, when I can't stand it, and can see that it's not right, a mistake, that it shouldn't have been written just that way, and I'm annoyed, feel rotten inside . . . (*Laughing.*) Then the public reads it: "Yes, charming, talented . . . Charming, but a far cry from Tolstoy," or "Lovely piece of work, but not up to Turgenev's *Fathers and Sons*."[56] And so until my dying day all I'll hear is charming and talented, charming and talented—, and when I die, my friends will file past my grave and say, "Here lies Trigorin. He wasn't so bad as a writer, but no Turgenev."

NINA. Forgive me, I refuse to accept that. You're simply spoiled by success.

TRIGORIN. What do you call success? I'm never satisfied with myself, I don't like myself as a writer. Worst of all is when I'm in some sort of trance and often I don't even understand what I'm writing . . . I love the water over there, the trees, sky, I have a feeling for nature; it inspires me with a passion, the irresistible urge to write. But I'm really more than just a landscape painter;[57] I do have a social conscience as well, I love my country, the people. I feel that if I'm a writer, I have an obligation to discuss the people, their suffering, their future, discuss science, human rights, et cetera, et cetera, and I do discuss all of it, trip over myself; I'm attacked from every side, I make people angry, I hurtle back and forth like a fox hunted down by hounds. I see that life and science keep moving farther and farther ahead, while I keep falling farther and farther behind, like a peasant who's missed his train and, when all's said and done, I feel that all I know how to write about is landscapes, and everything else I write is phony, phony to the nth degree!

NINA. You've been working too hard, and you've got no time or desire to admit your own importance. Even if you're dissatisfied with yourself, other people think you're great and beautiful! If I were a writer, like you, I would devote my whole life to the public, but I'd realize that their only happiness lay in being brought up to my level, and they would be yoked to my chariot.

---

56 The most famous novel (1862) of Ivan Sergeevich Turgenev (1818–1883), concerning a generational conflict, and offering a pattern of the "New Man." Chekhov gave the conflict between the generations a new twist in *The Seagull*.

57 Chekhov was the friend and admirer of the landscape painter Isaak Levitan, who tried to commit suicide in October 1895.

TRIGORIN. Well, well, a chariot . . . Am I Agamemnon or something?[58]

Both smile.

NINA. For the joy of being a writer or an actress, I would put up with my family disowning me, poverty, disappointment; I would live in a garret and eat nothing but black bread, suffer dissatisfaction with myself and realize my own imperfection, but in return I would insist on fame . . . real, resounding fame . . . (*Hides her face in her hands.*) My head's spinning . . . Oof!

ARKADINA's voice from the house: "Boris Alekseevich!"

TRIGORIN. They're calling me . . . I suppose it's about packing. But I don't feel like leaving. (*Looks around at the lake.*) Just look at this, God's country! . . . It's lovely!

NINA. You see the house and garden across the lake?

TRIGORIN. Yes.

NINA. That's my late mother's country house. I was born there. I've spent my whole life on the shores of this lake and I know every islet in it.

TRIGORIN. Must be nice over at your place! (*Having spotted the gull.*) But what's this?

NINA. A gull. Konstantin Gavrilych killed it.

TRIGORIN. Lovely bird. Honestly, I don't feel like leaving. Look here, go and talk Irina Nikolaevna into staying. (*Jots a note in his notebook.*)[59]

NINA. What's that you're writing?

TRIGORIN. Just jotting down a note . . . A subject came to mind . . . (*Putting away the notebook.*) Subject for a short story: on the shores of a lake a young girl grows up, just like you; loves the lake, like a gull, is happy and free, like a gull. But by chance a man comes along, sees her, and, having nothing better to do, destroys her, just like this gull here.

---

58 Agamemnon, leader of the Greek host in the Trojan war, was more familiar to Chekhov from Offenbach's comic opera *La Belle Hélène* (1864) than from Homer's *Iliad*.

59 Chekhov was against the indiscriminate use of notes in creative writing. "There's no reason to write down similes, tidy character sketches, or details of landscapes: they should appear of their own accord, whenever needed. But a bare fact, an unusual name, a technical term ought to be put down in a notebook; otherwise it will go astray and get lost."

Pause. ARKADINA appears in a window.

ARKADINA. Boris Alekseevich, where are you?

TRIGORIN. Coming! (*Goes and takes a glance round at Nina; at the window, to Arkadina.*)

What?

ARKADINA. We're staying.

TRIGORIN exits into the house.

NINA (*Crosses down to the footlights; after a moment's thought*). It's a dream!

Curtain

ACT THREE

*Dining room in Sorin's house. Doors right and left. Sideboard.
Cupboard with first-aid kit and medicine. Table center. Trunks
and cardboard boxes; signs of preparation for a departure.
TRIGORIN is eating lunch, MASHA stands by the table.*

MASHA. I'm telling you all this because you're a writer. You can put it to use. I swear to you: if he'd wounded himself seriously, I wouldn't have gone on living another minute. Not that I'm not brave. I've gone and made up my mind. I'll rip this love out of my heart, I'll rip it up by the roots.

TRIGORIN. How so?

MASHA. I'm getting married. To Medvedenko.

TRIGORIN. That's that schoolteacher?

MASHA. Yes.

TRIGORIN. I don't see the necessity.

MASHA. Loving hopelessly, waiting and waiting for years on end for something . . . But once I'm married, there'll be no room for love, new problems will blot out the old one. And anyhow, you know, it makes a change. Shall we have another?

TRIGORIN. Aren't you overdoing it?

MASHA. Oh, go ahead! (*Pours out a shot for each.*) Don't look at me like that. Women drink more often than you think. A few drink openly, like me, but most of them do it on the sly. Yes. And it's always vodka or brandy. (*Clinks glasses.*) Here's to you! You're a nice man. I'm sorry you're going away.

They drink.[60]

TRIGORIN. If it were up to me, I wouldn't be leaving.

MASHA. Then ask her to stay.

TRIGORIN. No, she won't stay now. Her son's been acting very tactlessly. First he tries to shoot himself,[61] and now I hear he intends to challenge me to a duel. And what for? He feuds and fusses, preaches about new forms . . . But there's room enough for everyone, isn't there? New and old—what's the point in shoving?

MASHA. Well, it's jealousy too. Though, that's no business of mine. (*Pause. YAKOV crosses left to right with a suitcase. NINA enters and stops by a window.*) My schoolteacher isn't very bright, but he's a decent sort, poor too, and he's awfully in love with me. I feel sorry for him. And I feel sorry for his poor old mother. Well, sir, please accept my best wishes. Think kindly of us. (*Shakes him firmly by the hand.*) Thanks a lot for your consideration. Do send me your book, and be sure there's an inscription. Only don't make it out "To dear madam," but simply "To Mariya, of no known family[62] and who lives in this world for no apparent reason." Good-bye. (*Exits.*)

NINA (*holding out her clenched fist to Trigorin*). Odds or evens?

TRIGORIN. Evens.

---

60 Vasily Kachalov wrote:

"Look, you know," Chekhov began, seeing how persistent I was, "when he, Trigorin, drinks vodka with Masha, I would definitely do it like this, definitely."
And with that he got up, adjusted his waistcoat, and awkwardly wheezed a couple of times.
"There you are, you know, I would definitely do it like that. When you've been sitting a long time, you always want to do that sort of thing . . ."

(*Shipovnik Almanac* 23 [1914])

61 The verb form in Russian makes it clear that he failed.

62 A common formula in police reports applied to vagrants without passports.

NINA (*sighing*). No. I've only got one bean in my hand. I was guessing whether to become an actress or not. If only someone would give me some advice.

TRIGORIN. You can't give advice about things like that.

Pause.

NINA. We're parting and . . . most likely we'll never see one another again. Please take a keepsake of me, here, this little medallion. I had them engrave your initials . . . and on this other side the title of your book: "Days and Nights."

TRIGORIN. How thoughtful! (*Kisses the medallion.*) A charming gift!

NINA. Remember me from time to time.

TRIGORIN. I will. I will remember you as you were on that sunny day—do *you* remember?—a week ago, when you were wearing a brightly colored dress . . . We were having a long talk . . . and something else, there was a white gull lying on the bench.

NINA (*pensively*). Yes, a gull . . . (*Pause.*) We can't go on talking, someone's coming . . . Before you go, save two minutes for me, please . . . (*Exits left.*)

At that very moment ARKADINA enters right, as does SORIN in a tailcoat with a star pinned to his chest,[63] then YAKOV, preoccupied with packing.

ARKADINA. You should stay home, you old man. With that rheumatism of yours what are you doing riding around paying calls? (*To Trigorin.*) Who went out just now? Nina?

TRIGORIN. Yes.

ARKADINA. *Excusez-moi*, we interrupted something . . . (*Sits down.*) I think everything's packed. I'm tired to death.

TRIGORIN (*reads the inscription on the medallion*). "Days and Nights," page 121, lines 11 and 12.

YAKOV (*clearing the table*). Do you want me to pack the fishing poles too?

TRIGORIN. Yes, I can use them again. But the books you can give away.

---

63 The decoration is an appurtenance of his status as an Actual State Councillor.

YAKOV. Yes, sir.

TRIGORIN (*to himself*). Page 121, lines 11 and 12. What is there in those lines? (*To Arkadina.*) Are there copies of my books anywhere in the house?

ARKADINA. In my brother's study, the corner bookcase.

TRIGORIN. Page 121 . . . (*Exits.*)

ARKADINA. Honestly, Petrusha, you ought to stay at home . . .

SORIN. You're leaving; with you gone it'll be boring at home . . .

ARKADINA And what's there to do in town?

SORIN. Nothing special, but even so. (*He laughs.*) They'll be laying the cornerstone for the town hall[64] and all the rest . . . Just for a couple of hours I'd like to stop feeling like a stick-in-the-mud,[65] I've been getting stale, like an old cigarette holder. I told them to send round my horses at one, we'll both go at the same time.

ARKADINA (*after a pause*). Oh, do stay here, don't be bored, don't catch cold. Look after my son. Keep an eye on him. Give him good advice.

Pause.

Now I've got to go and I still don't know how come Konstantin took a shot at himself. I suppose the main reason was jealousy, so the sooner I take Trigorin away from here, the better.

SORIN. How can I put this? There were other reasons too. Take my word for it, a man who's young, intelligent, living in the country, in the sticks, with no money, no position, no future. Nothing to keep him occupied. Gets ashamed of himself and alarmed by his own idleness. I love him dearly and he's very fond of me, but all the same, when all's said and done, he thinks he's unwanted at home, that he's a panhandler here, a charity case. Take my word for it, vanity . . .

ARKADINA. He's the cross I bear! (*Musing.*) He could get a desk job in the civil service, or something . . .

---

64 In the original, the new *zemstvo* building. See *Ivanov*, First Version, note 3.

65 Literally, this gudgeon's life (*peskarnaya zhizn*), a reference to Saltykov-Shchedrin's fable "The Wise Gudgeon," which deplores a conservative, philistine way of life.

SORIN (*whistles a tune, then tentatively*). I think it would be best if you . . . gave him some money. First of all, he ought to be dressed like a human being and all the rest. Just look, he's been wearing the same beat-up old frockcoat for the last three years, he has to go out without a topcoat . . . (*Laughs.*) Besides, it wouldn't hurt the boy to live it up a bit . . . Go abroad or something . . . It's not all that expensive.

ARKADINA. Even so . . . Possibly, I could manage the suit, but as for going abroad . . . No, at the moment I can't manage the suit either. (*Decisively.*) I have no money! (*SORIN laughs.*) None!

SORIN (*whistles a tune*). Yes, ma'am. Sorry, my dear, don't get angry. I believe you . . . You're a generous, selfless woman.

ARKADINA (*plaintively*). I have no money!

SORIN. If I had any money, take my word for it, I'd let him have it, but I haven't any, not a red cent. (*Laughs.*) The overseer snatches my whole pension from me, and wastes it on farming, livestock, beekeeping, and my money simply melts away. The bees die off, the cows die off, I can never get any horses . . .

ARKADINA. Yes, I do have some money, but I'm an actress, aren't I? My costumes alone are enough to ruin me.

SORIN. You're kind, affectionate . . . I respect you . . . Yes . . . But something's come over me again . . . (*Staggers.*) My head's spinning. (*Holds on to the table.*) I feel faint and all the rest.

ARKADINA (*alarmed*). Petrusha! (*Trying to hold him up.*) Petrusha, dear . . . (*Shouts.*) Help me! Help! (*Enter TREPLYOV, a bandage round his head, and MEDVEDENKO.*) He's fainting!

SORIN. Never mind, never mind . . . (*Smiles and drinks some water.*) It's all over . . . and all the rest.

TREPLYOV (*to his mother*). Don't be alarmed, Mama, it isn't serious. Uncle often gets like this these days. (*To his uncle.*) You ought to lie down for a while, Uncle.

SORIN. For a little while, yes . . . But all the same I'm driving to town . . . I'll go lie down and drive to town . . . Take it from me . . . (*He starts out, leaning on his stick.*)

MEDVEDENKO (*escorting him, holding his arm*). Here's a riddle: what goes on four legs in the morning, two at midday, three in the evening . . .[66]

SORIN (*laughs*). I know. And flat on its back at night. Thank you, I can walk on my own.

MEDVEDENKO. Now, now, don't show off! . . .

He and SORIN go out.

ARKADINA. He gave me such a fright!

TREPLYOV. Living in the country is bad for his health. He gets depressed. Now, Mama, if only you had a sudden fit of generosity and lent him a couple of thousand or so, he might be able to live in town all year long.

ARKADINA. I have no money. I'm an actress, not a banker.

Pause.

TREPLYOV. Mama, change my bandage. You do it so well.

ARKADINA (*gets iodoform and a drawerful of dressings from the first-aid cupboard*). The doctor's late.

TREPLYOV. He promised to be here by ten and it's already noon.

ARKADINA. Sit down. (*Removes the bandage from his head.*) Looks like a turban. Yesterday some tramp asked in the kitchen what your nationality was. It's almost completely healed. What's left is nothing. (*Kisses him on the head.*) And when I'm away, you won't do any more click-click?

TREPLYOV. No, Mama. It was a moment of insane desperation, when I lost control. It won't happen again. (*Kisses her hands.*) You've got wonderful hands. I remember long, long ago, when you were still working at the National Theatre[67]—I was a little boy then—there was a fight in our yard, a washerwoman who lived there got badly beaten up. Remember? She was picked up unconscious . . . You would go and see her, take her medicine, bathe her children in the washtub. Don't you remember?

ARKADINA. No. (*Putting on a fresh bandage.*)

---

66 The classical Greek riddle the Sphinx offers Oedipus. The answer is *man*.

67 The official Imperial theaters in St. Petersburg and Moscow.

TREPLYOV. At the time there were two ballerinas living in our building . . . They'd come and drink coffee with you . . .

ARKADINA. That I remember.

TREPLYOV. They were so religious.

Pause.

Just lately, these last few days, I love you every bit as tenderly and freely as when I was a child. Except for you, I've got no one left now. Only why, why do you give in to that man's influence?[68]

ARKADINA. You don't understand him, Konstantin. He's a person of the highest refinement.

TREPLYOV. But when they told him I was going to challenge him to a duel, his refinement didn't keep him from acting like a coward. He's going away. Retreating in disgrace!

ARKADINA. Don't be silly! I'm the one who's asked him to go away. Of course, I don't expect you to approve of our intimacy, but you're intelligent and sophisticated, I have the right to demand that you respect my independence.[69]

TREPLYOV. I do respect your independence, but you've got to let me be independent and treat that man any way I want.[70] The highest refinement! You and I are at one another's throats because of him, while he's somewhere in the drawing-room or the garden, laughing at us . . . cultivating Nina, trying to persuade her once and for all that he's a genius.

ARKADINA. You enjoy hurting my feelings. I respect that man and must ask you not to say nasty things about him to my face.

TREPLYOV. But I don't respect him. You want me to treat him like a genius too. Well, pardon me, I cannot tell a lie, his writing makes me sick.

---

68 This phrase was excised by the censor and replaced by Chekhov with "why does that man have to come between us?"

69 These two lines were excised by the censor and replaced with "He'll go right now. I will ask him to leave here myself."

70 This line was excised by the censor.

ARKADINA. That's jealousy. People with no talent but plenty of pretentions have nothing better to do than criticize really talented people. It's a comfort to them, I'm sure!

TREPLYOV (*sarcastically*). Really talented people! (*Angrily.*) I'm more talented than the lot of you put together, if it comes to that! (*Tears the bandage off his head.*) You dreary hacks hog the front-row seats in the arts and assume that the only legitimate and genuine things are what you do yourselves, so you suppress and stifle the rest! I don't believe in any of you! I don't believe in you or him!

ARKADINA. Mr. Avant-garde!. .

TREPLYOV. Go back to your darling theater and act in your pathetic, third-rate plays.

ARKADINA. I have never acted in that kind of play. Leave me out of it! You haven't got what it takes to write a miserable vaudeville sketch. You bourgeois from Kiev! You panhandler!

TREPLYOV. You skinflint!

ARKADINA. You scarecrow! (*TREPLYOV sits down and weeps quietly.*) You nobody! (*Walking up and down in agitation.*) Don't cry. You mustn't cry . . . (*She weeps.*) Don't do it . . . (*She kisses his forehead, cheeks, head.*) My darling boy, forgive me . . . Forgive your wicked mother. Forgive unhappy me.

TREPLYOV (*embraces her*). If only you knew! I've lost everything. She doesn't love me, I can't write any more . . . I've lost all hope . . .

ARKADINA. Don't lose heart. Everything will turn out all right. He'll be leaving soon, she'll love you again. (*Wipes away his tears.*) There now. We're friends again.

TREPLYOV (*kisses her hands*). Yes, Mama.

ARKADINA (*tenderly*). Make friends with him too. There's no need for duels . . . Is there?

TREPLYOV. All right . . . Only, Mama, don't make me see him again. It's too hard for me . . . I can't deal with it . . . (*TRIGORIN enters.*) There he is . . . I'm going . . . (*He rapidly throws the first-aid kit into the cupboard.*) The Doctor will do my bandage later on . . .

TRIGORIN (*leafing through a book*). Page 121 . . . lines 11 and 12 . . . Aha! . . . (*Reads.*) "If ever my life is of use to you, come and take it."[71]

TREPLYOV picks the bandage up off the floor and exits.

ARKADINA (*after a glance at her watch*). The horses will be here soon.

TRIGORIN (*to himself*). If ever my life is of use to you, come and take it.

ARKADINA. You've got all your things packed, I hope?

TRIGORIN (*impatiently*). Yes, yes . . . (*Musing.*) How come this appeal from a pure spirit has sounded a note of sorrow and my heart aches so poignantly? . . . If ever my life is of use to you, come and take it. (*To Arkadina.*) Let's stay just one more day! (*ARKADINA shakes her head no.*) Let's stay!

ARKADINA. Darling, I know what's keeping you here. But do show some self-control. You're a little tipsy, sober up.

TRIGORIN. Then you be sober too, be understanding, reasonable, please, come to terms with this like a true friend . . . (*Squeezes her hand.*) You're capable of sacrifice . . . Be my friend, let me go.

ARKADINA (*extremely upset*). You're that far gone?

TRIGORIN. I'm attracted to her! Maybe this is just what I need.

ARKADINA. The love of some country girl? Oh, how little you know yourself!

TRIGORIN. Sometimes people walk in their sleep, look, I'm here talking to you, but it's as if I'm asleep and seeing her in my dreams . . . I've succumbed to sweet, wonderful visions . . . Let me go.

---

71 Nemirovich-Danchenko wrote:

   While Chekhov was writing this play, the editors of *Russian Thought* sent him a bracelet charm in the shape of a book, on one side of which was engraved the title of his short story collection and on the other the numbers: p. 247, 1. 6 and 7. The gift was anonymous. In his collection Anton Pavlovich read: "You are the most generous, the noblest of men. I am eternally grateful to you. If you ever need my life come and take it." It is from the story "Neighbors" (1892), in which Grigory Vlasich says these words to his wife's brother. Anton Pavlovich vaguely surmised who had sent him this charm, and thought up an original way to send thanks and a reply: he had Nina give the same medallion to Trigorin and only changed the name of the book and the numbers. The answer arrived as intended at the first performance of *The Seagull*. The actors, of course, never suspected that, as they performed the play, they were simultaneously acting as letter-carriers."

   (*Out of the Past* [1938])

ARKADINA (*trembling*). No, no . . . I'm an ordinary woman, you mustn't talk to me that way . . . Don't tease me, Boris . . . It frightens me.

TRIGORIN. If you try, you can be extraordinary. A love that's young, charming, poetical, wafting me to a dream world—it's the one and only thing on this earth that can bring happiness. I've never yet experienced a love like that . . . When I was young I had no time, I was hanging around publishers' doorsteps, fighting off poverty . . . Now it's here, this love, it's come at last, luring me . . . What's the point of running away from it?

ARKADINA (*angrily*). You're out of your mind!

TRIGORIN. So what.

ARKADINA. You've all ganged up today to torture me! (*Weeps.*)

TRIGORIN (*puts his head in his hands*). She doesn't understand! She refuses to understand!

ARKADINA. Am I now so old and ugly that men don't think twice telling me about other women? (*Embraces and kisses him.*) Oh, you've gone crazy! My gorgeous, fabulous man . . . You're the last chapter in my life story! (*Kneels down.*) My joy, my pride, my blessedness . . . (*Embraces his knees.*) If you desert me for even a single hour, I won't survive. I'll go out of my mind, my incredible, magnificent man, my lord and master . . .

TRIGORIN. Somebody might come in. (*He helps her to rise.*)

ARKADINA. Let them, I'm not ashamed of my love for you. (*Kisses his hand.*) My precious, headstrong man, you want to do something reckless, but I won't have it, I won't let you . . . (*Laughs.*) You're mine . . . you're mine . . . And this forehead is mine, and these eyes are mine, and this beautiful silky hair is mine too . . . You're all mine. You're so talented, clever, our greatest living writer, you're Russia's only hope . . . You've got so much sincerity, clarity, originality, wholesome humor . . . With a single stroke you can pinpoint the most vital feature in a person or a landscape, your characters are so alive. Oh, no one can read you without going into ecstasy! You think this is soft soap?[72] Am I lying? Well, look into my eyes . . . look . . . Do I look like a liar? There, you see, I'm the only one who knows how to appreciate you; I'm the only one who tells you the truth, my darling, marvelous man . . . You will come? Won't you? You won't desert me?

---

72 *Finiam*, literally, incense; figuratively, gross flattery.

TRIGORIN. I've got no will of my own . . . I never had a will of my own . . .
Wishy-washy, spineless, always giving in—how can a woman find that
attractive? Take me, carry me off, but don't ever let me out of your sight . . .

ARKADINA (*to herself*). Now he is mine. (*Casually, as if nothing had happened.*) Of course, if you want to, you can stay. I'll go by myself, and you
can come later, in a week's time. After all, what's your rush?

TRIGORIN. No, let's go together.

ARKADINA. If you say so. Together, whatever you like, together . . . (*Pause.
TRIGORIN jots something in his notebook.*) What are you up to?

TRIGORIN. This morning I heard a good phrase: "the virgin grove" . . . It'll
come in handy. (*Stretching.*) Which means, we're on our way? More train
compartments, stations, lunch counters, fried food, smalltalk . . .

SHAMRAEV (*enters*). I have the melancholy honor of announcing that the
horses are here. The time has come, dear lady, to go to the station; the train
pulls in at two-o-five. By the way, Irina Nikolaevna, do me a favor, you won't
forget to find out what's become of the actor Suzdaltsev these days? Is he
alive? Is he well? Many's the drink we downed together once upon a time
. . . In "The Great Mail Robbery" his acting was inimitable . . . I recall he
was acting at the time in Elizavetgrad with the tragedian Izmailov, another
remarkable character[73] . . . Don't rush yourself, dear lady, we can spare
another five minutes. Once in some melodrama they were playing conspir-
ators, and when they were suddenly caught, the line was supposed to go:
"We've fallen into a trap," but Izmailov said, "We've trawlen into a flap" . . .
(*Roars with laughter.*) Into a flap!

> *While he is speaking, YAKOV fusses around the luggage, a
> HOUSEMAID brings ARKADINA her hat, coat, parasol, gloves;
> everyone helps Arkadina to dress. The COOK peers in through the
> door left, and after waiting a bit he enters hesitantly. POLINA
> ANDREEVNA enters, then SORIN and MEDVEDENKO.*

POLINA ANDREEVNA (*with a tiny basket*). Here are some plums for your
trip . . . Nice and ripe. You might want something for your sweet tooth.

---

73 Actors invented by Chekhov. *The Great Mail Robbery* is F. A. Burdin's adaptation of the French
melodrama *Le courrier de Lyon* (1850), by Eugène Lemoine-Moreau, Paul Siraudin, and Alfred
Delacour, well known to Victorian English audiences as *The Lyons Mail*. As an adolescent in Taganrog, Chekhov had seen and loved this play.

ARKADINA. That's very kind of you, Polina Andreevna.

POLINA ANDREEVNA. Good-bye, my dear! It anything wasn't right, do forgive me. (*Weeps.*)

ARKADINA (*embraces her*). Everything was fine, just fine. Only you mustn't cry.

POLINA ANDREEVNA. Time's running out for us!

ARKADINA. What can we do?

SORIN (*in an overcoat with a cape, wearing a hat and carrying a walking stick, enters from the door left; crosses the room*). Sister, it's time. You better not be late, when all's said and done. I'm going to get in. (*Exits.*)

MEDVEDENKO. And I'll go to the station on foot . . . to see you off. I'm a fast walker . . . (*He exits.*)

ARKADINA. Till we meet again, my dears . . . If we're alive and well, we'll see you again next summer . . . (*The HOUSEMAID, YAKOV, and the COOK kiss her hand.*) Don't forget me. (*Hands the COOK a ruble.*) Here's a ruble for the three of you.

COOK. Thank you kindly, ma'am. Have a pleasant trip! Mighty pleased to serve you!

YAKOV. God bless and keep you!

SHAMRAEV. Brighten our days with a little letter! Good-bye, Boris Alekseevich.

ARKADINA. Where's Konstantin? Tell him that I'm going. I've got to say good-bye. Well, think kindly of me. (*To Yakov.*) I gave a ruble to the cook. It's for the three of you.

> *Everyone goes out right. The stage is empty. Offstage there is the sort of noise that accompanies people seeing each other off. The HOUSEMAID returns to get the basket of plums from the table, and exits again.*

TRIGORIN (*returning*). I forgot my stick. I think it's out on the veranda. (*Crosses left and at the door runs into NINA, entering.*) Ah, it's you? We're leaving.

NINA. I felt we would meet again. (*Excited.*) Boris Alekseevich, I've made up my mind once and for all, the die is cast, I'm going on the stage. Tomorrow I'll be gone, I'm leaving my father, abandoning everything, starting a new life . . . I'm traveling like you . . . to Moscow. We shall meet there.

TRIGORIN (*glancing around*). Stay at the Slav Bazaar Hotel . . . Let me know the minute you're there . . . Molchanovka Street,[74] the Grokholsky Apartments . . . I'm in a hurry . . .

Pause.

NINA. Just one more minute.

TRIGORIN (*in an undertone*). You're so beautiful . . . Oh, how wonderful to think that we'll be seeing one another soon! (*She lays her head on his chest.*) I'll see these marvelous eyes again, that indescribably beautiful, tender smile . . . these delicate features, this look of angelic purity . . . My dearest . . . (*A prolonged kiss.*)

Curtain

ACT FOUR

Between Acts Three and Four two years have elapsed.

One of the drawing-rooms in Sorin's house, turned by Konstantin Treplyov into a workroom. Left and right doors, leading to inner rooms. Directly facing us, a glass door to the veranda. Besides the usual drawing-room furniture, in the right corner is a writing desk, near the left door a Turkish divan, a bookcase full of books, books on the windowsills, on chairs. — Evening. A single lamp with a shade is lit. Semi-darkness. We can hear the trees rustling and the wind wailing in the chimney. A WATCHMAN raps on a board.[75] MEDVEDENKO and MASHA enter.

---

74 *Slavyansky Bazar*, an elegant and fashionable hotel in central Moscow, rated one of the top three and much frequented by Chekhov. It was where Stanislavsky and Nemirovich-Danchenko held their epic lunch that resulted in the founding of the Moscow Art Theatre. Molchanovka is a street near Arbat Square in Moscow, in the center of the city, easy walking distance from the Slav Bazaar.

75 See *Ivanov*, First Version, note 19.

MASHA (*shouts out*). Konstantin Gavrilych! Konstantin Gavrilych! (*Looking around.*) Nobody here. The old man never stops asking, where's Kostya, where's Kostya . . . Can't live without him . . .

MEDVEDENKO. Afraid to be left alone. (*Listening hard.*) What awful weather! For two whole days now.

MASHA (*igniting the flame in a lamp*). There are waves on the lake. Enormous ones.

MEDVEDENKO. It's dark outside. Somebody should tell them to pull down that stage in the garden. It stands there bare, unsightly, like a skeleton, and the scene curtain flaps in the wind. When I was going by last night, I thought somebody was on it, crying . . .

MASHA. You don't say . . .

Pause.

MEDVEDENKO. Let's go home, Masha!

MASHA (*shakes her head no*). I'll stay and spend the night here.

MEDVEDENKO (*pleading*). Masha, let's go! Our baby's starving, I'll bet!

MASHA. Don't be silly. Matryona will feed him.

Pause.

MEDVEDENKO. It's a shame. The third night now without his mother.

MASHA. You're getting tiresome. In the old days at least you used to talk philosophy, but now it's all baby, home, baby, home—that's all anybody hears out of you.

MEDVEDENKO. Let's go, Masha!

MASHA. Go yourself.

MEDVEDENKO. Your father won't give me any horses.

MASHA. He will. Ask him and he'll give you.

MEDVEDENKO. Maybe so, I'll ask. That means, you'll be home tomorrow?

MASHA (*takes snuff*). All right, tomorrow. You're a pest . . .

Enter TREPLYOV and POLINA ANDREEVNA; TREPLYOV is carrying pillows and a blanket, and POLINA ANDREEVNA bedclothes; they lay them on the Turkish divan, after which TREPLYOV goes to his desk and sits.

MASHA. What's this for, Mama?

POLINA ANDREEVNA. Pyotr Nikolaevich asked for his bed to be made up in Kostya's room.

MASHA. Let me . . . (*Makes the bed.*)

POLINA ANDREEVNA (*sighs*). Old folks are like children . . . (*Walks over to the writing desk and, leaning on her elbows, looks at the manuscript.*)

Pause.

MEDVEDENKO. Well, I'm going. Good-bye, Masha. (*Kisses his wife's hand.*) Good-bye, Mama dear. (*Tries to kiss his mother-in-law's hand.*)

POLINA ANDREEVNA (*annoyed*). Well! Go if you're going.

MEDVEDENKO. Good-bye, Konstantin Gavrilych.

TREPLYOV silently offers his hand; MEDVEDENKO exits.

POLINA ANDREEVNA (*looking at the manuscript*). Nobody had the slightest idea, Kostya, that you would turn into a real writer. And now look, thank God, they've started sending you money from the magazines. (*Runs her hand over his hair.*) And you're handsome now . . . Dear, good Kostya, be a little more affectionate to my Mashenka.

MASHA (*making the bed*). Leave him be, Mama.

POLINA ANDREEVNA (*to Treplyov*). She's a wonderful little thing. (*Pause.*) Women, Kostya, ask nothing more than an occasional look of kindness. I know from experience.

TREPLYOV gets up from behind the desk and exits in silence.

MASHA. Now he's gone and got angry. You had to bring that up!

POLINA ANDREEVNA. I feel sorry for you, Mashenka.

MASHA. That's all I need!

POLINA ANDREEVNA. My heart bleeds for you. I do see everything, understand everything.

MASHA. It's all nonsense. Unrequited love—that's only in novels. Really silly. Just mustn't lose control or go on waiting for something, waiting for your ship to come in . . . If love ever burrows into your heart, you've got to get rid of it. They've just promised to transfer my husband to another school district. Once we've moved there—I'll forget all about it . . . I'll rip it out of my heart by the roots.

Two rooms away a melancholy waltz is played.

POLINA ANDREEVNA. Kostya's playing. That means he's depressed.

MASHA (*noiselessly makes a few waltz steps*). The main thing, Mama, is to have him out of sight. As soon as they transfer my Semyon, then believe you me, I'll forget in a month. This is all so silly.

The door left opens. DORN and MEDVEDENKO wheel in SORIN, in his armchair.

MEDVEDENKO. I've got six at home now. And flour almost two kopeks a pound.

DORN. It gets you going in circles.

MEDVEDENKO. It's all right for you to laugh. You've got more money than you could shake a stick at.

DORN. Money? After thirty years of practice, my friend, on constant call night and day, when I couldn't call my soul my own, all I managed to scrape together was two thousand; besides, I blew it all on my recent trip abroad. I haven't a penny.

MASHA (*to her husband*). Haven't you gone?

MEDVEDENKO (*apologetically*). How? If they don't give me horses!

MASHA (*bitterly annoyed, in an undertone*). I wish I'd never set eyes on you!

The wheelchair is halted in the left half of the room; POLINA ANDREEVNA, MASHA, and DORN sit down beside it; MEDVEDENKO, saddened, moves away to one side.

DORN. So many changes around here, I must say! They've turned the drawing-room into a study.

MASHA. It's more comfortable for Konstantin Gavrilych to work here. Whenever he likes, he can go out in the garden and think.

The WATCHMAN *taps his board.*

SORIN. Where's my sister?

DORN. Gone to the station to meet Trigorin. She'll be back any minute.

SORIN. If you found it necessary to write for my sister to come here, it means I'm seriously ill. (*After a silence.*) A fine state of affairs, I'm seriously ill, but meanwhile they won't give me any medicine.

DORN. And what would you like? Aspirin? Bicarbonate? Quinine?

SORIN. Uh-oh, here comes the philosophizing. Oh, what an affliction! (*Nodding his head towards the divan.*) That made up for me?

POLINA ANDREEVNA. For you, Pyotr Nikolaevich.

SORIN. Thank you.

DORN (*sings*). "The moon sails through the midnight sky . . ."[76]

SORIN. There's this subject for a story I want to give Kostya. The title should be: "The Man Who Wanted to." "*L'Homme qui a voulu.*"[77] In my youth I wanted to be an author—and wasn't; wanted to speak eloquently—and spoke abominably (*mimicking himself*) "and so on and so forth, this, that, and the other . . ." and in summing up used to ramble on and on, even broke out in a sweat; wanted to get married—and didn't; always wanted to live in town—and now am ending my life in the country and all the rest.

DORN. Wanted to become a senior civil servant—and did.

SORIN (*laughs*). That I never tried for. It came all by itself.

DORN. Complaining of life at age sixty-two is, you must agree—not very gracious.

SORIN. What a pigheaded fellow. Don't you realize, I'd like to live.

DORN. That's frivolous. By the laws of nature every life must come to an end.

SORIN. You argue like someone who's had it all. You've had it all and so you don't care about life, it doesn't matter to you. But even you will be afraid to die.

---

76 Beginning of a serenade by K. S. Shilovsky, popular at the time; its sheet music had gone through ten printings by 1882.

77 Chekhov may have been familiar with a series of comic monologues by the eccentric French writer Charles Cros, called *L'Homme Qui*, published between 1877 and 1882.

DORN. Fear of death is an animal fear . . . Have to repress it. A conscious fear of death is only for those who believe in life everlasting, which scares them because of their sins. But in the first place, you don't believe in religion, and in the second—what kind of sins have you got? You worked twenty-seven years in the Department of Justice—that's all.

SORIN (*laughs*). Twenty-eight.

> *TREPLYOV enters and sits on the footstool at Sorin's feet.*
> *MASHA never takes her eyes off him the whole time.*

DORN. We're keeping Konstantin Gavrilovich from working.

TREPLYOV. No, not at all.

Pause.

MEDVEDENKO. Might I ask, Doctor, which town abroad you liked most?

DORN. Genoa.

TREPLYOV. Why Genoa?

DORN. The superb crowds in the streets there. In the evening when you leave your hotel, the whole street is teeming with people. Then you slip into the crowd, aimlessly, zigzagging this way and that, you live along with it, you merge with it psychically and you start to believe that there may in fact be a universal soul, much like the one that Nina Zarechnaya acted in your play once.[78] By the way, where is Miss Zarechnaya these days? Where is she and how is she?

TREPLYOV. She's all right, I suppose.

DORN. I'm told she seems to be leading a rather peculiar life. What's that all about?

TREPLYOV. That, Doctor, is a long story.

DORN. Then you shorten it.

Pause.

---

78 Dr. Dorn's pleasure in fleeing the constraints of individual personality into multiple personality echoes Baudelaire: "The pleasure of being in crowds is a mysterious expression of the delight in the multiplication of numbers."

TREPLYOV. She ran away from home and went off with Trigorin. You know about that?

DORN. I do.

TREPLYOV. She had a baby. The baby died. Trigorin fell out of love with her and returned to his previous attachment, as might have been expected. In fact, he had never given up the previous one but, in his spineless way, somehow maintained both of them. So far as I can make out from my information, Nina's private life has not been a roaring success.

DORN. And the stage?

TREPLYOV. Even worse, it would seem. She made her debut outside Moscow at a summer theater, then toured the provinces. In those days I was keeping track of her and for a while wherever she was, I was there too. She would tackle the big roles, but her acting was crude, tasteless, her voice singsong and her gestures wooden. There were moments when she showed some talent at screaming or dying, but they were only moments.

DORN. In other words, she does have *some* talent?

TREPLYOV. It was hard to tell. I suppose she has. I saw her, but she didn't want to see me, and her maid wouldn't let me into her hotel room. I understood her mood and didn't insist on meeting. (*Pause.*) What else is there to tell you? Later, by the time I'd returned home, I would get letters from her. The letters were clever, affectionate, interesting; she never complained, but I felt that she was deeply unhappy; not a line but revealed frayed, strained nerves. And a somewhat deranged imagination. She would sign herself The Gull. In that play of Pushkin's, the miller says that he's a raven;[79] that's how she'd keep repeating in all her letters that she was a gull.[80] She's here now.

DORN. What do you mean here?

TREPLYOV. In town, at the railway hotel. About five days now she's been staying in a room there. I've been to see her, and Marya Ilyinishna drove over,

---

79 *Rusalka* (*The Naiad* or *Nixie*), a fragment of a verse drama by Aleksandr Pushkin (1799–1837), written sometime between 1826 and 1832; the story of a poor miller's daughter, seduced and abandoned by a prince. She drowns herself and turns into a water nymph, while her father goes mad and calls himself "the local raven." The tale was turned into an opera by A. S. Dargomyzhsky.

80 Since there are no definite or indefinite articles in Russian, this could also be translated "she is *the* gull."

but she won't receive anyone. Semyon Semyonych claims that yesterday after dinner he saw her in a field, a mile and a half from here.

MEDVEDENKO. Yes, I did see her. Heading for town. I bowed, asked her how come she didn't pay us a visit. She said she would.

TREPLYOV. She won't. (*Pause.*) Her father and stepmother have disowned her. They've set up watchmen all over so that she can't even get near the estate. (*Moves to the desk with the Doctor.*) How easy, Doctor, to be a philosopher on paper and how hard it is in fact!

SORIN. Splendid girl she was.

DORN. What's that again?

SORIN. Splendid girl, I said, she was. District Attorney Sorin was even a little bit in love with her for a while.

DORN. Old Casanova.[81]

> *SHAMRAEV's laugh is heard.*

POLINA ANDREEVNA. I think our folks are back from the station . . .

TREPLYOV. Yes, I hear Mama.

> *Enter ARKADINA, TRIGORIN, followed by SHAMRAEV.*

SHAMRAEV (*entering*). We're all growing old, weather-beaten by the elements, but you, dear lady, are just as young as ever . . . Colorful jacket, vivacity . . . grace . . .

ARKADINA. You want to put a hex on me again, you tiresome man!

TRIGORIN (*to Sorin*). Good evening, Pyotr Nikolaevich! How come you're still under the weather? That's not good! (*Having seen Masha, jovially.*) Marya Ilyinishna!

MASHA. You recognized me? (*Shakes his hand.*)

TRIGORIN. Married?

---

81 Literally, "old Lovelace," the voluptuary hero of Samuel Richardson's *Clarissa* (1748), whose sole purpose in life is to seduce the heroine. Its Russian version was hugely popular in the late eighteenth century, even among those who, like Tatyana's mother in *Yevgeny Onegin*, didn't read it. ("She loved Richardson / Not because she preferred Grandison to Lovelace; / But in the old days Princess Alina, / Her Moscow cousin, / Had often rambled on about them to her" [Act II, scene 30].) "Lovelace" gradually became a standard term for a philanderer.

MASHA. Long ago.

TRIGORIN. Happy? (*Exchanges bows with DORN and MEDVEDENKO, then hesitantly walks over to Treplyov.*) Irina Nikolaevna said that you've let bygones be bygones and no longer hold a grudge.

TREPLYOV extends his hand to him.

ARKADINA (*to her son*). Look, Boris Alekseevich brought the magazine with your new story.

TREPLYOV (*accepting the magazine, to Trigorin*). Thank you. Very kind of you.

They sit down.

TRIGORIN. Your fans send you their best wishes. In Petersburg and Moscow, mostly, they're starting to take an interest in you, and they're always asking me about you. Standard questions: what's he like, how old, dark or fair. For some reason they all think you're not young any more. And nobody knows your real name, since you publish under a pseudonym. You're a mystery, like the Man in the Iron Mask.[82]

TREPLYOV. You staying long?

TRIGORIN. No, tomorrow I think I'll go to Moscow. Have to. I'm tripping over myself to finish a novella, and after that I've promised to contribute something to an anthology. In short—the same old story.

While they're conversing, ARKADINA and POLINA ANDREEVNA put a card table in the middle of the room and open it up; SHAMRAEV lights candles, arranges chairs. They get a lotto set[83] from a cupboard.

TRIGORIN. The weather's given me a rude welcome. Ferocious wind. Tomorrow morning, if it's calmed down, I'll head out to the lake and do some fishing. By the way, I have to take a look round the garden and the

82 A mysterious political prisoner under Louis XIV, whose face was hidden by an iron mask. He was first mentioned in the *Mémoires secrets pour servir à l'histoire de Perse* (Amsterdam, 1745–1746), where he was alleged to be Louis's bastard. He is best known from *Le Vicomte de Bragelonne* (1848–1850), the third of Alexandre Dumas's musketeer novels, in which he is supposed to be Louis's twin.

83 An Italian import, known to Americans as Bingo, the game became fashionable in northern Russia in the 1840s and was briefly banned as a form of gambling. It was the common evening diversion on Chekhov's farm at Melikhovo.

place where—remember?—your play was performed. I've come up with a theme, just have to refresh my memory on the setting of the action.

MASHA (*to her father*). Papa, let my husband borrow a horse! He has to get home.

SHAMRAEV (*mimicking*). Horse . . . home . . . (*Severely.*) You saw yourself: they've just been to the station. They're not to go out again.

MASHA. But there must be other horses . . . (*Seeing that her father is not forthcoming, she waves her hand dismissively.*) I don't want anything to do with either of you . . .

MEDVEDENKO. I'll go on foot, Masha. Honestly.

POLINA ANDREEVNA (*sighs*). On foot in weather like this . . . (*Sits at the card table.*) If you please, ladies and gentlemen.

MEDVEDENKO. It's really only four miles in all . . . Good-bye . . . (*Kisses his wife's hand.*) Good-bye, Mama dear. (*His mother-in-law reluctantly extends her hand for him to kiss.*) I wouldn't have disturbed anybody, except that the baby . . . (*Bows to them all.*) Good-bye . . . (*He exits apologetically.*)

SHAMRAEV. Never fear, he'll get there. He's nobody special.

POLINA ANDREEVNA (*raps on the table*). If you please, ladies and gentlemen. Let's not waste time, they'll be calling us to supper soon.

SHAMRAEV, MASHA, and DORN sit at the table.

ARKADINA (*to Trigorin*). When the long autumn evenings draw on, they play lotto here. Come and have a look: the old-fashioned lotto set our late mother used to play with us when we were children. Wouldn't you like to play a round with us before supper? (*Sits at the table with Trigorin.*) The game's a bore, but once you get used to it, you don't mind. (*Deals three cards to each.*)

TREPLYOV (*leafing through the magazine*). His own story he's read, but on mine he hasn't even cut the pages. (*Puts the magazine on the desk, then starts for the door left; moving past his mother, he kisses her head.*)

ARKADINA. What about you, Kostya?

TREPLYOV. Sorry, I don't feel up to it . . . I'm going for a walk. (*Exits.*)

ARKADINA. The stakes are ten kopeks. Ante up for me, Doctor.

DORN. Your wish is my command.

MASHA. Everyone's ante'd up? I'm starting . . . Twenty-two!

ARKADINA. Got it.

MASHA. Three! . . .

DORN. Righto.

MASHA. Got three? Eight! Eighty-one! Ten!

SHAMRAEV. Not so fast.

ARKADINA. The reception they gave me in Kharkov, goodness gracious, my head's still spinning from it!

MASHA. Thirty-four!

A melancholy waltz is played offstage.

ARKADINA. The students organized an ovation . . . Three baskets of flowers, two bouquets, and look at this . . . (*Unpins a brooch from her bosom and throws it on the table.*)

SHAMRAEV. Yes, that's something, all right . . .

MASHA. Fifty! . . .

DORN. Just plain fifty?

ARKADINA. I was wearing a gorgeous outfit . . . Say what you like, when it comes to dressing I'm nobody's fool.

POLINA ANDREEVNA. Kostya's playing. The poor boy's depressed.

SHAMRAEV. The newspaper reviewers give him a hard time.

MASHA. Seventy-seven!

ARKADINA. Who cares about them.

TRIGORIN. He hasn't had any luck. His writing still can't manage to find its proper voice. There's something odd, indefinite about it, sometimes it's like gibberish . . . Not one living character.

MASHA. Eleven!

ARKADINA (*looking round at Sorin*). Petrusha, are you bored? (*Pause.*) He's asleep.

DORN. Sleep comes to the senior civil servant.

MASHA. Seven! Ninety!

TRIGORIN. If I lived on an estate like this, by a lake, you think I'd write? I'd kick this addiction and do nothing but fish.

MASHA. Twenty-eight!

TRIGORIN. To catch a chub or a perch—that's my idea of heaven!

DORN. Well, I have faith in Konstantin Gavrilych. There's something there! There's something there! He thinks in images, his stories are colorful, striking, and I have a real fondness for them. It's just a pity he doesn't have well-defined goals. He creates an impression, and leaves it at that, and of course by itself an impression doesn't get you very far. Irina Nikolaevna, are you glad your son's a writer?

ARKADINA. Imagine, I still haven't read him. Never any time.

MASHA. Twenty-six!

TREPLYOV quietly enters and goes to his desk.

SHAMRAEV (*to Trigorin*). Hey, Boris Alekseevich, that thing of yours is still here.

TRIGORIN. What thing?

SHAMRAEV. A while back Konstantin Gavrilych shot a gull, and you asked me to have it stuffed.

TRIGORIN. Don't remember. (*Thinking about it.*) Don't remember!

MASHA. Sixty-six! One!

TREPLYOV (*throws open the window, listens*). So dark! I can't understand how it is I feel so uneasy.

ARKADINA. Kostya, shut the window, it's drafty.

TREPLYOV closes the window.

MASHA. Eighty-eight!

TRIGORIN. It's my game, ladies and gentlemen.

ARKADINA (*merrily*). Bravo! Bravo!

SHAMRAEV. Bravo!

ARKADINA. This man has the most incredible luck, any time, any place. (*Rises.*) And now let's have a bite to eat. Our celebrity didn't have dinner today. After supper we'll resume our game. (*To her son.*) Kostya, put down your writing, we're eating.

TREPLYOV. I don't want any, Mama. I'm not hungry.

ARKADINA. You know best. (*Wakes Sorin.*) Petrusha, suppertime! (*Takes Shamraev's arm.*) I'll tell you about my reception in Kharkov . . .

> POLINA ANDREEVNA *blows out the candles on the table, then she and* DORN *wheel out the armchair. Everyone goes out the door left. Only* TREPLYOV *remains alone on stage at the writing desk.*

TREPLYOV (*prepares to write; scans what he's already written*). I've talked so much about new forms, but now I feel as if I'm gradually slipping into routine myself. (*Reads.*) "The poster on the fence proclaimed . . . A pale face, framed by dark hair . . ." Proclaimed, framed . . . It's trite.[84] (*Scratches it out.*) I'll start with the hero waking to the sound of rain, and get rid of all the rest. The description of the moonlit night's too long and contrived. Trigorin has perfected a technique for himself, it's easy for him . . . He has a shard of broken bottle glisten on the dam and a black shadow cast by the millwheel—and there's your moonlit night readymade.[85] But I've got to have the flickering light, and the dim twinkling of the stars, and the distant strains of a piano, dying away in the still, fragrant air . . . It's excruciating. (*Pause.*) Yes, I'm more and more convinced that the point isn't old or new forms, it's to write and not think about form, because it's flowing freely out of your soul. (*Someone knocks at the window closest to the desk.*) What's that? (*Looks out the window.*) Can't see anything . . . (*Opens the glass door and looks into the garden.*) Somebody's running down the steps. (*Calls out.*) Who's there? (*Goes out; he can be heard walking rapidly along the veranda; in a few seconds he returns with* NINA ZARECHNAYA.) Nina!

---

84 Chekhov used the same words in criticizing a story by Zhirkevich. "Nowadays ladies are the only writers who use 'the poster proclaimed,' 'a face framed by hair.'"

85 Compare Chekhov's story "The Wolf" (1886): "On the weir, drenched in moonlight, there was not a trace of shadow; in the middle the neck of a broken bottle shone like a star. The two millwheels, half sheltered in the shade of an outspread willow, looked angry and bad-tempered . . ." In a letter to his brother (May 10, 1886), he offers it as a facile technique.

Nina! (*NINA lays her head on his chest and sobs with restraint.*) (*Moved.*) Nina! Nina! it's you . . . you . . . I had a premonition, all day my heart was aching terribly. (*Removes her hat and knee-length cloak.*)[86] Oh, my sweet, my enchantress, she's here! We won't cry, we won't.

NINA. There's somebody here.

TREPLYOV. Nobody.

NINA. Lock the doors, or they'll come in.

TREPLYOV. No one will come in.

NINA. I know Irina Nikolaevna is here. Lock the doors.

TREPLYOV (*locks the door at right with a key, crosses left*). This one has no lock. I'll put a chair against it. (*Sets a chair against the door.*) Don't be afraid, no one will come in.

NINA (*stares fixedly at his face*). Let me look at you. (*Looking round.*) Warm, pleasant . . . This used to be a drawing-room. Have I changed a great deal?

TREPLYOV. Yes . . . You've lost weight, and your eyes are bigger. Nina, it feels so strange to be seeing you. How come you didn't let me in? How come you didn't show up before now? I know you've been living here almost a week . . . I've been over to your place several times every day, stood beneath your window like a beggar.

NINA. I was afraid you hated me. Every night I have the same dream that you look at me and don't recognize me. If you only knew! Ever since my arrival I keep coming here . . . to the lake. I was at your house lots of times and couldn't make up my mind to go in. Let's sit down. (*They sit.*) We'll sit and we'll talk and talk. It's nice here, warm, cozy . . . Do you hear—the wind? There's a passage in Turgenev: "Happy he who on such a night sits beneath his roof, and has a warm corner."[87] I'm a gull . . . No, that's wrong. (*Rubs her forehead.*) What was I on about? Yes . . . Turgenev . . . "And the Lord help all homeless wanderers . . ." Never mind. (*Sobs.*)

TREPLYOV. Nina, you still . . . Nina!

---

86 In the original, *talma.* A quilted, knee-length cloak with a wide, turned-down collar and silk lining, named after the French tragedian François Joseph Talma.

87 The last sentence is slightly misquoted from the epilogue of Turgenev's novel *Rudin* (1856).

NINA. Never mind, it makes me feel better . . . For two years now I haven't cried. Late last night I went to look at the garden, to see if our stage was still there. And it's standing to this day. I burst into tears for the first time in two years, and I felt relieved, my heart grew lighter. You see, I've stopped crying. (*Takes him by the hand.*) And so, now you're a writer. You're a writer, I'm an actress . . . We've both fallen into the maelstrom[88] . . . I used to live joyously, like a child—wake up in the morning and start to sing; I loved you, dreamed of fame, and now? First thing tomorrow morning I go to Yelets,[89] third class . . . traveling with peasants, and in Yelets art-loving businessmen will pester me with their propositions. A sordid kind of life!

TREPLYOV. Why Yelets?

NINA. I took an engagement for the whole winter. Time to go.

TREPLYOV. Nina, I cursed you, hated you, tore up your letters and photographs, but every moment I realized that my soul is bound to you forever. I haven't the power to stop loving you. From the time I lost you and began publishing, life for me has been unbearable—I'm in pain . . . My youth was suddenly somehow snatched away, and I felt as if I'd been living on this earth for ninety years. I appeal to you, kiss the ground you walk on; wherever I look, everywhere your face rises up before me, that caressing smile that shone on me in the best years of my life . . .

NINA (*perplexed*). Why does he say such things, why does he say such things?

TREPLYOV. I'm alone, unwarmed by anyone's affection. I'm cold as in a dungeon, and, no matter what I write, it's all arid, stale, gloomy. Stay here, Nina, I beg you, or let me go with you! (NINA *quickly puts on her hat and cloak.*) Nina, why? For God's sake, Nina . . . (*Watches her put on her wraps.*)

Pause.

NINA. My horses are standing at the gate. Don't see me out, I'll manage by myself . . . (*Tearfully.*) Give me some water . . .

TREPLYOV (*gives her something to drink*). Where are you off to now?

---

88 *Omut* can also be translated as "millrace," which would connect back to the *Rusalka* imagery. In Act Three of *Uncle Vanya*, it is translated as "millrace."

89 The Des Moines of tsarist Russia, a rapidly growing provincial trade center in the Oryol *guberniya*, south of Tula, noted for its grain elevators, tanneries, and brickyard, with a population of 52,000.

NINA. To town. (*Pause.*) Is Irina Nikolaevna here?

TREPLYOV. Yes . . . On Thursday Uncle wasn't well, we wired for her to come.

NINA. Why do you tell me you'd kiss the ground I walk on? I should be killed. (*Leans over the desk.*) I feel so tired! Have to get some rest . . . rest! (*Lifts her head.*) I'm a gull . . . That's wrong, I'm an actress. Ah, yes! (*Having heard Arkadina's and Trigorin's laughter, she listens, then runs to the door left and peeks through the keyhole.*) He's here too . . . (*Returning to Treplyov.*) Ah, yes . . . Never mind . . . Yes . . . He had no faith in the theater, he'd laugh at my dreams, and little by little I lost faith in it too, lost heart . . . But then the anxiety over our affair, jealousy, constant worrying about the baby . . . I became petty, trivial, acted mindlessly . . . I didn't know what to do with my hands, didn't know how to stand on stage, couldn't control my voice. You can't imagine what that's like, when you realize your acting is terrible. I'm a gull. No, that's wrong . . . Remember, you shot down a gull? By chance a man comes along, sees, and with nothing better to do destroys . . . Subject for a short story. That's wrong . . . (*Rubs her forehead.*) What was I saying? . . . I was talking about the stage. I'm not like that now . . . Now I'm a real actress, I like acting, I enjoy it, I'm intoxicated when I'm on stage and feel that I'm beautiful. And now that I'm living here, I go walking and walking and thinking and thinking and feel every day my spirit is growing stronger . . . Now I know, understand, Kostya, that in our work— it doesn't matter whether we act or we write—the main thing isn't fame, glamour, the things I dreamed about, it's knowing how to endure. I know how to shoulder my cross and I have faith. I have faith and it's not so painful for me, and when I think about my calling, I'm not afraid of life.

TREPLYOV (*mournfully*). You've found your path, you know where you're going, but I'm still drifting in a chaos of daydreams and images, without knowing what or whom it's for. I have no faith and I don't know what my calling is.[90]

NINA (*listening hard*). Ssh . . . I'm going. Good-bye. When I become a great actress, come to the city and have a look at me. Promise? But now . . . (*Squeezes his hand.*) Now it's late. I'm dead on my feet . . . I'm famished, I'd like a bite to eat . . .

---

90 From Chekhov's notebook: "Treplyov has no well-defined aims, and this is what destroyed him. His talent destroyed him. He says to Nina at the end: 'You have found your path, you are saved, but I am ruined.' "

TREPLYOV. Stay here, I'll bring you some supper . . .

NINA. No, no . . . Don't show me out, I'll manage by myself . . . My horses are close by . . . That means, she brought him with her? So what, it doesn't matter. When you see Trigorin, don't say anything to him . . . I love him. I love him even more than before . . . Subject for a short story . . . I love, love passionately, love to desperation. It used to be nice. Kostya! Remember? What a bright, warm, joyful, pure life, what feelings—feelings like tender, delicate flowers . . . Remember? . . . (*Recites.*) "Humans, lions, eagles, and partridges, antlered deer, geese, spiders, silent fishes that inhabit the waters, starfish, and those beings invisible to the naked eye,—in short, all living things, all living things, all living things, having completed the doleful cycle, are now extinct . . . Already thousands of centuries have passed since the earth bore any living creature, and this pale moon to no avail doth light her lamp. No more does the meadow awake to the cries of cranes, and the may flies are no longer to be heard in the linden groves . . ." (*Embraces Treplyov impulsively and runs to the glass door.*)

TREPLYOV (*after a pause*). I hope nobody runs into her in the garden and tells Mama. It might distress Mama . . . (*Over the course of two minutes, he silently tears up all his manuscripts and throws them under the desk, then unlocks the door and exits.*)

DORN (*trying to open the door left*). Funny. Door seems to be locked . . . (*Enters and puts the chair in its proper place.*) Obstacle course.

*Enter ARKADINA, POLINA ANDREEVNA, followed by
YAKOV with bottles and MASHA, then SHAMRAEV
and TRIGORIN.*

ARKADINA. Put the red wine and the beer for Boris Alekseevich here on the table. We'll drink while we play. Let's sit down, ladies and gentlemen.

POLINA ANDREEVNA (*to Yakov*). And bring the tea now. (*Lights the candles, sits at the card table.*)

SHAMRAEV (*leads Trigorin to the cupboard*). Here's that thing I was talking about before . . . (*Gets a stuffed gull out of the cupboard.*) You ordered it.

TRIGORIN (*staring at the gull*). Don't remember! (*Thinking about it.*) Don't remember!

A shot offstage right; everyone shudders.

ARKADINA (*alarmed*). What's that?

DORN. Nothing. I suppose something exploded in my first-aid kit. Don't worry. (*Exits through the door right, returns in a few seconds.*) That's what it is. A vial of ether exploded. (*Sings.*) "Once again I stand bewitched before thee . . ."

ARKADINA (*sitting at the table*). Phew, I was terrified. It reminded me of the time . . . (*Hides her face in her hands.*) Things even went black before my eyes . . .

DORN (*leafing through the magazine, to Trigorin*). About two months ago there was a certain article published in here . . . a letter from America, and I wanted to ask you, among other things . . . (*takes Trigorin round the waist and leads him down to the footlights*) because I'm very interested in this matter . . . (*Lowering his voice.*) Take Irina Nikolaevna somewhere away from here. The fact is, Konstantin Gavrilovich *has* shot himself . . .

Curtain

VARIANTS TO
The Seagull

These lines appeared in the censorship's copy (Cens.), the first publication in the journal *Russian Thought* (*Russkaya Mysl*, 1896) (RT), and the 1897 edition of Chekhov's plays (1897).

ACT ONE

page 744 / *After*: And tobacco? — Yesterday, ma'am, I had to get some flour, we look for the bag, high and low, and beggars had stolen it. Had to pay fifteen kopeks for another one. (Cens.)

page 745 / *Before*: Talk to my father yourself, because I won't. —

MASHA. Tell him yourself. The barn is full of millet now, and he says that if it weren't for the dogs thieves would carry it off.

TREPLYOV. To hell with him and his millet! (*Cens.*)

page 745 / *After*: I never get my way in the country — it's all millet one time, dogs another, no horses another, because they've gone to the mill and so on and so forth. (*Cens.*)

page 747 / *Before*: You've got it in your head — Horace said: *genus irritabile vatum.*[1] (*Cens., RT*)

page 748 / *After*: when all's said and done . . . — Once, about ten years ago, I published an article about trial lawyers, I just remembered, and, you know, it was pleasant, and meanwhile when I begin to remember that I worked twenty-eight years in the Justice Department, it's the other way round, I'd rather not think about it . . . (*Yawns.*) (*Cens.*)

page 752 / *Before*: TREPLYOV *enters from behind the platform.*

MEDVEDENKO (*to Sorin*). And before Europe achieves results, humanity, as Flammarion[2] writes, will perish as a consequence of the cooling of the earth's hemispheres.

SORIN. God bless us.

MASHA (*offering her snuffbox to Trigorin*). Do have some! You're always so silent, or do you ever talk?

TRIGORIN. Yes, I talk sometimes. (*Takes snuff.*) Disgusting. How can you!

MASHA. Well, you've got a nice smile. I suppose you're a simple man. (*Cens.*)

page 756 / *After*: I didn't mean to offend him. —

NINA (*peering out from behind the curtain*). Is it over already? We won't be going on?

ARKADINA. The author left. I suppose it is over. Come on out, my dear, and join us.

NINA. Right away. (*Disappears.*)

MEDVEDENKO (*to Masha*). It all depends on the substantiality of psychic matter and there's no basis. (*Cens.*)

page 756 / *After*: but in those days he was irresistible. —

     Polina Andreevna weeps quietly.

---

1 Latin: "Touchy is the tribe of poets," from Horace's *Epistles*, II, 2.

2 Camille Flammarion (1842–1925), French astronomer, prolific author of books on popular science, including *The Plurality of Inhabited Worlds* (1890). His astronomical fantasies inspired some of the features in Treplyov's play.

SHAMRAEV (*reproachfully*). Polina, Polina . . .

POLINA ANDREEVNA. Never mind . . . Forgive me . . . I suddenly got so depressed! (Cens.)

page 757 / *After*: Yes. —

SHAMRAEV. Bream and pike, for the most part. There are pike-perch as well, but not many. (Cens.)

page 758 / *After*: Credit where credit's due. —

MEDVEDENKO. A deplorable manifestation of atavism, worthy of the attention of Lombroso.[3]

DORN (*teasing*). "Lombroso" . . . You can't live without pedantic words. (Cens.)

page 758 / *After*: (*Takes him by the arm.*) — In some play there's a line: "Come to your senses, old man!" (Cens.)

page 760 / *Replace*: And will you all please leave me in peace! Stay here! Don't come after me!

with: MASHA. On what? My father will tell you that all the horses are busy.

TREPLYOV (*angrily*). He hasn't got the right! I don't keep anyone from living, so they can leave me in peace. (Cens.)

ACT TWO

page 762 / *After*: you don't live . . . —

MASHA. My mamma brought me up like that girl in the fairy tale who lived in a flower. I don't know how to do anything. (Cens.)

page 763 / *After*: just consider me and Trigorin. — I didn't pick out Boris Alekseevich, didn't lay siege, didn't enthrall, but when we met, everything in my head went topsy-turvy, my dears, and things turned green before my eyes. I used to stand and look at him and cry. I mean it, I'd howl and howl. What kind of master plan is that? (Cens.)

page 763 / *After*: "At Sea" by Maupassant, sweetheart. —

MEDVEDENKO. Never read it.

---

3 Cesare Lombroso (1856–1909), Italian criminologist, who published widely on the subject of decadence, sexual abnormality, and insanity; he believed that criminals and psychopaths could be identified by physical traits.

DORN. You only read what you don't understand.

MEDVEDENKO. Whatever books I can get I read.

DORN. All you read is Buckle and Spencer,[4] but you've got no more knowledge than a night watchman. According to you, the heart is made out of cartilage and the earth is held up by whales.

MEDVEDENKO. The earth is round.

DORN. Why do you say that so diffidently?

MEDVEDENKO (*taking offense*). When there's nothing to eat, it doesn't matter if the earth is round or square. Stop pestering me, will you please.

ARKADINA (*annoyed*). Stop it, gentlemen. (Cens.)

page 763 / *After*: It's so uninteresting! — (*Recites.*) Humans, lions, eagles and partridges, antlered deer, geese, spiders, silent fishes that inhabit the waters, starfish, and those beings invisible to the naked eye,—in short, all living things, all living things, all living things, having completed the doleful cycle, are now extinct . . . Already thousands of centuries have passed since the earth bore any living creature, and this pale moon to no avail doth light her lamp. No more does the meadow awake to the cries of cranes, and the may flies are no longer to be heard in the linden groves. (Cens.)

page 764 / *After*: stop smoking. —

DORN. You should have done it long ago. Tobacco and wine are so disgusting! (Cens.)

page 765 / *Replace*: You've lived in your lifetime, but what about me? I worked in the Department of Justice for twenty-eight years, but I still haven't lived.

with: You've lived your life, your room is full of embroidered pillows, slippers and all that, like some kind of museum, but I still haven't lived. (Cens.)

page 765 / *Replace*: So there and all the rest.

with: Everyone's right according to his own lights, everyone goes wherever his inclinations lead him. (Cens.)

page 765 / *Before*: A man should take life seriously, — It's precisely because everyone is right according to his own lights, that everyone suffers. (Cens.)

page 765 / *After*: ridiculous. — It's time to think about eternity.

---

4 For Buckle, see *The Cherry Orchard*, note 36. Herbert Spencer (1820–1903), English philosopher and sociologist, whose works were extensively translated into Russian.

TREPLYOV *walks past the house without a hat, a gun in one*
hand, and a dead gull in the other.

ARKADINA (*to her son*). Kostya, come join us!

TREPLYOV *glances at them and exits.*

DORN (*singing quietly*). "Tell her of love, flowers of mine . . ."

NINA. You're off-key, doctor.

DORN. It doesn't matter. (*To Sorin.*) As I was saying, Your Excellency. It's time to think about eternity. (*Pause.*) (Cens.)

page 765 / *Replace*: **DORN** (*sings*). "Tell her of love, flowers of mine . . ."

with: **DORN.** Well, say what you like, I cannot do without nature.

ARKADINA. What about books? In poetic images nature is more moving and refined than as is. (Cens.)

page 766 / *Replace*: Carriage horses?

with: A carriage horse? Did you say: a carriage horse? Go out there and see for yourself: the roan is lame, Cossack Lass is bloated with water . . . (Cens.)

page 766 / *After*: This is incredible! —

POLINA ANDREEVNA (*to her husband*). Stop it, I implore you.

ARKADINA. Horse-collars or rye are nothing to do with me . . . I am going and that's that.

SHAMRAEV. Irina Nikolaevna, have a heart, on what? (Cens.)

page 767 / *After*: What can I do? —

SORIN. He's going. He's leaving the farmwork at the busiest time and so on. I won't let him do it! I'll force him to stay!

DORN. Pyotr Nikolaevich, have a least a penny's worth of character! (Cens.)

page 767 / *Replace*: He even sent the carriage horses . . . his crudeness.

with: You know, he even sent the carriage horses into the fields. He does what he likes. His third year here he told the old man to mortgage the estate . . . What for? What was the need? He bought pedigreed turkeys and suckling pigs and they all died on his hands. He set up expensive beehives and in winter all the bees froze to death. The entire income from the estate he wastes on building, and on top of that takes the old man's pension away and sends Irina Nikolaevna six hundred rubles a year out of the old man's money, as if it were part of the income, and she's delighted, because she's stingy.

DORN (*distractedly*). Yes. (*Pause.*) (Cens.)

page 767 / *Replace*: stop lying . . . (*Pause.*)

with: stop lying . . . Twenty years I've been your wife, your friend . . . Take me
into your home.

page 767 / *Replace*: Forgive me, I'm getting on your nerves . . . **DORN** (*to
Nina, who walks by*)

with: **DORN** (*sings quietly*). "At the hour of parting, at the hour of farewell . . ."
    NINA *appears near the house; she picks flowers.*

POLINA ANDREEVNA (*to Dorn, in an undertone*). You spent all morning
again with Irina Nikolaevna!

DORN. I have to be with somebody.

POLINA ANDREEVNA. I'm suffering from jealousy. Forgive me. You're sick
and tired of me.

DORN. No, not at all.

POLINA ANDREEVNA. Of course, you're a doctor, there's no way you can
avoid women. That's how it is. But you know that this is torture. Be with
women, but at least try so that I don't notice it.

DORN. I'll try. (*To Nina.*) (Cens.)

page 768 / *After*: like anybody else . . . — They're modest. Yesterday I asked
him for an autograph, and he was naughty and wrote me bad poetry, deliberately bad, so that everyone would laugh . . . (Cens.)

ACT THREE

page 778 / *After*: I can never get any horses . . . — *Enter* MEDVEDENKO.
(Cens.)

page 778 / *Replace*: **SORIN.** You're kind, affectionate . . . I respect you . . . Yes
. . . (*Staggers.*)

with: **MEDVEDENKO** (*smokes a fat hand-rolled cigarette; addressing no one
in particular*). The schoolteacher at Telyatyev bought hay at a very good
price. Thirty-five pounds for nine kopeks, delivery included. And just last
week I paid eleven. It gets you going in circles. (*Noticing the star on Sorin's
chest.*) What's that you've got? Hm . . . I received a medal too, but they
should have given me money.

ARKADINA. Semyon Semyonych, be so kind, allow me to talk with my
brother. We would like to left in private.

MEDVEDENKO. Ah, fine! I understand . . . I understand . . . (*Exits.*)

SORIN. He comes here at the crack of dawn. Keeps coming and talking about something. (*Laughs.*) A kind man, but already a bit . . . makes you sick and tired. (*Staggers.*) (Cens.)

ACT FOUR

page 791 / *Replace*: **MEDVEDENKO.** Might I ask, Doctor, which town abroad you liked most?

with: **MEDVEDENKO** (*to Dorn*). Allow me to ask you, doctor, how much does a ream of writing paper cost abroad?

DORN. I don't know, I never bought any.

MEDVEDENKO. And what town did you like most? (Cens.)

page 795 / *After*: the setting of the action. —

SHAMRAEV (*to Arkadina*). Are they alive?

ARKADINA. I don't know.

SHAMRAEV. She was a highly talented actress, I must remark. Her like is not around nowadays! In *The Murder of Coverley*[5] she was just . . . (*Kisses the tips of his fingers.*) I'd give ten years of my life. (Cens.)

page 795 / *After*: with either of you . . . —

SHAMRAEV (*flaring up, in an undertone*). Well, cut my throat! Hang me! Let him go on foot! (Cens.)

page 795 / *After*: He's nobody special. —

DORN. You get married—you change. What's happened to atoms, substantiality, Flammarion.

        Sits at the card table. (Cens.)

page 797 / *After the stage direction*: TREPLYOV *closes the window.* —

SHAMRAEV. The wind's up. The wind's getting up . . . A certain young lady is standing by a window, conversing with an amorous young man, and her

---

5 A five-act melodrama adapted from the French by Nikolay Kireev; its climax involves a train speeding across the stage. Chekhov had seen it as a schoolboy in Taganrog and mentions it in several stories of the 1880s.

mamma says to her: "Come away from the window, Dashenka, or else you'll get the wind up . . ." The wind up! (*Roars with laughter.*)

DORN. Your jokes smell like an old, shabby waistcoat. (Cens.)

page 798 / *Replace: then she and DORN wheel out the armchair. Everyone goes out the door left. Only TREPLYOV remains alone on stage at the writing desk.*

with: *Everyone goes out left; on stage remain only SORIN in his chair and TREPLYOV at the desk.* (Cens.)

page 799 / *Replace*: Nobody. —

with: It's uncle. He's asleep. (Cens.)

page 799 / *Replace*: (*Looking round.*)

with: And now at him. (*Walks over to Sorin.*) He's asleep. (Cens.)

page 800 / *After*: Time to go. — (*Nodding at Sorin.*) Is he badly?

TREPLYOV. Yes. (*Pause.*) (Cens.)

page 802 / *Replace*: (*Recites.*)

with: (*Sits on the little bench, swathes herself in the bedsheet, which she has taken from the bed.*) (Cens.)

page 802 / *Replace: Embraces Treplyov impulsively*

with: *Tears off the sheet, embraces Treplyov impulsively, then Sorin* (Cens.)

page 802 / *After*: Obstacle course. —

POLINA ANDREEVNA (*following him*). You looked at her the whole time. I beg you, I entreat you by all that's holy, stop torturing me. Don't look at her, don't talk to her for so long.

DORN. All right, I'll try.

POLINA ANDREEVNA (*squeezing his hand to her breast*). I know, my jealousy's foolish, mindless, I'm embarrassed by it myself. You're fed up with me.

DORN. No, not at all. If it's hard for you to keep still, go on talking. (Cens.)

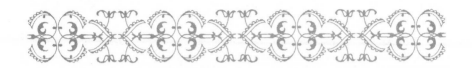

UNCLE VANYA

*M*any of Chekhov's contemporaries considered *Uncle Vanya* to be simply *The Wood Goblin* revised. For that reason, the Society for Russian Dramatic Authors denied it a prestigious prize in 1901. Scholars assume that Chekhov finished the play sometime in late 1896, after he had written *The Seagull*, but before that comedy had suffered the hapless opening that turned him off playwriting for years. When, in 1897, Nemirovich-Danchenko requested *Uncle Vanya* for the Moscow Art Theatre, which was fresh from its success with *The Seagull*, Chekhov had to explain that he had already promised it to the Maly Theatre. The literary-advisory committee there, whose members included a couple of professors, was offended by the slurs on Serebryakov's academic career and what it saw as a lack of motivation, and demanded revisions. Chekhov coolly withdrew *Uncle Vanya* and turned it over to the Art Theatre, which opened it on October 26, 1899. The opening night audience was less than enthusiastic, but the play gained in favor during its run. It became immensely popular in the provinces, where the audiences could identify with the plight of Vanya and Astrov. Gorky wrote to Chekhov, "I do not consider it a pearl, but I see in it a greater subject than others do; its subject is enormous, symbolic, and in its form it's something entirely original, something incomparable."[1]

A useful way of approaching *Uncle Vanya*, and indeed all of Chekhov's late plays, is that suggested by the poet Osip Mandelshtam in an unfinished article of 1936: starting with the cast list.

> What an inexpressive and colorless rebus. Why are they all together? How is the privy counselor related to anybody? Try and define the kinship or connection between Voinitsky, the son of a privy counselor's widow, the mother of the professor's first wife and Sofiya, the professor's young daughter by his first marriage. In order to establish that somebody happens to be somebody else's uncle, one must study the whole roster . . .

A biologist would call this Chekhovian principle ecological. Combination is the decisive factor in Chekhov. There is no action in his drama, there is only propinquity with its resultant unpleasantness.[2]

What Mandelshtam calls "propinquity" is more important than causal connections usually demanded by dramatic necessity, and distinct from naturalistic "environment." Chekhov brings his people together on special occasions to watch their collisions and evasions. Conjugal or blood ties prove to be a lesser determinant of the characters' behavior than the counter-irritants of their proximity to one another. They are rarely seen at work in their natural habitats: Arkadina was not on stage or Trigorin at his desk; the officers in *Three Sisters* are not in camp; here the Professor has been exiled from his lecture hall.

The principle is especially conspicuous in *Uncle Vanya*, where Chekhov stripped his cast down to the smallest number in any of his full-length plays. He achieved this primarily by conflating the cast of *The Wood Goblin*, combining the traits of two characters into one. By limiting the dramatis personae to eight (if we exclude the workman), Chekhov could present doublets of each character, to illustrate contrasting reactions to circumstances. Take the Serebryakov/Waffles dyad: the Professor, fond of his academic honors and perquisites, is an old man married to a young woman too repressed to betray him, yet he jealously tyrannizes over her. Waffles, whose pompous language aspires to erudition, and whose wife abandoned him almost immediately after their wedding, responded with loving generosity. His life, devoid of honors, is devoted to others. He feels strongly the opprobrium of being a "freeloader," while the Professor is oblivious to his own parasitism.

Of the old women, Marina is earthy, stolid in her obedience to the natural cycle, her life narrowly focused on the practical matters of barnyard and kitchen. Still, she is capable of shrewd comment on human behavior. Mariya Vasilyevna is equally static and narrow, but her eyes never rise from the pages of a pamphlet; she is totally blind to what goes on inside her fellow men. Her reading and Marina's knitting are both palliatives. One, meant for the betterment of all mankind, is sterile, while the other, meant for the comfort of individuals, is not.

The contrasts are more complex but just as vivid in the younger characters. Sonya and Yelena are both unhappy young women on the threshold of wasted lives; both are tentative and withdrawn in matters of the heart. Sonya, however, indulges in daydreams while eagerly drugging herself with work. Yelena is too inhibited to yield to her desires, managing to be both indolent and clumsily manipulative in her dealings with others. She declares her affinity to Vanya because they are both "exasperating" people.

Astrov and Vanya are the only two "educated persons in the district"; they started, like Ivanov, with exceptional promise, but grew disillusioned. Astrov's disillusionment was gradual, over years of drudgery as a country doctor; he has turned into a toper and a cynic but can still compartmentalize vestiges of his idealism in his reforestation projects. Vanya's disillusionment came as a thunderclap with the Professor's arrival; its suddenness negated any possibility of maintaining an ideal. Instead, he is diverted to fantasies of bedding Yelena and, even at a moment of crisis, considering himself a potential Dostoevsky or Schopenhauer. His impossible dreams are regularly deflated by Astrov's sarcasm, but both men are, to use a word repeated throughout the play, "crackpots" (*chudaki*).

Thus, the propinquity of the characters brings out their salient features: the existence of each puts the other in relief. As in *The Seagull*, they have been located by Chekhov on an estate where they are displaced persons. It has been in the family for little more than a generation. Vanya relinquished his patrimony to provide his sister's dowry, gave up his own career to cut expenses and work the estate on the Professor's behalf, taking his mother with him. They are acclimatized without being naturalized. The Professor and Yelena are obvious intruders, who disrupt the estate's settled rhythms and cannot accommodate themselves to it. Even Astrov seldom pays a call; he prefers his forests. Only Sonya, Marina, and Waffles are rooted in the estate's soil.

Again, the physical progression of the stage setting serves as an emblem of the inner development of the action. The play begins outside the house, with a tea table elaborately set to greet the Professor, who, on his entrance, walks right past it to closet himself in his study. The eruption of these dining room accessories into a natural setting suggests the upheaval caused by the Petersburgers' presence. Moreover, the samovar has gone cold during the long wait; it fails to serve its purpose. As is usual with Chekhov, the play begins with a couple of characters on stage, waiting for the others to precipitate an event. When it comes, the event—the tea party—is frustrated.

The second act moves indoors, its sense of claustrophobia enhanced by the impending storm and Yelena's need to throw open the window. The dining room too has been usurped by the Professor, who has turned it into a study *cum* sickroom, his medicine littering the sideboard. No family gathers to share a meal: midnight snacks, a clandestine glass of wine, tête-à-têtes rather than group encounters are standard. Nanny, who has already grumbled at the altered meal times, complains that the samovar has still not been cleared.

Later, she will rejoice that plain noodles have replaced the Professor's spicy curries.

In Act Three, the Professor thrusts the family into unfamiliar surroundings when he convenes them in a rarely used reception room. Cold, formal, empty, it suits the Professor's taste for his missing podium and further disorients the others. Nanny, cowed by the ambience, must be asked to sit down; for the sake of the occasion, she was prepared to stand by the door like a good servant. Anyone can wander through, like Vanya, who intrudes upon Astrov and Yelena with his bunch of roses. Another prop is rendered useless by circumstance.

Finally, in Act Four, we move, for the first time, to a room actually lived in, Vanya's combination bedchamber and estate office. The real life of the house has migrated to this small, cluttered area where day-to-day tasks are carried out, where Astrov keeps his drawing table, Sonya her ledgers. There is even a mat for peasants to wipe their feet on. Vanya, like Treplyov, has no personal space that is not encroached on, and none of his objects bespeaks a private being. Once the Professor and Yelena, the disruptive factor, are gone, the family comes together in this atmosphere of warmth generated by routine. For them to do so, however, Vanya must abandon his personal desires and ambitions; for good reason a caged starling chirps by the worktable. The absence of conversation is noteworthy is this symbiosis. Except for Vanya's impassioned outburst and Sonya's attempts to console him, the characters write, yawn, read, and strum the guitar voicelessly, with no need to communicate aloud, bound together by propinquity.

The more inward the play moves in terms of locale, the more the sense of oppression mounts. Chekhov uses weather and seasons along with certain verbal echoes to produce this feeling. In the first few lines of dialogue, Astrov declares, "It's stifling" (*dushno*), and variations on that sentiment occur with regularity. Vanya repeats it and speaks of Yelena's attempt to muffle her youth; the Professor begins Act Two by announcing that he cannot breathe, and Vanya speaks of being choked by the idea that his life is wasted. Astrov admits he would be suffocated if he had to live in the house for a month. The two young women fling open windows to be able to breathe freely. During the first two acts, a storm is brewing and then rages; and Vanya spends the last act moaning, *Tyazhelo mene*, literally "It is heavy on me," "I feel weighed down." At the very end, Sonya's "We shall rest" (*My otdokhnyom*), or "We'll be at peace," is etymologically related to *dushno* and connotes "breathing freely."

Yelena's repeated assertion that she is "shy," *zastenchivaya*, suggests etymologically that she is "hemmed in, walled up," and might, in context, be better translated "inhibited." The references to the Professor's gout, clouded vision, blood poisoning, and morphine contribute to the numbing atmosphere. This is intensified by the sense of isolation: constant reference is made to the great distances between places. Only Lopakhin the businessman in *The Cherry Orchard* is as insistent as Astrov on how many miles it takes to get somewhere. The cumulative effect is one of immobility and stagnation, oppression and frustration.

Time also acts as pressure. "What time is it?" or a statement of the hour is voiced at regular intervals, along with mention of years, months, seasons, mealtimes. The play begins with Astrov's asking Marina, "How long have we known one another?"—simple exposition but also an initiation of the motif of lives eroded by the steady passage of time. (Chekhov was to reuse this device to open *Three Sisters* and *The Cherry Orchard*.) *Uncle Vanya* opens at summer's end, proceeds through a wet and dismal autumn, and concludes with a bleak winter staring the characters in the face. The suggestion of summer's evanescence, the equation of middle age with the oncoming fall may seem hackneyed. Vanya certainly leaps at the obvious, with his bouquet of "mournful autumn roses" and his personalization of the storm as the pathetic fallacy of his own despair. Chekhov, however, used storms in his short stories as a premonition of a character's mental turmoil, and, in stage terms, the storm without and the storm within Vanya's brain effectively collaborate.

The play ends with Sonya's vision of "a long, long series of days, no end of evenings" to be lived through before the happy release of death. The sense of moments ticking away inexorably is much stronger here than in Chekhov's other plays, because there are no parties, balls, theatricals, railway journeys, or fires to break the monotony. The Professor and Yelena have destroyed routine, supplanting it with a more troubling sense of torpid leisure. Without the narcotic effect of their daily labor, Astrov, Vanya, and Sonya toy with erotic fantasies that make their present all the grimmer.

Beyond these apparent devices, Chekhov is presenting a temporal sequence that is only a segment of a whole conspectus of duration. The action of *Uncle Vanya* really began when Vanya gave up his inheritance for his sister's dowry years before; the consequences of that action fill Acts One through Four, but the further consequences remain unrevealed. How will the Professor and Yelena get along in the provincial university town of Kharkov? (In Chekhov, Kharkov is a symbol of nowhere: in *The Seagull* it acclaims Arkadina's acting and in *The Cherry Orchard* it is one of Lopakhin's destinations.)

How will Astrov manage to avoid dipsomania without the balm of Vanya's conversation and Sonya's solicitude? How will Vanya and Sonya salve their emotional wounds over the course of a lifetime? These questions are left to our imaginations.

Samuel Beckett, describing habit as a blissful painkiller, referred to "the perilous zones in the life of an individual, dangerous, precarious, painful, mysterious and fertile, when for a moment the boredom of living is replaced by the suffering of being.[3] Throughout *Uncle Vanya*, the characters, divorced from habit, suffer painful confrontations with being and, by the final curtain, must try hard to return to the humdrum but safe addiction to living.

Although the tautness of the play's structure, its triangles and confidants, might suggest neoclassic tragedy, *Uncle Vanya* comes closer to comedy, because no passion is ever pushed to an irremediable fulfillment. Yelena's name may refer to Helen of Troy, but, if so, Chekhov had Offenbach, not Homer, in mind. He may also have been thinking of the Russian fairy tale *Yelena the Fair*, a Cinderella story in which the sniveling booby Vanya woos and wins the beautiful princess with the aid of his dead father. Folklore has other echoes here: the Russian version of *Snow White* is quoted ("the fairest in the land") and Vanya characterizes Yelena as a *rusalka*, a water nymph of voluptuous beauty and destructive tendencies. Others may regard her as a dynamic force in their life, but she describes herself as a "secondary character," without any real impact. Her acceptance of a fleeting kiss and a souvenir pencil as trophies of a romantic upsurge is comically reductive.

The antitragic tendency of the play is apparent in the title. Most serious Russian drama at the turn of the nineteenth century bore titles of symbolic import or else the name of its protagonist or a central relationship. As a rule, Chekhov follows this convention. In *Uncle Vanya*, though, the title reveals that the center of attention is not Astrov, whose attractive qualities can upstage the title role in performance, but the self-pitying Voinitsky. Our Uncle Jack, as he might be in English, sounds peripheral, the archetype of mediocrity. Such a man is not serious enough to be called by a grownup name; he counts chiefly in his relationship to others. But who calls him Uncle Vanya? To the Professor, Yelena, and Astrov he is Ivan Petrovich, except when they mean to be slighting. "That Uncle Vanya" is how Yelena dismisses him in Act Three, and in Act Four Astrov flippantly calls for an embrace before "Uncle Vanya" comes in. To his mother, he is Jean, the "shining light" of his youth. He is Vanya primarily to Sonya and Waffles, who love him. Therefore, if Voinitsky matters most when he is Uncle Vanya, his self-realization lies not in compet-

ing with the Professor or winning Yelena but in his dealings with his dependents. He gave up trying to be Jean long ago; when he stops trying to be Ivan
Petrovich and fulfills himself as Uncle Vanya, a new life might commence.

NOTES

1 M. Gorky and A. Chekhov, *Stati, vyskazyvaniya, perepiska* (Moscow: Goslitizdat, 1951), pp.
63–65.

2 O. Mandelshtam, "O pyese A. Chekhova 'Dyadya Vanya,'" *Sobranie sochineniya* (Paris: YMCA
Press), IV, 107–109.

3 Samuel Beckett, *Proust* (London: Chatto and Windus, 1931), p. 8.

UNCLE VANYA

Дядя Ваня

Scenes from Country Life[1]
in Four Acts

[Bracketed footnote numerals refer to footnotes in *The Wood Goblin*.]

CHARACTERS[2]

SEREBRYAKOV, ALEKSANDR VLADIMIROVICH, *retired professor*

YELENA ANDREEVNA, *his wife*

SOFIYA ALEKSANDROVNA (SONYA), *his daughter by his first marriage*

VOINITSKAYA, MARIYA VASILYEVNA, *widow of a government official,[3] and mother of the Professor's first wife*

VOINITSKY, IVAN PETROVICH, *her son*

ASTROV, MIKHAIL LVOVICH, *a physician[4]*

TELEGIN, ILYA ILYICH, *an impoverished landowner*

MARINA, *an old nanny[5]*

A WORKMAN

---

1 The subtitle of Turgenev's earlier play *A Month in the Country*.

2 The names are suggestive but not explicit in their meanings. Serebryakov, "silvery"; Voinitsky, "warrior"; Astrov, "starry"; Telegin, "cart"; "Yelena" is Helen, with hints at Helen of Troy (Offenbach's rather than Homer's); and Sofiya is Greek for "wisdom."

3 Privy councillor, a relatively high civilian position in the table of official ranks, equivalent to a lieutenant-general in the army.

4 "Of course, the doctor has to be played suavely, nobly, in accord with the words of Sonya, who in Act Two calls him beautiful and refined" (Chekhov to his brother Mikhail, February 4, 1897).

5 The *nyanya* was the children's nursemaid, who would live in the household until her death, even when the children were grown up, and might care for their children in turn. Compare with Anfisa in *Three Sisters* and the deceased Nanny in *The Cherry Orchard*. Astrov banteringly calls her *nyanka*, a mildly folksy form.

The action takes place on Serebryakov's country estate.

ACT ONE

*The garden. Part of the house and its veranda are visible. Along
the path beneath an old poplar there is a table set for tea.
Benches, chairs; a guitar lies on one of the benches. Not far from
the table is a swing.—Between two and three in the afternoon.
Overcast.*

*MARINA, a corpulent, imperturbable old woman, sits by the
samovar knitting a stocking, while ASTROV paces nearby.*

MARINA (*pours a glass of tea*). Have a bite to eat, dearie.

ASTROV (*reluctantly takes the glass*). Somehow I don't feel like it.

MARINA. Maybe, you'll have a nip of vodka?

ASTROV. No. I don't drink vodka all the time. Besides, it's stifling.

Pause.

Nanny old girl, how long have we known one another?

MARINA (*thinking it over*). How long? God help my memory . . . You came
here, to these parts . . . when? . . . Vera Petrovna was still alive, dear little
Sonya's mother. In her time you visited us two winters . . . Well, that
means nigh onto eleven years have gone by. (*After giving it some thought.*)
Could be even more . . .

ASTROV. Have I changed terribly since then?

MARINA. Terribly. In those days you were young, good-looking, and now
you're old. And your good looks are gone too. And it's got to be said—you
like a nip of vodka.

ASTROV. Yes . . . In ten years' time I've turned into another man. And what's
the reason? I've been working too hard, nanny old girl. Morning to night

always on my feet, not a moment's rest, at night you lie under the blanket afraid you'll be hauled off to some patient.[6] In all the time we've known one another, I haven't had a single day to myself. Why wouldn't a man grow old? Besides, life itself is dreary, silly, filthy . . . It drags you down, this life. You're surrounded by crackpots, nothing but crackpots; you live with them for two, three years and, little by little, without noticing it, you turn into a crackpot yourself. (*Twirling his long moustache.*) Look at this interminable moustache I've been cultivating. A silly moustache. I've turned into a crackpot, nanny old girl . . . Speaking of silly, I'm still in my right mind, thank God, my brain's still intact, but my feelings are sort of numb. There's nothing I want, nothing I need, no one I love . . . Present company excepted. (*Kisses her on the head.*) When I was a child I had a dear old nanny just like you.

MARINA. Maybe you'd like a bite to eat?

ASTROV. No. In Lent, third week, I went to Malitskoe to deal with an epidemic . . . Spotted typhus[7] . . . In the huts the peasants were packed side by side . . . Mud, stench, smoke, bull calves on the floor right next to the sick . . . Piglets too . . . I was at it all day long, never sat down for a second, not a blessed drop passed my lips, and when I did get home, they wouldn't let me rest—they brought over a signalman from the railway; I put him on the table to operate, and he goes and dies on me under the chloroform. And just when they're least wanted, my feelings came back to life, and I felt a twinge of conscience, just as if I'd killed him on purpose . . . Down I sat, closed my eyes—just like this, and started thinking: the people who'll live one or two hundred years from now, the people we're blazing a trail for, will they remember us, have a kind word for us? Nanny old girl, they won't remember a thing!

MARINA. People won't remember, but God will remember.

ASTROV. Thank you for that. Just the right thing to say.

---

6 In the early 1890s the rural boards increased the number of medical outposts in the small villages, with several beds for in-patients and a dispensary for out-patients. Doctors were expected to look after all the peasants in a given district.

7 A highly contagious fever distinguished by purple spots, extreme prostration, and delirium.

*VOINITSKY emerges from the house; he has been napping after
lunch and looks rumpled; he sits on the bench,
adjusts his fancy tie.*[8]

VOINITSKY. Yes . . .

Pause.

Yes . . .

ASTROV. Had enough sleep?

VOINITSKY. Yes . . . Plenty. (*Yawns.*) Ever since the Professor and his lady
have been living here, our life's been shunted on to a siding . . . I sleep at
odd hours, for lunch and dinner eat all kinds of spicy food,[9] drink wine
. . . unhealthy, that's what I call it! Before, there wasn't a moment's leisure,
Sonya and I were always at work—now, lo and behold, Sonya does the
work on her own and I sleep, eat, drink . . . It's not right!

MARINA (*after shaking her head.*) No sense to it! The Professor gets up at
twelve o'clock, though the samovar's[10] been boiling away from early morning, waiting on him. Before they came we always had dinner between
noon and one, like everybody else, but now they're here it's going on seven.
At night the Professor reads and writes, and all of a sudden, round about
two, the bell rings . . . What's the matter, goodness gracious? Tea! Wake
folks up for him, set up the samovar . . . No sense to it!

ASTROV. And how much longer are they staying here?

---

8 According to Aleksandr Vishnevsky,

> Chekhov got very angry when a certain provincial theatre depicted Uncle Vanya as a
> landowner on the skids, i.e., dirty, tattered, in greased boots.
> "Well, what should he be like?" he was asked.
> "It's all written down in my play!" he replied.
> And this is in the stage direction with the remark that Uncle Vanya is wearing a fancy
> necktie. Chekhov considered that this was quite enough to designate his dress.
>
> > (*Scraps of Memory*, 1928)

Chekhov described Voinitsky as "an elegant cultivated man. It is counter to the truth to say that our
country squires walk around in boots that stink of grease" (Stanislavsky, *My Life in Art*, 1924). The
tie is mentioned specifically, because it is put on to impress Yelena Andreevna.

9 *Kabuli*, highly spiced Caucasian stews, similar to curries. Evidently, the Professor's biliousness
derives in part from his diet.

10 A metal urn, heated by charcoal, to keep water on the boiling point for making tea. The pot with
leaves is kept warm on top of the samovar, and filled with water from the tap as necessary.

VOINITSKY (*whistles*). A century. The Professor has decided to take root here.

MARINA. Just like now. The samovar's on the table two hours, and they go off for a walk.

VOINITSKY. Here they come, here they come . . . Don't fret yourself.

Voices are heard: from the bottom of the garden, returning from a walk, come SEREBRYAKOV, YELENA ANDREEVNA, SONYA, and TELEGIN.

SEREBRYAKOV. Beautiful, beautiful . . . Magnificent vistas.

TELEGIN. Outstanding, Your Excellency.

SONYA. Tomorrow we'll go to the forest preserve, Papa. Would you like that?

VOINITSKY. Ladies and gentlemen, it's tea time!

SEREBRYAKOV. My dear friends, send my tea to the study, if you'll be so kind! I have something more to do today.

SONYA. And you're sure to enjoy a visit to the forest preserve . . .

YELENA ANDREEVNA, SEREBRYAKOV, and SONYA go into the house; TELEGIN goes to the table and sits beside MARINA.

VOINITSKY. The weather's hot, stifling, but our prodigy of learning wears an overcoat and galoshes with an umbrella and gloves.[11]

ASTROV. Which shows he takes care of himself.

VOINITSKY. But isn't she fine! Really fine! In all my life I've never seen a more beautiful woman.

TELEGIN. I may be riding in the fields, Marina Timofeevna, or strolling in a shady garden, or looking at this table, and I have this feeling of inexplicable bliss![12] The weather is enchanting, the birdies are singing, we live, all

11 Chekhov wrote, in a notebook entry of August 20, 1896: "M[enshikov] in dry weather goes around in galoshes, carries an umbrella, so as not to die of sunstroke, is afraid to wash with cold water, complains about heart trouble."

12 Telegin's flowery way of speaking is typical of the old-fashioned landowner, trying to seem courtly and well educated. Chekhov uses a similar device in his first published story of 1879: "Letter of a Landowner to His Learned Neighbor Dr. Friedrich." Telegin's remark may be another of Chekhov's parodies of the famous Pushkin poem, "Whether I walk noisy streets . . ."

of us, in peace and harmony—what more could we ask? (*Accepting a glass.*) My heartfelt thanks!

VOINITSKY (*dreamily*). Her eyes . . . Wonderful woman!

ASTROV. Talk about something else, Ivan Petrovich.

VOINITSKY (*listlessly*). What am I supposed to talk about?

ASTROV. Nothing new?

VOINITSKY. Not a thing. The same old stuff. I'm just the same as ever I was, no, worse, I've got lazy, all I do is growl like an old grouch. My old magpie of a *maman* goes on babbling about women's rights; one eye peers into the grave, while the other pores over her high-minded pamphlets, looking for the dawn of a new life.

ASTROV. And the Professor?

VOINITSKY. And the Professor as usual sits alone in the study from morn to darkest night and writes. "With straining brain and furrowed brow, We write for nights and days, Yet all our poetry somehow Can never meet with praise."[5] I feel sorry for the paper! He'd be better off writing his autobiography. What a first-rate subject that is! A retired professor, you know what that means, a pedantic old fossil, a guppy with a terminal degree . . . Gout,[3] rheumatism, migraine, his poor old liver's bloated with envy and jealousy . . . Now this guppy lives on his first wife's estate, lives there reluctantly because he can't afford to live in town—Endlessly griping about his bad luck, although as a matter of fact he's incredibly lucky. (*Jittery.*) Just think about the luck he's had! The son of a humble sexton, a seminary student on a tuition scholarship, he's acquired academic degrees and chairs, the title "Your Excellency," married the daughter of a senator,[7] and so on and so forth. That's not the important thing, though. Check this out. For precisely twenty-five years the man reads and writes about art, although he understands absolutely nothing about art. For twenty-five years he chews over other people's ideas about realism, naturalism, and the rest of that rubbish; for twenty-five years he reads and writes about stuff that intelligent people have known for ages and fools couldn't care less about—which means, for twenty-five years he's been pouring the contents of one empty bottle into another, emptier bottle. And add to that, his conceit! His pretensions! He's gone into retirement and not a single living soul has ever heard of him, he is totally obscure; which means, for twenty-five years he took up someone else's place. But look at him! he struts about like a demigod!

ASTROV. Sounds like you're jealous.

VOINITSKY. Of course I'm jealous! Look at his success with women! Not even Don Juan enjoyed such unqualified success! His first wife, my sister, a beautiful, gentle creature, pure as that blue sky overhead, noble, open-hearted, with more admirers than he had students,—loved him as only pure angels can love beings as pure and beautiful as themselves. My mother, his mother-in-law, adores him to this day, and to this day he inspires her with awe and reverence. His second wife, a woman with looks, brains—you saw her just now—married him when he was an old man, made him a gift of her youth, beauty, independence, her brilliance. What for? Why?

ASTROV. She's faithful to the professor?

VOINITSKY. Sorry to say she is.

ASTROV. Why sorry?

VOINITSKY. Because this faithfulness is phony from start to finish. It's all sound and no sense. To cheat on an old husband you can't stand—that's immoral; to try and stifle the vestiges of pathetic youth and vital feeling in yourself—that's not immoral.

TELEGIN (*in a plaintive voice*). Vanya, I don't like it when you say things like that. Why, now, honestly . . . Anybody who cheats on a wife or husband is, I mean, a disloyal person, someone who might even betray his country!

VOINITSKY (*annoyed*). Turn off the waterworks, Waffles![8]

TELEGIN. Excuse me, Vanya. My wife ran away with the man she loved the day after our wedding on account of my unprepossessing looks. I didn't shirk my duty despite it all. I love her to this day, and I'm faithful to her, I help however I can, and sold my estate to educate the kiddies she bore to the man she loved. Happiness was denied me, but what I did have left was my pride. What about her? Her youth has gone now, her beauty, subject to the laws of nature, has faded, the man she loved has passed away . . . What does she have left?

> *Enter SONYA and YELENA ANDREEVNA; after a while, enter MARIYA VASILYEVNA with a book; she sits and reads; they give her tea and she drinks it without looking.*

SONYA (*hastily, to the nanny*). Nanny dear, some peasants have come. Go and talk to them, and I'll do the tea . . . (*Pours tea.*)

MARINA exits. YELENA ANDREEVNA takes her cup and sits in the swing, as she drinks.

ASTROV (*to Yelena Andreevna*). I came here to treat your husband. You wrote that he's very ill, rheumatism and something else, but it turns out he's as healthy as a horse.

YELENA ANDREEVNA. Last night he was moping, complaining of pains in his legs, but today they're gone . . .

ASTROV. And I was breaking my neck, forty-five miles at a gallop. Well, never mind, it's not the first time. So it won't be a total loss, I'll stay the night here, at least I'll get some sleep "to be taken as needed."[13]

SONYA. Why, that's lovely. It's so seldom you stay over with us. I don't suppose you've had dinner?

ASTROV. No, ma'am, I have not.

SONYA. Then you're just in time for some. Nowadays we dine between six and seven. (*Drinks.*) Tea's cold!

TELEGIN. There's been a perceptible drop in temperature in the samovar.

YELENA ANDREEVNA. Never mind, Ivan Ivanych, we'll drink it cold.

TELEGIN. Excuse me, ma'am . . . Not Ivan Ivanych, but Ilya Ilyich, ma'am . . . Ilya Ilyich Telegin, or, as some call me on account of my pockmarked face, Waffles. I once stood godfather to little Sonya, and His Excellency, your spouse, knows me very well. I'm now living with you, ma'am, on this estate, ma'am[14] . . . . If you will kindly notice, I dine with you every day.

SONYA. Ilya Ilyich is our assistant, our right-hand man. (*Affectionately.*) Here, Godfather, I'll pour you some more.

MARIYA VASILYEVNA. Ah!

SONYA. What's the matter, Granny?

---

13 In the original, he uses a Latin term often found in prescriptions: *quantum satis*, "as much as necessary."

14. *Ma'am* is to indicate that Telegin adds an *s* for *sudar* (sir) or *sudarinya* (madam) to his words, an old-fashioned and obsequious manner of speaking.

MARIYA VASILYEVNA. I forgot to tell *Alexandre*[15] . . . I must be losing my memory . . . today I got a letter from Kharkov from Pavel Alekseevich . . . He sent his new pamphlet.

ASTROV. Interesting?

MARIYA VASILYEVNA. Interesting, but rather peculiar. He opposes the very thing he was promoting seven years ago. It's appalling!

VOINITSKY. It's not at all appalling. Drink your tea, *maman*.

MARIYA VASILYEVNA. But I want to talk!

VOINITSKY. For fifty years now we've been talking and talking, and reading pamphlets. It's high time we stopped.

MARIYA VASILYEVNA. For some reason you don't like to listen when I talk. Pardon me, *Jean*, but this last year you have changed so much that I utterly fail to recognize you . . . You used to be a man of steadfast convictions, a shining light . . .

VOINITSKY. Oh, yes! I was a shining light but no one ever basked in my rays . . .

Pause.

I was a shining light . . . Don't rub salt in my wounds! Now I'm forty-seven. Before last year I was the same as you, deliberately trying to cloud my vision with this book learning of yours, to keep from seeing real life—and I thought I was doing the right thing. And now, if you had the least idea! I don't sleep nights out of frustration, out of spite for having wasted my time so stupidly when I could have had everything that's withheld from me now by my old age!

SONYA. Uncle Vanya, this is boring!

MARIYA VASILYEVNA (*to her son*). You seem to be blaming your former convictions for something . . . But they aren't to blame, *you* are. You have forgotten that convictions *per se* mean nothing, they're a dead letter . . . One must take action.[16]

---

15 Mariya Vasilyevna belongs to a generation of educated persons who conversed in French and referred to one another by the French forms of their names: hence, *Alexandre, Jean*.

16 *Nado delo delat,* "one must do something," "be active," "committed," "get involved." A motto of liberalism in the 1860s, it does *not* mean "One must work," as it is often translated.

VOINITSKY. Take action! Not everyone is capable of being a perpetual-motion writing machine like your Herr Professor.

MARIYA VASILYEVNA. What's that supposed to mean?

SONYA (*pleading*). Granny! Uncle Vanya! For pity's sake!

VOINITSKY. I'm mute. I'm mute and I apologize.

Pause.

YELENA ANDREEVNA. Lovely weather today . . . Not too hot . . .

Pause.

VOINITSKY. Good weather for hanging oneself . . .

TELEGIN strums his guitar. MARINA walks near the house and calls chickens.

MARINA. Chick, chick, chick . . .

SONYA. Nanny dear, what did the peasants come for?

MARINA. The same old thing, still on about those untilled fields. Chick, chick, chick . . .

SONYA. Who're you calling?

MARINA. Speckles's gone off with her chicks . . . The crows might get 'em. (*Exits.*)

TELEGIN plays a polka; all listen in silence.
Enter a WORKMAN.

WORKMAN. Is Mister Doctor here? (*To Astrov.*) 'Scuse me, Dr. Astrov, there's some folks here to fetch you.

ASTROV. Where from?

WORKMAN. The factory.[17]

ASTROV (*vexed*). Thanks a lot. That's that, got to go . . . (*Looking around for his peaked cap.*) What a nuisance, damn it . . .

---

17 Between 1887 and 1900 the number of factory workers in Russia increased from 1.5 to 2.1 million. Sanitary and housing conditions were very bad, since employers were not compelled to protect workers against dangerous machinery, and few factories provided medical attention.

SONYA. How unpleasant, honestly . . . After the factory you'll come to dinner.

ASTROV. No, it'll be too late. Now where in the world . . . where, oh where?[18] . . . (*To the Workman.*) Listen, my boy, bring me a shot of vodka, anyway.

WORKMAN exits.

Now where in the world . . . where, oh where . . . (*He has found his cap.*) In one of Ostrovsky's plays there's a man who's long on moustache and short on brains[19] . . . That's me all over. Well, my respects, ladies and gents . . . (*To Yelena Andreevna.*) If you drop in on me some time, along with Sofiya Aleksandrovna, of course, I'd be really delighted. I have a smallish estate, no more than eighty acres in all, but if you're interested, there's an experimental orchard and a tree nursery the like of which you'll not find a thousand miles around. Next door I've got the State forest preserve . . . The forest ranger there is old, always ailing, so, as a matter of fact, I do all the work.

YELENA ANDREEVNA. I've been told you're very fond of forests. Of course, they may be admirable, but really, don't they get in the way of your true calling? After all, you are a doctor.

ASTROV. God alone know what our true calling is.

YELENA ANDREEVNA. And is it interesting?

ASTROV. Yes, the work is interesting.

VOINITSKY (*sarcastically*). Very!

YELENA ANDREEVNA (*to Astrov*). You're still a young man, you look . . . well, thirty-six, thirty-seven . . . and I don't suppose it's as interesting as you say. Nothing but forest and more forest. I suppose it's monotonous.

SONYA. No, it's remarkably interesting. Mikhail Lvovich plants a new forest every year, and they've already honored him with a bronze medal and a testimonial. He's had a hand in preventing them from destroying the old-growth areas. If you hear him out, you'll agree with him completely. He

---

18 Astrov is imitating the manner of speaking of Anfusa Tikhonovna in Ostrovsky's 1875 comedy *Wolves and Sheep*.

19 The popular dramatist Aleksandr Ostrovsky (1823–1886). The character is Paratov in *The Girl without a Dowry* (1879), who, in Act Two, scene ix, says, "We already know one another. (*Bows.*) A man long on moustache and short on abilities."

says that forests beautify the land, that they teach people to understand beauty and inspire them with a sense of grandeur. Forests alleviate a harsh climate. In lands where the climate is mild, less energy is spent on the struggle with nature and therefore human beings there are milder and more delicate; there people are beautiful, athletic, very sensitive, their speech is refined, their movements graceful. There art and sciences flourish, their philosophy is not gloomy, their attitude to women is full of exquisite chivalry . . .

VOINITSKY (*laughing*). Bravo, bravo! . . . Which is all very charming, but not convincing, so (*To Astrov.*) allow me, my friend, to go on stoking my stoves with logs and building my sheds out of wood.

ASTROV. You can stoke your stoves with peat[20] and build sheds of stone. Well, all right, chop down forests when it's absolutely necessary, but why destroy them? Russian forests are toppling beneath the axe, the habitats of birds and beasts are dwindling, tens of thousands of trees are perishing, rivers are running shallow and drying up, gorgeous natural scenery is disappearing irretrievably, and all because lazy human beings can't be bothered to bend down and pick up fuel from the earth. (*To Yelena Andreevna.*) Am I right, madam? A person has to be an unreasoning barbarian to destroy what cannot be re-created. Human beings are endowed with reason and creative faculties in order to enhance what is given to them, but so far they have not created but destroyed. Forests are ever fewer and fewer, rivers dry up, wildlife is wiped out, the climate is spoiled, and every day the earth grows more impoverished and ugly. (*To Voinitsky.*) There you go, staring at me sarcastically, nothing I say is taken seriously, and . . . and, maybe I *am* talking like a crackpot, but, when I walk through the peasants' forests that I have saved from being chopped down, or when I hear the wind rustling in my stand of saplings, planted by my own hands, I realize that the climate is to some slight degree in my control, and if, a thousand years from now, humanity is happy, then even I will be partially responsible. When I plant a birch tree, and then see how it grows green and sways in the wind, my soul swells with pride, and I . . . (*Having seen the* WORKMAN, *who brings in a shot of vodka on a tray.*) Anyway . . . (*Drinks.*) My time's up. This is, most likely, crackpot talk, when's all said and done. And so I take my leave! (*Goes to the house.*)

---

20 In *The Wood Goblin*, the title character, Dr. Khrushchov, a liberal ecologist, says much the same thing.

SONYA (*takes him by the arm and accompanies him*). When *are* you coming back to see us?

ASTROV. Don't know . . .

SONYA. A whole month again? . . .

> ASTROV and SONYA *go into the house. MARIYA*
> VASILYEVNA *and* TELEGIN *remain near the table.* YELENA
> ANDREEVNA *and* VOINITSKY *walk toward the veranda.*

YELENA ANDREEVNA. Well, Ivan Petrovich, you behaved impossibly again. You had to provoke Mariya Vasilyevna with talk about perpetual motion! And today after lunch you picked a fight with Aleksandr again. It's all so petty!

VOINITSKY. And what if I hate him?

YELENA ANDREEVNA. There's no point in hating Aleksandr, he's the same as anybody else. No worse than you.

VOINITSKY. If you could see your face, your movements . . . What an indolent life you lead! Ah, the indolence of it!

YELENA ANDREEVNA. Ah, indolent and boring as well! Everyone insults my husband, everyone is so sympathetic with me: unhappy creature, she's got an old husband! This compassion for me—oh, how well I understand it! It's what Astrov was saying just now: you all recklessly chop down forests, and soon nothing will be left on earth. The very same way you recklessly destroy a human being, and soon, thanks to you, there won't be any loyalty or purity or capacity for self-sacrifice left on earth. Why can't you look at a woman with indifference if she isn't yours? Because—that doctor's right—inside all of you there lurks a demon of destruction. You have no pity for forests or birds or women or one another . . .

VOINITSKY. I don't like this philosophizing!

> *Pause.*

YELENA ANDREEVNA. That doctor has a weary, sensitive face. An interesting face. Sonya, it's obvious, likes him, she's in love with him, and I understand why. Since I've been here, he's dropped by three times now, but I'm inhibited and haven't once had a proper chat with him, haven't shown him much affection. He went away thinking I'm ill tempered. No doubt, Ivan

Petrovich, that's why we're such friends, you and I, we're both exasperating, tiresome people! Exasperating! Don't look at me that way, I don't like it.

VOINITSKY. How else can I look at you if I love you? You're my happiness, life, my youth! I know, my chances of reciprocity are minute, practically nil, but I don't want anything, just let me look at you, hear your voice . . .

YELENA ANDREEVNA. Hush, they can hear you!

Goes into the house.

VOINITSKY (*following her*). Let me talk about my love, don't drive me away, and that alone will be my greatest joy . . .

YELENA ANDREEVNA. This is agony . . .

They go into the house.

TELEGIN strums the strings and plays a polka; MARIYA VASILYEVNA jots a note in the margin of the pamphlet.

Curtain

ACT TWO

Dining room in Serebryakov's house. — Night. — We can hear the WATCHMAN tapping in the garden.[19]

SEREBRYAKOV sits in an armchair before an open window and drowses, and YELENA ANDREEVNA sits beside him and drowses too.

SEREBRYAKOV (*waking*). Who's there? Sonya, you?

YELENA ANDREEVNA. I'm here.

SEREBRYAKOV. You, Lenochka . . . The pain's unbearable!

YELENA ANDREEVNA. Your lap rug's fallen on the floor. (*Wraps up his legs.*) Aleksandr, I'll close the window.

SEREBRYAKOV. No, I'm suffocating . . . I just now started to doze off and dreamed that my left leg belonged to somebody else. I woke up with the agonizing pain. No, it isn't gout, more like rheumatism. What's the time now?

YELENA ANDREEVNA. Twenty past twelve.

Pause.

SEREBRYAKOV. In the morning see if we've got a Batyushkov[20] in the library. I think we have him.

YELENA ANDREEVNA. Huh? . . .

SEREBRYAKOV. Look for Batyushkov's poems in the morning. I seem to remember we had a copy. But why am I finding it so hard to breathe?

YELENA ANDREEVNA. You're tired. Second night without sleep.

SEREBRYAKOV. They say that Turgenev had gout that developed into *angina pectoris*.[21] I'm afraid I may have it too. Wretched, repulsive old age. Damn it to hell. When I got old, I began to disgust myself. Yes, and all the rest of you, I daresay, are disgusted to look at me.

YELENA ANDREEVNA. You talk about your old age as if it was our fault you're old.

SEREBRYAKOV. You're the first one to be disgusted by me.

> *YELENA ANDREEVNA moves away and sits at a distance.*

Of course, you're in the right. I'm no fool and I understand. You're young, healthy, beautiful, enjoy life, while I'm an old man, practically a corpse. That's it, isn't it? Have I got it right? And, of course, it was stupid of me to live this long. But wait a while, I'll soon liberate you all. I can't manage to hang on much longer.

YELENA ANDREEVNA. I'm worn out . . . For God's sake, be quiet.

SEREBRYAKOV. It turns out that thanks to me you're all worn out, bored, wasting your youth, I'm the only one enjoying life and having a good time. Oh, yes, of course!

YELENA ANDREEVNA. Do be quiet! You've run me ragged!

SEREBRYAKOV. I've run all of you ragged. Of course.

YELENA ANDREEVNA (*through tears*). This is unbearable! Say it, what do you want from me?

SEREBRYAKOV. Not a thing.

YELENA ANDREEVNA. Well then, be quiet. For pity's sake.

SEREBRYAKOV. Funny, isn't it: let Ivan Petrovich start talking or that old she-idiot Mariya Vasilyevna—and nothing happens, everyone listens, but let me say just one word, watch how they all start feeling sorry for themselves. Even my voice is disgusting. Well, suppose I am disgusting, I'm selfish, I'm a tyrant—but surely in my old age haven't I got a right to be selfish? Surely I've earned it? Surely, I ask you, I've earned the right to a peaceful old age, to have people pay me some attention?

YELENA ANDREEVNA. No one is disputing your rights.

The window rattles in the wind.

The wind's rising, I'll close the window. (*Closes it.*) It'll rain presently. No one is disputing your rights.

Pause. The WATCHMAN in the garden taps and sings a song.

SEREBRYAKOV. To labor all one's life in the cause of learning, to grow accustomed to one's study, to the lecture hall, to esteemed colleagues—and suddenly, for no rhyme or reason, to find oneself in this mausoleum, to spend every day seeing stupid people, listening to trivial chitchat . . . I want to live, I love success, I love celebrity, fame, and here—it's like being in exile. Every minute yearning for the past, watching the successes of others, fearing death . . . I can't do it! I haven't got the strength! And on top of that they won't forgive me my old age!

YELENA ANDREEVNA. Wait, be patient! In five or six years I too shall be old.

Enter SONYA.

SONYA. Papa, you specifically asked us to send for Doctor Astrov and when he came, you refused to let him in. That is discourteous. To disturb a man for no reason . . .

SEREBRYAKOV. What do I care about your Astrov? He understands as much about medicine as I do about astronomy.

SONYA. Just for your gout we can't send for a whole medical school.

SEREBRYAKOV. I won't even give that maniac[23] the time of day.

SONYA. Have it your way. (*Sits.*) It's all the same to me.

SEREBRYAKOV. What's the time now?

YELENA ANDREEVNA. Past twelve.

SEREBRYAKOV. It's stifling . . . Sonya, get me the drops from the table!

SONYA. Right away. (*Gives him the drops.*)

SEREBRYAKOV (*aggravated*). Ah, not those! A person can't ask for a thing!

SONYA. Please don't be crotchety. Some people may care for it, but don't try it on me, for goodness sake! I do not like it. And I have no time, I have to get up early tomorrow, I have hay to mow.

> *Enter VOINITSKY in dressing gown, holding a candle.*

VOINITSKY. Outside there's a storm brewing.

> *Lightning.*

Clear out now! *Hélène* and Sonya, go to bed. I've come to take over for you.

SEREBRYAKOV (*terrified*). No, no! Don't leave me with him! No. He'll talk me blue in the face.

VOINITSKY. But they've got to get some rest! This is the second night they've had no sleep.

SEREBRYAKOV. Let them go to bed, but you go away too. Thank you. I implore you. For the sake of our former friendship, don't protest. We'll talk later.

VOINITSKY (*with a sneer*). Our *former* friendship . . . Former . . .

SONYA. Be quiet, Uncle Vanya.

SEREBRYAKOV (*to his wife*). My dear, don't leave me alone with him! He'll talk me blue in the face!

VOINITSKY. This is starting to get ridiculous.

> *Enter MARINA with a candle.*

SONYA. You should be in bed, Nanny dear. It's very late.

MARINA. The samovar's not cleared from the table. Not likely a body'd be in bed.

SEREBRYAKOV. Nobody sleeps, everybody's worn out, I'm the only one who's deliriously happy.

MARINA (*walks over to Serebryakov; tenderly*). What is it, dearie? Achy? These legs o' mine got twinges too, such twinges. (*Adjusts the lap rug.*) This complaint o' yours goes back a long ways. Vera Petrovna, rest in peace, little Sonya's mother could never sleep nights, wasting away . . . Oh, how she loved you.

> *Pause.*

Old folks're like little 'uns, they want a body to feel sorry for 'em, but old folks got no one to feel sorry for 'em. (*Kisses Serebryakov on the shoulder.*)[21] Let's go, dearie, bedtime . . . Let's go, my sunshine . . . Some lime-flower tea I'll brew for you, your li'l legs I'll warm . . . God I'll pray to for you . . .

SEREBRYAKOV (*moved*). Let's go, Marina.

MARINA. These legs o' mine got twinges too, such twinges. (*Leads him with SONYA's help.*) Vera Petrovna never stopped wasting away, never stopped crying . . . You, Sonya darlin', were just a little 'un then, a silly . . . Come, come, dearie . . .

> *SEREBRYAKOV, SONYA, and MARINA leave.*

YELENA ANDREEVNA. I've worried myself sick over him. Can hardly stand on my feet.

VOINITSKY. He makes you sick and I make myself sick. This is the third night now I haven't slept.

YELENA ANDREEVNA. There's something oppressive about this house. Your mother hates everything except her pamphlets and the Professor; the Professor is irritable, won't trust me, is afraid of you; Sonya's nasty to her father, nasty to me, and hasn't spoken to me for two weeks now; you hate my husband and openly despise your mother; I'm irritable and today some twenty times I was ready to burst into tears . . . There's something oppressive about this house.

VOINITSKY. Let's drop the philosophizing!

---

21 A traditional form of greeting used by inferiors to their betters; a survival from the days of serfdom.

YELENA ANDREEVNA. Ivan Petrovich, you're an educated, intelligent man, I should think you'd understand that the world is being destroyed not by criminals, not by fires, but by hatred, animosities, all this petty bickering . . . You shouldn't be growling, you should be bringing everyone together.

VOINITSKY. First bring the two of us together! My darling . . . (*Clutches her hand.*)

YELENA ANDREEVNA. Stop it! (*Extricates her hand.*) Go away!

VOINITSKY. Any moment now the rain will end, and everything in nature will be refreshed and breathe easy. I'll be the only thing not refreshed by the storm. Day and night, like an incubus,[22] the idea chokes me that my life has been wasted irretrievably. I've got no past, it's been stupidly squandered on trivialities, and the present is horrible in its absurdity. Here, take my life and my love; what am I to do with them? My better feelings are fading away for no reason at all, like a sunbeam trapped at the bottom of a mineshaft, and I'm fading along with them.

YELENA ANDREEVNA. Whenever you talk to me about your love, it's as if I go numb and don't know what to say. Forgive me, there's nothing I can say to you. (*About to go.*) Goodnight.

VOINITSKY (*blocks her path*). And if only you had any idea how I suffer at the thought that right beside me in this house another life is fading away— yours! What are you waiting for? What damned philosophizing stands in your way? Seize the day, seize it . . .

YELENA ANDREEVNA (*stares fixedly at him*). Ivan Petrovich, you're drunk!

VOINITSKY. Could be, could be . . .

YELENA ANDREEVNA. Where's the doctor?

VOINITSKY. He's in there . . . spending the night in my room. Could be, could be . . . Anything could be!

YELENA ANDREEVNA. So you were drinking today? What for?

VOINITSKY. It makes me feel alive somehow . . . Don't stop me, *Hélène!*

---

22 Vanya uses the term *domovoy*, house goblin, which, like the English nightmare or European incubus, is reputed to interfere with the breathing of those who are sleeping. It connects with his reference to water sprites in Act Three.

YELENA ANDREEVNA. You never used to drink and you never used to talk so much . . . Go to bed! You're boring me.

VOINITSKY (*clutching her hand*). My darling . . . wonderful woman!

YELENA ANDREEVNA (*annoyed*). Leave me alone. Once and for all, this is disgusting. (*Exits.*)

VOINITSKY (*alone*). She walked out on me . . .

Pause.

Ten years ago I met her at my poor sister's. Then she was seventeen and I was thirty-seven. Why didn't I fall in love with her then and propose to her? After all it could have been! And now she'd be my wife . . . Yes . . . Now both of us would be awakened by the storm; she'd be frightened by the thunder and I'd hold her in my arms and whisper, "Don't be afraid, I'm here." Oh, marvelous thoughts, wonderful, it makes me laugh . . . but, my God, the thoughts are snarled up in my head . . . Why am I old? Why doesn't she understand me? Her speechifying, indolent morality, indolent drivel about destroying the world—it makes me profoundly sick.

Pause.

Oh, how I've been cheated! I idolized that professor, that pathetic martyr to gout, I worked for him like a beast of burden! Sonya and I squeezed every last drop out of this estate; like grasping peasants we drove a trade in vegetable oil, peas, cottage cheese, stinted ourselves on crumbs so we could scrape together the pennies and small change into thousands and send them to him. I was proud of him and his learning, I lived, I breathed for him! Everything he wrote or uttered seemed to me to emanate from a genius . . . God, and now? Now that he's retired you can see what his whole life adds up to: when he goes not a single page of his work will endure, he is utterly unknown, he's nothing! A soap bubble! And I've been cheated . . . I see it—stupidly cheated . . .

Enter ASTROV in a frockcoat without a waistcoat or necktie; he is tipsy; TELEGIN follows him with a guitar.

ASTROV. Play!

TELEGIN. They're all asleep, sir!

ASTROV. Play!

TELEGIN plays quietly.

ASTROV (*to Voinitsky*). You alone here? No ladies? (*Arms akimbo, sings softly.*) "My shack is fled, my fire is dead, I've got no place to lay my head . . ."[23] Well, the storm woke *me* up. An impressive little downpour. What's the time now?

VOINITSKY. How the hell should I know.

ASTROV. Could have sworn I heard the voice of Yelena Andreevna.

VOINITSKY. She was here a moment ago.

ASTROV. Magnificent woman. (*Spots the medicine bottles on the table.*) Medicine. Prescriptions galore! From Kharkov, from Moscow, from Tula . . . Every town in Russia must be fed up with his gout. Is he sick or faking?

VOINITSKY. Sick.

Pause.

ASTROV. Why're you so sad today? Sorry for the Professor or what?

VOINITSKY. Leave me alone.

ASTROV. Or else, maybe, in love with Mrs. Professor?

VOINITSKY. She's my friend.

ASTROV. Already?

VOINITSKY. What's that mean—already?

ASTROV. A woman can be a man's friend only in the following sequence: first, an acquaintance, next, a mistress, and thereafter a friend.

VOINITSKY. A vulgar philosophy.

ASTROV. What? Yes . . . Have to admit—I am turning vulgar. Y'see, I'm even drunk. Ordinarily I drink like this once a month. When I'm in this state, I become insolent and impertinent to the nth degree. Then nothing fazes me! I take on the most intricate operations and perform them beautifully; I outline the broadest plans for the future; at times like that I stop thinking of myself as a crackpot and believe that I'm doing humanity a stupendous favor . . . stupendous! And at times like that I have my own personal phi-

---

23 A folksong.

losophy, and all of you, my little brothers, seem to me to be tiny insects . . . microbes. (*To Telegin.*) Waffles, play!

TELEGIN. Dearest friend, I'd be glad to play for you with all my heart, but bear in mind—the family's asleep!

ASTROV. Play!

TELEGIN plays quietly.

ASTROV. A drink's what I need. Let's go back in, I think we've still got some cognac left. And when it's light, we'll head over to my place. Want to go for a rod? I've got an orderly[24] who never says "ride," always says, "rod."[25] Terrible crook. So, want to go for a rod? (*Seeing SONYA enter.*) 'Scuse me, I'm not wearing a tie. (*Quickly exits; TELEGIN follows him.*)

SONYA. So, Uncle Vanya, you and the Doctor got drunk together again. Birds of a feather flock together. Well, he's always been like that, but why should you? At your age it doesn't suit you at all.

VOINITSKY. Age has nothing to do with it. When life has no reality, people live on illusions. After all it's better than nothing.

SONYA. All our hay is mown, it rains every day, everything's rotting, and you're obsessed with illusions. You've given up farming for good . . . I'm the only one working, I'm completely worn out . . . (*Alarmed.*) Uncle, there are tears in your eyes!

VOINITSKY. What tears? Nothing of the sort . . . don't be silly . . . Just now the way you looked like your poor mother. My precious . . . (*Avidly kisses her hands and face.*) My dear sister . . . my darling sister . . . Where is she now? If only she knew! Ah, if only she knew!

SONYA. What? Uncle, knew what?

VOINITSKY. Oppressive, wrong . . . Never mind . . . Later . . . Never mind . . . I'm going . . . (*Goes.*)

SONYA (*knocks on the door*). Mikhail Lvovich! Are you asleep? May I see you for a moment!

---

24 *Feldsher* (from the German, *Feldscher*, an assistant medical officer), a medical attendant without a doctor's degree; in rural areas of Russia, the *feldsher* often stood in for a licensed physician.

25 In Russian, the wordplay is on *idet*, colloquially "shall we go," and *idyot*, which sounds like *idiot*, "imbecile," a pun Chekhov often used privately, especially in letters to his brother Aleksandr.

ASTROV (*behind the door*). Right away! (*After a slight delay, he enters; he is now wearing a waistcoat and a necktie.*) What can I do for you?

SONYA. Go ahead and drink, if it doesn't make you sick, but, please, don't let Uncle drink. It's no good for him.

ASTROV. Fine. We won't drink any more.

Pause.

I'll go home right now. No sooner said than done. By the time the horses are hitched, dawn'll be coming up.

SONYA. It's raining. Wait till morning.

ASTROV. The storm's passing over, we'll only catch the tail end of it. I'm going. And, please, do not invite me to visit your father any more. I tell him it's gout, and he says it's rheumatism; I ask him to lie down, he sits up. And today he wouldn't even see me.

SONYA. He's spoiled. (*Looks in the sideboard.*) Would you like a bite to eat?

ASTROV. I suppose so, sure.

SONYA. I love midnight snacks. I think there's something in the sideboard. In his lifetime, they say, he was a great success with women, and the ladies have spoiled him. Here, have some cheese.

Both stand at the sideboard and eat.

ASTROV. I didn't eat a thing today, just drank. Your father has a oppressive nature. (*Gets a bottle from the sideboard.*) May I? (*Drinks a shot.*) There's nobody around, so a man can speak frankly. You know, I have the feeling I wouldn't last a month in your house, I'd suffocate in this atmosphere . . . Your father, all wrapped up in his gout and his books, Uncle Vanya with his biliousness, your grandmother, lastly your stepmother . . .

SONYA. What about my stepmother?

ASTROV. Everything about a human being ought to be beautiful: face, dress, soul, ideas. She's the fairest in the land,[26] no argument there, but . . . all

---

26 Literally, "Fair is she," an allusion to the "Tale of the Tsar's Dead Daughter and the Seven Warriors," a Russian version of "Snow White," by Aleksandr Pushkin (1833); the evil Tsarina turns to her mirror with the question whether she is really the fairest in the land. The mirror replies: "Fair art thou, no contest there; but the Tsar's daughter's still more fair . . ."

she does is eat, sleep, go for walks, enchant us all with her beauty—and that's it. She has no responsibilities, others work for her . . . Am I right? And a life of idleness cannot be pure.

Pause.

Anyway, maybe I'm being too hard on her. I'm dissatisfied with life same as your Uncle Vanya, and we're both turning into grouches.

SONYA. So you're dissatisfied with life?

ASTROV. Life in the abstract I love, but our life, rural, Russian, humdrum, I cannot stand, and I despise it with every fiber of my being. And as to my own private life, honest to God, there's absolutely nothing good about it. You know how, when you walk through a forest on a dark night, if all the time in the distance there's a glimmer of light, you don't mind the fatigue or the dark or the prickly branches hitting you in the face . . . I work—as you know—harder than anyone else in the district, fate never stops hitting me in the face, at times I suffer unbearably, but in the distance there's no light glimmering for me. I've stopped expecting anything for myself, I don't love people . . . For a long time now I've loved no one.

SONYA. No one?

ASTROV. No one. I do feel a certain affection for your dear old nanny—for old time's sake. The peasants are very monotonous, backward, live in filth, and it's hard to get on with educated people. They're tedious. All of them, our good friends and acquaintances, think petty thoughts, feel petty feelings, and don't see beyond their noses—fools, plain and simple. And the ones who are a bit cleverer and a bit more earnest are hysterical, hung up on categories and clichés . . . Their sort whines, foments hatred, spreads contagious slander, they sidle up to a man, peer at him out of the corner of their eye and decide, "Oh, he's a psychopath!" or "He's a windbag!" And when they don't know what label to stick on my brow, they say, "He's peculiar, really peculiar!" I love forests—that's peculiar; I don't eat meat—that's peculiar too. A spontaneous, unpolluted, open relationship to nature and human beings no longer exists . . . Oh no, no! (*Is about to drink.*)

SONYA (*stops him*). No, for my sake, please, don't drink any more.

ASTROV. Why not?

SONYA. It's so out of character for you! You're refined, you have such a gentle voice . . . Besides, you, unlike anyone I know—you're beautiful. Why do you want to be like ordinary people who drink and play cards? Oh, don't do that, for my sake! You're always saying that people don't create, they only destroy what is given them from on high. Why then are you destroying yourself? You mustn't, you mustn't, I beg you, I implore you.

ASTROV (*extends a hand to her*). I won't drink any more.

SONYA. Give me your word.

ASTROV. Word of honor.

SONYA (*squeezes his hand firmly*). Thank you!

ASTROV. *Basta!*[27] I've sobered up. You see, I'm quite sober and will remain so to the end of my days. (*Looks at his watch.*) Well now, let's proceed. As I was saying: my time's long gone, it's too late for me . . . I'm growing old, overworked, coarsened, all my feelings are numb, and I don't believe I could form an attachment to anyone any more. I love no one and . . . have stopped falling in love. What still gets through to me is beauty. I'm not indifferent to it. It seems to me that if Yelena Andreevna here wanted to, she could turn my head in no time at all . . . But of course that's not love, not affection . . . (*Covers his eyes with his hand and shudders.*)

SONYA. What's wrong?

ASTROV. Just . . . In Lent a patient of mine died under the chloroform.

SONYA. It's time to forget that.

Pause.

Tell me, Mikhail Lvovich . . . If I happened to have a girlfriend or a younger sister, and you were to learn that she . . . well, let's suppose, she loves you, how would you deal with that?

ASTROV (*with a shrug*). I don't know, nohow, I suppose. I'd let her understand that I could not love her . . . besides, it's not the sort of thing that's on my mind. Anyway, if I'm to go, the time's come. Good-bye, my dear, otherwise we'll be at it till morning. (*Presses her hand.*) I'll go through the parlor, if you don't mind, or else I'm afraid your uncle will detain me.

Exits.

---

27 Italian: enough.

SONYA (*alone*). He didn't say anything to me . . . His heart and soul are still hidden from me, so why do I feel so happy? (*Laughs with delight.*) I said to him: you're refined, noble, you have such a gentle voice . . . Was that uncalled for? His voice throbs, caresses . . . I can feel it here in the air. And when I mentioned a younger sister, he didn't understand . . . (*Wringing her hands.*) Oh, it's an awful thing to be unattractive! Simply awful! And I know I'm unattractive, I know, I know . . . Last Sunday, when we were coming out of church, I heard the way they talked about me, and one woman said, "She's kind and good-natured, what a pity she's so unattractive . . ." Unattractive . . .

Enter YELENA ANDREEVNA.

YELENA ANDREEVNA (*opens a window*). The storm has passed. What lovely air!

Pause.

Where's the doctor?

SONYA. Gone.

Pause.

YELENA ANDREEVNA. *Sophie!*

SONYA. What?

YELENA ANDREEVNA. How long are you going to go on glowering at me? We haven't done one another any harm. Why do we have to be enemies? Enough is enough.

SONYA. I wanted to myself . . . (*Embraces her.*) No more tantrums.

YELENA ANDREEVNA. Splendid.

Both are agitated.

SONYA. Is Papa in bed?

YELENA ANDREEVNA. No, he's sitting in the parlor . . . We don't talk to one another for weeks on end and God knows why . . . (*Noticing the open sideboard.*) What's this?

SONYA. Mikhail Lvovich had some supper.

YELENA ANDREEVNA. And there's some wine . . . Let's pledge one another as sisters.[27]

SONYA. Let's.

YELENA ANDREEVNA. Out of the same glass . . . (*Pours.*) That's better. Well, here goes—friends?

SONYA. Friends.[28]

They drink and kiss.

For a long time now I've wanted to make it up, but somehow I was embarrassed . . .

Weeps.

YELENA ANDREEVNA. What are you crying for?

SONYA. No reason, it's the way I am.

YELENA ANDREEVNA. Well, never mind, never mind . . . (*Weeps.*) You little crackpot,[28] now you've got me crying . . .

Pause.

You're angry with me because you think I married your father for ulterior motives . . . If you'll believe an oath, I'll swear to you—I married him for love. I was attracted to him as a scholar and a celebrity. The love was unreal, artificial, but at the time I thought it was real. It's not my fault. But from the day we got married you've gone on punishing me with your shrewd, suspicious eyes.

SONYA. Well, truce, truce! We'll put it behind us.

YELENA ANDREEVNA. You mustn't look at people that way—it doesn't suit you. You must trust everyone, otherwise life becomes unliveable.

Pause.

SONYA. Tell me truthfully, friend to friend . . . Are you happy?

YELENA ANDREEVNA. No.

SONYA. I knew that. One more question. Tell me frankly—would you like to have a young husband?

YELENA ANDREEVNA. What a little girl you are still. Of course I would! (*Laughs.*) Go on, ask me something else, ask me . . .

---

28 Yelena has picked one of Astrov's favorite words; she's clearly been listening to him.

SONYA. Do you like the doctor?

YELENA ANDREEVNA. Yes, very much.

SONYA (*laughs*). I must look funny . . . don't I? Now he's gone, but I keep hearing his voice and footsteps, and I look out the dark window—and his face appears to me. Let me say what's on my mind . . . But I can't say it out loud, I'm embarrassed. Let's go to my room, we'll talk there. Do you think I'm being silly? Admit it . . . Tell me something about him . . .

YELENA ANDREEVNA. Such as?

SONYA. He's intelligent . . . He knows how to do everything, can do every-thing . . . He practices medicine and plants forests . . .

YELENA ANDREEVNA. Forests and medicine have nothing to do with it . . . Darling, what you have to understand is, he's got talent! Do you know the meaning of talent?[29] Daring, an uncluttered mind, breadth of vision . . . He plants a tree and already he's planning ahead, what the result will be in a thousand years, he's already imagining the happiness of generations to come. People like that are rare, one must love them . . . He drinks, he's uncouth—but what's the harm in that? A talented man in Russia cannot be a puritan. Just consider the life this doctor leads! Mud up to his waist on the roads, frosts, blizzards, vast distances, coarse, savage people, all around poverty, disease, and it's hard for a man working and struggling in sur-roundings like that day after day to reach the age of forty spotless and sober . . . (*Kisses her.*) I wish you happiness from the bottom of my heart, you deserve it . . . (*Rises.*) But mine is a dreary walk-on part . . . In the field of music and in my husband's house, in any of life's dramas—no matter where, in short, I've only had a walk-on part. Personally speaking, Sonya, when you think about it, I'm very, very unhappy! (*Walks nervously around the stage.*) No happiness for me in this world. No! Why are you laughing?

SONYA (*laughs, covering her face*). I'm so happy . . . happy!

YELENA ANDREEVNA. I'd like to play the piano . . . I want to play some-thing right now.

SONYA. Do play. (*Embraces her.*) I can't sleep. Play.

YELENA ANDREEVNA. Presently. Your father isn't asleep. When he's ill, music irritates him. Go and ask. If he doesn't object, I'll play. Go on.

SONYA. Right this minute. (*Exits.*)

In the garden the WATCHMAN is tapping.

YELENA ANDREEVNA. It's been a long time since I played. I'll play and weep, weep like a fool. (*Out the window.*) Is that you tapping, Yefim?

WATCHMAN'S VOICE. It's me!

YELENA ANDREEVNA. Don't tap, the master's not well.

WATCHMAN'S VOICE. I'll go right now! (*Whistles under his breath.*) Here, boys, Blacky, Laddy! Blacky![30]

Pause.

SONYA (*returning*). The answer's no!

Curtain

ACT THREE

Parlor in Serebryakov's house. Three doors: right, left, and center. — Daytime.

VOINITSKY, SONYA are sitting; YELENA ANDREEVNA walks about the stage with something on her mind.

VOINITSKY. Herr Professor has graciously expressed the desire that today we all congregate in this parlor at one o'clock P.M. (*Looks at his watch.*) A quarter to one. He's got something he wants to tell the world.

YELENA ANDREEVNA. Probably some business matter.

VOINITSKY. He has no business. He writes drivel, moans and groans and oozes envy, that's all.

SONYA (*reproachfully*). Uncle!

VOINITSKY. All right, sorry. (*Indicates Yelena Andreevna.*) Wonder at her: she can't walk, without tottering from sheer indolence. Very charming! Very!

YELENA ANDREEVNA. All you do all day is buzz, buzz — how come you don't get sick of it! (*Languorously.*) I'm dying of boredom, I don't know what I'm to do.

SONYA (*shrugging*). How about a little work? Only the lady has to make an effort.

YELENA ANDREEVNA. For instance?

SONYA. Get involved in running the farm, teach, tend the sick. Isn't that enough? Around here, before you and Papa arrived, Uncle Vanya and I used to go to the fair ourselves to market the flour.

YELENA ANDREEVNA. I don't know how. Besides, it's not interesting. Only in social-purpose novels do people teach and tend peasants, and how am I, out of the blue, supposed to go tend them or teach them?

SONYA. But then I can't understand what prevents you from going and teaching them. After a while it'll become second nature. (*Embraces her.*) Don't be bored, dear. (*Laughs.*) You're bored, you can't find a niche for yourself, but boredom and idleness are catching. Look: Uncle Vanya does nothing but follow you around, like a shadow, I've given up my chores and come running to you for a chat. I've got lazy, I can't help it! The Doctor used to stay with us very seldom, once a month, it wasn't easy to ask him, but now he rides over every day, he's abandoned his forests and his medicine. You must be a witch.

VOINITSKY. Why are you mooning about? (*Vigorously.*) Come, my elegant darling, show how clever you are! The blood of water nymphs courses through your veins, be a water nymph![33] Satisfy your desires at least once in your life, fall in love as fast as you can, head over heels, with some water sprite—plop! take a nosedive into the millrace, so that Herr Professor and the rest of us throw up our hands in amazement!

YELENA ANDREEVNA (*angrily*). Leave me alone! This is sadistic! (*About to go.*)

VOINITSKY (*doesn't let her go*). There, there, my sweet, forgive me . . . I apologize. (*Kisses her hands.*) Truce.

YELENA ANDREEVNA. You'd try the patience of a saint, you must admit.

VOINITSKY. As a token of peace and harmony, I'll bring you a bouquet of roses this very minute; I put it together for you this morning . . . Autumnal roses—superb, mournful roses . . . (*Exits.*)

SONYA. Autumnal roses—superb, mournful roses . . .

Both women look out the window.

YELENA ANDREEVNA. Here it is September already. How are we to get through the winter here?

Pause.

Where's the doctor?

SONYA. In Uncle Vanya's room. He's writing something. I'm glad Uncle Vanya went out, I have to talk to you.

YELENA ANDREEVNA. What about?

SONYA. What about? (*Lays her head on Yelena's breast.*).

YELENA ANDREEVNA. There, there . . . (*Smooths Sonya's hair.*) That'll do.

SONYA. I'm unattractive.

YELENA ANDREEVNA. You have beautiful hair.

SONYA. No! (*Looks round to view herself in a mirror.*) No! Whenever a woman's unattractive, they tell her, "You have beautiful eyes, you have beautiful hair!" . . . I've loved him now for six years, love him more than my own mother; every minute I can hear him, feel the pressure of his hand; and I stare at the door and wait, I get the sense he's just about to walk in. There, you see, I keep coming to you to talk about him. He's here every day now, but he doesn't look at me, doesn't see . . . It's so painful! There's no hope at all, no, none! (*In despair.*) Oh, God, my strength is gone . . . I was up all night praying . . . Lots of times I'll walk up to him, start to speak, look him in the eyes . . . I've got no pride left, no willpower . . . I couldn't help it and yesterday I confessed to Uncle Vanya that I love him . . . Even all the servants know I love him. Everyone knows.

YELENA ANDREEVNA. Does he?

SONYA. No. He doesn't notice me.

YELENA ANDREEVNA (*musing*). A peculiar sort of man . . . You know what? Let me talk to him . . . I'll be discreet, I'll hint . . .

Pause.

Honestly, how long can a person go on not knowing . . . Let me!

SONYA nods her head Yes.

That's splendid. Whether or not he's in love shouldn't be too hard to find out. Now don't be embarrassed, my pet, don't be upset—I'll question him discreetly, he won't even notice. All we have to find out is: yes or no?

Pause.

If no, then he should stop coming here. Right?

SONYA *nods her head Yes.*

It's easier when you don't see him. We won't file-and-forget it, we'll question him right now. He was planning to show me some drawings . . . Go and tell him I'd like to see him.

SONYA (*intensely excited*). You'll tell me the whole truth?

YELENA ANDREEVNA. Yes, of course. I should think that the truth, whatever it turns out to be, is nowhere near as awful as not knowing. Depend on me, my pet.

SONYA. Yes, yes . . . I'll say that you want to see his charts . . . (*Goes but stops near the door.*) No, not knowing is better . . . Then there's hope . . .

YELENA ANDREEVNA. What's that?

SONYA. Nothing. (*Exits.*)

YELENA ANDREEVNA (*alone*). Nothing's worse than knowing someone else's secret and being unable to help. (*Pondering.*) He's not in love with her—that's obvious, but why shouldn't he marry her? She's no beauty, but for a country doctor, at his age, she'd make a fine wife. A good head on her shoulders, so kind, unspoiled . . . No, that's not it, that's not it . . .

Pause.

I understand the poor girl. In the midst of howling boredom, when all she sees prowling around her are gray blurs, not people, all she hears are banalities, all they know is eating, drinking, sleeping, once in a while he'll show up, different from the others, handsome, interesting, attractive, like a full moon emerging from dark clouds . . . To yield to the embrace of such a man, to forget oneself . . . Apparently I'm a wee bit attracted myself. Yes, when he's not here, I'm bored, look, I'm smiling as I think about him . . . Uncle Vanya was saying the blood of water nymphs courses through my veins. "Satisfy your desires at least once in your life" . . . Should I? Maybe I have to . . . If I could fly like an uncaged bird away from you all, from your

drowsy expressions, from idle chatter, forget your very existence on earth
. . . But I'm a coward, inhibited . . . I'm having an attack of conscience . . .
There, he shows up every day, I can guess why he's here, and I'm starting
to feel guilty, any minute now I'll drop to my knees and beg Sonya's forgiveness, burst into tears . . .

ASTROV (*enters with a diagram*). Good afternoon! (*Shakes her hand.*) You
wanted to see my drawing?

YELENA ANDREEVNA. Yesterday you promised to show me your work . . .
You're free?

ASTROV. Oh, definitely. (*Unrolls the diagram on a card table and fastens it
with thumbtacks.*) Where were you born?

YELENA ANDREEVNA (*helping him*). In Petersburg.

ASTROV. And educated?

YELENA ANDREEVNA. At the Conservatory.[29]

ASTROV. Then you'll probably find this uninteresting.

YELENA ANDREEVNA. Why? True, I'm not familiar with country life, but
I've read quite a lot.

ASTROV. Here in the house I have my own table . . . In Ivan Petrovich's room.
When I'm utterly exhausted, to the point of total lethargy, I drop everything
and hurry over here, and then I amuse myself with this stuff for an hour or
two . . . Ivan Petrovich and Sofiya Aleksandrovna plug away at the accounts,
while I sit next them at my table and putter—and I feel warm, relaxed, and
the cricket chirps. But I don't allow myself this indulgence very often, once
a month . . . (*Pointing to the diagram.*)[30] Now look at this. A picture of our
district, as it was fifty years ago. The dark-green and light-green indicate forest; half the total area is covered with forest. Where the green is cross-

---

29 The St. Petersburg Conservatory, founded in 1862 by Anton Rubinstein, was an outstanding
nursery of brilliant musicians.

30 "The Art Theatre is putting on my *Uncle Vanya*; in the third act they need a survey map. Be so
kind as to pick out a suitable one and lend it or promise to donate a suitable one, when you find one
among those you don't need" (Chekhov to Dr. P. I. Kurkin, May 24, 1899). Kurkin sent him a
survey map of the Serpukhov region with the village of Melikhovo, where Chekhov lived, in the
middle.

hatched with red lines, there used to be elks, goats . . . I show both flora and fauna on this. In this lake lived swans, geese, ducks and, as the old-timers say, a power of birds of every description, more than the eye could see: they sailed by like a cloud. Besides hamlets and villages, you see, scattered here and there are different settlements, little farmsteads, monasteries of Old Believers,[31] water mills . . . Horned cattle and horses were numerous. The light-blue tells us that. For instance, in this county, the light-blue is laid on thick; there were whole herds of cattle, and in every stable there was an average of three horses.

Pause.

Now let's look further down. What it was like twenty-five years ago. Now only one-third the total area is under forestation. There are no more goats, but there are elks. The green and light-blue are much fainter. And so on and so on. Let's move to Part Three: a picture of the district at the present moment. The green is there in patches; the elks and swans and wood grouse have disappeared . . . Of the earlier settlements, small farmsteads, monasteries, mills, not a trace. Over all, a picture of gradual and indisputable decline, which will apparently take another ten or fifteen years to be complete. You will say that this is the result of civilization, that the old life must naturally give way to the new. Yes, I'd understand that, if these depleted forests were replaced by paved highways, railroads, if there were factories, mills, schools, — if the lower classes had become healthier, more prosperous, more intelligent, but there's certainly nothing like that here! In the district there're the same swamps, mosquitoes, the same impassable roads, indigence, typhus, diphtheria, fires . . . Here we're dealing with decline resulting from a struggle for survival beyond human strength; it's a decline caused by stagnation, ignorance, the most total absence of self-awareness, when a frostbitten, starving, sickly man, to preserve the last vestiges of life, to protect his children, instinctively, unthinkingly grabs hold of whatever can possibly satisfy his hunger, to warm himself he destroys everything, with no thought of the morrow . . . The destruction to date has been almost total, but to make up for it nothing has yet been created. (*Coldly.*) I see from your face that you find this uninteresting.

YELENA ANDREEVNA. But I understand so little of it.

---

31 Schismatics from the Russian Orthodox church, persecuted by the authorities from the seventeenth century, sought refuge in the countryside, and split into many sects.

ASTROV. There's nothing to understand, it's simply uninteresting.

YELENA ANDREEVNA. To tell the truth, my mind wasn't on it. Forgive me, I have to subject you to a slight interrogation, and I'm embarrassed, I don't know how to begin . . .

ASTROV. Interrogation?

YELENA ANDREEVNA. Yes, interrogation, but . . . quite a harmless one. Let's sit down.

They sit.

This concerns a certain young person. Let's talk openly, like friends, and not beat around the bush. All right?

ASTROV. All right.

YELENA ANDREEVNA. It concerns my stepdaughter Sonya. Do you like her?

ASTROV. Yes, I respect her.

YELENA ANDREEVNA. Do you like her as a woman?

ASTROV (*not immediately*). No.

YELENA ANDREEVNA. A few words more—and it's all over. Have you noticed anything?

ASTROV. No.

YELENA ANDREEVNA (*takes him by the hand*). You don't love her, I see it in your eyes . . . She is suffering . . . Understand that and . . . stop coming here.

ASTROV (*rises*). My time's up now . . . Actually, there's never any time . . . (*After a shrug.*) When could I? (*He is embarrassed.*)

YELENA ANDREEVNA. Oof! what a disagreeable conversation! I'm as relieved as if I'd been lugging around a twenty-ton weight. Well, thank goodness, that's over. We'll forget we ever had a talk and . . . and you will go away. You're an intelligent man, you understand . . .

Pause.

I'm blushing all over.

ASTROV. If you had said something a month or two ago, maybe I might have considered it, but now . . . (*Shrugs.*) But if she's suffering, well, of course . . . The only thing I don't understand is: why did *you* have to conduct this interrogation? (*Stares her in the face and wags his finger at her.*) You are a sly fox!

YELENA ANDREEVNA. What's that supposed to mean?

ASTROV (*laughing*). A sly fox! Suppose Sonya is suffering, I'm ready to accept that, but what's the point of your interrogation? (*Not letting her speak, energetically.*) Come now, don't act so surprised, you know perfectly well why I'm here every day . . . Why and for whose sake I'm here, you know very well indeed. Cunning little vixen, don't look at me like that, this chicken's an old hand . . .

YELENA ANDREEVNA (*bewildered*). Cunning vixen? I don't understand.

ASTROV. A beautiful, fluffy weasel . . . You need victims! For a whole month now I've done nothing, let everything slide, seek you out greedily—and you're awfully pleased by it—awfully . . . Well, what of it? I'm beaten, you knew that even without an interrogation. (*Crossing his hands over his chest and bowing his head.*) I surrender. Go ahead, eat me up.

YELENA ANDREEVNA. You're out of your mind!

ASTROV (*laughs through his teeth*). You're inhibited . . .

YELENA ANDREEVNA. Oh, I'm a better, more decent person than you think! I swear to you. (*About to go.*)

ASTROV (*blocking her path*). I will go today, I won't come here any more, but . . . (*takes her by the arm, looks around*) where shall we get together? Tell me quickly: where? Here someone might come in, tell me quickly . . . (*Passionately.*) What a wonderful, elegant . . . One kiss . . . Just let me kiss your fragrant hair . . .

YELENA ANDREEVNA. I swear to you . . .

ASTROV (*not letting her speak*). Why swear? There's no need to swear. There's no need for more words . . . Oh, what a beauty! What hands! (*Kisses her hands.*)

YELENA ANDREEVNA. That's enough, once and for all . . . go away . . . (*Extricates her hands.*) You're out of control.

ASTROV. Then tell me, tell me where we'll get together tomorrow? (*Takes her by the waist.*) You see, it's inevitable, we have to get together. (*Kisses her; at that moment VOINITSKY enters with a bouquet of roses and stops in the doorway.*)

YELENA ANDREEVNA (*not seeing Voinitsky*). For pity's sake . . . let go of me . . . (*Puts her head on Astrov's chest.*) No! (*Tries to go.*)

ASTROV (*restraining her by the waist*). Drive tomorrow to the forest preserve . . . around two o'clock . . . Yes? Yes? Will you?

YELENA ANDREEVNA (*having seen Voinitsky*). Let go! (*In intense embarrassment walks over to the window.*) This is horrible.

VOINITSKY (*puts the bouquet on a chair; agitated, wipes his face and the inside of his collar with a handkerchief*). Never mind . . . Yes . . . never mind . . .

ASTROV (*peeved*). Today, my dear Mr. Voinitsky, the weather's not too bad. It was overcast this morning, as if it was going to rain, but now it's sunny. To tell the truth, autumn's turned out lovely . . . and the winter wheat's doing all right. (*Rolls the diagram into a cylinder.*) Only trouble is: the days are getting shorter. (*Exits.*)

YELENA ANDREEVNA (*quickly goes over to Voinitsky*). You will make every effort, you will use all your influence to get my husband and me to leave here this very day! You hear? This very day!

VOINITSKY (*mopping his brow*). Huh? Well, yes . . . fine . . . *Hélène*, I saw it all, all of it . . .

YELENA ANDREEVNA (*on edge*). You hear? I must leave here this very day!

Enter SEREBRYAKOV, SONYA, TELEGIN, and MARINA.

TELEGIN. Your Excellency, I'm not in the best of health either. Why, for two days now, I've been under the weather. My head feels sort of, y'know . . .

SEREBRYAKOV. Where are the others? I do not like this house. Just like a labyrinth. Twenty-six enormous rooms, everyone scatters, and you can never find anyone. (*Rings.*) Request Mariya Vasilyevna and Yelena Andreevna to come here!

YELENA ANDREEVNA. I'm here.

SEREBRYAKOV. Please, ladies and gentlemen, be seated.

SONYA (*going over to Yelena Andreevna, impatiently*). What did he say?

YELENA ANDREEVNA. Later.

SONYA. You're trembling? You're upset? (*Looks searchingly into her face.*) I understand . . . He said he won't come here any more . . . Right?

Pause.

Tell me: am I right?

YELENA ANDREEVNA nods her head Yes.

SEREBRYAKOV (*to Telegin*). Ill health one might be reconciled to, if the worst came to the worst, but what I cannot stomach is this regimen of rustication. I have the feeling I've dropped off the earth on to some alien planet. Sit down, ladies and gentlemen, please. Sonya!

SONYA does not hear him, she stands with her head bowed in sorrow.

Sonya!

Pause.

She's not listening. (*To Marina.*) And you sit down too, Nanny.

The NANNY sits down and knits a stocking.

Please, my friends. Lend me your ears, as the saying goes. (*Laughs.*)

VOINITSKY (*getting excited*). Maybe I'm not needed? I can go?

SEREBRYAKOV. No, you are needed here more than anyone.

VOINITSKY. What do you want from me, sir?[36]

SEREBRYAKOV. Sir? . . . Why are you getting angry?

Pause.

If I've offended you in any way, then please forgive me.

VOINITSKY. Drop that tone. Let's get down to business . . . What do you want?

Enter MARIYA VASILYEVNA.

SEREBRYAKOV. And here's *Maman*. I shall begin, ladies and gentlemen.

Pause.

I have invited you here, my friends, to inform you that we are about to be visited by an Inspector General.[37] However, joking aside. The matter is a serious one. Ladies and gentlemen, I have convened you in order to solicit your aid and advice and, knowing your customary civility, I trust to receive them. I am a man of learning, a bookworm, and have ever been a stranger to practical life. I cannot do without the counsel of informed individuals, and so I ask you, Ivan Petrovich, and you too, Ilya Ilyich, you, *Maman* . . . . What it comes down to is *manet omnes una nox*,[38] we are all mortal in the sight of God; I am old, ill, and therefore deem it appropriate to regulate my material concerns insofar as they relate to my family. My life is over now, it's not myself I'm thinking of, but I have a young wife, an unmarried daughter.

Pause.

To go on living in the country I find impossible. We were not made for country life. To live in town on those funds which we earn from this estate is equally impossible. If we were to sell, say, our forest, that is an extraordinary measure which could not be repeated annually. We must seek out measures that will guarantee us a regular, more or less fixed amount of income. I have thought of one such measure and I have the honor to submit it for your discussion. Leaving aside the details, I set it forth in its general outlines. Our estate yields on average no more than two percent. I propose to sell it. If we turn the money thus acquired into interest-bearing securities, we shall receive from four to five percent, and I think there may even be a surplus of a few thousand, which will enable us to buy a small cottage in Finland.[39]

VOINITSKY. Hold on . . . my ears seem to be deceiving me. Repeat what you just said.

SEREBRYAKOV. Turn the money into interest-bearing securities and with the surplus left over buy a cottage in Finland.

VOINITSKY. Not Finland . . . You said something else.

SEREBRYAKOV. I propose to sell the estate.

VOINITSKY. There, that's it. You'll sell the estate, splendid, good thinking . . . And where do you propose I go with my old mother and Sonya there?

SEREBRYAKOV. All that will be discussed in due time. Not everything at once.

VOINITSKY. Hold on. Obviously, up to now I didn't have a grain of common sense. Up to now I was stupid enough to think that this estate belongs to Sonya. My late father bought this estate as a dowry for my sister. Up to now I was naive, I didn't interpret the laws like a heathen, and I thought the estate passed from my sister to Sonya.

SEREBRYAKOV. Yes, the estate belongs to Sonya. Who disputes it? Without Sonya's consent I will not resolve to sell it. Besides, I'm proposing to do this on Sonya's behalf.

VOINITSKY. This is incomprehensible, incomprehensible! Either I've gone out of my mind, or . . . or . . .

MARIYA VASILYEVNA. *Jean*, don't contradict *Alexandre*. Believe me, he knows better than we what is right and what is wrong.

VOINITSKY. No, give me some water. (*Drinks water.*) Say what it is you want, what do you want!

SEREBRYAKOV. I don't understand why you're getting so worked up. I don't say my project is ideal. If everyone finds it infeasible, I shall not insist.

Pause.

TELEGIN (*embarrassed*). Your Excellency, I cherish for learning not just reverence, but even a kindred feeling. My brother Grigory's wife's brother, maybe you deign to know him, Konstantin Trofimovich Spartakov,[32] had a master's degree . . .

VOINITSKY. Hold on, Waffles, we're talking business . . . Wait, later . . . (*To Serebryakov.*) You go ahead and ask *him*. This estate was bought from his uncle.

SEREBRYAKOV. Ah, why should I ask him? What for?

VOINITSKY. This estate was bought at that time for ninety-five thousand. Father paid only seventy down, so there was a mortgage of twenty-five thousand left. Now listen . . . This estate would not be free and clear if I hadn't relinquished an inheritance in favor of my sister, whom I loved devoutly. Moreover, for ten years I worked like an ox and paid off the whole debt . . .

---

32 In the original, *Lakedaimonov*, a joke name based on Lacedæmon, land of the Spartans.

SEREBRYAKOV. I'm sorry I brought up the subject.

VOINITSKY. The estate is clear of debt and turning a profit thanks only to my personal efforts. And now, when I'm growing old, they want to throw me out of here on my ear!

SEREBRYAKOV. I can't understand what you're driving at!

VOINITSKY. For twenty-five years I ran this estate, worked hard, sent you money like the most conscientious bookkeeper, and in all that time not once did you thank me. The whole time—both in my youth and now—you paid me a salary of five hundred rubles a year—a pittance!—and not once did you have the decency to raise it by even one ruble!

SEREBRYAKOV. Ivan Petrovich, how was I to know? I'm not a man of business and I have no head for such things. You could have raised it yourself as much as you liked.

VOINITSKY. Why didn't I steal? Why don't you all despise me because I didn't steal? That would have been the thing to do! and now I wouldn't be a pauper!

MARIYA VASILYEVNA (*sternly*). Jean!

TELEGIN (*getting upset*). Vanya, dear friend, you mustn't, you mustn't . . . . I'm all a-tremble . . . Why spoil good relations? (*Kisses him.*) You mustn't.

VOINITSKY. For twenty-five years I and my mother here, like moles, sat between these four walls . . . All our thoughts and feelings concerned no one but you. Days we talked about you, about your work, took pride in you, uttered your name with reverence; nights we wasted reading periodicals and books, which I now deeply despise!

TELEGIN. You mustn't, Vanya, you mustn't . . . I can't take it . . .

SEREBRYAKOV (*angrily*). I don't understand, what do you want?

VOINITSKY. To us you were a creature of a higher order, and we learned your articles by heart . . . But now my eyes have been opened! I see it all! You write about art, but not one thing do you understand about art! All your work, which I loved, isn't worth a tinker's dam! You bamboozled us!

SEREBRYAKOV. My friends! Try and calm him down, once and for all! I'm going!

YELENA ANDREEVNA. Ivan Petrovich, I insist that you keep quiet! You hear me?

VOINITSKY. I won't keep quiet! (*Blocking Serebryakov's path.*) Stop, I haven't finished! You ruined my life! I haven't lived, I haven't lived! Thanks to your charity I blighted, destroyed the best years of my life! You are my deadliest enemy!

TELEGIN. I can't take it . . . can't take it . . . I'm going. (*Exits in extreme consternation.*)

SEREBRYAKOV. What do you want from me? And what right do you have to take such a tone with me? A nobody! If the estate is yours, then take it, I have no use for it!

YELENA ANDREEVNA. I'm getting out of this hellhole this very minute! (*Screams.*) I can't take any more of this!

VOINITSKY. My life is wasted! I'm talented, intelligent, audacious . . . If I had had a normal life, I might have evolved into a Schopenhauer, a Dostoevsky[40] . . . What a damn fool thing to say! I'm losing my mind . . . Mommy, I'm desperate! Mommy!

MARIYA VASILYEVNA (*sternly*). Do as Aleksandr says!

SONYA (*kneels before the nanny and clings to her*). Nanny dear! Nanny dear!

VOINITSKY. Mommy! What am I to do? Don't, don't say anything! I know what I have to do! (*To Serebryakov.*) You're going to remember me! (*Goes to the center door.*)

MARIYA VASILYEVNA goes after him.

SEREBRYAKOV. Ladies and gentlemen, what is all this, I mean really? Get that madman away from me! I cannot live under the same roof with him! He lives right there (*indicates the center door*), practically on top of me . . . Move him into the village, to the servants' quarters, or I'll move, but to stay in the same house with him is out of the question . . .

YELENA ANDREEVNA (*to her husband*). We will leave here today! It is imperative you arrange it this very minute.

SEREBRYAKOV. The most insignificant creature!

SONYA (*kneeling, turns to her father; nervously, through tears*). Open your heart, Papa! Uncle Vanya and I are so unhappy! (*Mastering her despair.*)

Open your heart![33] Remember when you were younger, Uncle Vanya and Granny would spend nights translating books for you, copying out your writings . . . every night, every night! Uncle Vanya and I worked without a rest, afraid to spend a penny on ourselves, and sent everything to you . . . We had to pay our own way! I'm not saying this right, it's not what I mean, but you understand us, Papa. Open your heart!

YELENA ANDREEVNA (*distraught, to her husband*). Aleksandr, for heaven's sake, have it out with him . . . Please.

SEREBRYAKOV. Very well, I'll have it out with him . . . I'm not accusing him of anything, I'm not angry, but, you must agree, his behavior is just the slightest degree peculiar. If you insist, I'll go to him. (*Goes out the center door.*)

YELENA ANDREEVNA. Be gentler with him, calm him down . . . (*Goes out behind him.*)

SONYA (*clinging to the nanny*). Nanny dear! Nanny dear!

MARINA. Never mind, child. Honk, honk, go the geese—and then they stop . . . Honk, honk, honk—then they stop . . .

SONYA. Nanny dear!

MARINA (*smooths her hair*). You're shivery-shaky, just like you had a chill! Well, well, little orphan, God is merciful. Some lime-flower tea or raspberry, it'll pass . . . Don't grieve, little orphan . . . (*Looking at the center door, angrily.*) Fly off the handle, will you, you geese, dern ya all!

> *Offstage a gunshot; we hear YELENA ANDREEVNA scream; SONYA shudders.*

Ooh, what're you up to!

SEREBRYAKOV (*runs in, stumbling in fear*). Restrain him! Restrain him! He's gone out of his mind!

---

33 According to Nadezhda Butova:

Anton Pavlovich was once watching *Uncle Vanya.*

In the third act Sonya at the words "Papa, open your heart," got on her knees and kissed her father's hand.

"She mustn't do that, that's really not drama," said Anton Pavlovich. "All the sense, all the drama of a human being is inward, and not expressed in outward manifestations. There was drama in Sonya's life up to that moment, there will be drama after that, but this is simply an incident, the consequence of the gunshot. And a gunshot is really not drama, but an incident."

("From Memories of A. P. Chekhov at the Art Theatre," *Shipovnik Almanac* 23 [1914])

*YELENA ANDREEVNA and VOINITSKY are struggling in
the doorway.*

YELENA ANDREEVNA (*trying to wrest the revolver away from him*). Give it
to me! Give it to me, I tell you!

VOINITSKY. Let go, *Hélène!* Let go of me! (*Pulling loose, he runs in and looks
around for Serebryakov.*) Where is he? Ah, there he is? (*Fires at him.*) Bang!

Pause.

Missed him? Another fiasco?! (*Angrily.*) Oh, hell, hell . . . damn it to hell
. . . (*Throws the revolver on the floor and sits exhausted on a chair.*)

*SEREBRYAKOV is stunned; YELENA ANDREEVNA is
leaning against the wall, feeling faint.*

YELENA ANDREEVNA. Take me away from here! Take me away, kill me, but
. . . I cannot stay here, I cannot!

VOINITSKY (*in desperation*). Oh, what am I doing! What am I doing!

SONYA (*quietly*). Nanny dear! Nanny dear!

Curtain

ACT FOUR

*Ivan Petrovich's room; it is both his bedroom and the office of the
estate. By the window are a large table with ledgers and papers of
all sorts, a writing desk, cupboards, scales. A somewhat smaller
table for Astrov; on this table implements for drawing, paints;
beside it a cardboard portfolio. A starling in a cage. On the wall a
map of Africa, apparently of no use to anyone here. An enormous
divan, covered in oilcloth. At left a door leading to the bedroom;
at right a door in the wall. Beneath the right door is a doormat
to keep the peasants from tracking in mud.
—Autumn evening. Stillness.*

*TELEGIN and MARINA are seated face to face, winding a ball
of knitting yarn.*

TELEGIN. You be quick, Marina Timofeevna, or before you know it they'll
call us to say good-bye. They've already ordered the horses brought round.

MARINA (*trying to wind more quickly*). There's just a bit left.

TELEGIN. Kharkov's where they're going.[34] That's where they'll live.

MARINA. Good riddance.

TELEGIN. They got a scare . . . Yelena Andreevna says, "not one more hour,"
she says, "will I live here . . . let's go, let's go . . . We'll live," she says, "in
Kharkov, we'll give it the once-over and then we'll send for our things . . ."
Traveling light. Which means, Marina Timofeevna, they weren't destined
to live here. Not destined . . . Preordained by fate.

MARINA. Good riddance. Just now they were raising a rumpus, shooting
guns—a downright disgrace!

TELEGIN. Yes, a scene that deserves treatment by a painter of shipwrecks and
tempests.[43]

MARINA. That my eyes should see such a sight. (*Pause.*) Once again we'll live
as we used to, the old way. Tea in the morning between seven and eight,
dinner between noon and one, sit down to supper in the evening; everything in its place, the way folks do it . . . like Christians. (*With a sigh.*) It's
a long time, bless my soul, since I've had noodles.

TELEGIN. Yes, it's quite a little while since they served us noodles.

Pause.

Quite a little while . . . This morning, Marina Timofeevna, I go to the village and the shopkeeper yells at me, "Hey, you freeloader!" And it made
me feel so bitter!

MARINA. You pay it no mind, dearie. We're all freeloaders on God. You and
Sonya and Ivan Petrovich—no one sits idle, everyone gets down to work!
Everyone . . . where *is* Sonya?

TELEGIN. In the garden. She and the doctor are on the move, looking for
Ivan Petrovich. They're afraid he might lay hands on himself.

---

34 Capital of the Kharkov *guberniya* in the Ukraine, a university town of 220,000 inhabitants,
famous for its annual cattle and wool market. In the view of a Petersburger: back of the beyond.
Chekhov often uses it to suggest a humdrum way of life.

MARINA. And where's the pistol?

TELEGIN (*in a whisper*). I hid it in the cellar!

MARINA (*with a broad grin*). Bless us sinners!

Enter from outside VOINITSKY and ASTROV.

VOINITSKY. Leave me alone. (*To Marina and Telegin.*) Get out of here, leave me alone for just an hour! I can't stand being spied on.

TELEGIN. This minute, Vanya. (*Tiptoes out.*)

MARINA. Goosie-goosie-gander, honk, honk, honk! (*Gathers up the yarn and exits.*)

VOINITSKY. Leave me alone!

ASTROV. With the greatest of pleasure, I should have left here long ago, but, I repeat, I will not leave until you return what you took from me.

VOINITSKY. I took nothing from you.

ASTROV. I'm in earnest—don't detain me. It was time for me to leave hours ago.

VOINITSKY. Nothing, that's what I took from you.

Both sit down.

ASTROV. Is that so? All right, I'll wait a little longer, and then, sorry, I'll have to use force. We'll tie you up and frisk you. I mean this quite seriously.

VOINITSKY. Whatever you like.

Pause.

To act like such a fool; to shoot twice and miss both times! That's something I'll never forgive myself for!

ASTROV. When the urge to shoot came over you, you should have blown your brains out.

VOINITSKY (*after a shrug*). 'S funny. I attempted murder, but they don't arrest me, they don't put me on trial. Which means they think I'm insane. (*A malicious smile.*) I am insane, and the sane are the ones who pass themselves off as professors, learned sages, to conceal their lack of talent, their obtuseness, their blatant heartlessness. The sane are the ones who marry old men and then cheat on them in broad daylight, I saw, I saw the way you embraced her!

ASTROV. Yes, sir, embraced, sir,[35] what's it to you? (*Thumbs his nose at him.*)

VOINITSKY (*glancing at the door*). No, the earth is insane for supporting you.

ASTROV. Now, that's just stupid.

VOINITSKY. So what, I'm insane, not responsible in the eyes of the law. I have the right to say stupid things.

ASTROV. An old trick. You're not insane, you're just a crackpot. A baggy-pants clown.[36] There was a time when I considered every crackpot to be psychotic, abnormal, but now I'm of the opinion that the normal human condition is to be a crackpot.[37] You're perfectly normal.

VOINITSKY (*covers his face with his hands*). The shame! If you only knew the shame I feel! This stabbing sense of shame can't be compared to any pain there is. (*Plaintively.*) It's unbearable. (*Leans on the table.*) What am I to do? What am I to do?

ASTROV. Not a thing.

VOINITSKY. Give me something! Oh my God . . . I'm forty-seven; suppose I live to be sixty, I still have another thirteen years to get through. A long time! How can I live through those thirteen years! What will I do, how will I fill them? Oh, you understand . . . (*convulsively squeezes Astrov's hand*) you understand, if only one could live out the rest of one's life in a new way somehow. If one could wake up on a bright, still morning and feel that life had begun anew, that all the past is forgotten, has blown away like smoke. (*Weeps.*) To begin a new life . . . Write me a prescription, how to begin . . . where to begin . . .

ASTROV (*annoyed*). Aw, cut it out! What new life! Our condition, yours and mine, is hopeless.

VOINITSKY. Is it?

---

35 Astrov picks up Telegin's affected style of talking.

36 *Gorokhy shut*, literally "a pea-green jester," a generic term for a buffoon, like Shakespeare's "motley fool."

37 Compare Chekhov's notebooks: "He used to consider that a ridiculous crackpot was ill, but now he is of the opinion that it is the normal condition of mankind to be a ridiculous crackpot."

ASTROV. I'm convinced of it.

VOINITSKY. Give me something . . . (*Indicating his heart.*) It's searing inside.

ASTROV (*shouts in anger*). Stop it! (*Assuaging him.*) Those who will live a hundred, two hundred years from now and who will despise us because we lived our lives so stupidly and so gracelessly,—they may find a way to be happy, but we . . . For you and me there's only one hope. The hope that when we lie in our coffins, we'll be haunted by visions, maybe even pleasant ones. (*After a sigh.*) Yes, my boy. In the whole district there were only two decent, cultured men: you and I. But it took no more than ten years for humdrum life, despicable life to drag us down; its pestilential fumes poisoned our blood, and we became just as vulgar as everybody else. (*Vigorously.*) But don't try to charm away the toothache with talking. You give back what you took from me.

VOINITSKY. I didn't take anything from you.

ASTROV. What you took out of my portable medicine chest was a little jar of morphine.

Pause.

Listen, if you insist on putting an end to your life, no matter what, go out in the forest and shoot yourself there. But give back the morphine or else there'll be talk, inquests, they'll think I gave it to you . . . It'll be bad enough having to perform your autopsy . . . You think that'll be interesting?

Enter SONYA.

VOINITSKY. Leave me alone.

ASTROV (*to Sonya*). Sofiya Aleksandrovna, your uncle pilfered a little jar of morphine from my medicine chest and won't give it back. Tell him that it is . . . basically, not an intelligent thing to do.

SONYA. Uncle Vanya, did you take the morphine?

Pause.

ASTROV. He took it. I'm sure of it.

SONYA. Give it back. Why do you terrorize us? (*Tenderly.*) Give it back, Uncle Vanya. I may be just as unhappy as you are, but I don't give in to despair. I am patient and will be patient until my life comes to an end on its own . . . You be patient too.

Pause.

Give it back! (*Kisses his hands.*) Dear, wonderful uncle, dearest, give it back! (*Weeps.*) You're kind, you'll feel sorry for us and give it back. Have patience, uncle! Have patience!

VOINITSKY (*gets a little jar from the table and gives it to Astrov*). Go on, take it! (*To Sonya.*) But we must go to work quickly, do something quickly, or else I can't . . . I can't . . .

SONYA. Yes, yes, to work. As soon as we see them off, we'll get down to work . . . (*Nervously riffles through papers on the table.*) We've let everything go.

ASTROV (*puts the jar in the medicine chest and straps it tightly shut*). Now a man can be on his way.

YELENA ANDREEVNA (*enters*). Ivan Petrovich, you're here? We're leaving right away. Go to Aleksandr, he has something to say to you.

SONYA. Go, Uncle Vanya. (*Takes Voinitsky by the arm.*) Let's go. Papa and you ought to be reconciled. That's absolutely necessary.

SONYA and VOINITSKY leave.

YELENA ANDREEVNA. I'm leaving. (*Gives Astrov her hand.*) Good-bye.

ASTROV. So soon?

YELENA ANDREEVNA. The horses have already been brought round.

ASTROV. Good-bye.

YELENA ANDREEVNA. You promised me today that you would leave here.

ASTROV. I remember. I'm just leaving.

Pause.

Was the lady frightened? (*Takes her by the hand.*) Is this really so terrifying?

YELENA ANDREEVNA. Yes.

ASTROV. Otherwise the lady would have stayed! Ah? Tomorrow in the forest preserve . . .

YELENA ANDREEVNA. No . . . it's been settled . . . And that's why I can look at you so fearlessly, because our departure is definite . . . All I ask of you is: have a higher opinion of me. I would like you to respect me.

ASTROV. Ay! (*Gesture of impatience.*) Do stay, please. Admit it, you've got nothing to do in this world, no purpose in life, nothing to engage your attention, and, sooner or later, make no mistake, you'll give in to your feelings—it's inevitable. So it's far better not to let it happen in Kharkov or somewhere like Kursk but here, in the lap of nature . . . Poetically speaking, at least, autumn is a beautiful season . . . There are forest preserves, half-dilapidated manor houses out of a Turgenev novel . . .[38]

YELENA ANDREEVNA. What a funny man you are . . . I'm angry with you, but still . . . I'll remember you with pleasure. You're an interesting, original person. Never again will we meet, and so—why hide it? I was attracted to you a little . . . Well, let's shake hands and part as friends. Keep a kind thought for me.

ASTROV (*has shaken her hand*). Yes, go away . . . (*Pensively.*) You seem to be a decent, sincere person, but there also seems to be something odd about your basic nature. You and your husband show up, and everyone around here who used to work or putter or create things was compelled to lay aside his work and all summer long concentrate on nothing but your husband's gout and you. The two of you infected all the rest of us with your idleness. I was attracted, did nothing for a whole month, while people were falling ill, peasants grazed their cattle in my forest and stands of young trees . . . And so, wherever you and your husband set foot, destruction follows in your wake . . . I'm joking, of course, but all the same . . . it's odd, and I'm convinced that if you were to stay, the havoc wreaked would be stupendous. I would perish, and you would . . . wouldn't get off scot-free. Well, go away. *Finita la commedia!*[39]

YELENA ANDREEVNA (*takes a pencil from the table and quickly conceals it*). I'll take this pencil to remember you by.

ASTROV. It's kind of strange . . . We were getting to know one another and all of a sudden for no good reason . . . we'll never meet again. It's the way of the world . . . While nobody's here, before Uncle Vanya comes in with a bouquet, let me . . . kiss you . . . As a farewell . . . All right? (*Kisses her on the cheek.*) There now . . . Well done.

---

38 Allusion to such novels of Ivan Turgenev as *A Nest of Gentry*, which were proverbial by Chekhov's time.

39 Italian: "The play is over," an expression Chekhov often used in his letters to mean "it's all played out."

YELENA ANDREEVNA. I wish you the best of everything. (*Looking around.*) Whatever the cost, for once in my life! (*Embraces him impulsively, and both immediately and rapidly move away from one another.*) It's time to go.[40]

ASTROV. Go quickly. Now that the horses have been brought round, you'll be off.

YELENA ANDREEVNA. Here they come, I think.

Both listen hard.

ASTROV. *Finita!*

Enter SEREBRYAKOV, VOINITSKY, MARIYA VASILYEVNA with a book, TELEGIN, and SONYA.

SEREBRYAKOV (*to Voinitsky*). Let the dead past bury its dead.[41] After what has occurred in these last few hours, I have experienced so much and done so much thinking that I believe I could write a whole treatise on the art of living for the edification of posterity. I gladly accept your apologies and in turn ask you to forgive me. Good-bye! (*He and Vanya exchange kisses three times.*)

VOINITSKY. You will punctually receive the same amount as before. Everything will be as it was before.

YELENA ANDREEVNA embraces SONYA.

SEREBRYAKOV (*kisses Mariya Vasilyevna's hand*). Maman . . .

MARIYA VASILYEVNA (*kissing him*). *Alexandre*, have another picture taken and send me your photograph. You know how dear you are to me.

TELEGIN. Good-bye, Your Excellency! Don't forget us!

---

40 On September 30, 1899, Chekhov wrote Olga Knipper:

> At your command, I hasten to answer your letter in which you ask me about Astrov's last scene with Yelena. You write that Astrov addresses Yelena in that scene like the most passionate lover, "clutches at his feeling like a drowning man at a straw." But that's not right, not right at all! Astrov likes Yelena, she captivates him by her beauty, but in the last act he already knows that nothing will come of it, that Yelena is vanishing from him forever—and he talks to her in that scene in the same tone as about the heat in Africa, and kisses her quite casually, with nothing better to do. If Astrov carries on that scene tempestuously, the whole mood of the fourth act—quiet and despondent—will be lost."

41 I have chosen a quotation from Longfellow (from his *Psalm of Life*) to indicate the hackneyed nature of the Professor's remark. In the original Russian, Serebryakov quotes a proverb, "He who bears a grudge should have an eye plucked out."

SEREBRYAKOV (*after kissing his daughter*). Good-bye . . . Good-bye, all! (*Giving his hand to Astrov.*) Thank you for your pleasant company . . . I respect your way of thinking, your enthusiasms, effusions, but allow an old man to add to his valediction this one observation: one must take action, my friends! One must take action! (*Bows all round.*) My very best wishes! (*Exits, followed by MARIYA VASILYEVNA and SONYA.*)

VOINITSKY (*soundly kisses Yelena Andreevna's hand*). Good-bye . . . Forgive me . . . We'll never meet again.

YELENA ANDREEVNA (*moved*). Good-bye, my pet. (*Kisses him on the head and exits.*)

ASTROV (*to Telegin*). Waffles, tell them to bring round my horses too while they're at it.

TELEGIN. Right you are, dear friend. (*Exits.*)

Only ASTROV and VOINITSKY are left.

ASTROV (*takes the paints from the table and stuffs them into his suitcase*). Why don't you go and see them off?

VOINITSKY. Let them go, but I . . . I cannot. I feel depressed. Have to hurry and get involved in something . . . To work, to work! (*Burrows into the papers on the table.*)

Pause. The sound of harness bells.

ASTROV. They're gone. The Professor's relieved, I'll bet. You couldn't lure him back here again for all the tea in China.

MARINA (*enters*). They're gone. (*Sits in the easy chair and knits a stocking.*)

SONYA (*enters*). They're gone. (*Wipes her eyes.*) Pray God it's for the best. (*To Uncle.*) Well, Uncle Vanya, let's do something.

VOINITSKY. To work, to work . . .

SONYA. It's been ever so long since we sat together at this table. (*Lights a lamp on the table.*) There doesn't seem to be any ink . . . (*Takes the inkwell to the cupboard and fills it.*) But I feel down now that they're gone.

MARIYA VASILYEVNA (*enters slowly*). They're gone! (*Sits and gets absorbed in reading.*)

SONYA (*sits at the table and leafs through the ledgers*). First of all, Uncle Vanya, let's write up all the accounts. It's funny the way we've let things go. They sent for a bill again today. Write. You write one bill, I'll do another . . .

VOINITSKY (*writes*). "Account . . . of Mister . . ."

Both write in silence.

MARINA (*yawns*). Beddie-bye for me . . .

ASTROV. Stillness. The pens scratch, the cricket chirps. Warm, cozy . . . I don't feel like leaving here. (*The sound of harness bells.*) There, they've brought the horses . . . All that's left, therefore, is to say good-bye to you, my friends, to say good-bye to my table and — off we go! (*Places the diagram in the portfolio.*)

MARINA. Now what are you fussing for? You should sit a while.

ASTROV. Can't be done.

VOINITSKY (*writes*). "And carried over from the old debt two seventy-five . . ."

Enter the WORKMAN.

WORKMAN. Mikhail Lvovich, the horses are ready.

ASTROV. I heard. (*Gives him the medicine chest, suitcase, and portfolio.*) Here, take this. See that you don't crumple the portfolio.

WORKMAN. Yes, sir. (*Exits.*)

ASTROV. Well, now . . . (*Goes to say good-bye.*)

SONYA. When shall we see you again?

ASTROV. Not until summer, I should think. Hardly this winter . . . Naturally, if anything comes up, let me know — I'll stop by. (*Shakes hands.*) Thanks for the hospitality, the kindness . . . everything, in short. (*Goes to the nanny and kisses her on the head.*) Good-bye, old woman.

MARINA. So you're going without tea?

ASTROV. I don't want any, Nanny old girl.

MARINA. Maybe you'd like a nip of vodka?

ASTROV (*hesitantly*). Could be . . .

MARINA exits.

ASTROV (*after a pause*). For some reason my trace horse[42] started limping. I noticed it again yesterday, when Petrushka was leading him to water.

VOINITSKY. Needs a new shoe.

ASTROV. Have to stop at Rozhdestvennoe and look in at the blacksmith's. Can't be helped . . . (*Walks over to the map of Africa and looks at it.*) I suppose there must be a heat-wave over in Africa right now—something awful!

VOINITSKY. I suppose so.

MARINA (*returning with a saucer holding a shotglass of vodka and a little piece of bread*). Here you are. (*ASTROV drinks the vodka.*) Your health, dearie. (*Bows low.*) But you should have a bit o' bread.

ASTROV. No, this'll do . . . So, the best of everything! (*To Marina.*) Don't see me off, Nanny old girl, there's no need.

He leaves. SONYA follows with a candle to see him off; MARINA sits in her easy chair.

VOINITSKY (*writes*). "February second vegetable oil twenty pounds . . . February sixteenth another twenty pounds vegetable oil . . . buckwheat groats . . ."

Pause. The sound of harness bells.

MARINA. He's gone!

Pause.

SONYA (*returning, puts the candle on the table*). He's gone . . .

VOINITSKY (*checking over the accounts and making notations*). Total . . . fifty . . . twenty-five . . .

SONYA sits and writes.

MARINA (*yawns*). Uh, bless us sinners . . .

---

42 A troika consists of three horses harnessed together; the two harnessed by straps or traces to the outside shafts are called trace horses.

*TELEGIN tiptoes in, sits by the door, and quietly strums
the guitar.*

VOINITSKY (*to Sonya, running his hand through her hair*). Dearest child,
how hard it is! Oh, how hard it is!

SONYA. What can be done, we have to go on living!

Pause.

Uncle Vanya, we will go on living. We will live through a long, long series
of days, no end of evenings; we will patiently bear the ordeals that Fate sends
us; we will labor for others both now and in our old age, knowing no rest,
but when our time comes, we will die meekly and beyond the grave we will
tell how we suffered, how we wept, how bitter we felt, and God will take
pity on us, and you and I, Uncle Vanya, dear Uncle, shall see a life bright,
beautiful, exquisite, we shall rejoice and look upon our present unhappiness with forbearance, with a smile—and we'll be at peace.[43] I believe,
Uncle, I believe intensely, passionately . . . (*Kneels before him and lays her
head on his hands; in a weary voice.*) We'll be at peace!

TELEGIN quietly plays the guitar.

We'll be at peace! We shall hear the angels, we shall see heaven all diamonds, we shall see how all earthly woes, all our suffering will be sub-
merged in a compassion that will fill up the world, and our life will grow
serene, tender, sweet as a caress. I believe, believe . . . (*Wipes his tears
away with a handkerchief.*) Poor, poor Uncle Vanya, you're crying . . .
(*Through tears.*) You've known no joy in your life, but wait, Uncle Vanya,
wait . . . We'll be at peace . . . (*Embraces him.*) We'll be at peace!

The WATCHMAN taps.

*TELEGIN quietly goes on playing; MARIYA VASILYEVNA
writes in the margin of a pamphlet; MARINA knits a stocking.*

We'll be at peace!

Curtain slowly falls.

---

43 The Russian, *My otdokhnyom,* connotes, "We shall breathe easily" and is connected etymologically to words such as *dushno,* used by characters to say they are being stifled. The literal English
translation, "We shall rest," with its harsh dental ending, fails to convey Sonya's meaning sonically
or spiritually.

VARIANT TO

Uncle Vanya

Lines come from *Plays* (1897).

ACT ONE

page 829 / *After*: My time's up —
VOINITSKY (*to Yelena Andreevna*). He doesn't eat meat either.
ASTROV. Yes, I consider it a sin to kill living things.

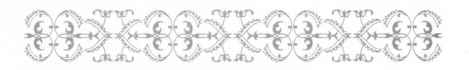

THREE SISTERS

At the urging of the Moscow Art Theatre, Chekhov set out to write them a play. With specific actors in mind for given roles, and mindful, too, of the Art Theatre's strengths, Chekhov spent more time in the composition of *Three Sisters* than on any of his earlier dramas. He was especially anxious to cut out superfluities in monologues and provide a sense of movement.

Unfortunately, when the Art Theatre actors heard the author read the play for the first time, in October 1900, they were sorely disappointed. "This is no play, it's only an outline" was the immediate reaction. Chekhov sedulously reworked all of it and in the process added many striking touches. The ironic counterpoint of Tusenbach's and Chebutykin's remarks in Acts One and Four, most of Solyony's pungent lines, Masha's quotation from *Ruslan and Lyudmila* about the curved seashore were added at this stage. It is amazing to think that only in revising the play did Chekhov decide to leave Masha on stage for the final tableau. He sat in on the early rehearsals and insisted that a colonel be in attendance to instruct the actors in proper military deportment; he personally orchestrated the fire-bell sound effects for Act Three. He put the greatest emphasis on that act, which, he insisted, must be performed quietly and wearily.

Three Sisters opened on January 31, 1901, with Stanislavsky as Vershinin, Olga Knipper as Masha, and the young Vsevolod Meyerhold as Tusenbach. Although many critics were put off by the play's seeming hopelessness and what struck them as vague motivation in the characters, the production was acclaimed by the public. "It's music, not acting," asserted Maksim Gorky.[1]

The writer Leonid Andreev attended the thirtieth performance, despite a friend's warning that its effect would be suicidally depressing. Quite against expectation, he found himself totally drawn into the play by the middle of Act One. No longer appraising the scenery or the actors, he became convinced that "the story of the three sisters . . . is not a fiction, not a fantasy, but a fact, an event, something every bit as real as stock options at the Savings Bank." By the end, he, with the rest of the audience, was in tears, but his dominant impression was not pessimistic. For Andreev, the residual effect, the pervasive mood, the play's basic "tragic melody" was a yearning for life. "Like steam, life can be compressed into a narrow little container, but, also like steam, it will endure pressure only to a certain point. And in *Three Sisters*, this pressure is brought to the limit, beyond which it will explode, — and don't you actually hear how life is seething, doesn't its angrily protesting voice reach your ears?"[2]

This reaction was due in part to the play's early run coinciding with student riots. Consequently, the characters' aspirations were identified with topical political protest. It was due as well to the theater's remarkably veristic production and its careful transmission of mood. Eventually, theatergoers would say not that they were going to the Art Theatre to view *Three Sisters* but that they were "paying a call on the Prozorovs." Chekhov's technique provided the premise for this illusion of reality.

This is the first time Chekhov employs a broad canvas devoid of exclusively foreground figures—no Ivanovs, not even Treplyovs or Vanyas. The sisters must share their space, in every sense, with Natasha, Tusenbach, and Solyony. There are no more soliloquys: almost never is a character left alone on stage. Andrey must pour out his discontents to deaf Ferapont, and Masha must proclaim her adulterous love to the stopped-up ears of her sister Olga. Têtes-à-têtes are of the briefest: no more Trigorin spinning out a description of a writer's career or Astrov explicating maps to a prospective paramour. Vershinin and Tusenbach spout their speeches about work and the future to a room full of auditors.

Those rhetorical paeans have been cited as Utopian alternatives to the dreary provincial life depicted on stage. True, the men who formulate them are ineffectual, with no chance of realizing their "thick-coming fantasies." But the monologues do work as a meliorative element. Unable in a play to use the narrative to offer a contrasting vision, Chekhov must put into the mouths of his characters visions of an improved life. The imagery of birds of passage, birch trees, flowing rivers sounds a note of freshness and harmony that highlights all the more acutely the characters' inability to get in touch with the spontaneous and the natural. The cranes are programmed to fly, "and whatever thoughts, sublime or trivial, drift through their heads, they'll go on flying, not knowing what for or where to."

The most blatant call for an alternative is the sisters' recurrent plaint, "To Moscow, to Moscow!" Almost from the play's premiere, critics wondered what was stopping the Prozorovs from buying a ticket to the big city. Moscow is an imaginary site, envisaged differently by each character. Andrey sees it not only as a university town but as the site of great restaurants, while for old Ferapont it marks the locale of a legendary pancake feast. Vershinin gloomily recalls a grim bridge and roaring water there, Solyony has invented a second university for it, and Olga looks back to a funeral. No clear image emerges from the medley of impressions, so that Moscow remains somewhere over the rainbow, just out of sight.

Because the sisters are fixated on this distant point, commentators and directors have regularly inflated them into heroines. Too frequently, the play is reduced to a conflict between three superwomen and a ravening bitch: the sensitive and high-strung Prozorov sorority can be no match for the ruthless life force embodied in Natasha, and so they succumb, albeit preserving their ideals. This common interpretation is not borne out by a close examination of the play, which Chekhov said had *four* heroines. As the Romanian critic Jovan Hristić has shrewdly noted, the three of the title are "true spiritual sisters of Hedda Gabler, who corrupt everything around them by dint of thinking themselves superior."[3] The analogy works on several levels, from the military upbringing (Masha's scorn of civilians is bitter) to the ultimate downfall, engineered partly by an instinctual bourgeoise (Natasha for Thea Elvsted), second-rate academics (Andrey and Kulygin for Tesman), and inept idealists (Vershinin and Tusenbach for Løvborg). Like Hedda, the three sisters are at variance with their environment, which, for them, represents common vulgarity.

The play maps the town's encroachment on their lives, as Olga becomes embedded in the educational hierarchy, Irina turns into a cog in the civil bureaucracy, Andrey a fixture on the County Council, and Masha a recalcitrant faculty wife. By the last act, the stage direction informs us that their backyard has become a kind of empty lot, across which the townsfolk tramp when necessary. It is the next step after the fire, when the townsfolk invaded their home and bore off their old clothes. And, of course, Natasha's depredations and that of her lover and the town's de facto head, the unseen Protopopov, began earliest of all.

To protect themselves against this encroachment, the sisters have erected a paling of culture, and within it, they have invited the military. For once, Chekhov does not use outsiders as a disruptive force; for the sisters, the soldiers spell color, excitement, life. But the factitiousness of this glamour quickly becomes apparent: a peacetime army is a symbol of idleness and pointless expense. Men trained to fight while away their time philosophizing and playing the piano, teaching gymnastics and reading the paper, carrying on backstairs love affairs and fighting duels. The sisters have pinned their hopes on a regiment of straw men. It is hard to determine who is the weakest: Vershinin, forecasting future happiness while unable to cope with his psychotic wife; Tusenbach, whose noble sentiments are belied by his unprepossessing looks and unassertive manner; or Solyony, veering crazily between blustering egotism and crippling introspection. These are carpet knights, suitable for dressing out a party but not for salvaging anyone's life. That the sisters should make such a fuss about them reveals at once the irreality of their values.

If culture, in the sense of refined feelings revealed through sensitivity and a cultivated understanding of art, is the touchstone for the Prozorovs, it will not sustain scrutiny either. The Prozorov family prides itself on the Russian intellectual's virtues of political awareness, social commitment, and artistic discrimination, and judges others by them. Many of the major characters are connected with the educational system. When tested by the realities of life, however, the fabric of their culture soon falls to pieces. They and their circle cling to the shreds and patches—Latin tags for Kulygin, quotations from Russian classics for Masha and Solyony, amateur music-making. Andrey's "sawing away" at the violin and Masha's untested prowess at the keyboard are mocked in the last act by Natasha's offstage rendition of the "Maiden's Prayer." Irina grieves that she cannot remember the Italian for window, as if a foreign vocabulary could buoy her up in a sea of despair. Solyony poses as the romantic poet Lermontov, but his behavior shows him to be more like Martynov, the bully who killed Lermontov in a duel. During the fire, it is Natasha who must remind Olga of the cultured person's duty "to help the poor, it's an obligation of the rich." Philosophizing (always a pejorative word for Chekhov) passes for thought, newspaper filler passes for knowledge, a superior attitude passes for delicacy of feeling, yet everyone's conduct sooner or later dissolves into rudeness or immorality.

Three Sisters does not simply demonstrate how three gifted women were defeated by a philistine environment, but rather how their unhappiness is of their own making. If they are subjugated and evicted by the Natashas of this world, it is because they have not recognized and dealt with their own shortcomings. At one point or another, each of the sisters is as callous and purblind as Natasha herself. Olga cattily criticizes Natasha's dress sense at a party, although she has been told that the girl is shy in company; in Act Three she refuses to listen to Masha's avowal of love, will not face facts. Her very removal to a garret is as much avoidance of involvement as it is an exile imposed by Natasha. Irina is remarkably unpleasant to both her suitors, Tusenbach and Solyony; as a telegraph clerk she is brusque with a grieving mother, and at the very last refuses to say the few words of love that might lighten the Baron's final moments, even though, as Chekhov informed Olga Knipper, she is prescient of the impending catastrophe. Masha swears like a trooper, drinks, abuses the old nanny nearly as badly and with less excuse than Natasha does. Her flagrant adultery with Vershinin may ultimately be more destructive than Natasha's with Protopopov, for Kulygin genuinely loves his wife, whereas Andrey tries to forget he has one.

This litany of faults is not meant to blacken the sisters or to exonerate Natasha, Solyony, and the others. It is meant to redress the balance: Chekhov selects the Prozorov family (who, along with the officers, were based on acquaintances) to sum up a way of life. With all the benefits of education, a loving home, and creature comforts, the sisters stagnate, not simply because they live in the sticks but because they keep deferring any activity that might give meaning to their existence. The ennobling labor that Tusenbach and Vershinin rhapsodize over, that inspires Irina, seems to have nothing in common with doing a job every day. Olga's teaching, Irina's work at the Council and the telegraph office, the position at the mines to which Tusenbach retires offer a prospect of meaningless drudgery.

The prevalent state of mind is to be "sick and tired" (*nadoelo*). In his brief moment alone with Masha in Act Two, Vershinin blames the average local educated Russian for being "sick and tired of his wife, sick and tired of his estate, sick and tired of his horses"; but he is clearly characterizing himself, for he soon draws a picture of his own wretched marriage. Masha, whom Vershinin would exempt as an exceptional person, is "sick and tired of winter," and when her husband proclaims his love with "I'm content, I'm content, I'm content!" she bitterly spits back, "I'm sick and tired, sick and tired, sick and tired." Even the genteel Olga pronounces herself "sick and tired" of the fire. The unanimous response to this spiritual malaise is a commonplace fatalism. Chebutykin's dismissive "It doesn't matter" (*Vsyo ravno*) is echoed by most of the characters. Vershinin quotes it when denying differences between the military and civilians; Tusenbach describes his resignation from the army in those words; Solyony denigrates his love for Irina with the phrase. According to Irina, Andrey's debts "don't matter" to Natasha. This deliberate insouciance is the counterbalance to the equally deliberate velleities about the future.

To represent the slow disintegration of these lives, *Three Sisters* unfolds over a longer period of time than any of Chekhov's other plays. It begins on the fifth of May, Irina's twentieth nameday, and ends in autumn, four years later. The characters talk incessantly about time, from the very first line. The passage of time is denoted by such obvious tokens as Natasha's growing children, Andrey's problem with overweight and debts, Olga's promotions. However, this is more than a family chronicle. Chekhov insists on the subjectivity of time. Each act indicates that what had gone before is now irrevocably swallowed up, not lost simply in the distant past, but in what had been yesterday. The youth in Moscow, aglow with promise, to which the sisters retrospect is tarnished by their initial response to its witness, Vershinin: "Oh, how you've aged!" The party in Act One is spoken of in Act Two, a few months later, as if it belonged to a bygone Golden Age. By Act Three, Tusenbach is referring to it as "Back in those days." Time measures the increasing negativity of life; it has been two years since the doctor took a drink, three years since Masha played the piano, or maybe four. It's been a long time since Andrey played cards—that is, the few months since Act Two. If time passes in a steady process of diminution, perspectives into the future are not enough to replace the losses. Chebutykin smashes a valuable clock, demolishing time, but his chiming watch in the last act continues to announce fresh departures.

Setting up markers for time, Chekhov constructs each act around a special event that catalyzes routine responses and sticks in the memory. Irina's name-day celebration serves a number of dramatic functions: it commemorates a date, assembles all the characters in one place, and is the highwater mark for the sisters' hopes. It is the last time we see them as sole mistresses in their own domain: each of them is on the verge of a promising situation. Coming of age opens the world to Irina; the arrival of Vershinin enlivens Masha; and Olga still enjoys teaching. The Shrovetide party in Act Two is in sharp contrast: it takes place after dark, with several habitués absent (Olga and Kulygin must work late, Vershinin is delayed by his wife's suicide attempt). Twice the party is broken up by the usurper Natasha, from whom no masqueraders are forthcoming any more than carriage horses were from Shamraev in *The Seagull*. Finally, the revelers realize that amusement must now be sought outside this home.

The eating at these events, a metaphor for shared experience, disintegrates as the play proceeds. Act One has ended with the cast gathered around the table, regaling themselves with roast turkey, apple pie, and too much vodka. The odd men out were Natasha and Andrey, furtively conducting their romance at a remove from the teasing family. In Act Two, however, Natasha is now seated at the festive board, criticizing the table manners of others and withholding tea; Solyony has eaten up all the chocolates. Once she gains a foothold, the indiscriminate feeding ends. Vershinin goes hungry.

The fire in Act Three is a real *coup de théâtre*: physical danger, mass hysteria and crowd movement, though kept offstage, have forced the characters into their present situation, both locally and emotionally. Like Andreev's image of steam rising in a boiler, they gradually are forced upward into the compressed space beneath the eaves. Even though the conflagration does not singe the Prozorov house, it creates this thermodynamic effect. Exhausted or drunk, in some way pushed to an extreme by the calamity, the characters pour out their feelings and then leave. It is the most hysterical of all the acts and the most confessional. To no avail does Olga protest, "I'm not listening, I'm not listening!" Unlike purifying fires in Ibsen and Strindberg, this blaze leaves the sisters uncleansed, as their world is rapidly being consumed. Amidst the desolation, they are simply charred.

Once again, Chekhov constrains his characters to come in contact by preventing privacy. One would expect the bedroom of an old-maid schoolmarm and a young virgin to be the most sacrosanct of chambers, but a concatenation of circumstances turns it into Grand Central Station, from which intruders like Solyony and Chebutykin must be forcibly ejected. The space is intimate, just right for playing out personal crises; but the secrets are made to detonate in public. The doctor's drunken creed of nihilism, Andrey's exasperation with his wife, Masha's blurting out of her adultery become public events.

Or else the private moment is neutralized by submersion in minutiae. Masha makes up her mind to elope with Vershinin. Traditionally, this would be a major dramatic turning point, the crux when the heroine undergoes her peripeteia. Here, the decision is muffled by plans for a charity recital, Tusenbach's snoring, and other people's personal problems. The chance tryst offered by the fire trivializes Masha's and Vershinin's love because it projects it against a background of civic crisis. Even their love song has been reduced to "trom-tom-tom," humming a theme from an operatic aria. What is crucial to some characters is always irrelevant or unknown to others, much as the seagull had been. As Chebutykin says, "It doesn't matter." Chekhov, however, does not insist on the impossibility of values and communication; he simply believes that the attribution of value is hard for myopic mortals to make.

The last act adjusts the angle of vantage. There is very little recollection in it, but a good deal of futile straining toward the future. A brief time has elapsed between Act Three, when the regiment's departure is offhandedly mentioned, and Act Four, when it takes place. The departure is so abrupt an end to the sisters' consoling illusion that they cannot bring themselves to allude to the past. Henceforth they will be thrown on their own resources. The play had begun with them lording it over the drawing room, but now they are cast into the yard. Olga lives at the school, Masha refuses to go into the house, Andrey wanders around with the baby carriage like a soul in limbo.

Food has lost its ability to comfort. The Baron must go off to his death without his morning coffee, while Andrey equates goose and cabbage with the deadly grip of matrimony. Each movement away is accompanied by music: the regiment leaves to the cheerful strains of a marching band, the piano tinkles to the cozy domesticity of Natasha and Protopopov, and the Doctor mockingly sings "Tarara boom de-ay." The bereft sisters standing in the yard are made to seem out of tune.

The final tableau, with the sisters clinging to one another, intoning "If only we knew, if only we knew," has been played optimistically, as if the dawn of a bright tomorrow did lie just beyond the horizon. But Olga's evocation of time to come has lost the rosy tinge of Vershinin's and Tusenbach's improvisation. Like Sonya's threnody in *Uncle Vanya*, it is whistling in the dark, predicting a void that must be filled. The disillusionment of the four hours' traffic on the stage and the four years' passage of time has aged the sisters but not enlightened them. They still, in William Blake's words, "nurse unacted desires." The music-hall chorus Chebutykin sings had lyrics (which would have been known to everyone in the original audience): "I'm sitting on a curbstone / And weeping bitterly / Because I know so little." The implied mockery shows Olga's "If only we knew" to be an absurd wish. Chekhov's antiphony of Olga and Chebutykin carols the impossibility of such awareness, and the need to soldier on, despite that disability.

NOTES

1 Maksim Gorky, *Sobranie sochineniya* (Moscow: Akademiya Nauk SSR, 1958), XXVIII, 159.

2 Leonid Andreev, "Tri sestry," *Polnoe sobranie sochineny* (St. Petersburg: A. F. Marks, 1913), VI, 321–25.

3 Jovan Hristić, *Le théâtre de Tchékhov*, trans. Harita Wybrands and Francis Wybrands (Lausanne: L'Âge d'homme, 1982), p. 166.

THREE SISTERS

Три сестры

A Drama in Four Acts

CAST OF CHARACTERS [1]

PROZOROV, ANDREY SERGEEVICH

NATALIYA IVANOVNA, *his fiancée, afterwards his wife*

OLGA

MASHA — *his sisters*

IRINA

KULYGIN, FYODOR ILYICH, *high school teacher, Masha's husband*

VERSHININ, ALEKSANDR IGNATYEVICH, *Lieutenant Colonel,
battery commander*

TUSENBACH, NIKOLAY LVOVICH, *Baron, Lieutenant*

SOLYONY, VASILY VASILYEVICH, *Staff Captain*

CHEBUTYKIN, IVAN ROMANOVICH, *army doctor*

FEDOTIK, ALEKSEY PETROVICH, *Second Lieutenant*

RODÉ,[2] VLADIMIR KARLOVICH, *Second Lieutenant*

FERAPONT, *messenger for the County Council,[3] an old timer*

ANFISA, *nanny, an old woman of 80*

---

1 There are fewer "speaking names" in this play than in the others. Ironically, Prozorov suggests "insight, perspicuity," and Vershinin "heights, summit." Solyony means "salty." The name of the unseen Protopopov hints at descent from a line of archpriests.

2 Chekhov may have taken this unusual name from a well-known family of balalaika players and dancers, who came to prominence in the 1880s.

3 *Zemskaya uprava,* the permanent executive council of the *zemstvo,* or Rural Board, elected from among the members, and not unlike a cabinet in its operations. For *zemstvo,* see *Ivanov,* First Version, note 3.

The action takes place in a county seat.[4]

ACT ONE

In the Prozorovs' home. A drawing-room with columns, behind which a large reception room can be seen. Midday: outside it's sunny and bright.[5] *In the reception room a table is being set for lunch.*

OLGA, wearing the dark blue uniform of a teacher at a high-school for girls,[6] *never stops correcting students' examination books, both standing still and on the move. MASHA, in a black dress, her hat in her lap, sits reading a book. IRINA, in a white dress, stands rapt in thought.*

OLGA. Father died just a year ago, this very day, the fifth of May, your saint's day,[7] Irina. It was very cold, snowing, in fact. I never thought I'd live through it, you had fainted dead away. But a year's gone by now, and we don't mind thinking about it, you're back to wearing white, your face is beaming. (*The clock strikes twelve.*) The clock struck then too. I remember, when Father was carried to his grave, there was music playing, they fired a salute at the cemetery. He was a general, commanded a whole brigade, but

---

4 The capital of the *guberniya* and hence the seat of the regional government.

5 According to V. V. Luzhsky:

> In *Three Sisters* on the rise of the curtain, as Stanislavsky's concept has it, birds are singing. These sounds were usually produced by Stanislavsky himself, A. L. Vishnevsky, I. M. Moskvin, V. F. Gribunin, N. G. Aleksandrov, and I, standing in the wings and cooing like doves. [Chekhov] listened to all these shenanigans and, walking over to me, said: "Listen, you bill and coo wonderfully, only it's an Egyptian dove!" And of the portrait of the sisters' father—General Prozorov (me in the makeup of an old general) he remarked, "Listen, that's a Japanese general, we don't have that kind in Russia."
>
> (*Solntse Rossii* 228/25 [1914])

6 Olga and Kulygin teach at a *gymnasium,* or four-year high school, open to all classes of society; in 1876, to slow down the upward mobility of the lower classes, a heavy dose of Latin, Greek, and Old Church Slavonic replaced the more dangerous subjects of history, literature, and geography in the extremely rigorous curriculum. Hence Kulygin's frequent citations from the classics.

7 Also known as a name day. Orthodox Russians celebrate the day of the saint after whom a person was named more commonly than they celebrate the person's birthday. St. Irina's day is May 5 in the Orthodox calendar.

very few people showed up. Of course, it was raining at the time. Pelting rain and snow too.

IRINA. Why remember?

> *Behind the columns, in the reception room near the table,*
> *BARON TUSENBACH, CHEBUTYKIN, and*
> *SOLYONY appear.*

OLGA. Today it's warm, the windows can be thrown open, and the birch trees aren't even budding yet. Father was put in charge of a brigade and we all left Moscow eleven years ago, and I distinctly remember, it was early May, why, just this time of year, everything in Moscow would already be in bloom, warm, everything would be bathed in sunlight. Eleven years have gone by, but I can remember everything there, as if we'd left yesterday. Oh my goodness! I woke up this morning, saw the light pouring in, the spring-time, and joy began to quicken in my heart, I began to long passionately for my beloved home.

CHEBUTYKIN. To hell with both of you!

TUSENBACH. You're right, it's ridiculous.

> *MASHA, brooding over her book, quietly whistles a tune under*
> *her breath.*[8]

OLGA. Don't whistle, Masha. How can you!

> *Pause.*

Because I'm at the high school all day long and then have to give tutorials well into the night, I've got this constant headache, and my thoughts are those of an old woman. As a matter of fact, the four years I've been working at the high school, I've felt as if every day my strength and youth were draining from me drop by drop. While that same old dream keeps growing bigger and stronger . . .

IRINA. To go to Moscow. To sell the house, wind up everything here and — go to Moscow . . .

---

8 "Don't pull a sorrowful face in any of the acts. Angry, yes, but not sorrowful. People who go about with inner sorrow a long time and are used to it only whistle and often grow pensive. So you may every so often grow pensive on stage in the course of the dialogue" (Chekhov to Olga Knipper, January 2 [15], 1901).

OLGA. Yes! Quick as you can to Moscow.

CHEBUTYKIN and TUSENBACH laugh.

IRINA. Brother will probably become a professor, he certainly won't go on living here. The only thing holding us back is our poor old Masha.

OLGA. Masha will come and spend all summer in Moscow, every year.

MASHA quietly whistles a tune.

IRINA. God willing, everything will work out. (*Looking out the window.*) Lovely weather today. I don't know why my heart feels so light! This morning I remembered that it was my saint's day, and suddenly I felt so happy, and remembered my childhood, when Mama was still alive. And such wonderful thoughts ran through my head, such thoughts!

OLGA. You're simply radiant today, you look especially pretty. And Masha's pretty too. Andrey'd be good looking, only he's putting on too much weight, and it doesn't suit him. And I'm aging just a bit and getting terribly thin, I suppose because I get cross with the girls at school. Well, today I'm free, I'm home, and my head doesn't ache, I feel younger than I did yesterday. I'm only twenty-eight . . . Everything is for the best, everything is God's will, but I do think that if I were married and could stay home all day, things might be better.

Pause.

I'd love my husband.

TUSENBACH (*to Solyony*). You talk such rubbish, a person gets sick and tired just listening to you. (*Entering the drawing-room.*) I forgot to mention. Today you'll be getting a visit from our new battery commander Vershinin. (*Sits at the baby grand piano.*)

OLGA. Is that so? That'll be nice.

IRINA. Is he old?

TUSENBACH. No, not really. Forty at most, forty-five. (*Quietly plays by ear.*) A splendid fellow, by all accounts. And no fool, that's for sure. Only he does talk a lot.

IRINA. Is he interesting?

TUSENBACH. Yes, so-so, but he's got a wife, a mother-in-law, and two little girls. His second wife at that. He goes visiting and tells everybody that he's got a wife and two little girls. He'll tell it here too. The wife's some kind of half-wit, with a long braid, like a schoolgirl, only talks about highfalutin stuff, philosophy, and she makes frequent attempts at suicide, apparently in order to give her husband a hard time. I would have left a woman like that ages ago, but he puts up with it and settles for complaining.

SOLYONY (*entering the drawing-room from the reception room with CHEBU-TYKIN*). With one hand I can't lift more than fifty pounds, but with both it goes up to two hundred pounds. Which leads me to conclude that two men are not twice as strong as one, but three times as strong, even stronger . . .

CHEBUTYKIN (*reads the paper as he walks*). For loss of hair . . . eight and a half grams of naphthalene in half a bottle of grain alcohol . . . dissolve and apply daily . . .[9] (*Makes a note in a memo book.*) Let's jot that down, shall we! (*To Solyony.*) Listen, as I was saying, you stick a tiny little cork in a tiny little bottle, and pass a tiny little glass tube through it . . . Then you take a tiny little pinch of the most common, ordinary alum . . .

IRINA. Ivan Romanych, dear Ivan Romanych!

CHEBUTYKIN. What, my darling girl, light of my life?

IRINA. Tell me, why am I so happy today? I feel as if I'm skimming along at full sail, with the wide blue sky above me and big white birds drifting by. Why is that? Why?

CHEBUTYKIN (*kissing both her hands, tenderly*). My own white bird . . .

IRINA. When I woke up today, I got out of bed and washed, and suddenly it dawned on me that I understand everything in the world and I know how a person ought to live. Dear Ivan Romanych, I know everything. A person has to work hard, work by the sweat of his brow, no matter who he is, and that's the only thing that gives meaning and purpose to his life, his happiness, his moments of ecstasy. Wouldn't it be wonderful to be a manual

---

9 Letter of Olga Knipper to Chekhov (September 12, 1900): "I'm going to give you a wonderful remedy to keep hair from falling out. Take ½ bottle of methylated spirits and mix in 8 grams of naphtalin and rub it in regularly—it's a big help. Will you do it? Because it's not a good idea to come to Moscow bald—people will think I pulled your hair out."

laborer who gets up while it's still dark out and breaks stones on the road, or a shepherd, or a schoolteacher, or an engineer on the railroad . . . My God, what's the point of being human, you might as well be an ox, an ordinary horse, so long as you're working, rather than a young woman who gets up at noon, has her coffee in bed, and takes two hours to dress . . . oh, isn't that awful! Sometimes when the weather's sultry, the way you long for a drink, well, that's the way I long for work. And if I don't get up early and work hard, stop being my friend, Ivan Romanych.

CHEBUTYKIN (*tenderly*). I will, I will . . .

OLGA. Father drilled us to get up at seven. Nowadays Irina wakes up at seven and stays in bed at least till nine, thinking about things. And the serious face on her! (*Laughs.*)

IRINA. You're used to treating me like a little girl, so you think it's strange when I put on a serious face. I'm twenty years old!

TUSENBACH. The longing for hard work, oh dear, how well I understand it! I've never worked in my life. I was born in Petersburg, cold, idle Petersburg, to a family that didn't know the meaning of hard work or hardship. I remember, whenever I came home from school, a lackey would pull off my boots, while I'd fidget and my mother would gaze at me in adoration and be surprised when anyone looked at me any other way. They tried to shield me from hard work. And they just about managed it, only just! The time has come, there's a thundercloud looming over us, there's a bracing, mighty tempest lying in wait, close at hand, and soon it will blow all the indolence, apathy, prejudice against hard work, putrid boredom out of our society. I shall work, and in twenty-five or thirty years everyone will be working. Every last one of us!

CHEBUTYKIN. I won't work.

TUSENBACH. You don't count.

SOLYONY. In twenty-five years you won't be on this earth, thank God. In two or three years you'll die of apoplexy, or I'll fly off the handle and put a bullet through your brain, angel mine. (*Takes a flask of perfume from his pocket and sprinkles his chest and hands.*)

CHEBUTYKIN (*laughs*). As a matter of fact, I've never done a thing. Ever since I left the university, I haven't lifted a finger, not even read a book, nothing but newspapers . . . (*Takes from his pocket a second newspaper.*) You see . . . I know by the papers that there was, let's say, somebody named Dobrolyubov,[10] but what he wrote—I don't know . . . God knows . . . (*Someone can be heard knocking on the floor from a lower story.*) There . . . They're calling for me downstairs, someone's come for me. I'll be right there . . . hold on . . . . (*Leaves hurriedly, combing his beard.*)

IRINA. This is something he's cooked up.

TUSENBACH. Yes. He went out with a look of triumph on his face, I'll bet he's about to deliver a present.

IRINA. How unpleasant!

OLGA. Yes, it's awful. He's always doing something silly.

MASHA. "On the curved seashore a green oak stands, a golden chain wound round that oak . . . A golden chain wound round that oak . . ."[11] (*Rises and hums quietly.*)

OLGA. You're in a funny mood today, Masha. (*MASHA, humming, adjusts her hat.*) Where are you off to?

MASHA. Home.

IRINA. Strange . . .

TUSENBACH. Leaving a saint's day party!

MASHA. Doesn't matter. . I'll be back this evening. Good-bye, my dearest . . . (*Kisses Irina.*) Best wishes once more, good health, be happy. In the old days, when Father was alive, every time we celebrated a saint's day some thirty or forty officers would show up, there was lots of noise, but today there's only a man and a half, and it's as desolate as a desert . . . I'm off . . .

---

10 Nikolay Aleksandrovich Dobrolyubov (1836–1861), Russian journalist of the radical democratic camp and proponent of realistic literature. He invented the concept of the "superfluous man."

11 Masha is quoting from the opening lines of the famous poetic fable *Ruslan and Lyudmila*, by Aleksandr Pushkin, a classic love story. On her wedding night, Lyudmila is abducted by a wizard and Ruslan finds her only after many adventures. The lines are: "On the curved seashore a green oak stands, / A golden chain wound round that oak; / And night and day a learned cat / Walks round and round upon that chain. / When he goes right a song he sings, / When he goes left a tale he tells." An English equivalent might be Edward Lear's " The owl and the pussy-cat went to sea, In a beautiful pea-green boat . . . A beautiful pea-green boat . . ."

I'm melancholeric[12] today, I don't feel very cheerful, and you musn't mind me. (*Laughs through tears.*) Later we'll have a talk, but good-bye for now, my darling, I'm off.

IRINA (*put out*). Well, that's just like you . . .

OLGA (*plaintively*). I understand you, Masha.

SOLYONY. If a man philosophizes, you could call it philosophistry or even sophisticuffs, but if a woman philosophizes or two women, that you could call—Polly want a cracker!

MASHA. What do you mean by that, you dreadfully awful man?

SOLYONY. Not a thing. "He scarcely had time to gasp, When the bear had him in its grasp."[13]

Pause.

MASHA (*to Olga, angrily*). Stop sniveling!

Enter ANFISA and FERAPONT with a layer cake.

ANFISA. Over here, dearie. Come on in, your feet're clean. (*To Irina.*) From the County Council, from Protopopov, from Mikhail Ivanych . . . A cake.

IRINA. Thank you. Thank him. (*Takes the cake.*)

FERAPONT. How's that?

IRINA (*louder*). Thank him!

OLGA. Nanny dear, give him some pie. Ferapont, go on, out there they'll give you some pie.

FERAPONT. How's that?

ANFISA. Let's go, dearie, Ferapont Spiridonych. Let's go . . . (*Exits with FERAPONT.*)

---

12 *Merlekhyundiya*, instead of *melankholiya.* A favorite word of Chekhov's, often used in private correspondence, as well as in "The Examining Magistrate" and *Ivanov.* " . . . your nerves are in bad shape and you're under the sway of a psychiatric semi-ailment, which seminarians calls melancholera" (to A. A. Suvorin, August 23, 1893).

13 Quotation from the fable "The Peasant and the Farmhand," by Ivan Krylov (1768–1844), which Chekhov also quotes in the story "Among Friends" (1898): "He had a habit, unsettling for his interlocutor, of pronouncing as an exclamation a certain phrase which had no relation to the conversation, while snapping his fingers."

MASHA. I do not like Protopopov, that bear bearing gifts. It isn't right to invite him.

IRINA. I didn't invite him.

MASHA. Good girl.

> Enter CHEBUTYKIN, *followed by a soldier carrying a silver*
> *samovar; a low murmur of astonishment and displeasure.*

OLGA (*hides her face in her hands*). A samovar! How dreadfully inappropriate.[14] (*Goes to the table in the reception room.*)

IRINA. Ivan Romanych, you darling, what are you doing!

TUSENBACH (*laughs*). I told you so.   — *Together*

MASHA. Ivan Romanych, you're simply shameless!

CHEBUTYKIN. My dears, my darlings, you're the only ones I have, for me you're more precious than anything on this earth. I'll be sixty soon, I'm an old man, a lonely, insignificant old man . . . There's nothing good about me, except this love for you, and if it weren't for you, I'd be dead and gone long ago . . . (*To Irina.*) My dearest child, I've known you since the day you were born . . . I held you in my arms . . . I loved your poor mama . . .

IRINA. But why such expensive presents?

CHEBUTYKIN (*through tears, angrily*). Expensive presents . . . You're the limit! (*To the orderly.*) Put the samovar over there . . . (*Mimics.*) Expensive presents . . . (*The orderly takes the samovar into the reception room.*)

ANFISA (*crossing the drawing-room*). My dears, a strange colonel! He's already took off his overcoat, boys and girls, he's coming in here. Arinushka, now you be a charming, polite little girl . . . (*Going out.*) Lunch should have been served a long time ago now . . . Honest to goodness . . .

TUSENBACH. Vershinin, I suppose.

> *Enter VERSHININ.*

Lieutenant Colonel Vershinin.

---

14 A samovar was traditionally given by a husband to his wife on their silver or golden anniversary.

VERSHININ (*to Masha and Irina*). May I introduce myself: Vershinin.[15] Very, very pleased to meet you at long last. How you've grown! My! my!

IRINA. Do sit down, please. We're glad to have you.

VERSHININ (*merrily*). I am delighted, delighted. But weren't you three sisters? I remember three little girls. I've stopped remembering faces, but your father, Colonel Prozorov, had three little girls, that I distinctly remember and I saw them with my own eyes. How time flies. Dear, dear, how time flies!

TUSENBACH. The Colonel is from Moscow.

IRINA. From Moscow? You're from Moscow?

VERSHININ. Yes, that's where I'm from. Your late father was battery commander there, I was an officer in the same brigade. (*To Masha.*) Now your face I do seem to remember.

MASHA. And I remember yours—not at all!

IRINA. Olya! Olya! (*Shouts into the reception room.*) Olya, come here! (*OLGA enters the drawing-room from the reception room.*) Lieutenant Colonel Vershinin, it turns out, is from Moscow.

VERSHININ. You must be Olga Sergeevna, the eldest . . . And you're Masha . . . And you're Irina—the youngest . . .

OLGA. You're from Moscow?

VERSHININ. Yes. I was at school in Moscow and entered the service in Moscow, served a long time there, was finally assigned a battery here—I've been transferred here, as you see. I don't remember you individually, I only remember that you were three sisters. Your father's stuck in my memory, why, I can close my eyes and see him as if he were alive. I used to visit you in Moscow . . .

OLGA. I was sure I remembered everyone, and suddenly . . .

VERSHININ. My name is Aleksandr Ignatyevich . . .

IRINA. Aleksandr Ignatyevich, you're from Moscow . . . That's a coincidence!

---

15 "When I played Vershinin, Chekhov said: 'Good, very good. Only don't salute like that, it's not like a colonel. You salute like a lieutenant. You have to do it more firmly, more confidently' " (Vasily Kachalov, *Shipovnik Almanac* 23 [1914]).

OLGA. In fact we'll be moving there.

IRINA. We think we'll be there as soon as autumn. Our home town, we were born there . . . On Old Basmanny Street . . .

Both women laugh for joy.

MASHA. We've unexpectedly come across someone from our neck of the woods! (*Vivaciously.*) Now I remember! I do remember. Olya, at home they used to talk about "the lovesick major." You were a lieutenant then and in love with someone, and everybody teased you, calling you major for some reason . . .

VERSHININ (*laughs*). That's right, that's right! . . . The lovesick major, right you are . . .

MASHA. Then you only had a moustache . . . Oh, how you've aged! (*Plaintively.*) How you've aged!

VERSHININ. Yes, in those days they called me the lovesick major, I was still young and in love. It's not the same now.

OLGA. But you don't have a single gray hair yet. You've aged, but you haven't grown old.

VERSHININ. Nevertheless I am forty-three. Have you been away from Moscow a long time?

IRINA. Eleven years. Why, what's wrong, Masha, you're crying, you crazy . . . (*Plaintively.*) Now I'm starting to cry . . .

MASHA. I'm all right. And what street did you live on?

VERSHININ. Old Basmanny.

OLGA. Why, we lived there too . . .

VERSHININ. At one time I lived on German Street. I'd walk from German Street to the Red Barracks. On the way there's this grim-looking bridge, with the water roaring beneath it. A lonely man begins to feel his heart bowed down.

Pause.

But here there's such a broad, such a fertile river! A wonderful river!

OLGA. Yes, only it's cold. It's cold here and there are mosquitoes . . .

VERSHININ. Why should you care? Here there's such a wholesome, bracing Russian climate. A forest, a river . . . and birch trees here too. Dear, humble birches, I love them more than any other tree. It's a good place to live. Only it's odd, the train station is over thirteen miles away . . . And nobody knows why that is.

SOLYONY. I know why that is. (*Everyone stares at him.*) Because if the station were nearby, it wouldn't be far away, and if it were far away, obviously it wouldn't be nearby.

An awkward silence.

TUSENBACH. Always clowning, Solyony.

OLGA. Now I've remembered you too. I do remember.

VERSHININ. I knew your dear mother.

CHEBUTYKIN. She was a good woman, rest her soul.

IRINA. Mama is buried in Moscow.

OLGA. In Novo-devichy churchyard . . .[16]

MASHA. Just imagine, I'm already beginning to forget what she looked like. No one will remember about us either. They'll forget.

VERSHININ. Yes. They'll forget. Such is our fate, nothing you can do about it. The things we take to be serious, meaningful, of great importance—a time will come when they will be forgotten or seem of no importance.

Pause.

And the interesting thing is, we have absolutely no way of knowing just what will be considered sublime and important, and what trivial and absurd. Didn't the discoveries of Copernicus or, say, Columbus at first sound pointless, absurd, while some idiotic nonsense written by a crank sounded true? And it may come about that our present life, which we're so used to, will in time seem strange, uncomfortable, unintelligent, devoid of purity, maybe even depraved . . .

---

16 Graveyard attached to the historic Moscow "New Virgin" convent, where many celebrities of politics, society, and culture, including Chekhov and his father, are buried.

TUSENBACH. Who knows? Maybe they'll call our life elevated and remember us with respect. Nowadays we don't have torture, executions, invasions, and yet there's so much suffering.

SOLYONY (*shrilly*). Cheep, cheep, cheep . . . Don't feed the Baron birdseed, just let 'im philosophize.

TUSENBACH. Solyony, please leave me in peace . . . (*Moves to another seat.*) It gets to be a bore, after a while.

SOLYONY (*shrilly*). Cheep, cheep, cheep . . .

TUSENBACH (*to Vershinin*). The suffering that's so conspicuous nowadays— and there's so much of it!—nevertheless betokens a certain moral progress which society has already achieved . . .

VERSHININ. Yes, yes, of course.

CHEBUTYKIN. You said just now, Baron, they'll call our life elevated, but all the same people are low . . . (*Rises.*) Look how low I am. My only consolation is you telling me my life is elevated and makes sense.

Offstage someone is playing a violin.

MASHA. That's Andrey playing, our brother.

IRINA. He's the scholar of the family. He's meant to be a professor. Papa was a military man, but his son chose an academic career.

MASHA. As Papa wished.

OLGA. Today we were teasing the life out of him. He's a bit infatuated, it seems.

IRINA. With a certain local miss. She'll show up here today, most likely.

MASHA. Ah, the way she dresses! It's not so much unbecoming or unfashionable as simply pathetic. Some strange, gaudy, yellowish skirt with a vulgar little fringe and a red jacket. And her cheeks are scrubbed so raw! Andrey is not in love—I won't allow that, after all he has taste, but he's simply, well, teasing us, playing the fool. Yesterday I heard she's marrying Protopopov, the chairman of the County Council. And a good thing too . . . (*Out the side door.*) Andrey, come here! Just for a second, dear!

Enter ANDREY.

OLGA. This is my brother, Andrey Sergeich.

VERSHININ. Vershinin.

ANDREY. Prozorov. (*Wipes his sweating face.*) You're here as battery commander?

OLGA. Imagine, the Colonel is from Moscow.

ANDREY. Really? Well, congratulations, now my sisters won't give you a moment's peace.

VERSHININ. I've had plenty of time already to bore your sisters.

IRINA. Just look at the portrait-frame Andrey gave me today! (*Displays the frame.*) He made it himself.

VERSHININ (*looking at the frame and not knowing what to say*). Yes . . . quite something . . .

IRINA. And there's that picture frame over the baby grand, he made that too.

ANDREY waves his hand in dismissal and moves away.

OLGA. He's the scholar in the family and plays the violin and makes all sorts of things with his fretsaw, in short, a jack-of-all-trades. Andrey, don't go away! He's funny that way—always wandering off. Come over here!

*MASHA and IRINA take him by the arms and laughingly escort
him back.*

MASHA. Come on, come on!

ANDREY. Leave me alone, for pity's sake.

MASHA. Don't be ridiculous! They used to call the Colonel the lovesick major and he didn't get the tiniest bit angry.

VERSHININ. Not the tiniest bit!

MASHA. And I want to call you: the lovesick fiddler!

IRINA. Or the lovesick professor! . . .

OLGA. He's lovesick! Andryusha's lovesick!

IRINA (*applauding*). Bravo, bravo! Encore! Little Andryusha's lovesick!

CHEBUTYKIN (*comes up behind Andrey and puts both arms around his waist*). "For love alone did Nature put us on this earth!"[17] (*Roars with laughter: he's still holding on to his newspaper.*)

ANDREY. All right, that's enough, that's enough . . . (*Wipes his face.*) I didn't get a wink of sleep last night and now I'm not quite myself, as they say. I read until four, then I went to bed, but it was no good. I kept thinking about this and that, and the next thing I knew it's dawn and the sun's creeping into my bedroom. This summer, while I'm still here, I want to translate a certain book from the English.

VERSHININ. So you read English?

ANDREY. Yes. Father, rest in peace, overstocked us with education. It sounds silly and absurd, but, still, I must admit, after his death I started putting on weight and, well, I put on so much weight in one year, it's as if my body were freeing itself of its constraints. Thanks to Father, my sisters and I know French, German, and English, and Irina also knows a little Italian. But what good is it?

MASHA. In this town knowing three languages is a superfluous luxury. Not even a luxury, but a kind of superfluous appendage, a bit like a sixth finger. We know a lot of useless stuff.

VERSHININ. Well, I'll be. (*Laughs.*) I don't think there is or can be a town so boring and dismal that an intelligent, educated person isn't of use. Let's assume that among the one hundred thousand inhabitants of this town, which is, I grant you, backward and crude, there are only three such as you. Naturally, it's not up to you to enlighten the benighted masses that surround you. In the course of your lifetime you must gradually surrender and be swallowed up in the crowd of a hundred thousand, you'll be smothered by life, but even so you won't disappear, won't sink without a trace. In your wake others like you will appear, maybe six, then twelve, and so on, until at last the likes of you will be the majority. In two hundred, three hundred years life on earth will be unimaginably beautiful, stupendous. Man needs a life like that, and if it isn't here and now, then he must look forward to it, wait, dream, prepare himself for it, and that's the reason he must see and

---

17 The opening of Taisiya's "Russian aria" in the old opera-vaudeville *Reversals* by Pyotr Kobryakov (1808): "For love alone did Nature / Put us on this earth; / As comfort to the mortal race / She gave the gift of tender feelings!"

know more than his father and grandfather saw and knew. (*Laughs.*) And you complain you know a lot of useless stuff.

MASHA (*takes off her hat*). I'm staying for lunch.

IRINA (*with a sigh*). Honestly, I should have taken notes . . .

ANDREY's gone, he left unnoticed.

TUSENBACH. Many years from now, you say, life on earth will be beautiful, stupendous. That's true. But to take part in it now, even remotely, a person has to prepare for it, a person has to work . . .

VERSHININ (*rises*). Yes. By the way, you have so many flowers! (*Looking around.*) And wonderful quarters! I'm jealous! All my life I've knocked around in cramped quarters with two chairs, the same old sofa, and stoves that invariably smoke. The main thing missing in my life has been flowers like these . . . (*Waves his hand in dismissal.*) Oh, well! That's how it is!

TUSENBACH. Yes, a person has to work. I suppose you're thinking: he's gushing all over the place like a typical sentimental German.[18] But, word of honor, I'm a Russian, I don't even speak German. My father belongs to the Orthodox Church . . .

Pause.

VERSHININ (*paces the stage back and forth*). I often think: what if a man were to begin life anew, and fully conscious at that? If one life, which has already been lived out, were, how shall I put it?, a rough draft, and the other—a final revision! Then each of us, I think, would, first of all, try hard not to repeat himself, at least we'd create a different setting for our life, we'd furnish quarters like these for ourselves with flowers, great bunches of flowers . . . I have a wife, two little girls, moreover my wife's not a well woman, et cetera, et cetera, yes, but if one were to begin life from the beginning, I wouldn't get married . . . No, no!

Enter KULYGIN in a uniform dresscoat.[19]

---

18 Tusenbach further explains his German ancestry in Act Two. In Chekhov's notebooks, Tusenbach's patronymic is Karlovich (son of Karl), which was later changed to Lvovich (son of Leo, a more Russian name).

19 "You wear the tailcoat only in Act One; as to the bandolier (a polished black strap) you are quite right. At least until Act Four you should wear the uniform such as it was before 1900" (Chekhov to Aleksandr Vishnevsky, January 6 [18], 1901).

KULYGIN (*comes up to Irina*). Dearest sister, may I congratulate you on your saint's day and sincerely wish you, from the bottom of my heart, the best of health and all those things proper to wish a young girl of your years. (*Gives her a book.*) The history of our high school over the past fifty years, written by yours truly. A frivolous little book, written when I had nothing better to do, but you go ahead and read it all the same. Greetings, ladies and gentlemen! (*To Vershinin.*) Kulygin, teacher in the local high school. Civil servant, seventh class. (*To Irina.*) In that book you'll find a list of all the alumni of our high school for the past fifty years. *Feci quod potui, faciant meliora potentes.*[20] (*Kisses Masha.*)

IRINA. But didn't you give me this book last Easter?

KULYGIN (*laughs*). Impossible! In that case give it back, or better yet, give it to the Colonel. Here you are, Colonel. Some day you'll read it when you're bored.

VERSHININ. Thank you. (*Prepares to go.*) I'm most happy to have made your acquaintance . . .

OLGA. You're going? No, no!

IRINA. You'll stay and have lunch with us. Please.

OLGA. I insist!

VERSHININ (*bows*). I seem to have dropped in on a saint's day party. Forgive me, I didn't know, I haven't congratulated you . . . (*Goes into the reception room with OLGA.*)

KULYGIN. Today, ladies and gentlemen, is Sunday, the day of rest, therefore let us rest, let us make merry each according to his age and station in life. The rugs will have to be taken up for summer and put away until winter . . . With moth balls or naphthalene . . . The Romans were a healthy people because they knew how to work hard and they knew how to relax, they had *mens sana in corpore sano.*[21] Their life moved according to a set pattern. Our headmaster says: the main thing in every man's life is its pattern . . . Whatever loses its pattern ceases to exist—and in our everyday life the same holds true. (*Takes Masha round the waist, laughing.*) Masha loves

---

20 Latin: I have done what I could, let those who can do better. A paraphrase of Cicero, when the Roman consulate conferred his powers on his successors.

21 Latin: "A healthy mind in a healthy body," quotation from the *Satires* of Juvenal.

me. My wife loves me. And the window curtains too along with the rugs
. . . Today I'm cheerful, in splendid spirits. Masha, at four o'clock today we
have to go to the headmaster's. An outing's been arranged for the faculty
and their families.

MASHA. I'm not going.

KULYGIN (*mortified*). Masha dear, whyever not?

MASHA. We'll discuss it later . . . (*Angrily.*) Very well, I'll go, but do leave me
alone, for pity's sake . . . (*Walks away.*)

KULYGIN. And then we'll spend the evening at the headmaster's. Despite his
failing health that man strives above all to be sociable. An outstanding, brilliant personality. A magnificent man. Yesterday after our meeting he says
to me, "I'm tired, Fyodor Ilyich! I'm tired!" (*Looks at the clock on the wall,
then at his watch.*) Your clock is seven minutes fast. Yes, says he, I'm tired!

Offstage someone is playing the violin.

OLGA. Ladies and gentlemen, please come to the table! There's a meat pie!

KULYGIN. Ah, my dear Olga, my dear! Yesterday I worked from morn to
eleven at night, I was exhausted and today I feel happy. (*Goes to the table
in the reception room.*) My dear . . .

CHEBUTYKIN (*puts the newspaper in his pocket, combs out his beard*). A
meat pie? Splendid!

MASHA (*sternly, to Chebutykin*). Just watch your step, don't have anything to
drink today. You hear? Drinking's bad for you.

CHEBUTYKIN. Bah! That's over and done with. Two years since I last was
drunk. (*Impatiently.*) Anyways, lady, it don't make no never mind!

MASHA. All the same don't you dare drink. Don't you dare. (*Angrily, but so
her husband can't hear.*) Damn it to hell, another boring evening at the
headmaster's!

TUSENBACH. If I were in your shoes, I wouldn't go . . . Plain and simple.

CHEBUTYKIN. Don't go, my lovely!

MASHA. 'S all very well to say: don't go . . . This damned life is unbearable
. . . (*Goes into the reception room.*)

CHEBUTYKIN (*following her*). Now, now!

SOLYONY (*crossing into the reception room*). Cheep, cheep, cheep . . .

TUSENBACH. That's enough, Solyony. Cut it out!

SOLYONY. Cheep, cheep, cheep . . .

KULYGIN (*merrily*). Your health, Colonel! I'm an educator, and here in this house one of the family, Masha's hubby . . . She's a kindhearted creature, really kind . . .

VERSHININ. I'll have some of that dark vodka[22] there . . . (*Drinks.*) Your health! (*To Olga.*) I feel so good being here with you! . . .

> In the drawing-room IRINA and TUSENBACH remain.

IRINA. Masha's in a funny mood today. She married at eighteen, when he seemed to her to be the cleverest of men. And now he doesn't. He's the kindest, but not the cleverest.

OLGA (*impatiently*). Andrey, are you coming?

ANDREY (*offstage*). Right away. (*Enters and goes to the table.*)

TUSENBACH. What are you thinking about?

IRINA. This. I don't like that Solyony of yours, I'm afraid of him. Everything he says is stupid . . .

TUSENBACH. He's a strange fellow. I feel sorry for him, and I get annoyed by him, but mostly sorry. I think he's shy . . . When we're alone together, he's often clever and pleasant enough, but in company he's rude, a bully. Don't go, let them sit at the table a little. Let me be near you for a while. What are you thinking about? (*Pause.*) You're twenty, I'm not yet thirty. How many years there are ahead of us, a long, long series of days, filled with my love for you . . .

IRINA. Nikolay Lvovich, don't talk to me about love . . .

TUSENBACH (*not listening*). I thirst so passionately for life, struggle, hard work, and this thirst of my heart has blended with my love of you, Irina,

---

22 Vodka is traditionally flavored with herbs and spices, such as buffalo grass, cardamom, and peppercorns.

and it all seems to fit, because you're beautiful and life looks just as beautiful to me! What are you thinking about?

IRINA. You say: life is beautiful. Yes, but what if it only seems that way! For us three sisters, life hasn't been beautiful, it's choked us, like weeds . . . There are tears running down my face. That's not what we need . . . (*Quickly wipes her face, smiles.*) What we need is work, work. That's why things look so gloomy to us, why we take such a dim view of life, because we don't know what hard work is. We're the children of people who despised hard work . . .

> *NATALIYA IVANOVNA enters, wearing a pink dress with a green belt.*

NATASHA.[23] They've already sat down to lunch . . . I'm late . . . (*Catches a glimpse of herself in a mirror, sets herself to rights.*) My hairdo looks all right . . . (*On seeing Irina.*) Dear Irina Sergeevna, congratulations! (*Kisses her energetically and at length.*) You've got a lot of guests, honestly, I'm embarrassed . . . Good afternoon, Baron!

OLGA (*entering the drawing-room*). Why, here's Nataliya Ivanovna too. Good afternoon, my dear!

> *They exchange kisses.*

NATASHA. With the party girl. You've got such a lot of company, I'm awfully nervous . . .

OLGA. Don't be silly, it's all family. (*In an undertone, shocked.*) You're wearing a green belt! My dear, that's a mistake!

NATASHA. Is it bad luck?

OLGA. No, it simply doesn't go . . . It's all wrong somehow . . .

NATASHA (*on the verge of tears*). Really? But actually it's not green, it's more a sort of beige.

> *Follows OLGA into the reception room. In the reception room everyone is seated at the table; not a soul is left in the drawing-room.*

---

23 "Natasha" is the usual diminutive of "Nataliya" and is used throughout by the sisters.

KULYGIN. I wish you, Irina, a proper fiancé. It's high time you got married.

CHEBUTYKIN. Nataliya Ivanovna, I wish you a tiny little fiancé.

KULYGIN. Nataliya Ivanovna already has a tiny little fiancé.

MASHA (*raps a fork on a plate*). I'll have a glass of wine! What the hell, life's for living, so let's live dangerously!

KULYGIN. Your conduct gets C minus.

VERSHININ. My, this is a tasty cordial. What's it flavored with?

SOLYONY. Cockroaches.

IRINA (*on the verge of tears*). Ick! Ick! That's disgusting! . . .

OLGA. For supper we're having roast turkey and apple pie.[24] Thank God, I'm home all day today, home this evening . . . Gentlemen, do come again this evening.

VERSHININ. May I come in the evening too?

IRINA. Please do.

NATASHA. It's do as you please around here.

CHEBUTYKIN. "For love alone did Nature put us on this earth." (*Laughs.*)

ANDREY (*angrily*). Will you stop it, gentlemen! Don't you get sick of it?

    FEDOTIK and RODÉ enter with a large basket of flowers.

FEDOTIK. They're already eating lunch.

RODÉ (*loudly, rolling his* rs). They're already eating? Yes, they are already eating . . .

FEDOTIK. Wait just a minute! (*Takes a snapshot.*) One! Hold it just a bit more . . . (*Takes another snapshot.*) Two! Now we're through!

    They take the basket and go into the reception room, where they are greeted boisterously.

RODÉ (*loudly*). Congratulations, I wish you the best of everything, the best of everything! Enchanting weather today, simply splendid. All this morn-

---

24 American though this sounds, the turkey would have been stuffed with liver and walnuts, sliced, and served with a Madeira sauce. The open-face apple pie would contain almonds, cherry jam, and raisins.

ing I was out on a hike with the high school students. I teach gymnastics at the high school . . .

FEDOTIK. You may move now, Irina Sergeevna, yes you may! (*Takes a snapshot.*) You are an interesting model today. (*Pulls a humming-top out of his pocket.*) And in addition, look, a humming-top . . . Makes a wonderful sound . . .

IRINA. What a treasure!

MASHA. "On the curved seashore a green oak stands, a golden chain wound round that oak . . . A golden chain wound round that oak . . ." (*Tearfully.*) Now, why do I keep saying that? Those lines have been stuck in my head since this morning . . .

KULYGIN. Thirteen at table!

RODÉ (*loudly*). Ladies and gentlemen, how can you possibly lend credence to superstitions?

Laughter.

KULYGIN. If there are thirteen at table, that means there are lovers here. Might you be one, Doctor, perish the thought . . .

Laughter.

CHEBUTYKIN. I've been a sinner from way back, but, look, why Nataliya Ivanovna should get embarrassed is something I simply cannot understand.

Loud laughter. NATASHA runs out of the reception room into the drawing-room, followed by ANDREY.

ANDREY. Never mind, don't pay any attention! Wait . . . Stop, please . . .

NATASHA. I'm embarrassed . . . I don't know what to do with myself, and they're all poking fun at me. I just left the table, and I know it's impolite, but I can't . . . I can't . . . (*Hides her face in her hands.*)

ANDREY. My dearest, please, I beg you, don't get upset. I swear to you, they're only joking, it's all in good fun. My dearest, my own, they're all kind, loving people, and they love me and you. Come over here to the window where they can't see us . . . (*Looking around.*)

NATASHA. I'm so unaccustomed to being in society! . . .

ANDREY. Oh, youth, wonderful, beautiful youth. My dearest, my own, don't get so upset! . . . Believe me, believe me . . . I feel so good, my heart is brimming over with love, delight . . . Oh, they can't see us! They can't see! Why I fell in love with you, when I fell in love with you—oh, I have no idea. My dearest, good, pure love, be my wife! I'd love you, love you . . . like no one ever . . . (*A kiss.*)

> *TWO OFFICERS enter and, on seeing the kissing couple, stop*
> *in amazement.*

Curtain

ACT TWO

Same set as in Act One.

Eight o'clock at night. From offstage, as if from the street, one can
faintly hear a concertina playing. No lights.

Enter NATALIYA IVANOVNA in a housecoat and carrying a
candle; she walks around and stops by the door leading to
Andrey's room.

NATASHA. Andryusha, what're you doing? Reading? Never mind, I'm just . . . (*Walks around, opens another door and, after peeping in, closes it again.*) Seeing if there's a light . . .

ANDREY (*enters, holding a book*). You what, Natasha?

NATASHA. I'm checking to see if there's a light . . . Now that it's carnival week,[25] the servants are out of control, you have to keep a sharp lookout to see that nothing goes wrong. Last night at midnight I was walking through the dining room and there was a candle burning. Who lit it, I never did manage to find out. (*Puts down the candle.*) What time is it?

ANDREY (*after a look at his watch*). Quarter past eight.

---

25 *Maslennitsa*, or Butter Week, the week preceding Lent, was traditionally devoted to eating and carousing. The consumption of pancakes (*blini*) and the invitation of musicians into homes were traditional activities. Evidently a year and nine months have passed since Act One.

NATASHA. And Olga and Irina not back yet. They aren't here. Still at work, poor things. Olga at the faculty meeting, Irina at the telegraph office . . . (*Sighs.*) Just this morning I was saying to your sister, "Take care of yourself," I say, "Irina, love." But she doesn't listen. A quarter past eight, you said? I'm worried our Bobik[26] isn't at all well. Why is he so cold? Yesterday he had a fever and today he's cold all over . . . I'm so worried!

ANDREY. It's nothing, Natasha. The boy's healthy.

NATASHA. But even so we'd better put him on a diet. I'm worried. And at nine o'clock tonight, they were saying, the masqueraders[27] will be here. It'd be better if they didn't put in an appearance, Andryusha.

ANDREY. I really don't know. After all, they were sent for.

NATASHA. This morning the little darling woke up and looks at me, and suddenly he smiled, which means he recognized me. "Bobik," I say, "morning! morning! darling!" And he laughs. Children do understand, they understand perfectly well. So, in that case, Andryusha, I'll tell the servants not to let the masqueraders in.

ANDREY (*indecisively*). But, after all, that's up to my sisters. They're in charge here.

NATASHA. Oh, they are too, I'll tell them. They're considerate . . . (*Walks around.*) For supper I ordered some yogurt. Doctor says you shouldn't eat anything but yogurt, otherwise you won't lose weight. (*Stops.*) Bobik is cold. I'm worried, it's too cold for him in his room, most likely. At least until the weather gets warmer we should put him in another room. For instance, Irina's room is just right for a baby, it's dry and sunny all day long. I'll have to tell her, meanwhile she can double up with Olga in the same room . . . It doesn't matter, she's not at home during the day, only spends the night here . . . (*Pause.*) Andryusha sweetie-pie, why don't you say something?

ANDREY. No reason, I was thinking . . . Besides there's nothing to be said . . .

---

26 Natasha is being pretentious but gets it wrong. An English name such as Bob was fashionable in high society, but at this time Bobik was usually applied to dogs.

27 *Ryazhenye* were well-behaved amateur performers in carnival costume who, after dusk, would go from house to house at Shrovetide, dancing and receiving food in return. Trick-or-treaters and carolers combined, they might be joined by professional bear leaders, storytellers, and beggars. For a description, see Tolstoy's *War and Peace*, II, part 4, ch. 10.

NATASHA. Right . . . Something I wanted to tell you . . . Oh, yes. Ferapont's out there, sent by the council, he's asking to see you.

ANDREY (*yawns*). Send him in.

> NATASHA *exits;* ANDREY, *hunched over the candle she's forgotten, reads a book. Enter* FERAPONT; *he is wearing an old threadbare overcoat with a turned-up collar, his ears covered by a kerchief.*

ANDREY. 'Evening, old-timer. What have you got to say for yourself?

FERAPONT. Chairman sent a book and a paper of some sort. Here . . . (*Hands over a book and a paper.*)

ANDREY. Thanks. Fine. But why didn't you get here earlier? After all, it's past eight already.

FERAPONT. How's that?

ANDREY (*Louder*). I said, you've come so late, it's already past eight.

FERAPONT. Right you are. When I got here it was still light, but they wouldn't let me in all this time. The master, they say, is busy. Well, that's that. Busy's busy, I got no cause to rush. (*Thinking that Andrey is asking him something.*) How's that?

ANDREY. Nothing. (*Examining the book.*) Tomorrow's Friday, we don't meet, but I'll go there all the same . . . I'll find something to do, it's boring at home . . .

> *Pause.*

You dear old man, it's funny the way things change, the way life isn't fair! Today out of boredom, with nothing to do, I picked up this book here — my old university lecture notes, and I had to laugh . . . Good grief, I'm secretary to the County Council, the council Protopopov presides over, I'm secretary and the most I can hope for — is to become a full member of the County Council! Me a member of the local County Council, me, who dreams every night that I'm a professor at Moscow University, a famous scholar, the pride of Russia!

FERAPONT. I couldn't say . . . I'm hard o' hearing . . .

ANDREY. If your hearing was good, I probably wouldn't be talking to you. I have to talk to someone, and my wife doesn't understand me, my sisters scare me for some reason, I'm afraid they'll make fun of me, embarrass me

... I don't drink, I've no great fondness for barrooms, but I'd love to be sitting in Moscow at Testov's tavern right now or the Grand Moscow restaurant, my friend.

FERAPONT. Why, in Moscow, a contractor at the Council was saying the other day, there was some shopkeepers eating pancakes;[28] one ate forty pancakes and like to died. May ha' been forty, may ha' been fifty. I don't rec'llect.

ANDREY. You sit in Moscow in the vast main dining room of a restaurant, you don't know anyone and no one knows you, and at the same time you don't feel like a stranger. Whereas here you know everyone and everyone knows you, but you're a stranger, a stranger ... A stranger and alone.

FERAPONT. How's that?

Pause.

And that same contractor was saying—lying too, mebbe—as how there's a rope stretched acrost all Moscow.

ANDREY. What for?

FERAPONT. How do I know? The contractor said so.

ANDREY. Don't be silly. (*Reads the book.*) Were you ever in Moscow?

FERAPONT (*after a pause*). I was not. 'Tweren't God's will.

Pause.

Can I go?

ANDREY. You may go. Keep well.

FERAPONT exits.

Keep well. (*Reading.*) Come back tomorrow morning, pick up the paper ... Go on ...

Pause.

He's gone. (*The doorbell rings.*) Yes, business ... (*Stretches and unhurriedly goes back into his room.*)

---

28 The classical dish for Butter Week is pancakes made of raised flour or buckwheat dough, fried in plenty of butter and filled with cottage cheese. The round shape was to represent the sun, since this was originally a pagan holiday.

Offstage a nursemaid is singing a lullaby to a baby. Enter
MASHA *and* VERSHININ. *Later, during their dialogue, the*
PARLOR MAID *lights a lamp and candles.*

MASHA. I don't know. (*Pause.*) I don't know. Of course, habit has a lot to do
with it. After Father died, for instance, it was a long time before we could
get used to not having orderlies any more. But, habit aside, I think I'm
being impartial. Maybe it isn't like this in other places, but in our town the
most decent, most honorable and cultured people are the military.

VERSHININ. I'd like something to drink. I could use some tea.

MASHA (*after a glance at the clock*). They'll bring some soon. They married
me off when I was eighteen, and I was afraid of my husband because he
was a schoolteacher and at the time I'd just graduated. At the time he
seemed to me to be terribly clever, learned, and important. But that's no
longer the case, sad to say.

VERSHININ. Is that so . . . yes.

MASHA. I'm not including my husband, I'm used to him, but among civilians in general there so many crude, uncongenial, uncouth people. I get
upset, I'm offended by crudeness, it pains me to see a man who's not as
refined or sensitive or congenial as he should be. When I have to be with
schoolteachers, my husband's colleagues, I'm just in agony.

VERSHININ. Yes, ma'am . . . But I don't think it matters much, civilian or
military, they're equally uninteresting, at least in this town. Makes no difference! If you listen to any educated man in this town, civilian or military,
he's sick and tired of his wife, sick and tired of his home, sick and tired
of his estate, sick and tired of his horses . . . A Russian is highly capable
of coming up with advanced ideas, so tell me, why is his aim in life so
low? Why?

MASHA. Why?

VERSHININ. Why is he sick and tired of his children, sick and tired of his
wife? And why are his wife and children sick and tired of him?

MASHA. You're in a bad mood today.

VERSHININ. Could be. I haven't had dinner today, I've eaten nothing since
this morning. One of my daughters is under the weather, and when my
little girls are ill, anxiety gets the better of me. My conscience bothers me

for giving them such a mother. Oh, if only you could have seen her today! So petty! We started bickering at seven in the morning, and at nine I slammed the door and went out.

Pause.

I never talk about this, and it's strange, you're the only one I complain to. (*Kisses her hand.*) Don't be angry with me. Except for you, only you, I have no one, no one . . .

Pause.

MASHA. What a racket in the stove! Not long before Father died, there was a whistling in our stovepipe. It was exactly like that.

VERSHININ. You're superstitious?

MASHA. Yes.

VERSHININ. 'S funny. (*Kisses her hand.*) You're a superb, a marvelous woman. Superb, marvelous woman! It's dark in here, but I can see the sparkle in your eyes.

MASHA (*moves to another chair*). There's more light over here . . .

VERSHININ. I love, love, love . . . I love your eyes, your movements, which come to me in my dreams . . . Superb, marvelous woman!

MASHA (*laughing quietly*). When you talk to me that way, for some reason I have to laugh, even though I feel terrified. Don't say it again, please don't . . . (*In an undertone.*) Go on, do talk, it doesn't matter to me . . . (*Hides her face in her hands.*) To me it doesn't matter. Someone's coming in here, talk about something else . . .

IRINA and TUSENBACH enter through the reception room.

TUSENBACH. I have a tripartite name. I'm called Baron Tusenbach-Krone-Altschauer, but I'm a Russian, of the Orthodox faith, same as you. There's only a bit of German left in me, actually only the dogged obstinacy I pester you with. I escort you home every single night.

IRINA. I'm so tired!

TUSENBACH. And every single night I'll come to the telegraph office and escort you home, I will for ten, twenty years, until you chase me away . . . (*On seeing Masha and Vershinin, gleefully.*) Is that you? Good evening.

IRINA. Here I am, home at last. (*To Masha.*) Just now a lady comes in, wires her brother in Saratov[29] to say that her son has died, and she couldn't manage to remember the address. So she sent it without an address, simply to Saratov. Crying the whole time. And I was rude to her for no reason at all. "I haven't got the time," I said. It sounded so stupid. Are the masqueraders dropping by tonight?

MASHA. Yes.

IRINA (*sits in an armchair*). Have to rest. I'm tired.

TUSENBACH (*with a smile*). Whenever you come home from work, you look so small, such a tiny little thing . . .

Pause.

IRINA. I'm tired. No, I don't like the telegraph office, I don't like it.

MASHA. You're getting thinner . . . (*Whistles under her breath.*) And younger, for your face looks just like a sweet little boy's.

TUSENBACH. It's the way she does her hair.

IRINA. I've got to look for another job, this one's not for me. What I so wanted, what I dream of is definitely missing in this one. Drudgery without poetry, without thought . . . (*A knock on the floor.*) The doctor's knocking. (*To Tusenbach.*) Knock back, my dear. I can't . . . I'm tired . . . (*TUSENBACH knocks on the floor.*) He'll be here in a minute. Somebody ought to do something about him. Yesterday the Doctor and Andrey were at the club and lost again. They say Andrey lost two hundred rubles.

MASHA (*indifferently*). What can you do now!

IRINA. Two weeks ago he lost, back in December he lost. If only he'd hurry up and lose everything, maybe we'd leave this town. Honest to God, I dream of Moscow every night, I'm getting to be a regular obsessive. (*Laughs.*) We'll move there in June, and till June there's still . . . February, March, April, May . . . almost half a year!

MASHA. Just so long as Natasha hasn't found out about his losses.

IRINA. I shouldn't think it matters to her.

---

29 A city on the Volga.

CHEBUTYKIN, *only just got out of bed—he was napping after dinner—enters the reception room and combs out his beard, then sits there at the table and pulls a newspaper out of his pocket.*

MASHA. Here he comes . . . Has he paid his room rent?

IRINA (*laughs*). No. For eight months not the slightest kopek. Apparently he's forgotten.

MASHA (*laughs*). How pompously he sits!

They all laugh; pause.

IRINA. Why are you so silent, Colonel?

VERSHININ. I don't know. I'd like some tea. Half my kingdom for a glass of tea![30] I haven't had anything to eat since this morning . . .

CHEBUTYKIN. Irina Sergeevna!

IRINA. What do you want?

CHEBUTYKIN. Please come over here. *Venez ici!*[31] (*IRINA goes and sits at the table.*) I can't live without you. (*IRINA lays out a game of solitaire.*)

VERSHININ. What do you say? If there's no tea, let's at least philosophize.

TUSENBACH. Let's. What about?

VERSHININ. What about? Let's dream a little . . . for instance, about the life to come after us, some two hundred or three hundred years from now.

TUSENBACH. How about this? The people who come after us will fly in hot-air balloons, suit jackets will be cut in a different style, maybe they'll discover a sixth sense and put it to use, but life will stay just the same, life will be hard, full of mysteries, and happy. And a thousand years from now men will sigh in just the same way: "Ah, life is a burden!"—and just as they do now, they'll be scared and resist having to die.

VERSHININ (*after giving it some thought*). How I can put this? I have the impression that everything on earth should be changing little by little and is already changing before our very eyes. In two hundred, three hundred,

---

30 Paraphrase of the famous line from Shakespeare's *Richard III*: "A horse! A horse! My kingdom for a horse!" (Act V, scene 4).

31 French: Come here.

all right, a thousand years—the time span's of no importance—a new and happy life will come into being. This life is something we won't take part in, of course, but we're living for it now, we work, oh, and we suffer, we are creating it—and this is the one and only purpose of our existence and, if you like, our happiness.

MASHA laughs quietly.

TUSENBACH. What's come over you?

MASHA. I don't know. All day long I've been laughing, ever since this morning.

VERSHININ. I finished school at the same grade you did, I didn't go to the Military Academy; I read a great deal, but I don't know how to choose books and maybe I don't read what I should, and yet the more I live, the more I want to know. My hair's turning gray, any day now I'll be an old man, but I know so little, ah, so little! But even so, I think what's most important, what really matters I do know, and know it through and through. If only I could prove to you that there is no happiness, there shouldn't be and will not be for any of us . . . All we should do is work and go on working, as for happiness, that's the lot of future generations.

Pause.

Not my lot but that of future generations of future generations.

*FEDOTIK and RODÉ appear in the reception room; they sit
down and sing quietly, strumming on the guitar.*

TUSENBACH. To your way of thinking, a person's not supposed to dream of happiness! But what if I am happy!

VERSHININ. No.

TUSENBACH (*clasping his hands together and laughing*). Obviously, we're not communicating. Well, how can I convince you? (*MASHA laughs quietly.*) (*Wagging a finger at her.*) Go ahead and laugh! (*To Vershinin.*) Not just two hundred or three hundred, but even a million years from now, life will be the same as it's always been; it won't change, it will stay constant, governed by its own laws, which are none of our business or, at least, which we'll never figure out. Birds of passage, cranes, for instance, fly on and on, and whatever thoughts, sublime or trivial, may drift through their heads, they'll keep on flying and never know what for or where to. They fly and will keep on flying, whatever philosopher they may hatch; and let them philosophize to their heart's content, so long as they keep on flying . . .

MASHA. Then what's the point?

TUSENBACH. The point . . . Look, there's snow falling. What's the point of that?

Pause.

MASHA. It seems to me, a person ought to believe in something or look for something to believe in; otherwise his life is empty, empty . . . To live and not know why cranes fly, why children are born, why stars are in the sky . . . Either you know why you live or else it's all senseless, gobbledy-gook.

Pause.

VERSHININ. Still it's a pity that youth has flown . . .

MASHA. In one of Gogol's stories, he says: It's a sad world, my masters![32]

TUSENBACH. And I say: it's hard to argue with you, my masters! You're too much . . .

CHEBUTYKIN (*reading the paper*). Balzac was married in Berdichev.[33] (IRINA *sings quietly.*) That's something to jot down in the book. (*Jots it down.*) Balzac was married in Berdichev. (*Reads the paper.*)

IRINA (*laying out a game of solitaire; pensively*). Balzac was married in Berdichev.

TUSENBACH. The die is cast.[34] You know, Mariya Sergeevna, I've turned in my resignation.

MASHA. So I've heard. And I doubt anything good will come of it. I don't like civilians.

---

32 Masha is quoting the last sentence of Gogol's "Story of How Ivan Ivanovich and Ivan Niki-forovich Fell Out" (1832): literally, "It's boring in this world, gentlemen." Like Gogol's heroes, Tusenbach and Vershinin will never agree.

33 The French novelist Honoré de Balzac (1799–1850) married the Polish landowner Ewelyna Hanska in Berdichev a few months before he died. Berdichev, a city in the Kiev *guberniya* in Ukraine, was almost entirely populated by Jews, hence the incongruity.

34 Spoken by Julius Caesar on crossing the Rubicon, as related in Suetonius, *Lives of the Twelve Caesars.*

TUSENBACH. Doesn't matter . . . (*Rises.*) I'm not good looking, what kind of military figure do I cut? Besides, it doesn't matter, anyway . . . I'll go to work. At least once in my life I'll do some work, so I can come home at night, collapse on my bed exhausted and fall fast asleep in an instant. (*Going into the reception room.*) I suppose workingmen sleep soundly!

FEDOTIK (*to Irina*). Just now at Pyzhikov's on Moscow Street I bought you some colored pencils. And here's a little penknife.

IRINA. You're used to treating me like a child, but I really am grown up now . . . (*Takes the pencils and penknife; with delight.*) What fun!

FEDOTIK. And for myself I bought a jackknife . . . here, have a look at it . . . one blade, then another blade, a third, that's for cleaning out the ears, this is a tiny scissors, this one's for trimming nails . . .

RODÉ (*loudly*). Doctor, how old are you?

CHEBUTYKIN. Me? Thirty-two.

Laughter.

FEDOTIK. Now I'm going to show you another kind of solitaire . . . (*Deals out a game of solitaire.*)

> *The samovar is brought in. ANFISA is by the samovar; a bit of a wait and then NATASHA enters and also fusses around the samovar. SOLYONY enters and, after exchanging greetings, sits at the table.*

VERSHININ. Incidentally, that's quite a wind!

MASHA. Yes. I'm sick and tired of winter. I've already forgot what summer's like.

IRINA. The solitaire's coming out, I see. We'll be in Moscow.

FEDOTIK. No it isn't. You see, the eight was on top of the deuce of spades. (*Laughs.*) That means, you won't be in Moscow.

CHEBUTYKIN (*reads the paper*). Tsitsikar.[35] Smallpox is raging there.

ANFISA (*coming over to Masha*). Masha, have some tea, dearie. (*To Vershinin.*) Please, your honor . . . forgive me, dearie, I've forgot your name . . .

---

35 Or Tsitisar or Qiqihar or Ho-lung-kiang, a province of Chinese Manchuria.

MASHA. Bring it here, Nanny. I refuse to go in there.

IRINA. Nanny!

ANFISA. Co-oming!

NATASHA (*to Solyony*). Breastfed children understand one perfectly. "Good morning," I'll say, "Good morning, Bobik darling!" He'll stare at me in a special sort of way. You probably think that's the mother in me talking but no, no, absolutely not! He's an exceptional baby.

SOLYONY. If that baby were mine, I'd fry him in a pan and eat him. (*Takes his glass into the drawing-room and sits in a corner.*)

NATASHA (*hiding her face in her hands*). Rude, uncouth man!

MASHA. Happy the man who doesn't notice whether it's summer or winter. I think if I were in Moscow, I wouldn't pay any attention to the weather . . .

VERSHININ. A few days ago I was reading the diary of a French cabinet minister, written in prison. The cabinet minister had been sentenced for taking bribes in the Panama scandal.[36] With what intoxication, what ecstasy he recalls the birds he saw from his prison window and which he failed to notice before when he was a cabinet minister. Of course, now that he's released and at liberty, he's stopped noticing birds, just as before. And you'll stop noticing Moscow once you're living there. We have no happiness, there is none, we only long for it.

TUSENBACH (*takes a little box from the table*). Where are the chocolates?

IRINA. Solyony ate them.

TUSENBACH. All of 'em?

ANFISA (*handing round the tea*). There's a letter for you, dearie.

VERSHININ. For me? (*Takes the letter.*) From my daughters. (*Reads.*) Yes, naturally . . . Excuse me, Mariya Sergeevna, I'll leave ever so quietly. I won't have any tea. (*Rises in great agitation.*) These everlasting scenes . . .

MASHA. What is it? Not a secret?

---

36 *Impressions cellulaires*, by Charles Baïhaut (1834–1905), French Minister for Panama, who was condemned to two years in prison in 1893. Chekhov had read this book during his stay in Nice in 1897. The bankruptcy in 1888 of the company organized to build the Panama canal resulted in the conviction of several French politicians for fraud.

VERSHININ (*quietly*). My wife poisoned herself again. I've got to go. I'll slip out without being noticed. Awfully unpleasant all this. (*Kisses Masha's hand.*) My dear, wonderful, lovely woman . . . I'll slip out of here ever so quietly . . . (*Exits.*)

ANFISA. Where's he off to? Why, I gave him tea . . . What a one.

MASHA (*losing her temper*). Stop it! Forever badgering us, you never give us a moment's peace . . . (*Goes with her cup to the table.*) I'm sick and tired of you, old woman!

ANFISA. Why are you so touchy? Sweetheart!

ANDREY'S VOICE. Anfisa!

ANFISA (*mimics*). Anfisa! There he sits . . . (*Exits.*)

MASHA (*in the reception room at the table, angrily*). Do let me sit down! (*Messes up the cards on the table.*) Sprawling all over with your cards. Drink your tea!

IRINA. Mashka, you're being nasty.

MASHA. If I'm nasty, don't talk to me. Don't touch me!

CHEBUTYKIN (*laughing*). Don't touch her, don't touch . . .

MASHA. You're sixty years old, but you're like a snotty little boy, nobody knows what the hell you're babbling about.

NATASHA (*sighs*). Masha dear, what's the point of using such expressions in polite conversation? With your lovely looks you'd be simply enchanting in decent society, I'll say that straight to your face, if it weren't for that vocabulary of yours. *Je vous prie, pardonnez moi, Marie, mais vous avez des manières un peu grossières.*[37]

TUSENBACH (*restraining his laughter*). May I . . . may I . . . I think there's some cognac . . .

NATASHA. *Il paraît, que mon Bobik déjà ne dort pas,*[38] he woke up. He isn't well today. I'll go to him, excuse me . . . (*Exits.*)

---

37 French: Please, forgive me, Marie, but you have rather rude manners. French was common in Russian intellectual circles, but it is pretentious on the part of Natasha, who makes frequent mistakes. Correctly, it would be *"je vous en prie."*

38 Bad French: It seems my Bobik is already not asleep.

IRINA. But where has the Colonel gone?

MASHA. Home. His wife again—something unexpected.

TUSENBACH (*goes to Solyony, carrying a decanter of cognac*). You always sit by yourself, thinking about something—and you have no idea what. Well, let's make peace. Let's have some cognac. (*They drink.*) I'll have to tickle the ivories all night tonight, I suppose, play all sorts of trash . . . Come what may!

SOLYONY. Why make peace? I haven't quarreled with you.

TUSENBACH. You always make me feel that something has happened between us. You've got a strange personality, you must admit.

SOLYONY (*declaiming*). "Strange I may be, but then who is not?"[39] "Contain your wrath, Aleko!"[40]

TUSENBACH. What's Aleko got to do with it . . .

Pause.

SOLYONY. When I'm alone with anyone, it's all right, I'm like everybody else, but in company I'm dejected, inhibited, and . . . I talk all sorts of rubbish. But all the same I'm more honest and decent than lots and lots of people. And I can prove it.

TUSENBACH. I often get angry with you, you're constantly needling me when we're in public, but all the same for some reason I have an affinity to you. Come what may, I'll get drunk tonight. Let's drink!

SOLYONY. Let's drink. (*They drink.*) I don't have anything against you, Baron. But my temperament is like Lermontov's. (*Quietly.*) I even look a little like Lermontov[41] . . . so they say . . . (*Takes the flask of perfume from his pocket and sprinkles it on his hands.*)

---

39 Quotation from the classic comedy *Woe from Wit* by Aleksandr Griboedov, a line of the protagonist Chatsky (Act V, scene 1), who is in opposition to Moscow's high society and its blind Francophilia.

40 Aleko is the hero of the romantic verse tale "The Gypsies," by Aleksandr Pushkin (1824), heavily influenced by Byronic romanticism. A Russian depressed by civilization, Aleko turns his back on elegant Petersburg and lives with gypsies; he falls in love with a gypsy girl and commits a murder out of jealousy. Rachmaninov turned it into an opera (1892).

41 Mikhail Yuryevich Lermontov (1814–1841), after Pushkin the most important lyric poet of Russian Romanticism. As an officer, Lermontov was twice exiled to the Caucasus, then killed in a

TUSENBACH. I've turned in my resignation. *Basta!* For five years I kept turning it over in my mind and finally I came to a decision. I shall go to work.

SOLYONY (*declaiming*). "Contain your wrath, Aleko . . . Forget, forget your dreams . . ."

> *While they talk, ANDREY enters with a book and sits by*
> *the candles.*

TUSENBACH. I shall go to work.

CHEBUTYKIN (*going into the drawing-room with IRINA*). And the refreshments were also authentic Caucasian dishes: onion soup and for the roast—chekhartma, a meat dish.

SOLYONY. Cheremsha[42] isn't meat at all, but a vegetable related to our onion.

CHEBUTYKIN. No sir, angel mine. Chekhartma is not an onion, but roast mutton.

SOLYONY. And I tell you, cheremsha is onion.

CHEBUTYKIN. And I tell you, chekhartma is mutton.

SOLYONY. And I tell you, cheremsha is onion.

CHEBUTYKIN. Why should I argue with you? You were never in the Caucasus and never ate chekhartma.

SOLYONY. I never ate it, because I can't stand it. Cheremsha reeks as badly as garlic.

ANDREY (*pleading*). That's enough, gentlemen! For pity's sake!

TUSENBACH. When do the masqueraders get here?

IRINA. They promised to be here by nine, which means any minute now.

TUSENBACH (*embraces Andrey*). "Ah, you gates, my gates, new gates . . ."

---

duel. "Actually, Solyony does think that he looks like Lermontov, but of course he doesn't—it's ridiculous just to think of . . . He should be made up to look like Lermontov. The resemblance to Lermontov is enormous, but only in Solyony's mind" (Chekhov to I. A. Tikhomirov, January 14, 1901).

42 *Chekhartma*, correctly, *chikhartma*, is a Caucasian soup of lamb or chicken, flavored with coriander and saffron. *Cheremsha* may refer to either *cheremitsa* (masculine, *Allium angulosum*), the sharp-edged leek, or *cheremitsa* (feminine, *Allium ursinum*), wild garlic.

ANDREY (*dances and sings*). "New gates, made of maple . . ."

CHEBUTYKIN (*dances*). "Lattice-grates upon my gates!"[43]

Laughter.

TUSENBACH (*kisses Andrey*). Damn it, let's have a drink. Andryusha, let's drink to being old pals. And I'm going with you, Andryusha, to Moscow, to the university.

SOLYONY. Which one? In Moscow there are two universities.

ANDREY. In Moscow there is one university.

SOLYONY. And I tell you—two.

ANDREY. Make it three. The more the merrier.

SOLYONY. In Moscow there are two universities! (*Grumbling and hissing.*) In Moscow there are two universities: the old one and the new one. And if you don't enjoy listening to me, if my words annoy you, then I can stop talking. I can even go off into another room . . . (*Exits through one of the doors.*)

TUSENBACH. Bravo, bravo! (*Laughs.*) Gentlemen, proceed, I shall commence to play! Laughable that Solyony . . . (*Sits down at the baby grand, plays a waltz.*)

MASHA (*dances a waltz by herself*). Baron's drunk, Baron's drunk, Baron's drunk!

Enter NATASHA.

NATASHA (*to Chebutykin*). Ivan Romanych! (*Mentions something to Chebutykin, then quietly exits.*)

CHEBUTYKIN taps Tusenbach on the shoulder and whispers something to him.

IRINA. What is it?

CHEBUTYKIN. Time for us to go. Be well.

TUSENBACH. Good night. Time to go.

IRINA. Excuse me . . . But what about the masqueraders? . . .

---

43 A folksong sung as accompaniment to vigorous dancing.

ANDREY (*embarrassed*). There won't be any masqueraders. You see, my dear, Natasha says that Bobik isn't very well, and so . . . To make a long story short, I don't know anything about it, it doesn't matter to me in the least.

IRINA (*shrugging*). Bobik isn't well!

MASHA. Now we've had it! They're kicking us out, so I suppose we've got to go. (*To Irina.*) It's not Bobik that's sick, it's her . . . Here! (*Taps her forehead with a finger.*) Small-town slut![44]

> ANDREY *exits through the door right, to his room,*
> CHEBUTYKIN *follows him; those in the reception room*
> *say good-bye.*

FEDOTIK. What a shame! I'd counted on spending a full night here, but if the little baby's ill, then, of course . . . Tomorrow I'll bring him a little toy . . .

RODÉ (*loudly*). I deliberately took a nap after dinner today, I thought I'd be up all night dancing. After all, it's only nine o'clock now!

MASHA. Let's go out in the street and discuss it there. We'll come up with something to do.

> *"Good-bye! Keep well!" can be heard, as well as the merry*
> *laughter of TUSENBACH. ANFISA and the PARLOR MAID*
> *clear the table and extinguish the lights. The nursemaid can be*
> *heard singing. Enter quietly ANDREY in an overcoat and hat*
> *and CHEBUTYKIN.*

CHEBUTYKIN. I didn't have a chance to get married, because life flashed by me like a streak of lightning, and besides I was madly in love with your dear mother, who was married already . . .

ANDREY. There's no reason to get married. No reason, because it's a bore.

CHEBUTYKIN. That may be so, but then there's the loneliness. However much you philosophize, loneliness is a terrible thing, my boy . . . Although, basically . . . Of course, it doesn't matter!

ANDREY. Let's go quickly.

---

44 *Meshchanka*, literally, petty-bourgeois female, commoner. Natasha is a social inferior to the Prozorovs, who come from the gentry.

CHEBUTYKIN. What's the rush? We've got time.

ANDREY. I'm afraid the wife might stop me.

CHEBUTYKIN. Ah!

ANDREY. I won't play tonight, I'll just sit and watch. I don't feel well . . . Doctor, what should I take for shortness of breath?

CHEBUTYKIN. Why ask! I don't remember, my boy. I don't know.

ANDREY. Let's go through the kitchen.

They leave.

The doorbell rings, then rings again: voices and laughter
are heard.

IRINA (*enters*). What's that?

ANFISA (*in a whisper*). Masqueraders!

The doorbell.

IRINA. Nanny dear, say no one's at home. Make excuses.

ANFISA exits. IRINA walks about the room in a revery; she is on
edge. Enter SOLYONY.

SOLYONY (*bewildered*). No one's here . . . But where are they all?

IRINA. They went home.

SOLYONY. Strange. You're alone here?

IRINA. Alone. (*Pause.*) Good-bye.

SOLYONY. A while ago I behaved without proper restraint and discretion. But you aren't like the rest, you're exalted and pure, you can discern the truth . . . You alone, only you can understand me. I love, I love profoundly, incessantly . . .

IRINA. Good-bye! Go away.

SOLYONY. I can't live without you. (*Following her around.*) Oh, my heaven on earth! (*Plaintively.*) Oh, happiness! exquisite, wonderful, bewitching eyes, I've never seen their like in any other woman . . .

IRINA (*coldly*). Stop it, Vasily Vasilich!

SOLYONY. This is the first time I'm talking to you of love, and it's exactly like being out of this world, on another planet. (*Rubs his forehead.*) Well, still, it doesn't matter. You can't be compelled to care for me, of course . . . But I won't tolerate any successful rivals . . . Won't tolerate it . . . I swear to you by all that's holy, I'll kill any rival . . . Oh, wonderful woman!

NATASHA passes through with a candle.

NATASHA (*peers through one door, then another, and passes the door leading to her husband's room*). Andrey's in there. Let him read. Do forgive me, Vasily Vasilich, I didn't know you were here, I'm in a housecoat.

SOLYONY. It doesn't matter to me. Good-bye! (*Exits.*)

NATASHA. And you're tired, darling, my poor little girl. (*Kisses Irina.*) You should have gone to bed much sooner.

IRINA. Is Bobik asleep?

NATASHA. He's asleep. But he sleeps so restlessly. By the way, darling, I wanted to tell you, but you're never around, or I never have the time . . . Bobik's present nursery seems to me to be cold and damp. But your room is so right for a baby. Dearest, sweetheart, move in with Olya for a while!

IRINA (*confused*). Where?

A troika with harness bells can be heard pulling up to the house.

NATASHA. You and Olya can be in one room for a while, and your room will go to Bobik. He's such a little darling, today I say to him, "Bobik, you're mine! All mine!" And he stares at me with his pretty little peepers. (*Doorbell.*) That's Olga, I suppose. Isn't she late! (*The PARLOR MAID walks over to Natasha and whispers in her ear.*) Protopopov? What a character. Protopopov's here and wants me to go for a ride with him in the troika.[45] (*Laughs.*) How funny men are . . . (*Doorbell.*) Someone's ringing . . . Olga's back, I suppose. (*Exits.*)

The PARLOR MAID runs out; IRINA sits rapt in thought; enter KULYGIN and OLGA, followed by VERSHININ.

KULYGIN. Would you look at this. But they said they'd be having a party.

---

45 Sleigh rides, preferably in a troika, decorated with colored ribbons and bells, were a favorite pastime during *Maslennitsa*. The sleighs would travel in wide semicircles to commemorate the sun's passage.

VERSHININ. Strange, I left not long ago, half an hour, and they were waiting for the masqueraders . . .

IRINA. They've all gone.

KULYGIN. Masha's gone too? Where did she go? And why is Protopopov downstairs waiting in a troika? Who's he waiting for?

IRINA. Don't give me a quiz . . . I'm tired.

KULYGIN. Temper, temper . . .

OLGA. The meeting only just ended. I'm exhausted. Our headmistress is ill, and I'm taking her place now. My head, my head aches, my head . . . (*Sits.*) Andrey lost two hundred rubles at cards yesterday . . . The whole town's talking about it.

KULYGIN. Yes, the meeting wore me out too. (*Sits.*)

VERSHININ. My wife just now took it into her head to give me a scare, she all but poisoned herself. It's all blown over, and I'm relieved, I can take it easy now . . . So, I suppose, we've got to go? Well then, let me wish you all the best. Fyodor Ilyich, walk somewhere with me! I can't stay at home, I simply cannot . . . Let's go for a walk!

KULYGIN. I'm tired. I'm going nowhere. (*Rises.*) I'm tired. Did my wife go home?

IRINA. I suppose so.

KULYGIN (*kisses Irina's hand*). Good-bye. Tomorrow and the day after I've got the whole day to relax. All the best! (*Goes.*) I'd really like some tea. I counted on spending the evening in congenial company and—*o, fallacem hominum spem!*[46] . . . Accusative case, used in the vocative . . .

VERSHININ. Which means, I'm on my own. (*Exits with KULYGIN, whistling.*)

OLGA. My head aches, my poor head . . . Andrey lost . . . the whole town's talking . . . I'll go lie down. (*Goes.*) Tomorrow I'm free . . . Oh, goodness, how nice it'll be! Free tomorrow, free the day after . . . My head aches, my poor head . . . (*Exits.*)

---

46 Latin: "oh, vain is human hope!" from Cicero, *The Orator* (III, ii).

IRINA (*alone*). They've all gone. No one's left.

In the street there's a concertina, the NURSEMAID sings a song.

NATASHA (*wearing a fur coat and hat walks through the reception room, followed by the PARLOR MAID*). I'll be back in half an hour. Just going for a little ride. (*Exits.*)

IRINA (*alone, yearning*). To Moscow! To Moscow! To Moscow!

Curtain

ACT THREE

Olga's and Irina's room. Beds at left and right, fenced round with screens. Between two and three o'clock in the morning. Offstage an alarm bell is ringing to fight a fire that started much earlier. Quite clearly no one in the house has been to bed yet. On a sofa lies MASHA, dressed, as usual, in black.

Enter OLGA and ANFISA.

ANFISA. They're sitting downstairs now under the staircase . . . And I says, "Please go upstairs," I says, "'tain't right for you to sit here,"—they're crying. "Papa," they says, "we don't know where he's at. God forbid," they says, "he ain't burnt up." Where they'd get a notion like that! And there's some more in the yard . . . undressed too.

OLGA (*pulls dresses out of a wardrobe*). Here, take this gray one . . . And this one too . . . The housecoat as well . . . And take this skirt, my dear . . . What a thing to happen, dear God! Kirsanov Lane is burnt to the ground, it seems. (*Flings the dresses into her arms.*) The poor Vershinins are in a panic . . . Their house was nearly burned down. Have them spend the night with us . . . we can't let them go home . . . At poor Fedotik's everything was burnt, nothing was saved . . .

ANFISA. You'd better call Ferapont, Olyushka, otherwise I can't handle it all . . .

OLGA (*rings*). I'm not getting through . . . (*Out the door.*) Come in here, somebody!

*Through the open door can be seen a window, red with the glow
in the sky, and the fire brigade can be heard driving past
the house.*

How horrible. And I'm sick and tired of it!

Enter FERAPONT.

Here, take this and carry it downstairs . . . The young Kolotilin ladies are
standing under the stairs . . . give it to them. And give them this . . .

FERAPONT. Yes, ma'am. In the year '12 Moscow was burned down too. Lord
God almighty! It sure surprised the Frenchies.[47]

OLGA. Go, go on . . .

FERAPONT. Yes ma'am. (*Exits.*)

OLGA. Nanny dear, darling, give it all away. We don't need any of it, give it all
away, nanny dear . . . I'm worn out, can barely stand on my feet . . . we
can't let the Vershinins go home . . . The little girls will sleep in the
drawing-room, have the Colonel go to the baron's . . . Fedotik can go to
the baron's too, or let him stay here with us in the reception room . . . The
Doctor, as if he did it on purpose, is drunk, hideously drunk, and no one
can be put in with him. And Vershinin's wife in the drawing-room too.

ANFISA (*faintly*). Olyushka darling, don't drive me away! Don't drive me
away!

OLGA. Don't be silly, Nanny. No one's going to drive you away.

ANFISA (*lays her head on Olga's bosom*). My love, my precious, I toil, I work
. . . I'm getting feeble, everybody says, get out! And where am I to go?
Where? In my eighties. My eighty-second year . . .

OLGA. You sit down, Nanny dear . . . You're tired, poor thing . . . (*Helps her
sit down.*) Have a rest, my dear. How pale she is!

NATASHA enters.

NATASHA. Downstairs they're saying somebody ought to hurry and organize
a committee in aid of the fire victims. Why not? It's a lovely idea. As a rule

---

47 Ferapont alludes to the burning of Moscow in 1812 during its occupation by Napoleon's troops.
No one knows for sure, but rumor had it that the Russians started the fire.

one ought to help the poor, it's an obligation of the rich. Bobik and Sophie-kins are asleep, asleep as if nothing had happened. We've got so many peo-ple all over the place, wherever you go, the house is packed. There's flu going around town now, I'm worried the children might catch it.

OLGA (*not listening to her*). You can't see the fire from this room, it's peace-ful here . . .

NATASHA. Yes . . . I suppose I look a mess. (*Before a mirror.*) They say I'm putting on weight . . . it's not true! Not a bit of it! And Masha's asleep, worn out, poor thing . . . (*To Anfisa, coldly.*) Don't you dare sit in my presence! Stand up! Get out of here! (*ANFISA exits; pause.*) And why you hold on to that old woman I cannot understand!

OLGA (*startled*). Excuse me, I can't understand either . . .

NATASHA. There's no reason for her to be here. She's a peasant, ought to live in the country . . . It's pampering them! I like a house to be in order! There shouldn't be any useless people in a house. (*Stroking Olga's cheek.*) You're tired, poor dear! Our headmistress is tired! Why, when my Sophiekins is a big girl and goes to high school, I'll be afraid of you.

OLGA. I'm not going to be headmistress.

NATASHA. They'll pick you, Olga sweetie. The decision's made.

OLGA. I'll turn it down. I cannot . . . I haven't the strength for it . . . (*Drinks some water.*) Just now you abused Nanny so rudely . . . Forgive me, I'm in no condition to put up with . . . It's going dark before my eyes . . .

NATASHA (*agitated*). Forgive me, Olya, forgive . . . I didn't mean to upset you.

　　　　MASHA gets up, takes a pillow and exits, angrily.

OLGA. Try to understand, dear . . . Perhaps we've had a strange upbringing, but I cannot tolerate this. That sort of behavior depresses me, it makes me ill . . . My heart just sinks!

NATASHA. Forgive me, forgive me . . . (*Kisses her.*)

OLGA. Any coarseness, even the slightest, an indelicately spoken word upsets me . . .

NATASHA. I often say too much, that's true, but you must agree, my dear, she could live in the country.

OLGA. She's been with us thirty years.

NATASHA. But she's incapable of working now! Either I don't understand you or else you refuse to understand me. She's not fit for housework, she only sleeps or sits.

OLGA. Then let her sit.

NATASHA (*in wonderment*). What do you mean, let her sit? Why, she's a servant, isn't she! (*Plaintively.*) I don't understand you, Olya. I have a nursemaid, I have a wetnurse, I have a parlor maid, a cook . . . what do we need this old woman for? What for?

Offstage the alarm bell is rung.

OLGA. I've aged ten years tonight.

NATASHA. We've got to thrash this out, Olya, once and for all . . . You're at the high school, I'm at home, you have your teaching, I have my housework. And when I put in a word about servants, I know what I'm talking about; I know what I am talking about . . . And so tomorrow will see the last of that thieving old crow, that nasty old hag . . . (*Stamps her foot.*) that witch! . . . Don't you dare provoke me! Don't you dare! (*Recollecting herself.*) Honestly, if you don't move downstairs, why, we'll always be quarreling. It's awful.

Enter KULYGIN.[48]

KULYGIN. Where's Masha? It's high time we went home. They say the fire's dying down. (*Stretching.*) Only one ward was burnt, but the wind was so strong that it looked at first as if the whole town would go up in flames. (*Sits down.*) I'm worn out. Olechka, my dear . . . I often think: if it hadn't been for Masha, I would have married you, Olechka. You're very good . . . I'm exhausted. (*Hearkening to something.*)

OLGA. What?

KULYGIN. To make matters even worse, the doctor's on a bender, he's awfully drunk. To make matters even worse! (*Stands up.*) There, sounds like he's coming in here . . . You hear him? Yes, in here . . . (*Laughs.*) What a one,

---

48 "In Act Three, of course, you can appear in a double-breasted uniform tunic, that's right, but why in Act Two should you come into the drawing-room in a fur coat?" (Chekhov to Aleksandr Vishnevsky, January 17 [30], 1901).

honestly . . . I'll hide. (*Goes in the corner next to the wardrobe.*) What a delinquent!

OLGA. For two years he hasn't touched a drop, and now all of a sudden he goes and gets drunk . . . (*Goes with NATASHA to the back of the room.*)

> *CHEBUTYKIN enters; not staggering, seemingly sober, he crosses
> the room, stops, looks, then walks over to the washbasin and starts
> to wash his hands.*

CHEBUTYKIN (*surly*). Damn 'em all to hell . . . ram 'em all . . .[49] They think I'm a doctor, know how to treat all sorts of ailments, but I don't know a blessed thing, forgot anything I ever knew, don't remember a thing, not a blessed thing.

> *OLGA and NATASHA leave, unnoticed by him.*

To hell with 'em. Last Wednesday I treated a woman at Zasyp—she died, and it's my fault she died. Yes . . . I did know something twenty-five years ago or so, but now I don't remember a thing. Not a thing . . . My head's empty, my soul's frozen. Maybe I'm not even a human being, but just seem to have arms and legs . . . and a head; maybe I don't even exist at all, but it just seems to me I walk, eat, sleep. (*Weeps.*) Oh, if only I didn't exist! (*Stops weeping, surly.*) Who the hell knows . . . Day before yesterday talk at the club; they're dropping names, Shakespeare, Voltaire . . . I haven't read 'em, haven't read 'em at all, but I made a face to show I'd read 'em. And the others did the same as me. Shabby and vulgar and vile! And that woman that died on Wednesday, I remembered her . . . and remembered it all, and my soul turned all twisted, repulsive, foul . . . I went out, started drinking . . .

> *IRINA, VERSHININ, and TUSENBACH enter; TUSENBACH
> is wearing civilian clothes, new and fashionable.*

IRINA. Let's sit down here. No one will come in here.

VERSHININ. If it hadn't been for the soldiers, the whole town would have burnt down. Fine lads! (*Rubs his hands in satisfaction.*) Sterling fellows! ah, what fine lads!

---

49 Rhyming wordplay in Russian, "*chyort by pobral . . . podral*" (May the devil carry you off, may the devil thrash you soundly).

KULYGIN (*walking over to them*). What time is it, gentlemen?

TUSENBACH. Four o'clock already. Getting light.

IRINA. Everyone's sitting in the reception room, no one will leave. That Solyony of yours is sitting there too . . . (*To Chebutykin.*) You should be in bed, Doctor.

CHEBUTYKIN. Never mind, ma'am . . . Thank you, ma'am. (*Combs out his beard.*)

KULYGIN (*laughs*). You're sploshified, Doctor! (*Claps him on the shoulder.*) Attaboy! *In vino veritas*,[50] said the ancients.

TUSENBACH. They keep asking me to organize a concert on behalf of the fire victims.

IRINA. Why, who could . . .

TUSENBACH. A person could organize one, if a person wanted to. Your sister Mariya, for instance, plays the piano marvelously.

KULYGIN. Marvelously is the way she plays!

IRINA. By now she's forgotten. She hasn't played for three years . . . or four.

TUSENBACH. Absolutely no one in this town understands music, not a single soul, but I do understand it and I give you my word of honor, your sister Mariya plays magnificently, there's talent there.

KULYGIN. You're right, Baron. I love her very much, my Masha. She's superb.

TUSENBACH. To be able to play so splendidly and at the same time to realize that no one, absolutely no one understands you!

KULYGIN (*sighs*). Yes . . . But is it proper for her to take part in a concert? (*Pause.*) Of course I know nothing about it, gentlemen. Perhaps it might even be a good thing. Still, I must confess, our headmaster is a good man, a very good man indeed, the most intelligent of men, but the views he holds . . . Of course, it's none of my business, but even so, if you like, I can probably talk to him about it.

> CHEBUTYKIN *picks up a porcelain clock in both hands and scrutinizes it.*

---

50 Latin: in wine lies truth.

VERSHININ. I got covered in filth at the fire, must look a sight. (*Pause.*) Yesterday I heard in passing that they intend to transfer our brigade somewhere far away. Some say, to the Kingdom of Poland, others—possibly to Chita.[51]

TUSENBACH. I heard that too. Then what? The town will be quite empty.

IRINA. And we shall go away!

CHEBUTYKIN (*drops the clock, which shatters in pieces*). Smithereens!

Pause; everyone is distressed and embarrassed.

KULYGIN (*picks up the fragments*). To break such an expensive object—ah, Ivan Romanych, Ivan Romanych! You get F minus for conduct![52]

IRINA. That clock was our poor mama's.

CHEBUTYKIN. Could be . . . If it's mama's, then it's mama's. Could be I didn't break it, it only seems like I broke it. Maybe it only seems to us that we exist, but as a matter of fact we don't. I don't know anything, nobody knows anything. (*At the door.*) What are you staring at? Natasha's having a cute little affair with Protopopov, and you don't see it . . . There you sit and don't see a thing, while Natasha's having a little affair with Protopopov . . . (*Sings.*) "A fig for you and tell me how you like it . . ."[53] (*Exits.*)

VERSHININ. Yes . . . (*Laughs.*) How altogether strange this is! When the fire broke out, I rushed home right away; I get there, take a look—our house is intact and unharmed and out of danger, but my two little girls are standing on the doorstep in nothing but their underwear, their mother's missing, people are milling about, horses running, dogs, and their little girl faces express alarm, panic, entreaty, I don't know what; my heart clenched when I saw those faces. My God, I think, what else will those girls have to live through in the course of a long life! I grab them, run, and keep thinking that thought: what else will they have to live through in this world!

51 Poland at this time was a vice-regency of the Russian Empire. Chita was far away in the opposite direction, the capital of the region of Transbaikal, Siberia, on the Chinese frontier.

52 In Russian schools, grades ran from five to one, with five being highest. In Chekhov's original, Kulygin gives Chebutykin "Zero minus."

53 "Chebutykin sings only the words 'A fig for you and tell me how you like it . . .' They're the words from an operetta that was once put on at the Hermitage Theatre. I don't remember the name . . . Chebutykin shouldn't sing any more than that, otherwise his exit will take too long" (Chekhov to I. A. Tikhomirov, January 14, 1901).

Alarm bell; pause.

I get here, and their mother's here, shouting, throwing a tantrum.

MASHA enters with a pillow and sits on the sofa.

And when my little girls were standing on the doorstep in nothing but their underwear, barefoot, and the street was red with flames, and there was a terrible racket, it occurred to me that things like that used to happen many years ago when there'd be a sudden enemy invasion, looting and burning . . . And yet, what a fundamental difference there is between how things are now and how they were then! And a little more time will go by, say two hundred, three hundred years, and our present life will be regarded in the same way with horror and contempt, everything that exists now will seem awkward and clumsy and very uncomfortable and strange. Oh, for all we know, what a life that's going to be, what a life! (*Laughs.*) Forgive me, I've started philosophizing again. Do let me go on, ladies and gentlemen. I very much want to philosophize, the fit is on me now.

Pause.

Absolutely everyone's asleep. As I was saying: what a life that's going to be! Can you imagine . . . in town now there are only three like you, in generations to come there'll be more, ever more and more, and there'll come a time when everything will change to be your way, people will live your way, and then even you will become obsolete, people will evolve and be superior to you . . . (*Laughs.*) There's this special fit come over me today. I want like hell to live . . . (*Sings.*) "All ages bend the knee to love, its pangs are blessings from above . . ."[54]

MASHA. Trom-tom-tom.

VERSHININ. Trom-tom . . .

MASHA. Tra-ra-ra?

VERSHININ. Tra-ta-ta. (*Laughs.*)[55]

---

54 Vershinin is singing the opening of Gremin's aria in Chaikovsky's opera *Yevgeny Onegin* (1877), from Pushkin's verse novel.

55 "Vershinin pronounces 'trom-tom-tom' in the form of a question, and you in the form of an answer, and this strikes you as such an original joke that you pronounce this 'trom-trom' with a grin . . . She would *utter* 'trom-trom'—and begin to laugh, but not loudly, just barely. You mustn't create the same kind of character as [Yelena in] *Uncle Vanya* at this point, but someone younger and

Enter FEDOTIK.

FEDOTIK (*dances*). All burned up, all burned up! Every last thing!

Laughter.

IRINA. What's so funny about that? Everything's burnt?

FEDOTIK (*laughs*). Every last thing. Nothing's left. Even the guitar was burnt, and the camera equipment burnt, and all my letters . . . And the notebook I wanted to give you—burnt too.

Enter SOLYONY.

IRINA. No, please, go away, Vasily Vasilich. You can't come in here.

SOLYONY. Why can the Baron, and not me?

VERSHININ. We'd all better leave, in fact. How's the fire?

SOLYONY. They say it's dying down. No, I find this particularly odd, why can the Baron and why can't I? (*Takes out the flask of perfume and sprinkles it about.*)

VERSHININ. Trom-tom-tom.

MASHA. Trom-tom.

VERSHININ (*laughs; to Solyony*). Let's go into the reception room.

SOLYONY. All right, sir, but we're making a note of it. "I'd make my meaning crystal clear, But 'twould upset the geese, I fear . . ."[56] (*Looking at Tusenbach.*) Cheep, cheep, cheep . . .

He exits with VERSHININ and FEDOTIK.

IRINA. That Solyony's smoked up the place . . . (*Startled.*) The Baron's asleep! Baron! Baron!

TUSENBACH (*coming to*). I was tired, though . . . The brickworks . . . I'm not raving, as a matter of fact I'll be going to the brickworks soon, I'll start working there . . . There's been some talk about it already. (*To Irina, ten-*

---

livelier. Remember that you're easily amused, angered" (Chekhov to Olga Knipper, January 20, [February 2], 1901).

56 The moral of Ivan Krylov's fable *The Geese* (1811), in which the barnyard fowl boast of their ancestors, the geese who saved Rome, but have no merits of their own.

derly.) You're so pale, beautiful, bewitching . . . I feel as if your pallor brightens the dark atmosphere like a beacon . . . You're sad, you're dissatisfied with life . . . Oh, come away with me, come away to work together!

MASHA. Nikolay Lvovich, get out of here.

TUSENBACH (*laughing*). You're here? I didn't see you. (*Kisses Irina's hand.*) Good-bye, I'll be going . . . I look at you now and call to mind how once, long ago, on your saint's day, you were confident and carefree and talked of the joys of hard work . . . And what a happy life flashed before me then! Where is it? (*Kisses her hand.*) You've got tears in your eyes. Go to bed, it's daylight already . . . here comes the morning . . . If only I might give my life for you!

MASHA. Nikolay Lvovich, go away! Now really, what . . .

TUSENBACH. I'm going . . . (*Exit.*)

MASHA (*lies down*). You asleep, Fyodor?

KULYGIN. Huh?

MASHA. You should go home.

KULYGIN. My dearest Masha, my dearest Masha . . .

IRINA. She's worn out. You should let her rest, Fedya.

KULYGIN. I'll go right away . . . My wife's lovely, splendid . . . I love you, my one and only . . .

MASHA (*angrily*). Amo, amas, amat, amamus, amatis, amant.[57]

KULYGIN (*laughs*). No, really, she's marvelous. I've been married to you for seven years, but it feels as if we were wed only yesterday. Word of honor. No, really, you're a marvelous woman. I'm content, I'm content, I'm content!

MASHA. I'm sick and tired, sick and tired, sick and tired . . . (*Rises to speak in a sitting position.*) I just can't get it out of my head . . . it's simply appalling. Stuck in my brain like a spike, I can't keep quiet. I mean about Andrey . . .

---

57 Latin: the basic conjugation of the verb *amare*, to love: I love, thou lovest, he, she, or it loves, we love, you love, they love.

He's mortgaged this house to the bank, and his wife snatched all the money, but in fact the house belongs not just to him but to the four of us! He ought to know that, if he's a decent human being.

KULYGIN. Why bother, Masha! What's it to you? Andryusha's in debt all around, so leave him alone.

MASHA. It's appalling in any case. (*Lies down.*)

KULYGIN. You and I aren't poor. I work, I'm at the high school, later in the day I give lessons . . . I'm an honest man. A simple man . . . *Omnia mea mecum porto,*[58] as the saying goes.

MASHA. It's not that I need the money, but the unfairness of it galls me.

Pause.

Get going, Fyodor.

KULYGIN (*kisses her*). You're tired, rest for just half an hour, while I sit outside and wait. Get some sleep . . . (*Goes.*) I'm content, I'm content, I'm content. (*Exits.*)

IRINA. As a matter of fact, our Andrey's become so shallow, so seedy and old living with that woman! He used to make plans to be a professor, but yesterday he was boasting that he's finally managed to make member of the County Council. He's a Council member, but Protopopov's the chairman . . . The whole town's talking, laughing, and he's the only one who sees and knows nothing . . . Here again, everybody runs off to the fire, but he sits by himself in his room and pays no attention. All he does is play the violin. (*On edge.*) Oh, it's horrible, horrible, horrible! (*Weeps.*) I cannot, cannot stand it any more! . . . I cannot, I cannot! . . .

OLGA enters and tidies her nighttable.

(*Sobs loudly.*) Throw me out, throw me out, I can't stand any more! . . .

OLGA (*alarmed*). What's wrong, what's wrong? Dearest!

58 Latin: "I carry all my goods on my person," Cicero in *Paradoxa*. Expression of a member of the family of the philosopher Bias fleeing their country before the Persians and refusing to take any worldly goods with him (ca. 570 B.C.).

IRINA (*sobbing*). Where? Where has it all gone? Where is it? Oh, my God, my God! I've forgotten everything, forgotten . . . It's all tangled up in my mind . . . I can't remember the Italian for window or, uh, ceiling . . . I forget everything, every day I forget, and life goes on and won't ever, ever come back, we'll never get to Moscow . . . I can see that we won't . . .

OLGA. Dearest, dearest . . .

IRINA (*under control*). Oh, I'm unhappy . . . I cannot work, I will not go on working. Enough, enough! I used to be a telegraph operator, now I work for the town council and I hate, despise whatever they give me to do . . . I'm twenty-four already, I've been working for a long time now, and my brain has dried up, I've got skinny and ugly and old, and I've got nothing, nothing, no sort of satisfaction, while time marches on, and I keep feeling that I'm moving away from a genuine, beautiful life, moving ever farther and farther into some kind of abyss. I'm desperate, I'm desperate! And why I'm still alive, why I haven't killed myself before now, I don't understand . . .

OLGA. Don't cry, my little girl, don't cry . . . It pains me.

IRINA. I'm not crying, not crying . . . Enough . . . There, look, I'm not crying any more. Enough . . . Enough!

OLGA. Dearest, I'm speaking to you as a sister, as a friend; if you want my advice, marry the Baron! (*IRINA weeps quietly.*) After all, you do respect him, think highly of him . . . True, he's not good looking, but he's so decent, so pure . . . After all, people don't marry for love, but just to do their duty. At least that's how I think of it, and I would marry without love. Anyone who came courting, I'd marry him all the same, I mean if he were a decent man. I'd even marry an old man . . .

IRINA. I kept waiting for us to move to Moscow, there my true love would find me, I would dream about him, love him . . . But it's all turned out to be foolishness, nothing but foolishness.

OLGA (*embraces her sister*). My darling, lovely sister, I understand it all; when the Baron resigned from military service and came calling on us in a suit jacket, he looked so homely I even started to cry . . . He asked me, "What are you crying for?" How could I tell him! But if it were God's will that he marry you, I'd be very happy. That would make a change, a complete change.

NATASHA, *carrying a candle, crosses the stage from the door*
right to the door left, in silence.[59]

MASHA (*sits up*). She prowls around as if she was the one who'd set the fire.

OLGA. Don't be silly, Masha. The silliest in our family, that's you. Forgive
me, please.

Pause.

MASHA. I want to make a confession, dear sisters. My heart is heavy, I'll confess to you and never again to anyone, ever . . . I'll speak my piece right
now. (*Quietly.*) This is my secret, but you ought to know it all . . . I can't
keep still . . .(*Pause.*) I love, love . . . I love that man . . . You just saw him
. . . Well, there you have it. In short, I love Vershinin.[60]

OLGA (*goes behind her screen*). Stop it. It doesn't matter, I'm not listening.

MASHA. What can I do? (*Clutches her head.*) At first he struck me as peculiar, then I felt sorry for him . . . then I fell in love . . .

OLGA (*behind the screen*). I'm not listening, it doesn't matter. Whatever silly
things you say, it doesn't matter, I'm not listening.

MASHA. Ay, you're incredible, Olya. I love—which means, it's my fate. Which
means, such is my lot . . . And he loves me . . . it's all terrible. Right? it's no
good, is it? (*Takes Irina by the hands and draws her to her.*) Oh my dear . .
. How are we to get through our lives, what's to become of us . . . When you
read a novel, it all seems so trite and so easy to understand, but when you
fall in love yourself, you realize that no one knows anything about it and
everyone has to decide for herself . . . My dears, my sisters . . . I've con-

---

59 "You write that in Act Three, Natasha, making the rounds of the house at night, puts out the
lights and looks under the furniture for burglars. But, it seems to me, it would be better to have her
walk across the stage in a straight line, without a glance at anyone or anything, à la Lady Macbeth,
with a candle—something a bit tighter and more frightening" (Chekhov to Olga Knipper, January
2 [15], 1901).

60 "Masha's confession in Act Three is not exactly a confession, but only a frank statement. Behave
nervously but not despondently, no shouting, even smiling now and then and for the most part
behave so that one can feel the weariness of the night. And so that one can feel that you are more
intelligent than your sisters, you think yourself more intelligent, at least. As to 'trom-tom-tom,' do it
your way" (Chekhov to Olga Knipper, January 21 [February 3], 1901).

fessed to you, now I'll keep still . . . Now I'll be like that madman in Gogol's story . . .[61] still . . . still . . .

Enter ANDREY, followed by FERAPONT.

ANDREY (*angrily*). What d'you want? I don't understand.

FERAPONT (*in the doorway, indecisively*). Andrey Sergeich, I already said ten times or so.

ANDREY. In the first place, I'm not Andrey Sergeich to you, I'm Your Honor!

FERAPONT. The firemen, your highness, want to know if you'll let 'em drive across the garden to the river. Otherwise they got to ride round and round in a circle—wears the daylights out of 'em.

ANDREY. All right. Tell them, it's all right. (*FERAPONT exits.*) They make me sick. Where's Olga? (*OLGA appears from behind her screen.*) I came here to get the key to the bookcase, I've lost mine. You've got one of those tiny little keys. (*OLGA gives him the key in silence. IRINA goes behind her screen; pause.*) What a terrific fire, eh! It's starting to die down now. Dammit, that Ferapont got on my nerves, I was talking nonsense . . . Your Honor . . .

Pause.

Why don't you say something, Olga?

Pause.

It's about time you stopped being so silly, pouting like this, acting so high and mighty . . . You're here, Masha, Irina's here, well, that's just fine—let's clear this up right in the open, once and for all. What do you have against me? What?

OLGA. Drop it, Andryusha. We'll clear it up tomorrow. (*Distraught.*) What an excruciating night!

ANDREY (*he's very embarrassed*). Don't get upset. I'm asking this perfectly calmly: what do you have against me? Say it straight out.

VERSHININ's voice: "Trom-tom-tom!"

---

61 Poprishchin, hero of Gogol's story *Diary of a Madman* (1835), is a victim of unrequited love. He continually repeats the phrase "Never mind, never mind . . . be still."

MASHA (*rises; loudly*). Tra-ta-ta! (*To Olga.*) Good-bye, Olya, God bless
you. (*Goes behind the screen, kisses Irina.*) Sleep in peace . . . Good-bye,
Andrey. Go away, they're exhausted . . . tomorrow you can clear things up
. . . (*Leaves.*)

OLGA. Really, Andryusha, let's put it off till tomorrow . . . (*Goes behind her
screen.*) It's time for bed.

ANDREY. I'll just say this and then I'll go. Right away . . . In the first place,
you've got something against Natasha, my wife, and I've noticed it from the
very day of our wedding. If you want to know, Natasha is a beautiful, honest person, forthright and upstanding—that's my opinion. I love and respect
my wife, understand me, respect her and I demand that she be respected
by others as well. I repeat, she's an honest, upstanding person, and all your
criticism, if you don't mind my saying so, is simply frivolous . . .

Pause.

In the second place, you seem to be angry because I'm not a professor,
don't have scholarly pursuits. But I serve the county, I'm a member of the
County Council and I consider this service of mine just as dedicated and
exalted as service to scholarship. I'm a member of the County Council and
proud of it, if you want to know . . .

Pause.

In the third place . . . I've got something else to say . . . I mortgaged the
house, without asking your permission . . . There I am at fault, yes, and I
beg you to forgive me. I was driven to it by my debts . . . thirty-five thousand . . . I've stopped playing cards, I gave it up a long time ago, but the
main thing I can say in my defense is that you're girls, you get Father's pension, but I don't have . . . any income, so to speak . . .

Pause.

KULYGIN (*in the doorway*). Masha's not here? (*Alarmed.*) Where is she? This
is odd . . . (*Exits.*)

ANDREY. They aren't listening. Natasha is an excellent, honest person.
(*Paces the stage in silence, then stops.*) When I got married, I thought we'd
be happy . . . everybody happy . . . But my God . . . (*Weeps.*) My dear sisters, precious sisters, don't believe me, don't believe me . . . (*Exits.*)

KULYGIN (*in the doorway, worried*). Where's Masha? Isn't Masha here then?
Amazing. (*Exits.*)

Alarm bell; the stage is empty.

IRINA (*behind a screen*). Olya! Who's that knocking on the floor?

OLGA. It's the Doctor. He's drunk.

IRINA. What a crazy night!

Pause.

Olya! (*Peers out from behind her screen.*) Did you hear? They're taking the brigade away from us, they're transferring it somewhere far away.

OLGA. That's mere rumor.

IRINA. We'll be here all alone then . . . Olya!

OLGA. Well?

IRINA. Dearest, precious, I respect, I think highly of the Baron, he's a fine man, I will marry him, agreed, only let's go to Moscow! Only please, please, let's go! There's nothing on earth better than Moscow! Let's go, Olya! Let's go!

Curtain

ACT FOUR

An old garden attached to the Prozorovs' house. A long path lined with fir trees, at whose end a river can be seen. On the farther bank of the river is a forest. To the right, the veranda of the house; here on a table are bottles and glasses; apparently someone has been drinking champagne. Twelve o'clock noon. Passersby occasionally cut through the garden from the street to the river; five or so soldiers pass quickly by.

CHEBUTYKIN, in an affable mood that stays with him throughout the whole act, is sitting in an armchair in the garden, waiting to be called; he wears a forage cap and has a walking stick. IRINA, KULYGIN with a medal round his neck and without his moustache, and TUSENBACH, sitting on the veranda, are seeing off FEDOTIK and RODÉ, who are coming down the steps, both officers in field kit.

TUSENBACH (*exchanging kisses with FEDOTIK*). You're a good man, we were such friends. (*Exchanges kisses with RODÉ.*) One more time . . . Good-bye, my dear friend!

IRINA. See you soon!

FEDOTIK. It isn't see-you-soon, it's good-bye, we'll never meet again!

KULYGIN. Who knows! (*Wipes his eyes, smiles.*) Look, I'm starting to cry.

IRINA. We'll meet some day.

FEDOTIK. In, say, ten or fifteen years? But then we'll barely recognize one another, we'll say a formal how-d'you-do. (*Takes a snapshot.*) Hold still . . . Once more, the last time.

RODÉ (*embraces Tusenbach*). We won't meet again . . . (*Kisses Irina's hand.*) Thanks for everything, everything!

FEDOTIK (*annoyed*). Just hold still!

TUSENBACH. God willing, we shall meet. Do write to us. Be sure and write.

RODÉ (*casts a glance round the garden*). Good-bye, trees! (*Shouts.*) Hop to it! (*Pause.*) Good-bye, echo!

KULYGIN. You'll get married out there in Poland, perish the thought . . . Your Polish wife will throw her arms around you and say, "Kochany!"[62] (*Laughs.*)

FEDOTIK (*after a glance at his watch*). There's less than an hour left. Solyony's the only one from our battery going on the barge, we're with the line unit. Three batteries are leaving today in battalions, another three tomorrow— and the town will surrender to peace and quiet.

TUSENBACH. And godawful boredom.

RODÉ. And where's Mariya Sergeevna?

KULYGIN. Masha's in the garden.

FEDOTIK. Have to say good-bye to her.

RODÉ. Good-bye, got to go, or else I'll start bawling . . . (*Quickly embraces Tusenbach and Kulygin, kisses Irina's hand.*) We had a wonderful time here . . .

---

62 Polish: beloved, dearest.

FEDOTIK (*to Kulygin*). Here's a souvenir for you . . . a notebook with a tiny little pencil . . . We'll go through here to the river . . .

> *They move away, both looking around.*

RODÉ (*shouts*). Hop to it!

KULYGIN (*shouts*). Good-bye!

> *Very far upstage FEDOTIK and RODÉ run into MASHA and say good-bye to her; she exits with them.*

IRINA. They've gone . . . (*Sits on the bottom step of the veranda.*)

CHEBUTYKIN. And forgot to say good-bye to me.

IRINA. And what about *you*?

CHEBUTYKIN. Yes, I forgot too somehow. However, I'll soon be seeing them, I leave tomorrow. Yes . . . Just one day left. In a year they'll let me retire, I'll come back here again and live out my life beside you. I've just got one little year left before my pension . . . (*Puts the newspaper in his pocket, takes out another.*) I'll come back here to you and I'll change my way of living through and through. I'll turn into such a nice, quiet, beni . . . benignant, well-behaved little fellow . . .

IRINA. Well, you ought to change your way of life, my love. You ought to somehow.

CHEBUTYKIN. Yes. I can feel it. (*Sings quietly.*) "Tarara . . . boom de-ay . . . I sit in gloom all day . . ."[63]

KULYGIN. Incorrigible, that's our Doctor! Incorrigible!

CHEBUTYKIN. Well then, it's up to you to teach me better. Then I'd be corrigible.

IRINA. Fyodor shaved off his moustache. I can't look at him!

KULYGIN. Why not?

CHEBUTYKIN. I'd love to tell you what your face looks like now, but I'd better not.

---

63 A British music-hall song, accompanied by a high-kicking dance, which had a certain vogue on the Continent. In the Russian translation, it goes, "Tarara boom de-ay / I'm sitting on a curbstone / And weeping bitterly / Because I know so little." The second verse is slightly racy. Compare Chekhov's story "Volodya the Great and Volodya the Little" (1893).

KULYGIN. So what! It's comfortable this way, it's the *modus vivendi*.[64] Our headmaster never lets his moustache grow, and so, when I was made school inspector, I shaved mine off. Nobody likes it, but it doesn't matter to me. I'm content. Moustache or no, I'm just as content . . . (*Sits down.*)

> *Far upstage ANDREY is wheeling a sleeping infant in a baby carriage.*

IRINA. Ivan Romanych, my dear, my darling, I'm awfully worried. You were downtown yesterday, tell me, what happened there?

CHEBUTYKIN. What happened? Nothing. Trivia. (*Reads the paper.*) Doesn't matter.

KULYGIN. The story goes that Solyony and the Baron met yesterday downtown outside the theater . . .

TUSENBACH. Stop! Well, really . . . (*Waves his hand in dismissal and goes inside the house.*)

KULYGIN. Outside the theater . . . Solyony started needling the Baron, and the Baron wouldn't stand for it, and said something insulting . . .

CHEBUTYKIN. I wouldn't know. 'S all hokum.

KULYGIN. In a seminary once a teacher wrote "Hokum" on a composition, and the student thought it was Latin, started to conjugate it—hokum, hokium, hokii, hokia.[65] (*Laughs.*) Wonderfully funny. They say Solyony's in love with Irina and sort of developed a hatred for the Baron . . . That's understandable. Irina's a very nice girl. She even resembles Masha, the same sort of moodiness. Only you've got the milder temper, Irina. Although Masha has a very nice temper too, of course. I do love her, my Masha.

> *Offstage, at the bottom of the garden:* "Yoo-hoo! Hop to it!"

IRINA (*startled*). Somehow everything frightens me today.

> *Pause.*

All my things are already packed, after dinner I'll send them off. Tomorrow the Baron and I will be married, tomorrow we move to the brickworks, and

---

64 Latin: a means of living, a temporary compromise.

65 The Russian joke is that *chepukha* ("nonsense," "rot") written out in Cyrillic script looks like a nonexistent but ostensible Latin word *renixa*.

by the day after tomorrow I'll be in school, starting a new life. Somehow God will help me. When I took the qualifying exam for the teaching certificate, I even wept for joy, at the integrity of it . . .

Pause.

Any minute now the horse and wagon will come by for my things . . .

KULYGIN. Well, that's how it goes, but somehow it isn't serious. Nothing but abstract idealism, and very little seriousness. Still, I wish you good luck from the bottom of my heart.

CHEBUTYKIN (*affectionately*). My miracle, my dearest . . . My treasure . . . You've moved far away from me, I can't catch up with you. I'm left far behind, like a bird of passage that's too old to fly. Fly away, my darlings, fly and God bless you!

Pause.

It was a mistake to shave off your moustache, Fyodor Ilyich.

KULYGIN. That's enough out of you! (*Sighs.*) So today the military departs and everything will go on again as it did in the past. Say what you like, Masha's a good, honorable woman, I love her very much and thank my lucky stars. People have such different fates . . . There's a certain Kozyryov[66] who works for internal revenue. He went to school with me, was expelled his senior year in high school because he could never manage to learn the *ut consecutivum* construction.[67] Now he's awfully poor, ill, and whenever we meet, I say to him, "Greetings, *ut consecutivum*" — "Yes," he says, "*consecutivum* indeed . . ." and then he coughs. But I've been lucky all my life, I'm happy, look, I've even got the Order of Stanislas second class[68] and now I'm teaching others that same *ut consecutivum*. Of course, I'm a clever man, cleverer than a great many others, but that's not what happiness is all about . . .

---

66 A speaking name, since *kozyr* means "ace."

67 The rule in Latin grammar that demands the use of the subjunctive mood in subordinate clauses beginning with the conjunction *ut* (that, so that). Chekhov had trouble with it as a schoolboy.

68 One of the decorations bestowed in pre-Revolutionary Russia on civil servants and military men. The least important, the Stanislas 3rd Class, was bestowed on Chekhov in 1899 for his work in educating the peasants.

In the house "The Maiden's Prayer"[69] is played on the piano.

IRINA. And tomorrow night I won't have to listen to "The Maiden's Prayer," I won't have to meet Protopopov . . .

Pause.

There's Protopopov sitting in the drawing-room; he came by again today . . .

KULYGIN. The headmistress still isn't here?

Far upstage MASHA saunters quietly across the stage.

IRINA. No. She's been sent for. If only you knew how hard it is for me to live here alone, without Olya . . . She lives at the high school; she's head-mistress, busy with her work all day, while I'm alone, I'm bored, nothing to do, and the hateful room I live in . . . So I came to a decision: if it's not my fate to live in Moscow, so be it. After all, it must be fate. Nothing to be done about it . . . Everything is God's will, true enough. The Baron proposed to me . . . Then what? I thought it over and decided. He's a good man, a wonderful man really, so good . . . And suddenly, just as if my heart had sprouted wings, I cheered up, I felt relieved and once again I started wanting to work, work . . . Only something happened yesterday, a kind of mystery has been hanging over me . . .

CHEBUTYKIN. Hokium. Hokum.

NATASHA (*out the window*). The headmistress!

KULYGIN. The headmistress is here . . . Let's go in.

Exits into the house with IRINA.

CHEBUTYKIN (*reads the papers and sings softly*). Tarara . . . boom de-ay . . . I sit in gloom all day . . .

MASHA comes up; upstage ANDREY wheels the baby carriage.

MASHA. Sitting by himself, taking it easy . . .

CHEBUTYKIN. So what?

---

69 Sentimental piano piece by the Polish composer T. Badarzewska-Baranovskaia (1838–1862), "La prière d'une vierge." Anyone who could read a note could play it. In Bertolt Brecht and Kurt Weill's opera *The Rise and Fall of the City of Mahagonny* (1929), after it is played by a whore in a brothel, a customer sighs deeply and says, "Ah! that is eternal art."

MASHA (*sits down*). Nothing . . .

Pause.

Did you love my mother?

CHEBUTYKIN. Very much.

MASHA. And she loved you?

CHEBUTYKIN (*after a pause*). I can't remember any more.

MASHA. Is my man here? That's how our cook Marfa used to refer to her policeman: my man. Is my man here?

CHEBUTYKIN. Not yet.

MASHA. When you get happiness in bits and pieces, in snatches, and then you lose it, as I do, you gradually toughen up, you get bitchy. (*Points to her bosom.*) I'm seething inside . . . (*Looking at her brother Andrey, wheeling the baby carriage.*) Look at our Andrey, our baby brother . . . All hope is lost. Thousands of people were hoisting a bell, a lot of energy and money was expended, and all of a sudden it fell to the ground and smashed. All of a sudden, without rhyme or reason. 'S just the same with Andrey . . .

ANDREY. When will the house finally quiet down? Such a rumpus.

CHEBUTYKIN. Soon. (*Looks at his watch, then winds it; the watch chimes.*) I've got an antique watch, with a chime . . . The first, second, and fifth batteries are leaving at one on the dot.

Pause.

And I go tomorrow.

ANDREY. Forever?

CHEBUTYKIN. I don't know. Maybe I'll be back within the year. Who the hell knows, though . . . Doesn't matter . . .

Somewhere far away a harp and a fiddle can be heard playing.

ANDREY. The town's emptying out. Just as if a dust-cover had been dropped over it.

Pause.

Something happened yesterday outside the theater: they're all talking about it, but I don't know what it was.

CHEBUTYKIN. Nothing. Trivia. Solyony started needling the Baron, so the Baron flared up and insulted him, and what with one thing and another in the end Solyony was obliged to challenge him to a duel. (*Looks at his watch.*) It's about time now, I think . . . Half past twelve, in the state forest preserve, that one over there, the one you can see on the far side of the river . . . Bing-bang. (*Laughs.*) Solyony imagines he's Lermontov, and even writes poetry. Look, a joke's a joke, but this is his third duel by now.

MASHA. Whose?

CHEBUTYKIN. Solyony's!

MASHA. And what about the Baron?

CHEBUTYKIN. What *about* the Baron?

Pause.

MASHA. My thoughts are all snarled . . . Even so, I say it's not right to let him do it. He might wound the Baron or even kill him.

CHEBUTYKIN. The Baron's all right, but one baron more or less—does it really matter? Let it be! It doesn't matter! (*Beyond the garden a shout: "Yoo-hoo! Hop to it!"*) You wait. That's Skvortsov shouting, one of the seconds. He's sitting in a rowboat.

ANDREY. In my opinion, even taking part in a duel, even being present at one, if only in the capacity of a medical man, is simply immoral.

CHEBUTYKIN. It only seems that way . . . There's nothing on this earth, we aren't here, we don't exist, but it only seems that we exist . . . So what does it matter?

MASHA. So they waste the whole day here talking and talking . . . (*Walks.*) You live in a climate like this, expecting it to snow any minute, and you still carry on these conversations . . . (*Stops.*) I won't go inside the house, I can't go in there . . . When Vershinin comes, let me know . . . (*Walks up the path.*) And the birds of passage are already on the wing . . . (*Looks upward.*) Swans, or geese . . . My beauties, my happy creatures . . . (*Exits.*)

ANDREY. Our house is emptying out. The officers are going, you're going, sister's getting married, and I'll be left alone in the house.

CHEBUTYKIN. What about your wife?

FERAPONT enters with papers.

ANDREY. A wife is a wife. She's honest, decent, oh, and kind, but for all that there's something in her that reduces her to a petty, blind sort of bristly animal. In any case, she's not human. I'm talking to you as a friend, the only person I can open my heart to. I love Natasha, I do, but sometimes she seems to me incredibly vulgar, and then I get mixed up, I don't understand how and why I love her so or, at least, loved her . . .

CHEBUTYKIN (*rises*). My boy, I'll be leaving tomorrow, maybe we'll never meet again, so here's my advice to you. Look, put on your hat, take up your stick, and leave . . . leave and go away, go without looking back. And the farther you go the better.

> SOLYONY *passes by upstage with* TWO OFFICERS; *catching sight of Chebutykin, he turns towards him; the officers walk farther on.*

SOLYONY. Doctor, it's time! Half past twelve already. (*Exchanges greetings with* ANDREY.)

CHEBUTYKIN. Right away. You all make me sick. (*To Andrey.*) If anyone asks for me, Andryusha, say I'll be right back . . . (*Sighs.*) Oy-oy-oy!

SOLYONY. "He scarcely had time to gasp, when the bear had him in its grasp." (*Walks with him.*) What are you groaning about, old man?

CHEBUTYKIN. Oh!

SOLYONY. Feeling healthy?

CHEBUTYKIN (*angrily*). Like a rich man's wealthy.

SOLYONY. The old man's getting upset for no good reason. I'll indulge myself a bit, I'll only wing him, like a wood-snipe. (*Takes out the perfume and sprinkles his hands.*) Look, I've poured a whole flask on them today, but they still smell. My hands smell like a corpse.

> *Pause.*

So, sir . . . You remember the poem? "But he, the rebel, seeks the storm, As if a storm could give him peace . . ."[70]

CHEBUTYKIN. Yes. "He scarcely had time to gasp, when the bear had him in its grasp."

---

70 Familiar quotation from the poem "The Sail" ("Parus," 1832), by Mikhail Lermontov. Chekhov quotes it also in *The Wedding*.

Exits with SOLYONY.

FERAPONT. Papers to sign . . .

ANDREY (*jittery*). Get away from me! Get away! For pity's sake! (*Exits with the baby carriage.*)

FERAPONT. But that's what papers is for, to be signed. (*Exits upstage.*)

Enter IRINA and TUSENBACH, wearing a straw hat.
KULYGIN crosses the stage, shouting "Yoo-hoo, Masha, yoo-hoo!"

TUSENBACH. It looks like he's the only man in town who's glad the military are leaving.

IRINA. That's understandable.

Pause.

Our town is emptying out now.

TUSENBACH. I'll be back in a minute, dear.

IRINA. Where are you off to?

TUSENBACH. I have to go downtown to . . . to see my comrades off.

IRINA. That's not true . . . Nikolay, why are you so on edge today?

Pause.

What happened yesterday outside the theater?

TUSENBACH (*gesture of impatience*). I'll be back in an hour and we'll be together again. (*Kisses her hand.*) Light of my life . . . (*Looks into her face.*) It's five years now since I started loving you, and I still can't get used to it, and you seem ever more beautiful to me. What lustrous, wonderful hair! What eyes! I'll take you away tomorrow, we shall work, we'll be rich, my dreams will come true. You shall be happy. There's just one thing, though, just one thing: you don't love me!

IRINA. It's not in my power! I'll be your wife, and a true one, an obedient one, but there's no love, what can I do! (*Weeps.*) I've never loved even once in my life. Oh, I've dreamt so much about love, I've been dreaming about it for so long now, day and night, but my heart is like an expensive piano, locked tight and the key is lost.

Pause.

You seem restless.

TUSENBACH. I didn't sleep all night. There's never been anything in my life so terrible that it could frighten me, and yet this lost key tears my heart to pieces, won't let me sleep. Tell me something.

Pause.

Tell me something . . .

IRINA. What? What? Everything around us is so mysterious, the old trees stand in silence . . . (*Puts her head on his chest.*)

TUSENBACH. Tell me something.

IRINA. What? What am I to say? What?

TUSENBACH. Something.

IRINA. Stop it! Stop it!

Pause.

TUSENBACH. What trivia, what foolish trifles sometimes start to matter in our lives, all of a sudden, for no good reason. At first you laugh at them, treat them as trifles, and all the same you go on and feel you haven't the power to stop. Oh, let's not talk about it! I feel cheerful, as if I'm seeing those spruces, maples, birches for the first time in my life, and they all stare curiously at me and wait. What beautiful trees, and, really, the life we lead in their shade ought to be so beautiful! (*A shout: "Yoo-hoo! Hop to it!"*) I have to go, it's time now . . . There's a tree that's withered and dead, but all the same it sways with the others in the breeze. So, I guess, if I die too, I'll still take part in life one way or another. Good-bye, my dear . . . (*Kisses her hand.*) Those papers you gave me are in my desk, under the almanac.

IRINA. I'll go with you.

TUSENBACH (*alarmed*). No, no. (*Goes quickly, stops on the path.*) Irina!

IRINA. What?

TUSENBACH (*not knowing what to say*). I haven't had any coffee today. Ask them to make me some . . . (*Exits quickly.*)

> *IRINA stands rapt in thought, then walks far upstage and sits on a swing. Enter ANDREY with the baby carriage; FERAPONT appears.*

FERAPONT. Andrey Sergeich, these here papers ain't mine, they're official. I didn't dream 'em up.

ANDREY. Oh, where is it, where has my past gone to, when I was young, cheerful, intelligent, when my dreams and thoughts were refined, when my present and future glistened with hope? Why, when we've barely begun to live, do we get boring, gray, uninteresting, lazy, apathetic, useless, unhappy . . . Our town has existed for two hundred years, it contains a hundred thousand inhabitants, and not one who isn't exactly like the others, not one dedicated person, past or present, not one scholar, not one artist, not one even faintly remarkable person who might stir up envy or a passionate desire to emulate him. All they do is eat, drink, sleep, then die . . . others are born and they too eat, drink, sleep and, to keep from being stultified by boredom, vary their lives with vicious gossip, vodka, cards, crooked deals, and the wives cheat on the husbands while the husbands lie, pretend to notice nothing, hear nothing, and an irresistibly vulgar influence is brought to bear on the children, and the divine spark in them flickers out, and they become the same miserable, identical dead things as their fathers and mothers . . .[71] (*To Ferapont, angrily.*) What d'you want?

FERAPONT. How's that? Papers to sign.

ANDREY. You make me sick.

FERAPONT (*handing him the papers*). A while ago the doorman at the town hall was saying . . . Looks like, says he, this winter in Petersburg there was ten degrees o' frost.

ANDREY. The present is repulsive, but when, on the other hand, I think of the future, it's so fine! I start to feel so relieved, so expansive; and a light begins to dawn in the distance, I can see freedom, I can see how my children and I will be freed from idleness, from beer drinking, from goose and cabbage, from after-dinner naps, from degrading sloth . . .

FERAPONT. Two thousand people froze, seems like. The common folks, says he, was scared to death. Either Petersburg or Moscow — I don't rec'llect.

ANDREY (*caught up in a feeling of tenderness*). My dear sisters, my wonderful sisters! (*Plaintively.*) Masha, sister dear . . .

---

71 "[Chekhov] demanded that in the last monologue Andrey be very excited. 'He should almost threaten the audience with his fists!' " (V. V. Luzhsky, *Solntse Rossii* 228/25 [1914]).

NATASHA (*out the window*). Who's talking so loudly out there? Is that you, Andryusha? You'll wake up Sophiekins. *Il ne faut pas faire du bruit, la Sophie est dormée déjà. Vous êtes un ours.*[72] (*Losing her temper.*) If you want to talk, then give the buggy and the baby to somebody else. Ferapont, take the baby buggy from the master!

FERAPONT. Yes'm. (*Takes the carriage.*)

ANDREY (*embarrassed*). I'm talking softly.

NATASHA (*back of the window, petting her little boy*). Bobik! Cunning Bobik! Naughty Bobik!

ANDREY (*glancing at the papers*). All right, I'll look them over and sign what's necessary, and you take them back to the council . . .

> *Exits into the house, reading the papers; FERAPONT wheels*
> *the carriage.*

NATASHA (*back of the window*). Bobik, what's your mommy's name? Cutie, cutie! And who's this? It's Auntie Olya. Say to auntie: Afternoon, Olya!

> *Itinerant MUSICIANS, a MAN and a GIRL, play the fiddle and*
> *the harp. Out of the house come VERSHININ, OLGA, and*
> *ANFISA and listen a moment in silence; IRINA comes up*
> *to them.*

OLGA. Our garden's like an empty lot, people walk and drive right through it. Nanny, give those musicians something! . . .

ANFISA (*gives something to the musicians*). God bless you, sweethearts. (*The MUSICIANS bow and leave.*) Hard-luck folks. When your belly's full, you don't have to play. (*To Irina.*) Afternoon, Arisha! (*Kisses her.*) My, my, child, lookit the way I live now! The way I live! In the high school in government housing, grand rooms, along with Olyushka—the Lord decreed that for my old age. I've not lived like that in all my born days, sinner that I am . . . The housing's big, on the government money, and I've got a whole little room and a little bed to myself. All on the government. I wake up at night and— oh Lord, oh Mother o' God, there's nobody happier'n me!

VERSHININ (*after a glance at his watch*). We'll be leaving any minute, Olga Sergeevna. My time's up.

---

72 Bad French for "Don't make any noise. Sophie is already asleep. You are a bear!"

Pause.

I wish you the best of luck, the best . . . Where's Mariya Sergeevna?

IRINA. She's somewhere in the garden. I'll go find her.

VERSHININ. Please do. I'm in a hurry.

ANFISA. I'll go and look too. (*Shouts.*) Mashenka, yoo-hoo! (*Goes with IRINA to the bottom of the garden.*) Yoo-hoo, yoo-hoo!

VERSHININ. Everything must come to an end. Here we are saying good-bye. (*Looks at his watch.*) The town gave us a kind of lunch, we drank champagne, the mayor made a speech, I ate and listened, but in spirit I was here with you . . . (*Looks around the garden.*) I've grown accustomed to you.

OLGA. Will we ever meet again?

VERSHININ. I don't suppose so.

Pause.

My wife and both my little girls will stay on here another two months or so; please, if anything happens or if anything's needed . . .

OLGA. Yes, yes, of course. Don't worry.

Pause.

Tomorrow there won't be a single military man left in town, it will all have turned into a memory, and, of course, a new life will begin for us . . .

Pause.

Nothing works out the way we'd like it to. I didn't want to be a headmistress, but even so I am one. Which means, not being in Moscow.

VERSHININ. Well . . . Thank you for everything. Forgive me, if anything wasn't right . . . I talked a lot, an awful lot—and forgive me for it, don't think badly of me.

OLGA (*wipes away tears*). What's keeping Masha . . .

VERSHININ. What more is there to say at parting? How about philosophizing? . . . (*Laughs.*) Life is hard. It appears to many of us to be lackluster and hopeless, but even so, you must admit, it will grow ever brighter and easier, and apparently the time's not far off when it will be very bright. (*Looks at his watch.*) My time's up, it's time! In olden days humanity was preoccupied with wars, its whole existence filled with campaigns, invasions, victories, now all that's out of date, but it's left behind an enormous vacuum, which so far has been impossible to fill; humanity is passionately seeking and will find it at last. Ah, the sooner the better!

Pause.

You know, if only hard work were supplemented by education, and education by hard work. (*Looks at his watch.*) However, my time's up . . .

OLGA. Here she comes.

MASHA enters.

VERSHININ. I came to say good-bye . . .

OLGA draws somewhat apart, not to intrude on their farewells.

MASHA (*gazes into his face*). Good-bye . . . (*A long, drawn-out kiss.*)

OLGA. That'll do, that'll do . . .

MASHA sobs vehemently.

VERSHININ. Write to me . . . Don't forget! Let me go . . . it's time . . . Olga Sergeevna, take her, I have to . . . It's time . . . I'm late . . . (*Much affected, he kisses Olga's hand, then embraces Masha once again and leaves quickly.*)

OLGA. That'll do, Masha! Stop it, dear . . .

Enter KULYGIN.

KULYGIN (*in consternation*). Never mind, let her go on crying, let her . . . My good Masha, my kind Masha . . . You're my wife, and I'm happy, no matter what went on here . . . I'm not complaining, I'm not reproaching you in the least . . . Olya there is a witness . . . Let's start over again living as we used to, and I won't say a single word to you, no recriminations . . .

MASHA (*controlling her sobbing*). On the curved seashore a green oak stands, a golden chain wound round that oak . . . A golden chain wound round that oak . . . I'm losing my mind . . . On the curved seashore . . . a green oak stands . . .[73]

---

73 The images are from the opening lines of Pushkin's *Ruslan and Lyudmila*. See note 11. Masha changes the rhyme words "green oak" (*dub zelyony*) and "learned cat" (*kot uchyony*) to "green cat" (*kot zelyony*).

OLGA. Calm down, Masha . . . Calm down . . . Get her some water.

MASHA. I'm not crying any more.

KULYGIN. She's not crying any more . . . she's being considerate . . .

A muffled shot is heard in the distance.

MASHA. On the curved seashore a green oak stands, a golden chain wound round that oak . . . A golden chain wound round that oak . . . A green cat stands . . . A green oak stands . . . I'm raving . . . (*Drinks some water.*) Life's a failure . . . I don't want anything now . . . I'll be all right presently . . . Doesn't matter . . . What does that mean, on the curved seashore? Why is that phrase in my head? My thoughts are running wild.

IRINA enters.

The harp- and fiddle-playing can be heard far away down the street.

OLGA. Calm down, Masha. Now, there's a good girl . . . Let's go inside.

MASHA (*angrily*). I will not go in there. (*Sobs, but instantly stops.*) I don't go in that house any more and I won't go . . .

IRINA. Let's sit down together, at least let's not say anything. After all, I'm going away tomorrow . . .

Pause.

KULYGIN. Yesterday in the sophomore class I took this moustache and beard away from some smart-aleck . . . (*Puts on the moustache and beard.*) Looks like the German teacher . . . (*Laughs.*) Doesn't it? Those kids are a caution.

MASHA. Actually it does look like your German.

OLGA (*laughs*). Yes.

MASHA weeps.

IRINA. That's enough, Masha!

KULYGIN. A lot like him . . .

Enter NATASHA.

NATASHA (*to the Parlor Maid*). What? Protopopov's going to sit with Sophiekins for a while—Mikhail Ivanych—and Andrey Sergeich can take Bobik for an airing. So much fuss over children . . . (*To Irina.*) You're going away tomorrow, Irina—such a shame. Do stay just another little week at least. (*Shrieks on seeing Kulygin; he laughs and removes the moustache and beard.*) Why, you gave me quite a shock! (*To Irina.*) I've got used to you and do you think parting from you is easy for me? I've told them to move Andrey and his fiddle into your room—he can saw away in there!—and we'll put Sophiekins in his room. A wonderful, fantastic baby! Such a little cutie! Today she stared at me with her little peepers and went—"Mama."

KULYGIN. A beautiful baby, true enough.

NATASHA. In other words, I'll be all on my own here tomorrow. (*Sighs.*) First of all I'll have them chop down that row of fir trees, then that maple over there. In the evenings it's so eerie, unattractive . . . (*To Irina.*) Dear, that belt doesn't suit your coloring at all . . . it's in bad taste. You need something perkier. And then I'll have them plant posies everywhere, posies, and they'll give off such a fragrance . . . (*Sternly.*) Why is there a fork lying on this bench? (*Crossing into the house, to the Parlor Maid.*) Why is there a fork lying on a bench, I'm asking you? (*Shouts.*) Hold your tongue!

KULYGIN. She's on the warpath again!

Offstage the music plays a march; everyone listens.

OLGA. They're leaving.

Enter CHEBUTYKIN.

MASHA. Our boys are leaving. Well, that's that . . . Happy journey to them! (*To her husband.*) We ought to go home . . . Where's my hat and cape . . .

KULYGIN. I took them into the house . . . I'll fetch 'em right away. (*Exits into the house.*)

OLGA. Yes, now we can head for home. It's time.

CHEBUTYKIN. Olga Sergeevna!

OLGA. What?

Pause.

What?

CHEBUTYKIN. Nothing . . . I don't know how to tell you . . . (*Whispers in her ear.*)

OLGA (*in shock*). That's impossible!

CHEBUTYKIN. Yes . . . what a fuss . . . I'm worn out, exhausted, that's all I'll say . . . (*Annoyed.*) Anyway, it doesn't matter!

MASHA. What happened?

OLGA (*embraces Irina*). Today is a dreadful day . . . I don't know how to tell you, my precious . . .

IRINA. What? Tell me quickly, what? For God's sake! (*Weeps.*)

CHEBUTYKIN. The Baron was just killed in a duel.

IRINA. I knew it, I knew it . . .[74]

CHEBUTYKIN (*sits far upstage on a bench*). I'm worn out . . . (*Pulls a newspaper out of his pocket.*) Let 'em have a good cry . . . (*Sings quietly.*) Tarara boom de-ay . . . I sit in gloom all day . . . What does it matter!

The three sisters stand, clutching one another.

MASHA. Oh, how the music plays! They're leaving us, one of them has gone forever and ever, we're left alone to begin our life anew. One has to go on living . . . One has to go on living . . .

IRINA (*lays her head on Olga's bosom*). A time will come when everyone will realize why all this is, what these sufferings are for, there won't be any mysteries, but in the meantime a person has to live . . . has to work, nothing but work! Tomorrow I'll go away by myself, I'll teach school and I'll devote my whole life to anyone who may possibly need it. It's autumn now, winter will be here soon, the snow will cover everything up, but I shall work, I shall work . . .

OLGA (*embraces both sisters*). The music is playing so gaily, cheerfully, and I feel like living! Oh, dear Lord! Time will pass, and we'll be gone forever, people will forget us, they'll forget our faces, voices and how many of us there were, but our suffering will turn to joy for those who live after us, happiness and peace will come into being on this earth, and those who live now will be remembered with a kind word and a blessing. Oh, dear sisters,

---

74 "Irina does not know that Tusenbach is off to fight a duel; but she surmises that something untoward happened the day before, which might have serious and therefore evil consequences. And whenever a woman surmises, she says 'I knew it, I knew it'" (Chekhov to I. A. Tikhomirov, January 14 [27], 1901).

this life of ours is not over yet. Let's go on living! The music plays so gaily, so cheerfully, and it seems as if, just a little while longer and we shall learn why we're alive, why we suffer . . . If only we knew, if only we knew!

The music plays ever more quietly; KULYGIN, smiling cheerfully, brings in the hat and cape, ANDREY wheels a different baby carriage, in which Bobik is sitting.

CHEBUTYKIN (*sings quietly*). Tara . . . ra . . . boom-de-ay . . . I sit in gloom all day . . . (*Reads the paper.*) Doesn't matter! Doesn't matter!

OLGA. If only we knew, if only we knew!

Curtain

VARIANTS TO

Three Sisters

Lines come from the censor's copies (Cens.), the fair copy (A), the publication in *Russian Thought* (*Russkaya Mysl*) (RT), and separate publication as *Three Sisters* (1901) (TS).

ACT ONE

page 883 / *Replace*: you've gone back to wearing white, your face is beaming.
with: you're in white, there's a smile on your face. (A)

page 885 / *After*: such thoughts! — I'm twenty, already grown up, how nice it is! (Cens.)

page 887 / *Replace*: from hard work. And they just about managed it, only just! . . . a bracing, mighty tempest
with: from hard work, but they haven't protected us from the influence of this massive thing advancing on all of us, this glorious healthy tempest (Cens.)

page 887 / *Before*: In twenty-five years — No offense meant, (Cens.)

page 889 / *Replace*: If a man philosophizes . . . Polly want a cracker!
with: All this is philosophistics, it's your sophistics, mystics, excuse me, not
   worth a tinker's dam. It's all crapistics. (Cens.)

page 894 / *Replace*: after a while.
SOLYONY (*shrilly*) . . . **VERSHININ**. Yes, yes, of course.
with: after a while.
SOLYONY. Suffering . . . For instance, bugs bite one another . . . (*Gets
   embarrassed.*)
OLGA (*embarrassed, aside*). He's talking vulgarity.
VERSHININ (*to Tusenbach*). Of course, he may be right. (Cens.)

page 894 / *Replace*: Ah, the way she dresses! It's not so much
with: You're from Moscow, you understand. I can't look at the way they dress
   here, the local fashionplates simply offend me. It's not so much. (A, RT)

page 896 / *Replace*: Well, I'll be! . . . I don't think there is
with: Superfluous? Who knows! Who among us has a sufficiently accurate
   point of view to tell what's superfluous from what's necessary? I don't think
   we do . . . (A, RT)

page 897 / *After*: even remotely — to look forward to it. (Cens.)

page 897 / *After*: that invariably smoke. — Never in my life have I had such
   flowers . . . (A)

page 899 / *Replace*: **TUSENBACH**. . . . I wouldn't go . . . Don't go, my lovely!
with: **TUSENBACH**. So don't go.
CHEBUTYKIN. Certainly not. (Cens.)

page 900 / *Replace*: **SOLYONY** (*crossing into the reception room*). Cheep,
   cheep, cheep . . .
with: **SOLYONY**. You're always singing, it's business, well, now, let's dance.
   (*Goes in the reception room.*) (Cens.)

ACT TWO

page 907 / *Replace*: Come back tomorrow morning . . . *unhurriedly goes back
   into his room.*)

with: I remember everything, I haven't forgotten a thing. I have a phenomenal memory, with a memory like mine another man in my place would long ago have stretched himself and not a rope across all Moscow . . . Across all Russia . . . I don't think anything can provide greater, sweeter pleasure than fame . . .

The doorbell rings.

Yes, business . . . Once I dreamed of fame . . . yes . . . (*Stretches.*) And it was so possible . . . (*Unhurriedly goes into his room.*) (Cens., A, RT)

page 909 / *Replace*: I pester you with. I escort you home every single night.
with: I'm waiting for my own happiness. I've been waiting for you four years now and I'm ready to wait at least another ten. (Cens.)

page 909 / *Replace*: And every single night I'll . . . until you chase me away . . .
with: And ten years running I'll come to the telegraph office every night and escort you home! (Cens.)

page 910 / *After*: this town. — Not a town, but a pathetic little hamlet . . . (Cens.)

page 911 / *Replace*: (*laughs*). How pompously he sits!
with: Attaboy, Doctor! (Cens.)

page 912 / *After*: our happiness. — If not mine, then at least that of my posterity's posterity. (Cens.)

page 912 / *After*: will not be for any of us . . . — and we mustn't waste time and strength chasing after it. (Cens.)

page 912 / *After*: *strumming on the guitar*: — "Did you know my soul's unrest." (Cens.)

page 912 / *After*: Well, how can I convince you? — We live our own real life, the future will live its own life, just the same as ours—no better, no worse . . . (A, RT)

page 913 / *After*: Balzac was married in Berdichev.—

FEDOTIK shuffles the cards.

IRINA (*angrily*). What are you doing?
FEDOTIK. Don't mess up my wheeling and dealing.
IRINA. I'm fed up with you and your jokes.
FEDOTIK. Makes no difference, the solitaire wouldn't have come out. I shall now show you another kind . . . (*Deals out a hand of solitaire.*)
RODÉ (*loudly*). Doctor, how old are you?
CHEBUTYKIN. Me? Thirty-two.

Laughter.

IRINA (*looking at the cards*). But what was Balzac doing in Russia?

Pause. (Cens.)

page 914 / *Before*: **VERSHININ.** Incidentally, that's quite a wind!—

IRINA. The solitaire is coming out, I see . . . I don't believe in telling fortunes by cards, but my heart is filled with joy. We will live in Moscow.

FEDOTIK. No, the solitaire is not coming out. You see, the eight was lying on the deuce of spades. (*Laughs.*) Which means, you won't live in Moscow. (Cens.)

page 918 / *Replace*: **SOLYONY** (*declaiming*) . . . forget your dreams . . .

with: **SOLYONY.** It's all right, no matter what you say.

TUSENBACH. I shall work. (Cens.)

page 920 / *Replace*: What a shame! . . . I'll bring him a little toy . . .

with: Where can I go now with a guitar? (Cens.)

page 923 / *After*: Don't give me a quiz . . . I'm tired. — (*Hides his face in his hands.*) (Cens., A, RT)

ACT THREE

page 931 / *After*: what a life that's going to be, what a life! — What a pity that my little girls won't live long enough to see that time! They're special creatures, and I devote all my strength to making sure they will be beautiful and strong. (Cens.)

page 931 / *After*: and be superior to you . . . (*Laughs.*) — How I'd like to live, if only you knew. (Cens.)

page 938 / *Replace*: is simply frivolous . . .

with: are only the whims of old maids. Old maids never love their sisters-in-law—that's a rule. (A, RT, TS)

ACT FOUR

page 940 / *Replace*: (*casts a glance round the garden*)
with: (*casts a glance round the garden*) Today I destroyed my guitar, there's
nowhere to play it any more, and I don't feel like it. (Cens.)

page 940 / *Replace*: **TUSENBACH.** And godawful boredom . . . And where's
Mariya Sergeevna?
with: **IRINA.** Aleksey Petrovich, what happened yesterday on the boulevard
near the theater? Tell me frankly.
FEDOTIK. Nothing happened.
IRINA. Word of honor?

Pause.

FEDOTIK. Nothing happened . . . Well, trivia . . . It'll all blow over. But
where's Mariya Sergeevna? (Cens.)

page 940 / *Replace*: Good-bye, got to go . . . *she exits with them.*
with: Let's go, or else I'll start to cry.

They both walk out, glancing around.

We had a fine life here . . . (*Shouts.*) Mariya Sergeevna! Hop to it! (*They
leave.*) (Cens.)

page 942 / *Replace*: She even resembles Masha . . . I do love her, my Masha.
with: When I was engaged to Masha , sometimes I'd simply walk around like
a crazy person, like a drunk, and talk hokum, hokium . . . I'm happy now
too, but in those days I was delirious with happiness. Well, the baron is
probably the same way . . . (Cens.)

page 943 / *After*: shave off your moustache, Fyodor Ilyich. —
KULYGIN. That's enough out of you.
CHEBUYTKIN. Now your wife will be scared of you. (Cens.; A, RT)

page 943 / *After*: that's not what happiness is all about . . . — (*Pause.*) Strange
the fates people have. (Cens.); (*Pause*) You don't understand anything in
this world. (A, RT); (*Pause.*) (TS)

page 944 / *Replace*: (*reads the papers and sings softly*) . . . I sit in gloom all
day . . ."
with: Yes, say what you like, Ivan Romanych, but it's high time to change your

way of life. (*Sings quietly*). "Ah, you, Sashka, my mischief maker, change my blue notes . . .They're all brand-new notes . . ." (Cens.)

page 945 / *After*: you get bitchy — like a cook. (A, RT)

page 945 / *Replace*: (*Looking at her brother* . . . Look at our Andrey, our baby brother
with: The one I'd like to give a good thrashing is Andrushka over there, our baby brother. Ridiculous dummy! (A, RT)

page 946 / *After*: Bing-bang. (*Laughs.*) — Spaniards, can you imagine, an hidalgo . . . (Cens.)

page 946 / *After*: I'll be left alone in the house. — I don't consider a wife a person.

Enter FERAPONT with papers.

CHEBUTYKIN. Why not? (Cens.)

page 947 / *After*: the farther you go the better. — (*Pause.*) Or, whatever you like! Doesn't matter . . . (TS)

page 947 / *Replace*: **SOLYONY.** The old man's getting upset for no good reason . . .

Exits with SOLYONY.

with: **SOLYONY.** And what's the Baron doing? Writing his will? Saying good-bye to his beloved, pledging her eternal love or already on the battlefield?

Pause.

I'll wing him all the same, like a wood-snipe . . .

They leave. Cries are heard of "Hop to it. Yoo-hoo!"
ANDREY and FERAPONT enter. (Cens.)

page 948 / *Replace*: **FERAPONT.** Papers to sign . . . "Yoo-hoo, Masha, yoo-hoo!"
with: **ANDREY.** Oh, where is it, where has my past gone to, when I was young, cheerful, clever, when I dreamed and had refined thoughts, when both my present and my future lit up with hope? Why do we, having barely begun life, become boring, gray, uninteresting, lazy, indifferent, useless . . . Our town has been in existence for two hundred year, in it—it's a joke!—are a hundred thousand inhabitants, and not one who isn't like another, neither in the past or the present, not a single enthusiast, not a single scholar, not a single artist, not the least remarkable person, who might arouse envy or a passionate desire to emulate him . . . They only eat, drink, sleep, then die; others are born and they too eat, drink, sleep, and, in order not to be stupefied with boredom, vary their lives with nasty gossip, vodka, cards, and

the women cheat on their husbands, and the husbands lie, pretend they don't see anything, don't hear anything, and irresistibly a vulgar influence weighs on the children—and the divine spark dies out in them, and they become the same pitiful, indistinguishable corpses as their fathers and mothers . . . (*To Ferapont.*) Whaddya you want?

FERAPONT. How's that? Papers to be signed.

ANDREY (*caught up in a feeling of tenderness*). My dear sisters, my wonderful sisters!

FERAPONT (*handing over the papers*). The doorman at the gummint offices was just saying. Seems, he says, winter in Petersburg there was two hundred degrees of frost. Two thousand people froze to death. Folks, he says, was scared to death. Could be Petersburg, could be Moscow—I don't rec'llect.

ANDREY. Every night now I lie awake and think . . . I think about how in two or three years I'll end up drowning in unpaid debts, I'll become a pauper, this house will be sold, my wife will run out on me—suddenly my soul becomes so buoyant, so airy, and in the distance a light begins to dawn, I have a presentiment of freedom, and then I'd like to run to my three sisters, run to them, and shout out: sisters, I'm saved, I'm saved!

NATASHA (*through the window*). You're making too much noise there, Andryusha. You'll wake Sophiekins. (*Losing her temper.*) If you want to talk, give the baby buggy to somebody else. Ferapont, take the buggy from the master!

FERAPONT. Yes, ma'am. (*Takes the carriage.*)

ANDREY (*embarrassed*). I'll talk quietly.

NATASHA (*behind the window, petting her little boy*). Bobik! Naughty Bobik! Bad Bobik!

ANDREY (*glancing at the papers*). I'll look over this rigmarole right now and sign whatever I have to, and you can take it back to the office . . .

> He exits into the house, reading the papers; FERAPONT pushes the baby carriage; in the garden in the distance IRINA and TUSENBACH appear, the Baron is dressed foppishly, in a straw hat.

NATASHA (*behind the window*). Bobik, what's your mommy's name? Darling, darling! And who's that? That's auntie Olya. Say to auntie: afternoon, Olya!

> Enter KULYGIN.

KULYGIN (*to Irina*). Where's Masha?

IRINA. Somewhere in the garden.

KULYGIN. I haven't seen her since this morning . . . She's in a bad mood today . . . (*Shakes his head.*) And they still haven't painted that bench!

What a bunch, really . . . (*Shouts.*) Yoo-hoo! Masha, yoo-hoo! (*Exits into the garden.*) (Cens.)

page 949 / *After*: in life one way or another. —

> *Itinerant musicians, a man and a girl, play the fiddle and the harp.* (Cens.)

page 952 / *Replace*: Which means, not being in Moscow . . . . (*Laughs.*) Life is hard.

with: It's not up to me . . . I'll do a bit of work and, I suppose, I'll go to Moscow.

VERSHININ. Now where . . .

> *Pause.*

Life follows its own laws, not ours. Yes. (Cens.)

page 954 / *Replace*: **KULYGIN.** She's not crying any more . . . *Enter NATASHA.*

with: **MASHA.** We took the town of Turtukay, And all of us were standing by, We beat the English, beat the Turks . . . Damn it, I'm raving. (*Drinks water.*) I don't need anything . . . I'll be calm right away . . . It doesn't matter . . . We took the town of Turtukay, And all of us were standing by . . . The ideas are whirling around in my head.

> *Enter IRINA; far away down the street a harp and fiddle are heard playing.*

OLGA. Calm down, Masha. Let's go to my room.

MASHA. It's past me by. There's nothing now. (*Smiles.*) Which means, fate does what it wants, there's nothing you can do about it . . . (*Sobs and immediately stops.*) Let it be.

> *A distant gunshot is heard.*

IRINA (*shudders*). Let's go to the bottom of the garden, we'll sit together, not saying a word . . .

> *A distant gunshot is heard. NATASHA enters.* (Cens.)

page 955 / *Replace*: **OLGA.** What? . . . For God's sake! (*Weeps.*)

with: **OLGA.** What?

CHEBUYTKIN (*whispers in her ear*). Yes . . . what a fuss . . . Well, sir, now I'll have a bit of a sitdown, rest, then pack it up . . . (*Sits far upstage on the bench.*) I'm worn out. (*Pulls a newspaper out of his pocket.*)

OLGA (*embraces Irina*). I don't know what to say . . . Today is a dreadful day.

IRINA. What's been going on? Tell me, what? I won't faint, I won't. I'll endure it all . . . (Cens.)

page 956 / *After*: and I feel like living! — I shall live, sisters! . . . A person has
to live . . . (*Looks upwards.*) The birds of passage are overhead, they fly by
every spring and fall, for a thousand years now, and they don't know why
but they'll go on flying for a long, long time to come, many thousands of
years — until God finally reveals the mystery to them . . . (A)

page 957 / *After*: *plays ever more quietly; — very far upstage a commotion, a
crowd can be seen watching as the body of the Baron, slain in the duel, is
borne past.* (Cens.)[1]

----

1 "Of course you're a thousand times right, Tusenbach's body should certainly not be shown; I felt
that myself when I wrote and told you about it, if you recall" (Chekhov to Stanislavsky, January 15
[28], 1901).

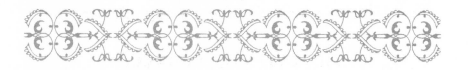

THE EVILS OF TOBACCO, FINAL VERSION

*S*ix distinct variants exist of this monologue, the more serious changes concomitant with the greater depth of psychology of Chekhov's works throughout the 1890s. Over the course of the recension, Chekhov heightened the emotional tone of the monologue, refined the comedy, and increased the pathos. The speaker's pseudo-scientific jargon became more attenuated, with a concurrent introduction of clichés.

The impetus for further revision may have come when, in 1898, Ya. Merpert, a Russian man of letters living in Paris, asked Chekhov for a one-act to be performed at an amateur recital. Although Chekhov asked his friends to send their plays instead, at the same time he made more revisions to *Tobacco* and presented it to his brother Ivan. In this version, a number of the grotesque details in the earlier variants are deleted. Nyukhin casts more aspersions on his unseen wife and reveals more pain at his enforced nullity. What Chekhov had earlier left the audience to deduce was now spelled out in tones of complaint. It was first performed by the writer A. I. Kuprin at a private club in Moscow in September 1901.

Chekhov did not intend to include the piece in his *Collected Works* but returned to it while working on *The Cherry Orchard* in 1902. To his publisher, Marks, he described it as "a new play" and insisted that it was intended exclusively for the stage, not for the reader. When Stanislavsky solicited Olga Knipper to ask Chekhov's permission to put it on, Chekhov replied to his wife, "Are you crazy!!! Give a vaudeville to the Art Theatre! A vaudeville with a single character who only talks, and does absolutely nothing!!" (October 8, 1902).

The final revision draws a more hateful portrait of Nyukhin's wife and consequently renders him more terrorized and pathetic. Chekhov turned the ridicule he had previously showered on his hero into pity, and suggested the spiritual vacuity of such a philistine existence. Nyukhin became the latest in the Russian tradition of the put-upon "little man."

THE EVILS OF TOBACCO

О вреде табака

A Stage Monologue in One Act

FINAL VERSION

C A S T

IVAN IVANOVICH NYUKHIN,[1] *the husband of his wife who runs a music school and a girls' boarding school.*

The stage represents the speaker's platform of a provincial club.

NYUKHIN (*with long side-whiskers, no moustache, in an old threadbare tailcoat, enters pompously, bows, and adjusts his waistcoat*). Kind ladies and, in a manner of speaking, gentlemen. (*Fluffs out his side-whiskers.*) Someone suggested to my wife that on behalf of charity I should give a lecture on a popular topic. Why not? You want a lecture, you'll get a lecture—I couldn't care less. Of course, I'm no professor and a stranger to academic degrees, but, nevertheless, all the same, for thirty years now, unceasingly, one might even say, at the cost of my own health and so on, I have been working on questions of a strictly scientific bent, I think deep thoughts and sometimes I even write, if you can picture such a thing, scholarly articles, I mean not exactly scholarly, but sort of, pardon the expression, along the scholarly line. Among others, a few days ago, I wrote a huge article entitled: "The Evils of Certain Insects." My daughters liked it a lot, especially the part about bedbugs, but I reread it and tore it up. After all, whatever you may write, you still can't do without insect powder. We've even got bugs in the grand piano . . . As the subject for today's lecture I chose, so to speak, the evils visited on humanity by the use of tobacco. I smoke myself, but my wife insisted that I lecture today about the evils of tobacco, and, so

---

1 Although the joke surname, from *nyukhat*, to take snuff, to sniffle, is retained, the absurd Christian name Markel is now changed to the common Ivan.

there's no point in arguing. If you want tobacco, you'll get tobacco — I really couldn't care less, but I suggest that you, kind ladies and gentlemen, attend to to my current lecture with due seriousness, otherwise who knows what will happen. Anyone who quails at the thought of a scientific lecture, doesn't care for it, doesn't have to listen and can leave. (*Adjusts his waist-coat.*) I especially solicit the attention of the medical professionals assembled here, who can glean a good deal of useful information from my lecture, because tobacco, besides its deleterious effects, can be also used as medicine. So, for instance, if you put a fly in a snuff box, it will drop dead, probably, from a nervous breakdown. Tobacco is, by and large, a plant . . . When I give a lecture, my right eye usually twitches, but pay it no mind: it's just from excitement. I'm a very nervous man, generally speaking, and my eye started to twitch on September 13th, 1889, the same day my wife gave birth, in a manner of speaking, to my fourth daughter, Varvara. All my daughters were born on the 13th. However (*after a glance at his watch*), considering the shortness of time, we will not digress from the subject of the lecture. I must remark that my wife runs a music school and a private boarding school, I mean not exactly a boarding school, but something along those lines. Just between ourselves, my wife loves to complain there's never enough of anything, but she's got a tidy sum tucked away, a good forty or fifty thousand, while I haven't got a kopek to my name, not a penny — well, what's the point of bringing that up? In the boarding school I'm in charge of the housekeeping department. I buy the provisions, supervise the servants, keep the accounts, stitch the composition books, exterminate the bedbugs, walk my wife's lapdog, catch the mice . . . Last night it fell to my duties to dole out flour and butter to the cook, because pancakes were on the menu. Well, sir, to make a long story short, today when the pancakes were already out of the pan, my wife came into the kitchen to say that three of the students won't eat pancakes, because they've got swollen glands. Therefore it would appear that we had fried a certain number of extra pancakes. What are we supposed to do with them? My wife at first ordered them put in the pantry, but then she thought about it and thought about it and says: "Eat those pancakes yourself, you dummy." When she's in a bad mood, that's the sort of thing she calls me: dummy, or viper, or Satan. And what kind of Satan am I? She's always in a bad mood. And I didn't so much eat them as gulp them down without chewing, because I'm always hungry. Yesterday, for instance, she didn't give me dinner. "Dummy," she says, "there's no point in feeding you . . ." But, however (*looks at his watch*), we have been wandering and digressed a bit from the subject. Let us proceed. Although, of course, you would much rather be listening to a ballad right now, or some symphony, or an aria . . . (*Starts to sing.*) "In the heat of battle we shall not blink an eye . . ." I don't know where that's from . . . Among other things, I forgot to tell you that in my wife's music school, besides doing the housekeeping, I'm also charged with teaching mathematics, physics, chemistry, geography, history, vocal exercises, literature, and so on. For dancing, singing, and drawing my wife charges special fees, although I'm also the one who teaches dancing and singing. Our musical academy is located at No. 13 Five Dog Lane. That's the reason, I suppose, that my life is such a failure, because I live at No. 13. And my daughters were born on the 13th, and our house has 13 window-panes . . . Well, what's the point of talking about it! To discuss terms my wife can be at home at any time, and the school's curriculum, if you like, can be purchased from the doorman for thirty kopeks a copy. (*Pulls a few brochures out of his pocket.*) And, if you like, I can let you have these. Thirty kopeks a piece! Anyone want one? (*Pause.*) Nobody wants one? Well, twenty kopeks! (*Pause.*) Annoying. Yes, No. 13! Nothing works out for me, I've got old, I've got stupid . . . Here I am giving a lecture, outwardly I'm cheerful, but in fact I'd like to scream my lungs out or fly somewhere to the ends of the earth. And there's no one to complain to, you just want to break down and cry . . . You'll say: your daughters . . . What about my daughters? I talk to them, but they only laugh . . . My wife has seven daughters . . . No, sorry, I think it's six . . . (*Briskly.*) Seven! The oldest of them, Anna, is twenty-seven, the youngest seventeen. Kind ladies and gentlemen! (*Glances around.*) I'm unhappy, I've turned into an idiot, a nonentity, but basically you see before you the happiest of fathers. Basically, that's the way it's supposed to be, and I don't dare say anything else. If only you knew! I've lived with my wife for thirty-three years, and, I may say, they were the best years of my life, well, not exactly the best, but by and large. They have flown by, in short, like one happy moment, personally speaking, damn them to hell. (*Glances around.*) However, she hasn't come yet, I don't think she's here, so I can say whatever I please . . . I am awfully scared . . . scared whenever she looks my way. Yes, here's what I have to say: my daughters have taken so long to get married probably because they're shy, and because no men ever get to see them. My wife doesn't want to throw parties, she never invites anyone to dinner, she's a very stingy, ill-tempered, bitchy lady, and therefore nobody calls on us, but . . . I can confide to you a secret . . . (*Comes down to the footlights.*) My wife's daughters can be seen on holidays at their auntie's, Natalya Semyonovna, the one who suffers from rheumatism and wears that yellow dress with the black polka-dots, as though she were sprinkled with spiders. They serve refreshments there. And when my wife isn't around, you might get a little . . . (*Flicks his throat to indicate drinking.*) I have to mention that I get drunk on a single shot, and it starts to put me in a good mood and at the same time makes me so depressed that I run out of words; for some reason I recall the days of my youth, and for some reason I want to run away, ah, if you only knew how much I want to run away! (*Passionately.*) Run away, cast off all of this and run away without a backward glance . . . where to? It doesn't matter where . . . just to run away from this shabby, vulgar, despicable life, which has turned me into an old, pathetic idiot, an old, pathetic imbecile, to run away from that stupid, shallow, penny-pinching bitch, bitch, bitch, my wife, who has made my life a living hell for thirty-three years, to run away from the music, the kitchen, my wife's money, from all that inanity and banality . . . and come to a halt somewhere far, far away in a meadow and stand like a tree, a pillar, a scarecrow in a cornfield, under the broad sky, and spend all night watching the quiet, bright moon hanging overhead, and forget, forget . . . Oh, how I'd like to forget it all! . . . How I'd like to tear off this vile old rag of a tailcoat I wore when I walked up the aisle thirty years ago . . . (*Tears off his tailcoat.*) which I wear whenever I give a lecture on behalf of charity . . . Take that! (*Tramples on the tailcoat.*) Take that! I'm old, poor, pathetic, like this waistcoat with its threadbare, shabby backing . . . (*Displays the back of it.*) I don't need anything! I am higher and purer than this, I was once young, intelligent, I studied at the university, I dreamed, I considered myself a human being . . . Now I don't need anything! Nothing except peace and quiet . . . peace and quiet! (*After a sidelong glance, quickly puts on his tailcoat.*) However, my wife is standing in the wings . . . She's arrived and is waiting there for me . . . (*Looks at his watch.*) Our time is up . . . If she asks, please, I beg you, tell her that the lecture was . . . that the dummy, I mean me, behaved with dignity. (*Looks to the side, coughs.*) She's looking this way . . . (*Raising his voice.*) Proceeding from the proposition that tobacco does contain a lethal poison, which I have already discussed, smoking is wrong whatever the circumstances, and I allow myself, in a manner of speaking, to hope that this lecture of mine "on the evils of tobacco" will be of some benefit. I have had my say. *Dixi et animam levavi!*[2]

He bows and pompously exits.

---

2 Latin: I have spoken and my soul is the easier for it!

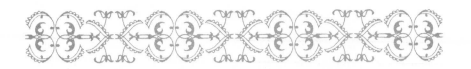

THE CHERRY ORCHARD

"The next play I write will definitely be funny, very funny, at least in concept," Chekhov declared to his wife, on March 7, 1901, after *Three Sisters* had opened. The concept, as the author sketched it to Stanislavsky, would incorporate a footman mad about fishing, a garrulous one-armed billiard player, and a situation in which a landowner is continually borrowing money from the footman. He also envisaged a branch of flowering cherry thrust through a window of the manor house.

Chekhov's notebooks reveal that *The Cherry Orchard* had taken root even earlier, with the governess Charlotta, another farcical type, and the idea that "the estate will soon go under the hammer" the next ramification. The theme had a personal application. For the boy Chekhov, the sale of his home after his father's bankruptcy had been painful. The imminent loss of one's residence looms over his early plays, becomes the (literal) trigger of *Uncle Vanya*, and gives an underlying dynamic to *Three Sisters*.

The endangered estate, in Chekhov's early plans, was to belong to a liberal-minded old lady who dressed like a girl, smoked, and couldn't do without society, a sympathetic sort tailored to the Maly Theatre's Olga Sadovskaya, who specialized in biddies and beldams. When the Maly Theatre refused to release her, Chekhov reshaped the role until it was suitable for someone of Olga Knipper's age. Only then did he conceive of Lopakhin. Varya first appeared as a grotesquely comic name, Varvara Nedotyopina (Varvara Left-in-the-Lurch): *nedotyopa* eventually became the catchphrase of old Firs.

As Chekhov's letters reveal, he stressed the play's comic nature, and was put out when the Moscow Art Theatre saw it as a tearful tragedy. Even if some of Chekhov's complaints can be dismissed as a side effect of his physical deterioration, there is no doubt that the Art Theatre misplaced many of his intended emphases. He seems to have meant the major role to be the peasant-turned-millionaire Lopakhin, played by Stanislavsky. However, Stanislavsky, a millionaire of peasant origins, preferred the part of the feckless aristocrat Gaev, and handed Lopakhin over to Leonid Leonidov, a less experienced actor. Olga Knipper, whom the author saw in the grotesque role of the German governess, was cast as the elegant Ranevskaya. Immediately the central focus shifted to the genteel family of landowners, because the strongest actors were in those parts. Later on, fugitives from the Revolution identified so closely with Ranevskaya and Gaev that they disseminated a nostalgic view of the gentry's plight throughout the West. Soviet productions then went to the opposite extreme, reinterpreting Lopakhin as a man of the people capable of building a progressive society, and the student Trofimov as an eloquent harbinger of that brave new world.

Choosing sides immediately reduces the play's complexity and ambiguity. Chekhov had no axe to grind, not even the one that chops down the orchard. Neither Lopakhin nor Trofimov is invested with greater validity than Ranevskaya or Gaev. Trofimov is constantly undercut by comic devices: after a melodramatic exit line, "All is over between us," he falls downstairs, and, despite his claim to be in the vanguard of progress, is too absent-minded to locate his own galoshes. Even his earnest speech about the idle upper classes and the benighted workers is addressed to the wrong audience: how can Ranevskaya possibly identify with the Asiatic bestiality that Trofimov indicts as a Russian characteristic? Only in the hearing of infatuated Anya do Trofimov's words seem prophetic; at other times, his inability to realize his situation renders them absurd.

Chekhov was anxious to avoid the stage clichés of the *kulak*, the hard-hearted, hard-fisted, loudmouthed merchant, in his portrayal of Lopakhin; after all, Lopakhin shares Chekhov's own background as a man of peasant background who worked his way up in a closed society. He can be the tactless boor that Gaev insists he is, exulting over his purchase of the orchard and starting its decimation even before the family leaves. But, in the same breath, he is aware of his shortcomings, longs for a more poetic existence, and has, in the words of his antagonist Trofimov, "delicate, gentle fingers, like an artist . . . a delicate, gentle soul." And for all his pragmatism, he too is comically inept when it comes to romance. His halfhearted wooing of Varya may result from a more deep-seated love of her foster mother.

Ironically, it is the impractical Ranevskaya who pricks Lopakhin's dreams of giants and vast horizons and suggests that he examine his own gray life rather than build castles in the air. She may be an incorrigible romantic about the orchard and totally scatterbrained about money, but on matters of sex she is more clear-sighted than Lopakhin, Trofimov, or Gaev, who considers her "depraved." Prudish as a young Komsomol, Trofimov is scandalized by her advice that he take a mistress; he had been annoyed that Varya should distrust his moments alone with Anya.

In short, any attempt to grade Chekhov's characters as "right-thinking" or "wrong-headed" ignores the multi-faceted nature of their portrayal. It would be a mistake to adopt wholeheartedly either the sentimental attitude of Gaev and Ranevskaya to the orchard or the pragmatic and "socially responsible" attitude of Lopakhin and Trofimov. By 1900 there were many works about uprooted gentlefolk and estates confiscated by *arrivistes*. Pyotr Nevezhin's *Second Youth* (1883), a popular melodrama dealing with the breakup of a nest of gentry, held the stage until the Revolution, and Chekhov had seen it. That same year Nikolay Solovyov's *Liquidation* appeared, in which an estate is saved by a rich peasant marrying the daughter of the family. Chekhov would not have been raking over these burnt-out themes if he did not have a fresh angle on them. *The Cherry Orchard* is the play in which Chekhov most successfully achieved a "new form," the amalgam of a symbolist outlook with the appurtenances of social comedy.

Perhaps the Russian critic A. R. Kugel was right when he wrote, "All the inhabitants of *The Cherry Orchard* are children and their behavior is childish."[1] Certainly, Chekhov seems to have abandoned his usual repertory company: there is no doctor, no mooning intellectual complaining of a wasted life (Yepikhodov may be a parody of that), no love triangles except the comic one of Yepikhodov-Dunyasha-Yasha. The only pistol is wielded by the hapless dolt Yepikhodov, and Nina's mysterious enveloping *"talma"* in *The Seagull* has dwindled into Dunyasha's *talmochka*, a fancy term for a shawl. Soliloquies have been replaced by monologues that are patently ridiculous (Gaev's speeches to the bookcase and the sunset) or misdirected (Trofimov's speech on progress). The absurdly named Simeonov-Pishchik, his "dear daughter Dashenka," and his rapid mood shifts would be out of place in *Three Sisters*. The upstart valet Yasha, who smells of chicken coops and cheap perfume, recalls Chichikov's servant Petrushka in *Dead Souls*, who permeates the ambience with his effluvium. Gogol, rather than Turgenev, is the presiding genius of this comedy.

All the characters are misfits, from Lopakhin, who dresses like a rich man but feels like a pig in a pastry shop, to Yasha and Dunyasha, servants who ape their betters, to the expelled student Trofimov, aimlessly hustled from place to place, to Yepikhodov, who puts simple ideas into inappropriate language, to Varya, who is an efficient manager but longs to be a pilgrim, to the most obvious example, the uprooted governess Charlotta, who has no notion who she is. Early on, we hear Lopakhin protest, "Got to remember who you are!" Jean-Louis Barrault, the French actor and director, suggested that the servants are satiric reflections of their master's ideals:[2] old Firs is the senile embodiment of the rosy past Gaev waxes lyrical over; Yasha, that pushing young particle, with his taste for Paris and champagne, is a parody of Lopakhin's upward mobility and Ranevskaya's sophistication; Trofimov's dreams of social betterment are mocked by Yepikhodov reading Buckle and beefing up his vocabulary.

If there is a norm here, it exists offstage, in town, at the bank, in the restaurant, in Mentone and Paris, where Ranevskaya's lover entreats her return, or in Yaroslavl, where Great Aunt frowns on the family's conduct. Chekhov peoples this unseen world with what Vladimir Nabokov might call "homunculi." Besides the lover and Auntie, there are Ranevskaya's alcoholic husband and drowned son; Pishchik's daughter and the Englishmen who find clay on his land; rich Deriganov, who might buy the estate; the Ragulins, who hire Varya; the famous Jewish orchestra; Gaev's deceased parents and servants; the staff, eating beans in the kitchen; and a host of others to indicate that the cherry orchard is a desert island in a teeming sea of life. Chekhov had used the device in *Uncle Vanya* and *Three Sisters*, where Vanya's dead sister, the prepotent Protopopov, Mrs. Colonel Vershinin, and Kulygin's headmaster shape the characters' fates but are never seen. In *The Cherry Orchard*, the plethora of invisible beings fortifies the sense of the estate's vulnerability, transience, and isolation.

Barrault also pointed out that "the action" of the play is measured by the outside pressures on the estate. In Act One, the cherry orchard is in danger of being sold, in Act Two it is on the verge of being sold, in Act Three it is sold, and in Act Four it has been sold. The characters are defined by their responses to these "events," which, because they are spoken of, intuited, feared, longed for, but never seen, automatically make the sale equivalent to Fate or Death in a play of Maeterlinck or Andreev. As Henri Bergson insisted,[3] any living being who tries to stand still in the evolving flow of time becomes mechanical and thus comical in action. How do the characters take a position in the temporal flow—are they delayed, do they moved with it, do they try to outrun it? Those who refuse to join in (Gaev and Firs) or who rush to get ahead of it (Trofimov) can end up looking ridiculous.

Viewed as traditional comedy, *The Cherry Orchard* thwarts our expectations: the lovers are not threatened except by their own impotence, the servants are uppity but no help to anyone, all the characters are expelled at the end, but their personal habits have undergone no reformation. Ranevskaya returns to her lover; Gaev, at his most doleful moment, pops another candy in his mouth; Lopakhin and Trofimov are back on the road, one on business, the other on a mission. Even the abandonment of Firs hints that he cannot exist off the estate but is, as Ranevskaya's greeting to him implies, a piece of furniture like "my dear little table." This resilience in the face of change, with the future yet to be revealed, is closest to the symbolist sense of human beings trapped in the involuntary processes of time, their own mortality insignificant within the broader current. A Bergsonian awareness that reality stands outside time, dwarfing the characters' mundane concerns, imbues Chekhov's comedy with its bemused objectivity.

It also bestows on *The Cherry Orchard* its sense of persons suspended for the nonce. The present barely exists, elbowed aside by memory and nostalgia on the one hand and by expectation and hope on the other. When the play first opened, the critic M. Nevedomsky remarked that the characters are "living persons, painted with the colors of vivid reality, and at the same time schemata of that reality, as it were its foregone conclusions." Or as Kugel put it more succinctly, "the inhabitants of *The Cherry Orchard* live, as if half asleep, spectrally, on the border line of the real and the mystical."[4]

Chekhov's friend the writer Ivan Bunin pointed out that there were no such cherry orchards to be found in Russia, that Chekhov was inventing an imaginary landscape.[5] The estate is a wasteland in which the characters drift among the trivia of their lives while expecting something dire or important to occur. As in Maeterlinck, the play opens with two persons waiting in a dimly lit space, and closes with the imminent demise of a character abandoned in emptiness. Chekhov's favorite scenarios of waiting are especially attenuated here, since the suspense of "What will happen to the orchard?" dominates the first three acts, and in the last act the wait for carriages to arrive and effect the diaspora frames the conclusion.

However, the symbolism goes hand-in-glove with carefully observed reality: they coexist. Hence the uneasiness caused by what seem to be humdrum characters or situations. Act Two, with its open-air setting, demonstrates this concurrence of reality and super-reality. Chekhov's people are seldom at ease in the open. The more egotistic they are, like Arkadina and Serebryakov, the sooner they head for the safe haven of the house or, like Natasha, renovate nature to suit their taste. The last act of *Three Sisters* strands its protagonists in an uncongenial vacancy, with yoo-hoos echoing across the expanse.

By removing the characters in *The Cherry Orchard* from the memory-laden atmosphere of the nursery (where children should feel at home), Chekhov strips them of their habitual defenses. In Act Two the characters meet on a road, one of those indeterminate locations, halfway between the railway station and the house but, symbolically, halfway between past and future, birth and death, being and nothingness. Something here impels them to deliver their innermost thoughts in monologues: Charlotta complains of her lack of identity, Yepikhodov declares his suicidal urges, Ranevskaya describes her "sinful" past, Gaev addresses the sunset, Trofimov speechifies about what's wrong with society, Lopakhin paints his hopes for Russia. As if hypnotized by the sound of their voices reverberating in the wilderness, they deliver up quintessences of themselves.

At this point comes the portentous moment of the snapped string. The moment is framed by those pauses that evoke the gaps in existence that Andrey Bely claimed were horrifying and that Beckett was to characterize as the transitional zone in which being made itself heard. Chekhov's characters again recall Maeterlinck's, faintly trying to surmise the nature of the potent force that hovers just outside the picture. The thought-filled pause, then the uncanny sound and the ensuing pause conjure up what lies beyond.

Even then, however, Chekhov does not forgo a realistic prextext for the inexplicable. Shortly before the moment, Yepikhodov crosses upstage, strumming his guitar. Might not the snapped spring be one broken by the clumsy bookkeeper? At the play's end, before we hear the sound plangently dying away, we are told by Lopakhin that he has left Yepikhodov on the grounds as a caretaker. Chekhov always overlays any symbolic inference with a patina of irreproachable reality.

The party scene in Act Three is the supreme example of Chekhov's intermingling of subliminal symbol and surface reality. Bely saw it as a "crystallization of Chekhov's devices." It so struck the imagination of the young director Meyerhold that he wrote to Chekhov, on May 8, 1904, that "the play is abstract like a symphony by Chaikovsky . . . in [the party scene] there is something Maeterlinckian, terrifying." He later referred to "this nightmarish dance of puppets in a farce" in "Chekhov's new mystical drama."[6]

The act takes place in three dimensions: the forestage, with its brief interchanges by individual characters, the forced gaiety of the dancing in the background, and the offstage auction whose outcome looms over it all. Without leaving the sphere of the mundane, we have what Novalis called "a sequence of ideal events running parallel to reality." Characters are thrust out from the indistinct background and then return to it. Scantily identified, the postal clerk and the stationmaster surge forward, unaware of the main characters' inner lives, and make unwitting ironic comment. The stationmaster recites Aleksey Tolstoy's orotund poem, "The Sinful Woman," about a courtesan's conversion

by Christ at a lavish orgy in Judaea. The opening lines, describing a sumptu-
ous banquet, cast a sardonic reflection on the frumps gathered on this dismal
occasion. They also show the earlier interview between the puritanical Trofimov and the self-confessed sinner Ranevskaya to be a parodic confrontation
between a Messiah in eyeglasses and a Magdalene in a Parisian ballgown. The
act culminates in the moving juxtaposition of Ranevskaya's weeping and
Lopakhin's laughter, as the unseen musicians play loudly at his behest.

The return to the nursery, now stripped of its evocative trappings, in Act
Four, confirms the inexorable expulsion. In Act One, it has been a room to
linger in; now it is a cheerless space in which characters loiter only momen-
tarily on their way to somewhere else. The old Russian tradition of sitting for
a moment before taking leave becomes especially meaningful when there are
no chairs, only trunks and bundles to perch on. The ghosts that Gaev and
Ranevskaya had seen in the orchard in the first act have now moved indoors,
in the person of Firs, who is doomed to haunt the scene of the past, since he
has no future.

The consummate mastery of *The Cherry Orchard* is revealed in an authorial shorthand that is both impressionistic and theatrical. The pull on Ranevskaya to return to Paris takes shape in the telegram prop: in Act One, she tears
up the telegrams; by Act Three, she has preserved them in her handbag; in
Act Four, the lodestones draw her back. The dialogue is similarly telegraphic,
as in Anya's short speech about her mother's flat in Paris. "Mama is living on
the sixth floor, I walk all the way up, there are some French people there,
ladies, an old Catholic priest with a pamphlet, and it's full of cigarette smoke,
not nice at all." In a few strokes, a past is encapsulated: a high walk-up, signi-
fying Ranevskaya's reduced circumstances, her toying with religious conversion, a *louche* atmosphere.

Each character is distinguished by an appropriate speech pattern. Ranevskaya constantly employs diminutives and terms of endearment; for her everyone is *golubchik*, "dovey." She is also vague, using adjectives like "some kind
of" (*kakoy-to*). Gaev is a parody of the after-dinner speaker: emotion can
be voiced only in fulsome oration, thick with platitudes. When his flow is
stanched, he falls back on billiard terms or stops his mouth with candy and
anchovies. Pishchik has high blood pressure, so Chekhov the doctor makes
sure he speaks in short, breathless phrases, a hodgepodge of old-world courtesy, hunting terms, and newspaper talk. Lopakhin's language is more varied,
according to his interlocutor: blunt and colloquial with servants, more
respectful with his former betters. As suits a businessman, he speaks concisely

and in well-structured sentences, citing exact numbers and a commercial vocabulary, with frequent glances at his watch. Only in dealing with Varya does he resort to ponderous facetiousness and even bleating.

Memorably, Firs's "half-baked bungler" is the last line in the play. Its periodic repetition suggests that Chekhov meant it to sum up all the characters. They are all inchoate, some, like Anya and Trofimov, in the process of taking shape, others, like Gaev and Yepikhodov, never to take shape. The whole play has been held in a similar state of contingency until the final moments, when real chopping begins in the orchard and, typically, it is heard from offstage, mingled with the more cryptic and reverberant sound of the snapped string.

NOTES

1 A. R. Kugel, *Russkie dramaturgi* (Moscow: Mir, 1934), p. 120.

2 Jean-Louis Barrault, "Pourquoi *La Cerisaie?*," *Cahiers de la Compagnie Barrault-Renaud* 6 (July 1954): 87–97.

3 Henri Bergson, *Laughter: An Essay on the Meaning of the Comic*, trans. Cloudesley Brereton and Fred Rothwell (New York: Macmillan, 1911), pp. 88–89.

4 M. Nevedomsky, "Simvolizm v posledney drame A. P. Chekhova," *Mir bozhy* 8, 2 (1904): 18–19. Kugel, op. cit., p. 125.

5 Ivan Bunin, *O Chekhove* (New York: Chekhov Publishing House, 1955), p. 216.

6 Andrey Bely, "Vishnyovy sad," *Vesy* (*Balances*) 5 (1904); Vsevolod Meyerhold, *Perepiska* (Moscow: Iskusstvo, 1976), p. 45; and "Teatr (k istorii tekhnike)," in *Teatr: kniga o novom teatre* (St. Petersburg: Shipovnik, 1908), pp.143–145.

THE CHERRY ORCHARD[1]

Вишнёвый сад

A Comedy[2]

CHARACTERS[3]

RANEVSKAYA, LYUBOV ANDREEVNA, *a landowner*

ANYA, *her daughter, 17*

VARYA, *her foster daughter, 24*

GAEV, LEONID ANDREEVICH, *Ranevskaya's brother*

LOPAKHIN, YERMOLAY ALEKSEICH, *a businessman*

TROFIMOV, PYOTR SERGEEVICH, *a university student*

SIMEONOV-PISHCHIK, BORIS BORISOVICH, *a landowner*

CHARLOTTA IVANOVA, *a governess*

YEPHIKHOV, SEMYON PANTELEEVICH, *a bookkeeper*

DUNYASHA, *a parlor maid*

FIRS[4] NIKOLAEVICH, *a valet, an old-timer of 87*

---

1 According to Stanislavsky, Chekhov wavered between the pronunciations *Vishnevy sad* (accentuated on the first syllable, "an orchard of cherries") and *Vishnyovy sad* (accentuated on the second syllable, "a cherry orchard"). He decided on the latter. "The former is a market garden, a plantation of cherry-trees, a profitable orchard which still had value. But the latter offers no profit, it does nothing but preserve within itself and its snow-white blossoms the poetry of the life of the masters of olden times" (*My Life in Art*).

2 This subtitle was used in the Marks edition of 1904. On the posters and publicity the play was denominated a drama.

3 To a Russian ear, certain associations can be made with the names. Lyubov means love, and a kind of indiscriminate love characterizes Ranevskaya. Gaev suggests *gaer*, buffoon, while Lopakhin may be derived from either *lopata*, shovel, or *lopat*, to shovel food down one's gullet—both earthy-sounding. Simeonov-Pishchik combines an ancient autocratic name with a silly one reminiscent of *pishchat*, to chirp, something like De Montfort-Tweet. A *pishchik* is a "swozzle," or pipe, used by puppeteers to produce the voice of Petrushka, the Russian Punch.

4 He is named for the Orthodox Saint Thyrsus (martyred 251).

YASHA, *a young valet*

A VAGRANT

THE STATION MASTER

A POSTAL CLERK

GUESTS, SERVANTS

The action takes place on Ranevskaya's country estate.[5]

ACT ONE

A room, which is still known as the nursery. One of the doors opens into Anya's bedroom. Dawn, soon the sun will be up. It is already May, the cherry trees are in bloom, but it is chilly in the orchard, there is an early morning frost. The windows in the room are shut. Enter DUNYASHA carrying a candle and LOPAKHIN holding a book.

LOPAKHIN. Train's pulled in, thank God. What time is it?

DUNYASHA. Almost two. (*Blows out the candle.*) Light already.

LOPAKHIN. But just how late was the train? A couple of hours at least. (*Yawns and stretches.*) That's me all over, had to do something stupid! Drove over here on purpose, to meet them at the station, and spent the time fast asleep . . . Sat down and dropped off. Annoying . . . Though you should have woke me up.

DUNYASHA. I thought you'd gone. (*Listening.*) There, sounds like they're driving up.

LOPAKHIN (*listening*). No . . . the luggage has to be loaded, one thing and another . . . (*Pause.*) Lyubov Andreevna's been living abroad five years

---

5. "It's an old manor house: once the life in it was very opulent, and this must be felt in the furnishings. Opulent and comfortable" (Chekhov to Olga Knipper, October 14, 1903). "The house in the play has two stories, is big. After all, in Act Three, there's talk about 'down the stairs' " (to Stanislavsky, November 5, 1903). Stanislavsky decided that the estate was located in the Oryol province near Kursk, possibly because the area is rich in potter's clay and would justify the Englishmen in Act Four finding "some sort of white clay" on Pishchik's land.

now, I don't know what she's like these days . . . A good sort of person, that's her. A kind-hearted, unpretentious person. I remember, when I was just a kid about fifteen,[6] my late father—he kept a shop in this village back then—punched me in the face with his fist, blood was gushing from my nose . . . We'd come into the yard back then for some reason, and he'd been drinking. Lyubov Andreevna, I remember as though it was yesterday, still a youngish lady, so slender, brought me to the washstand, here in this very room, the nursery. "Don't cry," she says, "my little peasant, it'll heal in time for your wedding . . ."

Pause.

My little peasant . . . My father, true, was a peasant, and here I am in a white waistcoat, yellow high-button shoes. Like a pig's snout on a tray of pastry . . .[7] Only difference is I'm rich, plenty of money, but if you think it over and work it out, once a peasant, always a peasant . . .[8] (*Leafs through the book.*) I was reading this here book and couldn't make head or tail of it. Reading and nodding off.

Pause.

DUNYASHA. The dogs didn't sleep all night, they can sense the mistress is coming home.

---

6 In an earlier version, the boy's age was five or six. At that time Chekhov still saw Ranevskaya as an old woman. He reduced her age when it became clear that Olga Knipper would play the part.

7 Literally, "with a pig's snout in White-Bread Row," the street in any city market where fine baked goods are sold.

8 "Lopakhin must be not be played as a loudmouth, that isn't the invariable sign of a merchant. He's a suave man" (Chekhov to Olga Knipper, October 30, 1903). "Lopakhin is a merchant, true; but a very decent person in every respect; he must behave with perfect decorum, like an educated man with no petty ways or tricks . . . In casting an actor in the part, you must remember that Varya, a serious and religious young girl, is in love with Lopakhin: she wouldn't be in love with some little moneygrubber . . ." (Chekhov to Stanislavsky, October 30, 1903). "Lopakhin—a white waistcoat and yellow high-button shoes; walks swinging his arms, a broad stride, thinks while walking, walks a straight line. Hair not short, and therefore often tosses back his head, while in thought he combs his beard, back to front, i.e., from his neck toward his mouth" (Chekhov to Nemirovich-Danchenko, November 2, 1903).
According to L. M. Leonidov,

> [Chekhov] told me that Lopakhin outwardly should either be like a merchant or like a medical professor at Moscow University. And later, at the rehearsals, after Act Three he said to me: "Listen, Lopakhin doesn't shout. He is rich, and rich men never shout." . . .
> When I inquired of Chekhov how to play Lopakhin, he replied: "In yellow high-button shoes."
> ("Past and Present," *Moscow Art Theatre Yearbook for 1944*, vol. 1 [1946])

LOPAKHIN. What's got into you, Dunyasha, you're so . . .

DUNYASHA. My hands are trembling. I'm going to swoon.

LOPAKHIN. Much too delicate, that's what you are, Dunyasha. Dressing up like a young lady, fixing your hair like one too. Mustn't do that. Got to remember who you are.

> *YEPIKHODOV* [9] *enters with a bouquet; he is wearing a jacket and brightly polished boots, which squeak noisily. On entering, he drops the bouquet.*

YEPIKHODOV (*picks up the bouquet*). Here, the gardener sent them, he says stick 'em in the dining room. (*He hands Dunyasha the bouquet.*)

LOPAKHIN. And bring me some kvas.[10]

DUNYASHA. Yes, sir. (*Exits.*)

YEPIKHODOV. There's a morning frost now, three degrees below, but the cherries are all in bloom. I can't condone our climate. (*Sighs.*) I can't. Our climate cannot be conducive in the right way. Look, Yermolay Alekseich, if I might append, day before yesterday I bought myself some boots and they, I venture to assure you, squeak so loud, it's quite out of the question. What's the best kind of grease?

LOPAKHIN. Leave me alone. You wear me out.

YEPIKHODOV. Every day I experience some kind of hard luck. But I don't complain, I'm used to it. I even smile.

> *DUNYASHA enters and gives Lopakhin a glass of kvas.*[11]

---

9 A parody of the self-made man represented by Lopakhin. Chekhov first envisaged the character as plump and elderly, but revised this to fit one of his favorite actors, Ivan Moskvin, who was young and trim. The character had several originals. Yepikhodov's autodidacticism, reading abstruse books to better his mind, originated when Chekhov suggested to one of his attendants in Yalta that he go in for self-improvement. So the man went out, bought a red tie, and announced his intention of learning French. Yepikhodov's clumsiness derives from a conjuring clown Chekhov saw perform at the Hermitage gardens. The act consisted of disasters: juggled eggs smashing on the clown's forehead, dishes crashing to the ground, while the woebegone wizard stood with an expression of bewilderment and embarrassment. Chekhov kept shouting, "Wonderful! It's wonderful!" (Stanislavsky, *Teatralnaya gazeta*, November 27, 1914).

10 See *The Bear,* note 6.

11 "Dunya and Yepikhodov stand in Lopakhin's presence, they do not sit. Lopakhin, after all, deports himself freely, like a lord, uses the familiar form in speaking to the housemaid, whereas she uses the formal form to him" (Chekhov to Stanislavsky, November 10, 1903).

YEPIKHODOV. I'm on my way. (*Bumps into a chair, which falls over.*) Look . . . (*As if in triumph.*) There, you see, pardon the expression, what a circumstance, one of many . . . It's simply incredible! (*He exits.*)

DUNYASHA. I have to confess, Yermolay Alekseich, Yepikhodov proposed to me.

LOPAKHIN. Ah!

DUNYASHA. I don't know how to handle it . . . He's a quiet sort, but sometimes he just starts talking, and you can't understand a word. It's nice and it's sensitive, only you can't understand a word. I kind of like him. He's madly in love with me. As a person he's always in trouble, something goes wrong every day. So around here we've taken to calling him Tons of Trouble . . .[12]

LOPAKHIN (*hearkening*). Listen, I think they're coming . . .

DUNYASHA. They're coming! What's the matter with me . . . I've got cold chills.

LOPAKHIN. They're coming. Let's go meet them. Will she recognize me? It's five years since last we met.

DUNYASHA (*flustered*). I'll faint this minute . . . Ah, I'll faint!

> *We hear the sound of two carriages drawing up to the house. LOPAKHIN and DUNYASHA go out quickly. The stage is empty. Noise begins in the adjoining rooms. FIRS, leaning on a stick, hurries across the stage; he has just been to meet Lyubov Andreevna; he is wearing an old suit of livery and a top hat; he mutters something to himself, but no words can be made out. A voice: "Let's go through here." LYUBOV ANDREEVNA,[13] ANYA, and CHARLOTTA IVANOVNA with a lapdog on a leash, all three dressed in traveling clothes, VARYA in an overcoat and kerchief, GAEV, SIMEONOV-PISHCHIK, LOPAKHIN,*

---

12 Literally, *Dvadtsat-dva neschastye*, Twenty-two Misfortunes, "twenty-two" being a number indicating "lots." *Neschastye* is a recurrent word throughout the play.

13 "No, I never wanted to suggest that Ranevskaya is chastened. The only thing that can chasten a woman like that is death . . . It isn't hard to play Ranevskaya; you only need from the beginning to take the right tone; you need to come up with a smile and a way of laughing, you have to know how to dress" (Chekhov to Olga Knipper, October 25, 1903).

DUNYASHA with a bundle and parasol, SERVANTS carrying
suitcases—all pass through the room.

ANYA.[14] Let's go through here. Mama, do you remember what room this is?

LYUBOV ANDREEVNA (*joyfully, through tears*). The nursery!

VARYA. It's cold, my hands are numb. (*To Lyubov Andreevna.*) Your rooms, the white and the violet, are still the same as ever, Mama dear.

LYUBOV ANDREEVNA. The nursery, my darling, beautiful room . . . I slept here when I was a little girl . . . (*Weeps.*) And now I feel like a little girl . . . (*She kisses her brother and Varya and then her brother again.*) And Varya is just the same as ever, looks like a nun. And I recognized Dunyasha . . . (*Kisses Dunyasha.*)

GAEV. The train was two hours late. What'd y' call that? What kind of system is that?

CHARLOTTA (*to Pishchik*). My dog eats nuts even.[15]

PISHCHIK (*astounded*).[16] Can you imagine!

They all go out, except for ANYA and DUNYASHA.

DUNYASHA. We're worn out with waiting . . . (*Helps Anya out of her overcoat and hat.*)

ANYA. I couldn't sleep the four nights on the train . . . now I'm so frozen.

---

14 "Anya [is] a bobtailed, uninteresting role. Varya [. . .] is a little nun, a little silly" (Chekhov to Nemirovich-Danchenko, October 30, 1903). "Anya can be played by anybody you like, even by an altogether unknown actress, only she must be young and look like a little girl, and talk in a young, ringing voice. This is not one of the major roles. Varya is a more important role . . . Varya does not resemble Sonya and Natasha; she is a figure in a black dress, a little nun, a little silly, a crybaby, etc., etc." (Chekhov to Nemirovich-Danchenko, November 2 , 1903).

15 "Charlotta is a major role . . . Charlotta speaks correct, not broken, Russian, but occasionally she pronounces the soft ending of a word hard, and she confuses the masculine and feminine gender of adjectives" (Chekhov to Nemirovich-Danchenko, November 2, 1903).
    "Muratova, who played Charlotta, asks Anton Pavlovich, might she wear a green necktie.
    "'You may but it's not necessary,' the author answers" (L. M. Leonidov, "Past and Present," *Moscow Art Theatre Yearbook for 1944*, vol. 1 [1946]).
    The character was based on an eccentric English governess, whom Chekhov had met while staying on Stanislavsky's estate. This acrobatic Miss Prism would leap up on Chekhov's shoulders and salute passersby by taking off his hat and forcing him to bow (*My Life in Art*, Russian ed.).

16 "Pishchik is a real Russian, an old man, debilitated by gout, old age, and over-indulgence, stout, dressed in a tight, long-waisted frockcoat . . . , boots without heels" (Chekhov to Nemirovich-Danchenko, November 2, 1903).

DUNYASHA. You left during Lent, there was snow then too, frost, and now? My darling! (*She laughs and kisses her.*) We're worn out with waiting for you, my pride and joy . . . I'll tell you now, I can't hold it back another minute . . .

ANYA (*weary*). Always something . . .

DUNYASHA. Yepikhodov the bookkeeper right after Easter proposed to me.

ANYA. You've got a one-track mind . . . (*Setting her hair to rights.*) I've lost all my hair pins . . . (*She is very tired, practically staggering.*)

DUNYASHA. I just don't know what to think. He loves me, loves me so much!

ANYA (*peering through the door to her room, tenderly*). My room, my windows, as if I'd never gone away. I'm home! Tomorrow morning I'll get up, run through the orchard . . . Oh, if only I could get some sleep! I couldn't sleep the whole way, I was worried to death.

DUNYASHA. Day before yesterday, Pyotr Sergeich arrived.

ANYA (*joyfully*). Petya!

DUNYASHA. The gent's sleeping in the bathhouse, the gent's staying there. "I'm afraid," says the gent, "to be a nuisance." (*Looking at her pocket watch.*) Somebody ought to wake the gent up, but Varvara Mikhailovna gave the order not to. "Don't you wake him up," she says.

Enter VARYA, with a key ring on her belt.

VARYA. Dunyasha, coffee right away . . . Mama dear is asking for coffee.

DUNYASHA. Just a minute. (*She exits.*)

VARYA. Well, thank God you're here. You're home again. (*Caressing her.*) My darling's here again! My beauty's here again!

ANYA. What I've been through.

VARYA. I can imagine!

ANYA. I left during Holy Week, it was so cold then. Charlotta kept talking the whole way, doing tricks. Why you stuck me with Charlotta . . .

VARYA. You couldn't have traveled by yourself, precious. Seventeen years old!

ANYA. We get to Paris, it was cold there too, snowing. My French is awful. Mama is living on the sixth floor, I walk all the way up, there are some

French people there, ladies, an old Catholic priest with a pamphlet, and it's full of cigarette smoke, not nice at all. And suddenly I started to feel sorry for Mama, so sorry for her, I took her head in my hands and couldn't let go. Then Mama kept hugging me, crying . . .

VARYA (*through tears*). Don't talk about it, don't talk about it . . .

ANYA. The villa near Mentone[17] she'd already sold, she had nothing left, nothing. And I hadn't a kopek left either, we barely got this far. And Mama doesn't understand! We sit down to dinner at a station, and she orders the most expensive meal and gives each waiter a ruble tip. Charlotta's the same. Yasha insists on his share too, it's simply awful. Of course Mama has a manservant, Yasha, we brought him back.

VARYA. I saw the low-life . . .

ANYA. Well, how are things? Have we paid the interest?

VARYA. What with.

ANYA. Oh dear, oh dear . . .

VARYA. In August the estate's to be auctioned off . . .

ANYA. Oh dear . . .

LOPAKHIN (*sticking his head in the doorway and bleating*). Me-e-eh . . . (*Exits.*)

VARYA (*through tears*). I'd like to smack him one . . . (*Shakes her fist.*)

ANYA (*embraces Varya, quietly*). Varya, has he proposed? (*VARYA shakes her head no.*) He *does* love you . . . Why don't you talk it over, what are you waiting for?

VARYA. I don't think it will work out for us. He has so much business, can't get around to me . . . and he pays me no mind. Forget about him, I can't stand to look at him . . . Everybody talks about our getting married, everybody says congratulations, but as a matter of fact, there's nothing to it, it's all like a dream . . . (*In a different tone.*) You've got a brooch like a bumblebee.

ANYA (*sadly*). Mama bought it. (*Goes to her room, speaks cheerfully, like a child.*) And in Paris I went up in a balloon!

---

17 Or Menton, a resort area on the Mediterranean coast of France. Nearby lies Monte Carlo, another suggestion of Ranevskaya's extravagance.

VARYA. My darling's here again! My beauty's here again!

DUNYASHA has returned with a coffeepot and is brewing coffee.

(*Stands near the door.*) The whole day long, darling, while I'm doing my chores, I keep dreaming. If only there were a rich man for you to marry, even I would be at peace, I'd go to a hermitage, then to Kiev . . . to Moscow, and I'd keep on going like that to holy shrines . . . I'd go on and on. Heaven! . . .[18]

ANYA. The birds are singing in the orchard. What time is it now?

VARYA. Must be three. Time for you to be asleep, dearest. (*Going into Anya's room.*) Heaven!

YASHA enters with a lap rug and a traveling bag.

YASHA (*crosses the stage; in a refined way*). May I come through, ma'am?

DUNYASHA. A person wouldn't recognize you, Yasha. You've really changed abroad.

YASHA. Mm . . . who are you?

DUNYASHA. When you left here, I was so high . . . (*Measures from the floor.*) Dunyasha, Fyodor Kozoedov's daughter. You don't remember!

YASHA. Mm . . . Tasty little pickle! (*Glances around and embraces her, she shrieks and drops a saucer. YASHA exits hurriedly.*)

VARYA (*in the doorway, crossly*). Now what was that?

DUNYASHA (*through tears*). I broke a saucer . . .

VARYA. That's good luck.

ANYA (*entering from her room*). We ought to warn Mama that Petya's here . . .

VARYA. I gave orders not to wake him.

ANYA (*thoughtfully*). Six years ago father died, a month later our brother Grisha drowned in the river, a sweet little boy, seven years old. Mama

18 Becoming a *bogomolets*, or pilgrim, was a common avocation in pre-Revolutionary Russia, especially for the rootless and outcast. One would trek from shrine to shrine, putting up at monasteries and living off alms. Varya's picture of such a life is highly idealized. Its picaresque side can be glimpsed in Nikolay Leskov's stories, such as "The Enchanted Pilgrim," in the ambiguous figure Luka in Gorky's 1902 play *The Lower Depths*, and in Chekhov's *Along the Highway*.

couldn't stand it, she went away, went away without looking back . . . (*Shivers.*) How well I understand her, if only she knew!

Pause.

Since Petya Trofimov was Grisha's tutor, he might remind her . . .

Enter FIRS in a jacket and white waistcoat.

FIRS (*goes to the coffeepot; preoccupied*). The mistress will take it in here . . . (*Putting on white gloves.*) Cawrfee ready? (*Sternly to Dunyasha.*) You! What about cream?

DUNYASHA. Oh, my goodness . . . (*Exits hurriedly.*)

FIRS (*fussing with the coffeepot*). Eh you, half-baked bungler[19] . . . (*Mumbles to himself.*) Come home from Paris . . . And the master went to Paris once upon a time . . . by coach and horses . . . (*Laughs.*)

VARYA. Firs, what are you on about?

FIRS. What's wanted, miss? (*Joyfully.*) My mistress has come home! I've been waiting! Now I can die . . . (*Weeps with joy.*)

Enter LYUBOV ANDREEVNA, GAEV, LOPAKHIN, and SIMEONOV-PISHCHIK, the last in a long-waisted coat of expensive cloth and baggy pantaloons.[20] GAEV, on entering, moves his arms and torso as if he were playing billiards.

LYUBOV ANDREEVNA. How does it go? Let me remember . . . Yellow in the corner! Doublette in the center![21]

---

19 *Nedotyopa* was not a Russian word when Chekhov used it; it was Ukrainian for an incompetent, a mental defective. Chekhov may have remembered hearing it in his childhood; it does not appear in Russian dictionaries until 1938, and then Chekhov is cited as the source. George Calderon perceived the etymology to derive from *ne*, not, and *dotyapat*, to finish chopping, which makes great sense in the context of the play. Translators grow gray over the word: earlier English versions have "good-for-nothing," "rogue," "duffer," "job-lot," "lummox," "silly young cuckoo," "silly old nothing," "nincompoop," "muddler," "silly galoot," "numbskull," "young flibbertigibbet." The critic Batyushkov considered the whole play to be a variation on the theme of "nedotyopery," each of the characters representing a different aspect of life unfulfilled.

20 Pishchik's costume makes him look more traditionally Russian than the others: the long coat and baggy pants tucked into boots are modern adaptations of medieval boyar dress.

21 In pre-Revolutionary Russia, billiards was played with five balls, one of them yellow. A doublette occurs when a player's ball hits the cushion, rebounds, and sinks the other player's ball. George Calderon ventured that Gaev "always plays a declaration game at billiards, no flukes allowed." Chekhov asked the actor he wanted to play Gaev to brush up on the terminology and add the proper

GAEV. Red in the corner! Once upon a time, sister, we used to sleep together here in this room, and now I've turned fifty-one, strange as it seems . . .

LOPAKHIN. Yes, time marches on.

GAEV. How's that?[22]

LOPAKHIN. Time, I say, marches on.

GAEV. It smells of cheap perfume[23] in here.

ANYA. I'm going to bed. Good night, Mama. (*Kisses her mother.*)

LYUBOV ANDREEVNA. My dazzling little princess.[24] (*Kisses her hands.*) Are you glad you're home? I can't get over it.

ANYA. Good night, Uncle.

GAEV (*kisses her face, hands*). God bless you. How like your mother you are! (*To his sister.*) Lyuba, at her age you were just the same.

> ANYA *gives her hand to Lopakhin and Pishchik, exits, and shuts the door behind her.*

LYUBOV ANDREEVNA. She's utterly exhausted.

PISHCHIK. Must be a long trip.

VARYA (*to Lopakhin and Pishchik*). Well, gentlemen? Three o'clock, by this time you've worn out your welcome.

LYUBOV ANDREEVNA (*laughing*). And you're still the same too, Varya. (*Draws Varya to her and kisses her.*) First I'll have some coffee, then everybody will go.

> FIRS *puts a cushion under her feet.*

---

phrases in rehearsal. "Ask Vishnevsky to listen in on people playing billiards and jot down as many billiard terms as he can. I don't play billiards, or did once, but now I've forgotten it all, and stick them in my play any old way. Later on Vishnevsky and I will talk it over, and I'll write in what's needed" (Chekhov to Olga Knipper, October 14, 1903).

22 The colloquial "*Kogo*" (literally, "Whom?") instead of "*chego*" ("What's that?"), the quirky locution of an aristocrat.

23 Patchouli, an oil made from an Asian plant, which has a very powerful aroma, prized in the Orient, but insufferable to many Westerners.

24 *Nenaglyadnaya ditsyusya moya*, literally, "blindingly beauteous bairn of mine," a formula found in fairy tales.

Thank you, dear. I've grown accustomed to coffee. I drink it night and day. Thank you, my old dear. (*Kisses Firs.*)

VARYA. I've got to see if all the luggage was brought in . . . (*Exits.*)

LYUBOV ANDREEVNA. Can I really be sitting here? (*Laughs.*) I feel like jumping up and down and swinging my arms. (*Covers her face with her hands.*) But suppose I'm dreaming! God knows, I love my country, love it dearly, I couldn't look at it from the train, couldn't stop crying. (*Through tears.*) However, we should have some coffee. Thank you, Firs, thank you, my old dear. I'm so glad you're still alive.

FIRS. Day before yesterday.

GAEV. He's hard of hearing.

LOPAKHIN. I've got to leave for Kharkov right away, around five. What a nuisance! I wanted to feast my eyes on you, have a chat . . . You're still as lovely as ever.

PISHCHIK (*breathing hard*). Even prettier . . . Dressed in Parisian fashions . . . "lost my cart with all four wheels . . ."[25]

LOPAKHIN. Your brother, Leonid Andreich here, says that I'm an oaf, I'm a money-grubbing peasant,[26] but it doesn't make the least bit of difference to me. Let him talk. The only thing I want is for you to believe in me as you once did, for your wonderful, heartbreaking eyes to look at me as they once did. Merciful God! My father was your grandfather's serf, and your father's, but you, you personally did so much for me once that I forgot all that and love you like my own kin . . . more than my own kin.

LYUBOV ANDREEVNA. I can't sit still, I just can't . . . (*Leaps up and walks about in great excitement.*) I won't survive this joy . . . Laugh at me, I'm silly . . . My dear little cupboard. (*Kisses the cupboard.*) My little table.

GAEV. While you were away Nanny died.

LYUBOV ANDREEVNA (*sits and drinks coffee*). Yes, rest in peace. They wrote me.

---

25 The rest of the folksong verse goes "lost my heart head over heels." It means "Going the whole hog."

26 *Kulak*, literally a fist, but figuratively a tight-fisted peasant or small dealer.

GAEV. And Anastasy died. Cross-eyed Petrusha left me and now he's working in town for the chief of police. (*Takes a little box of hard candies out of his pocket and sucks one.*)

PISHCHIK. My dear daughter Dashenka . . . sends her regards . . .

LOPAKHIN. I'd like to tell you something you'd enjoy, something to cheer you up. (*Looking at his watch.*) I have to go now, never time for a real conversation . . . well, here it is in a nutshell. As you already know, the cherry orchard will be sold to pay your debts, the auction is set for August twenty-second, but don't you worry, dear lady, don't lose any sleep, there's a way out . . . Here's my plan. Your attention, please! Your estate lies only thirteen miles from town, the railroad runs past it, and if the cherry orchard and the land along the river were subdivided into building lots and then leased out for summer cottages, you'd have an income of at the very least twenty-five thousand a year.

GAEV. Excuse me, what rubbish!

LYUBOV ANDREEVNA. I don't quite follow you, Yermolay Alekseich.

LOPAKHIN. You'll get out of the summer tenants at least twenty-five rubles a year for every two and a half acres, and if you advertise now, I'll bet whatever you like that by fall there won't be a single lot left vacant, they'll all be snapped up. In short, congratulations, you're saved. The location's wonderful, the river's deep. Only, of course, it'll have to be spruced up, cleared out . . . for example, tear down all the old sheds, and this house, say, which is absolutely worthless, chop down the old cherry orchard . . .

LYUBOV ANDREEVNA. Chop it down? My dear, forgive me, but you don't understand at all. If there's anything of interest in the entire district, even outstanding, it's none other than our cherry orchard.[27]

---

27 Chekhov's close friend, the writer Ivan Bunin, objected to this feature of the play. "I grew up in just such an impoverished 'nest of gentry,'" he wrote. "It was a desolate estate on the steppes, but with a large orchard, not cherry, of course, for, Chekhov to the contrary, nowhere in Russia were there orchards comprised *exclusively* of cherries; only *sections* of the orchards on these estates (though sometimes very vast sections) grew cherries, and nowhere, Chekhov to the contrary again, could these sections be *directly beside* the main house, nor was there anything wonderful about the cherry trees, which are quite unattractive, as everyone knows, gnarled with puny leaves, puny blossoms when in bloom (quite unlike those which blossom so enormously and lushly right under the very windows of the main house at the Art Theatre) . . ." (*O Chekhove* [New York, 1955], pp. 215–216).

LOPAKHIN. The only outstanding thing about this orchard is it's very big. The soil produces cherries every other year, and then there's no way to get rid of them, nobody buys them.

GAEV. The *Encyclopedia* makes reference to this orchard . . .

LOPAKHIN (*after a glance at his watch*). If we don't think up something and come to some decision, then on the twenty-second of August the cherry orchard and the whole estate will be sold at auction. Make up your mind! There's no other way out, I promise you. Absolutely none.

FIRS. In the old days, forty-fifty years back, cherries were dried, preserved, pickled, made into jam, and sometimes . . .

GAEV. Be quiet, Firs.

FIRS. And used to be whole cartloads of dried cherries were sent to Moscow and Kharkov. Then there was money! And in those days the dried cherries were tender, juicy, sweet, tasty . . . They had a recipe then . . .

LYUBOV ANDREEVNA. And where's that recipe today?

FIRS. It's forgot. Nobody remembers.

PISHCHIK (*to Lyubov*). What's going on in Paris? What was it like? You eat frogs?

LYUBOV ANDREEVNA. I ate crocodiles.

PISHCHIK. Can you imagine . . .

LOPAKHIN. So far there's only been gentry and peasants in the country, but now there's these vacationers. Every town, even the smallest, is surrounded these days by summer cottages. And I'll bet that over the next twenty-odd years the summer vacationer will multiply fantastically. Now all he does is drink tea on his balcony, but it might just happen that on his two and a half acres he starts growing things, and then your cherry orchard will become happy, rich, lush . . .

GAEV (*getting indignant*). What drivel!

Enter VARYA and YASHA.

VARYA. Mama dear, there are two telegrams for you. (*Selects a key; with a jangle opens the antique cupboard.*) Here they are.

LYUBOV ANDREEVNA. They're from Paris. (*Tears up the telegrams without reading them.*) I'm through with Paris . . .

GAEV. Lyuba, do you know how old that cupboard is? A week ago I pulled out the bottom drawer, took a look, and there are numbers branded on it. This cupboard was built exactly one hundred years ago. How d'you like that? Eh? Maybe we ought to celebrate its centenary. An inanimate object, but all the same, any way you look at it, this cupboard is a repository for books.

PISHCHIK (*astounded*). A hundred years . . . Can you imagine!

GAEV. Yes . . . This thing . . . (*Stroking the cupboard.*) Dear, venerated cupboard! I salute your existence, which for over a century has been dedicated to enlightened ideals of virtue and justice; your unspoken appeal to constructive endeavor has not faltered in the course of a century, sustaining (*through tears*) in generations of our line, courage, faith in a better future and nurturing within us ideals of decency and social consciousness.[28]

Pause.

LOPAKHIN. Right . . .

LYUBOV ANDREEVNA. You're still the same, Lyonya.

GAEV (*somewhat embarrassed*). Carom to the right corner! Red in the center!

LOPAKHIN (*glancing at his watch*). Well, my time's up.

YASHA (*handing medicine to Lyubov*). Maybe you'll take your pills now . . .

PISHCHIK. Shouldn't take medicine, dearest lady . . . It does no good, or harm . . . Hand 'em over . . . most respected lady. (*He takes the pills, shakes them into his palm, blows on them, pops them into his mouth, and drinks some kvas.*) There!

LYUBOV ANDREEVNA (*alarmed*). You've gone crazy!

PISHCHIK. I took all the pills.

---

28 Chekhov is making fun of the Russian mania for celebrating anniversaries. Stanislavsky reports that on the twenty-fifth anniversary of Chekhov's literary career, held during the third performance of *The Cherry Orchard*, "One of the men of letters began his speech of tribute with the same words that Gaev addresses to the old cupboard in Act One of *The Cherry Orchard*, 'Dear, venerated.' Only instead of cupboard, the orator said 'Anton Pavlovich.' Chekhov winked at me and smiled a wicked smile" (*Letters*).

LOPAKHIN. He's a bottomless pit.

They all laugh.

FIRS. The gent stayed with us Holy Week, ate half a bucket of pickles . . . (*Mumbles.*)

LYUBOV ANDREEVNA. What is he on about?

VARYA. For three years now he's been mumbling like that. We're used to it.

YASHA. Second childhood.

> *CHARLOTTA IVANOVNA crosses the stage in a white dress.*
> *She is very slender, tightly laced, with a pair of pince-nez on a*
> *cord at her waist.*

LOPAKHIN. Excuse me, Charlotta Ivanovna, I haven't had time yet to welcome you back. (*Tries to kiss her hand.*)

CHARLOTTA (*pulling her hand away*). If I let you kiss a hand, next you'd be after a elbow, then a shoulder . . .

LOPAKHIN. My unlucky day.

Everybody laughs.

Charlotta Ivanovna, show us a trick!

LYUBOV ANDREEVNA. Charlotta, show us a trick!

CHARLOTTA. Nothing doing. I want to go to bed. (*Exits.*)

LOPAKHIN. Three weeks from now we'll meet again. (*Kisses Lyubov Andreevna's hand.*) Meanwhile, good-bye. It's time. (*To Gaev.*) Be suing you.[29] (*Exchanges kisses with Pishchik.*) Be suing you. (*Gives his hand to Varya, then to Firs and Yasha.*) I don't want to go. (*To Lyubov Andreevna.*) If you reconsider this cottage business and come to a decision, then let me know, I'll arrange a loan of fifty thousand or so. Give it some serious thought.

VARYA (*angrily*). Well, go if you're going!

LOPAKHIN. I'm going, I'm going . . . (*He leaves.*)

GAEV. Oaf. All right, *pardon* . . . Varya's going to marry him, that's our Varya's little intended!

---

29 Instead of *Do svidaniya*, "Be seeing you," Lopakhin facetiously says *Do svidantsiya*.

VARYA. Don't say anything uncalled for, uncle dear.

LYUBOV ANDREEVNA. So what, Varya, I'll be very glad. He's a good man.

PISHCHIK. A man, you've got to tell the truth . . . most worthy . . . And my Dashenka . . . also says that . . . says all sorts of things. (*Snores but immediately wakes up.*) But by the way, most respected lady, lend me . . . . two hundred and forty rubles . . . tomorrow I've got to pay the interest on the mortgage . . .[30]

VARYA (*alarmed*). We're all out, all out!

LYUBOV ANDREEVNA. As a matter of fact, I haven't a thing.

PISHCHIK. It'll turn up. (*Laughs.*) I never lose hope. There, I think, all is lost, I'm a goner, lo and behold!—the railroad runs across my land and . . . pays me for it. And then, watch, something else will happen sooner or later . . . Dashenka will win two hundred thousand . . . she's got a lottery ticket.

LYUBOV ANDREEVNA. The coffee's finished, now we can go to bed.

FIRS (*brushes Gaev's clothes, scolding*). You didn't put on the right trousers again. What am I going to do with you!

VARYA (*quietly*). Anya's asleep. (*Quietly opens a window.*) The sun's up already, it's not so cold. Look, Mama dear, what wonderful trees! My goodness, the air! The starlings are singing!

GAEV (*opens another window*). The orchard's all white. You haven't forgotten, Lyuba? There's that long pathway leading straight on, straight on, like a stretched ribbon, it glistens on moonlit nights. You remember? You haven't forgotten?

LYUBOV ANDREEVNA (*looks through the window at the orchard*). O, my childhood, my innocence! I slept in this nursery, gazed out at the orchard, happiness awoke with me every morning, and it was just the same then, nothing has changed. (*Laughs with joy.*) All, all white! O, my orchard! After the dark, drizzly autumn and the cold winter, you're young again, full of happiness, the angels in heaven haven't forsaken you . . . If only I could

---

30 By 1903, almost one-half of all private land in Russia (excluding peasant land) was mortgaged, forcing the landed gentry to sell their estates and join the professional or commercial classes, as Gaev does at the end of this play.

lift off my chest and shoulders this heavy stone, if only I could forget my past!

GAEV. Yes, and the orchard will be sold for debts, strange as it seems . . .

LYUBOV ANDREEVNA. Look, our poor Mama is walking through the orchard . . . in a white dress! (*Laughs with joy.*) There she is.

GAEV. Where?

VARYA. God keep you, Mama dear.

LYUBOV ANDREEVNA. There's nobody there, it just seemed so to me. On the right, by the turning to the summerhouse, a white sapling was bending, it looked like a woman . . .

> *Enter TROFIMOV, in a shabby student's uniform*
> *and eyeglasses.*[31]

What a marvelous orchard! White bunches of blossoms, blue sky . . .

TROFIMOV. Lyubov Andreevna! (*She has stared round at him.*) I'll just pay my respects and then leave at once. (*Kisses her hand fervently.*) They told me to wait till morning, but I didn't have the patience . . .

> *LYUBOV ANDREEVNA stares in bewilderment.*

VARYA (*through tears*). This is Petya Trofimov.

TROFIMOV. Petya Trofimov, used to be tutor to your Grisha . . . Can I have changed so much?

> *LYUBOV ANDREEVNA embraces him and weeps quietly.*

GAEV (*embarrassed*). Come, come, Lyuba.

VARYA (*weeps*). Didn't I tell you, Petya, to wait till tomorrow.

LYUBOV ANDREEVNA. My Grisha . . . my little boy . . . Grisha . . . my son . . .

VARYA. There's no help for it, Mama dear, God's will be done.

---

31 "I'm worried about the second act's lack of action and a certain sketchy quality in Trofimov, the student. After all, time and again Trofimov is being sent into exile, time and again he is being expelled from the university, but how can you express stuff like that?" (Chekhov to Olga Knipper, October 19, 1903).

TROFIMOV (*gently, through tears*). There, there . . .

LYUBOV ANDREEVNA (*quietly weeping*). A little boy lost, drowned . . . What for? What for, my friend? (*More quietly.*) Anya's asleep in there, and I'm so loud . . . making noise . . . Well now, Petya? Why have you become so homely? Why have you got old?

TROFIMOV. On the train, a peasant woman called me: that scruffy gent.

LYUBOV ANDREEVNA. You were just a boy in those days, a dear little student, but now your hair is thinning, eyeglasses. Are you really still a student? (*Goes to the door.*)

TROFIMOV. I suppose I'll be a perpetual student.[32]

LYUBOV ANDREEVNA (*kisses her brother, then Varya*). Well, let's go to bed . . . You've got old too, Leonid.

PISHCHIK (*follows her*). That means it's time for bed . . . Ugh, my gout. I'll stay over with you . . . And if you would, Lyubov Andreevna, dear heart, tomorrow morning early . . . two hundred and forty rubles . . .

GAEV. He never gives up.

PISHCHIK. Two hundred and forty rubles . . . to pay the interest on the mortgage.

LYUBOV ANDREEVNA. I have no money, darling . . .

PISHCHIK. We'll pay it back, dear lady . . . The most trifling sum.

LYUBOV ANDREEVNA. Well, all right, Leonid will let you have it . . . Let him have it, Leonid.

GAEV. I'll let him have it, hold out your pockets.

LYUBOV ANDREEVNA. What can we do, let him have it . . . He needs it . . . He'll pay it back.

> *LYUBOV ANDREEVNA, TROFIMOV, PISHCHIK, and FIRS go out. GAEV, VARYA, and YASHA remain.*

GAEV. My sister still hasn't outgrown the habit of squandering money. (*To Yasha.*) Out of the way, my good man, you smell like a chicken coop.

---

32 Radical student dropouts were far from uncommon. The saying went, "It takes ten years to graduate—five in study, four in exile, and one wasted while the University is shut down."

YASHA (*with a sneer*). But you, Leonid Andreich, are just the same as you were.

GAEV. How's that? (*To Varya.*) What did he say?

VARYA (*to Yasha*). Your mother's come from the village, since yesterday she's been sitting in the servants' hall, she wants to see you . . .

YASHA. To hell with her!

VARYA. Ah, disgraceful!

YASHA. That's all I need. She could have come tomorrow. (*Exits.*)

VARYA. Mama dear is just as she was before, she hasn't changed a bit. If it were up to her, she'd give away everything.

GAEV. Yes . . .

Pause.

If a large number of cures is suggested for a particular disease, it means the disease is incurable. I think, wrack my brains, I've come up with all sorts of solutions, all sorts, which means, actually, none. It would be nice to inherit a fortune from somebody, nice if we married our Anya to a very rich man, nice to go to Yaroslavl and try our luck with our auntie the Countess. Auntie's really very, very wealthy.

VARYA (*weeps*). If only God would come to our aid.

GAEV. Stop sniveling. Auntie's very wealthy, but she isn't fond of us. In the first place, Sister married a lawyer, not a nobleman . . .

ANYA *appears in the doorway.*

Married a commoner and behaved herself, well, you can't say very virtuously. She's a good, kind, splendid person, I love her very much, but, no matter how you consider the extenuating circumstances, you still have to admit she's depraved. You can feel it in her slightest movement.

VARYA (*whispering*). Anya's standing in the doorway.

GAEV. How's that?

Pause.

Extraordinary, something's got in my right eye . . . my sight's beginning to fail. And Thursday, when I was at the county courthouse . . .

ANYA enters.

VARYA. Why aren't you asleep, Anya?

ANYA. I can't fall asleep. I can't.

GAEV. My teeny-weeny. (*Kisses Anya's face, hands.*) My little girl . . . (*Through tears.*) You're not my niece, you're my angel, you're everything to me. Believe me, believe . . .

ANYA. I believe you, Uncle. Everybody loves you, respects you . . . but dear Uncle, you must keep still, simply keep still. What were you saying just now about my Mama, your own sister? How come you said that?

GAEV. Yes, yes . . . (*Hides his face in her hands.*) It's an awful thing to say! My God! God help me! And today I made a speech to the cupboard . . . like a fool! And as soon as I'd finished, I realized what a fool I'd been.

VARYA. True, Uncle dear, you ought to keep still. Just keep still, that's all.

ANYA. If you keep still, you'll be more at peace with yourself.

GAEV. I'll keep still. (*Kisses Anya's and Varya's hands.*) I'll keep still. Only this is business. Thursday I was at the county courthouse, well, some friends gathered round, started talking about this and that, six of one, half a dozen of the other, and it turns out a person can sign a promissory note and borrow money to pay the interest to the bank.

VARYA. If only God would come to our aid!

GAEV. I'll go there on Tuesday and have another talk. (*To Varya.*) Stop sniveling. (*To Anya.*) Your Mama will talk to Lopakhin, he won't refuse her, of course . . . And you, after you've had a rest, will go to Yaroslavl to the Countess, your great-aunt . That way we'll have action on three fronts—and our business is in the bag! We'll pay off the interest, I'm sure of it . . . (*Pops a candy into his mouth.*) Word of honor, I'll swear by whatever you like, the estate won't be sold! (*Excited.*) I swear by my happiness! Here's my hand on it, call me a trashy, dishonorable man if I permit that auction! I swear with every fiber of my being!

ANYA (*a more peaceful mood comes over her, she is happy*). You're so good, Uncle, so clever! (*Embraces her uncle.*) Now I feel calm! I'm calm! I'm happy!

Enter FIRS.

FIRS (*scolding*). Leonid Andreich, have you no fear of God? When are you going to bed?

GAEV. Right away, right away. Go along, Firs. Have it your own way, I'll undress myself. Well, children, beddie-bye . . . Details tomorrow, but for now go to bed. (*Kisses Anya and Varya.*) I'm a man of the eighties . . . People don't put much stock in that period,[33] but all the same I can say I've suffered for my convictions to no small degree in my time. There's a good reason peasants love me. You've got to study peasants! You've got to know what . . .

ANYA. You're at it again, Uncle!

VARYA. Uncle dear, you must keep still.

FIRS (*angrily*). Leonid Andreich!

GAEV. Coming, coming . . . You two go to bed. Two cushion carom to the center! I sink the white . . . (*Exits followed by Firs, hobbling.*)

ANYA. Now I'm calm. I don't want to go to Yaroslavl. I don't like my great-aunt, but all the same, I'm calm. Thanks to Uncle. (*Sits down.*)

VARYA. Got to get some sleep. I'm off. Oh, while you were away there was a bit of an uprising. There's nobody living in the old servants' hall, as you know, except the old servants: Yefimushka, Polya, Yevstigney, oh, and Karp. They started letting these vagabonds spend the night there—I held my peace. Only then, I hear, they've spread the rumor that I gave orders to feed them nothing but beans. Out of stinginess, you see . . . And this was all Yevstigney's doing . . . Fine, I think. If that's how things are, I think, just you wait. I send for Yevstigney . . . (*Yawns.*) In he comes . . . What's wrong with you, I say, Yevstigney . . . you're such an idiot . . . (*Glancing at Anya.*) Anechka!

Pause.

Fast asleep! . . . (*Takes Anya by the arm.*) Let's go to bed . . . Let's go! . . . (*Leads her.*) My darling is fast asleep! Let's go! . . .

33 Under Alexander III, political reaction to reforms set in, the police and censorship became extremely repressive, and anti-Semitic pogroms broke out. Large-scale political reform became impossible, so that liberal intellectuals devoted themselves to local civilizing improvements in the villages, Tolstoyan passive resistance, and dabbling in "art for art's sake." This feeling of social and political impotence led to the torpid aimlessness common to Chekhov's characters.

They go out.

Far beyond the orchard a shepherd is playing his pipes.

*TROFIMOV crosses the stage, and, seeing Anya and Varya,
stops short.*

Ssh . . . She's asleep . . . asleep . . . Let's go, dearest.

ANYA (*softly, half-asleep*). I'm so tired . . . all the sleigh bells . . . Uncle . . .
dear . . . and Mama and Uncle . . .

VARYA. Let's go, dearest, let's go . . . (*They go into Anya's room.*)

TROFIMOV (*moved*). My sunshine! My springtime!

Curtain

ACT TWO

*A field. An old, long-abandoned shrine leaning to one side, beside
it a well, large slabs that were once, apparently, tombstones, and
an old bench. A road into Gaev's estate can be seen. At one side,
towering poplars cast their shadows; here the cherry orchard
begins. Farther off are telegraph poles, and way in the distance,
dimly sketched on the horizon, is a large town, which can be seen
only in the best and clearest weather. Soon the sun will set.
CHARLOTTA, YASHA, and DUNYASHA are sitting on the
bench. YEPIKHODOV stands nearby and strums a guitar;
everyone is rapt in thought. CHARLOTTA is wearing an old
peaked cap with a vizor; she has taken a rifle off her shoulder and
is adjusting a buckle on the strap.*

CHARLOTTA (*pensively*). I haven't got a valid passport,[34] I don't know how
old I am, and I always feel like I'm still oh so young. When I was a little
girl, my father and momma used to go from fairground to fairground, giving performances, pretty good ones. And I would do the death-defying

---

34 In the sense of an "internal passport," an identity document carried when traveling through the
Russian empire.

leap[35] and all sorts of stunts. And when Poppa and Momma died, a Ger-man gentlewoman took me home with her and started teaching me. Fine. I grew up, then turned into a governess. But where I'm from and who I am—I don't know . . . Who my parents were, maybe they weren't married . . . I don't know. (*Pulls a pickle out of her pocket and eats it.*) I don't know anything.

Pause.

It would be nice to talk to someone, but there is no one . . . I have no one.

YEPIKHODOV (*strums his guitar and sings*). "What care I for the noisy world, what are friends and foes to me . . ." How pleasant to play the mandolin!

DUNYASHA. That's a guitar, not a mandolin. (*Looks in a hand mirror and powders her nose.*)

YEPIKHODOV. To a lovesick lunatic, this is a mandolin . . . (*Sings quietly.*) "Were but my heart aflame with the spark of requited love . . ."

YASHA joins in.

CHARLOTTA. Horrible the way these people sing . . . Phooey! A pack of hyenas.

DUNYASHA (*to Yasha*). Anyway, how lucky to spend time abroad.

YASHA. Yes, of course. I can't disagree with you there. (*Yawns, then lights a cigar.*)

YEPIKHODOV. Stands to reason. Abroad everything long ago attained its complete complexification.

YASHA. Goes without saying.

YEPIKHODOV. I'm a cultured person, I read all kinds of remarkable books, but somehow I can't figure out my inclinations, what I want personally, to live or to shoot myself, speaking on my own behalf, nevertheless I always carry a revolver on my person. Here it is . . . (*Displays a revolver.*)

CHARLOTTA. I'm done. Now I'll go. (*Shoulders the gun.*) Yepikhodov, you're a very clever fellow, and a very frightening one; the women ought to love you madly. Brrr! (*On her way out.*) These clever people are all so stupid

---

35 In the original, Italian, *salto mortale.*

there's no one for me to talk to . . . No one . . . All alone, alone, I've got no one and . . . who I am, why I am, I don't know. (*Exits.*)

YEPIKHODOV. Speaking on my own behalf, not flying off on tangents, I must express myself about myself, among others, that Fate treats me ruthlessly, like a small storm-tossed ship. If, suppose, I'm wrong about this, then why when I woke up this morning, to give but a single example, I look and there on my chest is a ghastly enormity of a spider . . . Like so. (*Uses both hands to demonstrate.*) Or then again, I'll take some kvas, so as to drink it, and lo and behold, there'll be something indecent to the nth degree, along the lines of a cockroach . . .

Pause.

Have you read Buckle?[36]

Pause.

I should like to distress you, Avdotya Fyodorovna, with a couple of words.

DUNYASHA. Go ahead.

YEPIKHODOV. I would be desirous to see you in private . . . (*Sighs.*)

DUNYASHA (*embarrassed*). All right . . . only first bring me my wrap . . .[37] It's next to the cupboard . . . it's a bit damp here.

YEPIKHODOV. Yes, ma'am . . . I'll fetch it, ma'am . . . . Now I know what I have to do with my revolver . . . (*Takes the guitar and exits playing it.*)

YASHA. Tons of Trouble! Pretty stupid, take it from me. (*Yawns.*)

DUNYASHA. God forbid he should shoot himself.

Pause.

I've got jittery, nervous all the time. Just a little girl, they brought me to the master's house, now I'm out of touch with ordinary life, and my hands are

---

36 Henry Thomas Buckle (1821–1862), pronounced Buckly, whose *History of Civilization in England* (translated into Russian in 1861) posited that skepticism was the handmaiden of progress and that religion retards the advance of civilization. His materialist approach was much appreciated by progressive Russians in the 1870s, and Chekhov had read him as a student. By the end of the century Buckle's ideas seemed outmoded, so the reference suggests that Yepikhodov's efforts at self-education are behind the times.

37 Literally, *talmochka*, or little talma, a smaller version of the garment Nina wears in the last act of *The Seagull*.

white as white can be, like a young lady's. I've got sensitive, so delicate, ladylike, afraid of every little thing . . . Awfully so. And, Yasha, if you deceive me, then I don't know what'll happen to my nerves.

YASHA (*kisses her*). Tasty little pickle! Of course, a girl ought to know how far to go, and if there's one thing I hate, it's a girl who misbehaves . . .

DUNYASHA. I love you ever so much, you're educated, you can discuss anything.

Pause.

YASHA (*yawns*). Yes'm . . . The way I look at it, it's like this: if a girl loves somebody, that means she's immoral.

Pause.

Nice smoking a cigar in the fresh air . . . (*Listening.*) Someone's coming this way . . . The masters . . .

DUNYASHA impulsively embraces him.

Go home, pretend you'd been to the river for a swim, take this bypath or you'll run into them, and they'll think I've been going out with you. I couldn't stand that.

DUNYASHA (*coughs quietly*). Your cigar's given me a headache . . . (*Exits.*)

YASHA remains, seated beside the shrine. Enter LYUBOV ANDREEVNA, GAEV, and LOPAKHIN.

LOPAKHIN. You've got to decide once and for all—time won't stand still. The matter's really simple, after all. Do you agree to rent land for cottages or not? Give me a one-word answer: yes or no? Just one word!

LYUBOV ANDREEVNA. Who's been smoking those revolting cigars around here . . . (*Sits.*)

GAEV. Now that there's a railroad, things are convenient.[38] (*Sits.*) You ride to town and have lunch . . . yellow to the center! I should go home first, play one game . . .

LYUBOV ANDREEVNA. You'll have time.

---

38 There was a railway boom in Russia in the 1890s, although, owing to bribery and corruption, the stations were often some distance from the towns, and the service was far from efficient.

LOPAKHIN. Just one word! (*Pleading.*) Give me an answer!

GAEV (*yawning*). How's that?

LYUBOV ANDREEVNA (*looking into her purse*). Yesterday I had lots of money, but today there's very little left. My poor Varya feeds everybody milk soup to economize, in the kitchen the old people get nothing but beans, and somehow I'm spending recklessly . . . (*Drops the purse, scattering gold coins.*) Oh dear, they've spilled all over . . . (*Annoyed.*)

YASHA. Allow me, I'll pick them up at once. (*Gathers the money.*)

LYUBOV ANDREEVNA. That's sweet of you, Yasha. And why did I go out to lunch . . . That nasty restaurant of yours with its music, the tablecloths smelt of soap . . . Why drink so much, Lyonya? Why eat so much? Why talk so much? Today in the restaurant you started talking a lot again and all beside the point. About the seventies, about the decadents.[39] And who to? Talking to waiters about the decadents!

LOPAKHIN. Yes.

GAEV (*waves his hand in dismissal*). I'm incorrigible, it's obvious . . . (*Irritably, to Yasha.*) What's the matter, forever whirling around in front of us . . .

YASHA (*laughing*). I can't hear your voice without laughing.

GAEV (*to his sister*). Either he goes or I do . . .

LYUBOV ANDREEVNA. Go away, Yasha, run along . . .

YASHA (*handing the purse to Lyubov Andreevna*). I'll go right now. (*Barely keeping from laughing.*) Right this minute . . .

Exits.

LOPAKHIN. Deriganov the rich man intends to purchase your estate. They says he's coming to the auction in person.

LYUBOV ANDREEVNA. Where did you hear that?

LOPAKHIN. They were talking about it in town.

---

39 A period when the intelligentsia formed the *Narodniki*, or Populists, who preached a socialist doctrine and tried to educate the peasants. They were severely repressed in 1877–1878. Decadents here refers to writers of symbolist literature. See *The Seagull*, note 34.

GAEV. Our auntie in Yaroslavl promised to send something, but when or how much she'll send, we don't know . . .

LOPAKHIN. How much is she sending? A hundred thousand? Two hundred?

LYUBOV ANDREEVNA. Well . . . around ten or fifteen thousand, and we're glad to have it . . .

LOPAKHIN. Excuse me, such frivolous people as you, my friends, such unbusinesslike, peculiar people I've never run into before. Somebody tells you in plain words your estate is about to be sold, and you act as if you don't understand.

LYUBOV ANDREEVNA. But what are we supposed to do? Teach us, what?

LOPAKHIN. I teach you every day. Every day I tell you one and the same thing. Both the cherry orchard and the land have got to be leased as lots for cottages, do it right now, immediately—the auction is staring you in the face! Can't you understand! Decide once and for all that there'll be cottages, they'll lend you as much money as you want, and then you'll be saved.

LYUBOV ANDREEVNA. Cottages and vacationers—it's so vulgar, excuse me.

GAEV. I absolutely agree with you.

LOPAKHIN. I'll burst into tears or scream or fall down in a faint. It's too much for me! You're torturing me to death! (*To Gaev.*) You old biddy!

GAEV. How's that?

LOPAKHIN. Old biddy! (*Starts to exit.*)

LYUBOV ANDREEVNA (*frightened*). No, don't go, stay, dovey . . . Please. Maybe we'll think of something.

LOPAKHIN. What's there to think about?

LYUBOV ANDREEVNA. Don't go, please. With you here somehow it's more fun . . .

Pause.

I keep anticipating something, as if the house were about to collapse on top of us.

GAEV (*rapt in thought*). Off the cushion to the corner . . . doublette to the center . . .

LYUBOV ANDREEVNA. We've sinned so very much . . .

LOPAKHIN. What kind of sins have you got . . .

GAEV (*pops a hard candy into his mouth*). They say I've eaten up my whole estate in hard candies . . . (*Laughs.*)

LYUBOV ANDREEVNA. Oh, my sins . . . I've always thrown money around wildly, like a maniac, and married a man who produced nothing but debts. My husband died of champagne—he was a terrible drunkard,—and, then, to add to my troubles, I fell in love with another man, had an affair, and just at that time—this was my first punishment, dropped right on my head,—over there in the river . . . my little boy drowned, and I went abroad, went for good, never to return, never to see that river again . . . I shut my eyes, ran away, out of my mind, and *he* came after me . . . cruelly, brutally. I bought a villa near Mentone, because he fell ill there, and for three years I didn't know what it was to rest day or night: the invalid wore me out, my heart shriveled up. But last year, when the villa was sold to pay my debts, I went to Paris, and there he robbed me, ran off, had an affair with another woman, I tried to poison myself . . . so silly, so shameful . . . and suddenly I was drawn back to Russia, to my country, to my little girl . . . (*Wipes away her tears.*) Lord, Lord, be merciful, forgive me my sins! Don't punish me any more! (*Takes a telegram out of her pocket.*) I received this today from Paris . . . He begs my forgiveness, implores me to come back . . . (*Tears up telegram.*) Sounds like music somewhere. (*Listens.*)

GAEV. That's our famous Jewish orchestra. You remember, four fiddles, a flute, and a double bass.

LYUBOV ANDREEVNA. Does it still exist? We ought to hire them some time and throw a party.

LOPAKHIN (*listening*). I don't hear it . . . (*Sings softly.*) "And for cash the Prussians will frenchify the Russians." (*Laughs.*) That was some play I saw at the theater yesterday, very funny.

LYUBOV ANDREEVNA. And most likely there was nothing funny about it. You have no business looking at plays, you should look at yourselves more. You all live such gray lives, you talk such nonsense.

LOPAKHIN. That's true, I've got to admit, this life is of ours is idiotic . . .

Pause.

My dad was a peasant, an imbecile, he didn't understand anything, didn't teach me, all he did was get drunk and beat me, with the same old stick. Deep down, I'm the same kind of blockhead and imbecile. I never studied anything, my handwriting is disgusting, I write, I'm ashamed to show it to people, like a pig.

LYUBOV ANDREEVNA. You ought to get married, my friend.

LOPAKHIN. Yes . . . that's true.

LYUBOV ANDREEVNA. You should marry our Varya; she's a good girl.

LOPAKHIN. Yes.

LYUBOV ANDREEVNA. She came to me from peasant stock, she works all day long, but the main thing is she loves you. Besides, you've been fond of her a long time.

LOPAKHIN. Why not? I'm not against it . . . She's a good girl.

Pause.

GAEV. They're offering me a position at the bank. Six thousand a year . . . Have you heard?

LYUBOV ANDREEVNA. You indeed! Stay where you are . . .

FIRS enters, carrying an overcoat.

FIRS (*to Gaev*). Please, sir, put it on, or you'll get wet.

GAEV (*putting on the overcoat*). You're a pest, my man.

FIRS. Never you mind . . . This morning you went out, didn't tell nobody. (*Inspects him.*)

LYUBOV ANDREEVNA. How old you're getting, Firs!

FIRS. What's wanted?

LOPAKHIN. The mistress says, you're getting very old!

FIRS. I've lived a long time. They were making plans to marry me off, long before your daddy even saw the light . . . (*Laughs.*) And when freedom came,[40] I was already head footman. I didn't go along with freedom then, I stayed by the masters . . .

Pause.

And I recollect they was all glad, but what they was glad about, that they didn't know.

LOPAKHIN. It used to be nice all right. In those days you could at least get flogged.

FIRS (*not having heard*). I'll say. The peasants stood by the masters, the masters stood by the peasants, but now things is every which way, you can't figure it out.

GAEV. Keep quiet, Firs. Tomorrow I have to go to town. They promised to introduce me to some general, who might make us a loan on an I.O.U.

LOPAKHIN. Nothing'll come of it. And you won't pay the interest, never fear.

LYUBOV ANDREEVNA. He's raving. There are no such generals.

Enter TROFIMOV, ANYA, and VARYA.

GAEV. Look, here comes our crowd.

ANYA. Mama's sitting down.

LYUBOV ANDREEVNA (*tenderly*). Come here, come . . . My darlings . . . (*Embracing Anya and Varya.*) If only you both knew how much I love you. Sit beside me, that's right.

Everyone sits down.

LOPAKHIN. Our perpetual student is always stepping out with the young ladies.

TROFIMOV. None of your business.

LOPAKHIN. Soon he'll be fifty and he'll still be a student.

TROFIMOV. Stop your idiotic jokes.

LOPAKHIN. What are you getting angry about, you crank?

TROFIMOV. Stop pestering me.

---

40. Alexander II emancipated the serfs in 1861.

LOPAKHIN (*laughs*). And may I ask, what do you make of me?

TROFIMOV. This is what I make of you, Yermolay Alekseich: you're a rich man, soon you'll be a millionaire. And just as an essential component in the conversion of matter is the wild beast that devours whatever crosses its path, you're essential.

Everyone laughs.

VARYA. Petya, tell us about the planets instead.

LYUBOV ANDREEVNA. No, let's go on with yesterday's discussion.

TROFIMOV. What was that about?

GAEV. Human pride.[41]

TROFIMOV. Yesterday we talked for quite a while, but we didn't get anywhere. Human pride, as you see it, has something mystical about it. Maybe you're right from your point of view, but if we reason it out simply, without frills, what's the point of human pride, what's the sense of it, if man is poorly constructed physiologically, if the vast majority is crude, unthinking, profoundly wretched. We should stop admiring ourselves. We should just work.

GAEV. All the same you'll die.

TROFIMOV. Who knows? What does that mean—you'll die? Maybe man has a hundred senses and in death only the five we know perish, the remaining ninety-five live on.

LYUBOV ANDREEVNA. Aren't you clever, Petya! . . .

LOPAKHIN (*ironically*). Awfully!

TROFIMOV. Mankind is advancing, perfecting its powers. Everything that's unattainable for us now will some day come within our grasp and our understanding, only we've got to work, to help the truth seekers with all our might. So far here in Russia, very few people do any work. The vast majority of educated people, as I know them, pursues nothing, does nothing, and

---

41 A reference to Maksim Gorky's "Proud man" in the play *The Lower Depths* (1902). "Hu-man Be-ing! That's magnificent! That sounds . . . proud!" "Man is truth . . . He is the be-all and the end-all. Nothing exists but man, all the rest is the work of his hands and his brain. Man is something great, proud, man is."

so far isn't capable of work. They call themselves intellectuals, but they refer to the servants by pet names,[42] treat the peasants like animals, are poorly informed, read nothing serious, do absolutely nothing, just talk about science, barely understand art. They're all earnest, they all have serious faces, they all talk only about major issues, they philosophize, but meanwhile anybody can see that the working class is abominably fed, sleeps without pillows, thirty or forty to a room, everywhere bedbugs, stench,[43] damp, moral pollution . . . So obviously all our nice chitchat serves only to shut our eyes to ourselves and to others. Show me, where are the day-care centers we talk so much about, where are the reading rooms? People only write about them in novels, in fact there aren't any. There's only dirt, vulgarity, Asiatic inertia . . .[44] I'm afraid of, I don't like very earnest faces, I'm afraid of earnest discussions. It's better to keep still!

LOPAKHIN. You know, I get up before five every morning. I work from dawn to dusk, well, I always have money on hand, my own and other people's, and I can tell what the people around me are like. You only have to go into business to find out how few decent, honest people there are. Sometimes, when I can't sleep, I think: Lord, you gave us vast forests, boundless fields, the widest horizons, and living here, we really and truly ought to be giants . . .

LYUBOV ANDREEVNA. So you want to have giants . . . They're only good in fairy tales, anywhere else they're scary.

Far upstage YEPIKHODOV crosses and plays his guitar.

LYUBOV ANDREEVNA (*dreamily*). There goes Yepikhodov . . .

ANYA (*dreamily*). There goes Yepikhodov . . .

GAEV. The sun has set, ladies and gentlemen.

TROFIMOV. Yes.

---

42 Literally, "they address the servant girl with the familiar form of 'you,' " as Lopakhin does Dunyasha. It is typical of Trofimov's intellectual astigmatism that he demands token respect for the servant class but cannot foresee doing away with it entirely.

43 The line beginning "Anyone can see" and ending "moral pollution" was deleted by Chekhov to accommodate the censor, and restored only in 1917. It was replaced by a line reading, "the vast majority of us, ninety-nine percent, live like savages, at the least provocation swearing and punching one another in the mouth, eating nauseating food, sleeping in mud and foul air."

44 *Aziatchina*, a pre-Revolutionary term of abuse, referring to negative qualities in the Russian character such as laziness and inefficiency.

GAEV (*quietly, as if declaiming*). Oh Nature, wondrous creature, aglow with eternal radiance, beautiful yet impassive, you whom we call Mother, merging within yourself Life and Death, you nourish and you destroy . . .

VARYA (*pleading*). Uncle dear!

ANYA. Uncle, you're at it again!

TROFIMOV. You'd better bank the yellow in the center doublette.

GAEV. I'll be still, I'll be still.

> *Everyone sits, absorbed in thought. The only sound is* FIRS, *softly muttering. Suddenly a distant sound is heard, as if from the sky, the sound of a breaking string, dying away, mournfully.*[45]

LYUBOV ANDREEVNA. What's that?

LOPAKHIN. I don't know. Somewhere far off in a mineshaft the rope broke on a bucket.[46] But somewhere very far off.

GAEV. Or perhaps it was some kind of bird . . . something like a heron.

TROFIMOV. Or an owl . . .

LYUBOV ANDREEVNA (*shivers*). Unpleasant anyhow.

> *Pause.*

FIRS. Before the troubles, it was the same: the screech owl hooted and the samovar never stopped humming.

GAEV. Before what troubles?

FIRS. Before freedom.[47]

---

45 According to the literary critic Batyushkov, Chekhov put great stock in this sound. The author told him that Stanislavsky, not yet having read the play, asked him about the sound effects it ought to have. "'In one of the acts I have an offstage sound, a complicated kind of sound which cannot be described in a few words, but it is very important that this sound be exactly the way I want it.' . . . 'Is the sound really that important?' I asked. Anton Pavlovich looked at me sternly and said, 'It is.'"

46 This was a sound Chekhov remembered hearing as a boy. In his story "Happiness," he uses it ironically as a spectral laugh, presaging disappointment.

47 Under the terms of the Emancipation Act, field peasants were allotted land but had to pay back the government in annual installments the sum used to indemnify former landowners. House serfs, on the other hand, were allotted no land. Both these conditions caused tremendous hardship and were responsible for great unrest among the newly manumitted.

Pause.

LYUBOV ANDREEVNA. You know, everyone, we should go home. Evening's drawing on. (*To Anya.*) You've got tears in your eyes . . . What it is, little girl? (*Embraces her.*)

ANYA. Nothing special, Mama. Never mind.

TROFIMOV. Someone's coming.

> *A VAGRANT appears in a shabby white peaked cap and an overcoat; he is tipsy.*

VAGRANT. May I inquire, can I get directly to the station from here?

GAEV. You can. Follow that road.

VAGRANT. Obliged to you from the bottom of my heart. (*Coughs.*) Splendid weather we're having . . . (*Declaims.*) "Brother mine, suffering brother . . . come to the Volga, whose laments . . ."[48] (*To Varya.*) Mademoiselle, bestow a mere thirty kopeks on a famished fellow Russian . . .

> *VARYA is alarmed, screams.*

LOPAKHIN (*angrily*). A person's allowed to be rude only so far![49]

LYUBOV ANDREEVNA (*flustered*). Take this . . . here you are . . . (*Looks in her purse.*) No silver . . . Never mind, here's a gold piece for you . . .

VAGRANT. Obliged to you from the bottom of my heart! (*Exits.*)

> *Laughter.*

VARYA (*frightened*). I'm going . . . I'm going . . . Oh, Mama dear, there's nothing in the house for people to eat, and you gave him a gold piece.

LYUBOV ANDREEVNA. What can you do with a silly like me? I'll let you have all I've got when we get home. Yermolay Alekseich, lend me some more! . . .

LOPAKHIN. At your service.

---

48 The Vagrant quotes from a popular and populist poem of 1881 by Semyon Yakovlevich Nadson (1862–1887) and from Nekrasov's "Reflections at the Main Gate" (1858). The laments are supposed to come from barge haulers along the Volga. Quoting Nekrasov is always a sign of insincerity in Chekhov.

49 In Russian, Lopakin's remark is very awkwardly phrased.

LYUBOV ANDREEVNA. Come along, ladies and gentlemen, it's time. And look, Varya, we've made quite a match for you, congratulations.

VARYA (*through tears*). It's no joking matter, Mama.

LOPAKHIN. I'll feel ya,[50] get thee to a nunnery . . .

GAEV. My hands are trembling; it's been a long time since I played billiards.

LOPAKHIN. I'll feel ya, o nymph, in thy horizons be all my sins remembered![51]

LYUBOV ANDREEVNA. Come along, ladies and gentlemen. Almost time for supper.

VARYA. He scared me. My heart's pounding.

LOPAKHIN. I remind you, ladies and gentlemen, on the twenty-second of August the estate will be auctioned off. Think about that! . . . Think! . . .

Everyone leaves except TROFIMOV and ANYA.

ANYA (*laughing*). Thank the vagrant, he scared off Varya, now we're alone.

TROFIMOV. Varya's afraid we'll suddenly fall in love, so she hangs around us all day. Her narrow mind can't comprehend that we're above love. Avoiding the petty and specious that keeps us from being free and happy, that's the goal and meaning of our life. Forward! We march irresistibly toward the shining star, glowing there in the distance! Forward! No dropping behind, friends!

ANYA (*clapping her hands*). You speak so well!

Pause.

It's wonderful here today.

TROFIMOV. Yes, superb weather.

ANYA. What have you done to me, Petya, why have I stopped loving the cherry orchard as I used to? I loved it so tenderly, there seemed to me no finer place on earth than our orchard.

---

50 *Okhmeliya*, from *okhmelyat*, to get drunk, instead of Ophelia.

51 Lopakhin is misquoting Hamlet, "Nymph, in thy orisons, be all my sins remember'd" (Act III, scene 1).

TROFIMOV. All Russia is our orchard. The world is wide and beautiful and there are many wonderful places in it.

Pause.

Just think, Anya: your grandfather, great-grandfather, and all your ancestors were slave owners, they owned living souls, and from every cherry in the orchard, every leaf, every tree trunk there must be human beings watching you, you must hear voices . . . They owned living souls—it's corrupted all of you, honestly, those who lived before and those living now, so that your mother, you, your uncle, no longer notice that you're living in debt, at other people's expense, at the expense of those people whom you wouldn't even let beyond your front hall . . .[52] We're at least two hundred years behind the times, we've still got absolutely nothing, no definite attitude to the past, we just philosophize, complain of depression, or drink vodka. It's so clear, isn't it, that before we start living in the present, we must first atone for our past, put an end to it, and we can atone for it only through suffering, only through extraordinary, unremitting labor. Understand that, Anya.

ANYA. The house we live in hasn't been our house for a long time, and I'll go away, I give you my word.

TROFIMOV. If you have the housekeeper's keys, throw them down the well and go away. Be free as the wind.

ANYA (*enraptured*). You speak so well!

TROFIMOV. Believe me, Anya, believe! I'm not yet thirty, I'm young. I'm still a student, but I've already undergone so much! When winter comes, I'm starved, sick, anxious, poor as a beggar and—where haven't I been chased by Fate, where haven't I been! And yet always, every moment of the day and night, my soul has been full of inexplicable foreboding. I foresee happiness, Anya, I can see it already . . .

ANYA (*dreamily*). The moon's on the rise.

---

52 The line beginning "They owned living souls" and ending "your front hall" was deleted by Chekhov to accommodate the censor and restored only in 1917. It was replaced with this line: "Oh, it's dreadful, your orchard is terrifying. At evening or at night when you walk through the orchard, the old bark on the trees begins to glow and it seems as if the cherry trees are dreaming of what went on one or two hundred years ago, and painful nightmares make them droop. Why talk about it?"

*We can hear YEPIKHODOV playing the same gloomy tune
as before on his guitar. The moon comes up. Somewhere near
the poplars VARYA is looking for Anya and calling,
"Anya! Where are you?"*

TROFIMOV. Yes, the moon's on the rise.

Pause.

Here's happiness, here it comes, drawing closer and closer, I can already hear its footsteps. And if we don't see it, can't recognize it, what's wrong with that? Others will see it!

VARYA'S VOICE. Anya! Where are you?

TROFIMOV. That Varya again! (*Angrily.*) Aggravating!

ANYA. So what? Let's go down to the river. It's nice there.

TROFIMOV. Let's go.

They leave.

Varya's voice: "Anya! Anya!"

Curtain

ACT THREE

The drawing-room, separated from the ballroom by an arch. A chandelier is alight. We can hear a Jewish orchestra, the same one mentioned in Act Two, playing in the hallway. Evening. Grand-rond is being danced in the ballroom. SIMEONOV-PISHCHIK's voice: "Promenade à une paire!" The drawing-room is entered by: the first couple PISHCHIK and CHARLOTTA IVANOVNA, the second TROFIMOV and LYUBOV ANDREEVNA, the third ANYA and the POSTAL CLERK, the fourth VARYA and the STATION MASTER, etc. VARYA is weeping quietly and, as she dances, wipes away the tears. In the last couple DUNYASHA. They go around and through the drawing-room. PISHCHIK calls

out: "*Grand-rond, balançez!*" and "*Les cavaliers à genoux et
remerciez vos dames!*"[53]

*FIRS in a tailcoat crosses the room with a seltzer bottle on a tray.
PISHCHIK and TROFIMOV enter the room.*

PISHCHIK. I've got high blood pressure, I've already had two strokes, it's
tough dancing, but, as the saying goes, when you run with the pack,
whether you bark or not, keep on wagging your tail. Actually, I've got the
constitution of a horse. My late father, what a card, rest in peace, used to
talk of our ancestry as if our venerable line, the Simeonov-Pishchiks, was
descended from the very same horse Caligula made a senator . . .[54] (*Sits
down.*) But here's the problem: no money! A hungry dog believes only in
meat . . . (*Snores and immediately wakes up.*) Just like me . . . I can't think
of anything but money . . .

TROFIMOV. As a matter of fact, your build has something horsey about it.

PISHCHIK. So what . . . a horse is a noble beast . . . you could sell a horse . . .

*We hear billiards played in the next room. VARYA appears in the
archway to the ballroom.*

TROFIMOV (*teasing*). Madam Lopakhin! Madam Lopakhin!

VARYA (*angrily*). Scruffy gent!

TROFIMOV. Yes, I'm a scruffy gent and proud of it!

VARYA (*brooding bitterly*). Here we've hired musicians and what are we going
to pay them with? (*Exits.*)

TROFIMOV (*to Pishchik*). If the energy you've wasted in the course of a
lifetime tracking down money to pay off interest had been harnessed to
something else, you probably, ultimately could have turned the world
upside-down.

---

53 Figures in a quadrille: *Promenade à une paire!*: Promenade with your partner! *Grand-rond, balançez!*: reel around, swing your arms! *Les cavaliers à genoux et remerciez vos dames!*: Gentlemen, on
your knees and salute your ladies!

54 "To one of his chariot-steeds named Incitatus . . . besides a stable all-built of marble stone for
him, and a manger made of ivory, over and above his caparison also and harness of purple . . . he
allowed a house and family of servants, yea, and household stuff to furnish the same. . . . It is
reported, moreover, that he meant to prefer him into a consulship" (Suetonius, *History of Twelve
Caesars*, trans. Philemon Holland [1606]).

PISHCHIK. Nietzsche . . . a philosopher . . . the greatest, most famous . . . a man of immense intellect, says in his works that it's all right to counterfeit money.

TROFIMOV. So you've read Nietzsche?[55]

PISHCHIK. Well . . . Dashenka told me. But now I'm such straits that if it came to counterfeiting money . . . Day after tomorrow three hundred rubles to pay . . . I've already borrowed a hundred and thirty . . . (*Feeling his pockets, alarmed.*) The money's gone! I've lost the money! (*Through tears.*) Where's the money? (*Gleefully.*) Here it is, in the lining . . . I was really sweating for a minute . . .

Enter LYUBOV ANDREEVNA and
CHARLOTTA IVANOVNA.

LYUBOV ANDREEVNA (*humming a lezginka*).[56] Why is Lyonya taking so long? What's he doing in town? (*To Dunyasha.*) Dunyasha, offer the musicians some tea . . .

TROFIMOV. The auction didn't take place, in all likelihood.

LYUBOV ANDREEVNA. And the musicians showed up at the wrong time and we scheduled the ball for the wrong time . . . Well, never mind . . . (*Sits down and hums softly.*)

CHARLOTTA (*hands Pishchik a deck of cards*). Here's a deck of cards for you, think of a card, any card.

PISHCHIK. I've got one.

CHARLOTTA. Now shuffle the deck. Very good. Hand it over, oh my dear Mister Pishchik. *Ein, zwei, drei!*[57] Now look for it, it's in your side pocket . . .

---

55 Friedrich Wilhelm Nietzsche (1844–1900), whose philosophy encourages a new "master" morality for supermen and instigates revolt against the conventional constraints of Western civilization in his *Morgenröthe. Gedanken über die moralischen Vorurtheile* (*Dawns. Reflections on moral prejudices*, 1881). This recalls Chekhov's statement in a letter (February 25, 1895): "I should like to meet a philosopher like Nietzsche somewhere on a train or a steamer, and spend the whole night talking to him. I don't think his philosophy will last very long, though. It's more sensational than persuasive."

56 A lively Caucasian dance in two-four time, popularized by Glinka and by Rubinstein in his opera *The Demon*.

57 German: one, two, three.

PISHCHIK (*pulling a card from his side pocket*). Eight of spades, absolutely right! (*Astounded.*) Can you imagine!

CHARLOTTA (*holds deck of cards on her palm, to Trofimov*). Tell me quick, which card's on top?

TROFIMOV. What? Why, the queen of spades.

CHARLOTTA. Right! (*To Pishchik.*) Well? Which card's on top?

PISHCHIK. The ace of hearts.

CHARLOTTA. Right! (*Claps her hand over her palm, the deck of cards disappears.*) Isn't it lovely weather today!

> *She is answered by a mysterious female voice, as if from beneath the floor: "Oh yes, marvelous weather, Madam."*

You're so nice, my ideal . . .

> *Voice: "Madam, I been liking you very much too."*[58]

STATION MASTER (*applauding*). Lady ventriloquist, bravo!

PISHCHIK (*astounded*). Can you imagine! Bewitching Charlotta Ivanovna . . . I'm simply in love with you . . .

CHARLOTTA. In love? (*Shrugging.*) What do you know about love? *Guter Mensch, aber schlechter Musikant.*[59]

TROFIMOV (*claps Pishchik on the shoulder*). Good old horse . . .

CHARLOTTA. Your attention please, one more trick. (*Takes a laprug from a chair.*) Here is a very nice rug. I'd like to sell it . . . (*Shakes it out.*) What am I offered?

PISHCHIK (*astounded*). Can you imagine!

CHARLOTTA. *Ein, zwei, drei!* (*Quickly lifts the lowered rug.*)

> *Behind the rug stands ANYA, who curtsies, runs to her mother, embraces her, and runs back to the ballroom amid the general delight.*

---

58 In the Russian, Charlotta confuses her genders, using the masculine singular instead of the feminine plural.

59 German: A good man, but a bad musician. A catchphrase from the comedy *Ponce de Leon* by Clemens von Brentano (1804), meaning an incompetent, another version of *nedotyopa*.

LYUBOV ANDREEVNA (*applauding*). Bravo, bravo!

CHARLOTTA. One more time! *Ein, zwei, drei!* (*Lifts the rug.*)

> *Behind the rug stands VARYA, who bows.*

PISHCHIK (*astounded*). Can you imagine!

CHARLOTTA. The end! (*Throws the rug at Pishchik, curtsies, and runs into the ballroom.*)

PISHCHIK (*scurrying after her*). You little rascal! . . . How do you like that! How do you like that! (*Exits.*)

LYUBOV ANDREEVNA. And Leonid still isn't back. I don't understand what he can be doing in town all this time! Everything must be over there, either the estate is sold or the auction didn't take place, but why keep us in suspense so long?

VARYA (*trying to comfort her*). Uncle dear bought it, I'm sure of it.

TROFIMOV (*sarcastically*). Sure.

VARYA. Great-aunt sent him power of attorney, so he could buy it in her name and transfer the debt. She did it for Anya. And I'm sure, God willing, that Uncle dear bought it.

LYUBOV ANDREEVNA. Your great-aunt in Yaroslavl sent fifty thousand to buy the estate in her name—she doesn't trust us—but that money won't even pay off the interest. (*Hides her face in her hands.*) Today my fate will be decided, my fate . . .

TROFIMOV (*teases Varya*). Madam Lopakhin! Madam Lopakhin!

VARYA (*angrily*). Perpetual student! Twice already you've been expelled from the university.

LYUBOV ANDREEVNA. Why are you getting angry, Varya? He teases you about Lopakhin, what of it? You want to—then marry Lopakhin, he's a good, interesting person. You don't want to—don't get married; darling, nobody's forcing you.

VARYA. I take this seriously, Mama dear, I've got to speak frankly. He's a good man, I like him.

LYUBOV ANDREEVNA. Then marry him. What you're waiting for I cannot understand!

VARYA. Mama dear, I can't propose to him myself. For two years now people have been talking to me about him, everyone's talking, but he either keeps still or cracks jokes. I understand. He's getting rich, busy with his deals, no time for me. If only I'd had some money, even a little, just a hundred rubles, I'd have dropped everything, and gone far away. I'd have entered a convent.

TROFIMOV. Heaven!

VARYA (*to Trofimov*). A student ought to be intelligent! (*In a gentle voice, tearfully.*) You've got so homely, Petya, grown so old! (*To Lyubov Andreevna, no longer weeping.*) Only I can't do without work, Mama dear. I have to have something to do every minute.

Enter YASHA.

YASHA (*can hardly keep from laughing*). Yepikhodov broke a billiard cue!

He exits.

VARYA. What's Yepikhodov doing here? Who gave him permission to play billiards? I don't understand these people . . . (*Exits.*)

LYUBOV ANDREEVNA. Don't tease her, Petya, can't you see she's miserable enough without that?

TROFIMOV. She's just too officious, poking her nose into other people's affairs. All summer long she couldn't leave us in peace, me or Anya, she was afraid a romance might break out. What business is it of hers? And anyway, I didn't show any signs of it, I'm so removed from banality. We're above love!

LYUBOV ANDREEVNA. Well then, I must be beneath love. (*Extremely upset.*) Why isn't Leonid back? If only I knew: is the estate sold or not? Imagining trouble is so hard for me I don't even know what to think, I'm at a loss . . . I could scream right this minute . . . I could do something foolish. Save me, Petya. Say something, tell me . . .

TROFIMOV. Whether the estate's sold today or not—what's the difference? It's been over and done with for a long time now, no turning back, the bridges are burnt. Calm down, dear lady. You mustn't deceive yourself, for once in your life you've got to look the truth straight in the eye.

LYUBOV ANDREEVNA. What truth? You can see where truth is and where falsehood is, but I seem to have lost my sight. I can't see anything. You boldly solve all the major problems, but tell me, dovey, isn't that because you're young, because you haven't had time to suffer through any of your problems? You boldly look forward, but isn't that because you don't see, don't expect anything awful, because life is still hidden from your young eyes? You're more courageous, more sincere, more profound than we are, but stop and think, be indulgent if only in the tips of your fingers, spare me. This is where I was born, after all, this is where my father and my mother lived, my grandfather, I love this house, without the cherry orchard I couldn't make sense of my life, and if it really has to be sold, then sell me along with the orchard . . . (*Embraces Trofimov, kisses him on the forehead.*) Remember, my son was drowned here . . . (*Weeps.*) Show me some pity, dear, kind man.

TROFIMOV. You know I sympathize wholeheartedly.

LYUBOV ANDREEVNA. But you should say so differently, differently . . . (*Takes out a handkerchief, a telegram falls to the floor.*) My heart is so heavy today, you can't imagine. I can't take the noise here, my soul shudders at every sound, I shudder all over, but I can't go off by myself, I'd be terrified to be alone in silence. Don't blame me, Petya . . . I love you like my own flesh and blood. I'd gladly let you marry Anya, believe me, only, dovey, you've got to study, got to finish your degree. You don't do anything, Fate simply tosses you from place to place, it's so odd . . . Isn't that right? Isn't it? And something's got to be done about your beard, to make it grow somehow . . . (*Laughs.*) You look so funny!

TROFIMOV (*picks up the telegram*). I make no claim to be good looking . . .

LYUBOV ANDREEVNA. This telegram's from Paris. Every day I get one. Yesterday too and today. That wild man has fallen ill again, something's wrong with him again . . . He begs my forgiveness, implores me to come back, and actually I ought to go to Paris, stay with him a while. You look so disapproving, Petya, but what's to be done, dovey, what am I to do, he's ill, he's lonely, unhappy, and who's there to look after him, who'll keep him out of mischief, who'll give him his medicine at the right time? And what's there to hide or suppress, I love him, it's obvious, I love him, I love him . . . It's a millstone round my neck, it's dragging me down, but I love that stone and I can't live without it. (*Squeezes Trofimov's hand.*) Don't judge me harshly, Petya, don't say anything, don't talk . . .

TROFIMOV (*through tears*). Forgive my frankness, for God's sake: but he robbed you blind!

LYUBOV ANDREEVNA. No, no, no, you mustn't talk that way . . . (*Covers her ears.*)

TROFIMOV. Why, he's a scoundrel, you're the only one who doesn't realize it! He's a petty scoundrel, a nobody . . .

LYUBOV ANDREEVNA (*getting angry, but under control*). You're twenty-six or twenty-seven, but you're still a sophomoric schoolboy!

TROFIMOV. Is that so?

LYUBOV ANDREEVNA. You should act like a man, at your age you should understand people in love. And you should be in love yourself . . . you should fall in love! (*Angrily.*) Yes, yes! And there's no purity in you, you're simply a puritan, a funny crackpot, a freak . . .

TROFIMOV (*aghast*). What is she saying?

LYUBOV ANDREEVNA. "I am above love!" You're not above love, you're simply, as our Firs says, a half-baked bungler. At your age not to have a mistress! . . .

TROFIMOV (*aghast*). This is horrible! What is she saying! (*Rushes to the ballroom, clutching his head.*) This is horrible . . . I can't stand it, I'm going . . . (*Exits, but immediately returns.*) All is over between us! (*Exits to the hall.*)

LYUBOV ANDREEVNA (*shouting after him*). Petya, wait! You funny man, I was joking! Petya!

> *We hear in the hallway someone running up the stairs and suddenly falling back down with a crash. ANYA and VARYA shriek, but immediately there is the sound of laughter.*

LYUBOV ANDREEVNA. What's going on in there?

> *ANYA runs in.*

ANYA (*laughing*). Petya fell down the stairs! (*Runs out.*)

LYUBOV ANDREEVNA. What a crackpot that Petya is . . .

*The STATION MASTER stops in the middle of the ballroom and
recites Aleksey Tolstoy's "The Sinful Woman."* [60] *The guests listen,
but barely has he recited a few lines, when the strains of a waltz
reach them from the hallway, and the recitation breaks off.
Everyone dances. Enter from the hall, TROFIMOV, ANYA,
VARYA, and LYUBOV ANDREEVNA.*

Well, Petya . . . well, my pure-in-heart . . . I apologize . . . let's dance . . .
(*Dances with TROFIMOV.*)

ANYA and VARYA dance.

*FIRS enters, leaves his stick by the side door. YASHA also enters
the drawing-room, watching the dancers.*

YASHA. What's up, Gramps?

FIRS. I'm none too well. In the old days we had generals, barons, admirals
dancing at our parties, but now we send for the postal clerk and the station master, yes and they don't come a-running. Somehow I got weak.
The late master, the grandfather, doctored everybody with sealing wax for
every ailment. I've took sealing wax every day now for twenty-odd years,
and maybe more, maybe that's why I'm still alive.[61]

YASHA. You bore me stiff, Gramps. (*Yawns.*) How about dropping dead.

FIRS. Eh, you . . . half-baked bungler! (*Mutters.*)

*TROFIMOV and LYUBOV ANDREEVNA dance in the
ballroom, then in the drawing-room.*

---

60 Aleksey Konstantinovich Tolstoy (1817–1875), Russian poet; his fustian ballad "*Greshnitsa*"
(1858) was frequently recited at public gatherings, and even inspired a painting. It is about a Mag-
dalen and her repentance at a feast in Judaea under the influence of Christ. Chekhov, who had a
low opinion of Tolstoy's poetry, cites it in his stories to ironic effect. The title refers back to
Ranevskaya's catalogue of sins in Act Two. The opening lines of the poem also comment by contrast on the dowdiness of her ball:

> The people seethe; joy, laughter flash
> The lute is twanged, the cymbals clash.
> Fern fronds and flowers are strewn about,
> And 'twixt the columns in th'arcade
> In heavy folds the rich brocade
> With ribbon broderie is decked out . . .

61 The treatment is to soak the wax in water, and then drink the water.

LYUBOV ANDREEVNA. *Merci.* I'm going to sit for a bit . . . (*Sits down.*) I'm tired.

Enter ANYA.

ANYA (*upset*). Just now in the kitchen some man was saying the cherry orchard's been sold already.

LYUBOV ANDREEVNA. Sold to whom?

ANYA. He didn't say. He left. (*Dances with TROFIMOV; they both go into the ballroom.*)

YASHA. There was some old man muttering away. Not one of ours.

FIRS. And Leonid Andreich still isn't back, still not home. That topcoat he's got on's too flimsy, for between seasons, see if he don't catch cold. Eh, when they're young, they're green!

LYUBOV ANDREEVNA. I'll die this instant! Yasha, go and find out to whom it's been sold.

YASHA. He went away a long time ago, that old man. (*Laughs.*)

LYUBOV ANDREEVNA (*somewhat annoyed*). Well, what are you laughing about? What's made you so happy?

YASHA. Yepikhodov's awfully funny. The man's incompetent. Tons of Trouble.

LYUBOV ANDREEVNA. Firs, if the estate is sold, then where will you go?

FIRS. Wherever you order, there I'll go.

LYUBOV ANDREEVNA. Why is your face like that? Aren't you well? You know you ought to be in bed . . .

FIRS. Yes—(*with a grin*) I go to bed, and with me gone, who'll serve, who'll look after things? I'm the only one in the whole house.

YASHA (*to Lyubov Andreevna*). Lyubov Andreevna! Let me ask you a favor, be so kind! If you go off to Paris again, take me with you, please. For me to stick around here is absolutely out of the question. (*Glances around, lowers his voice.*) It goes without saying, you can see for yourself, the country's uncivilized, the people are immoral, not to mention the boredom, in the kitchen they feed us garbage and there's that Firs going around, muttering all kinds of improper remarks. Take me with you, be so kind!

Enter PISHCHIK.

PISHCHIK. May I request . . . a teeny waltz, loveliest of ladies . . . (*LYUBOV ANDREEVNA goes with him.*) Enchanting lady, I'll borrow a hundred and eighty little rubles off you just the same . . . Yes, I will . . . (*Dances.*) A hundred and eighty little rubles . . .

They have passed into the ballroom.

YASHA (*singing softly*). "Wilt thou learn my soul's unrest . . ."[62]

In the ballroom a figure in a gray top hat and checked trousers waves its arms and jumps up and down; shouts of "Bravo, Charlotta Ivanovna!"

DUNYASHA (*stops to powder her nose*). The young mistress orders me to dance—lots of gentlemen and few ladies—but dancing makes my head swim, my heart pound, Firs Nikolaevich, and just now the postal clerk told me something that took my breath away.

Music subsides.

FIRS. Well, what did he tell you?

DUNYASHA. You, he says, are like a flower.

YASHA (*yawns*). How uncouth . . . (*Exits.*)

DUNYASHA. Like a flower . . . I'm such a sensitive girl, I'm awfully fond of compliments.

FIRS. You'll get your head turned.

Enter YEPIKHODOV.

YEPIKHODOV. Avdotya Fyodorovna, you don't wish to see me . . . as if I were some sort of bug. (*Sighs.*) Ech, life!

DUNYASHA. What can I do for you?

YEPIKHODOV. Indubitably you may be right. (*Sighs.*) But, of course, if it's considered from a standpoint, then you, if I may venture the expression, pardon my outspokenness, positively drove me into a state of mind. I know my lot, every day I run into some kind of trouble, and I've grown accus-

---

62 Title and opening line of a ballad by N. S. Rzhevskaya (1869).

tomed to that long ago, so I look upon my destiny with a smile. You gave me your word, and even though I . . .

DUNYASHA. Please, let's talk later on, but leave me alone for now. I'm dreaming now. (*Toys with her fan.*)

YEPIKHODOV. Every day I run into trouble, and I, if I may venture the expression, merely smile, even laugh.

Enter VARYA from the ballroom.

VARYA. Haven't you gone yet, Semyon? Honestly, you are the most disrespectful man. (*To Dunyasha.*) Clear out of here, Dunyasha. (*To Yepikhodov.*) If you're not playing billiards and breaking the cue, you're lounging around the drawing-room like a guest.

YEPIKHODOV. To take me to task, if I may venture the expression, you can't.

VARYA. I'm not taking you to task, I'm just telling you. But you know all you do is walk around instead of attending to business. We keep a bookkeeper but nobody knows what for.

YEPIKHODOV (*offended*). Whether I work or whether I walk or whether I eat or whether I play billiards may be criticized only by my elders and betters who know what they're talking about.

VARYA. How dare you say such things to me! (*Flying into a rage.*) How dare you? You mean I don't know what I'm talking about? Get out of here! This minute!

YEPIKHODOV (*alarmed*). Please express yourself in a more refined manner.

VARYA (*beside herself*). This very minute, out of here! Out! (*He goes to the door, she follows him.*) Tons of Trouble! Don't draw another breath here! Don't let me set eyes on you!

YEPIKHODOV has gone, behind the door his voice: "I'm going to complain about you."

So, you're coming back? (*Seizes the stick Firs left near the door.*) Come on . . . come on . . . come on, I'll show you . . . Well, are you coming? Are you coming? Here's what you get . . . (*Swings the stick.*)

At the same moment, LOPAKHIN enters.

LOPAKHIN. My humble thanks.

VARYA (*angrily and sarcastically*). Sorry!

LOPAKHIN. Never mind, ma'am. Thank you kindly for the pleasant surprise.

VARYA. Don't mention it. (*Starts out, then looks back and asks gently.*) I didn't hurt you?

LOPAKHIN. No, it's nothing. The bump is going to be enormous, though.

> *Voices in the ballroom:* "Lopakhin's here, Yermolay Alekseich!"

PISHCHIK. Sights to be seen, sounds to be heard . . . (*He and LOPAKHIN exchange kisses.*) There's cognac on your breath, my dear boy, apple of my eye. But we were making merry here too.

> *Enter LYUBOV ANDREEVNA.*

LYUBOV ANDREEVNA. Is that you, Yermolay Alekseich? Why the delay? Where's Leonid?

LOPAKHIN. Leonid Andreich came back with me, he's on his way . . .

LYUBOV ANDREEVNA (*agitated*). Well, what? Was there an auction? Say something!

LOPAKHIN (*embarrassed, afraid to reveal his glee*). The auction was over by four o'clock . . . We missed the train, had to wait till half-past nine. (*Sighs heavily.*) Oof! My head's a little woozy . . .

> *Enter GAEV; his right hand is holding packages, his left is wiping away tears.*

LYUBOV ANDREEVNA. Lyonya, what? Well, Lyonya? (*Impatiently, tearfully.*) Hurry up, for God's sake . . .

GAEV (*not answering her, only waves his hand to Firs, weeping*). Here, take this . . . There's anchovies, smoked herring . . . I haven't had a thing to eat all day . . . What I've been through!

> *The door to the billiard room opens. We hear the click of the balls and YASHA's voice:* "Seven and eighteen!" *GAEV's expression alters, he stops crying.*

I'm awfully tired. Firs, help me change. (*Exits through the ballroom, followed by FIRS.*)

PISHCHIK. What about the auction? Tell us!

LYUBOV ANDREEVNA. Is the cherry orchard sold?

LOPAKHIN. Sold.

LYUBOV ANDREEVNA. Who bought it?

LOPAKHIN. I bought it.

> *Pause. LYUBOV ANDREEVNA is overcome; she would fall, were she not standing beside an armchair and a table. VARYA removes the keys from her belt, throws them on the floor in the middle of the drawing room and exits.*

LOPAKHIN. I bought it! Wait, ladies and gentlemen, do me a favor, my head's swimming, I can't talk . . . (*Laughs.*) We got to the auction, Deriganov's there already. Leonid Andreich only had fifteen thousand, and right off Deriganov bid thirty over and above the mortgage. I get the picture, I pitched into him, bid forty. He forty-five, I fifty-five. I mean, he kept upping it by fives, I by tens . . . Well, it ended. Over and above the mortgage I bid ninety thousand, it was knocked down to me. Now the cherry orchard's mine. Mine! (*Chuckling.*) My God, Lord, the cherry orchard's mine! Tell me I'm drunk, out of my mind, that I'm making it all up . . . (*Stamps his feet.*) Don't laugh at me! If only my father and grandfather could rise up from their graves and see all that's happened, how their Yermolay, beaten, barely literate Yermolay, who used to run around barefoot in the wintertime; how this same Yermolay bought the estate, the most beautiful thing in the world. I bought the estate where my grandfather and father were slaves, where they weren't even allowed in the kitchen. I'm dreaming, it's a hallucination, it only looks this way . . . This is a figment of your imagination, veiled by shadows of obscurity . . .[63] (*Picks up the keys, smiles gently.*) She threw down the keys, she wants to show that she's no longer in charge here . . . (*Jingles the keys.*) Well, it doesn't matter.

> *We hear the orchestra tuning up.*

Hey, musicians, play, I want to hear you! Come on, everybody, see how Yermolay Lopakhin will swing an axe in the cherry orchard, how the

---

63 George Calderon states that this is "a cant jocular phrase, a literary tag. Lopakhin is quoting out of some bad play, as usual when he is lively." Chekhov uses it in his correspondence.

trees'll come tumbling to the ground! We'll build cottages, and our grand-children and great-grandchildren will see a new life here . . . Music, play!

The music plays, LYUBOV ANDREEVNA has sunk into a chair,
crying bitterly.

(*Reproachfully.*) Why, oh, why didn't you listen to me? My poor, dear lady, you can't undo it now. (*Tearfully.*) Oh, if only this were all over quickly, if somehow our ungainly, unhappy life could be changed quickly.

PISHCHIK (*takes him by the arm; in an undertone*). She's crying. Let's go into the ballroom, leave her alone . . . Let's go . . . (*Drags him by the arm and leads him into the ballroom.*)

LOPAKHIN. So what? Music, play in tune! Let everything be the way I want it! (*Ironically.*) Here comes the new landlord, the owner of the cherry orchard! (*He accidentally bumps into a small table and almost knocks over the candelabrum.*) I can pay for everything!

Exits with PISHCHIK.

No one is left in the ballroom or drawing-room except LYUBOV
ANDREEVNA, who is sitting, all hunched up, weeping bitterly.
The music is playing softly. ANYA and TROFIMOV hurry in.
ANYA goes to her mother and kneels before her. TROFIMOV
remains at the entrance to the ballroom.

ANYA. Mama! . . . Mama, you're crying? Dear, kind, good Mama, my own, my beautiful, I love you . . . I bless you. The cherry orchard's sold, it's gone now, that's true, true, true, but don't cry, Mama, you've still got your life ahead of you, you've still got your good pure heart . . . Come with me, come, dearest, let's go away from here, let's go! . . . We'll plant a new orchard, more splendid than this one, you'll see it, you'll understand, and joy, peaceful, profound joy will sink into your heart, like the sun when night falls, and you'll smile, Mama! Let's go, dearest! Let's go! . . .

Curtain

ACT FOUR

*First act setting. Neither curtains on the windows nor pictures
on the wall, a few sticks of furniture remain, piled up in
a corner as if for sale. A feeling of emptiness. Near the door
to the outside and at the back of the stage are piles of suitcases,
traveling bags, etc. The door at left is open, and through it we can
hear the voices of Varya and Anya. LOPAKHIN stands, waiting.
YASHA is holding a tray of glasses filled with champagne.
In the hallway, YEPIKHODOV is tying up a carton.
Offstage, at the back, a murmur. It's the peasants come to say
good-bye. GAEV's voice: "Thank you, friends,
thank you."*

YASHA. The common folk have come to say good-bye. I'm of the opinion,
Yermolay Alekseich, they're decent enough people, but not very bright.

*The murmur subsides. Enter through the hall LYUBOV
ANDREEVNA and GAEV. She isn't crying, but is pale, her face
twitches, she can't talk.*

GAEV. You gave them your purse, Lyuba. You shouldn't have! You shouldn't
have!

LYUBOV ANDREEVNA. I couldn't help it! I couldn't help it!

They go out.

LOPAKHIN (*through the door, after them*). Please, I humbly beseech you! A
little drink at parting! It didn't occur to me to bring any from town, and at
the station I only found one bottle. Please!

Pause.

How about it, ladies and gentlemen? Don't you want any? (*Walks away
from the door.*) If I'd known, I wouldn't have bought it. Well, I won't drink
any either.

YASHA carefully sets the tray on a chair.

Drink up, Yasha, you have some.

YASHA. Greetings to those departing![64] And happy days to the stay-at-homes! (*Drinks.*) This champagne isn't the genuine article, you can take it from me.

LOPAKHIN. Eight rubles a bottle.

Pause.

It's cold as hell in here.

YASHA. They didn't stoke up today, it doesn't matter, we're leaving. (*Laughs.*)

LOPAKHIN. What's that for?

YASHA. Sheer satisfaction.

LOPAKHIN. Outside it's October, but sunny and mild, like summer. Good building weather. (*Glances at his watch, at the door.*) Ladies and gentlemen, remember, until the train leaves, there's forty-six minutes in all! Which means, in twenty minutes we start for the station. Get a move on.

Enter from outdoors TROFIMOV in an overcoat.

TROFIMOV. Seems to me it's time to go now. The horses are at the door. Where the hell are my galoshes? Disappeared. (*Through the door.*) Anya, my galoshes aren't here! I can't find them!

LOPAKHIN. And I have to be in Kharkov. I'll go with you on the same train. I'm spending all winter in Kharkov. I've been hanging around here with you, I'm worn out with nothing to do. I've got to be doing something, I don't even know where to put my hands; they dangle this funny way, like somebody else's.

TROFIMOV. We'll be going soon, and you can return to your productive labors.

LOPAKHIN. Do have a little drink.

TROFIMOV. None for me.

LOPAKHIN. In other words, back to Moscow now?

TROFIMOV. Yes, I'll go with them as far as town, but tomorrow back to Moscow.

---

64 Yasha is distorting a phrase usually applied to welcome arrivals.

LOPAKHIN. Yes . . . Hey, the professors are on a lecture strike, I'll bet they're waiting for you to show up!

TROFIMOV. None of your business.

LOPAKHIN. How many years have you been studying at the University?

TROFIMOV. Think up something fresher. That's old and stale. (*Looks for his galoshes.*) You know, it's unlikely we'll ever meet again, so let me give you a piece of advice as a farewell: don't wave your arms! Break yourself of that habit—arm-waving. And cottage-building as well, figuring that vacationers will eventually turn into property owners, figuring that way is just the same as arm-waving . . . Anyhow, I can't help liking you. You've got delicate, gentle fingers, like an artist, you've got a delicate, gentle heart . . .[65]

LOPAKHIN (*hugs him*). Good-bye, my boy. Thanks for everything. If you need it, borrow some money from me for the trip.

TROFIMOV. What for? Don't need it.

LOPAKHIN. But you don't have any!

TROFIMOV. I do. Thank you. I got some for a translation. Here it is, in my pocket. (*Anxiously.*) But my galoshes are missing!

VARYA (*from the next room*). Take your nasty things! (*She flings a pair of rubber galoshes on stage.*)

TROFIMOV. What are you upset about, Varya? Hm . . . But these aren't my galoshes!

LOPAKHIN. Last spring I planted nearly three thousand acres of poppies, and now I've cleared forty thousand net. And when my poppies bloomed, it was like a picture! So look, what I'm getting at is, I cleared forty thousand, which means I offer you a loan because I can afford it. Why turn up your nose? I'm a peasant . . . plain and simple.

TROFIMOV. Your father was a peasant, mine a druggist, and it all adds up to absolutely nothing.

LOPAKHIN pulls out his wallet.

---

65 These lines did not exist in the first version of the play but were added to support Chekhov's view of Lopakhin as a decent person.

Don't bother, don't bother . . . Even if you gave me two hundred thousand, I wouldn't take it. I'm a free man. And everything that you all value so highly and fondly, rich men and beggars alike, hasn't the slightest effect on me, it's like fluff floating in the air. I can manage without you, I can pass you by, I'm strong and proud. Humanity is moving toward the most sublime truth, the most sublime happiness possible on earth, and I'm in the front ranks!

LOPAKHIN. Will you get there?

TROFIMOV. I'll get there.

Pause.

I'll get there, or I'll blaze a trail for others to get there.

We hear in the distance an axe striking a tree.

LOPAKHIN. Well, good-bye, my boy. Time to go. We turn up our noses at one another, while life keeps slipping by. When I work a long time nonstop, then my thoughts are clearer, and I even seem to know why I exist. But, pal, how many people there are in Russia who don't know why they exist. Well, what's the difference, that's not what makes the world go round. Leonid Andreich, they say, took a job, he'll be in the bank, six thousand a year . . . Only he won't keep at it, too lazy . . .

ANYA (*in the doorway*). Mama begs you: until she's gone, not to chop down the orchard.

TROFIMOV. I mean really, haven't you got any tact . . . (*Exits through the hall.*)

LOPAKHIN. Right away, right away . . . These people, honestly! (*Exits after him.*)

ANYA. Did they take Firs to the hospital?

YASHA. I told them to this morning. They took him, I should think.

ANYA (*to Yepikhodov, who is crossing through the room*). Semyon Panteleich, please find out whether Firs was taken to the hospital.

YASHA (*offended*). I told Yegor this morning. Why ask a dozen times?

YEPIKHODOV. Superannuated Firs, in my conclusive opinion, is past all repairing, he should be gathered to his fathers. And I can only envy him.

(*Sets a suitcase on top of a cardboard hatbox and crushes it.*) Well, look at that, typical. I should have known.

YASHA (*scoffing*). Tons of Trouble . . .

YEPIKHODOV. Well, it could have happened to anybody.[66] (*Exits.*)

VARYA (*from behind the door*). Have they sent Firs to the hospital?

ANYA. They have.

VARYA. Then why didn't they take the letter to the doctor?

ANYA. We'll have to send someone after them . . . (*Exits.*)

VARYA (*from the next room*). Where's Yasha? Tell him his mother's here, wants to say good-bye to him.

YASHA (*waves his hand in dismissal*). They simply try my patience.

> DUNYASHA *in the meantime has been fussing with the luggage; now that* YASHA *is alone, she comes up to him.*

DUNYASHA. If only you'd take one little look at me, Yasha. You're going away . . . you're leaving me behind . . . (*Weeps and throws herself on his neck.*)

YASHA. What's the crying for? (*Drinks champagne.*) In six days I'll be in Paris again. Tomorrow we'll board an express train and dash away, we'll be gone in a flash. Somehow I can't believe it. Veev lah Franz! . . . It doesn't suit me here, I can't live . . . nothing going on. I've had an eyeful of uncouth behavior—I'm fed up with it. (*Drinks champagne.*) What's the crying for? Behave respectably, then you won't have to cry.[67]

DUNYASHA (*powdering her nose, looks in a hand mirror*). Drop me a line from Paris. I really loved you, Yasha, loved you so! I'm a soft-hearted creature, Yasha!

YASHA. Someone's coming in here. (*Fusses with the luggage, humming softly.*)

---

66 This line does not appear in any of the printed editions but was improvised in performance by Ivan Moskvin. It got a laugh, and he asked if he could keep it in. "Tell Moskvin he can insert the new lines, and I will put them in myself when I read the corrected proofs. I give him the most complete carte blanche" (Chekhov to Olga Knipper, March 20, 1904). Somehow, Chekhov never did insert the line in the proofs, but it appears penciled in to the Moscow Art Theatre prompt script.

67 Another echo of Hamlet to Ophelia: "If you are honest and fair, your honesty could admit no props to your fairness" (Act II, scene 1).

Enter LYUBOV ANDREEVNA, GAEV, ANYA, and
CHARLOTTA IVANOVNA.

GAEV. We should be off. Not much time left. (*Looking at Yasha.*) Who's that smelling of herring?

LYUBOV ANDREEVNA. In about ten minutes we ought to be getting into the carriages. (*Casting a glance round the room.*) Good-bye, dear old house, old grandfather. Winter will pass, spring will come again, but you won't be here any more, they'll tear you down. How much these walls have seen! (*Kissing her daughter ardently.*) My precious, you're radiant, your eyes are sparkling like two diamonds. Are you happy? Very?

ANYA. Very! A new life is beginning, Mama!

GAEV (*gaily*). As a matter of fact, everything's fine now. Before the sale of the cherry orchard, we were all upset, distressed, but then, once the matter was settled finally, irrevocably, everyone calmed down, even cheered up . . . I'm a bank employee, now I'm a financier . . . yellow to the center, and you, Lyuba, anyway, you're looking better, that's for sure.

LYUBOV ANDREEVNA. Yes. My nerves are better, that's true.

They help her on with her hat and coat.

I sleep well. Carry my things out, Yasha. It's time. (*To Anya.*) My little girl, we'll be back together soon . . . I'm off to Paris, I'll live there on that money your great-aunt in Yaroslavl sent us to buy the estate—hurray for Auntie!— but that money won't last long.

ANYA. Mama, you'll come back soon, soon . . . won't you? I'll study, pass the finals at the high school and then I'll work to help you. Mama, we'll be together and read all sorts of books . . . Won't we? (*Kisses her mother's hand.*) We'll read in the autumn evenings, we'll read lots of books, and before us a new, wonderful world will open up . . . (*Dreamily.*) Mama, come back . . .

LYUBOV ANDREEVNA. I'll come back, my precious. (*Embraces her daughter.*)

Enter LOPAKHIN. CHARLOTTA is quietly singing a song.

GAEV. Charlotta's happy! She's singing!

CHARLOTTA (*picks up a bundle that looks like a swaddled baby*). Rock-a-bye, baby, on the tree top . . .

We hear a baby crying: "Waa! Waa!"

Hush, my sweet, my dear little boy.

"Waa! . . . Waa! . . ."

I'm so sorry for you! (*Throws down the bundle.*) Will you please find me a position. I can't keep on this way.

LOPAKHIN. We'll find one, Charlotta Ivanovna, don't worry.

GAEV. Everyone's dropping us, Varya's leaving . . . we've suddenly become superfluous.

CHARLOTTA. There's nowhere for me to live in town. Have to go away . . . (*Hums.*) What difference does it make?

Enter PISHCHIK.

LOPAKHIN. The freak of nature!

PISHCHIK (*out of breath*). Oy, let me catch my breath . . . I'm winded . . . my most honored . . . Give me some water . . .

GAEV. After money, I suppose? Your humble servant, deliver me from temptation . . . (*Exits.*)

PISHCHIK (*out of breath*). I haven't been to see you for the longest time . . . loveliest of ladies . . . (*To Lopakhin.*) You here . . . glad to see you . . . a man of the most enormous intellect . . . take . . . go on . . . (*Hands money to Lopakhin.*) Four hundred rubles . . . I still owe you eight hundred and forty . . .

LOPAKHIN (*bewildered, shrugs*). It's like a dream . . . Where did you get this?

PISHCHIK. Wait . . . Hot . . . Most amazing thing happened. Some English-men[68] stopped by my place and found on my land some kind of white clay . . . (*To Lyubov Andreevna.*) And four hundred for you . . . beautiful lady, divine creature . . . (*Hands her money.*) The rest later. (*Drinks water.*) Just now some young man on the train was telling about some sort of . . . great

---

68 The British often appear in nineteenth-century Russian fiction as progressive and enterprising businessmen. They were often hired as estate managers, land surveyors, or experts in animal husbandry. The uncle of the writer Nikolay Leskov was a Scotsman who managed several vast Russian estates for their aristocratic owners.

philosopher who recommends jumping off roofs . . . "Jump!"—he says, and that solves the whole problem. (*Astounded*.) Can you imagine! Water! . . .

LOPAKHIN. Who were these Englishmen?

PISHCHIK. I leased them the lot with the clay for twenty-four years . . . But now, excuse me, no time . . . Have to run along . . . I'm going to Znoikov's . . . Kardamonov's . . . I owe everybody . . . (*Drinks*.) Your good health . . . On Thursday I'll drop by . . .

LYUBOV ANDREEVNA. We're just about to move to town, and tomorrow I'll be abroad.

PISHCHIK. What? (*Agitated*.) Why to town? Goodness, look at the furniture . . . the suitcases . . . well, never mind . . . (*Through tears*.) Never mind. Persons of the highest intelligence . . . those Englishmen . . . Never mind . . . Be happy . . . God will come to your aid . . . Never mind . . . Everything in this world comes to an end . . . (*Kisses Lyubov Andreevna's hand*.) And should rumor reach you that my end has come, just remember this very thing—a horse, and say: "Once there lived an old so-and-so . . . Simeonov-Pishchik . . . rest in peace" . . . The most incredible weather . . . yes . . . (*Exits, overcome with emotion, but immediately reappears in the doorway and says:*) Dashenka sends you her regards! (*Exits*.)

LYUBOV ANDREEVNA. Now we can go. I'm leaving with two things on my mind. First—that Firs is ill. (*Glancing at her watch*.) There's still five minutes . . .

ANYA. Mama, they've already sent Firs to the hospital. Yasha sent him this morning.

LYUBOV ANDREEVNA. My second anxiety is Varya. She's used to rising early and working, and now, without work, she's like a fish out of water. She's lost weight, she's got pale, she cries, poor soul . . .

Pause.

You know this perfectly well, Yermolay Alekseich; I had dreamt . . . of marrying her to you, yes, and it certainly looked as if you were going to get married. (*Whispers to Anya, who nods to Charlotta, and both leave*.) She loves you, you're fond of her, I don't know, I just don't know why you seem to sidestep one another. I don't understand!

LOPAKHIN. I don't understand either, I admit. It's all strange somehow . . . If there's still time, then I'm ready right now . . . Let's get it over with right away—and that'll be that, but if it wasn't for you, I have the feeling I wouldn't be proposing.

LYUBOV ANDREEVNA. That's wonderful. One little minute is all it takes. I'll call her right now . . .

LOPAKHIN. And there's champagne for the occasion. (*Looks in the glasses.*) Empty, somebody drank it already.

YASHA coughs.

I should say, lapped it up . . .

LYUBOV ANDREEVNA (*lively*). Fine! We'll go outside . . . Yasha, *allez!*[69] I'll call her . . . (*In the doorway.*) Varya, drop everything, come here. Come on! (*Exits with YASHA.*)

LOPAKHIN (*glancing at his watch.*) Yes . . .

Pause.

Behind the door a stifled laugh, whispering, finally VARYA enters.

VARYA (*inspects the luggage for a long time*). That's funny, I just can't find it . . .

LOPAKHIN. What are you looking for?

VARYA. I packed it myself and can't remember.

Pause.

LOPAKHIN. Where are you off to now, Varvara Mikhailovna?

VARYA. Me? To the Ragulins' . . . I've agreed to take charge of their household . . . as a housekeeper, sort of.

LOPAKHIN. That's in Yashnevo? About fifty miles from here.

Pause.

So ends life in this house . . .

---

69 French: go on!

VARYA (*examining the luggage*). Where in the world is it . . . Or maybe I packed it in the trunk . . . Yes, life in this house is over . . . there won't be any more . . .

LOPAKHIN. And I'll be riding to Kharkov soon . . . by the same train. Lots of business. But I'm leaving Yepikhodov on the grounds . . . I hired him.

VARYA. Is that so!

LOPAKHIN. Last year by this time it was already snowing, if you remember, but now it's mild, sunny. Except that it's cold . . . About three degrees of frost.

VARYA. I haven't noticed.

Pause.

And besides our thermometer is broken . . .

Pause.

Voice from outside through the door: "Yermolay Alekseich!"

LOPAKHIN (*as if expecting this call for a long time*). Right away! (*Rushes out.*)

VARYA, sitting on the floor, laying her head on a pile of dresses, quietly sobs. The door opens, LYUBOV ANDREEVNA enters cautiously.

LYUBOV ANDREEVNA. Well?

Pause.

We've got to go.

VARYA (*has stopped crying, wipes her eyes*). Yes, it's time, Mama dear. I'll get to the Ragulins' today, provided I don't miss the train . . .

LYUBOV ANDREEVNA (*in the doorway*). Anya, put your things on!

Enter ANYA, then GAEV, CHARLOTTA IVANOVNA. GAEV has on a heavy overcoat with a hood. The servants and coachmen gather. YEPIKHODOV fusses around the luggage.

Now we can be on our way.

ANYA (*joyously*). On our way!

GAEV. My friends, my dearly beloved friends! Abandoning this house forever, can I be silent, can I refrain from expressing at parting those feelings which now fill my whole being . . .

ANYA (*entreating*). Uncle! . . .

VARYA. Uncle dear, you mustn't!

GAEV (*downcast*). Bank the yellow to the center . . . I'll keep still . . .

Enter TROFIMOV, then LOPAKHIN.

TROFIMOV. Well, ladies and gentlemen, time to go!

LOPAKHIN. Yepikhodov, my overcoat!

LYUBOV ANDREEVNA. I'll sit just one little minute.[70] It's as if I never saw before what the walls in this house are like, what the ceilings are like, and now I gaze at them greedily, with such tender love . . .

GAEV. I remember when I was six, on Trinity Sunday[71] I sat in this window and watched my father driving to church . . .

LYUBOV ANDREEVNA. Is all the luggage loaded?

LOPAKHIN. Everything, I think. (*Putting on his overcoat, to Yepikhodov.*) You there, Yepikhodov, see that everything's in order.

YEPIKHODOV (*in a hoarse voice*). Don't worry, Yermolay Alekseich!

LOPAKHIN. What's the matter with you?

YEPIKHODOV. I just drank some water, swallowed something.

YASHA (*contemptuously*). How uncouth . . .

LYUBOV ANDREEVNA. We're going—and there won't be a soul left here.

LOPAKHIN. Not until spring.

VARYA (*pulls a parasol out of a bundle, looking as if she were about to hit someone*).

LOPAKHIN pretends to be scared.

What are you, what are you doing . . . it never entered my mind . . .

---

70 Sitting down for a brief while before leaving for a journey was an old Russian custom.

71 Pentecost or Whitsunday, always the Sunday that is closest to fifty days from Russian Easter.

TROFIMOV. Ladies and gentlemen, let's get into the carriages . . . It's high time! The train'll be here any minute!

VARYA. Petya, here they are, your galoshes, next to the suitcase. (*Tearfully.*) And yours are so muddy, so old . . .

TROFIMOV (*putting on his galoshes*). Let's go, ladies and gentlemen!

GAEV (*overcome with emotion, afraid he'll cry*). The train . . . the station . . . Follow-shot to the center, white doublette to the corner . . .

LYUBOV ANDREEVNA. Let's go!

LOPAKHIN. Everybody here? Nobody there? (*Locking the side door at the left.*) Things stored here, have to lock up. Let's go! . . .

ANYA. Good-bye, house! Good-bye, old life!

TROFIMOV. Hello, new life! (*Exits with ANYA.*)

> VARYA *casts a glance around the room and exits unhurriedly.*
> YASHA *and* CHARLOTTA *with her lapdog go out.*

LOPAKHIN. Which means, till spring. Come along, ladies and gentlemen . . . Till we meet again! . . . (*Exits.*)

> LYUBOV ANDREEVNA *and* GAEV *are left alone. As if they had been waiting for this, they throw their arms around one another's neck and sob with restraint, quietly, afraid of being heard.*

GAEV (*in despair*). Sister dear, sister dear . . .

LYUBOV ANDREEVNA. Oh, my darling, my sweet, beautiful orchard! . . . My life, my youth, my happiness, good-bye! . . . Good-bye! . . .

> ANYA's *voice (gaily, appealing):* "Mama! . . ."

> TROFIMOV's *voice (gaily, excited):* "Yoo-hoo! . . ."

LYUBOV ANDREEVNA. One last look at the walls, the windows . . . Our poor mother loved to walk in this room . . .

GAEV. Sister dear, sister dear! . . .

> ANYA's *voice:* "Mama! . . ."

> TROFIMOV's *voice:* "Yoo-hoo! . . ."

LYUBOV ANDREEVNA. We're coming! . . .

They go out.

The stage is empty. We hear all the doors being locked with a key, and then the carriages driving off. It grows quiet. In the stillness there is the dull thud of an axe against a tree, sounding forlorn and dismal.

We hear footsteps. From the door at right FIRS appears. He's dressed as always, in a jacket and white waistcoat, slippers on his feet. He is ill.

FIRS (*crosses to the door, tries the knob*). Locked. They've gone . . . (*Sits on the sofa.*) Forgot about me . . . Never mind . . . I'll sit here a spell . . . And Leonid Andreich, I'll bet, didn't put on his fur coat, went out in his topcoat . . . (*Sighs, anxiously.*) I didn't see to it . . . When they're young, they're green! (*Mutters something that cannot be understood.*) This life's gone by like I ain't lived. (*Lies down.*) I'll lie down a spell . . . Not a bit o' strength left in you, nothing left, nothing . . . Eh you . . . half-baked bungler! . . . (*Lies immobile.*)

We hear the distant sound, as if from the sky, the sound of a breaking string, dying away mournfully. Silence ensues, and all we hear far away in the orchard is the thud of an axe on a tree.

Curtain

VARIANTS TO

The Cherry Orchard

Lines come from the original manuscript version (A1), a subsequent set of corrections (A2), the manuscript with the addition to Act 2 (AA), and the first publication in the anthology *Knowledge* (*Znanie*) (K).

ACT ONE

page 986 / *Replace*: Everyone talks about our getting married . . . it's all like a
    dream . . .

with: Everyone talks about our getting married, everyone offers congratula-
    tions, and he looks just as if he was about to propose any minute now, but
    in fact there's nothing to it, it's all like a dream, an unsettling, bad dream . . .
    Sometimes it even gets scary, I don't know what to do with myself . . . (A2)

page 991 / *Replace*: I'd like to tell you . . . Here's my plan.

with: This is what I want to say before I go. (*After a glance at his watch.*) Now
    about the estate . . . in two words . . . I want to propose to you a means of
    finding a way out. So that your estate doesn't incur losses, you'd have to
    get up every day at four in the morning and work all day long. For you,
    of course, that's impossible, I understand . . . But there is another way
    out. (A1)

page 994 / *Replace*: Nothing doing. I want to go to bed. (*Exits.*)

with: (*walking over to the door*). Who is that standing in the doorway? Who's
    there? (*Knock on the door from that side.*) Who's that knocking? (*Knock.*)
    That gentleman is my fiancé. (*Exits.*) *Everyone laughs.* (A1 & 2)

page 995 / *After*: He's a good man. — By the way, how much do we owe him?
GAEV. For the second mortgage just a trifle—about forty thousand. (A1)
Stage direction: a peaceful mood has returned to her, she is happy. (A1 & 2)

page 1001 /   **ACT TWO**
*Opening stage direction: YASHA and DUNYASHA are sitting on
a bench, Yepikhodov stands nearby. From the estate along the
road TROFIMOV and ANYA pass by.*

ANYA. Great Aunt lives alone, she's very rich. She doesn't like Mamma. At
    first it was hard for me staying with her, she didn't talk much to me. Then
    nothing, she relented. She promised to send the money, gave me and
    Charlotta Ivanovna something for the trip. But how awful, how hard it is
    to feel that one is a poor relation.

TROFIMOV. There's somebody here already, it looks like . . . They're sitting
    down. In that case, let's walk along a little farther.

ANYA. Three weeks I've been away from home. I missed it so much!
   They leave. (A1 & 2)

page 1004 / *After*: Tasty little pickle! — *Pause.* (A2, AA)

page 1004 / *After*: a girl who misbehaves . . . — (*Sings quietly, and because he has no ear, extremely off-key*) "Would you know my soul's unrest." (A2)

page 1004 / *After*: The masters . . . — (*Rapidly.*) Come here today when it gets dark. Be sure to come . . . (A1 & 2)

page 1006 / *After*: Maybe we'll think of something. —
   *VARYA and CHARLOTTA IVANOVNA pass by on the road
   from the estate. CHARLOTTA is in a man's cap with a gun.*
VARYA. She's an intelligent, well-bred girl, nothing can happen, but all the same it's not right to leave her alone with a young man. Supper's at nine, Charlotta Ivanovna.
CHARLOTTA. I don't want to eat. (*Quietly hums a ditty.*)
VARYA. It doesn't matter. You have to for decency's sake. There, you see, they're sitting there on the riverbank . . .
   VARYA and CHARLOTTA leave. (A1 & 2)

page 1008 / *After*: (*Inspects him.*) — Today should be the lightweight gray suit, but this one's a disgrace. (A1)

page 1011 / *After*: **ANYA** (*dreamily*). There goes Yepikhodov . . . —
VARYA. How come he's living with us? He only eats on the run and drinks tea all day long . . .
LOPAKHIN. And makes plans to shoot himself.
LYUBOV ANDREEVNA. But I love Yepikhodov. When he talks about his troubles, it gets so funny. Don't discharge him, Varya.
VARYA. There's no other way, Mamma dear. We have to discharge him, the good-for-nothing. (A2)

page 1015 / *Replace*: **TROFIMOV.** Believe me, Anya, believe! . . . **Curtain**
with: **TROFIMOV.** Tsss . . . Someone's coming. That Varya again! (*Angrily.*) Exasperating!
ANYA. So what? Let's go to the river. It's nice there . . .
TROFIMOV. Let's go . . .
   They start out.

ANYA. Soon the moon will rise.

They leave.

Enter FIRS, then CHARLOTTA IVANOVNA. FIRS, muttering, is looking for something on the ground near the bench, lights a match.

CHARLOTTA. That you, Firs? What are you up to?

FIRS (*mutters*). Eh, you half-baked bungler!

CHARLOTTA (*sits on the bench and removes her cap*). That you, Firs? What are you looking for?

FIRS. Mistress mislaid her purse.

CHARLOTTA (*looking*). Here's a fan . . . And here's a hanky . . . smells of perfume.

Pause.

Nothing else. Lyubov Andreevna is constantly mislaying things. She's even mislaid her own life. (*Quietly sings a little song.*) I haven't got a valid passport, Granddad, I don't know how old I am, and I always feel like I'm still oh so young . . . (*Puts her cap on Firs; he sits motionless.*) O, I love you, my dear sir! (*Laughs.*) Ein, zwei, drei! (*Takes the cap off Firs and puts it on herself.*) When I was a little girl, my father and momma used to go from fairground to fairground, giving performances, pretty good ones. And I would be dressed as a boy and do the death-defying leap and all sorts of stunts, and so forth. And when Poppa and Momma died, a German gentlewoman took me home with her and started teaching me. Fine. I grew up, then turned into a governess. But where I'm from and who I am—I don't know . . . Who my parents were, maybe they weren't married . . . I don't know. (*Pulls a pickle from her pocket and eats it.*) I don't know anything.

FIRS. I was twenty or twenty-five, we're goin' along, me and the deacon's son and Vasily the cook, and there's this here man sittin' on a stone . . . a stranger like, don't know 'im . . . Somehow I git skeered and clear off, and when I'm gone they up and killed him . . . There was money on him.

CHARLOTTA. Well? *Weiter.*

FIRS. Then, I mean, comes a trial, they start askin' questions . . . They convict 'em . . . And me too . . . I sit in the penal colony two years or so . . . Then nothing, they let me go . . . A long time ago this was.

Pause.

You can't rec'llect all of it . . .

CHARLOTTA. It's time for you to die, Granddad. (*Eats the pickle.*)

FIRS. Huh? (*Mutters to himself.*) And then, I mean, we're all riding together, and there's a rest stop . . . Uncle leaped out of the wagon . . . took a sack

... and in that sack's another sack. And he looks, and there's something in there—jerk! jerk!

CHARLOTTA (*laughs, quietly*). Jerk, jerk! (*Eats the pickle.*)

> *We hear someone quickly walking along the road, playing a*
> *balalaika ... The moon comes up ... Somewhere near the poplars*
> VARYA *is looking for Anya and calling, "Anya! Where are you!"*
> *Curtain* (A1 & 2)

ACT THREE

page 1019 / *After*: *liking you very much, too.*
How are you?

> Voice: "O, when I seen you, my heart got very sore." (A)

page 1019 / *After*: *Guter Mensch, aber schlechter Musikant.* —

PISHCHIK. Well, I don't understand your schlechter-mechter. Lyubov Andreevna will favor me today with a loan of one hundred eighty rubles ... that I do understand ...

LYUBOV ANDREEVNA. What sort of money do I have? Leave off. (A)

page 1019 / *After*: Here is a very nice rug. — there are no moth-holes in it, no little stain. Very nice. (A)

page 1026 / *After*: *in a gray top hat* — *in a tailcoat* (A)

page 1026 / *After*: *to powder her nose* — *tries to do it without being noticed* (A)

page 1026 / *After*: my heart pound, Firs Nikolaevich — We've been drinking cognac, (A)

page 1027 / *After*: This very minute, out of here! Out! — Out! You riffraff! (A)

page 1029 / *After*: Don't laugh at me! — There's no need, no need, no need! (A)

ACT FOUR

page 1036 / *After*: but that money won't last long. — Well, Uncle got a job at the bank ... (A) page 1038 / *After*: twenty-four years . . . — (*Astounded.*) Can you imagine! (A)

page 1041 / *After*: fill my whole being . . . — My friends, you, who feel this as keenly as I do, who know . . . (A)

page 1041 / *After*: I'll sit just one little minute — I'll sit a while . . . This feels good, it feels grand . . . (A)

APPENDIX

LOST AND UNWRITTEN PLAYS

Taras Bulba [Тарас Бульба], 1873–1874

According to Scriba (E. A. Solovyev-Andreevich), "A. P. Chekhov as remembered by his relatives," *Priazovsky kray* 180 (1904), Chekhov's earliest literary effort was a dramatization of Nikolay Gogol's novel about Cossacks as a tragedy.

He Met His Match [Нашла коса на камень], 1878

From a letter of Aleksandr P. Chekhov to his younger brother Anton, October 14, 1878:

> *He Met His Match* is written in excellent language and very characteristic of each of the persons you introduce, but your plot is quite trifling. This latest manuscript of yours, which, for the sake of convenience, I passed off as my own, I read to my comrades, people of taste, including S. Solovyev, the author of [the comedy] *A Suburban Suitor.*[1] In every case the verdict was this: "The style is excellent, there's some know-how, but not much observation and no experience of everyday life. In time, *qui sait?*,[2] a professional writer might evolve."

The Hen Has Good Reason to Cluck [Недаром курица пела], early 1880s

Mikhail P. Chekhov, *Around Chekhov* (Moscow, 1964):

> When he was a student in the 7th class, Anton Pavlovich wrote [. . .] an awfully funny vaudeville *The Hen Has Good Reason to Cluck* and sent it [. . .] to us in Moscow to read aloud. [. . .] What became of the vaudeville, I don't know.

The Clean-Shaven Secretary with the Pistol [Бритвый секретаарь с пистолетом], early 1880s

Mikhail P. Chekhov, *On Chekhov* (Moscow, 1910):

He put into this vaudeville the editorial office of a newspaper with a double bed in it. One of the reporters brought an inept poem to be printed. And so Anton Pavlovich had to make up specially a particularly inept poem, in which the word "headlong" was to be repeated four times. Here is the poem:

> Forgive me, my angel white as snow,
> Friend of my days and my tender ideal,
> That I, love forgot, rush there headlong,
> Where death befalls . . . O, I am terrified! . . .
> (. . . .)
> I go back to the grave with tear-stained eyes.

"The last line is a bit morbid," says the editor to the hero of the vaudeville, "but the main thing is knowing how to recite."

Mikhail P. Chekhov, *Theatre, Actors and 'Tatyana Repina'* (Petrograd, 1924):

. . . Chekhov did not send this vaudeville to the theatrical censor and, unfortunately, I know nothing about its fate.

A *Parody of* Drugged by Life
[Пародия на пьесу "Чад жизни"], 1884.

Chekhov to Nikolay Leikin,[3] January 30, 1884:

Drugged by Life was written in the town of Voskresensk last summer, almost before my eyes. I also know the author, and his friends whom he mercilessly slights with his slander in his *Abysses* and *Crises* . . . Ashanin (former theater manager Begichev), Vycheslavtsev (former singer Vladislavtsev) and many other acquaintances of my family circle . . . It might be possible to do a little slandering of one's own, hiding behind a pseudonym.[4]

Leikin to Chekhov, February 19, 1884:

The parody of B. Markevich's play was already set up, when I got your letter not to print the parody, and I ordered the type to be dismantled.

Hamlet, Prince of Denmark [Намлет, Принц датский], 1887

Aleksandr P. Lazarev-Gruzinsky,[5] "Lost Novels and Plays of Chekhov," *Energy (Énergiya)* 3 (Petersburg, 1913):

> On one of my next visits he presented me with *Hamlet, Prince of Denmark.*
>
> "Take this playlet away with you to Kirzhach, A. S.! I began it, but I'm too lazy to finish it. I'm too busy and worn out by *Ivanov.* Write an ending, we'll work it over together."
>
> I pled that I had never written a play and was afraid to disappoint the hopes he invested in me as a dramatist.
>
> "Stuff and nonsense! You've got to begin some time, dear boy. Plays are our bread and butter. Write twenty plays, they'll make you a whole fortune!"
>
> *Hamlet, Prince of Denmark* had been begun by Chekhov on a quire of writing paper stitched into a notebook. This was Chekhov's favorite meed of paper for more or less major items. On similar quires *The Steppe* had been written. Shorter stories he most often wrote on long, narrow strips of thin writing or letter paper. For *Hamlet, Prince of Denmark,* Chekhov had written a list of the intended characters, to whom I might still add a few persons, as I wished, and about 200 to 250 lines of text [. . .] The criticism of theatrical manners was meant, among other things, to refer to the levity of backstage mores (Ophelia was supposed to appear to be cheating on Hamlet) and harshly tweak provincial impresarios for their stinginess, lack of culture, etc. Chekhov's view of them was the gloomiest.
>
> The action of the playlet took place behind the scenes of a provincial playhouse during the rehearsals of *Hamlet.* Hence the title *Hamlet, Prince of Denmark.* Act One began with the actors gathering to rehearse. The first to appear were two actors, one of whom, Tigrov (Chekhov came up with the name), who played Hamlet's father's ghost, told stories about his many years of trouping in backwoods provincial towns. His generally very funny account had one purely Chekhovian detail:
>
> "You arrive and put up at the 'Grand Hotel'—every dump in the sticks has its 'Hotel Europa' or 'Grand Hotel' . . ."
>
> The first act was to end with a scandal and general bedlam.
>
> The second act was supposed to show a scene from *Hamlet.*
>
> After thinking about the first act, I sketched out a few combinations and a plan for the first act to the end. My inexperience in writing for the stage was expressed in the fact that, instead of a scandal and general bedlam, the first act was filled with lots of dialogue, although comic and sufficiently lively. Having

kept a copy for myself, I sent the original *Hamlet, Prince of Denmark*, along with my rough drafts, to Chekhov and began to await the results of a letter.

Chekhov replied with a short postcard; admitting that my efforts to work out and finish the first act were not entirely hopeless, he promised after the production of *Ivanov* to send me a more detailed letter with notes on my supposed mistakes.

On November 27 I received that letter.

Chekhov to Lazarev-Gruzinsky, November 15, 1887:

The fact is that when I gave the actors a brief account of the plot of *Hamlet, Prince of Denmark*, they expressed a burning desire to play it no later than January, i.e., as soon as possible. Strike while the iron is hot. Have you written anything? Is it coming out as needed? Can you manage the plot and the stage conventions? Be that as it may, hurry and write me in detail what you have thought up, written down and have planned out. At the same time send me my manuscript (rolled into a scroll), keeping a copy for yourself. I will combine mine with yours, I will think up and immediately inform you of my intentions and projects. *Conditions:* 1) utter confusion, 2) each mug must be characteristic and speak its own language, 3) no dull spots, 4) uninterrupted action, 5) roles must be written for Gradov, Svetlov, Schmidthof, Kiselevsky, Solovtsov, Vyazovsky, Valentinov, Kosheva, Krasovskaya and Borozdina, 6) criticism of theatrical practices, without criticism our vaudeville would be meaningless.

While awaiting the speediest answer I recommend you, dear sir, to lie in bed, take your brains in hand and start cogitating; after long cogitation you will sit at your desk and sketch out your plan.

Lazarov-Gruzinsky to Chekhov, November 21, 1887:

I admit that your "Conditions" for a vaudeville are very clear, very correct and very necessary; what's needed are 1. complete mayhem, 2. absence of dull spots, 3. characteristics, 4. criticism, 5. action. As to the casting of roles, I am not familiar with the lines of business of Svetlov, Solovtsov, Vyazovsky, Valentinov and Kosheva.[6] Didn't Svetlov play Khlestakov, or am I wrong? Vyazovsky is a comic old man . . . *Kes ke say* Valentinov? Maybe this can all be worked out?

[. . .] I keep thinking about Act 2. True, it isn't suitable to present a scene from *Hamlet* (i.e., the early scenes). It would be better to set the second act of the vaudeville "backstage." Let *Hamlet* be going on, but our action unfolds behind the scenes: then the mixup with the wreathes is possible and anything you want, and even the general donnybrook. . . . In a best-case scenario the general fate of the vaudeville will be this: you will get Act 1 and the synopsis of Act 2 by November 29; you'll take a few days to read and consider it; meanwhile I will be busy with Act 2; on the 21st I'll come to Moscow (in the evening), on the 22 (Tuesday morning) I'll pay you a call, and 22–23–24 the vaudeville will receive its final form. [. . .] P.S. On second thought I'm changing the plan: first, you asked that I send you back your manuscript, I'm sending it; second, I'll hold on to the synopsis I have and planned (the ending), and wait for your answer, instructions, changes etc.

After your lines: Tigrov's speech; the impresario runs in and wants to carry off Tigrov *by force*, Tigrov is undaunted, the impresario disappears in horror; second attack on Borshchov; Borshchov lays into Tigrov and says that, as long as he lives, he will not yield; appearance of Tigrov's wife, incited by the impresario; she persuades Tigrov to leave the stage, entreats him, loses her temper, but when Tigrov reminds her of the impresario's insult, the old woman sides with her husband; Borshchov is exhausted; Tigrov sends his wife to help him; the reporter appears (on stage; how are we to put him in the orchestra?), approving of the unmasking of Tigrov and praising his exposure; but when Tigrov refers to the press—the reporter gets embarrassed etc. Tigrov shifts to the immorality of actr[esses]. The impresario for the second times wants to take him off by force and for the second time suffers defeat. Tigrov talks. Wishing to worm his way into the impresario's good graces, the prompter crawls out of his box, grabs the gaping Tigrov by the legs, stagehands run on and carry off Tigrov. The impresario is in transports of delight. But in a minute Tigrov appears again, devoid of fur coat and coattails ("Treachery may triumph for but a moment! . . ."). Unmasking of Ophelia, the engineer's procession, Hamlet's rage. Unmasking of Gertrude—Svireleva. Gertrude demands that the impresario shut Tigrov up; dialogue of Gertrude and the impresario; Gertrude faints. The impresario horrified agrees to do anything so long as Tigrov shuts up; Tigrov forces him to take an oath before the audience ("Swear" from *Hamlet*) and leaves the stage. Hamlet runs on stage, followed by Ophelia, who is trying in vain to convince him. Hamlet addresses himself to the now exultant (over his conclusion of the business with Tigrov) impresario and refuses to act. The impresario is dumb struck. Curtain.

In the second act I think there ought to be (as you already said) a fight between Babelmandebsky and the impresario and Tigrov, adding a different sort of confusion.

Chekhov to Lazarev-Gruzinsky, November 26, 1887:

Now about *Hamlet*

1) Your *Hamlet* consists entirely of dialogues, which have no organic connections. The dialogues are impossible. With each scene the number of characters has to increase progressively:

I

I I

I I I

I I I I

I I I I I

. . . .

By accumulating episodes and characters and connecting them, you will succeed in keeping the stage filled and noisy over the course of the whole act.

You forget that the Tigrovs and Co. feel the eyes of the audience on them at all times. Consequently, Hamlet's cross-examination of Ophelia as you've set it up is impossible. There's far too much outburst and noise at that point. Hamlet is upset, but at the same time he masks his unhappiness.

3) The press agent can speak only from the orchestra pit. What the hell's the point of dragging him on stage? He speaks curtly and firmly, Belyankin type.[7]

4) In Act II a scene from Hamlet has got to be played. In Act I the stage is set up in relation to the audience like this

. . . .

. . . .

⌣

But in Act II you want to set it up like this:

⌢

5) Your ending for Act I is stilted. It mustn't end like that . . . In the interests of Act II you have to end with the reconciliation of the parties. After all, in Act II Tigrov plays Hamlet's ghost!

6) By the way: the role of Trigrov is for Gradov.

7) Judging by your synopsis, you will be far from concise. Don't forget that half the time will be spent on the actors' business.

8) I'm afraid you're getting fed up with me and will start cursing me out for being an arrogant swine . . . But I am comforted by the thought that fussing over a vaudeville is good for you: you'll get the knack of it.

9) After the play [*Ivanov*] I was so worn out that I lost the ability to think straight and speak right. Don't be hard on me!

The Power of Hypnotism [Сила гипнотизма], 1887[8]

Ivan Leontiev-Shcheglov,[9] "Literary Supplement," *Niva* (*Cornfields*) 6–7 (1906):

> In those days Chekhov had not yet written plays, and the one-act joke *The Power of Hypnotism* which he thoroughly reminds me of in one of his letters also remained unrealized . . . This was almost the only one of Chekhov's improvisations of the time in dramatic form, from which, however, my memory has preserved only the "scenario" part. . . .
>
> A certain dark-eyed little widow has turned the heads of two of her admirers, a fat major with a superb majorial moustache and a youth with no moustache at all, a pharmacist's assistant. Both rivals, military and civilian, are crazy about her and ready to commit any folly for the sake of her flashing eyes, which possess, they are convinced, a certain special, demonic power. A funny love scene takes place between the seductive little widow and the fat major who, wheezing, gets down on his knees before the widow, offers her his hand and heart and swears that for love of her he will undergo the most awful sacrifices. The cruel little widow explains to the amorous major that she has nothing against his proposal and that the only obstacle to their march up the aisle . . . is the major's bushy moustache. And wishing to test the demonic power of her eyes, the little widow hypnotizes the major, and hypnotizes so successfully that the major silently heads for the door and hurries straight out of the parlor to the nearest available barber. Then there occurs a certain farcical mix-up, whose details have escaped my memory, but whose upshot is the complete triumph of the moustacheless pharmacist. (It would seem the enterprising suitor, taking advantage of his rival's absence, pours into the widow's cup of coffee a love potion of his own devising.) And at the very moment when the little widow falls into the pharmacist's embrace, the hypnotized major appears in the doorway in the most comic and silly plight: he has just got rid of his splendid moustache. . . . Of course, at the sight of the little widow's perfidy, "the power of hypnotism" ends in a moment and the vaudeville ends with it.
>
> I recall that the last scene, that is the major's appearance without his moustache, made us both laugh a lot. Evidently, *The Power of Hypnotism* had the

potential to become one of the most hilarious and popular of Russian farces, and I immediately made Chekhov promise that he would keep at it and not hide it away in a drawer.

"How's it going, *Antoine*, with *The Power of Hypnotism*?" I asked him in one of my next letters.

"I shall write *The Power of Hypnotism* next summer—I don't feel like it now!" *Antoine* negligently replied from his Moscow torpor.[10]

But summer went, winter came, then a number of years rolled by, and other, more melancholic themes eclipsed the brazenly funny joke of youth.

Leontiev-Shcheglov to Chekhov, September 30, 1888:

How is your *Power of Hypnotism*? Who knows—maybe, in defiance of all opinions, you are fated to become the more popular writer of vaudevilles.

Chekhov to Leontyev-Shcheglov, November 2, 1888:

Am I turning into a popular writer of vaudevilles? Goodness gracious, the way they clamor for them! If in my lifetime I just manage to scribble a dozen airy trifles for the stage, I'll be thankful for it. I have no love for the stage. I'll write *The Power of Hypnotism* during the summer—I don't feel like it right now. This season I'll write one little vaudeville and then rest until summer. Can you call this labor? Can you call this passion?

Thunder and Lightning [Гром и молиня],1888

Chekhov to A. S. Suvorin,[11] Moscow, December 23, 1888:

I've dreamed up for Savina, Davydov[12] and the ministers a vaudeville entitled *Thunder and Lightning*. During a thunderstorm at night I will have the country doctor Davydov drop in on the old maid Savina. Davydov's teeth will ache, and Savina will have an insufferable personality. Interesting dialogue, interrupted by thunder. At the end—I marry them. When I'm all written out, I'll start to write vaudevilles and live off them. I think I could write a hundred a year. Vaudeville plots gush up in me like oil in the wells of Baku. Why can't I give my oil fields to Shcheglov?

Untitled Comedies and Vaudevilles

Chekhov to his younger brother Ivan, late October 1883:

> I don't walk anywhere, I don't work. I keep busy with medicine and concocting a bad vaudeville.

Chekhov to Vladimir Tikhonov,[13] May 31, 1889:

> . . . I was starting a comedy, but wrote two acts and gave it up. It came out boring. There's nothing more boring than a boring play, but now, it would seem, I am capable of writing only boring stuff, so it's better to give it up.

Tatyana Shchepkina-Kupernik,[14] *Days of My Life*:

> I remember how once we were coming back to the estate [at Melikhovo] after a long walk. We were caught in the rain, and waited it out in an empty barn. Chekhov, holding a wet umbrella, said:
>
> "You know, somebody ought to write a vaudeville: two people are waiting out a rainstorm in an empty barn, they joke, they laugh, they dry out their umbrellas and make declarations of love—then the rain ends, the sun comes out—and suddenly the man dies of a heart attack!"
>
> "God save you!" I said in amazement. "How can you call that a vaudeville?"
>
> "Still, it's like life. You think things like that don't happen? Here we are joking, laughing—and suddenly—bang! The end!"
>
> Of course, he never wrote that "vaudeville."

Pavel Orlenev,[15] Memories of Chekhov in *Rabis* 29 (1929):

> I had just performed one of my vaudevilles—*From a Job to a Career*—at Korsh's Theatre. . . . After the intermission A. P. Chekhov came backstage. He walked into the dressing room and introduced himself.
>
> "You know," he said, smiling blandly at me, "as I watched you act, I wanted to write a vaudeville which would end in a suicide."

Pyotr Gnedich,[16] in *Istorichesky Vestnik (Historical Messenger)*, 1911:

> "Why do I write comedies!" Anton Pavlovich grieved. "Nobody needs them. The thing I should be writing is trivial vaudevilles! Ah, what can be better than a funny little, trivial little vaudeville, so funny that the spectators will burst their buttons roaring with laughter. And how healthy that would be for our hemorrhoidal organism!"

Aleksandr Vishnevsky,[17] *Scraps of Memory* (Leningrad, 1928):

> During a walk in [. . .] Tarasovka, Chekhov shared with me the plan for a play without a hero. The play was to be in four acts. During the first three acts people are waiting for the hero, they talk about him. He's on his way, he isn't on his way. And in Act Four, when everyone is fully prepared to meet him, a telegram arrives that he has died. This plan was very characteristic of Chekhov.

Chekhov to Olga Knipper-Chekhova,[18] October 1903:

> For the longest time now, I've been wanting to write the silliest possible vaudeville.

Untitled Dramas, 1903–1904

Mikhail P. Chekhov, "On A. P. Chekhov," *Everybody's Journal* (*Zhurnal dlya vsekh*) 7 (1906):

> My brother always had plenty of themes for plays. I remember, he told me the subject of a play he had thought up, in which there was supposed to be an enormous printing office on stage. My brother loved printing offices, even advised me to get a job at some big printing office, even loved the book trade, but believed most, I think, in selling books at railroad stations. While staying in Venice with Suvorin and the author Dmitry Merezhkovsky in March 1891, Chekhov considered writing a play about the tragic fate of the Doge Marino Faliero, who stood up for the honor of his young wife, insulted by a patrician slanderer, but was not supported by the senate, and, after an unsuccessful attempt at an uprising against the oligarchy, was executed in 1355.

Olga Knipper-Chekhova, memoirs in *Izvestiya*, July 14, 1934:

> In the last years of his life Anton Pavlovich had the idea of writing a play. It was still rather vague, but he told me that the hero of the play, a scholar, is in love with a woman who either doesn't love him or betrays him, and so this scholar goes to the Far North. This is how he imagined the third act: there is a steamship, lost in the ice, Northern lights, the scholar is standing alone on the deck, silence, serenity and long nights, and then against the background of the Northern lights he sees the shadow of the beloved woman skim by.

Konstantin Stanislavsky,[19] "A. P. Chekhov and the Art Theatre (Recollections)," *Yearbook of the Moscow Art Theatre 1943* (Moscow, 1945):

The Spring of 1904 passed. Anton Pavlovich's health kept getting worse. . . . However, despite his illness, he did not abandon his love of life. He was very interested in the Maeterlinck production which we were enthusiastically rehearsing at the time. He had to be kept abreast of the course of the work, shown the models for the sets, have the staging explained.

He himself dreamed of a play entirely new to his tendencies. Actually, the plot he concocted for the play was far from Chekhovian. Judge for yourself: two friends, both young, are in love with the same woman. This mutual love and jealousy creates complicated interrelationships. It ends up with them going on an expedition to the North Pole. The set for the last act depicts an enormous ship, lost in the ice. At the end of the play the two friends see a white ghost, gliding across the snow. Obviously, this is the phantom or soul of the beloved woman who has died far away in their homeland.

That was all that one could learn from Anton Pavlovich about his newly conceived play.

Aleksandr Kuprin,[20] memoirs in *Znanie* (*Knowledge*) 3 (St. Petersburg, 1905):

At the same time, he required of writers the most ordinary, true-to-life plots, simplicity of exposition and absence of tricky effects. "Why write," he wondered, "that somone got into a submarine and traveled to the North Pole to effect some reconciliation with people, while his beloved with a dramatic yelp throws herself off a bell-tower? All this is untrue, and doesn't happen in reality. One must write simply: about how Pyotr Semyonovich married Mariya Ivanovna. And that's all . . ."

NOTES

1 The actual author was A. M. Krasovsky. Solovyev had translated a comedy called *Too Few Suitors and Too Many Brides*.

2 French: who knows?

3 Nikolay Aleksandrovich Leikin (1841–1906), humorist and editor of the comic journal *Splinters* (*Oskolki*), to which Chekhov contributed from 1882 to 1887.

4 Instead of a parody, Chekhov wrote a damning review of the novel's dramatization (*Splinters of Moscow Life*, 7, February 18, 1884), and later refers to it in *The Seagull*.

5 Aleksandr Semyonovich Lazarev (1861–1927), a journalist and writer under the pseudonym A. Gruzinsky, was befriended by Chekhov, who tried to improve his style.

6 Members of Korsh's acting company in Moscow, many of whom appeared in the first production of *Ivanov*: Leonid Ivanovich Gradov-Sokolov (1840–1890) as Kosykh, Nikolay Vladimirovich Svetlov (d. 1909) as Borkin, and Bronislava Eduardovna Kosheva as Babakina. Chekhov's boyhood friend Nikolay Nikolaevich Solovtsov (1856–1902) created Smirnov in *The Bear*.

7 "Chekhov could do a very funny takeoff of L. L. Belyankin, far from the most vicious of the vicious Moscow journalists. By the words 'Belyankin type' he sketched for me a completely clear and finished type" (*Lazarev-Gruzinsky's note*)

8 For the final version of this play, see Collaboration, pp. 253–262.

9 See Collaboration, note 1.

10 Letter to Leontyev-Shcheglov, November 2, 1888.

11 Aleksey Sergeevich Suvorin (1834–1912), journalist and publisher, had risen from peasant origins to become a millionaire and influence monger in the conservative camp; he and Chekhov were good friends until they took opposite sides in the Dreyfus Affair.

12 Mariya Gavrilovna Savina (1850–1915), leading lady at the Alexandra Theatre in St. Petersburg, who created the role of Sarra there. Vladimir Nikolaevich Davydov (pseudonym of Ivan Nikolaevich Gorelov, 1849–1925), leading actor at the Maly Theatre, for whom Chekhov had written *Swan Song* and who created the role of *Ivanov* in both Moscow and Petersburg.

13 Vladimir Alekseevich Tikhonov (1857–1914), a fellow playwright, who wrote a review of *Ivanov*.

14 Tatyana Lvovich Shchepkina-Kupernik (1874–1934), writer and good friend of Chekhov's who introduced him to the actress Lidiya Yavorskaya, one of the models for Arkadina.

15 Pavel Nikolaeich Orlenev (Orlov, 1869–1932), an impassioned actor of neurotic roles such as Raskolnikov, who had begun his career at Suvorin's theater and corresponded with Chekhov in 1902–1904.

16 Pyotr Petrovich Gnedich (1855–1927), playwright; when he became manager of the Russian troupe of the Petersburg imperial theaters he tried to get Chekhov's plays onto the Alexandra stage.

17 Aleksandr Leonidovich Vishnevsky (Vishnevetsky, 1861–1943), former schoolmate of Chekhov and founding member of the Moscow Art Theatre, where he created the roles of Dorn, Voinitsky, and Kulygin.

18 Olga Leonardovna Knipper (1870–1959), actress at the Moscow Art Theatre, who played Arkadina, Yelena, Masha, Ranevskaya, and Sarra there; she met Chekhov in 1898 and married him in 1901.

19 Konstantin Sergeevich Alekseev, known as Stanislavsky (1863–1938), a wealthy industrialist and amateur actor-director, who, with Nemirovich-Danchenko, founded in 1898 the Moscow Art Theatre, where he directed the first Moscow revivals of *The Seagull* and *Uncle Vanya*, and the premieres of *Three Sisters* and *The Cherry Orchard*.

20 Aleksandr Ivanovich Kuprin (1870–1938), novelist and short story writer, became friendly with Chekhov in the 1890s, when Kuprin dabbled in playwriting.

1/3/11

10/20/14

15